**CASH FLOW
ANALYSIS**
CHAPTER 4, 6, & 17

**SUSTAINABLE
EARNINGS &
CASH FLOW
FORECASTS**
CHAPTERS 5, 6, & 7

DECISIONS

→ **DESIGNING FINANCIAL CONTRACTS**

→ **VALUATION & INVESTMENT**

→ **EVALUATING AUDIT RISKS**

→ **CREDIT ANALYSIS & RISK ASSESSMENT**

FINANCIAL REPORTING AND ANALYSIS

SECOND CANADIAN EDITION

Lawrence Revsine
Northwestern University

Daniel W. Collins
The University of Iowa

W. Bruce Johnson
The University of Iowa

Joel H. Amernic
University of Toronto

PEARSON
Prentice
Hall

Toronto

National Library of Canada Cataloguing in Publication

Financial reporting and analysis/Lawrence Revsine ... [et al.]. —
2nd Canadian ed.

Includes index.
ISBN 0-13-039793-8

1. Financial statements. 2. Financial statements—Case studies. 3. Corporations—Accounting. I. Revsine, Lawrence.

HF5681.B2F5277   2004   657'.3   C2002-904992-X

0-13-039793-8

Vice President, Editorial Director: Michael J. Young
Senior Acquisitions Editor: Samantha Scully
Executive Marketing Manager: Cas Sheilds
Developmental Editor: Toni Chahley
Production Editor: Marisa D'Andrea
Copy Editor: Susan Marshall
Proofreader: Laurel Sparrow
Production Coordinator: Deborah Starks
Page Layout: Nelson Gonzalez
Permissions Research: Amanda McCormick
Art Director: Julia Hall
Interior and Cover Design: Gillian Tsintziras
Cover Image: Shinichi Eguchi

1 2 3 4 5   08 07 06 05 04

Printed and bound in the United States.

Brief Contents

Contents

Preface

Objectives

We wrote *Financial Reporting and Analysis*, Second Canadian Edition, to help change the way in which the second-level course in financial accounting is taught. At many schools, this course often focuses on the details of GAAP and the accounting processes that underlie financial statements, and may lack emphasis on critical thinking and ignore the possible disparity between accounting numbers and words, and what we would perceive as economic and social "reality."

In contrast, our goal is to help students develop an understanding of the environment in which financial reporting choices are made, what the options are, how to use these data in making decisions, and—most importantly—how to avoid misusing financial statement data. We intend our book to provide instructors with an opportunity to present the "big picture" without sacrificing technical details. This user-oriented book shows students where the financial accounting numbers and words come from, and is consistent with the emergent "competency map" approach to accounting education based partly on the development of students' critical abilities. It also emphasizes the system of financial reporting in which management, boards of directors, audit committees, external auditors, standard-setters, and many others have a shared responsibility for transparent, ethical financial reporting. Our emphasis on the environment within which financial accounting operates is apt in this post-Enron era.

We convey what we believe to be the exciting nature of financial reporting in two stages. First, since business contracts are often linked to accounting numbers, we describe managers' incentives to "manage" numbers to benefit themselves and possibly shareholders. Second, we then employ real-world financial reports and events to illustrate vividly how alternatives to GAAP and unavoidable subjective estimates give managers discretion in reporting results.

We integrate the perspectives of accounting, corporate finance, economics, and a more critical analysis to help students grasp how business transactions get reported. In this approach, we first describe the business transaction and then show students the technical details of GAAP, how those details are applied in practice, and what the financial statements look like. Then we go a step further and ask: What do the numbers mean? Does the accounting process yield numbers and descriptions that seemingly reflect the ostensible economics of the transaction? And if not, what can users do to overcome this limitation?

This book is aimed at those who use financial statements for making decisions. Our definition of users includes auditors doing analytic reviews and establishing audit scope, lenders, equity analysts, investment bankers, members of the public monitoring corporate performance and behaviour, and others. We intend to help readers learn how to get behind the surface structure of accounting and conduct better audits, improve cash flow forecasts, undertake realistic valuations, and perhaps most importantly, participate effectively in holding corporations accountable.

Financial Reporting and Analysis provides instructors with a teaching/learning approach for achieving key goals in accounting and business education. Specifically, it helps instill capacities for: 1) abstract logical thinking, 2) solving unstructured problems, 3) understanding determining forces such as incentives, and 4) encouraging an integrated, cross-disciplinary view of financial reporting. The text discussions, as well as exercises, problems, and cases, were chosen or developed to help achieve these objectives.

Most of the exercises focus on learning the mechanics underlying GAAP and learning about financial statement "gymnastics," skills that we consider crucial for understanding. Virtually all problems and cases were written specifically for this book to provide instructors with assignment material that corresponds with our approach and allows students to build their analytical and critical abilities. Many new cases for the second Canadian edition reflect important recent developments.

Organization

Financial Reporting and Analysis is organized so that an understanding of the context of financial reporting is emphasized before applications involving intermediate-level topics are described. *Context* is provided by Chapters 1 through 7: In **Chapter 1,** we show that financial reporting is a creature of the society in which it exists and within which it evolved. We describe the demand and supply incentives for financial reporting and its institutional setting, and introduce the quality of earnings concept and Internet financial reporting. **Chapters 2, 3, and 4** review the four main financial statements, focusing on the contrasting and also complementary nature of accrual and cash-basis accounting. The concept of quality of earnings is expanded, especially in Chapter 2. These three chapters not only help refresh readers' memory of introductory financial accounting, but just as importantly show that financial reporting's context is rich in conceptual and technical detail.

Chapters 5, 6, and 7 provide perhaps the most crucial aspects of context, and are certainly the most innovative in intermediate-level texts.

The content of Chapter 5—financial statement analysis—is often placed towards the end of intermediate textbooks, but we have chosen to place this chapter close to the beginning in order to provide the "raw material" for financial analysis. An understanding of analytical concepts and techniques is first necessary for a more critical and complete understanding of the various intermediate financial accounting topics themselves. In this chapter, we also substantially reinforce the key idea of "quality of earnings."

Chapters 6 and 7 complete the introduction of context by describing the crucial role of financial accounting in valuation and contracting. We describe how valuation and similar models, and the economics of contracting, serve to provide important benchmarks to help evaluate the adequacy of reported financial accounting information. Chapters 8 through 18 then build on Chapters 1 through 7.

Chapters 8, 9, and 10 focus on topics often introduced in some detail in introductory textbooks, but with an emphasis on the quality of earnings and related strong user orientation constructed in Chapters 1 to 7. In these chapters, we consider not only intermediate, but also more advanced aspects of receivables, inventories, and capital assets.

Chapter 11 describes traditional aspects of accounting for long-term debt as liability financial instruments and emphasizes the impact of managerial incentives on debt accounting and disclosure. This chapter also describes derivative securities and hedges and the associated financial reporting.

Chapter 12 focuses on lease accounting, from both the lessee and lessor perspectives, and shows how users may analyze lease footnotes to adjust for off-balance-sheet leases. Again, the context provided in Chapters 1 through 7 provides useful benchmarks to critically evaluate and adjust for current accounting practice.

Chapter 13 focuses on accounting for income taxes. We emphasize the important roles of income tax footnotes and quality of earnings.

Chapter 14 focuses on an understanding of the building blocks of defined benefit pension accounting and other employee benefits, then introduces uncertainty as a link to understanding the choices made by standard-setters in this area. We stress analysis of pensions and postretirement benefits other than pensions, along with some of the apparent economics of pension accounting.

Chapter 15 describes accounting and reporting of owners' equity, including stock-based compensation. We provide further opportunities to consider the quality of earnings and other context perspectives, such as competing positions of managers, shareholders, regulators, and others that are played out.

Chapter 16 deals with the financial accounting and disclosure issues involved when one corporation acquires the shares of another corporation. **Chapter 17** describes in detail accounting standards and analytical issues involving cash flow statements, building on the base established in Chapter 4. The textbook ends with **Chapter 18**'s description of international financial reporting and inflation accounting.

New to This Edition

In the second Canadian edition of *Financial Reporting and Analysis*, we have incorporated many of the innovations included in the second U.S. edition, as well as additional learning materials. The years 2001 and 2002 represented a watershed for almost everyone and everything, and that includes even the arcane art of financial accounting and reporting. Major business and accounting scandals, represented most vividly by Enron, raised the bar on corporate accountability and therefore on the quality of information provided by companies about their activities.

The phrase "quality of earnings," used often over the past few years in connection with the overall assessment of a company's financial reporting, has become much more than mere words as capital markets in general and companies in particular struggled to restore their credibility. Therefore quality of earnings, introduced as an important concept in the first edition, has been elevated to a more central theme in the second Canadian edition. Material on Enron and other accounting-related crises have been included in **Chapter 1** (The Social Setting of Financial Reporting) and **Chapter 2** (Quality of Earnings, Accrual Accounting, and Income Determination), as well as a more systematic approach to teaching and learning about the quality of earnings. Students are encouraged to explore institutional similarities and differences between Canadian and U.S. financial reporting settings in order to understand the implications of Enron-like phenomena. And the widespread use of so-called adjusted or pro forma earnings numbers in financial reporting is raised as another factor affecting quality of earnings.

In addition, a greater emphasis has been placed on corporate financial reporting via the Internet. This emphasis not only recognizes that web-based reporting is becoming the norm, but also encourages accounting students to adopt a more sophisticated appreciation of the persuasive and rhetorical character of Internet financial and business reporting. In effect, the quality of a company's earnings has become an even more complex issue as we move away from a hard-copy, paper-based reporting system to one that seems accessible from anywhere and that is enveloped in a seductive new medium. It is not only the accounting measurement and disclosure choices that are now important, but also the way such choices are mediated by the Internet. This material is introduced in Chapter 1.

A new chapter—Additional Topics in Income Determination (**Chapter 3**)—has been added. This chapter is an expansion of the material in the former appendix of the first edition's Chapter 2. The central role of revenue accounting in determining a company's quality of earnings emphasizes that the balance-sheet approach of the first edition needed to be tempered by a strong focus on the income statement.

In **Chapter 4** (Structure of the Balance Sheet and Cash Flow Statement), the material on the structure of the balance sheet and cash flow statement has been updated.

Chapter 5 (Essentials of Financial Statement Analysis), **Chapter 6** (The Role of Financial Information in Valuation, Cash Flow Analysis, and Credit Risk Assessment), and **Chapter 7** (The Role of Financial Information in Contracting) have been updated but remain as the core driver rationalizing the demand for accounting information.

Chapter 8 (Receivables), **Chapter 9** (Inventories), and **Chapter 10** (Capital Assets and Amortization) have been updated with new material such as the CICA's accounting guideline on the transfer of receivables, additional material on securitizations, new CICA standards on goodwill and other intangibles, and proposed standards on long-lived asset impairment.

The material on financial instruments and hedging in **Chapter 11** (Financial Instruments as Liabilities) has been expanded and updated with current CICA positions (including Accounting Guideline 13, "Hedging Relationships"), and material on Enron. **Chapter 12** (Financial Reporting for Leases) on leases has also been updated.

Chapter 13 (Financial Reporting for Corporate Income Taxes) has been significantly changed, simplifying the exposition and placing more emphasis on the asset/liability approach. The material on the analysis of corporate income tax notes has been updated, and the link to quality of earnings has been expanded.

Chapter 14 (Reporting Employee Future Benefits) has a new introduction emphasizing the quality-of-earnings risks associated with the existing GAAP approach to accounting for, and reporting, employee future benefits, especially defined benefit pension plans. This chapter has been revised with a view to greater integration of material on defined benefit pension plans and employee future benefits other than pensions.

In **Chapter 15** (Financial Reporting for Owners' Equity), the material on earnings per share and stock-based compensation has been updated to reflect new Canadian accounting standards. Also, the controversy surrounding accounting for management stock option compensation has been incorporated into the chapter with an emphasis on the Canadian standard-setters and media reaction to the pressure over the latter part of 2002 to require companies to record these amounts in their financial statements.

Chapter 16 (Intercorporate Equity Investments, Consolidated Financial Statements, and Special Purpose Entities) has been updated to include proposed accounting standards about the consolidation of special purpose entities and disclosure of guarantees, as well as new standards on goodwill and the elimination of pooling accounting in Canada.

For all other chapters, we have updated many of the examples, added new cases, and also updated the Integrative Running Case Study on Bombardier by incorporating the annual report for the year ended January 31, 2002.

Features of this Textbook

Several features of *Financial Reporting and Analysis* contribute to the achievement of the objectives we described earlier:

- The organization of the text is a fundamental characteristic distinguishing this book. Introducing context at the start provides a powerful, coherent approach to the critical learning of financial reporting.
- Chapters devoted to valuation and contracting show in detail the realistic uses of financial accounting information as means of facilitating transactions in society.
- Introducing the quality of earnings construct provides a constant reminder to students of the importance of a critical analysis of GAAP.
- Use of real financial statements throughout not only shows the pervasiveness and social importance of financial reporting, but also stimulates interest and curiosity.
- Strong emphasis on analysis of the notes to financial statements shows the crucial information that might be derived as well as the integral nature of notes as part of financial statements.
- The incentives and disincentives facing the manager regarding financial accounting measurement and disclosure decisions are emphasized, illustrating that managers are human beings operating within an often complex web of competing pressures.
- The emerging force of corporate financial reporting on the Internet is acknowledged, with all the potential for change that it implies.

Pedagogy

Numerous pedagogical tools are used throughout this text to enhance the learning experience for students and to make the instructor's job easier:

- **Learning objectives** at the beginning of each chapter help students focus on the important points in the chapter.
- **Key terms** are in boldface type in the text and in the index so that students can easily find a term and its definition.
- Many **examples and exhibits** have been updated and replaced so students will have the most up-to-date and relevant data available.
- Untitled **sidebar boxes** and **endnotes** give students extra historical or international examples or references for further reading. Some of these boxes serve to expand on the discussion of the material in the text.
- The **URLs of companies and organizations** of interest to students using the book are placed in the margins of the text.
- **Recap boxes** appear at the end of each major section in the book. In a short paragraph they highlight the main points of the preceding material.

A Canadian company with 1 million pesos in the bank account of its Mexican manufacturing subsidiary would value the cash at 126,422.25 Canadian dollars in December 1996 when the exchange rate was 7.91 pesos to the dollar. This same bank account (with 1 million pesos) would have been valued at 200,000 Canadian dollars in 1995 when the exchange rate was 5 pesos to the dollar.

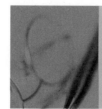

Recap
Financial statement information helps equity investors assess the value of companies and their securities; it helps creditors assess the company's ability both to meet its debt payments and to abide by loan terms; it helps financial advisors and securities analysts provide information and advice to investors and creditors; and it helps auditors both to recognize potential financial reporting abuses and to choose audit procedures to detect them.

- **Summary boxes** at the end of each chapter give students a brief wrap-up of the key ideas.

Summary

Conflicts of interest among managers, shareholders, lenders, or regulators are a natural feature of business. Contracts and regulations help address these conflicts of interest in ways that are mutually beneficial to the parties involved. Accounting numbers often play an important role in contracts and regulations because they provide useful information about the company's performance and financial condition, as well as about the management team's accomplishments.

Accounting-based lending agreements, compensation contracts, and regulations shape managers' incentives—after all, that's why accounting numbers are included in contracts and regulations. They also help explain the accounting choices managers make. Understanding why and how managers exercise their GAAP accounting discretion can be extremely helpful to those who are analyzing and interpreting a company's financial statements.

- End-of-chapter material includes **Exercises** that are a vehicle for learning GAAP mechanics and **Problems** and **Cases** that provide students with an opportunity to focus on analytical and critical-thinking skills at various levels of complexity.

- **Weblink Icons** in the end-of-chapter materials refer students to the Companion Website for further information such as financial reports and additional readings.
- **Additional Exercises, Problems, and Cases** are available on the Companion Website at **www.pearsoned.ca/revsine**.
- Several chapters contain a **Collaborative Learning Case** that can be assigned as a group project. This case helps build team-work skills valuable in the real world.

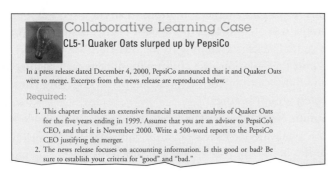

Collaborative Learning Case

CL5-1 Quaker Oats slurped up by PepsiCo

In a press release dated December 4, 2000, PepsiCo announced that it and Quaker Oats were to merge. Excerpts from the news release are reproduced below.

Required:

1. This chapter includes an extensive financial statement analysis of Quaker Oats for the five years ending in 1999. Assume that you are an advisor to PepsiCo's CEO, and that it is November 2000. Write a 500-word report to the PepsiCo CEO justifying the merger.
2. The news release focuses on accounting information. Is this good or bad? Be sure to establish your criteria for "good" and "bad."

- An **Integrative Running Case Study**, "Bombardier on the Web," is provided in many chapters. These cases require students to use the 2002 Bombardier Annual Report available on the Companion Website for this textbook at **www.pearsoned.ca/revsine**. Students are exposed to real-world issues such as finding specific data in a complete financial report and researching material on the web.

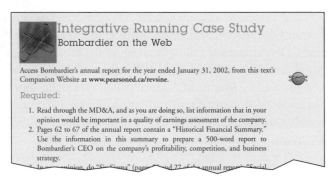

Integrative Running Case Study

Bombardier on the Web

Access Bombardier's annual report for the year ended January 31, 2002, from this text's Companion Website at **www.pearsoned.ca/revsine**.

Required:

1. Read through the MD&A, and as you are doing so, list information that in your opinion would be important in a quality of earnings assessment of the company.
2. Pages 62 to 67 of the annual report contain a "Historical Financial Summary." Use the information in this summary to prepare a 500-word report to Bombardier's CEO on the company's profitability, competition, and business strategy.
3. In your opinion, do "Six Sigma" (pages 26 and 27 of the annual report) "Social

Supplements

The following supplements are available from your Pearson Education Canada sales representative:

- **Instructor's Resource Manual with Solutions:** For each chapter of the text, this supplement contains a chapter overview, chapter outline, teaching tips, chapter quiz, and suggested readings. Instructors will also find additional Exercises, Problems, and Cases to supplement those available in the textbook and on the website. This supplement also provides detailed solutions to the chapter quiz and all of the Exercises, Problems, and Cases.
- **Test Item File:** Over 1,400 test questions, including multiple-choice questions, exercises, comprehensive problems, and short and long essay questions. Each question is tied to a learning objective, is assigned a difficulty level, provides a page reference, and identifies what skill (i.e., application, recall, etc.) is tested. Complete solutions are given.
- **Pearson TestGen:** The Pearson TestGen is a special computerized version of the Test Item File that enables instructors to view and edit the existing questions, add questions, generate tests, and print the tests in a variety of formats. Powerful search and sort functions make it easy to locate questions and arrange them in any order. TestGen also enables instructors to administer tests on a local area network, grade the tests electronically, and prepare the results in electronic or printed reports. Issued on a CD-ROM, the Pearson TestGen is compatible with Windows-based or Macintosh systems.
- **Solutions Acetates:** Complete solutions to all the Exercises, Problems, and Cases in the text are provided along with blank acetates so instructors can customize the package according to the questions they assign.
- **PowerPoint Presentations:** Key information from each chapter of the text, including figures and tables, are presented in an engaging visual format to enhance classroom lectures.
- **Companion Website:** Contains self-testing quizzes, weblinks, chapter summaries, additional Exercises, Problems, and Cases, material for the Bombardier on the Web exercises, and much more.

Acknowledgements for the Second Canadian Edition

The second Canadian edition is based on the innovative book written by Lawrence Revsine, Daniel Collins, and Bruce Johnson. I appreciate their willingness to share their work, and am privileged to participate in the preparation of both the first and second editions of the Canadian adaptation.

The research and writing of this adaptation was performed as part of a team put together by Pearson Education Canada. Samantha Scully, Senior Acquisitions Editor, and Toni Chahley, Developmental Editor, built upon the foundation provided by Pat Ferrier and Laurie Goebel in the first Canadian edition. My sincere thanks to them both, and to Söğüt Güleç, Marisa D'Andrea, Susan Marshall, and everyone who worked so hard to bring this edition to realization. I owe a special thanks to Toni Chahley, who with a cheerful disposition kept the project focused and on point over several crucial periods.

My colleagues Irene Wiecek, Ole-Kristian Hope, Sean Robb, Dan Segal, and Ramy Elitzur have provided good constructive and challenging conversation about teaching financial accounting, and the Rotman School of Management at the University of Toronto provided an environment that nourishes the development of teaching and curriculum.

Several reviewers graciously provided feedback on drafts of the manuscript. My thanks go out to

Leo Gallant
St. Francis Xavier University

Jim Hughes
British Columbia Institute of Technology

Jennifer L. Kao
University of Alberta

Kin Lo
University of British Columbia

Clifton Philpott
Kwantlen University College

Johan de Rooy
University of British Columbia

Wendy Roscow
Concordia University

A Great Way to Learn and Instruct Online

The Pearson Education Canada Companion Website is easy to navigate and is organized to correspond to the chapters in this textbook. Whether you are a student in the classroom or a distance learner you will discover helpful resources for in-depth study and research that empower you in your quest for greater knowledge and maximize your potential for success in the course.

Companion
Website

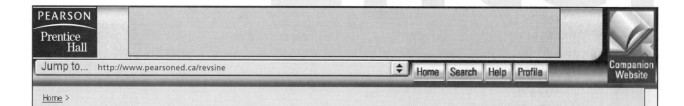

[**www.pearsoned.ca/revsine**]

PEARSON
Prentice Hall

Companion
Website

Jump to... http://www.pearsoned.ca/revsine   ▼   Home | Search | Help | Profile

Home >

PH Companion Website

Financial Reporting and Analysis, Second Canadian Edition, by Revsine, Collins, Johnson, and Amernic

Student Resources

The modules in this section provide students with tools for learning course material. These modules include:

- Chapter Objectives
- Destinations
- Self-Study Quizzes
- Internet Exercises
- Exercises

- Problems/Discussion Questions
- Cases
- Bombardier Annual Report
- Readings

In the quiz modules students can send answers to the grader and receive instant feedback on their progress through the Results Reporter. Coaching comments and references to the textbook may be available to ensure that students take advantage of all available resources to enhance their learning experience.

Instructor Resources

This section includes a link to InstructorCentral, our protected site where instructors will find items to facilitate teaching, such as downloadable PowerPoint Presentations. To get a password, simply contact your Pearson Education Canada Representative or call Faculty Sales and Services at 1-800-850-5813.

1

The Social Setting of Financial Reporting[1]

LEARNING OBJECTIVES

After studying this chapter, you should be able to:

1. Understand current dissatisfaction with accounting, due to situations involving companies such as Enron and Nortel

2. Explain why financial statements are a valuable, but potentially dangerous, source of information about companies, their current health, and their prospects for the future

3. Describe in general terms how financial statements can be used by investors, creditors, securities analysts, and auditors

4. Understand why accounting rules are established, and how management can shape the financial information communicated to outsiders

5. Describe how the demand for financial information comes from its potential ability to improve decision making and to make it possible to monitor managers' activities

6. Describe how the supply of financial information is influenced by the costs of producing and disseminating it and by the benefits it provides

7. Analyze corporate reporting on the Internet

"... accounting is not a science but an art."

R.G.H. Smails, "Economics and Accounting Concepts," *The Canadian Journal of Economics and Political Science,* 3(3), 1937, p. 449

Every once in a while an event comes along that creates a fundamental change in the way we think about things. For reasons to do with corporate governance and the efficient organization of economic activity, and especially for our purposes in examining financial reporting, the situation involving the Enron Corporation (Enron) was such an event. The bankruptcy of this company in late 2001, and the attendant revelations about insider deals, market manipulation, appalling accounting practices, and external audit failure, has had far-reaching effects, well beyond the confines of Enron's home in the United States. For example, the president and CEO of the Canadian Institute of Chartered Accountants released an "open letter" on "the Enron situation" on February 8, 2002, in which he wrote:

CICA
www.cica.ca

> *Here in Canada, our profession operates differently than it does in the United States. Our discipline and oversight regimes are significantly different and our practice inspection systems also differ from the American peer review process. Nonetheless, if change is needed in Canada, we have every confidence that we will be able to sit down together with the regulators and other stakeholders in the capital markets and get it done.*

[For an overview of Enron, its bankruptcy, and some of the accounting practices involved, see the PowerPoint slide presentation on the Companion Website for this textbook at **www.pearsoned.ca/revsine**.]

The reassurance that Canada's financial reporting and accountability system is different from the system in the United States is a bit comforting, but nevertheless we have little reason to be complacent. In recent years, we Canadians have had our own share of financial-reporting excitement. For example, consider the case of Nortel Networks Corporation (Nortel Networks or Nortel). Many business commentators, media pundits, and investment analysts regarded Nortel Networks as the epitome of the *New Economy*. In almost the twinkling of an eye, this company had transformed itself dramatically from a staid century-old telephone equipment manufacturing subsidiary of Canada's giant telephone company, BCE ("Ma Bell"), to a vibrant major global producer of fibre optic networks in its own right.[2] Nortel was a high-tech success story in search of a new cyberspace persona. It loudly proclaimed the intention to change from a *vertically* integrated company into a *virtually* integrated company[3]—a transformation it achieved very quickly between 1998 and 2000. To effect this transformation, Nortel placed saturation media advertisements in which it asked,

"What do you want the Internet to be?"

It seemed that Nortel was somehow almost intending to *become* the Internet—or some kind of physical epitome of the Internet in corporate North America.

In Nortel's annual report (known as the "10-K" report) filed with the U.S. Securities and Exchange Commission (SEC) for its halcyon year of 1999, Nortel described itself as:

> ... *incorporated under the laws of Canada on January 5, 1914 as the Northern Electric Company, Limited, a successor to ... Northern Electric and Manufacturing Company, Limited, a telephone set manufacturing subsidiary of Bell Canada incorporated in 1895. The Corporation changed its name to Northern Telecom Limited on March 1, 1976 and was amalgamated with two wholly-owned subsidiaries on January 4, 1982 under the Canada Business Corporations Act. On April 29, 1999, the Corporation changed its name to Nortel Networks Corporation in the English language ...*
>
> *Nortel Networks is a leading global supplier of networking solutions and services that support voice, data, and video transmission over wireless and wireline technologies. Nortel Networks is focused on building the infrastructure service enabling solutions and applications for the new, high-performance Internet. Nortel Networks' business consists of the design, development, assembly, manufacture, marketing, sale, financing, installation, servicing and support of networking solutions and services for Service Provider and Carrier customers, and Enterprise customers. Nortel Networks' solutions and services are used by customers to support the Internet and other public and private voice, data, and video networks. (p. 3)*

Nortel was a boom business in the emerging "dot.com" world. By July 2000, Nortel's common shares were trading at about CDN$120 (up from about CDN$20 in early 1999), with at times staggering volumes of shares traded daily. Nortel was the toast of mutual funds internationally. But then, soon after, the "Nortel bubble" burst and its share price collapsed to about CDN$10.[4]

Nortel's Accounting Fuelled an Acquisition Engine?

The process of accounting, "the language of business," has been long regarded as objective and factual. It is, after all, *quantitative*. And since debits must equal credits, how could accounting concern itself with anything other than solid facts? Accounting numbers, attested to by independent auditors, are commonly alleged to portray the "results of operations and financial position, and the cash flows" of an organization "in accordance with generally accepted accounting principles." But such an objective and factual view of accounting, which now seems somewhat old-fashioned and naive after *Enron* and *WorldCom Inc.*, ignores the fact that accounting should be regarded as rhetorical, as a means of persuasion. And it also ignores the caution that accounting is an "art" and not a "science" (see the introductory quote, originally made in 1937, to this chapter).

To radically remake itself, and to preempt competitors from beating it to newly emerging networking technologies, Nortel had embarked on a corporate buying spree. In its 1999 annual report, Nortel disclosed the following major acquisitions:

Acquisition	Date	Purchase Price	Cash or Nortel Shares?
Periphonics	Nov 12, 1999	US$650 million	Nortel shares
Shasta Networks	Apr 16, 1999	US$340 million	Nortel shares
Cambrian	Dec 15, 1998	US$248 million	cash
Bay Networks	Aug 31, 1998	US$6,873 million	Nortel shares
Aptis	Apr 22, 1998	US$286 million	mainly shares
BNI	Jan 9, 1998	US$433 million	mainly shares

Nortel largely used its common stock as "currency" to purchase these companies and acquire their technology. The higher Nortel's stock price, the higher the "price" Nortel could afford to "pay," and therefore the more likely Nortel could prevent competitors from making acquisitions that Nortel itself wanted to make. But what factors drive stock prices up? One theory is that a company's future expected earnings are the key factor. If expected future earnings are greater than what the market would normally require from a company (given the company's risk), the stock price will increase. Conversely, if expected future earnings are lower, the stock price will decrease. Another theory is that stock price movements are sometimes the result of "irrational exuberance."[5]

If the stock market had been "irrationally exuberant" about something, perhaps earnings, and if the capital markets had impounded (in the form of higher stock prices) continually increasingly optimistic expectations about continually increasing positive but abnormal earnings for Nortel, then Nortel (and presumably the capital markets) had a problem. Why? Because at the same time as Nortel was reporting ever-increasing *revenues* (US$15.5 billion in 1997; US$17.6 billion in 1998; and US$22.2 billion in 1999), under generally accepted accounting principles (GAAP) it was also reporting *losses* (a loss of US$569 million in 1998 and a loss of US$197 million in 1999)!

Nortel's reported losses arose mainly from the accounting requirement, enshrined in GAAP, to charge significant portions of the costs of the unproven technology and goodwill it had acquired on its corporate buying spree as expenses against revenue.

Thus, the more Nortel "paid" for high-tech acquisitions with its ever-increasing stock-cum-currency, the higher were these costs, and the lower were its reported earnings. So, if the capital markets had used current reported earnings as one of the inputs for predicting future earnings, these lower reported earnings would have dampened the growth engine. Consequently, the "currency" that Nortel was using to finance its strategic corporate acquisitions might collapse, taking the company (and executive stock options) along with it. In these circumstances, Nortel had good reason to redirect the capital markets' attention away from bottom-line GAAP "earnings" towards something it could control more easily. In other words, Nortel had a communications problem, which Nortel dealt with in two interrelated ways.

First, Nortel used denial. Nortel denied that bottom-line "earnings" were relevant—even "earnings" sanctified by GAAP and an unqualified audit opinion. This approach was implemented more prominently as shown in the following note in the audited financial statements:

3. Supplementary measures of net earnings and earnings per share [amounts in US$]

As a measure to assess financial performance, management utilizes supplementary measures of net earnings and earnings per common share which exclude the impact of Acquisition Related Costs and one-time gains and charges. The supplementary measures of net earnings and earnings per common share are as follows:

	1999	1998	1997
Net earnings (loss) applicable to common shares	$ (197)	$ (569)	$812
Add back:			
Acquisition-related amortization			
Purchased IPR&D	722	1,241	—
Acquired technology	686	228	—
Goodwill*	553	161	—
One-time gains	(264)	(441)	(102)
One-time charges	209	447	95
Net tax impact	16	(2)	(1)
Supplementary measure of net earnings	$1,725	$1,065	$804
Supplementary measure of net earnings per common share	$ 1.28	$ .93	$ .77

...

*Amortization for Bay Networks and all acquisitions subsequent to the acquisition of Bay Networks.
["Purchased IPR&D" refers to "in-process" research and development that Nortel acquired when it acquired these other companies.]

By means of this note, Nortel contended that the better measure of Nortel's financial performance was its "supplementary measure of net earnings" of US$1.725 billion in 1999 (and not the GAAP-computed loss of US$197 million). Nortel was also apparently contending that *real* earnings had increased to (then) present levels from US$804 million in 1997, a spectacular growth rate averaging 47% per year.

There is definitely some irony here. Note 3 is an integral part of the *audited* GAAP-compliant financial statements. Yet, in those audited financial statements, Nortel proclaims the irrelevance of the GAAP-computed and audited earnings number (a loss of US$197 million for 1999), and advocates its replacement by its supplementary or pro forma earnings number (a "profit" of US$1.725 billion for 1999)—and did so despite the auditors having attested to the "fairness" of the financial statements (and the GAAP-based net loss of US$197 million) in their unqualified audit opinion covering all of the audited financial statements, *including the notes.* In effect, what you see (a loss of US$197 million) is not what you really get (a profit of US$1.725 billion).

Nortel also dealt with its communication problem by emphasizing *revenue growth* rather than *current earnings* as the driver of the firm's value. There was nothing unusual about doing this in the heady Internet stock boom from 1997 to 2000. The stock market rhetoric at that time seemed to extol the merits of *revenues* rather than (typically nonexistent) *earnings* as the harbinger of stock value and corporate financial success.

Nortel was competing to acquire Internet technology, so-called "dot.com" companies, market share, and revenues. Yet, to be successful, the company's management needed to boost Nortel's share price—and to do that it had to portray significant revenue growth. Of course, *when* to formally recognize revenue and *how* much revenue to recognize in any accounting period are perennially delicate and ever-contentious points. Perhaps there was enough flexibility in revenue accounting for Nortel to stretch the accounting rules governing revenue recognition—or at least that's what major lawsuits against Nortel contend. The following headline, which appeared in the *Toronto Star,* summarizes one allegation[6]:

Nortel inflated sales, suit claims: 'Pulled forward' $500 million U.S., documents say

If you had invested in Nortel's shares partly on the basis of its financial statements, it would be understandable if you strongly resented the apparent plasticity in the reported accounting results. After all, isn't financial accounting information supposed to present fairly the results of a company's operations and its financial position? And just how widespread is this plasticity? To what extent can we really rely on reported financial results? A partial response to these questions was provided by the independent financial analysis organization Standard & Poor's in a news release dated May 14, 2002 ("Standard & Poor's To Change System For Evaluating Corporate Earnings: Widely-Supported "Core Earnings" Approach to be Applied to Earnings Analyses and Forecasts for US Indices, Company Data and Equity Research"), in which they defined their concept of "core earnings" as the basis upon which they would "evaluate corporate operating earnings of publicly held companies in the United States."

Standard & Poor's went on to define core earnings as GAAP earnings excluding discontinued operations and extraordinary items and "[i]ncluded in Standard & Poor's definition of Core Earnings are employee stock options grant expenses, restructuring charges from on-going operations, write-downs of depreciable or amortizable operating assets, pensions costs and purchased research and development. Excluded from this definition are impairment of goodwill charges, gains or losses from asset sales, pension gains, unrealized gains or losses from hedging activities, merger and acquisition related fees and litigation settlements."

S&P
www.
standardandpoors.
com

Nortel's "supplementary" net earnings, Standard & Poor's "core earnings," and many other earnings measures publicized recently lend an air of confusion to the financial reporting of earnings numbers. There is little doubt that GAAP have deficiencies, as we will show in this book, and thus the desire by companies to disclose and be evaluated by so-called **pro forma** earnings numbers is understandable.

However, this situation has led to a sort of "Wild West" of earnings numbers, prompting organizations such as Standard & Poor's establishment of their own conception of earnings numbers, as above.

Why Financial Statements Are Important

Without adequate high-quality accounting information, investors, employees, unions, creditors, suppliers, governments, and all others who must make decisions regarding companies cannot properly judge the opportunities and risks of investment alternatives, employment opportunities, and so on. To make informed decisions, investors, for example, rely on various kinds of information, including data on the economy, various industries, companies, and products. Complete information from competent sources enhances the ability to make the best decisions. Of course, only later will an investor be able to tell whether his or her investment decision was a good one, or will a supplier think it was wise to have shipped goods to a customer on extended credit terms. What we can tell you now is that *if you want to know more about a company, its current financial health, and its prospects for the future, the best source of information is probably the company's own financial statements. But financial statements require careful interpretation: they must not be accepted at "face value," even if they have an unqualified (i.e., favourable) audit opinion. Financial statements require careful and close reading.*

The economic events and activities that affect a company and that can be translated into accounting numbers are reflected in the company's financial statements. Some financial statements provide a picture of the company at a moment in time; others describe changes that took place over a period of time. Both types provide a basis for evaluating the past and predicting the future. For example, what is the annual rate of sales growth? Are accounts receivable increasing at an even greater rate than sales? How do sales and receivable growth rates compare to those of competitors? What rates of growth can be expected next year? These trends and relationships provide insights into a company's opportunities and risks, including growth and market acceptance, costs, productivity, profitability, and liquidity. Consequently, *a company's financial statements can serve various purposes: as an analytical tool, as a management report card, as an early warning signal, as a basis for prediction, and as a measure of accountability.*

Financial statements contain information that investors need to know in order to decide whether to invest in a company. Others need financial statement information to decide whether to extend credit, negotiate contract terms, or do business with the company. Financial statements serve a critical role in allocating capital in our society. Effective allocation of capital may promote efficient use of resources, encourage innovation, and provide a liquid market for buying and selling securities and for obtaining and granting credit.

Shareholders have learned that published financial statements do not always contain the most up-to-date information about a company's changing economic fortunes. To ensure that important financial news reaches interested parties as soon as possible, companies send press releases or hold meetings with analysts. Press releases typically announce things like contract awards, new product introductions, capital spending plans, or anticipated acquisitions or divestitures.

Although they are not as timely as press releases, periodic financial statements do provide an economic history that is comprehensive and quantitative—and that can therefore be used to gauge company performance. ***For this reason, financial statements are indispensable for developing an accurate profile of ongoing performance and prospects***. Financial reports also help in assessing the company's viability as changes occur in input and output markets, in production technologies, among competitors, or in other economic conditions.

The Nortel example illustrates an even more important lesson: financial statements may sometimes conceal more than they reveal. Indeed, the *Enron* phenomenon and situations like Nortel have created large-scale skepticism about financial accounting and reporting. Enron's external auditor, which was a major public accounting and professional services firm, has failed, with its clients moving to other firms and many of its employees being put out of work. And corporations that had been considered unassailable, such as the General Electric Company in the United States and BCE in Canada, have had their operations, strategies, and accounting subjected to much greater scrutiny.

Epilogue to Our Financial Reporting Vignette About Nortel

In the fall of 2000, one of the authors of this textbook assigned the following project to his students:

> *Read Nortel Networks' 1999 10-K report (filed with the U.S. Securities and Exchange Commission) and prepare a critical evaluation of the company's quality of earnings.*

The term *quality of earnings* will be used throughout this book. Although it will be described in much more detail in Chapter 2, just think of it for now as referring to the "fairness" of all the accounting measurement and disclosure decisions that a company has made, in relation to determination of earnings. For the assignment, the students examined the company's 10-K report in detail. This report, which Nortel had to file with U.S. authorities because it issued securities in the U.S., even though the company was headquartered in Canada, consisted of three main parts: a detailed description of the company, its products, markets, risks, and strategy; a management discussion and analysis; and a set of audited financial statements.

Although Nortel's stock was still being hyped in the marketplace, and its CEO, John Roth, was still regarded as a brilliant Canadian corporate icon, the students concluded that Nortel's quality of earnings was mediocre at best. This conclusion suggests that careful scrutiny of accounting information, in combination with knowledge of the company's operations and strategy gained from the 10-K report, can provide valuable insight into the financial picture that a company paints of itself.

Company-specific data used by investors, analysts, and others come primarily from published financial statements and the company's willingness to provide additional financial and operating data voluntarily. Management has some latitude in deciding what financial information will be made available and when it will be released. For example, even though financial statements must conform to accepted guidelines and standards, management has considerable discretion over the particular accounting procedures used in the statements and over the details contained in supplemental footnotes and related disclosures. To further complicate matters, ***accounting is absolutely not an exact science***. Some financial statement items are measured with a high degree of precision and reliability, such as the amount of cash on deposit in a company bank account. Other items are more judgmental and uncertain because they are derived from estimates of future events, such as product warranty claims.

People who read financial statements must:

- Understand that management can shape the financial information communicated to outside parties.

- Be able to distinguish between financial statement information that is highly reliable and information that is judgmental.

Both weigh heavily in determining the quality of the information in financial statements—and thus the extent to which it should be relied on for decision making. The analytical tools and perspectives in this book will enable you to understand and better interpret the information in financial statements and accompanying disclosures, as well as to appreciate fully the limitations of that information.

Economics of Accounting Information

An important role of financial accounting information is to facilitate economic transactions and thus to foster the efficient allocation of resources among businesses and individuals.[7] Perhaps the most familiar transactions involve raising financial capital. In these cases, a company seeks to attract additional financial resources by issuing common shares or debt securities. Here, financial reports provide information that can reduce investors' uncertainty about the company's opportunities and risks, thus lowering the company's cost of capital. If you think about this for a moment, you can imagine a sort of demand-and-supply model at work. Investors **demand** information regarding the company's opportunities and risks. Because companies wish to raise capital at the lowest possible cost, they have an economic incentive to **supply** the information investors want. In this section, we will see that the amount and type of financial accounting information provided by companies may depend on demand and supply forces much like those affecting any other economic commodity.

Financial statements are demanded because of their value as a source of information about the company's performance, financial condition, and stewardship of its resources. People demand financial statements because the data reported in them may improve decision making. *The supply of financial information is affected by the costs of producing and disseminating it and the benefits it will provide to the company.* Firms are thought to weigh the benefits they may gain from financial disclosures against the costs they incur in making those disclosures. Of course, regulatory bodies such as the provincial securities commissions and the Accounting Standards Board (AcSB) of the Canadian Institute of Chartered Accountants (CICA) influence the amount and type of financial information that companies disclose as well as when it is disclosed.

Demand for Enterprise Financial Statements

A company's financial statements are demanded by several groups, including:

1. Shareholders and other investors.
2. Managers and employees.
3. Lenders and suppliers.
4. Customers.
5. Government and regulatory agencies.

Shareholders and Other Investors

Shareholders and other investors, such as investors in a company's bonds, including investment advisors, use financial information to help choose a portfolio of securities consistent with their individual preferences for risk, return, dividend yield, and liquidity.

Financial statements are crucial in investment decisions that use **fundamental analysis** to identify mispriced securities. Fundamental analysis relies on balance sheet and income statement information, along with industry and macroeconomic data, to forecast future stock price movements. Investors who use this approach consider past sales, earnings, cash flow, product acceptance, and management performance to predict future trends in these financial indicators of a company's success or failure. Then they assess whether a particular stock or group of stocks is undervalued or overvalued at the current market price.

Investors who believe in the **efficient market hypothesis**—and who thus presume they have no insights about company value beyond the current security price—also find financial statement data to be useful. To efficient market investors, financial statement data provide a basis for assessing firm-specific variables, such as risk and dividend yield, that are important to portfolio selection decisions.

Technical analysis—another school of stock market analysis—relies on price and volume movements of stocks and does not concern itself with financial statement numbers.

Of course, investment analysis can be performed by shareholders and investors themselves—or by professional securities analysts who may possess specialized expertise or economies of scale in the acquisition, interpretation, and analysis of financial statements.

Shareholders and investors also use financial statement information when evaluating the performance of the company's top executives. When earnings and share price performance fall below acceptable levels, dissatisfied shareholders voice their complaints to management and outside directors. If this approach doesn't work, dissident shareholders may launch a campaign (proxy contest) to elect their own slate of directors at the next annual meeting. Activist investors often see this as a buying opportunity. By purchasing shares of the underperforming company at a bargain price, these investors hope to gain by joining forces with existing shareholders and "voting the incompetents out!"

Company performance as described in recent financial statements often becomes the focal point of the proxy contest. Management defends its record of past accomplishments while perhaps acknowledging a need for improvement in some areas of the business. Dissident shareholders point to management's past failures and the need to hire a new executive team. Of course, both sides are pointing to the same financial statements. Where one side sees success, the other sees only failure—and undecided shareholders must be capable of forming their own opinions on the matter.

The **efficient market hypothesis**, in its "semi-strong" form, says a share's current market price reflects all public information. Those who adhere to this theory consider it futile to seek undervalued or overvalued stocks or to forecast market movements using financial statements or other public data, because any new development is quickly reflected in a firm's share price. This perspective does not entirely preclude using financial statements for investment decisions, because financial information about a firm is still valuable for predicting the share's systematic risk (or Beta). Systematic risk remains important to the investment decision even if markets are efficient.

Managers, Employees, and Unions

Although managers regularly make operating and financing decisions based on information that is much more detailed and timely than the information found in financial statements, they also need—and therefore demand—financial statement data. Their demand arises from contracts, such as executive compensation agreements, that are linked to financial statement variables.

Executive compensation contracts frequently contain annual bonus and longer term pay components that are tied to financial statement results. Using accounting data in this manner may increase the efficiency of executive compensation contracts.

Rather than trying to determine whether a manager has performed capably during the year, and thus whether the manager deserves a bonus, the board of directors' compensation committee only needs to look at reported profitability or some other accounting measure that is an index of the company's, and thus the manager's, performance.

Employees demand financial statement information for several reasons: because of the increasing popularity of employee profit sharing and employee stock ownership plans (ESOPs); because of the need to monitor the health of company-sponsored pension plans and to gauge the likelihood that promised benefits will be provided upon retirement; because union contracts may link negotiated wage increases to the company's financial performance; and more generally because it helps them gauge their company's current and potential future profitability and solvency. In collective bargaining between a company and the union representing a group of its employees, accounting information about the company's earnings is often an important issue in assessing whether a company has the ability to pay a demanded compensation increase.

Lenders and Suppliers

Financial statements play several roles in the ongoing relationship between the company and those who supply financial capital. Commercial lenders (banks, trust companies, insurance companies, and pension funds) use financial statement information to help decide the loan amount, the interest rate, and the security that is needed for a business loan. Loan agreements contain contractual provisions (called **covenants**) that require the borrower to maintain minimum levels of working capital, interest coverage, or other key accounting variables that provide a safety net to the lender. Violation of these loan provisions can result in technical default and allow the lender to accelerate repayment, to request additional security, or to raise interest rates. So lenders monitor financial statement data to ascertain whether the covenants are being violated.

Suppliers demand financial statements for many reasons. A steel company may sell millions of dollars of rolled steel to an appliance manufacturer on credit. Before extending credit, careful suppliers scrutinize the buyer's financial position in much the same way that a commercial bank does—and for essentially the same reason. That is, suppliers assess the financial strength of their customers in order to determine whether they will be paid for goods shipped. Suppliers then continue to monitor the financial health of companies with whom they have a business relationship.

Customers

Repeat purchases and product guarantees or warranties create continuing relationships between a company and its customers. A buyer needs to know if its supplier has the financial strength to deliver a high-quality product on an agreed-upon schedule and if the supplier will be able to provide technical support after the sale. You wouldn't buy a personal computer from a door-to-door vendor without first checking out the product and the company that stands behind it. Financial statement information can help current and potential customers monitor a supplier's financial health and thus decide on whether to purchase that supplier's goods and services.

Government and Regulatory Agencies

Government and regulatory agencies demand financial statement information for various reasons.

Taxing authorities sometimes use financial statement information as a basis for establishing tax policies designed to enhance social welfare. For example, the Canadian government could use aggregate reported financial results as a means for

In most industrialized countries, the accounting rules that businesses are allowed to use for external reporting purposes differ from the accounting rules required for taxation purposes. Only in a few countries—most notably, France—are firms compelled to use financial reporting methods that conform to taxation rules. Canada allows divergence between the rules used to compute taxable income and those used for shareholder reports. As a consequence, corporate financial-reporting choices are seldom influenced by the *Income Tax Act.*

justifying tax policy changes such as instituting an investment tax credit during economic downturns.

Government organizations are often customers of businesses. For example, the Canadian army purchases weapons from suppliers whose contracts might guarantee an agreed-upon profit margin. In that setting, financial statement information is essential to the resolution of contractual disputes between the army and its suppliers, and for monitoring whether companies engaged in government business are earning profits beyond what the contracts allow.

Financial statement information is used to regulate businesses—especially public utilities, such as gas and electric companies. To achieve economies of scale in the production and distribution of natural gas and electricity, governments have historically granted exclusive franchises to individual gas and electric companies serving a specified area. In exchange for this monopoly privilege, the rates these companies are permitted to charge consumers are closely regulated. Accounting measures of profit and of asset values are essential because the accounting **rate of return**—reported profits divided by asset book value—is a key factor that regulators use in setting allowable charges.[8] (Recently, however, various Canadian provincial governments have moved to deregulate utilities and introduce competition.)

Banks, trust companies, insurance companies, and other financial institutions are also subject to regulation aimed at protecting individual customers and society from insolvency losses, for example, the inability of a bank to honour requests for the withdrawal of funds or the failure of an insurance company to provide compensation for covered damages as promised are undesirable outcomes to be avoided. Financial statements aid regulators in monitoring the health of these companies so that corrective action can be taken when needed.

Recap

Financial statement information can help to reduce uncertainty about a company's future profitability or economic health. This information also provides evidence about the quality of the company's management, about its ability to fulfill its obligations under supply agreements or labour contracts, or about other facets of the company's business activities. Financial statements are in demand because they provide information that may help improve decision making or make it possible to monitor managers' activities.

Disclosure Incentives and the Supply of Financial Information

Certain financial statement users, such as venture capitalists and bankers, sometimes possess enough bargaining power that they can compel companies to deliver the financial information they need for analysis. For example, a cash-starved company applying for a bank loan has strong incentives to provide all the data the lender requests. But most people who use financial statements are less fortunate. They must rely on mandated reporting, the willingness of a company to disclose more than what is required, and sources outside the company for the information needed to make decisions.

What forces prompt management's willingness to supply information? Browse through several corporate financial reports and you should notice substantial differences across companies—and perhaps over time—in the quality and quantity of the information they provide.

For example, some companies routinely disclose operating profits, production levels, and order backlogs by major product category so that analysts can quickly spot changes in product costs and market acceptance. Other companies provide rich verbal descriptions of their outstanding debt and their efforts to hedge interest rate risk or foreign currency risk. Still other companies seem to disclose only the bare minimum required. What might explain this apparent diversity in quality and quantity of financial information?

If the financial reporting environment were unregulated, disclosure might occur voluntarily as long as the incremental benefits to the company and its management from supplying financial information exceeded the incremental costs of providing that information. In other words, management's decisions about the scope, timing, and content of the company's financial statements and accompanying notes would be guided solely by the same cost and benefit considerations that influence the supply of any other commodity. Managers would assess the benefits created by voluntary disclosures and weigh these benefits against the costs of making the information available. Any differences in financial and nonfinancial disclosures across companies and over time would then be due to differences in the benefits or costs of voluntarily supplying financial information.

But, in fact, financial reporting in Canada and in many other developed countries is regulated by laws such as the *Canada Business Corporations Act* (CBCA) and by nongovernmental private sector organizations such as the CICA. The various public and private sector regulatory agencies establish and enforce financial reporting requirements **designed to ensure that companies meet certain minimum levels of financial disclosure.**[9] But companies frequently communicate financial information that exceeds these minimum levels. They apparently believe that the benefits of the "extra" disclosures outweigh the costs. What are the perceived benefits from voluntary disclosures that exceed minimum requirements?

Disclosure Benefits Companies compete with one another in capital, labour, output, and input markets. This competition creates incentives for management to reveal "good news" financial information about the firm. The news itself may be about a successful new product introduction, increased consumer demand for an existing product, an effective quality improvement, or other matters. By voluntarily disclosing otherwise unknown good news, the company may be able to obtain capital more cheaply or get better terms from suppliers.

To see how these incentives work, consider the market for financial capital. Companies try to raise capital at the lowest possible cost. They compete with one another both in terms of the returns they promise to capital suppliers and in terms of the characteristics of the financial instrument offered. Two important features of the capital market are:

1. Investors are uncertain about the quality of each offered instrument because the ultimate return from the security depends on future events.
2. It is costly for the company to be mistakenly perceived as offering a low-quality stock or bond—a "lemon."[10]

This lemon cost could be in the form of lower proceeds received from issuing shares, a higher interest rate that will have to be paid on a commercial loan, or more stringent conditions placed on that loan.

Given these market characteristics, owners and managers have an economic incentive to supply the amount and type of financial information that will enable them to raise capital on the best available terms. A company offering truly attractive, low-risk securities, for example, can avoid the lemon penalty by voluntarily supplying the amount and type of financial information that enables investors and lenders to properly gauge the risk and expected return of each instrument it offers. Of course, companies offering higher risk securities have incentives to mask their true condition by supplying overly optimistic financial information. However, there are offsetting forces that partially mitigate this tendency. Examples include requirements for audited financial statements and legal penalties associated with issuing false or misleading financial statements. Furthermore, managers want to maintain access to capital markets and establish a reputation for supplying credible financial information to capital market participants. ***Financial statement disclosures can convey economic benefits to firms—and thus to their owners and managers. However, firms cannot obtain these benefits at zero cost.***

Disclosure Costs Four potential costs can arise from informative financial disclosures:

1. Information collection, processing, and dissemination costs.
2. Competitive disadvantage costs.
3. Litigation costs.
4. Political costs.

The costs associated with **financial information collection, processing, and dissemination** can be large. Determining the company's obligation for postretirement employee health-care benefits provides an example. This disclosure requires numerous complicated actuarial computations as well as health-care cost projections for existing or anticipated medical treatments. Whether companies compile the data themselves or hire employee-benefit consultants to do it, the cost of generating a reasonable estimate of the company's postretirement obligation can be considerable. The costs of developing and presenting financial information also include the cost of auditing the accounting statement item (if the information is audited). Owners ultimately pay all of these costs, just as they ultimately bear all other company costs.

Another potential cost associated with financial disclosure is in the way competitors may use the information against the company that is providing the disclosure. Among the types of disclosures—financial and nonfinancial—that might create a **competitive disadvantage** are:

- Details about the company's strategies, plans, and tactics, such as new product development, pricing strategies, or new customer markets.

- Information about the company's technological and managerial innovations, such as innovative manufacturing and distribution systems, successful process redesign, continuous quality improvement techniques, or uniquely effective marketing approaches.

- Detailed information about company operations, such as sales and production cost figures for individual product lines or narrow geographical markets.

Disclosing sales and profitability by product line or geographical area may highlight opportunities previously unknown to competitors, thereby undermining a company's competitive advantage. And even though the *CICA Handbook* in Section 1520.04 urges (but doesn't require) companies to disclose "the amount of cost of goods sold," many Canadian companies do not. For example, Hudson's Bay

ALCAN ALUMINUM
LIMITED
www.alcan.com

Company and Alcan Aluminum Limited do not disclose this important number in their published income statements.

If labour unions or suppliers use the company's financial information to improve their bargaining power, the company's costs may increase and thus possibly weaken its competitive advantage.

Litigation costs result when shareholders, creditors, and other financial statement users initiate court actions against the company and its management for financial misrepresentation. For example, shareholders may initiate litigation when there's a sudden drop in stock price. If the price falls soon after the company has released new financial information to the marketplace, shareholders may sue the company and claim damages based on the share price decline. These shareholders argue they would not have committed financial capital to the company if they had known then (when they bought the stock) what they know now (after the company's disclosure). The Enron case is a recent example.

The costs of defending against suits, even those that are without merit, can be substantial. Apart from legal fees and settlement costs, there is the damage to corporate and personal reputations and the distraction of executives from productive activities that would otherwise add value to the company.

There are potential **political costs** of financial reporting, especially for companies in highly visible industries like oil or banking. Politically vulnerable firms with record high earnings are often attacked in the financial and popular press, which allege that those earnings constitute evidence of anticompetitive business practices. Politicians sometimes respond to (or exploit) heightened public opinion by proposing solutions to the "crisis" that is causing high earnings, thereby gaining media exposure for themselves and improving their chances for re-election or reappointment. Demands to roll back or regulate bank charges and to prevent bank mergers in the late 1990s were a direct result of what many in the media and elsewhere argued were excessive profits reported by the large Canadian banks.

Antimonopoly or combines litigation, environmental regulations, and the rescinding of protective import quotas are further examples of the costs politicians and government bureaucrats can impose on unpopular companies and industries. Financial reports are one source of information that politicians and bureaucrats can use to target firms or industries. For this reason, astute managers carefully weigh political considerations when choosing what financial information to report and how best to report it. As a result, some highly profitable—but politically vulnerable—firms may make themselves appear less profitable than they really are.[11]

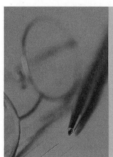

Recap

A company's financial reporting decisions are plausibly driven partly by economic considerations—and thus by cost-benefit tradeoffs. Companies that confront distinctly different competitive pressures in the marketplace and that face different financial reporting costs and benefits are likely to choose different accounting and reporting practices. A clear understanding of the economic factors that influence a company's financial reporting choices can help you to assess more keenly the quality of the information provided. That's what we'll help you do in this textbook.

A Closer Look at Professional Analysts

Different types of users of accounting information—investors, lenders, customers, suppliers, managers, employees, and so on—find corporate financial statements useful for their own decision-making needs. ***Financial statement users have diverse information needs because they face different decisions or may use different approaches to making the same kind of decision.*** For example, a retail customer deciding which brand of automobile to purchase needs far less financial information about each automotive manufacturer than a long-term equity investor who is planning to purchase common shares in one of those companies. Similarly, a commercial banker engaged in asset-based lending—meaning the loan is collateralized by the borrower's product inventory or receivables—needs far different financial information about the business than a banker who lends solely on the basis of the borrower's projected future cash flows.

It would be enormously difficult (perhaps impossible!) to frame our examination of corporate financial reporting and analysis around the diverse information needs of all potential users and the varied decisions they might possibly confront. So instead we will focus attention on professional analysts. But we define **analyst** broadly to include investors, creditors, union advisors, financial advisors, and auditors—anyone who uses financial statements to make decisions as part of his or her job. Let's see what professional analysts do.

Analysts' Decisions

The main task confronting **equity investors** (people who invest in a company's shares) is to form educated opinions about the absolute and relative value of companies and their equity securities (common and preferred stock), and then to make investment decisions based on those opinions. Investors who follow a *fundamental analysis approach* estimate the value of a security by assessing the amount, timing, and uncertainty of future cash flows that will accrue to the company issuing the security. The company's financial statements and other data are used to develop projections of its future cash flows. These cash flow estimates are then discounted for risk and the time value of money. Next, the discounted cash flow estimate is compared, on a per-share basis, to the current price of the company's stock, thus allowing the investor to decide whether to buy, hold, or sell the stock.[12]

Several other valuation approaches are used by investors. One is to estimate a company's **liquidation value**. For example, the investor would try to determine the total value of the company's assets if sold individually, and then subtract any debt the company owes. Another approach is to compute the price-to-earnings (or cash flow-to-earnings) ratio for other companies in the industry and then to apply that ratio to the company's current or projected earnings. Still other approaches rely on predictions of the company's quarterly earnings (or cash flow), changes in earnings, and changes in trends of earnings to identify possible short-term changes in the price of the company's equity securities.

Financial statement information is essential, in one way or another, to all these equity investment strategies.

The task confronting **creditors** is to assess the company's ability to meet its debt-related financial obligations through the timely payment of interest and principal, or through asset liquidation in the event that interest and principal cannot be repaid. Creditors include banks, trust companies, insurance companies, and other lenders, suppliers who sell to the company on credit, and those who invest in the company's publicly traded debt securities. Creditors form educated opinions about the company's **credit risk** by comparing principal and interest payments to estimates of the company's current and future cash flows. Companies that are good credit risks have projected operating cash flows that are more than sufficient to meet these debt payments. Credit risk assessments are also influenced by the company's **financial flexibility**, which is the ability to raise additional cash by selling assets, issuing stock, or borrowing more.

Companies judged to be high credit risks are charged higher rates of interest and may have more stringent conditions—referred to as **covenants**—placed on their loan agreements. These loan covenants may restrict the company from paying dividends, selling nonoperating assets, buying other companies, or borrowing additional funds without prior approval by the lender. Other types of covenants, particularly those based on reported accounting figures, protect the lender from a deterioration in the borrower's credit risk. Creditors use financial statement information to monitor the company's ongoing ability to comply with lending agreement covenants.

Financial advisors include securities analysts, brokers, portfolio managers, industry consultants, and others who provide information and advice to investors and creditors. They are often able to gather, process, and evaluate financial information more economically and accurately than individual investors and creditors, because they possess specialized skills or knowledge (e.g., industry expertise) or because they have access to specialized resources provided by their organizations. As a consequence, financial advisors can play a crucial role in the decision-making process of investors and creditors. Securities analysts, in particular, are among the most important and influential users of financial statements.

Independent auditors carefully examine financial statements prepared by the company prior to conducting an audit of those statements. An understanding of management's reporting incentives coupled with an understanding of reporting rules enables auditors to recognize vulnerable areas where financial reporting abuses are likely to occur. Astute auditors choose audit procedures designed to ensure that major improprieties can be detected.

Current auditing standards encourage independent auditors to use analytical review procedures on each engagement.[13] These tools are growing more popular and sophisticated each year. Why? Because they can help auditors and financial analysts avoid the embarrassment and economic loss of market "surprises," such as the one that occurred at Enron.

Independent auditors need to be well versed in the techniques of financial analysis in order to design effective audits. That's why auditors are included among those people we call analysts. Current auditing standards echo the lessons of past audit failures: *You can't build a foolproof audit unless you know how the game is played.* That means understanding the incentives of managers and knowing how to analyze financial information and conditions.

Analysts' Information Needs

What specific information about a company do professional analysts want? What types of information are most useful in predicting a company's earnings and cash flows when valuing its equity securities, assessing its debt repayment prospects, and evaluating audit vulnerabilities? Professional analysts say the following three types of financial information are needed:

1. Quarterly and annual financial statements along with nonfinancial operating and performance data that are used to manage the company's businesses.

2. Management's analysis of financial and nonfinancial data including reasons for changes in the financial and operating data along with key trends and a discussion of the past effect of those trends.

3. Information that makes it possible both to identify the future opportunities and risks confronting each of the company's businesses and to evaluate management's plans for the future.[14]

A company's financial statements provide professional investors, creditors, financial advisors, and auditors with information that heavily influences their decisions. Published financial reports of public companies also contain a **management's discussion and analysis (MD&A)** section that describes the financial condition of the company and the results of its operations. MD&A is one of the ways management communicates the reasons for changes in financial and operating data. Because management presumably understands the business, MD&A disclosures are an important information source for analysts. MD&A serves as the point where professional analysts start forming their own assessment of the business reasons for changes in financial condition or performance. This is especially true when the MD&A also contains forward-looking information about changing business opportunities and risks and about management's plans for the company.[15]

Some of the information needed by professional analysts is contained in nonfinancial statement documents. For example, annual proxy statements furnished to shareholders contain information about the credentials of senior corporate executives and directors, about management compensation and ownership, and about the identity of major shareholders. Trade journals, industry surveys, and various other sources contain information about current and potential competitors, changing technologies and markets, threats from substitute products or services, and the bargaining power of customers and suppliers. Such information is essential to those who want to form a complete picture of a company's opportunities and risks—and its prospects for the future.

> Companies and securities legislation require that corporations solicit votes of shareholders, since many shareholders will not be physically present at meetings to vote directly on corporate matters. This solicitation is called a proxy, and the information that accompanies it is called the **proxy statement** or **management information circular**. Annual meetings are required by corporation laws. The proxy statement for annual meetings will—among other things—provide information regarding nominees for directors, the recommended auditor for the ensuing year, the compensation of the five highest-paid executives, proposed changes in compensation plans, and other matters that periodically arise (such as shareholder proposals of various kinds).

Recap
Financial statement information helps equity investors assess the value of companies and their securities; it helps creditors assess the company's ability both to meet its debt payments and to abide by loan terms; it helps financial advisors and securities analysts provide information and advice to investors and creditors; and it helps auditors both to recognize potential financial reporting abuses and to choose audit procedures to detect them.

The Rules of the Financial Reporting Game

Professional analysts and other users of financial reporting are typically forward-looking. They consider future expectations when they assess the value of a company and its prospects for debt repayment. Financial statements and footnotes present an economic history of transactions and other events affecting the current condition of the company. Financial statements provide analysts with information about the past, thus giving them a basis for generating forecasts of future events, especially future earnings and cash flows.

To extrapolate into the future from financial statement data, investors, creditors, and their financial advisors must first understand the accounting measurement rules used to produce the data. Financial statements present a sort of financial picture of the company at a point in time, a picture that translates many (but not all) of the economic events affecting the business into financial terms. For example, the act of providing goods and services to customers in exchange for promised future cash payments is translated by the company's accounting system into financial statement amounts known as "sales revenue" and "accounts receivable." This linkage between economic events and how those events are depicted in a financial statement can sometimes seem mysterious or confusing to the analyst. For example, some companies record sales revenue in advance of actual delivery of the goods to customers. Other companies record revenue at the date of delivery to customers. And still others postpone recording revenue until payment for the goods is received from the customer. We'll now look more closely at the rules that govern accounting and financial reporting practices.

Generally Accepted Accounting Principles

Over time, the accounting profession in Canada and elsewhere has developed a network of conventions, rules, guidelines, and procedures, collectively referred to as **generally accepted accounting principles (GAAP)**. The principles and rules that govern financial reporting develop and evolve in response to changing business conditions. Consider, for example, the lease of retail store space at a shopping centre or mall. As people moved from the city to the suburbs, shopping centres emerged as convenient and accessible alternatives to traditional urban retail stores. Leasing became a popular alternative to ownership because it enabled retailing companies to gain access to store space without having to bear the burden of the large dollar outlay necessary to buy or build the store. Leasing was also attractive because it shared risks—like the competition provided by a new mall opening nearby—between the retailer and shopping mall owner. As leasing increased in popularity, it was left to the accounting profession to develop standards—some of which are quite complex—that were to be followed when accounting for leases. The guidelines that evolved are now part of GAAP and are discussed in detail in Chapter 12.

The overriding but rarely achieved goal of GAAP is to assure that financial statements represent faithfully and clearly the economic condition and performance of the company. To achieve this goal, accounting standard-setters contend that financial statements should possess certain qualitative characteristics that are important to the needs of professional analysts. These include:[16]

- **Relevance**. Financial information capable of making a difference in a decision. Relevant information helps users form more accurate predictions about the future, or it allows them to better understand how past economic events have affected the business.

- **Timeliness**. Making information available to decision makers before it loses its capacity to influence their decisions.

- **Reliability**. Financial information that is verifiable, faithfully represented, and reasonably free of error and bias.

    a. **Verifiability**. Independent measurers get similar results when using the same measurement methods. For example, the 2001 sales revenues of $6,152 million reported by Noranda Inc. are verifiable to the extent that knowledgeable accountants and auditors would agree on this amount after examining the company's sales transactions for the year. In this regard, verifiability refers to the degree of consensus among measurers.

b. **Representational faithfulness**. The degree to which the information represents what it purports to represent. It is the extent of correspondence between the accounting measurement and the underlying economic events represented by that measurement. If a company's balance sheet reports trade accounts payable of $423.8 million when the company actually owes suppliers $460.0 million, then the reported figure is not a faithful representation. One problem with Enron's accounting was that the company's financial statements didn't faithfully represent the totality of the company's financial position since certain assets and liabilities were only accounted for in so-called "special purpose entities" that were not consolidated into the Enron statements.

c. **Neutrality**. Information cannot be selected to favour one set of interested parties over another. For example, accountants cannot allow a company to suppress information in its financial statement footnotes about trademark infringement lawsuits against the company even though such disclosure is embarrassing. Thus, avoiding bias and error is crucial.

- **Comparability**. Financial information measured and reported in a similar manner among different companies. Comparability allows analysts to identify real economic similarities and differences among companies, because those differences and similarities are not obscured by accounting methods or disclosure practices.

- **Consistency**. The same accounting methods used to describe similar events from period to period. Consistency allows analysts to identify trends—and changes in trends—in the economic condition and performance of a company over time, because the trends are not obscured by changes in accounting methods or disclosure practices.

No single accounting method has all of these characteristics all of the time. In fact, GAAP frequently require financial statement users to accept a compromise that favours some qualitative characteristics over others. For example, GAAP financial statements would show an office building at its historical cost (original purchase price) minus accumulated depreciation. The most *relevant* measure of the office building for decisions, such as to keep or to sell, is often the discounted present value of its expected rental revenues. But this measure is argued to be not as *reliable* or *verifiable* as historical cost because future vacancy rates are unpredictable. GAAP's use of historical cost trades off increased reliability and verifiability for decreased relevance. Qualitative tradeoffs such as this often make it difficult to identify "good" accounting methods and disclosure practices.

> Companies can change accounting methods, but the changes are restricted to situations where it can be argued that the newly adopted accounting method is "preferable" to the old one. Companies that change accounting methods must disclose the nature and effect of the accounting change—as well as the justification for it—in the financial statements for the period in which the change is made. Common justifications include "to conform to industry practice" (i.e., improved comparability) and "more accurately represents the company's activities" (i.e., greater representational faithfulness).

Who Determines the Rules?

GAAP come from two main sources:

1. Written pronouncements by designated organizations.
2. Accounting practices that have evolved over time.

Written GAAP in Canada are produced by the CICA's AcSB, which has representation from all three professional accounting groups in Canada—the Canadian Institute of Chartered Accountants (CICA), the Certified General Accountants

CICA
www.cica.ca

CGA-CANADA
www.
cga-canada.org

CMA CANADA
www.
cma-canada.org

Association of Canada (CGA-Canada), and the Society of Management Accountants of Canada (CMA Canada)—as well as other constituents affected by accounting. In 1972, securities legislation administrators in several provinces issued an important document called National Policy No. 27, which:

> *stated that the securities administrators would regard* CICA Handbook *pronouncements as "generally accepted accounting principles" as that term was used in either securities legislation or companies legislation. ... As a result of this policy, the* CICA Handbook *has, in effect, taken on the status of law with respect to most filings under the jurisdiction of provincial securities acts. In 1975, the same result was brought about with respect to annual financial statements for companies under federal jurisdiction, as a result of the inclusion of a reference to the* CICA Handbook *in the regulations to the ... Canada Business Corporations Act.*[17]

In the United States, the federal government, through the SEC, has had the ultimate authority to determine the rules to be followed in preparing financial statements by companies whose securities are sold to the general public. This authority was given to the Commission when it was established in 1934 by Congress in response to the severe stock market decline of 1929. The SEC requires companies to file both annual *and* quarterly financial statements as well as other types of reports.

Although the SEC has the ultimate legal authority to set accounting principles in the U.S., it has delegated its authority to the accounting profession. The Financial Accounting Standards Board (FASB) is the organization that currently sets accounting standards in the United States. Although the FASB receives funding from various sources, it exists as an independent group.

The relative importance of *national* accounting standard setting (e.g., by the CICA's AcSB in Canada and the FASB in the United States) appears to be diminishing in favour of some system of *international* standard setting. The CICA went on record as supporting "the objective of harmonizing accounting standards internationally" in Section 1501 of the *CICA Handbook* ("International Accounting Standards"). An important caveat, however, is that while the United States is the most powerful supplier of capital and thus exerts tremendous influence over accounting standards worldwide, such harmonization of standards should not simply be the unquestioning acceptance of U.S. FASB pronouncements. Indeed, in its *Final Report* released in late summer 1998, the CICA Task Force on Standard Setting, while espousing the long-term goal of "one set of internationally accepted accounting standards in the private sector" (p. 2), was careful to explain that "harmonization" meant that such accounting standards were to be "arrived at following a process of input and negotiation among the relevant standard-setting bodies. This interpretation still allows a national body to set its own standards, but assumes that it will do so only in the event it can clearly demonstrate that its country's circumstances are unique" (p. 3).

Adversarial Nature of Financial Reporting

Many of the rules that comprise current GAAP are imprecise. They allow managers a degree of flexibility in choosing specific accounting techniques and reporting procedures—and therefore they are open to interpretation.

Managers frequently have reasons to exploit this flexibility. Their interests may conflict with the interests of shareholders, lenders, and others who rely on financial statement information to make decisions. Some companies adopt exemplary reporting standards, while others tend to be less forthright. Analysts who understand these conflicting incentives as well as the flexibility available under GAAP will see that a decision based on uncritical acceptance of financial statement data may turn out to be naive—and dangerous.

The flexibility of GAAP financial reporting standards provides opportunities to use accounting tricks that make the company seem less risky than it really is. For instance, some economic liabilities like equipment leases can be transformed into off-balance-sheet (and thus less visible) items. The company would then appear, from the balance sheet data, to have less debt and more borrowing capacity than is really the case. Commercial lenders who fail to spot off-balance-sheet liabilities of this sort can underestimate the risk inherent in their loan portfolios.

As another example, companies can **smooth** reported earnings by strategically timing the recognition of revenues and expenses. This strategy projects an image of a stable company that can easily service its debt, even in a severe business downturn. The benefits of such deceptions can be vast if lenders are fooled.[18] Furthermore, once the loan amount is received, the company has additional incentives to report its financial results in ways that circumvent default on loan covenants tied to accounting numbers.

Self-interest sometimes drives managers to manipulate the reported financial statement numbers in order to earn bonuses linked to sales or earnings targets. For example, if earnings are down late in the fiscal year, deliveries of product may be accelerated to increase recognized revenues and income before year's end. Similarly, managers can delay discretionary expenses like building repairs and maintenance if earnings are expected to be too low. On the other hand, if earnings are comfortably above the bonus goal, managers may write off obsolete equipment and inventory or increase reserves for uncollectible trade receivables, whereas those same accounting adjustments may be postponed if earnings are inadequate.

Another way in which financial reporting practices can be molded to suit management's interests is to downplay the significance of contingent liabilities—like unresolved product liability lawsuits—that may affect the value of the firm. There are many reasons why management's disclosure of a major legal contingency is likely to understate its true significance. In a lawsuit, candid disclosure could compromise the company's case. Similarly, public disclosure of impending financial hardships may harm the company if creditors respond by accelerating loan repayment schedules, by curtailing trade credit, or by seeking liquidation of the business.

This discussion states the case boldly and portrays the motives underlying financial reporting practices in an unflattering light. To be sure, most companies strive to provide fair and reasonable disclosure of their financial affairs. Of these companies, some are undoubtedly motivated as much by honour and integrity as by the knowledge that they will be rewarded for doing so. Nevertheless, there are companies that take full advantage of the leeway available under GAAP. The list includes Livent Inc., Philip Services Inc., and Cinar Corp., among others, in Canada, and Sunbeam Corp., Cendant Corp., and Waste Management Inc., in the U.S. And let's not forget Enron and WorldCom!

GAAP provide constraints that limit the range of financial statement manipulation. But these constraints are not always adequate and transparent. Auditors and the courts further counterbalance opportunistic financial reporting practices. Nevertheless, the analyst should recognize the adversarial nature of financial reporting, maintain a healthy skepticism, and understand that financial disclosures sometimes conceal more than they reveal. The flexibility inherent in GAAP can have dire consequences for those caught unawares.

Challenges Confronting Users of Financial Statement Information

Over the past several years, financial statements have become increasingly more complex partly because the business world has become more dynamic and complicated, and also partly because users of financial statements have demanded more information.

Global competition and the spread of various forms of capitalism throughout the world has prompted businesses to rely increasingly on foreign countries as a market for products and services, and as a source of capital. Competitive pressures have also contributed to a fundamental change in the way businesses organize and finance their activities. Corporate restructurings and mergers occur frequently. New types of financial instruments have become commonplace mechanisms through which companies raise capital and claim to manage risk. Financial service firms now represent a major portion of business activity. These and other features of the changing business landscape pose difficult challenges for contemporary financial reporting practices—and for an accounting model originally developed to fit companies engaged in local manufacturing and merchandising.

There has also been explosive growth in the use of electronic means to assemble and examine financial information in the last two decades. The accessibility of computers and software continues to rise as their cost falls. Quantitative analysis of financial data has become increasingly practicable, which in turn has meant increasing demand for and use of electronic databases containing financial information. Corporate press releases, analysts' research reports, historical financial data, and complete annual and quarterly financial reports are now readily available in electronic form through commercial vendors. Canadian public companies post considerable financial information on their websites. Also, many Canadian companies' financial documents are on file with the System for Electronic Document Analysis and Retrieval, or SEDAR. Documents filed with the U.S. SEC can now be accessed through its Electronic Data Gathering and Retrieval system (EDGAR).

SEDAR
www.sedar.com

EDGAR
www.sec.gov

In addition, accounting standards literature is now available on the Internet and on CD-ROM, with search capabilities.

These developments provide new opportunities for, and place new burdens on, analysts. On the one hand, there is a wealth of financial statement data and related information available to the analyst at relatively low cost. On the other hand, firms today operate in a dynamic environment that has made the task of assimilating and analyzing financial statements even more complex. The financial reporting practices of business firms are continually challenged on many fronts, and the astute analyst must remain vigilant to the possibility that financial reports sometimes do not capture underlying economic realities. Indeed, the advent of corporate financial reporting on the Internet suggests that the very *nature* of financial reporting may be undergoing profound changes.[19]

The Rhetoric of Financial Reporting on the Internet

The Internet is helping to create a new, rapidly growing, and influential corporate financial reporting environment. It was only as recently as 2001 that the CICA and the *National Post* introduced a category for "electronic disclosure" in their Annual

Report Awards. The website of Barrick Gold Corporation, the first Gold winner out of 92 companies entered in this category, was described by evaluators as "a true example of how corporations today need to embrace the web to forge deeper relationships with their stakeholders." Onex Corporation and Potash Corporation of Saskatchewan rounded out the top three companies in this new category.[20] With so many prestigious Canadian companies turning to the Internet for their financial reporting, it is important that stakeholders develop the tools to analyze the messages being directed to them.

In this part of Chapter 1, we describe "rhetorical" features of web-based financial reporting—in other words, the ways in which the messages conveyed by hypertext (including links to electronic documents such as text, graphics, photos, sound effects, and multimedia) are introduced to influence readers' perceptions of financial information posted on websites. Our particular focus is not on actual financial numbers and terminology, but on the "prelude" provided by a Chief Executive Officer's letter that is meant to enrich the narrative and condition the reader's response to the information about to be presented. In order to demonstrate how to start thinking about critically examining financial reporting on the web, we will use the Microsoft website as an example, employing the two key steps that are part of a close reading:

MICROSOFT INVESTOR RELATIONS
www.microsoft.com/ msft/ar.htm

1. Examine Placement of Hypertext.
2. Identify and Analyze Metaphors.

Case Study for Internet Reporting: The Microsoft Text[21]

Our analysis of Microsoft Corporation's web-based annual financial reporting information for 1999 was undertaken by accessing Microsoft's website on May 4 and July 19, 2000. (On both dates, most of the information accessed was reported as having been last updated on January 11, 2000.) This website was chosen because the information it contains has been crafted specifically for presentation in a web-based environment, and because Microsoft is a profoundly influential force in web-based technology. The rich range of technological tools used by Microsoft clearly illustrates the generational differences between Internet-based financial reporting, with its use of multimedia and nonlinear hypertext, and paper-based financial reporting. Microsoft has realized the communication power of the Internet as the major medium for its corporate reporting. We are interested in how Microsoft uses this technology to influence the interpretation of its financial reporting.

The following account of a close reading does not claim to be exhaustive. Its focus is on the hyperlink pathway in Microsoft's website that leads readers to the accounting reports. The intent is to provide examples of the variety of insights one can obtain through using the steps that make up a close reading. We used the "Investor Relations" part of Microsoft's website, specifically the 1999 annual report.

1. Examine Placement of Hypertext The first step in our "close reading" is to analyze the placement of hypertext. From the annual report page (www.microsoft.com/msft/ar.htm), we access the 1999 annual report and click on "Read Bill's Letter" (English), where we find a "handwritten" hypertext inscription that says "any time, any place, any device," seeming to float just to the right and above a photograph of Bill Gates.

It's significant that the hypertext "any time, any place, any device" is placed at the beginning of the annual report. We can thus regard this as one of the initial components of the cognitive map that Microsoft uses to prime readers' responses to the accounting information that follows. We'll look at the meanings conveyed by this hypertext when we discuss metaphors in Step 2.

Next, we note the placement of the photo of Bill Gates and the accompanying "Bill's Letter." Immediately they convey the message that "Bill Gates *IS* Microsoft." Gates' photo is positioned above a menu of 11 languages in which readers have the option of viewing the annual report. This positioning means some readers may see Microsoft (as represented by Gates) as being "on top of the world." This association is a subtle means of accentuating the power of Microsoft and of inviting readers to have confidence in their dealings with Microsoft and the corporate reporting to follow.

A key tool for putting Microsoft in a positive light is the president's letter. As usual, this letter is positioned near the beginning of the annual report. But what is unusual, however, is the informal title: *"Bill's Letter."* The role of this letter and Bill's smiling photo and handwritten inscription (discussed in Step 2) should not be ignored for their capacity to personalize Microsoft (through Gates) as a threat-free friend—a "buddy." So, even before encountering the main body of the accounting reports, readers are exposed to a "good news" overture—a "positive spin" on Microsoft. Readers could be forgiven for being comforted by them; for having been conditioned to place increased confidence in the accuracy and reliability of the financial information that is to follow on the website.

2. Identify and Analyze Metaphor

The second step in our "close reading" is to identify and analyze the meanings suggested by the images, visual or verbal, used in the website—in other words, its metaphors. By introducing these metaphors, what impression of the company is Microsoft trying to create? How is the reader's view of Microsoft shaped—consciously or unconsciously—by the messages conveyed by the images?

First, we look at the messages conveyed by visual imagery: the photo of "Bill," the "handwritten" message (is it Bill's very own handwriting?). They are softly seductive and seem intended to influence perception. After all, Bill looks and dresses ordinarily (tousled hair, eyeglasses, an "average" face, etc.). His handwriting is by no means a model for fashionable calligraphy. Thus, the visual metaphor is that "Bill (and through Bill, Microsoft) is human like you and me." However, Bill has at his fingertips an array of powerful Internet-based tools. Bill, an average-looking guy, can perform superior feats by taking advantage of the wonderful Internet world through the mediating influences of the products and worldview made possible by Microsoft. The implied message is that, like Bill, you'll be able to use *any device, any time, any place* to become a more productive (profitable) servant of the corporate economy, whether at work or at (alleged) leisure.

Let's think about the words themselves in the handwritten inscription: "any time, any place, any device." The inscription attempts to make a connection between Microsoft and the lives of the readers of the annual report. The phrase "any time, any place, any device" implies that the company will exist outside of time or place, and that it will be able to satisfy any requirements, at any moment, anywhere. It subliminally shapes readers' views of the company: we are invited to believe that Microsoft, by virtue of the dispersion of its products across the globe, is an inevitable part of life—that Microsoft is all powerful and all conquering, with the capacity to solve problems whenever and wherever they arise.

Next, we note that the inscription itself is a hyperlink; by clicking on it we access a moving montage of photographs. Although this graphic appears in the annual report, it is seemingly of little consequence to the substance of the accounting information and might even be regarded as a distraction to readers. But such apparent "irrelevance" makes it even more important to analyze the effects of the presence of this hypertext material. Why is it here?

Examining the visual content of the hyperlink more closely, we are confronted with a rotating montage of photos of seemingly diverse individuals. Apparently they are either contented customers or stakeholders, all with a common bond to Microsoft's technology. The photos reinforce social sex-role stereotypes, such as suited men in the office, women with children in household settings, and men playing golf. Despite the implied claims of the universal reach of Microsoft, all eight photos appear to be of North Americans, principally white males, and with token Americans of colour. There are seven males and four females depicted. Three of the four females (and none of the men) are depicted in the home.

The "safe," conventional images that Microsoft has selected can be interpreted as visual metaphors that deliberately attempt to make readers feel secure with the company. This is achieved indirectly by reinforcing these somewhat "comfortable" images in the minds of readers as quickly as possible. They are used to promote a feeling of security and, in turn, an affinity with Microsoft's "all-American" values. By denying the existence of other points of view, Microsoft reveals its resistance to any disruption of existing (or perceived) power relationships.

All the metaphors in "Bill's Letter" and the Microsoft website in general could be argued to contain at least partly hidden ideologies. The personification of Microsoft as some sort of friendly uncle, providing sage-like words of wisdom, reinforces a "family values" ideology. With the help of Microsoft in *extending your reach*, readers are encouraged to consider themselves as lesser persons who will thereby develop and become more capable and sophisticated. Finally, the friendly and approachable image of "Bill" is designed to reinforce the perception that such a clean-cut guy could only have sound, reliable, and trustworthy financial information to report. How could anyone not trust such a nice fellow?

Easily, perhaps! Looking critically at these metaphors, we speculate that the image of a friendly Bill Gates plays on the need for a stable grounding in people's lives—a need that is becoming more pronounced by the quickening pace of life in society. Ironically, many people would attribute this quickening to the "digital disturbance" created by the information technology that is Microsoft's lifeblood and that Microsoft largely made possible. Looking again at the photo, we note the depiction of a smiling Bill Gates is somewhat ironic considering the real threats posed by the major antitrust lawsuit that confronted Microsoft in the 1999 financial year. And, more importantly, as we examine these metaphors, we need to keep in mind the effects of the unprecedented domination of social and economic practices by Windows and other Microsoft products.

When interpreting the metaphors Microsoft invokes, then, readers should be aware that they are part of the prelude to the hard, number-based accounting data soon to be reported in the annual report. The metaphors are designed to shape users' views on the corporate information contained therein. Readers should be accordingly cautious.

User Beware!

This introduction to a close reading of Microsoft's web-based financial reporting has demonstrated the idiosyncrasies of an Internet reporting environment and the manner in which hypertext and the metaphors it conveys can be exploited to influence readers. Close reading of Internet-based reporting disclosures has profound implications for corporate disclosure regulation and accounting. Readers should be careful in examining Internet-based corporate reporting. Further, the presentation of the reporting should cause readers to re-evaluate the essential "objectivity" of financial accountability mechanisms.

Summary

Financial statements are an extremely important source of information about a company, its economic health, and its prospects. Equity investors use financial statements to form opinions about the value of a company and its stock. Creditors use statement information to assess a company's ability to make its debt payments and to comply with loan covenants. Stock analysts, brokers, and portfolio managers use financial statements as the basis for their recommendations to investors and creditors. Employees of a company use its financial statements to gain information about the prospects of their employment relationship, and unions are interested in a company's financial statements for many uses, including collective bargaining. Auditors use financial statements to help design more effective audits by spotting areas of potential reporting abuses.

That's why financial statements are in demand: they provide information that helps improve decision making, and they make it possible to monitor managers' activities. But what governs the supply of financial information?

Mandatory reporting is a partial answer. Most companies in Canada and other developed countries are required to produce and send out financial statements to shareholders as well as to file a copy with a government agency. This requirement allows all interested parties to view the statements. That's one reason companies supply financial information.

The other reason? It's because financial information that goes beyond the minimum requirements can often benefit the company, its managers, and owners. For example, voluntary financial disclosures can help the company obtain capital more cheaply or negotiate better terms from suppliers. But benefits like these come with potential costs: information collection, processing, and dissemination costs; competitive disadvantage costs; litigation costs; and political costs. This means that two companies with different financial reporting benefits and costs are likely to choose different accounting policies and reporting strategies.

Can they do so? Yes, because financial reporting standards are often imprecise and open to interpretation. This imprecision gives managers an opportunity to shape financial statements in ways that allow them to achieve specific reporting goals. Most managers use their accounting flexibility to paint a faithful picture of the company; other managers mold the financial statements to mask weaknesses and to hide problems. Analysts who understand financial reporting, managers' incentives, and the accounting flexibility available to managers will maintain a healthy skepticism about the numbers and recognize that financial statements sometimes conceal more than they reveal.

And the rise of Internet-based financial reporting adds more opportunities and complexity to the mix.

GAAP in Canada

Early Developments in Accounting

GAAP have been evolving in Canada for almost 150 years. The following is a brief description of how Canadian GAAP were molded into their present form and of the many organizations that influenced them over the years.

The need for some form of accountability system has been traced back thousands of years, and accounting scholars such as Richard Mattessich of the University of British Columbia offer argument and evidence that accounting existed at the dawn of history, some ten thousand years ago.[22] Professor Mattessich writes that the archeological evidence "suggests that accounting preceded abstract counting as well as writing." This tantalizing suggestion raises the importance of accounting's role in the establishment of civilizations a considerable notch or two! Ross Skinner, a Canadian accounting scholar and retired partner of a major accounting firm, asserts that there were three periods in accounting development:

> *In the first, from 4000 B.C. up to A.D. 1300, the record-keeping aspect was predominant. Accumulations of wealth require control, and for this some form of accounting is essential. The second period, from about 1300 up to 1850, was marked by the spread of commerce. … The distinguishing feature of this period was that accounting records became capable of dealing with masses of data and summarizing them so as to facilitate the business carried on … advances implicit in the technique of double entry mark the era as one of systematized bookkeeping rather than one of mere record keeping. The double-entry technique was further important in that it was capable of extension and refinement so as to meet the needs of the third era, from 1850 to the present.[23]*

From a business standpoint, in the part of North America that became known as Canada, accounting records—rudimentary as they were—helped organizations such as the Hudson's Bay Company (HBC) manage commerce over a far-flung, largely unknown land mass, where communication was inconsistent, hazardous, and uncertain. HBC, which is now Canada's largest retailer with its Zellers and The Bay stores, was granted a charter on May 2, 1670, by King Charles II of England that gave the "Governor and Company of Adventurers of England Trading into Hudson's Bay" a virtual monopoly on all commerce, especially the fur trade, in "what turned out to be an incredibly vast territory, the drainage basin of Hudson's Bay, which stretches from Ungava to the foothills of the Rockies."[24] Accounting, in the form of ledgers and other records of the company's far-flung fur-trading posts, provided vital information to the owners, who were usually located in England.

HUDSON'S BAY COMPANY
www.hbc.com

In this book, we are interested mainly in Skinner's third period of accounting's development, from about 1850 to the present. But isn't it nice to be aware of the possibility that accounting, far from being a dry-as-dust area of study, may have had profound impact on modern society? This is what the work of people like Mattessich and Skinner suggests.

The Modern Period, 1850 to the Present

Rather dramatically, Skinner writes about the beginnings of accounting's modern era in the following way:

> The groundwork for this final period was laid by the vast surge of economic activity in the preceding century known as the Industrial Revolution. The emergence of large-scale enterprise required the mobilization of large capital sums, which in turn led to the separation of the functions of ownership and management and to increasing use of the legal institution of the limited liability company. In time, accounting played its part by becoming a source of information about costs and profits to assist management. Also through financial statements it became a means of communicating information to investors, creditors and others who were separate from internal management but entitled to reports on enterprise progress.[25]

In the Canadian context in particular, accounting developed with strong influence from both England and the United States,[26] while still pursuing its own unique Canadian direction. Early Canadian colonial legislation in the 1850s and 1860s permitted companies to incorporate with limited liability, and imposed the first requirements for some form of financial reporting. For example, legislation passed in 1850 required banks "to forward to the Inspector General 'a full and clear statement of assets and liabilities,'" and in 1851 railway companies were required to file with the Legislature "a detailed and particular account ... of the moneys received and expended by the company."[27]

In 1874 and 1878, respectively, the Montreal and Toronto Stock Exchanges were incorporated, and between 1879 and 1886 the Association of Accountants in Montreal (which evolved into the Institute of Chartered Accountants of Quebec) and the Institutes of Chartered Accountants of Ontario and of Manitoba were established. The period 1885 to 1920 saw the emergence of an active accounting profession (with, for example, the Ontario Institute of CAs submitting briefs to legislative bodies on accounting and auditing matters), the publication of popular Canadian accounting textbooks, and the beginnings of accreditation of accounting courses in schools and colleges. The Ontario Institute was a leader in the development of what Professor Murphy calls "the pace-setting financial statement disclosure requirements of the provincial [Ontario] corporate legislation of 1907, [which was] later installed ... at the federal level in 1917."[28] This legislation "required, for presentation to shareholders at annual general meeting, a revenue and expenditure statement and balance sheet—the latter required the distinguishing of various asset, liability and equity accounts."[29]

In the early 1930s, the CICA began to submit briefs and submissions on accounting and auditing matters to government, which along with agitation in the financial press for improved disclosure in company financial statements and debates about stock promotion abuses, led to federal *Companies Act* legislation in 1934–35, which specified increased disclosure about income statement details and permitted consolidated statements, among other things.[30] The collapse of stock markets in 1929 strongly influenced this legislation.

The post-World War II years up to about 1960 saw continued activity in accounting. In 1946, the CICA's Accounting and Auditing Research Committee began to issue "Bulletins," which evolved over time into the *CICA Handbook* in 1968. Encouragement for improved accounting and disclosure was provided by the establishment in 1951 of the *Financial Post*'s annual financial statement awards, a steady stream of CICA bulletins, and further improvements in the disclosure and audit requirements in legislation.

But this postwar period was also important due to changes in the nature of accounting pronouncements issued by the CICA. At first, they were guidance, representing good practice. Now, however, they are mandatory standards. Skinner argues that this process towards mandatory standards in Canada got underway when the *Ontario Corporations Act* was revised in 1953, when the accounting profession persuaded the provincial government to include almost verbatim the CICA's Bulletin 1 on standards of disclosure. And "[a]s companies acts in the other provinces and in the federal jurisdiction came under review, there was a tendency to pick up provisions from other Canadian statutes. In this way the legal impact of the CICA recommendations on financial disclosure spread through much of the country."[31] Next, with the incorporation of the CICA bulletins into the new *CICA Handbook* in 1968, the CICA now recommended that any departure from the recommendations of the *Handbook* be disclosed in a company's footnotes, or, failing that, in the audit report. The *Handbook* was further entrenched as mandatory practice in 1972 when the provincial securities administrators issued national Policy No. 27, which said that CICA pronouncements would be regarded as "generally accepted accounting principles" for purposes of securities or companies legislation. And in 1975, the federal government essentially included the *Handbook* in the *Canada Business Corporations Act*, and several provinces have since followed suit. Thus, in Canada—in contrast to virtually every other country—the recommendations of the CICA's Accounting Standards Board (as it is now called) have virtually legal status. This gives the AcSB more authority than similar bodies in other countries, but also may result in the politicization of accounting standards.

During the 1970s and 1980s, there was considerable interest in developing a conceptual framework for financial accounting, much of it stimulated by American initiatives in this area. Edward Stamp, an accounting professor from England, was commissioned by the CICA to study the conceptual framework issue from a Canadian perspective, and in 1980 the CICA published his *Corporate Reporting: Its Future Evolution*. After much more deliberation, the Canadian accounting profession issued "Financial Statement Concepts" as Section 1000 of the *CICA Handbook*. The parts of financial accounting's currently accepted conceptual framework are described in Section 1000 of the *Handbook*. It is a "user-oriented" framework, since it is driven by the desire to satisfy the information needs that users might have about an organization.[32]

There has also been continual re-evaluation of the structure and process by which accounting standards are set in Canada, and the nature of those standards. For example, in 1981 the *Report* of the Special Committee on Standard Setting (SCOSS) was published, recommending that Canadian standards be written broadly as general principles rather than as detailed rules (as favoured by American standard setters). Until recently, Canadian standards have tended to be more general than American standards, but the differences in degree of detail are waning.

In the mid-1980s, in response to the failures of two Western Canada banks (Canadian Commercial Bank and Northland Bank) and the judicial inquiry that followed, the CICA established a commission to study the public's expectation of audits. Known as the Macdonald Commission (after its chair), the commission issued its report in 1988 and, among other things, included several recommendations regarding the setting of accounting standards. These recommendations reflected concern about: events and transactions for which written standards did not exist; existing standards that permitted too many alternatives; and the fast pace of change in how business was conducted, with new ways of structuring deals and securities, and the resulting lag in standards. Initiatives such as the CICA's Emerging Issues Committee (EIC), which issues nonbinding guidance on emerging accounting issues much more quickly than the Accounting Standards Board due-process approach, resulted from the report.

Accounting Standard Setting in Canada Today: Organizations and Process

Many organizations have an interest in, and influence on, accounting standard setting in Canada today. The most important are the various governments, provincial and federal, that provide the long-term legislative basis for accounting standards, and the CICA and the corresponding provincial CA institutes, who have often prodded legislators and who—at the CICA level—provide the standard-setting infrastructure. Other groups have also had important roles, however, including:

- The other major Canadian accounting professional bodies, particularly the Certified General Accountants Association of Canada (CGA-Canada) and the Society of Management Accountants of Canada (SMAC), both of which have representatives on the CICA's Accounting Standards Committee.

- Provincial securities commissions.

- The Canadian Academic Accounting Association (CAAA), which provides an academic and research perspective.

INTERNATIONAL
ACCOUNTING
STANDARDS BOARD
www.iasc.org.uk

- The International Accounting Standards Board (IASB), which is becoming more and more important in accounting standard setting as the global market entrenches itself.

- Major accounting firms and user groups.

- Stock exchanges; for example, the Toronto Stock Exchange issued guidelines in March 1999 for the Internet-based dissemination of information by TSX-listed companies.

As in most human systems, the tensions in corporate financial reporting seem to be a permanent feature. For example, on June 8, 1999, the chair of the Ontario Securities Commission (the OSC) gave a major speech in which he asserted that public trust in Canadian accounting and auditing was eroding, that pressure to report favourable earnings was leading at times to poor judgment, and that credibility was being damaged. The OSC chair, however, ended that speech on an optimistic note, suggesting that collective action by accountants, management, regulators, and others has the potential to positively reform the financial reporting system. But *Enron* and other recent situations have tempered such optimism. For example, on March 7, 2002, the OSC chair gave another, perhaps more sobering, speech entitled "Preventing Enron North: Improving Financial Reporting and Corporate Governance in Canada." Excerpts from the speech follow:

> ... In thinking about capital markets today, the issue that seems to be at the forefront of everyone's mind is the E-word—"Enron". This massive corporate failure has thrust into the spotlight many elements of the corporate disclosure system that underpin capital markets in Canada and around the world.
>
> In nearly every major country, the question being asked is: "Could it happen here?" Canada is no exception.
>
> At least in the short-term, public confidence in financial reporting, auditing and corporate governance structures has been damaged. The key issue now is to deter-

mine how to repair the damage—and restore public confidence. If we look to the marketplace, we begin to see the results of a search for solutions. We see the markets beginning to impose discipline in areas where previously many feared to tread. In some companies, management and boards of directors are re-examining the nature of their relationship with their external auditor. Public accounting firms are re-evaluating their business models.

Momentum is building in the marketplace. For regulators, the challenge is to harness this momentum to create positive and sustainable changes for the long-term. We need to move promptly—but not at the expense of a thorough and careful evaluation of the key lessons to be learned.

As I see it, Enron, as well as other major corporate failures in other parts of the world, have raised a wide range of issues.

Obviously, it has raised the issue of transparency and disclosure.

But it has also raised the issue of corporate governance structures: How adequate are they, and how effectively do boards of directors—and particularly audit committees—perform their responsibilities?

It has called into question the adequacy of financial statements as a relevant and reliable source of information about a company's financial condition.

In part, the issue is whether companies are complying fully with not just the letter but also the spirit of accounting standards. In part, it is whether the disclosure being provided by companies within the framework of generally accepted accounting principles is sufficiently clear for readers of financial statements. Can most readers readily understand the implications of the information they are being given?

But the more fundamental issue is the adequacy of the accounting principles themselves. Look at it this way: Is compliance with generally accepted accounting principles enough? Or are there areas in which financial statements may comply fully with established standards—and yet still obfuscate important information?

Finally, of course, any questioning of the adequacy of financial statements naturally and appropriately leads to questions about the role of the auditor and the effectiveness of the external audit process. It takes us into areas such as the independence of the auditor, and how we promote a system that strengthens the auditor's ability to maintain objectivity under pressure. For the public to have full confidence in the audit process, there must be an effective and transparent system for oversight and discipline of public accountants who practise as auditors of public companies.

Thus the Enron failure has focused attention on four of the underpinnings of our capital market structure:

- transparency and disclosure standards
- our reliance on financial statements
- corporate governance practices
- and the role of the external auditor.

I'll elaborate on each of these separately and put them into a Canadian context.

I'll start with the issue of transparency and disclosure. To get a sense of our relative vulnerability in Canada, it's important to recognize some of the significant differences between the U.S. disclosure system and the Canadian disclosure system.

First and foremost, in Canada we require continuous disclosure—ongoing public disclosure of material changes that affect a corporation as soon as those changes occur. This promotes a flow of information to the markets that continuously updates the public disclosure record. Once a company becomes a reporting issuer in Canada, it is subject to all of the continuous disclosure requirements and must meet them through electronic filings on our SEDAR system. All of those filings become readily accessible to the public through the SEDAR Website.

By contrast, the U.S. system relies on periodic disclosure at prescribed intervals. There is no general obligation in the United States to disclose all material changes—

only to be accurate about what is disclosed. In response to Enron, we're seeing proposals by the SEC that would move the U.S. system much closer to Canada's. Publicly-traded companies would be required to make immediate disclosure on the occurrence of any one of an expanded list of specifically identified events.

But we cannot allow the fact we may be ahead of the United States in this area to make us complacent. Indeed, I would urge all of you, both reporting issuers and advisors, to place a renewed emphasis on ensuring that you are meeting the goals of the continuous disclosure regime. When facing a decision as to whether an event is a material change, it's easy to see the fleeting advantage of rationalizing it away. But it makes more sense to recognize the long-term advantage—both to an individual company and to our capital markets—of maintaining a relevant and reliable stream of information to the marketplace.

Well-informed investors will recognize companies that fully disclose—and take that into account. Just ask Warren Buffet, the legendary leader of the Berkshire Hathaway empire. Buffet remarked earlier this week: "CEOs need to view themselves as the company's 'chief disclosure officer' and tell investors everything they need to know about the company's performance and accounting."

I can assure you that you won't be facing these challenges alone. At the OSC, we will continue to pursue our greatly enhanced initiatives in reviewing continuous disclosure of Ontario reporting issuers. You can fully expect that we will be asking pointed questions in the course of reviews of both continuous disclosure and prospectuses.

The adequacy of financial statements is the second issue. That has brought accounting standards in the United States under critical examination. Here, too, our situation in Canada is not identical to the United States. All of you who are involved with companies that raise money in the U.S. markets are well aware that there are many specific differences between Canadian and U.S. accounting standards. The difference I want to highlight is not one of detail but one of overall approach. Over many years, U.S. accounting standards have evolved into a set of detailed and prescriptive rules. In fact, some uncharitably characterize U.S. GAAP as "check the boxes accounting." Enron has highlighted this issue. Whether a debt-laden special-purpose entity was or was not required to be consolidated depended on the application of relatively arbitrary percentage thresholds.

Growing numbers of U.S. politicians and regulators are beginning to question whether the ever-exploding volume of narrowly written rules is actually contributing to better-quality financial reporting. Or is it simply providing a roadmap for investment bankers and others to design transactions with the specific objective of exploiting the rules and potentially obfuscating a company's financial position and performance? In Enron's case, for example, even if the boxes were checked accurately, did they add up to a full and complete picture of the company?

Historically, the approach to setting accounting standards in Canada has been different. Our Accounting Standards Board has emphasized the identification of sound principles. Both preparers and auditors of financial statements are required to exercise professional judgment based on those principles to reach sound conclusions as to the appropriate accounting for specific transactions.

But in recent years, we've moved a long way from this approach. As the pressure for convergence of accounting standards within North America has grown, we've begun to create what are essentially photocopies of detailed and rule-oriented U.S. standards. Similarly, the standards-setters have headed down a path of creating more and more specific and detailed interpretations of the application of particular standards.

I do not suggest that reverting to the principles-based Canadian standards of several years ago is the solution to all ills—it is not. However, I do believe we need to step back and re-evaluate the appropriate balance between principles and rules. And we also have to recognize that, to be effective, a principles-based approach has to be applied by professionals who look to the spirit and objective of the standards. In the words of the 1988 Macdonald Commission Report on the Public's Expectations of Audits: "It would be misleading 'to suggest that rules can replace the need for professional judgment'."

In dealing with this issue, we have to work with our international colleagues. In this regard, I would particularly look for leadership to the newly-established International Accounting Standards Board. Working with national standards setters, the Board has a unique opportunity to shape a body of high-quality accounting standards that will promote relevant and reliable financial reporting in which investors around the globe can have confidence.

As accounting standards-setters in the U.S. and Canada look closely at their standards to identify potential weaknesses exposed by the Enron fiasco, it is essential that they consider carefully what can be learned from their counterparts in other countries. For example, some argue that certain of the perceived financial reporting problems might have been avoided had Enron been reporting under allegedly more robust U.K. standards that focus on the substance of transactions.

Similarly, I have heard it suggested that current International Accounting Standards would require special-purpose entities to be consolidated into the financial statements of their sponsor in a wider range of circumstances than is the case under U.S. GAAP.

I make no judgment on the validity of these claims. My point is simply that we in Canada need to work with others to create the best of all possible accounting worlds. As Claude Lamoureux, the CEO of the Teachers' Pension Plan Board, put it the other day: "The best accounting standards—as opposed to the least offensive".

The Enron case may also cause us to think more carefully about what the audited statements tell us about the financial position of a company. Investors expect, and I believe are entitled to expect, that the totality of the financial disclosure in a set of financial statements fairly represents the company's financial position. Assurances on this score can only come from management or the external auditors or perhaps a combination of both.

If my memory serves me correctly, there was a time when the auditor's opinion included an assurance by the auditors that the financial statements presented fairly the company's financial position and the results of its operations. This requirement was dropped a few years ago. Now, all that is offered is an opinion that the financial statements are presented fairly in accordance with accounting principles. In today's increasingly complex business enterprises, we need to know that GAAP has been followed but this may no longer be enough. Investors also need to know that the auditor is satisfied the financial statements as a whole provide a fair and balanced representation of the company's financial situation. …

Source: David Brown, "Preventing Enron North: Improving Financial Reporting and Corporate Governance in Canada," www.osc.gov.on.ca/en/About/News/Speeches/spch_20020307_conf-board-enron.htm. With permission of the Ontario Securities Council.

Current Institutional Structure in the United States

In the United States, the SEC has broad statutory powers to define accounting terms, prescribe the methods of preparing financial reports, and specify the details to be presented in financial statements. Under the U.S. *Securities Act of 1933*, companies wanting to issue securities interstate must file a prospectus with the SEC. The prospectus is a public document—prepared for each new security offering—containing information about the company, its officers, and its financial affairs. The financial section of the prospectus must be audited by an independent CPA who is registered to practise before the SEC. Once securities have been sold to the public, the company is required to file with the SEC publicly accessible, audited financial statements each year. These annual statements are known as the 10-K report. In addition, unaudited quarterly financial reports (called 10-Q filings) are required. In most respects, the annual 10-K disclosure requirements closely overlap the information in the company's published financial statements.

Although the SEC has wide statutory authority to impose financial reporting rules, it continues to rely on the accounting profession to set and enforce accounting standards and to regulate the profession. The SEC has occasionally forced the accounting profession to tackle critical problems, and it once rejected an accounting standard issued by the FASB.[33] Such situations occur rarely.

Since July 1973, the Financial Accounting Standards Board (FASB) has been responsible for establishing accounting standards in the United States. The FASB has issued numerous Statements of Financial Accounting Standards, Statements of Financial Accounting Concepts, and technical bulletins. The FASB has neither the authority nor the responsibility to enforce compliance with GAAP. That responsibility rests with company management, the accounting profession, the SEC, and the courts. Some observers believe that compliance is the weak link in the private sector standard-setting chain. These critics point to frequent litigation on financial reporting matters in the courts, the escalating cost of liability insurance premiums paid by audit firms, and criticism by the SEC's chief accountant regarding the independence of external auditors.[34]

The FASB follows a "due process" procedure in developing accounting standards. This process is designed to ensure public input in the decision. Most accounting standards issued by the FASB go through three steps:

1. *Discussion–memorandum stage.* After the Board and its staff have considered a topic on its agenda—and perhaps consulted with experts and other interested parties—a discussion memorandum is issued. This memorandum outlines the key issues involved and the Board's preliminary views on those issues. The public is invited to comment in writing on the memorandum, and public hearings are sometimes held to permit interested individuals to express their views in person.

2. *Exposure–draft stage.* After further deliberation and modification by the Board and its staff, an exposure draft of the standard is issued. During the exposure period, which lasts not less than 30 days, further public comment is requested and evaluated.

3. *Voting stage.* Finally, the Board votes on whether to issue the standard as contained in the exposure draft or to revise it and issue a new exposure draft. For

a proposed standard to become official and a part of generally accepted accounting principles, five of the seven Board members must approve it.

Influential groups and organizations use the due process procedures of the FASB to plead their case for alternative solutions. The arguments often include cost-benefit considerations; claims that the proposed accounting treatment is not theoretically sound or will not be understood by users; implementation issues; and concerns that the proposed standard will be economically harmful to specific companies, industries, or the country.[35] Government agencies, preparer organizations such as the Business Roundtable, and industry trade organizations such as the Financial Executives Institute create substantial pressures on the Board. Some contend that the interests of investors, creditors, and other financial statement users are not always well represented in this political forum.

But, since Enron, the financial reporting political climate in the United States has changed radically. The Big Five accounting firm Andersen (formerly Arthur Andersen) has failed as, while the U.S. Department of Justice pursued criminal proceedings, many of the firm's clients left and its partner firms in other countries such as Canada joined one of the remaining large firms. More importantly, the U.S. House of Representatives and the U.S. Senate have both held extensive committee hearings not only on Enron's bankruptcy in particular but also on the entire scope of financial reporting, corporate accountability, and auditing. And the SEC, and even the president of the United States, have been active in response to Enron. For example, the U.S. president announced a ten-point plan in March 2002 (www.whitehouse.gov/infocus/corporateresponsibility).

For more Exercises, Problems/Discussion Questions, and Cases, visit the Companion Website for this textbook at **www.pearsoned.ca/revsine**.

Problems/Discussion Questions

P1-1 Demand for accounting information

Required:

1. Explain why each of the following groups might want financial accounting information. What type of financial information would each group find most useful and why?
   a. a corporation's existing shareholders
   b. prospective investors
   c. financial analysts who follow the company
   d. company managers
   e. current employees
   f. commercial lenders who have loaned money to the company
   g. current suppliers
   h. debt-rating agencies
   i. government regulatory agencies
   j. a union representing company employees

2. Identify at least one other group that might want financial accounting information about the company, and describe how the information would be used by this group.

P1-2 Incentives for voluntary disclosure

Required:

1. Describe how each of the following influences the supply of financial accounting information:
   a. debt and equity financial markets
   b. managerial labour market forces
   c. the market for corporate control (e.g., mergers, takeovers, and divestitures)

2. What other forces might cause managers to voluntarily release financial information about the company?

3. Identify five ways managers can voluntarily provide information about the company to outsiders. (You might consult the business news media for examples.) What advantages (if any) do these voluntary approaches have over the required financial disclosures contained in annual and quarterly reports to shareholders?

P1-3 Costs of disclosure

Required:

1. Describe each of the following disclosure costs associated with financial accounting information, and provide a concrete example of each cost:
   a. information collection, processing, and dissemination costs
   b. competitive disadvantage costs

     c.   litigation costs

     d.   political costs

  2. Identify at least one other potential disclosure cost.

P1-4 Proxy statement disclosures

A company's proxy statement or management information circular contains information about major shareholders, management compensation (salary, bonus, stock options, etc.), composition of the board of directors, and shares owned by top managers and members of the board of directors. Many Canadian companies file their proxy statements on the SEDAR website as pdf files.

Required:

Explain why this information could be useful to a financial analyst who is following the firm's activities.

P1-5 Your position on the issues

Provide a two- or three-sentence response that argues for or against each of these statements:

1. Accounting is an exact science.
2. Managers choose accounting procedures that produce the most accurate picture of the company's operating performance and financial condition.
3. Accounting standards in Canada are influenced more by politics than by science or economics.
4. If the CICA's AcSB and legislation supporting the *CICA Handbook* were not around to require and enforce minimum levels of financial disclosure by publicly held companies, most companies would provide little (if any) information to outsiders.
5. When managers possess good news about the company (i.e., information that will increase the share price), they have an incentive to publicly disclose the information as soon as possible.
6. When managers possess bad news about the company (i.e., information that will decrease the share price), they have an incentive to delay public disclosure as long as possible.
7. An investor who adopts a fundamental analysis approach to investment decisions has little use for financial statement information.
8. An investor who believes that capital markets are efficient has little use for financial statement information.
9. Managers who disclose only the minimum information required to meet GAAP and other regulatory requirements may be doing a disservice to shareholders.
10. Financial statements are not the only source of information analysts use when forecasting the company's future profitability and financial condition.

P1-6 How managers and professional investors rate information

A wide variety of financial and nonfinancial information is used in managing a company and in making decisions about whether to invest in a company. A recent survey of senior corporate managers and professional investors asked each group to rank the following information according to its importance ("1" being the most important and "14" being the least important). How do you think each item was ranked?

	Importance Ranking	
	Corporate Managers	**Professional Investors**
Business segment results	_____	_____
Capital expenditures	_____	_____
Cash flow	_____	_____
Cost control	_____	_____
Customer satisfaction	_____	_____
Earnings	_____	_____
Market growth	_____	_____
Market share	_____	_____
Measures of strategic achievement	_____	_____
New product development	_____	_____
Product and process quality	_____	_____
Research and development (R & D)	_____	_____
R & D productivity	_____	_____
Strategic goals	_____	_____

Cases

C1-1 The accounting instructor

During a class at the local university, an accounting instructor showed two slides as follows:

Slide 1:

Financial statements prepared according to GAAP

(i)   have at least a minimum, partly known level of quality assurance,
(ii) are subject to judgment (examples?),
(iii) are "general purpose," and may have to be "custom modified" to suit a specific purpose, and
(iv) are the output of a process involving a system of several players.

Slide 2:

As the instructor showed this slide, he said, "This 'system of several players' may be shown as the following."

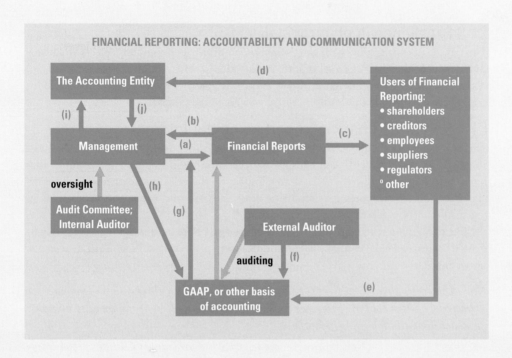

FINANCIAL REPORTING: ACCOUNTABILITY AND COMMUNICATION SYSTEM

The instructor went on to say that "*quality of earnings* is a judgment about the appropriateness of financial accounting information for a certain purpose, given the variety of technical accounting judgments and decisions that have been made, the adequacy of disclosure and transparency, and the context of the business entity and its environment. Adherence to GAAP, based upon an unqualified opinion of an independent external audit organization, is a necessary but insufficient condition to ensure a high QOE in a particular situation."

Required:

1. Develop an explanation for each arrow in Slide 2.
2. Are any arrows missing? Explain.
3. Based upon your general knowledge of Enron, which links in Slide 2 seemed to have "failed"?

C1-2 OSC Chair's speech

Excerpts from the OSC chair's March 7, 2002, speech entitled "Preventing Enron North: Improving Financial Reporting and Corporate Governance in Canada" are given in Appendix 1A to this chapter.

Required:

a. In his speech, the OSC chair said "the Enron failure has focused attention on four of the underpinnings of our capital market structure:
   • transparency and disclosure standards
   • our reliance on financial statements
   • corporate governance practices
   • and the role of the external auditor."

   Explain why, or why not, these are "four of the underpinnings of our capital market structure."

b. Do you agree with the comments on "transparency and disclosure"? Explain.

c. Do you agree with the comments on "reliance on financial statements"? Explain.

C1-3 Excellence in electronic disclosure

The CICA, in cooperation with the *National Post* newspaper, annually selects what they consider to be the "best" annual reports in Canada. In 2001, an award for excellence in electronic reporting was inaugurated. Go to the CICA website, and review the criteria for excellence in electronic disclosure. Critically evaluate the criteria.

C1-4 Corporate financial reporting on the Internet

There's a school of thought that says corporate financial reporting on the Internet is just an electronic version of disseminating financial information. This view assumes that Internet technology will have little, if any, impact on the very nature of financial reporting itself, and also assumes that reporting entities, users, and other parties involved in financial reporting will be essentially unchanged.

Technological change, however, is rarely if ever so polite, and is almost always downright disruptive. Neil Postman, a communications professor at New York University, argues that:

New technologies alter the structure of our interests: the things we think about. *They alter the character of our symbols: the things we think* with. *And they alter the nature of community: the arena in which thoughts develop.*

(Neil Postman, *Technopoly: The Surrender of Culture to Technology* [New York: Vintage Books, 1993], p. 20)

If we take Postman's comment seriously and apply this idea to financial reporting on the Internet, the suggestion is that this new technology might so disrupt what we think of as financial reporting that it might change beyond recognition. Here are ten reasons why this might be true.

1. *Immediacy.* Corporate financial reporting over the Internet is almost in real time (subject to bandwidth and other data-transfer constraints). Users' demand for information, including accountability information, will increase; managers may feel the "heat" of real-time monitoring. Will it make them more risk-averse than they might otherwise be? Will it make them more interested in *strategically* arranging transactions and contracts to control the (virtually constant and real-time) flow of information to outsiders?

2. *Broadening of existing audience for financial reporting.* The existing audience for financial reporting information has broadened and deepened. For example, shareholders and potential shareholders who previously may have relied almost exclusively on professional advisors now find barriers to accessing financial reporting information are significantly lowered—all they need is access to the Internet, plus a knowledge of business and financial accounting (a tall order, but less and less of a barrier). The more activist shareholders and stock-market participants might appear, the more (perhaps) volatility in the stock- and related financial instrument markets, since there is little time to reflect on and absorb information.

3. *Creation of a new audience for financial reporting.* The "public domain" in general (and not just shareholders and others who have a direct stake in the corporation) might be expected to take advantage of access to corporate financial reporting information on the Internet. Demands for "nonconventional" financial reporting information (environmental costs and liabilities; externalities; perhaps opportunity costs; more disaggregated disclosures; more detailed MD&A) might increase.

4. *Pressure to push back the boundary separating inside and outside information.* Demands for financial reporting might include transactions information and other information kept in various stages of disaggregation in corporate databases.

5. *Significant increase in volume of financial reporting and related information, and response of reporting entities with a wide array of new information.* This change is already happening, with companies such as Microsoft leading the way.

6. *A new dynamic created by hypertext webpages and wide real-time dissemination.* The hyperlinks may give users the illusion of more control over the information they consume (they can "choose" which links to follow through the corporate financial reporting portion of the website), but the links and the other media and multimedia features of the site are designed by management and management's consultants, with *some intent and strategy in mind.*

7. *Commodification of financial reporting information.* Financial reporting information becomes almost commodity-like, just part of a website (often extensive) that includes a wide variety of commercial information and corporate advertising. The distinction between financial reporting and other forms of corporate communications (such as self-promotion and advertising) becomes blurred, to the detriment of not only financial reporting, but more importantly the welfare of users and other stakeholders.

8. *Websites are alive with graphics, movement, different (multimedia) experiences, and therefore different metaphors.* Different metaphors become important to comprehending financial reporting on the Internet. Lakoff and Johnson's (George Lakoff and Mark Johnson, *Metaphors We Live By* [Chicago: University of Chicago Press, 1980], p. 157) comment that "people in power get to impose their metaphors" since metaphors "can have the power to define reality" has important implications for financial reporting on the Internet. Acknowledging that Internet corporate financial reporting is largely metaphorical and thus rhetorical in the classical sense will help us be better interpreters of financial accounting.

9. *The "presence" of financial reporting on the Internet.* Websites and their financial reporting content will move closer to fulfilling the concept of presence. The site may, almost virtually, *become* the company to the user.

10. *Strategic approach to website financial reporting.* Many organizations long ago adopted the view that financial reporting must be regarded as not merely a technical, but rather a more strategic exercise in compliance with GAAP and other regulations. If the previous nine observations make any sense whatsoever, then this view is made even more compelling within the context of financial reporting on the Internet. This view leads to questions such as "How does website financial reporting fit in with overall corporate strategy and corporate communications strategy?"

Required:

1. Do you agree that corporate financial reporting will be altered profoundly by the rise of the Internet? Evaluate the ten suggested reasons.

2. Bombardier Inc. is a Canadian global company with interests in the design, manufacturing, and marketing of transportation equipment, aerospace, and motorized consumer products. Visit the company's website and explore the webpages devoted to presenting financial and accounting information. Prepare a table listing these webpages, along with a brief description of the information on each webpage. Describe the main features of Bombardier's website, and assess its financial reporting in terms of design and usability.

Integrative Running Case Study
Bombardier on the Web

Required:

Access Bombardier's most recent annual report located on the Companion Website for this textbook (**www.pearsoned.ca/revsine**) and answer the following questions:

1. List the major sections of the report, and briefly indicate the function of each section.
2. Read the letter to shareholders. What important strategic information can you obtain from this section? Is the letter self-serving or straightforward? Recent research suggests that shareholders' letters are an important, carefully constructed part of the annual report, worthy of scrutiny to obtain insights into top management.[36]
3. Critically evaluate the sections entitled "Social Responsibility" and "Environment." What, if any, implications do these sections have for financial reporting?
4. Examine the section entitled "Management's Responsibility for Financial Reporting." What implications does the information in this section have for enhancing the quality of Bombardier's financial reporting?

Endnotes

1. The information contained in *Financial Reporting and Analysis* is of broad general usefulness to the accounting student and to those with an interest in accounting practices. Readers are cautioned, however, that this publication is sold with the understanding that the Publisher and the Authors are not engaged in rendering accounting, financial, or other professional services or advice. The examples used in this publication, and the references to, or opinions expressed about, financial reporting practices of companies identified in this book, are intended to serve educational purposes, including encouraging classroom discussion, and are not intended to serve as examples of effective or ineffective, or good or poor, practices.

2. Nortel reported revenues of US$22 billion in 1999. Former parent BCE's common share ownership had been reduced rapidly to about 3%, so Nortel was no longer beholden or accountable to BCE.

3. Nortel Networks Corporation, 1999 Annual Report, p. 10.

4. The share price has traded in the CDN$1.50 range in the fall of 2002.

5. Robert J. Shiller, *Irrational Exuberance* (Princeton, N.J.: Princeton University Press, 2000).

6. *The Toronto Star* (www.thestar.com).

7. A company may participate directly in an economic transaction when, for example, it issues debt or equity securities, or when it negotiates a loan or acquires equipment on credit. However, financial statement information also facilitates transactions in secondary markets like the Toronto Stock Exchange—where the company's financial securities are traded.

8. This regulation process is intended to enhance economic efficiency by precluding the construction of duplicate facilities that would otherwise occur in a competitive environment. Eliminating such redundancies presumably lowers the ultimate service cost to consumers. Regulatory agencies specify the accounting practices and disclosure policies that must be followed by companies under their jurisdiction. As a consequence, the accounting practices that utility companies use in preparing financial statements for regulatory agencies sometimes differ from those used in their shareholder reports.

9. In Canada, the Regulations of the CBCA specify that accounting standards established by the CICA's AcSB are to be used to fulfill the Act's financial reporting requirements. In the United States, corporate financial reporting is regulated by the SEC, which relies on private sector organizations such as the American Institute of Certified Public Accountants (AICPA) and the Financial Accounting Standards Board (FASB) to formulate financial accounting and reporting standards. In Germany, standards are prescribed by law in the *Commercial Code* (*Handelsgesetz*), the *Corporation Act* (*Aktiengesetz*), the *Cooperatives Act* (*Genossenschaftsgesetz*), and other laws related to specific types of business.

10. "Lemon" commonly refers to an automobile with hidden defects. In financial capital markets, "lemon" refers to an investment instrument with hidden risks.

11. There is another side to this "excessive profits" story. Politicians sometimes respond to public concern over

record losses at highly visible companies by providing various types of financial assistance (e.g., so-called *government bailouts* have occurred for Dome Petroleum, Canadair, Chrysler Canada, Ltd., and many other companies).

12. See Chapter 6 for additional details concerning this approach to deriving an estimate of a company's *fundamental* value.

13. "Analysis," *CICA Handbook,* Section 5301.

14. These findings are based on a comprehensive study of professional analysts' information needs conducted by the Special Committee on Financial Reporting of the AICPA. Further details about the study and the committee's recommendations can be found in *Improving Business Reporting—A Customer Focus: Meeting the Information Needs of Investors and Creditors* (New York: AICPA, 1994).

15. The MD&A is achieving more and more prominence. In its recent review draft publication entitled "MANAGEMENT DISCUSSION AND ANALYSIS: Guidance on Preparation and Disclosure," the Canadian Performance Reporting Initiative Board asserted that "the better a company communicates with those who assess its value in capital markets, the better the markets will understand and reward underlying potential prospects" (December 2001, p. 10).

16. A discussion of these qualitative characteristics and related issues is contained in "Financial Statement Concepts," *CICA Handbook*, Section 1000.

17. Ross M. Skinner, *Accounting Standards in Evolution* (Toronto: Holt, Rinehart, and Winston of Canada, Limited, 1987), pp. 35–36.

18. Lenders are fooled when they mistakenly assign too little risk (and thus charge too low an interest rate) to the borrowing. An interest cost savings of one-half of a percentage point on $1 billion of borrowings equates to $5 million (pre-tax) per year. If the company is in a 45% tax bracket and its shares trade at 15 times earnings, the payoff for concealing risk on financial statements is $41.25 million in share value. This value increase represents a wealth transfer to shareholders from creditors.

19. Joel H. Amernic, " 'Close Readings' of Internet Corporate Financial Reporting: Toward a More Critical Pedagogy on the Information Highway," *The Internet and Higher Education,* vol. 1 (1998), no. 2, pp. 87–112.

20. CICA and *National Post,* 2001 Annual Report Awards (available as a pdf file from the CICA website at www.cica.ca).

21. Based on R. Craig, L. Garrott, and J. Amernic, "A 'Close Reading' Protocol to Identify Perception-Fashioning Rhetoric in Website Financial Reporting: The Case of Microsoft," *Accounting and the Public Interest,* 1 (2001), pp. 1–16.

22. R. Mattessich, "Prehistoric Accounting and the Problem of Representation: On Recent Archeological Evidence of the Middle East from 8000 B.C. to 3000 B.C.," *The Accounting Historians Journal,* vol. 14, no. 2 (Fall 1987), pp. 71–91.

23. Ross M. Skinner, *Accounting Standards in Evolution* (Toronto: Holt, Rinehart, and Winston of Canada, Limited, 1987), p. 4.

24. Michael Bliss, *Northern Enterprise: Five Centuries of Canadian Business* (Toronto: McClelland and Stewart, 1987), p. 79.

25. Skinner, ibid., p. 4.

26. George J. Murphy, in "A Chronology of the Development of Corporate Financial Reporting in Canada: 1850 to 1983," *The Accounting Historians Journal,* vol. 13, no. 1 (Spring 1986), pp. 31–62, writes, "Prior to the turn of the century, actual legislated reporting requirements followed the English statutes quite closely; since that time, the Canadian requirements have generally been well in advance of those of England. Since the 1920s and 1930s, Canadian reporting practices and standards have been much more significantly influenced by the United States. That influence has been felt through the proximity and articulateness of the American accounting profession, the edicts of the Securities and Exchange Commission (SEC), the American parent–Canadian subsidiary relationships of many corporations, and the close ties amongst international public accounting firms" (pp. 31–32).

27. Murphy, ibid., p. 34.

28. Murphy, ibid., p. 36.

29. Murphy, ibid., p. 40.

30. Murphy, ibid., p. 44.

31. Skinner, op. cit., p. 35.

32. The need for a Canadian conceptual framework is analyzed in Joel Amernic and Morley Lemon, "Do We Need a Canadian Conceptual Framework?," *CA Magazine,* July 1984, pp. 22–27.

33. "Financial Accounting and Reporting by Oil and Gas Producing Companies," *Statement of Financial Accounting Standards (SFAS) No. 19* (Stamford, CT: FASB, 1977). This statement was issued after protracted deliberation, and it identified a single method of accounting that was to be followed by all affected companies. In August 1978, the SEC ruled that a new method of accounting for oil and gas reserves needed to be developed and that in the meantime companies could use any method that had been generally accepted prior to *SFAS No. 19.* This directly contradicted the FASB and required the issuance of both a statement suspending *SFAS No. 19* and a second FASB statement finally bringing the SEC and FASB into conformity with one another. SEC involvement was, in part, due to enactment of a public law requiring an investigation into and action on the state of oil and gas accounting rules by December 25, 1977. Such legal deadlines in connection with the accounting standard setting process are rare.

34. W. P. Schuetze, "A Mountain or a Molehill?" *Accounting Horizons,* March 1994, pp. 69–75.

35. For example, SEC reversal of *SFAS No. 19* was justified on the grounds that implementation of the proposed accounting standard would sharply inhibit petroleum exploration and development activities.

36. Joel H. Amernic and Russell J. Craig, "Accountability and Rhetoric During a Crisis: Walt Disney's 1940 Letter to Stockholders," *The Accounting Historians Journal,* 27(2) (2000), pp. 49–86.

2
Quality of Earnings, Accrual Accounting, and Income Determination

LEARNING OBJECTIVES
After studying this chapter, you should be able to:

1. Describe key aspects of *quality of earnings*, including how both accounting and nonaccounting decisions may affect this important concept

2. Explain the difference between cash-basis income and accrual income, and why the latter is generally a better measure of operating performance

3. Define the matching principle, and how it can be applied to recognize expenses under accrual accounting

4. Outline the difference between product and period costs, and why this distinction is important

5. Describe the format of, and classifications for, a multiple-step income statement, and how to differentiate sustainable earnings components from transitory earnings components

6. Explain the distinction between special and unusual items, discontinued operations, extraordinary items, and the cumulative effect of accounting changes

The concept of *quality of earnings*, which was introduced in Chapter 1, is examined more thoroughly in this chapter. This chapter and Chapter 3 also describe some key concepts and practices that govern the measurement of annual or quarterly income (or earnings) for financial reporting purposes. Income is the difference between **revenues** and **expenses**. The cornerstone of income measurement is **accrual accounting**. Under accrual accounting, *revenues are recorded in the period when they are "earned" and become "measurable"*—that is, when the seller has performed a service or conveyed an asset to a buyer, and the value to be received for that service or asset is reasonably assured and can be measured with a high degree of reliability. *Expenses are the expired costs or assets "used up" in producing those revenues, and they are recorded in the same accounting period in which the revenues are recognized, under the "matching principle."*

A natural consequence of accrual accounting is the decoupling of measured earnings from operating cash inflows and outflows. Reported revenues under accrual accounting generally do not correspond to cash receipts for the period; also, reported expenses do not always correspond to cash outlays for that period. In fact, *accrual accounting can produce large discrepancies between the firm's reported profit and the amount of cash generated from operations. Frequently, however, accrual accounting earnings provide a more reasonable measure of the economic value added during the period than do operating cash flows.*[1]

One of the many ways of thinking about quality of earnings is to focus on the relationship between a company's reported income for an accounting period and its cash flow from its activities for that same period. In order to illustrate this introductory way of looking at quality of earnings, we will use a demonstration case, *Office Equipment Inc.* But before we get to this case, we need to deal with two preliminaries.

First, in this chapter, and indeed throughout this textbook, we assume that you have completed a good introductory course in financial accounting. If your introductory financial accounting is a bit rusty, then perhaps you should examine the following learning materials that are available on the Companion Website for this textbook (**www.pearsoned.ca/revsine**):

COMPANION WEBSITE
www.pearsoned.ca/ revsine

- Using the accounting equation, Assets = Liabilities + Owners' Equity, to account for business transactions and events, and prepare a set of financial statements: see the "On Ice" case example;

- Reviewing debits and credits (this example builds on the "On Ice" case above): see "Transactions, events, and financial accounting: an introduction to double-entry bookkeeping";

- Reviewing the differences between accrual accounting and cash flow accounting: see "The accrual model, the cash flow model, and 'income.'"

Secondly, let's look at some aspects of *quality of earnings* from the perspective of both a manager and an analyst.

Quality of Earnings

How reliable is financial reporting? To what extent is a company's financial performance faithfully reflected by its financial statements? Does the information disclosed in financial reporting and the accounting policies and practices of a company contribute to a substantial understanding of the company? The concept of *quality of earnings* (QOE) is often employed to help analysts answer these and similar questions.

QOE is a complex concept, but here are some preliminary views of QOE:

Quality of earnings measures how much profits companies publicly report diverge from their true operating earnings. Low quality means the bottom line is padded with paper gains—such as the effect of inflation on a company's reported inventory values, or gains produced by "underdepreciation", when a company doesn't write off plant and equipment as fast as their real value is falling.

Because a decline in quality means companies' reported earnings are weaker and less sustainable than they appear, it indicates likely trouble for future earnings— whether or not a recession arrives. If history is any guide, those lower quality earnings also will come home to roost in lower stock prices ....[2]

...

The notion of earnings quality is multifaceted, and there is no consensus on how to measure it .... Basically, earnings are considered to be high quality when they are sustainable—for example, those that are generated from repeat customers or from a high quality product that enjoys steady customer demand based upon clear brand name identity. Examples of unsustainable earnings items include gains or losses resulting from debt retirement; write-offs of assets from corporate restructurings and plant closings; or reduction in discretionary expenditures for advertising, research and development, or management education.

Earnings quality is also affected by the accounting methods chosen by management to describe the routine, ongoing activities of a company (e.g., LIFO rather than FIFO inventory accounting, or the time period over which assets are amortized), and by the subjectivity—it's unavoidable!—of accounting estimates (e.g., allowance for future uncollectibles or assets' useful lives).[3]

Managers of reporting companies are key participants in the QOE story. Important aspects of managers' views about earnings-related behaviour in financial reporting were studied in a research article by Merchant and Rockness.[4]

The authors described their survey of managers in two companies and of a group of internal auditors. The survey asked respondents to indicate the degree to which they believed several different situations involving accounting and management decisions were ethical or unethical. Specifically, respondents were requested to select one of the following responses (on a five-point scale) to describe each situation:

- Ethical practice = 1.
- Questionable practice = 2. I would not say anything to the manager, but it makes me uncomfortable.
- Minor infraction = 3. The manager should be warned not to engage in the practice again.
- Serious infraction = 4. The manager should be severely reprimanded.
- Totally unethical = 5. The manager should be fired.

Here is an example of one situation in the questionnaire:

The general manager ordered his employees to defer all discretionary expenditures (e.g., travel, advertising, hiring, maintenance) into the next accounting period, so that his division could make its budgeted profit targets. Expected amount of deferral: $150,000. The expenses were postponed from November and December until January in order to make the annual target.

The average score of 308 responses to this situation was 2.09 (out of 5), suggesting that this deferring of all discretionary expenses was viewed as a questionable practice or minor infraction. However, the range of responses was from 1 to 5, and the standard deviation of 1.27 (which is a statistical measure of dispersion) was the highest of all the 13 scenarios presented in the questionnaire, indicating that there was considerable variance among the responses with respect to this item.

This research is useful since it helps provide some insight into managers' views about financial reporting. But questionnaire-based data gathering almost always suffers from being "context free" to varying degrees, which is a real problem in developing an understanding of managers' roles in financial reporting. Financial reporting is best viewed as a system in which managers play a key but only partial role and where they are subject to incentives, disincentives, and (imperfect) checks and balances.

In the aftermath of Enron, WorldCom, Nortel, and other highly publicized cases, issues relating to the ethics of earnings management are certainly recognized as being central to quality of earnings. Case C1-1 (The accounting instructor) in Chapter 1 provides a schematic representation of the "Financial Reporting: Accountability and Communication System," of which all components and processes must be operating harmoniously at a high ethical level for society to have confidence in accounting's quality of earnings. Surely the ethics of earnings management are a key aspect of QOE.

Office Equipment Inc.: A Simple Case of QOE

Office Equipment Inc. (OEI) is a small company whose common shares are held by 31 members of the Relack family. OEI, which sells high-quality office furniture, was founded 20 years ago by Ms S. Relack. She had the reputation among her relatives of being a sharp businessperson, if occasionally a little idiosyncratic, so they pretty much left the business in her hands. Besides, Ms Relack owned 40% of the shares up to near the end of 2002, while the remaining 60% were owned equally by each of the other 30 relatives, so spending the time and effort to watch out for their then individual interests of 2% each didn't seem worthwhile. In fact, they even thought it was too much of a bother to have a shareholders' agreement. The most recent financial data prepared under the supervision of Ms Relack are shown in Exhibit 2.1.

Abruptly just last month (January 2003), Ms Relack sold her share of the company (her management contract specified that she had the option of selling her shares to the other members of the family at "ten times the most recent net income"), resigned her position as CEO and also her position on the board of directors, and moved to a South Sea island. As one of the relatives exclaimed, "Why, she didn't even leave an e-mail address where she could be reached!"

Analysis (a) Cash flows and accrual income:

The degree of correlation between cash flow from operations and accrual income is an important indicator of QOE. Based upon the information provided in the case, the cash flow statement in Exhibit 2.2 may be reconstructed. (We strongly recommend that you attempt to prepare this cash flow statement from the case material provided, since it is a good review of some important introductory financial accounting. A complete solution is available on the Companion Website for this textbook at **www.pearsoned.ca/revsine**. Or, you can review the explanation of cash flow statements in Chapter 4.)

COMPANION WEBSITE
www.pearsoned.ca/ revsine

Reported net income is +$250,000, but the reconstructed cash flow from operating activities is –$140,000. Part of this dramatic difference is due to the company's accounting policy of including nonoperating-type disposal gains as part of operations, but the major factor is the huge increase in accounts receivable and inventories, as well as the very low amortization expense (see below). Comparing the details of cash flow and net income suggests that earnings of +$250,000 relative to operating cash flow seem hard to justify for this company, and thus QOE appears to be very low. But let's examine more details in part (b), which follows.

(b) Further comments on QOE: Now that we've prepared a cash flow statement for OEI, we want to learn as much as possible about the business and Ms Relack's decisions. Our assessment will be based upon the following two requirements.

1. The accounting policies that management chooses may provide an insight into management's attitudes and philosophies.

    Some comments on OEI's accounting policies:

    - Amortization is $20,000 per year, but building and equipment assets cost about $1,000,000, implying an average service life of 50 years. Doesn't 50 years seem excessively long? So is the $20,000 excessively understated, perhaps to inflate reported net income?

    - Should the accounting gains on the sale of land and buildings and equipment and the accounting loss on the sale of investments be classified as nonoperating items? If the answer is "yes," then the net income number misstates sustainable income from continuing operations.

Exhibit 2.1 OFFICE EQUIPMENT INC.

Balance Sheet and Other Information

	Years Ended December 31,	
	2002	2001
Cash	$ 0	$ 40,000
Accounts receivable	400,000	200,000
Inventory, at FIFO cost	600,000	250,000
Investments	10,000	110,000
Land	100,000	150,000
Buildings and equipment	1,000,000	1,060,000
Accumulated amortization	(760,000)	(800,000)
Patents	10,000	15,000
	$1,360,000	$1,025,000
Accounts payable	$ 160,000	$ 80,000
Accrued wages	80,000	0
Notes payable	300,000	320,000
Common shares	600,000	500,000
Retained earnings	220,000	125,000
	$1,360,000	$1,025,000

For 2002:

Net income was $250,000; there were no extraordinary gains or losses, and everything was accounted for as being due to operations.

Issued $100,000 in common shares for notes payable; a major supplier had accepted the notes payable late last year in lieu of payment.

Land was sold for $70,000 cash.

Capital asset amortization expense of $20,000 was recorded.

Amortizable capital assets that were fully amortized were sold for $30,000.

The "Investments" account consists mainly of blue-chip common shares that provided a steady if unspectacular stream of dividend income to OEI over the years. These shares were sold for $75,000 just after the stock market went into a tailspin.

Sales were $1,500,000, 10% higher than sales in 2001. The increase was due to Ms Relack's new policy of granting extended credit of 18 months to selected customers. The entire $1,500,000 was on account.

- Why is there apparently no allowance for doubtful accounts, especially since there is now a new, looser credit-granting policy? Is this another overstatement of net income? Accounts receivable have increased by 100%, but sales are up by only 10%.
- Inventory has increased by $350,000, but sales are up by 10% or a little over $136,000. How salable is the inventory on hand? What would be the result of a "lower-of-cost-and-market" approach to inventory valuation in this case? A FIFO cost flow assumption is being used; is this inflating reported net income as well?

Exhibit 2.2 OFFICE EQUIPMENT INC.

Cash Flow Statement

	Year Ended December 31, 2002
Operating activities:	
Net income	$250,000
Loss on sale of investments	25,000
Amortization of capital assets	20,000
Amortization of patents	5,000
Gain on land sale	(20,000)
Gain on buildings and equipment sale	(30,000)
	$250,000
Increase in accounts payable	$ 80,000
Increase in accrued wages	80,000
Increase in accounts receivable	(200,000)
Increase in inventories	(350,000)
Cash flows from operating activities (CFO)	($140,000)
Investing activities:	
Sale of long-term investments	$ 75,000
Sale of land	70,000
Sale of building and equipment	30,000
Cash flows from investing activities (CFI)	**$175,000**
Financing activities:	
Issue notes payable	$ 80,000
Dividends	(155,000)
Cash flows from financing activities (CFF)	$ (75,000)
Net decrease in cash and cash equivalents (CCE)	$ (40,000)
Cash and cash equivalents at beginning of period	40,000
Cash and cash equivalents at end of period	0
Other financing activities:	
Exchange of notes payable for common stock	**$100,000**

- Is the revenue recognition point for "selected" customers appropriate? Since they were granted extended credit terms, should we either delay revenue recognition, or at the very least account for possible sales returns?
- Why was no cash flow statement prepared and distributed to the owners?
- It seems that an audit was not performed. Why?

Overall, the array of accounting policies chosen by Ms Relack leads to serious questions about OEI's "quality of earnings." That is, how well does the income number, taking into consideration all the decisions that are behind it, represent the results of operations of the organization? Recall that CFO is $140,000, while net income is $250,000. The accounting decisions leading to the calculation of OEI's net income, along with the highly negative CFO, strongly suggest that Ms Relack was selecting accounting alternatives in an unethical manner, and that the quality of OEI's earnings is very poor indeed.

2. What nonaccounting business decisions made over the year are questionable?

Of course, we have just finished complaining about Ms Relack's accounting decisions, which are an important type of management decision. We now turn to the business decisions that were made:

- CFO is negative, CFI is positive, and CFF is negative. This cash flow pattern seems consistent with that of a downsizing company in a declining industry. Why are capital assets being sold off? Perhaps to generate cash flow when operations are not doing so?
- Why were the blue-chip stocks sold off, especially just after the market declined? Was this another attempt to generate cash flow when operations were not doing so?
- Was CFO artificially increased by deferring both accounts payable and (possibly) accrued wages?
- Why was the new credit policy adopted?
- Why was so much inventory purchased? Was there a link between Ms Relack and certain suppliers? If so, were the prices OEI paid fair?
- Why was such a large dividend paid out, in relation to CFO and the net decrease in cash? (This becomes especially troublesome if CFO was artificially overstated by deferring payments, and total cash flow by selling off possibly productive capital assets.)
- Why were some suppliers not paid last year? (Apparently, suppliers accepted notes payable in exchange for accounts payable.) This year (2001), they exchanged their notes payable for common shares so that the Relacks' shareholding was diluted.

There are lots of upsetting things to worry about in this short case. Perhaps the Relack relatives should think about hiring a lawyer! For our purposes, the case provides a nice little illustration of how an overall assessment of accounting and business decisions can help us to gain some insight into forming a judgment regarding QOE. And it reinforces the point that income under accrual accounting and cash flow are two quite different things. In the case of OEI, income as reported and cash flow from operations were even going in opposite directions! This "disconnect" between income and cash flow suggests strongly that accountants, managers, and analysts must be especially concerned with integrity in income measurement, and ensure that the generally accepted accounting principles (GAAP) standards in this area are applied in a straightforward way. We're now going to examine those guidelines.

Recap

The quality of earnings (QOE) of a company is a complex concept that analysts become familiar with as they gain experience. One aspect of QOE involves the relationship of a company's earnings number and its cash flow number, especially cash flow from operations. While it is expected that income and cash flow numbers will differ under accrual accounting, an examination of the reasons for this difference, as in the Office Equipment Inc. case, may reveal indications of poor QOE (or, conversely, good QOE).

Measuring Profit Performance: Revenues and Expenses

We have contrasted accrual accounting with cash-basis earnings in a simplified setting. Review the example on the Companion Website for this textbook at **www.pearsoned.ca/revsine** if you need to be convinced of the difference between measures of accrual income and cash flow. Now, in more realistic (and complex) settings, we will review some of the features associated with measuring revenues and expenses under accrual accounting.

For virtually all companies, income is not earned as a result of merely one activity. A manufacturing company, for example, earns income as a result of these separate and diverse activities, which may or may not occur in the sequence indicated:

1. Marketing the product.
2. Receiving customers' orders.
3. Negotiating and signing production contracts.
4. Ordering materials.
5. Manufacturing the product.
6. Delivering the product.
7. Collecting the cash from customers.

Since income is earned as a result of complex, multiple-stage processes, some guidelines are needed to determine at which stage income should be recognized in the financial statements. The key issue is the *timing* of income recognition: *When*, under GAAP, are revenues and expenses—and thus income—to be recognized?

The accounting process of recognizing income comprises two distinct steps. First, revenues must be recorded. This process of **revenue recognition** establishes the numbers that appear at the top of the income statement. The recognition of revenue then triggers the second step—the **matching** against revenue of the costs that expired (were used up) in generating the revenue. The difference between revenues and expired costs (expenses) is the **income** that should be recognized for the period.

Criteria for Revenue Recognition

According to GAAP, revenue is recognized at the *earliest* moment in time when *both* of the following conditions are satisfied:

Condition 1. The **critical event** in the process of earning the revenue has taken place.

Condition 2. The amount that will be collected is reasonably assured and is **measurable** with a reasonable degree of reliability.

The *CICA Handbook* sets out general GAAP for revenue recognition in its Section 3400. Our discussion is an interpretation of this section.

Condition 1: The Critical Event

While the earnings process is the result of many separate activities, there is usually one critical event considered to be absolutely essential to the ultimate increase in the net asset value of the firm. The exact nature of this critical event varies from industry to industry, as we will show in subsequent examples. Unless the critical event takes place, the value of the firm's net assets will not increase. Thus, the occurrence of the critical event is the first step that must be satisfied before revenue can be recognized. This step is a necessary, but not sufficient, condition for revenue to be recognized.

Condition 2: Measurability

Accountants do not immediately recognize revenue just because the critical event has taken place. There must be another condition: it must be possible to measure the amount of revenue that has been earned with a reasonable degree of assurance. Revenue cannot be recognized merely on the basis of an intuitive "feel" that certain events have added value to the firm's assets. There must be objective, verifiable evidence as to the amount of value that has been added. Unless the amount of value added can be reliably quantified, GAAP do not allow an increase in asset values to be recorded. Generally, this restriction translates into having a readily determinable price for the goods or service, which is a price established in the marketplace where buyers and sellers are free to negotiate the terms of trade. So-called list prices assigned to the good or service by the seller often do not satisfy the measurability condition, because they can deviate from the market-clearing price paid by the buyer.

Only after Conditions 1 and 2 are *both* met can revenue be recognized under GAAP. If an Internet service provider (ISP) markets a deal by which its customers receive two years of unlimited high-speed Internet access by paying an up-front fee of $240, certainly the measurability condition is satisfied. But the ISP hasn't provided the service as yet, and it hasn't earned the revenue, so when it receives $240 from a customer, it must record the following entry:

DR Cash	$240	
CR Unearned revenue		$240

The "Unearned revenue" account is a balance sheet account. Only as the service is provided will "Unearned revenue" be debited and "Revenue" be credited. For example, suppose that $240 was received from a customer in March 2003, for two years of service beginning April 1, 2003. By December 31, 2003 (the ISP's year end), the following adjusting entry must be recorded since both conditions have been met (9 out of the 24 months' worth = $90):

DR Unearned revenue	$90	
CR Revenue		$90

That is, in this example, the critical event in earning revenue is actually providing the ordered product (i.e., Internet high-speed access) to the customer. Stated somewhat differently, while revenue recognition Condition 2 is met in this example on initial receipt of the order with the prepayment (i.e., the amount of ultimate revenue—$240—is measurable with a high degree of assurance and reliability), Condition 1 is not met at that time and, therefore, no revenue is recognized because the critical event (i.e., provision of Internet access) has not yet occurred.

To further illustrate how the revenue recognition conditions can be applied, consider another example. On January 2, 2004, Gigantic Motors Corporation assembles 1,000 automobiles, each with a sticker price of $18,000. Since these cars have not yet been sold to dealers, they are parked in a lot adjacent to the plant. Let's examine how revenue recognition Conditions 1 and 2 operate in this setting.

Most observers would agree that the critical event in adding value in automobile manufacturing is production itself, since car manufacturers eventually sell all units produced. Accordingly, the critical event occurred as the automobiles rolled off the production line. However, no revenue would be recognized at that time. Although revenue recognition Condition 1 is satisfied, Condition 2 is *not* satisfied merely on completion of production. *This revenue recognition condition is not satisfied because the ultimate sale price of the automobiles is still unknown.* While Gigantic Motors has established a suggested list price of $18,000 per vehicle, the ultimate amount of cash that will actually be received in the future will depend upon general economic conditions, consumer tastes and preferences, and the availability and asking price of competing automobile models. Thus, the specific amount of value that has been added by production is not yet measurable with a reasonable degree of assurance. Revenue will be recognized only when the cars are sold to dealers at a known price. Only then is revenue recognition Condition 2 satisfied.

The financial reporting rules governing revenue recognition are often misunderstood. Because revenue is usually recognized at the time of sale in most industries, some observers erroneously conclude that the sale is itself the sole criterion for recognizing revenue. But this is not correct. The financial reporting rule for recognizing revenue is more complicated and subtle. Specifically, revenue is recognized as soon as Condition 1 (critical event) *and* Condition 2 (measurability) are *both* satisfied. *In most instances, the time of sale turns out to be the earliest moment at which both Conditions 1 and 2 are satisfied, which is why revenue is most frequently recognized at the time of sale of the product or service.*

But Conditions 1 and 2 are occasionally satisfied even before a legal sale (i.e., transfer of title) occurs. The following example illustrates where revenue can be recognized prior to sale.

Weld Shipyards has been building ocean-going oil tankers since 1951. In January 2003, Weld signs a contract to build a standard-design tanker for Humco Oil. The contract price is $60 million, and construction costs are estimated to total approximately $45 million. The tanker is expected to be completed by December 31, 2004. Weld intends to account for the project using the **percentage-of-completion** method.

Under the percentage-of-completion method (see Chapter 3 for a more detailed description), revenues and expenses are recognized as production takes place rather than at the time of completion (the sale). For example, if the tanker is 40% complete at the end of 2003 and finished in 2004, revenues and expenses would be recognized according to the following percentage-of-completion schedule:

($ in millions)	2003	2004	Two-Year Total
Percentage	40%	60%	100%
Revenue	$24	$36	$60
Expense	(18)	(27)	(45)
Income	$ 6	$ 9	$15

This method is permitted under GAAP when certain conditions—as in the Weld Shipyard example—are met. Condition 1 (critical event) is satisfied over time as the tanker is built—just as in Gigantic's automotive production example. But unlike the Gigantic Motors example, revenue recognition Condition 2 *is satisfied* for Weld Shipyards, since a firm contract with a known buyer at a set price of $60 million exists. Thus, the tanker example satisfies *both* of the two conditions necessary for revenue to be recognized. Additionally, expenses are also measurable with a reasonable degree of assurance since the tanker is of a standard design that Weld has built repeatedly in past years. This example provides an overview of why the percentage-of-completion method, when used properly, meets revenue recognition Conditions 1 and 2. Paragraph .08 of Section 3400 of the *CICA Handbook* sets out the GAAP for this situation.

In other circumstances, Conditions 1 and 2 may not both be satisfied until *after* the time of sale—for instance, until the cash is collected. In this case, it would be inappropriate to recognize income when the sale is made; instead, income recognition is deferred and is ultimately recognized in proportion to cash collections. Chapter 3 illustrates the **installment sales method**, an example in which revenue and expense are recognized at the time of cash collection rather than at the time of sale.

Figure 2.1 is a time-line diagram depicting the activities making up the revenue recognition process for some selected industries.

To justify recognizing revenue during the **production phase**, the following conditions must be met:

1. A specific customer must be identified and an exchange price agreed on. In most cases, a formal contract must be signed.
2. A significant portion of the services to be performed has been performed, and the expected costs of future services can be reliably estimated.
3. An assessment of the customer's credit standing permits a reasonably accurate estimate of the amount of cash that will be collected.

Situations where these conditions may be satisfied include long-term contracts for the construction of ships, bridges, and office buildings, as well as, for example, special-order government contracts for the production of military equipment.

As depicted in Figure 2.1, revenue may be recognized on **completion of production** in some industries. This recognition is justified when:

1. The product is immediately saleable at quoted market prices.
2. Units are homogeneous.
3. No significant uncertainty exists regarding the costs of distributing the product.

Examples where these circumstances exist include mining and harvesting of natural resources, as well as agricultural crops. These commodities are traded in active, organized markets, and thus a reliable market price can be determined at production even though the eventual buyer's identity is unknown at that time. Although GAAP permits mining and other natural resource companies to recognize revenue at completion of production, few actually do so. Instead, most delay revenue recognition until the time of sale.

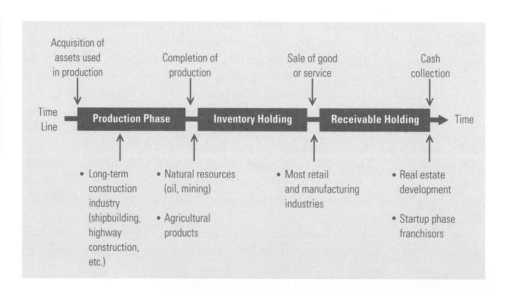

FIGURE 2.1
THE REVENUE RECOGNITION PROCESS

Industries recognizing revenue at indicated phases

Revenue recognition **at the time of sale** is the dominant practice in most retail and manufacturing industries. Occasionally, revenue is not recognized until **after the time of sale**. To justify postponing recognition of revenues, one or more of the following conditions must generally be present:

1. Extreme uncertainty exists regarding the amount of cash to be collected from customers. This uncertainty may be attributable to:

    - The customer's precarious financial condition.
    - Contingencies in the sales agreement that allow the buyer or seller to terminate the exchange.
    - The customer having the right to return the product and this right being frequently exercised.

2. Future services to be provided are substantial, and their costs cannot be estimated with reasonable precision.

These conditions exist in circumstances like real estate sales, where collection of the sale price occurs in protracted installments, and in sales of franchises for new or unproved concepts or products.

Regardless of which basis of revenue recognition is used, the recognition of expenses must always adhere to the matching principle—all costs incurred in generating the revenue must be recorded as expenses in the same period the related revenue is recognized. Matching expenses with revenues is the second step of the income recognition process.

Matching Expenses with Revenues

Once gross revenues for the period are determined, the next step in determining income is to accumulate and record the costs associated with generating those revenues. Some costs are easily traced to the revenues themselves. These **traceable** costs—also called **product** costs—are described as being **matched** with revenues. Other costs are clearly also important in generating revenue, but their contribution to a specific sale or to revenues of a particular period is more difficult to quantify. Such costs are expensed in the *time periods benefited*, which is why they are called **period** costs. Let's see how the matching principle is applied to traceable or product costs—as well as to period costs.

Traceable or Product Costs This next example illustrates how product costs are matched with revenue under GAAP income measurement rules.

Cory TV and Appliance, a retailer, sells one 24-inch colour television set on the last day of February for $500 cash. The TV set was purchased from the manufacturer for $240 cash in January of that same year. Cory provides a 60-day "parts and labour" warranty to the customer. A typical 24-inch colour TV requires $10 of warranty service during the first month following the sale and another $15 of service in the second month.

The expected (as well as the actually experienced) cash flows associated with this single transaction are depicted in Figure 2.2.

GAAP revenue recognition criteria are satisfied by the cash sale in February, so $500 of revenue is recorded in that month. The current and expected future costs of generating that revenue are $265, and these costs are recorded as expenses in the same month (February) that the revenue is recognized. Thus, accrual accounting trans-

FIGURE 2.2
CASH FLOW
DIAGRAM

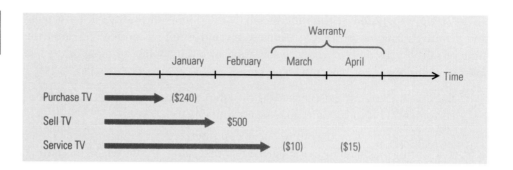

forms the cash flow diagram of Figure 2.2 into the revenue recognition and expense matching diagram shown in Figure 2.3.

Period Costs Cory TV and Appliance incurs other types of costs, which are also crucial in generating revenues. However, the link between these costs and individual sales is difficult to establish. One example of costs of this nature is advertising expenditures.

Assume Cory TV buys five minutes of advertising time on a local radio station each month for a monthly cost of $700. Obviously, the purpose of advertising is to generate sales. However, it is virtually impossible to associate any month's advertising expenditure with any specific sale, since consumer behaviour is the result of diverse influences and repeated advertising exposure. Consequently, GAAP does not try to match advertising expenditures with specific sales. Instead, the cost of advertising is charged as an expense in the period in which the ads run. Such costs are called **period costs**. No effort is made to link any particular advertising campaign with particular sales, since there exists no objective means for establishing this linkage.

The distinction between traceable (product) costs and period costs is discussed further in Chapter 9. At this point, it is important to understand that in applying the matching concept, some costs are directly matched against revenues while others are associated with time periods.

Recap
Matching involves associating expired costs (expenses) with the revenues recognized in a period or with the passage of time. Costs directly matched against revenues are called product costs, while costs matched with the passage of time are called period costs.

FIGURE 2.3
REVENUE
RECOGNITION
AND EXPENSE
MATCHING

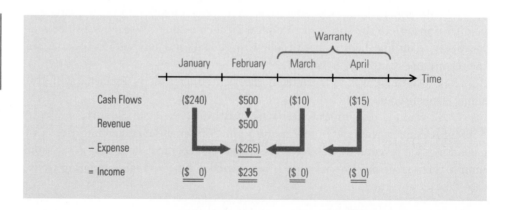

Income Statement Format and Classification

Virtually all decision models in modern corporate finance are based on future cash flows. One way to provide users with information about future cash flows is to present them with cash flow forecasts prepared by management. Traditional financial reporting rejects this approach because such numbers are too "soft" (i.e., too speculative or manipulable).

An alternative to satisfying users' needs for assessing future cash flows is to provide financial information based on past and current events in a format that gives users reliable and representative baseline numbers for generating *their own* forecasts of future cash flows. This format for income statements segregates components of income. The intent of this format is to classify income components as "transitory" or "sustainable" (i.e., likely to be repeated in future reporting periods).

As we survey the existing format and classification rules, we will see that the format of multiple-step income statements is intended to subdivide income in a manner which facilitates forecasting. Our discussion is based on the comparative income statements of Mythical Corporation for 2000–2002 that are presented in Exhibit 2.3. This exhibit illustrates how existing disclosure rules can help users predict future events.

The income statement isolates a key figure called **Income from continuing operations**. (See ① in Exhibit 2.3.) This component of income should include only the *normal, recurring, (presumably) more sustainable, ongoing economic activities* of the organization. As we'll discuss shortly, this intermediate income number can sometimes include gains and losses that occur relatively infrequently—called **special or unusual items** (item ② in Exhibit 2.3)—but nevertheless arise from a firm's ongoing, continuing operations. With the possible exception of some of these special or unusual items, "Income from continuing operations" summarizes the wealth effects of recurring transactions or activities that are expected to continue into the future. Therefore, this figure may serve as the anchor or jumping-off point for forecasting future profits.

Other components of income do not recur—and hence do not form a good basis for projecting future income. These other, (presumably) more transitory components of income are disclosed separately below the "Income from continuing operations" number (items ③ and ④ are shown net of tax). These nonrecurring earnings components fall into two general categories:

- Discontinued operations.
- Extraordinary items.

The rules for classification and placement of these nonrecurring items within the income statement are discussed in the following sections. These classification rules describe in detail what may be included in each statement category. As we will see, the rules standardize the format of disclosures as well as prevent certain "abuses" or distortions that might occur if firms were allowed to commingle these nonrecurring components of earnings with more sustainable, recurring revenue and expense items.

Discontinued Operations (Item ③)

Since a primary objective of financial reporting is to assist users in estimating future cash flows, transactions related to operations that the firm intends to discontinue, or

Exhibit 2.3 MYTHICAL CORPORATION

Income Statements for the Years Ended December 31, 2000–2002

(000,000 omitted)	2002	2001	2000
Net sales	$3,957	$3,478	$3,241
Costs of goods sold	(1,364)	(1,189)	(1,096)
Gross profit	$2,593	$2,289	$2,145
Selling, general, and administrative	(1,093)	(949)	(922)
② Special or unusual items (Note 1)	(251)	—	—
Income from continuing operations before income taxes	1,249	1,340	1,223
Income tax expense	(406)	(436)	(411)
① Income from continuing operations	$ 843	$ 904	$ 812
③ Discontinued operations (Note 2)			
Income from operation of discontinued business division, net of tax	203	393	528
Gain on disposal of discontinued division, net of tax	98	—	—
Income before extraordinary item	$1,144	$1,297	$1,340
④ Extraordinary loss, net of income tax effect (Note 3)	—	(170)	—
Net income	$1,144	$1,127	$1,340

Note 1: Special or Unusual Items—A strike closed the Pleasant Grove manufacturing facility for five months in mid-2002. The fixed costs incurred at the idle plant totalled $251 million.

Note 2: Discontinued Operations—The Company discontinued a business segment in 2002. The 2002 operating income and gain on disposal for this segment, net of tax, were $203 million and $98 million, respectively.

Note 3: Extraordinary Loss—A fire partially destroyed the chemical plant in River City in 2001. The Company had no insurance coverage for such losses, which amounted to $170 million.

CICA Handbook Section 3475 defines a discontinued operation as "the operations of a business segment that has been sold, abandoned, shut down, or otherwise disposed of, or that is the subject of a formal plan of disposal" (para. 3475.02).

has already discontinued, must be separated from other income items.[5] The reason is straightforward since, by definition, discontinued operations will not generate *future* operating cash flows.

In Exhibit 2.3, you can see that Mythical Corporation discontinued a business segment in 2002 (item ③). Notice that the operating results of this recently discontinued segment are not included in income from continuing operations in the current period (2002) when the decision to discontinue was made; nor are they included in any of the prior years (2001 and 2000) for which comparative data are provided. Also, notice that *income from discontinued operations is reported net of income tax effect, as are extraordinary losses* ④. This "net of tax" treatment is called **intraperiod income tax allocation**. The reason for this net of tax treatment is the belief that the income tax should be matched with the item that gave rise to it. This separation is widely thought to make the income figures more informative to users.

Here's why: If income tax were not matched with the item giving rise to it, then total reported income tax expense would combine taxes arising from both transitory items and from more sustainable items. Mixing the tax effect of continuing activities with the tax effect of single occurrence events would make it difficult for statement readers to forecast future tax outflows arising from ongoing events. Under intraperiod income tax allocation, the income tax associated with the (presumably) sustainable income from continuing operations before income taxes is separately disclosed as $406 million in 2002. Taxes arising from the (presumably) transitory items ③ and ④ are not included in the $406 million figure, thus facilitating forecasts of expected future flows after tax.

The revenues and expenses of the segment discontinued by Mythical Corporation in 2002 were also removed from the corresponding numbers reflecting 2001 and 2000 results (highlighted). This makes the "Income from continuing operations" number of $843 million in 2002, the year of discontinued operations, truly comparable with the "Income from continuing operations" numbers of $904 million and $812 million in 2001 and 2000, respectively. Restating the 2001 and 2000 results to make them comparable to the 2002 results means that all the numbers from the "Net sales" line through the "Income from continuing operations" line reported in the 2001 and 2000 columns of the 2002 annual report will be different from the corresponding numbers originally reported in the 2001 and 2000 statements. While initially confusing to analysts who wish to review the past sequence of earnings numbers to detect trends in a company's financial performance (often referred to as **time series analysis**), this adjustment to the numbers is essential for valid year-to-year comparisons.

Discontinuing an operating unit of the company invariably results in other gains or losses as assets in the discontinued segment are sold or scrapped. These gains or losses are disclosed separately, again net of their income tax effect, as illustrated by the $98 million gain in Exhibit 2.3.

Consider one last point on discontinued operations. Most firms are regularly disposing of assets and altering product lines in response to changes in competitive conditions and consumer tastes and preferences. Adjustments of these sorts are a *normal, recurring* part of doing business. Consequently, the financial results of these redeployments should be included in income from continuing operations. Disclosure rules for discontinued operations were formalized because accounting standard setters were somewhat mistrustful of firms' financial reporting motives. Apparently, there was fear that managers might be motivated to use abandonments or dispositions of minor segments or divisions as a way to manipulate the reported sequence or time series of earnings from *continuing* operations. Thus, guidelines for what constituted a discontinued segment were developed to reduce this possibility.

◀ *CICA Handbook* Section 3475.02 defines a business segment for purposes of identifying a discontinued operation as "a component of an entity, the activities of which represent a line of business significant to the entity as a whole and/or are directed to a particular class of customer significant to the entity as a whole."

Grey areas exist, despite these reporting rules for discontinued operations. However, the intent of the disclosure rules is to prevent firms from manipulating the number that purports to be income from continuing operations (item ①) by treating losses (or gains) on normal asset sales and dispositions as if they had arisen from discontinued operations. To qualify for exclusion from the continuing operations number and to be reported separately as discontinued operations, entire segments of readily distinguishable assets and/or customer groupings must be discontinued.

Extraordinary Items (Item ④)

Another category of transitory items reported separately on the income statement is extraordinary items (item ④ in Exhibit 2.3). To be treated as an extraordinary item, the event or transaction must fulfill all of the following criteria:[6]

1. *Unusual nature.* The underlying event or transaction possesses a high degree of abnormality and, taking into account the environment in which the company operates, that event or transaction is unrelated to the ordinary activities of the business.

The business environment in which an enterprise operates is a primary consideration in determining whether an underlying event or transaction is unusual and infrequent. The environment of an enterprise includes such factors as the characteristics of the industry or industries in which it operates, the geographical location of its operations, and the nature and extent of government regulation. For example, a plant explosion that results in uninsured losses would be considered an extraordinary loss by most businesses. But for a company that manufactures explosive materials (e.g., dynamite), losses from such an event may not be unusual or infrequent, given the environment in which the entity conducts its operations.

2. *Infrequent occurrence.* The underlying event or transaction is of a type that would not reasonably be expected to recur in the foreseeable future, again taking into account the environment in which the business operates.
3. *Independent of management.* The underlying event or transaction does "not depend primarily on decisions or determinations by management or owners" (para. 3480.02).

Like discontinued operations, extraordinary items are reported net of tax. Given the stringency of the criteria, few events qualify as extraordinary items. Examples of qualifying items include losses resulting from natural disasters (e.g., tornadoes) or losses arising from new laws or edicts (e.g., an expropriation by a foreign government).

As used in the authoritative accounting literature, an item is material if its magnitude or importance is sufficient to make a difference in one's decision.

Events that meet one or two—but not all—of the criteria do not qualify as extraordinary items. If material, these events must be disclosed as a separate line item on the income statement or in the footnotes to the financial reports. When separately reported on the income statement, they must be disclosed as a component of income from continuing operations in the section "Special or unusual items." For example, the Mythical Corporation income statement includes a "Special or unusual item" for losses incurred in conjunction with a labour strike, which is disclosed as a separate line item and discussed in a statement note. (See item ② and Note 1 in Exhibit 2.3.)

Other examples of special or unusual items include:[7]

1. Writedowns or writeoffs of receivables, inventories, equipment leased to others, and intangibles.
2. Gains or losses from the exchange or translation of foreign currencies.
3. Gains or losses from the sale or abandonment of property, plant, or equipment.
4. Special one-time charges resulting from corporate restructurings.
5. Gains or losses from the sale of investments.

Including special or unusual items as a component of income from continuing operations complicates financial forecasting and analysis. These special items are treated as a part of income from continuing operations because *collectively* they represent events that arise repeatedly as a normal part of ongoing business activities. However, some special items occur often while others recur sporadically. For example, firms are continuously selling or disposing of obsolete manufacturing assets as well as taking writedowns on inventory or selling investment securities. However, other special or unusual items—like strikes and reorganizations—occur less frequently. Consequently, the persistence of special or unusual items is likely to vary from period to period and from item to item. As a result, separate disclosure is provided for such special or unusual items to assist users in forecasting future results. Since these items are included as part of income from continuing operations *before* tax (sometimes referred to as being reported "above the line"), they are *not* disclosed net of tax effects.

The justification for defining extraordinary items so precisely and for requiring separate disclosure of special or nonrecurring items is to prevent statement manipulation. Without such requirements management might, in a "down" earnings year, be tempted to treat nonrecurring gains as part of income from continuing operations and nonrecurring losses as extraordinary. Precise guidelines preclude this.

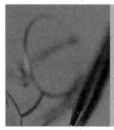

Recap

To be categorized as extraordinary and to appear below the "Income from continuing operations" line, an item must be unusual in nature *and* occur infrequently *and* be primarily beyond management's control. Special or unusual items that do not meet all these criteria, yet are considered material, are required to be disclosed separately as part of pre-tax income from continuing operations.

Usefulness of "Special" and Transitory Items

As Exhibit 2.3 illustrates, financial reporting rules for presenting operating results are designed to isolate transitory and nonsuitable components of earnings in order to assist users in predicting future earnings and cash flows. Research evidence confirms that the GAAP income statement classification framework we have discussed is useful to statement users. Specifically, subdividing earnings into three transitory components—special or unusual items, discontinued operations, and extraordinary items—and disclosing these amounts separately so that they are distinguished from the income that comes from continuing operations improves forecasts of future earnings.[8]

Accounting Changes

Aside from extraordinary and unusual items, and discontinued items, *accounting changes* are another group of accounting items that in some cases affect the income statement directly, and in others bypass the income statement and are recorded in the retained earnings statement. GAAP identify three categories of accounting changes in *CICA Handbook*, Section 1506:

1. A Change in Accounting Policy
This occurs when a company switches from one accounting policy or method to another. For example, a change from straight-line to accelerated amortization, or from LIFO to FIFO for inventory accounting, would each be an example of a change in accounting policy. These sorts of changes occur when a company adopts a new GAAP for the first time, or decides "that the change would result in a more appropriate presentation of events or transactions in the financial statements of the enterprise" (Section 1506.02). Canadian GAAP require that changes in accounting policies be accounted for retroactively, except when the information necessary for retroactive application is not reasonably available.[9] As an illustration, suppose that Imex Corporation began operations in January 2000, and had the following (highly simplified) income statements and retained earnings statements for the first three years of its corporate life:

	Periods Ended December 31,		
	2000	**2001**	**2002**
Revenues	$1,000,000	$1,200,000	$1,400,000
Expenses (except amortization)	400,000	700,000	750,000
Amortization of capital assets	100,000	100,000	100,000
Net income before income taxes	500,000	400,000	550,000
Less: Income taxes	200,000	160,000	220,000
Net income	$ 300,000	$ 240,000	$ 330,000
Retained earnings, start of period	0	250,000	440,000
	300,000	490,000	770,000
Less: Dividends	50,000	50,000	50,000
Retained earnings, end of period	$ 250,000	$ 440,000	$ 720,000

Imex's income tax rate is 40%. The company has used straight-line amortization of its capital assets up until the end of 2002. But early in 2003, management decides that accelerated amortization "would result in a more appropriate presentation of events or transactions in the financial statements of the enterprise" (Section 1506.02), and makes the change effective January 1, 2003. Amortization of capital assets using an accelerated method would have been $180,000, $150,000, and $130,000 in the years 2000, 2001, and 2002.

Up until the end of 2002 (the last period in which the old, straight-line method was used), cumulative amortization was $300,000; cumulative amortization would have been $460,000 under the newly adopted accelerated method. The difference of $160,000 would have resulted in retained earnings being *lower* by $160,000 × (1 − 0.40), or $96,000, and accumulated amortization on capital assets on the balance sheet being $160,000 higher, as at December 31, 2002. The journal entry to record this accounting change is:

DR	Retained earnings	$96,000	
DR	Future income tax liabilities	64,000	
	CR Accumulated amortization		$160,000

The debit to the account "Future income tax liabilities" records the income tax effect of the accounting change. This account will be explained in detail in Chapter 13, since our focus here is on how the accounting change is presented and not on the income tax effect.

GAAP in Canada require that *"[w]hen a change in an accounting policy is applied retroactively, the financial statements of all prior periods presented for comparative purposes should be restated to give effect to the new accounting policy ..."* (para. 1506.15), so the presentation in the 2003 comparative financial statements for Imex would be (we assumed that accelerated amortization for the current year, 2003, is $110,000):

	Periods Ended December 31,	
	2003	2002
Revenues	$1,410,000	$1,400,000
Expenses (except amortization)	800,000	750,000
Amortization of capital assets	110,000	130,000
Net income before income taxes	500,000	520,000
Less: Income taxes	200,000	208,000
Net income	$ 300,000	$ 312,000
Retained earnings, start of period	624,000	440,000
	924,000	752,000
Less: Accounting change (see footnote)	0	78,000
Retained earnings, start of period, as restated	924,000	674,000
Less: Dividends	50,000	50,000
Retained earnings, end of period	$ 874,000	$ 624,000

Notice that the new, accelerated amortization number is shown for both years presented ($130,000 for 2002, even though when the year 2002 results were first reported *in* 2002, the old, straight-line number of $100,000 was used). Also notice that the adjustment to the 2002 opening retained earnings is $78,000, not the $96,000 that we calculated above for the journal entry recording the accounting change. The $78,000 represents the cumulative effect on retained earnings of the accounting change up to the start of the first presented period, that is, 2002, and is calculated as follows:

New accelerated amortization up to the start of the first year shown (i.e., 2002):

$$\$180,000 \text{ (for 2000)} + \$150,000 \text{ (for 2001)} = \$330,000$$

Old straight-line amortization up to the start of the first year shown (i.e., 2002):

$$\$100,000 \text{ (for 2000)} + \$100,000 \text{ (for 2001)} = \underline{\ \ 200,000}$$

Increase in accumulated amortization of capital assets: $130,000

And, after the income tax effect, this is:

$$(1 - 0.40) \times \$130,000 = \$78,000$$

 A footnote to the financial statements would explain the rationale and the quantitative impact of the accounting change.

In contrast to the Canadian requirements, most changes in accounting principles in the United States must be accounted for by recording the cumulative effect of the change in the income statement of the year of the change.

2. Corrections of Errors in Prior Period Financial Statements

These result "from a mistake in computation affecting the financial statements, from a misinterpretation or misrepresentation of information, from an oversight of information available at the time the financial statements were prepared that ought to have been taken into account, or from a misappropriation of assets" (Section

1506.26). GAAP require that error corrections be accounted for technically in the same way as accounting changes are accounted for (i.e., retroactively, with restatement of prior periods shown), but with full disclosure about the nature and impact of the error (Section 1506.29 and .30). Corrections of errors are very uncommon, but when they do occur they are often a strong signal that there might be more than just financial accounting problems in the company. The case of Livent Inc. provides a vivid illustration.

Founded in 1989 by Canadian entertainment impresario Garth Drabinsky, Toronto-based Livent Inc. was the largest and fastest-growing producer of live theatre in North America. Livent produced original shows as well as theatrical classics, including musicals such as *Joseph and the Amazing Technicolor Dreamcoat, The Phantom of the Opera, Ragtime,* and *Showboat,* among others. The company's Broadway productions won 18 prestigious Tony Awards, including "best musical" for *Kiss of the Spider Woman.* But the music began to stop in the spring of 1998 when the company needed an injection of financial resources.

As part of the new management structure announced in April 1998, Drabinsky's control over the company was curtailed as he gave up his role of chairman, and was assigned the new title of "Chief Creative Director." In August, he was suspended from the company as media reports began to swirl regarding alleged unsavoury business practices. Then, on or about November 18, 1998, the following events occurred:

- Drabinsky was fired following allegations that he and his Livent colleague Myron Gottlieb took $7.5 million in secret kickbacks.

- Livent's new management accused Drabinsky of "fraudulently manipulating" the company's accounting records in order to hide $100 million in losses, and launched a $225 million lawsuit against Drabinsky and Gottlieb.

- Drabinsky and Gottlieb responded with countersuits, denying all charges.

- The company filed for bankruptcy protection in a U.S. court, and sought relief in Canada under the *Companies' Creditors Arrangements Act.*

- The company issued restated financial statements for 1996 and 1997, turning a reported profit for 1996 into a loss and significantly increasing the loss already reported for 1997. In a "Material Change Report" dated November 18, 1998, and filed to comply with provincial securities acts, Livent management provided details of its financial statement restatements, alleging (on pages 2–3) that:

Management Uncovers Pervasive, Systemic Accounting Irregularities

The company announced on August 10, 1998 that it had uncovered serious accounting irregularities and has conducted an intensive investigation of such irregularities since then. The company's investigation revealed massive, systemic accounting irregularities that permeated the company. These accounting irregularities included:

Transactions Improperly Recorded as Revenue Certain side agreements or other material terms between Livent and third parties were discovered as part of the company's investigation that were never disclosed to the Board of Directors or the Board's Audit Committee. These undisclosed side agreements materially altered the terms of transactions for which the company had recognized revenues. The discovery of these previously undisclosed side agreements required the reversal or modification of revenue recognition for the transactions.

In the company's restated financials, net income was reduced by $19.4 million (US$14.2 million) in 1996 and $23.3 million (US$17.0 million) in 1997 to correct for these irregularities.

Operating Costs Improperly Capitalized to Fixed Assets Millions of dollars of running costs for current productions (e.g., cast salaries, advertising, etc.), as well as G&A expenses, were inappropriately capitalized to fixed assets instead of being expensed as incurred. In the restated financials, net income was reduced by $3.1 million (US$2.3 million) in 1996 and $10.7 million (US$7.8 million) in 1997 to correct for these irregularities.

Improper Recording of Costs Millions of dollars of expenses were improperly shifted from one quarter to the next and were carried in an "expense roll." Effectively, the former senior management of the company directed that certain expenses and accounts payable be backed out, reversed in or withheld from the general ledger system in the quarter in which they should have been expensed. They were therefore not properly reflected in the company's financial statements for that period. In the restated financials, net income was reduced by $3.9 million (US$2.9 million) in 1996 and $0.5 million (US$0.3 million) in 1997 to correct for these irregularities.

Improper Recording of Preproduction Costs In some cases, preproduction costs for current shows were capitalized to preproduction accounts for shows that were not scheduled to be presented until a future time period, thereby deferring recognition of these costs until such future periods. In other cases, preproduction costs were improperly capitalized to fixed assets and preproduction costs were not recorded in the proper year. To correct for these irregularities, in the restated financials net income was reduced by $11.1 million (US$8.2 million) in 1996 and increased by $1.6 million (US$1.2 million) in 1997.

Improperly Accelerated Recognition of Revenue The timing of recognition of revenue was improperly accelerated for certain transactions. For example, in some cases, the entire amount of sponsorship was recorded at the time the sponsorship agreement was signed (or in some cases before the agreement was even executed) instead of properly amortizing the revenue over the relevant period of the agreement.

On December 16, 1998, a team of 35 Royal Canadian Mounted Police investigators raided Livent's Toronto headquarters and seized two truckloads of documents. Sadly, on June 1, 1999, it was announced that Livent's assets were to be sold to an American entertainment company.

3. Changes in Accounting Estimates

These occur frequently as part of the normal process of financial accounting, and do not require retroactive restatement (Section 1506.25). This makes sense, since such changes result from applying new information about an accounting item. For example, if a company increases its allowance for doubtful accounts in response to new information that the creditworthiness of the company's customers has slipped a bit, the effect of the increase should be accounted for only over the current and future periods that are impacted by the new economic situation of the customers.

When the economic circumstances underlying an accounting estimate change, GAAP require that the estimate also be changed. For instance, when unforeseen technological advances shorten the service life of an asset, the period over which the asset is amortized must be similarly shortened.

When accounting estimates are changed, past income is never adjusted; instead, the income effects of the changed estimate are accounted for in the period of change—and in future periods, if the change affects both. If the change in estimate has a material effect on current and future income, the dollar amount of the effect must be disclosed.

An example illustrates the process for adjusting current and future period numbers when a change in an accounting estimate is made. Miles Corporation purchased a production machine on January 1, 2000, for $6 million. The machine had no salvage value and an expected useful life of ten years. Amortization was on a straight-line basis. On January 1, 2002, the book value of the machine was $4.8 million (i.e., $6 million of original cost minus two years of accumulated amortization at $0.6 million per year). At that date, it became evident that due to changes in demand for the machine's output, its *remaining* useful life is six years, not eight years. If Miles Corporation had had perfect foresight, the annual amortization charge should have been $0.75 million ($6 million divided by eight years), amounting to $1.5 million over the first two years. Consequently, there was $0.3 million too little accumulated amortization ($1.5 million minus $1.2 million) on January 1, 2002, and pre-tax income for the previous two years was overstated by $0.3 million. Rather than forcing Miles to retroactively adjust reported past income, the GAAP disclosure rules require the change in estimate to be reflected in higher amortization charges over the new remaining life of the asset—in this case, from 2002 to 2005.[10] Depreciation in those years should be $0.8 million per year (i.e., the remaining book value of $4.8 million divided by the remaining useful life of six years). Over the entire eight-year life of the asset, amortization is calculated as follows:

2000–2001	2 years × $0.6 million per year	= $1.2 million
2002–2005	6 years × $0.8 million per year	= $4.8 million
Total cost of the asset		$6.0 million

From the perspective of perfect foresight, in which amortization would have been $0.75 million per year, amortization in the first two years was understated by $0.15 million annually, and in each of the last six years, it was overstated by $0.05 million annually. Obviously, over the eight-year life of the asset, the amortization charges total $6.0 million.

Why are changes in estimates "corrected" in this peculiar fashion? The reason is that accrual accounting requires many estimates; since the future is highly uncertain, a high proportion of these estimates turn out to be incorrect. If past income were corrected for every misestimate, income statements would be cluttered with numerous retroactive adjustments. The approach illustrated in this example provides an expedient way to deal with the uncertainty in financial statements without generating burdensome corrections.

Change in Reporting Entity

Another type of accounting change can arise when a company acquires or merges with another company. In such circumstances, the newly combined entity presents consolidated financial statements in place of the previously separate statements of each party to the transaction. Such combinations result in what is called a **change in reporting entity**, and are discussed in more detail in Chapter 16, Intercorporate Equity Investments, Consolidated Financial Statements, and Special Purpose Entities.

Recap

Accounting changes can dramatically affect reported earnings and distort year-to-year comparisons. For these reasons, GAAP require special disclosures to improve interperiod comparability and to help statement users understand what effect the accounting change has had on the current period's reported profits.

Comprehensive Income: An American Accounting Innovation

Generally, items included in net income are **closed transactions**. A closed transaction is one whose ultimate "payoff" results from events (1) that have already occurred and (2) whose dollar flows can be predicted fairly accurately. Recollect that income recognition automatically triggers a corresponding change in the carrying amount (book value) of net assets.

Sometimes balance sheet carrying amounts change even though the transaction is not yet closed. Let's consider a specific example, such as a bank or other financial institution that has investments in stocks or other financial instruments with readily determinable market values. Assume that these securities are held in the firm's "available for sale" portfolio and that their current market values exceed original purchase price. During the early 1990s, the Financial Accounting Standards Board (FASB) in the United States decided that the fair market value of the securities—rather than invested historical cost (the amount originally invested in them)—should appear on the balance sheet. To recognize the market value increase, the following accounting entry must be made:

```
DR   Marketable securities                          XXX
     CR   Owners' equity—unrealized holding
          gain on investment securities                       XXX
```

Obviously, the credit to offset the increase in the marketable securities account must be made to some sort of equity account. Notice, however, that this is not a closed transaction, since the securities have not been sold. Because such transactions are still **open**, the FASB does not require running the credit through the income statement. Instead, the owners' equity increase is reported directly as a separate component of equity in the balance sheet.[11] Thus, selected unrealized gains (or losses) arising from incomplete (or open) transactions sometimes bypass the income statement and are reported as direct adjustments to stockholders' equity. Such items are called **other comprehensive income** components and fall into one of the three following categories:[12]

1. Unrealized gains (losses) on marketable securities held in firms' "available for sale" portfolios.
2. Unrealized gains (losses) resulting from translating foreign currency financial statements of majority-owned subsidiaries into U.S. dollar amounts for the purpose of preparing consolidated financial statements.
3. In certain cases, unrealized losses resulting from recognition of minimum pension obligations under U.S. *SFAS No. 87*.

Figure 2.4 provides an overview of the elements that make up comprehensive income.

In "Elements of Financial Statements," *Statement of Financial Accounting Concepts Statement No. 6* (Stamford, CT: FASB, 1985), para. 70, comprehensive income is defined as "the change in equity (net assets) of a business enterprise during a period from transactions and other events and circumstances from nonowner sources. It includes all changes in equity during a period except those resulting from investments by owners and distributions to owners."

FIGURE 2.4
ELEMENTS OF
COMPREHENSIVE
INCOME

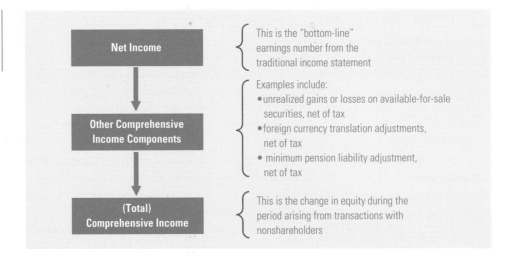

SFAS No. 130 requires firms to report comprehensive income in a statement that is displayed with the same prominence as other financial statements. Firms are permitted to display the components of other comprehensive income in one of several alternative formats:

1. In a single-statement format, one in which net income and other comprehensive income are added together to disclose (total) comprehensive income.
2. In a two-statement approach, one in which net income comprises one statement and a second, which presents a separate statement of comprehensive income.
3. As part of the statement of changes in stockholders' equity.

In the summer of 1999, the CICA's AcSB—in cooperation with standard setters from other countries—indicated that it was exploring an approach similar to FASB's comprehensive income. Exhibit 2.4 illustrates the one-statement approach and Exhibit 2.5 shows the two-statement approach for General Motors Corporation.

GENERAL MOTORS
www.gm.com

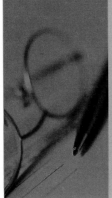

Recap

Comprehensive income measures the change in equity (net assets) of a company that results from all nonowner transactions and events. It comprises both bottom-line accrual income reported on the income statement and other comprehensive income components. Other comprehensive income comprises selected unrealized gains and losses on incomplete (or open) transactions that bypass the income statement and that are reported as direct credits or charges to stockholders' equity. U.S. companies are required to report comprehensive income in a statement that is displayed with the same prominence as other financial statements. But firms are free to choose the format of presentation—either as a separate statement or as part of a statement that is combined with the income statement or a statement of changes in stockholders' equity.

Exhibit 2.4 GENERAL MOTORS CORPORATION AND SUBSIDIARIES

Consolidated Statements of Income and Comprehensive Income
One-Statement Approach

	Years Ended December 31,		
(US$ in millions)	1996	1995	1994
Net sales and revenues			
Manufactured products	$145,341	$143,666	$134,760
Financial services	12,674	11,664	9,419
Other income	6,054	4,942	4,320
Total net sales and revenues	164,069	160,272	148,499
Costs and expenses			
Cost of sales and other operating charges, exclusive of items listed below	123,922	121,300	113,585
Selling, general, and administrative expenses	14,580	12,550	11,319
Amortization expenses	11,840	11,213	9,645
Interest expense	5,695	5,182	5,392
Plant closings reserve adjustments	(727)	—	—
Other deductions	2,083	1,678	1,460
Total costs and expenses	157,393	151,923	141,401
Income from continuing operations before income taxes	6,676	8,349	7,098
Income taxes	1,723	2,316	2,232
Income from continuing operations before cumulative effect of accounting changes	4,953	6,033	4,866
Income from discontinued operations	10	900	793
Cumulative effect of accounting changes	—	(52)	(758)
Net income	4,963	6,881	4,901
Other comprehensive income, net of tax			
Foreign currency translation adjustments	(336)	323	394
Unrealized holding gains (losses) arising during period	(70)	249	79
Minimum pension liability adjustment	1,246	(1,188)	1,763
Other comprehensive income	840	(616)	2,236
Comprehensive income	$ 5,803	$ 6,265	$ 7,137

Source: P. McConnell, *Accounting Issues*, Bear, Stearns & Co., Inc., August 27, 1997.

Exhibit 2.5 GENERAL MOTORS CORPORATION AND SUBSIDIARIES

Consolidated Statements of Income
Two-Statement Approach

	Years Ended December 31,		
(US$ in millions)	1996	1995	1994
Net sales and revenues			
Manufactured products	$145,341	$143,666	$134,760
Financial services	12,674	11,664	9,419
Other income	6,054	4,942	4,320
Total net sales and revenues	164,069	160,272	148,499
Costs and expenses			
Cost of sales and other operating charges, exclusive of items listed below	123,922	121,300	113,585
Selling, general, and administrative expenses	14,580	12,550	11,319
Amortization expenses	11,840	11,213	9,645
Interest expense	5,695	5,182	5,392
Plant closings reserve adjustments	(727)	—	—
Other deductions	2,083	1,678	1,460
Total costs and expenses	157,393	151,923	141,401
Income from continuing operations before income taxes	6,676	8,349	7,098
Income taxes	1,723	2,316	2,232
Income from continuing operations before cumulative effect of accounting changes	4,953	6,033	4,866
Income from discontinued operations	10	900	793
Cumulative effect of accounting changes	—	(52)	(758)
Net income	$ 4,963	$ 6,881	$ 4,901

Consolidated Statement of Comprehensive Income

	Years Ended December 31,		
(US$ in millions)	1996	1995	1994
Net income	$ 4,963	$ 6,881	$ 4,901
Other comprehensive income, net of tax			
Foreign currency translation adjustments	(336)	323	394
Unrealized holding gains (losses) arising during period	(70)	249	79
Minimum pension liability adjustment	1,246	(1,188)	1,763
Other comprehensive income	840	(616)	2,236
Comprehensive income	$ 5,803	$ 6,265	$ 7,137

Source: P. McConnell, *Accounting Issues*, Bear, Stearns & Co., Inc., August 27, 1997.

Summary

The concept of *quality of earnings*, introduced in Chapter 1, is more completely described in this chapter. The key differences between cash and accrual income measurement are highlighted, and the importance of these differences in understanding quality of earnings is described. In most instances, accrual-basis revenues do not coincide with cash receipts, and accrual expenses do not coincide with cash disbursements. The principles that govern revenue and expense recognition under accrual accounting are designed to alleviate the mismatching of cash inflows and cash outflows that occurs under cash-basis accounting, and to help analysts form a judgment on a company's quality of earnings.

Revenue is recognized when *both* the "critical event" and "measurability" conditions are satisfied. The critical event establishes when the entity has done something to "earn" the asset being received, and measurability is established when the revenue can be measured with a reasonable degree of assurance. These two conditions may be satisfied before or after the point of sale. The matching principle determines how and when the assets that are "used up" in generating the revenue—or that expire with the passage of time—are expensed. Relative to current operating cash flows, accrual earnings generally provide a more useful measure of firm performance, and serve as a more useful benchmark for predicting future cash flows.

Predicting future cash flows and earnings is critical to assessing the value of a firm's shares and its creditworthiness. Multiple-step income statements are designed to facilitate this forecasting process by isolating the more recurring or sustainable components of earnings from the nonrecurring or transitory earnings components. GAAP disclosure requirements for various types of accounting changes also facilitate the analysis of company performance over time.

For more Exercises, Problems/Discussion Questions, and Cases, visit the Companion Website for this textbook at **www.pearsoned.ca/revsine**.

Exercises

E2-1 Determining accrual- and cash-basis revenue

In November and December 2003, Now Company, a newly established magazine publisher, received $36,000 for 1,000 three-year subscriptions at $12 per year, starting with the January 2004 issue of the magazine.

Required:

How much should Now report in its 2003 income statement for subscriptions revenue on an accrual basis? How much revenue would be reported in 2003 on a cash basis?

E2-2 Determining unearned subscription revenue

Video Mart sells one- and two-year mail order subscriptions for its video-of-the-month business. Subscriptions are collected in advance and credited to sales. An analysis of the recorded sales activity revealed the following:

	2002	2003
Sales	$420,000	$500,000
Less cancellations	(20,000)	(30,000)
Net sales	$400,000	$470,000
Subscription expirations:		
2002	$120,000	
2003	155,000	$130,000
2004	125,000	200,000
2005		140,000
	$400,000	$470,000

Required:

At what amount should the company report unearned subscriptions revenue on the December 31, 2003, balance sheet?

E2-3 Converting from accrual- to cash-basis revenue

In its accrual-basis income statement for the year ended December 31, 2001, JK Company reported revenue of $1,750,000. Here is more information:

Accounts receivable 12/31/2000	$350,000
Uncollectible accounts written off during 2001	20,000
Accounts receivable 12/31/2001	505,000

Required:

Under the cash basis of income determination, how much should JK report as revenue for 2001?

E2-4 Converting from accrual- to cash-basis revenue

Pocket Company reported accrual-basis revenue of $2,100,000 in its income statement for the year ended December 31, 2001. Additional information was as follows:

	12/31/2000	12/31/2001
Accounts receivable	$415,000	$550,000
Allowance for doubtful accounts	25,000	40,000

No uncollectible accounts were written off during 2001.

Required:

Had the cash basis of accounting been used instead, how much revenue would Pocket Company have recognized for 2001?

E2-5 Converting from cash- to accrual-basis revenue

Milo Green, M.D., keeps her accounting records on the cash basis. During 2003, Dr. Green collected $150,000 in fees from her patients. At December 31, 2002, Dr. Green had accounts receivable of $20,000. At December 31, 2003, she had accounts receivable of $35,000 and unearned fees of $5,000.

Required:

On the accrual basis, how much was Dr. Green's patient service revenue for 2003?

E2-6 Converting from cash- to accrual-basis revenue

Zing Corporation reported rental revenue of $3,105,000 in its cash-basis income statement for the year ended November 30, 2003. Additional information is as follows:

Rents receivable, November 30, 2003	$1,060,000
Rents receivable, November 30, 2002	800,000
Uncollectible rents written off during the fiscal year	40,000

Required:

Under the accrual basis, Zing should report gross rental revenue of how much in 2003?

E2-7 Converting from accrual- to cash-basis expense

Under Rock Company's accounting system, all insurance premiums paid are debited to prepaid insurance. For interim financial reports, Rock makes monthly estimated charges to insurance expense with credits to prepaid insurance. Additional information for the year ended December 31, 2001, is as follows:

Prepaid insurance at December 31, 2000	$225,000
Charges to insurance expense during 2001, including a year-end adjustment of $35,000	875,000
Unexpired insurance premiums at December 31, 2001	245,000

Required:

What was the total amount of insurance premiums paid by Rock during 2001?

Problems/Discussion Questions

P2-1 Journal entries and statement preparation

- On January 1, 2001, Frances Corporation started doing business and the owners contributed $200,000 capital in cash.
- The company paid $24,000 to cover the rent for office space for the 24-month period from January 1, 2001, to December 31, 2002.
- On March 1, 2001, MSK Inc. entered into a consulting contract under which Frances Corporation promised to provide consulting to MSK Inc. for the ten-month period from March 1, 2001, to December 31, 2001. In return, MSK agreed to a monthly consulting fee of $15,000, which was all to be paid in January 2002. Frances Corporation fulfilled its contractual obligation during the year.
- On July 1, 2001, Frances Corporation purchased office equipment for $100,000 cash. The equipment has an estimated useful life of five years and no salvage value. The equipment was immediately placed into use. Frances Corporation uses the straight-line method of amortization. Frances Corporation records amortization expense in proportion to the number of months' usage.
- Through November 30, 2001, the company had paid $66,000 to its employees for 11 months of salaries. On December 31, 2001, Norbert Corporation advanced $20,000 to Frances Corporation for consulting services to be provided during 2002.

Required:

1. Provide journal entries for each of these transactions.
2. Provide adjusting entries at the end of the year.
3. Prepare an income statement for the year ended December 31, 2001.
4. Prepare a balance sheet as of December 31, 2001.

P2-2 Converting accounting records from cash basis to accrual basis

The following information pertains to Baron Flowers, a calendar-year sole proprietorship, which maintained its books on the cash basis during the year.

Baron Flowers
Trial Balance
December 31, 2002

	DR	CR
Cash	$ 25,600	
Accounts receivable 12/31/2001	16,200	
Inventory 12/31/2001	62,000	
Furniture and fixtures	118,200	
Land improvements	45,000	
Accumulated amortization 12/31/2001		$ 32,400
Accounts payable 12/31/2001		17,000
Baron, drawings		
Baron, capital 12/31/2001		124,600
Sales		653,000
Purchases	305,100	
Salaries	174,000	
Payroll taxes	12,400	
Insurance	8,700	
Rent	34,200	
Utilities	12,600	
Living expenses	13,000	
	$827,000	$827,000

The "Baron, drawings" account is used to record any distributions to Mr. Baron. The "Baron, capital" account is used to record any capital contributions that Mr. Baron makes to the business and any profits or losses retained in the business.

Baron has developed plans to expand into the wholesale flower market and is in the process of negotiating a bank loan to finance the expansion. The bank is requesting 2002 financial statements prepared on the accrual basis of accounting from Baron. During the course of a review engagement, Mr. Muir, Baron's accountant, obtained the following additional information:

1. Amounts due from customers totalled $32,000 at December 31, 2002.
2. An analysis of the receivables revealed that an allowance for uncollectible accounts of $3,800 should be provided.
3. Unpaid invoices for flower purchases totalled $30,500 and $17,000 at December 31, 2002, and December 31, 2001, respectively.
4. A physical count of the goods at December 31, 2002, determined that the inventory totalled $72,800. The inventory was priced at cost, which approximates market value.
5. On May 1, 2002, Baron paid $8,700 to renew its comprehensive insurance coverage for one year. The premium on the previous policy, which expired on April 30, 2002, was $7,800.

6. On January 2, 2002, Baron entered into a 25-year operating lease for the vacant lot adjacent to Baron's retail store, which was to be used as a parking lot. As agreed to in the lease, Baron paved and fenced the lot at a cost of $45,000. The improvements were completed on April 1, 2002, and they have an estimated useful life of 15 years. No provision for amortization has been recorded. Amortization on furniture and fixtures was $12,000 for 2002.

7. Accrued expenses at December 31, 2001 and 2002 were as follows:

	2001	2002
Utilities	$ 900	$1,500
Payroll taxes	1,100	1,600
	$2,000	$3,100

8. Baron was notified late in the year of a lawsuit filed against his business for an injury to a customer. Baron's attorney believes that an unfavourable outcome is probable and that a reasonable estimate of the settlement exclusive of amounts covered by insurance is $50,000.

9. The salaries account includes $4,000 per month paid to the proprietor. Baron also received $250 per week for living expenses.

Required:

1. Determine the adjustments that are required to convert the trial balance of Baron Flowers to the accrual basis of accounting for the year ended December 31, 2002. Prepare formal journal entries to support your adjustments.
2. Write a brief memo to Baron explaining why the bank would require financial statements prepared on the accrual basis instead of the cash basis.

P2-3 Adjusting entries and statement preparation

The following is the preclosing trial balance of Antonia Retailers, Inc.:

Antonia Retailers, Inc.
Preclosing Trial Balance as of December 31, 2003

	DR	CR
Cash	$ 42,000	
Accounts receivable	67,500	
Prepaid rent	15,000	
Inventory	100,000	
Equipment	60,000	
Building	90,000	
Allowance for doubtful accounts		$ 5,000
Accumulated amortization—equipment		30,000
Accumulated amortization—building		9,000
Advance from customers		25,000
Accounts payable		18,000
Salaries payable		4,000
Capital stock		70,000
Retained earnings 1/1/03		187,500
Sales revenue		350,000
Cost of goods sold	185,000	
Salaries expense	50,000	
Bad debt expense	10,500	
Rent expense	30,000	
Insurance expense	18,000	
Amortization expense—building	5,000	
Amortization expense—equipment	2,000	
Dividends	23,500	
Totals	$698,500	$698,500

The following additional information is provided to you:

1. The company paid a salary advance of $10,000 to one of its employees, an amount that was debited to the salaries expense account. This was an advance against the employee's salary for the year 2004.
2. On January 1, 2003, the company paid an insurance premium of $18,000, which was debited to the insurance expense account. The premium provided insurance coverage for 18 months beginning on January 1, 2003.
3. The company decided to revise its estimate of bad debts expense by calculating it at 10% of its sales revenue.
4. On January 1, 2004, the board of directors of the company declared an additional dividend of $10,000 for the year 2003.

Required:

1. Prepare the necessary adjusting entries for the year ended December 31, 2003.
2. Prepare an income statement for the year ended December 31, 2003.
3. Prepare a balance sheet as of December 31, 2003.

P2-4 Income measurement under alternative revenue recognition rules

Ms Fuji started a business on January 1, 2003. Key operating statistics for 2003 were:

Beginning inventory	–0–
Number of units produced	20,000
Number of units sold (delivery basis)	16,000
Number of units sold for which cash has been received by December 31, 2003	14,000

Direct production costs were $12 per unit. There were no fixed costs or selling/delivery expenses. The selling price per unit was $16.

On January 1, 2004, Ms Fuji decided to liquidate the business. She sold the remaining inventory at $13 per unit for cash. By January 15, 2004, she collected the amount due from customers for sales made during 2003.

Required:

Based on the preceding information, compute the net income of Ms Fuji for the years 2003 and 2004 under the:

1. Production basis.
2. Sales (or delivery) basis.
3. Cash collection basis.

P2-5 Income determination under alternative bases of revenue recognition

Agri Pro, a farm corporation, produced 15,000 bushels of wheat in its first year of operations. During the year, Agri Pro sold 10,000 bushels of the grain at $2.40/bushel, and collected three-fourths of the selling price on the grain sold; the balance is to be collected in equal amounts during each of the two following years. The local grain elevator is quoting a year-end market price of $3/bushel.

Additional Data for the First Year:

Amortization on equipment	$ 3,000
Other production costs (cash)—per bushel	$ 0.50
Miscellaneous administrative costs (cash)	$ 4,000
Selling and delivery costs (incurred and paid at time of sale), per bushel	$ 0.10
Dividends paid to stockholders during year one	$10,000
Interest on borrowed money (one-half paid in cash)	$ 5,000

Required:

Compute net income under each of the methods indicated as follows, and determine the carrying (book) value of inventory and accounts receivable at the end of the first year of operation for each of these methods:

1. Recognize revenues when production is complete.
2. Recognize revenues at point of sale.
3. Recognize revenues on an installment (cash collection) basis.

P2-6 Determining missing amounts on income statement

The following information was taken from a recent IBM Corporation income statement. IBM is a major producer of electronic computing equipment.

IBM CORPORATION
www.ibm.com

($ in millions)	
Restructuring charges	$11,645
Research, development, and engineering	6,522
Operating income	?
Software revenue	?
Interest expense	1,360
Cost of rentals and financing	?
Services revenue	7,352
Cost of sales	19,698
Cost of maintenance	3,430
Earnings before income taxes	?
Net earnings	?
Maintenance revenue	7,635
Total costs of sales and services	35,069
Gross profit	?
Selling, general, and administrative	?
Cost of software	3,924
Total revenues	64,523
Other income, principally interest	573
Cost of services	6,051
Rentals and financing revenue	4,678
Total operating expenses	37,693
Provision for income taxes	(2,161)
Sales revenue	33,755

Required:

1. Recast IBM's income statement and present it in good form. Fill in the missing blanks.
2. Determine what the gross profit percentage is from sales, software, maintenance, services, and from rentals and financing. Which is most profitable? Support your answer numerically.
3. Consider the item "Restructuring charges." What impact did this charge have on IBM's cash flow?
4. IBM's income statements report "Research, development, and engineering" expenses of about $6.5 billion each year. These expenses are incurred by IBM to enhance current products and to develop new products in the hope of generating higher future sales. GAAP usually require that all such costs be expensed in the year incurred.

   Consider the following statement: "Research, development, and engineering expenditures are really assets because they will benefit the future operations of the firm (i.e., lead to higher sales)." If you agree with this statement, suggest an alternative way to account for research, development, and engineering expenditures, one that does not expense them in the year incurred. If you disagree, what are your reasons?

5. Estimate IBM's cash flow from operations for the year using only data from the income statement. Justify the inclusion or exclusion of various income statement items from your calculation. Do the "Net earnings" and "Cash flow from operations" numbers provide a similar view of the results of IBM's operations for the year? Discuss.

P2-7 Quality of earnings

Required:

1. Conduct an online search for the phrases "quality of earnings" and "earnings quality," and save the five most useful results.
2. Explain your choices in Question 1.
3. Based upon your search, construct a comprehensive definition of quality of earnings. Explain why your definition is useful.
4. Does the perceived reputation of management affect a company's quality of earnings? Explain.
5. "Only accounting choices affect quality of earnings." Do you agree? Explain.
6. "*Disclosure* is a crucial aspect of quality of earnings." Do you agree? Explain.
7. "If a company's cash flow from operations is greater than its net income from operations, it must have a good quality of earnings." Do you agree? Explain.

Cases

C2-1 The Quaker Oats Company: Classification of gains versus losses

QUAKER OATS
www.quakeroats.
com

In 1991 and again in 1995, Quaker Oats Company, a U.S. company, disposed of business segments. The 1991 transaction was a spinoff of Fisher-Price (a toy manufacturing operation) to the company's shareholders. The 1995 transaction was principally composed of the sale of both the North American and the European pet food business.

Exhibit 1 contains the consolidated statements of income from the 1991 annual report as well as the financial statement footnote on discontinued operations, which also appeared in that report. Exhibit 2 reflects the consolidated statements of income from the 1995 annual report. In addition, Exhibit 2 also contains excerpts from two 1995 financial statement footnotes.

Notice that Quaker treated the 1991 transaction as a discontinued operation "below the line," while the 1995 transaction was treated differently.

Exhibit 1 THE QUAKER OATS COMPANY AND SUBSIDIARIES

Consolidated Statements of Income

	Year Ended June 30,		
(US$ in millions, except per-share data)	1991	1990	1989
Net sales	$5,491.2	$5,030.6	$4,879.4
Cost of goods sold	2,839.7	2,685.9	2,655.3
Gross profit	2,651.5	2,344.7	2,224.1
Selling, general, and administrative expenses	2,121.2	1,844.1	1,779.0
Interest expense—net of $9.0, $11.0, and $12.4 interest income	86.2	101.8	56.4
Other expense—net	32.6	16.4	149.6
Income from continuing operations before income taxes	411.5	382.4	239.1
Provision for income taxes	175.7	153.5	90.2
Income from continuing operations	235.8	228.9	148.9
Income (loss) from discontinued operations—net of tax	(30.0)	(59.9)	54.1
Net income	205.8	169.0	203.0
Preferred dividends—net of tax	4.3	4.5	—
Net income available for common	$ 201.5	$ 164.5	$ 203.0
Per common share:			
Income from continuing operations	$ 3.05	$ 2.93	$ 1.88
Income (loss) from discontinued operations	(0.40)	(0.78)	0.68
Net income	$ 2.65	$ 2.15	$ 2.56
Dividends declared	1.56	1.40	1.20
Average number of common shares outstanding (in thousands)	75,904	76,537	79,307

Note 2: Discontinued Operations—In April 1990 the Company's Board of Directors approved in principle the distribution of Fisher-Price to the Company's shareholders. Accordingly, Fisher-Price has been reflected as a discontinued operation in the accompanying financial statements for all periods presented. The tax-free distribution was completed on June 28, 1991 and Fisher-Price, Inc., an independent free-standing company, was created. The distribution reduced reinvested earnings by $200 million. The $29.6 million payable to Fisher-Price at June 30, 1991 represents an estimate of the final cash settlement pursuant to the Distribution Agreement. Each holder of Quaker common stock on July 8, 1991 received one share of Fisher-Price, Inc. common stock for every five shares of Quaker common stock held as of such date. Fisher-Price, Inc. common stock is publicly traded.

The loss from discontinued operations for fiscal 1990 was $59.9 million, or 78 cents per share, including $25.5 million, or 33 cents per share, for the loss from the first nine months of fiscal 1990 and an after-tax provision of $34.4 million, or 45 cents per share, recorded in the fourth quarter. The third-quarter results included charges of $10.7 million, or 8 cents per share, for the East Aurora, New York manufacturing facility closing and $17 million, or 23 cents per share, for anticipated transaction expenses of the planned spinoff and projected operating losses (including allocated interest expense) through the expected completion date of the spinoff. The fourth-quarter provision included charges of $8.6 million, or 7 cents per share, for the pending closing of Fisher-Price's Holland, New York manufacturing facility and $4.8 million, or 4 cents per share, for costs relating to staff reductions. The fourth-quarter provision also included $25.4 million, or 21 cents per share, for inventory writedowns and the cost of maintaining related trade programs and $18.1 million, or 13 cents per share, for higher projected operating losses through the spinoff date due to lower than previously anticipated sales volumes.

During fiscal 1991, the Company recorded an additional $50 million pre-tax charge ($30 million after tax), or 40 cents per share to discontinued operations. The charge related primarily to receivables credit risk exposure, product recall reserves and severance costs.

The following summarizes the results of operations for discontinued operations ($ in millions):

	1991	1990	1989
Sales	$601.0	$702.6	$844.8
Pretax earnings (loss)	$ (50.0)	$ (96.2)	$ 89.6
Income taxes (benefit)	(20.0)	(36.3)	35.5
Income (loss) from discontinued operations	$ (30.0)	$ (59.9)	$ 54.1

Fisher-Price operating loss for fiscal 1991 was approximately $35 million.

Fisher-Price operating losses for the fourth quarter of fiscal 1990, including the Holland, New York plant closing and severance charges, were $40 million, including allocated interest expense of $1.2 million. Interest expense of $6.7 million, $7.4 million, and $7.1 million was allocated to discontinued operations in fiscal 1991, 1990, and 1989, respectively.

Exhibit 2 THE QUAKER OATS COMPANY AND SUBSIDIARIES

Consolidated Statements of Income

	Year Ended June 30,		
(US$ in millions, except per-share data)	1995	1994	1993
Net sales	$6,365.2	$5,955.0	$5,730.6
Cost of goods sold	3,381.5	2,926.2	2,870.0
Gross profit	2,983.7	3,028.8	2,860.6
Selling, general, and administrative expenses	2,603.2	2,425.6	2,302.3
Gains on divestitures and restructuring charges—net	(1,094.3)	108.6	20.5
Interest expense—net of $6.3, $8.9, and $10.5 interest income, respectively	110.7	89.7	55.1
Foreign exchange loss—net	4.2	26.2	15.1
Income before income taxes and cumulative effect of accounting changes	1,359.9	378.7	467.6
Provision for income taxes	553.8	147.2	180.8
Income before cumulative effect of accounting changes	806.1	231.5	286.8
Cumulative effect of accounting changes—net of tax	(4.1)	—	(115.5)
Net income	802.0	231.5	171.3
Preferred dividends—net of tax	4.0	4.0	4.2
Net income available for common	$ 798.0	$227.5	$ 167.1
Per common share:			
Income before cumulative effect of accounting changes	$ 6.00	$ 1.68	$ 1.96
Cumulative effect of accounting changes	(0.03)	—	(0.79)
Net income	$ 5.97	$ 1.68	$ 1.17
Dividends declared	$ 1.14	$ 1.06	$ 0.96
Average number of common shares outstanding (in thousands)	133,763	135,236	143,948

Acquisitions and Divestitures Footnote Excerpt—On March 14, 1995 the Company completed the sale of its North American pet food business to H. J. Heinz Company for $725.0 million and realized a gain of $513.0 million. On April 24, 1995 the Company completed the sale of its European pet food business to Dalgety PLC for $700.0 million and realized a gain of $487.2 million. Other divestitures in fiscal 1995 included the Dutch honey business in February 1995, the Mexican chocolate business in May 1995, and the U.S. bean and chili businesses in June 1995. The Company realized gains on these divestitures of $4.9 million, $74.5 million, and $91.2 million, respectively.

The following table presents sales and operating income from the businesses divested in fiscal 1995 through the sale dates. Operating income includes certain allocations of overhead expenses and excludes gains on divestitures and restructuring charges in all fiscal years.

($ in millions)	1995	1994	1993
Sales			
U.S. and Canadian grocery products	$ 554.6	$ 757.3	$ 720.8
International grocery products	760.4	876.0	969.8
Sales from divested businesses	$1,315.0	$1,633.3	$1,690.6
Operating income			
U.S. and Canadian grocery products	$ 39.3	$ 54.2	$ 55.6
International grocery products	34.1	50.6	63.7
Operating income from divested businesses	$ 73.4	$ 104.8	$ 119.3

Restructuring Charges—In fiscal 1995 the Company recorded a restructuring charge of $76.5 million for cost-reduction and realignment activities in order to address the changes in its business portfolio and to allow it to quickly and effectively respond to the needs of trade customers and consumers. These changes result in the elimination of approximately 850 positions and primarily include the realignment of the corporate, shared services and business unit structures, the European cereals business, and the U.S. distribution center network. Savings from these activities are expected to be about $50 million annually beginning in calendar 1996. Approximately 90% of the annual savings will be in cash.

Required:

1. Why do you think the 1991 and 1995 divestiture transactions were treated so differently?
2. Do you agree with each year's financial statement placement?
3. What factors do you think were used to justify the fact that each treatment conformed to GAAP?
4. Comment on the company's quality of earnings.

C2-2 Baldwin Piano and Organ I (KR): Identifying critical events for revenue recognition

The following information is based on the 1993 annual report and 10-K report of Baldwin Piano and Organ Company:

BALDWIN PIANO
www.baldwinpiano.com

The company is the largest American manufacturer of keyboard musical instruments, and it manufactures and distributes all major product classes of pianos and electronic organs. The company believes that the breadth and quality of its line of keyboard musical instruments, its large and well-established dealer distribution networks, and its efficient and low-cost manufacturing capabilities have enabled it to maintain its strong market share in the keyboard musical instrument market.

Over the company's 131-year history, its principal products have been pianos and organs. The company significantly expanded its principal business lines through its 1988 acquisition of the keyboard operations of The Wurlitzer Company, which now operates as a wholly owned subsidiary of the company. Over the years, the company has also expanded and diversified its product line in order to utilize excess capacity and its woodworking, electronics, and technical expertise. The company manufactures printed circuit boards, electronic assemblies, grandfather and other quality clocks, and wooden cabinets.

The company ships keyboard instruments and clocks to its dealer network on a consignment basis. Accordingly, revenue is recognized at the time the dealer sells the instrument to a third party. The company charges a monthly display fee on all consigned inventory held by dealers longer than 90 days. This display fee, on an annual basis, ranged from 12% to 16% of the selling price of such inventory to the dealer. Display fee income is included under the component "Other operating income, net."

The company distributes its Baldwin keyboard musical instruments in the United States through approximately 500 independent dealers (600 outlets) and 11 company-owned stores operating in six major metropolitan areas. Most of the independent dealers carry Baldwin products as their principal line—and often their exclusive one.

The company has been engaged in financing the retail purchase of its products for over 80 years. In 1993, approximately 35% of the company's domestic sales were financed by the company in retail installment programs offered through the company's dealers. Installment contract receivables are recorded at the principal amount of the contracts. Interest on the contracts is recorded as income over the life of the contracts. The company has entered into agreements with an independent financial institution to sell substantially all its installment receivable contracts. The company continues to service (collect cash and perform other administrative services) all installment receivables sold. Over the lives of the contracts, the difference between the original interest earned on the contracts and the interest paid to the independent financial institution is recognized as the component labelled "Income on the sale of installment receivables." The installment contracts are written generally at fixed rates ranging from 12% to 16% with terms extending over three to five years. The interest paid to the independent financial institution is around 5%. Under the agreement with the independent financial institution, the company is required to repurchase either installment receivables that become more than 120 days past due or accounts that are deemed uncollectible.

Wurlitzer and the electronic contract business transfer title and recognize revenue at the time of shipment to their dealers and customers, respectively.

The company distributes its Wurlitzer products through approximately 400 independent dealers. The company's networks of Baldwin dealers and Wurlitzer dealers are separate and distinct, with no significant overlap. Certain Wurlitzer dealers finance their inventory from an independent bank. Dealers can borrow money from the bank on the basis of the value of the inventory purchased from Wurlitzer, with the musical instruments pledged as collateral. The dealers are also required to pay the bank monthly interest payments and pay the principal balance after inventory is sold or if it is held longer than 12 months. The bank may request Wurlitzer to repurchase notes due from delinquent dealers. The company believes that its financial statements contain adequate provisions for any loss that may be incurred as a result of this commitment.

The electronic contract business consists of manufacturing printed circuit boards and electromechanical assemblies for manufacturers outside the music industry. These products were a natural extension of the company's production and those research and development capabilities developed in connection with its electronic keyboard musical instrument business. The company currently produces printed circuit boards and other electronic assemblies for a diverse group of original equipment manufacturers, which sell to the medical electronics, telecommunications, computer peripheral, specialty consumer, data communications, and industrial control markets.

Required:

1. Baldwin uses different critical events to recognize revenue from the sale of inventory for its different business segments. Identify the critical events and rank them from the most to the least conservative policy according to your judgment of the circumstances. For each source of revenue, does the chosen revenue recognition method satisfy both the critical event and the measurability criteria? If you don't have enough information, discuss what additional information is needed to form a judgment on this issue.

2. In addition to income from the sale of inventory, Baldwin also earns income from financing the sale of some of its inventories. Identify the critical event used by Baldwin to record the financing income. Discuss whether the revenue recognition method for the financing income satisfies the critical event and measurability criteria. Total financing income includes gain or loss on sale of installment receivables and interest income.

Integrative Running Case Study
Bombardier on the Web

Access the Bombardier Inc. annual report for the year ended January 31, 2002, on the Companion Website for this textbook at **www.pearsoned.ca/revsine**. Bombardier manufactures several different types of products and provides several different types of services. Glance through the first 24 pages of the report to get a general idea of what the company does.

Required:

1. Suggest, with reasons, revenue recognition policies for each Bombardier product and service based upon your reading of the first 24 pages of the annual report. Should the revenue recognition policies for financial reporting to shareholders and others be the same as the policies for, say, management compensation plans based upon achieving sales targets?
2. Evaluate the company's revenue recognition policies set out in the audited financial statement notes on pages 76 and 78 of the report.
3. Suggest how the events of September 11, 2001, might affect the company's quality of earnings going forward.

Collaborative Learning Cases

CL2-1 Baldwin Piano and Organ II (KR): Analysis and interpretation of income statement

In addition to the information provided in Baldwin Piano I, consider the following information we've provided along with information from the 1993 annual report and the SEC 10-K report of Baldwin Piano and Organ Company (amounts in US$).

Baldwin Piano and Organ Company
Income Statements for the Year Ended December 31,

(US$)	1993	1992	1991
Net sales	$120,657,455	$110,076,904	$103,230,431
Cost of goods sold	(89,970,702)	(79,637,060)	(74,038,724)
Gross profit	30,686,753	30,439,844	29,191,707
Income on the sale of installment receivables	5,746,125	5,256,583	4,023,525
Interest income on installment receivables	443,431	308,220	350,058
Other operating income, net	3,530,751	3,803,228	3,768,760
	40,407,060	39,807,875	37,334,050
Operating expenses			
Selling, general, and administrative expense	(26,187,629)	(25,118,465)	(23,970,568)
Provision for doubtful accounts	(1,702,234)	(2,053,189)	(2,131,644)
Operating profit	12,517,197	12,636,221	11,231,838
Interest expense	(2,232,258)	(2,610,521)	(3,932,830)
Income before income taxes	10,284,939	10,025,700	7,299,008
Income taxes	(4,120,000)	(4,090,000)	(2,884,000)
Income before cumulative effects of change in accounting principles	6,164,939	5,935,700	4,415,008
Cumulative effect of changes in postretirement and postemployment benefits	(1,604,000)	—	—
Net income	$ 4,560,939	$ 5,935,700	$ 4,415,008

Interest income on installment receivables represents interest on receivables not sold to the independent financial institution.

The following summary table was prepared on the basis of the business segment data reported by Baldwin:

Business	Segment Revenue as a Percentage of Total Revenue		Segment Profit as a Percentage of Segment Revenue	
	1993	1992	1993	1992
Musical products	72.70%	81.50%	5.00%	7.60%
Electronic	22.20	13.30	14.80	13.90
Financing services	5.20	5.10	52.80	49.20

The cash flow statement indicates that the company has repaid long-term debt of about US$8.6 million, US$5.6 million, and US$8.3 million during the years 1991, 1992, and 1993, respectively. The balance sheet indicates that the book value of the company's finished goods inventory decreased by about 8% from 1992 to 1993.

In March 1993, the contents of one of the company's finished goods warehouses were damaged by exposure to smoke from a fire adjacent to the warehouse. The company has received insurance proceeds equal to the wholesale value of the destroyed inventory. Accordingly, a gain of approximately US$1,412,000 on the insurance settlement is included in the 1993 Consolidated Statements of Earnings in the component labelled "Other operating income, net."

On January 27, 1993, the company entered into an agreement in principle whereby Peridot Associates, Inc. (Peridot) would acquire all outstanding shares of the company's common stock at a per-share price of US$18.25, subject to certain contingencies. The agreement expired on May 16, 1993. Under the agreement, the company was obligated to reimburse Peridot US$800,000 for certain expenses incurred by Peridot. Additionally, the company incurred other expenses of approximately US$305,000 related to the proposed acquisition. These combined expenses are included in the 1993 Consolidated Statements of Earnings as the component labelled "Other operating income, net."

Required:

Identify and explain the sources of the change in Baldwin's profitability from 1992 to 1993 with a view to evaluating its current earnings quality and future prospects. To what extent can this change be attributed to changes in the management's estimates?

Hint: Preparing a common-size income statement and/or year-to-year percentage change analysis of income statement items will help you formulate your response. Additional information regarding Baldwin Piano can be found in Case C2-2.

CL2-2 Global Crossing's accounting and the quality of earnings

A news report in the *Toronto Star* of March 22, 2002, began as follows:

> *Global Crossing "no Enron"'*
>
> ...
>
> *Officials of insolvent fibre-optics giant Global Crossing Ltd. deny that deceptive accounting practices were part of the company's financial collapse. "Global Crossing is no Enron," chief executive officer John Legere and chief financial officer Dan Cohrs told skeptical lawmakers in a statement yesterday to a House of Representatives financial-services committee panel ..."*[13]

To read the testimonies of various witnesses who appeared before the financial-services committee hearings on Global Crossing's bankruptcy and the company's 2000 10-K report, access the Companion Website for this textbook at **www.pearsoned.ca/revsine**.

Required:

Assume that you are an analyst with a major pension fund, and answer the following questions:

1. Briefly describe the major accounting issues raised at the hearings.
2. Review Global Crossing's 2000 audited financial statements as published in the 2000 10-K report. Based on your review, comment on the allegations raised in the committee hearings.
3. Based upon your analyses above, prepare a memo (about three pages, double-spaced) for your supervisor assessing Global Crossing's quality of earnings.

Endnotes

1. Economic value added represents the increase in the value of a product or service as a consequence of operating activities. To illustrate: Consider that the value of an assembled automobile far exceeds the value of its separate steel, glass, plastic, rubber, and electronics components. The difference between the aggregate cost of manufacturing the automobile and the price at which the car is sold to the dealer represents economic value added (or lost).

2. Donnelly, "Profits: Quality Erodes, Making Them Less Reliable," *Wall Street Journal,* October 18, 1990, Section C.

3. This definition of quality of earnings was written by the textbook authors. Professor W. Smieliauskas of the University of Toronto suggests that "[t]here seems to be two meanings to QOE ... 1. The [company] is doing well; 2. Earnings capture economic substance independent of (1)."

4. K. A. Merchant and J. Rockness, "The Ethics of Managing Earnings: An Empirical Investigation," *Journal of Accounting and Public Policy,* vol. 13 (1994), pp. 79–94.

5. "Discontinued Operations," *CICA Handbook,* Section 3475, para. .06.

6. "Extraordinary Items," *CICA Handbook,* Section 3480.

7. See *CICA Handbook,* Section 3480.04.

8. P.M. Fairfield, R.J. Sweeney, and T.L. Yohn, "Accounting Classification and the Predictive Content of Earnings," *The Accounting Review,* July 1996, pp. 337–355.

9. There are also other limited exceptions to retroactive accounting for accounting changes. See Section 1506.11.

10. *CICA Handbook,* Section 1506.25.

11. "Accounting for Certain Investments in Debt and Equity Securities," *SFAS No. 115* (Norwalk, CT: FASB, 1993), para. 13.

12. "Reporting Comprehensive Income," *SFAS No. 130* (Norwalk, CT: FASB, 1997).

13. Jim Abrams, Associated Press, *Toronto Star,* March 22, 2002, p. E5.

3
Additional Topics in Income Determination

LEARNING OBJECTIVES
After studying this chapter, you should be able to:

1. Describe the conditions under which it is appropriate to recognize revenues and profits either before or after the point of sale

2. Describe the procedures for recognizing revenue and adjusting associated asset values in three specific settings—long-term construction contracts, agricultural commodities, and installment sales

3. Show how the flexibility in GAAP for income determination invites earnings management

4. Explain various techniques used by firms to manage earnings

5. Explain how regulatory institutions have focused on revenue recognition to curb earnings management and thereby improve the quality of earnings

6. Describe how GAAP for interim reporting and segment disclosures may assist analysts in understanding a company

This chapter covers special topics in income determination. The first part of the chapter outlines the conditions and describes the accounting procedures for recognizing revenue and profit either before or after a sale occurs. The second part builds on the introduction to quality of earnings in Chapter 2, and looks at earnings management and how firms can sometimes exploit the flexibility in generally accepted accounting principles (GAAP) to manage earnings up or down.

Because revenue is usually recognized at the time of sale in most industries, some people erroneously conclude that the sale is itself the *sole* criterion in recognizing revenue. This is not correct! The approach to recognizing revenue is more complicated and subtle. As noted in Chapter 2, revenue is recognized at the earliest moment in time that Condition 1 (the "critical event") *and* Condition 2 ("measurability") are *both* satisfied. ***The earliest moment at which Conditions 1 and 2 are both satisfied is usually the time of sale.*** That is why revenue is usually recognized when the sale is made.

But there are cases in which Conditions 1 and 2 are satisfied *before* the sale—for instance, as production takes place. When this happens and when expenses are *also* measurable with a reasonable degree of assurance, GAAP allow income to be recognized before the sale.

In other circumstances, Conditions 1 and 2 may not both be satisfied until *after* the time of sale—for instance, not until the cash is collected. In these cases, GAAP disallow revenue recognition when the sale occurs; instead, revenue recognition is often deferred until cash is received.

Revenue Recognition Prior to Sale

Percentage-of-Completion Method

Long-term construction projects—such as roads and bridges, military hardware, and costly items such as oil tankers—frequently satisfy both revenue recognition conditions prior to the time of sale.

These types of projects are usually begun only after a formal contract with a purchaser has been signed. Since a buyer for the completed project is assured, the critical event in the earning of revenue is the actual construction—that is, revenue recognition. Condition 1 is satisfied as construction progresses. Furthermore, since the contract price is specific, the amount of the revenue that has been earned is measurable with a reasonable degree of assurance, thus satisfying revenue recognition Condition 2.

In many construction projects, it is also possible to estimate with reasonable accuracy the cost of the project and to measure its stage of completion. Furthermore, construction contracts usually require purchasers to make payments to the contractor as construction progresses. These interim payments help ensure that the contractor will receive payment for the work performed.

When long-term construction contracts possess all these attributes, revenue recognition Conditions 1 and 2 are both satisfied as construction progresses, and expenses can be matched against revenues to determine income. This is called the **percentage-of-completion method** (*CICA Handbook* Section 3400.08). Here's an example of how it works.

Solid Construction Corporation signs a contract with the City of Springfield on January 1, 2001, to build a highway bridge over Stony Creek. The contract price is $1,000,000; construction costs are estimated to be $800,000; and the project is scheduled to be completed by December 31, 2003. Periodic cash payments are to be made by the City of Springfield as construction progresses.

	Actual experience on the project as of December 31,		
	2001	**2002**	**2003**
Costs incurred to date	$240,000	$544,000	$ 850,000
Estimated future costs	560,000	306,000	—
Billings to date	280,000	650,000	1,000,000
Cash collections to date	210,000	600,000	1,000,000

Under the percentage-of-completion method, the profit to be recognized in any year is based on the ratio of incurred contract costs divided by estimated total contract costs. Using the data in the example, we compute the profit for 2001 using the following steps:

Step 1   Compute the percentage-of-completion ratio by dividing costs incurred to date by estimated total costs.

This step is taken to estimate the percentage of completion at any given point during the project. At the end of 2001, estimated total costs on the project are $800,000—that is, $240,000 of costs incurred in 2001 plus $560,000 of estimated future costs. The cost ratio is:

$$\frac{\$240,000}{\$800,000} = 0.30 \text{ or } 30\%$$

Step 2 Determine the estimated total profit on the contract by comparing the contract price with the estimated total costs.

At the end of 2001, the estimated profit on the contract is still $200,000, which is the difference between the contract price of $1,000,000 and the estimated total costs of $800,000.

Step 3 Compute the estimated profit earned to date.

The estimated profit earned to date is the cost ratio (or percentage of completion) computed in Step 1 multiplied by the estimated profit computed in Step 2.

$$0.30 \times \$200,000 = \$60,000$$

Notice that 30% of the total estimated costs of $800,000 have been incurred by the end of 2001, so 30% of the total estimated profit of $200,000 can be recognized in that same year—that is, profit is recognized in proportion to costs incurred. Since no profit has been recognized prior to 2001, all the $60,000 is recognizable in 2001.

Because cost estimates and completion stages change, these computations must be repeated in each subsequent year. Furthermore, the profit computation for each subsequent contract year must add another step. The computation of profit in 2002 illustrates this point.

Step 1 Compute the completion ratio by dividing incurred costs by estimated total costs.

At the end of 2002, estimated total costs on this contract have risen to $850,000—$544,000 of costs incurred through 2002 plus $306,000 of estimated future costs. The cost ratio (or percentage of completion) is:

$$\frac{\$544,000}{\$850,000} = 0.64 \text{ or } 64\%$$

Step 2 Determine the estimated profit on the contract.

The estimated profit on the contract has now dropped to $150,000—the difference between the contract price of $1,000,000 and the newly estimated total costs of $850,000 as of the end of 2002.

Step 3 Compute the estimated profit earned to date.

Since 64% of the total estimated costs have already been incurred (Step 1), 64% of the revised estimated profit of $150,000 (Step 2), or $96,000, has been earned through December 31, 2002.

Notice that a portion of the profit on this contract—$60,000—has already been recognized in 2001. Therefore, only the *incremental profit* earned in 2002 should be recognized. This requires an additional computation.

Step 4 Compute the incremental profit earned in the current year.

The estimated total profit earned through December 31, 2002, is $96,000 (Step 3). Since $60,000 of the estimated profit was recognized on this contract in 2001, only $36,000 ($96,000 − $60,000) of additional profit can be recognized in 2002.

These four steps can be expressed succinctly using the following profit computation formula:

$$\left[\frac{\text{Costs incurred to date}}{\text{Estimated total costs}} \times \frac{\text{Estimated}}{\text{total profit}}\right] - \frac{\text{Profit recognized}}{\text{in previous years}} = \frac{\text{Profit recognized}}{\text{in current year}} \quad (3.1)$$

$$\underbrace{\hspace{4cm}}_{\text{Profit earned to date}} \qquad \underbrace{\hspace{3cm}}_{\substack{\text{Previously recognized} \\ \text{profit}}}$$

The previously recognized profit is the sum of all profits (or losses) recognized on the contract in prior years—that is, the sum of all profits (or losses) that were determined by multiplying the cost–completion ratio by the total profit estimated at those earlier dates. Again, the reason for subtracting this amount from the amount for profit earned to date is to avoid double-counting profits recognized in prior years.

Repeating the computations for 2001 and 2002 using the formula in equation (3.1) gives the following results:

Profit Computation

$$2001: \quad \left[\frac{\$240,000}{\$800,000} \times \$200,000\right] - \quad\quad 0 \quad\quad = \quad \$60,000$$

$$\underbrace{\hspace{4cm}}_{\text{Profit earned to date}} \qquad \underbrace{\hspace{3cm}}_{\substack{\text{Previously recognized} \\ \text{profit}}} \qquad \underbrace{\hspace{3cm}}_{\substack{\text{Profit recognized} \\ \text{in 2001}}}$$

$$2002: \quad \left[\frac{\$544,000}{\$850,000} \times \$150,000\right] - \quad \$60,000 \quad = \quad \$36,000$$

$$\underbrace{\hspace{4cm}}_{\text{Profit earned to date}} \qquad \underbrace{\hspace{3cm}}_{\substack{\text{Previously recognized} \\ \text{profit}}} \qquad \underbrace{\hspace{3cm}}_{\substack{\text{Profit recognized} \\ \text{in 2002}}}$$

Of course, these results are identical to those derived using the multiple-step approach illustrated previously. The computation for 2003 is:

$$2003: \quad \left[\frac{\$850,000}{\$850,000} \times \$150,000\right] - \quad \$96,000 \quad = \quad \$54,000$$

$$\underbrace{\hspace{4cm}}_{\text{Profit earned to date}} \qquad \underbrace{\hspace{3cm}}_{\substack{\text{Previously recognized} \\ \text{profit}}} \qquad \underbrace{\hspace{3cm}}_{\substack{\text{Profit recognized} \\ \text{in 2003}}}$$

Under the percentage-of-completion method, the cumulative profit recognized over the three years totals $150,000 ($60,000 + $36,000 + $54,000). This total equals the difference between the contract price of $1,000,000 and the actual costs of $850,000.

The journal entries shown in Exhibit 3.1 would be used to record these events on the books of Solid Construction Corporation.

Entries (2) and (3) of Exhibit 3.1 require elaboration. Income is recognized in entries using the income recognition formula of equation (3.1). An alternative to entry (2), which would provide more detailed information, is to separately record the construction expenses shown in Exhibit 3.1. The amount debited to "Construction expense" each period is the actual construction costs incurred in that period. The credit to "Construction revenue" is determined by multiplying the total contract price by the completion percentage and then subtracting any revenue recognized in

Exhibit 3.1 SOLID CONSTRUCTION CORPORATION

Journal Entries
Percentage-of-Completion Method

	2001	2002	2003
(1) To record costs incurred			
DR Inventory: Construction in progress	$240,000	$304,000	$ 306,000
CR Accounts payable, cash, etc.	$240,000	$304,000	$ 306,000
(2) To record income recognized			
DR Inventory: Construction in progress	$ 60,000	$ 36,000	$ 54,000
CR Income on long-term construction contract	$ 60,000	$ 36,000	$ 54,000
Alternative entry			
DR Inventory: Construction in progress[1]	$ 60,000[1]	$ 36,000[1]	$ 54,000[1]
DR Construction expense[2]	$240,000[2]	$304,000[2]	$ 306,000[2]
CR Construction revenue[3]	$300,000[3]	$340,000[3]	$ 360,000[3]
[1]Gross profit earned in current period	30% × ($1,000,000 – $800,000)	64% × ($1,000,000 – $850,000) – $60,000	($1,000,000 – $850,000) – $96,000
[2]Actual construction costs incurred in current period	$240,000	$544,000 – $240,000	$850,000 – $544,000
[3]Revenues earned in current period	30% × $1,000,000	(64% × $1,000,000) – $300,000	$1,000,000 – $300,000 – $340,000
(3) To record customer billings			
DR Accounts receivable	$280,000	$370,000	$ 350,000
CR Billings on construction in progress	$280,000	$370,000	$ 350,000
(4) To record cash received			
DR Cash	$210,000	$390,000	$ 400,000
CR Accounts receivable	$210,000	$390,000	$ 400,000
(5) To record completion and acceptance of the project			
DR Billings on construction in progress			$1,000,000
CR Construction in progress			$1,000,000

prior periods. For example, the revenue recognized in 2002 is determined by multiplying the contract price of $1,000,000 times the completion percentage as of the end of 2002 (64%), giving total revenue earned to date of $640,000. Subtracting the $300,000 of revenue recognized in 2001 yields "Construction revenue" of $340,000 recognized in 2002.

Consistent with asset valuation and income determination being linked together, as discussed in Chapter 2, the carrying value of net assets is also increased as income is recognized. This is why the entry (2) debit increases the "Construction in progress" account, which is a part of inventory. Thus, entry (2) reflects the dual financial statement impact of income recognition: *both net assets and income increase.*

In entry (3), the account "Billings on construction in progress" is treated as a contra account (reduction) to the inventory subcomponent labelled "Construction in progress." The net of these two accounts is shown as a current asset (if there is a debit balance) or as a current liability (if there is a credit balance). In our example, the balance sheet for Solid Construction Corporation for 2001 and 2002 is presented in this way:

2001		
Current Assets		
Accounts receivable		$70,000
Inventory: Construction in progress	$300,000	
Less: Billings on construction in progress	(280,000)	
		$20,000
2002		
Current Assets		
Accounts receivable		$50,000
Current Liabilities		
Inventory: Construction in progress	$640,000	
Less: Billings on construction in progress	(650,000)	
		$10,000

The component "Billings on construction in progress" must be treated as a contra-inventory account to avoid double-counting on the balance sheet. Typically, a sale results in a receivable being recognized and a simultaneous decrease in inventory. However, inventory is not reduced in long-term construction accounting since the sale is not made until completion. The contra-account treatment avoids including certain costs and profit twice—once in inventory ("Inventory: Construction in progress") and once in the receivables account.

Finally, although profits are recognized proportionately as construction progresses, *estimated losses on a contract are recognized in their entirety as soon as it becomes known that a contract loss will ensue.*

To illustrate, suppose that at the end of 2002, Solid Construction's management discovered that an unexpected geological feature of Stony Creek would require an additional expenditure of $200,000 in 2003. Had this construction problem not been discovered at the end of 2002, profit of $54,000 would have been recorded in 2003. Now, however, the *loss* of $146,000 ($200, 000 – $54,000) must be recorded immediately at the end of 2002. The journal entries in Exhibit 3.1 for 2002 would remain the same except that the following entry should be added:

DR	Loss on construction contract		
	due to additional costs	$146,000	
	CR Estimated liabilities		$146,000

This additional entry for 2002 would cause overall profit for 2002 (originally $36,000) to become a loss of $110,000 ($146,000 – $36,000). Since profit of $60,000 was recorded back in 2001, the expected overall contract profit as at the end of 2002 can be computed as follows:

Total contract price	$1,000,000
Actual costs incurred to end of 2002	(544,000)
Original future estimated costs for 2003	(306,000)
Unexpected additional costs for 2003	(200,000)
Revised estimated (loss) on contract	$ (50,000)

Now for 2003, in this situation of spending the extra $200,000, all the 2003 journal entries in Exhibit 3.1 would remain the same, except that there would be no entry to record the $54,000 gross profit.

In the original example, income is recognized by using the ratio of incurred costs divided by estimated total costs. This cost ratio is widely used since it provides a simple index of progress toward completion (i.e., work done to date). However, there are situations in which this cost ratio may not accurately reflect construction progress. For example, consider a case in which raw materials to be used in construction are stockpiled in advance of use. In such situations, costs are being incurred as the raw materials are received and recorded on the books. Yet these costs do not increase the stage of completion until the materials are actually *used*. In projects in which this stockpiling is significant, some other means for measuring progress toward completion would be preferable. Possibilities include labour hours worked or various output measures (such as miles of roadway completed).

Completed-Contract Method

There are cases in which it is not possible to determine expected costs with a high degree of reliability under long-term construction contracts, making the use of the percentage-of-completion method inappropriate. In these situations, the **completed-contract method** is used instead (*CICA Handbook* Section 3400.08).

The completed-contract method defers recognition of income until the project is completed. Journal entries under the completed-contract method are identical to those illustrated previously for the percentage-of-completion method except that entry (2) in Exhibit 3.1, which records income as construction progresses, is omitted. Instead, all the income on the contract is recognized in the period in which the contract is completed. Here is the entry for recognizing income in 2003 under the completed-contract method:

DR	Billings on construction in progress	$1,000,000	
	CR Construction in progress		$850,000
	CR Income on long-term construction contract		$150,000

Although income is recognized only on completion, losses are recognized in their entirety as soon as their probable existence is known.

Table 3.1 illustrates that total income for the three years is the same under both the completed-contract method and the percentage-of-completion method ($150,000). However, the timing of income recognition differs considerably.

Furthermore, the net asset balance at intermediate construction stages will also differ between the two methods. As shown in column (g) of Table 3.2, *the amount of this net asset balance difference in any year is precisely equal to the difference in cumulative profit recognized on each basis.* This difference in net asset balances exists because the recognition of income has a corresponding effect on net asset balances.

TABLE 3.1 YEARLY INCOME COMPARISON OF TWO LONG-TERM CONTRACT ACCOUNTING METHODS

Year	Completed-Contract Method	Percentage-of-Completion Method
2001	–0–	$ 60,000
2002	–0–	36,000
2003	$150,000	54,000
Total income	$150,000	$150,000

Revenue Recognition on Commodities

The timing of revenue recognition for producers of agricultural and mining commodities raises some interesting issues. There is general agreement that in both mining and farming, the critical event in adding value usually comes *before* the actual sale. The critical event in mining is extracting the resource from the ground. In agriculture, the critical event is harvest (since prior to harvest, the crop may still be lost because of drought, hail, insects, or disease—only after the crop is safely out of the field have these income-threatening possibilities been avoided.) Thus, revenue recognition Condition 1 is satisfied prior to the sale itself.

However, the precise time at which revenue recognition Condition 2 ("measurability") is satisfied for commodities producers is open to some dispute. The following example explores the issues.

> *A farmer harvests 110,000 bushels of corn on September 30, 2001. On this day, the posted market price per bushel was $3.50. The total cost of growing the crop was $220,000, or $2.00 per bushel. The farmer decides to sell 100,000 bushels for cash on September 30 at the posted price of $3.50 and stores the remaining 10,000 bushels. On January 2, 2002, the market price drops to $3.00. Fearing further price declines, the farmer immediately sells the bushels in storage at a price of $3.00 per bushel.*

TABLE 3.2 COMPARATIVE ACCOUNT BALANCES

Completed-Contract Method Versus Percentage-of-Completion Method

	December 31, Year-End Account Balances						
	Completed-Contract Method			Percentage-of-Completion Method			
	(a) Construction in Progress	(b) Billings	(c) Net Asset Balance Col. (a) – Col. (b)	(d) Construction in Progress	(e) Billings	(f) Net Asset Balance Col. (d) – Col. (e)	(g) Difference in Net Asset Balances Between Methods Col. (f) – Col. (c)
2001	$240,000	$280,000	–$40,000	$300,000	$280,000	$+20,000	$+60,000[1]
2002	544,000	650,000	–106,000	640,000	650,000	–10,000	+96,000[2]
2003	–0–	–0–	–0–	–0–	–0–	–0–	–0–

[1]Also equals difference between cumulative profit on percentage-of-completion method ($60,000) and the completed-contract method ($0) from Table 3.1.

[2]Also equals difference between cumulative profit on percentage-of-completion method ($60,000 + $36,000 = $96,000) and the completed-contract method ($0 + $0) from Table 3.1.

Completed-Transaction (Sales) Method

The timing of revenue recognition on the 100,000 bushels of corn that were sold on September 30 is straightforward. Revenue recognition Conditions 1 and 2 are both satisfied at September 30, and income would be recognized at the time of sale. The income statement would show:

2001 Income Statement	
Revenues (sale of 100,000 bushels at a market price of $3.50 per bushel)	$ 350,000
Expenses (costs of $2.00 per bushel for 100,000 bushels sold)	(200,000)
Income from sale	$ 150,000

Under the traditional view, which we call the **completed-transaction (sales) method**, no income would be recognized at September 30 on the 10,000 bushels that were harvested but not sold. For these 10,000 bushels, revenue recognition Condition 2 is considered not to have been met since the eventual selling price is still unknown (i.e., the sale transaction is not yet completed). The bushels in storage would be reflected on the farmer's balance sheet at their *cost* of $20,000 ($2.00 per bushel × 10,000 bushels).

When the bushels in storage are sold in 2002, the income statement would reflect a profit on the sale of the 10,000 bushels:

> As costs are incurred during the year, the direct costs of crop production—things like seed, fertilizer, fuel, and amortization on machinery—are charged to a "Production in process" or "Crop inventory" account with offsetting credits to Cash, Accounts payable, or Accumulated amortization.

2002 Income Statement	
Revenues (sale of 10,000 bushels at a market price of $3.00 per bushel)	$30,000
Expenses (costs of $2.00 per bushel for 10,000 bushels sold)	(20,000)
Income from sale	$10,000

Note that the traditional approach avoids recognizing any income on the 10,000 unsold bushels until the sales transaction is completed in 2002.

Market Price (Production) Method

There is another way of measuring income in the previous example. This alternative recognizes that well-organized markets exist for most agricultural and many mining commodities. Indeed, marketing boards may guarantee prices for certain agricultural commodities. In addition, the quantities offered for sale by any individual producer are usually very small in relation to the total size of the market. Producers face an established price for as many units as they choose to sell. These factors mean that a readily determinable market price at which output *could be sold* is continuously available. In this view, revenue recognition Condition 2 ("measurability") is satisfied prior to the actual sale of actively traded commodities.

Since revenue recognition Condition 1 ("critical event") occurs at harvest, both conditions necessary to recognize revenue are satisfied as soon as the crop is safely out of the field (i.e., at the point of production). Thus, farming income on all 110,000 bushels is recognized under this approach on September 30:

Revenues (100,000 bushels sold at a market price of $3.50)	$ 350,000
Expenses (costs of $2.00 per bushel for 100,000 bushels sold)	(200,000)
Market gain on unsold inventory (10,000 bushels times the difference between the $3.50 market price at the date of harvest and the $2.00 cost per bushel)	15,000
Total income from farming activities	$ 165,000

This **market price (or production) method** recognizes farming income on the 10,000 unsold bushels as well as on the 100,000 bushels sold. This view emphasizes the fact that the farmer *could have sold* these 10,000 bushels at the time of harvest for a readily determinable price of $3.50 per bushel. Since the critical event in farming is harvest and since the potential sales price at the time of harvest is known, both revenue recognition conditions relating to farming are deemed to be satisfied on September 30. Therefore, farming income of $165,000 is immediately determinable.

Under the market price method, the bushels in storage are reflected on the farmer's balance sheet at $35,000 ($3.50 market price at harvest times 10,000 bushels). If the corn was initially carried at its *cost* of $20,000 ($2.00 per bushel times 10,000 bushels), the entry necessary to reflect the value added by farming is:

DR	Crop inventory	$15,000	
	CR Market gain on unsold inventory		$15,000

The credit would appear as shown on the income statement for 2001.

After the corn is harvested, the activity called farming has ended. However, this farmer is actually engaged in another business in addition to farming. By withholding 10,000 bushels from the market, the farmer is also pursuing a separate (non-farming) activity called **speculation**. This speculation is undertaken in the hope that prices will rise above their September 30 level of $3.50 per bushel. Subsequent changes in the market price of corn will thus give rise to speculative gains or losses—also called **inventory holding gains and losses**.

To illustrate, recollect that at the start of 2002, the market price of corn drops from $3.50 to $3.00 per bushel. This decline in price gives rise to a speculative (holding) loss in 2002 of $5,000 (a decline of $0.50 per bushel times 10,000 bushels). The inventory is marked-to-market, and the journal entry to reflect the loss is:

DR	Inventory (holding) loss on speculation	$5,000	
	CR Crop inventory		$5,000

After this entry is posted, the carrying value of the inventory is now reduced to $30,000 (10,000 bushels times $3.00 per bushel).

Fearing further price declines, the farmer immediately sells the remaining 10,000 bushels at $3.00 on January 2. The corresponding entry is:

DR	Cost of goods sold	$30,000	
	CR Crop inventory		$30,000
DR	Cash	$30,000	
	CR Crop revenue		$30,000

Comparison: Completed-Transaction (Sales) and Market Price (Production) Methods

Although total income over the two periods is the same under the two approaches, the income recognized in each period is not the same, and the activities to which the income is attributed also differ:

Completed-Transaction (Sales) Method			Market Price (Production) Method	
Income from sales	$150,000	2001	Income from farming activities	$165,000
Income from sales	10,000	2002	Holding loss on speculation	(5,000)
Total income	$160,000		Total income	$160,000

The completed-transaction (sales) method avoids recognizing any income on the 10,000 unsold bushels until the transaction is completed (when the crop is sold). However, in emphasizing completed transactions, this traditional approach—the completed-transaction method—merges the results of the farmer's speculative and farming activities and does not reflect their separate results.

This example illustrates why income recognition can be controversial. In practice, the completed-transaction method is far more prevalent. However, the market price method would also be deemed to be in conformity with GAAP when readily determinable market values are continuously available. The market price method has the dual advantages of (1) explicitly recognizing the separate results arising from the farming and speculative activities that the farmer is engaged in, and (2) conforming more closely to the income recognition conditions introduced in Chapter 2.

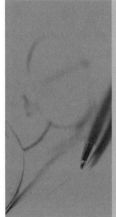

Recap

For long-term construction contracts and commodities (natural resources and agricultural products), the two conditions for revenue recognition—"critical event" and "measurability"—are frequently satisfied prior to sale. The percentage-of-completion method recognizes revenue and profits (losses) on long-term construction contracts as work progresses. The market price (production) method recognizes the difference between the cost of the natural resource or agricultural commodity and its prevailing market price as income at the time of production or harvest. In both cases, an inventory account— "Construction in progress" for long-term construction contracts and "Crop inventory" for commodities—is debited to reflect the increase in value that is recognized on the income statement, thereby maintaining the link between income determination and asset valuation.

Revenue Recognition Subsequent to Sale

Installment Sales Method

Sometimes revenue is not recognized even though a valid sale has taken place. This accounting treatment is acceptable only under highly unusual circumstances. One instance in which revenue recognition might be delayed beyond the point of sale is when sales are made under very extended cash collection terms. Examples include installment sales of consumer durables and retail land sales of vacation or retirement property. A lengthy collection period considerably increases the risk of nonpayment. *Where the risk of noncollection is unusually high and where the proportion of installment accounts that are likely to be uncollectible cannot be reasonably estimated, then revenue recognition may be deferred.*

When these extreme risk situations exist, neither of the two revenue recognition conditions is satisfied. Specifically, when it's highly uncertain whether customers will make the cash payments called for in the contract, then the sale itself is not the critical event in creating value. In such circumstances, the actual cash collection is the critical event, and revenue recognition Condition 1 is satisfied only as the amounts due from customers are received. Similarly, revenue recognition Condition 2 is not satisfied either since the amount ultimately collectible from customers cannot be measured with a reasonable degree of assurance at the time of sale.

Since Conditions 1 and 2 are both satisfied only over time as cash collections take place, a revenue recognition method tied to cash collections has been devised to deal with such situations. This revenue recognition approach is called the **installment sales method.**

Installment Sales Method Illustrated

The installment sales method recognizes revenue and income proportionately as cash is collected. The amount recognized in any period is based on two factors:

1. The installment-sales gross-profit percentage (gross profit/sales).
2. The amount of cash collected on installment accounts receivable.

Here's an example of revenue and income recognition under the installment sales method:

	2001	2002
Installment sales	$1,200,000	$1,300,000
Cost of installment goods sold	840,000	884,000
Gross profit	$ 360,000	$ 416,000
Gross profit percentage	30%	32%
Cash collections		
On 2001 installment sales	$ 300,000	$ 600,000
On 2002 installment sales		$ 340,000

During 2001, installment sales of $1,200,000 were made. The potential gross profit on these sales was $360,000. The installment contracts call for cash payments over each of the next four years. Because of the extreme uncertainties regarding ultimate collectibility, this gross profit will be recognized only as customers pay on their accounts. Since $300,000 of cash was collected in 2001, the gross profit recognized in 2001 will be $90,000 (30% × $300,000, where 30% is the gross profit percentage [gross profit/sales] on 2001 installment sales). This $90,000 is shown on the 2001 income statement as 2001 income from installment sales. The difference between the total potential gross profit of $360,000 and the $90,000 of recognized income—or $270,000—is deferred gross profit (see entries [4] and [5] in Exhibit 3.2).

Income recognized in the year 2002 from installment sales comprises two components:

1. A component relating to year 2002 cash collections on 2001 installment sales.
2. A component relating to year 2002 cash collections on 2002 installment sales.

The computation for installment sales income recognized in 2002 is:

Total 2002 Installment Sales Income

	Gross Profit Recognized
Component relating to 2001 sales	
Cash collections in year 2002 from 2001 sales	$600,000
Multiplied by year 2001 gross profit percentage	30%
	$180,000
Component relating to year 2002 sales	
Cash collections in year 2002 from 2002 sales	$340,000
Multiplied by year 2002 gross profit percentage	32%
	$108,800
Total installment sales income recognized in year 2002	$288,800

Journal entries to record these facts for years 2001 and 2002 are shown in Exhibit 3.2.

Exhibit 3.2 INSTALLMENT SALES METHOD

Journal Entries

	2001		2002	
(1) To record installment sales				
DR Accounts receivable—2001 installment sales	$1,200,000			
DR Accounts receivable—2002 installment sales			$1,300,000	
CR Installment sales revenue		$1,200,000		$1,300,000
(2) To record cost of goods sold				
DR Cost of installment goods sold	$ 840,000		$ 884,000	
CR Inventory		$ 840,000		$ 884,000
(3) To record cash collections				
DR Cash	$ 300,000		$ 940,000	
CR Accounts receivable—2001 installment sales		$ 300,000		$ 600,000
CR Accounts receivable—2002 installment sales				$ 340,000
(4) To defer gross profit on portion of current period sales that are not yet collected				
DR Deferred gross profit (income statement)	$270,000		$ 307,200	
CR Deferred gross profit—adjustment to accounts receivable		$ 270,000		$ 307,200
(5) To recognize realized gross profit on installment sales of prior periods				
DR Deferred gross profit—adjustment to accounts receivable			$ 180,000	
CR Recognized gross profit on installment sales—prior year				$ 180,000

The income statement would appear as follows:

	2001	2002
Installment sales	$1,200,000	$1,300,000
Cost of installment goods sold	(840,000)	(884,000)
Gross profit	360,000	416,000
Less: Deferred gross profit on installment sales of current year	(270,000)	(307,200)
Gross profit recognized on current year's sales	90,000	108,800
Plus: Gross profit recognized on installment sales of prior years	—	180,000
Total gross profit recognized this year	$ 90,000	$ 288,800

Some additional internal recordkeeping is necessary when applying the installment sales method. Installment sales and the related cost of goods sold must be tracked by individual year in order to compute the gross profit percentage that applies to each year. In addition, the accounting system must match cash collections with the specific sales year to which the cash collections relate. This matching is needed in order to apply the correct gross profit percentage to cash receipts.

On the balance sheet, the "Accounts receivable—installment sales" components are classified as current assets if they are due within 12 months of the balance sheet date. Amounts not expected to be collected within the next year may also be classified as current assets if installment sales are a normal part of the company's operations, since the company's operating cycle would include the installment collection period. Existing practice typically classifies the deferred gross profit account as a contra asset, which is shown as a reduction to accounts receivable.

Selling, general, and administrative expenses relating to installment sales are treated as period costs—that is, as costs that are expensed in the period in which they are incurred—because they provide no further benefits. This treatment is consistent with the manner in which period costs are handled for normal (noninstallment) sales.

Interest on Installment Contracts The essence of an installment sales contract is that the cash payments arising from the sale are spread over multiple periods. Because of this delay in receiving the sales proceeds, sellers charge interest on installment sales contracts. Consequently, the required monthly or quarterly installment payments include both interest and principal. This complication was omitted from the example we just illustrated. GAAP require that the interest component of the periodic cash proceeds must be recorded separately. This means that interest payments are not considered when computing the recognized gross profit on installment sales. Chapter 8 outlines the procedures for differentiating between principal and interest payments on customer receivables.

Cost-Recovery Method

This method does not recognize any gross profit until the cumulative amount of payments received by the company equals the cost of the sold item. The rationale is that, in risky situations where cash is received in installments and receipt of the final installments is doubtful, overall income or loss cannot be determined with any reasonable degree of assurance until all cash is received. Eldon S. Hendriksen, in *Accounting Theory* (fifth edition, with Michael F. Van Breda, Homewood, Illinois: Irwin, 1992) writes that, under the cost-recovery method, *the first installments are considered to be a return of invested costs, and income is recorded only after all costs have been recovered ... all additional installments are treated as income. (p. 367)*

Hendriksen also points out that a good example of when the cost-recovery method may be used "is where a bond is in default and payments of principal and interest are made as cash becomes available through liquidation of the mortgaged property or other means. Because of the uncertainty regarding future payments under the bond contract, all collections, whether considered payments of principal or interest ... are treated as a return of the bond investment until such investment has been fully recovered" (pp. 367–368).

Recap

The installment sales method of revenue recognition is used when the risk of noncollection is high or when it is impractical to estimate the amount of uncollectibles. Under the installment sales method, the gross profit on sales is deferred and recognized in income in subsequent periods—that is, when the installment receivables are collected in cash. The link between income determination and asset valuation is maintained by showing deferred gross profit as a contra account (reduction) to installment accounts receivable. The cost-recovery method may be viewed as the most extreme version of the installment sales method.

Earnings Management

The criteria for revenue and expense recognition outlined in Chapter 2 provide general guidelines for accrual accounting income determination. But applying these rules in specific settings still leaves room for considerable latitude and judgment. For example, determining when revenue has been earned (critical event) and is realizable (measurability)—the two conditions for revenue recognition—are often judgment calls. Managers can sometimes exploit the flexibility in GAAP to manipulate reported earnings in ways that mask the underlying performance of the company. Some managers have even resorted to outright financial fraud to inflate reported earnings, but this is relatively rare.

Earnings management is not a new concept. But the perception is that it has become increasingly more common in today's marketplace because of pressure to meet analysts' earnings forecasts. Companies that miss analysts' earnings per share (EPS) by even a few pennies frequently experience significant stock price declines. Several highly publicized examples of alleged accounting "irregularities" (as mentioned in Chapters 1 and 2) and recent research studies[1] lend support to concerns about earnings management.

One way to avoid a market penalty for reporting a loss is to make sure to report a profit—real or artificial. Results from a recent research study suggest that artificially inflating earnings is a common occurrence, especially for firms that would otherwise report small losses.[2] Figure 3.1(a) shows a frequency distribution of annual reported earnings for a large number of firms over a 20-year period. The horizontal axis represents groupings of reported earnings divided by beginning-of-year market value of equity. The interval width of grouping is 0.005. Thus, the grouping labelled −1 includes scaled earnings from −0.005 to just less than 0.000, grouping 0 contains values from 0.000 to just less than +0.005, while grouping +1 contains values from

Let's use a number example for clarity. Assume Hong Company reports 2001 earnings of $500,000 and the market value of its equity on January 1, 2001, was $62,500,000.

Thus, $500,000 ÷ $62,500,000 = 0.008. Since 0.008 is within the interval of 0.005 to 0.010, Hong Company would appear in earnings interval +1.

FIGURE 3.1(a)
DISTRIBUTION OF
ANNUAL NET
INCOME
Source: P. Dechow,
S. Richardson, and
A. Tuna (see
endnote 1).

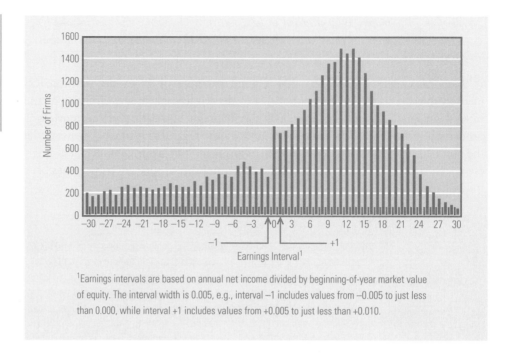

¹Earnings intervals are based on annual net income divided by beginning-of-year market value of equity. The interval width is 0.005, e.g., interval −1 includes values from −0.005 to just less than 0.000, while interval +1 includes values from +0.005 to just less than +0.010.

+0.005 to just less than +0.010. The vertical axis measures the number of firms whose reported earnings fall into the various categories.

The striking feature of this graph is the discontinuity in the number of firms reporting slightly negative earnings versus slightly positive earnings. Substantially fewer firms fall below zero (grouping −1) compared to those reporting earnings at or just above zero (groupings 0 and +1). This suggests that managers try to avoid reporting losses. One way of doing so even in troubled times is to exploit the flexibility in GAAP to push earnings into the positive range.

As noted above, investors often penalize companies that fail to meet analysts' earnings expectations. Figure 3.1(b) reflects the strong incentive managers have to meet or beat analysts' earnings estimates. This graph shows the distribution of analysts' annual EPS forecast errors (i.e., actual EPS minus analysts' consensus EPS estimate). The interval width of each bar is one cent. Thus, the forecast error bar −1 (+1) reflects the number of firm-years where actual earnings per share falls below (above) the analysts' consensus forecasts by one cent. Note the large number of observations clustered in the zero forecast error interval where actual EPS equals the consensus estimate. Also, note the much smaller number of forecast errors that fall in the bar just below zero (−1) compared to the number that fall just above zero (+1). One explanation of this result is that some companies are managing earnings upward to "meet or beat" analysts' earnings projections.

The analysts' consensus EPS estimates come from I/B/E/S. This acronym stands for the U.S. Institutional Brokers Estimate System and provides institutional analyst earnings per share forecasts (both annual and quarterly) for over 18,000 companies in over 50 countries.

Popular Earnings Management Devices

What are some of the more popular techniques firms use to manage earnings? Arthur Levitt has singled out five areas that the SEC finds particularly troublesome and pervasive.[3]

SEC
www.sec.gov

- *"Big Bath" restructuring charges:* The 1990s were the decade of **restructuring** in corporate America. To remain competitive and become more efficient,

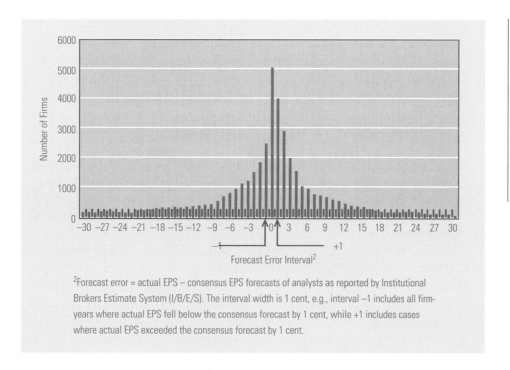

FIGURE 3.1(b)
DISTRIBUTION OF ANNUAL FORECAST ERRORS (IN CENTS) AS REPORTED BY I/B/E/S

Source: P. Dechow, S. Richardson, and A. Tuna (see endnote 1).

[2]Forecast error = actual EPS − consensus EPS forecasts of analysts as reported by Institutional Brokers Estimate System (I/B/E/S). The interval width is 1 cent, e.g., interval −1 includes all firm-years where actual EPS fell below the consensus forecast by 1 cent, while +1 includes cases where actual EPS exceeded the consensus forecast by 1 cent.

hundreds of companies closed plants, consolidated operations, reduced their labour force, and sold non-core business units. Once a decision to restructure is made, GAAP require companies to estimate the future costs they expect to incur to carry out the restructuring—for such things as employee severance payments and plant closings. These estimated restructuring costs are then charged to an expense account with an offsetting credit to a liability account ("Restructuring reserve" or "Estimated liability for restructuring") in the current period. In an effort to "clean up" company balance sheets, managers have often taken excessive restructuring writeoffs and overstated estimated charges for future expenditures. Examples of questionable items that the SEC has found in restructuring charges include services to be provided in some future period by lawyers, accountants, and investment bankers; special bonuses for officers; and expenses for retraining and relocating people. Amazingly, some companies even took charges for training people not yet hired!

Why are companies tempted to overstate restructuring charges? The conventional wisdom is that investors look beyond one-time special charges and writeoffs and, instead, value a company's stock based on sustainable operating earnings (see Chapter 6). So, many believe that taking "big bath" charges does not actually affect stock price.[4] Moreover, these restructuring charges and associated liability reserves are sometimes reversed in future years when earnings fall short of targets, thereby providing a boost to the bottom line at opportune times.

- *Creative acquisition accounting and purchased R&D:* When one company buys another company and uses the **purchase method** of accounting for the combination (see Chapter 16), the buyer must allocate a portion of the purchase price to the acquired firm's identifiable net assets, including intangibles like in-process (incomplete) research and development (R&D) activities.

Statement of Financial Standards (SFAS) No. 2, referred to in CICA's EIC-55, Identifiable Assets Acquired in a Business Combination, states that "while future benefits from a particular research and development project may be foreseen, they generally cannot be measured with a reasonable degree of certainty.[5] Accordingly, values assigned to R&D projects that have no alternative future use are immediately expensed (i.e., in the period in which the acquisition occurs). This treatment results in an economic asset (potential benefits from in-process R&D) that never appears on the balance sheet. If and when revenues from these R&D investments materialize, there are no offsetting charges to expense because the cost of the purchased R&D was written off in the period acquired. This is a classic example of mismatching revenues and expenses that gives the appearance of excessive profitability in later years.

The fair value of in-process R&D is difficult to measure and, therefore, difficult to verify. This creates considerable opportunity to manage post-acquisition earnings by allocating a disproportionate share of the initial purchase price to in-process R&D. This problem has been particularly acute for acquisitions of technology and software development companies where a major portion of the purchase price has been allocated to in-process R&D activities that are then immediately written off.

- *Miscellaneous "cookie jar reserves":* Accrual accounting allows companies to estimate and accrue for obligations that will be paid in *future periods* as a result of the transactions or events in the *current period.* Similar reserves are allowed for estimated declines in asset values. Examples include provisions for bad debts and loan losses, warranty costs, sales returns and reserves for various future expenditures related to corporate restructuring. Some companies use unrealistic assumptions to arrive at these estimated charges. They over-reserve in good times and cut back on estimated charges, or even reverse previous charges, in bad times. As a result, the "cookie jar reserves" become a convenient device for income smoothing.

- *Intentional errors deemed to be "immaterial" and intentional bias in estimates:* Materiality thresholds are another way of using financial reporting flexibility to influence earnings. Sometimes, companies intentionally misapply GAAP (e.g., capitalizing an expenditure that should be expensed). If this incorrect treatment is subsequently caught by the auditor, management might justify the error by arguing that the earnings effect is "immaterial" and, therefore, not worth correcting. The problem, of course, is that a series of these "immaterial" errors spread across several accounts can, in the aggregate, have a material effect on bottom line earnings.

Intentional misstatement of estimates is another area of abuse. Estimates abound in accrual accounting. Examples include estimated useful lives and salvage values for fixed assets, estimates of bad debts, and the amount of writedown for obsolete inventory. Management can often shade these estimates in one direction or the other to achieve a desired earnings target. As long as these estimates fall within "acceptable" ranges, the biased estimate is unlikely to draw attention from the external auditor.

- *Premature or aggressive revenue recognition:* Another common abuse is to recognize revenues before they have been "earned" (the critical event) or become "realized" (measurability). This important earnings management device is discussed in the next section.

Revenue Recognition Abuses

The SEC in the U.S. says that revenue is earned (critical event) and is realized or realizable (measurability)—and, therefore, can be recognized—when all of the following criteria are met:

1. Persuasive evidence of an exchange arrangement exists.
2. Delivery has occurred or services have been rendered.
3. The seller's price to the buyer is fixed or determinable.
4. Collectibility is reasonably assured.

"Arrangement" means there is a final understanding between the parties as to the specific nature and terms of the agreed-upon transaction.

The following scenarios taken from an SEC Staff Accounting Bulletin (SAB) illustrate some troublesome areas of revenue recognition as well as the SEC's interpretive response as to the appropriate treatment.[6]

- Scenario 1—Goods shipped on consignment: A software manufacturer (seller) ships 100,000 copies of a new video game to distributors, charging $50 per copy. Under the terms of the signed agreement, distributors have the right (a) to return unsold copies of the video game, and (b) not to pay the seller until they resell the product to final customers through their retail outlets. The software manufacturer wants to recognize $5,000,000 of revenue upon delivery of the video games to the distributors. Can the company do this?

    SEC interpretive response: No revenue can be recognized on delivery because the seller retains the risk and rewards of ownership of the product. Title does not pass to the distributor when the goods are shipped. Also, under criterion 4 above, there is considerable uncertainty as to ultimate collectibility of the sales price on the goods shipped.

- Scenario 2—Sales with delayed delivery: Prior to the close of its September 30 fiscal quarter, a manufacturer (seller) completes production of 50,000 specialized gas valves. The valves sell for $60 each and were ordered by customers that assemble and sell gas fireplaces. The customers are unable to take delivery by September 30 for reasons that include: (1) lack of available storage space, (2) having ample inventory on hand to cover production for the next month, and (3) delayed production schedules. The seller segregates the valves awaiting shipment from other unsold products in its own warehouse and wishes to recognize $3,000,000 of revenue in the current quarter from these goods produced, but not shipped.

    SEC interpretive response: Without further conditions being spelled out in the sales agreement (criterion 1), the seller cannot recognize revenue until delivery has taken place (criterion 2). Generally, delivery is *not* considered to have occurred unless the customer (a) takes title, and (b) assumes the risk and rewards of ownership of the products. Typically, delivery occurs when a product is received at the customer's place of business or when the product is shipped to the customer. If the buyer requests in the sales agreement that the transaction be on a "bill and hold" basis, and has a substantial business purpose for doing so, then the seller may recognize revenue when the production of the goods is complete.

- Scenario 3—Goods sold on layaway: Company R, a retailer, offers layaway sales to its customers. Company R collects an initial cash deposit from the customer, but retains the merchandise and sets it aside in its inventory.

Although a date may be specified within which the customer must finalize the purchase, Company R does not require the customer to sign a fixed payment agreement. The merchandise is not released to the customer until full payment is received. Company R wants to recognize revenue equal to a pro rata portion of the merchandise sales as cash is collected.

SEC interpretive response: Company R should postpone recognizing revenue until merchandise is delivered to the customer (criterion 2). Until then, the cash received to date should be recognized as a liability such as "Deposits from layaway customers." Because Company R retains the risks of ownership, receives only deposits, and does not have an enforceable right to the remainder of the purchase price, it is not entitled to recognize revenue until the sales price is received in full.

- Scenario 4—Nonrefundable up-front fees: Increasingly, service providers negotiate agreements with customers that require the customer to pay a nonrefundable up-front "initiation" or service "activation" fee. For example, companies that provide telecommunications services typically charge each new customer a nonrefundable activation fee. Once enrolled for service, customers then pay monthly usage fees that just cover the company's operating costs. The costs to activate the telecommunications service are minimal. Thus, the up-front fee more than covers these costs. The key question here is when should revenue from nonrefundable up-front activation fees be recognized?

  SEC interpretive response: Unless the up-front fee is in exchange for products delivered or services performed that represent the culmination of a separate earnings process, deferral of revenue is appropriate because service has not been rendered (criterion 2). In such circumstances, the up-front fees, even if nonrefundable, are deemed to be earned as the services are delivered over the full term of the service agreement. This means that the up-front fees should be deferred and recognized pro rata over the periods when services are provided because that's when the fees are earned.

- Scenario 5—Gross versus net basis for Internet resellers: Another troublesome area is the method used to record sales by certain Internet companies that simply act as an agent or broker in a transaction. For example, assume Dot.com Company operates an Internet site from which it sells airline tickets. Customers place orders by selecting a specific flight from Dot.com's website and providing a credit card number for payment. Dot.com receives the order and credit card authorization and passes this information along to the airline. The airline sends the tickets directly to the customer. Dot.com does not take title to the tickets and, therefore, has no ownership risk or other responsibility for the tickets. The airline is fully responsible for all returned tickets and disputed credit card charges. (So Dot.com is an agent or broker that facilitates the transaction between the customer and the airline.) The average ticket price is $500, of which Dot.com receives $25 as commission. In the event a credit card sale is rejected, Dot.com loses its $25 margin on the sale. Because the management of Dot.com believes that revenue growth is what drives its share price, it seeks to report the revenue from this transaction on a "gross" basis at $500, along with cost of sales of $475.

  SEC interpretive response: Dot.com should report the revenue from this transaction on a "net" basis—$25 as commission revenue and $0 for cost of sales. In determining whether revenue should be reported gross (with separate display of cost of sales) or on a net basis, the SEC stipulates that the following factors be considered:

1. Is Dot.com acting as a principal or as an agent/broker in the transaction?
2. Does Dot.com take title to the ticket?
3. Does Dot.com assume the risks of ownership such as possible losses from bad debts or returns?

If Dot.com acts as a principal in the transaction, takes title to the tickets, or assumes the ownership risks, then the gross method is deemed appropriate. Otherwise, the net method must be used.

It is important to note that SAB 101 was not meant to change GAAP. Instead, it is intended to close some loopholes and eliminate grey areas in how GAAP is being applied in practice. A recent survey of annual reports indicates that the SEC guidelines have diminished abuses.[7] However, aggressive revenue recognition still occurs. So analysts must be vigilant for firms that overstate true earnings performance by bending revenue recognition rules.

GAAP for Interim Reporting and Segment Disclosures

As part of our discussion of income determination, we must mention two additional sections of the *CICA Handbook* that are intended to improve the quality of reported income. Section 1701 ("Segment Disclosures") requires that public companies disclose information about the segments in which they operate, their products and services, geographic areas, and major customers. As the section points out in paragraph 1701.02, such information is useful in helping analysts understand a company's performance and its future cash-generating prospects. One key decision that management must make in discharging its obligations under this section is the determination of an *operating segment* that is also *reportable*, and the section includes guidelines to assist management in this endeavour. But, as always when reading accounting information, users must be alert to the possibility that the reportable segments chosen by the company might be selected for reasons other than full and fair disclosure, but of course the independent audit provides a considerable level of quality assurance on this issue.

Section 1751 ("Interim Financial Statements") establishes standards for reporting quarterly and other interim financial accounting information. In general, it requires that the same accounting policies that a company uses in its annual audited financial statements be used in its interim financials, and therefore each interim period be a stand-alone period.

Recap
The criteria for revenue and expense recognition are intended to provide general guidance for accrual accounting income determination. However, these general criteria leave ample room for judgment and interpretation that creates flexibility in GAAP. Analysts and investors must be alert for management's attempts to exploit this flexibility in ways that push the boundaries of acceptable revenue and expense recognition.

Summary

The "critical event" and "measurability" conditions for revenue recognition are typically satisfied at point of sale. However, there are circumstances—long-term construction contracts, production of natural resources, and agricultural commodities—where it is appropriate to recognize revenue prior to sale. Revenue recognition may also be delayed until after the sale—specifically, when cash is collected. This approach is used when there is considerable uncertainty about the collectibility of the sales price or where there are significant costs that will be incurred after the sale that are difficult to predict. This chapter outlines the special accounting procedures used when revenue recognition doesn't occur at the point of sale.

The broad criteria for revenue and expense recognition leave room for considerable latitude and judgment. This flexibility in GAAP can sometimes be exploited by management to hide or misrepresent the underlying economic performance of a company. This chapter outlines some of the more common ways of managing earnings that have come under SEC scrutiny. Later chapters provide further examples of how earnings can be manipulated. Auditors and financial statement users must be aware of management's incentives to manage earnings, and the ways in which this is accomplished. Armed with this knowledge, you will be in a much better position to spot "accounting irregularities" and to avoid their unpleasant consequences.

Exercises

E3-1 Long-term construction contract accounting

American Institute of Certified Public Accountants (AICPA) adapted

The following data pertain to Pell Company's construction jobs, which commenced during 2001:

	Project 1	Project 2
Contract price	$420,000	$300,000
Costs incurred during 2001	240,000	280,000
Estimated cost to complete	120,000	40,000
Billed to customers during 2001	150,000	270,000
Received from customers during 2001	90,000	250,000

Required:

1. If Pell used the completed-contract method, what amount of gross profit (loss) would be reported in its 2001 income statement?
2. If Pell used the percentage-of-completion method, what amount of gross profit (loss) would be reported in the 2001 income statement?

E3-2 Percentage-of-completion method of revenue recognition

CICA adapted

Construction Company started a contract in June 2000 to build a bridge at a fixed price of $10 million. The bridge was to be completed by October 2002 at a total estimated cost of $8 million. Total cumulative costs incurred by the end of December 2000 and 2001 were $2 million and $5.5 million, respectively. Because of cost overruns in 2001, it is now expected that the project will cost $800,000 more than originally estimated.

Required:

Compute the gross profit to be recognized for the year ended December 31, 2001, using the percentage-of-completion method of revenue recognition.

E3-3 Determining gross profit using installment sales

AICPA adapted

Lang Company uses the installment method of revenue recognition. The following data pertain to Lang's installment sales for the years ended December 31, 2001 and 2002.

	2001	2002
Installment receivables at year-end on 2001 sales	$60,000	$30,000
Installment receivables at year-end on 2002 sales	—	69,000
Installment sales	80,000	90,000
Cost of sales	40,000	60,000

What amount should Lang report as deferred gross profit in its December 31, 2001 and 2002 balance sheets?

E3-4 Determining gross profit using the installment sales method

AICPA method

Since there is no reasonable basis for estimating the degree of collectibility, Astor Company uses the installment method of revenue recognition for the following sales:

	2001	2000
Sales	$900,000	$600,000
Collections from:		
2000 sales	100,000	200,000
2001 sales	300,000	—
Accounts written off:		
2000 sales	150,000	50,000
2001 sales	50,000	—
Gross profit percentage	40%	30%

Required:

What amount should Astor report as deferred gross profit in its December 31, 2001 balance sheet for the 2000 and 2001 sales?

E3-5 Determining gross profit using the installment method

AICPA adapted

On January 2, 2001, Yardley Company sold a manufacturing plant to Ivory Inc. for $1,500,000. On that date, the plant's carrying cost was $1,000,000. Ivory gave Yardley $300,000 cash and a $1,200,000 note, payable in four annual installments of $300,000 cash plus 12% interest. Ivory made the first principal and interest payment of $444,000 on December 31, 2001. Yardley uses the installment method of revenue recognition.

Required:

In its 2001 income statement, what amount of realized gross profit should Yardley report?

E3-6 Determining installment accounts receivable

AICPA adapted

Taft Corporation, which began business on January 1, 2001, appropriately uses the installment sales method of accounting. The following data are available for December 31, 2001 and 2002:

	2001	2002
Balance of deferred gross profit on sales on account for:		
2001	$300,000	$120,000
2002		$440,000
Gross profit on sales	30%	40%

The installment accounts receivable balances at December 31, 2001 and 2002 would be how much?

E3-7 Determining realized gross profit on installment sales

AICPA adapted

Kul Company, which began operations on January 1, 2001, appropriately uses the installment sales method of accounting. The following information is available for 2001:

Installment accounts receivable, December 31, 2001	$400,000
Deferred gross profit, December 31, 2001 (before recognition of realized gross profit for 2001)	$280,000
Gross profit on sales	40%

For the year ended December 31, 2001, cash collections and realized gross profit on installment sales should be how much?

Problems/Discussion Questions

P3-1 Income measurement under alternative revenue recognition rules

Ms Fuji started a business on January 1, 2001. Key operating statistics for 2001 were as follows:

Beginning inventory	–0–
Number of units produced	20,000
Number of units sold (delivery basis)	16,000
Number of units sold for which cash has been received by December 31, 2001	14,000

Direct production costs were $12 per unit. There were no fixed costs or selling/delivery expenses. The selling price per unit was $16.00.

On January 1, 2002, Ms Fuji decided to liquidate the business. She sold the remaining inventory at $13.00 per unit for cash. By January 15, 2002, she collected the amount due from customers for sales made during 2001.

Based on the above information, compute the net income of Ms Fuji for the years 2001 and 2002 under:

1. Production basis.
2. Sales (or delivery) basis.
3. Cash collection basis.

P3-2 Income determination under alternative bases of revenue recognition

Agri Pro, a farm corporation, produced 15,000 bushels of wheat in its first year of operations. During the year, Agri Pro sold 10,000 bushels of the grain produced for $2.40 per bushel and collected three-fourths of the selling price on the grain sold; the balance is to be collected in equal amounts during each of the two following years. The local grain elevator is quoting a year-end market price of $3.00 per bushel. Additional data for the first year are as follows:

Amortization on equipment	$ 3,000
Other production costs (cash)—per bushel	$ 0.50
Miscellaneous administrative costs (cash)	$ 4,000
Selling and delivery costs (incurred and paid at time of sale), per bushel	$ 0.10
Dividends paid to stockholders during Year 1	$10,000
Interest on borrowed money (one-half paid in cash)	$ 5,000

Agri Pro is enthusiastic about the accountant's concept of matching product costs with revenues.

Required:

Compute net income under each of the indicated methods and determine the carrying (book) value of inventory and accounts receivable at the end of the first year of operation for each of these methods.

1. Recognize revenue when production is complete.
2. Recognize revenue at point of sale.
3. Recognize revenue on an installment (cash collection) basis.

P3-3 Determining pre-tax income, inventory carrying value, and accounts receivable under sales and production basis

Howe, Inc., a crude oil producer, started business on May 1, 2001. Howe sells all its production, f.o.b. shipping point, to a single customer at the current spot price for crude oil in the region where Howe is located. The customer pays Howe 60% of the selling price at the time of delivery with the remaining to be paid in 10 months. Throughout 2001, the spot market price for the oil was $28.00 per barrel; however, on December 31, 2001, the market price jumped to $31.00 per barrel, where it is expected to remain. Howe's direct production costs are $12.00 per barrel, drilling equipment amortization expense totalled $180,000 for the eight-month period ending December 31, and property taxes of $75,000 were paid during the year. Howe produced 30,000 barrels of oil, of which 6,000 barrels were included in January 1, 2002, opening inventory.

Required:

Compute Howe's 2001 pre-tax income and determine its inventory carrying value and accounts receivable balance at December 31, 2001, under the following:

1. Production basis.
2. Sales (completed transaction) basis.
3. Installment (cash collection) basis.

P3-4 Percentage-of-completion accounting
AICPA adapted

In 2001, Long Construction began work under a three-year contract. The contract price is $800,000. Long uses the percentage-of-completion method for financial accounting purposes. The income to be recognized each year is based on the proportion of cost incurred to total estimated costs for completing the contract. The financial statement presentations relating to this contract at December 31, 2001, follow:

Balance Sheet	
Accounts receivable—construction contract billings	$15,000
Construction in progress	50,000
Less contract billings	(47,000)
Construction in progress less billings	$ 3,000
Income Statement	
Income (before tax) on the contract recognized in 2001	$10,000

Required:

1. How much cash was collected in 2001 on this contract?
2. What was the initial estimated total cost on this project?
3. What is the estimated total income (before tax) on this contract?

P3-5 Revenue recognition for goods on consignment

Englewood Marine is a builder of fibreglass fishing boats. The boats are marketed through a network of third-party dealers on a consignment basis. The consignment agreement stipulates that Englewood retains title to the boats until final sale to the customer. Dealers can return unsold boats to Englewood by paying shipping expenses and a financing fee for the time held. Each boat's cost to dealers is fixed at $28,000. Englewood's gross profit margin per boat is 30%.

Englewood shipped 41 boats to dealers during the six months ending October 31. Shipments were:

Monthly Boat Shipments to Dealers

May	3	August	9
June	6	September	8
July	8	October	7

Dealers had three Englewood boats on hand for the quarter ended July 31 and two boats on hand at October 31.

Required:

1. Prepare a schedule showing Englewood Marine's revenues, cost of goods sold, and gross profit for the quarters ending July 31 and October 31.
2. Indicate how Englewood Marine would report the unsold boats and for how much at July 31 and October 31.

P3-6 Revenue recognition based on delivery performance

Composite, Inc. is a manufacturer of modular homes. Due to lack of storage space for raw material inventories, Composite implemented a just-in-time inventory process in early 1999. Composite contracts with qualified vendors to be sole suppliers for a given raw material. In return, the vendors guarantee performance in accordance with Composite's purchase order.

On Friday, November 2, 2001, Composite placed a purchase order with Mogul Chemical Company for plastic resins. Composite's purchase order specifically states that all material is shipped so that Composite takes title to the goods when they are received.

Delivery is to be made at 6:00 a.m. on the designated delivery date. Designated delivery date, kilograms, and selling price per kilogram are:

Delivery Date	Kilograms	Selling Price per Kilogram
Friday, November 30, 2001	75,000	$1.00
Friday, December 7, 2001	80,000	1.00
Friday, December 14, 2001	60,000	1.10
Friday, December 21, 2001	50,000	1.20
Friday, January 4, 2002	50,000	1.20

In December, Mogul Chemical was experiencing a slowdown in sales and decided to produce Composite's January 2002 order over the Christmas holidays. After completing the production on December 29, the material was promptly loaded on a trailer, which was immediately locked and sealed. An invoice and a bill of lading were prepared. The invoice was then sent to Composite on a "bill and hold" basis.

Upon receiving the invoice, Composite contacted Mogul and was told that the material was invoiced because Mogul wanted to include the sale in the quarter ended December 31, 2001. However, actual delivery would take place according to the purchase order terms. Composite accepted the explanation.

Required:

1. Determine the sales revenue that Mogul should recognize on transactions with Composite for the quarter ended December 31, 2001.
2. What would Mogul's justification be for including the production on December 29 in its December sales?
3. Should Mogul include the December 29 production in its December sales? Why or why not?

P3-7 Revenue recognition on layaways

DW Hooks is a customer-oriented retailer of high-definition televisions and other electronic and computer equipment. Hooks will accept layaway sales provided the customer makes a minimum down payment of 20% of the retail price and pays the balance off within 90 days. After the customer makes the initial deposit, Hooks transfers the merchandise from a "Retail Inventory" account to a "Layaway—Merchandise Inventory" account. Inventory is valued at approximately 80% of the retail-selling price. When the layaway sale is paid in full, Hooks will deliver the merchandise to the customer.

At January 31, 2001, Hooks had $72,000 of merchandise on layaway, for which customers have made cash deposits totalling $55,000. For the quarter ending April 30, Hooks had the following layaway transactions:

Month	Amounts Added to Layaway Inventory	Deposits Made During Month	Deliveries	
			Cost	Retail
February	$49,000	$45,000	$24,000	$30,000
March	50,000	67,000	56,000	70,000
April	40,000	51,000	48,000	60,000

Required:

1. Prepare the journal entries required to record these transactions.
2. Prepare a schedule showing sales revenue earned for the period, and reconcile balances in layaway and customer deposits at January 31, 2001, to April 30, 2001.
3. How should Hook report the customer deposits in its financial statements?

Cases

C3-1 Smith's Farm: Alternative bases of income determination

Teresa Smith owns and operates a farm in Saskatchewan. During 2001, she produced and harvested 40,000 bushels of wheat. Smith had no inventory of wheat at the start of the year. Immediately after harvesting the wheat in the late summer of 2001, Smith sold 30,000 bushels to a local grain elevator operator. As of December 31, 2001, Smith had received payment for 20,000 bushels. Additional information relating to the farm follows:

Price:	
Market price per bushel at the time of harvest and sale to the grain elevator operator	$ 3.60
Market price per bushel at December 31, 2001	$ 3.60
Costs:	
Variable production costs per bushel	$ 0.50
Delivery costs per bushel	$ 0.20
Annual fixed costs of operating the farm that are unrelated to the volume of production	$25,000

Required:

1. Prepare a 2001 income statement for Smith's Farm under each of the following assumptions regarding what constitutes the "critical event" in the process of recognizing income:
   a. Assuming that production is the critical event.
   b. Assuming that the sale is the critical event.
   c. Assuming that cash collection is the critical event.
   (For simplicity, treat the fixed operating costs as period—rather than product—costs.)
2. Determine the December 31, 2001, balances for wheat inventory and accounts receivable under each of the three income recognition methods in Question 1.
3. Assume that the farm is left idle during 2002. Since there is no harvest, Smith's only transaction consists of an October 2002 sale of the 10,000 bushels in inventory at a price of $2.80 per bushel. Further assume that no fixed costs are incurred while the farm is idle. Compute 2002 income on both the sale and production basis. Discuss the causes for any profit or loss reported under each income determination alternative.

C3-2 Stewart & Stevenson Services, Inc. (KR): Understanding accounts used for long-term construction contract accounting

Stewart & Stevenson Services, Inc. manufactures motors and generators. Here are the Year 2 financial statements of Stewart & Stevenson Services, Inc. (all dollar amounts are in U.S. dollars):

Stewart & Stevenson Services, Inc.		
	Year 2	**Year 1**
Balance Sheet Items		
Accounts receivable	$ 143,166	$121,030
Costs incurred on uncompleted contracts	190,670	70,766
Accrued profits	13,117	9,857
Cost incurred + accrued profits	203,787	80,623
Less: Customer progress payments	(164,078)	(55,258)
Cost in excess of billings (net)	$ 39,709	$ 25,365
Income Statement Items		
Sales revenue	$ 812,526	$686,363
Cost of sales	685,879	569,695
Gross margin	$ 126,647	$116,668
Gross margin rate	15.6%	17.0%

Assumption: All sales revenues are from long-term construction contracts.

Required:

1. Using the information provided above, reconstruct the following T-accounts, showing how the accounts changed from their beginning to ending balances in Year 2.

Stewart and Stevenson Services, Inc.

Construction in Process Inventory

Beginning balance	$ 80,623		
Ending balance	203,787		

Billings on Contract (Progress Payments)

		$ 55,258	Beginning balance
		164,078	Ending balance

Accounts Receivable

Beginning balance	$121,030		
Ending balance	143,166		

2. Compute sales revenue, cost of goods sold, and gross margin, assuming the company was using the completed-contract method during Year 2.
3. Assuming a tax effect rate of 40% and also that the company switched from the percentage-of-completion method to the completed-contract method at the end of Year 2, compute the effect of this change of accounting principle.

4. Assuming the information on accrued profits is not available, estimate the gross margin, assuming the company was using the completed-contract method during Year 2.
5. Explain the difference between the gross profits obtained for Questions 2 and 4.
6. Assuming the information on accrued profits is not available, estimate the margin if revenue were recognized on a cash collected basis.

 Collaborative Learning Cases

CL3-1 Earnings management: A potpourri of allegations, innuendos, and settlements involving measurement and disclosure

Several accounting situations involving prominent companies are listed below.

Required:

1. Select at least three of the following situations, and track down the source provided.
2. Briefly explain the earnings management issue(s) involved in the situations that you selected. As part of your explanation, describe the accounting details, as appropriate.
3. Explain how *quality of earnings* might be impacted.
4. In your opinion, is financial reporting adversarial? Explain why or why not, drawing upon the evidence in this case.

Situation	Company	Information and Source
1	Livent	A *Statement of Allegations* posted to the Ontario Securities Commission's (OSC) website begins as follows: "that Livent, for the fiscal years ending December 31, 1996 and December 31, 1997, and for the quarter ended March 31, 1998, made statements in its interim and audited annual financial statements required to be filed or furnished under Ontario securities law that, in a material respect and at the time and in the light of the circumstances under which they were made, were misleading or untrue or did not state a fact that was required to be stated or that was necessary to make the statements not misleading."
2.	Air Canada	A *Settlement Agreement* posted to the OSC's website summarized the facts in a case involving Air Canada's disclosure of earnings information to a select group of analysts prior to public disclosure.
3	General Electric (GE)	Gretchen Morgensen writes about the alleged serious charges against GE regarding income management in "Wait a Second: What Devils Lurk in the Details?" (*New York Times*, April 14, 2002). (See also the rejoinder issued by GE on April 15, 2002, by Richard F. Wacker, GE's Vice-President, Corporate Investor Communications, available on GE's website.)

4	Boeing	"Boeing's Secrets: Did the Aircraft Giant Exploit Accounting Rules to Conceal a Huge Factory Snafu?" by Stanley Holmes and Mike France (*BusinessWeek online*, May 20, 2002).
5	Xerox	A *Complaint* to the SEC dated April 11, 2002 (stored on the SEC website) begins as follows: "From at least 1997 through 2000, Xerox … defrauded investors … Xerox disguised its true operating performance by using undisclosed accounting maneuvers …"
6	Halliburton Company	This situation has political overtones, since current U.S. Vice-President Dick Cheney was CEO of the company at the time the alleged accounting infractions took place. See "Under Cheney, Halliburton Altered Policy on Accounting" by Alex Berenson and Lowell Bergman (*New York Times*, May 22, 2002).

CL3-2 The case of Canadian Airlines and the "Net Income–Wage Concession Swap"

Canadian Airlines (Canadian) was the smaller of two national airline passenger carriers in Canada, with its main routes in Western Canada and the Asia–Pacific region. However, the company had been undergoing tough times for some years, and after a bitter (by Canadian standards) corporate battle, Canadian Airlines was acquired by its larger rival, Air Canada in early 2000.

In the mid-1990s, during a series of earlier crises, Canadian had developed a close strategic relationship with AMR Corporation, the parent of American Airlines (see Exhibit 1), and had also instituted several cost-cutting initiatives, an important one being a unique negotiated wage concession with the company's employees. The company described this wage concession as follows:

Wage Concessions

All employees of CAI and its subsidiaries accepted a four year wage reduction program beginning January 1, 1997. The program reduces each employee's salary or wage by 10% for all amounts that would otherwise have been payable over $25,000 annually. This program saved the Company $31.4 million in salary and wage expenses in 1997. In return for these wage concessions, a profit sharing program was established whereby 10% of audited income before income taxes (before accounting for the profit sharing) of the Company in 1997 and 1998, and 20% in 1999 and 2000, is to be distributed to employees. Based on the Company's 1997 results of operations, employees became eligible to receive $0.8 million under this program. In addition, as part of the Operational Restructuring Plan, an agreement was reached with the Company's unions for the extension of all collective agreements to December 31, 2000 … (Canadian Airlines Corporation Prospectus, April 20, 1998)

Leaders of the Canadian union movement were always uneasy with this arrangement to swap wages for a share of future net income, and their unease proved especially well founded when Canadian reported losses in 1998 and 1999 and was swallowed by its rival Air Canada in 2000. One of the apparent problems involved the potential elasticity of the accounting measure called "audited income before income taxes (before accounting for the profit sharing)."

The 1997 audited financial statements for Canadian are presented on pages 122–135. Canadian received an unqualified audit opinion in 1997. Assume that you are an assistant to the research director for a national union. Since your expertise lies in the financial area, the research director has asked you to prepare a report analyzing Canadian's 1997 audited financial statements, with a focus on the quality of earnings. The director tells you the following:

"I'm not sure that I can prove it, but I believe that companies like Canadian can more or less control their financial accounting results, and manufacture a profit or loss when they need to. For example, since 1997 was the first year of the wage concession agreement, it makes sense that Canadian would want to show at least a small profit so that the employees would feel that they were getting something back for their wage concession which saved the company over $30 million that year. After that, they were hooked, and it didn't matter what the company reported in 1998 and after."

Even though you are aware that there are permissible alternatives within GAAP, you doubt that a set of audited financial statements could be flexible enough so that a profit or loss could be *manufactured*.

Required:

In this assignment, you will not actually prepare the report required by the research director. Instead, you will answer the following questions as if you were doing the background work for the report. In total, your submission should not be more than seven pages.

1. Prepare a comprehensive definition of quality of earnings that the research director would understand.
2. Identify and explain five accounting issues in the Canadian Airlines financials that might suggest that the company's quality of earnings is not as high as would be desirable.
3. What is your overall opinion of the company's disclosure? Explain.
4. Explain how, if at all, the income measure described in the wage concession arrangement could have been improved.

Exhibit 1 EXCERPTS FROM CANADIAN AIRLINES CORPORATION'S PROSPECTUS, APRIL 20, 1998

Relationship with AMR and American Airlines

Since the 1994 Financial Restructuring, AMR has played a critical role in the operations of the Company, culminating with the implementation of the Operational Restructuring Plan. This involvement has proven to be extremely beneficial to the Company in a variety of ways; among other things, it has enhanced the Company's route network, provided additional, higher-yielding business traffic to the Company's system, assisted with route and fleet analysis, reduced overhead costs and provided marketing and sales support. The Company has also benefited from the management expertise of the employees that have joined CAI from AMR and from the advisory role that AMR plays as a shareholder of CAI. A number of key corporate initiatives which form the basis of the Company's business strategy require the involvement of AMR and American Airlines. In addition, a substantial portion of the Company's operations are dependent upon services provided by AMR under the services agreement. As a result, the AMR relationship has a critical bearing on the Company's prospects for success in the future. The Company is unable to predict the manner in which the AMR relationship might change or the impact that any such change might have on the Company's financial condition or results of operations. However, such change could arise in a number of ways, including: (i) the exercise of any termination rights under the key AMR agreements including, without limitation, the services agreement and the cooperative service agreement (which establishes the codesharing arrangements); (ii) a divergence in corporate objectives resulting in conflict of interest on governance issues (including significant operational matters that require the approval of AMR); or (iii) the revocation of antitrust immunity by the U.S. Government. The occurrence of any of these events will have a material adverse effect on the Company's operations, financial condition and results of operations. In addition, in the event that American Airlines is granted additional rights to serve Asian destinations (American Airlines was recently able to secure additional rights to operate flights to Japan) and such rights significantly reduced the benefits to American Airlines provided by the Company's Asian route network and Vancouver hub, AMR's current level of support for the Company could be reduced. If AMR were to reduce or withdraw its support for the Company, the prospects for the Operational Restructuring Plan could be undermined and the Company's financial condition and results of operations could be materially adversely affected. Finally, AMR, through its indirect wholly-owned subsidiary, Aurora, purchased $246.0 million of preferred shares of CAI as part of the 1994 Financial Restructuring. While AMR's ability to resell those preferred shares is subject to certain restrictions, there can be no assurance that AMR will not sell part or all of its investment at any time in the future.

Exhibit 2 CANADIAN AIRLINES' 1997 AUDITED FINANCIAL STATEMENTS

Consolidated Financial Statements of
Canadian Airlines Corporation
Years ended December 31, 1997 and 1996

Management's Report

The consolidated financial statements are the responsibility of the management of Canadian Airlines Corporation and have been prepared in accordance with generally accepted accounting principles.

Management is responsible for the reliability and integrity of the consolidated financial statements, the notes to the consolidated financial statements, and other financial information contained in this report.

Management is also responsible for maintaining a system of internal control designed to provide reasonable assurance that assets are safeguarded and that accounting systems provide timely, accurate and reliable financial information.

The Board of Directors is responsible for ensuring that management fulfills its responsibilities for financial reporting and internal control. The Board is assisted in exercising its responsibilities through the Audit Committee of the Board, which is composed of five non-management directors. The Committee meets regularly with management and the auditors to satisfy itself that management's responsibilities are properly discharged, to review the consolidated financial statements and to recommend approval of the consolidated financial statements to the Board.

The Shareholders have appointed KPMG as the external auditors of the Company and, in that capacity, they have examined the consolidated financial statements for the years ended December 31, 1997 and 1996. The Auditors' Report to the Shareholders is presented herein.

(signed)   (signed)

K.E. Benson   D.A. Carty
President and Chief Executive Officer   Senior Vice President and
                                            Chief Financial Officer

Auditors' Report to the Shareholders

We have audited the consolidated balance sheets of Canadian Airlines Corporation as at December 31, 1997 and 1996 and the consolidated statements of operations, deficit and changes in financial position for the years then ended. These financial statements are the responsibility of the Corporation's management. Our responsibility is to express an opinion on these financial statements based on our audits.

We conducted our audits in accordance with generally accepted auditing standards. Those standards require that we plan and perform an audit to obtain reasonable assurance whether the financial statements are free of material misstatement. An audit includes examining, on a test basis, evidence supporting the amounts and disclosures in the financial statements. An audit also includes assessing the accounting principles used and significant estimates made by management, as well as evaluating the overall financial statement presentation.

In our opinion, these consolidated financial statements present fairly, in all material respects, the financial position of the Corporation as at December 31, 1997 and 1996 and the results of its operations and the changes in its financial position for the years then ended in accordance with generally accepted accounting principles.

KPMG

Chartered Accountants

Calgary, Canada
February 25, 1998

CANADIAN AIRLINES CORPORATION

Consolidated Balance Sheets

December 31, 1997 and 1996
(In Millions)

	1997	1996
Assets		
Cash and short-term investments	$ 193.9	$ 68.4
Accounts receivable	222.9	211.8
Materials and supplies	138.5	141.0
Deposits and prepaid expenses	38.4	35.3
	593.7	456.5
Property and equipment, at cost (note 2):		
Flight equipment	1,232.3	1,237.1
Land, buildings and ground equipment	248.8	246.4
Deposits on flight equipment (note 12)	30.7	49.7
	1,511.8	1,533.2
Less accumulated depreciation	397.7	304.1
	1,114.1	1,229.1
Other assets (note 3)	204.4	181.1
	$1,912.2	$1,866.7
Liabilities and Shareholders' Deficiency		
Accounts payable and accrued liabilities	$ 514.9	$ 539.9
Advance ticket sales	234.2	201.4
Current portion of long-term debt (note 4)	129.0	157.1
	878.1	898.4
Long-term debt (note 4)	697.8	683.9
Deferred credits	52.1	23.7
Preferred shares of subsidiary (note 6)	307.4	289.3
Shareholders' deficiency:		
Capital stock (note 7)	406.9	406.9
Deficit	(430.1)	(435.5)
	(23.2)	(28.6)
Commitments (note 12)		
Contingencies (note 13)		
	$1,912.2	$1,866.7

See accompanying notes to consolidated financial statements.

Approved by the Board:

(signed) H. R. Steele   Director

(signed) A. V. Mauro   Director

CANADIAN AIRLINES CORPORATION

Consolidated Statements of Operations

Years ended December 31, 1997 and 1996
(In Millions)

	1997	1996
Operating revenues:		
Passenger	$2,629.1	$2,570.7
Cargo and mail	242.6	227.2
Charter and tour	47.1	148.3
Contract services and other	156.7	150.2
	3,075.5	3,096.4
Operating expenses:		
Salaries, wages and benefits	757.6	804.6
Fuel	470.5	507.1
Aircraft rentals	303.0	302.5
Commissions	266.4	300.7
Maintenance materials and services	185.4	170.0
Passenger meals and amenities	150.8	157.3
Airport user fees	110.5	109.2
Depreciation and amortization	109.3	115.9
Other	624.9	723.2
	2,978.4	3,190.5
Operating income (loss) before undernoted items	97.1	(94.1)
Restructuring expenses	—	6.4
Operating income (loss)	97.1	(100.5)
Non-operating expense (income):		
Net interest expense (note 8)	69.8	65.4
Annual premium on preferred shares of subsidiary (note 6)	18.1	17.0
Loss (gain) on sale of property and equipment	(2.2)	2.6
Other	4.2	(0.1)
	89.9	84.9
Income (loss) before income taxes	7.2	(185.4)
Income tax expense (note 9)	1.8	1.7
Income (loss)	$ 5.4	$ (187.1)
Income (loss) per Common Share (note 7):		
Basic	$ 0.12	$ (4.23)
Fully diluted	0.11	(4.23)
Weighted average number of Common Shares outstanding (in thousands) (note 7)	44,663	44,200

See accompanying notes to consolidated financial statements.

CANADIAN AIRLINES CORPORATION

Consolidated Statements of Deficit

Years ended December 31, 1997 and 1996
(In Millions)

	1997	1996
Balance at beginning of year	$(435.5)	$(248.4)
Income (loss)	5.4	(187.1)
Balance at end of year	$(430.1)	$(435.5)

See accompanying notes to consolidated financial statements.

CANADIAN AIRLINES CORPORATION

Consolidated Statements of Changes in Financial Position

Years ended December 31, 1997 and 1996
(In Millions)

	1997	1996
Cash provided by (used in):		
Operations:		
Income (loss)	$ 5.4	$(187.1)
Add items not involving cash:		
Depreciation and amortization	109.3	115.9
Fuel tax recovery amortization	(31.0)	—
Employee share entitlement contributions (note 7)	—	24.5
Loss (gain) on sale of property and equipment	(2.2)	2.6
Annual premium on preferred shares of subsidiary (note 6)	18.1	17.0
Other	2.8	10.2
Funds from (used in) operations	102.4	(16.9)
Change in noncash working capital items related to operations	0.8	19.2
Net cash flow from operations	103.2	2.3
Financing activities:		
Issuance of long-term debt	7.3	23.9
Repayment of long-term debt	(94.8)	(201.8)
Deferred interest and aircraft lease payments (note 4)	87.1	—
Fuel tax recovery	54.8	—
	54.4	(177.9)
Investing activities:		
Disposal of property and equipment	32.0	149.6
Purchase of property and equipment	(32.3)	(43.3)
Deposits on flight equipment	—	(21.5)
Other	(31.8)	(41.1)
	(32.1)	43.7
Increase (decrease) in cash	125.5	(131.9)
Cash at beginning of year	68.4	200.3
Cash at end of year	$193.9	$ 68.4

"Cash" comprises cash and short-term investments.

See accompanying notes to consolidated financial statements.

CANADIAN AIRLINES CORPORATION

Notes to Consolidated Financial Statements

Years ended December 31, 1997 and 1996
(Tabular Amounts in Millions of Dollars)

1. **Significant accounting policies:**

   (a) **Basis of consolidation:**

   These consolidated financial statements include the accounts of Canadian Airlines Corporation and its subsidiary Canadian Airlines International Ltd. ("Canadian Airlines") and its subsidiaries, Canadian Holidays Ltd. up to its sale on August 9, 1996, and Canadian Regional Airlines Ltd. ("Canadian Regional"). Canadian Regional includes the accounts of its subsidiaries Time Air Inc., Ontario Express Ltd. and Inter-Canadien (1991) Inc.

   (b) **Translation of foreign currencies:**

   Monetary assets and liabilities denominated in foreign currency are translated into Canadian dollars at rates of exchange in effect at the balance sheet date. Other assets and revenue and expense items are translated at rates prevailing when they were acquired or incurred. Translation gains and losses are included in income except for unrealized gains and losses on long-term monetary items which are deferred and amortized over their term (note 4).

   (c) **Materials and supplies:**

   Materials and supplies are valued at the lower of cost and replacement cost.

   (d) **Property and equipment:**

   Depreciation is provided at straight-line rates to estimated residual values based on the following estimated useful lives:

Asset	Basis
Flight equipment	12–20 years
Buildings	10–40 years
Ground equipment	5–10 years

   (e) **Deferred charges:**

   Pre-operating costs related to the introduction of new types of aircraft and computer systems development costs are amortized over various periods up to 10 years.

   Costs incurred on the issue of long term obligations are amortized on a straight-line basis over the life of the related obligation.

   (f) **Maintenance and repairs:**

   Maintenance and repairs, including major flight equipment overhauls, for aircraft are charged to income as incurred.

   (g) **Revenue recognition:**

   Air transportation revenue is recognized when the transportation is provided. The value of unused tickets or portions thereof is included in the balance sheet as advance ticket sales under current liabilities.

   (h) **Frequent flyer program:**

   The incremental costs of providing travel awards under the Corporation's "Canadian Plus" and affiliated carrier's frequent flyer programs are accrued as the entitlements to such awards are earned and are included in accounts payable and accrued liabilities.

   (i) **Capitalization of interest:**

   Interest on funds used to finance payments made for the acquisition of flight equipment prior to entry into service and on other advance payments for capital acquisitions is capitalized and included in the cost of the related capital item.

1. **Significant accounting policies (continued):**

   (j) **Earnings per share:**

   Earnings per share are calculated based upon the weighted average number of common shares and earned entitlements to acquire common shares outstanding.

   (k) **Financial instruments:**

   The Corporation enters into forward contracts to manage its exposure to jet fuel price volatility. Gains and losses are recorded as adjustments to fuel expense when the contracts are closed.

   The Corporation manages its foreign exchange exposure on inflows and outflows of foreign currency through the use of forward contracts. Resulting gains and losses are recorded as adjustments to related revenue or expense as the contracts are closed.

   (l) **Use of estimates:**

   The preparation of financial statements requires management to make estimates and assumptions based on information available as of the date of the financial statements. Actual results could differ from those estimates.

   (m) **Comparative figures:**

   Certain balances have been reclassified to conform with current accounting presentation.

2. **Property and equipment:**

   The following assets under capital lease have been included in property and equipment:

	1997	1996
Flight equipment	$ 73.4	$ 85.1
Less accumulated depreciation	31.2	25.4
	$ 42.2	$ 59.7

3. **Other assets:**

	1997	1996
Deferred charges (note 10)	$197.4	$174.0
Agreements and leases receivable	4.8	5.0
Other	2.2	2.1
	$204.4	$181.1

4. Long-term debt:

	1997	1996
Bank loans drawn on committed credit facilities and bearing interest at floating rates which at December 31, 1997 averaged 6.4% (i)	$ 16.0	$ 21.9
Term loans (Cdn. $72,900,000, U.S. $125,300,000; 1996 - Cdn. $79,600,000, U.S. $137,009,000) due between 1998 and 2003, secured by certain flight equipment and aircraft spare parts and bearing interest at fixed and floating rates which at December 31, 1997 averaged 9.0%	252.0	267.2
Bank loans (U.S. $140,800,000; 1996 - $144,420,000) due between 1998 and 2010, secured by certain flight equipment and bearing interest at fixed and floating rates which at December 31, 1997 averaged 10.3%	201.2	197.8
Capital lease obligations (note 5)	77.4	86.9
Conditional sale agreements (U.S. $50,946,000; 1996 - $54,915,000) due between 1998 and 2002, secured by certain flight equipment and bearing interest at 11.0%	72.8	75.2
Term loans due in 2001, secured by certain flight equipment, real estate and other assets of which $11,174,000 is guaranteed by the Government of Canada and $15,774,000 by certain provincial governments, bearing interest at floating rates which at December 31, 1997 averaged 4.5%	26.9	29.9
Convertible non-interest bearing notes (U.S. $3,885,000; and Japanese Yen 3,315,482,000); due in 2002, secured by certain flight equipment (ii)	41.9	44.5
Other	151.4	117.6
	839.6	841.0
Deferred exchange losses (iii)	(12.7)	—
	$826.9	$841.0
Less amounts included in current liabilities	129.0	157.1
Long-term debt	$697.9	$683.9

(i) The Corporation has a $135,000,000 demand loan secured primarily by accounts receivable and inventory. At December 31, 1997 the Corporation has drawn $16,000,000 (1996 - $21,900,000) against this credit facility and there are outstanding letters of credit under the facility in the amount of $117,000,000 (1996 - $103,000,000).

(ii) The convertible notes are redeemable by the Corporation for cash at any time, and are convertible to non-voting shares or common shares:

    (a) at the option of the holder at a conversion price of $20.00 or at a conversion price equal to 95% of a weighted average trading price of the shares after April 1999; or

    (b) at the option of the Corporation at a conversion price of the shares of $20.00 provided that the weighted average trading price reaches $25.00.

(iii) At December 31, 1997, $12,784,0000 of losses on translation of foreign currency denominated debt have been deferred and are amortized over the remaining term of the obligations. Due to the occurrence of events of default and the lenders' ability to accelerate payment, the balance of the deferred exchange gains in the amount of $225,000 at December 31, 1996 has been credited to operations in restructuring expense. These events of default were remedied during 1997.

4. **Long-term debt (continued):**

(iv) During 1997, the Corporation negotiated a Payment Deferral Plan with certain creditors, designed to improve short-term liquidity in early 1997.

Under the terms of the Payment Deferral Plan, secured aircraft lenders and aircraft lessors accepted deferrals of principal, and lease payments, for up to six months between November 1996 and May 29, 1997. Under-secured lenders accepted deferrals of principal and interest. Principal, interest and lease payments deferred during this moratorium period are being repaid with interest.

Long-term debt repayments, excluding capital leases (note 5), during each of the next five years at current rates of exchange are as follows:

1998	$110.1
1999	113.7
2000	105.1
2001	109.7
2002	47.0

5. **Lease obligations:**

Future minimum lease payments at December 31, 1997 under capital leases and operating leases for aircraft in the fleet and other lease obligations, including airport terminal facilities are as follows:

		Operating Leases	
	Capital Leases	**Aircraft**	**Other**
1998	$ 13.0	$ 281.0	$ 49.1
1999	14.5	250.2	43.5
2000	14.2	257.4	34.5
2001	13.9	190.9	26.2
2002	9.9	166.1	23.4
Thereafter	45.0	727.2	149.1
Total minimum lease payments	110.5	$1,872.8	$325.8
Less amount representing interest	33.1		
Present value of obligations	$ 77.4		

The amount representing interest has been calculated at the rates implied by the terms of the leases (6.8% to 11.7%).

Certain future operating lease payments are evidenced by non-interest bearing notes due in 2002. The lease payments evidenced by the notes are accrued over the terms of the leases. Operating lease obligations include notes of $27,905,000 (Japanese Yen 2,474,525,000) less the amount accrued to December 31, 1997 of $7,838,000 which is included in long-term debt. The notes may be exchanged for common shares on the same terms as other non-interest bearing notes (note 4(ii)).

6. Preferred shares of subsidiary:

On April 27, 1994, the Corporation's then wholly-owned subsidiary, Canadian Airlines issued 827,016 voting and non-voting preferred shares of Canadian Airlines to a wholly-owned subsidiary of AMR Corporation for proceeds of $246,000,000.

The preferred shares are convertible at any time at AMR Corporation's option into voting and non-voting common shares of Canadian Airlines at an escalating conversion rate such that if conversion had occurred April 27, 1994 AMR Corporation would have received an approximate 27.5% equity interest in Canadian Airlines. Canadian Airlines is entitled to force conversion after five years if the value of a Canadian Airlines share (as determined by reference to the Corporation's market capitalization on a fully diluted basis) exceeds the conversion rate. Canadian Airlines' present intention is to force conversion at the earliest possible time. If converted at five years from issuance, AMR Corporation would hold an approximate 33.9% equity interest in Canadian Airlines. If conversion had occurred as at December 31, 1997 AMR Corporation would have held a 32.6% equity interest in Canadian Airlines. AMR Corporation is restricted under the Canada Transportation Act from holding more than 25% of the voting shares of Canadian Airlines.

If not previously converted, the preferred shares require redemption on April 27, 2014 at their issue price plus a compounding annual premium of 6.25% for the first ten years and 3.7% thereafter. The cumulative premium as at December 31, 1997 amounted to $61,400,000.

The Corporation may acquire the Canadian Airlines' shares held by AMR Corporation at any time, for an amount which would provide AMR Corporation with a 15% compounded annual rate of return on its investment.

Preferred shares as at December 31, 1995	$272.3
Annual premium on preferred shares	17.0
Preferred shares as at December 31, 1996	289.3
Annual premium on preferred shares	18.1
Preferred shares as at December 31, 1997	$307.4

7. Capital stock:

(a) Authorized capital:

The authorized share capital of the Corporation consists of an unlimited number of Common Shares without par value, an unlimited number of non-voting shares without par value, and an unlimited number of First and Second Preferred Shares without par value.

(b) Common Shares:

Common share capital is comprised of issued and outstanding common shares and non-voting shares and issued but unexercised entitlements issued to employees pursuant to the employee investment plan.

Non-voting shares rank equally in all respects with common shares except with respect to voting privileges at shareholders' meetings. Holders of non-voting shares within the meaning of the CTA (note 7(g)) have the right to convert the non-voting shares into common shares on a one to one basis.

In May 1995, holders of common shares of the Corporation voted in favour of consolidating the common shares, non-voting shares, and employee entitlements to receive common shares of the Corporation on a one-for-twenty basis. The number of common shares or non-voting shares issuable upon the exercise of outstanding options and redeemable warrants of the Corporation and the related option price and exercise price have been proportionately adjusted.

7. **Capital stock (continued):**

Details of changes in Common Shares during the period are as follows:

	Common Shares		Entitlements		Total	
	Number	**Amount**	**Number**	**Amount**	**Number**	**Amounts**
	(millions)		**(millions)**		**(millions)**	
Balance, December 31, 1995	37.8	$297.1	5.3	$85.3	43.1	$382.4
Earned under employee investment plan	—	—	1.5	24.5	1.5	24.5
Common shares issued in exchange for entitlements	1.6	26.2	(1.6)	(26.2)	—	—
Balance December 31, 1996	39.4	323.3	5.2	83.6	44.6	406.9
Common shares issued in exchange for entitlements (note 8(e))	0.9	14.4	(0.9)	(14.4)	—	—
Balance, December 31, 1997	40.3	$337.7	4.3	$69.2	44.6	$406.9

(c) **Second Preferred Shares:**

The Corporation has issued and outstanding the following Second Preferred Shares: one Series X-2, one Series Y-2, and one Series Z. These shares are held by various employee groups of the Corporation and permit the holders to nominate a total of four directors to the Board of the Corporation.

One Second Preferred Shares Series X and one Second Preferred Shares Series Y were redeemed for nominal consideration in 1997.

(d) **Redeemable warrants:**

The Corporation has issued and outstanding 327,971,000 warrants at December 31, 1997. The holders of the warrants may acquire common shares or non-voting shares on the basis of one common share or non-voting share for 20 warrants until April 1999 at $16.00 per share. Holders of the warrants are required to convert upon notice from the Corporation that the average trading price exceeds $32.00.

(e) **Employee investment plan:**

Between 1993 and 1996 substantially all of the Corporation's employees participated in a payroll reduction plan whereby employees received a portion of their wages in the form of entitlements to acquire common shares of the Corporation. Contributions over the four years amounted to $200,000,000 which resulted in a maximum of 12,500,000 common shares issuable at an agreed rate of $16.00 per common share.

At December 31, 1997, $69,200,000 of earned entitlements are yet to be converted to common shares representing a potential of 4,300,000 common shares. Holders of entitlements have until July 31, 2004 to convert entitlements to common shares. These entitlements are included in Common Shares in the consolidated financial statements.

(f) **Share option plans:**

Executive Plan:

The Corporation has established an Executive Incentive Share Option Plan under which 5,500,000 Common Shares have been reserved. At December 31, 1997, options to purchase an aggregate of 3,662,000 common shares at prices ranging from $1.68 to $12.00 per share are outstanding, exercisable at varying dates up to December, 2007.

Pilots' Plan:

As part of its collective agreement with the Airline Pilot Association, the Corporation has reserved 10,000,000 common shares for issuance pursuant to stock options to be granted to pilots employed by Canadian Airlines. At December 31, 1997, options to purchase an aggregate of 2,290,000 shares, at prices ranging from $2.78 to $8.00 per share, are outstanding. These options are exercisable at varying dates up to July 30, 2004.

7. Capital stock (continued):

(g) Legislative provisions:

The Canadian Airlines Corporation Act (Alberta) prohibits any person or group of associated persons, other than the Province of Alberta, from holding as shareholders or beneficial owners, more than 10% of the issued and outstanding voting shares of the Corporation. A bill is presently before the Alberta Legislature which, if passed, will remove this ownership restriction.

The Canada Transportation Act, 1987 (CTA) prohibits non-Canadians from owning more than 25% of the voting equity of the Corporation and its subsidiaries.

8. Net interest expense:

	1997	1996
Interest on long-term debt	$75.8	$73.1
Less interest capitalized	—	2.5
Interest expense	75.8	70.6
Less interest income	6.0	5.2
	$69.8	$65.4

9. Income taxes:

The following is a reconciliation of the income tax expense calculated at combined Federal and Provincial rates with the income tax expense in the consolidated statement of operations:

	1997	1996
Combined federal and provincial income tax rates	41.5%	41.5%
Provision for (reduction of) income taxes at combined federal and provincial rates	$ 2.9	$(76.9)
Tax effect of:		
Non-deductible expenses	11.1	21.7
Large corporation and capital tax	1.8	1.7
Benefit of prior years losses	(14.0)	55.2
	$ 1.8	$ 1.7

At December 31, 1997, the Corporation and its subsidiaries have income tax losses and differences between deductible amounts for accounting and tax purposes, aggregating $107,000,000, which have not been recognized for accounting purposes. In addition the Company is able to reinstate $355,000,000 and $34,000,000 of income tax losses upon repayment of excise tax rebates received in 1997 and 1992, respectively on the basis of $10.00 of losses reinstated for each $1.00 of rebate repaid. Repayment of rebates received in 1992 are subject to interest.

10. Pension plans:

The Corporation provides retirement benefits for substantially all of its employees under defined benefit and defined contribution pension plans. Current service costs for the defined contribution plans are recognized as retirement benefits are earned under the plans.

Based on the most recent reports prepared by independent actuaries, the present value of the accrued pension benefits of defined benefit plans at December 31, 1997 was $1,412,000,000 and the market value of related pension plan assets was $1,704,000,000.

The Corporation records a deferred charge which represents the cumulative amount of pension funding contributions over expenses recognized. At December 31, 1997 this deferred charge amounted to $144,600,000.

11. Financial instruments and risk management:

The Corporation's operating results are subject to variations due to volatility in interest rates, foreign exchange rates and jet fuel prices. The Corporation uses various derivative financial instruments for the purpose of hedging existing commitments or obligations.

(a) Interest Rate Management:

The Corporation maintains a general policy of financing aircraft for terms of 12 to 20 years at interest rates which are fixed for the terms of the financing. At December 31, 1997, approximately 35% of debt and capital lease obligations were subject to floating interest rates.

(b) Foreign Exchange Risk Management:

The Corporation periodically uses certain foreign exchange contracts to manage risks associated with the relative values of world currencies. As at December 31, 1997, the Corporation's unrealized gains on outstanding foreign currency hedges amounted to $500,000 (1996 - nil).

(c) Fuel Price Risk Management:

The Corporation enters into certain contracts to manage its exposure to jet fuel price volatility. Gains and losses resulting from fuel hedging transactions are recognized as a component of fuel expense. As at December 31, 1997, the Corporation had hedged 18% of its expected 1998 fuel requirements. As at December 31, 1997, the unrealized loss on outstanding fuel contracts amounted to $5,400,000, compared to a gain of $5,000,000 as at December 31, 1996.

(d) Consolidated Balance Sheet Financial Instruments Fair Values:

Cash and short-term investments are valued at their carrying amounts due to their short period to maturity.

The fair value of long-term debt, including current portion of long-term debt, is based on rates currently available to the Corporation for debt with similar terms and maturities. The fair value of long-term debt approximates the book value as at December 31, 1997.

12. Commitments:

The Corporation is committed to expenditures, estimated at U.S. $464,000,000 for 10 A320-200 aircraft and related support equipment with delivery dates between 2000 and 2001. Deposits of U.S. $17,200,000 have been made and recorded as property and equipment at December 31, 1997.

The Corporation has the option to acquire two B767-300ER aircraft, one B747-400 aircraft and ten A320-200 aircraft.

During 1994 Canadian Airlines entered into a 20 year agreement with AMR Corporation whereby Canadian Airlines will purchase certain decision support and information services from AMR Corporation including reservation services, accounting, data processing, and operations planning. The cost of services provided is estimated at U.S. $110,000,000 per annum. During 1997, AMR Corporation agreed to a reduction in these service fees for the years 1997 to 2000 estimated at $48,000,000 per year.

13. Contingencies:

The Corporation and its subsidiaries are involved in a number of legal proceedings. In the opinion of the Corporation's counsel, no significant liabilities are expected to arise from these proceedings.

Endnotes

1. D. Burgstahler and I. Dichev, "Earnings Management to Avoid Earnings Decreases and Losses," *Journal of Accounting and Economics,* December 1997, pp. 99–126; F. Degeorge, J. Patel, and R. Zeckhauser, "Earnings Management to Exceed Thresholds," *Journal of Business,* January 1999, pp. 1–33; P. Dechow, S. Richardson, and A. Tuna, "Are Benchmark Beaters Doing Anything Wrong?" working paper, University of Michigan Business School, April 2000.

2. Dechow et al., ibid.

3. These statements were made by Arthur Levitt (former Chair of the SEC) in a speech entitled "The Number Game," delivered at the New York University Center for Law and Business, September 28, 1998.

4. J. Elliott and D. Hanna, "Repeated Accounting Write-Offs and the Information Content of Earnings," *Journal of Accounting Research, Supplement* (1996), pp. 135–155.

5. "Accounting for Research and Development Costs," *Statement of Financial Accounting Standards (SFAS) No. 2* (Stamford, CT: Financial Accounting Standards Board [FASB], 1974), para. 45.

6. "Revenue Recognition in Financial Statements," *Staff Accounting Bulletin No. 101* (Washington, D.C., Securities and Exchange Commission, December 3, 1999).

7. P. McConnell, J. Pegg, and D. Zion, "Revenue Recognition 101," *Accounting Issues,* Bear, Stearns & Co. Inc., New York, March 10, 2000.

4

Structure of the Balance Sheet and Cash Flow Statement

LEARNING OBJECTIVES

After studying this chapter, you should be able to:

1. Describe the classification criteria and measurement methods used for the various asset, liability, and shareholders' equity accounts found on a typical corporate balance sheet

2. Explain how the information provided in successive balance sheets and the income statement can be used to explain the change in cash for a particular reporting period

3. Show how information provided in the cash flow statement can be used to explain changes in noncash accounts on the balance sheet

4. Understand and explain the significance of the distinction between operating, investing, and financing sources and uses of cash

5. Show how changes in current asset and liability accounts can be used to adjust accrual earnings to obtain cash flows from operations

The **balance sheet** contains a summary of the assets, liabilities, and owners' equity of a company, all measured at the same point in time. It provides useful information, subject to often severe limitations that we will discuss throughout this book, on how management has invested the resources of the company and where these resources came from. Information from the balance sheet is often used for assessing a company's rate of return, capital structure, liquidity, solvency, operating and financial flexibility,[1] and other important indicators of company success or failure, as we describe in Chapter 5.

The three main financial statements—the balance sheet, the income statement, and the cash flow statement—should be viewed as part of an integrated set of financial information about a company. In other words, just focusing on one of these statements to the exclusion of the others is an ineffective, and inefficient, approach to understanding and analyzing financial statements. But for pedagogical purposes, we provide an overview of only the balance sheet in the first part of this chapter.

We will use the financial statements of Potash Corporation of Saskatchewan, Inc. (PCS), a well-known Canadian natural resources company, to illustrate the classification criteria and measurement methods used in a typical balance sheet. PCS is one of the world's largest integrated fertilizer and related industrial and feed products companies with significant market share in each of the three primary nutrient products: potash, phosphate, and nitrogen. This company is the largest potash producer worldwide by capacity. In 2001, the company's potash operations represented an estimated 15% of global production, 23% of global potash capacity, and 59% of global potash excess capacity. PCS is the third largest producer of phosphates also worldwide by capacity. In 2001, its phosphate operations represented an estimated 5% of

POTASH CORPORATION OF SASKATCHEWAN www.potashcorp.com

world phosphoric acid production and 6% of world phosphoric acid capacity. This company is the second largest producer of nitrogen products in the Western hemisphere.

While many people characterize generally accepted accounting principles (GAAP) balance sheet carrying amounts as **historical costs**, what these carrying amounts really represent is more complicated. In fact, carrying amounts in a GAAP balance sheet are a mixture of historical costs, **current costs** (also called **fair value**), **net realizable value**, and **discounted present values**.

Exhibit 4.1 shows PCS's balance sheet, which uses a typical Canadian disclosure format. In the "Assets" section, cash and any other assets expected to be converted into cash within the next 12 months (or within the **operating cycle**, if the operating cycle is longer than 12 months) are classified as "Current assets." Assets not expected to be converted into cash within this period are categorized separately. Within the "Current assets" category, items are disclosed in descending order of liquidity—how quickly the items will be converted into cash through the normal course of business. In the "Liabilities" section of the balance sheet, items expected to be settled from current assets within the next 12 months (or within the operating cycle, if longer) are categorized as "Current liabilities." All other liabilities appear in a separate section as noncurrent or long-term obligations. Equity claims also appear in their own separate section of the balance sheet, which is often referred to as the "Shareholders' equity" section.

Classification Criteria and Measurement Conventions for Balance Sheet Accounts

To convey a feeling for the diversity of the measurement bases used in a typical balance sheet, we will select and discuss a few accounts from PCS's 2001 comparative balance sheet, which is reproduced in Exhibit 4.1. Many of the measurement issues introduced in this section are explored in greater depth in subsequent chapters.

One important feature of PCS's balance sheet is that the company reports in U.S. dollars. So even though its balance sheet and other financial statements are prepared in accordance with Canadian GAAP, like many Canadian companies with significant U.S. operations, PCS uses the U.S. dollar as its reporting currency.

Cash The balance sheet carrying amount for cash reflects the amount of money or currency the firm has on hand or in bank accounts. If cash consists exclusively of Canadian dollar amounts, the balance sheet cash account reflects the *historical* amount of net dollar units arising from past transactions (in PCS's case, the amount reported on its balance sheet would be the U.S. dollar equivalent at the balance sheet date). Due to the unique liquidity of cash, this historical amount of net dollar units is identical to the current market value of the cash.

For **monetary assets** like cash, accounts receivable, and notes receivable, the current rate of exchange in effect at the balance sheet date is used to translate one currency unit into another. As a consequence of using the current rate of exchange (rather than the historical rate of exchange that was in effect at the time of the foreign currency cash inflow), this portion of the cash account is carried at its **current market price**—*not* at its historical transaction amount. For foreign currency deposits, current market exchange values are used irrespective of whether they are higher or

---

A firm's **operating cycle** is the elapsed time beginning with the initiation of production and ending with the eventual cash collection of the receivables generated from the sale of the finished product.

Monetary assets are fixed in dollar amounts irrespective of price changes. A $300,000 cash deposit remains fixed at $300,000 even if the general level of prices goes up and the purchasing power of that $300,000 declines.

Nonmonetary assets like inventory and buildings are not fixed in dollar amounts—that is, inventory purchased for $300,000 can conceivably increase in value if prices go up. While not assured, this potential for changing value is the distinguishing characteristic of nonmonetary items—their value is not expressed in a fixed number of monetary units.

Exhibit 4.1 POTASH CORPORATION OF SASKATCHEWAN, INC.

Consolidated Statements of Financial Position

(in millions of U.S. dollars)	as at December 31,	
	2001	**2000**
Assets		
Current Assets		
Cash and cash equivalents	$ 45.3	$ 100.0
Accounts receivable (Note 4)	256.7	326.6
Inventories (Note 5)	481.1	406.2
Prepaid expenses	36.5	38.9
	819.6	871.7
Property, plant and equipment (Note 6)	3,245.6	2,910.1
Goodwill (Note 7)	97.0	106.4
Other assets (Note 8)	435.1	257.5
	$4,597.3	$4,145.7
Liabilities		
Current Liabilities		
Short-term debt (Note 9)	$ 501.1	$ 488.8
Accounts payable and accrued charges (Note 10)	271.4	525.9
Current portion of long-term debt (Note 11)	—	5.7
	772.5	1,020.4
Long-term debt (Note 11)	1,013.7	413.7
Future income tax liability (Note 21)	457.6	435.1
Accrued post-retirement/post-employment benefits (Note 13)	177.3	175.1
Accrued reclamation costs (Note 14)	83.0	83.0
Other non-current liabilities and deferred credits	6.7	6.3
	2,510.8	2,133.6
Contingencies (Note 25)		
Shareholders' Equity		
Share Capital (Note 15)	1,182.5	1,177.4
Unlimited authorization of common shares without par value; issued and outstanding 51,952,482 and 51,840,572 shares in 2001 and 2000, respectively		
Unlimited authorization of first preferred shares; none outstanding		
Contributed Surplus	264.2	264.2
Retained Earnings	639.8	570.5
	2,086.5	2,012.1
	$4,597.3	$4,145.7

(See Notes to the Consolidated Financial Statements)

Approved by the Board,

Dallas J. Howe (signed), Director E.   Robert Stromberg (signed), Director

A Canadian company
with 1 million pesos in
the bank account of its
Mexican manufacturing
subsidiary would value
the cash at 126,422.25
Canadian dollars in
December 1996 when
the exchange rate was
7.91 pesos to the dollar.
This same bank account
(with 1 million pesos)
would have been valued
at 200,000 Canadian
dollars in 1995 when the
exchange rate was 5
pesos to the dollar.

lower than the historical rate. Consequently, the GAAP measurement convention for cash is, in reality, current market price rather than historical cost.

The full caption for the balance sheet line item in PCS's balance sheet is "Cash and cash equivalents," which signals that the category is broader than cash itself. In PCS's case, Note 1 to its financial statements reveals the following: "Cash Equivalents: Highly liquid investments with an original maturity of three months or less are considered to be cash equivalents."

We can tell from the 2000 comparative figure for "Cash and cash equivalents" in PCS's balance sheet in Exhibit 4.1, that is, US$100.0 million, that "Cash and cash equivalents" *decreased* by US$54.7 million during 2001.

Net Accounts Receivable

The balance sheet carrying amount for gross accounts receivable is equal to the face amount arising from the past transaction. Thus, if a customer purchased goods with a sales price of US$100,000 on November 15, 2002, the following entry would be made:

DR Accounts receivable	$100,000	
CR Sales revenue		$100,000

If the receivable is still outstanding at December 31, 2002, it would be shown on the balance sheet at $100,000. However, accrual accounting requires that any future costs be matched against the revenues recognized in that period. When sales are made for credit (on account), some sales may unknowingly be made to customers who will not pay. The expense associated with these uncollectible accounts must be recognized—on an estimated basis—in the period in which the sales arise. This requirement compels companies to estimate the proportion of existing accounts receivable balances that they reasonably believe will ultimately not be collected. In PCS's case, the 2001 accounts receivable disclosure shows (in millions of U.S. dollars):

The accounting entry to recognize
estimated uncollectible accounts is:
DR Bad debt expense $XXX
   CR Allowance for
      doubtful accounts $XXX
The debited account reduces income
in the current period, while the credit appears as a deduction from gross
accounts receivable, as shown in
PCS's Note 4, which follows. Such
deductions from asset accounts are
called **contra-asset** accounts.
(Estimating and recognizing bad
debts expense is discussed in
Chapter 8.)

[Extracted and adapted from PCS's Note 4, 2001]:

	2001	2000
Gross accounts receivable	$263.7	$334.3
Less: Allowance for doubtful accounts	(7.0)	(7.7)
Net accounts receivable reported on balance sheet	$256.7	$326.6

Notice that as a consequence of these accounting techniques, the total for net accounts receivable is carried at expected **net realizable value** as of the balance sheet date, not at original historical cost.

Inventories

In the notes to the financial statements, PCS discloses the following:

[From the company's accounting policy note]:

Inventories

Inventories of finished product, raw materials and work in process are valued at the lower of cost and net realizable value. Cost for substantially all finished product, raw materials and work in process inventories is determined using the first in, first out (FIFO) method. Certain inventories of materials and supplies are valued at the lower of average cost and replacement cost and certain inventories of materials and supplies are valued at the lower of cost and market.

[from Note 5 (in millions of U.S. dollars)]:

5. INVENTORIES

	2001	2000
Finished product	$144.7	$176.6
Materials and supplies	113.9	114.5
Raw materials	65.6	16.9
Work in process	156.9	98.2
	$481.1	$406.2

This level of disclosure is typical, and leaves many questions open. For example, what are the details of the three different approaches to accounting for various types of "Materials and supplies"?

Property, Plant, and Equipment Although this item appears on the balance sheet at its net amount, PCS does provide information about the components of this figure in the financial statement notes, as follows (in millions of U.S. dollars):

6. PROPERTY, PLANT AND EQUIPMENT

	2001		
	Cost	Accumulated Depreciation and Amortization	Net Book Value
Land and improvements	$ 215.7	$ 31.3	$ 184.4
Buildings and improvements	448.7	196.9	251.8
Machinery and equipment	3,744.2	999.9	2,744.3
Mine development costs	111.3	46.2	65.1
	$4,519.9	$1,274.3	$3,425.6

	2000		
	Cost	Accumulated Depreciation and Amortization	Net Book Value
Land and improvements	$ 221.7	$ 30.2	$ 191.5
Buildings and improvements	448.8	139.4	309.4
Machinery and equipment	3,219.4	896.0	2,323.4
Mine development costs	132.0	46.2	85.8
	$4,021.9	$1,111.8	$2,910.1

Depreciation and amortization of property, plant and equipment included in Cost of Goods Sold and in Selling and Administrative was $170.4 (2000 – $170.6; 1999 – $161.1).

All items in this category are carried on the balance sheet at *historical cost minus accumulated amortization/depreciation*. However, when a capital asset becomes impaired (i.e., when its carrying amount may no longer be recoverable) the capital asset account is reduced to its lower **recoverable amount**.[2] If available, quoted current market prices are the best measure of fair value. However, market prices for capital assets are not always readily available. Consequently, fair value may need to be estimated by discounting expected future net operating cash flows. (This topic is covered in greater detail in Chapter 10.)

Goodwill In the notes, PCS indicates that "[g]oodwill represents the excess of the purchase price and related costs over the value assigned to the net tangible assets of businesses acquired and is carried at cost. Goodwill is being amortized on a straight-line basis over a period of 40 years. The company assesses impairment based on the estimated undiscounted future cash flows. Impairment is measured by comparing book value against the estimated undiscounted future cash flows and any such impairment is included in the statement of income."

In its Note 7, PCS discloses that goodwill amortization is grouped into selling and administrative expenses on the company's income statement. Goodwill GAAP has recently been dramatically changed. See the discussion of *CICA Handbook* Section 3062 ("Goodwill and Other Intangible Assets") in Chapter 16.

Other Assets PSC reports the details of the cryptically named "Other assets" in its Note 8 (in millions of U.S. dollars):

8. OTHER ASSETS

	2001	2000
Deferred charges – net of accumulated amortization	$ 129.3	$ 90.2
Prepaid pension costs	25.3	26.5
Land held for sale	2.6	3.5
Investments, at equity	17.8	20.7
Investments, at cost	223.2	92.8
Rotational plant maintenance costs – net of accumulated amortization	30.3	18.3
Other	6.6	5.5
	$435.1	$257.5

Amortization of deferred charges and rotational plant maintenance costs included in Cost of Goods Sold and in Selling and Administrative was $12.3 (2000 – $13.4; 1999 – $18.3).

This list is a grab-bag of items, all classified as noncurrent, with what seems like a variety of measurement bases. There is even an "Other" category in this "Other Assets" list, but its small amount seems innocuous enough.

Short-Term Debt PSC's Note 9 reveals that this category of financing had an interest rate, on average, of 2.29% in 2001, down from 6.98% in 2000.

Accounts Payable and Accrued Charges These items are reflected on the balance sheet at the amount of the original liability—that is, at the amount arising at the inception of the transactions. Consequently, the numbers are shown at historical cost.

Long-Term Debt When long-term debt (typically, notes or bonds) is issued, the initial balance sheet carrying amount is determined by computing the **present value** of the sum of (1) the future principal repayment plus (2) the periodic interest payments. The rate used for discounting these amounts is the effective yield on the notes or bonds at the date they were issued. Here, we'll simply provide a brief overview of the general measurement rules for long-term debt. More on bonds and other long-term debt instruments is presented in Chapter 11.

When bonds are sold at par, the amount received is equal to the recorded face amount of the debt. For example, if a company sells $100,000,000 of 15-year, 10% coupon bonds for $100,000,000, the accounting entry is:

DR Cash $100,000,000
     CR Bonds payable $100,000,000

The $100,000,000 carrying amount is, in fact, equal to the present value of the principal *and* interest payments over the life of the bond discounted at 10%, the effective yield at the time of issue. The effective yield is 10% since the effective yield on bonds sold at par is equal to the coupon rate. (We'll show why in Chapter 11.) When bonds are sold at a premium or at a discount, the initial carrying amount is again equal to the present value of the future payments, where the discount rate is the effective yield on the bonds. In general, at balance sheet dates after the bonds' issuance date, the subsequent carrying amount of *all* bonds outstanding is equal to the present value of the future principal and interest flows discounted at the *original effective yield rate*. This carrying amount will differ from the current market price of the bonds whenever interest rates have changed subsequent to issuance. Consequently, long-term debt is also carried at historical cost, where the carrying amount is determined by calculating the present value of the future cash flow using the original effective yield on the bonds as the discount rate.

We haven't examined the *details* of PCS's long-term debt here, but we will point out that PCS's balance sheet breaks up long-term debt into two categories: a current portion and a long-term debt portion. We can see that *none* of PCS's long-term debt is due within one year of the end of 2001.

Future Income Tax Liability
This account represents taxes on income recognized in PCS's income statement in current and prior periods that will not be paid to the government until future periods, if at all. Thus, this amount is reported as a **future income tax liability**. In Canada, the rules used to determine income for financial reporting purposes (called by several names, including: **book income; GAAP income; financial accounting income;** etc.) frequently do not conform to the rules used to determine income for taxation purposes (called **taxable income**). Book income also diverges from taxable income in many other industrialized countries. Income determination rules for financial reporting differ from rules for determining income for taxation purposes because of the very different objectives of the two computations. The objective in measuring book income is to reflect a firm's underlying economic success: Was the firm profitable during the period? The objective in measuring taxable income is to conform to laws designed to provide a basis for funding government operations. Since the rules governing taxable income computations result from a national political process, these rules do not necessarily measure changes in firms' underlying economic condition. Most companies maintain two sets of accounting records (or books) to facilitate both objectives:

1. Accurate financial reporting.
2. Compliance with tax laws.

The amount reported as book income forms the basis for the income tax expense reported on the income statement. However, the amount actually owed and paid to the government (i.e., the credit to cash and to income taxes payable on the balance sheet) is determined by a company's taxable income. As a consequence, the debit to the income statement account (tax expense) and the credit to the balance sheet account (cash or taxes payable) ***will usually be for different amounts.*** To balance the entry, future income taxes—reflecting the difference in the *timing* of revenue and expense in computing book income versus taxable income—must be debited or credited. (The measurement and reporting rules for future income taxes are covered in Chapter 13.)

Book income can exceed taxable income for at least two possible reasons:

1. The *Income Tax Act* rules allow a company to claim deductions for tax purposes before these items are reflected as GAAP expenses on the books.
2. GAAP allow a company to reflect revenues on the income statement before they are deemed to be taxable by the Act.

Since these timing differences are expected to reverse in subsequent years, *future* taxable income will exceed book income. Accordingly, credit balances in future income taxes reflect the expected future liability associated with these timing difference reversals. Even though these reversals may be expected to take place in, say, two or more years in the future, GAAP in Canada require that a company account for these amounts at their *undiscounted amount.* In other words, under existing GAAP, a company must treat expected reversals in the years 2004 and 2011 identically—that is, the time value of money is not taken into account.

The accounting treatment for future income taxes is in direct contrast to the measurement rules used to reflect long-term debt. The future outflows associated with long-term debt are reflected at their discounted present value; the future outflows associated with book–tax timing differences are reflected at their full undiscounted amounts. Our purpose in introducing this inconsistency is to reemphasize the fact that the measurement rules used to value different balance sheet accounts differ from item to item. Thus, balance sheet items are *not* all measured at historical costs. Some are, some aren't. And among those balance sheet amounts that are measured at historical cost, some—like long-term debt—are measured using a discounting approach; on the other hand, other accounts—like future taxes—are reflected at their full, undiscounted historical amounts.

Various Other Long-Term Liability Items on PCS's Balance Sheet

PCS's "Accrued post-retirement/post-employment benefits" are explained in Chapter 14 in the context of pensions and other post-employment benefits. The GAAP rules in this area are complex.

PCS's "Accrued reclamation costs" long-term liability relates to its resource extraction activities: PCS accrues restoration and reclamation costs as part of its normal operations.

Shareholders' Equity

We defer discussion of shareholders' equity until Chapter 15, except for some brief comments on retained earnings.

The "Retained earnings" account generally measures the net of cumulative earnings less cumulative dividend distributions of the company since its inception. Therefore, it represents the cumulative earnings that have been reinvested in the business. The "Retained earnings" account is increased (decreased) by the net income (net loss) for the period and is decreased for dividends that are declared in the period. For many firms, like PCS, retained earnings represent a major portion of shareholders' equity. Thus, the book value of equity is usually significantly determined by looking at the past earnings that have been retained and reinvested in the business. As we will see in Chapters 5 and 6, book value of equity is a key element of many performance measures—like return on equity (ROE)—and it plays an important role in equity valuation.

Because different measurement bases pervade the balance sheet, income is a mixture of historical costs, current values, and present values, which means that retained earnings is also a mixture of many different measurement bases.

International Differences in Balance Sheet Presentation
The account titles and the format of balance sheets prepared in other countries can differ very significantly from the account titles and format of the balance sheets prepared in Canada and the U.S. For example, although we are used to seeing assets presented in order of decreasing liquidity, balance sheets prepared in the U.K. and Germany show capital assets first followed by current assets in increasing order of liquidity. Chapter 18 describes some important international differences.

Balance Sheets, Disclosure, Transparency, and the Quality of Earnings
With the crisis in accounting and financial reporting of the early 2000s, balance sheets prepared with full disclosure and transparency uppermost in mind are essential to acquiring a corporate reputation of high quality of earnings. An editorial in the *Toronto Star* (the largest circulation daily newspaper in Canada, at www.thestar.com) dated July 3, 2002, lamented about a "new revelation almost every day of crooked accounting practices." So mere compliance with technical accounting rules under GAAP is clearly not sufficient: management, under the oversight of corporate boards of directors and their audit committees, must ensure proactively that balance sheets and other financial statements and accompanying notes are readable and understandable, and commit no errors of omission or commission.

Recap
The balance sheet provides a snapshot of the financial position of a company at a given point in time. It shows various types of assets held at the balance sheet date and the claims against those assets (i.e., how those assets have been financed).

Balance sheet accounts reflect a variety of measurement bases, including historical cost, current costs (also called fair value), net realizable value, and present value. Therefore, users of balance sheet information must be careful to recognize the effects these different measurement bases can have both when aggregating numbers across accounts and when computing ratios for making intercompany comparisons.

Cash Flow Statement

The balance sheet shows a firm's investments (assets) and financial structure (liabilities and shareholders' equity) at a given *point in time*. By contrast, the **cash flow statement** shows the user why a firm's investments and financial structure have *changed* between two balance sheet dates. The connection between successive balance sheet positions and the cash flow statement can be demonstrated through simple manipulation of the basic accounting equation:

$$\text{Assets} = \text{Liabilities} + \text{Shareholders' equity} \qquad (4.1)$$

Partitioning the assets into cash and all other assets yields:

$$\text{Cash} + \text{Noncash assets} = \text{Liabilities} + \text{Shareholders' equity} \qquad (4.2)$$

Rearranging yields:

$$\text{Cash} = \text{Liabilities} - \text{Noncash assets} + \text{Shareholders' equity} \qquad (4.3)$$

From basic algebra, we know that this equality must also hold for the algebraic sum of the changes on both sides of the equation. Recasting equation (4.3) in the form of the change (Δ) in each term results in:

$$\Delta \text{ Cash} = \Delta \text{ Liabilities} - \Delta \text{ Noncash assets} + \Delta \text{ Shareholders' equity} \qquad (4.4)$$

Thus, the cash flow statement—which provides an explanation of why a firm's cash position has changed between successive balance sheet dates—simultaneously explains the changes that have taken place in the firm's noncash asset, liability, and shareholders' equity accounts over the same time period.

The change in a firm's cash position between successive balance sheet dates will *not* equal the reported earnings for that period. There are three reasons for this:

1. Reported net income usually will not equal cash flow from **operating activities** because (a) noncash revenues and expenses are often recognized as part of accrual accounting, and (b) certain operating cash inflows and outflows are not recorded as revenues or expenses in the same period under accrual accounting.
2. Changes in cash are also caused by nonoperating **investing activities** like the purchase or sale of fixed assets.
3. Additional changes in cash are caused by **financing activities** like the issuance of stock or bonds or the repayment of a bank loan.

Cash flows are critical to assessing a company's liquidity and creditworthiness. Firms with cash flows that are lower than currently maturing obligations can be forced into liquidation or bankruptcy. Because cash flows and accrual earnings can differ dramatically, current reporting standards mandate that firms prepare a cash flow statement as well as an income statement and balance sheet. The cash flow statement is designed to explain the causes for year-to-year changes in the balance of cash and cash equivalents.[3] In this chapter, we briefly introduce the cash flow statement, focusing on the format of the statement and on some of the basic adjustments that are needed to convert accrual earnings to cash flow from operations. Later, after you have had a chance to review the accrual and cash flow effects of the transactions that affect various balance sheet and income statement accounts in the intervening chapters, you will find a more detailed explanation of the cash flow statement in Chapter 17.

The cash flow statement summarizes the cash inflows and outflows of a company broken down into its three principal activities:

- *Operating activities.* Cash flows from operating activities result from the cash effects of transactions and events that affect operating income—both production and delivery of goods and services.
- *Investing activities.* Cash flows from investing activities include: making and collecting loans; investing in and disposing of debt or equity securities; and purchasing and disposing of assets, like equipment, that are used by a company in the production of goods or services.
- *Financing activities.* Cash flows from financing activities include obtaining cash from new issues of stock or bonds, paying dividends or buying back a company's own shares (treasury stock), borrowing money, and repaying amounts borrowed.

Companies that are able to satisfy most of their cash needs from operating cash flows are generally considered to be in stronger financial health and better credit risks than companies that are not able to do so.

Cash Flows Versus Accrual Earnings

The following example illustrates the major differences between cash flows and accrual earnings and why a cash flow statement is needed to fully understand the distinction between the two.

HRB Advertising Company opened for business on April 1, 2003. The corporation's activities and transactions for the remainder of 2003 are summarized as follows:

1. Herb Wilson, Robin Hansen, and Barbara Reynolds each contributed $3,500 cash on April 1 for shares of the company's common stock.
2. HRB rented office space beginning April 1, and paid the full year's rental of $2,000 per month—or $24,000—in advance.
3. The company borrowed $10,000 from a local bank on April 1. The loan and accrued interest is payable on January 1, 2004, with interest at the rate of 12% per year.
4. HRB purchased office equipment with a five-year life for $15,000 cash on April 1. Salvage value is zero and the equipment is being amortized straight-line.
5. HRB sold and billed customers for $65,000 of advertising services rendered between April 1 and December 31. Of this amount, $20,000 was still uncollected by year-end.
6. By year-end, the company incurred and paid the following operating costs: (a) utilities, $650; (b) salaries, $36,250; and (c) supplies, $800.
7. The company had accrued (unpaid) expenses at year-end as follows: (a) utilities, $75; (b) salaries, $2,400; and (c) interest, $900.
8. Supplies purchased on account and unpaid at year-end amounted to $50.
9. Supplies inventory on hand at year-end amounted to $100.
10. Annual amortization on office equipment is $15,000 ÷ 5 years = $3,000. Since the equipment was acquired on April 1, the amortization expense for 2003 is $3,000 × 9/12 = $2,250.

Herb, Robin, and Barbara were delighted to discover that the company earned a profit (before taxes) of $3,725 in 2003. They were also shocked to learn that the company's chequing account was overdrawn by $11,200 at year-end, particularly since the bank loan was now due.

Is HRB Advertising Company profitable? Or is it about to go bankrupt? What are its prospects for the future? Exhibit 4.2 helps us examine these issues.

While HRB Advertising generated *positive* accrual accounting earnings during 2003 of $3,725, its operating cash flow was a *negative* $16,700. Columns (b) and (c) show the causes for the divergence between the components of accrual income [column (a)] and operating cash flows [column (d)]. Also note that because of a net infusion of cash from financing activities [column (d)], the net change in cash (a negative $11,200) was considerably smaller than the negative cash flow of $16,700 from operating activities.

We now discuss the rationale behind each of the adjustments in columns (b) and (c). We examine each adjustment in terms of how it affects "bottom-line" *accrual basis net income*—not how the item affects revenues or expenses that make up net

Exhibit 4.2 HRB ADVERTISING COMPANY

Analysis of Accrual Income Versus Change in Cash for Year Ended December 31, 2003

Item	(a) Accrual Income	(b) Noncash Accruals: Revenue Earned (or Expenses Incurred)	(c) Prepayments and Supplies Buildup	(d) a + b + c Cash Received (or Paid) During 2003
Operating Activities				
Advertising revenues	$65,000	−$20,000[5]		$45,000
Salaries	−38,650	+2,400[7b]		−36,250
Rent	−18,000		−$6,000[2]	−24,000
Utilities	−725	+75[7a]		−650
Supplies	−750	+50[8]	−100[9]	−800
Interest	−900	+900[7c]		—
Amortization	−2,250	+2,250[10]		—
Operating cash flow				−$16,700
Net income	$ 3,725			
Investing Activities				
Equipment purchase				−$15,000[4]
Financing Activities				
Share issuance				$10,500[1]
Bank borrowing				10,000[3]
				$20,500
Change in cash				−$11,200

Note: Numbers in parentheses refer to numbered transactions on page 147.

income. Thus, because expenses are treated as negative amounts in computing net income, an adjustment that reduces (increases) an expense is treated as a plus (negative) amount in columns (b) and (c).

- Advertising revenues recognized under accrual accounting totalled $65,000. However, $20,000 of this remains as uncollected accounts receivable at year-end. Thus, the ending balance in the "Accounts receivable" account must be *subtracted* from the accrual-basis revenues to obtain the cash received during the year for advertising services.

- The salaries expense of $38,650 for the year includes the $36,250 of salaries incurred and paid in cash plus the $2,400 of salary expense accrued at year-end. Therefore, the accrued (unpaid) salaries, which is the ending balance in the "Accrued salaries payable" (liability) account, must be *added back* to total salaries expense to obtain the salaries paid in cash.

- HRB recognized rent expense of $2,000 × 9 months = $18,000 in 2003. The difference between the amount paid out in cash and the amount recognized as expense under accrual accounting ($24,000 − $18,000 = $6,000) would be the ending balance in the "Prepaid rent" (asset) account. This amount is shown as a negative adjustment (*subtraction*) in column (c), since the cash outflow for rent was greater than the amount of rent expense recognized.

- The utilities expense of $725 for the year includes the $650 of utilities paid in cash plus $75 of utilities expense accrued at year-end. The utilities expense incurred but not yet paid, which is the ending balance in the "Accrued utilities payable" (liability) account, must be *added back* to the total utilities expense to obtain the cash payments for utilities in 2003.

- Total supplies purchased during the year included $800 paid in cash and $50 purchased on account ("Accounts payable"). Of the amount purchased, $100 of supplies remains on hand and shows up in the "Supplies inventory" account at the end of the year. Thus, supplies expense under accrual accounting is $800 + $50 – $100 = $750. To adjust the accrual-basis expense to obtain the cash outflow for supplies requires that we *add back* the ending balance in accounts payable (which was a noncash increase to the supplies expense) and *subtract* the $100 ending balance in supplies inventory (which was a noncash decrease to the supplies expense).

- Accrued interest expense for the year is $10,000 \times 12\% \times 9/12 = \$900$. Since none of this has been paid in cash, the ending balance in the "Accrued interest payable" (liability) account must be *added back* to the "Interest expense" account to obtain the cash paid out for interest in 2003.

- Amortization is a noncash expense under accrual accounting. Therefore, this amount, which is reflected in the increase in the "Accumulated amortization" (contra-asset) account, must be *added back* to amortization expense.

Except for amortization, each of the adjustments we have just outlined involves using the ending balance (which is also the *change* in the account balance in the first year) of a current asset account (e.g., "Accounts receivable," "Supplies inventory," or "Prepaid rent") or a current liability account (e.g., "Accounts payable," "Salaries payable," "Utilities payable," or "Interest payable") to adjust accrual-basis revenues or expenses in order to obtain cash flows from operations. The adjustments to accrual-basis income (revenues minus expenses) for changes in current asset and current liability accounts that represent accrued revenues, deferred (unearned) revenues, accrued expenses, or deferred (prepaid) expenses are summarized in Figure 4.1.

Exhibit 4.3 illustrates how the adjustments to accrual earnings due to *changes* in various current asset and liability accounts would be reflected in a GAAP cash flow statement. The item numbers appearing next to each element in the statement correspond to the numbers in columns (b), (c), and (d) of Exhibit 4.2. The presentation format illustrated is called the **indirect approach**, since it does not show the individual operating cash inflows and outflows directly [which is called the **direct approach** shown in column (d) of Exhibit 4.2]. Rather, net cash flows from operations is arrived at indirectly by adjusting earnings due to the differences between accrual-basis revenues and expenses and cash inflows and outflows during the period.

The cash flow statement in Exhibit 4.3 will help Herb, Robin, and Barbara understand the causes for their overdrawn chequing account. While the business was profitable from an accrual accounting standpoint, total cash flows were negative. This should not be surprising since startup companies often spend a large portion of their available cash on equipment purchases, inventory buildup, and the production of goods and services that are frequently sold on account—and, therefore, that generate no cash immediately. Although the company is profitable, it may be forced into bankruptcy unless quick action is taken to resolve the cash flow deficit. To remain in

FIGURE 4.1
ADJUSTMENT TO
ACCRUAL
EARNINGS FOR
CHANGES IN
WORKING
CAPITAL
ACCOUNTS TO
OBTAIN CASH
FLOWS FROM
OPERATIONS

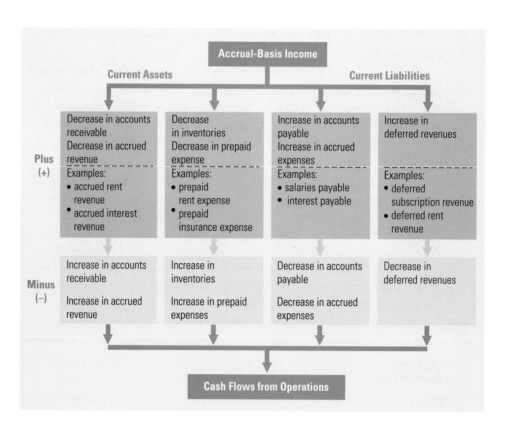

Exhibit 4.3 HRB ADVERTISING COMPANY

Cash Flow Statement for Year Ended December 31, 2003

Cash Flows from Operating Activities

Net income		$ 3,725
Plus:		
Amortization[10]	$ 2,250	
Increase in salaries payable[7b]	2,400	
Increase in accounts payable[8]	50	
Increase in utilities payable[7a]	75	
Increase in interest payable[7c]	900	5,675
Minus:		
Increase in receivables[5]	(20,000)	
Increase in prepaid rent[2]	(6,000)	
Increase in supplies inventory[9]	(100)	(26,100)
Cash flows from operating activities		($16,700)
Cash Flows from Investing Activities		
Equipment purchase[4]		(15,000)
Cash Flows from Financing Activities		
Share issuance[1]		$10,500
Bank borrowing[3]		10,000
		$20,500
Net decrease in cash		($11,200)

business, the owners must infuse more equity capital, arrange for an extension of their bank loan, or speed up cash collections.

Deriving Cash Flow Information

The three owners were able to convince their banker to refinance the loan but only after they each agreed to contribute another $2,000 to the company—a total of $6,000. The loan was replaced by a three-year note, but the interest rate was increased to 13.50% to reflect the additional risk associated with the refinanced borrowing. Herb, Robin, and Barbara felt confident that with careful attention to both earnings and cash flow, they could successfully grow the business and repay the note before its maturity.

During 2004—the second year of business—advertising revenues substantially increased and operating cash flows were positive, but the company recorded a loss for the year. Exhibit 4.4 contains HRB Advertising's comparative balance sheets for 2003 and 2004, and Exhibit 4.5 presents the company's earnings and cash flow statements for the two years.

We can see from the balance sheet that the $10,000 bank loan was refinanced as a note ("Note payable" in Exhibit 4.4) and that additional common stock of $6,000 was issued during 2004. Also notice that the company's cash account ended the year with a positive balance of $500.

Exhibit 4.4 HRB ADVERTISING COMPANY
Comparative Balance Sheets

	December 31,	
	2003	**2004**
Assets		
Cash	($11,200)	$ 500
Accounts receivable	20,000	15,775
Supplies inventory	100	225
Prepaid rent	6,000	6,000
Office equipment	15,000	16,500
Less: Accumulated amortization	(2,250)	(5,500)
Total assets	$27,650	$33,500
Liabilities and Equities		
Utilities payable	$ 75	$ 50
Interest payable	900	675
Accounts payable (supplies)	50	75
Salaries payable	2,400	4,200
Bank loan	10,000	–0–
Note payable	–0–	10,000
Total liabilities	$13,425	$15,000
Common shares	10,500	16,500
Retained earnings	3,725	2,000
Total liabilities and shareholders' equity	$27,650	$33,500

Exhibit 4.5 HRB ADVERTISING COMPANY

Comparative Income and Cash Flow Statements
For Years Ended December 31, 2003 and 2004

	2003	2004
Income Statement		
Revenue from advertising services	$65,000	$92,000
Less:		
Salaries expense	(38,650)	(62,875)
Supplies expense	(750)	(1,200)
Rent expense	(18,000)	(24,000)
Utilities expense	(725)	(1,050)
Interest expense	(900)	(1,350)
Amortization expense	(2,250)	(3,250)
Net income	$ 3,725	($ 1,725)

(a)

	2003	2004
Cash Flow Statement		
Cash flows from operating activities		
Net income	$ 3,725	($ 1,725)
Amortization	2,250	3,250
	5,975	1,525
Working capital adjustments:		
Accounts receivable decrease (increase)	(20,000)	4,225
Supplies inventory decrease (increase)	(100)	(125)
Prepaid rent decrease (increase)	(6,000)	–0–
Utilities payable increase (decrease)	75	(25)
Accounts payable (supplies) increase (decrease)	50	25
Interest payable increase (decrease)	900	(225)
Salaries payable increase (decrease)	2,400	1,800
Cash flow from operating activities	($16,700)	$ 7,200
Equipment purchases	($15,000)	($ 1,500)
Cash flow from investing activities	($15,000)	($ 1,500)
Bank loan (repayment)	$10,000	($10,000)
Note payable issued	–0–	10,000
Common shares issued	10,500	6,000
Cash flow from financing activities	$20,500	$ 6,000
Net increase (decrease) in cash balance	($11,200)	$11,700

(b)

Highlights from the income statement (Exhibit 4.5a) include a substantial growth in advertising revenues from $65,000 to $92,000, a 41.5% increase. At the same time, the company was able to speed up its collection of credit sales and reduce its "Accounts receivable" balance, as shown in Exhibit 4.4. Unfortunately, salary expense increased nearly 63%, from $38,650 to $62,875, which seems to be the major factor contributing to the company's $1,725 loss for the year. From the cash flow statement (see Exhibit 4.5b), we see that 2004 cash flows from operations totalled a positive $7,200 even though the business sustained a loss for the year. The company's overall cash balance increased by $11,700 during the year, with $6,000 of that amount representing cash contributed by the owners in exchange for additional common stock.

Although Canadian companies must now include cash flow statements similar to Exhibit 4.5b in their annual reports to shareholders and in their quarterly reports, it still might be useful to be able to derive the cash flow statement from a company's balance sheet and income statement to examine how the statements relate to one another. Indeed, useful information might be tracked down during such an exercise.

Deriving information about a company's cash receipts and disbursements from balance sheet and income statement information involves little more than a careful and systematic analysis of the changes in individual balance sheet accounts and their corresponding effects on the income statement, if the disclosure level is adequate. From this analysis, you can deduce individual cash flows and construct a summary schedule of cash receipts (inflows) and disbursements (outflows) that closely resembles the cash flow statement presented in Exhibit 4.5.

The starting point for this analysis is the cash account itself. Notice from the balance sheet (Exhibit 4.4) that the company's cash position increased by $11,700 during 2004, from the $11,200 deficit at the beginning of the year to a $500 positive balance at year-end. Consequently, we know that total cash receipts for the year must have been $11,700 greater than total cash payments. Now let's uncover some individual cash flow items.

Exhibit 4.6 illustrates the general T-account analysis that can be used to derive cash flow information from selected balance sheet accounts of HRB Advertising for 2004. From the comparative balance sheet in Exhibit 4.4, the beginning and ending balances can be obtained for each *balance sheet* account that is affected when a revenue or expense item is recorded. The accrual-basis revenue or expense that results in a debit or credit to the related balance sheet account can then be entered (see circled items in Exhibit 4.6). The cash received or cash paid, which results in an offsetting entry to each of these accounts, is the "plug" figure (in bold) that is needed to arrive at the ending balance which is given. We now illustrate this analysis for selected accounts in Exhibit 4.6.

The company's only source of operating cash inflows is customer receipts, so we begin with an analysis of the "Accounts receivable" account. As shown in Exhibit 4.6, the balance in the "Accounts receivable" account declined by $4,225 during 2004, from a beginning balance of $20,000 to a year-end balance of $15,775. Since billings for advertising services performed during 2004 totalled $92,000 (i.e., revenue from advertising services in the earnings statement of Exhibit 4.5), HRB must have collected $96,225 from its customers. Note that collections must have been $4,225 greater than new billings, because the "Accounts receivable" balance decreased by this amount during the year. Another way to think about this calculation is to assume that all customers pay on a timely basis. In this case, HRB would have collected $20,000 cash from customers billed in 2003 and another $76,225 from customers billed in 2004 (or $92,000 billings minus the $15,775 that was uncollected at year-end).

Salary payments represent the company's largest operating cash outflow. Exhibit 4.6 shows that salaries payable increased by $1,800 during the year, from a beginning balance of $2,400 to $4,200 at year-end. Consequently, salary payments must have been $61,075 for the year, or $1,800 less than the total salaries expense of $62,875 which shows up in the income statement in Exhibit 4.5.

Exhibit 4.6 HRB ADVERTISING COMPANY

Analysis of Income Statement and Balance Sheet Accounts
For Year Ended December 31, 2004

Income Statement	Balance Sheet

Revenue from Advertising Services | **Accounts Receivable**

		Beginning balance	$20,000	
$92,000				$96,225 — Collections (cash basis)
		Advertising revenues (accrual basis)	$92,000	
		Ending balance	$15,775	

Salaries Expense | **Salaries Payable**

		$ 2,400	Beginning balance
$62,875	Salaries paid $61,075 (cash basis)	$62,875	Salaries expense
	(accrual basis)	$ 4,200	Ending balance

Rent Expense | **Prepaid Rent**

Rent expense from 1/1/2004 to 3/31/2004	$ 6,000	Beginning balance	$ 6,000	Amortized from beginning balance — Rent expense from 1/1/2004 to 3/31/2004
Rent expense from 4/1/2004 to 12/31/2004	$18,000	Rent paid in advance on 4/1/2004 (cash basis) $24,000	$ 6,000	
		(accrual basis)	$18,000	Amortized from 4/1/2004 payment — Rent expense from 4/1/2004 to 12/31/2004
Total expense	$24,000	Ending balance	$ 6,000	

Utilities Expense | **Utilities Payable**

		$ 75	Beginning balance
$ 1,050	Payments (cash basis) $1,075	$1,050	Utilities expense
	(accrual basis)		
		$ 50	Ending balance

Some cash inflows and outflows involve more than one balance sheet account. This is illustrated in Exhibit 4.6 for the case of supplies. As shown there, "Accounts payable (supplies)" increased $25 during the year, from a beginning balance of $50 to $75 at year-end. This means that payments for supplies must have been $25 less than purchases. But, where can we find information about purchases? Certainly not from the income statement (Exhibit 4.5), because it reports the cost of supplies *used* during the year regardless of when they were purchased. Since purchases increase the total supplies on hand, we turn our attention to the "Supplies inventory" account. As we see from Exhibit 4.6, supplies inventory increased by $125 during the year, from $100 at the start to $225 at year-end. Purchases must therefore have been $125 greater than the amount of supplies used during the year (i.e., the supplies expense from Exhibit 4.5). In other words, purchases must have totalled $1,325 (or the $1,200 supplies expense plus the $125 inventory increase), and consequently, supplier payments must have totalled $1,300 (or $1,325 purchases minus the $25 accounts payable increase).

Exhibit 4.6 (CONT.)

Analysis of Income Statement and Balance Sheet Accounts
For Year Ended December 31, 2004

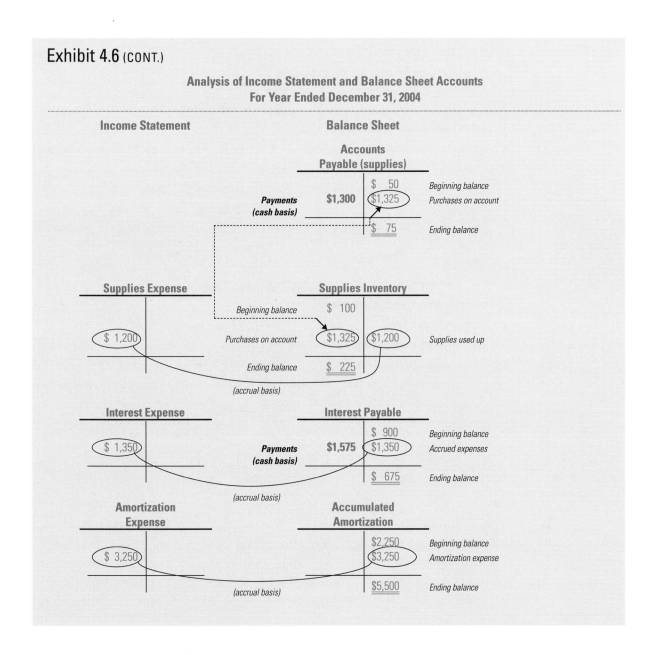

The same kind of analysis just outlined is illustrated for the "Prepaid rent," "Accounts payable (utilities)," and "Accrued interest payable" accounts in Exhibit 4.6. The process continues until all balance sheet accounts are fully reconciled and the company's cash receipts and disbursements are identified. In addition, analysis of changes in the "Notes payable," "Common shares," and "Equipment" accounts (not shown) can identify cash inflows and outflows from financing and investing activities.

The derived cash inflows and outflows for HRB Advertising are listed in Exhibit 4.7 by major source—operating, investing, or financing activities. This schedule explains how the company's cash balance increased by $11,700 during the year. Operating activities contributed $7,200 of cash, $1,500 was spent on new equipment, and financing activities added another $6,000. These are precisely the cash inflows and outflows described by the company's cash flow statement in Exhibit 4.5.

The analysis in Exhibit 4.7 has focused on the adjustments to accrual earnings that are required as a result of changes in various working capital (current assets

Exhibit 4.7 HRB ADVERTISING COMPANY

Schedule of Cash Receipts and Disbursements
For the Years Ended December 31, 2003 and 2004

	2003	2004	
Cash flows from operating activities			
Revenues from advertising services	$45,000	$96,225 ◄──	from Accounts Receivable
Salaries	(36,250)	(61,075) ◄──	from Salaries Payable
Rent	(24,000)	(24,000) ◄──	from Prepaid Rent
Utilities	(650)	(1,075) ◄──	from Utilities Payable
Supplies	(800)	(1,300) ◄──	from Accounts Payable (Supplies)
Interest	–0–	(1,575) ◄──	from Interest Payable
Operating cash flow	($16,700)	$ 7,200	
Cash flows from investing activities			
Equipment purchase	($15,000)	($ 1,500) ◄──	from Office Equipment
Cash flows from financing activities			
Bank borrowing	$10,000	($10,000) ◄──	from Bank Loan
Note issuance	–0–	10,000 ◄──	from Notes Payable
Share issuance	10,500	6,000 ◄──	from Common Shares
	20,500	6,000	
Net increase (decrease) in cash	($11,200)	$11,700 ◄──	from Cash

minus current liabilities) accounts in order to derive operating cash flows under the indirect method. Obviously, many other adjustments are required to fully reconcile accrual earnings and cash flows from operations. These will be discussed in Chapter 17 after you have had a chance to review in some detail the accrual accounting entries related to noncurrent asset and liability accounts.

Recap

Accrual earnings and cash flows capture different aspects of a firm's performance and can frequently differ by a wide margin from year to year. Cash flows are critical to assessing a company's liquidity and creditworthiness. The cash flow statement provides a detailed summary of the cash inflows and outflows that are derived from a company's three primary activities—operating, investing, and financing. This section has outlined the basic techniques for deriving operating cash flows from an analysis of comparative balance sheets and income statement information; in this regard, particular attention was given to changes in current asset and current liability accounts that capture differences between the cash flow effects and accrual earnings effects of revenue and expense transactions.

Summary

The balance sheet and the cash flow statement are two of the primary financial statements required under GAAP. The balance sheet shows the assets of a company at a given point in time and how those assets are financed (debt versus equity). A variety of measurement bases are used to report the various asset, liability, and shareholders' equity accounts. When making intercompany comparisons, financial statement users must be careful to recognize how the different measurement bases affect key financial ratios.

The cash flow statement shows the change in cash for a given period that is broken down into operating, investing, and financing activities. Successive balance sheets and the cash flow statements articulate with one another, because changes in noncash balance sheet accounts can be used to explain changes in cash for a period. Analysis of changes in selected balance sheet accounts also can be used to explain why operating cash flows differ from accrual income. Conversely, the cash flow statement provides information that enables users to understand changes in balance sheet accounts that have occurred over the reporting period. Understanding the interrelationships between successive balance sheets and the cash flow statements, and being able to exploit them to derive unknown account balances, are important skills for analysts and lending officers.

Full disclosure and transparency are key to a user's understanding of balance sheet and cash flow information, and thus to quality of earnings.

For more Exercises, Problems/Discussion Questions, and Cases, visit the Companion Website for this textbook at **www.pearsoned.ca/revsine**.

Exercises

E4-1 Determining collections on account

During 2001, Major Company, a service organization, had $200,000 in cash sales and $3,000,000 in credit sales. The accounts receivable balances were $500,000 and $585,000 at December 31, 2000 and 2001, respectively.

Required:

What was Major Company's cash receipts from sales in 2001?

E4-2 Determining cash from operations

The following information is available from Crystal Corporation's accounting records for the year ended December 31, 2001:

Cash received from customers	$950,000
Rent received	10,000
Cash paid to suppliers and employees	590,000
Taxes paid	110,000
Cash dividends paid	40,000

Required:

Compute cash flow provided by operations for 2001.

E4-3 Determining cash collections on account

Ziploc Company is preparing its cash budget for the month of June. The following information is available concerning its accounts receivable:

Estimated credit sales for June	$210,000
Actual credit sales for May	$150,000
Estimated collection in June for credit sales in June	20% of month's sales
Estimated collection in June for credit sales in May	70% of month's sales
Estimated collection in June for credit sales prior to May	$ 13,000
Estimated writeoffs in June for uncollectible credit sales	$ 8,000
Estimated bad debts expense in June for credit sales in June	$ 6,000

Required:

What are the estimated cash receipts from accounts receivable collections in June?

E4-4 Determining ending accounts receivable

The following information is available for Pete Corporation's first year of operation:

Payment for merchandise purchases	$300,000
Ending merchandise inventory	60,000
Accounts payable (balance at end of year)	40,000
Collections from customers during year	270,000

All merchandise items were marked to sell at 30% above cost.

What should be the ending balance in accounts receivable, assuming all accounts are deemed collectible?

E4-5 Determining cash disbursements

Serven Corporation has estimated its accrual-basis revenue and expenses for June 2003 and would like your help in estimating cash disbursements for the same month. Selected data from these estimated amounts are as follows:

• Sales	$750,000
Gross profit (based on sales)	30%
Increase in trade accounts receivable for the month	$ 25,000
Change in accounts payable during month	–0–
Increase in inventory during month	$ 10,000

- Variable selling, general, and administrative expenses include a charge for uncollectible accounts of 1% of sales.
- Total selling, general, and administrative expenses are $61,000 per month plus 15% of sales.
- Amortization expense of $30,000 per month is included in selling, general, and administrative expense.

Required:

On the basis of the preceding data, what are the estimated cash disbursements from operations for June?

E4-6 Determining cash collections on account

The following information was taken from the 2003 financial statement of Algor Corporation:

Accounts receivable, January 1, 2003	$ 24,200
Accounts receivable, December 31, 2003	32,600
Sales on account and cash sales	535,000

No accounts receivable were written off or recovered during the year, and there is a zero balance in the "Allowance for bad debts" account.

Required:

Determine the cash collected from customers by Algor Corporation in 2003.

E4-7 Determining cash received from customers

Lance Corporation's cash flow statement for the year ended December 31, 2003, was prepared using the indirect method, and it included the following items:

Net income	$67,000
Noncash adjustments:	
Amortization expense	9,000
Increase in accounts receivable	(10,000)
Decrease in inventory	40,000
Decrease in accounts payable	(12,000)
Net cash flows from operating activities	$94,000

Lance reported revenues from customers of $92,000 in its 2003 income statement.

What amount of cash did Lance receive from customers during the year ended December 31, 2003?

Problems/Discussion Questions

P4-1 Measurement conventions for balance sheet accounts

The information on page 163 is taken from Hudson's Bay Company's balance sheet as of January 31, 2002.

Required:

1. Identify the measurement basis underlying each of the items listed (excluding subtotals).
2. Adopt the role of a critical financial investigator and write a report (500 words) based upon the comparative balance sheet.

P4-2 Determining cash flows from operating and investing activities

HiTech Ltd. reported net income of $400,000 for 2001. Changes occurred in several balance sheet accounts as follows:

Equipment	$35,000 increase	Inventories	$30,000 decrease
Accumulated amortization	40,000 increase	Accounts receivable	15,000 increase
Note payable	30,000 increase	Accounts payable	5,000 decrease

Additional Information:

1. During 2001, HiTech sold equipment costing $25,000, with accumulated amortization of $12,000, for a gain of $8,000.
2. In December 2001, HiTech purchased equipment costing $60,000, with $30,000 cash and a 12% note payable of $30,000.
3. Amortization expense for the year was $60,000.

Required:

1. In HiTech's 2001 cash flow statement, calculate net cash provided by operating activities.
2. In HiTech's 2001 cash flow statement, calculate net cash used in investing activities.

Hudson's Bay Company
Consolidated Balance Sheets

January 31 (thousands of dollars)	Notes	2002	2001
Current assets			
Cash in stores		7,392	7,649
Short-term deposits		331,350	86,142
Credit card receivables	2	487,281	499,690
Other accounts receivable		73,494	103,302
Merchandise inventories		1,489,049	1,575,306
Prepaid expenses and other current assets		157,149	100,150
		2,545,715	2,372,239
Secured receivables	4	11,838	18,415
Fixed assets	5	1,292,519	1,336,348
Goodwill		160,436	180,069
Pensions	6	334,641	290,535
Other assets	7	189,049	178,444
		4,534,198	4,376,050
Current liabilities			
Short-term borrowings	8	24,188	22,000
Trade accounts payable		391,808	496,354
Other accounts payable and accrued expenses		576,335	584,114
Long-term debt due within one year	8	92,620	125,703
		1,084,951	1,228,171
Long-term debt	8	688,939	674,575
Employee future benefits other than pensions	6	58,579	58,621
Future income taxes	3	173,105	111,336
Shareholders' equity			
Subordinated debentures	9	400,507	201,466
Capital stock	10	1,418,995	1,430,376
Contributed surplus	10	40,818	37,793
Retained earnings		668,304	633,712
		2,528,624	2,303,347
		4,534,198	4,376,050

On behalf of the Board:

(signed)   (signed)

L. Yves Fortier, C.C., Q.C.   Peter W. Mills, Q.C.
Director   Director

P4-3 Understanding the relation between the income statement, cash flow statement, and changes in balance sheet accounts

The following cash flow information pertains to the 2001 operations of Matterhorn Inc., a maker of ski equipment:

Cash collections from customers	$16,670
Cash payments to suppliers	19,428
Cash payments for various operating expenses	7,148
Cash payments for current income taxes	200
Cash provided by operating activities	(10,106)

The following additional information comes from Matterhorn's 2001 income statement:

Net income	$ 609
Amortization of equipment	2,256
Amortization of patents	399
Loss on sale of equipment	169

The following additional information comes from Matterhorn's 2000 and 2001 comparative balance sheets (decreases are in parentheses):

Change in accounts receivable	$3,630
Change in inventory	3,250
Change in accounts payable	(3,998)
Change in accrued operating expenses	(2,788)
Change in future income tax liability	127

Required:

1. Use the preceding information to derive Matterhorn's 2001 income statement.
2. Use the same information to compute Matterhorn's 2001 cash flow from operating activities under the indirect method (i.e., derive cash flow from operating activities by making the necessary adjustments to net income).
3. Provide a brief explanation for the difference observed between net income and cash provided by operating activities.

P4-4 Understanding the relation between the income statement, cash flow statement, and changes in balance sheet accounts

The following cash flow information pertains to the 2002 operations of Diva Inc.:

Cash collections from customers	$72,481
Cash payments to suppliers	51,768
Cash payments for selling and administrative expenses	9,409
Cash payments for interest	1,344
Cash payments for current income taxes	671
Cash provided by operating activities	9,289

The following additional information comes from Diva's 2002 income statement:

Net income	$1,085
Amortization of equipment	7,380
Gain on sale of equipment	327

The following additional information comes from Diva's 2001 and 2002 comparative balance sheets (decreases are in parentheses):

Change in accounts receivable	($4,603)
Change in inventory	7,400
Change in accounts payable	3,146
Change in accrued selling and administrative expenses	772
Change in future income tax liability	(87)
Change in accrued interest payable	117

Required:

1. Use the preceding information to derive Diva's 2002 income statement.
2. Use the same information to compute Diva's 2002 cash flow from operating activities under the indirect method (i.e., derive cash flow from operating activities by making the necessary adjustments to net income).
3. Provide a brief explanation for the difference observed between net income and cash provided by operating activities.

P4-5 Understanding the relation between operating cash flows and accrual earnings

The following information is taken from the operating section of the cash flow statement (direct method) of Battery Builders, Inc.:

Collections from customers	$28,000
Payments to suppliers for purchases	(13,000)
Payments for operating expenses	(9,000)
Payments for current period income taxes	(4,000)
Cash provided by operating activities	$ 2,000

The following information is obtained from the income statement of Battery Builders:

Net income	$4,000
Amortization expense	4,000
Gain on sale of equipment	2,000
Writeoff of goodwill	1,000

In addition, the following information is obtained from the comparative balance sheets of Battery Builders (+/− refers to increase/decrease):

Change in accounts receivable	+$3,000
Change in inventory	+3,000
Change in accounts payable	+2,000
Change in accrued payable (related to operating expense)	−2,000
Change in future income tax liability	+1,000

1. Prepare a complete accrual-basis income statement for the current year.
2. Compute the cash flows from operations using the indirect approach (i.e., start with accrual-basis net income and adjust for various items to get cash flows from operations).

P4-6 Interpreting financial statement data: Alcan

ALCAN ALUMINUM
LIMITED
www.alcan.com

Alcan Aluminum Limited operates several companies in all aspects of the aluminum industry, from bauxite mining to manufacturing and recycling. Although a Canadian corporation that follows Canadian GAAP, Alcan reports in U.S. dollars, since it is an international company with a presence in more than 30 countries and significant American operations. Total sales and operating revenues for 1997 were US$7.8 billion, and net income was US$0.5 billion.

Alcan's consolidated statements of income, consolidated statements of retained earnings, consolidated balance sheets, and consolidated statements of cash flow, as they appeared in the company's 1997 annual report, are shown on pages 165–167.

Required:

1. Suppose the following items were not disclosed separately on Alcan's December 31, 1997, balance sheet. Show how they could each be derived from the given balance sheets alone.
   • aluminum inventories
   • accumulated depreciation
   • payables
   • debt not maturing within one year
   • retained earnings
2. Using information from only Alcan's balance sheets, judge the company's ability to make payments on its current liabilities.
3. Using information from only Alcan's balance sheets, describe the significant changes in the company's financial position over the three years shown.
4. Assume that you are a financial analyst. On the basis of the financial position of Alcan as portrayed in its balance sheets over the period 1995–1997, would you advise your clients to invest in the common shares of the company?
5. Would your answer to Question 4 change if you had also analyzed Alcan's income and cash flow statements? Explain.
6. Is it possible to derive the information on Alcan's cash flow statements from the income statements, balance sheets, and retained earnings statements? If this is possible, is the cash flow statement unnecessary?

Alcan Aluminum Limited
Consolidated Statement of Income

(in millions of US$, except per-share amounts)	Year Ended December 31, 1997	1996	1995
Revenues			
Sales and operating revenues	$7,777	$7,614	$9,287
Other income	88	75	100
	7,865	7,689	9,387
Costs and expenses			
Cost of sales and operating expenses	5,995	5,905	7,233
Depreciation (Note 2)	436	431	447
Selling, administrative, and general expenses	444	422	484
Research and development expenses	72	71	76
Interest	101	125	204
Other expenses	54	88	61
	7,102	7,042	8,505
Income before income taxes and other items	763	647	882
Income taxes (Note 5)	258	226	340
Income before other items	505	421	542
Equity loss (Note 7)	(33)	(10)	(3)
Minority interests	(4)	(1)	4
Net income before extraordinary item	$ 468	$ 410	$ 543
Extraordinary gain (loss) (Note 3)	17	—	(280)
Net income	$ 485	$ 410	$ 263
Dividends on preference shares	10	16	24
Net income attributable to common shareholders	$ 475	$394	$ 239
Net income per common share before extraordinary item (Note 2)	$ 2.02	$ 1.74	$ 2.30
Extraordinary gain (loss) per common share (Note 3)	0.07	—	(1.24)
Net income per common share (Note 2)	$ 2.09	$ 1.74	$ 1.06
Dividends per common share	$ 0.60	$ 0.60	$ 0.45

Consolidated Statement of Retained Earnings

(in millions of US$)	Year Ended December 31, 1997	1996	1995
Retained earnings—beginning of year	$3,217	$2,959	$2,821
Net income	485	410	263
	3,702	3,369	3,084
Dividends—Common	136	136	101
—Preference	10	16	24
Retained earnings—end of year (Note 14)	$3,556	$3,217	$2,959

Alcan Aluminum Limited
Consolidated Balance Sheet

(in millions of US$, except per-share amounts)	December 31, 1997	1996	1995
Assets			
Current assets:			
Cash and time deposits	$ 608	$ 546	$ 66
Receivables	1,292	1,262	1,449
Inventories:			
Aluminum	800	736	888
Raw materials	307	325	321
Other supplies	234	244	281
	1,341	1,305	1,490
	3,241	3,113	3,005
Deferred charges and other assets	424	314	364
Investments (Notes 7 and 9)	343	428	695
Property, plant, and equipment (Note 8):			
Cost	11,715	11,517	11,735
Accumulated depreciation	6,257	6,047	6,063
	5,458	5,470	5,672
Total assets	$9,466	$9,325	$9,736
Liabilities and shareholders' equity			
Current liabilities:			
Payables	$1,052	$1,008	$1,107
Short-term borrowings	238	178	212
Income and other taxes	98	98	101
Debt maturing within one year (Note 11)	36	19	28
	1,424	1,303	1,448
Debt not maturing within one year (Notes 11 and 16)	1,241	1,319	1,745
Deferred credits and other liabilities (Note 10)	715	770	701
Deferred income taxes	969	996	979
Minority interests (Note 9)	43	73	28
Shareholders' equity:			
Redeemable non-retractable preference shares (Note 12)	203	203	353
Common shareholders' equity:			
Common shares (Note 13)	1,251	1,235	1,219
Retained earnings (Note 14)	3,556	3,217	2,959
Deferred translation adjustments (Note 15)	64	209	304
	4,871	4,661	4,482
	5,074	4,864	4,835
Commitments and contingencies (Note 17)			
Total liabilities and shareholders' equity	$9,466	$9,325	$9,736

Alcan Aluminum Limited
Consolidated Statement of Cash Flows

(in millions of US$)	Year Ended December 31,		
	1997	1996	1995
Operating activities			
Net income	$485	$410	$ 263
Adjustments to determine cash from operating activities:			
Extraordinary loss	—	—	280
Depreciation	436	431	447
Deferred income taxes	(8)	15	174
Equity income—net of dividends	39	21	12
Change in receivables	(30)	187	(38)
Change in inventories	(37)	185	(107)
Change in payables	44	(99)	11
Change in income and other taxes payable	—	(3)	78
Changes in operating working capital due to:			
Deferred translation adjustments	(93)	(29)	33
Acquisitions, disposals, and consolidations/deconsolidations	(9)	(178)	(77)
Change in deferred charges, other assets, deferred credits, and other liabilities—net	(139)	25	30
Gain on sales of businesses—net	(12)	(8)	(34)
Other—net	43	24	(28)
Cash from operating activities	719	981	1,044
Financing activities			
New debt	22	56	90
Debt repayments	(25)	(459)	(738)
	(3)	(403)	(648)
Short-term borrowings—net	90	(11)	4
Common shares issued	16	16	24
Shares issued by subsidiary companies	—	—	1
Redemption of preference shares	—	(150)	—
Dividends—Alcan shareholders (including preference)	(146)	(152)	(125)
—Minority interests	(3)	—	—
Cash used for financing activities	(46)	(700)	(744)
Investment activities			
Property, plant and equipment	(641)	(482)	(390)
Investments	—	—	(38)
Other	—	—	(13)
	(641)	(482)	(441)
Net proceeds from disposal of businesses and other assets	54	660	168
Cash from (used for) investment activities	(587)	178	(273)
Effect of exchange rate changes on cash and time deposits	(12)	(1)	1
Increase in cash and time deposits	74	458	28
Cash of companies consolidated (deconsolidated)—net	(12)	22	11
Cash and time deposits—beginning of year	546	66	27
Cash and time deposits—end of year	$608	$546	$ 66

P4-7 Analyzing the difference between operating cash flows and accrual earnings

The following are Food Tiger's 2001 and 2002 balance sheets and 2002 income statement.

Food Tiger Inc. Comparative Balance Sheets		
	December 31,	
	2002	2001
Assets		
Current assets:		
Cash and cash equivalents	$ 6,804	$ 428
Receivables	97,106	76,961
Inventories	844,539	673,606
Prepaid expenses	9,401	16,684
Total current assets	957,850	767,679
Property at cost	1,446,896	1,094,804
Less: Accumulated amortization	(407,641)	(303,027)
	1,039,255	791,777
Total assets	$1,997,105	$1,559,456
Liabilities and Shareholders' Equity		
Current liabilities:		
Accounts payable—trade	$ 343,163	$ 290,064
Accrued expenses	184,017	138,921
Accrued interest payable	1,067	3,394
Income taxes payable	37,390	42,958
Total current liabilities	565,637	475,337
Long-term debt	504,913	415,561
Total liabilities	$1,070,550	$ 890,898
Shareholders' equity		
Common shares	263,155	162,298
Retained earnings	663,400	506,260
Total shareholders' equity	926,555	668,558
Total liabilities and shareholders' equity	$1,997,105	$1,559,456

Food Tiger Inc.	
Income Statement	
2002	
Net sales	$6,438,507
Cost of goods sold	5,102,977
Gross profit	1,335,530
Selling and administrative expenses	855,809
Interest expense	34,436
Amortization	104,614
Income before income taxes	340,671
Provision for income taxes	135,500
Net income	$ 205,171

Additional Information:

1. The "Accounts payable, trade" account is only used for purchases of merchandise inventory.
2. The balance in the "Prepaid expenses" account represents prepaid selling and administrative expenses for the following year.
3. Except for the prepaid selling and administrative expenses noted in (2), the company records all selling and administrative expenses in the accrued expenses account prior to making payment.
4. The company records all interest expense in the "Accrued interest payable" account prior to making payment.
5. The company records all income tax expense in the "Income taxes payable" account prior to making payment.
6. Cash dividends declared and paid during 2002 were $48,031.
7. No long-term assets were disposed of in 2002.

Required:

1. Prepare an analysis of Food Tiger's 2002 operating cash flows and accrual-based net income by completing the following table. The table follows the format of Exhibit 4.2 in this chapter.
2. Prepare Food Tiger's "cash flow statement" for 2002. Follow the format of Exhibit 4.3 also in this chapter.

	(a)	(b)	(c)	(d)
		Noncash Accruals	Prepayments/	(a + b + c)
	Accrual	Revenue Earned or	Buildups/Other	Cash Received (+)
Item	Income	Expenses Incurred	Adjustments	or Paid (−)
Operating Activities				
.				
.				
.				
Net income				
Operating cash flow				
Investing Activities				
.				
.				
.				
Financing Activities				
.				
.				
.				
Change in Cash				

Food Tiger Inc.
Analysis of Change in Cash Versus Income for 2002

Cases

C4-1 Debbie Dress Shops Inc.: Determine cash flow amounts from comparative balance sheets and income statement

The balance sheet and income statement for Debbie Dress Shops are presented along with some additional information about the accounts. You are to answer the questions that follow concerning cash flows for the period.

1. All accounts receivable and accounts payable are related to trade merchandise. Accounts payable are recorded net and always are paid to take all the discounts allowed. The allowance for doubtful accounts at the end of 2001 was the same as at the end of 2000; no receivables were charged against the allowance during 2001.
2. The proceeds from the note payable were used to finance a new store building. Capital stock was sold to provide additional working capital.

Required:

1. Calculate cash collected during 2001 from accounts receivable.
2. Calculate cash payments during 2001 on accounts payable to suppliers.
3. Calculate cash provided from operations for 2001.
4. Calculate cash inflows during 2001 from financing activities.
5. Calculate cash outflows from investing activities during 2001.

Debbie Dress Shops Inc.
Balance Sheet

	December 31,	
	2001	**2000**
Assets		
Current assets:		
Cash	$ 300,000	$ 200,000
Accounts receivable—net	840,000	580,000
Merchandise inventory	660,000	420,000
Prepaid expenses	100,000	50,000
Total current assets	1,900,000	1,250,000
Long-term investments	80,000	—
Land, building, and fixtures	1,130,000	600,000
Less: Accumulated amortization	(110,000)	(50,000)
	1,020,000	550,000
Total assets	$3,000,000	$1,800,000
Liabilities and Shareholders' Equity		
Current liabilities:		
Accounts payable	$ 530,000	$ 440,000
Accrued expenses	140,000	130,000
Dividends payable	70,000	—
Total current liabilities	740,000	570,000
Note payable—due year 2003	500,000	—
Shareholders' equity:		
Common shares	1,200,000	900,000
Retained earnings	560,000	330,000
Total shareholders' equity	1,760,000	1,230,000
Total liabilities and shareholders' equity	$3,000,000	$1,800,000

Debbie Dress Shops Inc.
Income Statements

	Year Ended December 31,	
	2001	**2000**
Net credit sales	$6,400,000	$4,000,000
Cost of goods sold	5,000,000	3,200,000
Gross profit	1,400,000	800,000
Expenses (including income taxes)	1,000,000	520,000
Net income	$ 400,000	$ 280,000

C4-2 Drop Zone Corporation (CW): Understanding the relation between successive balance sheets and the cash flow statement

Drop Zone manufactures equipment for sky divers. Here are Drop Zone Corporation's balance sheet at the end of 2001 and its cash flow statement for 2002.

Drop Zone Corporation Balance Sheet December 31, 2001	
Assets	
Current assets:	
Cash	$ 7,410
Accounts receivable—net	6,270
Inventory	13,395
Prepaid assets	1,995
Total current assets	29,070
Land	27,930
Buildings and equipment	194,655
Less: Accumulated amortization, buildings, and equipment	(40,185)
Total assets	$211,470
Liabilities and Shareholders' Equity	
Current liabilities:	
Accounts payable	$ 11,400
Accrued payables	3,135
Total current liabilities	14,535
Long-term debt	19,950
Shareholders' equity:	
Common shares	18,525
Contributed surplus	31,920
Retained earnings	144,780
Less: Treasury shares	(18,240)
Total liabilities and shareholders' equity	$211,470

Drop Zone Corporation
Cash Flow Statement
For the Year Ended December 31, 2002

Operating Activities

Net income	$ 11,400
Plus (minus) noncash items:	
+ Depreciation expense	5,415
Plus (minus) changes in current asset and liability accounts:	
+ Decrease in inventory	1,425
+ Decrease in prepaid assets	855
+ Increase in accrued payables	1,140
– Increase in accounts receivable	(3,990)
– Decrease in accounts payable	(2,850)
Cash provided by operating activities	$ 13,395
Investing Activities	
Purchase of equipment	$(39,615)
Proceeds from the sale of land	8,550
Cash used by investing activities	(31,065)
Financing Activities	
Issuance of long-term debt	$ 16,245
Issuance of common shares	12,825
Cash dividends paid	(6,270)
Purchase of treasury shares	(2,565)
Cash provided by financing activities	$ 20,235
Net cash flow	$ 2,565

Additional Information:

1. During 2002, 500 shares of common stock were sold to the public.
2. Land was sold during 2002 at an amount that equalled its original cost.

Required:

Use the preceding information to derive Drop Zone Corporation's balance sheet at the end of 2002.

Integrative Running Case Study
Bombardier on the Web

Locate Bombardier Inc.'s annual report for the year ended January 31, 2002, through this textbook's Companion Website at **www.pearsoned.ca/revsine**. Examine the consolidated statements of cash flows on page 72.

Required:

1. Explain why the company has presented cash flow information for both Bombardier Consolidated and separately for Bombardier operating companies and BC (Bombardier Capital).
2. Describe the companies' financing and investing activities for 2002 and 2001. What are the major differences?
3. Consolidated cash flow from operations decreased by $688.6 million in 2002, but cash and cash equivalents decreased by $911.1 million. How can this be?

Endnotes

1. "Operating and financial flexibility" refers to a company's ability to adjust to unexpected downturns in its environment or to take advantage of opportunities as they arise. Balance sheets provide some of the information for making these assessments. A company with most of its assets invested in specialized manufacturing facilities may have limited ability to adjust to a decline in demand for its output. Similarly, a company with little cash and high debt on its balance sheet may be unable to take advantage of opportunities.

2. "Property, Plant and Equipment," *CICA Handbook*, Section 3061, para. .38. The CICA's AcSB issued an exposure draft entitled "Impairment or Disposal of Long-Lived Assets" in February 2002. See Chapter 10.

3. The format for preparing the cash flow statement is specified in "Cash Flows Statements," *CICA Handbook*, Section 1540, which was revised effective June 1998. As defined in Section 1540, *cash equivalents* "are short-term, highly liquid investments that are readily convertible to known amounts of cash and which are subject to an insignificant risk of changes in value" (para. .06).

5
Essentials of Financial Statement Analysis

LEARNING OBJECTIVES
After studying this chapter, you should be able to:

1. Understand how competitive forces and a company's business strategy influence its operating profitability and the composition of its balance sheet

2. Appreciate why analysts worry about the quality of financial statement information and how quality is determined

3. Analyze a company's profitability using return on assets (ROA), and gain insights from separating ROA into its profit margin and asset turnover components

4. Use return on common equity (ROCE) to assess the impact of financial leverage on a company's profitability

5. Differentiate between short-term liquidity risk and long-term solvency risk, and use financial ratios to assess these two dimensions of credit risk

6. Interpret the results of an analysis of profitability and risk

7. Know why EBITDA (earnings before interest, taxes, depreciation, and amortization) can be a misleading indicator of profitability and cash flow

Investors would be well advised to shut out all the yammering about earnings expectations, consensus forecasts, and whisper numbers and focus instead on the financial information reported by companies themselves.[1]

A firm's financial statements are like a complex story. If you know how to interpret the story, you can more clearly understand what is going on at the firm. Has profitability improved? Are customers paying their bills more promptly? How was the new manufacturing plant financed? Financial statements hold many of the answers to these and other questions. They can help tell us how the company got to where it is today, and they can help us forecast where the company might be tomorrow.

This chapter provides an overview of three financial analysis tools—**common size statements**, **trend statements**, and **financial ratios**. We show how each tool is used, and we explain how to interpret the results from each. But the important message in this chapter is that all financial analysis tools are built around reported accounting data, and these tools can be no better than the data from which they are constructed. *What financial data a company chooses to report and how the data are reported affect not only the financial statements themselves but also the ratios and other numbers used to analyze those statements.*

Introducing financial analysis tools at this early point prepares you for later chapters where we describe various financial reporting alternatives and their impact on ratios, trends, and other comparisons.

Basic Approaches

Analysts use financial statements and financial data in many ways and for many different purposes. Two purposes you should know are time-series analysis and cross-sectional analysis.

Time-series analysis helps identify financial trends over time for a *single* company or business unit. The analyst might be interested in determining the rate of growth in revenues for Intel Corporation, or the degree to which Intel's earnings have fluctuated historically with inflation, business cycles, foreign currency exchange rates, or changes in economic growth in domestic or foreign markets.

Cross-sectional analysis helps identify similarities and differences *across* companies or business units at a single moment in time. The analyst might compare the current year profitability of one company in an industry to a competitor's profitability. A related analytic tool—**benchmark comparison**—measures a company's performance or health against some predetermined standard. For example, commercial lending agreements often require the borrowing company to maintain minimum dollar levels of working capital or tangible net worth. Once the loan has been granted, the lender—a bank or insurance company—monitors compliance by comparing the borrower's reported financial amounts and ratios to those specified in the loan agreement.

> **Tangible net worth** is usually defined as total *tangible* assets minus total liabilities, where tangible assets exclude things like goodwill, patents, trademarks, and other *intangible* items.

Analysts use a mixture of time-series and cross-sectional tools when evaluating a particular company or business unit. Using these tools can reveal meaningful details about current profitability and financial condition and can also reveal details about recent changes that might affect future profitability or financial condition. However, this analysis is based on financial statement data, and hence can be influenced by distortions of that data—if the data are indeed distorted.

Evaluating the "Quality" of Accounting Numbers

Analysts use financial statement information to "get behind the numbers" (i.e., to see more accurately the economic activities and condition of the company and its prospects) as depicted in Figure 5.1. However, financial statements do not always provide a complete and faithful picture of a company's activities and condition. The raw data needed for a complete and faithful picture do not always reach the financial reports because the information is filtered through generally accepted accounting principles (GAAP) and management's accounting discretion. Both factors can distort the quality of the reported information and the analyst's view of the company.

Let's see how the financial reporting "filter" phenomenon works with equipment leases. GAAP require that each lease be classified as either a **capital lease** or an **operating lease** and that only capital leases be reported as balance sheet assets and liabilities. Operating leases are "off-balance-sheet" items, which means they are not included in the reported asset and liability numbers but are instead disclosed in supplemental footnotes that accompany the financial statements. (We'll see how and why this is so in Chapter 12.) So the GAAP "filter" lets capital leases pass to the balance sheet but diverts operating leases to the statement footnotes. Analysts can—and do—use these footnotes to recast the balance sheet so that all equipment leases are treated the same way. The GAAP filter is then overcome.

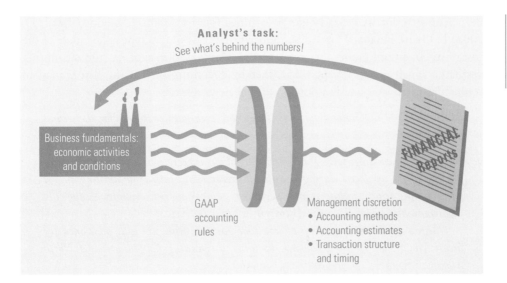

FIGURE 5.1
THE FINANCIAL
REPORTING
FILTER AND THE
ANALYST'S TASK

As we have seen in previous chapters, management discretion can cloud financial analysis in several ways. For example, managers who understand GAAP can use these principles to structure business transactions so that financial reporting goals are achieved. Do you, as a manager, want to keep equipment leases off the balance sheet? Then just make certain your company's lease contracts meet the GAAP rules for an operating lease. Doing so keeps your leases off the balance sheet and lowers your reported debt.

Management discretion can also complicate the analyst's task in areas like inventory accounting, where GAAP allow managers to freely choose from among several alternative reporting methods. Because each inventory method leads to a different set of reported earnings and asset numbers, an analyst can make financial comparisons. Here, too, the analyst can sometimes use footnote information to recast the reported financial results and thereby eliminate management discretion as an information filter.

Management also has discretion over accounting estimates and the timing of business transactions. Consider estimated "bad debt expense," which is management's forecast of the amount of current sales that will never be collected from credit customers. A reduction in estimated bad debt expense could mean customer credit quality has improved (i.e., more credit customers are now expected to pay their bills). Or, it could mean bad debt expense was temporarily reduced to meet a quarterly earnings goal. Similar questions arise over the timing of discretionary expenditures for advertising, research and development (R&D), or information technology. Did advertising expense decline because the current ad program was such a resounding success, or because management curtailed spending this quarter just to meet an earnings goal? In other words, have business fundamentals improved or is it simply "earnings management"?

So the quality of accounting numbers, what we referred to as the *quality of earnings* in Chapters 1, 2, and 3, is a crucial variable in financial statement analysis. The Enron affair and other apparent financial reporting failures (see Chapter 1) have served as stimuli to strengthen the underlying system that produces accounting numbers. Companies are aware that they must be perceived to be "as pure as Caesar's wife" when it comes to financial reporting, so they are in the process of improving the methods for disclosure and reporting of accounting information. For example, in a

GAAP and management discretion can sometimes make the analyst's task easier by illuminating aspects of the company's activities and condition. For example, GAAP require companies to disclose sales and operating income by business segment—information that some companies would not otherwise make available. Similarly, management sometimes goes far beyond GAAP's minimum reporting requirements by disclosing financial and non-financial operating details that are useful to analysts.

news release about its second-quarter earnings for the six months ended April 30, 2002, TD Bank Financial Group announced that it would include an estimate of the cost of stock options granted to employees as compensation expense (the accounting details of which are in Chapter 15), thereby becoming one of the first Canadian companies to do so. Here is a portion of that news release:

> *TORONTO* – *TD Bank Financial Group today announced results for the second quarter of fiscal 2002.*
>
> *"Overall TD's earnings fall significantly short of our expectations and are reflective of the challenges we faced during a difficult credit cycle, further weakening in the telecommunications industry and declining capital market activity," said TD Chairman and Chief Executive Officer A. Charles Baillie.*
>
> *"Despite these challenges, we believe that our businesses are well positioned for future growth as we work towards building the leading Canadian-based North American financial services company," he added.*
>
> *TD also announced today, effective November 1, 2002, it intends to report stock option awards as compensation expense. "With the introduction of a new Canadian standard on stock-based compensation, we believe the time is right to change the way in which we account for options," Baillie noted. "Option awards are a part of compensation and should be treated in a similar manner to other compensation expenses."*

Can we expect to see such a continuous improvement in the quality of earnings? In the short run, perhaps, but as the effect of Enron and similar phenomena wear off, it is almost a certainty that (perhaps subtle, perhaps overt) deteriorations in the quality of earnings will begin to appear. In other words, as a character in the TV series *The X-Files* advised, "Trust no one!"

Recap

Analysts need to understand what accounting data do and do not reveal about a company's economic activities and condition. They must also know how to adjust the reported numbers, when necessary, to overcome distortions caused by GAAP and generally by management's accounting and disclosure choices. The first step in making an informed analysis of financial statements is to carefully evaluate the quality of the reported accounting numbers. No tool of financial statement analysis is completely immune to distortions caused by GAAP or by management's reporting choices.

Quaker Oats Company— An Illustration

> *We have a unique combination of powerhouse food brands plus a growth engine like no other—Gatorade. In 1999, our business grew in all the right ways: volumes, revenues, margins, and ultimately profits. We are disciplined stewards of capital, using our resources effectively, reducing operating costs, and driving greater efficiencies in our businesses around the world.* [Quaker Oats Company 1999 Annual Report]

QUAKER OATS COMPANY www.quakeroats.com

With annual sales of US$5 billion and a market capitalization of over US$7 billion, the Quaker Oats Company is one of the world's largest food processors. The company was formed in 1901 as the successor to a company that was organized in 1891. Quaker Oats manufactures and sells grocery products in the United States, Canada,

Europe, Latin America, and the Pacific. The company operates 46 manufacturing plants in 15 countries, and it has distribution centres and sales offices in 21 countries.

In August 2001, Quaker Oats merged with PepsiCo, Inc., and so Quaker's financial statement presence disappeared from public view. The merger was, according to PepsiCo's 2001 audited financial statements, accounted for as a "pooling of interests," which is a method of accounting for consolidations described in Chapter 16. Ironically, this method has been forbidden recently in Canada and the United States, as we discuss in that chapter.

Quaker's portfolio of grocery products includes ready-to-eat and hot cereals, grain-based snacks, syrups, frozen breakfast products, thirst-quenching beverages, and rice and pasta products, as well as institutional and food service products. Included in the company's product line are such well-known brand names as Quaker Oatmeal, Cap'n Crunch cereal, Rice-A-Roni flavoured rice dishes, and Gatorade. Of Quaker's 1999 sales, 93% came from brands holding the number one or number two position in their product category, and nearly 40% of sales and profits came from Gatorade.

The food processing industry in North America is now quite mature. The amount of food consumed per person remains essentially unchanged from one year to the next. With the North American population growing at only about 1% annually, companies like Quaker have focused their attention on demographic shifts, on the growing ethnic diversity of the population, and on expanding their presence in foreign markets.

Labour is the largest component of food production costs; it represents about one-third of total manufacturing costs. Grains, sweeteners, and other food commodities that are the raw materials for Quaker's products account for another 20%. Other manufacturing costs include packaging, transportation, and energy. The business requires substantial investments in management and distribution facilities, but the pace of technological change in the industry is slow.

Competition centres around reinforcing established brands, developing new value-added products, and reducing manufacturing and logistics costs to achieve lower selling prices. Established brands are reinforced through marketing, advertising, and promotional programs that build brand awareness and increase repeat product purchases. The emphasis on cost reduction by food processing companies reflects intense competition both in the mature markets of North America and Europe, and among price-conscious consumers worldwide.

Now that you have a general overview of the business and the industry, let's take a look at the company's financial statements.

Quaker's Financial Statements

Comparative income statements for the Quaker Oats Company are shown in Exhibit 5.1(a). Sales decreased from roughly US$6 billion in 1995 to US$5 billion in 1997, and then they fell to US$4.7 billion in 1999. The company's pre-tax income was also erratic during these years: It declined from US$1,220.5 million in 1995 to only US$415.6 million the next year, and then declined again to a US$1,064.3 million loss in 1997. By 1999, pre-tax income had rebounded to US$618.3 million.

Why were sales and pre-tax earnings so volatile? After all, Quaker Oats is a mature company operating in a stable industry, one in which gyrations in sales and earnings are virtually nonexistent. What's been happening?

Exhibit 5.1(a) QUAKER OATS COMPANY

Comparative Income Statements
(US$ in millions)

	1999	1998	1997	1996	1995
Sales	$4,725.2	$4,842.5	$5,015.7	$5,199.0	$5,954.0
Cost of goods sold	2,136.8	2,374.4	2,564.9	2,807.5	3,294.4
Gross profit	2,588.4	2,468.1	2,450.8	2,391.5	2,659.6
Selling, general, and administrative expenses	1,904.1	1,872.5	1,938.9	1,981.0	2,358.6
(Gains) losses on divestitures, restructurings, and asset impairment	(2.3)	128.5	1,486.3	(113.4)	(1,053.5)
Interest expense	61.9	69.6	85.8	106.8	131.6
Other expenses	6.4	0.9	4.1	1.5	2.2
Pre-tax income	618.3	396.6	(1,064.3)	415.6	1,220.7
Income taxes	163.3	112.1	(133.4)	167.7	496.5
Net income (loss)	455.0	284.5	(930.9)	247.9	724.2
Preferred dividends	4.4	4.5	3.5	3.7	2.0
Net income (loss) available for common	$ 450.6	$ 280.0	($ 934.4)	$ 244.2	$ 722.2

A closer look at the income statements gives us part of the answer. Pre-tax earnings in 1995 benefited from a US$1,053.5 million pre-tax divestiture gain—the result of selling some product lines. Divestiture gains of US$113.4 million and US$2.3 million helped boost pre-tax earnings for 1996 and 1999, respectively. Pre-tax earnings in 1997 and 1998 suffered from divestiture and restructuring charges of US$1,486.3 million and US$128.5 million, respectively. Information elsewhere in the annual report tells us that the 1995 gain came from selling off several businesses—pet foods, bean and chili products, Mexican chocolate, and Dutch honey. Divestitures in 1996 included some of the company's frozen foods and Italian products business. The 1997 divestiture charge was for Snapple, a beverage business Quaker Oats bought in 1994 for US$1.7 billion and sold in 1997 for US$300 million.

Removing these divestiture and restructuring items from pre-tax income helps clarify matters: sales have been declining but *adjusted* pre-tax income has increased each year! Let's find the source of that improvement.

Adjustments to Remove Divestiture/Restructuring Gains and Losses

(US$ in millions)	1999	1998	1997	1996	1995
Pre-tax income	$618.3	$396.6	($1,064.3)	$415.6	$1,220.5
− Divestiture/restructuring (gains) losses	(2.3)	128.5	1,486.3	(113.4)	(1,053.5)
= Adjusted pre-tax income	$616.0	$525.1	$ 422.0	$302.2	$ 167.0

Financial analysts use *common size* and *trend* statements to help spot changes in a company's cost structure and profit performance. **Common size income statements**, shown in Exhibit 5.1(b), recast each statement item as a percentage of sales. For example, Quaker's expense for cost of goods sold for 1999 is shown as 45.2% of 1999 sales (45.2% = $2,136.8 cost of goods sold$_{99}$/$4,725.2 sales$_{99}$) instead of US$2,136.8 million. The **trend statements** shown in Exhibit 5.1(b) also recast each

Exhibit 5.1(b) QUAKER OATS COMPANY
Common Size and Trend Analysis of Income

Common size statements (% of sales)	1999	1998	1997	1996	1995
Sales	100.0	100.0	100.0	100.0	100.0
Cost of goods sold	45.2	49.0	51.1	54.0	55.3
Gross profit	54.8	51.0	48.9	46.0	44.7
Selling, general, and administrative expenses	40.3	38.7	38.7	38.1	39.6
(Gains) losses on divestitures, restructurings, and asset impairment	0.0	2.7	29.6	−2.2	−17.6
Interest expense	1.3	1.4	1.7	2.1	2.2
Other expenses	0.1	0.0	0.1	0.0	0.0
Pre-tax income	13.1	8.2	−21.2	8.0	20.5
Income taxes	3.5	2.3	−2.6	3.2	8.3
Net income (loss)	9.6	5.9	−18.6	4.8	12.2
Preferred dividends	0.1	0.1	0.1	0.1	0.0
Net income (loss) available for common	9.5	5.8	−18.5	4.7	12.2
Adjusted pre-tax income	13.0	10.8	8.4	5.8	2.8

Trend statements (1995 = 100%)	1999	1998	1997	1996	1995
Sales	79.4	81.3	84.2	87.3	100.0
Cost of goods sold	64.9	72.1	77.9	85.2	100.0
Gross profit	97.3	92.8	92.1	89.9	100.0
Selling, general, and administrative expenses	80.7	79.4	82.2	84.0	100.0
(Gains) losses on divestitures, restructurings, and asset impairment	0.2	−12.2	−141.1	10.8	100.0
Interest expense	47.0	52.9	65.2	81.2	100.0
Other expenses	290.9	40.9	186.4	68.2	100.0
Pre-tax income	50.7	32.5	−87.2	34.1	100.0
Income taxes	32.9	22.6	−26.9	33.8	100.0
Net income (loss)	62.8	39.3	−128.6	34.2	100.0
Preferred dividends	220.0	225.0	175.0	185.0	100.0
Net income (loss) available for common	62.4	38.8	−129.4	33.8	100.0
Adjusted pre-tax income	368.9	314.4	252.7	181.0	100.0

statement item in percentage terms, but they do so using a base year number rather than sales. For instance, a trend statement of income shows Quaker's 1999 expense for cost of goods sold as 64.9% of base year (1995) cost of goods sold (64.9% = $2,136.8 cost of goods sold$_{99}$/$3,294.4 cost of goods sold$_{95}$).

Several aspects of the company's profit performance are revealed by these statements:

- Sales in 1999 were only 79.4% of what they were in 1995, having fallen steadily since 1995 (trend statements).

- Cost of goods sold in 1999 was 64.9% of its 1995 level (trend statements).

- Quaker enjoyed a hefty gross profit—54.8% in 1999—up from 44.7% in 1995 (common size statements).

- Selling, general, and administrative expenses increased to 40.3% of each sales dollar in 1999 from a low in 1996 of 38.1% (common size statements).

- After divestiture/restructuring charges and gains are eliminated, pre-tax income in 1999 represented 13.0% of sales compared to only 2.8% in 1995 (common size statements).

The past several years have been difficult for the company and its employees. Quaker Oats sold several food businesses in 1995 and used the cash to pay for the Snapple acquisition, only to sell Snapple two years later. These divestitures explain why sales dropped more than 20% from 1995 to 1999. But there is some good news. By selling off its under-performing brands and by increasing operating efficiencies at its manufacturing plants, Quaker Oats was able to reduce cost of goods sold from 55.3% of sales in 1995 to only 45.2% of sales in 1999. This improvement explains why adjusted pre-tax income rose from 2.8% of sales to 13.0% of sales during the same period. While sales fell, more of each sales dollar hit the bottom line!

Now let's see what we can learn from the balance sheet.

Exhibit 5.2(a) shows Quaker's comparative balance sheets using reported dollar amounts. The company's assets are concentrated in cash, trade accounts receivable, finished goods (under "Inventories"), manufacturing and distribution facilities (called "Property, plant, and equipment"), and (before 1997) intangibles. To finance these assets, Quaker has relied on a combination of short-term and long-term debt, vendor payables, and preferred and common stock, along with internally generated resources (represented as "Retained earnings").

Several important changes in the company's asset mix and financial structure have occurred since 1995. These changes can be easily seen from the common size and trend statements in Exhibit 5.2(b) ("Assets") and Exhibit 5.2(c) ("Liabilities and Owners' Equity").

Consider the composition of Quaker's assets in 1999. The company's common size statements in Exhibit 5.2(b) show that trade accounts receivable made up 10.6% of total assets that year, up from 8.6% in 1995. Inventories represented another 11.1% of total 1999 assets, also up somewhat from 1995 levels. Quaker's gross (before depreciation) investment in property, plant, and equipment (PP&E) was 77.3% of total 1999 assets, but the net (after subtracting accumulated depreciation) book value of PP&E was only 46.2% of total assets. This asset mix of roughly 11% trade accounts receivable, 11% inventories, and 46% net PP&E was typical for an established manufacturing company operating in a mature industry where credit sales—and thus trade receivables—are an important component of the distribution channel. Quaker's other assets—cash, other assets, miscellaneous current assets, and intangibles—made up the remaining 32% of the company's total assets for 1999. The company's cash balance, 11.8% of 1999 total assets, was high for a manufacturing firm where 2% to 3% is the norm.

Quaker Oats had a substantial investment in intangible assets: US$2.3 billion (Exhibit 5.2[a]) in 1995, or 50% of total assets (Exhibit 5.2[b]). This investment is a natural result of the company's growth strategy. Faced with mature markets for its existing products, Quaker Oats and other large food processors have sought to increase market share by acquiring smaller companies with established and successful regional products. Quaker then uses its own manufacturing, distribution, and mar-

Exhibit 5.2(a) QUAKER OATS COMPANY

Comparative Balance Sheets

(US$ in millions)	1999	1998	1997	1996	1995
Assets					
Cash and cash equivalents	$ 282.9	$ 326.6	$ 84.2	$ 110.5	$ 93.2
Marketable securities	0.3	27.5	—	—	—
Trade accounts receivable—net of allowances	254.3	283.4	305.7	294.9	398.3
Inventories:					
Finished goods	186.6	189.1	172.6	181.8	203.6
Grains and raw materials	50.0	48.4	59.0	62.1	69.7
Packaging materials and supplies	29.6	23.9	24.5	31.0	33.4
Total inventories	266.2	261.4	256.1	274.9	306.7
Other current assets	193.0	216.1	487.0	209.4	281.9
Total current assets	996.7	1,115.0	1,133.0	889.7	1,080.1
Other assets	55.9	79.4	48.8	66.8	63.3
Property, plant, and equipment at cost	1,851.9	1,818.8	1,913.1	1,943.3	1,946.0
Less accumulated depreciation	(745.2)	(748.6)	(748.4)	(742.6)	(778.2)
	1,106.7	1,070.2	1,164.7	1,200.7	1,167.8
Intangible assets—net of amortization	236.9	245.7	350.5	2,237.2	2,309.2
Total assets	$2,396.2	$2,510.3	$2,697.0	$4,394.4	$4,620.4
Liabilities and Owners' Equity					
Short-term debt	$ 73.3	$ 41.3	$ 61.0	$ 517.0	$ 643.4
Current portion of long-term debt	81.2	95.2	108.4	51.1	68.6
Trade accounts payable	213.6	168.4	191.3	210.2	298.4
Various accrued payables	570.2	704.2	585.0	576.4	691.3
Total current liabilities	938.3	1,009.1	945.7	1,354.7	1,701.7
Long-term debt	715.0	795.1	887.6	993.5	1,051.8
Other liabilities	523.1	533.4	615.2	797.3	769.9
Preferred stock	61.0	70.1	77.7	19.0	17.7
Common stock	840.0	840.0	840.0	840.0	840.0
Treasury stock	(1,457.4)	(1,176.0)	(898.6)	(959.8)	(998.4)
Retained earnings	776.2	438.6	229.4	1,349.7	1,237.7
Total common shareholders' equity	158.8	102.6	170.8	1,229.9	1,079.3
Total liabilities and equity	$2,396.2	$2,510.3	$2,697.0	$4,394.4	$4,620.4

keting expertise to penetrate national or international markets. The company's investment in intangible assets includes amounts paid to acquire trademarks and patented processes from smaller firms. It also includes **goodwill**—the amount in the acquisition price that represents a premium paid for the target company over and above the value of its identifiable assets. (Chapter 16 has more on goodwill.) In fact, most of

Exhibit 5.2(b) QUAKER OATS COMPANY

Common Size and Trend Analysis of Assets

Common Size Statements (% of total assets)	1999	1998	1997	1996	1995
Assets					
Cash and cash equivalents	11.8	14.1	3.1	2.5	2.0
Trade accounts receivable—net of allowances	10.6	11.3	11.3	6.7	8.6
Inventories:					
Finished goods	7.8	7.5	6.4	4.2	4.4
Grains and raw materials	2.1	1.9	2.2	1.4	1.5
Packaging materials and supplies	1.2	1.0	0.9	0.7	0.7
Total inventories	11.1	10.4	9.5	6.3	6.6
Other current assets	8.1	8.6	18.1	4.8	6.1
Total current assets	41.6	44.4	42.0	20.3	23.3
Other assets	2.3	3.2	1.8	1.5	1.4
Property, plant, and equipment at cost	77.3	72.4	70.9	44.2	42.1
Less accumulated depreciation	−31.1	−29.8	−27.7	−16.9	−16.8
	46.2	42.6	43.2	27.3	25.3
Intangible assets—net of amortization	9.9	9.8	13.0	50.9	50.0
Total assets	100.0	100.0	100.0	100.0	100.0

Trend Statements (1995 = 100%)	1999	1998	1997	1996	1995
Assets					
Cash and cash equivalents	303.9	379.9	90.3	118.6	100.0
Trade accounts receivable—net of allowances	63.8	71.2	76.8	74.0	100.0
Inventories:					
Finished goods	91.7	92.9	84.8	89.3	100.0
Grains and raw materials	71.7	69.4	84.6	89.1	100.0
Packaging materials and supplies	88.6	71.6	73.4	92.8	100.0
Total inventories	86.8	85.2	83.5	89.6	100.0
Other current assets	68.5	76.7	172.8	74.3	100.0
Total current assets	92.3	103.2	104.9	82.4	100.0
Other assets	88.3	125.4	77.1	105.5	100.0
Property, plant, and equipment at cost	95.2	93.5	98.3	99.9	100.0
Less accumulated depreciation	95.8	96.2	96.2	95.4	100.0
	94.8	91.6	99.7	102.8	100.0
Intangible assets—net of amortization	10.3	10.6	15.2	96.9	100.0
Total assets	51.9	54.3	58.4	95.1	100.0

Exhibit 5.2(c) QUAKER OATS COMPANY

Common Size and Trend Analysis of Liabilities and Equity

Common Size Statements (% of total assets)	1999	1998	1997	1996	1995
Liabilities and Owners' Equity					
Short-term debt	3.1	1.6	2.3	11.8	13.9
Current portion of long-term debt	3.4	3.8	4.0	1.2	1.5
Trade accounts payable	8.9	6.7	7.1	4.8	6.4
Various accrued payables	23.8	28.1	21.7	13.1	15.0
Total current liabilities	39.2	40.2	35.1	30.9	36.8
Long-term debt	29.8	31.7	32.9	22.6	22.8
Other liabilities	21.8	21.2	22.8	18.1	16.6
Preferred stock	2.6	2.8	2.9	0.4	0.4
Common stock	35.0	33.4	31.1	19.1	18.2
Treasury stock	−60.8	−46.8	−33.3	−21.8	−21.6
Retained earnings	32.4	17.5	8.5	30.7	26.8
Total common shareholders' equity	6.6	4.1	6.3	28.0	23.4
Total liabilities and equity	100.0	100.0	100.0	100.0	100.0

Trend Statements (1995 = 100%)	1999	1998	1997	1996	1995
Liabilities and Owners' Equity					
Short-term debt	11.4	6.4	9.5	80.4	100.0
Current portion of long-term debt	118.4	138.8	158.0	74.5	100.0
Trade accounts payable	71.6	56.4	64.1	70.4	100.0
Various accrued payables	82.5	101.9	84.6	83.4	100.0
Total current liabilities	55.1	59.3	55.6	79.6	100.0
Long-term debt	68.0	75.6	84.4	94.5	100.0
Other liabilities	67.9	69.3	79.9	103.6	100.0
Preferred stock	344.6	396.0	439.0	107.3	100.0
Common stock	100.0	100.0	100.0	100.0	100.0
Treasury stock	146.0	117.8	90.0	96.1	100.0
Retained earnings	62.7	35.4	18.5	109.0	100.0
Total common shareholders' equity	14.7	9.5	15.8	114.0	100.0
Total liabilities and equity	51.9	54.3	58.4	95.1	100.0

the company's US$2.3 billion of intangible assets in 1995 could be traced to a single acquisition—the 1994 purchase of Snapple beverage for US$1.7 billion. This one transaction added US$1.4 billion to goodwill.

What happened in 1997 when Quaker's intangibles fell to US$350 million (Exhibit 5.2[a]) or only 13% of total assets (Exhibit 5.2[b])? If you guessed that the company sold a product line, you are correct. Quaker sold the Snapple beverage business for about US$300 million—that's US$1.4 billion less than it had paid for Snapple three years earlier. As a result, the company's intangible assets decreased

81.7% in that year alone (1996 intangible assets of 96.9% minus 1997 intangibles of 15.2% from the trend statements in Exhibit 5.2[b]).

Because of the company's huge investment in Snapple intangibles, trade receivables made up only 8.6% of 1995 total assets (Exhibit 5.2[b]). Inventories added 6.6%, with another 25.3% coming from net PP&E. But does this mean that Quaker Oats increased its investment in all of these assets after selling Snapple? Not necessarily! The trend statements show that trade receivables in 1999 were 63.8% and inventories were 86.8% of their 1995 levels—but PP&E changed very little (both gross and net book values in 1999 were about 95% of their 1995 levels). *Trend statements provide a clearer indication of growth and decline than do common size statements.*

What changes in the company's financial structure have occurred since 1995? Has the mix of debt and equity capital remained constant over the past five years? And what about the proportion of short-term versus long-term borrowing? The common size and trend statements in Exhibit 5.2(c) provide the answers. We can see the following from the common size statements:

- Current liabilities were 39.2% in 1999, up slightly from 36.8% in 1995, but short-term debt fell to 3.1% from 13.9% in 1995.

- Long-term debt grew to 29.8% in 1999, up from 22.8% in 1995, while the balance in the "Other liabilities" component increased to 21.8% from 16.6%.

- Preferred stock increased but common shareholders' equity decreased over these five years, especially in 1997 when "retained earnings" fell because of the Snapple divestiture loss.

So the common size statements show a relatively stable financial structure, with some decrease in short-term debt offset by an increase in the percentage of long-term debt. The trend statements show the following:

- Short-term debt in 1999 fell to only 11.4% of its 1995 level.

- Long-term debt fell to 68% of its 1995 level by 1999.

- Common stock was unchanged, but preferred stock grew 344.6%.

An unusual feature of Quaker's financial structure is its stock repurchase program, as indicated by the size of and growth in treasury stock on the balance sheet. This statement item represents the amount paid by Quaker Oats to buy back its own previously issued common and preferred stock. We can learn more about Quaker's stock repurchase program by examining the company's cash flow statements.

Exhibit 5.3(a) presents comparative cash flow statements, with some statement items reported as combined figures to simplify the presentation. Common size and trends for selected cash flow items are shown in Exhibit 5.3(b). The common size statements are constructed by dividing each cash flow item by sales for that year. For example, Quaker's operating activities generated US$631.1 million cash (Exhibit 5.3[a]) in 1999, or 13.4% of sales of US$4,725.2 million (Exhibit 5.1[a]). In other words, cash from operations in 1999 was 13.4 cents for each sales dollar, up from 6.8 cents in 1995 (Exhibit 5.3[b]).

How does Quaker use these operating cash flows? Like most manufacturing companies, Quaker must devote resources to plant modernization and improvement. In addition, as mentioned earlier, much of the company's growth comes from buying established product lines from others. Therefore, a major cash use is capital expenditures and acquisitions, which consumed US$194.3 million in 1999 (Exhibit 5.3[a]),

Exhibit 5.3(a) QUAKER OATS COMPANY

Comparative Cash Flow Statements

(US$ in millions)	1999	1998	1997	1996	1995
Net income	$455.0	$284.5	($ 930.9)	$ 247.9	$ 724.0
Adjustments	176.1	229.0	1,420.9	162.5	(316.9)
Cash from operations	631.1	513.5	490.0	410.4	407.1
Capital expenditures and acquisitions—net	(194.3)	68.9	84.3	(68.3)	920.2
Other investments	33.9	217.6	—	0.2	4.2
Cash used in investing activities	(160.4)	286.5	84.3	(68.1)	924.4
Cash dividends	(156.2)	(159.7)	(159.4)	(157.0)	(154.8)
Reduction of debt—net	(60.4)	(124.0)	(499.0)	(199.8)	(1,090.9)
Repurchase of common and preferred stock	(382.3)	(384.9)	(56.2)	(5.5)	(5.7)
Other financing activities	82.6	112.0	121.2	31.0	(91.6)
Cash used in financing activities	(516.3)	(556.6)	(593.4)	(331.3)	(1,343.0)
Effect of exchange rate changes on cash	1.9	(1.0)	(7.2)	6.3	1.7
Net increase (decrease) in cash	($ 43.7)	$242.4	($ 26.3)	$ 17.3	($ 9.8)

or 4.1 cents per sales dollar (4.1% in Exhibit 5.3[b]). The company's cash dividends, US$156.2 million in 1999, or 3.3 cents per sales dollar, are comparable to those of many other mature companies with substantial operating cash flows. Debt payments consumed another US$60.4 million of cash in 1999, or 1.3 cents per sales dollar. This left 4.7 cents (13.4 – 4.1 – 3.3 – 1.3) of operating cash flow per sales dollar to cover the company's stock repurchases, other financing and investing activities, exchange rate effects, and the net increase in cash.

Now that we understand where the cash came from and how it was used, let's take a closer look at Quaker's stock repurchasing activities. The company spent US$382.3 million (Exhibit 5.3[a]) buying back common and preferred stock in 1999, and another US$384.9 million in 1998. These cash payments to stockholders represented 8.1 cents (Exhibit 5.3[b]) per sales dollar in 1999 and 7.9 cents in 1998, compared to 13.4 cents and 10.6 cents, respectively, in operating cash flows. That means the company spent more than half of its operating cash flows in those two years on stock repurchases. Buybacks also occurred in 1995 through 1997, but the dollar amounts involved were substantially smaller.

Why did Quaker Oats accelerate its stock repurchases in 1998? *Buybacks often increase when companies no longer need to use operating cash flows for other purposes like business acquisitions and debt repayment.* That's exactly what happened at Quaker Oats.

The cash flow statements in Exhibit 5.3(a) show that Quaker Oats generated about US$920 million in 1995 by selling off some product lines. These funds, when combined with about US$407 million in cash from operations, were more than enough to cover the company's US$1,091 million debt repayment that year. Debt repayments of US$200 million in 1996 and US$499 million in 1997 were made primarily from operating cash flows. By 1998, Quaker's cash from operations (US$514 million) far exceeded its cash needs for debt repayment (US$124 million) and acquisitions (+US$69 million because the company sold more businesses that year). The problem: what should be done with the extra cash?

Exhibit 5.3(b) QUAKER OATS COMPANY

Common Size and Trend Analysis of Selected Cash Flow Items

Common Size Statements (% of sales)	1999	1998	1997	1996	1995
Selected Items					
Cash from operations	13.4	10.6	9.8	7.9	6.8
Capital expenditures and acquisitions—net	−4.1	1.4	1.7	−1.3	15.5
Other investments	0.7	4.5	0.0	0.0	0.1
Cash used in investing activities	−3.4	5.9	1.7	−1.3	15.6
Cash dividends	−3.3	−3.3	−3.2	−3.0	−2.6
Reduction of debt—net	−1.3	−2.6	−10.0	−3.9	−18.3
Repurchase of common and preferred stock	−8.1	−7.9	−1.1	−0.1	−0.1
Other financing activities	1.8	2.3	2.4	0.6	−1.6
Cash used in financing activities	−10.9	−11.5	−11.9	−6.4	−22.6
Effect of exchange rate changes on cash	0.0	0.0	−0.1	0.1	0.0
Net increase (decrease) in cash	−0.9	5.0	−0.5	0.3	−0.2

Trend Statements (1995 = 100%)	1999	1998	1997	1996	1995
Selected Items					
Cash from operations	155.0	126.1	120.4	100.8	100.0
Capital expenditures and acquisitions—net	−21.1	7.5	9.2	−7.4	100.0
Other investments	807.1	5181.0	0.0	4.8	100.0
Cash used in investing activities	−17.4	31.0	9.1	−7.4	100.0
Cash dividends	100.9	103.2	103.0	101.4	100.0
Reduction of debt—net	5.5	11.4	45.7	18.3	100.0
Repurchase of common and preferred stock	6707.0	6752.6	986.0	96.5	100.0
Other financing activities	−90.2	−122.3	−132.3	−33.8	100.0
Cash used in financing activities	38.4	41.4	44.2	24.7	100.0
Effect of exchange rate changes on cash	111.8	−58.8	−423.5	370.6	100.0
Net increase (decrease) in cash	445.9	−2473.5	268.4	−176.5	100.0

Cash dividends to common and preferred shareholders provide part of the answer. Quaker Oats paid out nearly US$160 million in dividends in 1998, about the same amount that was paid out in 1997 and 1996. But that left an operating cash flow surplus of US$299 million ($514 − $124 + $69 − $160). Rather than put the money in a bank account, Quaker used it and some other cash to buy back US$385 million of common stock from its shareholders. The company repurchased another US$382 million of its common shares in 1999. Returning excess cash to shareholders makes good business sense when there are no attractive investment opportunities available to the company.

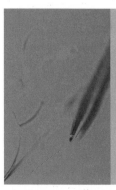

Profitability, Competition, and Business Strategy

The mechanics of running a business are not really very complicated when you get down to essentials. You have to make some stuff and sell it to somebody for more than it costs you. That's about all there is, except for a few million details.

[John L. McCaffey]

Financial ratios are another powerful tool analysts use in evaluating profit performance and assessing credit risk. Most evaluations of profit performance begin with the **return on assets (ROA)** ratio,

$$ROA = \frac{NOPAT}{Average\ assets}$$

where "NOPAT" refers to the company's **net operating profit after taxes** for a particular period (such as a year), and "average assets" is the average book value of total assets over the same time period. Before computing ROA, analysts adjust the company's reported earnings and asset figures. These adjustments fall into three broad categories:

1. Adjustments aimed at *isolating a company's sustainable operating profits* by removing nonoperating or nonrecurring items from reported income.
2. An adjustment that *eliminates after-tax interest expense* from the profit calculation so that *operating* profitability comparisons over time or across companies are not clouded by differences in financial structure.[2]
3. Adjustments for *distortions related to accounting quality concerns*, which involve potential adjustments to both income and assets for items such as nonoperating income from short-term investments or the off-balance-sheet operating leases mentioned earlier.

Exhibit 5.4 summarizes the ROA calculations for Quaker Oats using the company's earnings and balance sheet information from Exhibit 5.1(a) and Exhibit 5.2(a). The adjustments made to reported earnings each year eliminate the restructuring charges, gains and interest, on an after-tax basis. ROA for 1999 thus becomes:

$$ROA_{99} = \frac{Net\ income \pm Charges\ and\ gains \times (1 - Tax\ rate) + Interest \times (1 - Tax\ rate)}{Average\ assets}$$

$$= \frac{\$455.0 - \$2.3 \times (1 - 0.35) + \$61.9 \times (1 - 0.35)}{(\$2,510.3 + \$2,396.2)/2} = 0.201\ or\ 20.1\%$$

Exhibit 5.4 QUAKER OATS COMPANY

Return on Assets

(US$ in millions)	1999	1998	1997	1996
Net income as reported	$ 455.0	$ 284.5	($ 930.9)	$ 247.9
Restructuring/divestitures after-taxes	(1.5)	83.5	1,246.3	(73.7)
Interest expense after-taxes	40.2	45.2	55.8	69.4
Net operating profit after-tax (NOPAT)	$ 493.7	$ 413.3	$ 371.2	$ 243.6
Assets at year-end	$2,396.2	$2,510.3	$2,697.0	$4,394.4
Assets at beginning of year	2,510.3	2,697.0	4,394.4	4,620.4
Average assets	$2,453.3	$2,603.7	$3,545.7	$4,507.4
Return on assets (NOPAT/Average assets)	20.1%	15.9%	10.5%	5.4%

Note: Following common practice, an approximate tax rate (35% in this case) is used to compute after-tax restructuring charges (gains) and interest expense. For the 1997 restructuring loss, the income tax effect of US$240 million (or 16%) was taken directly from a footnote in the Quaker Oats annual report.

After all adjustments, Quaker's ROA increased from 5.4% in 1996 to 20.1% in 1999. Here's why.

There are just two ways a company can increase its operating profits per asset dollar. One way is to increase the profit yield on each sales dollar. The other is to expand the amount of sales generated from each asset dollar. In other words, a company that wants *to increase its rate of return on assets* can strive to do so in two different ways:

1. By increasing the operating profit margin.
2. By increasing the intensity of asset utilization.

Both approaches are embedded in the ROA calculation:

$$ROA = \frac{NOPAT}{Average\ assets} = \left(\frac{NOPAT}{Sales}\right) \times \left(\frac{Sales}{Average\ assets}\right)$$

$$= Operating\ profit\ margin \times Asset\ turnover$$

Changes in the profit yield per sales dollar show up as changes in the **operating profit margin**, and changes in the amount of sales generated from each asset dollar are reflected as **asset turnover** changes.

Consider a company that earns $9 million of NOPAT on sales of $100 million and that has an average asset base of $50 million. The ROA for this company is:

$$ROA = \left(\frac{NOPAT}{Sales}\right) \times \left(\frac{Sales}{Average\ assets}\right)$$

$$= (\$9/\$100) \times (\$100/\$50) = 0.09 \times 2 = 0.18\ or\ 18\%$$

Now suppose that some efficiencies in inventory and accounts receivable management exist so that average assets can be reduced to US$45 million without sacrificing sales. Assets turnover will increase to 2.22 and ROA will rise to 20%:

$$ROA = \left(\frac{NOPAT}{Sales}\right) \times \left(\frac{Sales}{Average\ assets}\right)$$

$$= \left(\frac{\$9}{\$100}\right) \times \left(\frac{\$100}{\$45}\right) = 0.09 \times 2.22 = 0.20\ or\ 20\%$$

However, there is another way to boost ROA from 18% to 20%—that is, increase the operating profit margin to 10% through aggressive cost reductions. Sales are unchanged and asset turnover stays at 2, but ROA is now:

$$ROA = \left(\frac{NOPAT}{Sales}\right) \times \left(\frac{Sales}{Average\ assets}\right)$$

$$= \left(\frac{\$10}{\$100}\right) \times \left(\frac{\$100}{\$50}\right) = 0.10 \times 2 = 0.20\ or\ 20\%$$

Exhibit 5.5 extends the ROA analysis of Quaker Oats by presenting margin and turnover figures for each of the four years. Here we learn that Quaker's improved profitability stemmed from a combination of better operating margins and increased turnover. For example, in 1996 the company was generating US$1.15 of sales from each asset dollar, and each sales dollar produced 4.7 cents of NOPAT for an ROA of 5.4%. By contrast, Quaker generated US$1.93 of sales per asset dollar in 1999, and each sales dollar produced 10.4 cents of NOPAT, so ROA that year was 20.1%.

The explanation for Quaker's profitability improvement lies in the numbers—and the business decisions that lurk behind the numbers. By shedding Snapple and other under-performing food brands, sales were reduced (Exhibit 5.1[a]) but the operating profit margin more than doubled. Manufacturing efficiency gains may have also played a role in the company's margin increase. But there is another part to the story. Fewer food brands means fewer resources tied up in receivables, inventories, and facilities (property, plant, and equipment). Quaker's asset base was considerably more productive in 1999 (US$1.93 of sales per dollar of assets) than it was in 1995 (US$1.15 of sales per asset dollar).

Can Quaker Oats sustain this level of profitability? It is hard to say. Increased manufacturing costs, brand erosion, and competitive price pressures could reduce the company's ROA. For example, an increase in the cost of cereal grains could easily cause the operating margin to decline to 10.0% from its 1999 level of 10.4%. This small change when amplified by the asset turnover would result in ROA declining from 20.1% to 19.3% (= 10.0% × 1.93). To sustain ROA at 20.1%, Quaker would then need to generate an additional US$0.08 of sales per asset dollar (20.1% = 10.0% × 2.01). However, growing sales is always difficult in a mature industry.

Some analysts find it helpful to further decompose ROA by isolating individual factors that contribute to a company's operating profit margin and asset turnover. For example, the operating profit margin for Quaker Oats can be expressed as:

$$Operating\ profit\ margin = \frac{NOPAT}{Sales} = \frac{(Sales - CGS - SG\&A - Other - Taxes)}{Sales}$$

$$= \left(\frac{Sales}{Sales}\right) - \left(\frac{CGS}{Sales}\right) - \left(\frac{SG\&A}{Sales}\right) - \left(\frac{Other}{Sales}\right) - \left(\frac{Taxes}{Sales}\right)$$

$$= 100\% - \left(\frac{CGS}{Sales}\right) - \left(\frac{SG\&A}{Sales}\right) - \left(\frac{Other}{Sales}\right) - \left(\frac{Taxes}{Sales}\right)$$

where, from Exhibit 5.1(a), "CGS" is the company's cost of goods sold expense, "CG&A" is Quaker's selling, general, and administrative expense; "Other" is other expenses and revenues, and "Taxes" is adjusted income tax expense. These margin components (which happen to correspond to the common size earnings statement items we've already described) can help the analyst identify areas where cost reductions have been achieved or where cost improvements are needed.

Using the information in Quaker's 1999 income statement to illustrate the tax expense adjustment, we find that adjusted taxes would equal $184.2 instead of the reported income tax expense of $163.3 shown in the statement. The various adjustments made in arriving at NOPAT also cause the tax component of ROA to differ from the reported figure. The correct figure for taxes is computed by solving:

NOPAT = Sales – CGS – SG&A – Other – Taxes

Substitution for NOPAT and the other statement items yields:

$493.7 = $4,725.2 – $2,136.8 – $1,904.1 – $6.4 – Taxes, meaning that Taxes = $184.2 that year.

Exhibit 5.5 QUAKER OATS COMPANY

ROA Decomposition

(US$ in millions)	1999	1998	1997	1996
Sales	$4,725.2	$4,842.5	$5,015.7	$5,199.0
NOPAT	493.7	413.2	371.2	243.6
Average assets	2,453.3	2,603.7	3,545.7	4,507.4
Operating profit margin (*NOPAT/Sales*)	10.4%	8.5%	7.4%	4.7%
Asset turnover *(Sales/Average assets)*	1.93	1.86	1.41	1.15
ROA = Margin × Asset turnover	20.1%	15.8%	10.4%	5.4%

The asset turnover component of ROA can be decomposed as:

$$\frac{1}{\text{Asset turnover}} = \frac{\text{Average assets}}{\text{Sales}} = \left(\frac{\text{Average current assets} + \text{Average long-term assets}}{\text{Sales}} \right)$$

$$= \left(\frac{\text{Average current assets}}{\text{Sales}} \right) + \left(\frac{\text{Average long-term assets}}{\text{Sales}} \right)$$

$$= \left(\frac{1}{\text{Current asset turnover}} \right) + \left(\frac{1}{\text{Long-term asset turnover}} \right)$$

The **current asset turnover** ratio helps the analyst spot efficiency gains from improved accounts receivable and inventory management, while the **long-term asset turnover** ratio captures information about property, plant, and equipment utilization.

ROA and Competitive Advantage

Our analysis of Quaker's profit performance has thus far revealed that the company's ROA for 1999 was 20.1%, up from 5.4% in 1996. This profitability increase was traced to a combination of higher operating margins and increased asset utilization. Now we want to know how Quaker's profit performance compares with other companies in the industry.

Exhibit 5.6 presents a decomposition of 1999 ROA for Quaker and one of its competitors, Kellogg Company, a manufacturer of ready-to-eat cereals and convenience foods. Also shown are average ROA and component values for the industry—grain mill products—to which Quaker and Kellogg belong. Industry data like these are available from a variety of sources, including Standard & Poor's *Industry Survey*, Robert Morris and Associates' *Annual Statement Studies*, and many online financial information services.

Exhibit 5.6 QUAKER OATS AND THE COMPETITION

1999 ROA Decomposition

	Quaker	Kellogg	Grain Mill Products Industry
Operating profit margin (NOPAT/Sales)	10.4%	9.8%	4.1%
Asset turnover (Sales/Average assets)	1.93	1.42	1.38
Return on assets (ROA)	**20.1%**	**13.9%**	**5.7%**

Quaker Oats was more profitable then Kellogg in 1999, earning an ROA of 20.1% compared to Kellogg's 13.9%. Moreover, both companies beat the industry average ROA of 5.7%. How did Quaker achieve superior profit performance? The ROA decomposition reveals that Quaker's NOPAT margin was 10.4 cents per sales dollar—slightly better than Kellogg's 9.8% margin but considerably above the industry-wide margin of 4.1 cents. A strong operating margin was key to the success of both companies. And the reason Quaker Oats outperformed Kellogg? Better asset turnover. Quaker generated $1.93 in sales per dollar compared to only $1.42 in sales per asset dollar at Kellogg and just $1.38 for the industry.

The key to Quaker's success in 1999 is found in both its profit margin and its asset turnover. Quaker outperformed the competition by earning a higher operating profit margin on each dollar of sales and by generating more sales per asset dollar.

Can Quaker maintain this level of ROA performance? The answer can be found only by identifying Quaker's competitive advantage—that is, the source of its superior operating profit margin and turnover rate—and by determining whether that competitive advantage is sustainable over time. Several factors can explain why companies operating in the same industry—and which therefore are confronting similar economic conditions—can earn markedly different rates of return on their assets. Some companies gain a competitive advantage over rivals by developing unique products or services. Others do so by providing consistent quality or exceptional customer service and convenience. Still others get ahead because of their innovative production technologies, distribution channels, or sales and marketing efforts. The sustainability of these advantages, however, varies.

Competition in an industry continually works to drive down the rate of return on assets toward the competitive floor—that is, the rate of return that would be earned in an economist's "perfectly competitive" industry. This competitive floor is approximated by the yield on long-term government securities (i.e., the **risk-free rate of return**), adjusting upward for the risk of business failure and capital loss in the industry. Companies that consistently earn rates of return above the floor are said to have a **competitive advantage**. However, rates of return that are higher than the industry floor stimulate more competition as existing companies innovate and expand their market reach or as new companies enter the industry. These developments lead to an erosion of profitability and advantage.

To see how these forces work, consider the simplified representation of the ready-to-eat cereals industry comprising four firms in Figure 5.2. Firm A and Firm B earn exactly the same competitive floor rate of return, which we assume to be 12%, but they do so in different ways. Firm A earns a 12% ROA by combining a high margin (say 8%) with low turnover (say 1.5). Firm B, on the other hand, has a low margin (say 2%) and a high turnover (6 times). Despite their differences, both companies achieve the same level of economic success: ROA = 12% = 8% × 1.5 = 2% × 6.

Company C enjoys a competitive advantage that allows it to earn a return greater than 12%; Company D is disadvantaged and earns a return less than 12%.

Company C's superior profitability stems from the wide acceptance of its successful new breakfast cereal (Vita-Flakes) among health-conscious consumers. C's current edge is that Vita-Flakes are unique in the marketplace.

The particular competitive advantage C now enjoys may not persist. Other cereal companies can and will develop products that rival Vita-Flakes in taste and nutritional benefits. As rival products become available, they will compete directly with Vita-Flakes for each consumer dollar, and C's sales volume will thus decline. This will prompt a reduction in C's asset turnover, and it will shift C leftward (dotted arrow)

FIGURE 5.2
ILUSTRATION OF
HOW MARGIN
AND TURNOVER
AFFECT RETURN
ON ASSETS (ROA)

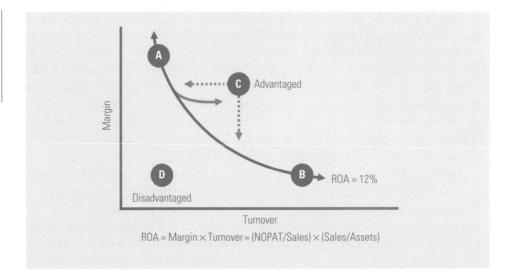

ROA = Margin × Turnover = (NOPAT/Sales) × (Sales/Assets)

in Figure 5.2 toward the competitive ROA of 12%. Of course, C's management is unlikely to ignore the introduction of rival breakfast products. Faced with the threatened loss of its competitive advantage, C could respond by reducing product prices or by increasing advertising expenditures. Both responses could stimulate additional consumer sales and increase turnover, causing a shift back to the right (as depicted by the curved arrow in Figure 5.2). However, price reductions and increased advertising costs also lower the company's NOPAT margin, and thus they produce a downward shift (dotted arrow) toward the competitive ROA floor.

While the challenge to C is sustaining its Vita-Flakes advantage in the face of escalating competition, Company D is facing different challenges. D's current level of profitability is below the industry floor of 12%. Investors and creditors will be reluctant to commit additional financial resources to D unless its profit picture improves. Why? Because D is not currently earning a rate of return large enough to compensate investors for business and financial risk. If D is unable to rectify the situation quickly, its cost of capital will increase, its profit margin will become even lower, and its long-term financial viability may be threatened. What turnaround strategies can D pursue?

According to most observers, there are only two strategies for achieving superior performance in any business. One strategy is product and service **differentiation**; the other is **low-cost leadership**.[3] A differentiation strategy focuses customer attention on "unique" product or service attributes to gain brand loyalty and attractive profit margins. The idea is quite simple: People are willing to pay premium prices for things they value and can't get elsewhere.

Differentiation can take several forms. Examples include advanced technology and performance capabilities, consistent quality, availability in multiple colours or sizes, prompt delivery, technical support services, customer financing, distribution channels, or some other factor of real or perceived importance to customers. Our hypothetical cereal companies, for instance, are likely to focus customer attention on superior taste and nutritional benefits when introducing products intended to compete with Vita-Flakes. High-end retailers like Holt-Renfrew and Nordstrom achieve differentiation by emphasizing customer service, merchandise quality, and a "unique" shopping experience.

A low-cost leadership strategy focuses customer attention on product pricing, often using slogans like "everyday low prices" or "the lowest price in town." The goal is to become the lowest cost producer in the marketplace so that you can underprice the competition, achieve the highest sales volume, and still make a profit on each sale. Companies can attain a low-cost position in various ways. Examples include quantity discount purchases, a lean administrative structure, and production efficiencies from outsourcing or vigorous cost containment. Large retailing companies like Wal-Mart are able to negotiate steep quantity discounts with manufacturers because their size gives them more bargaining power; such discounts then allow the retailer to offer merchandise to customers at comparatively low prices.

Few companies actually pursue one strategy to the exclusion of the other. Most companies try to do both—developing customer loyalty while controlling costs. Understanding the relative emphasis a company places on differentiation versus low-cost leadership can be important for competitive analysis. *Differences in the business strategies companies adopt give rise to economic differences, which are reflected in differences in operating margins, earnings, and asset utilization.* For example, in Figure 5.2 the two cereal companies, A and B, earn exactly the same 12% competitive ROA. Company A achieved this profitability level through a combination of high margin (8%) and low asset turnover (1.5), a combination often associated with companies that adopt a differentiation strategy. Company B achieved the same ROA through a combination of low margin (2%) and high turnover (6), a pattern consistent with low-cost leadership.

The choice confronting D company's management should now be clear. There are three ways D can return to a competitive profit level: (1) improve the operating margin, (2) increase asset turnover (more sales volume or fewer assets), or (3) both. Margin improvements will shift D upward in Figure 5.2, whereas better turnover will shift it horizontally to the right. In both cases, D moves closer to the industry ROA of 12%. So management must choose one path or the other—or a combination of the two. That's all they need to do—and attend to a few million details to do it.

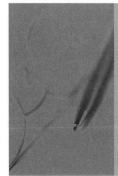

Recap

Not every company in an industry earns the same rate of return on its assets. Some earn more than the industry average ROA while others earn less. Companies that fall below the industry average ROA strive to grow sales, improve operating efficiency, and better manage assets so that they can become competitive again. Those who are fortunate enough to earn more than the industry average ROA struggle to maintain their competitive advantage—through differentiation or low-cost leadership—and to stay on top. This ebb and flow of competition shows up as differences in ROA and in its profit margin and asset turnover components.

Credit Risk and Capital Structure

Credit risk refers to the ability and willingness of a borrower (an individual or organization) to pay its debt. Ability and willingness influence the likelihood that the lender (typically a bank or insurance company) will receive promised principal and interest payments when due. In the corporate arena, two factors must be kept in mind:

- A company's *ability to repay debt* is determined by its capacity to generate cash from operations, asset sales, or external financial markets in excess of its cash needs.

- A company's *willingness to pay* depends on which of the competing cash needs is viewed by management as most pressing at the moment. Those needs include working capital and plant capacity requirements to sustain current operating activities, capital expenditures for new product and service development or market expansion, and shareholder dividends or debt service requirements.

Numerous and interrelated risks influence a company's ability to generate cash. Multinational companies, for example, must cope with possible changes in host government regulations, potential political unrest, and fluctuating currency exchange rates. Domestic companies are exposed to the kind of risk associated with political or demographic changes, recession, inflation, and interest rate fluctuations. Companies within a particular industry confront risks related to technological change, shifting competition, regulation, and availability of raw materials and labour. Management competency, litigation, and the company's strategic direction are additional sources of risk. Each of these risks ultimately affects a company's operating performance, net income, and cash flows. In fact, the cash flow statement—which reports the net amount of cash generated or used by operating, investing, and financing activities—is an important source of information for analyzing a company's credit risk.

For instance, the comparative cash flow statements for Quaker Oats in Exhibit 5.3(a) reveal strong, and growing, operating cash flows. The company's US$631 million of operating cash flows in 1999 were more than sufficient to cover its net investing needs (US$160 million), leaving a cash surplus of US$471 million ($631 – $160) available for other purposes. How did the company use this cash surplus? Quaker spent US$156 million that year on cash dividend payments and US$382 million on stock repurchases while also paying down its short-term and long-term debt by over US$60 million. Some of the money for these payments came from other financing activities (US$83 million) and Quaker's existing cash reserves (US$44 million). Based on this cursory analysis, it appears that Quaker is a low credit risk company because it generates operating cash flows substantially in excess of what is required to sustain its business activities.

Although cash flow statements contain information enabling a user to assess a company's credit risk, financial ratios are also useful for this purpose. *Credit risk analysis using financial ratios typically involves an assessment of liquidity and solvency.* **Liquidity** refers to the company's *short-term* ability to generate cash for working capital needs and immediate debt repayment needs. **Solvency** refers to the *long-term* ability to generate cash internally or from external sources in order to satisfy plant capacity needs, fuel growth, and repay debt when due. Our discussion of financial ratios as an analytical tool for assessing credit risk is based on the distinction between concerns for short-term liquidity and for long-term solvency.

Short-Term Liquidity

Short-term liquidity problems arise because operating cash inflows don't match outflows. To illustrate the mismatching problem, let's consider the *operating cycle* of a retailer like Wal-Mart. It acquires merchandise from suppliers on credit, promising to pay within 30 to 60 days. The merchandise is first shipped to Wal-Mart warehouses. Later it is sent on to Wal-Mart stores where it is displayed for purchase and promoted through in-store and regular advertising. Wal-Mart pays for some transportation, labour, and advertising costs immediately and delays payment of other costs. Eventually, Wal-Mart sells the merchandise to customers, who pay by cash or credit card; receivables (if any) are collected some time later; and the company then pays the remaining amounts owed to suppliers and others. Liquidity problems arise when cash inflows from customers lag behind the cash outflows to employees, suppliers, and others.

The operating cycle must not only generate sufficient cash to supply working capital needs, it must also provide cash to service debt as payments become due. For some companies, interest expense is their largest single cost. Such companies may discover that operating cash flows are sufficient to cover periodic interest payments but that the need to repay loan principal causes a liquidity problem. Companies that are not liquid—and are therefore not able to pay obligations as they come due—may be forced into bankruptcy.

One index of a company's short-term liquidity is its **current ratio:**

$$\text{Current ratio} = \frac{\text{Current assets}}{\text{Current liabilities}}$$

Current assets include cash and "near cash" items. For example, receivables become cash as they are collected, so they are only one step removed from cash. Inventories are converted into cash in two steps:

1. They must be sold, usually on credit.
2. The resulting receivable must later be collected.

By including receivables and inventory in current assets, the current ratio reflects existing cash as well as amounts soon to be converted to cash in the normal operating cycle.

A more short-run reflection of liquidity is the **quick ratio:**

$$\text{Quick ratio} = \frac{\text{Cash + Marketable securities + Receivables}}{\text{Current liabilities}}$$

Few businesses can instantaneously convert their inventories into cash. So the quick ratio does not include inventory in the numerator and thus provides a measure of *very* immediate liquidity.

Activity ratios tell us how efficiently the company is using its assets. Activity ratios can highlight causes for operating cash flow mismatches. For example, the **accounts receivable turnover** ratio is an activity ratio that can help analysts determine whether receivables are excessive when compared to existing levels of credit sales:

$$\text{Accounts receivable turnover} = \frac{\text{Net credit sales}}{\text{Average accounts receivable}}$$

To illustrate how to interpret this ratio, suppose annual credit sales totalled $10 million and that customer accounts receivable were $2 million at the beginning of the year and $3 million at year-end. The accounts receivable turnover ratio value is calculated as:

$$\frac{\$10}{(\$2 + \$3)/2} = 4 \text{ times per year}$$

The average annual balance of receivables ($2.5 million) represents one-fourth of yearly credit sales ($2.5/$10 = 1/4), so receivables must turn over four times per year.

The accounts receivable turnover ratio can also be used by the analyst to spot changes in customer payment patterns. For example, dividing the accounts receivable turnover ratio into 365 days tells us the number of days that the average customer receivable is "on the books" before it is collected—that is:

Most companies just report a single "Sales" number that is the sum of cash plus credit sales. Using total "Sales" instead of "Credit sales" in the accounts receivable turnover calculation can sometimes produce misleading results. Companies for which cash sales comprise a large proportion of total "Sales" will have relatively low accounts receivable balances and correspondingly large receivable turnover ratios. Fortunately, cash sales are rare in a surprisingly large number of businesses today. In certain industries like discount retailing, however, cash sales are the rule rather than the exception.

$$\text{Days accounts receivable outstanding} = \frac{365 \text{ days}}{\text{Accounts receivable turnover}} = \frac{365 \text{ days}}{4}$$
$$= 91.25 \text{ days}$$

In our example, the average accounts receivable is collected about 91 days after the credit sale occurs. This is the same as saying accounts receivable "turn over" four times per year.

Another activity ratio is the **inventory turnover ratio**, which tells us how effectively inventories are managed:

$$\text{Inventory turnover} = \frac{\text{Cost of goods sold}}{\text{Average inventory}}$$

Assume that beginning inventory was $8 million, that year-end inventory was $9 million, and that cost of goods sold was $43.35 million. Therefore, inventory turnover is:

$$\frac{\$43.350}{(\$8 + \$9)/2} = 5.1 \text{ times per year}$$

Amazon.com and other e-commerce retailing companies exhibit large inventory turnover ratios as a consequence of adopting business models that emphasize high sales volume and avoid the need to stock inventory in brick-and-mortar stores. As a result, Amazon's inventory turnover ratio (24.4 in 1998) has a large numerator (US$476 million, reflecting high volume) and a small denominator (US$19.5 million, reflecting low inventory levels).

The inventory turnover ratio can also be used to determine the average **days inventory held** as follows:

$$\text{Days inventory held} = \frac{365 \text{ days}}{\text{Inventory turnover}} = \frac{365 \text{ days}}{5.1} = 71.57 \text{ days}$$

In our example, it takes about 72 days for inventory to move from the company to its customers. In other words, average inventory is sufficient to cover almost 72 days of customer sales. This is just another way of saying that inventory turns over 5.1 times (i.e., 365 days/71.57 days) each year.

The **accounts payable turnover** ratio—and its **days payable outstanding** counterpart—helps the analyst understand the company's pattern of payments to suppliers:

$$\text{Accounts payable turnover} = \frac{\text{Inventory purchases}}{\text{Average accounts payable}}$$

$$\text{Days accounts payable outstanding} = \frac{365 \text{ days}}{\text{Accounts payable turnover}}$$

Suppose trade accounts payable averaged $7.4 million and inventory purchases totalled $44.350 million during the year. The accounts payable turnover ratio would then equal almost 6 (i.e., turnover occurs six times per year), and the days accounts payable outstanding would be almost 61 days. (You should verify both calculations!) *More timely payment of accounts payable would lead to a lower average payable balance, a higher turnover ratio, and fewer days outstanding.*

Let's piece these activity ratios together to get a picture that will help us analyze the financial condition of our company.

- Inventory remains on hand for about 72 days.

For retail companies like Amazon.com and Wal-Mart, inventory purchases equal cost of goods sold expense plus the year's inventory increase—that is, $44.350 = $43.350 + ($9 – $8) in our example.

Financial Reporting and Analysis

- Inventory is sold and another 91 days elapse before cash is collected from the customer.
- Suppliers are paid about 60 days after inventory is purchased.

Cash outflows and inflows seem dangerously mismatched by 103 days (72 + 91 − 60). This hypothetical company's **operating cycle** spans 163 days—that is how long it takes to sell inventory (72 days) and collect cash from the customers (91 days). But the company pays for inventory purchases in just 60 days, so its **cash cycle** is 103 days—suppliers are paid 103 days before the company has received cash from product sales. This company may face a short-term liquidity problem because cash outflows and inflows are mismatched by 103 days. It must rely on other cash sources—like bank notes—to sustain its operating working capital requirements over the 103-day gap.

Exhibit 5.7 reports the operating cycle and cash cycle for three retailers: Amazon.com, Wal-Mart, and Nordstrom. Each company has adopted a different business model, and differences in these business models show up as differences in working capital activity ratios, operating cycles, and cash cycles. Amazon.com is an e-commerce retailer that doesn't have to stock inventory on store shelves. Consequently, inventory levels at Amazon.com are quite low—just 15.0 days. Amazon's customers pay by bank credit card so Amazon gets cash (from the customer's credit card company) almost instantaneously when it makes a sale. The operating cycle at Amazon.com is 15.0 days but the cash cycle is *minus* 139.7 days. That's because Amazon waits 154.7 days after buying inventory to pay its suppliers.

Wal-Mart and Nordstrom are traditional brick-and-mortar retailers that target different market segments. Wal-Mart carries a broad line of merchandise, emphasizes low prices, and most customers pay cash or use a credit card. Nordstrom is known for its fashion apparel and shoes. The company emphasizes product quality and customer service, including its in-store credit card. Wal-Mart has a 76.1 day operating cycle compared to 163.5 days at Nordstrom. It takes Nordstrom longer to sell inventory (120.9 days compared to 72.1 days at Wal-Mart), and longer to collect cash from customers once the sale has been made (42.6 days, compared to 4.0 days at Wal-Mart). However, both companies pay suppliers in about 34 days. So the difference in cash cycle at the two companies— 42.7 days at Wal-Mart compared to 129.2 days at Nordstrom—can be traced back to Nordstrom's emphasis on fashion apparel (slower to sell) and its in-store

The calculation of inventory turnover and days inventory held for a manufacturing firm is more complicated than for the merchandising firm illustrated here. That's because inventory in a manufacturing firm must pass through three stages of the operating cycle:

1. As *raw material*, from purchase to the start of production.
2. As *work-in-process*, over the length of the production cycle.
3. As *finished goods*, from completion of production until it is sold.

Inventory in a merchandising firm passes only through Stage 3.

To calculate how long inventory is held at each stage, analysts use the following:

Raw materials: 365 days × Average raw materials inventory/Raw materials used

Work-in-process: 365 days × Average work-in-process inventory/Cost of goods manufactured

Finished goods: 365 days × Average finished goods inventory/Cost of goods sold

Cost of goods sold and the breakdown of inventory into raw materials, work-in-process, and finished goods is reported in the financial statements. Cost of goods manufactured can be calculated as "cost of goods sold" *plus* ending "finished goods inventory" *minus* beginning "finished goods inventory." However, the amount of raw materials used in production is rarely disclosed in financial statements. It may be available in the company's fact book or obtained by contacting the company's investor relations group.

Exhibit 5.7 AMAZON.COM, WAL-MART, AND NORDSTROM

Comparison of 1998 Operating and Cash Cycles

	Amazon.com	Wal-Mart	Nordstrom
Working capital activity ratios:			
1. Days inventory held	15.0	72.1	120.9
2. Days accounts receivable outstanding	0.0	4.0	42.6
3. Days accounts payable outstanding	154.7	33.4	34.3
Operating cycle (1 + 2)	15.0	76.1	163.5
Cash cycle (1 + 2 − 3)	(139.7)	42.7	129.2

credit card (slower to collect cash). Both companies must carefully manage their short-term liquidity because cash outflows and inflows are mismatched.

Let's return to our analysis of the Quaker Oats Company. Exhibit 5.8 reports data on the company's short-term liquidity ratios. Quaker's current ratio was 1.06 in 1999, down from 1.20 two years earlier. The quick ratio was 0.57 in 1999, suggesting some improvements since 1997. The quick ratio means cash and receivables at Quaker were sufficient to cover 57% of the company's 1999 current liabilities. Adding inventories further improves the picture—the current ratio of 1.06 means that total current assets covered 106% of Quaker's current liabilities.

Quaker's credit customers were paying more promptly in 1999 than they did in 1997, with days receivable outstanding at 20.8 compared to 21.9 two years earlier. However, Quaker was paying its bills less promptly—days payable outstanding rose from 28.4 in 1997 to 33.1 in 1999. Inventory turnover also deteriorated, and inventory levels were up from 37.8 days of inventory held in 1997 to 45.1 days in 1999.

There is some misalignment of operating cash flows, since payments to suppliers occur about 33 days after purchase; in contrast, it takes 66 days (20.8 + 45.1) to generate a sale and collect cash from customers. In view of the company's overall level of positive operating cash flows, this misalignment is unlikely to cause concerns.

Long-Term Solvency
Solvency refers to the ability of a company to generate a stream of cash inflows sufficient to maintain its productive capacity and still meet the interest and principal payments on its long-term debt. A company that cannot make timely payments in the amount required becomes insolvent and may be compelled to reorganize or liquidate.

Debt ratios provide information about the amount of long-term debt in a company's financial structure. The more a company relies on long-term borrowing to finance its business activities, the higher its debt ratio and the greater the long-term solvency risk. There are several variations in debt ratios. Two commonly used ratios are:

$$\text{Long-term debt to assets} = \frac{\text{Long-term debt}}{\text{Total assets}}$$

$$\text{Long-term debt to tangible assets} = \frac{\text{Long-term debt}}{\text{Total tangible assets}}$$

Exhibit 5.8 QUAKER OATS COMPANY
Credit Risk Analysis: Short-Term Liquidity

	1999	1998	1997
Current ratio	1.06	1.10	1.20
Quick ratio	0.57	0.63	0.41
Working capital activity ratios			
1. Days inventory held	45.1	39.8	37.8
2. Days accounts receivable outstanding	20.8	22.2	21.9
3. Days accounts payable outstanding	33.1	27.9	28.4
Operating cycle (1 + 2)	65.9	62.0	59.7
Cash cycle (1 + 2 − 3)	32.8	34.1	31.3

Suppose a company has $20 million of outstanding long-term debt and $100 million of total assets, of which $35 million are intangibles like goodwill or purchased patents, trademarks, or copyrights. The two debt ratios would be:

$$\text{Long-term debt to assets} = \frac{\$20}{\$100} = 0.200$$

$$\text{Long-term debt to tangible assets} = \frac{\$20}{\$100 - \$35} = 0.308$$

These results tell us that only 20 cents of each asset dollar was financed using long-term debt. The remaining 80 cents came from other sources—internally generated resources, short-term borrowing, or equity capital in the form of common and preferred stock. This level of debt—only 20 cents of each asset dollar—would be surprisingly high for a discount retailer like Wal-Mart but surprisingly low for an electric utility company. Retailers use short-term debt and trade credit to finance their inventory purchases, and they usually lease (but don't own) their retail stores. Electric utilities, on the other hand, rely on long-term debt to support their sizable investment in power-generating facilities and transmission lines. Electric utilities also have relatively predictable operating cash flows because energy demand is reasonably stable and competition is limited by regulators. Companies whose sales fluctuate widely due to changing economic conditions generally prefer to avoid debt, since the fixed interest charges are difficult to meet during bad times. These cyclical companies tend to have smaller debt-to-asset ratios.

Analysts devote considerable attention to refining both the numerator and denominator of debt ratios. For example, analysts include in the numerator hybrid securities having the cash flow characteristics of debt even though these hybrids are not classified as long-term debt on the balance sheet. Operating leases and other off-balance-sheet obligations are routinely included as debt equivalents. The exclusion of intangible assets from the ratio's denominator is also common. This adjustment is intended to remove "soft" assets—those difficult to value reliably—from the analysis.

Comparative debt ratios for Quaker Oats are shown in Exhibit 5.9. The company's ratio of long-term debt to total assets was 0.33 in 1999, a slight decrease from the 0.37 level in 1997. The ratio of long-term debt to tangible assets stood at 0.37, also down from 0.42 in 1997. The two ratios moved in the same direction and are consistent with a manufacturing company that requires significant long-term financing to support its business and yet is financially sound.

Although debt ratios are useful for understanding the financial structure of a company, they provide no information about its ability to generate a stream of inflows sufficient to make principal and interest payments. One financial ratio commonly used for this purpose is the **interest coverage ratio**:

$$\text{Interest coverage} = \frac{\text{Operating income before taxes and interest}}{\text{Interest expense}}$$

This ratio indicates how many times interest expense is covered by operating profits before taxes and interest are factored in. It reflects the cushion between operating profit inflows and required interest payments. If the company must also make periodic principal payments, then the analyst could include those amounts in the calculation.

Many analysts use an *adjusted* operating income figure that removes nonoperating and nonrecurring items from reported income and that corrects for accounting quality distortions. But, be careful, since terms like "adjusted income" may be used in other ways as well. See Chapter 1's description of Nortel Networks' "supplementary measure of net earnings."

Exhibit 5.9 QUAKER OATS COMPANY

Credit Risk Analysis: Long-Term Solvency

	1999	1998	1997
Ratio of long-term debt to assets	0.33	0.36	0.37
Ratio of long-term debt to tangible assets	0.37	0.39	0.42
Interest coverage ratio	11.05	8.56	5.97
Ratio of operating cash flow to total liabilities	0.29	0.22	0.20

Suppose a company has $200 million of operating income before taxes and interest, and $50 million of interest expense. The company's **interest coverage ratio** is:

$$\frac{\$200}{\$50} = 4$$

This shows that operating profit is four times larger than interest expense—a substantial cushion for the lender. But now suppose our company is also required to make a $100 million debt principal payment. The revised interest coverage ratio is:

$$\frac{\$200}{\$50 + \$100} = 1.33$$

When required debt payments are factored in, the lender's cushion now looks thin.

A criticism of the traditional interest coverage ratio is that it uses earnings rather than operating cash flows in the numerator. Some analysts prefer to compute a **cash flow coverage ratio** in which the numerator represents operating cash flows before interest and tax payments are factored in. When operating profits and cash flows move in tandem, both versions of the ratio will yield similar results. However, when the two measures do diverge—as during a period of rapid growth—income may be a poor substitute for cash flow, and in that case the cash flow coverage ratio is preferable.

Another useful measure of long-term solvency compares **operating cash flow** to the company's **total liabilities** (excluding deferred taxes):

$$\frac{\text{Operating cash flow}}{\text{to total liabilities}} = \frac{\text{Cash flow from continuing operations}}{\text{Average current liabilities plus long-term debt}}$$

This ratio shows the ability of a company to generate cash from operations in order to service both short-term and long-term borrowings.

Referring to Exhibit 5.9, we see an interest coverage ratio of 11.05 in 1999—a significant improvement from the 5.97 in 1997. Two factors help explain this. Net income was up in 1999 compared to that in 1997, and interest expense was down because Quaker repaid some of the long-term borrowing used to finance its Snapple purchase. As a result, interest coverage in 1999 benefited from a larger income flow and a lower level of interest expense.

Quaker's ratio of operating cash flow to total liabilities clearly demonstrates why the company is regarded by most analysts as financially solvent and a low credit risk. Operating cash flow in 1999 was sufficient to repay 29% of the company's total debt, up somewhat from the 1997 level. It is remarkable that a company of Quaker's size can generate enough cash from operations to repay all borrowings in three and one-half years (1 year/0.29 repayment per year = 3.45 years).

Recap

When lenders want to know about a company's ability to pay debts on time, they assess its credit risk. A cash flow statement is often the starting point for credit risk assessment because it shows the company's operating cash flows along with its financing and investment needs. A company with low credit risk generates operating cash flows substantially in excess of what are required to sustain its business activities. Liquidity and solvency ratios are additional tools the lender can use to assess credit risk.

Return on Equity and Financial Leverage

Profitability and credit risk both influence the return that common shareholders earn on their investment in the company. To see how, let's look at what happens when a successful company borrows money to fund its growth.

ParsTech develops and distributes home financial planning software nationwide. Assume the company has $1 million in assets and no debt—ParsTech is an "all equity" firm. Earnings in 2001 are $150,000 and the entire amount is paid to shareholders as a dividend. These events are summarized in the first row of Exhibit 5.10.

ParsTech's ROA for 2001 is 15% ($150,000 in earnings/$1 million in assets). Since the company has no debt, all the earnings belong to shareholders, so **return on common equity** (ROCE) is also 15% ($150,000 in earnings/$1 million in common equity).

Early in 2002, the company borrows $1 million to expand its manufacturing, distribution, and customer support facilities. Lenders charge only 10% interest on the loan because the company has steady cash flows and a track record of successful new product introductions.

Strong consumer demand plus expanded plant capacity produce a banner year for the company. Earnings before interest total $300,000 in 2002, and ParsTech's ROA is again 15% (shown in the second row of Exhibit 5.10). Who gets the $300,000? Lenders must receive their share—$100,000 in interest on the loan—but the rest belongs to common shareholders. Shareholders receive $200,000 and ROCE is 20%.

Why did ROCE increase while ROA was unchanged? The answer is **financial leverage**. ParsTech borrowed $1 million at 10% (or $100,000 annual interest) but earned 15% (or $150,000) on the money. After the company paid interest charges, common shareholders gained $50,000 without investing more of their own money in the company. Financial leverage benefits shareholders whenever the cost of debt

Exhibit 5.10 PARSTECH

Financial Leverage

	Earnings Before Interest[1]	Assets	Common Shareholders' Equity	Return on Assets (ROA)	Interest Charges	Net Income Available to Common Stockholders	Return on Common Equity (ROCE)
2001	$150,000	$1 million	$1 million	15%	—	$150,000	15%
2002	300,000	2 million	1 million	15	$100,000	200,000	20
2003	450,000	3 million	1 million	15	300,000	150,000	15

[1]Earnings are before interest but after taxes, and they are distributed to lenders (as interest) and shareholders (as dividends) each year.

More precisely, it's the *after-tax* cost of debt that must be less than what the company earns on borrowed funds. If the corporate income tax rate is 35%, ParsTech has an after-tax cost of debt of 6.5% [10% × (1 – 0.35)] even though lenders are charging 10% interest. Financial leverage benefits ParsTech shareholders as long as the company earns more than 6.5% after tax on its debt-financed investment.

(10% in our example) is less than what the company earns on the borrowed funds (15% in our example).

The downside here, however, is that financial leverage can sometimes be costly to shareholders. For instance, suppose that ParsTech borrows another $1 million in 2003 to further expand its facilities. But this time, lenders assign a higher credit risk to the company and charge 20% interest. Earnings before interest but after taxes are $450,000 in 2003, and ParsTech's ROA is again 15%. What is ROCE?

Now lenders receive $300,000 in interest—$100,000 for the first loan plus $200,000 for the second—leaving only $150,000 of earnings for common shareholders. ROCE in 2003 is 15% ($150,000/$1 million in common equity), down from the previous year. Stockholders are no better off now than they were two years earlier when the company was smaller and earnings were lower. What happened?

The second loan cost more (20% or $200,000 in annual interest) than ParsTech was able to earn ($150,000) on the borrowed funds, and shareholders had to make up the difference. *Financial leverage is beneficial—but only when the company earns more than the incremental after-tax cost of debt.* If the cost of debt becomes too high, increasing leverage can actually harm shareholders.

If you want to gauge a company's profit performance from its shareholders' viewpoint, use ROCE.

$$ROCE = \frac{\text{Net income available to common shareholders}}{\text{Average common shareholders' equity}}$$

ROCE measures a company's performance in using capital provided by common shareholders to generate earnings.[4] It explicitly considers how the company's assets are financed. Interest charged on loans and dividends on preferred stock are both subtracted in arriving at "Net income available to common shareholders." The capital provided by common shareholders during the period can be computed by averaging the total capital attributable to the common shares at the beginning and end of the period. For example, using the data in Exhibits 5.1(a) and 5.2(a), the ROCE for Quaker Oats in 1999 is:

$$ROCE = \frac{\text{Net income} - \text{Restructuring charges and gains} - \text{Preferred dividends}}{\text{Average common shareholders' equity}}$$

$$= \frac{\$455.0 - \$1.5 - \$4.4}{(\$158.8 + \$102.6)/2} = \frac{\$449.1}{\$130.7} = 3.436 \text{ or } 343.6\%$$

where $455.0 is reported net income, $1.5 is the after-tax restructuring charges and gains (i.e., $2.3 × 65%), and $4.4 is preferred dividends. A 35% tax rate has been assumed. The restructuring charges and gains are eliminated from reported net income so that ROCE reflects only continuing operations. Quaker's ROCE was uncommonly high in 1999 compared to the industry average of 12.0% or the company's 14.8% ROCE in 1996. The reason? Common shareholders' equity was reduced by about US$1.3 billion when Quaker sold Snapple back in 1997. Average common shareholders' equity was US$131 million in 1999, compared to US$1,155 million in 1996. This smaller equity base, when combined with strong earnings, produced an exceptionally high ROCE.

Components of ROCE

We can break ROCE into several components to aid in our interpretation, much as we did earlier with ROA. The components of ROCE are ROA, common earnings leverage, and financial leverage:

ROCE = ROA × Common earnings leverage × Financial structure leverage

$$= \left(\frac{\text{NOPAT}}{\text{Average assets}}\right) \times \left(\frac{\text{Net income available to common shareholders}}{\text{NOPAT}}\right)$$

$$\times \left(\frac{\text{Average assets}}{\text{Average common shareholders' equity}}\right)$$

$$= \frac{\text{Net income available to common shareholders}}{\text{Average common shareholders' equity}}$$

ROA measures the profitability of operations before considering how the company's assets are financed. The **common earnings leverage ratio** shows the proportion of NOPAT (net operating profits before interest but after taxes) that belongs to common shareholders. The **financial structure leverage ratio** measures the degree to which the company uses common shareholders' capital to finance assets.

The ROCE breakdown for Quaker Oats in 1999 is:

ROCE = ROA × Common earnings leverage × Financial structure leverage

$$= \left(\frac{\$493.7}{(\$2,396.2 + \$2,510.3)/2}\right) \times \left(\frac{\$449.1}{\$493.7}\right) \times \left(\frac{(\$2,510.3 + \$2,396.2)/2}{(\$158.8 + \$102.6)/2}\right)$$

$$= 0.2012 \times 0.910 \times 18.7701$$

$$= 3.436 \text{ or } 343.6\%$$

Quaker's higher ROCE (343.6%) compared to ROA (20.1%) occurred because the company had a lot of debt in its financial structure, resulting in a high financial structure leverage ratio (18.77). (Recall from Exhibit 5.2(c) that common shareholders' equity represented only 6.6% of total assets in 1999.) Interest on this debt contributed to a moderate common earnings leverage ratio (0.910). The two factors in combination produced a return on common equity that was 17.1 times (0.910 × 18.770) greater than what the company earned on all assets (20.1% ROA).

To see how the components of ROCE work together, consider two companies—NoDebt and HiDebt—both having $2 million in assets. NoDebt raised all its capital from common shareholders; HiDebt borrowed $1 million at 10% interest. Both companies pay income taxes at a combined federal and provincial rate of 40%.

Exhibit 5.11 shows how the two companies compare in different earnings years. Let's start with a good earnings year, one in which both companies earn $240,000 before interest but after taxes. This represents an ROA of 12% for both companies, and 12% is also NoDebt's ROCE. HiDebt's ROCE is 18%, since $180,000 of earnings ($240,000 – $60,000) is available to common shareholders. Leverage increased the return to HiDebt's shareholders because the capital contributed by lenders earned 12% but required an after-tax interest payment of only 6%—that is, (1 – 40%) × 10%. The extra 6% earned on each borrowed dollar of assets increased the return to common shareholders.

But what happens when earnings are low? That situation is illustrated by the bad earnings year shown in Exhibit 5.11. Both companies earn $60,000 before interest but after taxes, for a 3% ROA. All of these earnings are available to NoDebt shareholders, so ROCE at the company is also 3%. At HiDebt, after-tax interest charges wipe out earnings and ROCE becomes 0% because there's nothing left for shareholders. HiDebt earns 3% on each asset dollar but must pay 6% to lenders for each dollar borrowed. Here leverage decreases the return to common equity.

Exhibit 5.11 NODEBT AND HIDEBT

Profitability and Financial Leverage

	Total Assets	Shareholders' Equity	Earnings Before Interest[1]	After-Tax Interest	Available to Common Shareholders	ROA	ROCE
Good Earnings Year							
HiDebt	$2 million	$1 million	$240,000	$60,000	$180,000	12.0%	18.0%
NoDebt	2 million	2 million	240,000	—	240,000	12.0	12.0
Neutral Earnings Year							
HiDebt	2 million	1 million	120,000	60,000	60,000	6.0	6.0
NoDebt	2 million	2 million	120,000	—	120,000	6.0	6.0
Bad Earnings Year							
HiDebt	2 million	1 million	60,000	60,000	—	3.0	0.0
NoDebt	2 million	2 million	60,000	—	60,000	3.0	3.0

[1]Earnings are before interest but after taxes. HiDebt has after-tax interest charges of $60,000—that is, $1 million × 10% × (1 – 40%)—each year.

In the neutral year, leverage neither helps nor hurts shareholders. That's because the 6% return earned on each asset dollar just equals the 6% after-tax cost of borrowing. Figure 5.3 illustrates the key results from this example.

FIGURE 5.3
FINANCIAL LEVERAGE AND ROCE

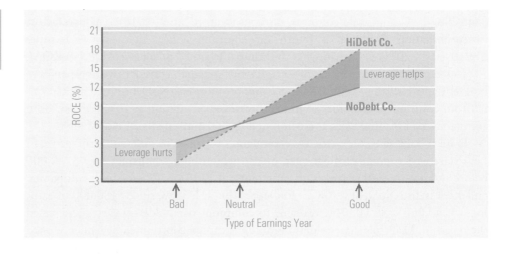

Recap

Financial leverage works two ways. It can make good years better by increasing the shareholders' return, but it can also make bad years worse by decreasing the shareholders' return. It all depends on whether the company earns more on each borrowed dollar than it pays out in interest.

Exhibit 5.12 MARCONI COMMUNICATIONS

GAAP Earnings, "Pro forma" Earnings, EBITDA, and "Cash" Earnings

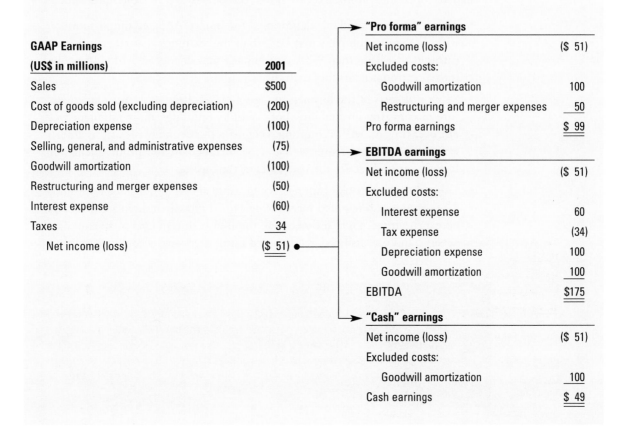

GAAP Earnings

(US$ in millions)	2001
Sales	$500
Cost of goods sold (excluding depreciation)	(200)
Depreciation expense	(100)
Selling, general, and administrative expenses	(75)
Goodwill amortization	(100)
Restructuring and merger expenses	(50)
Interest expense	(60)
Taxes	34
Net income (loss)	($ 51)

"Pro forma" earnings

Net income (loss)	($ 51)
Excluded costs:	
Goodwill amortization	100
Restructuring and merger expenses	50
Pro forma earnings	$ 99

EBITDA earnings

Net income (loss)	($ 51)
Excluded costs:	
Interest expense	60
Tax expense	(34)
Depreciation expense	100
Goodwill amortization	100
EBITDA	$175

"Cash" earnings

Net income (loss)	($ 51)
Excluded costs:	
Goodwill amortization	100
Cash earnings	$ 49

profitability. Skeptics argue that "pro forma" profits are nothing more than EEBS—earnings excluding bad stuff![6]

"Cash" earnings also emerged in the late 1990s as a term used to describe GAAP earnings without goodwill amortization, although it is sometimes mistakenly used as a synonym for EBITDA. Goodwill is now a significant balance sheet asset for many U.S. companies, often representing more than 50% of total assets. The growing importance of goodwill on balance sheets reflects a shift in the economy away from companies built around physical capital ("bricks and mortar") and toward companies built around intellectual capital (knowledge and information). As more companies grow through buying other firms, and more goodwill accumulates on the balance sheet, GAAP earnings fall because of escalating goodwill amortization. "Cash" earnings ignore the goodwill charge to income and thus provide, proponents argue, a clearer picture of profitability for acquisitive growth companies. In fact, the Accounting Standards Board has eliminated the requirement for amortizing goodwill.[7]

Why are companies resorting to EBITDA and "pro forma" earnings instead of just highlighting their GAAP earnings performance? The answer is simple—impression management! It's a whole lot easier to transform a GAAP loss into a "profit" by changing how profits are measured rather than by changing the economics of the business itself. Just cross out a few

Accounting goodwill arises when one company purchases another, and the price paid exceeds the fair market value of the seller's bricks-and-mortar net assets (see Chapter 16). Suppose Bidder.com bought Target.com for $40 million cash. Target's net bricks-and-mortar assets—cash, receivables, inventories, buildings, and equipment *minus* current liabilities and debt—total only $5 million. Why is Bidder willing to pay $35 million more than the book value of Target's net assets? Because Bidder will get access to a valuable technology, subscriber base, or market opportunity that is not currently reflected on Target's balance sheet. The *excess* purchase price ($35 million) will show up on Bidder's books as goodwill, which will—if it is impaired—be charged against future earnings.

expense items here and there, and suddenly the business looks profitable again. Sometimes the adjustments are well-intentioned attempts to describe the company's sustainable operating profits and cash flows. But not always. In either case, remember:

- There are no standard definitions for non-GAAP earnings numbers. EBITDA at one company may be "pro forma" earnings at another and "cash" earnings at still another. Worse, a company may change its EBITDA or "pro forma" earnings definition each quarter.

- Some real costs of the business are ignored, resulting in an incomplete picture of company profitability. For example, buildings and equipment wear out over time. GAAP accounting recognizes this economic reality as amortization expense and requires that it be included in the profit calculation. Ignoring it understates the true costs of the business.

- Using these non-GAAP earnings as a measure of cash flow can be misleading. They ignore cash required for working capital growth and replacement capital expenditures. They also overlook the non-cash elements of revenues and expense and can easily be manipulated using aggressive accounting policies.

Recap

Despite the growing acceptance of these non-GAAP profit measures on Bay Street, in corporate boardrooms, and among credit analysts, informed financial statement readers must be wary and look behind the numbers to understand what's really going on in the business. For the credit analyst, the message is simple: You can't buy a cup of coffee with EBITDA, "pro forma" earnings, or "cash" earnings. It takes real cash!

Summary

Financial ratios, along with common size and trend statements, provide analysts with powerful tools for tracking a company's performance over time, for making comparisons among different companies, and for assessing compliance with contractual benchmarks.

Alternative accounting methods can produce very different balance sheet and income statement figures, and as a result, numerous financial ratios can be affected. Analysts must be alert to this possibility and know how to recognize when differences in the GAAP accounting methods that a company uses, rather than economic fundamentals, are affecting the analysis.

Another problem arises because under GAAP, fixed assets are measured using the historical cost convention. Two companies with identical assets that were purchased at different times will show those assets at different amounts. The company with the older (presumably lower cost) assets would likely report a higher ROA as well as a higher asset turnover ratio. Here, too, the analyst must guard against accounting distortions that mask economic fundamentals.

These and other accounting influences complicate financial analysis and the interpretation of differences in ratios. That's why we examine the effects of accounting method choices, inflation, and other potential distortions of reported financial statement numbers in subsequent chapters.

Exercises

E5-1 Inventory turnover

Motley Company's merchandise inventory and other related accounts for 2001 follow:

Sales	$3,000,000
Cost of goods sold	2,200,000
Merchandise inventory	
Beginning of year	500,000
End of year	600,000

Required:

Assuming that the buildup of merchandise inventory was relatively constant during the year, how many times did the merchandise inventory turn over during 2001?

E5-2 Receivable and inventory turnover

Selected data of the Islander Company follow:

	As of December 31,	
Balance Sheet Data	**2001**	**2000**
Accounts receivable	$ 500,000	$ 470,000
Allowance for doubtful accounts	(25,000)	(20,000)
Net accounts receivable	$ 475,000	$ 450,000
Inventories—lower of cost or market	$ 600,000	$ 550,000

	Year Ended December 31,	
Income Statement Data	**2001**	**2000**
Net credit sales	$2,500,000	$2,200,000
Net cash sales	500,000	400,000
Net sales	$3,000,000	$2,600,000
Cost of goods sold	$2,000,000	$1,800,000
Selling, general, and administrative expenses	300,000	270,000
Other	50,000	30,000
Total operating expenses	$2,350,000	$2,100,000

Required:

1. What is the accounts receivable turnover for 2001?
2. What is the inventory turnover for 2001?

E5-3 Inventory turnover

On January 1, 2001, River Company's beginning inventory was $400,000. During 2001, the company purchased $1,900,000 of additional inventory, and on December 31, 2001, River's ending inventory was $500,000.

Required:

What is the inventory turnover for 2001?

E5-4 Receivable turnover

Utica Company's net accounts receivable was $250,000 at December 31, 2001, and $300,000 at December 31, 2002. Net cash sales for 2002 were $100,000. The accounts receivable turnover for 2002 was 5.0, and this turnover figure was computed from net credit sales for the year.

Required:

What were Utica's total net sales for 2002?

E5-5 Current and quick ratios

Todd Corporation wrote off $100,000 of obsolete inventory at December 31, 2001.

Required:

What effect did this writeoff have on the company's 2001 current and quick ratios?

E5-6 Current ratio

Gil Corporation has current assets of $90,000 and current liabilities of $180,000.

Required:

Compute the effect of each of the following transactions on Gil's current ratio:

1. Refinancing a $30,000 long-term mortgage with a short-term note
2. Purchasing $50,000 of merchandise inventory with short-term accounts payable
3. Paying $20,000 of short-term accounts payable
4. Collecting $10,000 of short-term accounts receivable

E5-7 Interest coverage

The following data were taken from the financial records of Glum Corporation for 2002:

Sales	$3,600,000
Bond interest expense	120,000
Income taxes	600,000
Net income	800,000

Required:

How many times was bond interest earned in 2002?

Problems/Discussion Questions

P5-1 Financial ratios and the balance sheet

Required:

Use the following information along with your knowledge of financial ratios and balance sheet relationships to fill in the missing items on the balance sheet of Clapton Corporation. Round all amounts to the nearest dollar.

Additional Information:

1. Days accounts payable outstanding was 45.6 days in 2001, compared to 66.3 days in 2000.
2. The current ratio at the end of 2001 was 2.5, compared to 2.0 at the end of 2000.
3. The firm's gross profit rate was 25% in 2001 and 28% in 2000.
4. Net income for 2001 was $1,250,000, compared to $1,000,000 in 2000.
5. No common or preferred stock was issued during 2001.
6. Return on average assets was 5% for 2001, compared to 8% in 2000.
7. Cash dividends declared and paid in 2001 were $250,000; in 2000 they were $200,000.
8. Days accounts receivable outstanding was 36.5 days in 2001 and 50.5 days in 2000.
9. The long-term debt to total asset ratio at the end of 2001 was 0.40, compared to 0.30 at the end of 2000.
10. The quick ratio at the end of 2001 was 1.6875, compared to 1.5 at the end of 2000.
11. Days inventory held was 60.8 days in 2001 and 75.7 days in 2000.
12. Net sales in 2001 were $20,000,000, compared to $18,000,000 in 2000.
13. Net operating profit after taxes—but before interest—for 2001 was $1,750,000, compared to $1,400,000 in 2000.

Clapton Corporation
Consolidated Balance Sheets

	As of December 31,	
	2001	2000
Assets		
Current assets		
Cash	$ (a)	$ 500,000
Marketable securities	3,200,000	(b)
Accounts receivable	(c)	1,800,000
Inventories	(d)	(e)
Prepaid expenses	550,000	450,000
Total current assets	10,000,000	(f)
Property, plant, and equipment (net)	(g)	18,000,000
Noncurrent assets		
Long-term receivables	2,500,000	2,000,000
Investments	1,500,000	1,000,000
Other	1,000,000	(h)
Total assets	$ (i)	$ (j)
Liabilities and Stockholders' Equity		
Current liabilities		
Accounts payable	$ (k)	$ (l)
Wages and employee benefits payable	775,000	(m)
Income taxes	300,000	750,000
Advances and deposits	100,000	200,000
Other current liabilities	200,000	400,000
Total current liabilities	(n)	(o)
Long-term liabilities		
Long-term debt	(p)	9,000,000
Deferred income taxes	3,000,000	2,000,000
Other	(q)	500,000
Total liabilities	(r)	15,000,000
Stockholders' equity		
Preferred stock	1,000,000	(s)
Common stock	(t)	2,000,000
Paid-in capital	(u)	9,000,000
Retained earnings	(v)	(w)
Total stockholders' equity	(x)	(y)
Total liabilities and stockholders' equity	$ (z)	$ (zz)

- Start by calculating the missing values for common and preferred stock. Then compute total assets for 2000.
- Find total assets for 2001 using 2000 total assets with the information in items (6) and (13).
- Accounts receivable for 2001 can be found using 2000 accounts receivable along with the information in items (8) and (12).

P5-2 Why financial ratios change

AICPA adapted

Daley, Inc. is consistently profitable. Daley's normal financial statement relationships are as follows:

Current ratio	3 to 1
Inventory turnover	4 times
Total debt/total assets ratio	0.5 to 1

Required:

Determine whether each transaction or event that follows increased, decreased, or had no effect on each ratio.

1. Daley declared, but did not pay, a cash dividend.
2. Customers returned invoiced goods for which they had not paid.
3. Accounts payable were paid at year-end.
4. Daley recorded both a receivable from an insurance company and a loss from fire damage to a factory building.
5. Early in the year, Daley increased the selling price of one of its products because customer demand far exceeded production capacity. The number of units sold that year was the same as last year.

P5-3 Working backward to the statements

AICPA adapted

The December 31, 2001, balance sheet of Ratio, Inc. is presented next. These are the *only* accounts in Ratio's balance sheet. Amounts indicated by a question mark (?) can be calculated from the additional information given.

Assets

Cash	$ 25,000
Accounts receivable (net)	?
Inventory	?
Property, plant, and equipment (net)	294,000
	$432,000

Liabilities and Stockholders' Equity

Accounts payable (trade)	?
Income taxes payable (current)	25,000
Long-term debt	?
Common stock	300,000
Retained earnings	?
	$432,000

Additional Information:

Current ratio at year-end	1.5 to 1
Total liabilities divided by total stockholders' equity	0.8
Inventory turnover based on sales and ending inventory	15 times
Inventory turnover based on cost of goods sold and ending inventory	10.5 times
Gross margin for 2001	$315,000

Required:

Compute the December 31, 2001, balance for each missing item.

$$\textit{Hint: } \frac{\text{Gross margin}}{\text{Inventory}} = \frac{\text{Sales} - \text{CGS}}{\text{Inventory}} = \left(\frac{\text{Sales}}{\text{Inventory}}\right) - \left(\frac{\text{CGS}}{\text{Inventory}}\right)$$

P5-4 EBITDA and revenue recognition

GIDDINGS & LEWIS
www.giddings.com

Giddings & Lewis, Inc. (G&L) supplies industrial automation equipment and machine tools to the automotive industry. G&L uses the percentage-of-completion method for recognizing revenue on its long-term contracts. Customer orders have long lead times because they involve multi-year capital investment programs. Sometimes orders are cancelled. Selected items from the company's financial statements are shown below.

(US$ in millions)	1993	1994	1995
Sales	$571.5	$619.5	$730.6
Accounts receivable—billed	141.6	94.5	147.9
Accounts receivable—unbilled	104.5	249.4	202.7
Total accounts receivable	246.1	343.9	350.6
Inventory	57.4	74.8	102.3
Earnings before interest and taxes (EBIT)	74.8	75.8	38.1
Depreciation and amortization	14.8	15.4	19.3
Plant writedown	–0–	–0–	30.3

Required:

1. Compute EBITDA and "adjusted EBITDA"—after excluding the plant write-down—for each year shown in the schedule.
2. Are profits at G&L keeping pace with sales?
3. Compute "days receivables outstanding"—use year-end receivables—for each year shown in the schedule.
4. Why might analysts be concerned about earnings quality at G&L?

P5-5 Maytag Corporation: Profitability analysis

Maytag Corporation manufactures and distributes a broad line of home appliances including gas and electric ranges, dishwashers, refrigerators, freezers, laundry equipment, and vacuum-cleaning products. The home appliance segment contributes about 87% of Maytag's total sales. The company's other two segments are commercial appliances and international appliances, both of which have grown over the last three years. Roughly 89% of Maytag's sales come from North American markets.

MAYTAG
CORPORATION
www.maytagcorp.
com

Refer to Maytag's 1999 financial statements. As shown, consolidated sales increased 19.4% from 1997 to 1998 and 6.3% from 1998 to 1999. Earnings varied considerably over these years with net income (before extraordinary items) increasing from US$183.49 million in 1997 to US$286.51 million in 1998 and to US$328.53 million in 1999.

Required:

Prepare an analysis of Maytag's profitability for 1999, 1998, and 1997 following the steps outlined below. For all ratios requiring balance sheet values, use the average of beginning and ending balances. Ratios using earnings numbers should be based on income before extraordinary items. Assume a 35% tax rate.

Step 1. Calculate average total assets, liabilities, and stockholders' equity for 1999.

	1999	1998	1997
Average total assets	?	$2,550,909	$2,422,047
Average total liabilities and minority interest	?	1,989,222	1,827,148
Average total shareholders' equity	?	561,687	594,900

Step 2. Calculate Maytag's return on assets (ROA) for each year. Use margin and turnover analysis together with common size income statements to explain the year-to-year change in ROA.

Step 3. What after-tax interest rate has Maytag been paying for its total debt? Analyze the portion of average total assets that Maytag has been financing with debt over the last three years and comment on any apparent strategy.

Step 4. Calculate Maytag's return on common equity (ROCE) for each year. Has leverage benefited Maytag's shareholders? How can you tell?

Maytag Corporation
Consolidated Statements of Income

(US$ in thousands)	1999	1998	1997
Net sales	$4,323,673	$4,069,290	$3,407,911
Cost of sales	3,072,253	2,887,663	2,471,623
Gross profit	1,251,420	1,181,627	936,288
Selling, general, and administrative expense	675,927	658,889	578,015
Operating income	575,493	522,738	358,273
Interest expense	(59,259)	(62,765)	(58,995)
Other, net	14,617	10,912	1,277
Income before taxes, minority interest, and extraordinary item	530,851	470,885	300,555
Income taxes	195,100	176,100	109,800
Income before minority interest and extraordinary item	335,751	294,785	190,755
Minority interest	(7,223)	(8,275)	(7,265)
Income before extraordinary item	328,528	286,510	183,490
Extraordinary item—loss on early retirement of debt	—	(5,900)	(3,200)
Net income	$ 328,528	$ 280,610	$ 180,290

Maytag Corporation
Consolidated Balance Sheets

(US$ in thousands)	1999	1998
Assets		
Current assets		
Cash and cash equivalents	$ 28,815	$ 28,642
Accounts receivable	494,747	472,979
Inventory	404,120	383,753
Deferred income taxes	35,484	39,014
Other current assets	58,350	44,474
Total current assets	1,021,516	968,862
Noncurrent assets		
Deferred income taxes	106,600	120,273
Prepaid pension costs	1,487	1,399
Intangible pension asset	48,668	62,811
Other intangible assets	427,212	424,312
Other noncurrent assets	54,896	44,412
Total noncurrent assets	638,863	653,207

Maytag Corporation
Consolidated Balance Sheets

(US$ in thousands)	1999	1998
Property, plant, and equipment		
Land	$ 19,660	$ 19,317
Buildings and improvements	349,369	333,032
Machinery and equipment	1,622,764	1,499,872
Construction in progress	74,057	102,042
	2,065,850	1,954,263
Less allowance for depreciation	1,089,742	988,669
Total property, plant, and equipment	976,108	965,594
Total assets	$2,636,487	$2,587,663
Liabilities and Shareholders' Equity		
Current liabilities		
Notes payable	$ 133,041	$ 112,898
Accounts payable	277,780	279,086
Accrued liabilities	271,729	258,537
Current portion of long-term debt	170,473	140,176
Total current liabilities	853,023	790,697
Noncurrent liabilities		
Deferred income taxes	22,842	21,191
Long-term debt	337,764	446,505
Postretirement benefit obligations	467,386	460,599
Accrued pension cost	56,528	69,660
Other noncurrent liabilities	101,776	117,392
Total noncurrent liabilities	986,296	1,115,347
Mandatorily redeemable preferred securities	200,000	–0–
Minority interest	169,788	174,055
Shareholders' equity		
Common stock	146,438	146,438
Additional paid-in capital	503,346	467,192
Retained earnings	1,026,288	760,115
Treasury stock	(1,190,894)	(805,802)
Employee stock plans	(38,836)	(45,331)
Accumulated comprehensive income	(18,962)	(15,048)
Total shareholders' equity	427,380	507,564
Total liabilities and equity	$2,636,487	$2,587,663

P5-6 Nike and Reebok: Comparative analysis of footwear manufacturers

NIKE, INC.
www.nikebiz.com
REEBOK
INTERNATIONAL LTD.
www.reebok.com

Nike designs, develops, and markets quality footwear, apparel, athletic equipment, and accessories worldwide. The company sells its products to approximately 20,000 retail accounts in the United States and through a mix of independent distributors, licensees, and subsidiaries in approximately 110 countries around the world.

Reebok International Ltd. designs and markets sports, fitness, and "casual use" footwear and apparel. The company has four major brands: Reebok, Greg Norman, Rockport (shoes), and the Ralph Lauren Footwear Company, which manufactures footwear sold under the Ralph Lauren and Polo Shirt brands. Financial statements for Nike and Reebok follow.

Additional Information:

1. Reebok's cash flow from operations was US$281,625 in 1999, US$151,777 in 1998, and US$126,925 in 1997. Nike's cash flow from operations was US$961,000, US$517,500, and US$323,100, respectively.
2. If a tax rate is needed, use a rate of 35%.

Required:

1. Using the information in the financial statements, calculate the following financial ratios for fiscal 1999 for each company. Financial ratio values for 1998 have already been computed.

	1999		1998	
	Nike	Reebok	Nike	Reebok
Current ratio	?	?	2.07	2.22
Quick ratio	?	?	1.25	1.35
Accounts receivable turnover	?	?	5.57	5.97
Days receivable outstanding	?	?	65.5	61.1
Inventory turnover	?	?	4.44	3.71
Days inventory held	?	?	82.2	98.4
Accounts payable turnover	?	?	9.63	10.16
Days accounts payable outstanding	?	?	37.9	35.9
Return on assets	?	?	9.7%	4.9%
Long-term debt to total assets	?	?	7.0%	31.9%
Long-term debt to total tangible assets	?	?	7.6%	33.2%
Interest coverage	?	?	11.9	1.6
Operating cash flow to total liabilities	?	?	23.9%	13.2%
Operating profit margin	?	?	5.5%	2.7%
Asset turnover	?	?	1.78	1.84

2. Use the results of the ratio analysis to identify similarities and differences in the profitability, liquidity, and long-term solvency of the two firms.
3. As a financial analyst following the two firms, what other information (beyond what's in the financial statements) would you seek to supplement the ratio analysis?

Reebok International Ltd.
Consolidated Statements of Income

(US$ in thousands)	1999	1998	1997
Net sales	$2,899,872	$3,224,592	$3,643,599
Other income (expenses)	(8,635)	(19,167)	(6,158)
	2,891,237	3,205,425	3,637,441
Cost and expenses			
Cost of sales	1,783,914	2,037,465	2,294,049
Selling, general, and administrative expenses	971,945	1,043,199	1,069,433
Special charges	61,625	35,000	58,161
Amortization of intangibles	5,183	3,432	4,157
Minority interest	6,900	1,178	10,476
Interest expense	49,691	60,671	64,366
Interest income	(9,159)	(11,372)	(10,810)
	2,870,099	3,169,573	3,489,832
Income before income taxes	21,138	35,852	147,609
Income taxes	10,093	11,925	12,490
Net income	$ 11,045	$ 23,927	$ 135,119

Nike, Inc.
Consolidated Statements of Income

(US$ in thousands)	1999	1998	1997
Revenues	$8,776,900	$9,553,100	$9,186,500
Cost and expenses			
Cost of sales	5,493,500	6,065,500	5,503,000
Selling and administrative expenses	2,426,600	2,623,800	2,303,700
Interest expense	44,100	60,000	52,300
Other (income) expense (net)	21,500	20,900	32,300
Restructuring charges	45,100	129,900	–0–
	8,030,800	8,900,100	7,891,300
Income before income taxes	746,100	653,000	1,295,200
Income taxes	294,700	253,400	499,400
Net income	$ 451,400	$ 399,600	$ 795,800

Reebok International Ltd.
Consolidated Balance Sheets

(US$ in thousands)	1999	1998
Assets		
Current assets		
Cash and cash equivalents	$ 281,744	$ 180,070
Accounts receivable (net)	417,404	517,830
Inventories	414,616	535,168
Deferred income taxes	88,127	78,419
Prepaid expenses	41,227	50,309
Total current assets	1,243,118	1,361,796
Property and equipment (net)	178,111	172,585
Intangibles (net)	68,892	68,648
Deferred income taxes	43,868	99,212
Other	30,139	37,383
Total assets	$1,564,128	$1,739,624
Liabilities and Stockholders' Equity		
Current liabilities		
Notes payable to bank	$ 27,614	$ 48,070
Current portion of long-term debt	185,167	86,640
Accounts payable	153,998	203,144
Accrued expenses	248,822	191,833
Income taxes payable	8,302	82,597
Total current liabilities	623,903	612,284
Long-term debt (net)	370,302	554,432
Minority interest	41,107	31,972
Outstanding redemption value of equity put options	–0–	16,559
Shareholders' equity		
Common stock	930	933
Retained earnings	1,170,885	1,156,739
Treasury stock	(617,620)	(617,620)
Unearned compensation	–0–	(26)
Accumulated comprehensive income	(25,379)	(15,649)
Total shareholders' equity	528,816	524,377
Total liabilities and shareholders' equity	$1,564,128	$1,739,624

Nike, Inc.
Consolidated Balance Sheets

(US$ in thousands)	1999	1998
Assets		
Current assets		
Cash and cash equivalents	$ 198,100	$ 108,600
Accounts receivable (net)	1,540,100	1,674,400
Inventories	1,199,300	1,396,600
Deferred income taxes	120,600	156,800
Income tax receivable	15,900	–0–
Prepaid expenses	190,900	196,200
Total current assets	3,264,900	3,532,600
Property and equipment (net)	1,265,800	1,153,100
Identifiable intangible assets and goodwill	426,600	435,800
Deferred income taxes	290,400	275,900
Total assets	$5,247,700	$5,397,400
Liabilities and Stockholders' Equity		
Current liabilities		
Current portion of long-term debt	$ 1,000	$ 1,600
Notes payable	419,100	480,200
Accounts payable	373,200	584,600
Accrued liabilities	653,600	608,500
Income taxes payable	–0–	28,900
Total current liabilities	1,446,900	1,703,800
Long-term debt (net)	386,100	379,400
Deferred income taxes and other liabilities	79,800	52,300
Redeemable preferred stock	300	300
Shareholders' equity		
Common stock, Class A convertible	200	200
Common stock, Class B	2,700	2,700
Capital in excess of stated value	334,100	262,500
Foreign currency translation adjustment	(68,900)	(47,200)
Retained earnings	3,066,500	3,043,400
Total shareholders' equity	3,334,600	3,261,600
Total liabilities and shareholders' equity	$5,247,700	$5,397,400

P5-7 Toys "R" Us, Inc: Common size statements of cash flow

TOYS "R" US
www.toysrus.com

Shown below are the consolidated statements of cash flows for Toys "R" Us, Inc. for 2000, 1999, and 1998. The company reported sales (in millions) of US$11,862, US$11,170, and US$11,038, respectively, in these years.

Toys "R" Us, Inc. and Subsidiaries			
Consolidated Statements of Cash Flows			
(US$ in millions)	2000	1999	1998
Cash Flows from Operating Activities			
Net (loss) earnings	$ 279	$ (132)	$ 490
Adjustments:			
Depreciation, amortization, and asset write-offs	278	255	253
Deferred income taxes	156	(90)	18
Restructuring and other charges	–0–	546	–0–
Changes in operating assets and liabilities:			
Accounts and other receivables	35	(43)	(40)
Merchandise inventories	(192)	233	(265)
Prepaid expenses and other operating assets	(69)	(27)	(9)
Accounts payable, accrued expenses, and other liabilities	497	229	22
Income taxes payable	(119)	(7)	40
Net cash provided by operating activities	865	964	509
Cash Flows from Investing Activities			
Capital expenditures (net)	(533)	(373)	(494)
Other assets	(28)	(49)	(22)
Purchase of Imaginarium, net of cash acquired	(43)	–0–	–0–
Net cash used in investing activities	(604)	(422)	(516)
Cash Flows from Financing Activities			
Short-term borrowings (net)	95	4	(142)
Long-term borrowings	593	771	11
Long-term debt repayments	(604)	(412)	(176)
Exercise of stock options	14	16	62
Share repurchase program	(200)	(723)	(253)
Net cash used in financing activities	(102)	(344)	(498)
Effect of exchange rate changes	15	(2)	(42)
Cash and Cash Equivalents			
Increase (decrease) during year	174	196	(547)
Beginning of year	410	214	761
End of year	$ 584	$ 410	$ 214

1. What is the purpose of preparing common size statements of cash flows? For example, what can a financial analyst learn about a firm by preparing a set of common size statements of cash flows?
2. Prepare common size statements of cash flows (expressed as a percentage of sales) for the fiscal years ending 2000, 1999, and 1998 for Toys "R" Us, Inc.
3. Interpret your common size statements of cash flows. For example, what interesting features of the company's operating, financing, and investing activities do they reveal?

Cases

C5-1 Sun Microsystems and Micron Electronics (CW): Comparative financial statement analysis

Micron Electronics develops, markets, manufactures, sells, and supports personal computer (PC) systems for consumer, government, and business use. The company provides end-users with memory intensive PC systems that include the latest hardware and software features commercially at competitive prices.

Sun Microsystems is a leading supplier of network computing products including workstations, servers, software, microprocessors, and a full range of services and support. Sun's products command a significant share of a rapidly growing segment of the computer industry—networked workstations and servers. The company's products are used for many demanding commercial and technical applications. Sun has differentiated itself from its competitors by its commitment to the network computing model and the UNIX operating system, its rapid innovation, and its open systems architecture.

SUN MICROSYSTEMS
www.sun.com

The accompanying exhibits contain the comparative income statements and balance sheets of Micron Electronics and Sun Microsystems for 1997 through 1999. The statements are presented on a common size basis and on a trend basis (with 1997 data omitted for trend statement brevity).

MICRON ELECTRONICS
www.micronpc.com

Sun Microsystems, Inc. and Micron Electronics, Inc.
Comparative Common Size and Trend Analysis of Earnings

	Sun Microsystems			Micron Electronics		
Common Size Statements (% of sales)	**1999**	**1998**	**1997**	**1999**	**1998**	**1997**
Net sales	100.0	100.0	100.0	100.0	100.0	100.0
Cost of sales	48.2	47.9	50.3	81.2	87.2	82.7
Gross profit	51.8	52.1	49.7	18.8	12.8	17.3
R&D expenditures	11.8	12.2	9.9	0.3	0.6	0.5
Selling, general, and administrative expenses	27.0	28.4	27.9	15.2	16.4	10.1
Other operating expenses (income)	–0–	–0–	–0–	0.3	0.6	(0.3)
Operating income (loss)	13.0	11.5	11.9	3.0	(4.8)	7.0
Non-operating (income) expense	(0.7)	(0.5)	(1.2)	(1.1)	(9.8)	(0.4)
Interest expense	–0–	–0–	0.1	–0–	–0–	–0–
Income before tax	13.7	12.0	13.0	4.1	5.0	7.4
Provision for income taxes	4.9	4.2	4.2	1.6	2.2	2.9
Net income	8.8	7.8	8.8	2.5	2.8	4.5
Trend Statements (1997 = 100%)	**1999**	**1998**		**1999**	**1998**	
Net sales	136.4	113.9		73.5	88.6	
Cost of sales	130.7	108.6		72.2	93.4	
Gross profit	142.1	119.2		80.0	65.8	
R&D expenditures	162.9	140.2		47.0	105.4	
Selling, general, and administrative expenses	132.1	115.6		110.5	143.4	
Other operating expenses (income)	–0–	–0–		(0.5)	(1.8)	
Operating income (loss)	148.2	110.1		31.7	(61.5)	
Non-operating (income) expense	82.8	46.7		201.3	2,153.0	
Interest expense	–0–	–0–		–0–	–0–	
Income before tax	143.2	104.9		41.0	59.6	
Provision for income taxes	160.1	115.2		39.6	66.8	
Net income	135.3	100.1		41.9	55.0	

Sun Microsystems, Inc. and Micron Electronics, Inc.
Comparative Common Size Analysis of Balance Sheets

Common Size Statements (% of assets)	Sun Microsystems			Micron Electronics		
	1999	1998	1997	1999	1998	1997
Cash and cash equivalents	12.9	14.4	14.1	27.5	47.4	24.3
Marketable securities	18.7	8.3	9.6	18.7	4.2	1.3
Receivables	27.2	32.3	35.5	20.8	18.5	29.5
Inventories	3.7	6.1	9.3	2.4	4.5	15.2
Deferred income taxes	5.8	6.5	6.1	2.0	2.8	3.5
Other current assets	4.3	5.0	4.8	2.8	0.4	0.5
Total current assets	72.6	72.6	79.4	74.2	77.8	74.3
Net property, plant, and equipment	19.1	22.8	17.0	21.8	21.3	25.2
Other assets	8.3	4.6	3.6	4.0	0.9	0.5
Total assets	100.0	100.0	100.0	100.0	100.0	100.0
Notes payable	0.0	0.9	2.1	1.0	2.4	2.5
Accounts payable	9.0	8.7	10.0	30.0	31.0	40.1
Accrued payroll	6.2	5.5	7.2	–0–	–0–	–0–
Deferred revenue	5.0	4.6	4.2	–0–	–0–	–0–
Accrued liabilities and other	18.2	17.5	15.8	2.8	2.7	4.8
Total current liabilities	38.4	37.2	39.3	33.8	36.1	47.4
Long-term debt and other obligations	4.5	1.3	2.3	3.8	3.7	4.4
Total liabilities	42.9	38.5	41.6	37.6	39.8	51.8
Common stock (net)	0.0	0.0	0.0	0.1	0.1	0.1
Capital surplus	20.7	23.6	26.2	17.4	17.7	15.8
Retained earnings	49.0	55.2	51.3	44.9	42.3	32.3
Treasury stock	(12.3)	(17.7)	(19.5)	–0–	–0–	–0–
Other comprehensive income (loss)	(0.1)	0.4	0.4	–0–	0.1	–0–
Stockholders' equity	57.1	61.5	58.4	62.4	60.2	48.2
Total liabilities and net worth	100.0	100.0	100.0	100.0	100.0	100.0

Sun Microsystems, Inc. and Micron Electronics, Inc.
Comparative Trend Analysis of Balance Sheets

Trend Statements (1997 = 100%)	Sun Microsystems		Micron Electronics	
	1999	1998	1999	1998
Cash and cash equivalents	165.0	124.6	109.3	178.6
Marketable securities	348.2	105.2	1,366.0	290.1
Receivables	137.2	110.8	68.3	57.4
Inventories	70.3	79.1	15.2	26.7
Deferred income taxes	169.9	129.7	56.5	73.1
Other current assets	164.6	127.0	524.2	61.9
Total current assets	164.0	111.2	96.6	95.6
Net property, plant, and equipment	201.1	162.6	83.5	77.2
Other assets	411.5	155.6	808.5	165.7
Total assets	179.3	121.6	96.7	91.3
Notes payable	1.6	46.7	37.6	90.2
Accounts payable	160.8	105.7	72.3	70.6
Accrued payroll	154.1	93.6	–0–	–0–
Deferred revenue	213.6	134.1	–0–	–0–
Accrued liabilities and other	205.5	134.3	56.1	51.6
Total current liabilities	174.5	114.8	68.8	69.7
Long-term debt and other obligations	359.0	70.1	82.7	75.3
Total liabilities	184.5	112.4	70.0	70.2
Common stock (net)	201.7	100.0	100.7	100.3
Capital surplus	141.7	109.4	106.5	102.3
Retained earnings	171.2	130.8	134.4	119.5
Treasury stock	114.3	109.6	–0–	–0–
Other comprehensive income (loss)	(57.9)	115.3	–0–	(5.9)
Stockholders' equity	175.5	128.1	125.4	114.0
Total liabilities and net worth	179.3	121.6	96.7	91.3

Required:

1. What similarities and differences about the companies do the common size and trend statements reveal? Which company has the stronger profit performance?
2. As an equity research analyst working for one of Micron Electronics' institutional investors, what questions would you ask of Micron management?

C5-2 Sun Microsystems and Micron Electronics, Inc. (CW): Management discussion and analysis

This builds on the preceding case (C5-1). The MD&A section of a company's annual report to shareholders contains an interpretive review of operating results, liquidity, and capital resources. One can think of the MD&A section as a narrative discussion of the firm's financial past, one that can help investors chart the future. Management is encouraged to disclose prospective or forward-looking data. These data might include specific earnings or sales forecasts, or a discussion of recent trends and events and how they may affect future operations and cash flows.

Required:

1. Access the EDGAR system at the SEC (www.sec.gov or www.freeedgar.com) and obtain the MD&A sections of the annual reports of Sun Microsystems (year-ended June 30, 1999) and Micron Electronics (year-ended September 2, 1999).
2. What key themes are stressed in each company's MD&A? For example, what positives and negatives about past performance or about the future outlook of each company are mentioned?
3. Does the MD&A complement or reinforce your financial ratio analysis in C5-1? What contradictions surface, if any?
4. As an analyst, is there anything not discussed in the MD&A that you feel should have been mentioned?

Integrative Running Case Study
Bombardier on the Web

Access Bombardier's annual report for the year ended January 31, 2002, from this text's Companion Website at **www.pearsoned.ca/revsine**.

Required:

1. Read through the MD&A, and as you are doing so, list information that in your opinion would be important in a quality of earnings assessment of the company.
2. Pages 62 to 67 of the annual report contain a "Historical Financial Summary." Use the information in this summary to prepare a 500-word report to Bombardier's CEO on the company's profitability, competition, and business strategy.
3. In your opinion, do "Six Sigma" (pages 26 and 27 of the annual report), "Social Responsibility" (pages 28 and 29), and "Environment, Health and Safety" (page 30) contribute to the quality of Bombardier's earnings? Explain.
4. The CEO of Vancouver City Savings Credit Union (VanCity) wrote in "The VanCity Difference—A Case for the Triple Bottom Line Approach to Business" (published in *Corporate Environmental Strategy*, 9[1], 2002, pp. 24–29) that "[t]he 'triple bottom line' approach to business—taking environmental, social and financial results into consideration in the development and implementation of a corporate business strategy—is a movement gaining momentum around the world." Do you believe this statement is true? Why? If it is true, what implications might it have for Bombardier's quality of earnings?

CL5-1 Quaker Oats slurped up by PepsiCo

In a press release dated December 4, 2000, PepsiCo announced that it and Quaker Oats were to merge. Excerpts from the news release are reproduced below.

Required:

1. This chapter includes an extensive financial statement analysis of Quaker Oats for the five years ending in 1999. Assume that you are an advisor to PepsiCo's CEO, and that it is November 2000. Write a 500-word report to the PepsiCo CEO justifying the merger.
2. The news release focuses on accounting information. Is this good or bad? Be sure to establish your criteria for "good" and "bad."
3. Access the PepsiCo website. Based upon the most recent PepsiCo financial information, has the Quaker merger been successful for PepsiCo?

NEWS RELEASE: PepsiCo To Acquire The Quaker Oats Company

Acquisition Creates Big Growth Opportunities and Synergies Across Snack and Beverage Portfolio; Combination Also To Accelerate Leadership Changes

PURCHASE, NY and CHICAGO, IL, Dec. 4, 2000 – PepsiCo, Inc. and the Quaker Oats Company said today they have reached an agreement for PepsiCo to acquire Quaker in a tax-free transaction which features PepsiCo exchanging 2.3 shares of its stock for each share of Quaker, up to a maximum value of [US]$105 for each Quaker share. There is no guaranteed price protection or "collar." However, if the value to Quaker shareholders falls below [US]$92 per share, there is a provision for Quaker to exit the deal without penalty.

The addition of Quaker is expected to be accretive to PepsiCo's earnings per share in the first full year and thereafter. The acquisition will immediately improve PepsiCo's return on invested capital by 200 basis points. The addition of Quaker will also enhance PepsiCo's ongoing sales and profit growth rates. The transaction will be accounted for as a pooling of interests and is expected to close in the first half of next year, subject to approval by PepsiCo and Quaker shareholders and expiration of the Hart-Scott-Rodino Antitrust waiting period and other customary approvals. PepsiCo also said the stock transaction would require the issuance of approximately 315 million new shares to Quaker shareholders.

"This will be a truly outstanding combination," said Roger A. Enrico, PepsiCo Chairman and Chief Executive Officer. "Bringing together Quaker and PepsiCo creates a wealth of exciting growth opportunities as well as important cost and selling synergies. It is also very consistent with our sharp focus on convenient food and beverages."

Quaker Chairman Robert S. Morrison said, "Over the last three years, The Quaker Oats Company has outpaced the growth of the U.S. food and beverage industry. It's a testament to our strong brands, talented people and operating effectiveness. Combining with the world-renowned PepsiCo organization will unleash the tremendous global growth potential of the Gatorade brand and leverage the strengths of our foods business."

...[...]...

The acquisition of Quaker provides PepsiCo with several key strategic and economic benefits:

Quaker's powerful Gatorade brand, the world's number one sports drink, will make PepsiCo the clear leader in non-carbonated beverages, the fastest growing sector of the beverage industry. Additionally, leveraging the much larger scale of Gatorade's vast ware-house distribution system will enable PepsiCo's Tropicana juice unit to gain the scale it needs to make its ambient juice brands stronger and more profitable.

Quaker's rapidly expanding snack business—including granola bars, rice snacks and fruit and oatmeal bars—is highly complementary to PepsiCo's Frito-Lay unit, the world leader in salty snacks. The Quaker brand will extend PepsiCo's reach into morning on-the-go meal occasions, snacks aimed at kids and grain-based snacks. Distributing Quaker's snacks through Frito-Lay's vast distribution system will create very substantial growth opportunities both in the U.S. and internationally.

Quaker's highly profitable non-snack food business (with leading brands like Quaker Oatmeal, Life and Cap'n Crunch cereals, Rice a Roni and Aunt Jemima syrup) generates hundreds of millions of dollars in cash, and through increased innovation and efficiencies can continue to provide steady profit growth and substantial free cash flow.

Combining PepsiCo and Quaker will create a company with an exceptionally strong position in the rapidly growing market for convenience foods and beverages. The combined company, which will retain the PepsiCo name, will have pro forma revenues of [US]$25 billion. Its expected market capitalization of more than [US]$80 billion will place it among the world's five largest consumer products companies.

Merrill Lynch served as advisor to PepsiCo, Inc. and Goldman Sachs served as lead advisor to Quaker Oats. JP Morgan also served as an advisor to Quaker Oats.

…[…]…

Endnotes

1. G. Morgenson, "Flying Blind in a Fog of Data," *New York Times*, June 18, 2000.

2. To illustrate how financial structure can affect profitability comparisons, consider two companies that have (a) identical after-tax operating profits of $500 before interest expense is considered, and (b) the same total asset base of $5,000. One company has no interest-bearing debt; the other has $2,000 of 12% debt outstanding. Annual interest expense on this debt is $240 = $2,000 × 0.12, but the deductibility of interest expense for tax purposes saves the company $84 = $240 × 0.35 each year when the corporate income tax rate is 35%. Consequently, the company with debt would report net income of $344 or $500 − $240 × (1 − 0.35). If financing costs are ignored, the all-equity company would have an ROA of 10% ($500/$5,000), while the company with debt would have an ROA of 6.88% ($344/$5,000). The analyst might mistakenly conclude that one company's profit performance is superior to that of the other company when, in fact, the only difference between these two companies is their choice of financing. The "adjusted" ROA for the company with debt would confirm that identical levels of *operating* profit performance had been achieved:

$$\text{ROA} = \frac{\text{After-tax operating profits} + \text{Interest expense} \times (1 - \text{Tax rate})}{\text{Average assets}}$$

$$= \frac{\$344 + \$240 \times (1 - 0.35)}{\$5,000} = 0.10 \text{ or } 10\%$$

3. See W.K. Hall, "Survival Strategies in a Hostile Environment," *Harvard Business Review*, September–October 1980, pp. 78–85; and M.E. Porter, *Competitive Strategy* (New York: Free Press, 1980). Porter also describes a "niche" or "focused" strategy whereby companies achieve uniqueness within a narrowly defined market segment.

4. If the analysts' goal is to isolate *sustainable* ROCE, "Net income available to common shareholders" should be purged of nonoperating and nonrecurring items and corrected for accounting quality distortions. These are discussed in later chapters.

5. P. Stumpp, T. Marshella, M. Rowan, R. McCreary, and M. Coppola, "Putting EBITDA in Perspective: Ten Critical Failings of EBITDA as the Principal Determinant of Cash Flow," *Global Credit Research Report*, Moody's Investors Service (June 2000).

6. J. Fox, "Forget Earnings—Try Fully Diluted EEBS!" *Fortune*, May 11, 1998.

7. See Chapter 16.

6

The Role of Financial Information in Valuation, Cash Flow Analysis, and Credit Risk Assessment

LEARNING OBJECTIVES

After studying this chapter, you should be able to:

1. Describe the basic steps in corporate valuation

2. Explain what free cash flows are and how they are used to value a company

3. Explain the importance of accounting earnings in valuation and why *current* accrual accounting earnings are considered more useful than *current* cash flows for assessing *future* cash flows

4. Describe what an earnings multiple is and what factors contribute to variation in price to earnings multiples

5. Understand how useful accounting earnings are in assessing share prices

6. Understand the distinction among permanent, transitory, and valuation-irrelevant components of earnings and how each affects price-earnings multiples

7. Describe the combined equity book value and abnormal earnings approach to valuation and how it is applied in practice

8. Explain the notion of "earnings surprises" and how stock returns relate to "good news" and "bad news" earnings surprises

9. Explain the importance of cash flow analysis and credit risk assessment in lending decisions

We introduced the key financial ratios used to assess an entity's operating performance, liquidity, solvency, and financial condition in the previous chapter. In this chapter, we examine in more detail the role that financial accounting information plays in valuation, cash flow analysis, and credit risk assessment. Along the way, we will also build a framework for understanding what academic and professional research has to say about the usefulness of accounting numbers to investors and creditors.

Corporate valuation involves estimating the worth or price of a company, one of its operating units, or its ownership shares. Although there are several approaches to valuation, equity investors and analysts often use **fundamental analysis** to estimate the value of a company by assessing the amount, timing, and uncertainty of its future operating cash flows or earnings. The data in a firm's financial statements, along with industry and economywide data, are used to develop projections of the firm's future

> Fundamental analysis refers to the process of using basic accounting measures or "fundamentals" like accounting earnings, cash flows, or book values to estimate a company's worth.

earnings or cash flows, which are then discounted at a risk-adjusted cost of capital to arrive at an initial valuation estimate. This initial estimate is further refined by adding the current value of nonoperating assets (such as a corporate art collection) and subtracting off-balance-sheet obligations. This refined valuation becomes the basis for buy, hold, or sell decisions.

Cash flow assessment plays a central role in analyzing the **credit risk** of a company. Lenders use a firm's financial statements and other information external to the firm to estimate its future cash flows, which are then compared to its future debt service requirements. Companies with projected operating cash flows that comfortably exceed debt principal and interest payments are deemed good credit risks. Less favourable operating cash flow prospects may suggest that the firm is a high credit risk and, therefore, should be charged higher rates of interest, have more stringent conditions placed on its loans, or be refused credit.

Corporate Valuation

Valuing an entire company, an operating division of that company, or its ownership shares involves the following three basic steps:

1. **Forecasting** future values of some financial attributes—hereafter, we refer to these attributes as **value-relevant attributes**—that drive a firm's value. Common value-relevant attributes include:
   - distributable or free cash flows (defined and discussed later)
   - accounting earnings
   - balance sheet book values

2. Determining the **risk** or **uncertainty** associated with the value-relevant attribute.

3. Determining the **discounted present value** of the expected future values of the value-relevant attribute, where the discount rate reflects the risk or uncertainty inherent in the value attribute of interest.

The Discounted Free Cash Flow Approach

The **distributable—or free—cash flow valuation model** combines the elements in these three steps to express current stock price as the discounted present value of expected future distributable cash flows. **Free cash flow**—a term gaining increasing popularity among analysts—is sometimes defined as the company's operating cash flows (before interest) minus cash outlays for the replacement of existing operating capacity like buildings, equipment, and furnishings. It's the amount available to finance planned expansion of operating capacity, to reduce debt, to pay dividends, or to repurchase stock. This is the best way to measure free cash flows if you are interested in valuing the company as a whole and without regard to its capital structure.

But what if you want to value just the company's common stock? Then we need to refine our free cash flow measure by also subtracting cash interest payments, debt repayments, and preferred dividends. What's left is the free cash flow (denoted CF) that's available to common stockholders.[1] Of course, CF can be used to pay common dividends, buy back common stock, or expand operating capacity. Accordingly, the free cash flow equity valuation model can be written as:[2]

Dividends are another value-relevant attribute commonly discussed in finance texts. However, the "divided discount" approach to valuation is of limited practical use despite its intuitive appeal. This is because dividends represent the *distribution* of wealth and can be arbitrarily determined by the board of directors up to the final liquidating dividend. The accounting measures considered here focus on wealth *creation*, and they are not arbitrarily determined. Therefore, we (and others) consider them to be more meaningful attributes for determining value.

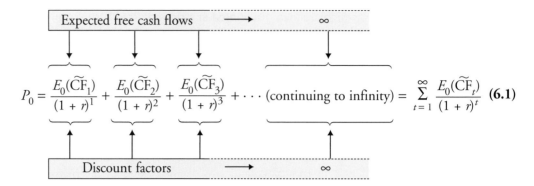

$$P_0 = \frac{E_0(\widetilde{CF}_1)}{(1+r)^1} + \frac{E_0(\widetilde{CF}_2)}{(1+r)^2} + \frac{E_0(\widetilde{CF}_3)}{(1+r)^3} + \cdots \text{(continuing to infinity)} = \sum_{t=1}^{\infty} \frac{E_0(\widetilde{CF}_t)}{(1+r)^t} \quad (6.1)$$

The price, P_0, that the market sets today (at time $t = 0$) for a company's stock equals the sum (Σ) of the stream of *expected future distributable—or free—cash flows* [the $E_0(\widetilde{CF})$ terms in the numerators] per share of stock *discounted back to the present* [the $(1 + r)^t$ terms in the denominators].[3] The E_0 signifies that the cash flows are *expected*. The subscript 0 on E indicates that today's stock price (P_0) is based on investors' *current assessment* (at time $t = 0$) of the company's expected future cash flows.

The cash flow stream begins one period from now at $t = 1$, and it continues over an infinite horizon to $t = \infty$, but each future free cash flow is currently unknown and therefore uncertain.[4]

The discount rate, r, commonly referred to as the **equity cost of capital**, is adjusted to reflect the uncertainty or riskiness of the cash flow stream.[5] Streams that are more uncertain or risky will be discounted at a higher rate.

Multiplying the estimated stock price, P_0, by the number of common shares outstanding produces an estimate of the total common equity value of the company.

Simply put, the discounted free cash flow valuation model in equation (6.1) says that today's market price of each common share depends on investors' current *expectations* about the future economic prospects of the firm as measured by free cash flows. These future cash flows are discounted by a factor that reflects the risk (or uncertainty) and timing of the anticipated flows.

To apply this valuation model as represented, we would have to estimate free cash flows for each and every future period, starting one year hence and going forward forever. Obviously, this would be a daunting task. In practice, the valuation process can be simplified by making some assumptions.[6]

For a mature firm with a stable cash flow, you can assume that the *current level* of cash flows (CF_0) will continue in perpetuity—a zero-growth perpetuity. This means the *expected* free cash flows in each future period can be replaced with the *known* current period cash flow so that equation (6.1) becomes:

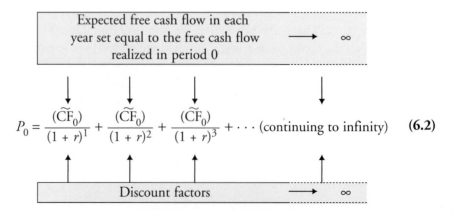

$$P_0 = \frac{(\widetilde{CF}_0)}{(1+r)^1} + \frac{(\widetilde{CF}_0)}{(1+r)^2} + \frac{(\widetilde{CF}_0)}{(1+r)^3} + \cdots \text{(continuing to infinity)} \quad (6.2)$$

The present value of the same dollar cash flow over an infinite horizon—called a **constant perpetuity**—simplifies to:[7]

$$P_0 = \frac{CF_0}{r} \qquad\qquad (6.3)$$

Thus, if a company is currently generating a free cash flow of $5 per share, which is expected to continue indefinitely, and if the discount rate is 10%, the estimated share price would be $5/0.10 = $50.

The Role of Earnings in Valuation

We have just described a free cash flow valuation model linking investors' beliefs or expectations about a company's future cash flow prospects to today's stock price. *But what role does earnings play in valuation?* If investors are truly interested in knowing the company's future cash flows, why would they care about current earnings? The answer hinges on the belief that *current* accrual accounting earnings are more useful than measures of *current* cash flows in predicting *future* cash flows.[8] In Section 1000, para. 12 of the *CICA Handbook,* the AcSB emphasizes the role of accounting information in prediction:

> *Investors and creditors of profit oriented enterprises are interested, for the purpose of making resource allocation decisions, in predicting the ability of the entity to earn income and generate cash flows in the future to meet its obligations and to generate a return on investment.*

And the Financial Accounting Standards Board (FASB) in the United States makes an explicit assertion about current accrual income versus current cash flows:

> *Information about enterprise earnings and its components measured by accrual accounting generally provides a better indication of enterprise performance than information about current cash receipts and payments.*[9]

The FASB stresses that the primary objective of financial reporting is to provide useful information to investors and creditors for assessing the *amount, timing,* and *uncertainty* of prospective enterprise net cash flows.[10] The FASB contends that users pay attention to a firm's accounting earnings because these measures of periodic firm performance improve their ability to forecast companies' future cash flows.

The belief that *current* earnings are better than *current* cash flows for predicting *future* cash flows arises from the *forward-looking* nature of accrual accounting. To illustrate, consider this example. Under generally accepted accounting principles (GAAP), a $100,000 cash expenditure for production equipment would not be expensed in its entirety when purchased. Instead, that expenditure is charged to an asset account and the asset is amortized over future years as it produces the products sold to customers. Both the depreciable life and amortization method are chosen to reflect the *expected future benefit pattern* that arises from the use of the asset. Accrual accounting automatically incorporates this long-horizon, multiple-period view for such capital expenditure transactions.

Consider another example. Under accrual accounting, an up-front cash advance from a customer is recognized as income, not when the cash is received, but rather over a series of future periods as the advance is earned. Cash flows are "lumpy," but—as illustrated in these examples—accrual accounting earnings measurement takes a long-horizon perspective that smooths out the "lumpiness" in year-to-year cash flows.

This explains why we contend that current earnings provide a much better measure of long-run expected operating performance than current cash flows.

An empirical study found that stock returns correlate better with accrual earnings than with realized operating cash flows. This finding supports the above contention[11] and implies that investors are better able to predict a company's future free cash flows using the company's accrual earnings than by using realized cash flows.

Figure 6.1 illustrates the link between a company's current earnings, future free cash flows, and current stock price, as suggested by the FASB and by the empirical evidence.[12] The analyst combines information about the company's current earnings, its business strategy, and the industry's competitive dynamics to forecast sustainable future free cash flows. ***Through the use of accruals and deferrals, accrual accounting produces an earnings number that smooths out the unevenness or "lumpiness" in year-to-year cash flows, and it provides an estimate of sustainable "annualized" long-run future free cash flows.*** The final step in this process involves using the annualized free cash flow estimate together with the risk-adjusted discount rate to arrive at an estimated value for the firm's stock.

To appreciate the implications of these links, let's revisit the simplified zero-growth perpetuity setting and our free cash flow valuation model in equation (6.3). Assuming zero growth means that one way to estimate a firm's equity value (or stock price) is to use its free cash flow in the current period (CF_0) as our forecast of free cash flow in each future period. But according to the FASB's assertion, the current period accrual income is a better proxy for sustainable or annualized future cash flows than the current period free cash flow. This means replacing the current period free cash flow, CF_0 in equation (6.3), with the current period's earnings (denoted X_0). In this case, the free cash flow valuation model simplifies to:

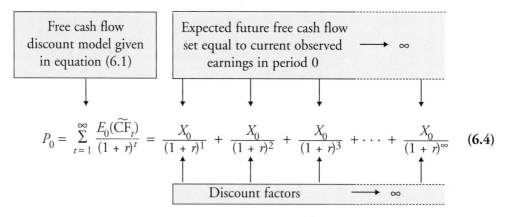

$$P_0 = \sum_{t=1}^{\infty} \frac{E_0(\widetilde{CF}_t)}{(1+r)^t} = \frac{X_0}{(1+r)^1} + \frac{X_0}{(1+r)^2} + \frac{X_0}{(1+r)^3} + \cdots + \frac{X_0}{(1+r)^\infty} \quad (6.4)$$

FIGURE 6.1
LINKAGE BETWEEN SHARE PRICE AND ACCRUAL EARNINGS

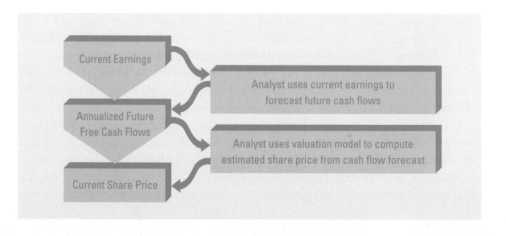

As in equation (6.3), the right side of equation (6.4) is a perpetuity with a discounted present value of X_0/r. Thus, given our simplifying assumptions, the current stock price estimate can be expressed as a capitalized rate ($1/r$) times a perpetuity equal to the current period earnings:

$$P_0 = \frac{1}{r}(X_0) = \frac{X_0}{r} \qquad \qquad (6.5)$$

or alternatively:

$$\frac{P_0}{X_0} = \frac{1}{r} \qquad \qquad (6.6)$$

The left side of equation (6.6) is the **price-earnings (P/E) ratio**, also called the **earnings multiple**, which is a measure of the relation between a firm's current earnings and its share price. Under the assumption of zero growth, the price-earnings ratio in equation (6.6) is the reciprocal of the risk-adjusted interest rate (equity cost of capital) used to discount future earnings. If the current risk-adjusted interest rate is 8%, the earnings multiple is $1/0.08 = 12.5$, which is the rate at which $1 of current earnings is capitalized into price. If the company reports current earnings of $5 per share and if investors believe this earnings level will persist in perpetuity at $5 per share, then the capitalized value of the future earnings stream implies a share price of $5 \times 12.5 = $62.50.

Recap

In theory, equity valuation involves discounting the expected value of some measure of wealth creation—like free cash flow or earnings—over an infinite horizon using a risk-adjusted discount rate (equity cost of capital). In practice, simplifying assumptions are often made to facilitate the valuation process. One simplification is to assume that future periods' free cash flows will be a perpetuity equal to the current period's accrual earnings. Accrual accounting produces an earnings number that smooths out the unevenness in the year-to-year cash flows, thereby providing a measure of periodic firm performance that is generally a better indicator of the long-run sustainable free cash flows of an enterprise. Using this valuation approach, stock price is stated as a multiple of current period earnings, where the multiple (in the no-growth case) is the reciprocal of the firm's equity cost of capital. But, keep in mind that we are describing *models* here, constructed by human beings, and not some underlying natural "reality."

Research on Earnings and Equity Valuation

Over the past 30 years, researchers have investigated the **value-relevance** of financial accounting information mainly in U.S. settings.[13] Many of these studies seek to further our understanding of the relation between share prices and companies' earnings.

To illustrate, let's consider equation (6.5). That equation suggests that current earnings (X_0) can "explain" current share price (P_0) in the sense that perpetual earnings of $5 per share give rise to a $62.50 share price. It immediately follows that *differences* in current earnings across firms should help explain *differences* in share prices across firms at a particular point in time. *That is, if accounting earnings are viewed by investors as an important piece of information for assessing firm value, then earnings differences across firms should help explain differences in these firms' share prices.* This is just another way of saying that earnings are value-relevant.

One way to test whether reported earnings are value-relevant is to examine the statistical association between share prices and earnings across many firms at a given point in time. Studies of this type are called **cross-sectional tests**. Researchers explored this statistical association using the following simple earnings valuation equation:

$$P_i = \alpha + \beta X_i + e_i \tag{6.7}$$

where

- P_i is the end-of-period closing share price for firm i, and X_i is the firm's reported accounting earnings for that period.

- The intercept, (α), and slope (β) terms in the equation represent coefficients to be estimated using standard regression analysis or similar techniques.

- e_i denotes a random error which reflects the variation in share prices that cannot be explained by that firm's earnings.

If accounting earnings are relevant for determining share prices, then the value of the estimated slope coefficient (β), which measures the covariance between earnings and prices, should be positive. That is, a statistically positive β means that differences in earnings across firms explain a significant portion of the variation in share prices across firms. Moreover, if current earnings were a perfect forecast of future free cash flows, and if all companies had the same cost of equity capital and conformed to the zero-growth assumption, current earnings would explain 100% of the cross-sectional variation in share prices.

Figure 6.2 plots 1999 year-end share prices (the vertical axis) against annual earnings per share (EPS) (the horizontal axis) for 39 retail grocery companies. The upward-sloping line represents the estimated price-earnings relation for the general-form regression equation (6.7) for this group of companies at the end of 1999. The regression line has a vertical axis intercept (α) estimate of $9.80 per share and a slope (β) coefficient estimate of 9.55[14]—that is:

FIGURE 6.2

1999 P/E RELATION FOR RETAIL GROCERY STORES

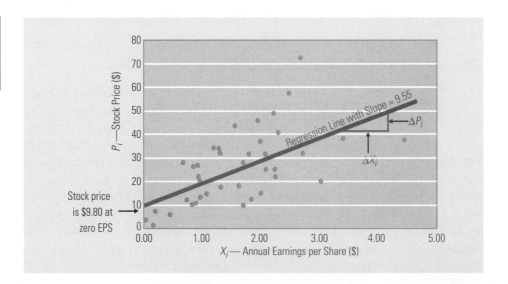

$$P_i = \underset{\substack{\uparrow \\ \text{Stock} \\ \text{price at} \\ \text{\$0 EPS}}}{\overset{\overset{\text{intercept}}{\downarrow}}{\$9.80}} + \underset{\substack{\uparrow \\ \text{Earnings} \\ \text{multiple}}}{\overset{\overset{\text{slope}}{\downarrow}}{9.55}} \times \underset{\substack{\uparrow \\ \text{EPS}}}{(\$X_i)} \qquad \textbf{(6.8)}$$

So the predicted share price for one of these grocery companies that reported earnings per share of $X_i = \$1$ in 1999 would be $\$19.35 = \$9.80 + \$9.55 \times \$1$. The estimated slope coefficient ($\beta = 9.55$) is positive and statistically significant, indicating that reported earnings explains, in a statistical sense, some of the cross-sectional variation in share prices of the grocery companies. However, the proportion of variation in share prices explained by earnings (the adjusted R^2 for the regression) is only 34.2%. Some points lie well above the average price-earnings relation depicted in Figure 6.2, while others fall far below the regression line. The next section discusses reasons why current earnings do not explain 100% of the variation in current prices and why some firms' P/E ratios are well above (below) average.

Sources of Variation in P/E Multiples

Risk Differences The shares of two firms with the same level of current and future earnings can sell for different prices because of differences in risk or uncertainty associated with those earnings. Where the risk is greater for one firm, the risk-adjusted cost of capital will be higher, which means that the discount rate used in capitalizing earnings will also be *higher*, resulting in a *lower* stock price.

To illustrate, let's assume that Firm A and Firm B both report current earnings of $10 per share and it is expected, on average, that these earnings will persist into the future. An analysis of the two firms reveals that Firm A's earnings exhibit greater volatility or dispersion over time—therefore, greater risk—thus, resulting in a 15% cost of equity capital. Firm B's earnings exhibit lower dispersion—thus, lower risk—and a 10% cost of equity capital is determined to be appropriate. The estimated prices for these two firms' shares would be computed as:

Firm A	Firm B
$\dfrac{\$10}{0.15} = \$66.67$	$\dfrac{\$10}{0.10} = \$100$

Thus, despite having equal earnings, Firm A's stock price will be one-third less than Firm B's ($66.67 versus $100) because the risk associated with Firm A is greater and its cost of capital (15%) is higher than Firm B's (10%).

Growth Opportunities Most firms' P/E ratios run between 10 and 20. However, it was not uncommon before the dot-com meltdown to find startup companies like Netscape and high-tech companies like Oracle trading at prices that were 50 (or more) times current earnings. What could explain these exceptionally high P/E ratios?

In addition to valuing earnings generated from existing assets, the market also may be assumed to value a firm's **growth opportunities**—that is, the potential earnings from reinvesting current earnings in new projects that will earn a rate of return in excess of the cost of equity capital. The net present value of growth opportunities

(NPVGO) from the reinvestment of current earnings adds a positive increment to a firm's stock price, resulting in above-average P/E multiples. For a firm with positive growth opportunities, the pricing function in equation (6.5) can be rewritten as:

$$P_0 \quad = \quad \frac{X_0}{r} \quad + \quad \text{NPVGO} \qquad \textbf{(6.9)}$$

Present value of earnings from assets in place	Net present value of future growth opportunities

The first term on the right side of the equation is the value of the firm that has no growth opportunities and distributes all its earnings to shareholders in the form of dividends. The second term is the *additional* value if the firm retains earnings to fund new investment projects that have positive net present values.

To illustrate the incremental value derived from growth opportunities, let's assume that Firm A has 100,000 shares outstanding and can generate earnings of $1 million per year in perpetuity if it undertakes no new investment projects. Thus, its earnings per share is $10 ($1 million/100,000 shares). If Firm A's cost of equity capital is 10%, the price per share would be:

$$P_0 = \frac{X_0}{r} = \frac{\$10}{0.10} = \$100$$

Now assume that Firm A can reinvest at the start of period 1 the entire amount of earnings from period 0 in a project that is expected to increase earnings in period 1 and *in every subsequent period* by $150,000, or $1.50 per share, which represents a 15% return on the reinvested earnings ($150,000/$1 million). If Firm A's cost of capital remains at 10%, the net present value of this investment as of the start of period 1 is:

$$-\$1,000,000 \quad + \quad \frac{\$150,000}{0.10} \quad = \quad \$500,000$$

Earnings invested at beginning of period 1	Present value at beginning of period 1 of incremental return from reinvested earnings

Since $500,000 is the net present value as of the beginning of period 1, the value at time 0 can be determined by discounting back one period as follows:

$$\frac{\$500,000}{(1 + 0.10)^1} = \$454,545$$

Thus, NPVGO per share is $454,545/100,000 = $4.55. The price per share of Firm A with growth opportunities is:

$$P_0 = \frac{X_0}{r} + \text{NPVGO}$$

$$= \frac{\$10}{0.10} + \$4.55 = \$104.55$$

240

Note that the stock price increases over what it was with no-growth ($100), because the firm is able to reinvest earnings in a project expected to earn a 15% rate of return (forever) when the firm's cost of capital or discount rate is only 10%. In this simplified example, the retention rate on earnings was 100%—meaning that none of the earnings was paid as dividends to shareholders. But this need not be the case for a firm to have growing earnings.

In general, the growth rate in earnings will depend on:

- the portion of earnings reinvested each period, called the **retention ratio** (k)[15]

- the rate of return earned on new investment (r^*)

As long as the retention ratio is positive and as long as the return earned on new investment is greater than the firm's cost of equity capital $(r^* > r)$, NPVGO will be positive and will contribute to an above-average P/E multiple. Return on equity (ROCE), one of the key accounting performance measures introduced in Chapter 5, can be used to assess whether a firm is likely to earn a return on reinvested earnings that exceeds its cost of equity capital.

Permanent, Transitory, and Valuation-Irrelevant Components of Earnings

If investors view firms' current earnings levels as likely to persist in perpetuity, then the slope coefficient (β) in equation (6.7) should equal the average earnings multiple for the particular companies and time period being examined. This prediction follows directly from the equity valuation model in equation (6.5), where current earnings are translated into share price using an earnings multiple based on the risk-adjusted cost of equity capital. For example, if the average risk-adjusted cost of capital is 8%, then β should be $1/0.08$ or 12.5. However, for many firms, the earnings multiple falls well below this theoretical value.[16] Why?

One explanation is that reported earnings numbers often contain three distinctly different components, each subject to different earnings capitalization rates:[17]

1. A **permanent earnings** component (X_i^P) that is valuation-relevant and expected to persist into the future. In theory, the multiple for this component should approach $1/r$.
2. A **transitory earnings** component (X_i^T) that is valuation-relevant but is not expected to persist into the future. Since transitory earnings result from one-time events or transactions, the multiple for this component should approach 1.0.
3. A **value-irrelevant or noise** component (X_i^0) that is unrelated to future free cash flows or future earnings and, therefore, is *not* pertinent to assessing current share price. Such earnings components should carry a multiple of zero.

These three earnings components correspond roughly to two broad classifications in the multiple-step income statements as described in Chapter 2 and a retained earnings adjustment item. For example:

- *Income from continuing operations (exclusive of special or nonrecurring items)* is generally regarded as a recurring, sustainable component of a company's profit performance, and thus it would fall into the permanent earnings category.

Some items that make up income from continuing operations may correctly be viewed by investors as highly transitory and/or price-irrelevant, and therefore they would be capitalized accordingly. Examples include inventory holding gains and losses embedded in first-in, first-out (FIFO) earnings, last-in-first-out (LIFO) liquidation profits that result when old LIFO inventory layers are sold, and gains or losses from the sale of fixed assets and special one-time reorganization costs. Later chapters discuss the value-relevance of these and other earnings and balance sheet items in considerable detail.

- *Income (loss) from discontinued operations and extraordinary gains and losses*, on the other hand, are nonrecurring in nature. These items are more likely to be viewed as transitory components of earnings and, therefore, they are valued at a much lower multiple than those items associated with permanent earnings components.

- A *change in accounting principles*, which gives rise to a *cumulative effect adjustment* to retained earnings that has no future cash flow consequences to shareholders, may be viewed as "noise" that is valuation-irrelevant. Under U.S. GAAP, such adjustments may be reported in the income statement.

The idea that reported earnings may sometimes contain permanent, transitory, and value-irrelevant components suggests that X_i (total earnings) in the simple price-earnings regression model of equation (6.7) should be rewritten as the sum of permanent, transitory, and valuation-irrelevant components—that is:

$$X_i = X_i^P + X_i^T + X_i^0$$

This modification allows for a different multiple or capitalization rate for each earnings component, as follows:[18]

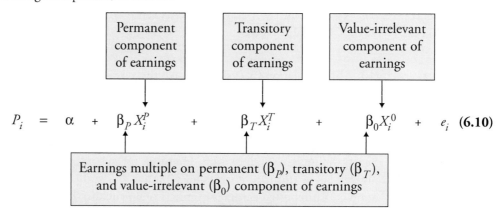

The equation in (6.10) expresses share price as a function of the permanent, transitory, and valuation-irrelevant components of earnings. Each earnings component has a different earnings multiple—β_P, β_T, and β_0, respectively.

In theory, permanent (sustainable) earnings should have a higher earnings multiple than transitory earnings because we expect the former to persist longer into the future—that is, β_P should be greater than β_T.[19] Likewise, the multiple for transitory earnings should exceed the multiple for price-irrelevant earnings since the latter have no bearing on future cash flows and, therefore, have no bearing on price—that is, β_0 should be 0 while β_T should be approximately 1.0. Figure 6.3 illustrates these predictions about earnings multiples for different earnings components. The slope of each line corresponds to the earnings multiple for that particular earnings component, where r equals 20%.

To illustrate the importance of distinguishing between permanent, transitory, and price-irrelevant earnings components, let's suppose two companies report identical bottom-line earnings of $10 per share. Does this mean they would necessarily sell for the same price? Perhaps not, as we will see.

A careful analysis of the financial statements and related footnotes of Firm A reveals that total earnings can be decomposed into three categories: (1) 60% that is judged to be price-relevant and permanent, (2) 30% that is price-relevant but transi-

TABLE 6.1 APPLYING PRICE-EARNINGS MULTIPLES TO EARNINGS COMPONENTS

	Firm A	Firm B
EPS as reported	$10	$10
Analyst's EPS decomposition		
Permanent component	60% of $10 = $6	50% of $10 = $5
Transitory component	30% of $10 = $3	20% of $10 = $2
Value-irrelevant component	10% of $10 = $1	30% of $10 = $3
Earnings multiple applied to each earnings component at cost of capital of $r = 20\%$		
Permanent component ($\beta_p = 5 = 1/0.20$)	$5 \times \$6 = 30$	$5 \times \$5 = 25$
Transitory component ($\beta_T = 1$)	$1 \times \$3 = 3$	$1 \times \$2 = 2$
Value-irrelevant component ($\beta_0 = 0$)	$0 \times \$1 = 0$	$0 \times \$3 = 0$
Implied Share Price	**$33**	**$27**
Implied total earnings multiple (Share price/EPS as reported)	3.3	2.7

tory, and (3) 10% that is considered price-irrelevant. Analysis of Firm B's financial reports indicates its earnings composition is 50% permanent, 20% transitory, and 30% value-irrelevant. This decomposition of each firm's reported EPS is shown in Table 6.1.

Using a 20% cost of capital to capitalize the permanent component of earnings, we find that the valuation model in equation (6.10) implies a share price of $33 for Firm A and $27 for Firm B. Firm A's share price is approximately 20% greater than Firm B's price, even though both companies report the same earnings per share. In the vernacular of the analyst community, Firm A's stock sells for a higher earnings multiple because investors perceive its **earnings quality** to be superior to that of Firm B.

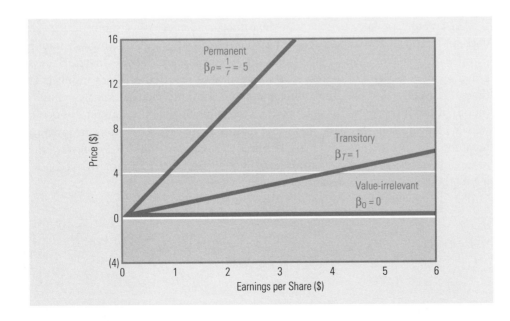

FIGURE 6.3
PRICE-EARNINGS MULTIPLES FOR PERMANENT, TRANSITORY, AND VALUE-IRRELEVANT EARNINGS COMPONENTS WITH $r = 20\%$

The Concept of Earnings Quality ... Again!

You will recall from the discussion in previous chapters that the notion of earnings quality is multifaceted, and there is no consensus on how to measure it.[20] Basically, earnings are considered to be high quality when they are sustainable—for example, those that are generated from repeat customers or from a high-quality product that enjoys steady customer demand based on clear brand name identity. Examples of unsustainable earnings items include: gains or losses resulting from debt retirement; writeoff of assets from corporate restructuring and plant closings; or reduction in discretionary expenditures for advertising, research and development, or management education.

One study found that when reported earnings are adjusted for quality differences—for example, subtracting (adding back) transitory gains (losses) or adjusting for differences in inventory methods (FIFO versus LIFO)—the resultant "quality-adjusted" earnings numbers better explain why firms' shares sell for different prices.[21] These results suggest that differences in earnings quality are associated with differences in the overall earnings capitalization rate (earnings multiple) that investors assign to reported earnings when determining share prices. It should be easy enough to see that, as transitory (X_i^T) or price-irrelevant (X_i^0) components become a more important part of a firm's reported earnings, then

- the quality of those reported earnings is eroded and
- reported earnings become a less reliable indicator of the company's long-run sustainable cash flows.
- Hence, earnings are a less reliable indicator of fundamental value.

These relationships are illustrated in Table 6.1, where we see that Firm B (with a higher proportion of transitory or price-irrelevant components of earnings) has an overall earnings multiple of 2.7 while Firm A has one of 3.3. Suppose all the reported earnings were considered permanent. Then the shares would sell for $10/0.20 = $50, and the earnings multiple would be 5. Low-quality earnings comprising transitory or value-irrelevant components will therefore be assigned a lower overall earnings multiple (i.e., they will be capitalized at a lower rate). Ignoring these differences in earnings quality will lower the association between reported earnings and stock prices across firms.

The research to date suggests that the capital market is rather sophisticated—it does not react naively to reported earnings, but instead, appears to distinguish among permanent, transitory, and value-irrelevant earnings components. Investors as a group seem to recognize differences in the quality of reported earnings numbers at times, on average, and take these differences into account when assessing the implications of earnings reports for share prices. From time to time throughout this book, we will come back to this basic idea as we discuss alternative accounting treatments, both for ongoing events and for specialized transactions, and as we review the research literature that seeks to assess the valuation relevance of alternative accounting methods and footnote disclosures.

These discretionary expenditures are treated as expenses under accrual accounting. Therefore, a firm can provide a temporary boost to earnings by cutting back on the amount spent for these activities. However, such earnings increases are not sustainable, because these expenditures are critical to creating future demand for the firm's products, and to creating new products or developing competent management—all important determinants of long-run sustainable earnings.

The Abnormal Earnings Approach to Equity Valuation

In the previous section, we found that the role of accounting earnings information is *indirect*—earnings are only useful because they help generate improved forecasts of future free cash flows. Recently, another valuation approach has emerged in practice that uses earnings and equity book value numbers *themselves* as direct inputs to the valuation process. Under many circumstances, this approach leads to valuation estimates that are equivalent to those that arise from using the discounted free cash flow approach. But this new model helps us better understand what factors influence share price behaviour over time and share price differences across firms.

This model is based on the notion that share prices are driven not by the level of earnings themselves but by the level of earnings relative to some benchmark. That benchmark is the cost of capital, expressed in dollars, and it reflects the level of earnings investors demand from the company as compensation for the risks of investment. The notion is that investors willingly pay a premium only for those firms that earn more than the cost of capital—meaning firms that produce **positive abnormal** earnings. For firms whose earnings are "ordinary" or "normal"—that is, where an earnings rate is equal to the cost of capital—investors are only willing to pay an amount equal to the underlying book value of assets. Firms that earn less than the cost of capital—that produce **negative abnormal earnings**—would have a share price *below* book value. This relationship between share prices, book value, and abnormal earnings performance is expressed mathematically in the following valuation model:[22]

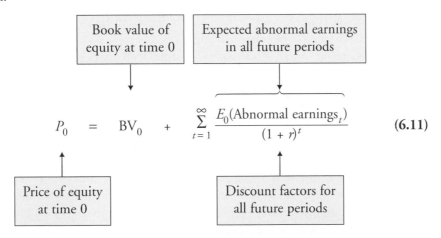

$$P_0 \quad = \quad BV_0 \quad + \quad \sum_{t=1}^{\infty} \frac{E_0(\text{Abnormal earnings}_t)}{(1+r)^t} \qquad \textbf{(6.11)}$$

where

- BV denotes equity book value (assets minus liabilities) that shareholders have invested in the firm.

- E_0 denotes the expectation about future abnormal earnings formed at time 0.

- r is the cost of equity capital.

The cost of equity capital, r, also corresponds to the risk-adjusted return that shareholders require from their investment. Therefore, $r \times BV_{t-1}$—or shareholders' required rate of return multiplied by beginning-of-period invested capital—denotes the earnings level the company must generate in period t to satisfy shareholders. Any difference between actual earnings for period t (X_t) and shareholders' required dollar return on invested capital at the beginning of the period $r \times BV_{t-1}$ represents **abnormal earnings**.

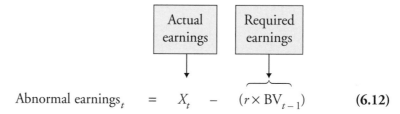

$$\text{Abnormal earnings}_t \quad = \quad X_t \quad - \quad (r \times BV_{t-1}) \qquad \textbf{(6.12)}$$

To illustrate, suppose a company's equity book value (BV) at the beginning of the year is $100 per share, and the cost of equity, r, is 15%. Shareholders therefore require earnings of at least $100 × 15% or $15 per share. If the market expects the company to report earnings equal to the benchmark earnings but it actually earns $20 per share for the year—thus exceeding the benchmark—the price will increase to reflect the company's superior performance. If actual earnings are only $10—thus falling short of the benchmark expected earnings—the price will fall. The amount of the increase (or decline) depends on the degree to which shareholders believe that abnormal (or below normal) earnings are permanent rather than transitory.

Financial statements and related footnotes provide a wealth of information for assessing the relationships expressed by equations (6.11) and (6.12). The balance sheet provides detailed information on the book value of equity (assets minus liabilities). The income statement provides detailed information for assessing a firm's earnings. Chapter 5 describes how asset and equity book values and earnings numbers can be combined into two key ratios—return on assets (ROA) and return on equity (ROCE)—for assessing a firm's performance.

If ROCE exceeds ROA, then the firm has the ability to earn a return on its investments that exceeds its cost of debt financing. This is because ROA measures the company's earnings return on all invested capital (since total assets must equal debt plus equity), whereas ROCE is the return on equity capital. Recall from the previous chapter that interest paid on debt financing (net of taxes) is added back to net income to form the numerator of the ROA calculation. Thus, this adjusted earnings number measures the return on all invested capital—both debt and equity—which equals total assets.

A firm's ROCE can be compared to its required rate of return on equity (cost of equity capital) or to the ROCEs of other companies in the industry to evaluate its prospects for generating "abnormal earnings." Companies with ROCEs that consistently exceed the industry average generally will have shares that sell for a higher premium relative to book value (i.e., a higher market-to-book ratio).

In making comparisons across firms, the analyst must be careful to gauge the quality and comparability of the accounting policies or methods used. For example, does the company being analyzed tend to select liberal accounting methods (i.e., those that may increase earnings and net asset values) or more conservative methods (i.e., those that may decrease earnings and net asset values)? The degree of conservatism associated with a firm's accounting choices will have a direct bearing on the relationship among share price, earnings, and equity book value components of equation (6.11). To see this, let us consider a company that has a $10 share price and an $8 per share equity book value. Analysts who understand the accounting complexities described later in this book know there are two reasons why this company's stock may be valued at a $2 premium relative to equity book value. One reason is that shareholders believe the company will produce abnormal earnings in the future and those future earnings are valued—according to equation (6.11)—at $2 today. A second possibility, however, is that they only expect the company to produce "normal" earnings in the future (i.e., zero abnormal earnings), but recognize that the company's conservative accounting methods understate equity book value by $2 per share.[23]

Much of the information needed for assessing the quality and value-relevance of a company's reported accounting numbers appears in footnotes that accompany the financial statements. These footnotes describe accounting policies for such matters as amortization (straight-line versus accelerated methods), inventory valuation (LIFO versus FIFO), and methods of accounting for business combinations (purchase versus pooling of interests). Later chapters will clarify the important differences in these and other accounting methods and their impact on earnings and balance sheet book values. In certain instances, we will show how users of this information can adjust reported numbers to put firms that use different methods on a more equal footing before using those numbers for valuation purposes.

The abnormal earnings valuation model is illustrated in Appendix 6A to this chapter with Reebok International Ltd.

Recap

The intuition underlying the combined book value–abnormal earnings approach to valuation assumes that there are two basic determinants of future earnings: (1) the resources (net assets) that are invested to generate returns for shareholders; and (2) the rate of return or profitability earned on those net assets. If a firm can earn a return on net assets (equity book value) that exceeds (falls below) its cost of equity capital, then it will generate positive (negative) abnormal earnings, and its shares will sell at a premium (discount) relative to book value. A key feature of this valuation model is that it explicitly takes into account a cost for the capital provided by the owners of the business. Value is added only if the earnings generated by the net assets exceed the equity cost of capital benchmark. Application of this model for a short horizon setting is discussed and illustrated in Appendix 6A to this chapter.

Earnings Surprises

The earnings capitalization model [equation (6.5)] and the abnormal earnings model [equation (6.11)] share a common characteristic: each requires estimates of future earnings. But estimates can (and usually do) prove to be incorrect. When this happens, an "earnings surprise" results.

If securities markets are rational and efficient in the sense of fully (and correctly) impounding available information into prices, then share values will reflect investors' unbiased expectations about the company's future earnings and cash flows. These expectations incorporate a vast array of information, including knowledge of the company's earnings and cash flow history, product market conditions, competitor actions, and other factors. For example, the share prices of General Motors and Ford incorporate information about unit sales figures published weekly in the financial press, as well as expectations about changes in interest rates, because interest rates influence consumers' car-buying behaviour. Share price changes occur as investors receive new information and then revise their expectations about the future earnings and cash flow prospects of the company.[24] Financial reports are an important source of information that investors use in updating their expectations.

Consider a typical General Motors quarterly earnings announcement that is released through major financial wire services. If reported quarterly earnings correspond exactly to the earnings investors expected before the announcement, they have no reason to alter their expectations about GM's future earnings or cash flows. The reported quarterly earnings would simply *confirm* market expectations. The earnings release may resolve market uncertainty about current earnings—but it does not provide new information to investors. On the other hand, if reported quarterly earnings deviate from investors' expectations, this **earnings surprise** represents new information that investors will use to revise their expectations about the company's future earnings and cash flow prospects. Of course, this change in investor expectations will cause the company's share price to change following the earnings announcement.

The way share prices change in response to new information about earnings can be expressed mathematically as follows:

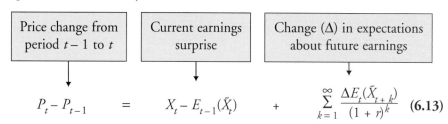

$$P_t - P_{t-1} = X_t - E_{t-1}(\bar{X}_t) + \sum_{k=1}^{\infty} \frac{\Delta E_t(\bar{X}_{t+k})}{(1+r)^k} \quad \textbf{(6.13)}$$

where

- $P_t - P_{t-1}$ is the share price change from just before to just after the earnings announcement.

- $X_t - E_{t-1}(\bar{X}_t)$ is the current period t's "earnings surprise" or deviation of reported earnings from the market's expectation at the beginning of the period.

- $\sum_{k=1}^{\infty} \frac{\Delta E_t(\bar{X}_{t+k})}{(1+r)^k}$, the summation term, represents the valuation impact of revised expectations about future earnings.

Figure 6.4 illustrates the typical behaviour of share returns leading up to and following quarterly earnings announcements for three different scenarios:

1. Reported earnings are viewed as a "*good news*" earnings surprise because they exceed market expectations.
2. Reported earnings contain "*no news*" because they correspond exactly to market expectations.

FIGURE 6.4
SHARE RETURNS
AND QUARTERLY
EARNINGS
"SURPRISES"

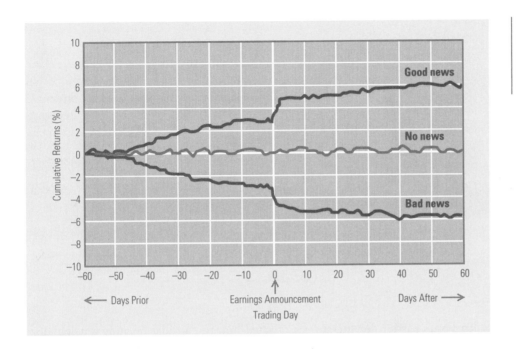

3. Reported earnings are viewed as a "*bad news*" earnings surprise because they fall below market expectations.[25]

Companies that report "good news" earnings (a positive earnings surprise) tend to have an upward drift in share returns prior to the actual earnings announcement date (day 0 in Figure 6.4), followed by another share return increase on announcement. The share returns of companies reporting "bad news" earnings surprises exhibit a negative drift prior to the announcement, followed by another decrease in returns at the announcement date. Modest post-announcement drifts in share returns are also not uncommon, especially when the earnings surprise is quite large.[26] Quarterly earnings announcements that contain "no news" lead to stock returns that hover around zero before and after announcement.

It's easy to explain why share prices sometimes exhibit a positive or negative drift *prior* to the actual earnings announcement date. Take the case of General Motors. Investors learn about the company's automobile sales on a weekly basis and therefore can anticipate fairly well the actual quarterly earnings number prior to its formal announcement by GM. The fact that GM's share price changes at the announcement date indicates that not all the information contained in the earnings release is fully anticipated by investors. Small companies—and those not closely followed by securities analysts—tend to exhibit less pre-announcement share return drift because investors usually have very limited information about the company and its earnings prospects for the quarter. Large companies, whose performance is closely followed by analysts, are more likely to exhibit the share return behaviour illustrated in Figure 6.4.

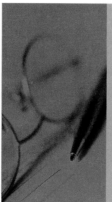

Recap

Share price at any given point in time is assumed to reflect investors' aggregate expectations about the company's future earnings. Information that changes investors' expectations about future earnings will cause prices to rise or fall depending on whether the information represents "good news" or "bad news." Research evidence demonstrates that quarterly and annual earnings announcements are important information events that cause share prices to increase (positive returns) or decrease (negative returns) when the reported earnings turn out to be greater (less) than expected. The amount of surprise conveyed by earnings announcements depends on the amount of pre-announcement information about company operations that is provided elsewhere in the financial press.

Valuing a Business Opportunity (An Illustration)

Allen Ford's passion for literature motivated him to consider opening a neighbourhood bookstore. Allen convinced a colleague who was an expert in market research to look at the economic viability of a general-title neighbourhood bookstore. The results of his analysis further fuelled Allen's enthusiasm: the market demographics were favourable, and there was little direct competition. Annual sales were projected to ultimately reach $350,000.

Allen rejected the notion of opening his own independent store, and instead focused on several franchise opportunities. By affiliating with a national or regional company, Allen would enjoy the benefits of brand name recognition, economies of scale in purchasing and advertising, and employee training and support programs. After investigating several possibilities, Allen settled on The BookWorm, an expanding regional chain of franchised bookstores that emphasized convenience, price, selection, and neighbourhood friendliness. Each store had a coffee bar surrounded by ample soft seating, with abundant natural light encouraging patrons to browse leisurely. This concept had a proven track record of success in similar communities, and it appealed to Allen's tastes.

A BookWorm franchise could be established with a franchise investment of about $100,000, including the initial franchise fee of $21,000, fixtures of $20,000 to $25,000, and an inventory cost of $40,000 to $60,000. The inventory and fixtures would be purchased from the corporate parent, BookWorm, Inc. Corporate staff would conduct a site location study, assist in negotiating competitive lease terms for retail space, help with store layout and renovation, train employees on operating policies and procedures, and provide all grand opening advertising and promotional materials. Once a new BookWorm franchise opens, the corporate parent receives royalties (typically as a percentage of sales) which are determined in accordance with a 15-year renewable franchise contract.

The prospectus that Allen obtained from the parent company contained the selected financial highlights for a typical BookWorm franchise store shown in Table 6.2. The notes accompanying the table indicated: that store fixtures are amortized over 10 years using the straight-line method; that the initial franchise fee is amortized over 15 years; that operating expenses include a competitive salary for a store manager; and that income taxes have been ignored because they are owner-specific, thus making them highly variable across locations.

	Year 1	Year 2	Year 3	Year 4	Year 5
Sales	$200,000	$250,000	$300,000	$325,000	$350,000
Franchise royalty (5%)	10,000	12,500	15,000	16,250	17,500
Pre-tax earnings	(6,900)	3,600	13,750	22,000	26,250
Free cash flows	(3,000)	5,500	15,000	15,000	24,500
Assets at year-end	100,000	100,000	100,000	100,000	100,000
Owner's investment:					
Beginning of year	100,000	100,000	100,000	100,000	100,000
+ Pre-tax earnings	(6,900)	3,600	13,750	22,000	26,250
− Distribution to owner	6,900	(3,600)	(13,750)	(22,000)	(26,250)
= End of year	$100,000	$100,000	$100,000	$100,000	$100,000

With these financial projections and his understanding of the marketplace, Allen Ford must decide whether to invest $100,000 in a BookWorm franchise. Influencing the decision may be several nonfinancial considerations, such as the degree of confidence Allen has in BookWorm's corporate staff or the proposed interior design and ambiance of the shop. However, viewed through the stark and partial lens of economics, Allen's decision problem simplifies to the standard net present value rule—invest if the estimated value of the franchise (adjusted for the risk of investment) exceeds its $100,000 cost. From trade sources, Allen learned that 16% was a reasonable approximation of the cost of equity capital for franchised neighbourhood bookstores. Allen used two different approaches to estimate the value of the bookstore, relying on predictions contained in the **pro forma** (i.e., forecasted) financial statements whenever possible.

The first approach, based on expected future *free cash flows*, is summarized in Table 6.3. Sales and free cash flow projections for Years 1 through 5 are taken directly from the pro forma financial statement data in Table 6.2. Allen believes that sales will remain flat after Year 5 and that free cash flows will average about $25,000 per year. These assumptions produce a Year 5 **terminal value** estimate of $156,250—that is, the present value (at the end of Year 5) of the perpetual $25,000 free cash flow per year, discounted at a 16% cost of equity capital (= 25,000/0.16).

When the terminal value at the end of Year 5 is discounted back to the present (beginning of Year 1) and added to the sum of the present value of expected free cash flows for Year 1 through Year 5, the result is a free cash flow value estimate for the bookstore of $105,453, as shown in Table 6.3. This amount is *greater* than Allen's required capital investment of $100,000—this means Allen will be earning a return in excess of 16% per year on his investment *if* he opens the bookstore and the financial projections underlying the valuation estimate prove correct.

A second approach for estimating the value of Allen's business opportunity relies on expected future *abnormal earnings*—the amount by which operating earnings each year exceed the dollar cost of capital for the bookstore. This valuation approach, also based on projections contained in the pro forma financial statements, is summarized in Table 6.4.

TABLE 6.3 BOOKWORM FRANCHISE VALUATION OF EXPECTED FUTURE CASH FLOWS

	Year 1	Year 2	Year 3	Year 4	Year 5	Beyond Year 5
a) Financial Projections						
Sales	$200,000	$250,000	$300,000	$325,000	$350,000	$350,000
Free Cash Flows	($3,000)	$ 5,500	$ 15,000	$ 15,000	$ 24,500	$ 25,000
As a Percentage of Sales	*−1.5%*	*2.2%*	*5.0%*	*4.6%*	*7.0%*	*7.1%*
						Estimated terminal value ↓
b) Valuation Estimate at 16%						
Expected Future Cash Flow	($3,000)	$ 5,500	$ 15,000	$ 15,000	$ 24,500	$156,250
× Discount Factor at 16%	0.86207	0.74316	0.64066	0.55229	0.47611	0.47611
= Present Value of Each Flow	($2,586)	$ 4,087	$ 9,610	$ 8,284	$ 11,665	$ 74,393
c) Estimated value (sum of all present values above)	$105,453					

Terminal value = $25,000/0.16

TABLE 6.4 BOOKWORM FRANCHISE VALUATION OF EXPECTED ABNORMAL EARNINGS

	Year 1	Year 2	Year 3	Year 4	Year 5	Beyond Year 5
a) Financial Projections						
Sales	$200,000	$250,000	$300,000	$325,000	$350,000	$350,000
Pre-tax Earnings (loss)	($6,900)	$ 3,600	$ 13,750	$ 22,000	$ 26,250	$ 25,000
As a Percentage of Sales	*−3.5%*	*1.4%*	*4.6%*	*6.8%*	*7.5%*	*7.1%*
b) Computation of Abnormal Earnings						
Equity book value (beginning of year)	$100,000	$100,000	$100,000	$100,000	$100,000	$100,000
× Cost of equity capital = 16%	0.16	0.16	0.16	0.16	0.16	0.16
= Normal earnings	$ 16,000	$ 16,000	$ 16,000	$ 16,000	$ 16,000	$ 16,000
c) Projected Pre-tax Earnings (Loss)	$ (6,900)	$ 3,600	$ 13,750	$ 22,000	$ 26,250	$ 25,000
− Normal earnings	($16,000)	($16,000)	($16,000)	($16,000)	($16,000)	($16,000)
= **Abnormal earnings (loss)**	**($ 22,900)**	**($ 12,400)**	**($ 2,250)**	**$ 6,000**	**$ 10,250**	**$ 9,000**
d) Valuation Estimate at 16%						Estimated terminal value ↓
Expected abnormal earnings (loss)	($ 22,900)	($ 12,400)	($ 2,250)	$ 6,000	$ 10,250	$ 56,250
× Discount factor at 16%	0.86207	0.74316	0.64066	0.55229	0.47611	0.47611
= **Present value of each abnormal earnings flow**	($ 19,741)	($ 9,215)	($ 1,441)	$ 3,314	$ 4,880	$ 26,781
e) Sum of All Present Values	$ 4,578					
+ **Capital to start the business**	100,000					
= **Estimated value**	$104,578					

Terminal value = $9,000/0.16 = $56,250

Part (a) of Table 6.4 summarizes the pro forma earnings forecasts for the bookstore. As before, Allen believes sales and pre-tax earnings will be flat beyond Year 5.

Part (b) describes the calculation of yearly abnormal earnings. First, the 16% "Cost of equity capital" is multiplied by the beginning book value of equity to produce a figure called "**normal earnings**" in each year. The component "Normal earnings" represents the level of profit performance that investors (including Allen) demand from the business in order to earn their 16% per year required rate of return.

Next, in part (c), the component "Normal earnings" is subtracted from "Projected pre-tax earnings" to produce an estimate of expected "Abnormal earnings" for each year.

In part (d), the Year 5 "Terminal value" estimate of $56,250 represents the present value (at the end of Year 5) of the perpetual $9,000 per year abnormal earnings flow from Year 6 to infinity, discounted at a 16% cost of equity capital. The present value (as of the beginning of Year 1) of all abnormal earnings sums to $4,578. This amount, when added to the $100,000 of capital required to start the business, yields a valuation estimate for the bookstore of $104,578. Once again, the analysis supports opening the bookstore.

Cash Flow Analysis and Credit Risk

Equity investors analyze financial statements to determine the value of a firm's shares. Creditors, on the other hand, are primarily concerned with assessing a firm's ability to meet its debt obligations through timely payment of principal and interest. Commercial banks, insurance companies, pension funds, and other lenders form opinions about a company's **credit risk** by comparing current and future debt service requirements to estimates of the company's current and expected future cash flows.

Financing the BookWorm Franchise
After carefully reviewing the investment opportunity, Allen Ford decided to purchase a BookWorm franchise. The evaluation process was lengthy; it included personal interviews with ten current franchise owners. These interviews enabled Allen to gain a deeper understanding of the business and its key risks and success factors. In addition, he was able to identify several proven marketing and promotional strategies for launching the franchise. With this information and an assessment of local market conditions, Allen refined the financial projections supplied by the corporate parent, performed a valuation analysis, and concluded that the franchise was likely to earn an acceptable risk-adjusted rate of return over time. There was still one hurdle—financing a portion of the $100,000 franchise purchase price.

Allen needed a bank loan for two reasons. First, the total market value of Allen's personal investment portfolio was $50,000. Second, Allen's interviews with other franchise owners revealed that a $100,000 initial investment might not provide an adequate cash cushion for the first year of operations.

After describing to a local banker the business opportunity and his cash needs in the $50,000 to $100,000 range, Allen learned that ample funds were currently available at attractive interest rates. Allen was asked to complete a detailed loan application, including a personal credit history and business plan, and to prepare monthly earnings and cash flow projections for the first two years of franchise operations. Filled with optimism, Allen began assembling the financial and other information required and thinking about the kind of loan he would seek from the bank.

Before investing, Allen should perform a **sensitivity analysis** of the free cash flow and abnormal earnings valuation estimates. Sensitivity analysis involves constructing "best case" and "worst case" scenarios for the business that incorporate alternative assumptions about sales, costs, and competitor behaviour. Each scenario produces financial forecasts that become the basis for revised free cash flow and abnormal earnings valuation estimates. In this way, Allen could learn how alternative economic conditions might affect the bookstore's value and his return on investment.

Seasonal lines of credit are commonly used by companies with sales cycles that are also seasonal (e.g., lawn and garden equipment retailers). These loans provide the cash to support increases in current assets during the peak selling period. The borrower draws on the seasonal credit line as funds are required and repays as seasonal sales produce net cash inflows. **Special-purpose business loans** are often used to finance, on a temporary basis, increases in current assets resulting from unusual or unexpected circumstances.

Traditional Lending Products

Commercial Bank Loans Commercial bank loans are a common source of cash for most business enterprises today. These loans can be structured as short-term or long-term, fixed or floating rate, payable on demand or with fixed maturity, and secured or unsecured.

Short-Term Loans: Loans with maturities of one year or less, called short-term loans, make up more than half of all commercial bank loans. Seasonal lines of credit and special-purpose loans are the most common short-term borrowing. Short-term loans are used primarily to finance working capital needs resulting from temporary inventory or receivables increases. They may be **secured** by the inventories or receivables themselves, or they may be **unsecured**. Loan repayment usually comes from the routine conversion of these current assets into cash.

Long-Term Loans: Called **term lending agreements**, long-term loans have an original maturity of more than one year, with maturities ranging from two to five years being the most common. The principal and interest repayment schedules, along with other conditions of the loan, are detailed in a signed contractual agreement between the borrower and the bank. Term loans are often used to finance the purchase of fixed assets, the acquisition of another company, the refinancing of existing long-term debt, or permanent working capital needs. They are also frequently secured by pledging the assets acquired with the loan proceeds, although lenders rarely look to asset liquidation as the primary source of funds for loan repayment. Scheduled principal and interest payments are generally presumed to come from the borrower's future operating cash flows.

Revolving Loans: Revolving loans are a variation on the seasonal credit line, have a commitment period extending beyond one year, and allow borrowing up to a maximum level at any time over the life of the loan. Revolving loans are often used to finance cash imbalances that arise in day-to-day operations, seasonal needs, or permanent working capital needs when normal trade credit is inadequate to support a company's sales volume. Borrowers have the right to prepay the revolving loan and later re-borrow those funds, but they must comply with the terms and conditions specified in the loan agreement. The interest rate on the revolving line of credit is usually the bank's prime lending rate plus an additional percentage, and the rate will usually change (or "float") as the prime rate rises or falls over the life of the credit line. In addition to interest, the borrower pays a "commitment fee" based on the total amount of the credit extended.

Other Sources of Debt Financing

Commercial banks are not the only source of debt financing for businesses. Another source of financing is **commercial paper**, which consists of short-term notes sold directly to investors by large and highly rated companies. These notes usually mature in 270 days or less and carry a fixed interest rate. Because commercial paper is issued directly to investors and is usually secured by a bank credit line, the interest rate the company pays is often significantly below the rate a bank would charge for a direct loan.

Long-term forms of public debt financing include **bonds, debentures,** or **notes**.[27] Long-term debt securities are promises made by the issuing company to pay principal when due and to make timely interest payments on the unpaid balance. Bonds can have numerous special features. For example, **secured bonds** specify collateral that protects the bondholder if and when the borrower defaults. Other bonds contain **seniority** features that specify which bondholders will be paid off first in the event of bankruptcy. Some may contain **sinking fund provisions** that require the borrowing company to make annual payments to the trustee, who then uses the funds to retire a portion of the debt prior to its maturity. Still others may contain **call provisions,** which allow the company to repurchase or "call" part or all of the debt issue at stated prices over a specific period.

Regardless of the special features attached, virtually all bonds or notes contain numerous **protective covenants** tied to financial performance measures that are designed to protect the interests of the creditor. These covenants place restrictions on the borrower's activity and are described in the **indenture**, a written agreement between the borrowing company and its creditors. The role that accounting numbers play in these debt covenants will be discussed in greater detail in Chapter 7.

Credit Analysis

To lend funds to a company, a commercial loan officer of a bank must first evaluate the prospective borrower's ability to repay the proposed loan at maturity. This evaluation typically involves financial analysis and includes the preparation of forecasted financial statements, "due diligence" (a qualitative assessment of management's character and capability), and analysis of credit risk.

Financial analysis of a potential borrower begins with an understanding of the firm, its business, its key risks and success factors, and the competitive dynamics of the industry. Next, an evaluation of the quality of its accounting earnings and financial reporting choices is made to determine whether traditional ratios and statistics derived from the financial statements can be relied on to measure accurately the company's economic performance and financial condition. Lenders and credit analysts frequently adjust reported financial statement numbers. For example, nonrecurring gains and losses and other transitory components of earnings are removed from the reported bottom-line earnings number to arrive at a measure of operating performance that is more representative of a firm's long-run sustainable profitability. Off-balance-sheet obligations (e.g., operating lease commitments) are frequently added to a firm's reported debt. Finally, other adjustments are made to improve the comparability of the financial data across potential loan candidates.

The next step is evaluating the company's profit performance and balance sheet strength. Financial, operating, and leverage ratios (discussed in Chapter 5) as well as trends in revenues and expenses are examined over time and compared to industry averages. This phase of the analysis is intended to identify positive and negative changes in the prospective borrower's profitability, financial health, and industry position. However, the historical performance and condition of the borrower is only a partial indication of creditworthiness. Loan approval is largely determined by the borrower's ability to repay the proposed loan from *future* operating cash flows. *Consequently, an estimate of the company's future financial condition is indispensable to most lending decisions.*

Pro forma (i.e., forecasted) financial statements are prepared by the credit analyst to assess the borrower's ability to generate sufficient cash flows to make interest and principal payments when due.[28] These projections incorporate the analyst's understanding of the company's plans and business strategy, the potential responses of rival companies, and other factors that shape the prospective borrower's economic environment. The pro forma financial statements and their underlying assumptions are then tested to establish the borrower's vulnerability to changing economic circumstances. This testing involves examining plausible "worst-case" scenarios that indicate just how poorly the company can perform before it defaults. This enables the analyst to gauge the company's **financial flexibility**—that is, the degree to which a company can satisfy its cash needs during periods of fiscal stress by drawing on existing credit lines, by accessing capital markets, by curtailing discretionary cash expenditures, or by selling assets.

Due diligence evaluation is like "kicking the tires" of the prospective borrower by conducting plant tours, trade checks, and interviews with competitors, suppliers, customers, and employees. Comprehensive due diligence may also include asset appraisals, reviews of the company's other debt obligations, internal controls, planned capital expenditures, potential environmental liabilities, and other matters that bear on the company's future success and ability to repay debt at maturity.

The final step of credit analysis is a **comprehensive risk assessment** that involves evaluating and summarizing the various individual risks associated with the loan. Some risks will be unique to the specific borrower; others will be associated with potential changes in the economy or industry, new regulations, or unanticipated events. The credit analyst evaluates the severity of each risk in terms of (1) its probability of occurrence, (2) how it could affect the borrower's ability or willingness to repay, and (3) the bank's estimated costs if the borrower defaults.

If the prospective borrower is judged to be creditworthy, the final terms and conditions of the loan are negotiated with the borrower. Obviously, lenders are compensated for anticipated credit risks through the interest rate charged on the loan. The yield on a loan must be sufficient to cover the lender's (1) cost of borrowing funds; (2) costs of administering, monitoring, and servicing the loan; (3) normal (competitive) return on the equity capital needed to support lending operations; and (4) premium for exposure to default risk. However, collateralized loans or loans with personal guarantees lower credit risk and enable lenders to lower the borrower's cost of debt. Credit evaluations performed by rating agencies such as Standard & Poor's or Moody's closely resemble the process described here for commercial bank loans. Ratings are assigned to long-term debt, medium-term notes, and commercial paper based on analysts' evaluations of (1) the likelihood of default, (2) the nature and provisions of the debt, and (3) the protection afforded debtholders in the event of bankruptcy.[29]

Interpretation of Cash Flow Components

Cash flow analyses and forecasts are central to all credit evaluations and lending decisions. A company's obligation to make interest and principal payments cannot be satisfied out of earnings, because accrual earnings includes many noncash accruals and deferrals. Rather, payment has to be made with cash! Consider the situation confronting your client, G. T. Wilson Company.

Wilson Company has been a client of your bank for over 40 years. The company owns and operates nearly 850 retail furniture stores and has over 38,000 employees. Sales and earnings growth have exceeded the industry average until recently, and the company has paid dividends consistently since 1906. Prior to 1992, Wilson built its reputation on sales of moderately priced upholstered furniture, case goods (wooden tables, chairs, and bookcases), and decorative accessories. The company's stores were located in large, urban centres where occupancy costs were quite low. Increased competition and changing consumer tastes caused Wilson to alter its strategy beginning in 1992. One aspect of this strategic shift involved expanding the company's product line to include higher-quality furniture, consumer electronics, and home entertainment systems. To complement this expanded product line, Wilson also introduced a credit card system so that customers could more easily make payment for their purchases. Wilson used commercial paper, bank loans, and trade credit to finance the growth of receivables and inventories. The company's strategy also focused on closing unprofitable downtown stores; at the same time it chose a route of rapid expansion by opening new stores in suburban shopping centres.

Your bank has extended two loans to Wilson, a $50 million secured construction loan that matures in 2004 and a $200 million revolving credit line that is currently up for renewal. Wilson has always been in compliance with the terms of the revolving line of credit, but the company's borrowing has been at or near the maximum amount allowed for the past two years. Exhibit 6.1 presents comparative cash flow statements for the company and Exhibit 6.2 reports selected financial statistics. What do these cash flow statements and summary statistics tell us about the company's credit risk?

Cash Flow from Operations

The net cash flow from operations indicates the amount of cash the company was able to generate from its ongoing core business activities. Generating cash from operations is essential to the long-term economic viability of the business. However, not every company can be expected to produce positive operating cash flows every year. Even financially healthy companies must sometimes spend more cash on their operating activities than they receive from customers.

As we can see from the comparative cash flow statements in Exhibit 6.1, Wilson produced positive operating cash flows in 1993 and 1994. After that, its operating cash flows have been consistently negative and declining, with the average level for the last three years approximately equal to *minus* $100 million. This performance sharply contrasts with the company's sales and earnings performance as shown in Exhibit 6.2. Sales have grown steadily from $920 million in 1992 to $1.85 billion in 1999, with a small decline in 2000. Net income increased from $31.6 million in 1992 to a peak of $41.9 million in 1995, followed by three years of relative stability where earnings averaged about $33 million each year. Net income declined in 1999 to $10.9 million, and the company reported a $145 million loss in 2000.

What aspects of Wilson's operations consumed cash during the company's profitable years? Exhibit 6.1 reveals that the primary factors contributing to the company's negative operating cash flows are increases in accounts receivable and increases in inventories. Some growth in receivables and inventories is to be expected as a natural consequence of the company's decision to expand its product line and to introduce a customer credit card. However, increases in receivables or inventories can sometimes signal unfavourable business conditions. For example, the average collection period for customer accounts ("Days receivable" in Exhibit 6.2) increased from 91.3 days in 1992 to 142.5 days in 2000. This trend could reflect expanded credit card use, more lenient credit policies toward customers, or a deterioration in customers' ability to pay. Similarly, the increase in "Days inventory" (Exhibit 6.2) from 100.9 in 1992 to 130.5 in 2000 could be due to product line extensions, escalating merchandise costs, or slack consumer demand. The credit analyst must carefully evaluate each possible explanation to discover what economic forces are responsible for the company's negative operating cash flows and whether positive cash flows from operating activities are likely to be generated in the future.

It is interesting to note that Wilson's allowance for uncollectibles actually declines in percentage terms (Exhibit 6.2) even though the average collection period increased. Why do you suppose this happens?

Exhibit 6.1 G. T. WILSON COMPANY

Comparative Cash Flow Statements

($ in thousands)	1992	1993	1994	1995	1996	1997	1998	1999	2000
Operating									
Net income	$ 31,600	$ 33,000	$ 38,200	$ 41,900	$ 36,400	$ 31,600	$ 34,950	$ 10,900	$(145,400)
Amortization	7,500	8,200	8,400	9,000	9,600	10,600	12,000	13,600	14,600
Other adjustments to income	70	(850)	(1,100)	(1,600)	(2,500)	(1,800)	(1,700)	(1,350)	(17,000)
(Increase) Decrease in receivables	(57,700)	(42,000)	(40,300)	(55,500)	(12,000)	(49,900)	(60,300)	(72,200)	9,600
(Increase) Decrease in inventories	(23,300)	(9,100)	(24,900)	(13,500)	(38,400)	(38,200)	(100,850)	(51,100)	(4,350)
(Increase) Decrease in prepayments	(450)	100	(400)	(650)	(200)	(150)	(1,250)	(650)	700
Increase (Decrease) in accounts payable	17,600	3,800	22,400	2,050	13,900	6,900	(12,100)	(8,000)	42,400
Increase (Decrease) in other current liabilities	8,100	11,900	8,500	15,400	(21,900)	13,900	14,950	15,650	(1,500)
Cash flow from operations	**$(16,580)**	**$ 5,050**	**$ 10,800**	**$ (2,900)**	**$(15,100)**	**$(27,050)**	**$(114,300)**	**$ (93,150)**	**$(100,950)**
Investing									
Acquisition of property, plant, and equipment	(15,250)	(7,800)	(10,600)	(14,400)	(16,100)	(25,900)	(26,250)	(23,150)	(15,500)
Acquisition of investments	(250)	(400)	—	—	(450)	(6,000)	(2,200)	(5,700)	(5,300)
Cash flow from investing	**(15,500)**	**$ (8,200)**	**$(10,600)**	**$(14,400)**	**$ (16,550)**	**$(31,900)**	**$ (28,450)**	**$ (28,850)**	**$ (20,800)**
Financing									
Increase (Decrease) in short-term borrowing	60,300	1,600	18,900	64,000	64,300	(8,650)	152,300	63,050	147,600
Increase (Decrease) in long-term borrowing	—	(1,500)	(1,500)	(1,650)	(1,500)	98,450	(1,600)	93,900	(4,000)
Increase (Decrease) in capital stock	2,700	4,000	850	(17,900)	(8,900)	7,400	(8,200)	1,800	850
Dividends	(14,100)	(14,400)	(17,700)	(19,700)	(20,800)	(21,100)	(21,150)	(21,100)	(4,500)
Cash flow from financing	**$ 48,900**	**$(10,300)**	**$ 550**	**$ 24,750**	**$ 33,100**	**$ 76,100**	**$ 121,350**	**$137,650**	**$ 139,950**
Other	(450)	(400)	(100)	—	(400)	(1,350)	2,450	(650)	(700)
Change in cash	**$ 16,370**	**$(13,850)**	**$ 650**	**$ 7,450**	**$ 1,050**	**$ 15,800**	**$ (18,950)**	**$ 15,000**	**$ 17,500**

Year Ended January 31,

Exhibit 6.2 G. T. WILSON COMPANY SELECTED FINANCIAL STATISTICS

| | Year Ended January 31, | | | | | | | | |
	1992	1993	1994	1995	1996	1997	1998	1999	2000
Operations									
Sales ($ millions)	$920	$980	$1,095	$1,210	$1,250	$1,375	$1,665	$1,850	$1,762
Number of new stores (net of closures)	4	6	13	21	52	40	37	41	21
Gross profit/sales	31.8%	32.1%	32.8%	33.0%	36.5%	35.8%	35.3%	35.1%	30.1%
Selling, general, and administrative/sales	24.8%	25.1%	25.2%	25.2%	29.9%	30.7%	30.6%	30.4%	41.3%
Net income/sales	3.4%	3.4%	3.5%	3.5%	2.9%	2.3%	2.1%	0.6%	−8.3%
Dividends/net income	44.6%	43.6%	46.3%	47.0%	57.1%	66.8%	60.5%	193.6%	n.a.
Short-Term Liquidity									
Current assets/current liabilities	3.7	3.6	3.3	3.4	3.7	4.6	4.5	5.0	6.2
Operating cash flows as a % of sales	−1.8%	0.5%	1.0%	−0.2%	−1.2%	−2.0%	−6.9%	−5.0%	−5.7%
Days receivable	91.3	95.3	104.1	115.1	126.2	131.1	130.5	140.0	142.5
% allowance for uncollectibles	3.8%	4.1%	3.8%	4.0%	3.6%	3.2%	2.8%	3.0%	3.3%
Days inventory	100.9	100.2	102.7	104.3	112.8	117.1	129.6	131.2	130.5
Days payable	42.4	42.5	48.6	45.7	48.9	47.1	33.6	30.7	42.6
Long-Term Solvency									
Total debt as a % of assets	32.7%	29.3%	25.9%	30.8%	37.3%	41.8%	49.8%	56.4%	75.7%
Interest coverage	8.8	8.1	8.7	6.4	4.7	4.5	3.9	1.2	(2.4)
Short-term debt as a % of total debt	33.3%	46.5%	59.4%	70.8%	81.6%	64.0%	75.8%	70.0%	78.3%

A business that spends more cash on its operating activities than it generates must find ways to finance the operating cash shortfall. Typically, this means using up cash reserves, borrowing additional cash, issuing additional equity, or liquidating investments like real estate and other fixed assets. None of these options can be sustained for long. For example, Wilson could finance the company's continued operating cash flow deficit by selling some retail stores to another company. Doing this might jeopardize the company's ability to generate positive operating cash flows in the future. Similarly, creditors are unlikely to keep lending to a business that continously does not generate an acceptable level of cash flow from its operations. In this regard, Wilson's inability to generate positive operating cash flows in recent years is particularly troublesome.

Investing Activities
In this section of the cash flow statement, companies disclose capital expenditures, acquisitions of other firms, and investments in marketable securities. Of course, disinvestment generates cash (examples include the sale of equipment or investment securities).

The cash flow statements of Wilson Company (Exhibit 6.1) show sustained investment in property, plant, and equipment that is consistent with the company's expansion in new stores (Exhibit 6.2). Analysts should carefully investigate the capital expenditures of the company and any fixed asset retirements during the year.

Capital expenditures and asset sales should be consistent with the company's business strategy and growth opportunities. For example, consider the following scenarios.

- *Emerging companies* require substantial investments in property, plant, and equipment at a stage when operating cash flows are typically negative.

- *Established growth companies* also require substantial fixed asset investments to further expand their market presence. Operating cash flows for established growth companies can be positive or negative, depending on the pace of expansion, the degree to which expansion also requires working capital investment, and the ability of the company to generate a positive operating cash flow from established markets.

- *Mature companies'* capital expenditures, on the other hand, are limited to the amount needed to sustain current levels of operation. Mature companies usually rely on internal sources (operating cash flows and fixed asset sales) to finance their capital expenditure needs.

Changes in a company's capital expenditures or fixed asset sales over time must be carefully analyzed. For example, a sharp reduction in capital expenditures for an emerging growth company may indicate that the company is suffering from a temporary cash shortage. Decreased capital expenditures may also signal a more fundamental change in management's expectations about the company's growth opportunities and competitive environment. Similarly, an unexplained increase in fixed asset sales could mean that management needs to raise cash quickly or that it is eliminating excess production capacity. The analyst needs to evaluate each of these possibilities because they have very different implications for the company's future operating cash flows.

Financing Activities

The most significant source of external financing for most companies is debt. There is a large research literature in finance which explores the "optimal" amount of debt financing that companies should include in their capital structure. Determining this optimal debt level involves a tradeoff between two competing economic forces—taxes and bankruptcy costs.[30] The advantage of debt financing is that interest on debt is tax-deductible. The disadvantage is that highly leveraged firms have a greater risk of bankruptcy. The precise point at which these two forces counterbalance one another varies from company to company and over time. One way analysts can assess the optimal level of debt is to evaluate the company's historical and estimated future ability to meet scheduled debt payments. In this regard the situation at G. T. Wilson Company would appear bleak.

The financing section of Wilson's cash flow statements (Exhibit 6.1) reveals a heavy reliance on short-term debt that is used to finance the company's capital expenditures and operating cash flow deficits. The company issued $98.45 million of long-term debt in 1997 and $93.9 million in 1999. But the vast majority of Wilson's external financing has been in the form of short-term debt. Total debt as a percentage of assets (Exhibit 6.2) has grown from 32.7% in 1992 to 75.7% in 2000; short-term debt as a percentage of total debt has increased from 33.3% in 1992 to 78.3% in 2000; and the company's interest coverage ratio has deteriorated from 8.8 times to *minus* 2.4 times.

Wilson's cash flow needs and the company's growing debt burden raise questions about the wisdom of its dividend policy. Recall that Wilson has paid cash dividends to shareholders since 1906, and it continued to do so during 2000 when the company reported a $145 million loss. Cash dividend payments totalled $14.1 million in

1992, grew to about $21 million in 1996, and then held steady at that level until falling to $4.5 million in 2000. These cash flows could instead have been used to finance the company's operating deficits and capital expenditures—or to pay down debt.

Why was management so reluctant to curtail dividends? The payment of a cash dividend is viewed as an important signal by many financial analysts and investors. Management presumably "signals" its expectations about the future through its dividend policy. A cash dividend increase is viewed as an indication that management expects future operating cash flows to be favourable—to the extent it can sustain the higher dividend. A reduction in cash dividends is interpreted as an indication that management expects future operating cash flows to decrease and remain at this decreased level. Research tends to corroborate dividend signalling. Increases and decreases in cash dividend payments are (on average) associated with subsequent earnings and operating cash flow changes in the same direction. Of course, the degree of association between dividend changes and future earnings or operating cash flow performance is less than perfect. Consequently, financial analysts and investors must carefully evaluate the specific circumstances confronting each company.

Recommendation Wilson's use of short-term debt financing, coupled with its inability to generate positive cash flows from operations, places the company in a precarious position. Unless other external sources of financing are identified or unless operating activities start to generate positive cash flows, the company will be forced to declare bankruptcy if short-term creditors demand payment on existing loans. In short, Wilson Company is a serious credit risk to the bank, and renewal of the $200 million revolving credit line is probably not justified. In fact, the bank may well consider taking immediate steps to improve the likelihood of loan repayment and to protect its creditor position in the event of bankruptcy.

This illustration is based loosely on the financial statements of W. T. Grant for the years 1967 through 1975. At the time that it filed for bankruptcy in late 1975, Grant was the 17th-largest retailer in the United States. The company's collapse has been traced to a failed business strategy that involved rapid store expansion, product line extensions, and customer credit terms that contributed to delayed payment and increased customer default risk.[31]

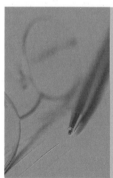

Recap

Timing differences between cash inflows and outflows create the need to borrow money. Cash flow analysis helps lenders identify why cash flow imbalances occur and whether the imbalance is temporary. Commercial banks, insurance companies, pension funds, and other lenders are willing to lend the needed cash only if there is a high probability that the borrower's future cash inflows will be sufficient to repay the loan. Credit analysts rely on their understanding of the company, its business strategy and the competitive environment, and the adequacy of its past cash flows as a basis for forecasting future cash flows and assessing the company's financial flexibility under stress.

Summary

In Section 1000 of the *CICA Handbook*, the AcSB emphasizes that:

Investors and creditors of profit-oriented enterprises are interested, for the purpose of making resource allocation decisions, in predicting the ability of the entity to earn income and generate cash flows in the future to meet its obligations and to generate a return on investment.[32]

This chapter provides a framework for understanding how financial reporting tries to meet this important need. Specifically, we analyze the role that accounting numbers might play in valuation, cash flow analysis, and credit risk assessment. Alternative valuation models and approaches to credit risk assessment are presented to provide some structure and concreteness.

A critical part of understanding the **decision-relevance**[33] of accounting information—a major focus of this book—is understanding *which* accounting numbers are used, *why* they are used, and *how* they are used in investment and credit decisions. Knowing how earnings, book values, and cash flows are used in investment and credit decisions will help you to assess the value-relevance of alternative accounting measures discussed in subsequent chapters of this book—not only those recognized in the body of the financial statements but also those disclosed in financial statement footnotes.

Knowing what accounting numbers are used in investment and credit decisions and how these numbers are affected by certain transactions or accounting methods is important for understanding the incentives that management has for structuring transactions in certain ways or for choosing among alternative generally accepted accounting treatments for a particular event or transaction. We will come back to this point repeatedly as we explore the underlying economics of transactions and the alternative accounting methods used to describe them.

Appendix 6A

Abnormal Earnings Valuation

This appendix illustrates how the abnormal earnings valuation model can be combined with security analysts' published earnings forecasts to produce an **intrinsic share price estimate** for a company. To make this illustration real, we focus on Reebok International Ltd. and those analysts' earnings forecasts that were available in March 2000 when the company's common stock was trading at US$9.25 per share. Then we show how this valuation model can also be used to understand the market's expectations for an Internet company, Amazon.com.

REEBOK
INTERNATIONAL LTD.
www.reebok.com

Reebok (named after the *reebok*, a swift and agile African gazelle) entered the U.S. market in 1979 following several decades of success as a designer and manufacturer of high-performance running shoes marketed in the United Kingdom. By merging high-performance technology with style and fashion, the company successfully rode the sports and fitness wave in the United States in the mid-1980s. In 1989, Reebok introduced "The Pump" technology into its basketball shoes. Today, the company continues to emphasize both high performance and fashion in its products.

Share Price Valuation There are five steps to deriving a share price estimate using analysts' earnings forecasts and the abnormal earnings valuation model:

1. Obtain analysts' earnings-per-share (EPS) forecasts for some finite horizon, say the next five years.
2. Combine the EPS forecasts with projected dividends to forecast common equity book value over the horizon.
3. Compute yearly *abnormal* earnings by subtracting *normal* earnings (i.e., beginning equity book value multiplied by the equity cost of capital) from analysts' EPS forecasts.
4. Forecast the perpetual (terminal year) *abnormal* earnings flow that will occur beyond the explicit forecast horizon.

5. Add the current book value and the present value of the two abnormal earnings components—the first five years and for years beyond the terminal period—to obtain an intrinsic value estimate of the company's share price.

Each of these steps is illustrated in the Reebok valuation in Table 6.5.

TABLE 6.5 REEBOK INTERNATIONAL LTD.

Abnormal Earnings Valuation as of March 1, 2000

(US$)	Historical Results		Forecasted Results					Beyond
	1998	1999	2000	2001	2002	2003	2004	2004
(a) Earnings Forecasts								
Reported earnings per share[1]	$1.04	$1.30						
Last year's earnings per share			$ 1.30	$ 1.19	$ 1.39	$ 1.53	$ 1.69	
× (1 + Forecasted earnings growth)			0.9154	1.1681	1.1020	1.1020	1.1020	
= Forecasted earnings per share			$ 1.19	$ 1.39	$ 1.53	$ 1.69	$ 1.86	
(b) Equity Book Value Forecasts								
Equity book value at beginning of year	$8.99	$9.56	$ 9.40	$10.59	$11.98	$13.51	$15.20	
+ Earnings per share from (a)	1.04	1.30	1.19	1.39	1.53	1.69	1.86	
+ Stock issued (repurchased)	0.03	(0.24)	0.00	0.00	0.00	0.00	0.00	
+ Other comprehensive income per share	(0.50)	(1.22)	0.00	0.00	0.00	0.00	0.00	
− Dividends per share	0.00	0.00	0.00	0.00	0.00	0.00	0.00	
= Equity book value at year-end	$9.56	$9.40	$10.59	$11.98	$13.51	$15.20	$17.06	
ROE = EPS/Equity book value at beginning of year	11.6%	13.6%	12.7%	13.1%	12.8%	12.5%	12.2%	
(c) Abnormal Earnings								
Equity book value at beginning of year	$8.99	$9.56	$ 9.40	$10.59	$11.98	$13.51	$15.20	
× Equity cost of capital	13.0%	13.0%	13.0%	13.0%	13.0%	13.0%	13.0%	
= Normal earnings	$1.17	$1.24	$1.22	$1.38	$1.56	$1.76	$1.98	
Actual or forecasted earnings	$1.04	$1.30	$1.19	$1.39	$1.53	$1.69	$1.86	
− Normal earnings	1.17	1.24	1.22	1.38	1.56	1.76	1.98	
= Abnormal earnings	($0.13)	$0.06	($0.03)	$0.01	($0.03)	($0.07)	($0.12)	
(d) Valuation								
Future abnormal earnings in forecast horizon			($0.03)	$0.01	($0.03)	($0.07)	($0.12)	
× Discount factor at 13%			0.88496	0.78315	0.69305	0.61332	0.54276	
= Abnormal earnings discounted to present			($0.03)	$0.01	($0.02)	($0.04)	($0.06)	
Abnormal earnings in year 2005[2]								($ 0.12)
Assumed long-term growth rate								3.0%
Perpetuity factor for year 2004								10.0
Discount factor at 13%								0.54276
Present value of terminal year abnormal earnings[3]								($ 0.67)
(e) Estimated Share Price								
Sum of discounted abnormal earnings over horizon			($ 0.14)					
+ Present value of terminal year abnormal earnings			(0.67)					
= Present value of all abnormal earnings			(0.81)					
+ Current equity book value			9.40					
= Estimated current share price at March 1, 2000			$ 8.59					
Actual share price at March 1, 2000			$ 9.25					

[1]Adjusted for nonrecurring gains and losses.

[2]This is forecasted abnormal earnings for 2004, multiplied by one plus the long-term growth rate: ($0.12) × (1 + 0.03) = ($0.1236), or ($0.12) rounded.

[3]This is just ($0.1236) × 10.0 × 0.54276 = ($0.6709), or ($0.67) rounded.

Our forecast horizon—and the one used by analysts covering the company—is the five-year period from 2000 through 2004. There are at least three reasons why analysts focus on the short-to-intermediate term in valuing a company. First, competitive pressures may make it difficult for the company to sustain growth in sales, profits, and cash flows in the long run. Thus, it is unrealistic to forecast that a growing company can maintain high short-term growth rates for an indefinite period. Second, long-range projections are more uncertain and, therefore, subject to greater error. Simply put, projected earnings or dividend payouts to shareholders become less and less reliable the further removed they are from the current forecast date. And third, because of the time value of money, the discounted present values of future abnormal earnings or free cash flows become smaller as the forecast horizon increases. In other words, longer-range forecasts simply do not matter very much in terms of determining current share price. For example, the present value of a dollar received 25 years from now discounted at 15%—a very realistic estimate for the cost of equity capital—is equal to $\$1 \div (1 + 0.15)^{25} = \$0.03$.

In late March 2000, securities analysts who covered Reebok were forecasting EPS of US$1.19 for 2000 and US$1.39 for 2001. These same analysts were forecasting annual EPS growth of 10.2% for 2002 through 2004. Based on the company's projected EPS of US$1.39 for 2001, this means that analysts were forecasting 2002 EPS of US$1.53 (or $\$1.39 \times 1.1020$). These same analysts were forecasting 2003 EPS of US$1.69 (or $\$1.53 \times 1.1020$), and so on. These EPS forecasts are presented in part (a) of Table 6.5.

Next, we need to compute the book value of common equity for each year of the five-year forecast horizon. From the historical information contained in part (b) of the table, we learn that Reebok has not been paying dividends for the last two years or buying back much of its common stock. We assume that no dividend distributions or additional stock repurchases will occur over the next five years. These assumptions are combined with the EPS forecasts from part (a) to produce the equity book value forecasts of US$10.59 per share at the end of 2000 and US$17.06 per share at the end of 2004.

The abnormal earnings calculation for each of the five years in our forecast horizon is shown in part (c) of Table 6.5. Here, "normal" earnings are subtracted from the annual EPS forecasts. Normal earnings are just Reebok's common equity book value at the *beginning* of each year—as computed in part (b)—multiplied by the company's cost of equity capital, which is 13%.[34] For example, the –US$0.03 per share of abnormal earnings for 2000 is simply analysts' US$1.19 EPS forecast minus the US$1.22 normal earnings (13% × $9.40 beginning book value) for the year.

These abnormal earnings forecasts from part (c) become the basic inputs to the valuation calculation in part (d), where abnormal earnings are discounted at the company's 13% equity cost of capital. A *terminal value* calculation intended to represent the value of the company's abnormal earnings flow beyond our five-year forecast horizon is also shown in part (d). To arrive at this terminal value estimate, we assume that Reebok's abnormal earnings of –US$0.12 in year 2004 will continue to grow by 3% each year for the foreseeable future.[35] The present value of this growing perpetual flow at the beginning of year 2005 is –US$1.236, which is year 2004 earnings multiplied by the long-term growth rate (1 + 0.03), and then multiplied again by the perpetuity factor 10.0.[36] This quantity is then discounted using the present value factor for five periods discounted at 13% (0.54276), which translates the present value of abnormal earnings at the beginning of 2005 into a current-day present value of –US$0.67. Part (e) shows that the sum of all discounted abnormal earnings flows (–US$0.81) plus the company's current equity book value (US$9.40) produces an estimated share price of US$8.59; this contrasts with Reebok's actual US$9.25 share price.

What does this tell us? For one thing, Reebok's US$9.25 per share stock price on March 1, 2000, was somewhat higher than that implied by securities analysts' five-year EPS and dividend payout forecasts coupled with our own predictions about earnings growth beyond the forecast horizon (year 2004). In this regard, Reebok's stock may appear to be somewhat overpriced in the marketplace. However, the market may have been anticipating abnormal earnings to stop declining beyond year 2004 and instead return to breakeven (US$0.00) or become slightly positive. The rub, of course, is that we cannot know at the time which of the forecasts will prove correct in the future.

The abnormal earnings valuation model in Table 6.5 can be used to value almost any publicly traded company. It's easy to implement because it requires just a hand-ful of items—earnings forecasts from analysts, a beginning book value of equity, fore-casts of dividends and stock repurchases, an equity cost of capital (discount rate), and a long-term growth rate for abnormal earnings beyond the terminal year. But how well does it work?

There are several ways to answer this question. One approach compares the accu-racy of stock price estimates from several different valuation models—for example, the abnormal earnings model versus the free cash flow valuation model. A recent study did just that using a sample of nearly 3,000 firm-year observations over 1989 through 1993.[37] Earnings, dividends, and cash flow forecasts were gathered from *Value Line* for each sample firm and year. These forecasts were then used as inputs to an abnormal earnings valuation model (like the one in Table 6.5) and as inputs to a separate free cash flow valuation model. The two value estimates—one based on abnormal earnings and the other based on free cash flows—were then compared to actual stock prices. Which valuation model was best? Abnormal earnings value esti-mates were more accurate and explained more of the variation in actual stock prices than did free cash flow value estimates.

> In theory, both valua-tion models should produce the same stock price estimate. But in practice, the two valuation models often do not produce the same stock price estimate.

A related study asked if money can be made from the abnormal earnings valua-tion model in Table 6.5.[38] Using a sample of nearly 18,000 firm-year observations covering 1979 to 1991, the researchers computed valuation estimates for each firm and year. These estimates were then used to construct a *value index*—it's the esti-mated value divided by the actual share price—for each company and year. (The value index for Reebok would be $8.59/$9.25 = 0.929.) The simulated trading strat-egy involved "buying" the most undervalued companies (high value index) and "sell-ing short" the most overvalued companies (low value index). This strategy produced a three-year portfolio return of 35%, which implies investors can profit from using the abnormal earnings valuation model.

Valuing a Dot-Com "Trying to get your arms around the value of an Internet stock is like trying to hug the air."[39]

Determining a company's worth is difficult enough for firms like Reebok or Wal-Mart, which have an established business model, a solid customer base, and a proven record of profit and cash flows. But how do you value an Internet company like Amazon.com—a company with no profits to date? Is Amazon.com really worth the US$40 billion the stock market gave it in December 1999 when the company's shares were selling for US$113 each? the US$6.7 billion the stock market gave it in January 2001 (US$19 per share)? Or, is it worth something else?

Internet stocks and other emerging growth companies are difficult to value using the free cash flow or abnormal earnings models described in this chapter. The problem is that these valuation methods require forecasts of future revenue growth, profit margins, cash investment needs, and other important inputs. But how do you forecast the future when it's a company with little history and an unproven business plan? Even thoughtful forecasts are still guesses, and a bad one will throw a valuation off-kilter—making the stock seem either too cheap or too expensive. To overcome this problem, some analysts have turned to so-called new economy valuation metrics (e.g., eyeballs, Internet time, and page views) intended to minimize the guesswork.[40]

YAHOO!
www.yahoo.com

Here's how one "new economy" valuation metric is used. Let's suppose 25.2 million people visited the Yahoo! website at least once in January. If you divide the number of Yahoo! visitors into the company's market capitalization of US$18.4 billion—that's just January's US$33 stock price multiplied by 558.4 million Yahoo! shares outstanding—you get a market value of US$731 per visitor. In other words, the stock market says each Yahoo! visitor is worth US$731. Compare that to one of Yahoo's rivals, Lycos Inc., where the numbers work out to be about US$135 per visitor. According to analysts who use the new metrics, this disparity in visitor value means Yahoo! shares are expensive while Lycos shares are cheap—even though neither company is currently making a profit on its visitors!

A different approach to valuation turns the whole process on its head.[41] Instead of forecasting all the inputs to come up with a number for what the stock should be worth, this method starts with the stock price and works backward to answer the question: What kind of profitability and growth does this company have to deliver to justify the price? This method does not avoid making some assumptions, but it's a way to perform a reality check on the stock market.

AMAZON.COM
www.amazon.com

To see how this approach works, let's take a closer look at Amazon.com. For the 12 months ended September 30, 2000, the company had a net loss of US$1.2 billion on sales of US$2.5 billion. (That's a loss of US$0.48 on each sales dollar.) Amazon's stock price fell from a record US$113 in December 1999 to US$19 by January 2001. But even at the price of US$19, the stock market had lofty expectations for the company—a one-year leap to profitability followed by revenue and earnings growth of 39% a year for the next 10 years, as we show you next.

To arrive at that conclusion, we derived the market-implied growth rate from the current stock price. Here's how. From our discussion earlier in this chapter, a company's market value has two components. One relates to assets in place and the other to future growth opportunities—see equation (6.9). In the context of the abnormal earnings valuation model, these two components are called *current operations value* (COV), a measure of the worth of the company as it now operates, and *future growth value* (FGV), a measure of the company's expected growth.

Market value (MV) = Current operations value (COV) + Future growth value (FGV)

Once you determine the COV—and that's the easier of the two—you can figure out the market-implied future growth value. And once you know the FGV, you can determine the implied revenue and earnings growth rate. Then you can make a judgment about whether that growth rate is achievable.

Sounds easy enough, although some aspects of the analysis can be troublesome. The details behind our Amazon.com calculations are in Table 6.6. To keep things simple, let's focus only on the highlights. First, we determine the company's *total* market value—the value of common stock, preferred stock, and debt. At the price of US$19, Amazon's common stock is worth US$6,762 million (US$19 per share times

TABLE 6.6 AMAZON.COM

Valuing an Internet Company

A. Determining the Market-Implied Growth Rate (US$ in millions, except per share amounts)

(a) Market Value of the Company

Stock price per share—January 2001	$19.00	
× Common shares outstanding (in millions)	355.9	
= Market value of common stock		$6,762
+ Value of preferred stock		—
+ Value of interest-bearing debt		2,100
= Market value of the company		$8,862

(b) Operating Assumptions and Capital

Sales for the next 12 months	$3,600	
× Long-term average operating margin	10%	
= Long-term average NOPAT		$ 360
Book value of interest-bearing debt	$2,100	
+ Book value of stockholder's equity	(229)	
= Capital invested in the company	$1,871	
Cost of capital	15%	
Required NOPAT (rounded)		281
Abnormal NOPAT		$ 79

(c) Current Operations Value (COV)

Abnormal NOPAT from current operations	$ 79	
÷ Cost of capital (discount rate)	15%	
= Value of abnormal NOPAT from current operations (rounded)	$ 527	
+ Current capital in the company	1,871	
= Current operations value of the company		$2,398

(d) Future Growth Value (FGV)

Market value of the company	$8,862
Current operations value of the company	(2,398)
Future growth value of the company	$6,464
Implied annual growth rate	39.0%

B. Getting Behind the Numbers

The abnormal earnings valuation model is used as our benchmark for evaluating Amazon.com's US$19 stock price. But two modifications are made to adapt the abnormal earnings valuation equation (6.11) for our purposes here. The first modification involves isolating the COV and FGV components of the model:

$$P_0 = BV_0 + \sum_{t=1}^{\infty} \frac{E_0 \, (\text{Abnormal earnings}_t)}{(1 + r)^t}$$

$$= BV_0 + \frac{E_0 \, (\text{Current abnormal earnings})}{r} + FGV \tag{6.11}$$

$$= COV + FGV$$

The second modification is made because Amazon.com has a deficit balance in stockholders' equity. To overcome problems associated with a negative value for BV_0 and its impact on the abnormal earnings calculation, we redefine all components of the valuation model to reflect *total* capital (debt plus equity). A weighted-average cost of capital for debt and equity is used, with the cost of equity capital calculated as described in endnote 34.

The implied annual growth rate is found by solving a complex expression that equates FGV with the present value of abnormal earnings growth over a ten-year horizon.

the 355.9 million shares outstanding). The company has no preferred stock and US$2,100 million in debt. So, the company's *total* market value is US$8,862 million.

Next to be determined is the company's COV—what Amazon would be worth if there were no further growth. But hold on—it's not making money now. Sure, but that's because of large startup costs—dollars spent on information technology, e-commerce software, and on acquiring customers. Once those costs are out of the way, assume that the company will earn an operating margin of 10%. So, to determine COV, we will assume the company is now earning its average long-term margin and is thus profitable.

To get COV from the abnormal earnings valuation model, we start with expected sales for the next 12 months of US$3,600 million (obtained from management or from analysts who follow the company—we used an analyst's forecast). Then we multiply the sales forecast by the long-term operating margin of 10% to arrive at expected operating profits (required NOPAT) of US$360 million per year. Next, we need to find out how much capital—shareholders' equity and debt—is invested currently in the company. Amazon's most recent balance sheet showed US$2,100 million of debt and a deficit of US$229 million in stockholders' equity, so total capital is US$1,871 million. What level of profits must the company generate to satisfy its debt and equity investors? To get that number, we need a cost of capital estimate so that we can compute normal earnings. Because the stock is volatile, we assume a high cost of capital—15% (endnote 34 describes our approach). The company thus needs to generate US$281 million in earnings (or US$1,871 million multiplied by 15%) to satisfy its investors. That's less than the US$360 million of expected operating profits, so abnormal earnings are US$79 million more than investors require ($360 million minus $281 million).

To get the COV, we divide expected abnormal earnings by 15%—which yields US$527 million—and then add current investor capital of US$1,871 million. This gives Amazon a current operations value of US$2,398 million. With no future growth, that's what the company would be worth.

Now it's easy to determine Amazon's future growth value (FGV). We simply subtract US$2,398 million from the total market value (US$8,862 million), which gives an FGV of US$6,464 million. How fast do revenues and operating profits have to grow over the next 10 years to give you a future growth value of US$6,464 million? The answer is 39% a year, assuming margins of 10% and a 15% cost of capital.

Can Amazon achieve a 39% average annual revenue (and profit) growth rate over 10 years? That's where investors and analysts must turn to industry fundamentals and common sense. For instance, Amazon's sales would need to reach US$96 billion, and its operating profits US$9.6 billion, in 10 years. Is that realistic? Not if the company sells only books. The total of all U.S. retail book sales in 1999 was about US$12 billion. Even if book sales expanded by 3% a year, total retail sales would be only about US$16 billion ten years out. If Amazon captured the entire U.S. retail book market, it would still fall US$86 billion short of the projected sales target.

Clearly, Amazon must sell more than just books if it is to achieve the market-implied growth rate. And it does sell more—including CDs, consumer electronics, and a variety of other items on a global basis. So, let's turn to Wal-Mart, a "bricks and mortar" retailer, for a different perspective on Amazon's growth prospects. Wal-Mart had sales of US$165 billion and operating profits of US$622 million in 1999. Can Amazon become more than half as large as Wal-Mart in 10 years? Some analysts clearly think so because the consensus five-year earnings growth rate forecast for Amazon was 41% in January 2001. On the other hand, as e-commerce draws more competitors—including Wal-Mart—it may be unrealistic to assume that Amazon can achieve the levels of growth and profitability needed to sustain its US$19 stock price. Of the 29 Wall Street analysts who covered the company in January 2001, 18 rated Amazon a "buy" or "strong buy" and 11 said investors should continue to "hold" the stock. Stay tuned.

Appendix 6B

Measuring Cash Flow at Standard & Poor's (S&P)

Discussions about cash flow often suffer from lack of uniform definition of terms. The table illustrates S&P's terminology with respect to specific cash flow concepts. At the top is the item from the funds flow statement usually labelled "**funds from operations**" (FFO) or "**working capital from operations.**" This quantity is net income adjusted for amortization and other noncash debits and credits factored into it. Back out the changes in working capital investment to arrive at "**operating cash flow.**"

STANDARD & POOR'S
www.
standardandpoors.
com

Next, capital expenditures and cash dividends are subtracted out to arrive at "**free operating cash flow**" and "**discretionary cash flow,**" respectively. Finally, the purchase cost of acquisitions is subtracted from the running total, proceeds from asset disposals added, and other miscellaneous sources and uses of cash netted together. "**Prefinancing cash flow**" is the end result of these computations, which represents the extent to which company cash flow from all internal sources has been sufficient to cover all internal needs.

The bottom part of the table reconciles prefinancing cash flow to various categories of external financing and changes in the company's own cash balances. In the example, XYZ Corporation experienced a $35.7 million cash shortfall in Year 1, which had to be met with a combination of additional borrowings and a drawdown of its own cash.

XYZ Corporation Cash Flow Summary		
($ in millions)	Year 1	Year 2
Funds from operations (FFO)	$18.58	$22.34
Decrease (increase) in noncash current assets	(33.12)	1.05
Increase (decrease) in noncash current liabilities	15.07	(12.61)
Operating cash flow	$ 0.53	$10.78
Capital expenditures	(11.06)	(9.74)
Free operating cash flow	($10.53)	$ 1.04
Cash dividends	(4.45)	(5.14)
Discretionary cash flow	($14.98)	($ 4.10)
Acquisitions	(21.00)	—
Asset disposals	0.73	0.24
Net other sources (uses) of cash	(0.44)	(0.09)
Prefinancing cash flow	($35.69)	($ 3.95)
Increase (decrease) in short-term debt	$23.00	—
Increase (decrease) in long-term debt	6.12	13.02
Net sale (repurchase) of equity	0.32	(7.07)
Decrease (increase) in cash and securities	6.25	(2.00)
	$35.69	$ 3.95

Source: Standard & Poor's Corporate Finance Criteria (New York: Standard & Poor's Rating Group), 1994, p. 25.

Appendix 6C

Measuring "Core Earnings" at Standard & Poor's (S&P)

STANDARD & POOR'S
www.
standardandpoors.
com

Recall from Chapter 1 that S&P has initiated a program of adjusting reported GAAP-based earnings numbers in order to get closer to what the company terms "core" earnings. More information on this initiative may be found at the company's website.

Problems/Discussion Questions

P6-1 Explaining differences in P/E ratios

The P/E ratios in July 1999 for two groups of companies were:

Company	P/E Ratio
Group A	
General Motors	6.3
Merck & Company	26.3
Microsoft	38.6
Group B	
Compaq Computer	40.0
Dell Computer	64.6
Gateway	35.4

Required:

1. What factors might explain the differences in the P/E ratios of the companies in Group A?
2. What factors might explain the differences in the P/E ratios of the companies in Group B?

P6-2 Abnormal earnings—some simple examples

As discussed in the chapter, abnormal earnings (AE) are:

$$AE_t = \text{Actual earnings} - \text{Required earnings}$$

which may be expressed as:

$$NOPAT - (r \times BV_{t-1})$$

where NOPAT is the firm's net operating profit after taxes, r is the cost of equity capital, and BV_{t-1} is book value of equity at $t-1$.

Required:

Solve the following problems:

1. If NOPAT is $5,000, $r = 15\%$, and BV_{t-1} is $50,000, what is AE?
2. If NOPAT is $25,000, $r = 18\%$, and BV_{t-1} is $125,000, what is AE?
3. Assume that the firm in Question 2 can increase NOPAT to $30,000 by instituting some cost-cutting measures. What would be the new AE?
4. Assume that the firm in Question 2 can divest $25,000 of unproductive capital, with NOPAT falling by only $2,000. What would be the new AE?
5. Assume that the firm in Question 2 can add a new division at a cost of $40,000, which will increase NOPAT by $7,600 per year. Would adding the new division increase AE?
6. Assume that the firm in Question 1 can add a new division at a cost of $25,000, which will increase NOPAT by $3,500 per year. Would adding the new division increase AE?

P6-3 Value creation by two companies

As discussed in the chapter, abnormal earnings (AE) are:

$$AE_t = \text{Actual earnings} - \text{Required earnings}$$

which may be expressed as:

$$AE_t = NOPAT_t - (r \times BV_{t-1})$$

where NOPAT is the firm's net operating profit after taxes, r is the cost of equity capital, and BV_{t-1} is book value of equity at $t-1$.

The following lists the NOPAT, BV_{t-1}, and cost of equity for two companies.

Company A	2000	2001	2002	2003	2004
NOPAT	$ 66,920	$ 79,632	$ 83,314	$ 89,920	$ 92,690
BV_{t-1}	$478,000	$504,000	$541,000	$ 562,000	$ 598,000
Cost of equity capital	0.152	0.167	0.159	0.172	0.166

Company B	2000	2001	2002	2003	2004
NOPAT	$192,940	$176,341	$227,700	$ 198,900	$ 282,964
BV_{t-1}	$877,000	$943,000	$989,999	$1,020,000	$1,199,000
Cost of equity capital	0.188	0.179	0.183	0.175	0.186

Required:

1. Calculate each firm's AE each year from 2000 to 2004.
2. Which firm was a better investment for its shareholders over the 2000–2004 period? Why?

P6-4 Determinants of P/E ratios

A firm's P/E ratio can be written as:

$$P/E = \frac{\text{Market price per share}}{\text{Earnings per share}} = \frac{1}{r} + \frac{\text{Present value of growth opportunities (per share)}}{\text{Earnings per share}}$$

where r is the required rate of return (discount rate).

Required:

Briefly discuss how a firm's P/E ratio is related to (a) the present value of the firm's growth opportunities, (b) the firm's risk, and (c) the firm's choice of accounting methods.

P6-5 Abnormal earnings valuation—Dell Computer example

DELL COMPUTER
CORPORATION
www.dell.ca

Dell Computer Corporation (Dell) designs, develops, manufactures, markets, services, and supports a wide range of computer systems, including desktops, notebooks, and network servers; it also markets software, peripherals, and service and support programs. With revenue of US$7.8 billion for fiscal 1997 (which ended on January 31, 1997), the company is the world's leading direct computer systems company and one of the top five computer vendors in the world.

The company was founded on the principle that delivering computers custom-built to customer order is the best business model for providing solutions that are truly relevant to end user needs. This build-to-order, flexible manufacturing process enables the company to achieve faster inventory turnover and reduced inventory levels, and it allows the company to rapidly incorporate new technologies and components into its product offerings. In the same way that the company's computer products are built to order, service and support programs are designed to fit specific customer requirements. The company offers a broad range of service and support programs through its own technical personnel and its direct management of specialized service suppliers. These services range from telephone support to on-site customer-dedicated systems engineers.

1. Appearing in the accompanying table are Dell's earnings per share and equity book value per share for the 1995–1997 fiscal years (Dell's fiscal year ends on January 31).
2. Dell has not been paying any dividends on its common shares. Assume that this will continue in the future.
3. In the past two years, Dell has repurchased some common shares in the open market. Assume that this will not continue in the future.
4. On February 1, 1997, the financial analysts following Dell were projecting annual earnings per share growth for the next five years (i.e., fiscal years 1998–2002), ranging from 15% to 45%, with an average of 25%.
5. After an initial five-year horizon, assume that Dell's abnormal earnings will grow by 7.5% per year.
6. On February 1, 1997, the Value Line Investment Survey estimated Dell's beta to be 1.05. Assume that on February 1, 1997, the risk-free rate of return is 6%. Use this information, along with a market risk premium of 7.5%, to estimate Dell's cost of equity capital as of February 1, 1997. (See the Reebok example in Appendix 6A of this chapter for calculation of the equity cost of capital using the capital asset pricing model.)
7. On February 1, 1997, Dell's actual share price is US$66.125.

Dell Computer

(US$)	January 31, 1995	1996	1997
As reported earnings per share	$0.85	$1.34	$2.77
Equity book value beginning of year	$3.08	$4.08	$5.20
+ Earnings per share	0.85	1.34	2.77
+ Stock issued (repurchased)	0.15	(0.22)	(3.31)
− Dividends per share	0	0	0
= Equity book value, end of year	$4.08	$5.20	$4.66

Required:

1. Use the abnormal earnings valuation model demonstrated in Appendix 6A of this chapter to derive an estimate of Dell's share price as of February 1, 1997. Use the average of analysts' earnings per share growth estimates of 25% in your calculation. How does the price you derive compare to the actual share price previously mentioned?
2. Respond to Question 1 again, except use the highest of the analysts' earnings per share growth estimates of 45% in your calculation. How does the price you derive compare to the actual share price just mentioned?
3. What factors might explain the differences in the prices derived in Questions 1 and 2 from Dell's actual share price?
4. What impact would varying the assumptions about the growth rate of earnings per share, cost of equity capital, and growth in abnormal earnings after the initial five-year horizon have on the valuations made earlier?

P6-6 Discussion questions on the role of accounting numbers in valuation

1. Describe the role of accounting numbers in corporate valuation.
2. Describe the role of accounting numbers in cash flow assessment.
3. What is meant by sustainable earnings? What types of earnings are not sustainable?
4. Briefly describe what the process of valuation involves.
5. What are free cash flows? Describe the key features of the free cash flow approach to valuation.
6. What are abnormal earnings? Describe the key features of the abnormal earnings approach to valuation.
7. What is an earnings surprise? How does an earnings surprise impact the value of a firm's equity? Be specific.

P6-7 Earnings-based equity valuations

In each of the following cases, assume that the firm's new investments earn a return of 15%, that the firm pays out 50% of its earnings as dividends, and that an earnings-based valuation model is being used.

Hint: The following two equations will facilitate your solution to this problem.[42]

$$g = (1 - k) \times \text{ROI}$$

$$P = [k \times E_0(1 + g)]/(r - g)$$

where:

g = growth rate of earnings
ROI = return on new investments (i.e., return on reinvested earnings)
k = the dividend payout ratio
E_0 = earnings for the most recent year
r = investor's required rate of return
P = estimated stock value

1. Based on the preceding information, what is the growth rate of the firm's earnings?
2. If Jackson Corp.'s most recent earnings per share are $5 and the current share price is $40, what is the firm's required rate of return on equity?
3. If Wilson's most recent earnings per share are $9 and if its required rate of return on equity is 22.5%, what is the current share price?

Cases

C6-1 ATI Technologies Inc.'s 1998 financial results

ATI TECHNOLOGIES
www.ati.com

Mr. K. Y. Ho, President and CEO of ATI Technologies Inc. (ATI), a technology company based in Thornhill, Ontario, began his 1998 "Message to Shareholders" with the following statement: "We are proud that ATI rose to a new level of success. ATI is now *the* world leader in our industry and ranks among the few truly outstanding Canadian technology companies."

1998 was a banner year for ATI. Sales exceeded $1 billion for the first time (almost doubling from 1997), net income increased 253.2% from 1997 to $168 million, and the company's closing share price at fiscal year end was $16.65 (an increase of 185.6% from the $5.83 of one year earlier). *Business Week* magazine named ATI's Mr. Ho as one of the "Top 25 Executives of the Year" in its January 11, 1999 issue.

A five-year historical review, as published in the 1998 annual report (page 51) appears below.

ATI Technologies Inc. Five-Year Historical Review					
(thousands of Canadian dollars, except per share amounts and other statistics)	Years Ended August 31,				
	1998	1997	1996	1995	1994
Operating Results					
Sales	$1,156,921	$602,839	$466,598	$359,732	$232,280
Gross margin	427,990	193,686	122,899	84,233	47,246
Net income	168,424	47,689	27,347	15,868	(2,691)
Operating cash flow	34,650	28,534	61,503	19,262	(54,935)
Financial Position					
Cash*	$ 68,900	$ 71,763	$ 73,855	$ 30,845	$ 29,275
Total assets	597,208	291,735	208,484	178,605	146,700
Bank indebtedness	—	—	10,270	12,425	23,734
Shareholders' equity	389,309	206,000	148,149	119,301	103,303
Working capital	297,678	152,435	111,470	92,655	75,960
Per Share Data					
Net income per Share					
Basic	$ 0.86	$ 0.25	$ 0.15	$ 0.09	$ (0.02)
Fully diluted	$ 0.79	$ 0.24	$ 0.14	$ 0.09	$ (0.02)
Market price:					
High	$ 19.65	$ 5.83	$ 3.21	$ 2.72	$ 4.97
Low	$ 6.04	$ 2.70	$ 2.19	$ 1.14	$ 1.25
Close	$ 16.65	$ 5.83	$ 2.75	$ 2.25	$ 1.28
Other					
Total number of employees	1,477	1,074	757	669	594
Number of employees in R&D	634	473	303	251	204
Shares outstanding:					
End of year	199,174,293	193,998,148	189,984,740	189,080,000	189,000,000
Weighted average	196,478,550	191,573,328	189,576,980	189,028,668	184,166,668

*Cash is defined as cash, cash equivalents, and short-term investments.

Additional Information:

ATI was founded in 1985. At fiscal year-end 1998 (August 31), it employed more than 1,400 people in Canada, the United States, Europe, and elsewhere. Its shares trade on the Toronto Stock Exchange under the symbol "ATY." The company is the world's largest supplier of 3D graphics and multimedia technology. Over the past five years, the company has made a remarkable turnaround; its 1994 results showed a net loss of $2.7 million and operating cash flow of minus $54.9 million, with share price at fiscal 1994 closing (August 31, 1994) of $1.28.

Comparative income statements and balance sheets for ATI for fiscal 1998 are also presented below.

ATI Technologies Inc.			
Consolidated Statements of Operations and Retained Earnings			
	Years Ended August 31,		
(thousands of Canadian dollars, except per share amounts)	**1998**	**1997**	**1996**
Sales	$1,156,921	$602,839	$466,598
Cost of goods sold	728,931	409,153	343,699
Gross margin	427,990	193,686	122,899
Expenses			
Selling and marketing	101,411	58,936	45,174
Research and development	66,574	44,459	27,507
Administrative	30,247	21,848	14,933
	198,232	125,243	87,614
Income from operations	229,758	68,443	35,285
Interest and other income	5,908	3,733	3,683
Interest expense	(155)	(382)	(179)
Income before income taxes	235,511	71,794	38,789
Income taxes (Note 9)	67,087	24,105	11,442
Net Income	$ 168,424	$ 47,689	$ 27,347
Retained Earnings, beginning of year	96,249	48,560	21,213
Retained Earnings, end of year	$ 264,673	$ 96,249	$ 48,560
Net Income per Share			
Basic	$ 0.86	$ 0.25	$ 0.15
Fully diluted	$ 0.79	$ 0.24	$ 0.14

ATI Technologies Inc.		
Consolidated Balance Sheets		
	August 31,	
(thousands of Canadian dollars)	1998	1997
Assets		
Current assets:		
Cash and cash equivalents	$ 7,400	$ 71,763
Short-term investments	61,500	—
Accounts receivable	235,782	113,744
Inventories (note 4)	173,145	41,591
Prepayments and sundry receivables	19,250	6,072
Total current assets	497,077	233,170
Capital assets (note 5)	55,365	31,085
Other assets (note 6)	44,766	27,480
Total Assets	$597,208	$291,735
Liabilities and Shareholders' Equity		
Current liabilities:		
Accounts payable	$114,769	$ 55,537
Accrued liabilities	38,176	17,687
Income taxes payable	46,454	7,511
Total current liabilities	199,399	80,735
Deferred income taxes	8,500	5,000
Shareholders' equity—Share capital (Note 8)		
Common shares:		
Authorized—unlimited number of common shares		
Issued and outstanding—199,174,293		
(1997—193,988,148)	124,636	109,751
Preferred shares:		
Authorized—unlimited number of preferred shares		
Issued and outstanding—Nil (1997—Nil)	—	—
Retained earnings	264,673	96,249
Total shareholders' equity	389,309	206,000
Total Liabilities and Shareholders' Equity	$597,208	$291,735
Commitments and Contingencies (Notes 11 and 12)		
Subsequent Event (Note 14)		

Required:

Assume a ten-year forecasting horizon, and make any other needed assumptions in order to estimate ATI's August 31, 1998 common share value using the following earnings model:

$$P_0 = BV_0 + \sum_{t=1}^{\infty} \frac{E_0(X_t - r\,BV_{t-1})}{(1+r)^t}$$

where (omitting the time subscripts) P denotes the total value of all shares outstanding, BV denotes the book value of shareholders' equity, r denotes the cost of equity capital,

E denotes the expectations operator, and X denotes net income. Make your estimate for all the shares outstanding, and also on a per-share basis (199,174,293 common shares were issued and outstanding as of August 31, 1998).

C6-2 The T. Eaton Company Limited's initial public offering (IPO)

Eaton's was Canada's largest privately owned department store until 1998, when it was forced to raise funds through a public share offering after a financial restructuring and corporate reorganization due to poor financial performance. Since its establishment in 1869, the company's "Eaton's" name has been almost synonymous with retailing in Canada: "the name is one of the most recognized brand names in Canadian retailing," according to the company's June 1, 1998 IPO prospectus. The cover sheet of the prospectus indicated that the offering price for the common shares to be issued was $15, with $14.25 net proceeds to Eaton's after the underwriting fee, thus raising $166,933,004 for the company. The offering price per share exceeded the net tangible book value per common share as at January 1, 1998 by $1.13.

The "Prospectus Summary" is shown (abridged) in Appendix 1 to this case, and selected historical and forecasted financial information, as disclosed in the IPO prospectus, is shown in Appendix 2. The company issued the following warning (shown here in summary form): "In evaluating the Company and its business, prospective investors should consider carefully the following risks ... : Implementation of Business Strategy ... Recent Management Changes ... Fashion Apparel Industry Risks ... Competitive Considerations ... Relationships with Suppliers ... Store Locations ... Availability of Capital Resources ... Security Interests [all of the Company's assets are subject to various security interests and liens securing certain indebtedness] ... Performance Warranty Obligations [certain of the Company's assets have been pledged as security for certain performance warranty obligations ... in connection with the sale of the Company's credit operations] ... Unresolved Companies' Creditors Arrangement Act Claims ... Principal Shareholders [the 'Eaton Family' ... will, indirectly, be the ... owners of approximately 53.9% of the outstanding Common Shares] ... Year 2000 Exposure ... Shrinkage [Eaton's rate of inventory shrinkage has averaged 3.5% of ... 'net sales over the last two years, well above the industry average of less than 2.0% of sales']."

The IPO prospectus included the following industry overview (abridged):

Industry Overview

General

The Canadian retail industry has become increasingly competitive in recent years due to continued downsizing, consolidations and an influx of foreign competition. Nonetheless, according to data compiled by Statistics Canada, the size of the Canadian department store market has been increasing by approximately 4% annually over the past five years. Statistics Canada compiles retail data according to a number of categories, including Department Store Sales ("DSS") and Department Store Type Merchandise ("DSTM") sales. DSS is further divided into DSS Discount (Kmart Canada, Wal-Mart Canada and Zellers) and DSS Major (The Bay, Eaton's and Sears Canada). While DSS is limited to sale by department stores, DSTM is calculated from all retail sales excluding automobiles, gas, food and restaurant sales. In 1997, DSS was $15.9 billion while DSTM sales were $77.5 billion. The following is a summary of Eaton's market share of these indices for the last five years:

(in millions)	1993	1994	% Change	1995	% Change	1996	% Change	1997	% Change
DSS Major[1]	$ 6,838	$ 6,764	(1.1%)	$ 6,430	(4.9%)	$ 6,402	(0.4%)	$ 6,925[2]	8.2%
Eaton's Share	28.8%	27.4%		26.5%		26.0%		24.4%	
DSS Total[1]	$12,794	$13,299	3.9%	$13,840	4.1%	$14,447	4.4%	$15,929	10.3%
Eaton's Share	15.4%	14.0%		12.3%		11.5%		10.6%	
DSTM	$66,316	$69,558	4.9%	$70,682	1.6%	$72,484	2.5%	$77,422	6.8%
Eaton's Share	3.0%	2.7%		2.4%		2.3%		2.2%	

Source: Adapted from Statistics Canada.

Notes:

(1) DSS Major and DSS Total exclude credit operations and catalogue sales.

(2) Estimate based on fiscal 1997 retail sales of Eaton's, The Bay and Sears Canada.

Over the last five years, Eaton's market share as a percentage of both DSTM and DSS has declined. Unsuccessful pricing strategies, an inadequate capital investment in retail operations and increased competition all contributed to a decline in Eaton's market share. See "Restructuring—Factors Leading up to the Restructuring."

Competition

Eaton's competes with retailers that operate in the moderate, moderate-better and better designer merchandise categories. Eaton's primary competitor is The Bay. However, Eaton's also competes with Canada's other traditional department store, Sears Canada, and a few regional department stores. To a lesser and declining extent, Eaton's also competes with the discount department stores, Kmart Canada, Wal-Mart Canada and Zellers. In early 1998, Hudson's Bay Company, owner of The Bay and Zellers chains, announced the acquisition of Kmart Canada, further concentrating the competition among the relatively few large Canadian retail companies. Other competitors include specialty retailers, Canadian non-department store retailers, catalogue operations and some United States retailers (especially in cross-border towns) and direct response marketers.

An analysis of "unusual items" expensed from 1995 to 1997 revealed the following (IPO prospectus, June 1, 1998, p. 40) (abridged):

Unusual items

The significant components of unusual items are as follows:

($ amounts in millions)	1997	1996	1995
Restructuring costs:			
Store closure and other restructuring costs	$(124.6)	$(18.3)	$(38.1)
CCAA costs	(56.8)	—	—
Write-off of fixed assets	(4.6)	(63.7)	—
	(186.0)	(82.0)	(38.1)
Gain on settlement of pension surplus	41.9	—	—
Gain (loss) on sale of assets	18.3	(0.1)	6.7
Other	1.3	1.7	0.3
	$(124.5)	$(80.4)	$(31.1)

Fiscal 1997 restructuring costs include the costs to close 21 stores in fiscal 1997 and in the first quarter of fiscal 1998, the costs of reducing the Company's workforce and the costs to implement other administrative and operational restructuring initiatives. The CCAA costs relate to various expenses incurred by the Company during the CCAA period, as well as costs related to the CCAA claims settlement process.

During the 1997 fiscal year, the Company realized approximately $202 million under various pension surplus sharing programs. The excess of these proceeds over the recorded value of the pension assets gave rise to the gain on settlement set out above.

The Company's restructuring charges in fiscal 1995 and 1996 primarily reflect severance and voluntary retirement costs. In fiscal 1996, the restructuring charge also included a significant write-down of system development costs related to its unsuccessful information systems development initiatives. In addition, the Company wrote down the carrying value of various fixed assets used in its retail operations (for example, store fixtures, equipment, computer assets and certain corporate assets) based on management's assessment of the recoverability of the carrying value of such assets through sale or continued use based on planned restructuring activities.

Required:

1. Given the information provided, how is the per share offering price of $15 justified?
2. Attempt to justify the share price by using ideas based upon an abnormal earning valuation, assuming the company's cost of equity capital is in the range of 17% to 22%.
3. Unfortunately, in August 1999 Eaton's went bankrupt; the final price of the company's common shares was $0.40. An article in the financial press blamed the company's managers, the underwriters, and the public accountants for producing an overly optimistic IPO prospectus 14 months earlier. Do you agree?

APPENDIX 1

Prospectus Summary

The following is a summary only, the contents of which are necessarily selective, and should be read in conjunction with, and is qualified in its entirety by, the more detailed information and financial statements (including the notes thereto) appearing elsewhere in this prospectus. Unless the context indicates otherwise, all references to the "Company" or "Eaton's" refer to The T. Eaton Company Limited and its subsidiaries. The company's year-end is the last Saturday in January of each year. References to fiscal years 1997, 1996 and 1995 are to the 53-week period ended January 31, 1998 and the 52-week periods ended January 25, 1997 and January 27, 1996, respectively.

The Company

Eaton's is Canada's largest privately-owned department store retailer. Eaton's mission is to become Canada's leading national fashion department store. Since 1869, the "EATON'S" name has been associated with the retail business of the Company and is one of the most recognized brand names in Canadian retailing. The Company's 64 department stores are located in major shopping centres and select downtown locations in every province in Canada other than Newfoundland and Prince Edward Island. Eaton's department stores offer a full range of soft goods and a narrower range of hard goods merchandise in the moderate, moderate-better and better designer merchandise categories. Eaton's merchandise is focused on apparel, accessories, cosmetics and soft home fashions.

After many years of profitability, Eaton's financial performance declined during the 1990s as a result of a combination of a number of internal and external factors, including an unsuccessful pricing strategy, inadequate capital investment in retail operations, certain unprofitable stores, weak consumer spending and increased competition. In 1997, Eaton's effected a financial restructuring under the *Companies' Creditors Arrangement Act* (the "CCAA") and a corporate reorganization under the *Business Corporations Act* (Ontario) (together, the "Restructuring"). The Restructuring enabled the Company to close 18 unprofitable stores, to relocate its head office to unused Eaton's premises in the Toronto area and to restructure approximately $450 million of secured and unsecured debt. See "Restructuring." As a result of the Restructuring, the Company established an improved financial and operational basis on which to build its business strategy.

Following Eaton's emergence from the CCAA proceedings, the Company obtained a three-year operating line of credit, implemented a new corporate governance structure and began developing Eaton's new business strategy (the "Business Strategy"). The Business Strategy includes new merchandising initiatives, marketing strategies, investments in inventory and store renovations and cost reduction initiatives. The Business Strategy is designed to establish Eaton's as Canada's leading national fashion department store and to significantly increase its market share and profitability.

The Business Strategy builds on Eaton's many strengths, which include:

- *Prime store locations in key Canadian markets*—Eaton's operates 64 department stores located in virtually every major shopping centre and select downtown locations in Canada. The Company believes that neither existing competitors nor new entrants can easily replicate the Company's prime store locations.

- *Strong franchise value and customer goodwill*—For 129 years, the "EATON'S" name has been associated with the retail business of the Company and is one of the most recognized names in Canadian retailing. According to independent market research of Canada's six largest markets prepared by Kubas Consultants and ACNielsen of Canada in February 1997, Eaton's ranked ahead of The Bay and Sears Canada in the following categories: "customer service," "variety and selection," "store layout and decor" and "merchandise quality."

- *Strong supplier relationships*—Eaton's has maintained strong relationships with a number of national brand name and designer brand name suppliers. In addition, Eaton's has negotiated exclusive arrangements with several high-profile suppliers. Many of the Company's suppliers assist the Company with the promotion and marketing of their merchandise. See "Business of the Company—Merchandising" and "—Supplier Arrangements."

- *Experienced new management team*—Eaton's has assembled a new senior management team, led by George Kosich, a 38-year veteran of Canadian retail-ing, that has extensive experience in the Canadian retail industry. See "Management—Management Team."

In addition to capitalizing on its current strengths, Eaton's Business Strategy addresses the Company's previous weaknesses. Key elements of the Business Strategy include the following:

- *Market Positioning*—Eaton's is implementing merchandising, marketing and customer service strategies that are intended to differentiate the Company from its competition and establish Eaton's as a fashion department store retailer of moderate, moderate-better and better designer merchandise. The Company will have a wide assortment of "moderate" merchandise, which offers quality and style at prices appealing to most customers, and "moderate-better" merchandise, which appeals to customers who are oriented more towards fashion and quality than price. In addition, select Eaton's stores will carry a selection of "better designer" merchandise which is upscale and differentiated with limited distribution and is supported by a particular designer. ...

- *Expansion and Rationalization of the Merchandise Mix*—In-store merchandise inventory density is being raised to what management believes are industry levels. Inventory density per square foot for continuing stores is being increased by 35% to an average of $97 per square foot during fiscal 1998 compared to fiscal 1997. Top-selling national and designer brands and exclusive goods are being distributed throughout the Eaton's store chain. At the same time, Eaton's is expanding the development and promotion of its own private brands which are expected to provide greater margin opportunities and thereby increase overall product margins. In addition, Eaton's is substantially reducing its hard goods business which has been generating low margins and expanding its merchandising mix in soft goods which typically have higher margins. ...

- *Supplier Shop Arrangements*—Eaton's has entered into a significant number of new initiatives with leading suppliers of national and designer brands involving the installation of supplier sponsored in-store specialty shops. Such shops consist of installations involving permanent or semi-permanent in-store renovations ("hard shops") and installations involving promotional banners, shelving and other materials which may be easily assembled, disassembled and reconfigured ("soft shops"), to display and promote merchandise and improve the appearance of its stores. ...

- *Renovation Program*—Eaton's has begun to implement a renovation program to improve the appearance of its stores and update displays to reflect a contemporary image. Renovations have been and will continue to be based on clear sightlines, ease of shopping, wider aisles, comfortable lighting and an environment that reflects quality and style. The Business Strategy contemplates significant capital expenditures for store renovations over the next few years. ...

- *Gross Margin Improvement*—Eaton's merchandising initiatives are expected to substantially improve gross margins. In addition, discussions with suppliers in the development of the Business Plan have, in many instances, resulted in improved supplier terms in the form of volume and other rebates, discounts and shared-cost programs. Major initiatives have been undertaken to address Eaton's relatively high rate of inventory shrinkage. ...

- *Expense Reductions*—Expenses will be reduced as a result of initiatives implemented during the Restructuring, including the closing of certain unprofitable stores, the relocation of the Company's head office and personnel reductions. The Company continues to evaluate and monitor store profitability. In addition, overhead expenses are expected to be further reduced during fiscal 1998 as a result of the redistribution and reduction of personnel, principally from non-selling areas. Further expense reductions are expected to be achieved through the re-engineering of business processes and improved business systems. ...

Recent Operating Results

The Company's net sales for comparable stores for the 12-week period ended April 25, 1998 were $317.0 million compared to $285.7 million for the comparable period in 1997, representing an 11.0% increase. Comparable store sales increased 10.3% for February 1998 compared to February 1997, 13.7% for March 1998 compared to March 1997 and 9.1% for April 1998 compared to April 1997.

The Company's loss from retail operations for the 12-week period ended April 25, 1998 was $19.9 million compared to $55.9 million for the comparable period in 1997.

The Company's results of operations for the 12-week period ended April 25, 1998 are not necessarily indicative of its results of operations for the entire fiscal year.

The Company's net sales for comparable stores for the four-week period ended May 23, 1998 were $104.7 million compared to $108.8 million for the comparable period in 1997, representing a 3.8% decrease. Taking into account actual net sales results for the four-week period ended May 23, 1998, the forecast contained in this prospectus was reviewed by management of the Company. Management concluded that the forecast represents its best judgment as to the most probable set of

future industry and economic conditions and the Company's intended course of action under those conditions based on information existing at June 1, 1998. The forecast was approved by the board of directors on June 1, 1998.

The Company's net sales for comparable stores for the first quarter (16-week period from February 1, 1998 to May 23, 1998) were $421.7 million compared to $394.5 million for the first quarter of 1997, representing an increase of 6.9%.

The foregoing information for the 12-week period ended April 25, 1998, the four-week period ended May 23, 1998 and the 16-week period ended May 23, 1998 is unaudited and has not been subject to review level or audit review by the auditors of the Company.

The Offering

Offering: 11,666,667 Common Shares. Up to an additional 1,750,000 Common Shares may be offered on the exercise of the Over-Allotment Option granted by the Company to the Underwriters. In connection with this offering, the Eaton Family has agreed to purchase an aggregate of 2,754,600 Common Shares, of which 830,000 Common Shares will be purchased from the Underwriters for cash and 1,924,600 Common Shares will be purchased using approximately $28.9 million aggregate principal amount of subordinated notes of the Company due February 1, 2000 which are held by the Eaton Family.

Price: $15.00 per Common Share.

Amount: $175,000,005

Use of Proceeds: The estimated net proceeds to the Company from this offering, after deducting the fee payable to the Underwriters and the estimated expenses of this offering, will be approximately $166 million. The net proceeds are intended to be used to finance store renovations and supplier shop installations. Pending such use, the Company will either apply such proceeds to the outstanding balance under its revolving Credit Facility or will invest such proceeds in short-term government securities. See "Use of Proceeds" and "Business of the Company—Capital Expenditures."

Dividend Policy: The Company's intention is to reinvest its earnings in the business. The Company does not anticipate the payment of dividends on the Common Shares in the near future. Any future determination to pay dividends will be at the discretion of the board of directors of the Company and will depend on the Company's financial condition, capital requirements and such other factors as the board of directors may deem relevant.

Risk Factors: An investment in the Common Shares is subject to a number of risk factors which potential investors should carefully consider, including risks relating to: implementation of the Business Strategy, recent management changes, reliance on management, fashion apparel industry risks, competitive considerations, relationships with suppliers, store locations, availability of capital resources, security interests, performance warranty obligations, unresolved Companies' Creditors Arrangement Act claims, principal shareholders, Year 2000 exposure, importance of information systems, shrinkage, dilution, no prior market, market risk and environmental matters. See "Risk Factors."

APPENDIX 2

Prospectus Summary

Selected Historical and Forecast Consolidated Financial Information, Balance Sheet Data, and Operating Statistics

The following is a summary of certain selected historical and forecast consolidated financial information, balance sheet data and operating statistics for the Company and is qualified in its entirety by the detailed provisions of the Company's Consolidated Financial Statements and the Forecast Consolidated Statement of Earnings and the respective notes thereto and Management's Discussion and Analysis of Financial Condition and Results of Operations contained in this prospectus:

(thousands of dollars except per share data)	Forecast[1] 52 weeks Ending January 30, 1999	Historical 53 weeks Ended January 31, 1998	52 weeks Ended January 25, 1997	52 weeks Ended January 27, 1996
Earnings Data				
Revenue:				
Continuing stores[2]	$1,822,000	$1,599,400	$1,514,400	$1,517,400
Stores closed[3]	—	88,800	152,134	189,264
Total revenue	1,822,000	1,688,200	1,666,534	1,706,664
Cost of merchandise sold	1,199,000	1,162,322	1,129,498	1,113,656
Gross margin	623,000	525,878	537,036	593,008
Operating, administrative and selling expenses	545,000	602,431	588,861	600,820
EBITDA[4]	78,000	(76,553)	(51,825)	(7,812)
Depreciation and amortization	31,000	32,090	40,647	38,459
EBIT[5]	47,000	(108,643)	(92,472)	(46,271)
Interest expense	13,000	17,279	20,693	24,226
Earnings (loss) before income taxes and unusual items	34,000	(125,922)	(113,165)	(70,497)
Unusual items	(16,000)	(124,543)	(80,361)	(31,126)
Earnings (loss) before income taxes	18,000	(250,465)	(193,526)	(101,623)
Income tax recovery	(12,000)	(83,170)	(23,364)	(44,801)
Earnings (loss) before earnings from discontinued operations	30,000	(167,295)	(170,162)	(56,822)
Earnings from discontinued operations	28,000	11,435	44	40,175
Net earnings (loss) for the fiscal year	$ 58,000	$ (155,860)	$ (170,118)	$ (16,647)

(thousands of dollars except per share data)	Forecast[1] 52 weeks Ending January 30, 1999	Historical		
		53 weeks Ended January 31, 1998	52 weeks Ended January 25, 1997	52 weeks Ended January 27, 1996
Fully diluted earnings (loss) per common share:				
Before discontinued operations[6]	$ 1.57	$(20.77)	$(21.12)	$(7.05)
Discontinued operations[6]	1.37	1.42	—	4.99
Net fully diluted earnings (loss) per common share[6]	$ 2.94	$(19.35)	$(21.12)	$(2.06)
Weighted average number of common shares outstanding (thousands)[6]	20,371	8,055	8,055	8,055
Operating Statistics—Continuing Stores[2]				
Sales growth	13.9%	5.6%	0.0%	—
Sales per square foot	$ 197	$ 173	$ 163	$ 164

(thousands of dollars)	As at January 31, 1998	As at January 25, 1997
Balance Sheet Data—Retail Operations		
Total current assets	$414,870	$391,766
Total current liabilities[7]	301,265	441,145
Working capital	113,605	(49,379)
Merchandise inventories	350,619	272,536
Fixed assets and deferred pension and other assets	161,709	404,040
Notes payable	132,978	—
Long-term obligations[7]	31,317	129,917
Shareholders' equity	130,845	226,705

Notes:

(1) **The reader is cautioned that, as the forecast is based upon assumptions regarding future events, actual results will vary from the forecast results and the variations may be material. See "Financial Forecast."**

(2) Based on the Company's 64 department stores, one home store (specializing in furniture, appliances and home fashions) and two smaller stores offering clearance and factory outlet merchandise.

(3) Consists of 21 closed department stores.

(4) Earnings before interest, taxes, depreciation and amortization.

(5) Earnings before interest and taxes.

(6) After giving effect to the subdivision of the Common Shares on a 16.11 for one basis and, for the fiscal year ending January 30, 1999, to (i) the purchase by the Company of the Class A shares of the Company for an aggregate of 1,833,333 Common Shares, (ii) the purchase by the Eaton Family of 1,924,600 Common Shares using approximately $28.9 million principal amount of subordinated notes of the Company which are held by the Eaton Family, (iii) the issuance of 11,666,667 Common Shares pursuant to this offering, and (iv) 1,645,034 Common Shares issuable pursuant to the exercise of options granted under the Company's stock option plan.

(7) Excludes notes payable. See note 2 to the Company's Consolidated Financial Statements as at January 31, 1998 contained in this prospectus.

Integrative Running Case Study
Bombardier on the Web

The combined book value/abnormal earnings model for estimating common share value is:

$$P_0 = BV_0 + \sum_{t=1}^{\infty} \frac{E_0\,(X_t - rBV_{t-1})}{(1+r)^t}$$

where (omitting the time subscripts) P denotes the total value of all outstanding shares, BV denotes the book value of shareholders' equity, r denotes the cost of equity capital, E denotes the expectations operator, and X denotes net income. In words, the model states that share value is the book value of shareholders' equity plus the present value of future expected abnormal net income (where abnormal net income is net income less the cost of equity capital multiplied by the beginning-of-period book value of shareholders' equity).

The model is amazingly simple. Two "rubs" are that the model is silent on just how one comes up with expected net income for future periods (and therefore future expected abnormal net income) and just how many future periods should be used. Owing to the way present value is calculated, abnormal net income amounts expected for periods in the distant future have a trivial present value and are essentially irrelevant to valuation. In addition, competitive market forces tend eventually to drive abnormal net income to zero. Thus, it isn't important to make the forecasting horizon terribly long. Professional analysts rarely use more than 15 years, often fewer than 10.

Access the Bombardier Inc. annual report for the year ended January 31, 2002, from the Companion Website for this textbook at **www. pearsoned.ca/revsine**.

Required:

1. Assume a five-year forecasting horizon. Use the combined book value/abnormal earnings model to predict the total value of Bombardier Inc.'s common shares as of January 31, 2002.
2. Convert your estimate in question 1 to a per-share estimate. Compare your per-share estimate with the company's actual share price.
3. How sensitive is your valuation in question 1 above to changes in key parameters?
4. The events of September 11, 2001, had a profound impact on companies such as Bombardier. Discuss in general terms how this would affect your use of the valuation model. Would your response be different if your valuation were being performed as of January 31, 2001?

Endnotes

1. One of the earliest accounting treatments of this concept appeared in L. Revsine, *Replacement Cost Accounting* (Englewood Cliffs, NJ: Prentice Hall, 1973), pp. 33–5 and 95–100. There, free cash flow was defined as "the portion of net operating flows that can be distributed as a dividend without reducing the level of future physical operations" (p. 34).

2. See E. F. Fama and M. H. Miller, *The Theory of Finance* (New York: Holt, Rinehart & Winston, 1972), Chapter 2; R. Brealey and S. Myers, *Principles of Corporate Finance* (New York: McGraw-Hill, 1988), Chapter 4; S. A. Ross, R. W. Westerfield, and J. F. Jaffee, *Corporate Finance* (Homewood, IL: Richard D. Irwin, 1993), Chapter 5. The common equity value of a company is the company's total value minus an amount representing claims of debtholders and preferred shareholders.

3. We depict uncertain future amounts with a tilde (~). Thus, $E_0\widetilde{CF}_3$ indicates the currently expected uncertain free cash flow for period 3 in the future. By contrast, the already known past cash flow in period 0 would be shown without the tilde (i.e., CF_0).

4. An alternative representation of the discounted cash flow valuation model presumes that the future cash flow stream continues only through some finite terminal period, T, at which point the company is liquidated and a liquidating or terminal distribution, $\widetilde{CF}_T$, is paid to shareholders:

$$P_0 = \sum_{t=1}^{T-1} \frac{E_0(\widetilde{CF}_T)}{(1+r)^t} + \frac{E_0(\widetilde{CF}_T)}{(1+r)^T}$$

5. There is no clear consensus in the finance literature on how to best estimate the cost of equity capital. However, one popular approach is to use the capital asset pricing model (CAPM), which expresses the equity cost of capital as the sum of the return on a riskless asset (r_f) plus an equity risk premium $[E(r_M) - r_f]$ multiplied by the company's systematic (beta) risk—that is:

$$r_e = r_f + [E(r_M) - r_f]\beta.$$

6. These simplifying assumptions and other detailed aspects of the valuation process are described in B. Cornell, *Corporate Valuation* (Homewood, IL: R. D. Irwin, 1993); and T. Copeland, T. Koller, and J. Murin, *Valuation* (New York: Wiley, 1994).

7. A constant perpetuity is a stream of constant cash flows without end. To see why the present value of a cash flow perpetuity, that is

$$PV = \frac{CF}{(1+r)^1} + \frac{CF}{(1+r)^2} + \frac{CF}{(1+r)^3} + \cdots + \frac{CF}{(1+r)^\infty}$$

reduces to

$$PV = \frac{CF}{r}$$

Consider the following example. Assume that the market price (i.e., present value) of an investment is $1,000 and that this investment will yield a return of 9%, or $90, in perpetuity. Since the amount of this perpetual cash flow is PV × r, we can express the amount of the perpetuity as:

$$PV \times r = CF$$

Dividing both sides of the equation by r immediately yields the formula for the present value of a perpetuity:

$$PV = \frac{CF}{r}$$

In our example:

$$\$1,000 = \frac{\$90}{0.09}$$

8. Evidence on the usefulness of *current earnings* in predicting *future cash flows* is provided by R. Greenberg, G. Johnson, and K. Ramesh, "Earnings Versus Cash Flow as a Predictor of Future Cash Flow," *Journal of Accounting, Auditing and Finance*, Fall 1986, pp. 266–77.

9. "Objectives of Financial Reporting by Business Enterprises," *Statement of Financial Accounting Concepts No. 1* (Stamford, CT: FASB, 1978), para. 43.

10. Ibid., para. 37. The term **net cash flows** refers to the difference between cash receipts (inflows) and cash payments (outflows).

11. P. Dechow, "Accounting Earnings and Cash Flows as Measures of Firm Performance: The Role of Accounting Accruals," *Journal of Accounting and Economics*, July 1994, pp. 3–42.

12. For a slightly different discussion of these links, see W. H. Beaver, *Financial Reporting: An Accounting Revolution* (Englewood Cliffs, NJ: Prentice Hall, 1981), Chapter 4.

13. For an overview of this research, see B. Lev and J. Ohlson, "Market-Based Empirical Research in Accounting: A Review, Interpretation, and Extension," *Journal of Accounting Research* (Supplement, 1982), pp. 249–322: and B. Lev, "On the Usefulness of Earnings and Earnings Research: Lessons and Directions from Two Decades of Empirical Research," *Journal of Accounting Research* (Supplement, 1989), pp. 153–92.

14. The error term (e_i) in equation (6.7) does not appear in equation (6.8) since the latter equation provides the expression for the fitted regression line. The vertical deviations from the fitted regression line and the data points that plot the combination of earnings and price for individual firms are the e_i error terms in equation (6.7).

15. One minus the retention ratio $(1 - k)$ is the dividend payout ratio.

16. Notice that the slope coefficient of 9.55 for retail grocery stores in Figure 6.2 suggests an earnings capitalization rate of 10.47% because $1/0.1047 = 9.55$.

17. For a more formal discussion of these three earnings components and their valuation implication, see R. Ramakrishnan and J. Thomas, "Valuation of Permanent, Transitory, and Price-Irrelevant Components of Reported Earnings," *Journal of Accounting, Auditing & Finance*, vol. 13, no. 3 (Summer 1998), pp. 301–336.

18. You may wonder about the distinction between the value-irrelevant component (X_i^0) and the error term (e_i) in equation (6.10). X_i^0 is a component of earnings that is not relevant to assessing price, while e_i is not a component of current earnings but is relevant to assessing price. For example, e_i may represent news about a new scientific breakthrough or discovery the firm has just made that would have a positive effect on price, but it would not yet be reflected in current earnings.

19. Lipe presents evidence consistent with this conjecture. He finds a greater share price reaction to earnings components that exhibit greater permanence than to those components that are more transitory in nature. See R. Lipe, "The Information Contained in the Components of Earnings," *Journal of Accounting Research* (Supplement, 1986), pp. 33–64.

20. See L. Bernstein and J. Siegel, "The Concept of Earnings Quality," *Financial Analysts Journal*, July–August 1979, pp. 72–5; J. Siegel, "The Quality of Earnings Concept—A Survey," *Financial Analysts Journal*, March–April 1982, pp. 60–8.

21. See B. Lev and R. Thiagarajan, "Fundamental Information Analysis," *Journal of Accounting Research*, Autumn 1993, pp. 190–215. To arrive at "quality-adjusted" earnings, the researchers started with reported earnings and then eliminated revenue or expense items thought to be transitory or value-irrelevant.

22. Several variations of the abnormal earnings valuation model have appeared in the literature. Recent examples include J. Ohlson, "Earnings, Book Values, and Dividends in Equity Valuation," *Contemporary Accounting Research*, Spring 1995, pp. 681–87; T. Copeland, T. Koller, and J. Murrin, *Valuation: Measuring and Managing the Value of Companies* (New York: Wiley, 1994); and G. B. Stewart, III, *The Quest for Value* (New York: Harper Business, 1991).

23. For a further discussion of these points and the implications of the abnormal earnings valuation model, see G. Feltham and J. Ohlson, "Valuation and Clean Surplus Accounting for Operating and Financial Assets," *Contemporary Accounting Research*, Spring 1995, pp. 689–731; V. Bernard, "The Feltham–Ohlson Framework: Implications for Empiricists," *Contemporary Accounting Research*, Spring 1995, pp. 733–47, and Stewart, ibid.

24. Share price changes can also occur because of unanticipated changes in interest (discount) rates over time.

25. For research on the association between earnings surprises and share returns, see R. Ball and P. Brown, "An Empirical Evaluation of Accounting Income Numbers," *Journal of Accounting Research*, Autumn 1968, pp. 159–78; and G. Foster, C. Olsen, and T. Shevlin, "Earnings Releases, Anomalies, and the Behavior of Security Returns," *Accounting Review*, October 1984, pp. 574–603.

26. A number of studies investigate whether post-earnings announcement drift provides opportunities to earn abnormal returns in the stock market. For a review of this literature, see V. Bernard, "Stock Price Reactions to Earnings Announcements: A Summary of Recent Anomalous Evidence and Possible Explanations," in R. Thaler (ed.), *Advances in Behavioral Finance* (New York: Russell Sage Foundation, 1992).

27. The word **bond** is commonly used to refer to all kinds of secured and unsecured debt although, strictly speaking, a bond is a secured debt. A **debenture** is an unsecured bond, one in which no specific pledge of property is made, although the debenture holder does have a claim on property not otherwise pledged as collateral or security. The term **note** is generally used for unsecured debt instruments issued with an original maturity of ten years or less.

28. Techniques for constructing financial statement forecasts are described in T. Copeland et al., op. cit.; K. Palepu, V. Bernard, and P. Healy, *Business Analysis and Valuation* (Cincinnati, OH: South-Western Publishing, 1996); and C. Stickney, *Financial Statement Analysis: A Strategic Perspective* (Fort Worth, TX: Dryden Press, 1993).

29. A detailed description of the rating process used at Standard & Poor's is contained in the company's monograph *Corporate Finance Criteria* (New York: Standard & Poor's, 1994).

30. See Ross, Westerfield, and Jaffe, op. cit., Chapter 16. These and other authors identify a third economic force that influences firms' capital structure decisions—that is, agency costs. These costs will be considered in more detail in Chapter 7.

31. See J. Largay and C. Stickney, "Cash Flows, Ratio Analysis and the W. T. Grant Company Bankruptcy," *Financial Analysts Journal*, July–August 1980, pp. 51–84.

32. "Financial Statement Concepts," Section 1000, *CICA Handbook*, para. 12.

33. The AcSB writes: "For the information provided in financial statements to be useful, it must be relevant to the decisions made by users" (ibid., para. 20).

34. This figure was derived from the capital asset pricing model (CAPM) using the then-current risk-free rate of 6.33% for 30-year treasury bonds, Reebok's equity beta of 1.10 as reported by *Zacks Investment Research*, and a long-term market risk premium of 6%. The CAPM formula applied to Reebok is: $6.33\% + (1.10 \times 6\%) = 12.93\%$ or about 13%.

35. Because of competitive pressures, the assumed growth rate of abnormal earnings beyond year 2004 is less than the growth rate in abnormal earnings from 2000 to 2004, which averages 7.8%.

36. This discount factor is equal to one divided by the difference between the equity cost of capital (13%) and the abnormal earnings growth rate (3%), or $1/(0.13 - 0.03)$.

37. J. Francis, P. Olsson, and D. R. Oswald, "Comparing the Accuracy and Explainability of Dividends, Free Cash Flow, and Abnormal Earnings Equity Value Estimates," *Journal of Accounting Research*, Spring 2000, pp. 45–70.

38. R. Frankel and C. Lee, "Accounting Valuation, Market Expectation, and Cross-Sectional Stock Returns," *Journal of Accounting and Economics*, June 1998, pp. 283–320.

39. R. D. Hof, E. Neuborne, and H. Green, "Internet Stocks: What's Their Real Worth," *Business Week* (December 14, 1998).

40. N. Byrnes, "Eyeballs, Bah! Figuring Dot-Coms' Real Worth," *Business Week*, October 30, 2000.

41. G. Milano, "EVA and the 'New' Economy," *Journal of Applied Corporate Finance*, Summer 2000, pp. 118–28.

42. See G. White, A. Sondhi, and D. Fried, *The Analysis and Use of Financial Statements* (New York: John Wiley & Sons, Inc., 1998), Chapter 19, pp. 1045–50.

43. For a detailed discussion of the EVA™ model, see G. B. Stewart, III, *The Quest for Value* (New York: HarperBusiness, 1991).

7
The Role of Financial Information in Contracting

LEARNING OBJECTIVES
After studying this chapter, you should be able to:

1. Describe the conflicts of interest that arise between managers and shareholders, lenders, or regulators

2. Explain how and why accounting numbers are used in debt agreements, in compensation contracts, and for regulatory purposes

3. Explain how managerial incentives are influenced by the use of accounting-based contracts and regulations

4. Understand what role contracts and regulations play in shaping managers' accounting choices

Business contracts include formal written agreements, such as Allen Ford's franchise contract with BookWorm Inc. (Chapter 6 explains why Allen Ford decided to purchase a BookWorm franchise. In this chapter, Allen must obtain a bank loan to finance the purchase.)

Financial accounting numbers are often used to define contract terms and to monitor compliance with those terms.

Commercial lending agreements, for example, may require the borrower to maintain a current ratio or interest coverage ratio above a certain level. This requirement protects the lender from a deterioration of the borrower's credit risk. The lender then uses earnings, cash flow, and balance sheet data to monitor the borrower's compliance with the loan covenants. Financial data are also used in executive compensation contracts and in formal agreements with government agencies, joint-venture partners, suppliers, distributors, and customers. Figure 7.1 identifies the parties in each of these kinds of contracts. The value of financial statement data for contracting purposes depends on the accounting methods used by the company and its freedom to change them. For example, an interest coverage provision is *unlikely* to protect the lender if the borrowing company can achieve the required coverage level by simply changing its accounting methods or through other artificial means. Contracting parties understand that financial reporting flexibility affects how contracts are written and enforced. In this chapter we describe these influences and address these questions:

- What role do accounting numbers play in these contracts?

- What incentives do accounting-based contracts create for the parties involved?

- How do these incentives help us understand why managers choose certain accounting methods and avoid others?

- How do these incentives influence when transactions are recorded on the books?

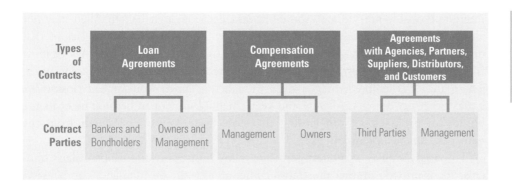

FIGURE 7.1
SIGNIFICANT
CONTRACTING
RELATIONSHIPS
IN CORPORATE
ORGANIZATIONS

Finalizing the BookWorm Loan

Allen Ford assembled the monthly cash flow projections and other materials requested by the loan officer. This was not easy, but it produced an unintended benefit: Allen was forced again to evaluate the economic viability of the bookstore and the financial challenges ahead. His detailed cash flow projections revealed the need for a revolving credit line, one that was slightly larger than he anticipated originally. Otherwise, the prospects for the business seemed bright, and Allen was eager to finalize the two loans.

Several days after Allen completed the loan application, the bank phoned him to indicate preliminary approval of both the term loan and the revolving credit line. Allen was elated with the approval but surprised by the interest rate. It seemed higher than the interest rates that other local banks were charging for similar business loans. Allen and the loan officer agreed to meet to discuss the final terms and conditions of both loans. The loan officer advised Allen to consider accepting more stringent loan covenant restrictions in exchange for a lower rate of interest. Allen was not quite sure what the loan officer had in mind, but it seemed worth exploring. Allen knew that some loan covenants were tied directly to the borrower's financial statements, and he wanted to be certain that the accounting-based covenants proposed by the bank were consistent with his financial projections for the bookstore. In preparation for this negotiation, Allen reviewed the types of covenants commonly used in commercial bank loans.

Conflicts of Interest in Business Relationships

Delegating decision-making authority is an essential feature of the modern corporation and most business relationships. Capital providers (shareholders and lenders) delegate authority to professional managers. In turn, managers delegate authority over aspects of a company's business affairs to others—inside and even outside the company—who have expertise or timely access to information that is critical for decision making. (Wal-Mart, for example, allows some suppliers to monitor product sales electronically at its checkout stands and to ship new inventory stock without first seeking company approval.) But delegation of authority can cause **conflicts of interest**. The conflicts arise when one party to the business relationship can take actions that benefit him or her but harm the other party.

WAL-MART
www.walmart.com

Suppose that rather than operating the store himself, Allen Ford hired a bookstore manager. Would the bookstore manager always make decisions that are in Allen's best interest? Probably not, because some business decisions that benefit Allen may not always benefit the manager. Conversely, there will be other business decisions that directly benefit the manager at Allen's expense. Consider this example: A long-time friend of the manager arrives in town unexpectedly and suggests a leisurely lunch. The manager is tempted to agree even though that lunch would mean closing the bookstore for two hours. Allen would keep the bookstore open because he bears the burden of profits lost from closing the store and receives no benefit from the manager's luncheon reunion.

Potential conflicts of interest permeate many business relationships. Allen's franchise loans provide another illustration. The interest rate on each loan compensates the bank for credit risk and the other costs associated with providing financial capital to the BookWorm business. Once the loans have been granted, however, Allen might be tempted to divert the cash toward other, more risky investment opportunities—like buying tickets in a lottery. The chance of winning $40 million may be quite remote, but his obligation to repay the loan remains the same whether the cash is invested in the bookstore or in lottery tickets.

Contract terms can be designed to reduce or eliminate conflicting incentives that arise in business relationships. Allen's loan agreements will describe the business purpose for each loan and require that the borrowed funds be used only for those purposes. By agreeing to such conditions, Allen is providing the bank with a written assurance that borrowed funds will not be diverted to other (unspecified) uses—such as buying lottery tickets. Business contracts specify the mutual expectations—the rights and responsibilities—of each participant in the relationship, and thus they provide a low-cost mechanism for addressing any conflicts of interest that may arise.

Lending Agreements and Debt Covenants

Most companies have debt, in the form of either commercial bank loans or bonds. In addition, managers frequently own shares of the companies they manage. As we will see, the interests of creditors and shareholders often diverge, particularly after the lender has made the loan proceeds available. This divergence creates incentives for managers to take actions that transfer part of the company's value from creditors to the managers themselves as well as to other shareholders. *These incentives arise because business decisions affect not only the value of the firm, but also the relative share of that value which belongs to owners rather than to creditors.*

Two sources of conflict can arise between creditors and owners:

1. **Asset substitution.** If a company borrows to engage in low-risk investment projects and the interest rate charged by the lender is commensurate with that low risk, the value of the business to owners is increased—and the value to creditors is reduced—by substituting higher-risk projects.
2. **Repayment.** If a company borrows money for a new project and the interest rate charged presumes the company's current dividend policy will be maintained, the value of the business to creditors is reduced when the borrowed funds are used instead to pay larger dividends. At the extreme, if the company sells all its assets and pays owners a liquidating dividend, creditors are left with a worthless business.[1]

We begin by looking at **asset substitution** and the conflicting incentives of creditors and owners. Figure 7.2 shows the probability distribution of dollar returns associated with two investment projects.[2] Each curve spans the entire range of possible dollar returns for the project, with the height of the curve at any given point indicating the probability of receiving that particular dollar return. Both investment projects have the same cost ($M), the same expected dollar return ($E), the same investment horizon (one year), and the same market risk.[3] But, as shown, the potential returns from Project 2 have greater dispersion (higher variance) than do those from Project 1. In other words, the extreme dollar returns—those at the far left and right in the figure—have a greater probability of occurrence for Project 2 than for Project 1. If the two projects require the same dollar investment, which would the owner-manager select?

With no debt outstanding, shareholders—including the owner-manager—would be indifferent between the two projects. That's because the value of the company is the same no matter which project is chosen, since both projects have the same cost ($M), the same expected dollar return ($E), and the same market risk.

But what if the company had debt that required principal and interest payments of $M one year from now? Would shareholders still be indifferent between the two projects? What about creditors who supplied debt financing to the company? Would they too be indifferent?

When companies have debt outstanding, the dispersion of dollar returns for each investment project—the likelihood of extreme outcomes—has a bearing on the **relative value** of the project to creditors and stockholders. So even though the two projects in Figure 7.2 have the same expected value ($E), one will now be worth more than the other because they don't have the same dispersion.

To see this, consider the viewpoint of creditors who expect to be paid from the dollars earned by the chosen project. Notice that the *probability* of Project 1 generating dollar returns less than the required loan payment of $M is given by the area d_1 under the Project 1 curve. We refer to this region as the "default zone" because if Project 1 produces returns to the left of $M, the company will default on part or all of its required loan payment. Since the probability of all possible dollar returns from a given project must sum to one, the probability that creditors will receive *full*

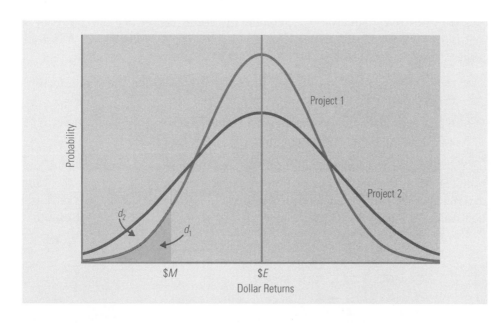

FIGURE 7.2
PROBABILITY
DISTRIBUTIONS
OF DOLLAR
RETURNS FOR
TWO
INVESTMENT
PROJECTS

payment is $(1 - d_1)$; this is shown by the *unshaded area* under the Project 1 curve to the right of $M.

The default zone for Project 2 is the area d_2. The probability that creditors will receive full payment from Project 2 is $(1 - d_2)$, and because d_2 is larger than d_1, the probability of repayment for Project 1 is greater than the probability of repayment for Project 2.

Compare the default regions of the two investments. It is clear why creditors prefer Project 1 over Project 2. This is because Project 2 has a higher default probability than does Project 1—and thus, it has a correspondingly lower probability that creditors will be paid in full. Obviously, the value of the business to creditors will be greater if Project 1 is chosen because it has less default risk.

But what do shareholders prefer? Shareholders are not obligated to pay a company's debts when corporate cash flows are inadequate to cover what is owed. This limits their "downside" exposure: when project returns fall below $M, shareholders don't have to make up the shortfall so that creditors can be paid. Creditors, on the other hand, have limited "upside potential" because their **fixed claim** (the $M in our example) to corporate cash flows does not get larger when project returns exceed $M. *All other things being equal, shareholders of companies with debt financing prefer investment projects with high dispersion (like Project 2), because they receive all payoffs greater than $M while creditors absorb the loss associated with payoffs less than $M.*

If the company borrows $M for low-risk Project 1 but then invests those funds in high-risk Project 2, shareholder value is increased but creditor value falls. Substituting the high-risk Project 2 for the low-risk Project 1 leaves shareholders with more upside potential—but creditors have more "downside potential" of default. Asset substitution transfers wealth from creditors to shareholders but leaves the total value of the business unchanged. This result is illustrated in Figure 7.3(a).

The situation we've just described involved projects with the same cost, expected return, and market risk—and thus, the same total value. We've also seen that asset substitution changes how the company's total value is shared between owners and creditors—but that it does not change the value of the company.

A more serious problem for creditors is when owners gain (and creditors lose) by making the company itself less valuable. This kind of asset substitution—illustrated in Figure 7.3(b)—occurs when the high-risk Project 2 has a lower expected value (or greater market risk) than Project 1. Skipping the details, we see that the end result is that borrowing for Project 1 but then putting the money into Project 2 instead makes:

- the company worth less because Project 2 has a smaller total value than Project 1
- the owners' share of the company worth more (and the creditors' share worth less) because Project 2 has more dispersion than Project 1

Shareholders are willing to substitute projects that *reduce* the total value of the company when the wealth transfer from creditors more than compensates them for the overall value loss. The company is worth less ($950 versus $1,000), but substitution results in more value for shareholders ($770 versus $750) and less for creditors ($180 versus $250).

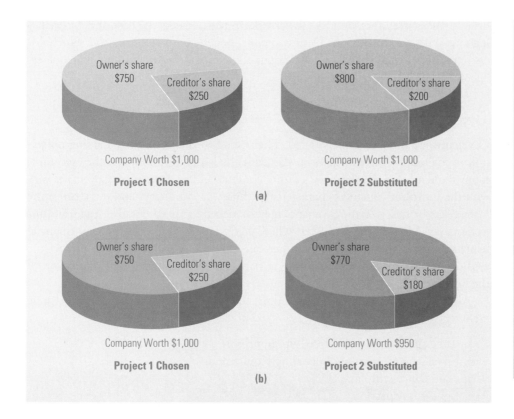

(a) Investment projects with the same expected dollar returns (and market risk) but different dispersions

(b) Investment projects with different expected dollar returns (and market risk) and different dispersions

The **repayment problem** involves how to use the cash generated by the company's operating activities. Management has three choices:

1. reinvest the cash back into the business
2. repay amounts owed to lenders
3. pay dividends to or buy back shares from shareholders

When companies are financed partially with debt, owner-managers have incentives to distribute cash to shareholders (including themselves).[4] This could be done in several ways. Management could forgo investments in positive net present value projects and instead pay dividends to shareholders or repurchase outstanding shares; or management could sell existing business assets and distribute the proceeds to shareholders (again by means of dividends or share repurchases). Both actions leave creditors with a company of greatly reduced value or worse—an "empty corporate shell." The value of the business to creditors is reduced because there are fewer total corporate resources available for debt repayment, making loan default more likely.

Creditors know that their interests will sometimes conflict with the interests of shareholders and owner-managers. Without protections granted by borrowers, creditors will demand a higher return (interest rate) on business loans as compensation for the added risk of asset substitution and repayment. This higher interest rate is the way creditors obtain **price protection** against the possibility that owner-managers will take actions that benefit shareholders but harm creditors. But price protection increases the cost of debt financing and shifts $M to the right in Figure 7.2—thus causing shareholder value to fall!

Another way to reduce conflicts of interest between creditors and shareholders is by writing contracts that restrict—explicitly or implicitly—the owner-manager's ability to harm creditors.[5] To do this, loan provisions are specifically designed to address asset substitution and repayment. These covenants effectively lower the default risk of creditors, and this lower risk, in turn, lowers the cost of debt financing and shifts $M to the left. Debt covenants benefit both creditors and shareholders. Creditors benefit because debt covenants reduce default risk, and shareholders benefit from the lowered cost of debt.

The Structure of Debt Covenants

Covenants are intensively negotiated. They establish the borrower's ongoing obligation to maintain a certain financial status for the loan's duration, and they set minimum standards for the borrower's future conduct and performance. Covenants vary with the borrower's business characteristics, financial condition, and the term of the loan. If credit risk is high, covenants may be tied directly to detailed financial projections provided by the borrower; where credit risk is low, a few general financial benchmarks may be sufficient. In either case, covenants are designed to protect the creditor and to give an early warning of deterioration in the financial condition of the borrower.

Affirmative covenants stipulate actions the borrower *must* take. Generally, these include:

1. using the loan for the agreed-upon purpose
2. financial covenants and reporting requirements
3. compliance with laws
4. rights of inspection
5. maintenance of insurance, properties, and records

Financial covenants establish minimum financial tests with which a borrower must comply. These tests can specify dollar amounts (such as required minimum levels of net worth and working capital) or ratios (such as minimum debt-to-equity and interest coverage ratios). Financial covenants are intended to signal financial difficulty and to trigger intervention by the creditor—we explain how later—long before liquidation or bankruptcy becomes necessary. To keep the lender informed about the company's financial and operating performance, the borrower is required to meet certain reporting requirements (e.g., to produce annual financial statements) and to provide financial reports to the lender in a timely manner.

Here is an example from a credit agreement between Philip Services (an integrated metals recovery and industrial services company formerly headquartered in Hamilton) and a group of banks:

> *Financial Statements. Furnish to the Administrative Agent: as soon as available, but in any event within 120 days after the end of each Financial Year a copy of the audited consolidated balance sheet of the Cdn. Borrower and its Subsidiaries as at the end of such Financial Year, together with the related audited consolidated statements of earnings, changes in financial position and shareholders' equity of the Cdn. Borrower and its Subsidiaries for such Financial Year, setting forth in each case in comparative form the figures for the previous Financial Year and reported on by [a firm of] independent internationally recognized firm of chartered accountants or certified public accountants ...*

Note that not only do the financial statements have to be submitted, but they must be audited as well.

Financial covenants often do not stipulate the accounting methods to be used, except that they must comply with GAAP, as shown by these excerpts from the Philip Services agreement:

DEFINITIONS

In this Agreement, unless the context otherwise requires:

...

"CAPITAL EXPENDITURES" of any Person shall mean any expenditures by such Person made in connection with the purchase, lease, acquisition, erection or construction of property (including any such property acquired pursuant to a Capitalized Lease Obligation) or any other expenditures, in any such case which are required to be capitalized in accordance with GAAP ...

"CAPITALIZED LEASE OBLIGATION" shall mean, for any Person, any payment obligation of such Person under an agreement for the lease or rental of, or providing such Person with the right to use, property that, in accordance with GAAP, is required to be capitalized....

"CURRENT ASSETS" shall mean, at any time, all current assets ... in accordance with GAAP.

"CURRENT LIABILITIES" shall mean, at any time, all current liabilities ... in accordance with GAAP.

Loan agreements guard against asset substitution by placing restrictions on how the money can be used—here is an example from TCBY Enterprises ("The Country's Best Yogurt"):

TCBY ENTERPRISES
www.tcby.com

> *Borrower will use the proceeds of the term loans for the loan purposes set forth ... in Section 1.1 of this agreement. (para. 5.5 of TCBY term loan agreement)*

The financial covenants establish specific levels of performance as well as conditions that must be met, and they give precise meaning to the financial terms and ratios mentioned in the contract—for example:

> *Borrower will at all times maintain a ratio of Current Assets to Current Liabilities ... that is greater than 2.0 to 1.0 ... a Profitability Ratio greater than 1.5 to 1.0 ... [defined as] the ratio of Net Income for the immediately preceding period of twelve calendar months to Current Maturities of Long Term Debt ... a Fixed Charge Coverage Ratio greater than 1.0 to 1.0 ... [defined as] the ratio of Net Income of the Borrower and Subsidiaries for the immediately preceding period of twelve calendar months plus Noncash Charges of the Borrower and Subsidiaries for the same period to Current Maturities of Long Term Debt of the Borrower and Subsidiaries plus cash dividends paid by TCBY to the shareholders of TCBY for the preceding period of twelve calendar months plus Replacement CapEx of the Borrower and Subsidiaries for the preceding twelve calendar months. ... (paras. 5.7, 5.8, and 5.9 of TCBY term loan agreement)*

Notice that TCBY is required to maintain a **fixed charge coverage** ratio greater than 1.0, and the ratio is defined as:

$$\text{Fixed charge coverage} = \frac{\text{Net income} + \text{Noncash charges}}{\text{Current maturities} + \text{Dividends} + \text{Replacement CapEx}}$$

all measured over the most recent 12 months. Noncash charges—like depreciation and goodwill amortization—are added back to net income because they don't reduce the cash available for debt repayment. Replacement CapEx—capital expenditures required to maintain (but not expand) the business—is viewed by TCBY's lender as a necessary cash outflow, like debt repayment.

Also notice how the fixed charge coverage requirement indirectly limits the company's ability to pay dividends. Suppose TCBY had net income of $50, noncash charges of $35, current loan maturities of $40, and replacement capital expenditures of $30. How large of a dividend could TCBY pay to shareholders?

A simple calculation shows the answer to be $15.

$$\text{Fixed charge coverage} = \frac{\$50 + \$35}{\$40 + \text{Dividend} + \$30} = 1.0$$

$$= \frac{\$50 + \$35}{\$40 + \$15 + \$30} = 1.0$$

Dividends in excess of $15 would put TCBY in violation of its fixed charge coverage requirement.

Negative covenants tend to be more significant and even more intensively negotiated than affirmative covenants, because they place direct restrictions on managerial decisions. These restrictions prevent actions that might impair the lender's claims against the company's cash flows, earnings, and assets. Negative covenants commonly include limits on total indebtedness, investment of funds, capital expenditures, leases, and corporate loans and advances, as well as restrictions on the payment of cash dividends, share repurchases, mergers, asset sales, voluntary prepayment of other indebtedness, and on new business ventures. Note this example from the TCBY loan agreement:

> *[Borrower agrees that it will not] sell, lease, transfer, or otherwise dispose of any assets … except the sale of inventory in the ordinary course of business and disposition of obsolete or worn-out equipment upon the replacement thereof … [or to] repurchase the stock of TCBY using, directly or indirectly, the proceeds of any loan. (paras. 6.6 and 6.12 of TCBY term loan agreement)*

The prohibition on stock repurchases addresses the repayment problem described earlier in the chapter.

Restrictions on total indebtedness limit the amount of additional debt the company may incur over the term of the loan. These restrictions are usually stated as a dollar amount or in the form of a ratio (e.g., total debt to assets, or working capital, or tangible net worth)—for example:

> *[Borrower agrees that it will not take on any new loans if] the aggregate amount of all such loans, advances and extensions of credit … would exceed twenty-five percent (25%) of the consolidated Tangible Net Worth of the Borrower. … (para. 6.3 of TCBY term loan agreement)*

Covenants restricting the use of funds for dividend payments, share repurchases, capital expenditures, and other business purposes are often included so the creditor has greater assurance that cash will be available to make interest and principal payments when due. In limiting the borrower's ability to sell, merge, or transfer operating assets (including subsidiaries), the creditor is ensuring the survival of the borrower's repayment potential.

It is also common for a borrower to agree not to use any of its existing property as collateral on future loans without first obtaining consent from the current lender—for example:

> *[Borrower agrees that it will not] [c]reate, incur, assume or suffer to exist any Lien, encumbrance, or charge of any kind (including any lease required to be capitalized*

under GAAP) upon any of its properties and/or assets other than Permitted Liens.
(para. 6.1 of TCBY term loan agreement)

An unusual feature of this **negative pledge**—a promise to not take a particular action—is that TCBY agrees to limit its property leasing activities, but it does so only for leases required to be capitalized under GAAP. The agreement does not restrict TCBY from entering into more operating leases.

The "**events of default**" section of a loan agreement describes circumstances in which the creditor has the right to terminate the lending relationship. Situations leading to default include the failure to pay interest or principal when due, inaccuracy in representations, failure to abide by a covenant, failure to pay other debts when due (known as "cross default"), impairment of collateral, change in management or ownership, and bankruptcy.

Most lending agreements require the borrower to provide a **Certificate of Compliance,** which affirms that management has reviewed the financial statements and found no violation of any covenant provision. If a covenant has been violated, the nature and status of the violation must be specified.[6] Remedies for breach of covenant restrictions include renegotiation of the debt contract terms (e.g., an increase in the interest rate), seizure of collateral, acceleration of the maturity of the debt, or initiation of legal bankruptcy proceedings.

The common remedy creditors exercise in the event of default is renegotiation of the loan agreement. All aspects of the loan—payment schedule, interest rate, collateral, affirmative and negative covenants—may be renegotiated. In cases where the default circumstances are considered less significant, the creditor may waive the violation or give the borrower a period of time—a "grace period"—to correct its covenant breach. In cases where the default is severe, the creditor may accelerate loan repayment (with interest) and terminate its relationship with the borrower. Although creditors rarely exercise the right to accelerate repayment, having this right substantially strengthens a lender's negotiating position with the borrower if problems arise.

Recap

When it comes to a company's business decisions, what's best for managers and shareholders isn't always best for creditors. Debt convenants—including those based on accounting numbers—help reduce this conflict of interest. Creditors benefit because debt covenants reduce default risk, and shareholders benefit from the lowered cost of debt financing.

Managers' Responses to Potential Debt Covenant Violations

Violating a covenant is costly. So managers have strong incentives to make accounting choices that reduce the likelihood of technical default. Such choices include not only the selection of alternative accounting techniques (e.g., LIFO versus FIFO inventory methods) but also discretionary expenditures (e.g., research and development or advertising), accrual adjustments (e.g., bad debt provisions), and decisions about when to initiate transactions that result in accounting gains or losses (e.g., asset disposal or corporate restructuring). Readers of financial statements must be able to recognize and understand these incentives and their effect on managers' accounting choices.

A number of studies have examined how incentives arising out of debt contracts affect managers' accounting choices. One study looked at voluntary accounting

A **technical default** occurs when the borrower violates one or more loan covenants but has made all interest and principal payments. A **payment default** occurs when the borrower is unable to make the scheduled interest or principal payment.

changes made by 130 companies reporting covenant violations from 1980 to 1989. This study found that net worth and working capital restrictions are the most frequently violated accounting-based covenants and that companies approaching default often made accounting changes that increased reported earnings.[7] Common techniques used to increase earnings are changes in pension cost assumptions (to be discussed later in Chapter 14), the liquidation of LIFO layers, and the adoption of the FIFO inventory method (Chapter 9).

Another study examined what are called **discretionary accounting accruals**—noncash financial statement adjustments which "accrue" revenue (e.g., debits to accounts receivable and credits to sales) or accrue expenses (e.g., debits to warranty expenses and credits to accrued warranties payable).[8] This study, which looked at discretionary accruals by 94 companies reporting covenant violations from 1985 to 1988, found that "abnormal" accruals in the year prior to violation significantly increased reported earnings. (Normal accruals were determined by examining each company's past accruals and by benchmarking against average accruals reported by other firms in the same industry that year.) Moreover, these accrual adjustments were also more likely to increase working capital in the year of covenant violation.

These and other studies suggest that *management tends to make accounting changes and/or to manipulate discretionary accruals to avoid violating debt covenants.* Earnings increases that arise from management's efforts to avoid violating covenant provisions are unlikely to reflect fairly the underlying economic condition of the company and, therefore, are not likely to be sustainable. Unsustainable earnings increases are unlikely to translate into permanent cash flow increases (Chapter 2). These "tenuous" earnings components should be interpreted with caution.

Throughout the remainder of the book, we highlight how alternative accounting methods and accrual adjustments affect earnings and key financial ratios. We'll alert you to accounting choices that can have substantial implications for debt covenants—implications you should keep in mind as you go about interpreting and using accounting numbers for making economic decisions.

Management Compensation

Most modern corporations are not run by descendants of those who founded the organization but instead are controlled by professional managers—that is, "hired hands" who may lack the passion for corporate excellence that comes with substantial share ownership. This separation of ownership and control creates potential conflicts of interest between shareholders and managers.

Consider a top executive whose job requires extensive travel and who, for reasons of "comfort and convenience," prefers the corporate jet to a commercial airline. Who receives the benefits of the comfort and convenience? And who pays the cost? If the comfort and convenience that comes from using the corporate jet leads to increased managerial productivity, both parties stand to gain. Shareholders lose, however, when both the benefits of comfort and convenience accrue only to the executive and there are no productivity improvements. That's because shareholders alone bear the added cost of travel by corporate jet.

Obviously, managers have incentives to use corporate assets for their personal benefit at the expense of owners. Potential conflicts of interest can be overcome if managers are given incentives that cause them to behave like owners. One means is a compensation package that links managerial pay to improvements in firm value.[9] If the manager's compensation goes up as the organization's value increases, managers

The corporate jet example illustrates one type of conflict between shareholders and managers—the tendency of managers to "overconsume" corporate resources. Professional managers also have incentives both to retain cash rather than pay dividends and to accept negative net present value investment projects that reduce the volatility (or variance) of firm cash flows. Managers who are close to retirement age may have little incentive to adopt a long-term focus. Shareholders' interests can be compromised by these incentives.

have an incentive to take actions that lead to increased firm value—that is, managers and owners benefit simultaneously.

Two ways of aligning managers' incentives with owners' interests are to link compensation to stock returns and/or financial performance measures such as accounting earnings. Both are widely used. Neither is perfect.

Consider stock returns. Managerial strategies and decisions clearly affect share prices in the long run. But in the short run, share prices could rise or fall due to factors like interest rate changes that are beyond management's control.

Similar problems cloud the link between compensation and financial performance measures like earnings. On the positive side, earnings are probably less susceptible to the influence of temporary and external economic forces, and unlike stock returns, accounting-based financial performance measures can be tied to a manager's specific responsibilities, such as the profitability of a single product line or geographical region. On the other hand, using accounting earnings as a measure is frequently criticized for its reliance on accruals, deferrals, allocations, and valuations that involve varying degrees of subjectivity and judgment.

A good compensation plan must overcome the incentive alignment problems we have discussed and motivate managers to act like owners. But this is not the whole story, of course, because good compensation plans for managers must also take into account the effects of management decisions on parties other than the owners. For example, if a compensation plan is designed in such a way as to encourage managers to make decisions that ignore environmental issues, firm value might increase (at least in the short run) but clearly the incentives in the plan are not "good."

How Executives Are Paid

Most compensation packages involve a base salary, an annual (or short-term) incentive, and a long-term incentive:

- **Base salary** is typically dictated by industry norms and the executive's specialized skills.

- **Short-term incentives** set financial performance goals that must be achieved if the executive is to earn various bonus awards. For example, a plan may stipulate that a bonus of 10% of salary is earned only if the after-tax return on assets for the company exceeds 12%. But a 20% bonus can be earned if return on assets is 15% or more. Such plans link pay to performance; since compensation is "at risk," managers have an incentive to achieve plan goals.

- **Long-term incentives** motivate and reward executives for the company's long-term growth and prosperity (typically three to seven years). Long-term incentives are designed to counterbalance the inherently short-term orientation of annual incentives.

Two studies of executive compensation in Canada illustrate trends in the mix among base salary, short-term incentives, and long-term incentives. KPMG examined 236 proxy statements filed by TSE 300 companies and concluded:

Compensation Mix
The introduction by the [Ontario Securities Commission] in 1993 of detailed disclosure of executive compensation for the five highest-paid executives placed pressure on board compensation committees to explain the rationale for executive pay. Similar regulations introduced earlier in the United States slowed the growth of base salaries

◄ Changes in interest rates affect share prices for two reasons. To see why, consider the effect of a *decrease* in marketwide interest rates. First notice that a decrease in marketwide interest rates will reduce the company's cost of equity capital. As shown in equation (6.5), this will increase share price. Second, as interest rates decrease, the yields on fixed-rate bond investments fall, making them less attractive to investors. This increases the demand for stocks in general and, ceteris paribus, leads to an increase in stock prices.

◄ Certain features of executive compensation packages are also designed to reduce the combined tax liability of the company and its managers. Tax considerations undoubtedly contribute to the popularity of certain pay practices and help explain their use by some companies and not others.

KPMG
www.kpmg.com

and increased the growth of annual bonus/incentive targets. Today, in the United States, base pay for executives plays a much smaller role in relation to total annual cash compensation than it did 10 years ago. Now that we have completed five years under the detailed OSC disclosure regulations, we find a similar shift in emphasis from base pay to incentive pay taking place in Canada. In 1993, CEO average base pay amounted to 72% of total annual cash compensation (base pay and bonus/ incentive). In 1997, average base pay represented 54% of total annual cash compensation. Similar but less pronounced changes have occurred in the base/incentive mix of the other executives whose compensation has been disclosed.[10]

ERNST AND YOUNG
www.ey.com

In a similar study of TSE 300 companies, Ernst and Young found that 53% of annual total remuneration of CEOs was salary, 21% was annual bonus, and 21% was long-term incentive (the remaining 5% was classified as "other cash"). Similar patterns were found for chief financial officers and for profit centre heads. Also, over 85% of CEOs had stock options as part of their compensation mix.[11] In the KPMG study, another interesting finding was that the higher-performing companies[12] on average paid their CEOs less base salary and higher annual bonus/incentive than low-performing companies.

Stock options are by far the most frequently used long-term incentive device. Because the option only has value if the market price of the underlying stock rises, the executive has an incentive to strive to increase shareholder value as measured by stock price.

Stock appreciation rights (SARs) are a stock option variation developed to ease the cash flow burden faced by executives when stock options are exercised. The executive does not have to pay anything to receive the cash value of an appreciated SAR, since he or she receives the money equivalent of the increase in the company's share price.

Restricted stock is typically an award of stock that is nontransferable or subject to forfeiture for a period of years. Restricted stock grants provide an effective set of "golden handcuffs" for retaining executives with desirable skills, at least during the restriction period. **Phantom stock** has all the characteristics of restricted stock, except that the executive receives the cash value of shares "earned out" rather than the shares themselves.

Performance plans award shares or cash units earned (in whole or in part) according to the degree of achievement of predetermined performance goals. From a financial reporting perspective, these plans are important because performance goals are often tied to financial targets (e.g., earnings-per-share growth or return-on-equity hurdles). Occasionally, the performance goals are strategic—increasing market share, reducing costs, or raising product quality. Performance goals are established at the beginning of the award period, which usually ranges from four to seven years and may be stated in absolute terms or relative to those performance levels achieved by a group of peer companies.

Performance unit (or cash) plans allocate to each executive a given number of "units" of fixed dollar value at the start of the award period. At the end of the award period, the executive receives cash equal to the number of units "earned out" times the fixed dollar value, with the proportion of units earned determined by the degree to which performance goals have been achieved.

Performance shares are similar to unit plans insofar as each executive is allocated a fixed number of common shares, with the proportion earned out again contingent upon the extent to which financial and strategic goals are met. Since performance plans are an important element of long-term incentive compensation, analysts and other statement readers must be aware that financial reporting choices can impact managers' long-term compensation.

Compensation Disclosure—What's the Impact?

In an article published in the *Ivey Business Journal*, the authors wrote:

> *In 1993, the Ontario Securities Commission issued a mandate requiring all firms listed on the Toronto stock exchange to disclose the compensation plans for each of their top-five paid executives. The OSC ruling made the disclosure of executive compensation in Canada a reality. The requirements, similar to those in the United States, were expected to change the compensation/performance relationship, as shareholders sought to maximize value. In fact, did shareholders win? Or did executives?* [13]

IVEY BUSINESS JOURNAL ONLINE www. iveybusinessjournal. com.

The authors found some evidence, based on an analysis of the 100 largest Canadian companies by market capitalization, that mandatory executive compensation disclosure results in *both* higher executive total compensation (salary plus bonus) *and* bonuses apparently "more closely aligned with market ... performance after [the introduction of the disclosure requirements]". Such results seem to be consistent with the idea that executive compensation plans should encourage executives to increase company market value (albeit a limited notion of "performance," which ignores the social realm!), and that the introduction of mandatory disclosure of executives' compensation in Canada tends to cause "the shift from internal (board) to external (shareholder) monitoring"[14] of management. But things rarely work out in the way that changes in policies and laws, such as the compensation disclosure requirement, anticipate.

For example, a *Globe and Mail* article reported that a survey that examined CEO compensation for 100 of the largest TSE-listed companies found that "CEOs saw a 54-per-cent rise in total compensation [in 2001] ... when the TSE 100-stock index fell 16 per cent and when final profits in the survey group dropped 13 per cent on average."[15] And in the same article, Jane Courtemanche of the Ontario Municipal Employees Retirement Board (OMERS, which has a major investment portfolio) is quoted as saying,

> It's pretty clear that directors have let down their shareholders in a lot of cases. The numbers speak for themselves.

The article goes on to report that "Ms. Courtemanche said that 'OMERS has proxy voting guidelines that call on companies to link bonuses to specific performance targets.'"

So executive compensation disclosure in Canada, while not without its critics and supporters, is at least putting some pressure on the need to ensure that boards of directors of companies consider carefully the detailed design of compensation plans, including of course how accounting information fits in.

Information about a company's executive compensation practices can be found in the annual proxy statement, a notification of the annual shareholders meeting, filed with the provincial securities commissions. Among other disclosures, this document describes both the compensation payments and awards made to the five highest-paid executives of the company and any new executive compensation plans submitted for shareholder approval. Exhibit 7.1 presents excerpts from the 2002 proxy statement of Bombardier Inc.

BOMBARDIER INC. www.bombardier.com

Exhibit 7.1 BOMBARDIER INC.

Excerpts from 2002 Proxy Statement

Remuneration of Named Executive Officers

Summary Compensation Table

The Summary Compensation Table shows certain compensation information for the Chairman of the Board and of the Executive Committee and the four other most highly compensated corporate management executive officers (collectively, the "Named Executive Officers") for services rendered in all capacities during the financial years ended January 31, 2002, 2001 and 2000. This information includes the base salaries, bonus awards, the number of stock options granted and certain other compensations, whether paid or deferred.

| | | Annual Compensation | | | Long-Term Compensation | | | |
| | | | | | Awards | | | |
Name and Principal Position	As at January 31	Salary ($)	Bonuses ($)	Other Annual Compensation ($)[1]	Securities Under Options Granted (#)	Restricted Share or Restricted Share Units ($)	LTP Payouts ($)	All other Compensation ($)
Laurent Beaudoin Chairman of the Board and of the Executive Committee	2002	1,000,000	—	115,992[2]	—	—	—	—
	2001	1,000,000	—	144,634	—	—	—	—
	2000	1,000,000	—	86,891	2,000,000	—	—	—
Jean-Louis Fontaine Vice Chairman	2002	400,000	200,000	—	—	—	—	—
	2001	375,000	542,062	—	—	—	—	—
	2000	350,000	311,500	—	200,000	—	—	—
Robert E. Brown President and Chief Executive Officer	2002	1,250,000	950,000	—	1,000,000	—	—	—
	2001	1,100,000	2,862,090	—	—	—	—	—
	2000	1,000,000	1,800,000	—	—	—	—	—
Carroll L'Italien Senior Vice President	2002	460,000	300,000	—	—	—	—	—
	2001	420,000	849,954	—	—	—	—	—
	2000	207,692[3]	302,900	—	400,000	—	—	—
Louis Morin Senior Vice President and Chief Financial Officer	2002	450,000	300,000	—	—	—	—	—
	2001	400,000	809,480	—	80,000	—	—	—
	2000	300,000	347,245	—	120,000	—	—	—

(1) The value of benefits not exceeding the lesser of $50,000 or 10% of the sum of salary and bonuses has been omitted.

(2) This sum includes $83,648 for personal use of the Corporation's aircraft.

(3) For the period from July 24, 1999 to January 31, 2000.

Stock Option Plan

The Stock Option Plan (the "Plan") of the Corporation provides for the granting to key employees of the Corporation and its subsidiaries of non-assignable options to purchase an aggregate number of Class B subordinate shares which could not exceed 133,782,688 outstanding Class B subordinate shares; of this number, 69,536,694 shares are available for granting.

The option price is the weighted average trading price of the Class B subordinate shares traded on the Toronto Stock Exchange on the five trading days immediately preceding the day on which the option is granted. The option price is payable in full at the time of exercise of the option. Unless otherwise determined by the Board of Directors of the Corporation, the options are exercisable during periods commencing not earlier than two years following the date of granting and terminating not later than ten years after such date of granting.

Furthermore, an optionee shall not have purchased more than 25% of the aggregate number of shares covered by his option at the expiration of the third year following the date of granting of such option, more than 50% of the aggregate number of shares covered by his option at the expiration of the fourth year following the date of granting of such option and more than 75% of the aggregate number of shares covered by his option at the expiration of the fifth year following the date of granting of such option. As a general rule, the number Class B subordinate shares granted to each key employee is based on a multiple being directly related to the key employee's management level in the Corporation or one of its subsidiaries.

As at January 31, 2002, options for a total of 43,493,984 Class B subordinate shares had been granted and were outstanding.

Granting of Stock Options to the Named Executive Officers for the Financial Year Ended January 31, 2002

The following table sets forth various information with respect to stock options granted to the named Executive Officers during the financial year ended January 31, 2002.

Name	Securities Under Options Granted (#)	$ of Total Options Granted to Employees in the Financial Year	Exercise or Base Price ($/Security)	Market Value of Securities Underlying Options on the Date of Grant ($/Security)	Expiration Date
Laurent Beaudoin	—	—	—	—	—
Jean-Louis Fontaine	—	—	—	—	—
Robert E. Brown	1,000,000	17.2%	$22.79	$22.30	February 14, 2011
Carroll L'Italien	—	—	—	—	—
Louis Morin	—	—	—	—	—

Options Exercised in Last Completed Financial Year

The following table summarizes for each of the Named Executive Officers the number of stock options exercised during the financial year ended January 31, 2002, the aggregate value realized upon exercise and the total number and value of unexercised options held at January 31, 2002. Value

realized upon exercise is the difference between the closing price of the Class B subordinate share on the exercise date and the exercise price of the option. Value of unexercised options at financial year end is the difference between the closing price of the Class B subordinate share on January 31, 2002 ($14.70) and the exercise price.

Name	Shares Acquired on Exercise (#)	Aggregate Value Realized ($)	Unexercised Options at Financial Year End		Value of Unexercised Options at Financial Year End	
			Exercisable (#)	Unexercisable (#)	Exercisable ($)	Unexercisable ($)
Laurent Beaudoin	—	—	9,300,000	1,500,000	102,597,500	6,142,500
Jean-Louis Fontaine	—	—	650,000	150,000	7,106,625	614,250
Robert E. Brown	—	—	2,000,000	2,000,000	17,837,480	7,272,500
Carroll L'Italien	—	—	100,000	300,000	348,000	1,044,000
Louis Morin	—	—	170,000	230,000	1,307,050	752,250

The number of shares indicated in the foregoing tables reflect, in part, adjustments following two-for-one stock splits which took place on July 7, 1995, July 10, 1998, and July 7, 2000.

The value of unexercised options, unlike the amounts set forth in the column "Aggregate Value Realized", has not been, and may never be, realized. The actual gains, if any, on exercise will depend on the value of the Class B subordinate shares of the Corporation on the date of exercise.

Pension Plan

Senior Officers, including the Named Executive Officers, participate in two non-contributory defined benefit pension plans. Benefits payable from the basic plan correspond to 2% of average earnings in the three continuous years of service during which they were paid their highest salary (up to a maximum salary of $86,111) times the number of years of credited service.

Since January 1, 2001, the supplemental plan provides (depending on the management level) for additional benefits of 1.75% of average earnings in excess of $86,111 times the number of years of credited service or 2.25% or 2.50% of average earnings times the number of years of credited service, less the pension payable from the basic plan and any benefits payable from other pension plans of the Corporation. Benefits are reduced by 1/3 of 1% for each month between the date of early retirement and the date of a participant's 60th birthday or, if earlier, the date at which the participant's age plus his years of credited service total 85. No benefits are payable from the supplemental plan if a participant has not completed five years of service.

The following table shows total annual benefits payable at age 60 from the basic plan and the supplemental plan computed on a percentage of 2.25%. Upon the death of a participant, the spouse will be entitled to a benefit equal to 60% of the benefit to which such participant was entitled. If the participant has no spouse at the time of retirement, the benefits will be paid, after death, to the designated beneficiary until such time as 120 monthly installments, in the aggregate, have been paid to the participant and to the designated beneficiary.

All benefits payable from these plans are in addition to government social security benefits. Only base salary is taken into consideration in calculating pension benefits.

Annual Benefits Payable at the Normal Retirement Age of 60

	Years of Service			
Average remuneration	20	25	30	35
$200,000	$ 90,000	$112,500	$135,000	$157,500
$300,000	$135,000	$168,750	$202,500	$236,250
$400,000	$180,000	$225,000	$270,000	$315,000
$500,000	$225,000	$281,250	$337,500	$393,750
$600,000	$270,000	$337,500	$405,000	$472,500
$700,000	$315,000	$393,750	$472,500	$551,250
$800,000	$360,000	$450,000	$540,000	$630,000
$900,000	$405,000	$506,250	$607,500	$708,750
$1,000,000	$450,000	$562,500	$675,000	$787,500
$1,100,000	$495,000	$618,750	$742,500	$866,250
$1,200,000	$540,000	$675,000	$810,000	$945,000

Years of credited service as at January 31, 2002 for each of the Named Executive Officers hereafter mentioned are:

Robert E. Brown	15 years
Carroll L'Italien	8 years and 1 month
Louis Morin	19 years and 4 months

At the normal retirement age of 60, the three Named Executive Officers whose names appear below will have the following number of years of credited service:

Robert E. Brown	18 years and 1 month
Carroll L'Italien	11 years and 1 month
Louis Morin	34 years and 6 months

The Chairman, Laurent Beaudoin, reached the age of 60 in May 1998. Pursuant to the basic pension plan and the supplemental pension plan, he would have been entitled, should he have retired on January 31, 2002, to an allowance which would have been $1,049,479 according to average pensionable earnings in the amount of $1,083,333 as to that date. The allowance to which he will be entitled at age 65 will be based on his pensionable earnings and his years of credited service as of that date. As at January 31, 2002,

Laurent Beaudoin had 38 years and 9 months of credited service. Upon his death, his wife will be entitled to a benefit equal to 60% of the benefits to which he was entitled.

The Vice Chairman, Jean-Louis Fontaine, reached the age of 60 in December 1999. Pursuant to the basic pension plan and the supplemental pension plan, he would have been entitled, should he have retired on January 31, 2002, to an allowance which would have been $354,687 according to average pensionable earnings in the amount of $375,000 as to that date. The allowance to which he will be entitled at age 65 will be based on his pensionable earnings and his years of credited service as of that date. As at January 31, 2002, Jean-Louis Fontaine had 37 years and 10 months of credited service. Upon his death, his wife will be entitled to a benefit equal to 60% of the benefits to which he was entitled.

The President and Chief Executive Officer, Robert E. Brown, will be entitled, in addition to his annual benefit as described in the chart above, to an additional allowance of 2% of his average pensionable earnings multiplied by his years of credited service from January 1, 1998.

Change-of-Control Agreement

The President and Chief Executive Officer, Robert E. Brown, and the Corporation have entered into an agreement which outlines the respective rights and obligations of each of them in respect of situations which might lead to a change in control of the Corporation. No such situation is currently pending and Management is not aware of any existing circumstances that could lead to such a situation.

In order to ensure the continued involvement of Mr. Brown in the business and affairs of the Corporation during negotiations which might lead to a change in control, Mr. Brown has agreed that, if he were to then choose to leave the employment of the Corporation, he would not do so for a period of at least four months after either an actual change in control or the date on which the discussions or negotiations relating to same would end or would be abandoned.

If, within six months following a change in control, Mr. Brown's employment were to be terminated by the Corporation (except if such termination results from death, retirement or cause), Mr. Brown would be entitled to receive from the Corporation, in addition to accrued base salary and pro rata share of his annual target bonus, an amount in cash equal to the lesser of (a) three times his annual salary and bonus (based on prior years) and (b) his base salary that would have been payable for the period from the date of termination until his normal retirement date (being, in a change of control context, Mr. Brown's 60th birthday) plus a proportionate bonus.

If, within six months following a change in control, Mr. Brown's employment were to be terminated by him (except if such termination were the result from death or retirement), Mr. Brown would be entitled to receive from the Corporation, in addition to accrued base salary and pro rata share of his annual target bonus, an amount in cash equal to the lesser of (a) the greater of (i) three times his annual salary (based on prior years) and (ii) two times his annual salary and bonus (based on prior years) and (b) his base salary that would have been payable for the period from the date of termination until the normal retirement date plus a proportionate bonus.

The amounts that would be payable to Mr. Brown after a change in control upon termination of employment where such termination would arise from disability, retirement or cause are also outlined in the agreement.

In addition to the foregoing, upon termination of Mr. Brown's employment within six months after a change in control, all options held by Mr. Brown which would not have yet vested would become fully vested and would be exercisable by him for a period of 60 days.

For the purposes of the agreement, change in control means the fact that a majority of the Directors of the Corporation cease to be nominees of the Bombardier family.

Report of the Compensation Committee

As at January 31, 2002, the Compensation Committee consisted of five Directors, two of whom are Officers of the Corporation, namely, the Chairman, Laurent Beaudoin, and one of the Vice Chairmen, J.R. André Bombardier, and three of whom are outside Directors, namely André Desmarais, Pierre Legrand and Jean C. Monty. The committee meets at least three times a year.

The aggregate compensation of the Senior Officers of the Corporation, including the Named Executive Officers, consists of three components: base salary, the incentive (short-term) plan and the stock option plan.

The Compensation Committee has responsibility for defining compensation conditions, salary classes, the extent and levels of participation in the incentive (short-term) program and the stock option plan. The Committee monitors succession planning and determines the compensation of the Senior Officers in light of annual earnings.

To assist it in achieving its goals, the Committee calls on the services of compensation consultants who are responsible for gathering information on the policies in effect in companies comparable with the Corporation. The Corporation's policy is to offer its Senior Officers competitive salaries and to hire employees who are experts in their field at their market value in order to achieve annual financial performance targets. In addition to market surveys, the Compensation Committee takes into consideration the profitability of the Corporation. Thus, growth in base salary is a function of individual performance, the results obtained by the Corporation and comparisons with the industry in general.

In addition to the base salary, the Corporation offers an incentive plan which emphasizes the creation of economic value for the Shareholders of the Corporation and which is linked to the performance objectives of each group or division. A bonus target is set as a percentage of the salary of a Senior Officer and the program allows for a maximum amount of bonuses for each group. The incentive plan encourages employees to try to outperform the earnings forecasts contained in annual operating budgets.

In the case of the Senior Officers at the Corporate Office, the incentive plan is based on the return obtained on the Shareholders' equity during a given year. For the Senior Officers to earn a bonus, such return must have exceeded 12.5% at year-end. Any percentage point in excess is multiplied by a factor which is in turn based on the management level of the Senior Officer.

The performance of the Corporation and sustained growth in the value of its shares depend on striking a balance between short and long-term considerations. To this end a stock option plan was introduced in 1986 to allow options on Class B subordinate shares of the Corporation to be granted to key employees of the Corporation and its sub- sidiaries. This plan is described on pages 6 and 7.

The Compensation Committee determines the number of stock options to be granted based, as a general rule, on a multiple of salary which is established according to the management level held by the key employee of the Corporation or one of its subsidiaries. The application of the formula is flexible and the Compensation Committee takes into account all relevant circumstances when making its decisions. Barring circumstances involving an exceptional contribution or a promotion, the status of each key employee as regards stock options is reviewed every three years.

The determination of the base salaries of the Chief Executive Officer and the other Senior Officers takes into account salary comparisons with positions involving similar responsibility and complexity, as per information obtained from outside consultants, and considerations of internal equity.

In brief, all of the Senior Officers receive a compensa- tion that is based on their individual performance, the per- formance of the Corporation and market forces.

Laurent Beaudoin André Desmarais
J.R. André Bombardier Pierre Legrand
Jean C. Monty

Incentives Tied to Accounting Numbers

Many companies use performance plans, which are usually tied to accounting num- bers, as *long-term* compensation incentives. For *annual* bonus plans, accounting numbers become overwhelmingly important. Let's take a closer look at these "at risk" compensation components—annual bonus plans and long-term compensation— that are tied to accounting numbers.

The common performance measures used in *annual* incentive plans for senior corporate executives are shown in Figure 7.4. Virtually every company included in the survey from which the figure is taken has an annual performance-based incentive compensation plan for executives. Most plans link bonus awards to one or more accounting-based performance measures, such as earnings per share, or return on equity. Operating cash flows are the performance measure in 15% of the bonus plans. Total return to shareholders—dividends plus share price appreciation—is the per- formance measure in 8% of the bonus plans. Figure 7.5 paints a similar picture of the performance measures used in *long-term* incentive plans. Although some companies (14%) tie long-term incentive awards to total return to shareholders, most use earn- ings performance to determine long-term compensation awards. Together, Figures 7.4 and 7.5 show how extensively accounting numbers serve as the basis for annual

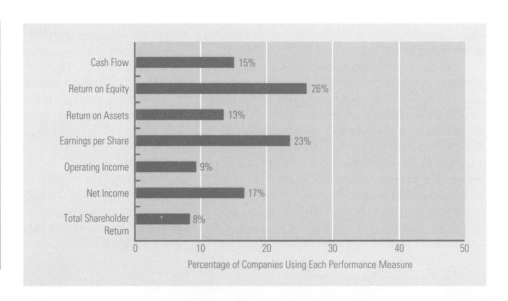

FIGURE 7.4
ANNUAL PERFORMANCE- BASED PLANS (1993)

The individual percentages add up to more than 100% because some companies use multiple measures of performance.

Source: Hay Group, Inc., 1993.

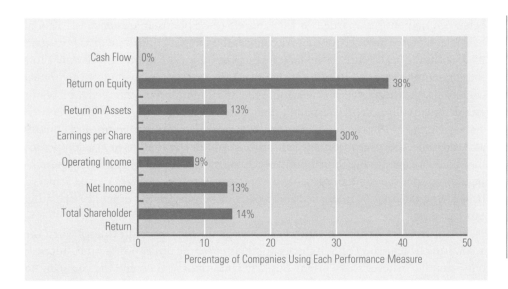

FIGURE 7.5
LONG-TERM
PERFORMANCE-
BASED PLANS
(1993)

The individual
percentages add
up to more than
100% because
some companies
use multiple
measures of
performance.

Source: Hay Group,
Inc., 1993.

bonus and long-term performance awards. This widespread use of accounting-based incentives is controversial for at least three reasons.

First, earnings growth does not automatically translate into increased shareholder value. Management can "grow" earnings by expanding the size of the business through acquisitions or new investment. This strategy can produce substantial dollar increases in sales volume, operating earnings, and EPS. But these added profits don't always increase shareholder value. For shareholder value to increase, the company must earn more on new investments than its incremental cost of capital. Unfortunately, not all acquisitions and investments clear the cost-of-capital "hurdle" even though they may show an accounting profit. So earnings-based incentive compensation plans can sometimes reward managers for launching new investments that increase earnings but not shareholder value.

Second, accounting-based incentive plans can encourage managers to adopt a short-term business focus. Consider the typical bonus plan illustrated in Figure 7.6. The executive receives a bonus equal to 100% of base salary if annual EPS reaches the $3.50 target. The bonus award declines to 50% of base salary for EPS performance at the $3 level, and it escalates to 150% for EPS at the $4 level. If EPS falls

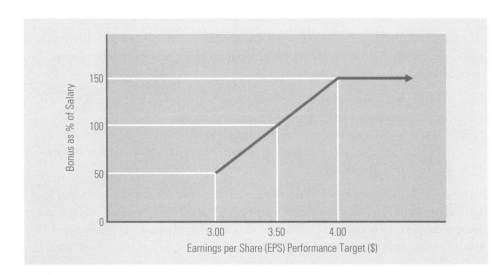

FIGURE 7.6
STRUCTURE OF
ANNUAL
PERFORMANCE
BONUS

below $3, no bonus is awarded; at EPS above $4, the bonus award remains 150% of base salary. To see how accounting-based incentives might contribute to a short-term focus, consider an executive who believes current business conditions will only allow the company to earn $2.80 EPS for the year. Despite these unfavourable (no bonus) conditions, the executive can still achieve the $3 EPS minimum required for a bonus award by curtailing needed expenditures—simply cutting back on critical research and development. Research expenses go down, reported earnings go up, and bonuses are paid! This short-term strategy can prove costly in the long term if a competitor introduces a new product based on the technology the company had been research-ing. Of course, the same unsustainable short-run earnings increase can be achieved by delaying essential maintenance and repairs or by postponing other key operating expenditures.

Executives also have an incentive to "manage down" reported earnings when the accounting benchmark (EPS in this example) is *above* the upper bonus limit. Suppose our executive believes that current business conditions will enable the company to earn $4.20 EPS this year. Here the executive has an incentive to reduce reported earn-ings to $4, deferring the excess to the future. After all, the same bonus award is granted no matter whether EPS is at the $4 or the $4.20 level!

How can excess earnings be deferred? It's easy! Delay some fourth-quarter cus-tomer shipments until the beginning of next year. Current year's sales decline and earnings fall without affecting this year's bonus award; the delayed sales and earnings count toward next year's bonus, and the probability of earning the bonus next year increases too!

Third, executives have some discretion over the company's accounting policies, and they can use that discretion to achieve bonus goals. For example, an executive falling short of the $3 EPS minimum might reduce fourth-quarter inventories, report a "LIFO liquidation" gain, and boost earnings to a level above the bonus threshold. (LIFO liquidations are discussed in Chapter 9.) On the other hand, if earnings per-formance is so low that reaching the bonus threshold is impossible, the manager has an incentive to further reduce earnings. The objective of these deliberate earnings reductions—called "big baths"—is simple. Today's writeoffs lower future expenses, thereby increasing future earnings—and future bonuses! Examples of "big bath" writeoffs include higher bad debt allowances, large restructuring charges, and good-will reductions. Accounting discretion also allows managers who believe earnings will exceed the $4 ceiling to play bonus "games"—reduce reported earnings down to the bonus maximum and defer the excess.

Research Evidence Do managers use accounting flexibility to achieve bonus goals? One study, which looked at annual bonus plans like the one in Figure 7.6, revealed two things:[16]

1. When annual earnings already exceeded the $4 bonus ceiling, managers used discretionary accounting options to *reduce* earnings.
2. When it was clearly evident that earnings would be below the bonus thresh-old ($3 in Figure 7.6), managers used their financial reporting flexibility to reduce earnings still further.

These reductions in earnings had no impact on that year's bonus but improved man-agers' chances of receiving bonuses the following year. That's because taking a larger discretionary expense this year often meant a smaller expense next year—and that helped to ensure that next year's earnings would meet or beat the bonus target.

Another research study found evidence that R&D expenditures tend to decline during the years immediately prior to a CEO's retirement.[17] Existing GAAP require R&D expenditures to be expensed as incurred, thereby reducing income and bonuses. By reducing R&D expenditures prior to retirement, these CEOs were able to increase the payout from their bonus contracts.

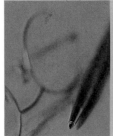

Recap

Compensation plans should align managers' incentives with the objectives of shareholders. Many compensation plans link incentive pay to accounting numbers; this link is an effective management incentive since improved financial performance generally translates into greater shareholder wealth. Unfortunately, accounting numbers can be manipulated. Consequently, compensation plans tied to financial goals sometimes backfire because of the short-term, self-interested focus of executives.

Protection Against Short-Term Focus Compensation plans must also be designed to include long-term incentive components (primarily stock options) that are specifically intended to mitigate the short-term focus of executives. Stock options give managers a strong incentive to avoid shortsighted business decisions and instead operate the company in ways that create shareholder value.

Another factor that can reduce short-term focus involves the fact that incentive compensation plans are administered by a committee of the board of directors, called the **Compensation Committee.** This committee comprises the company's outside (nonmanagement) directors. It can intervene when circumstances warrant modification of the scheduled incentive award. In general, the compensation committee can adjust the incentive award whenever it believes that current earnings have been unduly influenced by special items.

For example, language of the following sort is typical in many compensation agreements:

> *At any time prior to the payment of performance awards, the compensation committee may adjust previously established performance targets and other terms and conditions... to reflect major unforeseen events such as changes in laws, regulations, or accounting practices, mergers, acquisitions, divestitures, or extraordinary, unusual, or nonrecurring items or events.*[18]

Also, innovative ways of designing accounting-based incentive measures are appearing that purportedly better align managers' and shareholders' interests than conventional accounting measures. A prominent example is Economic Value Added (EVA[TM] for short; New York-based consultants Stern Stewart have registered the name), which is based upon net operating profit after taxes (NOPAT in Chapter 5), minus a charge for the use of capital. Some companies are beginning to include information about their EVA[TM] in their annual reports, and *CA Magazine* reports that the CFO for a major Canadian accounting firm believes that reporting this new measure will shortly become commonplace (see Exhibit 7.2).

STERN STEWART & CO.
www.eva.com

CA MAGAZINE
www.camagazine.com

Exhibit 7.2 EXCERPT FROM *CA MAGAZINE* ON ECONOMIC VALUE ADDED

Performance-Measurement Takeover Bid!

The New Year is here, a seemingly logical time for business watchers to reflect about the financial performance of companies in 1997. Among the newest financial performance measurements many are eyeing are Economic Value Added (EVA) and Market Value Added (MVA)—the brainchildren of the New York financial consulting firm Stern Stewart & Co.

Investors, analysts and money managers are paying increasing attention to these measurements to find stock market bargains. In fact, Dave Pollard, chief knowledge officer for Ernst and Young in Canada, predicts that accountants will one day be including EVA and MVA on all balance sheets. "I would say that we are probably five years away from having EVA and MVA as part of the staple of financial calculations that CAs produce as a matter of course," he says.

EVA is essentially a company's net income less the implicit cost of equity and debt for a given period. Instead of measuring profitability in terms of, say, earnings per share, EVA does so in terms of the return on all capital employed.

MVA is the company's cumulative economic value added over a period of time. It represents the difference between the value that the shareholders place on a public company and the company's [shareholders'] equity. If investors can take out more than the total capital invested during the life of the company, then MVA will be positive. In such a case, the company will have created wealth. If the reverse is true, the company will have destroyed wealth. This can occur even if the company has turned a profit in terms of earnings per share.

Studies show that a company that has a positive EVA year after year will see its MVA rise. Conversely, a persistently negative EVA will lead to a lowered MVA because the market will have no confidence that the company can produce a good return on its invested capital. As a result, companies can appear in completely different positions in the respective rankings for EVA and MVA.

The 1997 EVA/MVA rankings for Canadian companies will be released in June (1998) by Stern Stewart. In 1996, the top five EVA-ranked Canadian companies were Magna International Inc., Agrium Inc., Newbridge Networks Corp., Quebecor Inc. and Bombardier Inc. The top five MVA-ranked Canadian companies were The Thomson Corp., Barrick Gold Corp., Bombardier Inc., Placer Dome Inc. and Rogers Communications Inc.

Source: *CA Magazine*, January–February 1998, p. 15.

Capital Requirements in the Banking Industry

Banks and other financial institutions are required to meet **minimum capital requirements.** The purpose of these requirements is to ensure that the bank (or institution) remains financially sound and can meet its obligations to depositors.

The test for capital adequacy is a simple one: Does the amount of investor capital or the ratio of investor capital to gross assets—both defined by accounting principles specified for these institutions—exceed the minimum level allowed by the regulator? If it does, the bank is in compliance and considered to have adequate capital. If bank capital falls below the minimum allowed, regulatory intervention can be triggered.

Suppose Hometown Bank had gross assets of $900 million and investor capital of $135 million, and suppose the bank's regulators had set a 10% minimum capital ratio. Hometown would be in compliance with the capital requirement because it has a capital adequacy ratio of 15%, calculated as:

$$\text{Capital adequacy ratio} = \frac{\text{Invested capital}}{\text{Gross assets}}$$

$$= \frac{\$135 \text{ million}}{\$900 \text{ million}} = 0.15 \text{ or } 15\%$$

which is above the 10% minimum allowed.

Regulators have a powerful weapon to encourage compliance with minimum capital guidelines. They can impose costs on banks and financial institutions found to be in noncompliance. For example, a noncomplying bank:

- is required to submit a comprehensive plan describing how and when its capital will be increased
- can be examined more frequently by the regulator
- can be denied a request to merge, open new branches, or expand its services
- can be subject to more stringently applied dividend restrictions if it has inadequate or "potentially inadequate" capital (e.g., Hometown Bank might be prohibited from paying any dividends if its capital adequacy ratio falls to the minimum level allowed, 10%)

Because regulators can restrict bank operations, a bank with "inadequate" capital incurs greater regulatory costs than a bank with adequate capital.

There are several ways bank managers can avoid costly noncompliance penalties as a result of failing to meet minimum capital requirements. The best approach is to operate profitably and invest wisely so that the bank remains financially sound. Another way is to choose accounting policies that increase capital or decrease gross assets (both computed according to accounting principles specified for their institutions) so that the bank can pass its capital adequacy test. Let's look more closely at this "artificial" approach to regulatory compliance.

The cash that banks receive from depositors is used to make customer loans. These loans show up as balance sheet receivables, and often they represent the bank's single largest asset. **Uncollected loans** are a significant cost of business in the banking industry, and bank managers have some discretion over the timing and amount of recorded uncollectibles. This discretion can be used to improve the bank's capital adequacy ratio. How?

It's really very simple: Understate the true loan loss provision and loan charge-offs for the year. This not only improves the bank's capital adequacy ratio; it also increases the net income figure reported to shareholders. But these improvements are just an illusion. In reality, the bank manager forecasts more uncollectibles than are shown on the financial reports. Understating loan loss provisions and charge-offs may help avoid noncompliance with bank capital requirements, but this strategy hides the bank's true performance and condition from both regulators and shareholders.

> A bank's **loan loss provision** is just the estimated bad debt expense associated with its loan receivables. **Loan charge-offs** are loans the bank no longer expects to collect. Loan loss provisions decrease net income while loan charge-offs decrease bank capital.

Rate Regulation in the Utilities Industries

Utility companies like Manitoba Hydro, Hydro-Québec, and Bell Canada have traditionally had their prices set or monitored by government regulatory agencies—that is, by public utility commissions and boards. The rate formulas of most commissions used accounting-determined costs and asset values. A typical rate formula for an electric utility looked like this:

HYDRO-QUÉBEC
www.hydroquebec.com

MANITOBA HYDRO
www.hydro.mb.ca

BELL CANADA
www.bell.ca

Allowed revenue = Operating costs + Amortization + Taxes + (ROA × Asset base)

where ROA was the **return on assets** allowed by the regulator. The rate formula set total allowed revenues equal to an amount that covered the company's operating costs (fuel, labour, and administrative expenses plus amortization and taxes) and provided a "fair" return on the capital invested in operating assets (things like generating stations, transmission lines, fuel inventory, and so on).

Rate regulation of public utilities is giving way to a move toward a more competition-based model across Canada. For example, in May 1997 the Canadian Radio-television and Telecommunications Commission (CRTC)—the government body that oversees telephone and communications industries in Canada—announced that competition would replace rate of return regulation in the local telephone services market. And in December 1997, the CRTC announced the deregulation of Bell Canada's voice long-distance services. However, since the competition-based approach is in its infancy, and since rate regulation is still in effect for many utilities (for example, the CRTC still uses traditional rate of return regulation for smaller Ontario and Quebec-based telephone companies, as does the Public Utilities Board of Manitoba for certain parts of that province's electricity generating system), it is important to at least briefly examine the impact of rate regulation on accounting choices. As we do, we must keep in mind that every regulatory body usually has (and has had) the power to specify **regulatory accounting principles,** or RAP, the accounting methods and procedures that must be followed when putting together financial statements for submission to the regulatory agency. RAP often differ from GAAP.

Suppose Canwest Power & Light has annual operating costs, amortization, and taxes of $300 million. Suppose also that $500 million of capital is invested in operating assets. Finally, suppose that the public utilities commission sets ROA at 10%. The annual revenue allowed would be:

$$\text{Allowed revenue} = \$300 \text{ million} + (10\% \times \$500 \text{ million})$$
$$= \$300 \text{ million} + \$50 \text{ million} = \$350 \text{ million}$$

To arrive at a rate per kilowatt-hour of electricity, the $350 million of revenue allowed is divided by the company's **estimate** of total kilowatt-hours to be sold during the year.

Industry RAP govern which items can be included in a regulated utility's operating costs and asset base—and which cannot be included. The difference is important, because included items are charged to customers but disallowed items are charged to shareholders if the utility is shareholder-owned. Consider this example: Suppose Canwest Power & Light spends $10 million on customer safety advertising and $50 million on "corporate image" advertising. Customer safety advertising is an allowed operating cost, so it is included in the rate formula. Customers ultimately pay for the $10 million spent on safety advertising through higher electricity rates.

Corporate image advertising is not an allowed cost in most jurisdictions, so the $50 million that Canwest Power & Light spent promoting itself cannot be passed on to customers in the form of higher electricity rates. Who pays the bill? Shareholders do, because there's $50 million less cash in the company. Regulators see image advertising as unnecessary. Consequently, they do not require customers to pay for it through higher electricity rates.

The example illustrates how RAP can influence rate regulation and the revenues ultimately received by utility companies. But there's another important point to the example. Industry RAP treat customer safety advertising and corporate image advertising differently. GAAP do not—both kinds of advertising would be included in operating costs on the company's income statement. Other differences between public utility RAP and GAAP are:

- **deferring costs** that would otherwise be charged to expense by nonregulated companies—utilities can postpone expensing storm damage costs, for example, as long as it is probable that those specific deferred costs are subject to recovery in future revenues

- **capitalization of equity costs** on construction projects when interest alone can be capitalized by nonregulated companies

Rate regulation also creates incentives for public utility managers to artificially increase the asset base. Suppose Canwest Power & Light signs a $700,000 one-year rental agreement for service vehicles. If the rental payment is an allowed operating cost for rate-making purposes, customers would pay $700,000 in higher electricity rates. On the other hand, if the rental could be included in the company's asset base, customers would pay $770,000, or 10% more—$700,000 for amortization (the full cost of the one-year asset) plus another $70,000 so that shareholders receive the allowed 10% return on the $700,000 asset.

Given the choice, shareholders would prefer to have the rental payment treated as an asset for rate-making purposes. The company could then charge customers an extra $70,000 and use the cash to cover "disallowed" costs—like image advertising—or to pay shareholder dividends. One way to make this happen is to design the rental contract so that it qualifies for RAP (and GAAP) treatment as an asset.

Taxation

All companies are "regulated" by provincial and federal tax authorities. When it comes to income taxes and the Canadian government, the regulators are Parliament and the Canada Customs and Revenue Agency (CCRA). Parliament writes the law, but CCRA interprets and administers it and collects the income tax.

The *Income Tax Act* and its regulations govern the computation of net income for tax purposes. These accounting rules are just another type of RAP. Many tax act accounting rules agree with GAAP. Consider this example: Revenue is generally recognized for tax and GAAP purposes at the time of sale and not later, when cash is collected from customers. However, there are situations in which tax act accounting rules differ from GAAP.

A case in point is "goodwill"—the excess price paid to acquire a business over and above its net asset value. GAAP allow companies to expense goodwill gradually over a period of time—up to 40 years. Tax act rules do not permit companies to expense goodwill (and thereby reduce taxable income) except in very rare circumstances. For many companies, this means that taxable net income (computed without goodwill expense) is higher than the GAAP net income figure (computed after subtracting goodwill expense) reported to shareholders. This may explain why some managers avoid recorded goodwill—it lowers GAAP net income but it doesn't lower the company's income tax payments.

Another example of differences between GAAP and tax legislation and regulations is the treatment of inventory. The Canada Customs and Revenue Agency will not permit the use of the LIFO inventory method, even though it is of course very acceptable under GAAP (see Section 3030 of the *CICA Handbook*). We will examine the effect of differences between GAAP and *Income Tax Act* treatments of a wide range of items in Chapter 13. However, it is important to keep in mind the following key point about differences between Canadian income

CCRA
www.ccra-adrc.gc.ca

To see how **goodwill** arises, suppose a business with assets worth $80 million and debt of $40 million is purchased by Raider Corporation for $55 million. Raider will record the purchase as:

DR	Assets purchased (at fair value)	$80 million	
DR	Goodwill (excess purchase price)	$15 million	
	CR Cash paid out		$55 million
	CR Liabilities assumed by Raider		$40 million

Notice that the goodwill increase of $15 million is required to make the journal entry balance. (Goodwill is discussed in Chapter 16.)

tax regulations and Canadian GAAP: "in determining income from a business [for income tax purposes], generally accepted accounting principles ... must be applied unless specific rules are provided for in the Act."[19]

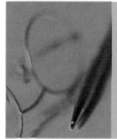

Recap

Government regulatory agencies and taxing authorities can write their own accounting rules, and many do. The result is that some financial statements for shareholders and creditors contain special regulatory items or use regulatory accounting methods which deviate from normal GAAP. Accounting-based regulations—including the *Income Tax Act*—also influence the choice of GAAP accounting methods for shareholder reports and when transactions are recorded.

Analytical Insights: Identifying "Managed" Earnings

It is essential for financial statement users to identify companies that achieve incremental increases in earnings resulting from strength in business fundamentals rather than earnings management techniques or accounting "gimmickry."[20]

We said in Chapter 6 that the key measure of corporate value is **permanent** ("sustainable") **earnings** from core businesses—the "above the line" income from continuing operations as discussed in Chapter 2. Most analysts, investors, and lenders agree. Compared to botttom-line net income, core earnings provide a truer picture of a company's ability to generate profits from its major business activities. Core earnings are also more predictive of the company's sustainable economic performance, its long-term growth trends, and its financial viability.

But uncovering a company's core earnings and assessing its overall performance is not easy. The challenge comes from several sources. As an analyst, you must do the following:

- Wrestle with differences in accounting methods and reporting practices across companies—even in the same industry.

- Identify areas where accounting choices can hide potential earnings surprises—so-called accounting torpedoes—such as a major writeoff of bad debts or intangibles.

- Assess the degree to which the firm has "managed" earnings and used accounting gimmickry.

- Adjust the reported financial statement amounts to eliminate the impact of these potential accounting "abuses."

This book is devoted to helping you meet the challenge.

The message from this chapter and from Chapter 3 is that managers sometimes have powerful incentives to "manage" the reported profitability and financial condition of their companies. These incentives are motivated by loan covenants, compensation contracts, regulatory agency oversight, tax avoidance efforts, a desire to "meet or beat" analysts' quarterly earnings forecasts, and to increase the company's stock price. Financial statement gimmicks are likely to be most prevalent when these accounting incentives are especially strong. For example, when the company is in danger of violating its debt covenants; or when a large portion of top management

Accounting gimmicks sometimes backfire. In 1997, top officers and directors at Leslie Fay agreed to pay back US$34.7 million to shareholders of the company. The payment settled lawsuits filed by shareholders because of alleged accounting gimmicks used in 1991 and 1992. Among other things, the suits charged that earnings gimmicks artificially increased officers' bonuses in those years. See L. Vickery, "Leslie Fay's Ex-Financial Chief, Polishan, is Found Guilty of Fraud," *Wall Street Journal*, July 7, 2000.

pay comes from bonuses tied to earnings per share or sales growth; or when management has a lengthy record of beating "the Street's" earnings forecast by a penny. What's the penalty for failing to "make" the numbers? Loan default, lost bonuses, and an abrupt stock price decline.

So now you know *when* to look for potential accounting distortions, but what exactly do you look *for* and *where* do you look? How do companies "manage" earnings? What accounting gimmicks are used?

The remaining chapters of this book explore the topics in detail. For now, we'll simply give you a "broad-brush" overview to sensitize you to the danger areas.

Look to areas where subjective judgments or estimates have a significant impact on the financial statements. For some companies, the areas to scrutinize might be revenue recognition, deferred marketing and customer acquisition costs, or reserves for bad debts and inventory obsolescence. For other companies, the critical areas may involve intangible asset valuation, asset impairment, warranty and product liability reserves, restructuring charges, or litigation and environmental contingencies. Also take a close look at areas where it is difficult to evaluate the company's accounting practices because no authoritative standards exist or because established practices are controversial. And watch out for large business transactions, especially those that are unusually complex in structure or in their financial statement effects. And take a magnifying glass to the financial statement footnotes and other financial disclosures. They should be complete and transparent—allowing you to look behind the numbers to see what's really going on in the company. If not, there may be an accounting torpedo headed in your direction.[21]

Exhibit 7.3 contains a partial list of tell-tale signs for identifying "aggressive" accounting choices. Keep this list handy as you read the rest of the book. We have a lot more to say about the "red flags" in Exhibit 7.3 and why they are helpful. Each chapter discusses other warning signals that you may want to add to the list.

Exhibit 7.3 TELL-TALE SIGNS OF POTENTIAL ACCOUNTING DISTORTIONS

- Unexplained changes in accounting methods like a switch from LIFO to FIFO inventory methods.
- LIFO "dipping" or excessive year-end inventory purchases for LIFO companies when prices are rising.
- Changes in the estimate of an asset's useful life, lease residual value, and pension or post-retirement health care benefit assumptions.
- Receivables or inventory growth that outpaces sales growth.
- Bad debt reserves that are low relative to receivables, past credit losses, or peer companies.
- Sudden "off-loading" of receivables by sale or securitization.
- Unusually long depreciation lives and amortization periods.
- Increasing gap between earnings and operating cash flows.
- Increasing gap between earnings and taxable income.
- Unexplained large increases or decreases in deferred income tax balances.
- Off-balance-sheet financing arrangements including significant use of joint ventures, "take-or-pay" contracts, or operating leases.
- Unexpected writeoffs of receivables and loans, inventories, buildings and equipment, or intangibles.
- Large changes in discretionary expenses such as advertising and R&D.
- Unusual business transactions that boost earnings.
- Audit qualifications or changes in the outside auditor.

Note: These (and other) accounting "red flags" are described more fully in later chapters.

Summary

Conflicts of interest among managers, shareholders, lenders, or regulators are a natural feature of business. Contracts and regulations help address these conflicts of interest in ways that are mutually beneficial to the parties involved. Accounting numbers often play an important role in contracts and regulations because they provide useful information about the company's performance and financial condition, as well as about the management team's accomplishments.

Accounting-based lending agreements, compensation contracts, and regulations shape managers' incentives—after all, that's why accounting numbers are included in contracts and regulations. They also help explain the accounting choices managers make. Understanding why and how managers exercise their GAAP accounting discretion can be extremely helpful to those who are analyzing and interpreting a company's financial statements.

And what happened to Allen Ford? The bank provided the loans Allen needed to open his first BookWorm, and the concept proved so successful he now owns three stores. Allen is currently developing a business plan for a used-book store to be called Second Time Around.

For more Exercises, Problems/Discussion Questions, and Cases, visit the Companion Website for this textbook at **www.pearsoned.ca/revsine**.

Exercises

E7-1 Conflicts of interest and agency costs

Suppose you and two friends each invested $100,000 in an oil and gas partnership. The general partner—Huge Gamble, Inc.—invests no cash but makes all operating decisions for the partnership, including where and how deep to drill for oil. Drilling costs plus a management fee are charged against the $300,000 of cash you and your friends invested. If oil is found, you each get 15% of partnership net income, with the remaining 55% going to Huge Gamble. But if the wells are dry, you get nothing except any cash that remains.

Required:

What is an agency relationship and what are agency costs? How do these concepts apply to your investment in the oil and gas partnership?

E7-2 Understanding debt covenants

Required:

What is a debt covenant? Why do lenders include them in loan agreements? Why do borrowers agree to include covenants in loan agreements?

E7-3 Debt covenants and accounting methods

Typically, the debt covenants in loan agreements do not explicitly mention the accounting methods that must be used when the company prepares financial statements for submission to the lender.

Required:

Why don't lenders require the use of specific accounting methods rather than letting management pick from among GAAP alternatives?

E7-4 Contracts and accounting numbers

Required:

What are the advantages of loan agreements that contain covenants tied to accounting numbers? Are there any disadvantages? Explain.

E7-5 Conflict of interest and accounting information

Required:

1. Explain and outline the significance of "asset substitution" and the "repayment problem."
2. Explain how "price protection" can be used to compensate lenders for the added risk of asset substitution and repayment.
3. Explain why price protection may cause shareholder value to fall.
4. Explain why writing contracts that restrict the owner-manager's ability to harm creditors may be a better way than price protection to reduce creditor-versus-shareholder conflicts.
5. Explain the advantages and disadvantages of using accounting-based numbers in covenants to the contracts mentioned in part 4 above.

E7-6 Equipment repairs and rate regulation

Power & Light, a shareholder-owned, regulated electricity company, has just spent $5 million repairing one of its electrical generating stations, which was damaged by a tornado. The loss was uninsured. Management has asked the public service commission for approval to treat the $5 million as an asset for rate-making purposes rather than as an allowed expense.

Required:

What difference will this make to customers and shareholders?

E7-7 Incentive design

The top five executives at Marvel Manufacturing are paid annual bonuses based on pre-determined earnings goals. These bonuses can be as much as 500% of salary. As a member of the company's compensation committee, you've been asked to comment on the following proposed changes to the annual bonus plan:

- Use after-tax income from continuing operations as the earnings performance measure instead of bottom-line net income.
- Set performance goals on the basis of return on assets (ROA) rather than earnings.
- Set performance goals—net income or ROA—with the goal of beating the industry average rather than meeting an absolute performance target.

Required:

What are the advantages and disadvantages of each suggested change?

E7-8 Medical malprofits

Required:

Explain the potential conflict of interest that arises when doctors own the hospitals in which they work. The following U.S. news article may help.

COLUMBIA/HCA
HEALTHCARE
CORPORATION
www.columbia.net

The executive who became the most visible symbol of profit-driven medical care stepped down yesterday as the top officer of the Columbia/HCA Healthcare Corporation amid a criminal investigation of whether the company's pursuit of profits has stretched beyond the legal limits … [he] will be replaced by Thomas F. Frist Jr., a surgeon by training, who has made his career in the hospital business. … Dr. Frist said he was ending Columbia's practice of selling ownership stakes in its hospitals to its doctors. That has been a critical piece of the strategy that helped propel Colombia's growth but led to great legal and ethical criticism that the company was compromising the medical independence of its doctors.

Source: *New York Times,* July 26, 1997.

E7-9 Bonus tied to EPS performance

Mr. John Brincat is the president and chief executive of Mercury Finance, an auto lender that specializes in lending to high credit-risk customers.

Mr. Brincat is eligible for an annual bonus equal to 1% of Net After-tax Earnings of the Company and is eligible for an additional bonus based upon annual increases in Net After-tax Earnings per share only after earnings exceed 20% over the prior year. The additional bonus is determined as follows:

- *Earnings per share increases of 0% to 19.99%, no additional bonus is paid.*

- *Earnings per share increases of 20% to 29.99%, additional bonus will be equal to 2.5% of the amount of increase from the prior year.*
- *Earnings per share increases of 30% to 39.99%, additional bonus will be equal to 3.0% of the amount of increase from the prior year.*
- *Earnings per share increases of 40% or more, additional bonus will be equal to 3.5% of the amount of increase from the prior year.*

In addition, at the time the employment contract was entered into, Mr. Brincat was issued a stock option grant ... of 2,500,000 shares at a price of $17.375 per share, the fair market value on the date of the grant. The options vest equally during the next five years of the contract and are exercisable in increments of 500,000 shares annually only if earnings per share each year exceeds the prior year's earnings per share by 20%. If earnings per share do not increase by 20%, Mr. Brincat forfeits that year's options and has no further right or claim to that year's options.

Source: Mercury Finance 1995 proxy.

Required:

As a shareholder, how comfortable would you be if your company's managers had contracts with these types of incentives? Why?

Problems/Discussion Questions

P7-1 Managerial incentives and stock ownership

Campbell Soup Executives Must Own Firm's Stock

CAMPBELL SOUP CO.
www.campbellsoup.
com

Campbell Soup Co. said Tuesday it is introducing a stock ownership plan for its chief executive and about 70 other senior executives. Under the plan, David Johnson, president and chief executive officer, is required to hold three times his 1992 base salary of [US]$757,500 in shares by the end of 1994. He must maintain the three times-earnings stake every year until he leaves the company. Executive or senior vice presidents are expected to buy and hold at least two times their annual base salary by 1994. Corporate vice presidents who have been with the company for three or more years will buy and hold the equivalent of one year's base salary. Senior executives will buy shares equal to at least one-half their annual salary. All corporate officers must hold at least 1,000 shares of Campbell stock by the end of this year.

Source: Bloomberg Business News, May 1993.

Required:

1. Suppose Mr. Johnson received a base salary (before personal income taxes) of $800,000 in 1993. His personal tax rate was 35% that year, and the year-end value of his Campbell stock was $1.6 million. How much of his after-tax salary for 1993 would go toward buying more stock in the company?
2. What are the advantages and disadvantages of Campbell's stock ownership plan?
3. Do you think that institutional investors (e.g., pension portfolio managers and mutual fund managers) would favour or oppose Campbell's plan? Why?

Chapter 7: The Role of Financial Information in Contracting   319

P7-2 Managerial incentives and pay

(a) In 1996, Canadian Airlines Corporation and its employees agreed that the employees would grant the airline a 10% wage concession as a key component of a restructuring plan to save the beleaguered company. In return, beginning in 1997, employees would each year divide up an amount equal to 10% of the airline's net income computed according to GAAP.

(b) When Abitibi-Price and Stone Consolidated merged in 1997 to form the pulp and paper giant Abitibi-Consolidated, about 300 managers and executives of the merged organization were eligible for bonuses under the "Synergy Achievement Compensation Plan." This plan is described as follows in the company's 1998 Management Proxy Circular:

Synergy Achievement Compensation Plan

The Company has also implemented a Synergy Achievement Compensation Plan to reward employees who played and continue to play a strategic implementation role in achieving annualized synergies as part of the amalgamation process. Approximately 300 senior managers and operators will be able to earn significant one-time bonuses should the Company achieve annualized synergies in excess of $100 million. Synergy compensation payments will be paid on the basis of total synergies achieved by the Company during the period from June, 1997 to August, 1999 (the "Entitlement Period"). Synergies included in any calculation for compensation payment must be based on economic advantages or cost savings to the Company as demonstrated in three consecutive monthly run-rates during the Entitlement Period. The synergy compensation payment ranges from 25% to 100% of the participant's salary depending on the categorization of the participant and the level and nature of synergies achieved. (p. 15)

(c) When Canadian National Railway was privatized in 1995, an important component of executive compensation depended on achievement of operating ratio targets. A railway's operating ratio is calculated by dividing railway operating costs by railway revenues.

Required:

For each of the above situations, answer the following:

1. Explain how accounting information is important.
2. Discuss how accounting decisions might become controversial.
3. List, with reasons, strengths and weaknesses of each example.
4. What other components of a compensation plan would you include, given the particular circumstance of each business?

P7-3 Corporate governance

In June 1997, the Calpers pension fund announced that it wanted to strengthen the power and independence of corporate boards by urging companies to:

1. Adopt a tougher definition of independent director. To count as independent, for example, a board member couldn't serve more than ten years, hold a personal-services contract with a senior executive, or be affiliated with a nonprofit group that gets "significant contributions" from the company.
2. Appoint these independent directors to a majority of board seats. Only those directors meeting ten strict measures of independence could serve on key board committees, such as the audit, nominating, and compensation panels.

3. Pick an independent "lead" director, who would help the chairman run the board. About 36% of the biggest industrial companies had lead directors last year, up from 21% in 1995, according to a survey of 1,058 directors by recruiters Korn/Ferry International in New York.
4. Publish guidelines in the annual proxy statement describing how the board handles competing time commitments when directors serve on multiple boards.
5. Decide what proportion of board members may exceed a certain age.

Calpers to Back Corporate Governance Standards

The nation's biggest public pension fund soon will demand that the nation's biggest businesses bolster the board's power and independence through much stronger corporate-governance practices.

Directors of the California Public Employees' Retirement System [Calpers] today are expected to endorse corporate-governance standards for the first time. The standards, which define board independence more rigidly than ever before, mark the latest burst of activism by a giant fund that played an influential role in the departure of chief executives from General Motors Corp., Eastman Kodak Co., International Business Machine Corp. and other companies.

Calpers will grade the 300 largest U.S. companies in its [US]$113 billion stock portfolio on whether they meet its new minimum standards, dubbed "fundamental principles." Fund officials say they plan to withhold votes for the re-election of directors at concerns scoring the worst grades. Though other activist investors praised the standards, some executives said full compliance could be difficult. ...

A majority of the 300 companies that Calpers will grade probably don't meet every fundamental principle, suggested Kayla Gillan, the fund's general counsel. But many will revamp their corporate-governance practices "simply because they don't want to get a bad grade." ...

Some boards undoubtedly will resist Calper's sweeping corporate-governance push. The stricter definition of direct independence "doesn't make sense at all," said Terence J. Gallagher, corporate-governance vice president at Pfizer Inc. For instance, he noted, about four of Pfizer's 13 nonemployee directors have served more than a decade and they're all highly valued. ...

The Calpers board today probably also will approve a set of tougher "ideal" principles, which Ms. Gillan said she may use to grade the 300 companies again in the future. These standards include: a) appointment of an independent director as chairman; b) board term limits; c) removal of directors who don't achieve certain performance criteria; d) limiting employees' board seats to just the chief executive officer; and e) a 10% limit on the number of directors more than 70 years old.

Source: Wall Street Journal, June 16, 1997.

CALIFORNIA PUBLIC EMPLOYEES' RETIREMENT SYSTEM
www.calpers.org

IBM CORP.
www.ibm.com

PFIZER INC.
www.pfizer.com

EASTMAN KODAK CO.
www.kodak.com

Required:

1. Why do companies have boards of directors?
2. Outside board members at some companies are longtime personal friends of the CEO and own no company shares. Some serve on ten or more boards and earn substantial fees from doing so. Company-funded retirement plans for board members are also common. How might each of these factors weaken corporate governance?
3. How will each of Calpers' proposals improve corporate governance?
4. Will these corporate governance changes help companies achieve better financial performance?

P7-4 Compensation of outside directors

Required:

1. The news article that follows says Times Mirror pays its outside directors in stock and stock options. What are the advantages of linking directors' compensation to share price performance? Are there any disadvantages?
2. Share prices are influenced by a variety of factors that are beyond management's control—like interest rates, the health of the economy and industry, changing consumer tastes, and so on. Should directors' pay be influenced by these factors?
3. As a director of Times Mirror, would you vote in favour of a management proposal to eliminate all dividends on the company's common stock? Why?

Times Mirror Joins Companies That Pay Outside Directors by Stock Performance

Times Mirror Co., joining a small group of publicly traded companies, ended fixed pay for outside directors in favor of a more risk-prone, entirely stock-based compensation plan. The new program, which gives directors a substantial raise this year, reflects the market-minded views of Chairman and Chief Executive Officer Mark Willes.

Under the media company's revised pay plan, directors who aren't company employees receive as an annual retainer 500 shares of Times Mirror common stock and a cash payment equal to the value of 500 shares, effective January 1, 1997, the company said. Although the proxy information didn't set a value, the package adds up to [US]$50,375 for each director, based on the [US]$59.375 per-share price of Times Mirror shares on January 2, the first trading day of the year. That's a 68% raise from the [US]$30,000 fixed retainer paid half in cash and half in stock during 1996.

The new plan eliminates fees of [US]$1,000 for each board and committee meeting, along with pensions, for nonemployee directors. Instead, nonemployee board members will each be granted options of 5,000 shares of common stock annually, this year at an option price of [US]$46.6875 a share. Times Mirror shares closed down [US]$1.625 Thursday at [US]$57.25 in New York Stock Exchange composite trading.

Switching to such risk-based pay for directors puts Times Mirror in a small group of major companies that have taken similar steps, including Sunbeam Corp. and Scott Paper Co. Advocates of shareholders' rights have long urged widespread use of stock-linked compensation for directors.

Half the compensation is in cash in order to cover taxes, Mr. Willes said, adding that the company wanted to set up a system under which "it didn't cost you money to be a director." While the package for directors may appear richer than those used by some other firms, Mr. Willes said that's largely because "it accounts for the risk involved."

Source: Wall Street Journal, March 31, 1997.

P7-5 Earnings quality and pay

Following your retirement as senior vice-president of finance for a large company, you joined the board of B.C. Grand Cruises Inc. You serve on the compensation committee and help set the bonuses paid to the company's top five executives. According to the annual bonus plan, each executive can earn a bonus of 1% of annual net income.

No bonuses were paid in 2000 because the company reported a net loss of $6,588,000.

Shortly after the end of the year, the compensation committee received a letter signed by all five executives, indicating that they felt the company had performed well in 2000. The letter identified the following items from the 2000 income statement which the executives felt painted a less favourable view of their performance than was actually the case:

Proposed Adjustments to 2000 Earnings
($ in thousands)

Restructuring and other nonrecurring charges	$63,000
Loss from discontinued operations	$22,851
Extraordinary charge, asset writedowns	$92,032

The letter asked the compensation committee to add these items back to the reported net loss and then to recalculate the bonus awards for 2000. The fiscal year 2000 income statement follows.

B.C. Grand Cruises Inc.
Consolidated Statement of Income

($ in thousands)	Year Ended June 30, 2000
Net revenues	$1,024,467
Cost of sales	535,178
Gross margin	489,289
Selling, general, and administrative	299,101
Research, development, and engineering	94,172
Gain on sale of joint venture	(33,000)
Restructuring and other nonrecurring charges	63,000
Operating income	66,016
Gain on sale of investment	40,800
Interest expense	(7,145)
Interest income	2,382
Other income (expense)—net	(2,121)
Income before income taxes	99,932
Provision for income taxes	(29,980)
Income from continuing operations	69,952
Income (loss) for discontinued operations (net of tax effect)	(22,851)
Gain on disposal of discontinued operations (net of tax effect)	38,343
Extraordinary charge, asset writedowns (net of tax effect)	(92,032)
Net income	$ (6,588)

Required:

1. As a member of the compensation committee, how would you respond to each suggested adjustment? Why?
2. What 2000 net income figure do you suggest be used to determine bonuses for the year?

P7-6 Avoiding debt covenant violations

Food Lion, Inc. operates a chain of retail supermarkets principally in the southeastern United States. The company's stores sell a wide variety of groceries, produce, meats, dairy products, seafood, frozen food, deli/bakery, and nonfood items (such as tobacco, health and beauty aids, and other household and personal products). The supermarket business is highly competitive, and it is characterized by low profit margins. Food Lion competes with national, regional, and local supermarket chains; discount food stores; single unit stores; convenience stores; and warehouse clubs.

FOOD LION, INC.
www.foodlion.com

On June 4, 1993, Food Lion entered into a credit agreement with a group of banks. Excerpts taken from the loan agreement follow.

Section 5.19 Limitation on Incurrence of Funded Debt

The Borrower will not create, assume or incur or in any manner be or become liable in respect of any Funded Debt, except: (i) Funded Debt arising under the Senior Note Agreement; (ii) Funded Debt outstanding on the Closing Date and reflected on Schedule 5.19; (iii) Funded Debt, provided that at the time of the creation, assumption or incurrence thereof and after giving effect thereto and to the application of the proceeds thereof: (a) in the case of the creation, assumption or incurrence of any Funded Debt at any time on or before January 1, 1994, the ratio of Income Available for Fixed Charges for the immediately preceding four Fiscal Quarters to Pro Forma Fixed Charges for such four Fiscal Quarters shall have been at least 1.75 to 1.00, and (b) in the case of the creation, assumption or incurrence of any Funded Debt at any time after January 1, 1994, the ratio of Income Available for Fixed Charges for the immediately preceding four Fiscal Quarters to Pro Forma Fixed Charges for such four Fiscal Quarters shall have been at least 2.00 to 1.00.

Section 5.20. Fixed Charges Coverage

At the end of each Fiscal Quarter, commencing with the Fiscal Quarter ending June 19, 1993, the ratio of Income Available for Fixed Charges for the immediately preceding four Fiscal Quarters then ended to Consolidated Fixed Charges for the immediately preceding four Fiscal Quarters then ended, shall not have been less than (i) 1.65 to 1.0 for the Fiscal Quarters ending on or before September 10, 1994 and (ii) 1.75 to 1.0 at all times thereafter.

Section 5.21. Minimum Consolidated Tangible Net Worth

Consolidated Tangible Net Worth will at no time be less than (i) [US]$706,575,475 plus (ii) 30.0% of the cumulative Consolidated Net income of the Borrower during any period after January 2, 1993, calculated quarterly but excluding from such calculations of Consolidated Net Income for purposes of this clause (ii), any quarter in which the Consolidated Net Income of the Borrower and its Consolidated Subsidiaries is negative.

Source: Food Lion, Inc. loan agreement.

Required:

1. In two more weeks, the company's books are closed for the quarter and the *fixed charges coverage* might fall below the level required by the loan agreement. How can management avoid violating this covenant?
2. The company's *tangible net worth* may also fall below the amount specified in the loan agreement. How can management avoid violating this covenant?
3. Elsewhere in the loan agreement it says that the company's *ratio of consolidated debt to total capitalization* must be at least 0.75 to 1.0. How can management avoid violating this covenant?
4. Suppose you were one of Food Lion's bankers, and you were thinking about making changes to the loan covenants. What management activities would you most want to limit? Why?

P7-7 The privatization of CN

In 1995, the Government of Canada privatized (sold to the general public) Canadian National Railway Company (CN) by means of an initial public offering of common shares. Up until that time, CN had been a Crown corporation, wholly owned by the federal government. As part of the privatization, CN instituted the new executive compensation policy described in the excerpt, below, from the October 1995 prospectus.

Required:

1. Discuss the advantages and disadvantages of the new CN compensation policy, given the new strategic direction of the company.
2. Explain how the various parts of the compensation policy work together.
3. Explain how accounting information is an important part of the new compensation policy, and discuss accounting controversies that might arise.

Canadian National Railway Company
Excerpt from October 1995 Prospectus

Remuneration of Directors and Officers

Executive Compensation

The following table sets forth the annual compensation for the Chief Executive Officer and for each of the other four most highly compensated executive officers for the year ended December 31, 1994 and for each of the two preceding years, to the extent that those officers were in the employ of the Company. Columns relating to long-term compensation have been omitted from the table as the Company did not have capital stock related award plans and there has been no compensation arising from long-term incentive plans during the years reflected in the table.

| | | Annual Compensation | | | |
Name and Principal Position	Year	Salary $	Bonus $	Other Annual Compensation $	All Other Compensation $
P. M. Tellier[1] President and Chief Executive Officer	1994	345,000	—	45,443	—
	1993	345,000	—	51,752	—
	1992	86,250	—	—	—
G. K. Davies[2] Senior Vice-President Marketing	1994	300,498	75,125	112,191	223,693
	1993	48,888	—	28,483	205,995
	1992	—	—	—	—
Y. H. Masse Executive Vice-President & Chief Financial Officer	1994	284,338	69,300	—	—
	1993	290,245	—	—	—
	1992	263,530	—	—	—
J. T. McBain[3] Senior Vice-President Operations	1994	200,051	54,700	—	—
	1993	191,201	—	—	—
	1992	136,896	—	—	—
M. J. Sabia[4] Senior Vice-President Corporate Development	1994	191,784	48,400	—	—
	1993	141,670	—	—	—
	1992	—	—	—	—

(1) Mr. Tellier joined the Company as President and Chief Executive Officer on October 1, 1992. His annual salary was established by the Government of Canada. The amounts shown as "Other Annual Compensation" include $32,114 and $39,495 for housing assistance for the years 1994 and 1993 respectively.

(2) Mr. Davies joined the Company on November 1, 1993. His annual compensation is paid in U.S. currency and, for the purposes of the above table, has been converted to Canadian currency at Revenue Canada's average rate of exchange for 1994 of 1.3659. Other Annual Compensation includes $99,887 and $28,483 for 1994 and 1993 respectively for tax equalization payments to compensate for higher tax liabilities in Canada compared to those applicable to his previous residence. All Other Compensation consists entirely of payments for loss of emoluments of previous employment. Mr. Davies' right to receive payments for loss of emoluments will terminate in 1996.

(3) Mr. McBain was promoted to his present position in January 1993.

(4) Mr. Sabia joined the Company on March 1, 1993.

Aggregate Compensation

The aggregate amount of compensation paid in 1994 by the Company and its subsidiaries to all officers and directors as a group was $5,263,846.

New CN Compensation Policy

In 1995, in the context of the Company's goal of creating a competitive market-oriented railroad with performance levels more comparable to major U.S. railroads, the Company has adopted a new compensation policy whereby a significant proportion of annual and long-term compensation of all non-union employees is variable and tied directly to the financial performance of the Company and the enhancement of shareholder value.

The first element of this new policy consists of annual variable incentive compensation in the form of cash bonuses based on the achievement of key financial targets, including targets based on the operating ratio, pre-tax rail income and total operating expense reductions.

The second element of the compensation policy is intended to align executive compensation with the interests of shareholders and the enhancement of shareholder value. Stock options to be granted to executive officers, at an exercise price equal to the initial public offering price, will create a direct linkage between executive rewards and shareholder value as the benefit of this compensation element will not be realized unless stock appreciation occurs over a number of years. See "Management Stock Option Plan."

The Company's compensation plans are administered by the Human Resources Committee of the Board of Directors, which is also responsible for the ongoing development of compensation policies. The primary focus of the Company in terms of compensation is to provide executives with strong incentives to create shareholder value and improve the financial performance of the Company. In addition, by the implementation of employee and management stock purchase plans, the Company intends to encourage broad stock ownership by executives and employees.

Management Matching Offer

In connection with the Offerings, the Company is implementing a one-time management share participation plan whereby approximately 200 management employees will have the opportunity to purchase Common Shares from the Company at the public offering price (i.e., the sum of the instalment payments) with financial assistance from the Company and to receive a certain number of matched shares from the Company for a nominal amount (the "Management Matching Offer"). ...

Management Stock Option Plan

In connection with the Offerings, the Company is also implementing a management stock option plan (the "Option Plan"). Under the Option Plan, managers of the Company eligible for the Management Matching Offer will be granted options to acquire Common Shares at a price equal to the initial public offering price of the Common Shares (the sum of the instalment payments). One-third of the options will vest over four years if the manager remains with the Company (the "Conventional Options"), and two-thirds will vest only if additional conditions in the form of the attainment by the Company of operating ratio targets decreasing from 85.6% to 82.0% in the period from 1996 to 2000 are met (the "Performance Options"). If the operating ratio for any particular year is within 0.5% of the target established in the Option Plan for that year, then the manager may exercise up to 75% of the Performance Options which could otherwise be exercised. Options will be non-transferable except, in certain circumstances, upon the death of the holder of such options. Conventional Options will have a maximum term of 10 years from the date of the grant and any Performance Options which become exercisable will expire in 2001. Under the Option Plan, options will be cancelled upon the termination of a participant's employment for cause or if the participant voluntarily terminates employment. In the event of the death of a participant, all options held by such participant will be cancelled 180 days after the participant's death. In the event that the participant's employment is terminated by the Company other than for cause, all options held by such participant will be cancelled 30 days after termination of the participant's employment. A manager may exercise vested Conventional Options for up to three years after retirement, but Performance Options expire on retirement.

The Option Plan will be administered by the Board of Directors, and the Human Resources Committee will determine the number of shares to be covered by options granted to participants. An aggregate of 1,103,750 Common Shares have been reserved for issuance to holders of options granted under the Option Plan (based on an assumed offering price of $24.00 per Common Share).

Cases

C7-1 Potash Corporation of Saskatchewan's executive compensation disclosure

Potash Corporation of Saskatchewan (PCS), the largest integrated fertilizer company in the world, was formed by the Saskatchewan government in 1975. It became a shareholder-owned company in 1989, and is listed on the TSX and NYSE. Strong phosphate sales volumes and potash prices made 1998 a record year for the company's reported gross margin and cash flow. Net income for 1998 was US$261.0 million (12% below 1997). Net sales for 1998 were US$2.3 billion.

Excerpts from PCS's 1998 proxy circular are reproduced below.

Potash Corporation of Saskatchewan
Excerpts from 1998 Proxy Circular

Executive Compensation

Summary Compensation Table

The following table sets forth compensation in respect of the individuals who were, as at December 31, 1997, the Chief Executive Officer and the other four most highly compensated executive officers of the Corporation (the "Named Executive Officers").

Summary Compensation Table[1]

| Name and Principal Position | Year | Annual Compensation | | | Long-Term Compensation | | All Other Compensation $ |
| | | Salary $ | Bonus[2] $ | Other Annual Compensation $ | Awards | Payouts | |
					Securities Underlying Options Granted[3] #	LTIP Payouts $	
Charles E. Childers,	1997	1,100,000	2,100,000	181,631[2]	80,000	1,677,671	10,961[4]
Chairman, President and	1996	1,000,000	1,000,000	659,582	80,000	1,274,431	11,000[4]
Chief Executive Officer	1995	900,000	900,000	246,541	60,000	452,694	10,617[4]
	1997	374,083	280,000	[3]	40,000	81,938	8,072
William J. Doyle,	1996	356,500	500,000	273,011	40,000	770,715	7,857
President, PCS Sales	1995	330,000	276,000	—	40,000	164,189	14,603
Thomas J. Wright,	1997	433,200	325,000	—	35,000	81,938	8,840
President, PCS Phosphate	1996	418,200	300,000	—	35,000	303,056	8,437
Company, Inc.	1995	297,250	238,000	—	30,000	51,368	6,318
Gary E. Carlson, President, PCS Nitrogen, Inc.	1997	246,800	225,000	—	37,500	61,453	12,902
John Gugulyn,	1997	184,684	149,689	—	25,000	47,797	6,428
Senior Vice President,	1996	164,515	144,480	—	20,000	336,970	6,300
Administration	1995	150,808	143,323	—	13,000	70,851	6,839

(1) All amounts, which were denominated in Canadian dollars, have been converted to United States dollars using the average exchange rate for the month prior to the date of payment. ...

(2) Reports amounts awarded pursuant to the Corporation's Short-Term Incentive Plan and, where applicable, contractual bonuses. See "Compensation Committee—Short-Term Incentive Compensation."

(3) Options granted pursuant to the Corporation's Stock Option Plan—Officers and Key Employees.

(4) The reported amounts for 1997, 1996 and 1995 consist, respectively, of:

   (i) $4,957, $4,930 and $5,533 which represents the Corporation's contribution to the Corporation's defined contribution pension plan (see "Pension Plans"); and

   (ii) $6,004, $6,070 and $5,084 which represents the value of the benefit for group term life insurance premiums paid by the Corporation.

Options

The following table sets forth the grants of stock options to the Named Executive Officers pursuant to the Corporation's Stock Option Plan—Officers and Key Employees for the year ended December 31, 1997. ...

Option Grants During the Most Recently Completed Fiscal Year

Individual Grants

Name	Number of Securities Underlying Options Granted #	% of Total Options Granted to Employees in Fiscal Year	Exercise or Base Price $/Share	Expiration Date	Grant Date Present Value (3) (4) (5) $
Charles E. Childers	80,000[1]	9.40	86.75	Nov. 6, 2007	2,179,200
William J. Doyle	40,000[1]	4.70	86.75	Nov. 6, 2007	1,089,600
Thomas J. Wright	35,000[1]	4.11	86.75	Nov. 6, 2007	953,400
Gary Carlson	25,000[1]	4.41	86.75	Nov. 6, 2007	681,000
	12,500[2]		81.75	May 7, 2007	345,125
John Gugulyn	25,000[1]	2.94	CDN$121.50	Nov. 6, 2007	657,041

(1) Options granted on November 6, 1997. Each option is exercisable with respect to one-half of the indicated number on or after November 6, 1998 and with respect to the balance of the indicated number on or after November 6, 1999 (or earlier in the event of a "change of control" of the Corporation as defined in the Corporation's Stock Option Plan—Officers and Key Employees). All options are transferable (without consideration) to the spouse, children and grandchildren of the original optionee (or to a trust, partnership or limited liability company, the entire beneficial interest of which is held by one or more of the foregoing persons), in accordance with the terms and conditions of the Stock Option Plan—Officers and Key Employees.

(2) Option granted on May 7, 1997. The option is exercisable with respect to one-half of the indicated number on or after May 7, 1998 and with respect to the balance of the indicated number on or after May 7, 1999 (or earlier in the event of a "change of control" of the Corporation as defined in the Corporation's Stock Option Plan—Officers and Key Employees).

(3) The Modified Black-Scholes Option Pricing Model was used to determine the grant date present value of the stock options granted in November, 1997 by the Corporation to the Named Executive Officers. Under the Modified Black-Scholes Option Pricing Model, the grant date present value of the stock options

referred to in the table was CDN$36.84 per Share for Mr. Gugulyn and $27.24 per Share for Mr. Childers, Mr. Doyle. Mr. Wright and Mr. Carlson. The material assumptions and adjustments incorporated in the Modified Black-Scholes Option Pricing Model in estimating the value of options reflected in the above table include the following:

   (i) with respect to the option held by Mr. Gugulyn, an interest rate of 5.49% (representing the interest rate on a Canadian Treasury security with a maturity date corresponding to that of the option term) and with respect to options held by Mr. Childers, Mr. Doyle, Mr. Wright and Mr. Carlson, an interest rate of 5.88% (representing the interest rate on a U.S. Treasury security with a maturity date corresponding to that of the option term);

   (ii) with respect to the option held by Mr. Gugulyn, volatility of 25.85% (calculated using daily stock prices on The Toronto Stock Exchange for the one-year period prior to the grant date) and with respect to options held by Mr. Childers, Mr. Doyle, Mr. Wright and Mr. Carlson, volatility of 25.48% (calculated using daily stock prices on the New York Stock Exchange for the one-year period prior to the grant date);

   (iii) with respect to the option held by Mr. Gugulyn, dividends at the rate of CDN$1.44 per Share and with respect to Mr. Childers, Mr. Doyle, Mr. Wright and Mr. Carlson, dividends at the rate of $1.03 per Share (representing the annualized dividends paid with respect to a Share at the date of grant); and

(iv) a reduction of approximately 26% to reflect the probability of forfeiture due to termination prior to vesting, and the probability of a shortened option term due to termination of employment prior to the option expiration date.

The ultimate values of the options will depend on the future market price of the Shares, which cannot be forecast with reasonable accuracy. The actual value, if any, an optionee will realize upon exercise of an option will depend on the excess of the market value of the Shares over the exercise price on the date the option is exercised.

(4) With respect to Mr. Carlson's May, 1997 stock option grant, the methodology employed in footnote (3) is applicable, except that the grant date present value of the stock options referred to in the table was $27.61 per Share, the interest rate applied was 6.71% and the volatility factor applied was 27.25%.

(5) Amounts denominated in Canadian dollars are converted to United States dollars at the exchange rate in effect at the date of grant of the options. ...

Long-Term Incentive Plan

The following table shows the awards made in the most recently completed financial year pursuant to the Corporation's Long-Term Incentive Plan ("LTIP").

Long-Term Incentive Plan Awards During the Most Recently Completed Fiscal Year

Name	Securities, Units or Other Rights		Performance or Other Period Until Maturation of Payout
Charles E. Childers	12,500	(1)	(1)
	8,333.33	(2)	(2)
William J. Doyle	3,000	(1)	(1)
	2,000	(2)	(2)
Thomas J. Wright	3,000	(1)	(1)
	2,000	(2)	(2)
Gary E. Carlson	2,250	(1)	(1)
	1,500	(2)	(2)
John Gugulyn	1,750	(1)	(1)
	1,166.67	(2)	(2)

(1) Represents part one units granted effective January 1, 1997. Such units will be redeemed on a redemption date selected by the Compensation Committee, which date will be no later than December 31, 1999 (see "Compensation Committee Report on Executive Compensation"). Each unit will be redeemed on a redemption date for an amount equal to the closing price of the Corporation's Shares on the New York Stock Exchange on the first day preceding the redemption date in which a round lot of Shares was traded on such exchange. The units eligible to be redeemed may, on or before the redemption date, be reduced or increased by up to 50% based on the performance of the Corporation and the employee, in accordance with criteria established by the Compensation Committee from time to time.

(2) Represents part two units granted effective January 1, 1997, less units redeemed on December 30, 1997. One-half of the remaining part two units must be redeemed on or before January 1, 1999 and the remaining one-half must be redeemed no later than December 31, 1999 on redemption dates as determined by the Compensation Committee (see "Compensation Committee Report on Executive Compensation"). Each unit will be redeemed for an amount equal to the closing price of the Corporation's common shares on the New York Stock Exchange on the day first preceding the redemption date in which a round lot of shares was traded on such exchange.

Compensation Committee

Composition of the Compensation Committee

The following individuals served as members of the Compensation Committee during the fiscal year which ended on December 31, 1997.

- Denis J. Coté (Chairman)
- Donald E. Phillips
- Daryl K. Seaman
- Barrie A. Wigmore

Compensation Committee Report on Executive Compensation

The Compensation Committee of the Board (the "Committee") is, at present, composed of four directors who are neither officers nor former officers of the Corporation. The Committee is charged with formulating and making recommendations to the Board in respect of compensation issues relating to directors and senior officers of the Corporation. The Committee also makes recommendations regarding the Corporation's Stock Option Plans and administers its Short and Long-Term Incentive Plans, each in accordance with its terms. In addition, the Committee, in consultation with the Chief Executive Officer, considers and reports to the Board regarding corporate succession matters.

Executive compensation policies are designed with the objective of attracting and retaining qualified executives by providing compensation packages which are competitive within the marketplace and by compensating them in a manner which encourages individual performance consistent with shareholder expectations.

Salary

In 1995 the Corporation adopted a "broad band" salary system for senior executives (i.e. vice presidents and above, but not including the chief executive officer) of the Corporation. Under the broad band system a salary range is established by the Compensation Committee for each senior executive level after consultation with independent compensation consultants. Each individual's salary is set within the applicable range taking into account the individual's duties, performance and experience. Individual executive salaries are subject to approval by the Chief Executive Officer and the Compensation Committee of the Board.

Short-Term Incentive Compensation

The Corporation's Short-Term Incentive Plan is intended to aid in developing strong corporate management by providing financial incentives to key employees to meet or achieve objectives which contribute materially to the Corporation's success. The plan provides for incentive awards based on an individual's performance, position with the Corporation and the financial results of the Corporation. Ranges of incentive awards are established for each position, which awards are expressed as a percentage of annual salary. The actual percentage used in cal-

culating the award is determined by the Corporation's return on equity in relation to a pre-established target, subject to adjustment based upon the individual's performance. Under the terms of the plan, generally no payments are made when the return on equity is less than 50% of the target set by the Board for that year. For senior executives, which include the Named Executive Officers, incentive awards range from 20% to 100% of salary depending upon actual return on equity as compared to target return on equity once the minimum threshold requirement has been met, all subject to a plus or minus 10% adjustment based on the Executive's performance.

Long-Term Incentive Compensation

The Corporation's Long-Term Incentive Plan, as amended, is designed to retain high-potential, high-value employees, to recognize and reward their significant contributions to the long-term success of the Corporation, and to align their interests more closely with the shareholders of the Corporation. The plan provides for the discretionary grant of units to eligible employees effective January 1, 1994 and January 1 every three years thereafter and on such other dates as circumstances warrant. A unit is a notional amount equal to the market value of a common share of the Corporation. The units are divided equally into "part one" and "part two" units upon their grant. The number of units granted to an eligible employee is approximately three times the amount determined by dividing the employee's target bonus by the closing price of the shares on the New York Stock Exchange on the first day preceding the date of the grant of the units in which a round lot of shares was traded on such Exchange.

The units are redeemed for cash on the basis of their "market value" on a redemption date. The "market value" of a unit is the closing price of the shares on the New York Stock Exchange on the first day preceding the redemption date in which a round lot of shares was traded on such Exchange. Cash amounts payable under the plan to employees who receive salary in Canadian currency shall be converted to Canadian currency on the redemption date, based on the published exchange rate of the Bank of Canada in effect as of the close of business on the business day immediately preceding the redemption date. Redemption dates are determined by the Committee in accordance with the terms of the plan. The redemption date for the part one units may not be later than the last day of the second calendar year following the calendar year of the grant of the units. One-third of the part two units must be redeemed on or before each of the first, second and third anniversary of the grant of the units. However, in no event shall the redemption date for the part two units be later than the end of the second calendar year following the calendar year of the grant of units.

The number of part one units eligible to be redeemed on a redemption date is subject to adjustment based upon the performance of the Corporation and the employee, in accordance with criteria established by the Committee from time to time. The

Committee may, on or before, a redemption date for part one units, reduce or increase an employee's part one units by a maximum of 50%.

The interests of management are also tied to the interests of the Corporation's shareholders through the annual grant of options to executives and other key employees pursuant to the Corporation's Stock Option Plan—Officers and Key Employees. The options are granted at 100% of market value, become exercisable over two years (or earlier in the event of a "change of control" as defined in the plan) and expire after ten years. Options are granted having regard to the position in and contribution made to the Corporation by the individual involved. The aggregate number of Shares issuable pursuant to options granted under the Corporation's Stock Option Plan—Officers and Key Employees is 3,842,000, although the Board is proposing to increase the aggregate number of Shares issuable pursuant to options granted under the plan (see "Amendment to Stock Option Plan"). The number of shares subject to options granted to an individual is a function of the individual's position within the Corporation and his or her ability to affect corporate performance.

In considering whether to grant options and how many shares are to be subject to options, the Committee considers the aggregate number of options outstanding and is also guided in such matters by applicable regulatory constraints.

In relative terms, greater emphasis within the compensation package is given to annual cash compensation (salary and short-term incentives) than to long-term incentives and options. However, each element of the package is designed to complement the others in enabling the Corporation to achieve the objectives of its compensation policies.

Chief Executive Officer Compensation

The terms and conditions of Mr. Childers' employment with the Corporation are governed by an employment agreement. Among other things, the agreement provides that, in addition to receiving an annual salary, Mr. Childers is entitled to participate in other compensation programs of general applicability to senior corporate management.

The Committee reviews annually the CEO's salary, any awards under the Short and Long-Term Incentive Plans and any grant of options under the Corporation's Stock Option Plan—Officers and Key Employees. The CEO's annual salary is determined primarily on the basis of the individual's performance and the performance of the Corporation. While no mathematical weighting formula exists, the Committee considers all factors which it deems relevant including the net income of the Corporation, the Corporation's share price, the duties and responsibilities of the CEO and current compensation levels. Awards pursuant to the Short and Long-Term Incentive Plans and under the Corporation's Stock Option Plan—Officers and Key Employees are made in accordance with the plans as outlined above.

Reference is also made to the compensation of chief executive officers of an appropriate comparable group of fertilizer producers and marketers selected by the Corporation. The comparison of Mr. Childers' compensation to the comparable group incorporates many factors including the relative size of the companies, their profitability and share price, the duties of the chief executive officer and any other extenuating or special circumstances.

Required:

1. Disclosure of the details of executive compensation is a relatively recent requirement in Canada. Discuss the benefits and costs of such disclosure from the perspectives of the following groups:

   - corporate management
   - corporate employees other than senior management
   - shareholders
   - creditors
   - competitors
   - other relevant groups

2. Describe the various components of PCS's executive compensation scheme. What is the rationale for each component?

3. Describe how the components are apparently intended to work together.

4. What are the strengths and weaknesses of the scheme? Would you have altered any part of it?

5. What are the financial implications of the scheme?

C7-2 Maxcor Manufacturing: Compensation and earnings quality

Margaret Magee has served both as an outside director to Maxcor Manufacturing since 1980 and as a member of the company's compensation committee since 1987. Margaret has been reviewing Maxcor's 1998 preliminary earnings statement (reproduced below) in preparation for the February 1999 board and compensation committee meetings. She is uneasy about the company's computation of "operating profits" for 1998, particularly since management bonuses at Maxcor are based on achieving specific operating profit goals.

Maxcor Manufacturing Consolidated Results of Operations		
	Year Ended December 31,	
(US$ in millions)	1998	1997
Sales	$98.4	$111.2
Operating costs:		
Cost of goods sold	(81.5)	(92.2)
Selling, general, and administrative expenses	(12.5)	(12.9)
Operating profit	4.4	6.1
Research and development expenses (see note)	(5.7)	(2.4)
Provision for plant closings (see note)	(2.6)	—
Interest expense	(2.9)	(2.6)
Other income	0.7	1.2
Profit (loss) before taxes	(6.1)	2.3
Provision (credit) for income taxes	2.1	(0.8)
Profit (loss) of consolidated companies	(4.0)	1.5
Equity in profit of affiliated companies	0.2	0.3
Profit (loss)	$ (3.8)	$ 1.8

The preliminary financial statements also contained the following footnotes:

Research and Engineering Expenses. Research and engineering expenses include both "Research and development expenses" for new product development and charges to "Cost of goods sold" for ongoing efforts to improve existing products. The amounts (in millions) for 1998 and 1997 were:

	1998	1997
Research and development expenses	$5.7	$2.4
Cost of goods sold	2.9	6.3
Research and engineering expense	$8.6	$8.7

Plant Closing Costs. In 1998, the Company recorded provisions for plant closing and staff consolidation costs totalling [US]$2.62 million. Included in this total are charges related to the probable closing of the Company's York, Pennsylvania facility ([US]$1.75 million), the consolidation of the North American operations of the Building Construction Products Division ([US]$0.63 million), and charges to reflect lower estimates of the market value of previously closed U.S. facilities ([US]$0.24 million). These costs include the estimated costs of employee severance benefits, the estimated net losses on disposal of land, buildings, machinery and equipment, and other costs incidental to the closing and planned consolidation.

Maxcor Manufacturing is an established, privately held manufacturer that operates in two principal business segments: *Building Construction Products*, which involves the design, manufacturing, and marketing of construction and materials-handling machinery; and *Engines* for various off-highway applications. Before 1998, the company had experienced 15 years of steadily increasing sales and operating profits.

The company was founded in 1938 by Hugh Maxwell, a former Ford Motor Company engineer. Neither Mr. Maxwell nor any member of his family is currently an officer of the company. Maxcor's common stock is held by the Maxwell Family Trust (35%), the Maxwell Employee Stock Ownership Plan (ESOP) Trust (50%), a venture capital firm (13%), and current management (2%). Margaret Magee also serves as an outside trustee for the Maxwell ESOP Trust.

Maxcor's senior management participates in an incentive bonus plan that was adopted in 1986. The bonus formula for 1998 was approved by the compensation committee at its February 1997 meeting. According to the plan, each senior manager's 1998 bonus is to be determined as follows:

Bonus as Percentage of 1998 Salary	1998 Operating Profits (US$ in millions)
0%	Below $4.0
100	At least $4.0
200	At least $6.0
300	At least $8.0

The compensation committee can award a lesser amount than that indicated by the plan formula if circumstances warrant such action. No bonus reductions have occurred since the plan was adopted in 1986.

Required:

Why might Ms Magee feel uneasy about Maxcor's computation of 1998 operating profits? Should Ms Magee approve the 100% bonus payment for 1998 as specified by the plan formula? What changes (if any) would you recommend be made to the bonus formula for next year?

Endnotes

1. Descriptions of these—and other—creditor–shareholder conflicts of interest are contained in A. Barnea, R. Haugen, and L. Senbet, *Agency Problems and Financial Contracting* (Englewood Cliffs, NJ: Prentice Hall, 1985); C. Smith and J. Warner, "On Financial Contracting: An Analysis of Bond Covenants," *Journal of Financial Economics*, 1979, pp. 117–61; and R. Watts and J. Zimmerman, *Positive Accounting Theory* (Englewood Cliffs, NJ: Prentice Hall, 1986).

2. Investment outcomes cannot be known in advance with certainty. So it is convenient to represent outcome possibilities using a **probability distribution** like the one in Figure 7.2, which shows the likelihood that the investment project will yield a particular dollar outcome. For example, one project may have a 10% chance of earning $5,000 or less, a 40% chance of earning from $5,000 to $20,000, a 40% chance of earning between $20,000 and $35,000, and a 10% chance of earning more than $35,000. This illustration of asset substitution is adapted from R. Watts and J. Zimmerman, *Positive Accounting Theory* (Englewood Cliffs, NJ: Prentice Hall, 1986), p. 187.

3. These project attributes greatly simplify the discussion. **Market risk** is the covariance of project returns with market returns in the sense commonly used when discussing capital asset pricing models. See, for example, S. A. Ross, R. W. Westerfield, and J. F. Jaffe, *Corporate Finance* (Homewood, IL: Irwin, 1993), p. 295.

4. S. C. Myers, "Determinants of Corporate Borrowing," *Journal of Financial Economics*, November 1977, pp. 147–75.

5. M. C. Jensen and W. H. Meckling, "Theory of the Firm: Managerial Behavior, Agency Costs and Ownership Structure," *Journal of Financial Economics*, October 1976, pp. 305–60. Op. cit., Smith and Warner.

6. Paragraph 52 of Section 3860 of the *CICA Handbook*, "Financial Instruments—Disclosure and Presentation," states that companies complying with GAAP should "*disclose information about the extent and nature of the financial instruments [such as a bond], including signifi-*

cant terms and conditions that may affect the amount, timing and certainty of future cash flows." The section goes on to give as an example "any condition of the instrument or an associated covenant that, if contravened, would significantly alter any of the other terms (for example, a maximum debt-to-equity ratio in a bond covenant that, if contravened, would make the full principal amount of the bond due and payable immediately" (para. 3860.54 (j)). Any such amounts "due and payable immediately" must be classified as a current liability (Section 1510.03), with appropriate disclosure of the default.

7. A. P. Sweeney, "Debt-Covenant Violations and Managers' Accounting Responses," *Journal of Accounting and Economics*, May 1994, pp. 281–308.

8. M. L. DeFond and J. Jiambalvo, "Debt Covenant Violation and Manipulation of Accruals," *Journal of Accounting and Economics,* January 1994, pp. 145–76.

9. Although we limit our attention to the incentive role of compensation, several other factors lessen (but do not eliminate) a manager's tendency to take actions that yield personal benefits but reduce firm value. A more complete discussion of these issues is contained in Jensen and Meckling, op. cit., and Watts and Zimmerman, op. cit.

10. KPMG, *Executive Compensation Practices in the TSE 300 Companies 1998*, p. 3.

11. Ernst and Young, *Executive and Directors' Compensation—Recent Trends*, December 9, 1998.

12. "Higher-performing companies" were "companies whose cumulative return index exceeded the TSE 300 cumulative return index by more than 10%." Op cit., p. 6.

13. J. Craighead, M. Magnan, and L. Thorne, "Compensation Disclosure: Who Wins*?", Ivey Business Journal,* September/October 2000, pp. 11–13. The quote is from page 11.

14. Ibid., p. 13.

15. J. McFarland, "Boards rapped over CEO Compensation," *The Globe and Mail,* online edition, April 24, 2001.

16. P. Healy, "The Effect of Bonus Schemes on Accounting Decisions," *Journal of Accounting and Economics,* April 1985, pp. 85–108.

17. P. M. Dechow and R. G. Sloan, "Executive Incentives and the Horizon Problem: An Empirical Investigation," *Journal of Accounting and Economics,* March 1991, pp. 51–89.

18. J. D. England, "Executive Pay, Incentives and Performance," in D. E. Logue (ed.), *Handbook of Modern Finance* (Boston: Warren, Gorham & Lamont, 1996), p. E9–18.

19. René Huot, *Understanding Income Tax* (Scarborough, Ont.: Carswell, 1994), p. 318.

20. G. Napolitano, *Earnings Management Revisited: Minimizing the Torpedoes in Financial Reports* (New York: Goldman Sachs, November 1998), p. 3.

21. Recent examples of accounting torpedoes can be found in N. Byrnes and J. M. Laderman, "Help for Investors: How to Spot Trouble," *Business Week*, October 5, 1998; N. Byrnes, R. A. Melcher, and D. Sparks, "Earnings Hocus-Pocus," *Business Week,* October 5, 1998; C. Loomis, "Lies, Damned Lies, and Managed Earnings," *Fortune,* August 2, 1999; M. Maremount, "Anatomy of a Fraud," *Business Week,* September 16, 1996; S. Pulliam, "Earnings Management Spurs Selloffs Now," *Wall Street Journal,* October 29, 1999; and S. Tully, "The Earnings Illusion," *Fortune,* April 20, 1999.

8
Receivables

LEARNING OBJECTIVES
After studying this chapter, you should be able to:

1. Understand the methods used to estimate uncollectible accounts in order to determine the expected net realizable value of accounts receivable

2. Describe how firms estimate and record sales returns and adjustments

3. Explain how to evaluate whether or not reported receivables arose from real sales and to recognize various danger signals

4. Show how to impute and record interest when notes receivable yield either no explicit interest or an unrealistically low interest rate

5. Describe how companies transfer or dispose of receivables in order to accelerate cash collection and how to distinguish between transactions that represent sales of receivables and transactions that represent borrowings

6. Understand that receivables are sometimes restructured when a customer experiences financial difficulty and show how the troubled-debt restructuring is accounted for

Receivables are amounts owed to a business firm by outsiders. In U.K. financial reports, receivables are called "debtors"—a term clearly connoting the legal obligation of outsiders to make payments to a firm. Most receivables arise from credit sales and are called **trade receivables or accounts receivable.** Receivables that result from other types of transactions and events (e.g., insurance claims from casualty losses) are separately disclosed, if significant, on the balance sheet to facilitate informed financial analysis.

Assessing the Net Realizable Value of Accounts Receivable

Generally accepted accounting principles (GAAP) require that accounts receivable be reflected in the balance sheet at their **net realizable value.**[1] Two things must be estimated to determine the net realizable value of receivables:

1. the amount that will not be collected because customers are unable to pay—called **uncollectibles**

2. the amount that will not be collected because customers return the merchandise for credit or are allowed a reduction in the amount owed—called **returns** and **adjustments**

The next sections discuss financial reporting issues relating to uncollectibles, returns, and adjustments.

Estimating Uncollectibles

Some credit sales never get collected. These losses are an unavoidable cost of doing business. Companies could adopt such stringent credit standards that "bad debt" losses would be virtually zero. But if they only sold to customers with impeccable credit records, they would forgo many otherwise profitable sales opportunities.

Most companies establish credit policies by weighing the expected cost of credit sales—customer billing and collection costs plus potential bad debt losses—against the benefit of increased sales. Companies choose what they believe is a profit-maximizing balance. This tradeoff between increased costs and additional profits from credit sales illustrates that bad debts are often unavoidable. Consequently, the accrual accounting matching principle requires that some *estimate* of uncollectible accounts be associated with current period sales—that is, *estimated losses from customers who are ultimately unable to pay are treated as an expense of the period in which the sale is made.* Obviously, companies can't know at the time of sale which customers will ultimately be unable to pay. So proper matching of revenues and expenses is achieved by estimating the proportion of current period credit sales that will not be collected in the future, and then by charging this amount as an expense.

Suppose Bristol Corporation estimates, on the basis of current industry trends and the company's experience, that bad debt losses arising from first quarter 2001 sales are expected to be $30,000. The entry Bristol would make under GAAP is:

DR	Bad debt expense	$30,000
CR	Allowance for uncollectibles	$30,000

The allowance for uncollectibles is a contra-asset account, and this amount is subtracted from gross accounts receivable. If Bristol's gross accounts receivable and allowance for uncollectibles balances *before* recording this bad debt entry were $1,500,000 and $15,000, respectively, then after recording bad debts, its balance sheet would show:

Accounts receivable (gross)	$1,500,000	
Less: Allowance for uncollectibles	(45,000)	{ (15,000) Initial balance
Accounts receivable (net)	$1,455,000	(30,000) Addition

There are two approaches for estimating uncollectible accounts. One involves multiplying a specific loss percentage by sales revenues; the other involves multiplying a (usually different) loss percentage by gross accounts receivable. Each approach is illustrated as follows.

1. *The sales revenue approach.* Assume that Bristol Corporation prepares quarterly financial statements and must estimate bad debt expense at the end of each quarter. Analyzing customer payment patterns, Bristol determined that bad debt losses average about 1% of sales. If first quarter sales in 2001 total $3,000,000, then bad debt losses from those sales are expected to total $30,000. The entry previously illustrated would then be made to record the company's estimate of bad debt expenses arising from current quarter sales.

2. *The gross accounts receivable approach.* Suppose that instead of estimating bad debts as a percentage of sales, Bristol determined that at any given time approximately 3% of gross accounts receivable eventually prove uncollectible. Gross receivables at March 31, 2001, total $1,500,000, which means that on that date the required allowance for uncollectibles is 3% of this amount, or $45,000. Because the allowance-account balance is only $15,000, $30,000 must be added to the uncollectibles account at the end of the quarter. Doing this would bring the allowance for uncollectibles balance up to $45,000.

Writing Off Bad Debts

When a specific account receivable is known to be definitely uncollectible, the entire account must be removed from the books. For example, if Bristol determines that a $750 receivable from Ralph Company cannot be collected, the following entry is made:

DR   Allowance for uncollectibles $750
    CR   Account receivable—Ralph Company $750

Notice that this entry has no effect on income. A specific account receivable (Ralph Company) is eliminated from the books and the allowance contra account is reduced, *but no bad debt is recorded.* This is consistent with the accrual accounting philosophy of recording estimated bad debt expense when the sale was made rather than at some later date when the nonpaying customer is identified. Of course, Bristol Corporation does not know at the time of each sale which particular customers will be unable to pay. That's why the offsetting credit for bad debt expense was originally made to the contra asset "Allowance for uncollectibles." *Only when the seller knows which specific receivable is uncollectible can the individual account (Ralph Company) be written off.* This is what the preceding entry accomplishes.

Assessing the Adequacy of the Allowance for Uncollectibles Account Balance

No matter which method—percentage of sales or percentage of gross receivables—is used to estimate bad debts, management must periodically assess the reasonableness of the allowance for uncollectibles balance. Given existing economic conditions and customer circumstances, a manager should ask "Is the balance in the allowance-for-uncollectibles account adequate, excessive, or insufficient?"

To make this judgment, management performs an **aging of accounts receivable.** As the name implies, an aging of receivables is simply a determination of how long each receivable has been on the books. Receivables that are long past due often arise because customers are experiencing financial difficulties and may ultimately be unable to pay. An aging is performed by subdividing total accounts receivable into several categories, as shown in Exhibit 8.1.

Obviously, considerable judgment goes into evaluating the adequacy of the allowance-for-uncollectibles balance. Most companies make careful appraisals in this area, since audit guidelines are well developed and auditors' scrutiny is intense.

Exhibit 8.2 contains selected financial statement figures taken from the 1996 annual report of Heilig-Meyers Company, the largest furniture retailer in the United States. Over 80% of all Heilig-Meyers customers buy on credit using the company's

---

Exhibit 8.1 BRISTOL CORPORATION

Allowance for Uncollectibles Based on Aging of Receivables

On December 31, 2001 Bristol Corporation's gross accounts receivable are $1,600,000, and the allowance-for-uncollectibles balance is $39,000. Bristol's normal sales terms require payments within 30 days after the sale is made and the goods are received by the buyer. Bristol determines that the receivables have the following age distribution:

	Current	31–90 Days Old	91–180 Days Old	Over 180 Days Old	Total
Amount	$1,450,000	$125,000	$15,000	$10,000	$1,600,000

Once the receivables have been grouped by age category, a separate estimate of uncollectibles by category is developed. On the basis of past experience, Bristol determines the following estimate of expected bad debt losses by category:

	Current	31–90 Days Old	91–180 Days Old	Over 180 Days Old
Estimated % of bad debt losses	2.5%	6%	20%	40%

The required balance in the allowance-for-uncollectibles account would then be:

	Current	31–90 Days Old	91–180 Days Old	Over 180 Days Old	Total
Amount	$1,450,000	$125,000	$15,000	$10,000	$1,600,000
Estimated % of bad debt losses	2.5%	6%	20%	40%	
Allowance for uncollectibles	$ 36,250	$ 7,500	$ 3,000	$ 4,000	$ 50,750

Because the allowance-for-uncollectibles balance is only $39,000, the account must be increased by $11,750. To bring the balance up to the $50,750 figure indicated by the aging, Bristol would make the following adjusting entry:

DR Bad debt expense $11,750
 CR Allowance for uncollectibles $11,750

Exhibit 8.2 HEILIG-MEYERS COMPANY

Analysis of Uncollectible Accounts Receivable

(US$ in millions)	1996	1995
A. Reported Amounts		
Sales of merchandise	$1,138.5	$956.0
Pre-tax earnings	64.5	105.9
Customer receivables (gross)	573.7	584.9
Allowance for uncollectibles	54.7	46.7
Bad debt expense	65.4	45.4
B. Analysis		
Bad debt expense as % of sales	5.7%	4.8%
Allowance as % of customer receivables	9.5%	8.0%

Source: Heilig-Meyers 1996 annual report to shareholders.

in-house installment financing plan. Store managers are authorized to make customer credit decisions within corporate guidelines.

1996 was a difficult year for Heilig-Meyers. Sales increased 19% (from US$956.0 million to US$1,138.5 million), but pre-tax earnings fell 39% (from US$105.9 million to US$64.5 million). Earnings declined because aggressive price competition caused margins to narrow throughout the industry, and the company's growth strategy resulted in high costs for new-store openings. Bad debt expense for the year (US$65.4 million) roughly equalled the company's pre-tax earnings (US$64.5 million). Despite a poor profit performance, both bad debt expense (as a percentage of sales) and the allowance for uncollectibles (as a percentage of gross customer receivables) increased in 1996. This suggests that Heilig-Meyers was taking a more conservative view of receivable collections than it had in the past, perhaps because the customer credit quality had recently deteriorated.

What impact did this conservative view have on the company's 1996 pre-tax earnings? The data in Exhibit 8.2 provide the answer.

Suppose Heilig-Meyers had maintained its 1996 bad debt expense at 4.8% of sales (the rate used in 1995). Bad debt expense would then have been US$54.6 million (4.8% of US$1,138.5 million sales)—or US$10.8 million lower. This would have meant a corresponding US$10.8 million (or 16.7%) increase in pre-tax earnings for the year.

Now suppose Heilig-Meyers had kept the allowance for uncollectibles at 8% of gross receivables (the rate used in 1995). In this case, the allowance account balance for 1996 would have been US$45.9 million (8% of US$573.7 million gross customer receivables)—or US$8.8 million lower than what the company actually reported. Of course, this would have meant a US$8.8 million reduction in bad debt expense for the year, and an US$8.8 million (or 13.6%) increase in pre-tax earnings.

This analysis demonstrates that the company's decision to be more conservative about receivable collections penalized reported earnings in what was already a poor profit year.

For companies like Heilig-Meyers, where most customer purchases are financed with in-house credit, a small change in the percentage rate used to estimate bad debt expense or the allowance for uncollectibles can have a big impact on reported earnings.

Determining whether the allowance for uncollectibles is adequate requires careful judgment. Consequently, the temptation to "manage" earnings by using bad debt accruals can be strong. As the Heilig-Meyers example illustrates, not all companies succumb to this temptation. However, research evidence does show that companies tend to reduce bad debt expense when earnings are otherwise low—and then to increase the expense when earnings are high.[2]

Estimating Sales Returns and Adjustments

It is inevitable that sometimes the wrong goods are shipped to customers or the correct goods arrive damaged. In either case, the customer will return the item or request a price adjustment. When goods are returned or price adjustments granted, the customer's account receivable must be reduced and an income statement charge made. Assume that Bristol Corporation agrees to reduce by $8,000 the price of goods that arrived damaged at Bath Company. Bristol would make the following entry to record this price adjustment:

DR Sales returns and adjustments	$8,000	
CR Account receivable—Bath Company		$8,000

Bath now owes $8,000 less than the amount it was previously billed, as reflected by the reduction to accounts receivable. The account that is debited here is an offset to sales revenues—termed a contra-revenue account. Sales revenues are not reduced directly; the contra-revenue account allows Bristol Corporation to monitor the frequency and amount of returns and price adjustments, since these events represent potential breakdowns in customer relations.

At the end of the reporting period, companies estimate the expected amount of future returns and adjustments arising from receivables currently on the books. If the estimated number is large in relation to the accounts receivable balance or to earnings, then the following adjusting entry should be made:

DR Sales returns and adjustments	$$$$	
CR Allowance for sales returns and adjustments		$$$$

Ignoring estimated future returns and adjustments has a trivial effect on income when the amount of actual returns and adjustments does not vary greatly from year to year.

The debit is again to a contra-revenue account that reduces net sales by the estimated amount. Since it is not yet known which specific customer accounts will involve future returns and adjustments, the credit entry must be made to a contra-asset account that offsets accounts receivable. In practice, estimated sales returns and adjustments are seldom material in relation to receivables. Consequently, no end-of-period accrual is typically made for these items.

Ordinary returns and adjustments are seldom a major issue in financial reporting. On the other hand, companies occasionally adopt "aggressive" revenue recognition practices—meaning that revenue is recognized either prematurely or inappropriately. This revenue recognition aggressiveness generates significant returns in later periods. Aggressive revenue recognition overstates both accounts receivable and income. Consequently, analysts must understand that a sudden spurt in accounts receivable may be a danger signal, as we see next.

Do Existing Receivables Represent Real Sales?

When a company's sales terms, customer credit standing, and accounting methods do not change from period to period, the growth rates in sales and in accounts receivable will be roughly equal. If sales grow by 10%, accounts receivable should also grow by about 10%. Understanding this fact, astute statement readers carefully monitor the relationship between sales growth and receivables growth. Any disparity between the two growth rates raises a "red flag." Receivables that grow at a higher rate than sales could reflect a number of significant causes. For example, the disparity in growth rates might reflect something positive like a deliberate change in sales terms designed to attract new customers. Suppose that instead of requiring payment within 30 days of shipment, the company allows customers to pay in four months. Changes like this broaden the potential market for the company's products and services by allowing slightly less creditworthy customers to transact with the firm. In this case, receivables growth will far outpace sales growth. (Assume that before introducing more lenient credit terms, the company had annual sales of $12 million and customers, on average, paid within 30 days. Outstanding accounts receivable, therefore, represent one month's sales, or $1 million. Under the new credit program, customer receivables would represent four months' sales, or $4 million; this represents a 300% increase even if total sales remain unchanged.)

Alternatively, receivables growth exceeding sales growth could be an early warning signal of emerging problems. One explanation is deteriorating creditworthiness among existing customers. If customers are unable to pay, sales will not be collected when due and accounts receivable will grow at a faster rate than sales. However, this problem should be uncovered in careful audits by the company's independent auditor. Accordingly, when the unusual growth in receivables is due to an inability of customers to pay on time, GAAP financial statements would ordinarily show a large increase in estimated uncollectibles.

Vendor financing, in which a company provides extended credit terms to a customer during, perhaps, periods when the customer is in some economic difficulty, may also result in unusual increases in receivables, including long-term receivables, and thus must be carefully monitored. As Nortel Networks' vendor financing program accelerated, its provision for uncollectibles on its long-term receivables increased significantly over the 1997–2000 period.

Another reason why receivables growth might exceed sales growth is that the firm has changed its financial reporting procedures, which determine *when* sales are recognized. Consider Table 8.1, which presents selected financial statement data for Bausch & Lomb Inc. for the period 1990–1993.

Table 8.1 shows that net trade accounts receivable grew dramatically in both 1992 and 1993. This growth shows up in absolute dollar amounts (an increase of US$72,076 in 1992 and US$107,635 in 1993) as well as in relation to total balance sheet assets (11.8% in 1991 versus 14.8% in 1992 and 15.3% in 1993). But what makes this growth seem "unusual" is the disparity between sales and receivables growth rates. While sales grew at 12.43% in 1992 and 9.54% in 1993, receivables jumped by 35.11% and 38.81% in those same years, respectively (highlighted areas in Table 8.1). Clearly, something unusual was happening in both years.

A partial explanation was provided one year later in the company's 1994 annual report, which stated:

> *In the fourth quarter of 1993, the Company adopted a business strategy to shift responsibility for the sale and distribution of a portion of the U.S. traditional contact lens business to optical distributors. A 1993 fourth quarter marketing program to implement this strategy was developed, contributing one-time net income of approximately [US]$10 million. Subsequently, this strategy proved unsuccessful.*

Prior to this change in Bausch & Lomb's business strategy, revenue and associated receivables were recognized when sales were made to retailers or ultimate consumers.

Collectibility of receivables requires forecasts of future conditions. Such forecasts could prove incorrect. However, existing auditing procedures for accounts receivable are very detailed and stringent, requiring auditors to send confirmations to customers verifying the legitimacy of the recorded receivables. Aging schedules to uncover payment problems are also required. Furthermore, auditors undertake credit checks on the company's largest customers to ascertain the probability of eventual collection. As a consequence of these procedures, while collectibility requires forecasts that could prove to be wrong, extreme overstatement of net (collectible) receivables is rare.

BAUSCH & LOMB INC.
www.bausch.com

TABLE 8.1 BAUSCH & LOMB INC

Selected Financial Statement Data, 1990–93

(US$000 omitted)	1990	1991	1992	1993
Net sales	$1,368,580	$1,520,104	$1,709,086	$1,872,184
Net trade accounts receivable	$ 202,967	$ 205,262	$ 277,338	$ 384,973
Days sales outstanding[1]	54 days[1]	49 days	59 days	75 days
Receivables as a % of total assets	12.1%	11.8%	14.8%	15.3%
Year-to-year growth in:				
Net sales		$151,524	$188,982	$163,098
Net trade accounts receivable		$ 2,295	$ 72,076	$107,635
Net sales		11.07%	12.43%	9.54%
Net trade accounts receivable		1.13%	35.11%	38.81%

[1]"Days sales outstanding" is "Net trade accounts receivables" divided by "Net sales" per day. For example, the calculation for 1990 "Days sales outstanding" is:

$$\$202,967 \text{ net trade receivables}/(\$1,368,580 \text{ net sales}/365 \text{ days}) = 54 \text{ days}$$

Source: Bausch & Lomb Inc. annual reports.

In the fourth quarter of 1993, however, shipments to distributors appear to have been treated as sales. This change in revenue recognition was in keeping with the shift in sales strategy, but the worry might have been that distributors would be unable to sell their inventory and then have to return it to Bausch & Lomb for credit. This is exactly what ultimately happened, as described in the company's 1994 annual report:

> *In October 1994, the Company announced it had implemented a new pricing policy for traditional contact lenses and agreed on a one-time basis to accept returns from these distributors.* As a result, the Company recorded sales reserves and pricing adjustments which reduced operating earnings by approximately $20 million in the third quarter. The new pricing policy sought to enhance the Company's competitive position in a market segment where industry prices had declined since the business strategy was implemented. *The returns program allowed U.S. distributors to send back the excess portion of unsold traditional lenses and balance their overall contact lens inventories. [Emphasis added.]*

This statement suggests that the changes in sales strategy and revenue recognition only began in 1993. Yet the data in Table 8.1 reveal that a large disparity between sales and receivables growth rates occurred earlier. What explains this pre-1993 disparity?

A *Business Week* article published six months after Bausch & Lomb released its 1994 annual report suggests several possible explanations.[3] The article asserts that top-down pressure to achieve sales and profit goals caused Bausch & Lomb managers to loosen revenue recognition standards in the early 1990s, an assertion that has been vehemently denied by top Bausch & Lomb executives. Specifically, Bausch & Lomb sales representatives allegedly "gave customers extraordinarily long payment terms, knowingly fed gray markets, and threatened to cut off distributors unless they took on huge quantities of unwanted products. Some also shipped goods before customers ordered them and booked the shipments as sales...."[4] The article further contends that this type of deal making "became frantic" from the last quarter of 1992 through to early 1994 and that the U.S. contact lens division "had a habit of constantly rolling over unpaid bills so that customers wouldn't return unwanted goods for credit."[5] If true, these practices would explain the unusual pre-1993 receivables growth.

Figure 8.1 depicts the company's days sales outstanding (DSO) for receivables by quarter for March 1989 through to the end of 1995. DSO receivables is just the dollar amount of outstanding receivables divided by average daily sales. From March 1989 to March 1992, DSO receivables at Bausch & Lomb averaged about 50 days and fluctuated little from quarter to quarter. By the end of 1992, however, outstanding receivables had grown to 59 days, and by the fourth quarter of 1993 they stood at 72 days. This unusual pattern of growth in DSO receivables at Bausch & Lomb undoubtedly caused some financial statement readers to become skeptical about the company's revenue recognition practices.

One last point regarding Bausch & Lomb. The *Business Week* article contends that the reported December 31, 1993 accounts receivable number of US$385 million (see Table 8.1) *understates* the real growth of outstanding customer credit. The understatement occurs, according to the article, because Bausch & Lomb sold some receivables to a third-party financing company for cash. Receivable sales of this sort are called **factoring.** If the receivables had not been factored, then the reported disparity in sales and receivables growth rates for 1992 and 1993 would have been even larger!

Scrutiny of changes in accounts receivable balances is essential. Large increases in accounts receivable relative to sales frequently represent a danger signal. The two most likely causes are (1) collection difficulties and (2) sales contingencies or disputes that may lead to potential returns.

Many revenue recognition "irregularities" can be discovered by tracking the relationship between changes in sales and receivables. Another example is provided by the 1997 Sunbeam Corporation annual report.

Albert J. Dunlap joined Sunbeam Corporation as Chairman and Chief Executive Officer in July 1996. He had earned a reputation as a "turnaround" specialist because of his aggressiveness in restructuring and downsizing companies he previously ran, such as Scott Paper. By cutting costs and eliminating waste, Dunlap restored these companies to profitability. Sunbeam had mediocre performance in the years prior to Dunlap's arrival. But reported 1997 quarterly and annual financial results seemed to indicate considerable improvement.

SUNBEAM
www.sunbeam.com

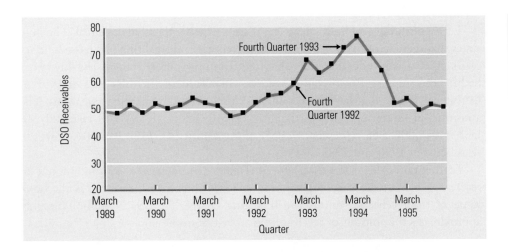

FIGURE 8.1
BAUSCH & LOMB
INC.

DSO receivables
by quarter

At the start of his letter to shareholders in the 1997 annual report, Dunlap stated:

We had an amazing year in 1997! During the past 12 months we set new records in almost every facet of the Company's operations. We experienced significant sales growth and concurrently increased margins and earnings.

The letter concluded:

Stay tuned, the best is yet to come!

Soon after the 1997 Sunbeam annual report appeared, some analysts raised questions about the quality of the reported earnings and the economic validity of the results.[6] Sales for 1997 and 1996 and year-end receivables were as follows:

($000 omitted)	1997	1996
Net sales	$1,168,182	$984,236
Gross trade accounts receivable	305,219	227,043

Sales grew by 18.69% ([$1,168,182 − $984,236] ÷ $984,236) while receivables grew by 34.43% ([$305,219 − $227,043] ÷ $227,043). The disparity in growth rates is a clue that there may have been a problem. Investigation was warranted since the following notes to the 1997 annual report disclose "bill and hold sales" and disposal of receivables—events that affect both sales and receivables.

Revenue Recognition

The Company recognizes revenues from product sales principally at the time of shipment to customers. In limited circumstances, at the customer's request the Company may sell seasonal product on a bill and hold basis provided that the goods are completed, packaged and ready for shipment, such goods are segregated and the risks of ownership and legal title have passed to the customer. The amount of such bill and hold sales at December 29, 1997 was approximately 3% of consolidated revenues. *[Emphasis and highlighting added.]*

Credit Facilities

In December 1997, the Company entered into a revolving trade accounts receivable securitization program to sell without recourse, through a wholly-owned subsidiary, certain trade accounts receivable. The maximum amount of receivables that can be sold through this program is [US]$70 million. At December 28, 1997, the Company had received approximately [US]$59 million from the sale of trade accounts receivable. *[Emphasis and highlighting added.]*

Source: Sunbeam Corporation 1997 Annual Report.

Let's look at **bill and hold** sales. One issue is whether these sales are real. The note states that these terms were at the customer's request and legal title had passed. So it's reasonable to conclude that the sales were legitimate even though the inventory hadn't been shipped. But the other issue is whether these are really sales of 1997 or instead 1998 sales that have been pulled into 1997 by the bill and hold terms. The amount in question isn't trivial—3% of sales (US$1,168,182,000) is US$35,045,000. This represents 19.05% of the reported US$183,946,000 growth in sales between 1996 and 1997.

Furthermore, the true growth in receivables is understated by the amount of receivables sold at the end of 1997. The US$59 million cash received is the book value of the receivables minus the financing charge. So US$59 million roughly approximates the amount of receivables removed from the books.

In a bill and hold sale, the company recognizes revenue and the associated account receivable, but does not ship the product to the customer until later.

Let's summarize the clues that were available to the careful analyst:

1. Receivables growth greatly exceeded sales growth.
2. Bill and hold sales raise the possibility that some of this disparity is because sales were booked too early, thus generating receivables that won't be collected quickly. Worse yet, collection may never occur if delivery of "sold" items is ultimately refused.
3. Had Sunbeam not sold approximately US$59 million of receivables, the "real" growth rate of receivables would have exceeded the reported rate of 34.43%, further increasing the disparity between sales and receivables growth rates. This even larger disparity increases the likelihood that some "channel stuffing"—that is, overly aggressive revenue recognition on items "sold" to dealers—was occurring.

These, as well as other issues unrelated to receivables, prompted a reaudit of Sunbeam's financial statements from the fourth quarter of 1996 through the first quarter of 1998. The reaudit disclosed that 1997 sales were overstated by US$95,092,000 and profits were US$38,301,000 rather than US$109,415,000, as reported.[7]

And it was careful scrutiny by informed analysts that led to inquiries which resulted in these corrections!

Albert J. Dunlap was fired by Sunbeam's board of directors on June 15, 1998.

Recap

Evaluating the net realizable value of accounts receivable requires an analysis of the adequacy of estimated uncollectibles and provisions for returns and adjustments. When receivables growth exceeds sales growth, this could be an indication of aggressive revenue recognition policies. Statement readers who carefully examine receivables trends and levels can discern potential problems as they evolve.

Imputed Interest on Trade Notes Receivable

In certain industries, the seller sometimes extends long-term credit to the buyer, who then signs a note. If the note bears an interest rate approximating prevailing borrowing and lending rates, the accounting is straightforward. Assume that Elle Corporation manufactures and sells a machine to Alberta Products Company. The cash selling price of the machine is $50,000. Elle accepts a three-year $50,000 note signed by Alberta Products, with interest of 10% per annum to be paid in quarterly installments each year. Assume that 10% approximates prevailing borrowing rates for companies as creditworthy as Alberta Products. Upon making the sale, Elle would record the following:

```
DR  Note receivable—Alberta Products Company      $50,000
      CR  Sales revenues                                    $50,000
```

Interest income would accrue each quarter, and when the cash payment is received, the accrued interest receivable would be reduced. These are the entries:

```
DR  Accrued interest receivable                    $1,250
      CR  Interest income                                    $1,250
(To accrue three months' interest = [$50,000 × 0.10] ÷ 4.)
```

```
DR   Cash                                                    $1,250
     CR   Accrued interest receivable                                      $1,250
(To record receipt of the interest payment.)
```

A complication arises for a note that does not state an interest rate or when the stated rate is lower than prevailing rates for loans of similar risk. Suppose Monson Corporation sells equipment it manufactured to Davenport Products Corporation in exchange for a $50,000 note due in three years. The note bears no explicit interest. It just says that the entire $50,000 is to be paid at the end of three years. Monson's published cash selling price for the equipment is $37,566, and the current borrowing rate for companies like Davenport is 10%.

Reference to Appendix I Table 1 at the back of this textbook indicates that the present value factor for a payment three years away at a 10% rate is 0.75132. Therefore, the present value of the note is $50,000 times 0.75132, or $37,566— which is exactly equal to the cash selling price of the equipment. Although the $50,000 note itself does not contain any mention of interest, Monson will earn a return of 10% per year for financing Davenport's long-term credit purchase. This is easily demonstrated as follows:

Present value of $50,000 payment in 3 years (cash sales price)	$37,566.00
Plus: Year 1 interest: 10% × $37,566.00	3,756.60
Equals: Present value of $50,000 payment in 2 years	41,322.60
Plus: Year 2 interest: 10% × $41,322.60	4,132.26
Equals: Present value of $50,000 payment in 1 year	45,454.86
Plus: Year 3 interest: 10% × $45,454.86	4,545.14[1]
Equals: Payment by Davenport at the end of year 3	$50,000.00

[1]Rounded.

At the end of year 3, Monson receives a payment of $50,000, which consists of the cash sales price ($37,566) plus interest ($12,434 = $3,756.60 + $4,132.26 + $4,545.14).

Monson Corporation would make the following entry at the time of the sale to Davenport Products Corporation:

```
DR   Note receivable—Davenport                  $37,566.00
     CR   Sales revenue                                      $37,566.00
```

Over the next three years, the note receivable is increased and interest income is recognized. For example, at the end of year 1, the following entry would be made:[8]

```
DR   Note receivable—Davenport                  $3,756.60
     CR   Interest income                                    $3,756.60
```

Notice that after Monson records interest income of $4,132.26 in year 2 and $4,545.14 in year 3, the carrying amount of the note receivable will be exactly $50,000. When Davenport makes the required payment at maturity of the note, Monson Corporation would record the following:

```
DR   Cash                                       $50,000.00
     CR   Note receivable—Davenport                         $50,000.00
```

An additional complication arises when the note receivable contains a stated interest rate *but the stated rate is lower than prevailing borrowing rates at the time of the transaction.* When this happens, interest must again be imputed. Assume that Quinones Corporation sells a machine to Martin Manufacturing in exchange for a

$40,000, three-year, 2.5% note from Martin. At the time of the sale, the interest rate normally charged to companies with Martin's credit rating is 10%. Since the note's stated interest rate is far below Martin's normal borrowing rate, Quinones must determine the machine's implied sales price by computing the note's present value at the 10% rate:

Nominal Interest-Bearing Note
Calculation of Present Value at 10% Effective Interest Rate

Present value of $40,000 principal repayment in three years at 10%:

$40,000	×	0.75132	=	$30,052.80

Present value of three interest payments of $1,000 (i.e., $40,000 × 0.025), each at 10%:

Year 1:	$ 1,000	×	0.90909	=	909.09
Year 2:	$ 1,000	×	0.82645	=	826.45
Year 3:	$ 1,000	×	0.75132	=	751.32
TOTAL					$32,539.66

This computation shows that the implied cash selling price of the machine is $32,539.66, because this amount equals the discounted present value of the note Quinones received in exchange for the machine. So Quinones would make the following entry:

DR	Note receivable—Martin Manufacturing	$32,539.66	
	CR Sales revenue		$32,539.66

Since payment was deferred, Quinones will earn 10% over the duration of the note on the amount of the credit sale ($32,539.66). The interest earned consists of three $1,000 payments over each of the ensuing years and another imputed interest payment of $7,460.34 ($40,000 minus the $32,539.66 implied cash selling price) at maturity. The composition of yearly interest income is shown in Table 8.2, and Figure 8.2 shows the note receivable from the time of sale to maturity.

As shown in Table 8.2 and Figure 8.2, the present value, and thus the carrying value, of the note—column (d) of Table 8.2—increases each year. The increase equals the difference between the annual 10% interest income earned—column (a)—and

TABLE 8.2 QUINONES CORPORATION

Computation of Interest on Note Receivable

	(a) Interest Income— 10% of Column (d) Balance for Prior Year	(b) Cash Interest Received	(c) Increase in Present Value of Note (a) Minus (b)	(d) End of Year Present Value of Note
Inception	—	—	—	$32,539.66
Year 1	$3,253.97	1,000.00	$2,253.97	34,793.63
Year 2	3,479.36	1,000.00	2,479.36	37,272.99
Year 3	3,727.01[1]	1,000.00	2,727.01	40,000.00

[1]Rounded.

FIGURE 8.2

QUINONES
CORPORATION

Carrying value of
note receivable

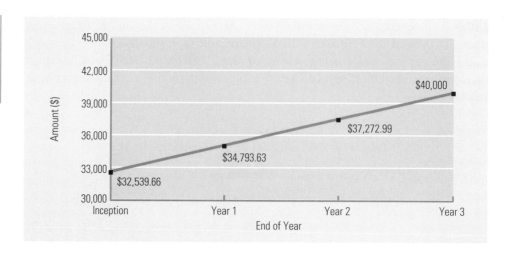

the cash received—column (b). For example, in Year 1 Quinones would make the following entry:

DR	Note receivable—Martin Manufacturing	$2,253.97	
DR	Cash	1,000.00	
	CR Interest income		$3,253.97

Similar entries would be made in years 2 and 3 using the amounts shown in Table 8.2. At the end of year 3, the carrying amount of the note will be $40,000. When Martin pays the note on maturity, Quinones will record the payment as follows:

DR	Cash	$40,000.00	
	CR Note receivable—Martin Manufacturing		$40,000.00

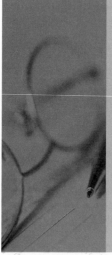

Recap

For long-term credit sales transactions utilizing notes receivable:

- Sales revenue is recorded at the known cash price (Monson Corporation) or at the implied cash price (Quinones Corporation) of the item sold. The implied cash price is determined by computing the note receivable's present value using the prevailing borrowing rate.
- Interest income is recorded each period over the note's term to maturity using the prevailing borrowing rate (i.e., effective market rate of interest).

This approach achieves a clear separation between the two income sources—credit sales and interest earned. Income from the credit sale is recorded when the sale is made. Interest income from financing the customer's purchase, on the other hand, is recorded over time as it is earned. This separation of income sources makes it possible to assess the degree to which a company's overall earnings are due to profitable credit sales versus profitable customer financing—a potentially important distinction.

Accelerating Cash Collection: Transfers and Dispositions of Receivables

Companies collect cash from their credit customers according to the payment schedule for the note or trade receivable. Sometimes companies prefer not to wait until customer payments arrive in the normal course of business. Instead, they accelerate cash collection with the help of a bank or financial institution.

There are two ways to accelerate cash collections, as depicted in Figure 8.3. One is **factoring,** where the company sells its receivables outright to the bank or some other financial institution in exchange for cash. Customer payments flow directly to the bank in most cases. Factoring can be **without recourse,** meaning that the bank cannot turn to the company for payment in the event that some customer receivables prove uncollectible. Factoring can also be **with recourse,** meaning that the company is willing to buy back any bad receivables from the bank. The other way to accelerate cash collection is **assignment** of receivables, which is a loan collateralized by receivables. The company gets cash from the bank, and the company is responsible for all loan payments.

There are several reasons why companies might want to accelerate cash collections from customers:

1. *Competitive conditions require credit sales but the company is unwilling to bear the cost of processing and collecting receivables.* Restaurants illustrate this phenomenon. Customers of upscale restaurants expect to be able to charge meals rather than pay cash. Yet most restaurants are reluctant to incur the costs of servicing receivables. Consequently, restaurants rely on third parties like TD VISA, Bank of Montreal MasterCard, American Express, and Diners Club, companies which, in effect, "buy" the customer receivable from the restaurant.

2. *There may be an imbalance between the credit terms of the company's suppliers and the time required to collect customer receivables.* Suppliers might extend credit on six-month terms to a company while inventory turnover plus receivables turnover totals 210 days. To pay suppliers within the due date, early cash collection is necessary.

3. *The company may have an immediate need for cash but be short of it.* Selling receivables to a financial institution allows the company to raise cash quickly. Using receivables as collateral for a bank loan also represents a way to obtain quick cash (and perhaps low-cost financing).

Let's take a look at the accounting issues that arise when receivables are sold or assigned.

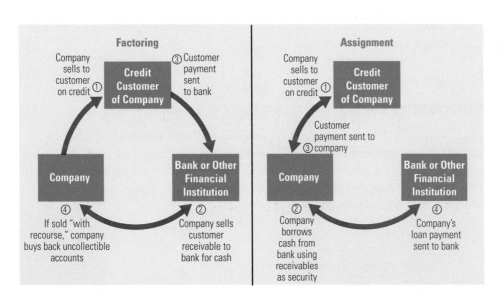

FIGURE 8.3
TRANSFERS AND
DISPOSITIONS OF
RECEIVABLES

Sale of Receivables (Factoring)

To illustrate a factoring transaction without recourse, suppose Hervey Corporation sells $80,000 of its customer receivables to Leslie Financing Corporation. The purchaser (Leslie Financing) is called the **factor**. Leslie charges a 5% fee (5% × $80,000 = $4,000) for this service and pays Hervey $76,000. The entry to record the **nonrecourse** sale of the receivables on Hervey Corporation's books is:

DR	Cash	$76,000	
DR	Interest expense	4,000	
	CR Accounts receivable		$80,000

The $4,000 is charged to interest expense because this amount represents the financing charge Hervey incurred to accelerate cash collection. In a sale without recourse, if some of Hervey Corporation's customers fail to pay the amount owed, Leslie Financing has no recourse against Hervey (hence the term)—and thus, Leslie bears the loss.

Next we illustrate the sale of accounts receivable with recourse. Again, assume Hervey Corporation sells $80,000 of trade receivables to Leslie Financing. If any of the receivables are not paid, Hervey bears the loss. Leslie's fee is reduced to 4% with a recourse transaction rather than 5% because the risk to Leslie is lower. Assume Leslie withholds $5,000 to cover possible noncollections. The entry on Hervey Corporation's books is:

DR	Cash	$71,800	
DR	Interest expense	3,200	
DR	Due from Leslie Financing	5,000	
	CR Accounts receivable		$80,000

The $5,000 holdback account "Due from Leslie Financing" represents a cushion to absorb credit losses that must ultimately be borne by Hervey in a sale with recourse.

Next assume that all but $3,750 of receivables are ultimately collected. Once collections are known, the financing company remits the final settlement amount. The entry on Hervey Corporation's books would be:

DR	Cash	$1,250	
DR	Allowance for uncollectibles	3,750	
	CR Due from Leslie Financing		$5,000

> Usually, the bank or financing company refuses to bear the costs of sales returns, discounts, or price adjustments. Consequently, a holdback to cover these items may be included in the transaction. For example, if the holdback is $3,000 and if all other facts regarding the nonrecourse sale are unchanged, the entry on Hervey's books would be:
>
> | | | |
> |---|---|---|
> | DR Cash | $73,000 | |
> | DR Interest expense | 4,000 | |
> | DR Due from Leslie Financing | 3,000 | |
> | CR Accounts receivable | | $80,000 |
>
> Any returns, discounts, or adjustments reduce the amount paid to Hervey by Leslie. If these items totalled $1,800 on the sold receivables, Leslie would ultimately pay an additional $1,200 to Hervey and Hervey would make the following entry:
>
> | | | |
> |---|---|---|
> | DR Cash | $1,200 | |
> | DR Sales returns, adjustments, and discounts | 1,800 | |
> | CR Due from Leslie Financing | | $3,000 |

> The $3,750 debit to allowance for uncollectibles is appropriate if normal allowances had been accrued on the receivables that were sold. If this isn't the case, then the debit of $3,750 would be made to an account entitled "Loss on sale of receivables" or some other similarly titled income statement loss account.

Borrowing Using Receivables as Collateral

If the transaction between Hervey Corporation and Leslie Financing had been a collateralized loan rather than a sale of receivables, then the accounts receivable would not be removed from Hervey's books. Instead, a liability account would be created to reflect the loan. Suppose that $80,000 of receivables were pledged as collateral for a 4% loan; then the entry would be:

DR	Cash	$76,800	
DR	Prepaid interest	3,200	
	CR Loan payable—Leslie Financing		$80,000

The fact that the receivables have been pledged as collateral for this loan must be disclosed in the notes to the financial statements, if material.[9] Once the loan is due, Hervey would make the following entries:

DR	Loan payable—Leslie Financing	$80,000	
	CR Cash		$80,000
DR	Interest expense	3,200	
	CR Prepaid interest		3,200

Notes receivable can also be assigned or sold. Accelerating cash collection on notes in this way is called **discounting**, because the financial institution advances cash to the company based on the *discounted present value* of the notes. For example, suppose Abbott Manufacturing received a $9,000, six-month, 8% per annum interest-bearing note from Weaver Company, a customer. That same day, Abbott discounted the note at CanaBank. If the bank discounts the note at 12%, Abbott would receive only $8,798.40. The cash proceeds to Abbott are determined as follows:

Face amount of the note	$9,000.00
Interest on note ($9,000 × 0.08 × ½*)	360.00
Maturity amount of the note	9,360.00
Interest charged by bank:	
($9,360 × 0.12 × ½*)	561.60
Cash proceeds	$8,798.40

*Multiplication by ½ represents 6 months' interest.

At maturity, the bank will present the note to Weaver Company for payment. Abbott would make the following entry when the note is discounted:

DR	Cash	$8,798.40	
DR	Interest expense	201.60	
	CR Note receivable		$9,000

Accelerating cash collection generates interest expense of $201.60, the difference between the book value of the note and the cash proceeds.

Notes can be discounted either with or without recourse. If discounted with recourse, then CanaBank would collect $9,360 ($9,000 principal plus $360 interest) from Abbott if Weaver failed to pay the note at maturity. When notes are discounted with recourse and the note is removed from the books of the seller, a contingent liability must be disclosed in the footnotes.[10]

Ambiguities Abound: Is It a Sale or a Borrowing?

Usually, the nature of the transaction is clear when receivables are sold or assigned. But in some situations, it is not obvious whether the receivables have been sold or are instead being used as collateral in a borrowing transaction. The ambiguity arises whenever certain obligations, duties, or rights regarding the transferred receivables are retained by the transferor (i.e., the company whose receivables are being transferred).

In 2001, the CICA issued an Accounting Guideline on transfers of receivables. The Guideline, *AcG-12* ("Transfers of Receivables"), replaces two EICs (*EIC-9* and *EIC-54*), and more or less harmonizes Canadian practice with the U.S. standard in this area, *SFAS 140*. *AcG-12*, which became effective for receivables transfers occurring after June 30, 2001, sets out financial accounting and reporting standards for sales, securitizations, and also servicing of receivables and other financial assets.

This guideline has the following important features:

- *control* should determine how a receivables transfer is accounted for;
- when a transaction results in a disaggregation of receivables into separate components, companies should account for the financial assets and liabilities according to the variety of components which result (the so-called financial-components approach).

This guideline also sets out criteria by which a transfer of all or a portion of receivables should be accounted for as a **sale**:

- The transferred assets have been placed beyond the reach of the transferor, even in bankruptcy;
- Transferees have the right to pledge or dispose of the assets;
- No agreements exist that would cause the transferor to reacquire the assets (from paragraph 9, *AcG–12*, "Transfer of Receivables," March 2001).

Transfers of receivables have assumed great importance with the growth of **financial asset securitization.** *Securitization occurs when receivables (like mortgages or automobile loans) are bundled and sold or transferred to another organization, which issues securities that are collateralized by the transferred receivables.*

For example, the financing subsidiary of Bombardier Inc. (Bombardier Capital) sells so-called Floating Rate Asset-Backed Certificates to investors. The collateral supporting these certificates is bundled finance loans on Bombardier recreational and other products. By bundling large numbers of receivables, the seller creates value because the risk of loss is reduced by the portfolio effect of the bundling itself.

Home mortgages, car loans, credit card debt, and health club membership fees are just a few of the receivables that have been securitized and sold to investors. Ambiguities arise, for example, when a bank transfers a group of mortgages (which, to the bank, are receivables) to some other organization but retains the responsibility for servicing the mortgages. The bank often continues to collect the mortgage payments or to handle customer inquiries, or it even promises to buy back the mortgages at some future date if certain conditions occur. How these transactions are treated has important financial reporting implications. For example:

1. If the transaction is really a borrowing but is erroneously treated as a sale, then both assets and liabilities are understated (i.e., the loan does not appear on the company's balance sheet and neither do the receivables). Ratios like debt-to-equity and rate of return on assets are consequently distorted.
2. If the transaction is really a sale, then a gain or loss on the transaction should be recognized. To erroneously treat such transactions as borrowings misrepresents the company's net assets.

Here's how the accounting would be handled under *AcG–12* for a transaction involving a sale of a portion of a receivables asset.

Company X, which has common shares listed on the TSX and annual revenues of about $150 million, has $1,000,000 of loans receivable that yield 10% per annum interest for their remaining lives of nine years. The company has just broken even on a reported income basis this past year, and since it is experiencing a bit of a cash squeeze, is contemplating transferring the $1,000,000 loans receivable principal plus the right to receive interest income of 8% on the loans to another entity for $1,000,000. However, Company X will continue to service the loans, and the proposed contract between Company X and the other entity stipulates that Company X's compensation for performing the loan servicing is the right to receive half the interest income not transferred. The remaining half of the interest income not transferred is considered an interest-only strip receivable with a fair value of $60,000 on the date of the transfer. At the date of the transfer, the fair value of the loans, including servicing, is agreed to be $1,100,000. The fair value of the servicing asset is $40,000. Company X's chief accountant has prepared the following analysis of the transactions, along with her recommendations, for purposes of external financial reporting:

Carrying amount according to fair values

	Fair Value	Percentage Sold	Allocated Carrying Amount
Loans transferred	$1,000,000	91.0%	$910,000
Servicing asset	40,000	3.6%	36,000
Interest-only strip receivable	60,000	5.4%	54,000
Totals	$1,100,000	100.0%	$1,000,000

Gain on transfer:

Net proceeds	$1,000,000
Carrying amount of loans transferred	910,000
Gain on transfer	$ 90,000

Recommended journal entries for external financial reporting purposes:

DR	Cash	$1,000,000	
	CR Loans receivable		$910,000
	CR Gain		90,000

To record transfer.

DR	Servicing asset	36,000	
DR	Interest-only strip receivable	54,000	
	CR Loans receivable		90,000

To record servicing asset and interest-only strip receivable.

A Closer Look at Securitizations

Securitizations are popular for two reasons. First, investors have a strong appetite for acquiring securitized assets. Second, firms with large amounts of receivables have powerful incentives to engage in securitizations. It's a "win-win" situation for investors and firms; both parties benefit.

Investors benefit because they are able to obtain highly liquid financial instruments that diversify their risk. A simple example shows this. Suppose the prevailing rate of return on debt instruments with "moderate" risk is 9% per annum. The 9% yield is determined by the credit standing of large corporate and government issuers of bonds and other instruments. By contrast, people who take out home mortgages with banks do not have the same high credit standing as the bond issuers. Understandably, the rates people pay on mortgages are higher—let's say 10% per year.

Assume that a bank forms a bundled portfolio of these home mortgages and is prepared to sell them at a price that yields the investor a return of 9%. The risk associated with the individual mortgages ranges from "low" to "moderately high" *but the risk of the bundled portfolio in the aggregate is "moderate."* So the investors have an investment option that also provides a 9% per year yield at the same "moderate" risk level but responds differently than other debt instruments to changes in interest rates and other economic events. This diversifies risk and that's attractive. Furthermore, the investors could not form a "moderate" risk, 9% return mortgage portfolio themselves since the costs of identifying potential mortgagees and doing a credit analysis are high and would lower their return below 9%. And even if they could construct their own portfolio, if investors later wanted to liquidate the investment, they'd have difficulty finding buyers for individual mortgages. So investors benefit from securitizations by gaining liquid portfolio diversification opportunities that they could not achieve on their own.

If you don't understand this now, it's too early to panic. We'll explain why there's a gain in Chapter 11. You'll be able to follow the discussion in this section without a detailed understanding of the specifics underlying the gain.

It's even better for the investors! To make the securities more attractive, the bank will provide investors with a return that slightly exceeds 9%.

But the bank also wins! If the bank sells the 10% mortgages at a price that yields the purchasers a return of 9%, this means that the selling price is higher than the carrying value of the mortgages on the bank's books. So the bank records a gain on the sale of the receivables. ***This gain exists because the bank has created value.*** As we just saw, the individual investors would never consider lending directly to, say, two or three home purchasers. (It's too risky. Who knows how many will default?) But the large portfolio is much less risky. So investors who are unable to duplicate the bank's return on their own without assuming high risks (and costs) are very willing to accept the 9% return.

Banks and other firms that engage in securitization transactions do not transact directly with the investors. The format of securitizations is somewhat convoluted, for reasons we'll soon explain. Figure 8.4 shows how a typical securitization is structured. The firm doing the securitization (the transferor) forms what is called a **special purpose entity** or **SPE.** We discuss SPEs and their involvement in the Enron debacle more broadly in Chapter 16; for now, we concentrate on SPEs involving securitization transactions. The SPE is usually a trust or corporation that is legally distinct from the transferor and is created solely for the purpose of undertaking the securitization transaction. The transferor then sells the receivables (mortgages in our example) to the SPE. The SPE creates and issues debt securities (with the mortgages as collateral) that are sold to outside investors. The cash received from the investors by

FIGURE 8.4
THE STRUCTURE OF SECURITIZATION

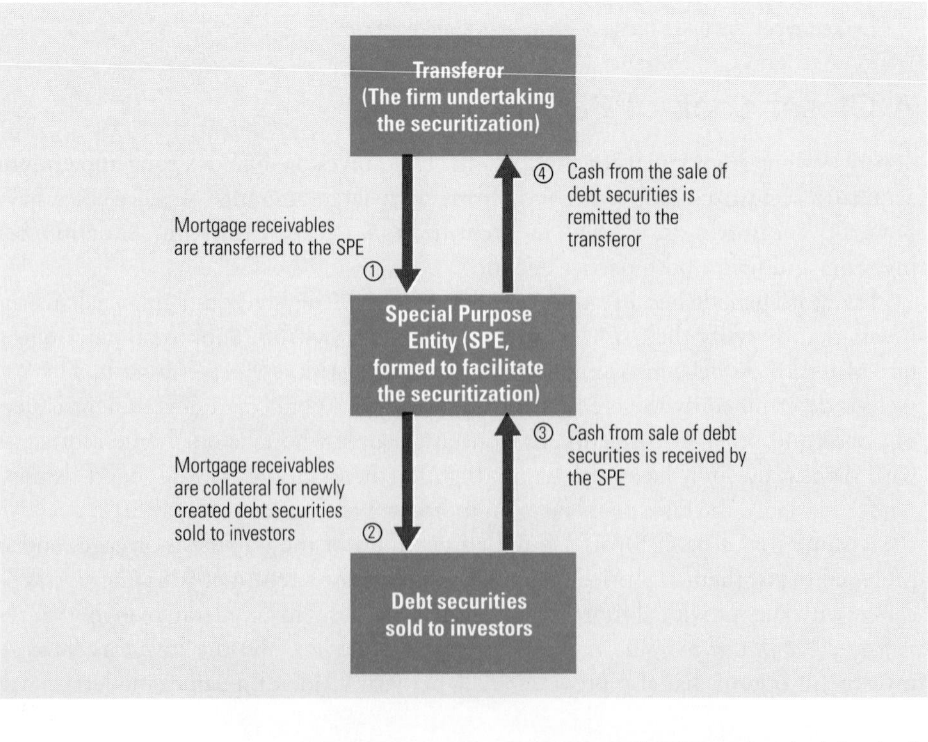

the SPE is then remitted to the transferor. In many situations, the transferor continues to service the assets (i.e., handle cash collections, record keeping, etc.) usually for a fee that is paid by the SPE.

The cash flows from the mortgages themselves (i.e., principal repayment and interest) are later used to make the periodic interest and principal repayments to the investors who bought the debt securities.

The SPE is created for two reasons. One is to protect the investors who bought the debt securities. Because the receivables were sold to the SPE, they are beyond the reach of the transferor and its creditors. *So even if the transferor were to declare bankruptcy, the collateral underlying the notes is safe from seizure.* The other reason for creating the SPE is that its existence allows the transferor to receive favourable financial reporting treatment for the transaction. Here's why. If there were no SPE, the transferor would issue the notes directly to investors. This would constitute a collateralized borrowing; the receivables would appear on the transferor's books and so would the notes (as a liability). But by creating the legally distinct entity, the receivables are removed from the transferor's books. Furthermore, the notes are the SPE's debt, not the transferor's. Since the SPE is not consolidated, the debt securities never appear on the transferor's balance sheet. *So both the receivables and the debt are "off-balance-sheet."*

Some Cautions for Statement Readers

Factoring and assignment of receivables raise some issues for those who analyze financial statements. The main issue is the level of disclosure in statement footnotes when receivables have been transferred during the reporting period. When the transfer is with recourse (and the "selling" company is still responsible for uncollected receivables), GAAP requires footnote disclosure of the contingent liability.[11] *But there is no similar unequivocal disclosure requirement when receivables are sold without recourse.*

What this means for statement readers is simply this. Earlier in the chapter, we saw that one way to assess whether reported receivables arose from legitimate sales was to compare the growth rate of sales and the growth rate of receivables. This comparison in Table 8.1 for Bausch & Lomb showed that receivables growth far outstripped sales growth between 1991 and 1993. Our conclusion—based on disclosures from the 1994 Bausch & Lomb annual report—was that the leap in receivables growth arose from "forcing" inventory on distributors and treating these shipments as sales. The way to recognize these potential trouble areas is to monitor receivables growth. *But if firms can sell receivables to a factor and not disclose the transaction, the number representing receivables as reported in the balance sheet will understate the true growth in receivables over the period.*

This is precisely what *Business Week* says happened at Bausch & Lomb, whose "internal financial documents," they claim, show year-end 1993 receivables to be US$506 million rather than the US$385 million reported on the company's balance sheet (see Table 8.1). According to *Business Week*, Bausch & Lomb felt the factored receivables didn't need to be disclosed under GAAP.[12]

The opportunity to sell receivables provides a way for companies to disguise the *real* extent of receivables growth. Suppose a company is "aggressively" booking sales to artificially raise current earnings. To avoid discovery, the company could factor some of its "good" receivables—those that don't arise from the questionable sales—and thus understate the true disparity in the growth of receivables and sales.

Securitizations are carefully designed to enable the transferor to avoid consolidating the SPE. To accomplish this, the SPE must meet four conditions stated in *SFAS No. 140,* para. 35:
1. *It is demonstrably distinct from the transferor.* This condition is met if the transferor cannot unilaterally dissolve the SPE and either of two other highly technical circumstances apply.
2. *Its activities are narrowly limited.* These are restricted to holding title to the transferred assets, issuing the collateralized debt securities, collecting cash flows from the transferred assets, and making interest and principal payments to holders of the debt securities.
3. *It holds only rigidly defined types of assets.* The assets must not require decision making by the SPE.
4. *Its ability to dispose of assets is limited to narrowly defined circumstances.* This means that the SPE must be an unthinking robot that cannot exercise discretion.

Why does the FASB allow favourable off-balance-sheet treatment for these contorted transactions? One reason is because they are economically beneficial. That is, the transferor creates value through the portfolio effect of bundling the assets, and the investors diversify their risk and earn slightly higher returns.

Consequently, statement readers must scrutinize footnotes and the financing activities section of the cash flow statement for any evidence of dispositions of receivables that may be masking overly aggressive revenue recognition policies.

Troubled Debt Restructuring

What happens to a lender when a customer is financially unable to make the interest and principal payments required by an installment loan or other receivable? Rather than force the customer into bankruptcy, lenders frequently agree to **restructure** the loan receivable, thus allowing the customer to remain in business. The restructured loan can differ from the original loan in several ways:

- Scheduled interest and principal payments may be reduced or eliminated.
- The repayment schedule may be extended over a longer time period.
- The customer and lender can settle the loan for cash, other assets, or equity interests.

Lenders are willing to restructure a customer's loan to help the customer resolve present financial difficulties and stay in business. And lenders often receive more through restructuring than through foreclosure or bankruptcy.

Consider the bank debt restructuring described in Exhibit 8.3. White Rose Crafts and Nursery Sales Limited operated several gardening and crafts retail stores in Ontario and Quebec. In fiscal 1997 (which ended July 27, 1997), the company found itself unable to repay its term bank loan. The bank agreed to restructure the debt as described in the exhibit, deferred the first principal payment, and ignored the fact that White Rose had breached covenant default. In exchange, the bank received 1,060,000 Class B non-voting convertible market shares in the company, a commitment that it would raise additional equity (or debt ranking lower than the bank's term loan), and a "cash sweep test" by which excess cash would be applied to the term loan.

Troubled debt restructurings can be accomplished in two fundamentally different ways:

- **settlement,** where the original loan is cancelled by a transfer of cash or other assets to the lender
- **continuation with modification** of debt terms, where the original loan is cancelled and a new loan agreement is signed

Of course, some troubled debt restructurings contain elements of both settlement and modification.

The accounting issues related to troubled debt restructuring involve both the measurement of the new (modified) loan and a report of any gain or loss. The following examples illustrate these issues.

Suppose that Harper Companies purchased $75,000 of equipment from Farmers Suppliers Ltd. on January 1, 1998. Harper paid $25,000 cash and signed a five-year 10% installment note for the remaining $50,000 of the purchase price. The note calls for annual payments of $10,000 plus interest on December 31 of each year. Harper Companies made the first two installment payments on time but was unable to make the third annual payment on December 31, 2000. After much negotiation, Farmers agreed to restructure the note receivable. At that time, Harper owed $30,000 in unpaid principal plus $3,000 in accrued interest. We will also assume that the

Exhibit 8.3 WHITE ROSE CRAFTS AND NURSERY SALES LIMITED

Bank Debt Restructuring Notes to Financial Statements

8. Restructuring of Existing Bank Facilities

In October 1996, the Company signed an Amended and Restated Credit Agreement, "Amended Credit Agreement" with its Bank which superseded its original loan agreement. The Bank waived its rights in respect of a covenant default which had occurred under the original loan agreement at July 28, 1996. The Company deferred its first principal payment in exchange for:

i) a restructuring fee of $1,590,000 which was satisfied in November 1996 by the issuance of 1,060,000 Class B non-voting convertible shares at $1.50, at the current market price, prevailing at that date.

ii) a commitment to raise a minimum of $3,000,000 in additional equity and/or debt fully subordinated to the Bank by January 15, 1997. The Company subsequently issued 3,540,206 Common Shares, for cash of $3,746,500.

At July 27, 1997, the Bank waived its rights in respect of covenant defaults which occurred under the Amended Credit Agreement.

The terms of the Amended Credit Agreement are as follows:

A. Cash Sweep

Commencing in Fiscal 1998, under the Amended Credit Agreement, the Company will be subject to an annual cash sweep test in which excess cash will be applied to the term loan in inverse order of payment maturity, until the balance is reduced to $14,979,500.

B. Term Loan

Minimum repayments are as follows:

1998	$ 2,100
1999	4,200
2000	4,200
2001	4,200
2002	15,259
	$29,959

To reduce exposure on the term loan from increases in interest rates, the Company has utilized banker's acceptances. The remainder of the term loan bears interest at prime plus 1/2%.

C. Operating Facility

The Company has available a bank line of credit of $38 million at an interest rate of prime, to service seasonal liquidity and letter of credit requirements throughout the year.

D. Security

Both the term and operating facilities are secured by a fixed and floating charge debenture of $90 million, a moveable hypothec in the amount of $15 million for the assets in the province of Quebec, a charge on inventories, a registered general assignment of book debts and the assignment of proceeds from fire and life insurance.

Subsequent to year-end, the Company obtained an additional $7.4 million (1996—$8 million) operating line of credit at an interest rate of prime plus 6% (1996—prime) for seasonal liquidity requirements, bringing the total operating credit line to $45.4 million until November 30, 1997. Also, to reduce the Company's exposure to fluctuating interest rates, the Company financed $30 million of the operating credit facility with short-term banker's acceptances at a rate of 3.6%. As part of the amendment, two new covenants were added.

restructuring was agreed to on January 1, 2001 and that both companies had already recorded interest up to that date.

Settlement

Suppose Farmers agrees to cancel the loan if Harper pays $5,000 cash and turns over the company car. The car was purchased 18 months ago for $21,000 cash, has a current fair market value of $18,000, and is carried on Harper's books at $16,000

($21,000 original cost minus $5,000 accumulated amortization). Notice that the combined economic value of the cash ($5,000) and automobile ($18,000) is $23,000—or $10,000 less than the $33,000 Harper owes Farmers.

The January 1, 2001 entries made to record settlement of the troubled debt are:

Harper Companies (Borrower)

(a) To increase the net carrying amount of the automobile ($16,000) to its fair market value ($18,000):

DR	Automobile	$ 2,000	
	CR Gain on disposal of asset		$ 2,000

(b) To record the settlement:

DR	Note payable	$30,000	
DR	Interest payable	3,000	
DR	Accumulated amortization	5,000	
	CR Cash		$ 5,000
	CR Automobile		23,000
	CR Gain on debt restructuring		10,000

Farmers Suppliers Ltd. (Lender)

(a) To record the settlement:

DR	Cash	$ 5,000	
DR	Automobile	18,000	
DR	Loss on receivable restructuring	10,000	
	CR Note receivable		$30,000
	CR Interest receivable		3,000

What do these entries accomplish? The settlement creates two earnings gains for Harper: (1) a gain on asset disposal of $2,000, which is the difference between the car's fair market value ($18,000) and its book value ($16,000); and (2) a debt restructuring gain of $10,000, representing the difference between the note's book value plus accrued interest ($30,000 plus $3,000) and the fair market value of assets transferred ($5,000 cash plus $18,000 automobile). Farmers has a debt restructuring loss for the same $10,000 figure.[13] Both companies record all interest up to the restructuring date and then cancel the note and related interest receivable and payable.

Continuation with Modification of Debt Terms

Instead of reaching a negotiated settlement of the note receivable, Harper and Farmers could have resolved the troubled debt by modifying the terms of the original loan. The possibilities are endless. For accounting purposes, the only thing that matters is whether the ***undiscounted sum of future cash flows under the restructured note is above or below the note's book value (including accrued interest) at the restructuring date.***

Suppose Farmers agrees to defer all principal and interest payments on the note receivable to maturity. Harper's final (and only) payment on December 31, 2002 would total $39,000 (the $30,000 principal plus $9,000 representing three years' interest at 10%). Harper and Farmers have already recorded $3,000 in accrued interest as of January 1, 2001. So the book value of the note plus accrued interest is $33,000 at the restructuring date.

Because the sum of future cash flows on the restructured note ($39,000) is *greater* than the carrying value of the original payable ($33,000), Harper will not show a restructuring gain. Instead, Harper will compute a new (and lower) effective interest

To see this, notice that the restructured note calls for Harper Companies to make a single payment of $39,000 on December 31, 2002—two years from the January 1, 2001 restructuring date. We need to find a discount rate that equates the present value of this $39,000 payment with the $33,000 carrying value of the note receivable. This means finding the rate r that solves the following equation:

$$\underbrace{\text{Carrying value}}_{\$33,000} = \underbrace{\frac{\text{Present value of future cash flows}}{\$39,000}}_{\dfrac{\$39,000}{(1 + r)^2}}$$

The value of r is 0.087. The present value factor for a single payment due in two periods at 8.7% is 0.84615, and $39,000 multiplied by this factor equals $33,000 (rounded).

rate for the restructured note and accrue interest at that rate until the loan is fully paid. The new effective interest rate is that rate which equates the present value of the restructured cash flows to the carrying value of the debt at the date of restructure. The new effective interest rate for Harper Companies is 8.7% per year.

Farmers will continue using the 10% interest rate on the original note. To do so, it must value the restructured note payments using a 10% effective interest rate. Farmers then shows a loss for the difference between the present value of the restructured note, which is $32,232, and the carrying value of the original note ($33,000).[14]

The entries made by both companies are:

The present value factor for a single payment due in two years at 10% is 0.82645. The value of the note is $39,000 × 0.82645, or $32,232 (rounded).

Harper Companies (Borrower)

(a) To record the modified note (when sum of restructured cash flows is greater than note book value plus accrued interest):

DR	Note payable	$30,000	
DR	Interest payable	3,000	
	CR Restructured note payable		$33,000

Farmers Suppliers Ltd. (Lender)

(a) To record the modified note (when sum of restructured cash flows is greater than note book value plus accrued interest):

DR	Restructured note receivable	$32,232	
DR	Loss on receivable restructuring	768	
	CR Note receivable		$30,000
	CR Interest receivable		3,000

Both companies accrue interest beginning on the debt restructuring date (January 1, 2001) and ending on the maturity date of the restructured note (December 31, 2002). But they will *not* use the same interest rate. The borrower, Harper, will record annual interest at 8.7% of the note's carrying value at the beginning of each year, whereas Farmers will use a 10% annual rate. The entries for the next two years would be:

Harper Companies (Borrower)

(a) To record interest on December 31, 2001:

DR	Interest expense	$2,871	
	CR Restructured note payable		$2,871

($2,871 = $33,000 × 8.7%)

(b) To record interest on December 31, 2002:

DR	Interest expense	$3,121	
	CR Restructured note payable		$3,121

($3,121 = [$33,000 + $2,871] × 8.7%)

Farmers Suppliers Ltd. (Lender)

(a) To record interest on December 31, 2001:

DR	Restructured note receivable	$3,223	
	CR Interest income		$3,223

($3,223 = $32,232 × 10%)

(b) To record interest on December 31, 2002:

DR	Restructured note receivable	$3,546	
	CR Interest income		$3,546

($3,546 = [$32,232 + $3,223] × 10%)

Over time, the note payable at Harper and the note receivable at Farmers grow to the final balance of $39,000, the required payment at maturity.

	Harper	Farmers
Restructured note, initial carrying amount	$33,000	$32,232
Accrued interest expense, Harper:		
2001	2,871	
2002	3,121	
Accrued interest revenue, Farmers:		
2001		3,223
2002		3,546
Note carrying amount, December 31, 2002	$39,000*	$39,000*

*Rounded.

The previous example involves a restructured loan in which the total restructured cash flows are greater than the carrying value of the troubled debt. Now let's examine a situation in which the sum of the future cash flows is *less* than the carrying value of the troubled debt.

Suppose Farmers waives all interest payments and defers all principal payments until December 31, 2002 (as in the White Rose example in Exhibit 8.3). The restructured cash payments ($30,000) are *less* than the carrying value of the original receivable ($33,000). Harper will show a gain on the debt restructuring, and all subsequent payments will be treated as a reduction of the restructured principal. No interest expense is recorded by Harper. Farmers, on the other hand, follows the procedures outlined in the previous example. The restructured note is valued at $24,794 (using the 10% effective interest rate from the original note), a debt restructuring loss is recorded, and interest income is accrued to maturity. The entries made at the restructuring date would be:

> The $24,794 is just the present value of $30,000 received in two years at 10%, or $24,794 = $30,000 × 0.82645.

Harper Companies (Borrower)

(a) To record the modified note (restructured cash flows less than note book value):

DR	Note payable	$30,000	
DR	Interest payable	3,000	
	CR Restructured note payable		$30,000
	CR Gain on debt restructuring		3,000

Farmers Suppliers Ltd. (Lender)

(a) To record the modified note (restructured cash flows less than note book value):

DR	Restructured note receivable	$24,794	
DR	Loss on receivable restructuring	8,206	
	CR Note receivable		$30,000
	CR Interest receivable		3,000

Harper would not record any interest over the life of the restructured note. The $30,000 cash payment on December 31, 2002 would reduce the outstanding balance of Harper's restructured note payable. Farmers still records interest income over the life of the note. These entries would be:

Harper Companies (Borrower)
(No entries are made until the cash payment at maturity.)

Farmers Suppliers Ltd. (Lender)

(a) To record interest on December 31, 2001:

    DR   Restructured note receivable $2,479

        CR   Interest income $2,479

    ($2,479 = $24,794 × 10%)

(b) To record interest on December 31, 2002:

    DR   Restructured note receivable $2,727

        CR   Interest income $2,727

    ($2,727 = [$24,794 + $2,479] × 10%)

The note receivable balance at Farmers will grow to $30,000 at maturity.

Summary

GAAP require that accounts receivable be shown at their net realizable value. This means that gross accounts receivable must be reduced by the amount of estimated uncollectibles and returns/adjustments. Companies use one of two methods to estimate uncollectible accounts, (1) the sales revenue approach or (2) the gross accounts receivable approach. Under either approach, firms must periodically assess the reasonableness of the uncollectibles balance by performing an aging of accounts receivable.

When receivables growth exceeds sales growth, this could indicate that aggressive revenue recognition practices are being used. For this reason, careful analysis of period-to-period trends is necessary to determine whether the reported receivables arise from real sales.

In certain long-term credit sales transactions, interest must be imputed by determining the note receivable's present value. This is necessary to distinguish between income from the sale and interest income, which might be recognized in different periods.

Firms sometimes transfer or dispose of receivables before their due date in order to accelerate cash collection. Sales of receivables—also called factoring—can be with or without recourse. Receivables are also occasionally used as collateral for a loan. In analyzing these transactions, it is sometimes not obvious whether the transaction to accelerate cash collection represents a sale or a borrowing; however, the AcSB has provided guidelines for distinguishing between sales (where the transferor surrenders control over the receivables) and borrowings (where control is not surrendered). Receivables that are transferred get removed from the balance sheet. Analysts must be alert to the possibility that the "missing" receivables distort the true relationship between receivables' and sales' growth rates.

Banks and other holders of receivables will frequently restructure the terms of the receivable when a customer is unable to make required payments. These troubled debt restructurings can take one of two forms, (1) settlement or (2) continuation with modification of debt terms. When terms are modified, the precise accounting treatment depends on whether the sum of future cash flows under the restructured note is above or below the note's book value at the restructuring date.

Self-Study Problem: Roomkin & Juris Department Stores Securitization

Roomkin & Juris is a department store chain in the western United States. In September 2001, it created a legally separate trust (R & J Trust) to serve as the special purpose entity for securitizing US$1,000,000 of customer receivables. Customers are charged an interest rate of 12% per year on unpaid receivable balances. The receivables were sold to the trust that in turn issued US$1,000,000 of two-year 9% per annum notes collateralized by the receivables. Interest on the notes is paid quarterly. Roomkin & Juris services the accounts and remits a portion of the cash collected to the trust. The R & J Trust uses this cash to make all required payments to the investors. Because the receivables are constantly turning over, this is what is called a **revolving securitization.** The amount of collateral must be maintained at the original amount (here US$1,000,000) less any credit losses (which, assume, are borne by the investors). Three transactions in 2001 were related to the securitization:

- *September 30:* Roomkin & Juris sells receivables with a book value of US$980,000 (i.e., gross receivables of US$1,000,000 and an allowance for uncollectibles of US$20,000) to the trust for US$995,000.

- *October 1–December 29:* Roomkin & Juris collects US$692,500 from customers on the receivables sold to the trust. This amount represents payment of both the principal portion of the receivables and interest.

- *December 30:* Roomkin & Juris transfers US$692,500 of new receivables and cash to the trust to replenish the collateral base and to allow it to make required interest payments.

1. **Record the sale of the receivables on Roomkin & Juris' books.**
   The journal entry is:

DR Cash	$995,000	
DR Allowance for uncollectibles	20,000	
CR Accounts receivable		$1,000,000
CR Gain on sale of receivables		15,000

   Because the investors bear all credit losses, the allowance that relates to the sold receivables is removed from the books. The journal entry presumes that Roomkin & Juris do not charge a fee for servicing the accounts. The US$15,000 gain is the value created by securitization—it's what investors are willing to pay over and above the book value of the receivables.

2. **Record Roomkin & Juris' cash collections on the sold receivables.**
   The journal entry is:

DR Cash	$692,500	
CR Due to R & J Trust		$692,500

   The collateral must be maintained at US$1,000,000 less any credit losses. (Remember, investors bear all credit losses in this securitization.) So Roomkin & Juris must replace the receivables principal that has been repaid by the customers, plus US$22,500 cash to cover the fourth quarter 2001 interest payment on the notes ($1,000,000 × 9% × $\frac{1}{4}$ = $22,500). This total is US$692,500.

3. **Record the asset transfer to the R & J Trust.**

   The journal entry is:

DR	Due to R & J Trust	$692,500	
	CR Accounts receivable		$670,000
	CR Cash		22,500

   Since some of the original accounts receivable have been collected, the collateral is now replenished by a transfer of US$670,000 of *new* receivables to the R & J Trust. US$22,500 cash enables the trust to make the quarterly interest payment on the notes.

4. **What happens in September 2003 when the R & J Trust repays the principal amount of the notes?**

   Over the two years, the collateral has been maintained at US$1,000,000 minus any credit losses. Let's assume that the receivables collateral balance is US$984,000 on September 30, 2003, when the notes are due; that is, credit losses were US$16,000 ($1,000,000 – $984,000). The amount of principal repayment that the investors will receive is US$984,000. Roomkin & Juris will remit that amount in cash to the R & J Trust. Since the securitization has terminated, collateral is no longer needed and the receivables are transferred back from the R & J Trust to the department store. The entry on Roomkin & Juris' books is:

DR	Accounts receivable	$984,000	
	CR Cash		$984,000

Exercises

E8-1 Account analysis

For the month of December 2001, the records of Pilot Corporation show the following information:

Cash received on accounts receivable	$135,000
Cash sales	30,000
Accounts receivable, December 1, 2001	80,000
Accounts receivable, December 31, 2001	84,000
Accounts receivable written off as uncollectible	2,000

Required:

Determine the gross sales for the month of December 2001.

E8-2 Account analysis

At the close of its first year of operations, on December 31, 2001, Alpha Company had accounts receivable of $250,000, which were *net* of the related allowance for doubtful accounts. During 2001, the company had charges to bad debt expense of $40,000 and wrote off, as uncollectible, accounts receivable of $10,000.

Required:

What should the company report on its balance sheet at December 31, 2001, as accounts receivable *before* the allowance for doubtful accounts?

E8-3 Ratio effects of writeoffs

Pen Company wrote off a $1,000 bad debt against the $14,000 balance in its allowance account.

Required:

For the following amounts or ratios, determine the relationship between the amount or ratio before the writeoff (x) and the amount or ratio after the writeoff (y):

Amount or Ratio	Possibilities
1. Current ratio	a. x greater than y
2. Net accounts receivable balance	b. x equals y
3. Gross accounts receivable balance	c. x less than y
4. Return on assets	d. Cannot be determined

E8-4 Bad debt expense

The following information is available for the Milano Company:

Credit sales during 2001	$175,000
Allowance for doubtful accounts at December 31, 2000	3,100
Accounts receivable deemed worthless and written off during 2001	1,900

During 2001, Milano estimated that its bad debt expense should be 1% of all credit sales.

As a result of a review and aging of accounts receivable in early January 2002, it has been determined that an allowance for doubtful accounts of $1,800 is needed at December 31, 2001.

Required:

What is the total amount that Milano should record as bad debt expense for the year ended December 31, 2001?

E8-5 Amortization table

Booker Company sold some machinery to Pam Company on January 1, 2002, for which the cash selling price was $822,240. Pam entered into an installment sales contract with Booker at an interest rate of 6.9%. The contract required payments of $200,000 a year over five years, with the first payment due on December 31, 2002.

Required:

Prepare an amortization schedule that shows what portion of each $200,000 payment will be shown as interest income over the period 2002–2006.

E8-6 Discounted note

Bye Company received a $75,000, six-month, 12% interest-bearing note from a customer. The note was discounted the same day at National Bank at 13%.

Required:

Compute the amount of cash received by Bye from the bank.

E8-7 Accounts receivable and bad debt

Lumonics Inc. reported accounts receivable of $31,673,000 and $45,096,000 as at December 31, 1998 and 1997, net of an allowance for doubtful accounts of $311,000 and $191,000, respectively. The company provided the following analysis of the allowance account:

Description	Balance at Beginning of Period	Charged to Costs and Expenses	Charged to Other Accounts	Deductions	Balance at End of Period
Lumonics Inc.					
Schedule II—Valuation and Qualifying Accounts					
Year ended December 31, 1996, allowance for doubtful accounts	$293	$59	—	$131	$221
Year ended December 31, 1997, allowance for doubtful accounts	221	15	—	45	191
Year ended December 31, 1998, allowance for doubtful accounts	191	109	—	(11)	311

Required:

1. Prepare all journal entries associated with receivables.
2. The company reported sales of $144,192,000 and $177,328,000 in fiscal 1998 and 1997, with gross profits of $40,673,000 and $65,922,000, respectively. Any comments?

Problems/Discussion Questions

P8-1 Comprehensive receivables and allowance analysis

On January 1, 2002, Hussain Corporation reports the following information pertaining to its accounts receivable:

Accounts receivable (gross)	$20,000
Less: Allowance for uncollectibles	(2,000)
Accounts receivable (net)	$18,000

For the year ended December 31, 2002, Hussain Corporation had credit sales of $100,000. Collections for the year amounted to $92,000, of which $16,000 was from 2001 sales and $76,000 was from current year's sales. Bad debts written off during the year totalled $9,000; $4,000 of this total pertained to receivables outstanding as of January 1, 2002, and $5,000 was from this year's sales. On December 31, 2002, the company prepared the following aging schedule to determine the ending balance in the allowance for uncollectibles:

Aging Information	Book Value	Expected Bad Debts
Over 90 days old	$2,000	30%
31–90 days old	7,000	20
Current (0–30 days)	(To be computed by you)	10

Required:

1. Provide journal entries to record the preceding transactions as well as year-end bad debt expense. Compute the ending accounts receivable and allowance balances.
2. Show how the accounts receivable balance you computed will be disclosed in the balance sheet as of December 31, 2002.
3. Show how much of the bad debt expense for 2002 relates to actual and expected future writeoffs from 2002 sales versus prior years' sales.

P8-2 Interest schedule

On December 31, 2002, Sea Containers Ltd., a company located in Hamilton, Bermuda, reported notes receivable of US$63,930,000. This amount represents the present value of future cash flows (both principal and interest) discounted at a rate of 11.12% per annum. The schedule of collections of the receivables is provided next (US$ in thousands).

Year Ending December	Collections
2003	$20,724
2004	15,896
2005	11,559
2006	7,179
2007	8,559
2008	13
	$63,930

Assume that the interest due is paid along with the face value of the receivables at the end of each year.

Required:

Provide journal entries to record the interest received as well as the collection of the notes receivable.

P8-3 Account analysis

The following information is adapted from the financial statements of Buck Hill Falls Company. The company provides recreational facilities, water and sewage services, miscellaneous maintenance services, etc. to residents of Buck Hill Falls, Monroe County, Pennsylvania.

	Buck Hill Falls Company Fiscal Years Ended October 31		
(US$)	1996	1995	1994
From Income Statements			
Revenues	$2,175,475	$2,218,139	$2,203,529
Provision for doubtful accounts	20,585	150,631	95,241
From Balance Sheets			
Gross accounts receivable	$ 353,723	$ 325,229	$ 210,758
(–) Allowance for doubtful accounts	(100,445)	(79,860)	(35,000)
Net accounts receivable	$ 253,278	$ 245,369	$ 175,758

Note: Bad debt expense is frequently referred to as "provision for doubtful accounts."

Required:

1. Reconstruct all the journal entries pertaining to "Gross accounts receivable" and "Allowance for doubtful accounts" (i.e., "Allowance for uncollectibles") for the fiscal years ended October 31, 1995 and October 31, 1996. You may assume that all revenues are from credit sales.
2. Try to identify scenarios consistent with the allowance and writeoff activity reported over the 1994–96 period.

P8-4 Cash discounts and returns

On January 1, 2002, Hillock Brewing Company sold 50,000 bottles of beer to various customers for $45,000 using credit terms of 3/10, n/30. These credit terms mean that customers will get a cash discount of 3% of invoice price for payments made within 10 days of the sale (this is what the 3/10 signifies). If payment is not made within 10 days, then the entire invoice price is due no later than the 30th day (this is what the n/30 signifies). At the time of sale, Hillock expects sales returns of 5%. On January 9, 2002, customers made payment on one-half of the total receivables. They returned goods with a selling price of $2,000 on January 15, 2002. The balance due was paid on January 28, 2002.

Required:

1. Provide journal entries to record the preceding transactions in the books of Hillock Company; assume that Hillock records *expected* sales returns at the time of sales.
2. Redo Question 1 assuming that customers returned goods with a selling price of $3,000 on January 15, 2002.
3. Provide journal entries to record the preceding transactions in the books of Hillock Company; assume that Hillock records sales returns when customers actually return the goods.
4. Since the net sales revenue is the same under both methods—Questions 1 and 3—what is the advantage of recording anticipated sales returns rather than waiting to record them when the customers actually return the goods?
5. Assuming that the incremental annualized borrowing rate for a customer is 18%, are customers better off paying within 10 days to get the discount or should they wait to pay until the 30th day?

P8-5 Factoring receivables

Atherton Manufacturing Company sold $200,000 of accounts receivable (with a corresponding balance of $4,000 in the allowance for uncollectibles) without recourse to a factor with notification (i.e., the customers were instructed to mail their cheques directly to the factor). While the factor was liable for all bad debts, Atherton was responsible for sales returns. The factor charged 12% per annum interest on the gross receivables for a period of one month (which is the expected weighted average time to maturity of the receivables) plus a factoring fee of 6%, both of which were deducted by the factor from the value of receivables. A 5% holdback was retained by the factor for expected sales returns. The customers returned inventory with a selling price of $3,000. All remaining accounts were settled and the factor paid the balance due. The factor incurred actual bad debts of $7,500. Assume that Atherton records sales returns only when goods are returned (i.e., it does not record an allowance for sales returns).

Required:

1. Provide journal entries to record the preceding transactions.

In answering Questions 2 and 3, make the following modified assumptions:

- Atherton Manufacturing Company transfers $200,000 of accounts receivable (with a corresponding balance of $4,000 in the allowance for uncollectibles) *with full recourse* to a factor *without notification* (i.e., the customers continue to mail the cheques to Atherton). Using the cash collected from the customers, Atherton repays the factor.

- The factor charged a factoring fee of 2.5%.
- A 7% holdback was retained by the factor; 5% of this holdback pertained to expected sales returns and the additional 2% to bad debts.
- The actual bad debts were $5,500.

2. Now assume that the transfer of receivables was considered a "sale." Provide journal entries to record the preceding transactions.
3. Now assume that the transfer of receivables was considered a "borrowing." Provide journal entries to record the preceding transactions.

P8-6 Reconstructing T-accounts

The following information is taken from the financial statements of Vibrant Health Care Inc.:

	Excerpts from Balance Sheets as of:	
	June 30, 2001	June 30, 2000
Gross accounts receivable	$26,944,000	$31,651,000
Allowance for doubtful accounts	(3,925,000)	(4,955,000)
Net accounts receivable	$23,019,000	$26,696,000

	Excerpts from Income Statements for the Years Ended:		
	June 30, 2001	June 30, 2000	June 30, 1999
Revenue	$137,002,000	$136,354,000	$136,946,000
Provision for doubtful accounts	5,846,000	8,148,000	8,628,000
Operating income before taxes	6,900,000	(1,048,000)	9,321,000

Note: Bad debt expense is frequently referred to as "provision for doubtful accounts."

Required:

1. Reconstruct all the journal entries relating to "Gross accounts receivable" and "Allowance for doubtful accounts" (i.e., "Allowance for uncollectibles") for the fiscal year ended June 30, 2001. You may assume that all revenues are from credit sales.
2. Assume that the company computes its bad debt expense by multiplying sales revenues by some percentage. (This is called the sales revenue approach.) Recalculate the bad debt expense (i.e., "Provision for doubtful accounts") for the fiscal year 2001; assume that Vibrant estimated the 2001 bad debts at the same percentage of revenue as it did in 2000. Using the revised figure, show how "Gross accounts receivable" and "Allowance for doubtful accounts" would be presented as of the end of the fiscal year 2001. Also calculate a revised operating income before taxes using the revised figure for bad debt expense.
3. In answering this question, assume that the company is using the gross accounts receivable approach to estimate its bad debt expense (i.e., for convenience, assume that "Allowance for doubtful accounts" is fixed as a percentage of gross receivables). Recalculate the bad debts expense for the fiscal year 2001 *and* the ending balance in "Allowance for doubtful accounts" at the end of the fiscal year 2001; assume that Vibrant estimated the expected bad debts at the same percentage of receivables as it did in 2000. Also, calculate the revised operating income before taxes using the revised figure for bad debt expense.

4. On the basis of your answers to Questions 2 and 3, what inferences can be drawn about Vibrant's accounts receivables management and the adequacy of the allowance for doubtful accounts?

P8-7 Accounting for transfer of receivables

The following footnotes are excerpted from the financial statements of five companies:

Hudson's Bay Company, January 31, 1998

Note No. 7—Credit Card Receivables

Under a securitization program the Company has sold, with limited recourse, undivided co-ownership interests in certain of its credit card receivables to an independent Trust, amounting to $500 million: $200 million on January 30, 1998 and $300 million on January 27, 1997. No gain or loss has been recorded by the Company as a result of these transactions. The Company services these accounts and pays to the Trust a portion of service charge revenues derived from the sold co-ownership interests equal to the Trust's stipulated share thereof.

Canadian National Railway Company, December 31, 1998

Note No. 5—Accounts Receivable

(in millions)	December 31, 1998	1997
Freight:		
Trade	$217	$504
Accrued	48	43
Non-freight	180	178
	445	725
Provision for doubtful accounts	(41)	(44)
	$404	$681

On June 25, 1998, the Company entered into a revolving agreement to sell eligible freight trade receivables. The agreement, which expires in June 2003, allows for sales of freight trade receivables up to a maximum of $250 million. At December 31, 1998, $150 million and US$45 million (CDN$69 million) had been sold on a limited recourse basis, pursuant to the agreement. The Company has retained the responsibility for servicing and collecting the accounts receivable sold. Costs related to the agreement, which fluctuates with changes in prevailing interest rates, are included in Other income.

Ricoh Company Ltd., March 31, 1994

Note No. 7—Short-Term Borrowings and Trade Notes Receivable Discounted with Banks

The Company and certain of its domestic subsidiaries regularly discount trade notes receivable on a full recourse basis with banks. These trade notes receivable discounted are contingent liabilities. The weighted average interest rates on these trade notes receivable discounted were 4.2% and 3.2% as of March 31, 1993 and 1994, respectively.

Crown Crafts Inc., March 31, 1994

Note No. 4—Financing Arrangements

Factoring Agreement
The Company assigns substantially all of its trade accounts receivable to a commercial factor. Under the terms of the factoring agreement, the factor remits invoiced amounts to the Company on the approximate due dates of the factored invoices. The Company does not borrow funds from its fac- tor or take advances against its factored receivables bal- ances. Accounts are factored without recourse as to credit losses but with recourse as to returns, allowances, dis- putes and discounts. Factoring fees included in marketing and administrative expenses in the consolidated state- ments of earnings were: US$1,501,000 (1994), US$1,223,000 (1993) and US$1,077,000 (1992).

Foxmeyer Corporation, March 31, 1994

Note C—Accounts Receivable Financing
On October 29, 1993, the Corporation entered into a one year agreement to sell a percentage ownership interest in a defined pool of the Corporation's trade accounts receiv- able with limited recourse. Proceeds of $125.0 million from the sale were used to reduce amounts outstanding under the Corporation's revolving credit facilities. Generally, an undivided interest in new accounts receivable will be sold daily as existing accounts receivable are collected to main- tain the participation interest at $125.0 million. Such accounts receivable sold are not included in the accompa- nying consolidated balance sheet at March 31, 1994. An allowance for doubtful accounts has been retained on the participation interest sold based on estimates of the Corporation's risk of credit loss from its obligation under the recourse provisions. The cost of the accounts receivable financing program is based on a 30-day commercial paper rate plus certain fees. The total cost of the program in 1994 was $2.2 million and was charged against "Other income" in the accompanying consolidated statements of income. Under the agreement, the Corporation also acts as agent for the purchaser by performing recordkeeping and collec- tion functions on the participation interest sold. The agree- ment contains certain covenants regarding the quality of the accounts receivable portfolio, as well as other covenants which are substantially identical to those con- tained in the Corporation's credit facilities.

Required:

How do the five companies record the transfer of their receivables—that is, as a sale or borrowing? Is their accounting treatment consistent with the economics of the transac- tions? Explain.

Cases

C8-1 Inco Limited: Comprehensive receivables

Appearing next is information pertaining to the "Allowance for doubtful accounts" account of Inco Limited. Examine this information and answer the following questions (thousands of $US).

INCO LIMITED
www.inco.com

	1997	1996	1995
Allowance for Doubtful Accounts			
Balance, beginning of year	7,424	?	?
Provision charged to expense	?	567	689
Writeoffs, less recoveries	1,132	?	898
Balance, end of year	7,769	?	7,165

Required:

1. Solve for the unknowns in the schedule given above.
2. Make all entries related to the "Allowance for doubtful accounts" account for fiscal years 1995–97.
3. Make all entries for bad debts for fiscal years 1995–97 assuming Inco did not accrue for estimated bad debt losses but instead recorded bad debt expense once receivables were determined to be uncollectible. (This is called the direct writeoff method.)
4. Discuss the rationale for preferring the allowance method over the direct write-off method.
5. Calculate the cumulative difference in reported income under the allowance and direct writeoff methods over the 1995–97 period. Comment on your finding.
6. Assume that it is the end of 1998 and Inco's managers are trying to decide on the amount of the bad debt expense for 1998. On the basis of an aging of accounts receivable, the accounting department feels that a provision of US$7.0 million is appropriate. However, the company just found out that a customer with an outstanding account receivable of US$10.0 million may have to file for bankruptcy. The decision facing Inco managers is whether to increase the initial provision of US$7.0 million by US$10.0 million, by some lesser amount, or by nothing at all. What is your recommendation?
7. Consider the following information. Assume that you are a manager of Inco Limited and have a cash bonus plan that is a function of reported earnings before income taxes. In particular, assume that you receive an annual cash bonus of zero if earnings before income taxes is below US$100 million and 1.0% of the amount by which earnings before income taxes exceeds US$100 million up to a maximum bonus of US$1 million (i.e., when net income reaches US$200 million, no further bonus can be earned). What adjustment to the initial US$7.0-million bad debt provision might you decide on in each of the following scenarios?
   (a) Earnings before income taxes (including the initial US$7.0-million provision for bad debts) is US$65.0 million.
   (b) Earnings before income taxes (including the initial US$7.0-million provision for bad debts) is US$110.0 million.
   (c) Earnings before income taxes (including the initial US$7.0-million provision for bad debts) is US$225.0 million.
   (d) Earnings before income taxes (including the initial US$7.0-million provision for bad debts) is US$205.0 million.

8. What other settings/situations can you identify in which managers may use the provision for bad debts to accomplish some contract-related strategy?
9. Identify other items in the financial statements (besides the bad debt provision) that managers have the ability to "manage."
10. Discuss how each of the following may permit managers to "manage" earnings:
    (a) selecting accounting principles
    (b) classifying income statement items
    (c) timing transactions

C8-2 Spiegel Inc. (KR): Analyzing receivables growth

You have recently been hired as an equity analyst at a large mutual fund. During your first week, you receive the following memo:

> Welcome to Vitality Mutual Funds. I am sure you are excited to join our firm as a financial analyst. I am currently looking at the financial statements of Spiegel Inc., which is a multi-channel specialty company that owns Spiegel, Eddie Bauer and Newport News. The company also owns First Consumers National Bank ("FCNB"). FCNB is a special purpose bank limited to the issuance of credit cards, primarily FCNB Preferred Charge cards for use by Spiegel, Eddie Bauer and Newport News customers. I need your assistance in analyzing the company's accounts receivable. I did some cursory analysis and identified some very interesting trends. During 1994 and 1995, the growth in sales has outpaced the growth in receivables. In fact, during 1995, while the company's net sales grew at around 7%, its receivables decreased by more than 30%! I am quite pleased with the improvement in receivables management. In fact, the receivables collection period has dropped from around 140 days to less than 120 days. This is quite impressive given that the company relies very heavily on installment sales to generate a substantial majority of its revenue. However, I am not sure how Spiegel is accounting for the sale of receivables or how the factoring of receivables impacts my calculations. One additional thing that I can't understand is why Spiegel is showing a portion of the allowance for sales returns under accrued liabilities. I am under the impression that such allowance accounts are contra-asset accounts. What I need from you is a succinct report (with supporting analysis) addressing the issues that I have raised in this memo. To help you in your analysis, I have included below some information that I have on the company. Good luck.
>
> Sincerely,
>
> Maria S. Kang
> Senior Analyst
> Vitality Mutual Funds

The following table provides an adapted breakdown of the net receivables balance reported in comparative balance sheets:

	As of December 31,		
(in US$)	1995	1994	1993
Receivables generated from operations	$2,001,081	$1,683,444	$1,403,618
Receivables sold	(1,180,000)	(480,000)	(330,000)
Receivables owned	821,081	1,203,444	1,073,618
Less: Allowance for returns	(37,769)	(27,762)	(28,238)
Less: Allowance for doubtful accounts	(40,832)	(49,954)	(46,855)
Receivables—net (from balance sheet)	$ 742,480	$1,125,728	$ 998,525

During 1995, 1994, and 1993, the company transferred portions of its customer receivables to trusts which, in turn, sold certificates representing undivided interests in the trusts to investors. These transactions are similar to the factoring of receivables, except that a group of investors, as opposed to a single factor, is investing in the receivables of Spiegel. Certificates sold were US$700,000 in 1995 (under two separate transactions of US$350,000 each) and US$150,000 and US$330,000 (in 1994 and 1993, respectively). As a result of these transactions, other revenue increased by US$18,637 and US$10,658 in 1995 and 1994, respectively, representing the gain on only the sold receivables that existed at the date of the sale. The receivables were *sold without recourse,* and the bad debt reserve related to the net receivables sold has been reduced accordingly. Note that Spiegel is still responsible for sales returns, although the investors in the securitized receivables bear the bad debt risk. As cash is collected from the customers, Spiegel pays only the required interest portion to the investors and reinvests the remaining cash flows in new accounts receivable that are generated (i.e., the investors are continually refinancing the receivables of Spiegel over the duration of the securitization agreement). The company owns the remaining undivided interest in the trusts not represented by the certificates (i.e., Spiegel is retaining ownership of a portion of the securitized receivables which is included under "Receivables owned"). In addition, the company *will service all receivables for the trusts* (i.e., Spiegel is performing the administrative aspects of collecting and distributing the cash flows from the receivables).

The company reported the following sales figures over the three-year period:

	For the Years Ended December 31,		
(in US$)	1995	1994	1993
Net sales	$2,886,225	$2,706,791	$2,337,235

In addition, the following table provides information on the company's allowance for doubtful accounts over the same period:

	Allowance for Doubtful Accounts		
(in US$)	1995	1994	1993
Beginning balance	$49,954	$46,855	$37,231
Charged to earnings	91,612	79,183	69,160
Reduction for receivables sold	(33,600)	(6,300)	(1,609)
Other	—	—	695
Accounts written off	(67,134)	(69,784)	(58,622)
Ending balance	$40,832	$49,954	$46,855

"Other" represents the beginning balance of Newport News, which was acquired in 1993.

The company's accrued liabilities at the end of 1995 include "Allowance for returns" of US$31,927. Such breakdown is not available for the prior two years.

The following footnote describes the company's revenue recognition policy:

Revenue Recognition

Sales made under installment accounts represent a substantial portion of net sales. The Company provides for returns at the time of sale based upon projected merchandise returns.

Required:

Provide the analysis requested by Ms Kang including journal entries which show how Spiegel accounts for the sale of receivables.

C8-3 Sears Canada's credit operations

Sears is regarded as Canada's largest single full-line retailer of general merchandise. It has department and specialty stores, and catalogue selling locations, across the country. In its 1998 annual report for the 52-week period ended January 2, 1999, Sears Canada Inc. included the following, each of which is presented below:

- an 11-year summary of results
- an MD&A analysis of the company's credit operation
- a discussion of its securitization of charge account receivables

Assume the dollar amounts are in Canadian dollars throughout this case.

SEARS CANADA INC.
www.sears.ca

Required:

1. Has the quality of Sears' accounts receivables increased or decreased over the past year? What is your evidence?
2. Comment on Sears' financial results over the past several years.
3. What impact have the following had on the company?
   (a) acceptance of third-party credit cards
   (b) acceptance of debit cards
4. Explain the details of the securitization of charge accounts receivable, perhaps using a diagram.
5. What is the economic motivation for the securitization program?
6. Explain why, as shown in the company's discussion of its securitization of charge account receivables, Sears Canada Inc.'s debt ratings are *less than* Sears Canada Receivables Trust's.
7. Has the securitization program affected the interpretation of Sears Canada's financial results in the 11-year summary? Explain.

Eleven Year Summary[1]

Fiscal Year	1998	1997	1996	1995	1994	1993	1992	1991	1990	1989	1988
Results for the Year (in millions)											
Total revenues	$4,967	$4,584	$3,956	$3,918	$4,066	$4,032	$4,042	$4,169	$4,642	$4,621	$4,377
Depreciation	96	78	78	74	67	69	70	56	55	48	47
Earnings (loss) before unusual items and income taxes	269	215	70	43	88	15	(101)	(31)	70	186	175
Unusual items gain (loss)	0	0	(45)	(21)	(5)	(5)	(46)	(8)	(31)	0	0
Earnings (loss) before income taxes	269	215	25	22	83	10	(147)	(39)	39	186	175
Income taxes (recovery)	123	99	16	10	38	6	(56)	(10)	19	83	82
Net earnings (loss)	146	116	9	12	45	4	(91)	(29)	20	103	93
Dividends declared	25	25	23	23	23	23	21	20	20	21	21
Capital expenditures	142	160	63	76	60	37	55	235	204	116	118
Year End Position (in millions)											
Accounts receivable	$1,100	$1,225	$1,033	$ 926	$1,324	$1,101	$ 909	$1,090	$1,877	$1,784	$1,496
Inventories	739	640	491	507	559	563	628	693	665	807	747
Net capital assets	868	825	744	763	800	813	941	997	803	665	572
Total assets	3,198	3,007	2,734	2,554	2,949	2,746	2,796	3,069	3,581	3,512	3,103
Working capital	898	971	741	661	1,016	888	885	1,112	1,486	1,451	1,177
Long-term obligations	681	836	634	662	1,032	947	1,063	1,245	1,362	1,185	964
Shareholders' equity	1,164	1,042	949	856	867	845	863	900	948	970	883
Per Share of Capital Stock (in dollars)											
Net earnings (loss)	$ 1.38	$ 1.10	$ 0.09	$ 0.13	$ 0.47	$ 0.05	$(1.04)	$(0.34)	$ 0.25	$ 1.23	$ 1.11
Dividends declared	0.24	0.24	0.24	0.24	0.24	0.24	0.24	0.24	0.24	0.24	0.24
Shareholders' equity	10.98	9.84	8.98	9.02	9.13	8.90	9.10	10.67	11.25	11.26	10.27
Financial Ratios											
Return on average shareholders' equity (%)	13.3	11.7	1.0	1.4	5.2	0.5	(10.3)	(3.1)	2.2	11.4	11.2
Current ratio	1.7	1.9	1.7	1.7	2.0	2.0	2.1	2.4	2.3	2.1	2.0
Return on total revenues (%)	2.9	2.5	0.2	0.3	1.1	0.1	(2.2)	(0.7)	0.5	2.3	2.2
Debt/Equity ratio	42/58	45/55	46/54	48/52	59/41	58/42	59/41	61/39	67/33	66/134	65/35
Pre-tax margin (%)	5.4	4.7	0.6	0.6	2.0	0.3	(3.6)	(0.9)	0.8	4.0	4.0
Number of Selling Units											
Full-line department stores	109	110	110	110	110	110	109	106	97	92	84
Furniture stores	20	8	4	1	0	0	0	0	0	0	0
Outlet stores	12	8	9	10	11	12	13	15	18	17	16
Dealer stores	93	79	60	19	4	0	0	0	0	0	0
Catalogue selling locations	1,898	1,752	1,746	1,623	1,542	1,483	1,579	1,701	1,701	1,708	1,726

1. Certain amounts have been restated to reflect accounting changes related to the consolidation of the Company's proportionate share of the assets, liabilities, revenues and expenses of real estate joint ventures as recommended by the Canadian Institute of Chartered Accountants. The change in policy, effective in 1995, has been applied retroactively.

Management's Discussion and Analysis Extracts
Sears Canada Inc., January 2, 1999

Credit Operations ...

Sears credit operations finance and manage customer charge account receivables generated from the sale of goods and services charged on the Sears Card.

(in millions)	1998	1997
Total service charge revenues	$ 371.3	$ 364.8
Less: SCRT[2] share of revenues	(65.4)	(54.2)
Net service charge revenues	305.9	310.6
Earnings before interest and income taxes	$ 126.7	$ 127.5
Capital employed	$1,020.3	$1,090.8

[2]Refer to the section entitled "Securitization of Charge Account Receivables."

... Credit operations contributed $126.7 million to the Company's 1998 consolidated earnings before interest and income taxes, compared to $127.5 million in fiscal 1997.

Total service charge revenues earned on customer charge account receivables increased by $6.5 million or 1.8% in 1998. Fiscal 1997 contained 53 weeks. On a comparable 52 week basis, total service charge revenues increased by 3.8%. Through its securitization program, the Company securitizes customer charge account receivables in order to obtain a more favourable cost of funding. The cost of this funding is deducted from the total service charge revenues earned on the portfolio. (Refer to the section entitled "Securitization of Charge Account Receivables" ... .)

Charge Account Receivables Analysis

(in millions—except average outstanding account balance per customer)	1998	1997
Active customer accounts	3.9	3.8
Average outstanding balance per customer account at year end	$441	$439
Charge account receivables written-off during the year (net of recoveries)	$44.4	$46.4

Net write-offs as a percentage of the monthly average amounts outstanding were 2.9% in 1998 compared to 3.2% in 1997 and 3.4% in 1996. This write-off rate continues to be at the low end of industry norms. The Company maintains a low write-off rate through continued innovation of its portfolio management strategies.

Since October, 1993, Sears has been accepting third party credit cards in addition to the Sears Card. 1998 was the first full year debit cards were accepted in all of the Company's full-line stores, Sears Furniture Stores, and outlet stores. The chart below details the trend in method of payment.

	1998	1997	1996
Sears Card	62%	64%	66%
Third Party Credit Cards	13	13	11
Cash & Debit Cards	25	23	23
Total	100%	100%	100%

... Financing Activities

The Company has the flexibility to raise funds through bank borrowings, by issuing equity and corporate debt securities, and through the securitization of charge account receivables.

In 1998, the Company carried out the following significant financing activities:

→ On December 23, 1998, Sears filed a shelf prospectus with securities commissions in Canada that qualifies the issuance of up to $500 million in medium-term notes (debt with a term to maturity in excess of one year) over the next two years.

→ During 1998, long-term financing for new capital projects of real estate joint ventures was obtained in the amount of $3.4 million. In addition, $15.5 million of joint venture debt matured in 1998, of which $9.4 million was refinanced.

Securitization of Charge Account Receivables

Sears Acceptance Company Inc. ("Acceptance"), a wholly owned subsidiary of Sears, purchases all Sears Card charge account receivables (including deferred receivables) generated by merchandise and service sales. Through the Company's securitization program, Acceptance sells undivided co-ownership interests in the charge account receivables (excluding deferred receivables) to Sears Canada Receivables Trust (Trust 1) and Sears Canada Receivables Trust—1992 (Trust 2). In addition, Acceptance sells undivided co-ownership interests in its portfolio of charge account receivables (including deferred receivables) to Sears Canada Receivables Trust—1996 (Trust 3). Trust 1, Trust 2 and Trust 3 are collectively referred to as SCRT.

As the equity units of these trusts are held by independent parties, the assets and liabilities of SCRT are not reflected in the Company's consolidated financial statements. The cost to the Company of the securitization program is reflected as a reduction in the Company's share of Sears Card service charge revenues.

SCRT is an important financing vehicle which is able to obtain favourable interest rates because of its structure and the high quality of the portfolio of charge account receivables backing its debt. Securitization provides the Company with a diversified source of funds for the operation of its business.

→ *Trust 1*—Trust 1, which was established in 1991, issues short-term commercial paper to finance the purchase of undivided co-ownership interests in charge account receivables (excluding deferred receivables).

→ *Trust 2*—Trust 2, which was established in 1993, issues long-term senior and subordinated debentures to finance the purchase of undivided co-ownership interests in charge account receivables (excluding deferred receivables).

→ *Trust 3*—Trust 3, which was established in 1996, finances the purchase of undivided co-ownership interests in Acceptance's portfolio of charge account receivables (including deferred receivables) through drawdowns under revolving senior and subordinated note facilities.

Summary of Debt Ratings

	CBRS	DBRS
Sears Canada Inc.:		
Unsecured debentures	B++ (High)	BBB
SCRT:		
Commercial paper (Trust 1)[4]	A-1+	R-1 (High)
Senior debentures (Trust 2)[4]	A++	AAA
Subordinated debentures (Trust 2)	A	A (High)
Senior notes (Trust 3)[4]	A++	AAA
Subordinated notes (Trust 3)	A+	A

[4]Highest rating assigned by CBRS Inc. (CBRS) and Dominion Bond Rating Service Limited (DBRS) for this debt category.

Summary of SCRT Obligations

(in millions)	1998	1997
Commercial paper	$487.3	$374.8
Senior debt:		
6.50%, due December 16, 1998	—	150.0
5.34%, due December 16, 2003	150.0	—
8.95%, due June 1, 2004	175.0	175.0
Floating rate, due April 1, 2001	150.0	150.0
Floating rate, due June 30, 2006	122.7	43.1
	597.7	518.1

Subordinated debt:		
7.67% to 9.18%, due 1998 to 2004	3.9	7.2
Floating rate, due 1998 to 2004	31.0	13.7
Floating rate, due June 30, 2006	1.3	0.4
	36.2	21.3
Accrued liabilities	5.2	3.5
Trust units (floating rate due 1998 to 2006)	44.3	72.3
Total SCRT obligations	$1,170.7	$990.0

Capital Structure

The chart below highlights the improving trend in the debt to equity ratio, due primarily to the contribution of net earnings in 1998.

(in millions)	1998	% of Total	1997	% of Total
Long-term debt due within one year	$ 163.4	8.1	$ 11.6	0.6
Long-term debt	680.5	33.9	836.1	44.2
Total debt	843.9	42.0	847.7	44.8
Shareholders' equity	1,164.3	58.0	1,042.4	55.2
Total capital	$2,008.2	100.0	$1,890.1	100.0

Analysis of Funding Costs

The following table summarizes the Company's total funding costs including the cost of the securitization program:

(in millions)	1998	1997
Interest Costs		
Total debt at end of year	$ 843.9	$ 847.7
Average debt for year	845.5	758.4
Interest on long-term debt	$ 78.6	$ 74.5
Other interest (net)[5]	7.0	11.6
Interest expense	$ 85.6	$ 86.1
Average rate of debt[6]	10.2%	11.2%
Securitization Costs		
Amount securitized at end of year	$1,170.7	$ 990.0
Average amount securitized for year	1,056.9	1,019.6
Cost of funding	65.4	54.2
Average rate of securitized funding[6]	6.2%	5.2%
Total Funding		
Total funding at end of year	$2,014.6	$1,837.7
Total average funding for year	1,902.4	1,778.0
Total funding costs for year	151.0	140.3
Average rate of total funding[6]	8.0%	7.8%

⁵Other interest includes $8.9 million in 1998 ($13.2 million—1997) for payment of the interest rate differential on floating-to-fixed interest rate swaps.

⁶1997 calculation based on 365 day year rather than fiscal period of 53 weeks.

Total funding costs for 1998 increased by $10.7 million due primarily to higher average funding levels and higher interest rates applicable to floating rate funding outstanding in SCRT.

Integrative Running Case Study
Bombardier on the Web

The annual report for the year ended January 31, 2002 for Bombardier Inc. is located on the Companion Website at **www.pearsoned.ca/revsine**. Bombardier Capital (BC) is the financing arm of Bombardier, and information about its activities is on pages 22–23 and 50–53 of the annual report.

BC sells various loans and finance receivables, and information on these activities is disclosed on pages 57–58 of the annual report, and footnote 4.

Required:

1. Suggest economic rationales for BC's sales of loans and finance receivables. What is the role of the "Special Purpose Entities"?
2. Is it possible to conclude, on the basis of the information disclosed, whether "sales" have actually taken place?
3. Why did Bombardier Inc. set up BC as a separate entity to perform its business functions? How has BC's business changed over the past year?
4. Explain the significance of the information disclosed in footnote 4, from the perspective of assessing Bombardier Inc.'s quality of earnings.

Endnotes

1. "Net realizable value" means the selling price of an item minus reasonable further costs both to make the item ready to sell and to sell it. When applied to trade receivables, net realizable value means the amount of money the business can reasonably expect to collect from its credit customers ("Accounts and Notes Receivable," *CICA Handbook,* Section 3020).

2. See M. McNichols and G. P. Wilson, "Evidence of Earnings Management from the Provision for Bad Debts," *Journal of Accounting Research,* Supplement 1988, pp. 1–31; S. Moyer, "Capital Adequacy Ratio Regulations and Accounting Choices in Commercial Banks," *Journal of Accounting and Economics,* July 1990, pp. 123–54; M. Scholes, P. Wilson, and M. Wolfson, "Tax Planning, Regulatory Capital Planning and Financial Reporting Strategy for Commercial Banks," *Review of Financial Studies,* vol. 3, no. 4, 1990, pp. 625–50; J. Collins, D. Shackelford, and J. Wahlen, "Bank Differences in the Coordination of Regulatory Capital, Earnings, and Taxes," *Journal of Accounting Research,* Autumn 1995, pp. 263–91; A. Beatty, S. Chamberlain, and J. Magliolo, "Managing Financial Reports of Commercial Banks: The Influence of Taxes,

Regulatory Capital, and Earnings," *Journal of Accounting Research,* Autumn 1995, pp. 231–61. As the titles of these studies suggest, regulatory capital requirements in commercial banks and financial services companies also seem to exert an important influence on bad debt accruals.

3. M. Maremont, "Blind Ambition," *Business Week,* October 23, 1995, pp. 78–92.

4. Ibid., pp. 79–80.

5. Ibid., p. 86.

6. See Jonathan R. Laing, "Dangerous Games," *Barron's,* June 8, 1998.

7. See Dana Canedy, "Sunbeam Restates Results, and 'Fix' Shows Significant Warts," *New York Times,* October 21, 1998.

8. For simplicity, we ignore the periodic recording of interest on a monthly or quarterly basis during the year. In reality, if quarterly statements were prepared, the first-year interest income of $3,756.60 would be apportioned to each quarter.

9. "General Standards of Financial Statement Presentation," *CICA Handbook,* Section 1500, para. 1500.12.

10. "Contingencies," *CICA Handbook*, Section 3290.

11. *CICA Handbook*, Sections 1500 and 3290.

12. M. Maremont, op. cit., p. 90.

13. Farmers' settlement loss would be included in the computation of income from continuing operations.

14. "Impaired Loans," *CICA Handbook*, Section 3025.

9
Inventories

LEARNING OBJECTIVES
After studying this chapter, you should be able to:

1. Understand and implement the two methods used to determine inventory quantities—the perpetual inventory system and the periodic inventory system

2. Know what specific items and kinds of costs are included in inventory

3. Understand what absorption costing is and how it complicates financial analysis

4. Explain the difference between various cost flow assumptions—weighted average, FIFO, and LIFO

5. Understand how LIFO liquidations distort gross profit and how to adjust for these distortions to improve forecasts

6. Eliminate realized holding gains from FIFO income

7. Apply the lower of cost and market method and know on what assumptions the choice of method rests

A wholesaler or retailer buys assets like suits or shoes that are immediately saleable in their current form. Assets held for sale are called **inventories**. A typical wholesaler or retailer will have only one inventory account, called merchandise inventory, on its balance sheet.

A manufacturing firm makes a final product (e.g., a dishwasher) from many different inputs. A manufacturer's balance sheet typically has three categories for inventories—raw materials, work in process, and finished goods.

- **Raw materials inventory** consists of components (e.g., steel) that will eventually be used in the completed product.

- **Work-in-process inventory** includes the aggregate cost of units that have been started but not completed at the balance sheet date. This inventory category includes the costs of the raw materials, direct labour, and overhead[1] that have been incurred in the manufacture of the partially completed units.

- **Finished goods inventory** represents the total costs incorporated in completed but unsold units.

Inventories are usually a significant asset, both in absolute size and in proportion to all other assets. Indeed, with respect to a company's quality of earnings, inventory accounting is crucial. For example, Bombardier Inc.'s aerospace division manufactures regional and business jets that take many years to develop, construct, and market, thus making inventory accounting for such companies a multi-period problem.

BOMBARDIER INC.
www.bombardier.com

Mining companies, forest products companies, telecoms, and the many other types of businesses in the Canadian economy all have significant accounting issues related to inventory. Furthermore, selling inventories for a price greater than their cost represents the main source of a firm's total long-run income. For these reasons, inventory accounting is exceedingly important.

An Overview of Inventory Accounting Issues

We will use an example of a retailer who sells refrigerators to illustrate the basic issues in inventory accounting. Assume the retailer starts the year with a beginning inventory of one refrigerator, which costs $300. During the year, the cost of an identical refrigerator increases to $340, and the retailer purchases another refrigerator at this $340 cost. At the end of the year, the retailer sells one of the refrigerators for $500. Further assume that it is not possible to ascertain which of the two refrigerators was actually sold.

It is easy to determine the total cost of the goods that were available for sale by adding the cost of the beginning inventory and the cost of any purchases during the period—that is:

$$\boxed{\begin{array}{c}\text{Beginning Inventory}\\ \$300\end{array}} \;+\; \boxed{\begin{array}{c}\text{Inventory Purchases}\\ \$340\end{array}} \;=\; \boxed{\begin{array}{c}\text{Goods Available for Sale}\\ \$640\end{array}}$$

The total cost of the goods available for sale during the period was $640, which represents the aggregate *historical cost* of the two refrigerators.

The cost of the sold refrigerator must be removed from the inventory account and charged to cost of goods sold, while the cost of the other refrigerator remains in inventory. In other words, the total cost of the goods available for sale ($640) must be allocated between ending inventory and cost of goods sold. This allocation process can be represented as follows:

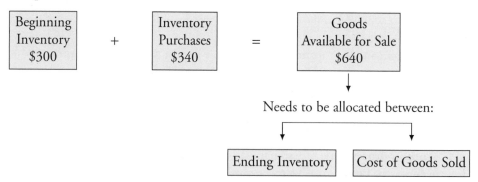

The choice of the method for making this allocation between ending inventory and cost of goods sold represents the major issue in inventory accounting.

Even in this simple case, there are at least three different ways that the total for the goods available for sale ($640) can be allocated between ending inventory and cost of goods sold:

1. Assume that the cost of the sold refrigerator should reflect the average cost of the two refrigerators (i.e., $640/2 = $320). In this case, the allocation would be:

This is called the **weighted average** inventory costing method.

2. Or, assume that the cost of the sold refrigerator should reflect the cost of the oldest refrigerator in stock—the $300 unit from the beginning inventory. So the cost assigned to the refrigerator still on hand at the end of the year would be $340, which is the cost of the most recently purchased unit. Here, the allocation would be:

This method assumes the first unit purchased is the first unit sold. Accountants call this **first-in, first-out**, or **FIFO.**

3. Yet another way is to assume the cost of the sold refrigerator should reflect the cost of the most recently purchased refrigerator—the one costing $340. So the cost assigned to the refrigerator still on hand at the end of the year would be $300, the cost of the oldest available unit in inventory at the start of the year, making the allocation:

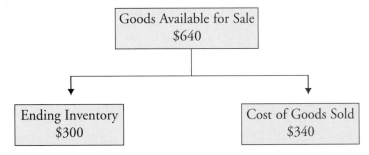

This method assumes the last unit purchased is the first unit sold. This is called **last-in, first-out**, or **LIFO.**

Each of these cost allocations assumes a different flow of inventory costs—average cost, FIFO, or LIFO—from the inventory account to the cost of goods sold expense account; this is why these methods are called *cost flow assumptions*. Generally accepted accounting principles (GAAP) do not require the *cost* flow assumption to correspond to the *physical* flow of inventory.[2] *If the cost of inventory never changed, all three cost flow assumptions would yield the same result.* Also, under historical cost accounting and no matter what cost flow assumption is used, the total dollar amount allocated between cost of goods sold and ending inventory always equals the historical dollar cost of the goods available for sale ($640 in this case). This important point is represented in the following table:

Cost Flow Assumption	Total Historical Cost of Goods Available for Sale	=	Amount Allocated to Ending Inventory	+	Amount Allocated to Cost of Goods Sold
Weighted average	$640	=	$320	+	$320
First-in, first-out (FIFO)	$640	=	$340	+	$300
Last-in, first-out (LIFO)	$640	=	$300	+	$340

Once an inventory cost flow assumption is selected, the cost of goods sold can be determined using the following formulas:

$$\boxed{\text{Beginning Inventory}} + \boxed{\text{Inventory Purchases}} = \boxed{\text{Goods Available for Sale}}$$

$$\boxed{\text{Goods Available for Sale}} - \boxed{\text{Ending Inventory}} = \boxed{\text{Cost of Goods Sold}}$$

For example, assume the ending inventory is $340. Then, under the FIFO cost flow assumption, cost of goods sold is calculated as:

Beginning inventory	$300
Merchandise purchases	+340
Goods available for sale	640
Ending FIFO inventory	−340
Cost of goods sold	$300

We kept this example simple to refresh your memory about basic inventory accounting points. Because actual business situations are more complex, questions like these may arise:

- How should physical quantities in inventory be determined?
- What items should be included in ending inventory?
- What costs should be included in inventory purchases (and eventually in ending inventory)?
- What cost flow assumption should be used for allocating goods available for sale between cost of goods sold and ending inventory?

Determining Inventory Quantities

There are two different methods for determining inventory *quantities*. A **perpetual inventory system** keeps a running (or "perpetual") record of the amount in inventory. Purchases are debited to the inventory account itself, and the cost of units sold is removed from the inventory account as sales are made. Usually, inventory quantities are recorded in both physical units and dollars. The amount of inventory on hand at any point in time should correspond to the unit balance in the inventory account.

The inventory T-account under a perpetual inventory system would contain the following information at any point in time:

Inventory	
Beginning inventory (units and $)	
Plus:	Minus:

Cost of units
    purchased (units and $)
	Cost of units
	    transferred to cost
	    of goods sold (units and $)

Equals:	
Ending inventory on hand (units and $)	

A **periodic inventory system** does not keep a running record of the amount of inventory on hand. Purchases are accumulated in a separate purchases account and no entry is made at the time of sale to reflect cost of goods sold. The records for a periodic inventory system look like this:

Inventory Purchases		Inventory	
Cost of units purchased ($ only)		Beginning inventory ($ only)	

In a periodic inventory system, ending inventory must be determined by physically counting the goods on hand at the end of the period. The computation for cost of goods sold is:

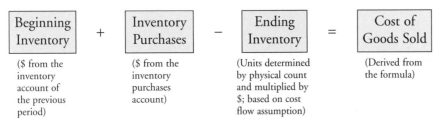

Beginning Inventory	+	Inventory Purchases	−	Ending Inventory	=	Cost of Goods Sold
($ from the inventory account of the previous period)		($ from the inventory purchases account)		(Units determined by physical count and multiplied by $; based on cost flow assumption)		(Derived from the formula)

To illustrate the accounting entries under each system, assume the following data:

Sales	$10,000
Beginning inventory	1,400
Inventory purchases	9,100
Ending inventory	3,500

The entries under the perpetual and periodic inventory systems are compared on the next page.

Comparison of Entries—Perpetual Versus Periodic Inventory System

Perpetual Inventory System		Periodic Inventory System	

Entry (1)

To Record Purchases:

DR Inventory	$ 9,100	DR Inventory purchases	$ 9,100
CR Accounts payable (or cash)	$ 9,100	CR Accounts payable (or cash)	$ 9,100

Entry (2)

To Record Sales:

DR Cash or Accounts receivable	$10,000	DR Cash or Accounts receivable	$10,000
CR Sales revenues	$10,000	CR Sales revenues	$10,000
DR Cost of goods sold	$ 7,000*		
CR Inventory	$ 7,000	(NO ENTRY)	

* Beginning inventory ($1,400) + Purchases ($9,100) – Ending inventory ($3,500) = Cost of goods sold ($7,000).

Entry (3)

To Close the Accounts:

(NO ENTRY)		DR Inventory (ending)	$ 3,500
		DR Cost of goods sold	$ 7,000
		CR Inventory (beginning)	$ 1,400
		CR Inventory purchases	$ 9,100

The inventory-related accounts would appear as follows under each method (entry numbers are indicated):

Perpetual Inventory System

Inventory			Cost of Goods Sold	
Beg. bal.	$1,400		(2)	$7,000
(1)	9,100	(2) $7,000		

			Sales	
End. bal.	$3,500			(2) $10,000

Periodic Inventory System

Inventory			Inventory Purchases	
Beg. bal.	$1,400		(1)	$9,100	(3) $ 9,100
(3)	3,500	(3) $1,400		

End. bal.	$3,500		Bal.	–0–

Cost of Goods Sold			Sales	
(3)	$7,000			(2) $10,000

Periodic inventory systems reduce record keeping, making these systems less costly to maintain. However, this cost advantage is achieved at the expense of far less management control over inventory. Under a periodic inventory system, there is no running inventory record, and quantities on hand must be determined by physical count. Furthermore, the cost of goods sold number under this system is a "plug" figure—that is, the computation assumes that goods not on hand when the physical count is taken were sold. But some of the goods not on hand may have been stolen or wasted. Under the periodic system, there is no way to determine the extent of these potential losses.

A perpetual inventory system is more complex and usually more expensive. It does not eliminate the need for a physical inventory, since the book inventory figures must be verified at least annually. But a perpetual system gives management greater control over inventories. For example, the running balance in inventory allows careful monitoring of stock levels, which is useful in avoiding stock-outs, particularly in manufacturing where "just-in-time" inventory purchasing is practised. Furthermore, comparing book inventories and physical count figures reveals discrepancies that may be due to theft, employee carelessness, or natural shrinkage.[3]

A choice between the two systems depends on their respective costs and benefits. Perpetual inventory systems are typically used where:

- *a small number of inventory units with high unit value exists.* An example is the inventory records for vehicles in an automobile dealership.

- *continuous monitoring of inventory levels is essential.* An example is a continuous production line where raw materials shortages would shut the operation down.

Periodic systems are used in situations of high-volume and low per-unit cost. However, the widespread use of computerized optical scanning equipment has led to the adoption of perpetual systems in supermarkets and other high-volume settings where such systems were previously not cost-effective. Wal-Mart and Costco were two of the first companies to utilize optical scanning and perpetual inventory systems. Wal-Mart shares the information captured by its electronic inventory management system with suppliers who are authorized to automatically ship new merchandise directly to Wal-Mart stores when inventory levels fall below prescribed minimum levels. This approach shortens inventory restocking cycles at Wal-Mart and reduces the need for warehouse inventories, thus reducing costs.

WAL-MART
www.walmart.com

COSTCO
www.costco.com

Items Included in Inventory

All tangible current assets not subject to amortization to which the firm has legal title should appear in the inventory account. However, in day-to-day operations, most firms do not attempt to use the passage of legal title as the criterion for including items in the inventory records, since this would be a time-consuming process. Instead, firms only record inventory when it is physically received.

Recording inventory when it is physically received creates no difficulties except when it comes time to prepare financial statements. At that time, the firm must determine whether all goods that were in fact legally owned have been included in the inventory account. Goods in transit are the primary concern, since legal title to such goods may transfer to the purchaser before they are physically received by the purchaser. The purchaser determines the legal status of goods in transit by examining invoices pertaining to goods received during the first few days of the next accounting period, and then uses this information to determine precisely when title passed.

Sometimes goods may be physically in the possession of a firm but not legally owned by the firm. One example is goods shipped on **consignment**. Here, the firm that holds the goods (the consignee) acts as an agent for the owner (the consignor) in selling the goods. The consignee receives a sales commission and forwards the net sales price (after deducting the commission and any selling expenses) to the consignor. Consignment goods should not be included in the inventory of the consignee; instead, they must appear as part of the inventory of the consignor.[4]

Costs Included in Inventory

The carrying cost of inventory should include all costs required to obtain physical possession and to put the merchandise in saleable condition. These costs include the purchase cost, sales taxes and transportation costs paid by the purchaser, insurance costs, and storage costs. For a manufacturing firm, inventory costs would also include those production costs—such as labour and overhead—that were incurred in making a finished saleable product.[5]

In principle, inventory costs should also include the costs of the purchasing department and other general administrative costs associated with the acquisition and disbursement of inventory. Realistically, however, such costs are extremely difficult to associate with individual purchases and would have to be allocated arbitrarily. From a cost-benefit perspective, the effort that would be expended in trying to assign these indirect inventory costs to unit purchases generally exceeds the benefits. That's why inventory cost shown in the accounting records is usually limited to *direct* acquisition and processing costs that can be objectively associated with specific goods. Costs that do not meet this criterion—such as purchasing department costs—are generally treated as period costs and expensed in the period in which they arise. Cash purchase discounts that are lost because of late payment represent interest expense rather than a cost of acquiring inventory. These costs are excluded from inventory and expensed.

Manufacturing Costs

The inventory costs of a manufacturer include raw material, labour, and certain overhead items. Costs of this type are called **product costs.** Product costs are assigned to inventory and treated as assets until the inventory is sold. When sold, the inventory carrying value is charged to cost of goods sold, and at that point all inventoried costs become an expense.

A manufacturer also incurs other costs that are not closely associated with production. Examples include general administrative costs (such as the president's salary) and selling costs. These costs are not inventoried. Instead, they are treated as expenses of the period in which they are incurred, and are called **period costs.**

The flow of product costs through the inventory accounts and, eventually, to the cost of goods sold account is illustrated in Exhibit 9.1.

Absorption Costing Versus Variable Costing

As indicated in Exhibit 9.1, manufacturing overhead costs are one element of product costs and accordingly included in inventory. However, there are two views regarding the appropriate treatment of *fixed* manufacturing overhead costs. One view is called **variable costing** (or direct costing); the other is called **absorption costing** (or full costing).

Variable costing includes only variable costs of production in inventory. **Variable costs** are those that change in proportion to the level of production. Examples include raw materials cost, direct labour, and certain overhead items such as the electricity used in running production equipment. **Fixed costs** of production do not change as

Exhibit 9.1 FLOW OF PRODUCT COSTS FOR MANUFACTURING BUSINESSES

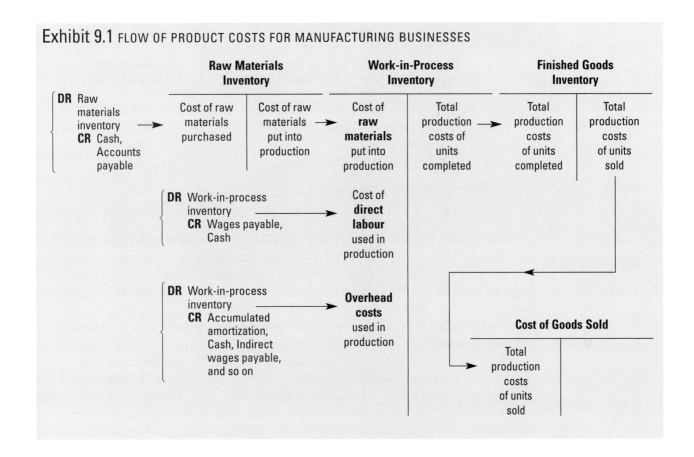

production levels change. Examples include rental of production facilities, amortization of production equipment, and property taxes. *When variable costing is used, these fixed overhead costs are not included in inventory cost.* Instead, fixed production overhead costs are treated as period costs and are expensed in the period in which they are incurred.

Under variable costing, incurred costs should only be included in inventory if they provide future benefits to the firm. Fixed production overhead costs are *not* assets since they expire in the period in which they are incurred and thus do not provide future benefit to the firm. For example, factory insurance carried in June provides no benefit to the firm after June 30; for insurance protection in July, another month's premium must be paid. But future benefits *do* derive from variable costs such as materials used in production; once materials have been purchased and used in making an inventory unit, that cost can be "stored" and will provide a future benefit when the inventory is eventually sold. These kinds of costs can be included in inventory under variable costing.

Under absorption costing, *all* production costs are inventoried. Fixed production overhead costs are not written off to expense as incurred. Instead they are treated as product costs and carried as assets in the appropriate inventory accounts. The rationale is that *both* variable and fixed production costs are assets since *both* are needed to produce a saleable product.

Both absorption costing and variable costing treat all selling, general, and administrative (SG&A) costs as period costs. These SG&A costs are *never* inventoried under *any* circumstances under either method. Table 9.1 represents the treatment of costs by category under each inventory costing approach. The only cost category treated differently is fixed production overhead.

TABLE 9.1 SUMMARY OF COST TREATMENT BY CATEGORY UNDER VARIABLE AND ABSORPTION COSTING

Cost Category	Inventoried Under Variable Costing?	Inventoried Under Absorption Costing?
Production materials	Yes	Yes
Production labour	Yes	Yes
Variable production overhead	Yes	Yes
Fixed production overhead	No	Yes
Selling, general, and administrative	No	No

The variable- and absorption-costing approaches provide statement readers with potentially very different pictures of year-to-year changes in performance—that is, the trend of earnings over a series of years can differ markedly under the two approaches, as we will show. These different earnings trends could influence analysts' forecasts. Analysts must understand the effects on financial statements of *both* methods even though ***GAAP does not encourage variable costing to be used in external financial statements.***

Unfortunately, absorption costing makes it difficult to interpret year-to-year changes in reported income. These problems arise when inventory levels change from one year to the next, which is illustrated in Exhibit 9.2.

Over the two years, there was a constant selling price, constant variable production costs per unit (e.g., material, labour, and variable overhead), and constant total fixed production costs. Units produced increased in 2003 (125,000 versus 100,000 in 2002), but units sold in 2003 dropped (90,000 versus 110,000 units in 2002).

Exhibit 9.3 shows that reported gross margin under absorption costing increased from $110,000 in 2002 to $130,000 in 2003—an 18.2% increase. Income *increased* despite the fact that variable production costs and selling price per unit were constant, fixed production costs did not change in total, and unit sales decreased.

Exhibit 9.2 ABSORPTION COSTING VERSUS VARIABLE COSTING

Selling price and cost data

Selling price = $8 per unit in both 2002 and 2003

Variable production costs = $3 per unit in both 2002 and 2003

Fixed production costs = $400,000 per year in both 2002 and 2003

Beginning inventory (FIFO basis), January 1, 2002 = 50,000 units @ $7

Production and sales volume data

	2002	2003
Units produced	100,000	125,000
Units sold	110,000	90,000
Ending inventory (in units)*	40,000	75,000

*Computations:
2002: 50,000 + 100,000 − 110,000 = 40,000 units
2003: 40,000 + 125,000 − 90,000 = 75,000 units

Exhibit 9.3 ABSORPTION VERSUS VARIABLE COSTING STATEMENTS: CONTRASTING THE OUTCOMES

Absorption Cost Income Statements

	2002		2003
Sales revenues (110,000 @ $8)	$880,000	Sales revenues (90,000 @ $8)	$720,000
Cost of goods sold:		Cost of goods sold:	
From beginning inventory (50,000 @ $7) $350,000		From beginning inventory (40,000 @ $7) $280,000	
From 2002 production (60,000 @ $7*) 420,000		From 2003 production (50,000 @ $6.20**) 310,000	
	(770,000)		(590,000)
Gross margin	$110,000	Gross margin	$130,000
Gross margin %	12.50%	Gross margin %	18.06%
Ending inventory: 40,000 units @ $7*	$280,000	Ending inventory: 75,000 units @ $6.20**	$465,000

*This cost is determined as follows:

Variable production costs (given)	$3.00/unit
Fixed production costs, unitized $400,000/100,000 =	4.00/unit
Total production cost for 2002	$7.00/unit

**This cost is determined as follows:

Variable production costs (given)	$3.00/unit
Fixed production costs, unitized $400,000/125,000 =	3.20/unit
Total production cost for 2003	$6.20/unit

Variable Cost Income Statements

	2002		2003
Sales revenues (110,000 @ $8)	$880,000	Sales revenues (90,000 @ $8)	$720,000
Variable cost of goods sold:		Variable cost of goods sold:	
From beginning inventory (50,000 @ $3) $150,000		From beginning inventory (40,000 @ $3) $120,000	
From 2002 production (60,000 @ $3) 180,000		From 2003 production (50,000 @ $3) 150,000	
	(330,000)		(270,000)
Variable contribution margin	550,000	Variable contribution margin	450,000
Less: Fixed production costs treated as a period expense	(400,000)	Less: Fixed production costs treated as a period expense	(400,000)
Variable cost gross margin	$150,000	Variable cost gross margin	$ 50,000
Gross margin %	17.05%	Gross margin %	6.94%
Ending inventory: 40,000 units @ $3	$120,000	Ending inventory: 75,000 units @ $3	$225,000

Why do we get this strange result? The answer reveals a major deficiency of financial statements prepared under absorption costing. Production increased in 2003 to 125,000 units and exceeded sales, which totalled 90,000 units. Inventory therefore increased by 35,000 units (125,000 minus 90,000) to a year-end total of 75,000 units. When inventory increases under absorption costing, as in this illustration, the amount of fixed cost assigned to inventory increases. *As inventory absorbs more fixed*

In Exhibit 9.3, the fixed costs in inventory at January 1, 2003, totalled $160,000 (i.e., 40,000 units times $4 of fixed cost per unit). At December 31, 2003, fixed cost included in inventory had risen to $240,000 (i.e., 75,000 units times $3.20 of fixed cost per unit).

cost, less fixed cost gets charged to the income statement and income goes up. Very large inventory increases produce a favourable income effect that can offset an unfavourable income effect caused, say, by a sales decrease. This is precisely what happened in the situation shown in Exhibit 9.3, and it is this effect that explains the jump in 2003 income.

By contrast, variable cost income in Exhibit 9.3 fell from $150,000 in 2002 to $50,000 in 2003. Critics of absorption costing contend that in situations similar to this example, variable costing better reflects the underlying economics.

Generalizing from this example, the mechanics of absorption costing can lead to year-to-year income changes that may delude the unwary. This is possible whenever production and sales are not in balance—that is, whenever physical inventory levels (in units) are either increasing or decreasing. When the number of units in inventory is increasing, gross margins under absorption costing tend to rise. This effect may be so large that it could obscure offsetting unfavourable effects (for example, sales decreases or deteriorating efficiency) that are taking place simultaneously. When physical inventory levels are decreasing, income under absorption costing tends to fall, since fixed overhead that was previously in inventory gets charged against income as part of the cost of goods sold.

Recap

To analyze comparative income statements, you must understand the mechanics of absorption costing and bear in mind that any imbalance between units produced and units sold may have a pronounced effect on reported income. Furthermore, the effect on income under absorption costing can obscure underlying changes of interest to statement readers. For example, a sudden, unexpected sales jump—clearly a good news event—may cause an inventory depletion. Under GAAP absorption costing, the reduction in inventory forces an additional dose of fixed overhead through the income statement, thereby masking part of the income benefit arising from the sales jump.

Cost Flow Assumptions: The Concepts

For most publicly held firms, inventory is continuously purchased in large quantities. It is very difficult to determine the precise purchase lot from which units have been sold, especially in firms where manufacturing alters the form of the raw materials acquired.

In a few industries, it is possible to identify which particular units have been sold. In retail businesses like jewellery stores and automobile dealerships, which sell a small number of high-value items, cost of goods sold can be measured by reference to the known cost of the actual units sold. This inventory accounting method is called **specific identification**. But this method suffers from a serious deficiency, since specific identification makes it relatively easy to manipulate income. Consider a large jewellery dealer with three identical watches in inventory that were acquired at three different purchase costs. Under specific identification, the reported profit on sale can be raised (or lowered) by simply delivering the lowest- (or highest-) cost watch. An inventory method allowing this kind of latitude is open to criticism.

Specific identification is usually not feasible for most businesses. Even when it is feasible, it has some serious drawbacks, as just illustrated. For these reasons, a **cost flow assumption** is usually required to allocate goods available for sale between ending inventory and cost of goods sold—that is:

It is important to understand that GAAP do not require the cost flow assumption to conform to the actual physical flow of the goods.

In a sample of companies surveyed by the Canadian Institute of Chartered Accountants (CICA), the inventory cost flow assumptions that the companies used, as shown in Table 9.2, indicate that the most popular inventory costing method is average cost, followed by FIFO, with LIFO far behind.

TABLE 9.2 FREQUENCY OF INVENTORY COST FLOW ASSUMPTIONS, 2000 AND 1999

	Number of Companies	
Methods	**2000**	**1999**
First-in, first-out (FIFO)	52	50
Last-in, first-out (LIFO)	3	3
Average cost	55	59
Other	4	3
Companies using more than one method	32	30

Source: Financial Reporting in Canada, 26th edition (Toronto: CICA, 2001).

In contrast to Canadian practice, LIFO is much more popular in the United States. Its relative lack of popularity in Canada is due largely to its not being acceptable for income tax return purposes, and the desire on the part of Canadian companies not to keep two sets of inventory accounts, one for GAAP reporting and one for income tax filing.

Let's revisit the refrigerator situation to explore the underlying cost flow concepts. This simple example highlights key issues. Recall the facts: The retailer started the year with a beginning inventory of one refrigerator, which had an invoice cost of $300. During the year, the dealer-cost of each identical refrigerator increased to $340. Assume that the retailer purchases another refrigerator at this $340 cost. At the end of the year, one of the two refrigerators is sold for $500.

First-In, First-Out (FIFO) Cost Flow

The first-in, first-out (FIFO) method assumes the oldest units available in inventory are the first units to be sold. This means that the ending inventory on the FIFO basis will always consist of the cost of the most recently acquired units. In the refrigerator example, the computations are:

Income statement

Sales revenues	$500
Cost of goods sold	300 (Cost of oldest unit)
Net income	$200

Balance sheet

Ending inventory	$340 (Cost of newest unit)

A FIFO cost flow for a more realistic case, one in which numerous purchases and sales are made throughout the year, is graphically shown in Figure 9.1. The FIFO cost flow in this diagram presumes that sales were made from the oldest available goods (in this case, the beginning inventory and the goods purchased from January through September) and that ending inventory is made up of the most recently acquired goods (October through December).

FIFO charges the oldest costs against revenues on the income statement. This characteristic is often viewed as a deficiency of the FIFO method, since current costs of replacing the units sold are not being matched with current revenues. However, on the balance sheet, FIFO inventory represents the most recent purchases and—if inventory turnover is reasonably rapid—will usually approximate current replacement costs.

Last-In, First-Out (LIFO) Cost Flow

The last-in, first-out (LIFO) method presumes sales were made from the most recently acquired units. In the refrigerator example, the computations are:

Income statement

Sales revenues	$500
Cost of goods sold	340 (Cost of newest unit)
Net income	$160

Balance sheet

Ending inventory	$300 (Cost of oldest unit)

This method will seldom correspond to the actual physical flow of goods, but GAAP does not require conformity between the assumed cost flow and the physical flow of units.

FIGURE 9.1
FIFO COST FLOW

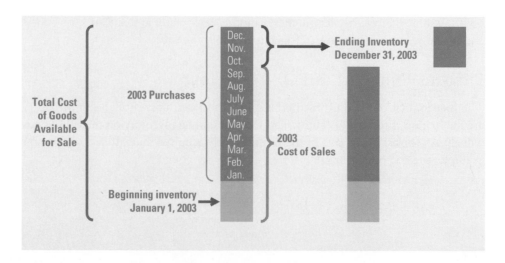

LIFO matches the most recently incurred costs against revenues. When purchases and sales occur continuously, the most recently incurred costs will be virtually identical to current replacement costs. So LIFO provides a good match between current costs and current revenues. But on the balance sheet, LIFO inventory consists of the oldest costs ($300 in the refrigerator example), which usually will not approximate the current replacement cost of inventory.

For firms that have used the LIFO method for many years, the LIFO inventory amount may reflect only a small fraction of what it would cost to replace this inventory at today's prices. A diagram of LIFO cost flow in Figure 9.2 shows how old **layers** can accumulate in ending inventory. As Figure 9.2 shows, when purchases exceed sales in any year, a new LIFO layer is formed. New inventory layers are valued using the *oldest* costs incurred during that year. For example, the LIFO layer added in 2003 is made up of the inventory purchase costs expended from January through March 2003. Since sales under LIFO are always presumed to have been made from the most recent purchases, the 2003 LIFO layer will remain on the books at the end of 2004 as long as units sold in 2004 do not exceed units purchased in 2004. As Figure 9.2 shows, not only did the 2003 LIFO layer remain, but a small additional LIFO layer was added in 2004, because unit purchases exceeded unit sales. A firm that has been on LIFO since, say, 1954 could still be carrying a portion of its inventory at 1954 costs, a portion at 1955 costs, and so on.

FIFO, LIFO, and Inventory Holding Gains

FIFO and LIFO give different financial statement results because each method treats inventory holding gains and losses in a different way. To understand the differences, we first need to understand inventory holding gains and losses.

Inventory holding gains and losses are the changes in input costs that occur following the purchase of inventory. Let's go back to the refrigerator example. Assume the replacement cost of each refrigerator at the end of the year was $340. However,

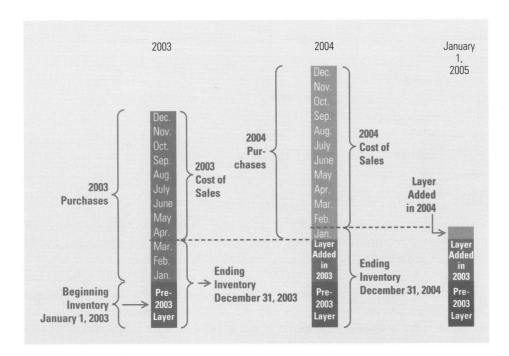

FIGURE 9.2
INVENTORY
DETERMINATION
UNDER LIFO
COST FLOW
ASSUMPTION

both FIFO and LIFO are historical cost methods, and therefore goods available for sale will reflect only the *historical cost* that was paid to acquire the two units on hand:

Beginning inventory (1 unit @ $300)	$300
Purchases (1 unit @ $340)	+340
Historical cost of goods available for sale	$640

Notice that historical cost accounting ignores the $40 holding gain that arose on the unit of beginning inventory as its replacement cost increased from $300 to $340. Thus, goods available for sale are shown at their historical cost of $640 rather than at their current replacement cost of $680 (i.e., to replace the two units would cost $340 each).

There is an accounting method that records holding gains on financial statements as they arise. This method is called **current cost accounting,** and it is not generally permitted for preparing the basic financial statements. However, in previous years when inflation and price changes were high, some Canadian firms disclosed such information.

In a current cost accounting system, the following entry would be made at the time that inventory replacement cost increased:

DR	Inventory	$40
CR	Unrealized holding gains	$40

The "unrealized holding gains" account represents an increase in owners' equity. Whether these holding gains should be treated as a component of net income or instead included directly in retained earnings is a controversial issue. In this chapter, we ignore the controversy and treat holding gains as an element of income.

Once the holding gains entry has been made, the *current* cost of goods available for sale is:

Beginning inventory (1 unit @ $300)	$300
Increase in the replacement cost of beginning inventory	+ 40
Purchases (1 unit @ $340)	+340
Current cost of goods available for sale (2 units @ $340)	$680

When the one unit is sold for $500, the partial financial statements under current cost would be:

Income statement

Sales revenues	$500
Replacement cost of goods sold (1 unit @ $340)	340
Current cost operating profit	$160

Balance sheet

Ending inventory	$340

The current cost operating profit figure is the margin that results from matching current replacement cost against current revenues. It reflects the expected ongoing profitability of current operations at current levels of costs and selling prices.

Figure 9.3 contrasts the treatment of total goods available for sale under (a) historical costing and (b) current costing. Notice that the total amount to be allocated between inventory and cost of goods sold is $40 higher under current costing. This difference is due to the **holding gain** that was added to goods available for sale under

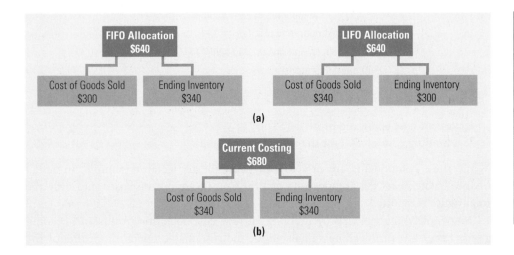

FIGURE 9.3
ALLOCATION OF
GOODS AVAILABLE
FOR SALE:
HISTORICAL
COSTING VERSUS
CURRENT COSTING

(a) Historical cost of goods available for sale = $640; and

(b) Current cost of goods available for sale = $680

current costing. Thus, in current costing, the total to be allocated is carried at current cost (two units at $340 each, for a total of $680). *This means that the balance sheet inventory number and the cost of goods sold number are both shown at current cost.* By contrast, the historical cost figure for goods available for sale ($640) is $40 less than the total current cost of the two units available ($680). This means that under LIFO, FIFO, or average cost, it is impossible to simultaneously reflect both inventory *and* cost of goods sold at current cost: one can be shown at (almost) current cost, but the other must then be shown at historical cost. *The primary difference between FIFO and LIFO is that each method requires a different choice about which element to show at the more out-of-date cost.* FIFO shows inventory at approximately[6] current cost but is then forced to reflect cost of goods sold at historical cost. LIFO shows cost of goods sold at approximately current cost but is then forced to reflect inventory on the balance sheet at historical cost.

During periods of rising input costs, FIFO income will be higher than LIFO income as long as inventory quantities remain constant or increase. (Decreases in inventory quantity—reductions in physical units in inventory—can produce a distortion known as a LIFO liquidation. This is discussed later in the chapter.) In the refrigerator example, FIFO income is $200, whereas LIFO income is $160. Income is *higher under FIFO because FIFO charges the old, lower cost units to cost of goods sold. By charging the oldest costs to the income statement, FIFO automatically includes in income the holding gain on the unit that was sold.* This result is easily seen by comparing the total income figures under FIFO and current costing.

FIFO Income		Current Cost Income	
Sales revenues	$500	Sales revenue	$500
Cost of goods sold	300	Replacement cost of goods sold	340
FIFO operating profit	$200	Current cost operating profit	$160

A comparison of the two income numbers shows that FIFO income is $40 higher. This $40 difference is, of course, the holding gain on the oldest refrigerator, which is the one that the FIFO assumption considers to have been sold. Another way to visualize this income difference is to decompose FIFO income into its component parts.

Components of FIFO Income

Current cost operating profit	$160
Holding gain on unit considered sold	40
FIFO operating profit	$200

This decomposition tells us that FIFO income comprises two components:

1. current cost operating profit of $160
2. a holding gain of $40 on the unit that was sold

The notion of "current cost operating profit" represents a matching against sales revenue of the then-current replacement cost of the inventory at the time of sale.

While these components are easy to extract in the refrigerator example, in actual financial statements the components of FIFO profit are not disclosed and only the total figure is reported.

Some analysts argue that by merging current cost operating profits and holding gains, FIFO gives misleading signals about the sustainable operating profits of the company. For example, operating profit is generally considered to be potentially sustainable if existing conditions continue. By contrast, holding gains are dependent on external price increases, which may or may not be sustainable. But FIFO gives the impression that operating profit is $200, thus suggesting that $200—not $160—is sustainable.

FIFO allocates the oldest costs incurred to the income statement and the newest costs to the balance sheet. When prices are rising, this results in an income number that is higher than the one produced by LIFO as well as a higher inventory value. Because the higher income number includes potentially unsustainable gains, that portion of FIFO income is considered to represent low-quality earnings.

The income number under LIFO will *usually* closely approximate the income number under current costing:

LIFO Income		**Current Cost Income**	
Sales revenue	$500	Sales revenue	$500
Cost of goods sold	340	Replacement cost of goods sold	340
LIFO operating profit	$160	Current cost operating profit	$160

When purchases occur continuously, this near equivalence exists because LIFO charges the most recently acquired goods to cost of goods sold. However, since LIFO is a historical cost accounting method, there is only $640 (rather than $680) to allocate between cost of goods sold and inventory in our refrigerator example. Because LIFO allocates the most recent cost of $340 to the income statement, that leaves only $300—the original historical cost—for allocation to the balance sheet. Therefore, the LIFO balance sheet inventory number will not reflect current replacement cost.

The LIFO Reserve Disclosure

As was mentioned earlier in this chapter, though LIFO is rare in Canadian financial statements, it is very popular in the United States, where it also can be used for income tax filing purposes.[7] Canadian users of the financial statements of American companies need to understand some additional effects of LIFO in order to better compare Canadian and U.S. companies, so this and subsequent sections focus on such issues.

Because LIFO inventory costs on the balance sheet frequently include old inventory layers, they are carried at amounts which are much lower than FIFO inventory amounts. This can make it very difficult to compare LIFO versus FIFO firms meaningfully. To remedy this difficulty, the Securities and Exchange Commission (SEC) in the United States adopted a disclosure policy in 1974 that requires LIFO firms to disclose the dollar magnitude of the difference between LIFO and FIFO inventory costs. This disclosure is called the **LIFO reserve** and must be reported at each balance sheet date. Exhibit 9.4, from the Vacu-Dry Company 1996 annual report, illustrates a typical disclosure of this divergence between LIFO and FIFO inventory amounts.

The disclosure in Exhibit 9.4 provides statement readers with an important tool. By adding the reported LIFO reserve amount at June 30, 1996, to the June 30, 1996, balance sheet LIFO inventory number, one can estimate June 30, 1996, FIFO inventory. Specifically, the sum of the ending LIFO inventory (US$3,430,000) and the fiscal year-end LIFO reserve (US$2,114,000) totals US$5,544,000. This sum represents an estimate of June 30, 1996, FIFO ending inventory of Vacu-Dry. Notice that this result immediately follows from the definition of the LIFO reserve, which is the difference between FIFO inventory amounts and LIFO inventory amounts—that is:

$$\text{Inventory}_{\text{FIFO}} \quad - \quad \text{Inventory}_{\text{LIFO}} \quad = \quad \text{LIFO reserve}$$
$$(\$5,544,000) \quad - \quad (\$3,430,000) \quad = \quad (\$2,114,000)$$

Therefore, rearranging the equation yields the following:

$$\text{Inventory}_{\text{FIFO}} \quad = \quad \text{Inventory}_{\text{LIFO}} \quad + \quad \text{LIFO reserve}$$
$$(\$5,544,000) \quad = \quad (\$3,430,000) \quad + \quad (\$2,114,000)$$

Thus, one can think of the FIFO inventory cost on the balance sheet as comprising LIFO inventory cost plus a LIFO reserve adjustment that measures the difference between the current cost of inventory units and the historical cost of all LIFO layers. The LIFO reserve disclosure allows the analyst to convert reported LIFO inventory amounts to FIFO amounts.[8] This adjustment can be performed for all dates for which LIFO reserve amounts are disclosed by American companies. To illustrate this point specifically, a similar adjustment using the beginning LIFO reserve disclosure in Exhibit 9.4 can also be made to estimate Vacu-Dry's June 30, 1995, FIFO inventory:

$$\text{Inventory}_{\text{FIFO}} \quad = \quad \text{Inventory}_{\text{LIFO}} \quad + \quad \text{LIFO reserve}$$
$$\$6,748,000 \quad = \quad \$5,414,000 \quad + \quad \$1,334,000$$

Technically, the SEC rule requires firms to disclose "the excess of replacement cost or current cost over stated LIFO value ..." (see Regulation S-X, Rule 5-02). In practice, most firms do measure the LIFO reserve as the difference between the LIFO inventory carrying amount and the replacement cost of the inventory. However, some firms compute the LIFO reserve by taking the difference between inventory book value at LIFO and inventory book value at FIFO. Presumably, this is justified if inventory turnover is reasonably rapid. In such situations, FIFO inventory will approximate replacement cost. Consequently, both of these alternative definitions of the LIFO reserve will usually result in similar amounts and thus comply with the SEC directive.

Exhibit 9.4 VACU-DRY COMPANY'S 1996 ANNUAL REPORT DISCLOSURES

Inventories Footnote Disclosure

	June 30,	
(US$)	1996	1995
Inventories [at LIFO]:		
Finished goods	$2,757,000	$4,926,000
Work in process	233,000	239,000
Raw materials and containers	440,000	249,000
Total	$3,430,000	$5,414,000

Disclosure on the Face of the Balance Sheet

	June 30,	
	1996	1995
Inventories, less LIFO reserves of $2,114,000 and $1,334,000 in 1996 and 1995, respectively	$3,430,000	$5,414,000

FIFO inventory at June 30, 1995, equals US$6,748,000. This number is, of course, the FIFO beginning inventory for fiscal year 1996.

Using the LIFO reserve disclosure in this way also makes it possible for analysts to convert cost of goods sold from LIFO to FIFO, and thus make the American company perhaps more comparable to a corresponding Canadian company (which would more likely be using FIFO). This is more easily understood by looking at the basic cost-of-goods-sold formula in column (1) of Exhibit 9.5. Notice that both the beginning and ending inventory *and* the cost of goods sold amounts in column (1) are measured at LIFO. (Inventory purchases represent the actual events of the period and do not require a cost flow assumption.) Column (2) shows the addition of the respective LIFO reserves to the beginning and ending LIFO inventories. As we just saw, the resulting sums yield FIFO inventory amounts, which are shown in column (3). Using the basic cost-of-goods-sold formula on the column (3) FIFO numbers yields FIFO cost of goods sold. Thus, the LIFO reserve disclosures make it possible to convert cost of goods sold from LIFO to FIFO.

Exhibit 9.6 shows how to convert cost of goods sold from LIFO to FIFO for the Vacu-Dry Company. FIFO cost of goods sold is US$23,362,000. To make valid comparisons across firms that use different inventory accounting methods, you must make adjustments like those in Exhibit 9.6.

You can use a shortcut to convert cost of goods sold from LIFO to FIFO. The shortcut focuses on the *change* in the LIFO reserve between the beginning and the end of the year, as reflected at the bottom of column (2) in Exhibit 9.5. (This shortcut avoids the need to successively add the respective LIFO reserve amounts to beginning and ending inventories.) Applying this shortcut to the Vacu-Dry data in Exhibit 9.6, we see that the change in the LIFO reserve was an *increase* of US$780,000 (i.e., US$1,334,000 at the start of the fiscal year versus US$2,114,000 at the end of the year) and that LIFO cost of goods sold exceeds FIFO cost of goods sold by US$780,000. Therefore, when the LIFO reserve amount *increases*, the shortcut calculation is:

$$\text{Cost of goods sold}_{LIFO} - \text{Increase in LIFO reserve} = \text{Cost of goods sold}_{FIFO}$$

Exhibit 9.5 ADJUSTING COST OF GOODS SOLD FROM LIFO TO FIFO

(1)	(2)	(3)
Beginning Inventory$_{LIFO}$	+ Beginning LIFO Reserve	= Beginning Inventory$_{FIFO}$
Plus:		Plus:
Purchases		Purchases
Equals:		Equals:
Goods Available$_{LIFO}$		Goods Available$_{FIFO}$
Minus:		Minus:
Ending Inventory$_{LIFO}$	+ Ending LIFO Reserve	Ending Inventory$_{FIFO}$
Equals:		= Equals:
	− Increase in LIFO Reserve	
Cost of Goods Sold$_{LIFO}$	or	= Cost of Goods Sold$_{FIFO}$
	+ Decrease in LIFO Reserve	

Exhibit 9.6 ADJUSTING FROM LIFO COST OF GOODS SOLD TO FIFO COST OF GOODS SOLD FOR THE VACU-DRY COMPANY

(US$ in thousands)	As Reported in Financial Statements (LIFO)		LIFO Reserve		Adjusted to FIFO Basis
Beginning inventory, June 30, 1995	$ 5,414	+	$1,334	=	$ 6,748
Purchases	22,158				22,158
Goods available	27,572				28,906
Ending inventory, June 30, 1996	3,430	+	2,114	=	5,544
Cost of goods sold	$24,142	−	$ 780 increase	=	$23,362

When the LIFO reserve amount *decreases*, the conversion is:

$$\text{Cost of goods sold}_{LIFO} + \text{Decrease in LIFO reserve} = \text{Cost of goods sold}_{FIFO}$$

The adjustment process can provide insights about inventory price movements. For example, since LIFO cost of goods sold is higher than FIFO cost of goods sold, we know that inventory purchase costs incurred by Vacu-Dry were rising during 1996.

Vacu-Dry uses LIFO for all of its inventory. But many American companies use a combination of inventory cost flow assumptions. The LIFO-to-FIFO adjustment for a company that uses LIFO for only a portion of its inventory is identical to the method used in Exhibit 9.6 for Vacu-Dry. The beginning and ending LIFO reserves, respectively, are added to beginning and ending reported inventory amounts. It doesn't matter that LIFO was used for only 60% to 62% of the inventory. By adding the LIFO reserve to the reported inventory, *the LIFO portion is adjusted* and what results is inventory calculated on a 100% FIFO basis. *Caveat:* When analysts use publicly available information, such as the U.S. LIFO reserve disclosure, to convert LIFO inventory accounting companies to (an approximation of) what the company's results would have been under FIFO inventory accounting, they are making an important, implicit assumption. They are assuming that management would have made the same operating and other business decisions under FIFO as were actually made under LIFO.

Recap

Under both FIFO and LIFO, the allocation of costs between ending inventory and cost of goods sold is limited to the *historical* costs incurred. As costs change, LIFO puts the "oldest" costs on the balance sheet, while FIFO runs the "oldest" costs through the income statement. The U.S. LIFO reserve disclosure permits analysts to transform financial statements from a LIFO to a FIFO basis, thus making comparisons between firms more meaningful when one firm is using LIFO and the other FIFO.

LIFO Liquidation

When a LIFO firm liquidates old LIFO layers, the net income number under LIFO can be seriously distorted. This is because the older (and usually lower) costs in the LIFO layers that are liquidated are "matched" against sales dollars which are stated at higher current prices. This results in an inflated or illusory profit margin. The following example illustrates the point.

The Bernazard Company had the following layers in its LIFO inventory at January 1, 2003, at which time the replacement cost of the inventory was $600 per unit.

Year LIFO Layer Added	Units	Unit Cost	Total	LIFO Reserve as of 1/1/03	
2000	10	$300	$ 3,000	($600 − $300) × 10 =	$ 3,000
2001	20	400	8,000	($600 − $400) × 20 =	4,000
2002	30	500	15,000	($600 − $500) × 30 =	3,000
	60		$26,000		$10,000

Bernazard sets its selling price by adding a $400 per unit markup to replacement cost at the time of sale. As of January 1, 2003, this cost was $600 per unit; this cost remained constant throughout 2003. During 2003, the company purchased 45 units at a cost of $600 per unit, and it sold 80 units at a price of $1,000 per unit. Pre-tax LIFO income for 2003 would be:

Sales revenue, 80 @ $1,000		$80,000
Cost of goods sold:		
2003 purchases, 45 @ $600	$27,000	
2002 purchases, 30 @ $500	15,000	
2001 purchases, 5 @ $400	2,000	
		44,000
LIFO gross margin		$36,000

Because the number of units sold (80) exceeded the number of units purchased (45) in 2003, Bernazard was forced to liquidate its entire 2002 LIFO layer and one-quarter of its 2001 LIFO layer. In such situations, the matching advantages of LIFO for the income statement disappear. Indeed, a "mismatching" occurs since LIFO income overstates the current cost or "real" operating margin of $400 per unit. (Notice that the reported LIFO margin per unit is $36,000 ÷ 80, or $450.) This $50 per unit overstatement of the margin occurs because some 2001 and 2002 purchase costs are being matched against 2003 revenues. Insofar as analysts use past margin numbers as a starting point in generating future cash flow estimates, the LIFO income number is misleading when dipping occurs. That is, the $450 *reported* unit margin overstates the current cost "*real*" margin of $400 used for pricing and thus does not represent a sustainable expected future per-unit margin number. LIFO earnings that include LIFO dipping profits are lower quality earnings. The illusory profit elements would generally be assigned a lower earnings multiple for valuation purposes. Research shows that security price reactions to earnings numbers that contain LIFO liquidation profits are smaller than the price reactions to earnings numbers that are devoid of these illusory profits.[9]

To understand better what happens when LIFO dipping occurs, we will examine the reported current cost operating margin for 2003 on a replacement cost basis. The current replacement cost margin is:

Sales revenues (80 × $1,000)	$80,000
Replacement cost of goods sold (80 × $600)	48,000
Current cost operating margin (80 × $400)	$32,000

The 2003 LIFO income of $36,000 exceeds the 2003 current cost margin of $32,000. This "extra" LIFO income of $4,000 is the result of mismatching. In more technical terms, as LIFO layers are liquidated, some of the inventory holding gains of 2002 and 2001 that were ignored under historical cost LIFO in the years they occurred suddenly get recognized as income as the old, lower cost inventory layers are matched against current selling prices. This can be seen by examining the December 31, 2003, LIFO inventory computation:

Year LIFO Layer Added	Remaining Units	Unit Cost	Ending Inventory 12/31/03 Total	LIFO Reserve as of 12/31/03	
2000	10	$300	$3,000	($600 − $300) × 10 =	$3,000
2001	15	$400	6,000	($600 − $400) × 15 =	3,000
	25		$9,000		$6,000

The LIFO reserve was $10,000 at January 1, 2003. Notice that the LIFO dipping has reduced the LIFO reserve to $6,000 at December 31, 2003. This $4,000 reduction in the LIFO reserve represents another way of visualizing how LIFO dipping creates a mismatching on the income statement. Previously ignored holding gains get included in income as old LIFO layers are liquidated. The earnings "boost" of $4,000 is equal to the difference between the current cost (at date of sale) to replace the liquidated layer of LIFO inventory and the original cost of those units. This is demonstrated in Exhibit 9.7.

Exhibit 9.7 CALCULATION OF LIFO LIQUIDATION PROFITS

LIFO Layer Liquidated							LIFO Liquidation Effect on Earnings
Year Added	Units Liquidated		Current Cost		Historical Cost		
2002	30	×	($600	−	$500)	=	$3,000
2001	5	×	($600	−	$400)	=	1,000
Total increase in pre-tax earnings due to LIFO liquidation							$4,000

When old LIFO layers are liquidated, LIFO income jumps, but the increase is not sustainable.

When the income effect of a LIFO liquidation is material, the SEC requires that the 10-K report disclose the dollar impact of LIFO dipping on income. Most companies that provide the 10-K disclosure also disclose the dollar impact of dipping in the annual report. The statement user should be alert to the fact that the earnings effect of LIFO dipping can be reported on either a *before-tax* or an *after-tax* basis. Exhibit 9.8 shows this disclosure (on both a before- and an after-tax basis) from Vacu-Dry Company's 1996 annual report.

The LIFO dipping disclosure in Exhibit 9.8 indicates that 1996 earnings before income taxes were increased by US$642,000 as a consequence of matching old LIFO layer costs against 1996 revenues. This number represents the *pre-tax* effect of LIFO liquidation, indicating that the reported LIFO gross margin in 1996 overstated sustainable earnings by US$642,000. Equivalently, the LIFO cost of goods sold was lower than current cost of goods sold by US$642,000.

We can now explain more precisely the LIFO-FIFO cost of goods sold (CGS) difference computed in Exhibit 9.6:

(US$ in thousands)

Excess of 1996 LIFO CGS ($24,142) over FIFO CGS ($23,362)	=	$ 780
Decrease in LIFO CGS attributable to LIFO dipping		642
Portion of excess attributable to rising input costs		$1,422

We know that LIFO cost of goods sold exceeded FIFO cost of goods sold by US$780,000. We also know that LIFO dipping *decreased* LIFO cost of goods sold by US$642,000. Therefore, input costs rose during 1996 and *increased* LIFO cost of goods sold by US$1,422,000.

The LIFO to FIFO adjustment is also used in trend analysis, as illustrated in Exhibit 9.9, where comparative gross profit data for Vacu-Dry are shown for 1994–96.

The Exhibit 9.9 data show that the gross profit percentage dropped sharply in 1995 and slightly in 1996. But we have also seen in Exhibit 9.8 that there was LIFO dipping in 1996, which had the effect of increasing the reported gross profit in 1996 over what it would have been without the liquidation. You might ask what the profit trend looks like after adjusting for LIFO dipping. We can extend the previous analysis to address this question, as shown in Exhibit 9.10.

The computations reveal that after removing the illusory income effect arising from LIFO dipping, the gross profit percentage for Vacu-Dry shows a dramatic downward trend over the 1994–96 period. The adjusted gross profit percentage fell from 15.3% in 1994 to 6.6% in 1996. This continuing deterioration is not immediately evident in the reported gross margin figures. Analysis of trend data provides potentially important information regarding management's performance in adapting to new market conditions. Neglecting to adjust the year-to-year data for nonsustainable factors (such as the artificial margin improvement that results from LIFO dipping) could easily lead to erroneous conclusions.

Consider one final point regarding Exhibit 9.10. Many analysts believe that the most recent margin percentage provides the least-biased estimate of the next year's

Exhibit 9.9 VACU-DRY COMPANY

Comparative Gross Profit Data

	Year Ended June 30,		
(US$ in thousands)	1996	1995	1994
Net sales	$26,533	$21,438	$27,773
Cost of goods sold	24,142	19,270	23,521
Gross profit	$ 2,391	$ 2,168	$ 4,252
Gross profit as a % of sales	9.0%	10.1%	15.3%

Exhibit 9.10 VACU-DRY COMPANY

Gross Profit Data Adjusted for LIFO Dipping

(US$ in thousands)	Year Ended June 30,		
	1996	1995	1994
Gross profit as reported	$ 2,391	$ 2,168	$ 4,252
Pre-tax effect of LIFO dipping on gross profit	642	—	—
Gross profit after eliminating LIFO dipping effect	$ 1,749	$ 2,168	$ 4,252
Net sales (as reported)	$26,533	$21,438	$27,773
Adjusted gross profit %	6.6%	10.1%	15.3%
Exhibit 9.9 gross profit %	9.0%	10.1%	15.3%
Difference	−2.4	N/A	N/A

margin percentage.[10] After the effects of LIFO dipping are eliminated, the adjusted gross margin percentage provides a clearer picture of the underlying real sustainable gross margin in each year. Analysts trying to estimate Vacu-Dry's future performance must understand that it is the 6.6% adjusted margin percentage—not the 9.0% unadjusted fig- ◄ ure—that represents the starting point for estimating the sustainable margin in subsequent periods.

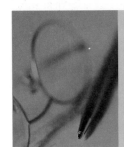

Recap

LIFO liquidations occur frequently and often have a large impact on reported earnings. The earnings effect arises from a mismatching, since LIFO layers carried at "old" costs are matched against current period revenues. Reported margins are distorted and so is the income trend.

Vacu-Dry disclosed both the pre-tax *and* after-tax income effect of LIFO dipping. Some companies only disclose the increase in net (after-tax) earnings. In these instances, analysts can still easily convert the LIFO dipping effect to a pre-tax basis and evaluate year-to-year changes in gross margin.

Here's how. Assume that a company discloses that LIFO dipping increased its net income by $3,055,000. Further assume that the income tax rate is 35%. Then:

$$\text{After-tax effect} = \text{Pre-tax effect} \times (1 - \text{marginal tax rate})$$
$$= \text{Pre-tax effect} \times (1 - 0.35)$$
$$= \frac{\$3,055,000}{0.65}$$
$$= \text{Pre-tax effect of } \$4,700,000$$

The $4,700,000 pre-tax impact of LIFO dipping would then be used to undertake an analysis like Exhibit 9.10.

Eliminating LIFO Ratio Distortions

LIFO inventory costing can lead to easily corrected ratio distortions. For example, on its June 30, 1996, balance sheet, Vacu-Dry Company reported total current assets of US$6,669,000 and total current liabilities of US$2,533,000. Utilizing these num- bers, the current ratio at June 30, 1996, is:

$$\frac{\text{Current assets}}{\text{Current liabilities}} = \frac{\$6,669,000}{\$2,533,000} = 2.63$$

However, Exhibit 9.4 disclosed that the LIFO inventory carrying amount under- stated FIFO (and replacement cost) inventory by US$2,114,000. This is the LIFO reserve which we must add to the numerator to reflect the current ratio in truly cur- rent terms. The adjusted current ratio is ($000 omitted):

$$\frac{\$6,669 + \$2,114}{\$2,533} = 3.47$$

The current ratio improves after making the LIFO adjustment. Most other ratios deteriorate once the adjustments for LIFO effects are recognized. To illustrate the general deterioration, consider the inventory turnover ratio:

$$\frac{\text{Cost of goods sold}}{\text{Average inventory}} = \text{Inventory turnover}$$

The inventory turnover ratio is designed to reflect the physical turnover of product—that is, how long the typical unit remains in inventory. Most firms have many inventory categories. This diversity renders unit measures of inventory turnover meaningless since unit turnover is difficult to interpret in a diversified firm. That's why dollar—rather than unit—inventory measures are used to compute the turnover ratio. For Vacu-Dry, using the inventory amounts from Exhibit 9.4 and cost of goods sold from Exhibit 9.9, inventory turnover for 1996 is ($000 omitted):

$$\frac{\$24,142}{(\$3,430 + \$5,414)/2} = 5.5 \text{ times per year}$$

The typical unit turns over 5.5 times per year. Another way to understand what this means is to divide 5.5 into 365, the number of days in a year. The result, 365/5.5 = 66.4, shows that the typical unit remains in inventory for 66.4 days.

The inventory turnover ratio is structured to approximate physical unit flow. The numerator is the cumulative dollar cost of units that have been sold; the denominator is the average cost of units on hand during the year. Under "normal" circumstances, the quotient should reflect the physical unit turnover. Unfortunately, LIFO frequently distorts the representation of physical unit flow. To see why, consider the denominator of the Vacu-Dry ratio; it does *not* reflect the then-current cost of the inventory at the beginning and end of fiscal year 1996, since the LIFO reserve at these times was, respectively, US$1,334,000 and US$2,114,000. For a firm using LIFO:

- The numerator of the ratio—cost of goods sold—is dominantly made up of 1996 costs.
- The denominator—average inventory—comprises old LIFO costs.

The quotient will not capture physical unit turnover unless an adjustment is made to the denominator. Furthermore, an adjustment to the numerator is also required because the pre-tax impact of the LIFO dipping (US$642,000) leads to a situation in which the cost of goods sold numerator understates *current* cost of goods sold by this amount. To correctly gauge physical turnover, the analyst must *always* adjust the denominator of LIFO firms' turnover by adding the LIFO reserve amounts to beginning and ending inventory. In addition, the numerator must also be adjusted for LIFO liquidation profits whenever LIFO dipping occurs. The Vacu-Dry 1996 inventory turnover ratio adjusting both the numerator and the denominator is ($000 omitted):

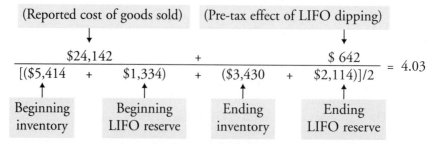

Dividing this LIFO adjusted turnover (4.03) into 365 days reveals that the typical unit, in fact, remains in inventory for 90.6 days—considerably longer than the 66.4 days suggested by the unadjusted analysis.

Recall that the LIFO reserve is only required to be disclosed by American companies; so performing such a distortion correction for Canadian companies using LIFO may not be possible.

Eliminating Realized Holding Gains for FIFO Firms

LIFO puts realized holding gains into income when old LIFO layers are eliminated. In contrast, reported income for FIFO firms *always* includes some realized holding gains during periods of rising inventory costs. In other words, FIFO cost of goods sold is too *low* by the amount of the inventory holding gains that have occurred during the period. Since holding gains are potentially unsustainable, astute analysts try to remove them from reported FIFO income (or, equivalently, add them to FIFO cost of goods sold).

The size of the divergence between FIFO cost of goods sold and replacement cost of goods sold depends on two factors:

1. *The significance of input cost changes.* All other factors being equal, the greater the amount of cost change, the larger the divergence between FIFO and replacement cost of goods sold.
2. *The rapidity of physical inventory turnover.* The slower the inventory turnover, the larger the divergence.

We illustrate a simple way to convert cost of goods sold from FIFO to replacement cost—and thereby eliminate realized holding gains from FIFO income.[11] This method requires an estimate of inventory cost change and assumes rapid inventory turnover. Consider the following example.

Ray Department Store experienced the following inventory transactions during 2001:

Beginning inventory (FIFO basis)	$1,000,000
Merchandise purchases	+8,000,000
Goods available for sale	9,000,000
Ending inventory (FIFO basis)	−1,100,000
Cost of goods sold (FIFO basis)	$7,900,000

On average, Ray's input costs for inventory increased by 10% during 2001.

This adjustment has three steps:

1. Determine FIFO cost of goods sold. In the example, it is $7,900,000. This amount is *not* adjusted.
2. Adjust the beginning inventory for one full year of specific price change. In the example, this is $1,000,000 times 10% or $100,000.
3. Replacement cost of goods sold is the sum of the amount in step 1 ($7,900,000) and the amount in step 2 ($100,000)—that is, $8,000,000.

The difference between the computed replacement cost of goods sold ($8,000,000) and the FIFO cost of goods sold ($7,900,000) equals the estimated amount of realized holding gains included in the FIFO income figure ($100,000). This simple method gives results that closely approximate those yielded by tedious calculation approaches.

(In Appendix 9A to this chapter, we provide an intuitive explanation for why this procedure for isolating realized holding gains for FIFO firms "works." We also discuss how analysts can use either price indices or competitors' data to estimate the rate of inventory cost change—10% in the example.)

Inventory Errors

Errors in computing inventory are rare and almost always accidental. For example, a computer programming mistake might assign the wrong costs to inventory items. But there are also occasional instances where companies deliberately (and fraudulently) misstate inventories to manipulate reported earnings. You must first understand how inventory errors affect reported results in order to understand why some managers use this misrepresentation technique.

To visualize the effect of inventory errors, let's assume that due to a miscount in the 2001 year-end physical inventory, Jones Corporation's ending inventory is *overstated* by $1 million. Further assume there are no other inventory errors. Using the cost-of-goods-sold formula, we see that this error *understates* 2001 cost of goods sold by $1 million:

Effect of 2001 Error on:

Beginning inventory	No error
Plus: Purchases	No error
Equals: Goods available	No error
Minus: Ending inventory	Overstated by $1 million
Equals: Cost of goods sold	Understated by $1 million

Because ending inventory is subtracted in the cost-of-goods-sold computation, an overstatement of ending inventory leads to an understatement of cost of goods sold. By understating cost of goods sold by $1 million, pre-tax income is overstated by $1 million. Furthermore, if the error is not detected and corrected in 2001, the error will also cause 2002 pre-tax income to be misstated. The reason that the error carries over into 2002 is because the December 31, 2001, ending inventory becomes the January 1, 2002, beginning inventory. So the carryforward effect (assuming no other 2002 inventory errors) is:

Effect of 2001 Error on the 2002 COGS Computation

Beginning inventory	Overstated by $1 million
Plus: Purchases	No error
Equals: Goods available	Overstated by $1 million
Minus: Ending inventory	No error
Equals: Cost of goods sold	Overstated by $1 million

The overstatement of 2002 cost of goods sold (COGS) results in a $1 million understatement of 2002 pre-tax income. The carryforward effect in 2002 is equal in amount but in the opposite direction from the 2001 effect. Because the first year's income is overstated by $1 million and the second year's income is understated by the same amount, by December 31, 2002—the end of the two-year cycle—the retained earnings account (which is cumulative, of course) will be correct.

If an inventory error is discovered during the reporting year, it is corrected immediately. However, if an error is not discovered until a subsequent year (say 2002 in our example), then the retained earnings balance as of the beginning of the discovery year (2002) is corrected. If the error has a material effect on the company's financial statements, it must be separately disclosed.

If we assume that Jones Corporation's inventory error was discovered in January 2002 and that the income tax rate is 35%, the entry to correct the error is:

DR Retained earnings	$650,000	
DR Income tax payable	350,000	
CR Inventory		$1,000,000

In recent years, the media have coined the phrase "accounting irregularities." Some of these irregularities simply relate to exuberant use of the flexibility within GAAP; others involve fraud. Accounting fraud is relatively rare, but it does happen. And some of the more spectacular frauds involve inventory misstatement. Leslie Fay Companies, Inc., is an example. The company manufactures women's apparel. 1992 was expected to be a difficult year for the firm because of pricing and style issues. To offset the emerging profit shortfall, quarter-end inventory was overstated. As we just saw, overstating ending inventory decreases cost of goods sold, increases income, and masks the adverse real conditions facing the company. Subsequent shareholder litigation alleged that this behaviour was partly motivated by a bonus plan tied to reported profits.[12] But as our numerical example illustrates, the phony earnings boost in the overstatement year reverses in the following year. So if the economic adversity that motivated the deliberate initial inventory overstatement continues, the inventory overstatements have to continue as well.

This is exactly what happened at Comptronix Corporation, an electronics manufacturer who lost an important customer in 1989.[13] After succumbing to the temptation of overstating profits by overstating inventory, the practice could not be abandoned without causing a reversal. So the overstatement continued until late 1992.[14] The fraud was eventually discovered at both companies. Can analysts do the same? For outsiders, fraud is difficult to detect. But, there are sometimes clues.[15] For example, the reduction in cost of goods sold arising from inventory overstatement increases gross margins. So an unexplained increase in gross margins during troubled economic times warrants investigation.

Summary

Financial reporting rules allow firms latitude in selecting a cost flow assumption for the purpose of determining the cost of goods sold reported on the income statement and the inventory values reported on the balance sheet. Some firms use FIFO, some (mainly American) use LIFO, and some use weighted average; others use a combination of these methods. This diversity in practice can severely hinder both interfirm and intrafirm comparability when inventory purchase costs are changing over time, which is the usual case. FIFO gross margins may embed sizeable inventory holding gains which may not be sustainable without continued inventory price increases. Similarly, LIFO gross margins can be distorted when LIFO liquidations occur. Working capital ratios and inventory turnover ratios of companies that are similarly situated can look quite different under LIFO versus FIFO inventory costing. Users of financial statements must understand these differences and know how to adjust for them using various footnote disclosures. Only by doing so can valid comparisons be made across firms that utilize different inventory cost flow assumptions. This chapter is designed to allow users to understand existing GAAP inventory methods and disclosures; it can also help users conduct informed comparisons and analysis of profitability and net asset positions across firms with varying inventory methods.

Self-Study Problem: Mitsuru Corporation

Mitsuru Corporation began business operations on January 1, 2001, as a wholesaler of macadamia nuts. Its purchase and sales transactions for 2001 are listed in Exhibit 9.11. Mitsuru uses a periodic inventory system.

1. **Compute 2001 ending inventory and cost of goods sold for Mitsuru Corporation using the weighted average cost flow assumption.**

Ending inventory totals 4,000 kg—that is, purchases of 23,000 kg minus sales of 19,000 kg. The average cost per kilogram (rounded) is:

$$\frac{\text{Total cost of goods available for sale} \to \$238,900}{\text{Kilograms} \to 23,000} = \$10.39/\text{kilogram}$$

Ending inventory is 4,000 kg times $10.39 or $41,560. Cost of goods sold is then determined as follows:

Total cost of goods available for sale	$238,900
Less: Ending inventory computed above	41,560
Cost of goods sold (weighted average method)	$197,340

2. **Compute 2001 ending inventory and cost of goods sold for Mitsuru Corporation using the FIFO cost flow assumption.**

Under the FIFO cost flow assumption, the ending inventory comprises the 4,000 most recently purchased kilograms of macadamia nuts. This ending inventory amount consists entirely of the December 18 purchase of 4,000 kg for $42,400.

Exhibit 9.11 MITSURU CORPORATION

Inventory Purchases and Sales

Date	Purchases			Sales (kg)
	Kilograms	Dollars/Kilogram	Total Dollars	
January 1	1,000	$10.00	$ 10,000	
February 3	4,000	10.20	40,800	
February 9				3,600
April 1	4,000	10.30	41,200	
May 29				3,500
June 28	5,000	10.40	52,000	
July 20				4,100
September 14	5,000	10.50	52,500	
September 17				4,200
December 18	4,000	10.60	42,400	
December 22				3,600
	23,000		$238,900	19,000

Accordingly, FIFO cost of goods sold is:

Total cost of goods available for sale	$238,900
Less: Ending FIFO inventory	42,400
FIFO cost of goods sold	$196,500

3. **Compute 2001 ending inventory and cost of goods sold for Mitsuru Corporation using the LIFO cost flow assumption.**

Under LIFO, the ending inventory comprises 4,000 kg of the oldest macadamia nut purchases. This 4,000 kg would consist of two layers:

January 1	1,000 kg	@	$10.00	=	$10,000
February 3	3,000 kg	@	$10.20	=	30,600
	4,000 kg				$40,600

Then, LIFO cost of goods sold is:

Total cost of goods available for sale	$238,900
Less: Ending LIFO inventory	40,600
LIFO cost of goods sold	$198,300

4. **Assume that the December 31, 2001, macadamia nut replacement cost is $10.60 per kilogram. Compute Mitsuru's LIFO reserve and use the beginning and ending LIFO reserve amounts to reconcile the LIFO cost of goods sold and the FIFO cost of goods sold.**

The LIFO reserve at a given point in time is the difference between the LIFO inventory book value and its then-current replacement cost. At January 1, 2001, Mitsuru Corporation's LIFO reserve was $0 since the LIFO book value and replacement cost both equalled $10,000. At December 31, 2001, the LIFO reserve was $1,800, computed as follows:

December 31, 2001, inventory replacement cost:	
4,000 kg @ $10.60	$42,400
December 31, 2001, LIFO inventory	40,600
December 31, 2001, LIFO reserve	$ 1,800

Using the formula for converting cost of goods sold from LIFO to FIFO in conjunction with the answers to Questions 2 and 3 of this Self-Study Problem yields:

$$CGS_{LIFO} + \begin{array}{c} Beginning \\ LIFO\ reserve \end{array} - \begin{array}{c} Ending \\ LIFO\ reserve \end{array} = CGS_{FIFO}$$

$$\$198,300 + 0 - \$1,800 = \$196,500$$

Notice that $196,500 equals the FIFO cost-of-goods-sold number computed in Question 2.

As discussed in the text, the reconciliation procedure is an approximation. Adding the LIFO reserve to the LIFO inventory equals replacement cost. If the inventory turns quickly, then inventory replacement cost *approximates* FIFO inventory. In this Self-Study Problem, ending FIFO inventory at $10.60 per kilogram exactly equals replacement cost. Hence, the adjustment is precise.

Appendix 9A

Eliminating Realized Holding Gains from FIFO Income

In this chapter, we show a simple way to estimate the amount of realized holding gains included in the FIFO income figure. In this appendix, we provide a simple example of this method.

Consider a firm buying and selling inventory in equal amounts daily as you contemplate Figure 9.4. The *quantity* of inventory purchased during the year is the area denoted "*P*." Beginning inventory *quantity* is the area denoted "*B*," and ending inventory *quantity* is the area denoted "*E*." Let's assume that *B* equals *E*—that is, inventory quantity did not change over the year. Under these conditions, the *units* making up FIFO cost of goods sold would consist of the area $B + (P - E)$. In other words, under the FIFO cost flow assumption, cost of goods sold consists of the first— or oldest—units available, which is beginning inventory plus the earliest purchases. Since purchases and sales occurred in equal amounts daily, the replacement cost of goods sold—in units—is made up of the area *P*. That is, under replacement cost, the units considered sold were the units purchased on the day of the sale. The difference between the units comprising the two cost of goods sold measures is the area *E* minus *B*. Expressed in units:

$$\text{CGS}_{RC} = \text{CGS}_{FIFO} + E - B \qquad (9.1)$$

Expressed in dollars:

$$\$\text{CGS}_{RC} = \$\text{CGS}_{FIFO} + \$E - \$B \qquad (9.2)$$

Notice that if inventory costs do not change over the year, $\$E = \$B$ and $\$\text{CGS}_{RC} = \$\text{CGS}_{FIFO}$. In general, it's reasonable to expect inventory costs to change from the beginning to the end of the year. If we assume that inventory purchase costs changed over the year at the rate *r*, then $\$E$ will not equal $\$B$, even though *E* units equals *B* units. Specifically, the dollar amount of ending inventory will equal $(1 + r)$ times the dollar amount of beginning inventory—that is:

$$\$E = \$B \times (1 + r) \qquad (9.3)$$

FIGURE 9.4 | DIAGRAM OF FIFO TO REPLACEMENT COST OF GOODS SOLD APPROXIMATION TECHNIQUE

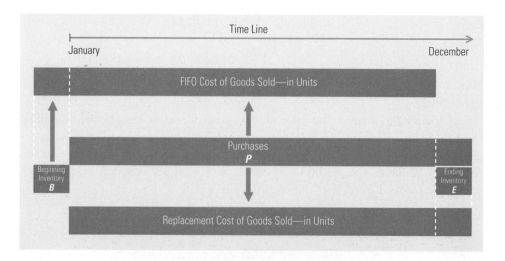

Substituting the value of $\$E$ from equation (9.3) into equation (9.2) yields:

$$\$CGS_{RC} = \$CGS_{FIFO} + \$B \times (1 + r) - \$B \qquad (9.4)$$

or:

$$\$CGS_{RC} = \$CGS_{FIFO} + \$B \times r \qquad (9.5)$$

Thus, the product $\$B \times r$ provides an estimate of the inventory holding profit (loss) that is embedded in the FIFO earnings number.

Notice that equation (9.5) is equivalent to the simple procedure used in the chapter. This approximation "works" as long as inventory unit quantities do not change very much over the year and as long as inventory purchases and sales take place frequently. If these conditions aren't met for a specific firm, the conversion from FIFO cost of goods sold to replacement cost of goods sold will not be accurate.

Eliminating realized holding gains from FIFO income requires estimates of r, the percentage change in inventory purchase costs. One means for estimating this rate is to use some input cost price index, such as one of the various price indices prepared by Statistics Canada.

Appendix 9B

Lower of Cost and Market Method

This appendix covers a widely used method in inventory accounting called the lower of cost and market method.

An asset represents a cost that has been incurred and which possesses future service potential value to the firm. If subsequent events cause the future service potential value of an asset to drop below its cost, then the asset's carrying value must be reduced. In inventory accounting, this is called the **lower of cost and market method.**

This GAAP inventory accounting method involves two phases. First, we need an answer to the question "Should inventory be accounted for on a company's balance sheet at *cost* (average, FIFO, LIFO) if the cost exceeds the market value of the inventory?" Let's make this easy to answer by assuming that the difference between the cost and market value is material, and we expect that the decline of the market value will be permanent. Under these conditions, if we left the inventory at cost on the balance sheet, the resulting financial statement measure of inventory would not be representationally faithful (Chapter 1). So writing the inventory down to market value seems reasonable and fair. For example, suppose FIFO cost was $2,000, and market value was $1,700. A journal entry such as the following would record the writedown, at the financial statement date at which the market decline below cost was decided by management to be material and permanent:

DR	Loss from decline in market value of inventory	$300	
	CR	Inventory	$300

where the account "Loss due to decline in market value of inventory" is an expense account appearing on the income statement.

A second question is "What 'market value' should be used? The replacement cost of the inventory (an input market number), or the 'net realizable value' (NRV) of the inventory (an output market number)?" Canadian GAAP permit either, although most companies use NRV.

The NRV and replacement cost could, in any given situation, be quite different. NRV is equal to the estimated selling price of inventory under normal business conditions, after deducting estimated costs of completion and sale. Replacement cost is equal to the cost of replacing the inventory. Both quantities—NRV and replacement cost—must be estimated at the same date.

American accounting practice in this area has evolved differently from Canadian practice, and the difference is worth describing, since it brings to light some difficulties. American practice focuses attention on the inventory's replacement cost. Whenever the replacement cost of inventory declines below its original cost, the presumption is that the service potential value of the inventory has been impaired and a writedown is warranted. If a unit of inventory originally cost $10 but if its replacement cost falls to $8, a decrease in carrying value of $2 would be required. *What's implied here is that inventory cost and eventual selling price move together.* The decline in replacement cost is presumed to signal that the price at which the inventory can be sold—its future service potential value—has fallen. Thus, a loss has occurred which must be recognized in the accounts.

In practice, the relationship between cost decreases and selling price decreases is unlikely to be perfect. For this reason, the market value used in applying lower of cost and market is subject to two constraints in American accounting practice:

1. **Ceiling.** "Market" should not exceed the net realizable value—that is, the estimated selling price in the ordinary course of business less reasonably predictable costs of completion and disposal.
2. **Floor.** "Market" should not be less than net realizable value reduced by an allowance for an approximately normal profit margin.[16]

The constraint that market should not exceed net realizable value represents a ceiling designed to avoid overstating obsolete goods. For example, a motor originally cost $80 but is now obsolete and has a net realizable value of only $50. Even if its replacement cost is $65, the inventory should be valued at its net realizable value of $50. To value it at replacement cost of $65 would fail to recognize the full extent of the expected loss that has occurred.

The floor constraint covers situations in which declines in input replacement cost do not move perfectly with declines in selling price. To illustrate, assume the following:

	Original Cost	Replacement Cost	Net Realizable Value	Net Realizable Value Less Normal Profit of $11
Inventory item	$60	$46	$70	$59

An inventory writedown to $46 would lead to an abnormally high profit of $24 (i.e., net realizable value of $70 less $46) when the inventory is sold in a later period. This $24 profit exceeds the $11 normal profit margin. A writedown to $59 would still afford the company a normal profit margin; any larger writedown would result in excess profits in future periods. The floor provides a lower bound for writedowns in situations where input replacement cost and selling price do not move together.

Together, these two constraints mean that the market value used in applying the lower of cost and market rule is the *middle value* of (1) replacement cost, (2) net realizable value, and (3) net realizable value less a normal profit margin. This is depicted in Figure 9.5. Applying the lower of cost and market rule is illustrated in Exhibit 9.12 using four scenarios.

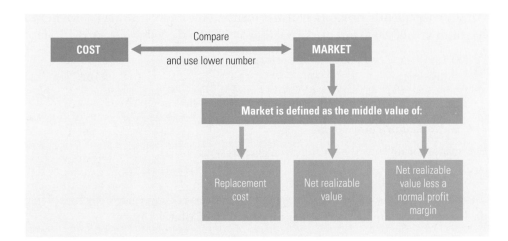

FIGURE 9.5
LOWER OF COST
AND MARKET
RULE FOR
INVENTORIES

Exhibit 9.12 APPLICATION OF LOWER OF COST AND MARKET RULE

		Market				
Scenario	Original Cost	Replacement Cost	Net Realizable Value	Net Realizable Value Less a Normal Profit Margin	Middle of the Three Market Values	Inventory Value Used
1	$20	$23	$27	$21	$23	$20
2	20	19	24	18	19	19
3	20	19	18	12	18	18
4	20	15	25	19	19	19

Scenario 1. Inventory is valued at cost ($20) since cost is lower than the middle of the three market values ($23). This illustrates the traditional rule for inventory carrying values in historical cost accounting: Inventories are carried at original cost unless the future service potential value of this cost has been impaired.

Scenario 2. Inventory is carried at replacement cost ($19). Market is defined as the middle value of the three definitions in Figure 9.5. The values are 18, 19, and 24, and 19 is between 18 and 24. Since market is less than original cost, it is presumed that a portion of the original service potential value of the inventory has been impaired. Therefore, the inventory is written down.

Scenario 3. Inventory is valued at net realizable value ($18) since net realizable value is the middle "market" value (i.e., 18 is between 12 and 19) and is below cost. Here we see the operation of the ceiling. This rule is intended to avoid carrying obsolete goods at a cost in excess of the net value that will be realized upon sale. If the rule were not invoked, inventory would be carried at $19 (its replacement cost), which is more than the $18 that it is expected to yield.

Scenario 4. Inventory is valued at net realizable value less a normal profit margin ($19) since this number is lower than original cost and is the middle value of the market price constraints. This illustrates the floor. If the rule were not invoked, inventory would be carried at $15 (its replacement cost). This would be an excessive writedown, since a $15 carrying cost would result in an above-normal margin when the goods are sold.

When a perpetual inventory system is used and inventory is written down from a cost of, say, $1,000,000 to a market value of $970,000, the following entry is made:[17]

DR Loss from decline in market value of inventory $30,000
     CR   Inventory $30,000

The lower of cost and market method can be applied to:

- individual inventory items
- classes of inventory—say, fertilizers versus weed killers
- the inventory as a whole

Companies have discretion regarding how inventories are aggregated when applying the lower of cost and market rule, as illustrated in Exhibit 9.13.

Exhibit 9.13 AGGREGATION ALTERNATIVES IN APPLYING THE LOWER OF COST AND MARKET RULE

Inventory Item	Cost	Market	Item	Class	Total
			Item	Class	Total
Class 1:					
Item 1	$10,000	$ 6,000	$ 6,000		
Item 2	3,000	8,000	3,000		
	$13,000	$14,000	$ 9,000	$13,000	
Class 2:					
Item 3	20,000	18,000	18,000	18,000	
	$33,000	$32,000	$27,000	$31,000	$32,000

Depending on whether the aggregation is by item of inventory, inventory class, or total inventory, the lower of cost and market value could be $27,000, $31,000, or $32,000.

The Contracting Origins of the Lower of Cost and Market Method

The lower of cost and market method for inventories evolved in the formative years of modern financial reporting to satisfy the information needs of what was then the most important external user group—commercial lenders. Banking in that era consisted mainly of securitized lending. Loans required collateral from the borrower, primarily in the form of inventory, accounts receivable, or fixed assets. Clearly, lenders wanted to avoid basing their decisions on overstated asset values, since overstated asset values resulted in inadequate amounts of collateral. The conservatism inherent in lower of cost and market represented a mechanism for protecting the then-dominant user group from unpleasant surprises—lower than expected collateral values. Thus, the lower of cost and market rule evolved because of the dominant form of lending contracts in use years ago.

Evaluation of the Lower of Cost and Market Rule

Individual and institutional equity investors are now important users of financial statements. The conservative bias built into the lower of cost and market rule protects lenders but it may sometimes harm these other users. Consider a prospective seller of an equity security of a company whose inventory is written down to market. If the writedown was unwarranted (e.g., because the decline in replacement cost did not presage a decline in eventual selling price), the prospective seller's position is worsened by lower of cost and market accounting, since the share price obtainable may be lower than the price that would exist with less conservative accounting. Clearly, conservative rules designed to systematically understate asset amounts favour lenders and equity purchasers over borrowers and equity sellers. This absence of neutrality which pervades lower of cost and market has troubled numerous financial reporting experts and has led to repeated criticisms of the approach.

In addition to its bias against those seeking loans and those selling equity securities, the lower of cost and market rule has another deficiency. It assumes that input costs and output prices generally move together. Therefore, a decline in input cost triggers a loss recognition because it is presumed that the cost decrease presages a selling price decrease. But there is little empirical evidence to corroborate this assumption. It is possible that input costs and output prices will move together. It is also possible that they may not. When input costs and selling prices do not move together, a loss may be recognized when, in fact, no loss has occurred. Consider, for example, the following illustration:

	Original Cost	Replacement Cost	Net Realizable Value	Net Realizable Value Less Normal Profit Margin
Cost relationships on January 1, 2001	$100	$100	$115	$90
Cost relationships on December 31, 2001	100	95	115	90

Strict application of the lower of cost and market rule using replacement cost as market would require a writedown of the inventory to $95 from its original cost of $100. However, the selling price of the inventory has not changed, since its net realizable value is still $115. Therefore, no loss exists but GAAP would require a $5 writedown!

In summary, the lower of cost and market rule reflects conservatism. As financial statement users have become more diverse, the rule has been subjected to mounting criticism. First, conservatism is itself an elusive concept; while inventory writedowns may initially be conservative, the resulting higher margin in the period following the writedown provides opportunities for earnings management. Second, as the use of published financial statements has broadened over the years, conservatism strikes many observers as a violation of the neutrality posture that reporting rules are designed to achieve. For example, if downward changes in replacement cost are considered to be reliable evidence of a loss, logic suggests that upward changes in replacement cost should similarly be considered reliable evidence of a gain. Finally, the lower of cost and market rule relies on an implicit relationship between input costs and output prices that may not prevail. When the input/output relationship does not exist, inventory losses may be recognized even though no real loss has occurred. As a consequence of these limitations, the lower of cost and market approach constitutes GAAP but it does not hold a secure place in accounting theory.

For more Exercises, Problems/Discussion Questions, and Cases, visit the Companion Website for this textbook at **www.pearsoned.ca/revsine**.

Exercises

E9-1 Account analysis

On January 1, 2001, the merchandise inventory of Citizen Company was $390,000. During 2001, Citizen purchased $1,900,000 of merchandise and recorded sales of $2,000,000. The gross profit (gross margin) on these sales was 20%.

Required:

What is the merchandise inventory of Citizen at December 31, 2001?

E9-2 Cost flow computations

Home Lighting had 200 lamps on hand at January 1, 2000, costing $18 each. Purchases and sales of lamps during the month of January were as follows:

Date	Purchases	Sales
January 12		150 @ $28
15	100 @ $20	
29	100 @ $22	
30		100 @ $32

Home does not maintain perpetual inventory records. According to a physical count, 150 lamps were on hand at January 31, 2000.

Required:

1. What is the cost of inventory at January 31, 2000, under the FIFO method?
2. What is the cost of the inventory at January 31, 2000, under the LIFO method?
3. How would your answers change, if at all, if a physical count showed that only 140 lamps were on hand at January 31, 2000?

E9-3 Account analysis

The following information is available for Day Company for 2001:

Cash disbursements for purchases of merchandise	$300,000
Increase in trade accounts payable	25,000
Decrease in merchandise inventory	10,000

Required:

What is the cost of goods sold for 2001?

E9-4 Account analysis

Retail Company's records indicate the following information:

Merchandise inventory, January 1, 2000	$ 550,000
Purchases, January 1 through December 31, 2000	2,250,000
Sales, January 1 through December 31, 2000	3,000,000

On December 31, 2000, a physical inventory determined that ending inventory of $650,000 was in the warehouse. Retail's gross profit on sales has remained constant at 30%. The company suspects some of the inventory may have been taken by some new employees.

Required:

At December 31, 2000, what is the estimated cost of missing inventory?

E9-5 Account analysis

On June 30, 2003, a flash flood damaged the warehouse and factory of Padway Corporation, completely destroying the work-in-process inventory. There was no damage to either the raw materials or finished goods inventories. A physical inventory taken after the flood revealed the following valuations:

Raw materials	$ 62,000
Work in process	–0–
Finished goods	119,000

The inventory of January 1, 2003, consisted of the following:

Raw materials	$ 30,000
Work in process	100,000
Finished goods	140,000
	$270,000

A review of the books and records disclosed that the gross profit margin historically approximated 25% of sales. The sales for the first six months of 2003 were $340,000. Raw material purchases were $115,000. Direct labour costs for this period were $80,000, and manufacturing overhead has historically been applied at 50% of direct labour.

Required:

Compute the value of the work-in-process inventory lost at June 30, 2003. Show supporting computations in good form.

E9-6 Cost flow computations

The Frate Company was formed on January 1, 2003. The following information is available from Frate's inventory records for Product Ply:

	Units	Unit Cost
January 1, 2003 (beginning inventory)	800	$ 9.00
Purchases:		
January 5, 2003	1,500	$10.00
May 25, 2003	1,200	$10.50
July 16, 2003	600	$11.00
November 26, 2003	900	$11.50

A physical inventory on December 31, 2003, showed 1,600 units on hand.

Required:

Prepare schedules to compute the ending inventory at December 31, 2003 under each of the following inventory methods:

   1. FIFO   2. LIFO   3. weighted average

Show supporting computations in good form.

E9-7 Absorption versus variable costing

Information from Green Company's records for the year ended December 31, 2001, is available as follows:

Net sales	$1,400,000
Cost of goods manufactured:	
Variable	$ 630,000
Fixed	$ 315,000
Operating expenses:	
Variable	$ 98,000
Fixed	$ 147,000
Units manufactured	70,000
Units sold	60,000
Finished goods inventory, 1/1/2001	–0–

There were no work-in-process inventories at the beginning or end of 2001.

Required:

1. What would be Green's finished goods inventory cost at December 31, 2001, under the variable (direct) costing method?
2. Under the absorption costing method, what would Green's operating income be?

Problems/Discussion Questions

P9-1 Inventory accounting—comprehensive

Alex Wholesalers Inc. began its business on January 1, 2002. Information on its inventory purchases and sales during 2002 is provided below. Assume a tax rate of 40%.

	Inventory Purchases		
	Units	Cost/Unit	Total
January 1	10,000	$4.00	$ 40,000
March 10	8,000	4.10	32,800
April 12	12,000	4.30	51,600
September 15	7,500	4.45	33,375
November 11	6,000	4.75	28,500
December 29	6,500	5.00	32,500
Units Available for Sale	**50,000**		**$218,775**

	Inventory Sales		
	Units	Price/Unit	Total
March 1	7,000	$8.00	$ 56,000
September 1	20,000	8.50	170,000
December 1	11,000	9.00	99,000
Units Sold	**38,000**		**$325,000**

1. Compute the cost of ending inventory and cost of goods sold under each of the following methods: (1) FIFO, (2) weighted average cost, and (3) LIFO. Assume Alex uses the periodic inventory procedure.
2. Assume that Alex uses the periodic LIFO method.

   (a) Calculate the replacement cost of the ending inventory and the American LIFO reserve as of the end of the year.
   (b) Provide an estimate of Alex's cost of goods sold under the periodic FIFO method based only on the information that would be publicly available to the investors of Alex under U.S. rules. Explain why your answer differs from FIFO cost of goods sold computed in Question 1.
   (c) The purchasing manager of Alex was planning to acquire 10,000 units of inventory on January 5, 2003, at $5 per unit. The accountant for Alex suggests that the company will be better off if Alex acquires the inventory on December 31, 2002. What are the pros and cons of the accountant's suggestion? Wherever possible, show supporting calculations.

3. Calculate cost of goods sold assuming that Alex uses the perpetual FIFO method.

P9-2 LIFO liquidation

The inventory footnote to the 2001 annual report of the Ruedy Company reads in part as follows:

> Because of a prolonged strike in one of our supplier's plants, inventories were unavoidably reduced during 2001. Under the LIFO system of accounting, this "eating into LIFO layers" resulted in an increase in after-tax net income of $36,000 over what it would have been had inventories been maintained at their physical levels which existed at the start of the year.

The price of Ruedy Company's merchandise purchases was $22 per unit for 20,000 units during 2001. Prior to 2001, inventory prices had risen steadily for many years. Ruedy Company uses a periodic inventory method. The company's inventory positions at the beginning and end of the year are summarized below. Ruedy's income tax rate is 40%.

Date	Physical Count of Inventory	LIFO Cost of Inventory
January 1, 2001	30,000 units	$?
December 31, 2001	20,000 units	260,000

Required:

1. Was 2001 cost of goods sold higher or lower as a result of "eating into LIFO layers"? By how much?
2. Were 2001 income taxes higher or lower as a result of "eating into LIFO layers"? By how much? (Keep in mind that LIFO may not be used in Canada for income tax filing purposes.)
3. What was the average cost per unit of the 10,000 units removed from the January 1, 2001, LIFO inventory?
4. What was the January 1, 2001, LIFO cost of inventory?
5. What was the reported 2001 cost of goods sold for Ruedy Company?

P9-3 Criteria for choosing a cost flow assumption

The president of Jeanette Corporation is in a dilemma regarding which inventory method (FIFO, average cost, or LIFO) to use. The controller of Jeanette Corporation provides the following list of factors that should be considered before making a choice.

1. Jeanette Corporation has borrowed money during the current month and has entered into a debt contract. The covenants of this contract require Jeanette Corporation to achieve a certain amount of net income and maintain a certain amount of working capital.

2. The board of directors of Jeanette is contemplating a proposal to reward the top management of Jeanette Corporation with an incentive bonus based on accounting net income.

3. The vice-president of finance suggests using the average cost method for financial reporting purposes. She argues that this method is a "good and fair compromise between FIFO and LIFO."

4. The president would like to adopt the method that provides both a better application of the matching principle and a more current measure of inventory on the balance sheet.

5. The controller suggests that Jeanette should adopt the FIFO method since "higher accounting income means higher stock price."

6. The assistant controller mentioned a bit sarcastically that "it doesn't matter what method we choose. The bottom line is just the result of a whole bunch of historical cost, arbitrary allocations anyway."

Required:

The president of Jeanette has asked you to write a report evaluating the pros and cons of each of the issues raised above. Given her busy schedule, she would like the report to be brief. Assume that Jeanette Corporation expects an upward trend in inventory prices.

P9-4 Inventory turnover

The following is excerpted from the financial statements of Tuneless Piano and Organ Company:

Consolidated Statements of Earnings

| | Years Ended December 31, | | |
	2002	2001	2000
Net sales	$120,657,455	$110,076,904	$103,230,431
Cost of goods sold	89,970,702	79,637,060	74,038,724
Gross profit	30,686,753	30,439,844	29,191,707

Inventories consist of the following:

	2002	2001
FIFO cost:		
Raw materials	$ 9,930,923	$ 9,500,765
Work in process	7,081,883	5,943,672
Finished goods	36,149,809	39,328,177
	53,162,615	54,772,614
Excess of FIFO cost over		
LIFO inventory value	(8,085,250)	(6,828,615)
	$45,077,365	$47,943,999

At December 31, 2002, approximately 77% of the company's inventories were valued on the LIFO method.

During the past three years, certain inventories were reduced. This reduction resulted in the liquidation of LIFO inventory layers carried at the lower costs prevailing in prior years as compared with the current cost of inventories. The effect of these inventory liquidations was to increase net earnings for 2002, 2001, and 2000 by approximately $694,000 ($0.20 per share), $519,000 ($0.15 per share) and $265,000 ($0.08 per share), respectively.

Required:

1. Estimate Tuneless' cost of goods sold and the cost of goods manufactured for the year 2002; assume the company had used FIFO instead of LIFO.
2. On the basis of these FIFO numbers, compute Tuneless' finished goods and work-in-process inventory turnovers (expressed in days) for the year 2002. What do these turnovers tell you about Tuneless' operating cycle?

P9-5 Interfirm comparisons

Fraser Corporation uses the LIFO method of inventory valuation and is in the process of preparing its financial statements for the year 2002. The controller of Fraser Corporation provided the following income statement for the year ended December 31, 2002, to the top management for review:

Sales Revenue		$1,000,000
Less: Cost of goods sold		
Beginning Inventory	150,000	
Add: Purchases	650,000	
Less: Ending Inventory	(200,000)	(600,000)
Gross Margin		400,000
Less: Selling and administrative expenses		(150,000)
Net Income Before Taxes		250,000
Less: Income taxes		(75,000)
Net Income		$ 175,000

The CEO of Fraser had mixed emotions after examining the income statement. He wanted to know how Fraser compares with its closest rival, KAS Corp., and he instructed the controller to "compute some ratios for both companies." KAS uses the FIFO method of inventory valuation. The following are excerpts from the controller's report:

	Fraser	**KAS**
Gross margin rate	?	49%
(Gross margin/sales)		
Return on sales	?	21%
(Net income/sales)		
Inventory turnover	?	1.8
CGS/average inventory		

Required:

1. Complete the controller's report by computing the ratios for Fraser from the information given in the income statement above. For each ratio, how does

Fraser compare with KAS? Explain how the choice of inventory methods biases the comparisons in favour of either Fraser or KAS.

2. After reviewing the controller's report, the CEO was concerned about Fraser's performance relative to KAS on two out of the three ratios. However, the controller pointed out to the CEO that the "perceived underperformance" of Fraser is primarily driven by differences in accounting methods. The CEO asked the controller, "Why don't you show me how an analyst might adjust our income statement to make it comparable to that of KAS?" Your task is to help the controller by preparing a pro forma income statement for Fraser, one that is comparable to that of KAS. Assume that if Fraser had used the FIFO method, the beginning and ending inventories would have been higher by $50,000 and $150,000, respectively. On the basis of the "adjusted" income statement, recompute the three ratios given in the controller's report, and explain how and why the CEO's earlier conclusions are altered by the revised figures.

P9-6 Identifying FIFO holding gains

Caldwell Corporation operates an ice cream processing plant and uses the FIFO inventory cost flow assumption. A partial income statement for the year ended December 31, 2003, appears below:

Caldwell Corporation
Statement of Income
For the Year Ended December 31, 2003

Sales revenues	$680,000,000
Cost of goods sold	360,000,000
Gross margin	320,000,000
SG&A expenses	200,000,000
Income before taxes	$120,000,000

Caldwell's physical inventory levels were virtually constant throughout 2003. The FIFO dollar amount of inventory at January 1, 2003, was $60,000,000. During 2003, the Consumer Price Index (an index of overall average purchasing power for typical urban-dwelling consumers) increased by 4%.

Caldwell Corporation's largest competitor, Fischer Confections, uses LIFO for inventory accounting. Here are excerpts from its December 31, 2003, inventory footnote:

Inventories are computed using the LIFO cost flow assumption. Comparative amounts were:

	December 31,	
	2003	2002
Raw materials	$ 8,100,000	$ 8,000,000
Finished goods	76,000,000	80,000,000
	$84,100,000	$88,000,000

The difference between the LIFO inventory amounts and the replacement cost of the inventory at December 31, 2003 and 2002, respectively, was $18,000,000 and $12,000,000. A LIFO liquidation occurred in 2003 which increased the reported gross margin by $1,000,000.

Required:

Using the above information, determine the *best* estimate of the amount of realized holding gains (or inventory profits) included in Caldwell Corporation's "income before taxes."

Cases

C9-1 Barbara Trading Company (KR): Understanding LIFO distortions

Barbara Trading Company has used the LIFO method of inventory accounting since its inception in 1970. At December 31, 1999, the ending inventory was:

Base layer	10,000 units @ $ 7	$ 70,000
1985 layer	5,000 units @ $12	60,000
		$130,000

The company uses the periodic inventory method, in which sales are assumed to have been made from the last inventory units acquired during the year (periodic LIFO). The purchase and sales prices change only once a year (i.e., on January 1). The operating expenses are $600,000 per year and the income tax rate is 40%.

Year	Units Purchased	Units Sold
2000	100,000 units @ $25	100,000 units @ $35
2001	90,000 units @ $30	100,000 units @ $40

During 2001, Barbara Trading implemented a new inventory management program to reduce the level of inventory holdings on hand.

Required:

1. Prepare Barbara's income statements for the years 2000 and 2001.
2. The CEO of Barbara, Ms I. M. Greedy, examined the effect of the new inventory management program on the company's inventory turnover. After doing some back-of-the-envelope calculations, Ms Greedy was overjoyed. "When our competitors are turning the inventory over 12–15 times a year, our inventory turnover for 2001 has exceeded 30!" How did the CEO estimate the inventory turnover ratio for 2001? From all the available information, provide an estimate of the "true" inventory turnover of Barbara during 2001. Assume the competitors' turnovers were based on data from their financial statements. What might be the potential limitations of comparing Barbara's inventory turnover with its competitors'? Show supporting figures where necessary.
3. The CEO was also ecstatic about the company's overall performance during the year 2001. "I am extremely pleased with the growth in our bottom line. Although some of the growth is probably due to the increase in selling price, most of it appears to be the result of our new inventory management program." Prepare a memo to the CEO explaining the "true" reasons behind the change in net income from 2000 to 2001. Show supporting figures where necessary. Also critically evaluate the rationale provided by the CEO for the growth in earnings.

C9-2 Baines Corporation: Absorption versus variable costing

Baines Corporation is a medium-sized manufacturer of fireplace grates. The company has been prosperous since its incorporation in 1960, largely due to a small, exceptionally skilled, and highly motivated managerial staff. Baines has been able to attract and retain its excellent management team because of a very attractive managerial incentive plan. The plan allocates 23% of total pre-tax FIFO-absorption cost profits into a pool which is distributed to managers as a year-end bonus. The bonus pool is allocated to individual managers using a point system based upon each manager's performance relative to a budgeted goal.

Data relating to 2002 operations were as follows:

Beginning inventory	1,500,000 units @ $2.95
Ending inventory	1,500,000 units @ $2.95
Production	4,000,000 units
Sales	4,000,000 units @ $3.50
Variable production costs	$1.45/unit
Fixed production costs	$6,000,000/year

Reported pre-tax profit for 2002 was:

Sales revenues	(4,000,000 @ $3.50)		$14,000,000
Costs of goods sold:			
Variable production costs	(4,000,000 @ $1.45)	$5,800,000	
Fixed production costs	(4,000,000 @ $1.50)	6,000,000	
			11,800,000
Operating profit			2,200,000
Interest expense			200,000
Pre-tax profit			$ 2,000,000

Early in 2003, interest rates increased and the president of Baines Corporation, Mr. Carleton, was concerned about the rising cost of financing the inventory. After a careful study of the situation, Mr. Carleton became convinced that inventory levels could be reduced considerably without adversely affecting sales or delivery performance, provided certain changes in purchasing, production, and sales procedures were adopted. Accordingly, Mr. Carleton called a meeting of the management group in February 2003 and outlined his multifaceted plan for reducing inventories.

His basic strategy met with immediate acceptance, and various additional efficiencies and other inventory management improvements were suggested by several of the participants. The meeting adjourned with each manager resolving to do all that was possible to decrease inventory levels and thereby reduce interest expenses.

As the year progressed, Mr. Carleton's proposals and the refinements suggested by the other managers were put into practice; as a result, inventory levels were significantly reduced by December 31, 2003. The managers were quite pleased with their successful implementation of the new strategy, and morale was quite high.

Basic facts concerning 2003 performance were:

Beginning inventory	1,500,000 units @ $2.95
Ending inventory	700,000 units @ $3.325
Production	3,200,000 units
Sales	4,000,000 units @ $3.50
Variable production costs	$1.45/unit
Fixed production costs	$6,000,000/year
Interest expense	$100,000/year

Shortly after the final 2003 profit figures were reported early in 2004, a general management meeting was held. As he walked into the room, Mr. Carleton was somewhat surprised to see a rather sullen and dispirited group of managers confronting him. One was heard to mumble, "Well, I wonder what this year's double-cross will be!"

Required:

1. What do you think caused the abrupt change in the mood of the management team at Baines Corporation? Cite figures to support your explanation.
2. How might this problem have been prevented? Cite figures to support your explanation.

Integrative Running Case Study
Bombardier on the Web

Inventory accounting information was published in the audited financial statements of Bombardier Inc. for the year ended January 31, 2002, on pages 76, 77 and in footnote 6 of the audited financial statements in the annual report. See this text's Companion Website at **www.pearsoned.ca/revsine**.

One of the aerospace businesses acquired by Bombardier was Canadair Ltd., which was sold to Bombardier by the government of Canada in 1986. In 1982, Canadair had reported huge losses in relation to the development of its Challenger aircraft; a newspaper article written at the time suggested that Canadair had made overly aggressive use of so-called program inventory accounting, resulting in a billion-dollar writedown of inventory against income as "Unusual items relating to Challenger program." Note 3 and Note 4 from the 1982 audited financial statements of Canadair Ltd. follow:

Excerpt from Notes to Consolidated Financial Statements
Years Ended December 31, 1982 and 1981

3. Challenger Program—Commercial Production and Unusual Items

The Challenger 600 program commenced in late 1976 with first flight in November 1978 and type certification in November 1980. Modifications developed through the certification process were incorporated in the aircraft in production during 1981. As a result of continual review and monitoring of production throughout 1982, management has determined that the program development process was completed by December 31, 1981 and that commercial production commenced in 1982. Type certification of the Challenger 601 was received in March 1983. At December 31, 1982, 67 aircraft had been delivered under the program.

Prior to 1982, costs such as development, finance, marketing, product support and general and administrative expenses had been included as part of contracts in process inventory as the management of the company believed at the time that all such inventoried costs would be recovered in the future. Concurrently with the commencement of commercial production, the company ceased charging these costs to contracts in process inventory and such costs incurred since January 1, 1982, have been expensed in the year. Before the commencement of commercial production, the cost of each aircraft delivered was removed from contracts in process and charged to cost of sales in an amount which equalled the selling price of the aircraft delivered.

Management no longer believes that there is reasonable assurance that the inventoried costs discussed in the preceding paragraph will be recovered from future sales. Thus, these costs have been written off to 1982 earnings as unusual items. Unusual items written off in the amount of $1,054.3 million also include estimated excess early production cost, development costs incurred in 1982 for the Challenger 601, provisions for claims, surplus and obsolete materials and other related estimated losses, aggregating $361.2 million.

4. Contracts in Process and Inventories

(in thousands of dollars)	1982	1981
Finished goods including aircraft, less advances and progress billings of $19.1 million (1981—nil)	$ 68,553	$ 5,820
Government contracts in process	1,749	5,461
Commercial programs and contracts in process, less advances and progress billings of $180.9 million (1981—$201.4 million)	44,446	1,008,766
Inventories of commercial products, materials and spare parts	12,903	11,572
	$127,651	$1,031,619

Required:

1. Describe in your own words the method of inventory accounting used by Canadair.
2. Assuming the allegation in the newspaper article was correct, explain why this method was used too aggressively.
3. Describe in detail Bombardier's inventory accounting policy.
4. Explain why the accounting for Bombardier's long-term contracts and programs may not be susceptible to the same risks today as its Canadair operations before Bombardier acquired it back in 1982.
5. How susceptible to "earnings management" is program inventory accounting?

Collaborative Learning Case

CL9-1 Weldotron Corporation (KR): Strategic choice of accounting methods

The following excerpts are taken from Weldotron's financial statements (US$).

Weldotron Corporation and Subsidiaries		
Condensed Consolidated Balance Sheets **February 28, 1994 and February 28, 1993**		
(US$ in thousands)	**1994**	**1993**
Assets		
Total current assets	$15,449	$16,162
Net property, plant, and equipment	3,417	3,725
Other assets	220	170
Total assets	$19,086	$20,057
Liabilities and stockholders' equity		
Total current liabilities	7,144	7,021
Long-term debt less current portion	1,527	1,585
Other long-term liabilities	683	637
Total liabilities	9,354	9,243
Minority interest	722	700
Stockholders' equity:		
Common stock, par value $0.05 per share; issued 2,352,720 in 1994 and 1,882,720 in 1993	118	94
Additional paid-in capital	9,798	8,715
(Deficit) Retained earnings	(783)	1,428
	9,133	10,237
Less: Common stock in treasury	(123)	(123)
Total stockholders' equity	9,010	10,114
Total liabilities & stockholders' equity	$19,086	$20,057

Weldotron Corporation and Subsidiaries

Condensed Consolidated Statements of Operations
For the Years Ended February 28, 1994, February 28, 1993, and February 29, 1992

(US$ in thousands)	1994	1993	1992
Net sales	$30,440	$26,400	$29,061
Costs and expenses:			
Cost of sales	22,375	19,322	21,372
Selling, general, and administrative	9,258	9,471	8,902
Depreciation and amortization	558	612	678
Restructuring charges	625	—	—
	32,816	29,405	30,952
Loss from operations	(2,376)	(3,005)	(1,891)
Other income (expenses)	128	(33)	606
Income tax (benefit) provision	59	(26)	—
Minority interest share of (income) loss	(22)	(57)	123
Loss from continuing operations	(2,211)	(3,121)	(1,162)
Discontinued operations	—	—	(1,059)
Net loss	$(2,211)	$(3,121)	$(2,221)

Excerpts from Footnotes:

(US$ in thousands)

1. Summary of Significant Account Policies

Inventories: Substantially all inventories are valued at the lower of cost, determined by the use of the first in, first out method (FIFO) or market (see Note 2).

Income Taxes: Weldotron Corporation and its subsidiaries file a consolidated federal income tax return. Accumulated undistributed earnings of the Company's foreign subsidiary were approximately $352 at February 28, 1994. No provision has been made for U.S. income taxes on these earnings as the Company has reinvested or plans to reinvest overseas.

2. Change in Accounting Principle for Inventories

Effective February 28, 1994, the Company changed its basis of valuing inventories from the last in, first out (LIFO) method to the first in, first out (FIFO) method.

In previous years, the Company experienced significant operating losses and has addressed these problems by discontinuing certain products and related parts. The results of inventory reductions in previous years resulted in the liquidation of LIFO layers which resulted in a mismatching of older costs with current revenues, which defeats the primary objective of LIFO. Further reductions of inventory levels are expected from the discontinuance of products and parts as well as better manufacturing methods which will reduce production lead times. Under these circumstances, the FIFO method of inventory valuation is the preferable method due to the improved matching of revenues and expenses and the current industry practice.

The change has been applied retroactively by restating prior years' financial statements. The effects of the reversal of the previous LIFO reserve were partially offset by the appropriate application of FIFO costing requirements. The effects of this change in the method of valuing inventory were to increase the net loss previously reported in

1993 by $128 and to decrease the net loss previously reported in 1992 by $97. The effects on 1994 were not material. The effects of this restatement were also to increase retained earnings as of March 1, 1991 by $2,356 (i.e., the retroactive effect). ...

7. Long Term Debt and Short Term Borrowings

On June 25, 1991, the Company entered into a credit facility (the "Credit Facility") with Congress Financial Corporation ("Congress"), a CoreStates Company, to provide a revolving line of credit and term loan for working capital purposes not to exceed $5,000, which replaced the Company's existing credit facility. The interest rate is 3.75% over the CoreStates floating base rate, which was 6% at February 28, 1994. The Credit Facility further requires that the Company pay fees on the unused line of credit, for administration and upon early termination of the Credit Facility. On April 13, 1994, the Credit Facility was extended for one year. It expires and is due and payable on or before June 25, 1995.

The Credit Facility is collateralized by substantially all of the assets of the Company and its domestic subsidiaries. Borrowings under the Credit Facility are limited to certain percentages of eligible inventory and accounts receivable including stipulations as to the ratio of advances collateralized by receivables compared to advances collateralized by inventory.

The Credit Facility's covenants stipulate that tangible domestic net worth of greater than $8,200 and consolidated working capital greater than $9,500 be maintained. In addition, the Credit Facility restricts the payment of dividends, limits the amount of the advances to and guarantees for the Company's foreign subsidiary and limits annual capital expenditures to $500. At February 28, 1994 the Company was in compliance with the covenants of the Credit Facility.

Borrowings under the Credit Facility aggregated $3,215, including a $1,500 long-term loan at February 28, 1994. The remaining borrowing under the Credit Facility is included in current liabilities.

Tax Note:

At February 28, 1994, $8,400 of federal tax loss carryforwards are available for regular income tax purposes.

Note 2 states that Weldotron changed its inventory method from LIFO to FIFO effective February 28, 1994. In the same note, the company has provided justifications for the change in the inventory cost flow assumptions. Note 7 discloses details of the company's credit facility and covenants. This note states that the company was in compliance with the covenants on February 28, 1994.

Required:

Financial reporting choices can sometimes allow companies to achieve strategic objectives and benefit shareholders. Using this perspective, evaluate the effect of Weldotron's inventory accounting change on its debt covenants, specifically on the tangible domestic net worth constraint of US$8,200.

Endnotes

1. Manufacturing overhead includes items such as amortization of production equipment and buildings, power, indirect labour, and so on.

2. "Inventories," *CICA Handbook,* Section 3030.

3. When the physical count reveals inventory shortages, the accounting records must be adjusted to conform to the actual amount on hand. For instance, if a shortage of $310 was indicated, the adjustment would be:

DR Loss from inventory shortage
    (or cost of goods sold) $310
    CR Inventory $310

4. Consignment goods also raise potential revenue recognition issues for the consignor that analysts must consider. For example, manufacturers may ship products to their dealers on consignment and nevertheless try to treat such shipments as sales, thereby recognizing income prematurely. Consequently, if "sales" terms provide the "purchaser" with the right to return unsold goods or if the cash payment terms on the "sale" are unusually long, it is possible that the manufacturer has treated consignment shipments as sales, thereby overstating both sales revenues and income and understating inventory.

5. In certain cases, interest incurred while inventory is being developed for sale can be capitalized, as described in Chapter 10. Examples include discrete projects such as shipbuilding or real estate development—that is, cases in which money is borrowed to finance construction over several reporting periods.

6. In our example, FIFO inventory is shown at *exactly* current cost. In more complicated situations that occur in real organizations, FIFO inventory amounts will *approximate* current costs. The faster the inventory turnover (cost of goods sold divided by average inventory), the closer the correspondence between inventory at FIFO cost and inventory at replacement cost.

7. But American companies that use LIFO for income tax filing purposes are required under U.S. tax rules to use LIFO for financial reporting (GAAP) purposes. This is called the **LIFO conformity rule**.

8. This conversion to FIFO will be an approximation when the LIFO reserve definition used by a particular company is the difference between inventory at LIFO and at replacement cost. As long as inventory turns fairly rapidly, the approximation is close.

9. T. Carroll, D. W. Collins, and W. B. Johnson, "The LIFO–FIFO Choice and the Quality of Earnings Signals," working paper, University of Iowa, August 1997.

10. This belief is correct when margins follow a random-walk pattern. In this type of environment, the least-biased estimate of the next period's value is generated by simply extrapolating the most recently observed past value.

11. See A. Falkenstein and R. L. Weil, "Replacement Cost Accounting: What Will Income Statements Based on the SEC Disclosures Show?—Part II," *Financial Analysts Journal,* March–April 1977, pp. 48–57. We have altered the Falkenstein and Weil procedural description slightly to simplify the exposition.

12. L. Vickery, "Leslie Fay's Ex-Financial Chief, Polishan, Is Found Guilty of Fraud," *Wall Street Journal,* July 7, 2000.

13. See C. Mulford and E. Comiskey, *Financial Warnings* (New York: John Wiley & Sons, Inc., 1996), pp. 228–233.

14. For a comprehensive discussion of the accounting issues at Comptronix, see J. L. Boockholdt, "Comptronix, Inc.: An Audit Case Involving Fraud," *Issues in Accounting Education,* February 2000, pp. 105–128.

15. For a discussion of these clues, see Mulford and Comiskey, op. cit.

16. "Restatement and Revision of Accounting Research Bulletins," *Accounting Research Bulletin No. 43* (New York: AICPA, 1953), Chapter 4, para. 8.

17. If a periodic inventory system is used, this entry would not be made. Instead, the ending *market* value of inventory ($970,000) would be used as ending inventory in the cost-of-goods-sold computation. However, this treatment essentially "buries" the $30,000 loss as an undisclosed element of cost of goods sold.

10
Capital Assets and Amortization

LEARNING OBJECTIVES
After studying this chapter, you should be able to:

1. Determine the measurement base used in accounting for capital assets and understand why this base was used

2. Identify which specific costs can be capitalized and choose which joint costs should be allocated among assets

3. Understand how generally accepted accounting principles (GAAP) measurement rules can complicate trend analysis and how to avoid misinterpretations

4. Know why balance sheet carrying amounts for internally developed intangibles usually differ from their real value

5. Recognize capital asset impairment

6. Understand computations for different amortization methods

7. Adjust for different amortization assumptions in order to improve interfirm comparisons

8. Know the international differences between capital asset accounting and amortization practices

An asset is something that generates future economic benefits and is under the exclusive control of a single entity. Assets can be tangible items like inventories or buildings and intangible items like patents and trademarks.

The previous two chapters—receivables and inventories—examined current assets. Current assets represent a large part of total assets for many companies. Recollect that a current asset is expected to be converted into cash within one year or within the operating cycle, whichever is longer.

This chapter concentrates on operating assets expected to yield their economic benefits (or service potential) over a period longer than one year. Such assets are called **capital** or **long-lived assets** to differentiate them from current assets. In practice, the term "fixed assets" is often used.

Inappropriate accounting for capital assets can have a very material impact on reported financial results, and therefore on the quality of earnings. This was perhaps most dramatically shown in the case of WorldCom Inc., the major American company that announced incorrect capital asset accounting on June 25, 2002, and subsequently filed for bankruptcy on July 21, 2002.

To get a flavour of the issues involving capital asset accounting in the WorldCom case, read this excerpt from the claim that the Securities Exchange Commission (SEC) filed in the United States District Court for the Southern District of New York on June 26, 2002:

> The operating cycle begins with the receipt of raw materials inventory and ends when the cash is received for the completed product that has been sold. If inventory turns over every 90 days and if the average receivables collection period is 50 days, then the operating cycle is 140 days (i.e., 90 + 50).

The Securities and Exchange Commission ("the Commission") alleges for its Complaint as follows:

1. From at least the first quarter of 2001 through the first quarter of 2002, defendant WorldCom Inc. ("WorldCom") defrauded investors. In a scheme directed and approved by its senior management, WorldCom disguised its true operating performance by using undisclosed and improper accounting that materially overstated its income before income taxes and minority interests by approximately [US]$3.055 billion in 2001 and [US]$797 million during the first quarter of 2002.

2. By improperly transferring certain costs to its capital accounts, WorldCom falsely portrayed itself as a profitable business during 2001 and the first quarter of 2002. WorldCom's transfer of its costs to its capital accounts violated the established standards of generally accepted accounting principles ("GAAP"). WorldCom's improper transfer of certain costs to its capital accounts was not disclosed to investors in a timely fashion, and misled investors about WorldCom's reported earnings. This improper accounting action was intended to manipulate WorldCom's earnings in the year ending 2001 and in the first quarter of 2002 to keep them in line with estimates by Wall Street analysts.

   …

THE FRAUDULENT SCHEME

4. WorldCom is a major global communications provider, operating in more than 65 countries. WorldCom provides data transmission and Internet services for businesses, and, through its MCI unit, provides telecommunications services for businesses and consumers. WorldCom became an important player in the telecommunications industry in the 1990s. However, as the economy cooled in 2001, WorldCom's earnings and profits similarly declined, making it difficult to keep WorldCom's earnings in line with expectations by industry analysts.

5. Starting at least in 2001, WorldCom engaged in an improper accounting scheme intended to manipulate its earnings to keep them in line with Wall Street's expectations, and to support WorldCom's stock price. One of WorldCom's major operating expenses was its so-called "line costs." In general, "line costs" represent fees WorldCom paid to third party telecommunication network providers for the right to access the third parties' networks. Under GAAP, these fees must be expensed and may not be capitalized. Nevertheless, beginning at least as early as the first quarter of 2001, WorldCom's senior management improperly directed the transfer of line costs to WorldCom's capital accounts in amounts sufficient to keep WorldCom's earnings in line with the analysts' consensus on WorldCom's earnings. Thus, in this manner, WorldCom materially understated its expenses, and materially overstated its earnings, thereby defrauding investors.

6. As a result of this improper accounting scheme, WorldCom materially underreported its expenses and materially overstated its earnings in its filings with the Commission, specifically, on its Form 10-K for the fiscal December 31, 2001, and on its Form 10-Q for the quarter ending on March 31, 2002.

7. In particular, WorldCom reported on its Consolidated Statement of Operations contained in its 2001 Form 10-K that its line costs for 2001 totaled $14.739 billion, and that its earnings before income taxes and minority interests totaled $2.393 billion, whereas, in truth and in fact, WorldCom's line costs for that period totaled approximately $17.794 billion, and it suffered a loss of approximately $662 million.

8. Further, WorldCom reported on its Consolidated Statement of Operations contained in its Form 10-Q for the first quarter of 2002 that its line costs for that quarter totaled $3.479 billion, and that its income before income taxes and minority interests totaled $240 million, whereas, in truth and in fact, WorldCom's line costs for that period totaled approximately $4.276 billion and it suffered a loss of approximately $557 million.

9. WorldCom's disclosures in its 2001 Form 10-K and in its Form 10-Q for the first quarter of 2002 failed to include material facts necessary to make the statements made in light of the circumstances in which they were made not misleading. In particular, these filings failed to disclose the company's accounting treatment of its line costs, that such treatment had changed from prior periods, and that the company's line costs were actually increasing substantially as a percentage of its revenues.

Capital assets represent a significant percentage of total assets in industries like oil exploration and refining, automotive manufacturing, and energy utilities. Exhibit 10.1 shows a condensed version of the asset portion of B.C. Gas Inc.'s balance sheet in both dollar and common-sized terms at December 31, 2001. Notice that property, plant, and equipment (or capital assets) comprise 83.1% of total assets. Firms have latitude in how much detail they provide about separate capital asset components. B.C. Gas chose to provide a footnote breakdown, as shown in Exhibit 10.2. Notice that the total from Exhibit 10.1 ($3,079.9) appears again in Exhibit 10.2. Statement readers can then see the breakdown of net property, plant, and equipment.

B.C. GAS INC.
www.bcgas.com

The *CICA Handbook* distinguishes between capital assets which are property, plant, and equipment, and other capital assets. Property, plant and equipment are identifiable tangible assets that meet all of the following criteria:

(a) are held for use in the production or supply of goods and services, for rental to others, for administrative purposes or for the development, construction, maintenance or repair of other property, plant and equipment;

(b) have been acquired, constructed or developed with the intention of being used on a continuing basis; and

(c) are not intended for sale in the ordinary course of business.

Property, plant, and equipment and intangible assets other than goodwill (see "Goodwill and Other Intangible Assets" Section 3062) are referred to collectively as "capital assets."[1]

Clearly, there's a high proportion of capital or long-lived assets in certain industries. However, the GAAP rules for measuring the carrying amounts of capital assets are frequently criticized, and we'll see why next.

Exhibit 10.1 B.C. GAS INC.

Condensed Partial Consolidated Statement of Financial Position

	December 31, 2001	
	Millions of Dollars	**Percentage**
Assets:		
Current assets	$ 503.5	13.6%
Other assets	122.3	3.3
Property, plant, and equipment	3,079.9	83.1
Total assets	$3,705.7	100.0%

Source: B.C. Gas Inc., 2001 annual report.

Exhibit 10.2 B.C. GAS INC.

Condensed Footnote Breakdown of Property, Plant, and Equipment (as adapted)

Years Ended December 31, 2001 and 2000

(millions of dollars, except per-share amounts)

1. Property, Plant, and Equipment

2001	Depreciation Rates	Cost	Accumulated Depreciation	Net Book Value
Natural gas and petroleum pipeline systems	1%–10%	$2,935.3	$628.2	$2,307.1
Pipeline under construction	0%	418.7	—	418.7
Plant, buildings, and equipment	1%–33%	358.9	122.6	236.3
Land and land rights	0%–5%	118.9	1.1	117.8
		$3,831.8	$751.9	$3,079.9

2000	Depreciation Rates	Cost	Accumulated Depreciation	Net Book Value
Natural gas and petroleum pipeline systems	1%–10%	$2,859.1	$585.9	$2,273.2
Pipeline under construction	0%	127.6	—	127.6
Plant, buildings, and equipment	1%–33%	324.7	112.5	212.2
Land and land rights	0%–5%	115.8	1.2	114.6
		$3,427.2	$699.6	$2,727.6

The composite depreciation rate on regulated property, plant and equipment for the year ended December 31, 2001 is approximately 2.9% (2000—3.0%).

Measuring the Carrying Amount of Capital Assets

There are two ways that assets could be measured:

1. Assets could be reflected at their estimated value in an *output* market. An output market refers to a market where assets are *sold*. We will call measures that use output market numbers **expected benefit approaches.**
2. Assets could be measured at their estimated cost in an *input* market. An input market refers to a market where assets are *purchased*. Measures that use input costs will be called **economic sacrifice approaches** to asset measurement.

Expected benefit approaches recognize that assets are valuable because of the *future cash inflows* they are expected to generate. Consequently, these approaches attempt to measure various definitions of an asset's future cash inflows. One example of an expected benefit approach is **discounted present value.** Here, the value of a piece of manufacturing equipment would be measured by estimating the discounted present value of the future net operating cash inflows expected to be generated from using it. Another example of an expected benefit approach is the cash flow amount that the asset would yield if it were sold instead of being used in operations. Under this approach, the value of a capital asset would be reflected at its **net realizable value**—the amount that would be received if the asset were sold in the used asset market.

Economic sacrifice approaches to asset measurement focus on the amount of resource expenditure necessary to acquire an asset. One example of an economic sacrifice approach is historical cost (the dominant GAAP measurement method)[2]—that is, the historical amount that was expended to buy the asset constitutes the past sacrifice incurred to bring the asset into the firm.

Another example of an economic sacrifice approach involves measuring the current (or replacement) cost of the asset. Under a **replacement cost** approach, an asset would be carried at its current purchase cost—the expenditure (*sacrifice*) necessary to obtain the asset today.

The Approach Used by GAAP

Table 10.1 shows a hypothetical range of capital asset carrying amounts as measured under each approach. Assume the asset is a vehicle used by a freight hauler to transport heavy industrial equipment. Let's say the truck originally cost $100,000, is two years old, has a remaining useful life of eight years, is being amortized straight-line, and has no salvage value.

GAAP uses historical cost—an economic sacrifice approach—for measuring capital assets in almost all circumstances. The choice of historical cost is not an accident. It results from several pragmatic aspects of the existing financial reporting environment.

As discussed in Chapter 1, financial reports play a critical role in resource allocation decisions such as equity investing and lending. Furthermore, accounting numbers are widely used in contracts such as loan agreements, incentive compensation plans, and union contracts. Because of these uses, *those parties whose transactions are explicitly or implicitly tied to accounting numbers expect them to be reliable numbers.* By *reliable*, we mean the numbers must not be open to manipulation. If the numbers were not reliable (e.g., if they could be easily manipulated by one party to the contract), then cautious decision makers would be reluctant to enter into contracts using

---

TABLE 10.1 HYPOTHETICAL CAPITAL ASSET CARRYING AMOUNTS

Expected Benefit Approaches

1. Discounted present value:
   Expected net operating cash inflows = $18,000 per year (assumed) for eight remaining years, discounted at a 10% (assumed) rate

$$5.33493^1 \times \$18,000 = \$96,029$$

2. Net realizable value:
   Current resale price from an over-the-road equipment listing for the specific vehicle model

$$\$85,000 \text{ (assumed)}$$

Economic Sacrifice Approaches

3. Historical cost less accumulated amortization:

$$\$100,000 - \left(\frac{\$100,000}{10 \text{ years}} \times 2 \text{ years} \right) = \$80,000$$

4. Replacement cost:
   Replacement cost of a two-year-old vehicle in equivalent condition

$$\$90,000 \text{ (assumed)}$$

---

[1] Discount factor for an ordinary annuity for eight years at 10%.

such "soft" numbers. The reason is that manipulation by one party could circumvent the contract terms.

Auditors also prefer that financial numbers have certain characteristics. The primary concern of auditors is that the numbers be objective. **Objectivity** means that the numbers should be verifiable; they should arise from readily observable, corroborable facts, rather than from subjective beliefs. Objective numbers are important to auditors because of the prevalence of legal suits arising from audited financial statements. Auditors believe that objective data help provide a defence in court and thus reduce potential litigation losses.

As modern financial reporting evolved, reliability and objectivity became qualitative criteria, or guidelines, for selecting acceptable capital asset measurement rules. Expected benefit approaches, such as discounted present value reporting, were discarded because the resulting numbers were neither reliable nor objective. That was because present value computations require inherently subjective forecasts of future net cash flows as well as an assumed discount rate. This is illustrated in Table 10.1 where alternative 1—the discounted present value/expected benefit approach—requires an estimate of expected net operating cash inflows ($18,000) and a choice of discount rate (10%). Most decision makers are reluctant to base contracts on such numbers since the other party to the contract could easily evade certain contract terms by simply altering the cash flow forecast amounts or the discount rate.

Another expected benefit approach—the net realizable value from selling the asset—has also been rejected as a measurement base because of its frequent lack of objectivity. Our example in Table 10.1 assumes that the capital asset has a readily determinable market price, as some do. However, many capital assets are immobile (e.g., buildings), and others are highly specialized and therefore traded in thin markets; consequently, selling prices are often not readily determinable. The current selling price of capital assets like these would need to be estimated on the basis of past transaction prices or transactions involving similar (but not necessarily identical) assets. Numbers obtained from such procedures are widely believed to fail the objectivity test.

The economic sacrifice approach that uses replacement cost (i.e., the estimated current cost of *replacing* the asset), has also been disqualified on the basis that the numbers lack objectivity.

The only capital asset measurement method that is reliable and objective is the economic sacrifice approach called historical cost. Consequently, capital assets are generally reflected in Canadian financial statements at the original historical cost of acquiring the asset (minus accumulated amortization[3]). Capital assets typically last for many years, and their replacement cost tends to increase. But GAAP prohibit adjustment for upward revisions in the replacement cost of the asset. However, when asset values are impaired, GAAP mandate writedowns. This is obviously inconsistent, and shows a downward bias. However, in light of Enron, WorldCom, and similar accounting scandals, some users of accounting information may appreciate such a bias, if handled prudently.

However important *reliability* and *objectivity* are for making specific decisions, *relevance* seems even more fundamental for selecting measurement bases for capital assets. If we could ignore issues of reliability and objectivity, measurement bases such as the net realizable value from selling a capital asset—as described above—would seem to be relevant for providing information about a company's command over resources and ability to operate. (See, for example, Professor Raymond Chambers' *Accounting, Evaluation, and Economic Behavior*, (Englewood Cliffs, New Jersey:

> Amortization is an allocation of historical cost to time periods. Except by coincidence, the net book value number at a point in time—original cost less accumulated amortization—does not reflect the "worth" of the asset at that point in time.

Prentice-Hall, 1966), which elaborates an accounting measurement theory based upon *relevance*.)

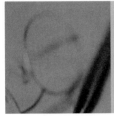

Recap

Since property, plant and equipment capital assets are predominantly carried at amortized historical cost, statement users should not expect balance sheet numbers for such assets to necessarily approximate their apparent economic worth. This is a serious deficiency (with important implications for statement users) that we will explore later in this chapter.

Capital Asset Measurement Rules Illustrated

Two rules govern the determination of the initial carrying amount of a capital asset:

1. All costs necessary to acquire the asset and make it ready for use are included in the asset account. (Costs included in the asset account are called **capitalized costs.** Expenditures excluded from asset categories are said to be "charged off," or expensed.)

2. **Joint costs** incurred in acquiring more than one asset are apportioned among the acquired assets.

Both rules are illustrated in the following example.

Canyon Corporation acquired a tract of land on June 1, 2003, by paying $6,000,000 and by assuming an existing mortgage of $1,000,000 on the land. The company demolished an empty structure on the property at a cost of $650,000. It was able to sell bricks and other materials from the demolished building for $10,000. Regrading and clearing the land cost $35,000.

Canyon then began constructing a new factory on the site. Architectural fees were $800,000, and the payments to contractors for building the factory totalled $12,000,000. Canyon negotiated a bank loan to help ease the cash flow crunch during construction. Interest payments over the period of construction totalled $715,000. Legal fees incurred in the transaction totalled $57,000, of which $17,000 was attributable to both examination of title covering the land purchase and legal issues relating to the assumption of the existing mortgage. The remaining $40,000 of legal fees were incurred as a consequence of contracts with the architect and the construction companies.

The amounts allocated to the land and building accounts, respectively, were determined as follows.

Canyon Corporation		
Joint Cost Allocation		
Fixed Asset Purchase		
Land		
Cash payment		$ 6,000,000
Mortgage assumed		1,000,000
Demolition of existing structure	$650,000	
Less: Salvage value of material	(10,000)	
		640,000
Regrading and clearing land		35,000
Legal fees allocated		17,000
Capitalized land costs		$ 7,692,000
Building		
Architectural fees		$ 800,000
Building costs		12,000,000
Interest capitalized		715,000
Legal fees allocated		40,000
Capitalized building costs		$13,555,000

Capitalized land costs include many items in addition to the $6,000,000 cash payment. For example, the cost of demolishing the existing structure (net of salvaged materials) is added to the land account, since the land had to be cleared before the building could be erected. This illustrates initial carrying amount Rule 1—all costs necessary to prepare the land for its intended use are capitalized as land costs. The legal fees illustrate Rule 2—joint costs are apportioned among assets, both the land and building in this case.

The costs allocated to the building include the interest arising from a loan Canyon negotiated to finance construction. GAAP permit capitalizing interest payments when the borrowing is undertaken to finance assets that have a long construction period. This treatment views interest as a cost of acquiring an asset. However, *capitalization is limited to interest arising from actual borrowings from outsiders*.

For example, in its 2001 financial statements, IPSCO Inc., a Regina-based mini-mill producer of steel and steel products, disclosed that one of its "Significant Accounting Policies" was that "Capital assets are stated at cost. For major projects under construction, the company capitalizes interest based on expenditures incurred to a maximum of interest costs on debt." The company also disclosed that $20,523,000 of interest costs were capitalized as part of capital assets in 2001.

Now, let's switch back to the hypothetical Canyon Corporation example. Rather than assuming that Canyon borrowed from a bank, assume Canyon had issued more common shares and used the proceeds to finance construction. Further assume that Canyon had absolutely no interest-bearing debt outstanding. Equity funds are not "free"—shareholders expect to earn a return, and they get angry when it doesn't materialize! Despite this, GAAP do not allow Canyon to calculate an artificial interest charge on the equity financing and capitalize this "imputed interest" as a part of the cost of the building. *So the way the construction is financed can alter the cost capitalized under GAAP.*

Treating equity that is issued to finance construction as "free" (when there is no interest-bearing debt outstanding) ignores the cost of capital provided by owners when periodic income is computed—that is, GAAP allow no expense recognition for the cost associated with capital provided by shareholders. These funds are treated as

Apportionment is also necessary when more than one asset is acquired for a lump-sum price. Assume two tracts of land are acquired for $1,000,000. For property tax purposes, the land tracts are assessed as follows:

Tract 1	$240,000
Tract 2	360,000
Total	$600,000

The $1,000,000 purchase price might be apportioned between the tracts in proportion to their assessed value—40% to tract 1 and 60% to tract 2.

IPSCO INC.
www.ipsco.com

if they were costless. In summary, the cost of equity capital is ignored in both income determination and asset costing.

Tax Versus Financial Reporting Incentives
The way incurred costs are allocated between land and building has an impact on the amount of income that will be reported in future periods. Land is a permanent asset—that's why it's not amortized. A factory building has a finite life and is amortized over future years. For financial reporting purposes, the manner in which costs are allocated—between, say, land and building—is guided by which one (land or building) generated the cost.

For *tax purposes*, the incentives for allocating costs between land and building asset categories are completely different, because the objective of most firms is to minimize tax payments, not to "correctly" allocate costs. The larger are the costs allocated to land for tax purposes, the *higher* the future taxable income becomes since land cannot be amortized. Aggressive taxpayers seek to minimize the amount of joint expenditures allocated to nonamortizable assets like land. Similarly, taxpayers would prefer not to capitalize interest payments for tax purposes since the benefits of the deduction would be spread over the amortizable life of the asset rather than being deductible immediately.

Capitalization Criteria—An Extension
See the example of Winger Enterprises, which follows, to help further clarify which costs are included in the determination of asset carrying amounts and which are not.

Total expenditures that are capitalized—that is, those that are included in the carrying amount of the machine—include *all* of the costs ($88,500) associated with getting the machine ready for production use, not just the invoice cost of $80,000.

To further illustrate capitalization criteria, consider the following extension of the example. Assume that in January 2004 Winger spent an additional $8,000 on the machine. The total expenditure comprised:

- $2,000 for ordinary repairs and maintenance expenditures required every several years
- $6,000 for the installation of a new component that allowed the machine to consume less raw material and operate more efficiently

In this example, the $2,000 would be treated as a period expense, while the $6,000 would be capitalized in 2004 and added to the carrying amount of the machine.

Winger Enterprises: Determination of Capitalized Costs

On January 1, 1999, Winger Enterprises purchased a machine that will be used in operations. The cash purchase invoice price of the machine was $80,000. The freight cost to transport the machine to Winger's factory was $1,200. During the month of January 1999 Winger's employees spent considerable time calibrating the machine and making adjustments and test runs to get it ready for production. Costs incurred in doing this were:

Allocated portion of production manager's salary for coordinating machine adjustments	$2,200
Hourly wages of production workers engaged in test runs of the machine	3,600
Cost of raw materials that were used in test runs (the output was not saleable)	1,500

Given these facts, the capitalized amount of the machine would be the total of all of the costs ($80,000 + 1,200 + 2,200 + 3,600 + 1,500 = $88,500).

As will be discussed in Chapter 15, GAAP utilize what is called the proprietary view of the firm. The proprietary view deems the firm and its owners to be indistinguishable. Consequently, funds contributed by owners do not come from "outsiders." *The firm can't charge itself interest on contributed ownership capital.*

GAAP capitalize an expenditure on property, plant, and equipment capital assets when the expenditure causes any of the following conditions:[4]

- The useful life of the asset is extended.

- The capacity of the asset is increased (i.e., when there is an increase in attainable units of output).

- The efficiency of the asset is increased (i.e., when fewer labour hours or raw material inputs are required).

- The quality of output is increased.

- Any other type of increase in the future service potential value of the asset results.

Financial Analysis and Capital Asset Reporting

Using amortized historical cost as the measure of fixed asset values introduces many pitfalls for unwary statement readers. Here's a simple example.

Chen Corporation purchases capital assets and begins operations on January 1, 1999. The assets cost $1,000,000, have a ten-year expected life and no salvage value, and will be amortized using the straight-line method. Assume that net operating cash flows (i.e., revenues minus variable operating expenses) for 1999 are $220,000. Chen's reported pre-tax return on start-of-period assets for 1999 is 12%, computed as:

Pre-tax net operating cash flows	$220,000
Amortization ($1,000,000/10 years)	100,000
Pre-tax profit	$120,000

The pre-tax return on start-of-period net assets is calculated as:

$$\frac{\text{Pre-tax profit}}{\text{Start-of-period net assets}} = \frac{\$120,000}{\$1,000,000} = 12\%$$

Let's assume Chen makes no additional capital expenditures over the ensuing four years. Consequently, the average age of its operating assets increases over this period. Further assume that, on average, prices in the economy are increasing at 3% per year and that Chen is able to keep pace by increasing its net operating cash flows by 3%. Our example incorporates two features—aging assets and inflation—which complicate statement analysis. Table 10.2 shows why.

Notice that the return on start-of-period assets rises from 12% to 24.6% over the five-year period as highlighted in Table 10.2. As we are about to explain, this increase is caused by two factors:

1. an aging asset base
2. increasing costs and prices

While our example is contrived, it does help us understand how historical cost reporting for fixed assets may make trend analyses misleading. Specifically, how should the increasing return be interpreted? Is Chen's year-to-year performance really improving? Is the 2003 rate of return sustainable?

"Is year-to-year performance improving?" Probably not. The upward drift in reported return on assets is caused by operating cash flows that automatically increase

TABLE 10.2 CHEN CORPORATION

Time-Series Distortions from Aging Assets and Inflation

	January 1, 1999	December 31, 1999	December 31, 2000	December 31, 2001	December 31, 2002	December 31, 2003
Asset book value	$1,000,000	$900,000	$800,000	$700,000	$600,000	$500,000
Net operating cash flow (increasing by 3% per year)		220,000	226,600	233,398	240,400	247,612
Amortization		100,000	100,000	100,000	100,000	100,000
Pre-tax profit		120,000	126,600	133,398	140,400	147,612
Return on start-of-period assets		12%	14.1%	16.7%	20.1%	24.6%
Average age of assets		1 year	2 years	3 years	4 years	5 years

with inflation, while amortization and net asset book value do not change under historical cost reporting. To know whether the rate of return increase is "real," we need each year's numbers expressed in terms of current-year prices. That is, to determine whether the return increase from 12% to 14.1% (in 2000) represents real improvement, we would need to know the replacement cost of the assets and we would need to recompute the rate of return using replacement cost amortization and asset value. Only then could we assess whether some portion of the year-to-year "improvement" is real—as opposed to being an artifact of the historical cost basis of accounting for fixed assets.

"Is the 2003 return sustainable?" No, it's not. If the rate of return for 2003 were recomputed on a replacement cost basis, it would not be 24.6%. Statement readers seldom have enough information to adjust for year-to-year distortions like those in Table 10.2. However, they must understand that *when asset reinvestment is not continuous, the increasing age of the asset base in conjunction with rising prices introduces distortions* like those in Table 10.2—and thus, projections must be made with caution.

Historical cost accounting for capital assets also creates problems for statement readers who try to make comparisons between companies like Chen Corporation and its competitors. To see why, suppose Chen's biggest competitor is Rizzo Corporation. As of January 1, 1999, Rizzo had assets with a net book value of $1,000,000. Recollect that Chen also had an asset net book value of $1,000,000 on that same date. While Chen's assets were new, let's assume Rizzo's were, on average, five years old and had a ten-year expected life. Rizzo also uses straight-line amortization with no salvage value. Given these assumptions, Rizzo's asset net book value comprised:

Long-lived assets at original cost	$2,000,000
Less: Accumulated amortization	1,000,000
Net asset book value	$1,000,000

Rizzo's policy is to replace 10% of its assets each year at the end of their useful lives. Assume that Rizzo's pre-tax net operating cash flow for 1999 is $320,000 and that its pre-tax return on start-of-period net assets is 12%, as shown on the next page.

Pre-tax net operating cash flow	$320,000
Amortization ($2,000,000/10 years)	200,000
Pre-tax profit	$120,000

The pre-tax return on start-of-period net assets is calculated as:

$$\frac{\text{Pre-tax profit}}{\text{Start-of-period net assets}} = \frac{\$120,000}{(\$2,000,000 - \$1,000,000)} = 12\%$$

Rizzo's 1999 pre-tax return on assets is 12%, the same as Chen's. Rizzo is also able to keep pace with inflation by increasing its net operating cash flows by 3% each year. We will assume that its annual capital expenditures to replace 10% of its January 1, 1999, asset base ($2,000,000 × 10% = $200,000) also increase at the inflation rate of 3% and that the new assets are purchased on the last day of the year. These assumptions yield the performance data for 1999–2003 in Table 10.3.

Here's what our Chen (Table 10.2) versus Rizzo Corporation (Table 10.3) example illustrates. The two firms start in identical financial reporting positions on January 1, 1999. Each has assets with a *net* book value of $1,000,000. The *only* difference is that Chen's assets are new and Rizzo's are five years old, on average. Rizzo constantly replaces its assets and maintains an average asset age of five years, while the average

TABLE 10.3 RIZZO CORPORATION

Time Series Without Distortion from Aging Assets

	January 1, 1999	December 31, 1999	December 31, 2000	December 31, 2001	December 31, 2002	December 31, 2003
				Year Ended		
Asset net book value	$1,000,000	$1,006,000	$1,017,580	$1,034,307	$1,055,736	$1,081,408
Capital expenditures (increasing by 3% per year)		206,000	212,180	218,545	225,102	231,855
Net operating cash flow (increasing by 3% per year)		$ 320,000	$ 329,600	$ 339,488	$ 349,673	$ 360,163
Amortization (see details below)		200,000	200,600	201,818	203,673	206,183
Pre-tax profit		120,000	129,000	137,670	146,000	153,980
Return on start-of period assets		12%	12.8%	13.5%	14.1%	14.6%
Average age of assets		5 years	5 years	5 years	5 years	5 years

	1999	2000	2001	2002	2003
Amortization details explained:					
1. Start of year **gross** original cost of assets	$2,000,000	$2,006,000	$2,018,180	$2,036,725	$2,061,827
2. Gross cost of assets retired at year-end	(200,000)	(200,000)	(200,000)	(200,000)	(200,000)
3. Capital expenditure on new assets (increases by 3%)	206,000	212,180	218,545	225,102	231,855
4. End of year **gross** original cost of assets	$2,006,000	$2,018,180	$2,036,725	$2,061,827	$2,093,682
Amortization for year:					
Item 1 × 10%	$ 200,000	$ 200,600	$ 201,818	$ 203,673	$ 206,183

age of Chen Corporation's assets is increasing, as highlighted in Table 10.2. Rizzo's reported return on start-of-period assets at the end of 2003 is 14.6%, Chen's is 24.6%. The firms experienced identical economic conditions and were able to respond identically. The only difference is that over this period Rizzo constantly maintained a capital asset age of five years, while the average age of Chen's assets increased from one year to five years. An analyst who is unaware of the asset age differential might erroneously conclude that Chen is more profitable than Rizzo in 2003 (a 24.6% versus a 14.6% return on assets) and that Chen's more dramatic upward trend presages a rosier future. As we have just seen, such inferences are unwarranted since the difference across firms is driven by the way that historical cost, fixed asset accounting rules affect firms with aging assets.

Table 10.2 is intended to convey the problems analysts face in doing trend analyses. These problems exist because of the GAAP rules used in capital asset financial reporting. Table 10.3 extends this critique of GAAP rules by focusing on problems these rules create when analysts make comparisons *across* firms.

While the issues raised in Tables 10.2 and 10.3 are real, the problems confronting analysts in practice are not usually so extreme. To understand why, let's first focus on year-to-year (time series) analyses, like those in Table 10.2. Unlike Chen, most firms replace some assets each year. Established firms with continuous capital expenditures do not experience the increasing average asset age shown in Table 10.2. Instead, with regular replacement, the average age of capital assets remains fairly constant from year to year. For these firms, the year-to-year pattern of returns more closely resembles that of Rizzo Corporation (in Table 10.3). That is why we introduced an example of a firm whose average asset age remained constant, like Rizzo's. As long as the rate of asset price increases is relatively low (like 3% in our example), the distortions caused by GAAP are small. If the *average age* of assets is relatively constant and if prices change at a constant rate, the reported rate of return ultimately stabilizes.[5] Of course, in those instances in which capital expenditures are "lumpy," statement readers must recognize the possibility that an aging asset base can lead to distorted returns on assets, like those of Table 10.2.

GAAP for capital assets do significantly impede rate-of-return comparisons across companies in certain situations. Within the same industry, differences like those between Chen and Rizzo would be unusual, since competition often leads firms to pursue similar investment and operating strategies. Firms that don't modernize or innovate are ultimately left behind. Consequently, market forces lead to commonalities that usually make comparisons across firms *within the same industry* meaningful.

The historical cost basis used for capital assets does create potentially significant problems for those comparing firms in *different industries*. Operating conditions, capital expenditure policies, and the rate of input cost change can vary significantly across industries. For example, if there is little technological change in one industry, there is little incentive for firms to replace old—but still functional—assets. In stagnating industries, the average age of assets can increase, and this tendency contrasts with industries in which technological advancements have proliferated. This average age differential can lead to misleading comparisons, like those illustrated in Table 10.2 (where Chen experienced an increase in asset age) as compared to Table 10.3 (where Rizzo's asset age remained stable).

Recap

GAAP rules for capital asset accounting complicate financial analysis. Statement readers need to understand what factors might cause distortions in trends and/or across firms and adjust for these distortions. Often, information to make the adjustment is unavailable. In these circumstances, knowing the approximate direction of any biases may help the statement reader avoid unwarranted inferences.

Intangible Assets

Intangible assets, like patents, trademarks, and copyrights, convey future benefits to their owners. When one organization purchases an intangible asset from some other organization—for example, a valuable trademark—few new accounting or reporting issues arise. The acquired intangible asset is recorded at the arm's-length transaction price and is amortized over its expected useful life, as described later in the chapter. (Another category of acquired intangible assets, called goodwill, arises as a consequence of certain types of corporate takeovers. This category of intangible is discussed in Chapter 16.)

Difficult financial reporting issues exist when the intangible asset is developed internally instead of being purchased from another company. These difficulties arise from the accounting treatment of the expenditures that ultimately create the valuable intangible asset (such as a patent or trademark). A patent, for example, may be the result of successful research and development expenditures; a valuable trademark is the result of successful advertising, clever packaging, or other processes that create brand loyalty.

The recoverability of research and development expenditures may be highly uncertain at the start of a project. Consequently, the Accounting Standards Board (AcSB) requires that all research and most development expenditures be expensed as incurred.[6] This mandated financial reporting uniformity was viewed as a practical way of dealing with the risk of nonrecoverability of R&D expenditures. Similarly, prevailing accounting principles have long required companies to treat advertising and creative product development expenditures as period costs, again because of the highly uncertain, difficult-to-predict, future benefits.

The major categories of cash outflows most likely to result in the creation of intangibles are usually immediately expensed (e.g., R&D, advertising, etc.). *When past outflows successfully create assets, the outflows have already been expensed and there are usually few remaining future outflows to capitalize!* Consequently, the carrying amount on the balance sheet for this type of intangible asset is often far below the value of the property right. For example, the 1991 annual report of Polaroid Corporation indicates that "Patents and Trademarks" are valued at US$1. However, a footnote in that same report discloses that Polaroid was awarded a court judgment arising from a suit which alleged that Eastman Kodak Company's instant cameras and film infringed on Polaroid patents. The judgment was ultimately settled for US$924.5 million. The size of the judgment and settlement indicates that the Polaroid patents are extremely valuable. Nevertheless, the real economic value of these internally developed intangible assets does not appear on Polaroid's balance sheet, since the costs incurred in developing the valuable patents were expensed as incurred. This situation is not unusual.

POLAROID
CORPORATION
www.polaroid.com

The GAAP bias that leads to an understatement of internally developed intangible assets has hindered financial analysis for many years, and the problem has worsened as modern economic activity shifted in the 1980s. In high-technology industries like software development and biotechnology, research has contributed to large increases in the value of intellectual property rights such as patents and trademarks. Yet accounting rules for internally developed intangibles have not always kept pace. However, the application of GAAP does evolve as economic situations change. For example, the so-called *year 2000 issue*[7] created several problems for businesses, one of which relates to accounting for expenditures made in order to ensure that a company's internally used computer software is Y2K-compliant. The CICA's Emerging Issues Committee (EIC) posed the question: "Should the external and internal costs specifically associated with modifying internal use computer software for the year 2000, be accounted for as an asset or expense as incurred?"[8] The EIC concluded that existing *Handbook* Section 3061 on capital assets, and particularly the paragraph on betterments (3061.26 and .27), "provide appropriate guidance for determining whether internal use software modification costs should be accounted for as an asset or expensed. ... For example, if the software modifications merely ensure the continued effectiveness of the affected software for its originally assessed useful life, the costs would be expensed. If, however, year 2000 software compliance is effected by rewriting software applications that enhance their service potential by extending the life of the software beyond its originally assessed useful life, the costs would be accounted for as a betterment."[9]

In 2001, the CICA issued Section 3062, "Goodwill and Other Intangible Assets," and Section 1581, "Business Combinations," which moved Canadian standards close to the U.S. position for these capital assets. Leaving our discussion of goodwill to Chapter 16, we will summarize the CICA's new standards on accounting for intangibles.

When one company acquires another and must therefore prepare consolidated financial statements as discussed in Chapter 16, acquired intangible assets may result (in addition to goodwill) (see also Section 1581). When Nortel Networks, for example, went on a corporate "shopping spree" in the late 1990s, it acquired a number of companies with so-called *in-process R&D*, which was then amortized quickly on Nortel's resulting consolidated financial statements. New Section 3062 specifically requires that intangibles such as in-process R&D not be written off, or written down, in the period of acquisition, unless they become impaired during that period. This section also provides (in para. 10) that intangible assets should be amortized over their useful lives, unless that life is indefinite, in which case no amortization is to be recorded. These new rules would have the following implications for a Nortel-like situation.

To set the scene, here's a summary of the intangibles (i.e., purchased in-process R&D (IPR&D) and acquired technology) that Nortel acquired in 1999 and 1998 (from Nortel's 1999 audited financial statements; recall this example from Chapter 1):

(All amounts are in $US.)

Acquisition	Date	Purchase Price	Acquired Technology	Purchased IPR&D	Goodwill
1999					
Periphonics (i)	November 12	$ 650	$ 66	$ 8	$ 414
Shasta Networks (ii)	April 16	$ 340	$ —	$ 180	$ 158
1998					
Cambrian (iii)	December 15	$ 248	$ —	$ 204	$ 48
Bay Networks (iv)	August 31	$6,873	$2,050	$1,000	$2,417
r³ (v)	June 8	$24	$ —	$ 20	$ 4
Aptis (vi)	April 22	$ 286	$ —	$ 203	$ 75
BNI (vii)	January 9	$ 433	$ —	$ 329	$ 75
Other (viii)	Various	$ 83	$ —	$ —	$ —

Here's Note 3 to those same financial statements:

3. Supplementary measures of net earnings and earnings per share [amounts in $US]

As a measure to assess financial performance, management utilizes supplementary measures of net earnings and earnings per common share which exclude the impact of Acquisition Related Costs and one-time gains and charges. The supplementary measures of net earnings and earnings per common share are as follows:

	1999	1998	1997
Net earnings (loss) applicable to common shares	$ (197)	$ (569)	$812
Add back:			
Acquisition-related amortization			
Purchased IPR&D	722	1,241	—
Acquired technology	686	228	—
Goodwill*	553	161	—
One-time gains	(264)	(441)	(102)
One-time charges	209	447	95
Net tax impact	16	(2)	(1)
Supplementary measure of net earnings	$1,725	$1,065	$804
Supplementary measure of earnings per common share	$ 1.28	$ .93	$ .77

...

*Amortization for Bay Networks and all acquisitions subsequent to the acquisition of Bay Networks.

...

Notice that the total amortization for 1998 and 1999 for the intangible asset "Purchased IPR&D" is US$1,963 million ($722 + $1,241). From the summary of purchases in those two years, the total "Purchased IPR&D" was US$2,004 million ($68 + $180 + $204 + $1,000 + $20 + $203 + $329), so the entire IPR&D intangible asset category was virtually fully amortized by the end of 1999. This treatment, in combination with the rather strange Note 3 above (which de-emphasizes GAAP earnings), implies that such intangible asset amortizations are not value-relevant (Chapter 6). Then, of course, why make the corporate acquisition? The new rules would seem to encourage managers to focus more carefully on determining such intangible asset costs and their useful lives.

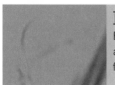

Recap

Balance sheet carrying amounts for internally developed intangible assets such as patents or trademarks are not dependable indicators of their value to the firm. Recent pronouncements seek to improve accounting for intangibles.

Intangibles Accounting in the United Kingdom: Similarities and Differences

The financial reporting rules for research and development in the United Kingdom are generally similar to those in Canada. Marketing and advertising costs are treated as period costs in the United Kingdom, just as they are in Canada. As a result, U.K. balance sheet numbers for patents, trademarks, and similar intangibles are subject to the same type of understatement as those in Canada.

However, there is a difference between the application of the historical cost accounting principle in the United Kingdom and Canada. United Kingdom accounting rules allow companies to write capital assets up to new higher carrying values when market value exceeds cost—making adherence to the cost principle more flexible in the United Kingdom. The understatement of intangibles on U.K. firms' books prompted a few U.K. companies to abandon the historical cost treatment of trademarks (called "brands" in the U.K.) and to write these intangible assets up to their estimated fair value. One author summarizes the U.K. treatment of brands as follows:

> *A case can be made that the brand value should be placed on the balance sheet or at least reported to shareholders as part of a firm's financial report. In fact, several British firms have added brand equity to the balance sheet. For example, in 1988 Ranks Hovis McDougall decided to put a balance sheet value of [US]$1.2 billion on its 60 brands. First, such an intangible asset can easily exceed in value that of tangible assets which are scrupulously reported and affect shareholders' valuation of firms. Second, reported brand equity can focus attention upon intangible assets and thus make it easier to justify brand building activities that are likely to pay off in the long term. Without such information, shareholders must rely upon short-term financials.*
>
> *The major difficulty involves a question of whether any valuation of brand equity can be both objective and verifiable. Unless brand valuation can be defended, it will not be helpful and can result in legal liability. It is no coincidence that in England, where brand value has been placed upon the balance sheet, there is a less litigious environment.*[10]

While only a few U.K. firms have actually written brands up to fair value, the fact that some have chosen to do so indicates the perceived limitations of existing accounting for intangibles.

A Case Study of Ambiguities in Capitalization Criteria: Oil and Gas Exploration Costs

Earlier, we described two characteristics that tend to make the book values of capital assets unreliable indicators of their value to the firm. First, for pragmatic reasons historical cost is used as the primary basis for measuring such assets. So past economic sacrifice—rather than current expected benefit—determines balance sheet carrying amounts. Second, the ultimate benefit from research and product development expenditures cannot be forecast at the start of a project; this uncertainty causes these items to be written off as period costs even if they eventually lead to the creation of an asset. That's why many development expenditures designed to create intangible assets never get capitalized, unless they qualify for capitalization under Section 3450.21.

Now we explain a third cause for the discrepancy between capital asset numbers and economic reality—*ambiguities in capitalization criteria.* These arise in several settings, including the treatment of oil and gas exploration costs. Consider the following example.

> ### Capitalization of Exploration Cost
>
> *Calaboga Oil paid $50 million for a large oil field in Alberta. During 2002, Calaboga explored for oil throughout the field. Twenty wells were drilled at a total cost of $200 million, or $10 million per well. Nineteen of the wells proved to be unproductive dry holes, while one was found to contain a considerable amount of oil. The financial reporting question is this: What is the appropriate carrying amount of the producing well?*

Two different approaches to determining the cost of the producing well have emerged. They differ in their treatment of the $190 million that was spent in drilling the 19 dry holes.

One alternative, called the **full-cost approach,** considers the $190 million to be a necessary cost of finding the one producing oil well. That well would be carried on the books at $250 million using the full-cost approach—the $50 million land purchase price plus the $200 million of total drilling costs.

Another alternative, the **successful-efforts approach,** would reflect the producing well at only $60 million. This is the sum of the $50 million land purchase price plus the $10 million cost of drilling the specific well that became a producer. The $190 million of drilling costs incurred on the unproductive wells would be written off to the 2002 income statement as a period expense.

The two approaches in this example can be summarized as follows:

Full Cost

Balance Sheet

Petroleum production property:

Land cost	$ 50,000,000
Drilling costs on dry holes	190,000,000
Drilling costs on producer	10,000,000
Capitalized amount	$250,000,000

Income Statement

2002 charge =	–0–

Successful Efforts

Balance Sheet

Petroleum production property:

Land cost	$ 50,000,000
Drilling costs on producer	10,000,000
Capitalized amount	$ 60,000,000

Income Statement

2002 charge =	$190,000,000

From year to year, reported profits would be more volatile using the successful-efforts approach, especially for small firms that do not have a large portfolio of drilling projects. Furthermore, small-growth firms that engage in extensive exploration activities would tend to report lower profits under successful efforts. To avoid this volatility and potentially lower average earnings, most smaller oil companies use the full-cost approach. Notice that under the full-cost option, unsuccessful drilling outcomes do not penalize current periods' earnings.

We focus on accounting options for oil and gas exploration because they involve typical financial reporting controversies. Specifically:

- The reporting options have the potential to influence managerial behaviour.
- The differing managerial incentives have implications for valuing firms.

We will now address these issues.

Influence of Reporting Options on Managerial Behaviour

Because the successful-efforts method results in more volatile earnings numbers for small oil and gas producers, managers' bonuses tied to reported earnings would be lost in certain years. Also, the lower near-term profits under the successful-efforts method could lead to violation of loan covenants tied to debt-to-equity ratios.

If one basis for the objection to successful-efforts accounting was managers' fears of losing bonuses, then it is likely that managers would adapt their behaviour if successful-efforts accounting were mandated. For example, managers of small companies might decide to forgo riskier drilling projects to avoid lower successful-efforts earnings if the riskier projects failed. By limiting their drilling efforts to "surer things," the managers would increase the probability of achieving bonus targets.

What we have just suggested underscores how reporting choices exert a potentially powerful impact on the behaviour of managers, as discussed in Chapters 1 and 7. Since bonus contracts are often tied to accounting numbers like net income, managers' operating decisions can be influenced by financial reporting rules.

The Implications of the Securities Markets and Valuation If securities markets are reasonably efficient, participants would be aware of the effect of the previously discussed incentives on managers' behaviour (i.e., to cut back on drilling if successful efforts were mandated). Indeed, the anticipated cutback in drilling levels would be expected to lower the discounted value of affected firms' future cash flows. Why? Because the riskier drilling projects that would be eliminated would still, in the aggregate, have had positive expected payoffs. Following this logic, we would expect to observe an adverse price reaction.

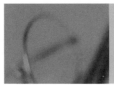

Recap
GAAP capitalization criteria for capital assets are sometimes ambiguous. Managers have an incentive to exploit this ambiguity in order to derive benefits for themselves and the firm in various contractual arrangements.

Asset Impairment

In this section, we review guidelines for determining when and how assets that have already been capitalized should be treated once their value subsequently becomes impaired.

The notion of **asset impairment** is straightforward. A firm acquires an asset because the future value expected to be generated by that asset exceeds its cost. Subsequently, if the asset's remaining expected future value falls below its net book value, that asset's value may have become impaired.

The magnitude of writedowns due to asset impairment can be very large, as illustrated in the excerpt from a press release issued by Inco Limited that appears in Exhibit 10.3.

INCO LIMITED
www.inco.com

Exhibit 10.3 EXCERPT FROM A PRESS RELEASE: INCO LIMITED

Inco Limited Reports Second Quarter 2002 Normalized Earnings of US$65 Million Before Non-Cash Charge

Non-Cash Net Asset Impairment Charge of US$1,613 Million Recorded in Quarter to Reduce Carrying Value of Voisey's Bay and Certain Other Assets

(All dollar amounts are expressed in US$.)

Toronto, July 23, 2002—Inco Limited reported normalized net earnings of $65 million, or 31 cents per common share (31 cents per share on a diluted basis), for the second quarter of 2002, compared with normalized net earnings of $45 million, or 20 cents per share (20 cents per share on a diluted basis), for the second quarter of 2001. The normalized net earnings for the second quarter of 2002 exclude (1) a non-cash net asset impairment charge, as discussed under "Non-Cash Asset Impairment Charge" below, of $1,613 million, or $8.82 per share, to reduce the carrying value of the Voisey's Bay project and certain other assets, and (2) unfavourable non-cash currency translation adjustments of $34 million, or 19 cents per share. Second quarter 2001 normalized net earnings excluded an unusual non-cash deferred tax benefit of $173 million, or 95 cents per share, and unfavourable non-cash currency translation adjustments of $26 million, or 14 cents per share. Results for

these two quarters, as calculated in accordance with Canadian generally accepted accounting principles ("Canadian GAAP"), which take into account these non-cash charges, including the net asset impairment charge, reflected a net loss of $1,582 million, or $8.70 per share ($8.70 per share on a diluted basis), for the second quarter of 2002, compared with net earnings of $192 million, or $1.01 per share (95 cents per share on a diluted basis), in the second quarter of 2001.

Non-Cash Asset Impairment Charge

As previously indicated on June 11, 2002, the Company announced that it would be undertaking a review of the net carrying value for Voisey's Bay in view of the Statement of Principles reached with the Government of the Province of Newfoundland and Labrador and other arrangements with key stakeholders that would enable the development of the

Voisey's Bay project to proceed. The Company has noted on a number of occasions in the Company's public filings and other documents that such events, if and when they were to occur, might require a significant reduction in the carrying value of Voisey's Bay and in the related deferred income and mining tax liability and in shareholders' equity. This review, which has now been completed, included an analysis of the key assumptions which the Company has utilized in evaluating this net carrying value on a quarter-to-quarter basis relating to a number of important factors, including the Company's best assessment of the expected cash flows from the project, how the development of Voisey's Bay, taking into account the agreements which have been reached, fits within the Company's overall long-term development plans and updated mining and other cost assumptions. As a result of this review, the Company recorded a non-cash charge of $1,552 million, net of deferred income and mining taxes of $770 million, in the second quarter of 2002 to reduce the $3,753 million net carrying value of the Voisey's Bay project to $2,201 million. In 2000, as a result of a change in Canadian GAAP, the deferred income and mining tax liability associated with Voisey's Bay was increased by $2,222 million and the carrying value of Voisey's Bay was also increased by this same amount.

Under Canadian GAAP, the carrying value of an impaired asset is required to be reduced to the amount of the estimated undiscounted future net cash flows from the use of the asset together with the asset's residual value. An asset impairment charge is measured differently under United States GAAP and would, under United States GAAP, result in a substantially higher non-cash asset impairment charge for the Voisey's Bay project. Disclosure of such differences between Canadian and United States GAAP will, in accordance with applicable requirements, be included in the Company's regulatory filings for the second quarter of 2002. This non-cash asset impairment charge does not result in a breach of any of the financial or other covenants under the Company's bank credit facilities or indentures covering its publicly held debt.

"We have taken this impairment charge following a complete review of the carrying value of Voisey's Bay with our Audit Committee, our full Board and our independent auditors," said Scott Hand, Chairman and CEO. "With Goro and Voisey's Bay, we are aggressively moving forward to achieve our goal of profitable growth," he added.

The following table summarizes the Voisey's Bay carrying value and related deferred income and mining tax liability at June 30, 2002 both before and after the asset impairment charge:

(in millions)	Gross Carrying Value (A)	Related Deferred Income and Mining Tax Liability (B)	Net Carrying Value ((A) – (B))
Before Impairment Charge	$5,616	$1,863	$3,753
After Impairment Charge	$3,294	$1,093	$2,201

Source: Canada Newswire, July 23, 2002.

In addition, the Company recorded a non-cash charge of $61 million, net of income and mining taxes of $15 million, in the second quarter of 2002 to reduce the carrying values of certain plant, equipment and non-core assets. The primary component of this charge concerns capitalized exploration and development costs relating to the Company's Victor Deep exploration project that, principally as a result of the development of the Voisey's Bay deposits, is not currently expected to be put into production in the foreseeable future.

For the first half of 2002, the Company's normalized net earnings, excluding currency translation adjustments and asset impairment charges, were $90 million, or 41 cents per share (41 cents per share on a diluted basis), compared with $96 million, or 45 cents per share (45 cents per share on a diluted basis), in the corresponding 2001 period. Results, calculated in accordance with Canadian GAAP, were a net loss of $1,571 million, or $8.69 per share ($8.69 per share on a diluted basis), for the first half of 2002, compared with net earnings of $277 million, or $1.44 per share ($1.38 per share on a diluted basis), in the corresponding 2001 period.

Notice in the Inco press release that the company mentions that "[a]n asset impairment charge is measured differently under United States GAAP ...." In 2002, the CICA issued an exposure draft ("Impairment or Disposal of Long-Lived Assets"), one goal of which was to harmonize in this area. The U.S. approach uses present values, while the existing (as of 2002) Canadian approach uses—as noted in the Inco press release—undiscounted future net cash flows. As one might expect, and as Inco mentions, the U.S. approach "result[s] in a substantially higher non-cash asset impairment charge."

Measuring impairment involves two stages. First, some threshold loss level must be established to determine when a writedown must be made. Second, once the threshold is triggered, the amount of the writedown must be determined and recorded.

The emergent standards for determining when an asset is impaired and the guidelines for reporting it are contained in the exposure draft mentioned earlier ("Impairment or Disposal of Long-Lived Assets"), and summarized in Figure 10.1.

We will now explain the impairment guidelines step-by-step through the lettered stages in Figure 10.1.

Stage A. The exposure draft recommends that an impairment review be made whenever external events raise the possibility that an asset has become impaired. Examples of such external events include a significant decrease in the asset's market value or in the business climate.

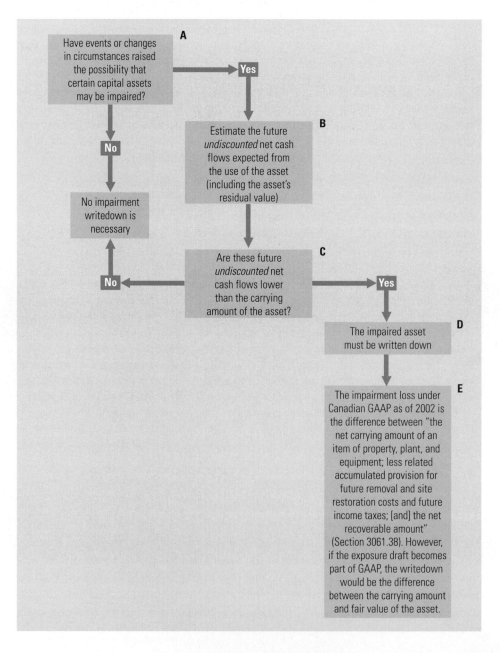

FIGURE 10.1
CAPITAL ASSET
IMPAIRMENT
GUIDELINES

Stage B. *This stage defines the threshold loss level which triggers the writedown (see Figure 10.1).*

Stage C. The threshold is triggered whenever the expected future *net* cash inflow—undiscounted total future inflows minus future outflows—is *lower* than the current carrying amount of the asset.

Stage D. When an impairment loss is recognized, the capital asset is written down. The income statement debit is included "above the line"—that is, as a component of income from continuing operations before income taxes.

Stage E. *This stage defines the amount of the writedown that must be recognized.* The writedown loss is currently measured as the difference between the net recoverable amount of the asset and the current carrying amount of the asset, less related accumulated provision for future removal and site restoration costs and future income taxes. The exposure draft calls for a writedown equal to the difference between the carrying amount of the asset and its fair value, where the "fair value" of an impaired asset would normally be measured using the present value of expected cash flows.

Impairment writedowns present managers with another set of potential earnings management opportunities. For example, in a very good earnings year, managers might be tempted to take an impairment writedown and then write the asset back up (through earnings) in some subsequent year when earnings are down. In Section 3061, the AcSB eliminated this opportunity for earnings management across years; this section prohibits firms from reversing a writedown (3061.39). Once an asset is written down, it cannot later be written up to a new, higher carrying amount. The exposure draft ("Impairment or Disposal of Long-Lived Assets") would continue this prohibition.

There is also research evidence regarding the timing of impairment writeoffs. This research indicates that managers used the previous absence of clear guidelines regarding the timing of impairment recognition to influence users' perceptions of how the firm was performing. One study that examined recognition of asset impairment found that these writeoffs were often made during periods of sustained economic difficulty—that is, the observed behaviour tended to conform to "big bath" bunching of expenses and losses.[11] This finding reinforces the need for clear guidelines in this area.

Asset Retirement Obligations

When an electric utility builds a nuclear plant, or an oil company constructs an offshore drilling rig, regulatory authorities require public welfare and safety expenditures at the end of the asset's life. Nuclear plants must be decontaminated and drilling rigs must be disassembled. This costs money. And by law, these expenditures must take place. *So when certain kinds of assets are built, a liability simultaneously arises.* Until recently, GAAP often ignored these required outflows at the end of an asset's life and the liability rarely appeared on firms' books. But this is changing. The CICA has issued an exposure draft ("Asset Retirement Obligations") that would require firms to record a liability when such assets are placed into service.[12]

Here's how the proposal works. Firms would be required to estimate the expected present value of the outflows that will occur when assets are eventually retired. These outflows would be discounted using an **adjusted risk-free rate**. The discounted pres-

Sometimes the liability arises *after* the asset is placed into service. For example, suppose a new law is passed requiring removal of gasoline storage tanks at the end of their useful lives. For firms utilizing these tanks, the liability arises when the law is passed, not when the tank was first placed into service. Also, liabilities may arise over time, as the asset is used. If a coal strip mine must be reclaimed, the liability arises proportionately as the mining occurs.

This is a risk-free interest rate adjusted to reflect the market's evaluation of the company's creditworthiness.

The present value factor for a payment five years away at 8% is 0.68058. So rounded to the nearest thousand, the present value is $12 million × 0.68058 = $8,167,000.

ent value of the liability would be recorded along with an increase in the carrying amount of the related long-lived asset. Consider the following example:

Kalai Oil Corporation constructs an oil drilling rig off the Atlantic coast which is placed into service on January 1, 2002. The rig cost $300 million to build. Suppose the law requires that the rig be removed at the end of its estimated useful life of five years. Kalai estimates that the cost of dismantling the rig will be $12 million and its credit adjusted risk-free rate is 8%. The discounted present value of the liability is $8,167,000. Assume that Kalai has already capitalized the $300 million cost of the rig in an account called "Drilling rig."

When the asset is placed into service, Kalai records the asset retirement obligation (ARO) as:

DR	Drilling rig (asset retirement cost)	$8,167,000	
	CR ARO liability		$8,167,000

The $8,167,000 debit to the asset account is allocated to expense using some systematic method. Assuming straight-line amortization over the expected useful life of five years, the entry is:

DR	Amortization expense	$1,633,400	
	CR Accumulated amortization—drilling rig		$1,633,400

The liability is initially recorded at its present value but grows over time as retirement nears. The present value of the liability will be increased by 8% per year, as the following schedule shows.

	(a) Present Value of the Liability at Start of Year	(b) Interest Expense [8% × Column (a) Amount]	(c) Present Value of the Liability at End of Year [Column (a) + Column (b)]
2002	$ 8,167,000	$653,360	$ 8,820,360
2003	8,820,360	705,629	9,525,989
2004	9,525,989	762,079	10,288,068
2005	10,288,068	823,045	11,111,113
2006	11,111,113	888,887*	12,000,000
*Rounded.			

The entry to record the increase in liability in 2002 is:

DR	Interest expense	$653,360	
	CR ARO liability		$653,360

Assume that an outside contractor dismantles the rig early in January 2007 at a cost of $11,750,000. The journal entry is:

DR	ARO liability	$12,000,000	
	CR Cash		$11,750,000
	CR Gain on settlement of ARO liability		250,000

As this book goes to press, the AcSB has not issued a final document regarding asset retirement obligations. It may tweak the existing exposure draft before issuing final rules, which are expected in late 2002 or early 2003.

Amortization

Productive assets like buildings, equipment, and machinery eventually wear out. So do assets like patents, which have a finite economic life. Consequently, the cost of these assets must be apportioned to the periods in which they provide benefits. This is the application of the matching principle (Chapter 2) to capital assets.

This matching process has been called **depreciation.** For intangible assets, the allocation of costs to periods was referred to as **amortization.** For mineral deposits and other wasting assets, the assignment of expired costs to periods was called **depletion.** However, in Canada, the AcSB, in Section 3061, has moved to broaden the use of the term "amortization" to include that of the term "depreciation." (However, in the United States, the word "depreciation" remains popular.)

In financial reporting, the cost allocated to periods through the amortization process is the asset's original historical cost minus its expected salvage value. The objective is to spread the original cost over the period of asset use; *amortization is not intended to track the capital asset's declining market value.* The asset's remaining end-of-period book value (its original cost minus cumulative amortization) would approximate its market value only by sheer coincidence. We stress this *absence* of correspondence between accounting measures of amortization and value decrement because accounting amortization, under GAAP, is a process of cost allocation, *not* asset valuation.

When applied to capital (or "long-lived") assets, the matching process requires the reporting entity to choose three parameters:

1. the expected useful life of the asset
2. the amortization pattern that will reflect the asset's declining service potential
3. the salvage value that is expected to exist at the time the asset is retired

Each requires predictions of future events, especially the pace of technological change and shifts in consumer tastes and preferences. Assets whose service potential expires evenly over time are amortized on a straight-line basis, while those that provide more valuable services in the early years are amortized on an accelerated basis. The following example illustrates the procedures.

Amortization Example

Facts

Cost of the asset	$10,500
Expected salvage value (i.e., net realizable value)	$ 500
Expected useful life	5 years

Straight-Line Amortization

$$(\text{Constant rate} \times \text{Constant base}) = \frac{\text{Cost} - \text{Salvage value}}{\text{Estimated life}}$$

$$\left(\frac{1}{5}\right) \times (\$10,500 - \$500) = \$2,000 \text{ per year for all 5 years}$$

Double-Declining-Balance Amortization

$(\text{Constant rate} \times \text{Changing base}) =$ Fixed percentage of straight-line rate $\times$ Book value at beginning of period

Straight-line rate	= 20%
Double straight-line rate	= 20% × 2 = 40%

Year	Beginning-of-Year Book Value	Amortization (40% of Beginning Book Value)	End-of-Year Book Value
1	$10,500.00	$4,200.00	$6,300.00
2	6,300.00	2,520.00	3,780.00

Year 3: Switch to straight-line method (as explained in the text)

$3,780 − $500 = $3,280; $3,280 ÷ 3 = $1,093.33

Year	Beginning-of-Year Book Value	Amortization (40% of Beginning Book Value)	End-of-Year Book Value
3	$3,780.00	$1,093.33	$2,686.67
4	2,686.67	1,093.33	1,593.34
5	1,593.34	1,093.34	500.00

Sum-of-the-Years' Digits Amortization

$$(\text{Changing rate} \times \text{Constant base}) = \frac{\text{Years remaining in life}}{\text{Sum-of-the-years'-digits}^{1}} \times (\text{Cost} - \text{Salvage})$$

Sum-of-the-years'-digits = 5 + 4 + 3 + 2 + 1 = 15

Year	Depreciable Basis ($10,500 − $500)	Applicable Fraction	Amortization
1	$10,000	5/15	$ 3,333.33
2	$10,000	4/15	2,666.67
3	$10,000	3/15	2,000.00
4	$10,000	2/15	1,333.33
5	$10,000	1/15	666.67
	Total	15/15	$10,000.00

[1] The formula for determining the sum-of-the-years'-digits is: $n(n + 1) \div 2$, where n equals the estimated life of the asset. In our example: $5(5 + 1) \div 2 = 15$. This, of course, is the answer we would get by tediously summing the years' digits—that is, 5 + 4 + 3 + 2 + 1 = 15.

The **straight-line** (SL) amortization method simply allocates cost minus salvage value evenly over the asset's expected useful life.

The amortization rate for the **double-declining-balance** method (DDB) is double the straight-line rate (20% per year for SL, 40% per year for DDB). Applying a constant DDB percentage to a declining balance will never cause book value to equal salvage value. To amortize down to an asset's expected salvage value using DDB, two "tricks" must be employed. First, in years 1 and 2, the 40% rate is applied to the book value of the assets, without subtracting the salvage value. Second, once the DDB amount falls below what it would be with the straight-line rate, a switch to the straight-line method is made. This happens in year 3, when DDB amortization would have been $3,780 × 40%, or $1,512, which is less than the straight-line amount of $2,000. Therefore, straight-line is used beginning in year 3. The SL amount is determined by taking the end of year 2 remaining book value, subtracting the salvage value ($3,780 − $500), and dividing the answer by 3.

Sum-of-the-years' digits (SYD) is another accelerated method used by firms. SYD will amortize an asset to precisely its salvage value, so a switch to SL is unnecessary.

Figure 10.2(a) shows the annual amortization charges under the alternative methods; Figure 10.2(b) shows the resulting net book value at each year-end. In preparing external financial reports, companies are free to select the amortization method they believe best reflects both the pattern of an asset's use and the services it provides. Within the same industry, different companies may use different methods. Even

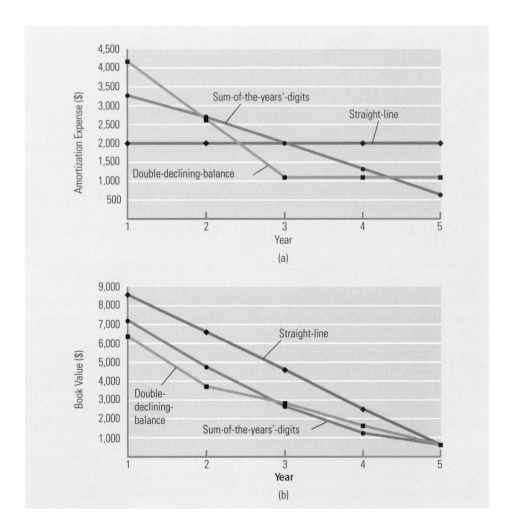

FIGURE 10.2

ILLUSTRATION OF ALTERNATIVE AMORTIZATION METHODS

(a) Annual amortization expense
(b) Net book value

TABLE 10.4 AMORTIZATION CHOICES

	Number of Companies	
	2000	**1999**
Straight-line	89	84
Declining-balance or accelarated (diminishing balance)	12	2
Units of production	5	5
Sinking fund	3	2

Source: Financial Reporting in Canada, 26th edition.

Units of production amortization methods charge off a constant dollar amount for each *unit* of product manufactured or sold.

within the same company, different types of assets may be amortized using different methods. For example, buildings might be amortized using the straight-line method, while trucks might be amortized using the sum-of-the-years'-digits method. Table 10.4 illustrates an annual survey of book amortization choices disclosed by a sample of companies.

Sinking fund amortization produces a pattern of *increasing* amortization over the capital asset's life. Some highly leveraged real estate companies prefer the net effect of low capital asset amortization and high interest charges early in the financed asset's life.

The Canadian Capital Cost Allowance (CCA) System: Another Accelerated Amortization Method

For purposes of preparing a tax return, Canadian taxpayers are permitted to deduct CCA *in lieu of* depreciation or amortization as computed under GAAP. CCA must be computed according to the rules set down in the *Income Tax Act's* Regulations. Instead of calculating CCA for each asset, the Regulations establish so-called classes, which group assets that have some similarities. For example, most types of buildings are included in Class 1, and cars and trucks are in Class 10. Most classes require that CCA be computed using the declining- (or diminishing-) balance method (an accelerated method), while some classes require the straight-line method. For example, Class 1 uses 4% declining balance and Class 10 uses 30% declining balance. The CCA calculation determines the *maximum* amount that can be deducted for purposes of deriving taxable income during the year; the taxpayer may deduct any amount up to this maximum.

To see how this system works for a simple example, assume that a new company called ABC Corporation purchased machinery costing $7,500 in 2003. According to the Regulations of the *Income Tax Act*, machinery is in Class 8, which requires that CCA be computed using 20% declining balance. This means that a maximum of 20% × $7,500, or $1,500, seemingly may be deducted as CCA on the corporate income tax return in respect of this asset for the year 2003. Unfortunately, normally only half of the CCA otherwise deductible may be deducted in the year in which an asset is acquired, so ABC Corporation's CCA in 2003 is only $750. The CCA of $750 reduces the remaining amount available for the next year's (2004) CCA calculation. This reduced amount is called in income tax jargon the undepreciated capital cost, or UCC. The following shows the maximum CCA that may be deducted by ABC Corporation over the first five years 2003 to 2007, for illustrative purposes:

Year	UCC at Start	CCA	UCC at End
2003	$7,500	$ 750*	$6,750
2004	6,750	1,350**	5,400
2005	5,400	1,080**	4,320
2006	4,320	864**	3,456
2007	3,456	691** (rounded)	2,765

*The "half-year rule" is in effect.

**Computed using 20% times the opening UCC.

Disposition of Capital Assets

When capital assets are disposed of before their useful lives are completed, any difference between the net book value of the asset and the disposition proceeds is treated as a gain or loss. Assume a capital asset is sold at the end of year 2 for $5,000 when its book value is $3,780. The asset's cost was $10,500. The following entry would be made:

DR	Cash	$5,000	
DR	Accumulated amortization	6,720	
	CR Capital asset		$10,500
	CR Gain on sale of asset		1,220

Dispositions of assets take place frequently as firms respond to changing production and consumer demand conditions. For this reason, gains and losses from asset sales do not satisfy the criteria for the extraordinary item treatment described in Chapter 2. Accordingly, such items are included in the income statement "above the line" as an element of pre-tax income from continuing operations.

Financial Analysis and Amortization Differences

Most Canadian firms use straight-line amortization for financial reporting purposes. Nevertheless, making valid comparisons across firms is often hindered by other amortization assumptions, especially differences in useful lives. Two firms in the same industry often amortize their otherwise similar assets over different estimated lives. When this happens, potentially significant income differences arise.

We now illustrate this problem and discuss ways to adjust amortization to achieve greater comparability across firms. Exhibit 10.4(a) shows information extracted from the 1999 annual report of UAL Corporation (an American company and parent of United Air Lines, Inc.); Exhibit 10.4(b) contains similar data from the 1999 annual report of Southwest Airlines Co. (another American company), one of United's competitors. Both companies amortize all their capital assets using the straight-line method. However, United amortizes aircraft over useful lives of 4 to 30 years; for Southwest useful lives range from 20 to 25 years. A similar difference in useful-life assumptions exists for ground equipment; United's estimated lives range from 3 to 45 years, while Southwest's are from 3 to 30 years. (See highlighted sections in Exhibit 10.4(a) and (b).)

UAL CORPORATION
www.ual.com

Clear differences exist but the level of disclosure is too cryptic to allow analysts to compute precise adjustments. Despite this drawback, by making reasonable assumptions, we can estimate the effect on income arising from the differences in asset lives for United and Southwest. Let's see how.

Exhibit 10.4(a) FINANCIAL STATEMENT EXCERPTS: FIXED ASSETS AND AMORTIZABLE LIVES

UAL Corporation
Balance Sheet Fixed Assets

	December 31,	
(US$ in millions)	1999	1998
Operating property and equipment		
Owned:		
Flight equipment	$13,518	$12,006
Advances on flight equipment	809	985
Other property and equipment	3,368	3,134
	17,695	16,125
Less: Accumulated depreciation and amortization	5,207	5,174
	12,488	10,951
Capital leases:		
Flight equipment	2,929	2,605
Other property and equipment	93	97
	3,022	2,702
Less: Accumulated amortization	645	599
	2,377	2,103
	$14,865	$13,054

Partial Footnote on Operating Property and Equipment

Depreciation and amortization of owned depreciable assets is based on the straight-line method over their estimated service lives. Leasehold improvements are amortized over the remaining period of the lease or the estimated service life of the related asset, whichever is less. Aircraft are depreciated to estimated salvage values, generally over lives of 4 to 30 years; buildings are depreciated over lives of 25 to 45 years; and other property and equipment are depreciated over lives of 3 to 15 years.

Properties under capital leases are amortized on the straight-line method over the life of the lease, or in the case of certain aircraft, over their estimated service lives. Lease terms are 10 to 30 years for aircraft and flight simulators and 25 years for buildings. Amortization of capital leases is included in depreciation and amortization expense.

Selected Income Statement Information

	Year Ended December 31,	
(US$ in millions)	1999	1998
Depreciation and amortization	$ 867	$793
Earnings before taxes, distributions on preferred securities and extraordinary items	$1,243	$827

Because both companies use straight-line amortization, the ratio of average gross property, plant, and equipment divided by amortization expense gives us a rough approximation of the estimated useful (amortizable) life of the average asset. Here's why. Straight-line amortization expense (SL) is computed as:

$$SL = \frac{\text{Gross property, plant, and equipment [minus salvage value]}}{\text{Average useful life}} \qquad (10.1)$$

Exhibit 10.4(b) FINANCIAL STATEMENT EXCERPTS: FIXED ASSETS AND AMORTIZABLE LIVES

Southwest Airlines Co.
Balance Sheet Fixed Assets

	December 31,	
(US$ in thousands)	1999	1998
Property and equipment, at cost		
Flight equipment	$5,768,506	$4,709,059
Ground property and equipment	742,230	720,604
Deposits on flight equipment purchase contracts	338,229	309,356
	6,848,965	5,739,019
Less: Allowance for depreciation	1,840,799	1,601,409
	$5,008,166	$4,137,610

Footnote on Property and Equipment Accounting Policy

PROPERTY AND EQUIPMENT Depreciation is provided by the straight-line method to residual values over periods ranging from 20 to 25 years for flight equipment and 3 to 30 years for ground property and equipment. Property under capital leases and related obligations are recorded at an amount equal to the present value of future minimum lease payments computed on the basis of the Company's incremental borrowing rate or, when known, the interest rate implicit in the lease. Amortization of property under capital leases is on a straight-line basis over the lease term and is included in depreciation expense.

Selected Income Statement Information

	Year Ended December 31,	
(US$ in thousands)	1999	1998
Depreciation	$248,660	$225,212
Income before income taxes	$773,611	$705,112

Rearranging terms:

$$SL \times (\text{Average useful life}) = \text{Gross property, plant, and equipment} \quad (10.2)$$
$$[\text{minus salvage value}]$$

Further rearranging yields:

$$\text{Average useful life} = \frac{\text{Gross property, plant, and equipment [minus salvage value]}}{SL} \quad (10.3)$$

The ratio in equation (10.3) is only a rough approximation for many reasons. One is that we cannot estimate the salvage values assumed by United and Southwest. Other factors which make the computation approximate are discussed next. The computation of average useful lives using the equation (10.3) approximation is shown in Exhibit 10.5.

End-of-year and start-of-year gross property are added together in Exhibit 10.5 and then divided by 2 in order to estimate average gross property for 1999. This computation suggests that, *on average*, United is using shorter estimated lives (21.8 years) than Southwest (24.0) years.[13]

Exhibit 10.5 COMPUTING APPROXIMATE AVERAGE USEFUL LIVES

(US$ in millions)	United	Southwest
Average gross property, plant, and equipment[1]	$\dfrac{\$19{,}908 + \$17{,}842}{2}$	$\dfrac{\$6{,}510.7 + \$5{,}429.7}{2}$
Depreciation expense	$\$867$	$\$248.7$
	$\dfrac{\$18{,}875}{\$867} = 21.8 \text{ years}$	$\dfrac{\$5{,}970.2}{\$248.7} = 24.0 \text{ years}$

[1]Excludes deposits and advances on flight equipment. For example, year-end 1999 numbers were computed as follows using Exhibit 10.4(a) and 10.4(b) data:

United: $13,518 + $3,368 + $2,929 + $93 = $19,908

Southwest: $5,768.5 + $742.2 = $6,510.7

To improve comparisons of profitability between United and Southwest, the analyst would like to undo these differences in amortization lives.[14] One way to undo these differences is to divide United's average gross property number by Southwest's estimated amortizable life—that is:

$$\frac{\$18{,}875}{24.0 \text{ years}} = \$786.5$$

The quotient, US$786.5 million, is the approximate annual United amortization expense number that would result from using Southwest's longer estimated useful life assumption. If these rough approximations are correct, United's 1999 amortization would fall by US$80.5 million (i.e., $867 million – $786.5 million) and earnings before taxes, extraordinary items, and the cumulative effect of accounting change would rise by the same amount. This represents a pre-tax earnings increase of 6.5%.

This adjustment process is crude and relies on assumptions. It assumes that the useful life differences are artificial. It further assumes that the dollar breakdown within asset categories is similar for both United and Southwest—that is, the computation assumes that United and Southwest Airlines both have roughly the same proportionate dollar amount of trucks, gate equipment, aircraft, and so on. If these assumptions are incorrect, then the average age computation for one airline cannot legitimately be applied to the other's asset base to estimate "adjusted" amortization. However, if these assumptions hold, the adjusted numbers should make a comparison of United and Southwest more accurate.

International Perspective

In Canada, the purpose of financial reporting rules is to capture the underlying economic activities of a firm. In the auditor's opinion, this is indicated by the phrase "these statements **present fairly.**" A similar overriding principle governs the preparation of financial statements in the United Kingdom, where the auditor opines that "these statements give a **true and fair view.**" The underlying economic position of the reporting entity also dominates the accounting principles in other countries, such as the Netherlands, the United States, Australia, and New Zealand.[15]

But this reporting perspective is not universal. In many other countries, publicly disseminated financial reports have other, overriding objectives. In France, all companies' financial reports must conform to a specified format using tax accounting measurement rules. Constraining companies to use a specific set of accounts and narrow measurement rules is thought to provide comparable data to government decision makers, thus enabling them to better regulate the economy. A similar philosophy governs financial reporting in other European countries, such as Italy and Belgium.

The United Kingdom has reporting rules similar to those in Canada. Nevertheless, there are differences in capital asset measurement procedures between the two countries. United Kingdom companies are permitted to periodically revalue land and buildings. When this is done, the accumulated amortization account is removed and the revalued amount becomes the new book value. The amount of the writeup is credited to an equity account called **revaluation reserve.** Assume a building that originally cost £20,000,000 and has an accumulated amortization balance of £10,000,000 is appraised at £35,000,000 and accordingly written up, as permitted by U.K. standards. The accounting entry would be:

DR	Building	£15,000,000	
DR	Accumulated amortization	10,000,000	
	CR Revaluation reserve		£25,000,000

Notice that the new net book value becomes £35,000,000 after this entry is made. This is seen as follows:

	Net Book Value Prior to Revaluation	Revaluation	Net Book Value After Revaluation
Building	£20,000,000	DR £15,000,000	£35,000,000
Less: Accumulated amortization	(10,000,000)	DR 10,000,000	—
Net book value	£10,000,000		£35,000,000

The revaluation reserve account that is credited in the previous entry is an owners' equity account. Under GAAP in the United Kingdom, this amount would be disclosed as a separate line item in the owners' equity section of the balance sheet.

Amortization in subsequent periods is based on the revaluation net book value (£35,000,000). If the building has an expected remaining useful life of 20 years at the time of the revaluation, annual amortization on the income statement will be £1,750,000 (i.e., £35,000,000 ÷ 20).[16]

Revaluations are not uncommon among U.K. companies. A report has indicated that approximately 25% of surveyed U.K. companies revalued at least some of their capital assets in 1993 and 1994.[17] While U.K. reporting rules encourage companies to update revaluations periodically, they do not require it. Consequently, even when balance sheets show revaluation reserves, readers cannot assume that a *recent* revaluation occurred or that the reported net book values approximate current cost. In addition to the updating problem, many U.K. firms never revalue fixed assets at all. This complicates comparisons across companies in the United Kingdom.

The International Accounting Standards Committee (succeeded by the International Accounting Standards Board—see Chapter 18), a group formed to bring uniformity to global financial reporting, also allows fixed asset revaluations. The revaluation procedure in *International Accounting Standard (IAS) 16* roughly parallels the U.K. approach.[18] However, *IAS 16* requires that revaluations be updated periodically—that is, whenever the revalued carrying amount differs materially from fair value.[19]

This example illustrates that despite the general similarities among Canadian, U.K., and international financial reporting rules, important differences do exist.

Writing up fixed assets to reflect reappraisal increases is forbidden in Canada as well as in the United States. Differences of this sort make financial analyses of foreign companies—even companies in "similar" reporting environments—a perilous activity.

Summary

GAAP for capital assets (property, plant, and equipment; intangible assets; and—as in Chapter 16—goodwill) is far from perfect. The need for reliable and objective numbers causes these assets to be measured generally in terms of an estimate of the economic sacrifice incurred to obtain them—their historical cost—rather than in terms of their current expected benefit—or worth—to the firm. Since it is uncertain whether future benefits result from research and brand development costs, these costs are generally expensed in the period incurred. Consequently, the balance sheet carrying amounts for intangible assets often differ from what might be argued to be more reasonable values.

A thorough understanding of how the GAAP measurement rules are applied allows statement readers to avoid pitfalls in trend analysis when investment in new assets is sporadic. Similarly, an understanding of differences in amortization choices across firms permits better interfirm comparisons. Finally, international practices for long-lived assets and book amortization charges are sometimes very different from those in Canada. Statement users who make comparisons across countries must exercise caution.

For more Exercises, Problems/Discussion Questions, and Cases, visit the Companion Website for this textbook at **www.pearsoned.ca/revsine**.

Exercises

E10-1 Determining asset cost and amortization expense

In January 2001, Beta Corporation entered into a contract to acquire a new machine for its factory. The machine, which had a cash price of $165,000, was paid for as follows:

Down payment	$ 30,000
Note payable due June 1, 2001	120,000
500 Shares of Beta common stock with an estimated value of $50 per share	25,000
Total	$175,000

Prior to the machine's use, installation costs of $4,000 were incurred. The machine has an estimated useful life of ten years and an estimated salvage value of $5,000.

Required:

What should Beta record as amortization expense for 2001 under the straight-line method, if GAAP are followed? (*Note:* Beta's common shares trade thinly; the $50 per share is a consultant's estimate.)

E10-2 Components of the cost of a capital asset under GAAP
CICA adapted

In accordance with its expansion plan, in 2002 Gamma Company acquired a large piece of land in a location about 500 kilometres from its headquarters. After demolishing the three old buildings on the land, the company undertook to build a plant. The construction contract has been awarded to a contractor. Several employees of Gamma have been assigned various tasks related to the construction project. The cost to construct the plant, approximately $25 million, is to be partly financed by a mortgage. According to the mortgage agreement, the bank will advance the funds as the construction disbursements are made. Management expects construction to be completed by June 2003.

Required:

Which one of the following items *cannot* be included in the cost of the plant, under GAAP? How sensible is the GAAP treatment?

1. the cost of demolishing the three old buildings that were on the land
2. any direct costs of the building assumed by Gamma beyond those anticipated in the construction contract
3. the interest cost accrued in 2002 on the mortgage loan
4. the salaries of employees assigned directly to the construction project
5. the fees paid to a firm of lawyers, members of which advised Gamma's in-house legal team on the wording of the mortgage agreement
6. amortization and other operating costs of Gamma's corporate jet that was used for transporting Gamma executives to numerous meetings to arrange (a) the mortgage financing and (b) the construction contract
7. a pro rata portion of the salaries and all other compensation (including bonuses and stock options) of the top managers who were involved in negotiating the contracts

8. a pro rata share of what Gamma's chief financial officer (CFO) calls "the cost of equity" (according to the CFO, this is an estimate of the cost of common shares and other equity financing used to run Gamma's business, and unlike the cost of debt [such as the mortgage], it is subject to considerable estimation error)

E10-3 Amortization base

The Pete Company purchased a tooling machine in 1992 for $30,000. The machine was being amortized on the straight-line method over an estimated useful life of 20 years, with no salvage value.

At the beginning of 2002, when the machine had been in use for 10 years, the company paid $5,000 to overhaul it. As a result of this improvement, the company estimated that the remaining useful life of the machine was now 15 years.

Required:

What amortization expense should be recorded for this machine in 2002?

E10-4 Analysis of various costs

In December 2001, Roger Printing Company incurred the following costs for one of its printing presses:

Purchase of collating and stapling attachment	$80,000
Installation of attachment	30,000
Replacement parts for overhaul of press	26,000
Labour and overhead in connection with overhaul	35,000

The overhaul resulted in a significant increase in production capability. Neither the attachment nor the overhaul increased the estimated useful life of the press.

Required:

What is the total amount of the preceding costs that should be capitalized under GAAP? Explain.

E10-5 Deferred payment contract

On January 1, 2001, Hardy Inc. purchased certain plant assets under a deferred payment contract. The agreement called for making annual payments of $10,000 per year for five years. The first payment is due on January 1, 2001, and the remainder of the payments are due on January 1 of each of the next four years. Assume an imputed interest rate of 10%.

Required:

Determine the entry to record the purchase of these plant assets on January 1, 2001. Explain your decisions.

E10-6 Analysis of various costs

Maco Manufacturing Company, a calendar-year company, purchased a machine for $65,000 on January 1, 2001. At the date of purchase, Maco incurred the following additional costs:

Loss on sale of old machinery	$2,000
Freight-in	500
Installation cost	2,000
Testing costs prior to regular operation	300

The estimated salvage value of the machine was $5,000, and Maco estimated the machine would have a useful life of 20 years, with amortization being computed on the straight-line method. In January 2003, accessories costing $3,600 were added to the machine in order to reduce its operating costs. These accessories neither prolonged the machine's life nor provided any additional salvage value.

Required:

What should Maco record as amortization expense for 2003?

Problems/Discussion Questions

P10-1 Allocation of acquisition costs among asset accounts

On April 23, 2002, Starlight Department Stores Inc. acquired a 75-hectare tract of land by paying $25,000,000 in cash, issuing a six-month note payable for $5,000,000, and by issuing 1,000,000 common shares. Also on April 23, 2002, Starlight's common stock was selling for $80 a share. The land had two existing buildings, one that Starlight intended to renovate and use as a warehouse, and another that Starlight intended to demolish to make way for the construction of a new department store. At the time of the purchase, the fair market values of the land and building were $105,000,000 and $20,000,000, respectively. To complete the purchase, Starlight incurred legal fees of $25,000. The land had two existing structures, one that Starlight intended to renovate and use as a warehouse, and another that Starlight intended to demolish to make way for the construction of a new department store. The cost of demolishing the building was $50,000. Starlight paid $250,000 to have the land graded so that the new store could be built. Starlight paid a total of $100,000,000 to have the new department store built and another $25,000,000 to renovate the old building. To fund the work on the two buildings, Starlight obtained a loan from City Bank. Starlight made interest payments of $10,000,000 on a construction loan during the period the buildings were being completed. (Assume that all of the interest payments qualify for capitalization.) Since parking would be needed for both the new department store and the warehouse, Starlight had a portion of the land covered with asphalt at a cost of $450,000. Starlight also paid $200,000 to install lighting for the parking lots and $75,000 to landscape the parking lots with trees and shrubs. During 2002, Starlight was assessed and paid property taxes of $150,000 on the new property. All work was completed by December 31, 2002, and the new store and warehouse were placed in service on January 1, 2003.

Required:

Determine what costs should be assigned to the (1) land, (2) building, and (3) land improvements asset accounts. (*Hint:* The allocation of the original purchase price between the land and building should be made in proportion to the relative fair market values of the land and building at the time of the purchase.)

P10-2 Capitalize or expense various costs

Formidable Express provides overnight delivery of letters and small parcels to numerous locations throughout Canada, Mexico, and the United States. As part of its operations, the company maintains a sizeable fleet of delivery trucks. Assume that Formidable Express made the following expenditures related to the fleet during 2001:

1. The company has the engines in its trucks serviced (i.e., tuned up) once every two years. The cost of the servicing in 2001 was $11.0 million.
2. Due to the high mileage put on the delivery vehicles, the company normally replaces 20% of its fleet's engines every year. In 2001, the cost incurred to replace engines amounted to $7.8 million.
3. The tires on each vehicle are replaced once every three years. The cost of the new tires installed in 2001 amounted to $1.0 million.
4. In 2001, the company paid $3.5 million to have the trucks in the fleet rust-proofed. Management expects that the trucks will now last an extra three years.
5. Because each truck was out of service for about a week due to the rustproofing in part 4, the company estimates that it lost $12.0 million in revenue during the course of the year.

Required:

How should Formidable Express account for each of these expenditures?

P10-3 Capitalize or expense various costs

Fly-by-Night is an international airline company. Its fleet includes Boeing 757s, 747s, 727s, Lockheed L-1011s, and McDonnell Douglas MD-83s, MD-80s, and DC-9s. Assume that Fly-by-Night made the following expenditures related to these aircraft in 2003:

1. New jet engines were installed on some of the MD-80s and MD-83s at a cost of $25.0 million.
2. The company paid $2.0 million to paint one-eighth of the fleet with the firm's new colours in order to create a new public image. The company intends to paint the remainder of the fleet over the next seven years.
3. Routine maintenance and repairs on various aircraft cost $8.0 million.
4. Noise abatement equipment (i.e., "hush kits") was installed on the fleet of DC-9s to meet maximum allowable noise levels upon takeoff. Equipment and installation cost $7.5 million.
5. The avionics systems were replaced on the Lockheed L-1011s. This will allow the aircraft to be used four more years than originally expected.
6. The existing seats on all 747s were replaced with new, more comfortable seats at a cost of $0.5 million.
7. The jet engines of 50% of the Boeing 727s received a major overhaul at a cost of $5.0 million. As a result, the aircraft should be more fuel-efficient.

Required:

1. Which of these expenditures should Fly-by-Night capitalize? Why? Assume GAAP are to be followed.
2. How might a firm like Fly-by-Night use expenditures like these to manage its earnings?

P10-4 Asset impairment

National Sweetener Company owns the patent to the artificial sweetener known as Supersweet. Assume that National Sweetener acquired the patent on January 1, 2002, at a cost of $300 million, expected the patent to have an economic useful life of 12 years, and has been amortizing the patent on a straight-line basis. Assume that at the time the patent was acquired, National Sweetener expected that the process would generate future net cash flows of $30 million in the first year of its useful life and that the cash flows would grow at a rate of 10% each year over the remainder of its useful life. By the year 2014 (i.e., after 12 years), National Sweetener expected that there would be several other artificial sweeteners on the market and therefore that it would sell the Supersweet patent at that time for about $75.0 million.

Year	Expected Future Cash Flows ($ in millions)	Year	Expected Future Cash Flows ($ in millions)
2002	$30.0	2009	$ 58.4
2003	33.0	2010	64.3
2004	36.3	2011	70.7
2005	39.9	2012	77.8
2006	43.9	2013	85.6
2007	48.3	Total	$641.3
2008	53.1		

On December 31, 2008, when the patent's book value was $125.0 million ($300.0 million – $175.0 million), National Sweetener learned that one of its competitors had come up with a revolutionary new sweetener that could be produced much more cheaply than Supersweet. National Sweetener expects that the introduction of this product on January 1, 2009, will substantially reduce the cash flows from its Supersweet patent process.

Consider the following two independent scenarios:

- *Scenario I.* National Sweetener expects that the cash flows from Supersweet over the 2009–2013 period will only be 50% of those originally projected and that the sale of the Supersweet patent will only bring $25 million when sold as originally planned. When discounted at a rate of 15% (which National Sweetener feels is appropriate), these amounts yield a present value of $129.0 million. National Sweetener estimates that the market value of the Supersweet patent on December 31, 2008, is $125.0 million.
- *Scenario II.* National Sweetener expects that the cash flows from Supersweet over the 2009–2013 period will only be 25% of those originally projected and that the sale of the Supersweet patent will only bring $25 million when sold as originally planned. When discounted at a rate of 15%, these amounts yield a present value of $70.7 million. National Sweetener estimates that the market value of the Supersweet patent on December 31, 2008, is $68.0 million.

Required:

1. Should National Sweetener recognize an impairment of its Supersweet patent in Scenario I? If so, what is the amount of the loss and at what amount should the patent be reported in National Sweetener's 2008 ending balance sheet?
2. Repeat Question 1 for the second scenario.

P10-5 Inco Limited's asset impairment

Recall the press release excerpt announcing Inco's asset impairment writedown, included in this chapter. In this press release, Inco states that the company will disclose the difference between the Canadian and U.S. measures of the impairment "in the Company's regulatory filings for the second quarter of 2002."

INCO LIMITED
www.inco.com

Required:

1. Explain why there is a difference between the Canadian and U.S. measures.
2. If the Canadian exposure draft becomes GAAP, would there still be a difference if the writedown took place after the effective date of a new standard?
3. Prepare a 500-word memo to your company's audit committee explaining why the U.S. method (and the proposed Canadian method) is *inferior* to current Canadian GAAP.

P10-6 Straight-line versus accelerated amortization ratio effects

The 2002 income statement and other information for Mallard Corporation, which is about to purchase a new machine at a cost of $500 and a new computer system at a cost of $300, appears below.

Sales	$1,000
Cost of goods sold	600
Gross profit	$ 400
Operating expenses	$ 150
Income before tax	$ 250
Income taxes	85
Net income	$ 165

Additional Information:

1. The two new assets are expected to generate a 25% annual rate of growth in the firm's sales.
2. The firm will include the amortization expense on the machine as part of cost of goods sold and the amortization expense on the computer system as part of operating expenses.
3. *Excluding* the amortization on the new machine, the firm's cost of goods sold is expected to increase at an annual rate of 7.5%.
4. *Excluding* the amortization on the new computer system, the firm's operating expenses are expected to increase at an annual rate of 4.0%.
5. The firm's gross total assets are expected to grow at a rate of 20% per year. Average gross total assets in 2002 were $1,000.
6. Both the machine and the computer system have a three-year useful life and a zero salvage value.
7. Assume an income tax rate of 34%.

Required:

1. Assume that the assets are purchased on January 1, 2003. Prepare pro forma income statements for 2003 through 2005. Assume the firm elects to use straight-line amortization.
2. Repeat Question 1, assuming instead that the firm elects to use the sum-of-the-years'-digits method.
3. For both questions 1 and 2, calculate the firm's gross profit rate (gross profit divided by sales), NOPAT margin (net operating profit after tax divided by sales), and return on assets (NOPAT divided by average total assets). How does the use of the different amortization methods affect the behaviour of the ratios over the 2003–2005 period?

P10-7 Approaches to capital asset valuation

1. Contrast the economic sacrifice and expected benefit approaches to capital asset valuation.
2. Current GAAP require firms to use historical cost (in most cases) to report the value of capital assets. As a statement reader, do you think that firms should be encouraged to voluntarily report their asset values under alternative valuation approaches? Why or why not?
3. As the manager of a publicly held company, what costs and benefits do you see associated with the voluntary disclosure of asset values using approaches other than historical cost?

Cases

C10-1 Microsoft (CW): Capitalization versus expensing of R&D

Microsoft develops, manufactures, licenses, sells, and supports a wide range of software products, including operating systems for personal computers (PCs) and servers; server applications for client/server environments; business and consumer productivity applications; interactive media programs; and Internet platform and development tools. Microsoft also offers online services, sells PC books and input devices, and researches and develops advanced technology software products. Microsoft products are available for most PCs, including Intel microprocessor-based computers and Apple computers. Microsoft's business strategy emphasizes the development of a broad line of PC software products for business and personal use.

MICROSOFT
CORPORATION
**www.microsoft.
com**

Income statement and balance sheet information taken from Microsoft's recent annual reports to shareholders follows. Assume an income tax rate of 35%.

Microsoft: Selected Financial Information

(US$ in millions)	1996	1997	1998	1999	2000
Sales	$ 8,671	$11,358	$15,262	$19,747	$22,956
Net income (NOPAT)	2,195	3,454	4,490	7,785	9,421
Total assets	10,093	14,387	22,357	38,625	52,150
Total shareholders' equity	6,908	10,777	16,627	28,438	41,368
Research and development	$ 1,432	$ 1,925	$ 2,897	$ 2,970	$ 3,775

Required:

1. How does current GAAP require firms to account for their research and development expenditures?
2. Use the reported information to calculate Microsoft's NOPAT margin (net operating profit after taxes divided by sales), asset turnover (sales divided by average total assets), return on assets (NOPAT divided by average total assets), and return on shareholders' equity (NOPAT divided by average shareholders' equity) for 1998, 1999, and 2000.
3. Assume that Microsoft expects its research and development expenditures to benefit the current accounting period as well as the next two accounting periods. Briefly describe how Microsoft's 1998 income statement and balance sheet would have been different if it had capitalized rather than expensed its research and development expenditures.

4. Repeat Question 2 after capitalizing the relevant portion of each period's research and development expenditures. As a statement reader, would you find the differences in the ratios in Questions 2 and 4 to be significant? Why?

C10-2 Target Corporation and Kmart (CW): Depreciation differences and financial statement analysis

TARGET
www.targetstores.
com

KMART
www.kmart.com

Target Corporation is a general merchandise retailer in the United States. Its divisions include Target, an upscale discount chain; Mervyn's, a middle-market promotional department store; and upscale department stores in the U.S. Midwest (Dayton's, Hudson's, and Marshall Field's).

Kmart Corporation is one of the world's largest mass merchandise retailers. The dominant portion of the firm's operations is general merchandise retailing through the operation of a chain of 2,170 Kmart discount stores in each of the 50 United States, Puerto Rico, the U.S. Virgin Islands, and Guam.

Information taken from both firms' 2000 annual reports to shareholders follows.

Target Corporation

(US$ in millions)	January 29 2000	January 30 1999
Property and Equipment		
Land	$ 2,069	$ 1,868
Buildings and improvements	7,807	7,217
Fixtures and equipment	3,422	3,274
Construction in progress	526	378
Accumulated depreciation	(3,925)	(3,768)
Property and equipment—net	$ 9,899	$ 8,969

Property and long-lived assets are recorded at cost less accumulated depreciation or amortization. Depreciation and amortization are computed using the straight-line method over estimated useful lives. Accelerated depreciation methods are generally used for income tax purposes.

Estimated useful lives by major asset category are as follows:

Asset	Life (in Years)
Buildings and improvements	8–50
Fixtures and equipment	5–8
Computer hardware and software	4
Intangible assets and goodwill	3–20

On an ongoing basis, we evaluate our long-lived assets for impairment using undiscounted cash flow analysis.

(US$ in millions)	January 29 2000	January 30 1999
Depreciation and amortization	$ 854	$ 780
Earnings before income taxes and extraordinary charge	1,936	1,556
Net earnings	$1,144	$ 935

Kmart Corporation

(US$ in millions)	January 26 2000	January 27 1999
Property:		
Land	$ 374	$ 334
Buildings	1,008	944
Leasehold improvements	2,502	2,156
Furniture and fixtures	5,509	5,142
Construction in progress	123	62
Property under capital leases	2,038	2,140
	$11,554	$10,778
Less-accumulated depreciation and amortization:		
Property owned	(3,977)	(3,674)
Property under capital leases	(1,167)	(1,190)
Total	$ 6,410	$ 5,914

Depreciation and amortization, including amortization of property held under capital leases, are computed on the basis of the estimated useful lives of the respective assets using the straight-line method for financial statement purposes and accelerated methods for tax purposes. The general ranges of lives are 25 to 50 years for buildings, 5 to 25 years for leasehold improvements, 3 to 5 years for computer systems and equipment and 3 to 17 years for furniture and fixtures.

Selected income statement information follows.

(US$ in millions)	January 26 2000	January 27 1999
Depreciation and amortization	$ 770	$671
Income before income taxes, dividends on convertible		
preferred securities, and discontinued operations	1,020	798
Net income	$ 403	$518

Required:

Assume a 35% tax rate.

1. Estimate the average useful life of each firm's long-lived assets.
2. Calculate a revised estimate of Kmart's 2000 depreciation expense using the estimated average useful life of Target's assets. Use this amount to recalculate Kmart's 2000 income before taxes and net income.
3. Calculate a revised estimate of Target's 2000 amortization expense using the estimated average useful life of Kmart's assets. Use this amount to recalculate Target's 2000 income before taxes and net income.
4. Why might a financial analyst want to make the adjustments in Questions 2 or 3?
5. What factors will affect the reliability and accuracy of the adjustments performed in Questions 2 and 3?

Endnotes

1. *CICA Handbook,* Section 3061, para. 3061.04.

2. "Property, Plant and Equipment," *CICA Handbook,* Section 3061, mandates that "Property, plant and equipment should be recorded at cost" (para. 3061.16). Section 3062 ("Goodwill and Other Intangible Assets") makes similar assertions.

3. Recent Canadian accounting standards prefer the term "amortization" over "depreciation."

4. *CICA Handbook,* Section 3061, para. 3061.26.

5. Continuing the assumptions of Table 10.3 to December 31, 2009, shows that the rate of return on assets ultimately stabilizes at approximately 15.4%. Thus, with constant (and relatively small) rates of price change, the distortion caused by historical cost accounting for capital assets is small.

6. *CICA Handbook,* Section 3450. Certain development costs, satisfying the criteria in para. 3450.21, may be deferred to future periods.

7. The Emerging Issues Committee has described the issue as follows: "Many computer systems process transactions based on storing two digits for the year of a transaction …, rather than a full four digits. A significant number of the computer systems based on two-digit years are not programmed to consider the start of a new century, unless they have recently been modified" ("Accounting for the Costs of Modifying Internal Use Computer Software for Year 2000 Compliance," *EIC-80,* April 10, 1997, p. 80.1).

8. Ibid.

9. Op. cit., p. 80.2.

10. D. A. Aaker, *Managing Brand Equity* (New York: Free Press, 1991), p. 28.

11. J. A. Elliott and W. H. Shaw, "Write-Offs as Accounting Procedures to Manage Perceptions," *Journal of Accounting Research,* Supplement 1988, pp. 91–119.

12. "Asset Retirement Obligations," April 2002, which is substantially the same as the recently issued U.S. standard *SFAS 143,* and is similar to the international standard *IAS 37.*

13. To understand why the Exhibit 10.5 answer is in years (i.e., 21.8 years and 24.0 years), let's express average gross property divided by amortization expense in terms of the underlying measurement dimensions:

Average gross property, plant, and equipment ← The underlying measurement dimension is $s

Amortization expense ← The underlying measurement dimension is $s per year

Expressing the computation in underlying measurement dimensions, the division in Exhibit 10.5 becomes:

$$\frac{\$s}{\$s/\text{Year}}$$

Following algebraic rules for division by fractions, we invert the denominator and multiply it by the numerator:

$$\$s \times \frac{\text{Year}}{\$s}$$

The $s cancel and the answer is expressed dimensionally in years (e.g., 21.8 years and 24.0 years).

14. It is possible that the useful-life differences reflect real economic variables rather than accounting choices. For example, Southwest's aircraft might be newer and, on average, have longer useful lives. If the useful lives differences are "real," then analysts' attempts to "undo" the differences may impede, rather than improve, profit comparisons.

15. Notice that the purpose of financial reporting, to capture the underlying economic activities of the firm, is *assumed* to be achievable. For some evidence that it is *not,* see Kevin J. Delaney, "The Organizational Construction of the 'Bottom Line,' " *Social Problems,* vol. 41, no. 4, 1994, pp. 497–518. But the U.S. case is truly governed by a desire to report "economic reality" only insofar as U.S. GAAP standards require companies to do so. But since we know that complying with U.S. GAAP causes deviation from "economic reality" in many instances (think of the requirement to expense R&D costs), we know that this compliance does not ensure "fair presentation." Since U.S. managers and auditors are motivated (largely by legal sanctions) to ensure compliance with U.S. GAAP, the result is a situation strongly driven by a "letter of the law" culture (witness the attempt to "fit" Enron's special purpose entities into compliance with U.S. quantitative requirements on nonconsolidation). Existing Canadian standards in Section 1500 ("General Standards of Financial Statement Presentation") do provide, however, for deviation from the *CICA Handbook* recommendations in order to achieve fair presentation. Such deviations are rare, and the AcSB is currently (July 2002) revising an exposure draft on this issue.

16. The amount in the owners' equity revaluation reserve account would be transferred year by year to retained earnings as the revalued asset is amortized. For example, if we assume that the asset is not subsequently revalued over the ensuing 20 years, £1,250,000 (i.e., £25,000,000 ÷ 20) would be reclassified each year. The entry would be:

DR Revaluation reserve	£1,250,000	
CR Retained earnings		£1,250,000

This reclassification entry is made in order to reduce the revaluation reserve as the asset ages. If no entry were made, there would still be a revaluation reserve amount on the books even after the asset was removed from service. The year-by-year transfer ultimately reduces the reserve to zero.

17. L. C. L. Skerratt and D. J. Tonkin (eds.), *Financial Reporting 1993–1994: A Survey of U.K. Reporting Practice* (London: The Institute of Chartered Accountants in England and Wales, 1994), p. 195.

18. "Property, Plant and Equipment," *IAS 16* (London: International Accounting Standards Committee, 1993).

19. Ibid., para. 34.

11
Financial Instruments as Liabilities

LEARNING OBJECTIVES
After studying this chapter, you should be able to:

1. Compute a bond's issue price from its effective yield to investors

2. Construct an amortization table for calculating bond interest expense and net carrying value

3. Understand why and how bond interest expense and net carrying value change over time

4. Understand how and when floating-rate debt protects lenders

5. Describe how debt extinguishment gains and losses arise, and what they mean

6. Find the future cash payments for a company's debt

7. Understand why off-balance-sheet financing and loss contingencies are important concerns for statement readers

8. Describe how futures, swaps, and options contracts help manage risk, and how they are reported

9. Understand important aspects of hedge accounting

S ection 1000 of the *CICA Handbook* defines "liabilities" in the following way:[1]

> *Liabilities are obligations of an entity arising from past transactions or events, the settlement of which may result in the transfer or use of assets, provision of services or other yielding of economic benefits in the future.* (para. 1000.32)

The *Handbook* section goes on to expand this definition by explaining that:

> *Liabilities have three essential characteristics:*
>
> *(a) they embody a duty or responsibility to others that entails settlement by future transfer or use of assets, provision of services or other yielding of economic benefits, at a specified or determinable date, on occurrence of a specified event, or on demand;*
>
> *(b) the duty or responsibility obligates the entity leaving it little or no discretion to avoid it; and*
>
> *(c) the transaction or event obligating the entity has already occurred.* (para. 1000.33)

Liabilities help businesses conduct their affairs by permitting delay—delay in payment or performance. But since "time is money," **interest** is a common feature of delayed payment liabilities. Interest represents the price charged for the privilege of delaying payment.

Most liabilities are **monetary liabilities** because they will be paid using cash. There are nonmonetary liabilities that are satisfied by the delivery of things other than cash, such as merchandise or services. An example is a product warranty. If the product fails during the warranty period, the warranty liability is satisfied by either repairing or replacing the product. The liability is extinguished by providing nonmonetary assets—labour and replacement parts from inventory or a new product—but not cash.

The title of this chapter, "Financial Instruments as Liabilities," emphasizes terminology introduced in Section 3860 of the *CICA Handbook*. That section uses the following terms: **financial instrument** ("any contract that gives rise to both a financial asset of one party and a financial liability or equity instrument of another party" (3860.05(a)); **financial liability** ("any liability that is a contractual obligation: (i) to deliver cash or another financial asset to another party; or (ii) to exchange financial instruments with another party under conditions that are potentially unfavourable" (3860.05 (c)). So the general definition of "liabilities" in Section 1000 is narrowed for purposes of both Section 3860 and our discussion in this chapter, focusing on "contractual" obligations, and more particularly, contractual monetary obligations.

Conceptually, monetary liabilities should be shown in the financial statements at the discounted present value of the future cash outflows required to satisfy the obligation. This allows interest to accumulate over time through accounting entries that assign interest expense—the cost of delay—to the time period(s) over which payment is delayed. In practice, this is what is done with long-term monetary liabilities.

However, current liabilities—obligations due within a year or within the company's operating cycle, whichever is longer—are not discounted. This is because the short maturity of current liabilities makes the difference between the amount due at maturity and present value immaterial. So current liabilities are shown at the undiscounted amount due. This treatment of current liabilities departs from the conceptual "ideal" solely on pragmatic grounds.

Noncurrent monetary liabilities, however, are initially recorded at present value when incurred. There are occasional exceptions. One is the future income tax account, which is reported at an undiscounted amount for reasons explained in Chapter 13. But the general rule is that noncurrent monetary liabilities are first recorded at their present value. The next section explains why.

Bonds Payable

Firms issue bonds to raise cash. A **bond** is a financial instrument that represents a formal promise to repay *both* the amount borrowed and interest. The precise terms of the borrowing are specified in the **bond indenture agreement**—the contract between the issuer and investors. In this section, we look at how companies account for this debt instrument and how to interpret debt disclosures in financial statements.

Characteristics of Bond Cash Flows

Bonds are usually issued with a **principal** amount of $1,000 per bond certificate. The principal amount—also called the **par value**, **maturity value**, or **face value**—represents the amount that will be repaid to the investor at the maturity date specified in the indenture agreement. The bond certificate also displays the **stated interest rate**—sometimes called the **coupon** or **nominal rate**.

The annual cash interest payments on the bond are computed by multiplying the principal amount by the stated interest rate. A bond with $1,000 principal and a 9%

Debentures, the most common type of corporate bond, are backed only by the general credit of the company. **Mortgage bonds** have real estate as collateral for the repayment of the loan. **Serial bonds** specify periodic payment of interest and a portion of the principal (e.g., an equal proportion each year to maturity). Despite these and other differences, the accounting for these financial instruments follows the general approach described here.

Investors must be careful to read the details of a bond's interest payment terms. For example, a bond that pays "9% interest annually" yields a single payment of $90 (per $1,000 of face value) each year. A bond that pays "9% interest semiannually" yields two payments of $45 each year (9% ÷ 2 = 4.5% each payment period). Although the total dollar interest payment is $90 per year in both cases, the semiannual bond is slightly more valuable because the investor receives half of the cash earlier than in the case of the annual payment bond.

per year stated interest rate will have an annual cash interest payment of $90. Typically, the total annual cash interest is paid in installments, either quarterly or semiannually.

While the face value is typically $1,000 per bond, the price at which it is issued can be equal to, below, or above the face value.

- When the issue price exactly equals the face value, the bond is sold **at par.**
- If the issue price is below face value, the bond is sold **at a discount.**
- If the issue price is greater than the face value, the bond is sold **at a premium.**

Market conditions dictate the relationship between what investors are willing to pay—the issue price—and the bond's face value.

Bonds Issued at Par

A bond's issue price determines its **effective yield**—or true rate of return. When the issue price of the bond equals its par value, the yield to investors is exactly equal to the coupon (or stated) rate. Consider the following example.

On January 1, 2001, Huff Corporation issued $1,000,000 face value of 10% per year bonds at par—that is, Huff got $1,000,000 cash from investors and promised to make interest and principal payments in the future. Since the cash interest payments on the bonds are always equal to the stated interest rate (10%) times the bond principal amount ($1,000,000), cash interest will total $100,000 per year. The bonds mature in ten years (on December 31, 2010), and interest is paid annually on December 31 of each year.

The accounting entry to record the issuance of these bonds on the books of Huff Corporation is:

DR Cash	$1,000,000	
CR Long-term bonds payable		$1,000,000

The bond is recorded at its issue price—the $1,000,000 cash received by Huff.

When bonds are sold at par (or face value), their effective yield to the investor is exactly equal to the coupon interest rate, which is 10% in this example. To show this, we list the cash payments and compute their present value as of the issue date—January 1, 2001—in Table 11.1. The effective yield is precisely 10% since the present value of the ten annual interest payments ($614,456) plus the present value of the principal repayment ($385,544) is equal to the issue proceeds received on January 1, 2001 ($1,000,000) when discounted at a 10% rate.

For bonds issued at par, the coupon rate on the bond is equal to the effective yield earned by bond investors. Furthermore, recording the bonds at par on the issuer's books automatically records them at their discounted present value.

In the example, the amount received for the bonds ($1,000,000) is precisely equal to the present value of the future debt-related cash outflows discounted at the 10% effective yield on the bonds.

Subsequent accounting for bonds issued at par is straightforward. Let's say Huff prepared monthly financial statements; the monthly journal entry for the accrual of interest would be:

The cash interest payments on the Huff bond are an **annuity,** which just means a series of equal payments made at equally spaced time intervals. If the first payment is made at the start of period 1, then it's an **annuity due.** Apartment leases often have this feature—the first month's payment is due when the lease is signed. The cash interest payments on Huff's bonds are an **ordinary annuity** (in arrears) because the first payment is due at the end of period 1 (December 31, 2001).

DR Interest expense	$8,333.33	
CR Accrued interest payable		$8,333.33

TABLE 11.1 HUFF CORPORATION

Demonstration That the Yield on Bonds Issued at Par Is Equal to the Coupon Rate (here 10%)

Date of Payment	Type of Payment	Amount of Payment	10% Present Value Factor	Discounted Present Value
12/31/01	Interest	$ 100,000	0.90909	$ 90,909
12/31/02	Interest	100,000	0.82645	82,645
12/31/03	Interest	100,000	0.75131	75,131
12/31/04	Interest	100,000	0.68301	68,301
12/31/05	Interest	100,000	0.62092	62,092
12/31/06	Interest	100,000	0.56447	56,447
12/31/07	Interest	100,000	0.51316	51,316
12/31/08	Interest	100,000	0.46651	46,651
12/31/09	Interest	100,000	0.42410	42,410
12/31/10	Interest	100,000	0.38554	38,554
Total present value of interest payments				**$ 614,456**
12/31/10	Principal	$1,000,000	0.385544	385,544
Total issue price on January 1, 2001				**$1,000,000**

This (rounded) amount represents one-twelfth of the $100,000 annual interest. At the end of the year, the accrued interest would total $100,000; upon payment of the interest by Huff, the following entry would be made:

DR   Accrued interest payable $100,000.00
   CR   Cash $100,000.00

Bonds Issued at a Discount

Arranging for the sale of bonds can take considerable time. The terms of the indenture—the bond contract—must be drafted and printed, an investment banker must be found, and the bond certificates themselves must be engraved. Market interest rates may change during the time it takes to do this and before the bonds are ready to be issued.

Assume those Huff bonds are printed during late 2000 and carry a 10% coupon interest rate. The 10% coupon rate immediately establishes the yearly cash interest payout of $100,000 (10% multiplied by the $1,000,000 face amount of the bonds).

But let's say there's a sudden change in the anticipated rate of inflation, causing investors to demand 11% for the bonds on the January 1, 2001, issue date. To provide the 11% return that investors demand, the bonds must be sold at a *discount* relative to face value. Consider why this is true. Since the annual cash interest payments are fixed at $100,000, the bond issue price must be lower than the $1,000,000 face amount to attract purchasers. How much lower than $1,000,000 must the issue price be? It must be reduced to a level that gives prospective investors exactly the 11% return they require. ***The price is determined by discounting the contractual cash flows at 11%***, as shown in Table 11.2. Lowering the issue price gives investors the extra interest they demand.

Bonds are seldom sold directly to investors by the issuing company. Instead, the bonds are sold through a financial intermediary—an **investment banker.** In most cases, the investment banker purchases the bonds and resells them to institutional investors (e.g., pension funds) at whatever price the market will bear. The investment banker's profit (or loss) is the difference between the price for which it buys the bonds from the issuing company and the price for which it sells them to investors, plus any fees paid by the company.

TABLE 11.2 HUFF CORPORATION

Determining the Issue Price for 10% Coupon Bonds When the Market Rate Is 11%

Date of Payment	Type of Payment	Amount of Payment	11% Present Value Factor	Discounted Present Value
12/31/01	Interest	$ 100,000	0.90090	$ 90,090
12/31/02	Interest	100,000	0.81162	81,162
12/31/03	Interest	100,000	0.73119	73,119
12/31/04	Interest	100,000	0.65873	65,873
12/31/05	Interest	100,000	0.59345	59,345
12/31/06	Interest	100,000	0.53464	53,464
12/31/07	Interest	100,000	0.48166	48,166
12/31/08	Interest	100,000	0.43393	43,393
12/31/09	Interest	100,000	0.39093	39,093
12/31/10	Interest	100,000	0.35218	35,218
Total present value of interest payments				**$588,923**
12/31/10	Principal	$1,000,000	0.352185	352,185
Total issue price on January 1, 2001				**$941,108**

Equivalently

December 31	2000	2001	2002	2003	2004	2005	2006	2007	2008	2009	2010
Cash interest payments	●	$100k	$100k	$100k	$100k	$100k	$100k	$100k	$100k	$100k	$100k
Cash principal payment	●	•	•	•	•	•	•	•	•	•	$1 m

Present value of single payment at 11%: $1 million × 0.352185 = $352,185

Present value of 10-period ordinary annuity at 11%: $100 thousand × 5.88923 = $588,923

The price that yields the required 11% return, given the stipulated $100,000 annual contractual interest payments, is $941,108. Investors seeking an 11% return will not be willing to pay more than $941,108 for ten-year bonds with a face value of $1,000,000 and a coupon rate of 10%. Why? Because if they paid more than this amount, they would be earning less than 11% on the bond's fixed cash flow stream. And Huff will not be willing to issue the bonds for less than $941,108 because to do so would mean paying more than 11% to investors. Thus, market forces will effectively set the issue price at $941,108.

The accounting entry that would be made on issuance of the bonds under these terms is:

DR	Cash	$941,108	
DR	Bond discount	58,892	
	CR Bonds payable		$1,000,000

The bond discount is a **liability valuation account** that is deducted from the bonds payable account for financial reporting purposes. The net balance sheet value for the bonds when they are issued will be $941,108 ($1,000,000 – $58,892)—the amount of cash Huff received. This again illustrates the basic principle that newly issued bonds are recorded at the present value of the contractual cash outflows for interest and principal repayment—where *the discount rate is the effective yield on the bonds at the issuance date* (here 11%).

When bonds are not sold at par, the calculation of annual interest expense and the accounting entry that records that expense are slightly more complicated. Consider the nature of the bond discount of $58,892. The discount amount is the difference between the cash Huff received and the amount Huff promised to repay on December 31, 2010. This $58,892 is really just additional interest—beyond the stated cash interest of $100,000 per year—that will be paid over the term of the loan. Cumulative interest expense over the ten years will total $1,058,892—the coupon interest of $1,000,000 paid out over the life of the bond plus the issue discount of $58,892 paid at maturity.

How should this "extra" interest of $58,892 be allocated across the ten years? GAAP permit bond discount to be allocated to interest expense on an **effective interest basis or a straight-line basis.** The effective interest basis requires the use of an amortization table, as shown in Table 11.3. In column (a), Huff received $941,108 on January 1, 2001, in exchange for issuing the bond certificates. Bondholders require an 11% return on the amount invested. Therefore, their interest income—and Huff's interest expense—in 2001 must be 11% of $941,108 or $103,521.88, as shown in column (b). The difference between $103,521.88 and the cash interest of $100,000 must also be included in interest expense during 2001. If interest is recorded annually, the entry is:

DR	Interest expense	$103,521.88
CR	Accrued interest payable	$100,000.00
CR	Bond discount	3,521.88

The process of "spreading" the discount on bonds to increase interest expense over the life of the bonds is called **discount amortization.** The yearly amortization amount is shown in column (c) of Table 11.3. After the amortization is recorded, the

> **Cumulative interest expense** can also be thought of as follows: The investor will ultimately receive total debt-related cash flows of $2,000,000, comprising principal plus cash interest. Huff received only $941,108 when the bonds were issued. The difference ($2,000,000 minus $941,108) equals $1,058,892, which must be the cumulative total interest expense over the life of the bond issue.

TABLE 11.3 HUFF CORPORATION

Bond Discount Amortization Schedule

Year	(a) Bond Net Carrying Amount at Start of Year	(b) Interest Expense (Column a × 11%)	(c) Bond Discount Amortized (Column b − $100,000)	(d) Bond Discount Balance at End of Year	(e) Bond Net Carrying Amount at End of Year (Column a + Column c)
2001	$941,108.00	$ 103,521.88	$ 3,521.88	$55,370.12	$ 944,629.88
2002	944,629.88	103,909.29	3,909.29	51,460.83	948,539.17
2003	948,539.17	104,339.31	4,339.31	47,121.52	952,878.48
2004	952,878.48	104,816.63	4,816.63	42,304.89	957,695.11
2005	957,695.11	105,346.46	5,346.46	36,958.43	963,041.57
2006	963,041.57	105,934.57	5,934.57	31,023.86	968,976.14
2007	968,976.14	106,587.38	6,587.38	24,436.48	975,563.52
2008	975,563.52	107,311.99	7,311.99	17,124.49	982,875.51
2009	982,875.51	108,116.31	8,116.31	9,008.18	990,991.82
2010	990,991.82	109,008.18*	9,008.18	–0–	$1,000,000.00
		$1,058,892.00	$58,892.00		

*Rounded.

year-end balance in the bond discount account—shown in column (d)—will be $55,370.12 (the original discount of $58,892 minus the 2001 amortization of $3,521.88). Also notice that the smaller the balance in the bond discount account, shown in column (d), the higher the **net carrying value** of the bond liability in column (e). The balance sheet value of the bond increases as the discount is amortized.

The bond amortization schedule illustrates that annual interest expense, column (b), is always equal to the effective interest rate (here 11%) multiplied by the start-of-year borrowing balance, column (a). The difference between the accrual accounting interest expense, column (b), and the $100,000 cash interest paid each year is the discount amortization, column (c). This amortization process is represented in Table 11.4.

While used in Canada, the straight-line basis seems less conceptually appropriate than the effective interest basis. Under the straight-line approach, the bond discount of $58,892 would be allocated equally over the ten-year term to maturity of the bond, with each year's interest expense debited for one-tenth of $58,892, or $5,889.20, as follows:

DR	Interest expense	$5,889.20
	CR Bond discount	$5,889.20

Therefore, total annual interest expense under the straight-line method would be the same each year, $105,889.20 (i.e., $5,889.20 + $100,000). And while the total interest expense over the ten years would be the same under both the straight-line method and the effective interest method (i.e., $1,058,892.00), the annual interest expense computed using the effective interest method more faithfully represents the cost of using debt, since it results in an interest expense that corresponds to the amount of the carrying value of that debt.

Bonds Issued at a Premium

Recording bonds that are issued at a premium is similar to the accounting for bonds issued at a discount. Assume that after the Huff Corporation bonds were printed late in 2000, interest rates *fell* to 9%. If the bonds were sold at par, Huff would be paying investors 10%—the coupon rate as printed—when investors are willing to accept 9% interest. Instead, Huff will issue the bonds at a **premium**—that is, at an amount sufficiently higher than the $1,000,000 face value so that investors will get only a 9% return. The exact amount is determined, as in the discount example, by taking the bond-related cash flows and discounting them at the effective yield rate (here 9%), as shown in Table 11.5.

The bonds would be issued for $1,064,177—the present value of the contractual principal and interest payments at a discount rate of 9%. Buying the bonds at this price will give investors a 9% effective yield.

TABLE 11.4

Determining the Amortization Amount

Interest expense	−	Cash interest payment	=	Amortization amount
$\begin{pmatrix} \text{Beginning of period} \\ \text{carrying amount} \times \text{yield at} \\ \text{of bonds} & \text{issuance} \end{pmatrix}$	−	$\begin{pmatrix} \text{Principal} & \text{Stated} \\ \text{amount of} \times \text{(coupon)} \\ \text{bonds} & \text{rate} \end{pmatrix}$	=	Amortization amount

TABLE 11.5 HUFF CORPORATION

Determining the Issue Price for 10% Coupon Bonds When the Market Rate Is 9%

Date of Payment	Type of Payment	Amount of Payment	9% Present Value Factor	Discounted Present Value
12/31/01	Interest	$ 100,000	0.91743	$ 91,743
12/31/02	Interest	100,000	0.84168	84,168
12/31/03	Interest	100,000	0.77218	77,218
12/31/04	Interest	100,000	0.70843	70,843
12/31/05	Interest	100,000	0.64993	64,993
12/31/06	Interest	100,000	0.59627	59,627
12/31/07	Interest	100,000	0.54703	54,703
12/31/08	Interest	100,000	0.50187	50,187
12/31/09	Interest	100,000	0.46043	46,043
12/31/10	Interest	100,000	0.42241	42,241
Total present value of interest payments				**$ 641,766**
12/31/10	Principal	$1,000,000	0.42241	**422,411**
Total issue price on January 1, 2001				**$1,064,177**

Equivalently:

December 31

	2000	2001	2002	2003	2004	2005	2006	2007	2008	2009	2010
Cash interest payments	●	$100k	$100k	$100k	$100k	$100k	$100k	$100k	$100k	$100k	$100k
Cash principal payment	●	●	●	●	●	●	●	●	●	●	$1 m

Present value of single payment at 9%: $1 million × 0.422411 = $422,411

Present value of 10-period ordinary annuity at 9%: $100 thousand × 6.41766 = $641,766

The entry to record the bond issuance would be:

```
DR  Cash                        $1,064,177
    CR   Bond premium                          $   64,177
    CR   Bonds payable                          1,000,000
```

The bond premium (like the bond discount) is also a liability valuation account; the premium balance is added to the bonds payable account to increase the balance sheet carrying value of the bonds. The Huff bonds will initially have a carrying value of $1,064,177. *When bonds are sold at a premium, amortization of the premium reduces interest expense.* Table 11.6 shows the amortization schedule. For example, the 2001 interest expense entry shows interest expense (from column (b)) equal to the $100,000 cash interest payment minus the premium amortization (from column (c))—that is:

```
DR   Interest expense            $95,775.93
DR   Bond premium                  4,224.07
    CR   Cash                                    $100,000.00
```

TABLE 11.6 HUFF CORPORATION

Bond Premium Amortization Schedule

Year	(a) Bond Net Carrying Amount at Start of Year	(b) Interest Expense (Column a × 9%)	(c) Bond Premium Amortized ($100,000 − Column b)	(d) Bond Premium Balance at End of Year	(e) Bond Net Carrying Amount at End of Year (Column a − Column c)
2001	$1,064,177.00	$ 95,775.93	$ 4,224.07	$59,952.93	$1,059,952.93
2002	1,059,952.93	95,395.76	4,604.24	55,348.69	1,055,348.69
2003	1,055,348.69	94,981.38	5,018.62	50,330.07	1,050,330.07
2004	1,050,330.07	94,529.71	5,470.29	44,859.78	1,044,859.78
2005	1,044,859.78	94,037.38	5,962.62	38,897.16	1,038,897.16
2006	1,038,897.16	93,500.74	6,499.26	32,397.90	1,032,397.90
2007	1,032,397.90	92,915.81	7,084.19	25,313.71	1,025,313.71
2008	1,025,313.71	92,278.23	7,721.77	17,591.94	1,017,591.94
2009	1,017,591.94	91,583.27	8,416.73	9,175.21	1,009,175.21
2010	1,009,175.21	90,824.79*	9,175.21*	−0−	1,000,000.00
		$935,823.00	$64,177.00		

*Rounded.

Amortizing the bond premium lowers the interest expense each year below the $100,000 annual cash interest payment. In other words, Huff initially received more cash than it promised to pay back at the end of ten years ($1,064,177 versus $1,000,000). The difference—or premium—is a reduction in interest expense over the period of the borrowing. And, as with bond discounts, the straight-line method of bond premium amortization—while acceptable in practice—would not be as conceptually appropriate as the effective interest method.

Looking at Bonds Graphically

The bar graphs in Figure 11.1 depict the components of issue price for Huff Corporation bonds when the interest rate is 10% (data from Table 11.1), 11% (data from Table 11.2), and 9% (data from Table 11.4). These bar graphs illustrate that *the issue price is determined by discounting the contractual principal and interest flows at the market yield rate.* Figure 11.2 is based on the numbers from Table 11.3, where the Huff bonds were sold at a discount because the market interest rate was 11%. Figure 11.2(a) shows interest expense and cash interest payments, and the difference between the two is the discount amortization. For example, $3,521.88, the discount amortized in 2001, is the highlighted amount from column (c) of Table 11.3. Figure 11.2(b) shows that the carrying value of the bonds increases as the discount is amortized each year. Figure 11.3 depicts the bond sold at a premium due to a 9% market interest rate. Figure 11.3(a) shows that interest expense is less than the coupon cash payment of $100,000. Figure 11.3(b) shows that the carrying value of the bond falls as the premium is amortized.

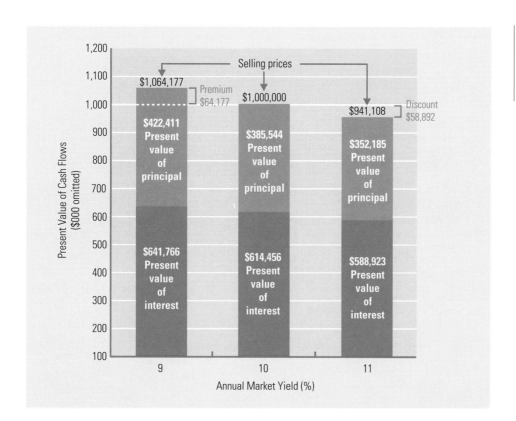

FIGURE 11.1
ILLUSTRATION OF SELLING PRICES OF 10% COUPON BONDS

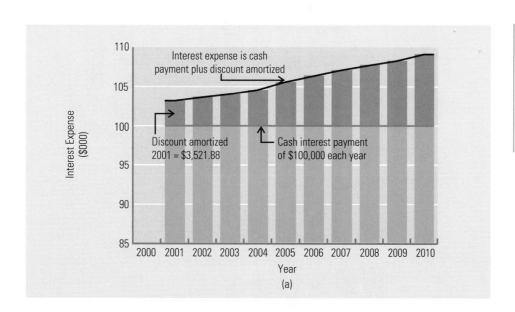

FIGURE 11.2(a)
ILLUSTRATION OF (a) CASH INTEREST PAYMENT, INTEREST EXPENSE

Market yield 11%

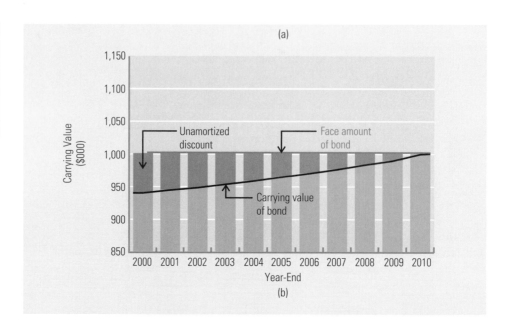

FIGURE 11.2(b)
ILLUSTRATION OF
(b) CARRYING
VALUE FOR 10%
BONDS SOLD AT
DISCOUNT

Market yield 11%

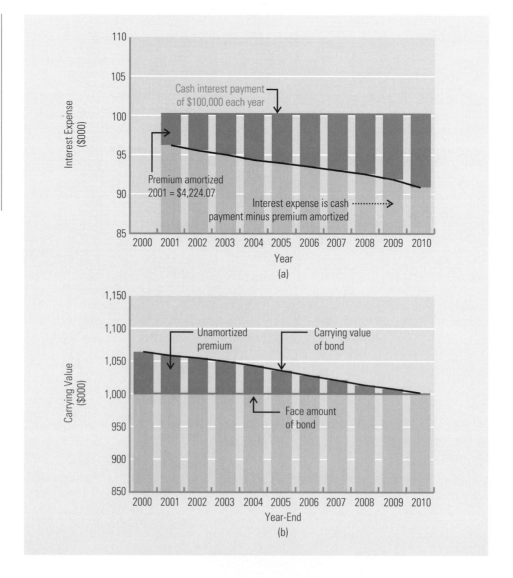

FIGURE 11.3
ILLUSTRATION OF
(a) CASH
INTEREST
PAYMENT,
INTEREST
EXPENSE, AND
(b) CARRYING
VALUE FOR 10%
BONDS SOLD AT
PREMIUM

Market yield 9%

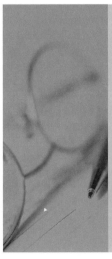

Recap

The cash interest and principal payments on a bond are set before the bond is issued, but market forces determine the issue price and thus the effective yield to investors. All bonds are first recorded on the issuer's books at the issue price. The effective interest rate is then used to compute interest expense and the net carrying value of the bond.

When bonds are sold at a discount, the effective interest rate is above the coupon rate. Amortization of the discount increases interest expense and adds to the bond's net carrying value. When bonds are sold at a premium, the effective interest rate is below the coupon rate. Amortization of the premium decreases interest expense and reduces the bond's net carrying value. Amortization of bond discount or premium using the effective interest rate method results in an annual interest expense that is correlated with the carrying value of the debt to which it relates. While the (alternative) straight-line method is acceptable, it is conceptually inferior.

Book Value Versus Market Value After Issuance

Although bonds payable are shown at their market value (meaning their present value) when they are first issued, their balance sheet value will not necessarily equal their market value later. That's because GAAP require bonds payable to be carried on the books at **amortized historical cost**. Since market interest rates often change, bond market prices also often change. *Thus, after issuance, the reported book value of bonds payable and their market value will frequently differ.*

To see this, let's return to the Huff Corporation example where 10% coupon bonds were issued at par on January 1, 2001. Because the bonds were issued at par, there is no discount or premium to amortize. Hence, the book value of the bonds will always equal the principal amount of $1,000,000 each year the bonds are outstanding. Bonds payable would be shown on the balance sheet at $1,000,000 at December 31, 2001, one year after being issued.

Now it's January 1, 2002, and market interest rates suddenly jump to 11%. Remember, prevailing interest rates "set" the price at which bonds are originally issued. It's no different after bonds have been issued—the market price is still set by prevailing interest rates. So the market price of Huff bonds after interest rates jump on January 1, 2002, is the remaining cash payments for interest and principal discounted at the new 11% effective yield that investors now require. The market price on January 1, 2002, would be $944,630, as shown in Table 11.7. However, under GAAP, the bond payable would still be shown on the books at the original $1,000,000 amount. In general, then, *reported book values after issuance will not necessarily equal the market value of the bonds, since market interest rates fluctuate over time.*

Floating Rate Debt
Table 11.7 illustrates another point—fluctuations in market interest rates change the value of financial instruments like Huff's 10% coupon bond. In our example, a one-percentage-point increase in the market rate of interest (from 10% to 11%) at the end of 2001 would cause the value of Huff's bond to fall by $55,370 (from $1,000,000 to $944,630). Investors who buy Huff bonds are exposed to market value losses because the coupon (stated) interest rate is fixed at 10% for the life of the bonds. When market interest rates increase, Huff bonds continue to pay only the fixed rate of 10% even though investors could do better elsewhere.

TABLE 11.7 HUFF CORPORATION

Calculation of Bond Price After an Interest Rate Increase from 10% to 11% on January 1, 2002

Date of Payment	Type of Payment	Amount of Payment	11% Present Value Factor	Discounted Present Value
12/31/02	Interest	$ 100,000	0.90090	$ 90,090
12/31/03	Interest	100,000	0.81162	81,162
12/31/04	Interest	100,000	0.73119	73,119
12/31/05	Interest	100,000	0.65873	65,873
12/31/06	Interest	100,000	0.59345	59,345
12/31/07	Interest	100,000	0.53464	53,464
12/31/08	Interest	100,000	0.48166	48,166
12/31/09	Interest	100,000	0.43393	43,393
12/31/10	Interest	100,000	0.39093	39,093
Total present value of interest payments				**$553,705**
12/31/10	Principal	$1,000,000	0.390925	390,925
Total market price on January 1, 2002				**$944,630**

There are several ways investors can protect themselves from such losses; the most common is **floating rate** debt. In contrast to the Huff Corporation bond, floating rate debt has a stated interest rate that fluctuates in tandem with some interest rate benchmark like the **London Interbank Offered Rate (LIBOR)**. This widely used benchmark for floating rate debt is the base interest rate paid on deposits between European banks.

Suppose both that the contractual interest rate on Huff's bonds was "LIBOR plus 4%, reset annually" and that the bonds were issued on January 1, 2001, when the LIBOR was 6%. Investors would receive a cash interest payment of $100,000 during 2001 because the contractual interest rate is 10% (LIBOR of 6% plus another 4%). If the LIBOR increased to 7% by January 1, 2002, investors would receive a cash interest payment of $110,000 (or 11%) that year because of the annual "reset" provision. The new rate equals the LIBOR of 7% plus another 4% by contract. The additional $10,000 cash payment, if maintained over the life of the bond, would exactly offset in present value terms the $55,370 value decline we computed from Table 11.7. *The market value of Huff's floating rate debt would remain $1,000,000 and investors would be protected from losses like those associated with Huff's fixed rate debt.*

Floating rate debt can also benefit the issuing company. If the LIBOR falls to 5%, Huff Corporation would be able to reduce its cash interest payments to $90,000, since the contractual interest rate would be reset to 9% (LIBOR of 5% plus another 4% by contract).

Investors benefit from floating rate debt when market interest rates increase, and issuing corporations benefit when market rates fall. Floating rate debt allows investors and issuing companies to share in the risks and rewards of changing market interest rates. Risk sharing lowers the company's overall borrowing costs, and this translates into floating rate debt that has a lower (expected) interest rate than would be charged on comparable fixed rate debt.

Since virtually all floating rate debt is issued at par, the accounting entries required are simple. Interest expense and accrued interest payable are recorded using the contractual rate in effect during the period. The following entries would have been made by Huff if it had issued the "LIBOR plus 4%, reset annually" bond on January 1, 2001:

1/1/01:	DR	Cash	$1,000,000	
		CR Bond payable		$1,000,000
12/31/01:	DR	Interest expense	$100,000	
		CR Accrued interest payable		$100,000
		2001 interest rate set at 10% (LIBOR of 6% plus another 4%).		
12/31/02:	DR	Interest expense	$110,000	
		CR Accrued interest payable		$110,000
		2002 interest rate reset to 11% (LIBOR of 7% plus another 4%).		

The balance sheet would continue to show bonds payable at $1,000,000, which also equals the market value of the floating rate debt.

Extinguishment of Debt

Interest rates constantly adjust to changes in levels of economic activity and changes in expected inflation rates, among many other factors. When interest rates change, the market price of fixed rate debt changes—as interest rates rise, the market price falls; as interest rates fall, the price rises. However, as we just saw, GAAP accounting for debt is at the price originally transacted. Subsequent market price changes are not recorded on the financial statements. This means that there will be differences (nearly always) between the book carrying amount of debt and its market value. This divergence creates no accounting gain or loss for debt that is not retired before maturity, since book value and debt market value are equal on the maturity date.

> **Book value** equals **market value** on the maturity date because the principal payment is then due immediately and, consequently, is not discounted.

However, when debt is retired before maturity, book value and market value are not typically equal at the retirement date, generating an accounting gain or loss.

To see this, let's go back to Huff's $1,000,000 of 10% fixed rate debt. On January 1, 2002, immediately after interest rates jump to 11%, Huff repurchases the 10% coupon bonds issued one year earlier. At the repurchase date, the market value of the bonds is $944,630, as we saw from Table 11.7. The book value is $1,000,000. The entry to record the repurchase (ignoring possible income taxes) is:

DR	Bonds payable	$1,000,000	
	CR Cash		$944,630
	CR Gain on debt extinguishment		55,370

The accounting gain (or loss) at retirement—more commonly called **extinguishment**—is the difference between the cash paid to extinguish the debt and the book value of the debt. Any extinguishment gain or loss does not meet the criteria for an extraordinary item, and so is shown on the income statement as part of income before extraordinary items. However, in the United States the FASB *requires* such gains or losses to be accounted for as "extraordinary."[2]

> When bonds are initially sold at a premium or discount, the book value is equal to the face value plus the premium or minus the discount. The premium or discount account must also be closed when debt is retired. Remember that interest expense and accrued interest payable may need to be brought up to date before recording the extinguishment itself.

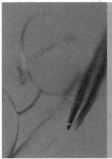
Managerial Incentives and Financial Reporting for Debt

In Chapters 1 and 7, we explained that accounting numbers are widely used to enforce contracts. One example is debt covenants, which could motivate managers to manipulate accounting numbers to evade contract restrictions. Critics suggest that GAAP accounting for long-term debt makes it possible to "manage" accounting numbers to achieve this evasion.

Debt Is Carried at Amortized Historical Cost

In a **debt-for-debt swap**, investors are offered the opportunity to exchange existing (old) debt for new debt issued by the company. **Equity-for-debt swaps** give investors the opportunity to exchange old debt for the company's common shares.

Some analysts contend that reporting debt at amortized historical cost—rather than at current market value—makes it easier to manipulate accounting numbers. **Debt-for-debt swaps** and **debt-for-equity swaps** illustrate the kinds of transactions which may be driven more by the financial statement effects they elicit than by any underlying economic benefits.

To illustrate, consider a highly simplified version of a debt-for-debt swap. Shifty Corporation has $1 million of outstanding 10% coupon debt originally issued at par. This debt will mature in exactly one year. Interest is paid annually. Since the debt was sold at par, its book value is $1 million. Assume that the current market rate for bonds of this risk class is 12%; therefore, the market price of the bonds is $982,146. Shifty induces the holders of the bonds to swap them for new bonds—also maturing in exactly one year—with a coupon rate of 12%. For simplicity, assume that the face value of the 12% bonds given to investors is exactly $982,146; this would also be the market value of the bonds, since the coupon rate of 12% equals the prevailing market rate. This debt-for-debt swap is illustrated in Figure 11.4.

The holders of the bonds will be indifferent between the old bonds and the new bonds because their market values are identical. (To induce the bondholders to exchange the 10% bonds for 12% bonds, some "sweetener" would have to be provided in the real world.)

This $982,146 figure is computed as follows:

Present value of $1,000,000 principal repayment due in one year at a 12% discount rate: $1,000,000 × 0.89286 = $892,860

Present value of $100,000 interest payment due in one year at a 12% discount rate: $100,000 × 0.89286 = $ 89,286

Market price $982,146

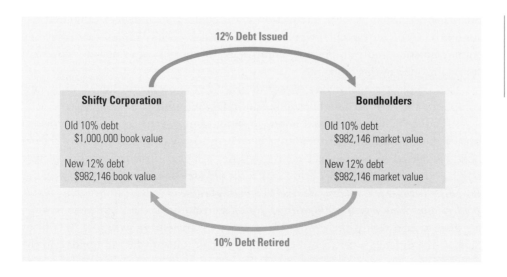

FIGURE 11.4
SHIFTY
CORPORATION
Debt-for-debt
swap

The market values are identical precisely because the present values of the two cash flow streams are identical when discounted at the prevailing 12% market interest rate:

Old 10% Bonds			New 12% Bonds		
Principal Repayment			**Principal Repayment**		
$1,000,000 × 0.89286 =	$892,860		$ 982,146 × 0.89286 =	$876,918*	
Interest Payment			**Interest Payment**		
$ 100,000 × 0.89286 =	$ 89,286		$ 117,858 × 0.89286 =	$105,228*	
$1,100,000	$982,146		$1,100,000*	$982,146	
Interest Computation			**Interest Computation**		
$1,000,000 × 10%	= $100,000		$ 982,146 × 12%	= $117,858*	

Note: The present value of $1 due in one year at 12% is 0.89286.
*Rounded.

As the computation reveals, even the **undiscounted** cash flows are identical (principal payment plus interest payment is $1,100,000). Ignoring tax effects, we find that a debt-for-debt swap like this has no real economic benefit to Shifty. However, if the swap were consummated, the entry on Shifty's books would be:

DR	Bonds payable (old)	$1,000,000	
CR	Bonds payable (new)		$982,146
CR	Gain on debt extinguishment		17,854

Despite the absence of real economic substance, an accounting "gain" would be reported. The gain really arose in prior periods as unanticipated inflation or other factors caused the market rate on the bonds to rise above the coupon rate. Because Shifty was paying interest at 10% when prevailing rates were higher, a year-by-year wealth transfer out of the pockets of the original bondholders and into the pockets of Shifty's shareholders was taking place. Historical cost accounting ignores this wealth transfer until the "artificial" swap transaction triggers recognition of the gain.

This example was designed to show the potential incentive for managerial opportunism that is introduced by historical cost accounting for debt. Critics of historical cost accounting raise the possibility that managers whose bonuses are tied to reported earnings might use swap gains to boost earnings (and bonuses) in years of poor

The wealth transfer gain from bondholders to shareholders does get reflected obliquely in historical cost statements, since historical cost interest expense is lower than interest expense at current market rates. Accordingly, *net income is higher than it would have been at current interest rates.*

operating performance. Also, a reduction in the book value of debt ($1,000,000 versus $982,146 in our example) would improve the debt–equity ratio—thus providing "opportunistic" motivations for companies in danger of violating covenant restrictions tied to this ratio.

This simple example makes it easy to visualize the problem. But we must now complicate the example so it corresponds to real-world swaps.

To induce holders of the old bonds to swap, some sweeteners must be provided because the transaction costs them time and energy. Since the market value of the old bonds is $982,146, one inducement is to offer a higher principal amount of new bonds—say, $990,000. *This change makes the net present value of the swap negative for Shifty because it is retiring debt with a market value of $982,146 by giving bondholders something worth $990,000.* Despite this real loss, if the swap went through on these altered terms, there would be a reported *accounting gain* of $10,000 for Shifty—the difference between the $1 million book value of the old bonds and the $990,000 market value of the new bonds. Extinguishment gains are generally taxable, and there are fees that must be paid to investment bankers or others who orchestrate the transaction. These added costs further increase the potential disparity between the reported accounting gain and the economic effects of the transaction.

On the other hand, there are sometimes real economic benefits associated with debt-for-debt exchanges. In contrast to our simple example, debt-for-debt swaps are rarely designed to be a "wash," one involving debt instruments with identical maturities and market values. Typical swaps are structured to extend debt maturity, alter the mix of interest and principal payments (postponing cash outflows), and take advantage of operating loss carryforwards (making the swap tax-free). On balance, therefore, it is entirely possible that some debt-for-debt exchanges generate real economic benefits even after factoring in the costs of doing the transaction.

This is precisely what a study of debt swaps in the U.S. airline industry found. Analyzing the economic effects of swaps structured by American Airlines, Eastern Airlines, and TWA revealed economic benefits for each company in the range of US$4.6 million to US$5.0 million.[3] However, *the reported book gain (net of tax) for each airline was substantially higher*—for example, it was US$24.65 million for Eastern, US$47.1 million for TWA, and US$48.4 million for American. Therefore, a large disparity exists between the historical cost book profits and the estimated economic benefits. If the economic benefits of debt-for-debt exchanges are small (on average), stock prices should change little when swaps are announced. In fact, that is the case.[4]

Differences between book profits and real profits have aroused curiosity about the motives underlying another—somewhat similar—debt extinguishment transaction: debt-for-equity swaps.

The conditions for a debt-for-equity swap exist when a company has low-coupon-rate debt outstanding (say, 4%) and market rates are much higher (say, 12%). *The market value of that debt is much lower than its book value.* As Figure 11.5 shows, Company X retires its low coupon debt by issuing common stock of equal market value. The difference between the book value of the debt and the market value of the stock that is issued is recorded as an accounting gain. The convoluted nature of the transaction, as well as the investment banker's involvement as an intermediary, is required to make the gain on debt extinguishment tax-free.

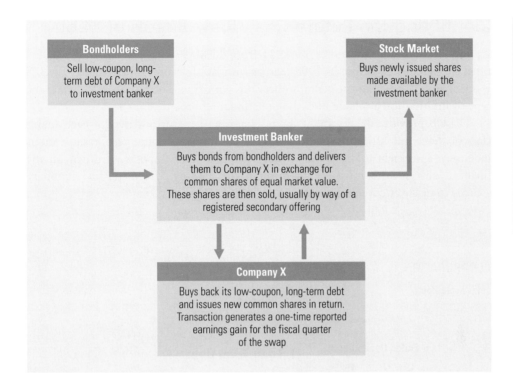

FIGURE 11.5
THE SEQUENCE OF EVENTS IN A DEBT-FOR-EQUITY SWAP

Source: J.R.M. Hand, "Did Firms Undertake Debt-Equity Swaps for an Accounting Paper Profit or True Financial Gain?" *The Accounting Review,* October 1989, pp. 587–623.

The accounting entry on the books of Company X would be:

DR Bonds payable	$ Book value	
CR Common shares		$ Market value
CR Gain on debt extinguishment		$ Difference

Debt book value is greater than the market value of shares issued because the debt has a low coupon rate but the market interest rate is high.

Debt-for-equity swaps alter the company's capital structure and undoubtedly precipitate real economic effects. One study found that debt-for-equity swaps were associated with a 9.9% share price decline (on average) at the transaction's announcement.[5] However, most debt-for-equity transactions result in extinguishment gains rather than losses. This prevalence of gains raises the suspicion that earnings enhancement—rather than capital structure alteration—may be the motivation behind these transactions. Some evidence suggests that companies may undertake debt-for-equity swaps to smooth otherwise unexpected and transitory decreases in quarterly earnings per share or to relax otherwise binding covenant constraints.[6]

Debt-for-debt swaps, debt-for-equity swaps, and other, similar transactions may serve valid economic purposes in certain instances. Nevertheless, the belief persists that the dominant motivation for these transactions is to increase reported income. This income effect results from the difference between the book value and market value of the liabilities.

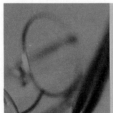

Recap

GAAP for long-term debt create opportunities for managing reported earnings and balance sheet numbers using debt-for-debt or debt-for-equity swaps. So statement readers must be alert to the possibility that reported swap gains (and losses) are just window dressing. How can you tell? Look behind the accounting numbers and see if there are real economic benefits from the swap.

Identifying the Future Cash Flow Effects of Debt

TELUS CORPORATION
www.telus.com

Exhibit 11.1 contains footnotes 3 and 11 from TELUS Corporation's 1997 audited financial statements. Before its 1998 merger with BC Telecom, Alberta-based TELUS was Canada's third-largest telecommunications company. The footnotes illustrate the type of information available in corporate annual reports.

TELUS provides details about interest rates and maturity dates for each major class of debt, but little information about the covenants contained in the various indenture agreements. This nondisclosure is typical and imposes a burden on the financial analyst who must search through the lending agreements or secondary sources to discover covenant details.

Exhibit 11.1 TELUS CORPORATION

Footnotes from 1997 Financial Statements

3. Interest Expense

(thousands)	Year Ended December 31, 1997	1996
Interest:		
Long-term debt	$115,827	$157,363
Other	2,218	1,075
	118,045	158,438
Less:		
Sinking fund income	10,039	9,134
Allowance for funds used during construction	2,706	2,526
Interest income	8,133	6,597
	20,078	18,257
	$ 97,167	$140,181

...

11. Long-Term Debt

(thousands)	December 31, 1997	1996
Notes payable:		
9.30% due January 1997	$ —	$200,000
9.80% due July 1997	—	200,000
9.90% due July 1998	200,000	200,000
12 00% due November 1999 (see **a** below)	50,000	50,000
11.80% due May 2003 (see **a** below)	150,000	150,000
Other notes with interest between 7.375% and 12.00% and maturing between 1996 and 2004 (see **b** below)	98,331	116,852
	498,331	916,852
9.50% Series A Debentures due August 2004 (see **c** below)	200,000	200,000
8.80% Series B Debentures due September 2025 (see **c** below)	200,000	200,000
Non-interest-bearing loans	4,895	4,442
Capital leases payable (see **d** below)	5,000	32,604
Non-recourse bank loans	—	35,181
Bank Credit Facility (see **e** below)	385,000	385,000
Other	2,663	3,518
	797,558	860,745
	1,295,889	1,777,597
Less: Current portion	265,418	266,009
	$1,030,471	$1,511,588

a. The outstanding 12.00% (due November 1999) and 11.80% (due May 2003) notes are secured by sinking fund assets of the Company. In accordance with note terms, these notes require annual sinking fund contributions of 1.00% of the principal amounts outstanding until one year prior to maturity. The 11.80% note has an early redemption provision at the Company's option during the three years prior to maturity. The other notes are unsecured.

b. The Other Notes with interest between 7.375% and 12.00% are unsecured debt obligations of TELUS Edmonton Holdings Inc. which are supported by a negative pledge respecting that Company's assets and certain new issue tests. TELUS Edmonton Holdings Inc. has undertaken to defease by December 31, 1999 all payments of principal and interest which would otherwise occur after January 1, 2000. The defeasance of these notes has been reflected in the long-term debt repayments.

c. The outstanding 9.50% Series A Debentures (due August 2004) and 8.80% Series B Debentures (due September 2025) are issued under the TELUS Communications Inc. trust indenture dated August 24, 1994 and a supplemental trust indenture dated September 22, 1995 relating to Series B Debentures only. These debentures are not secured by any mortgage, pledge or other charge. During 1995 the Company terminated an interest rate swap contract relating to the Series A Debentures and realized a gain on early termination in the amount of $16,760,000 which is being amortized and credited to interest expense over the remaining term of the Series A Debentures. The amortization of the gain resulted in an effective rate of interest on Series A

Debentures in the current year of 8.79% (1996—8.79%).

d. The capital leases have a weighted average interest rate of 6.00% (1996—9.42%).

e. The Company established a $500,000,000 five year variable interest rate unsecured credit facility on January 4, 1995. The composite interest rate, on the outstanding credit facility balance as at December 31, 1997 was 4.32% (1996—3.64%). During 1996 an additional $200,000,000 revolving credit facility was established and a $400,000,000 shelf prospectus, to permit public issues of medium term notes, was registered by TELUS Communications Inc.

f. The estimated fair value of the long-term debt at December 31, 1997 is $1,439,366,000 (1996—$1,886,209,000).

g. Anticipated requirements to meet long-term debt repayments and sinking fund provisions during the next five years from December 31, 1997 are as follows:

(thousands)	Requirement for Long-Term Debt Repayments and Sinking Fund Provisions	Requirement to Be Met by Sinking Fund Assets
1998	$267,418	$ —
1999	191,759	33,984
2000	291,241	—
2001	2,518	—
2002	3,072	—

There is, however, a wealth of information in these footnotes useful for determining the future cash flow implications of the company's long-term debt. For example, footnote 11 reveals current maturities of $265,418,000 as at the end of fiscal 1997. This is the amount that must be repaid in 1998.

We also learn from footnote 3 that TELUS incurred $115,827,000 in interest costs on long-term debt in 1997. Dividing this amount by the average book value of outstanding long-term debt ($1,295,889,000 + $1,777,597,000)/2 suggests that the effective interest rate for 1997 for TELUS was about 7.5%. Using this rate as the basis for forecasting 1998 interest payments, we discover that TELUS will have to spend about $97.2 million (7.5% multiplied by $1,295,889,000 total long-term debt outstanding as at the end of 1997) for interest next year. This cash outflow is in addition to the principal repayment of $265,418,000.

Cash flow forecasts of this sort can be constructed for each year from 1998 to 2002, since companies disclose scheduled debt repayments for each of the next five years after the balance sheet date (see footnote 11 (g) in Exhibit 11.1). For TELUS, long-term debt repayments scheduled for the year 2000 are particularly large, at $291,241,000. Statement readers will want to ascertain the extent to which TELUS's anticipated operating cash flows for that year will be sufficient to meet its scheduled debt interest and principal payments. Any shortfalls will necessitate asset sales or additional financing.

Incentives for Off-Balance-Sheet Liabilities

In Chapters 1 and 7, we described modern business contracts linked to (among other things) the amount of liabilities on a company's balance sheet. Examples include loans and bond indentures. These kinds of contracts usually contain terms and conditions for protecting the lender against loss. These contract terms are tied to the borrower's debt-to-equity ratio, debt-to-tangible-asset ratio, or some other financial ratio measured using reported liabilities. Accounting-related covenants typically contain language like "if the debt-to-equity ratio exceeds 1.7 in any quarter, the loan must immediately be repaid." The intent of these covenants is to provide an early warning signal regarding deteriorating credit worthiness. In principle, the early warning allows the lender to call in the loan before the borrower's condition deteriorates further.

These kinds of terms in loan contracts create incentives for managers of borrowing companies to minimize *reported* financial statement liabilities. Reducing the total amount of reported liabilities in the contractual ratio reduces the probability of covenant violations.

Enron provides an interesting case study of the effect of managerial incentives on the financial reporting of debt. The details of this effect were revealed in the U.S. Senate's hearing "The Role of the Financial Institutions in Enron's Collapse" (Permanent Subcommittee on Investigations, July 23, 2002). Huge financial institutions—such as JP Morgan Chase ("Chase") and Citigroup (and even the Toronto-Dominion!)—set up separate entities (known as special purpose entities or SPEs) to conduct transactions that resulted in the suppressing of debt as follows:

- Chase set up an SPE, which it named Mahonia Ltd., to act as an "independent" third party in a Chase–Enron deal. Chase and Mahonia entered into a contract in which Mahonia received money from Chase. In exchange, Mahonia agreed to deliver a fixed amount of gas at specified dates and locations (this contract is called a prepaid forward contract). Keep in mind that Mahonia was essentially a shell company. The money Mahonia received from Chase was the estimated future price of the gas on the expected delivery date.

- Then, Mahonia and Enron executed a "mirror contract" by which Enron received an amount of money from Mahonia (equal to the original amount that Mahonia received from Chase), and in exchange agreed to deliver to Mahonia a fixed amount of gas at specified dates and locations agreed to in advance. So Chase had title to a contract to receive gas that was transferred from Enron to Mahonia and then from Mahonia to Enron.

- At the same time that the above two prepaid contracts were executed, Enron and Chase executed a commodity swap agreement, as well as other transactions. The end result was that Enron received cash up front from Mahonia, a transaction that was funded entirely by the Chase bank. Subsequently, Enron paid the cash plus interest back to Chase according to a prearranged schedule.

Now here's the key: even though, in substance, Enron borrowed money from Chase, Enron accounted for these events as if it had received a prepayment on an agreement to sell gas in the future. Therefore, the total up-front cash received by Enron appeared on its cash flow statement as cash flow from operations (and not a financing cash flow), and no debt was shown on its balance sheet, just a deferred revenue. Our description of these so-called Enron "prepay" transaction sequences is just one example; more detail is provided in Case C11-2 (Enron accounting magic) at the end of this chapter.

Recap

The motivation for off-balance-sheet financing transactions is strong. Managers continue to develop innovative strategies to understate reported liabilities and to ensure that certain items remain "off the balance sheet." Financial analysts and auditors must remember the motivations behind off-balance-sheet financing, know how to identify peculiar and contorted borrowing arrangements, and adjust the reported financial statement numbers to better reflect economic reality. It is truly astonishing the lengths to which Enron apparently went to keep debt "off-balance-sheet."

Hedging[7]

Business organizations are exposed to **market risks** from many sources—changes in interest rates, foreign currency exchange rates, and commodity prices. Suppose a bank makes numerous five-year term loans at an annual interest rate of 8%. The earnings from those loans generate the cash needed to pay interest to "money-market" account depositors. The bank is exposed to interest rate risk: If money-market interest rates rise, the 8% fixed return from the loans may not be adequate to pay the new higher rates promised to depositors.

Similar risks confront manufacturers. Consider Ridge Development, a real estate development company that simultaneously constructs many single-family homes. Buyers make a down payment and agree to a fixed contract price to be paid upon completion of the home. The typical home is completed in four months or less, and lumber comprises the bulk of construction costs. Since lumber prices are volatile, the builder is at risk that profits could erode (or disappear) if lumber prices were to soar during the four-month construction cycle.

Managing market risk is essential to the overall business strategies of most companies today. This trend has been driven by the need to reduce cash flow volatility that arises from factors beyond management's control—the exchange rate of dollars to Japanese yen, the LIBOR interest rate (the benchmark interbank interest rate for European banks), or the price of natural gas to run a factory. In response to these and other financial market risks, many companies engage in **hedging**—business transactions designed to insulate them from commodity price, interest, or exchange rate risk. **Derivative securities** are often used to accomplish this insulation.

Businesses are also exposed to **operating risks** from severe weather conditions, industrial accidents, raw material shortages, labour strikes, and so on. Insurance contracts, financial guarantees, and other business arrangements are used to hedge operating risks—but these risks do not qualify for the special hedge accounting rules described later in this section. Only certain financial risks qualify for hedge accounting (see *AcG–13*, "Hedging Relationships").

Typical Derivative Securities and the Benefits of Hedging

Derivative securities get their name from the fact that they have no inherent value but instead represent a claim against some other asset—their value is *derived* from the value of the asset underlying that claim.[8]

A **forward contract** is an example of a derivative security. In a forward contract, two parties agree to the sale of some asset or commodity on some *future* date—called the settlement date—at a price specified *today*. You have been dealing with forward contracts your whole life, perhaps without knowing it. Suppose you walk into a bookstore on October 5 to buy the bestseller *Seven Unbeatable Strategies for Identifying Debt*. The book is sold out, but the clerk will reorder it for you and call you when it arrives. The clerk says that the book should arrive in about 15 days and will cost $39.95. If you agree on October 5 to pick up and pay for the book when called, you and the clerk have agreed to a forward contract. Three elements of this contract are key: the agreed upon price ($39.95) to be paid in the future; the delivery date ("in about 15 days"); and that you will "take delivery" by paying for the book and picking it up when notified. The clerk has "sold" you a forward contract for the bestseller.

What happens if you pay for the book on October 5? Then it's a simple cash sales transaction (with a promised future delivery date) but there is no forward contract involved. As long as both parties are *obligated* to perform under the agreement, it's a forward contract. Here that means the clerk is required to obtain a copy of the bestseller and deliver it to you within the specified time. And you are required to pay the agreed upon price and to take delivery.

Futures Contracts A variation of a forward contract takes place on financial exchanges like the New York Mercantile Exchange (COMEX) where **futures contracts** are traded daily in a market with many buyers and sellers. Futures contracts exist for commodities like corn, wheat, live hogs and cattle, cotton, copper, crude oil, lumber, and even electricity. Here is how they work.

Suppose on October 5 you "write" (meaning sell) a futures contract for 10 million pounds of February copper at 95 cents per pound—we'll show why you might want to do so in just a moment. By selling the contract, you are obligated to deliver the copper at the agreed-upon price in February. The buyer (or contract counterparty) is obliged to pay the fixed price per pound and take delivery of the copper. So far this looks like a forward contract because both parties have an obligation to perform in the future (February).

But there's more! Futures contracts do not have a predetermined settlement date—you (the seller) can choose to deliver the copper on any day during the delivery month (February). This gives sellers additional flexibility in settling the contract. When you decide to deliver the copper, you notify the COMEX clearinghouse, which then notifies an individual—let's call her Anne Smythe—who bought February copper contracts. (The clearinghouse selected Anne at random from all individuals who bought February copper contracts.) Anne is then told to be ready to accept delivery within the next several days. But what if she bought the contract as a speculative investment, has no real use for the copper and doesn't want delivery? Futures contracts have an added advantage over forward contracts because futures are actively traded on an exchange. This means Smythe can avoid delivery by selling a February copper contract for 10 million pounds thus creating a zero net position. The first contract obligates Smythe to accept delivery of 10 million pounds of copper, but the second contract obligates her to turn over 10 million pounds to someone else. One contract cancels the other, and Smythe avoids the embarrassment of having all that copper dumped on the floor of her garage.

How can you (the seller) avoid having to deliver the copper? Form a zero net position of your own by purchasing a February copper contract from someone else—perhaps even from Anne Smythe.

Now that you understand how futures contracts work, let's see how they can be used to hedge financial risk. Consider the opportunities confronting Rombauer Metals, a copper mining company. On October 1, 2001, Rombauer has 10 million pounds of copper inventory on hand at an average cost of 65 cents per pound. The "spot" (current delivery) price for copper on October 1 is 90 cents a pound. Rombauer could receive $9 million (10 million pounds times $0.90 per pound) by selling the entire copper inventory today. Selling the copper on October 1 would yield a $2.5 million gross profit ($0.90 selling price minus $0.65 average cost per pound, multiplied by 10 million pounds). However, Rombauer has decided to hold on to its copper until February 2002 when management believes the price will return to a normal level of 95 cents a pound. The commodities market seems to agree since February copper futures are priced as though copper will sell for 95 cents in February. The decision not to sell copper in October exposes Rombaurer to **commodity price risk** from a possible future decline in copper prices.

Figure 11.6(a) illustrates the company's commodity price risk exposure. If copper prices increase to 95 cents by February as expected, Rombaurer will receive $9.5 million for its copper and earn a gross profit of $3 million ($0.95 selling price minus $0.65 average cost per pound, multiplied by 10 million pounds). That's $0.5 million more gross profit than Rombaurer would earn by selling the copper on October 1. But what if the February price of copper falls to 85 cents? The cash received from selling copper would then be only $8.5 million, and the gross profit would be only $2 million. Each 10-cent decline in the February copper price lowers the company's cash flows and expected gross profits by $1 million. At 65 cents per pound, Rombaurer just breaks even (zero gross profit) and, at any price below 65 cents, the company has a loss. These potential cash flow and gross profit declines represent the *downside risk* associated with the February price of copper. There is *upside potential* as well. Each 10-cent increase in the February copper price will produce a $1 million increase in the company's cash flows and gross profits.

One way Rombaurer can protect itself from a decline in the price of copper is to hedge its position with futures contracts. Suppose Rombaurer sells 400 copper contracts—each contract is for 25,000 pounds—at 95 cents a pound for February delivery. The delivery month is chosen to coincide with the company's expected physical sale of the copper. The ultimate value of these contracts depends on the February price of copper as shown in Figure 11.6(b). For example, if the February copper price is 85 cents, the contracts will have provided $1 million of cash flow and profit protection ($0.95 contract price minus $0.85 February spot market price, multiplied by the 10 million pounds of copper). If the February spot price is 65 cents, the contracts

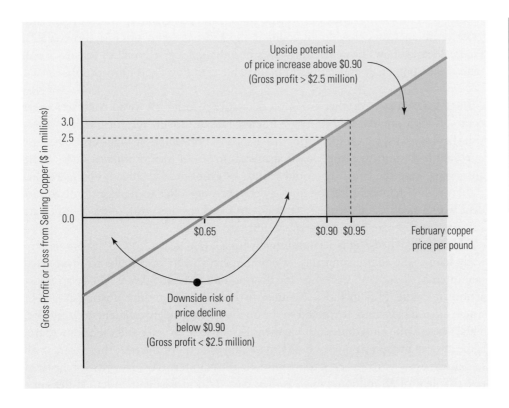

FIGURE 11.6(a)
ROMBAURER METALS

Using Futures Contracts to Hedge Copper Inventory

Before the hedge:

Potential gross profit and loss from the sale of copper in February

FIGURE 11.6(b)
ROMBAURER
METALS

Using Futures
Contracts to
Hedge Copper
Inventory

The hedging
instrument:

Potential value of
forward contract for
February copper

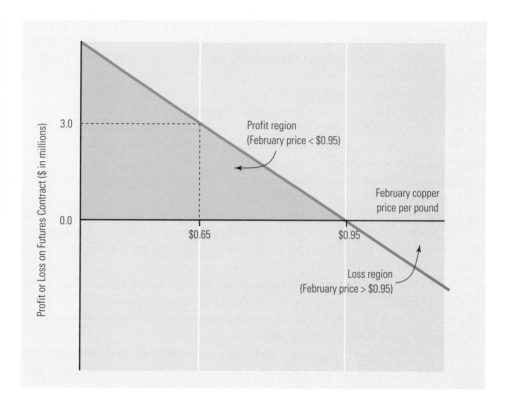

Profit or Loss on Futures Contract ($ in millions)

3.0

0.0

$0.65

$0.95

February copper
price per pound

Profit region
(February price < $0.95)

Loss region
(February price > $0.95)

Indeed, the futures contracts provide an immediate 5 cent benefit (ignoring present value considerations, inventory holding costs, and fees and commissions on the contracts) since the October 1 price of copper is only 90 cents.

One reason protection might be needed is that Kistler's operating cash flows are positively correlated with interest rates. In this case a decline in market rates would be accompanied by a decrease in operating cash flows, and the company may lack the cash flow needed to meet its payment obligations under the 8% fixed rate loan.

will have provided $3 million of protection. The futures contracts "lock in" a February price of 95 cents and eliminate the company's downside exposure to a decline in copper prices. February cash receipts will be $9.5 million, and profits will total $3.0 million, no matter what the February spot price for copper turns out to be. Of course, there is another side to the story. By hedging its original exposure to commodity price risk with futures contracts, Rombaurer has given up the cash flow and gross profit increases that could result if the February spot price is above $0.95. Figure 11.6(c) shows how the company's hedging strategy eliminates downside risk (and upside potential) and results in predictable cash flows and gross profits.

Swap Contract Another common derivative security is a **swap contract.** These contracts are a popular way to hedge interest rate or foreign currency exchange rate risk. Let's say Kistler Manufacturing has issued $100 million of long-term 8% fixed rate debt and wants to protect itself against a *decline* in market interest rates. There are several ways the company could reduce its exposure. We already discussed one earlier in this chapter, using a debt-for-debt exchange offer to replace the fixed rate debt with a floating rate loan. A second—and perhaps less costly—way is to create *synthetic* floating rate debt using an interest rate swap.

This form of hedging is accomplished with a "swap dealer." Swap dealers are typically banks who locate someone—a counterparty—who would like to make fixed rate interest *payments* in exchange for floating rate interest *receipts*. The swap transaction in Figure 11.7 includes a counterparty with outstanding floating rate debt where interest payments are linked to the one-year low-risk government-security rate. This is exactly the kind of interest payment Kistler seeks. Kistler and the counterparty agree to swap interest payments on $100 million of debt for the next three years, with settlement every year. At the settlement date, the counterparty gives Kistler the fixed rate payment of $8 million, which is then passed on to Kistler's lender. At the same

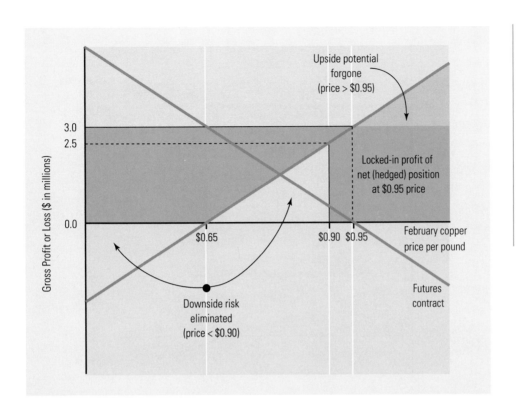

FIGURE 11.6(c)
ROMBAURER
METALS

Using Futures
Contracts to
Hedge Copper
Inventory

After the hedge:

Gross profit from
hedge position:
Combination of
unhedged copper
inventory and
forward contract

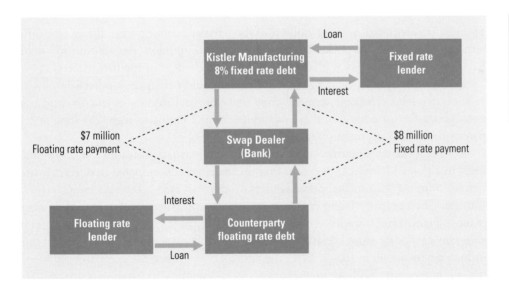

FIGURE 11.7
KISTLER
MANUFACTURING

An Interest Rate
Swap that Creates
Synthetic Floating
Rate Debt

time, Kistler gives the counterparty cash equal to the floating rate payment (say $7 million based on a government-security rate of 7%), and this too is passed on to the floating rate lender. In reality, only the $1 million difference in interest payments would be exchanged between the two parties to the swap.

The swap transforms Kistler's debt into floating rate, because receipts from the counterparty offset the fixed payment it is obligated to make. Figure 11.8 shows how the swap transaction eliminates Kistler's downside exposure to interest rate risk. If the government-security rate falls to 7%, Kistler will receive a net cash inflow of $1 million from the swap counterparty. This net cash inflow is the $8 million fixed rate payment minus the $7 million floating rate payment. Kistler then pays its lender

What's in it for the counterparty? By replacing the floating rate interest payments with synthetic fixed rate payments, the counterparty has reduced its exposure to cash flow volatility from interest rate changes.

FIGURE 11.8

KISTLER
MANUFACTURING

Using a Swap to
Hedge Interest
Rate Risk

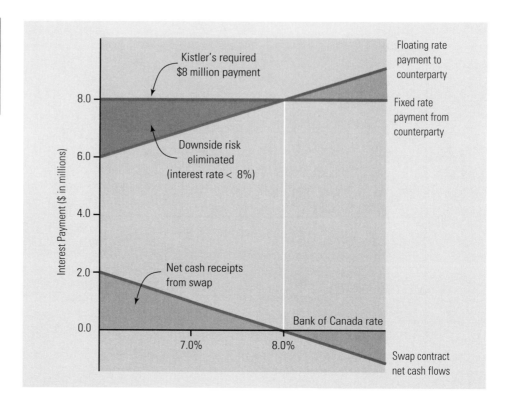

$8 million as required, with $1 million of the payment coming from the swap counterparty. Kistler's out-of-pocket interest cost is just $7 million, the amount it would have been required to pay if it had issued floating rate debt in the first place.[9]

Kistler ends up with floating rate debt that it could perhaps not otherwise obtain at attractive rates. The counterparty ends up with fixed interest payments, and the bank gets a fee for arranging the swap transaction. Everybody wins—as long as all parties fulfill their payment obligations.

A foreign exchange (currency) swap has the same structural features as those outlined in Figures 11.7 and 11.8 except that the loans are denominated in different currencies. Suppose St. Jean Inc. manufactures products in France but sells exclusively in Canada. The company borrows francs to finance construction of a manufacturing plant in France, and it wants to hedge its foreign exchange exposure on the loan. The company's exposure arises because its operating cash flows are in Canadian dollars but its loan payments are in francs. With the aid of a swap dealer, the company can identify a counterparty willing to exchange franc-denominated payments for dollar-denominated payments. The pattern of swapped cash flows would be identical to the flows depicted in Figure 11.7. St. Jean ends up with synthetic dollar-denominated debt and eliminates its exposure to fluctuations in the franc–dollar exchange rate.

But what happens if a swap goes wrong? A Dutch financial institution, Rabobank, balked at honouring a swap transaction with Royal Bank of Canada (in June 2002), the country's largest bank, because the original Royal Bank loan was made to one of the companies in the collapsed Enron empire. Royal counteracted by contending that Rabobank was engaging in "highly irresponsible and unwarranted" behaviour. (See Case C11-1 at the end of this chapter.)

Options Contract Futures and swaps are derivatives that require each party to the contract to engage in the agreed-upon transaction. But other types of derivative securities exist. One example is an option contract, which gives the holder an "option"—the right but not the obligation—to do something. To illustrate how options work, let's revisit our homebuilder discussed on page 499.

Suppose it is now January and Ridge Development needs 10 million board feet of lumber on hand in three months (April) to construct homes that the company has already sold to residential homebuyers. Lumber currently sells for $250 per 1,000 board feet, so Ridge would have to purchase $2.5 million of lumber at the current (January) price in order to meet its April commitment. But Ridge has no place to store the lumber and lumber prices are expected to increase over the next few months. How can the company eliminate its commodity price risk from its *anticipated* lumber purchase three months from now?

One approach is to buy a futures contract for April lumber. Ridge can "lock in" the profit margin on unbuilt homes it has sold by agreeing to pay a set price now (in January) for lumber delivered in April. But if lumber prices fall during the next three months, the builder—now locked into higher lumber prices by the futures contract— would forgo the increased profits from lower lumber prices.

By using options instead of futures, the builder can protect against lumber cost increases without sacrificing potential gains if lumber prices decline. This can be done by purchasing a call option on lumber—an option to buy lumber at a specified price over the option period. The call option protects the builder against lumber cost increases. But because it is an option, Ridge is not obligated to exercise the option should lumber prices fall. Options enable Ridge to hedge unfavourable price movements and still participate in the upside possibility of increased margins if lumber prices fall. Figure 11.9 shows how.

Some option contracts give the holder the right to *buy* a specific underlying asset at a specified price during a specified time. These are termed **call options.** Other option contracts give the holder the option to *sell* an asset at a specified price during a specified time period. These are **put options.**

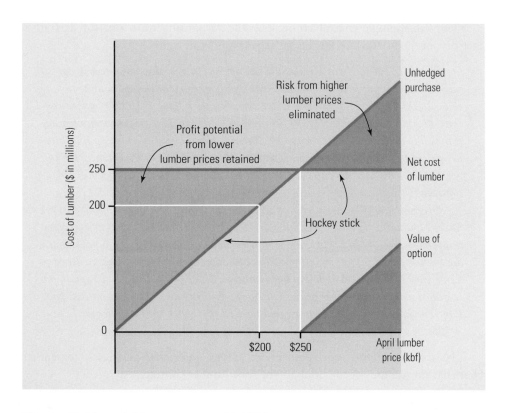

FIGURE 11.9
RIDGE DEVELOPMENT COMPANY

Using an Option to Hedge Commodity Price Risk

Without hedging its anticipated lumber purchase, Ridge is exposed to commodity price risk if lumber prices rise above the current $250 level over the next three months. To eliminate this exposure, Ridge buys a call option for 10 million board feet of April lumber at $250 per 1,000 board feet. If the April price of lumber is more than $250 per 1,000 board feet, Ridge will exercise the option and pay just the $250 contract price. But if the April price is, say, $200, Ridge will let the option expire and instead buy lumber in the open market—saving $500,000 in lumber costs ($50 per 1,000 board feet). The net result of the option hedge is a "hockey stick" shape (see Figure 11.9)—the *downside risk* of a lumber price increase is eliminated but the *upside potential* of a lumber price decrease is retained.

When options are used in this way, they do not necessarily "lock in" a specified profit margin or price. Instead, they provide a hedge that resembles insurance. Options allow companies to hedge against downside risk—value losses—while retaining the opportunity to benefit from favourable price movements.

Financial Reporting for Derivative Securities

Before we turn our attention to hedge accounting, let's consider first how stand-alone derivative securities in the absence of a hedging transaction might be accounted for if:

- All derivatives were to be carried on the balance sheet at fair value—no exceptions.

- Generally, changes in the fair value of derivatives were to be recognized in income when they occur. The only exception is for derivatives that qualify as hedges (explained below).

This is essentially the U.S. position currently; in Canada, GAAP is still in flux as of August 2002, but the CICA has issued some guidance (see *AcG–13*, "Hedging Relationships," and *EIC–128* on accounting for trading, speculative, or non-hedging derivatives).

Here's an example that illustrates possible accounting treatment for derivatives that do not qualify for special "hedge accounting" rules:

*On March 1, 2001, Heitz Metals buys call options (i.e., options to purchase) for 10 million board feet of June lumber. Each call option gives Heitz the opportunity to purchase 1,000 board feet of lumber, so the firm bought a total of 10,000 options contracts (10 million board feet/1,000 per contract). Heitz has no use for the lumber nor is the company hedging a financial risk. **Instead, Heitz is just speculating that lumber prices will increase during the next several months.** The settlement price is $240 per 1,000 board feet, the current spot price is $240, and Heitz pays $5,000 for the contracts.*

Over the next 30 days, a series of winter storms dump several feet of snow in the Rocky Mountains. This late snowfall delays the timber-harvesting season and creates a lumber shortage. By March 31, the spot price for lumber is $245 and June contracts are trading for $7,500 at the commodities exchange. Lumber prices have increased to $245 but Heitz owns an option to buy lumber at $240, so the value of the option has increased along with lumber prices. On April 15, Heitz decides to liquidate its position. The June lumber contracts are sold for $12,000 when the spot price for lumber is $252.

The accounting entry to record Heitz Metals' *speculative* purchase—remember, Heitz has no real use for the lumber—of June lumber contracts is:

DR	Marketable securities—lumber options	$5,000	
	CR Cash		$5,000

The derivative is recorded as an asset at its fair value—the purchase price. At the end of March, Heitz records the *change* in fair value of the derivative ($7,500 − $5,000 = $2,500):

DR	Market adjustment—lumber options	$2,500	
	CR Unrealized holding gain on lumber options (to income)		$2,500

The "Market adjustment" of $2,500 is added to the $5,000 balance in "Marketable securities." The contracts are now carried on the balance sheet at $7,500—which is their fair market value—and a $2,500 unrealized gain has been recorded in income for March. (If the options had declined in value, an unrealized holding loss would have been recorded along with a downward adjustment in the carrying value of the options.) Heitz then liquidates the options contracts on April 15:

> The unrealized gain (or loss) would be included in "Income from continuing operations" on the Heitz income statement.

DR	Cash	$12,000	
	CR Marketable securities—lumber options		$5,000
	CR Market adjustment—lumber options		2,500
	CR Realized holding gain on lumber options (to income)		4,500

A final entry reclassifies the unrealized holding gain:

DR	Unrealized holding gain on lumber options	$2,500	
	CR Realized holding gain on lumber options		$2,500

These accounting entries are used for all types of derivatives—forwards, futures, swaps and options—unless the special "hedge accounting" rules described in the next section apply. Three key points should be remembered:

1. Derivative contracts represent balance sheet assets and liabilities.
2. The carrying value of the derivative is adjusted to fair value at each balance sheet date.
3. The amount of the adjustment—the change in fair value—flows to the income statement as an unrealized holding gain (or loss).

As a result, speculative investments in derivative contracts can increase the volatility of reported earnings. But the earnings volatility that results from this accounting treatment perfectly reflects the derivative's inherent economic risk.

Hedge Accounting

In late 2001, the Accounting Standards Board (AcSB) issued the accounting guideline *AcG–13*, "Hedging Relationships," which, while it does not specify hedge-accounting methods—sets out when hedge accounting should be followed. *AcG–13* says that a company may use hedge accounting if all of the following conditions are fulfilled:

1. At the inception of the hedging relationship, the company—in accordance with its risk management policies—identifies the specific risk being hedged;
2. The hedging relationship must be fully documented, including all the key terms of the relationships, the method for assessing the effectiveness of the hedge, and the method for recognizing gains, losses, revenues, and expenses;
3. There is reasonable assurance the hedge will be effective.

When a company successfully hedges its exposure to market risk, any economic loss on the hedged item (e.g., copper inventory) will be offset by an economic gain on the derivative security (e.g., copper futures contracts). ***To accurately reflect the underlying economics of the hedge, the company should match the loss on the hedged item with the derivative's offsetting gain in the income statement of the same period.*** This matching is what the rules governing hedge accounting try to accomplish.[10] These special hedge accounting rules eliminate or reduce the earnings volatility that would otherwise result from reporting the change in the derivative's fair value in income. The type of hedge accounting to be applied varies depending on the nature of the exposure that is being hedged. In some cases, changes in the fair value of the derivative are reported in income as they occur, but the earnings impact is then offset by a corresponding charge (or credit) from adjusting the carrying value of the asset or liability being hedged. In other cases, earnings volatility is avoided by recording changes in the fair value of the derivative directly in "Other comprehensive income" in the United States.

When can hedge accounting be used? The answer depends on four considerations:

- Hedged item
- Hedging instrument
- Risk being hedged
- Effectiveness of hedge

In the United States, stringent GAAP criteria must be met to qualify for hedge accounting. Management must designate the derivative security as a hedging instrument, describe the hedging strategy, and document its effectiveness in eliminating a specific market risk for a specific hedged item. The details are voluminous and complex and illustrate an extreme example of setting accounting standards of detailed rules rather than more general principles, so we cannot possibly cover all the bases here. What we can do is provide an overview of the most common hedging situations and how hedge accounting works. The basics are outlined in Figure 11.10.

The **hedged item** can be (1) an existing asset or liability on the company's books, (2) a firm commitment, or (3) an anticipated (forecasted) transaction. Inventories of commodities like copper and lumber, receivables and loans, and debt obligations are examples of *existing assets and liabilities* that qualify as hedged items. If Hess Company agrees in June to buy network storage equipment from another company at a specific price with delivery in the future (say, August), that's a *firm commitment*. If, on the other hand, Hess just knows in June that it must buy the equipment by August but no purchase agreement has been signed, then it's a *forecasted transaction*.

The **hedging instrument** is most often a derivative security, although not all derivatives meet the GAAP rules and some qualifying hedges (e.g., the call provision of a callable bond) do not involve derivatives as the term is commonly used. Qualifying hedging instruments include options to purchase or sell an exchange-traded security, futures and forward contracts, and interest-rate and currency swaps. ***Insurance contracts, options to purchase real estate, equity and debt securities, and financial guarantee contracts do not qualify as hedging instruments.***

The **risk being hedged** must meet certain GAAP criteria. The eligible market risks are limited to those arising from overall changes in the fair value or cash flow of the hedged item, or from changes in benchmark interest rates (e.g., LIBOR), commodity prices (e.g., copper), foreign-currency exchange rates (e.g., Japanese yen to Canadian dollar), and the creditworthiness of the party (a company, institution, or

FIGURE 11.10
FINANCIAL
REPORTING FOR
DERIVATIVE
SECURITIES

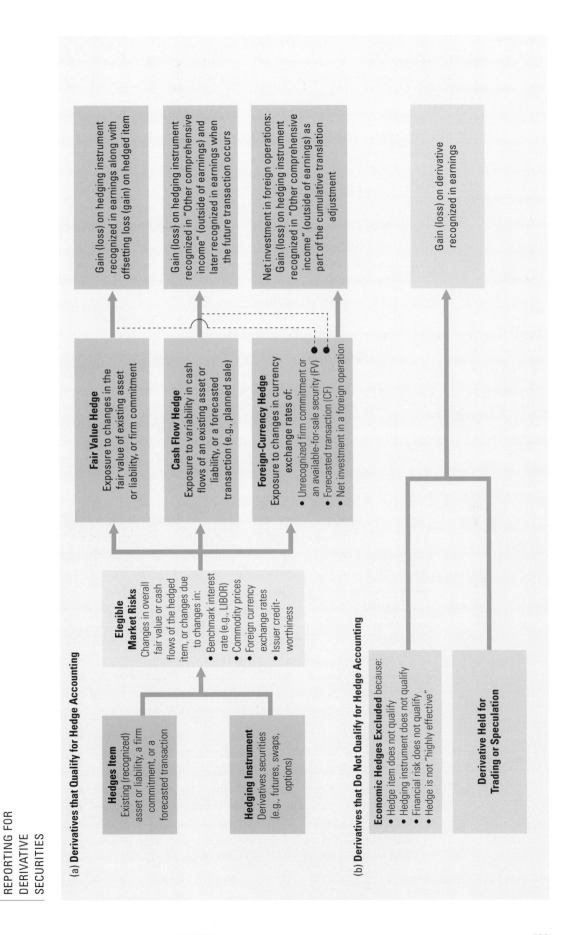

(a) **Derivatives that Qualify for Hedge Accounting**

(b) **Derivatives that Do Not Qualify for Hedge Accounting**

government agency) that issued a financial security. Other sorts of financial and operating risks (e.g., risks from weather conditions, industrial accidents, or labour strikes) do not qualify for hedge accounting. (We will discuss the effectiveness of the hedge later.)

GAAP groups the risks being hedged into three general categories:

1. A **fair value hedge** is a hedge of the exposure to changes in the fair market value of:
   - an *existing* asset or liability (e.g., the interest-rate risk exposure of a company's existing fixed rate debt), or
   - a *firm commitment* (e.g., the price risk exposure of a gold mining company that has agreed to sell refined gold to a jewellery manufacturer next year at a fixed price)

2. A **cash flow hedge** is a hedge of the exposure to changes in cash flows of:
   - an *existing* asset or liability (e.g., the interest-rate risk exposure of a company's existing floating rate debt), or
   - an *anticipated transaction* (e.g., a building contractor's exposure to the price risk of future lumber purchases)

3. A **foreign currency exposure hedge** is a hedge of the exposure to changes in currency exchange rates of an existing asset or liability, a firm commitment, a forecasted transaction, or a multinational company's net investment in a foreign operation. Here GAAP apply the fair value and cash flow hedge accounting rules to foreign currency exchange exposure. The one unique element of this exposure is a net investment in foreign operations. In Chapter 16, we describe the accounting and reporting issues unique to foreign subsidiaries.

Figure 11.10 describes the accounting procedures for (a) derivatives that qualify for hedge accounting, and (b) derivatives that do not qualify for hedge accounting. In the U.S., GAAP require all derivative securities—whether held for trading and speculation or as financial hedges—to be **marked-to-market,** meaning that they are carried at fair value on the balance sheet as assets or liabilities. The offsetting debit or credit that results from mark-to-market accounting then flows either to current income (for fair value hedges, certain foreign currency hedges, and derivatives that do not qualify for hedge accounting) or to "Other comprehensive income" in the U.S. (for cash flow hedges and most other foreign currency hedges).

Hedge accounting makes it possible for companies engaged in financial risk management to recognize the gain (or loss) on the hedged item in the same period as the offsetting loss (or gain) on the derivative security. To see how this is done, let's return to Rombaurer Metals and its copper inventory hedge:

On October 1, 2001, Rombaurer has 10 million pounds of copper inventory on hand at an average cost of $0.65 a pound. The spot price for copper is $0.90 a pound. Instead of selling copper now, Rombaurer decides to hold on to the inventory until February 2002 when management believes the price will return to a normal level of $0.95 a pound. To hedge its position, Rombaurer sells futures contracts for 10 million pounds at $0.95 for February delivery. The margin deposit on the contracts is $280,000. This is the amount the commodities broker requires as a good-faith cash deposit on the contracts. Spot and future prices over the next several months are:

	COMEX Copper Prices	
	Spot Price	February 2002 Futures Price
October 1, 2001	$0.90	$0.95
December 31, 2001	0.85	0.91
February 26, 2002	0.94	0.94

Rombaurer has successfully hedged its exposure to commodity price risk—and the fair value of its copper inventory—by selling the futures contracts. Then, for GAAP purposes, Rombaurer designates the futures contracts (the hedging instrument) as a **fair value hedge** of its exposure to market price fluctuations (the hedged risk) for existing copper inventory (the hedged item). As long as the futures contracts pass the GAAP test for hedge effectiveness—and they do, as we will see later—Rombaurer can use the special **fair value hedge accounting** rules. Here are the accounting entries.

On October 1, 2001, Rombaurer records the initial margin deposit on its fair value hedge:

DR Amount due from broker (a receivable) $280,000
    CR   Cash $280,000

No entry is made that day for the futures contracts themselves because they have zero value at inception—the February contract price ($0.95) equals the current $0.95 market price of February copper.

The spot price and the February futures price of copper both decline over the next several months. Rombaurer makes two journal entries at year-end, December 31. The first entry records the fair value increase for the hedging instrument:

DR Amount due from broker $400,000
    CR   Gain on hedge activity (to income) $400,000

The futures contracts are worth $400,000 on December 31, 2001. This amount is the difference between the copper price guaranteed by the contracts ($0.95) and the current futures price of February copper ($0.91), multiplied by the 10 million pounds of copper being hedged. Copper prices have fallen, but the hedge has provided $400,000 of commodity price protection.

The second year-end entry adjusts the carrying value of the hedged item—copper inventory—for the change in fair value ($0.91 minus $0.95, a $0.04 loss, multiplied by 10 million pounds):

DR Loss on hedge activity (to income) $400,000
    CR   Copper inventory $400,000

The carrying value of the copper inventory is now $6.1 million: that's the inventory's $6.5 million historical cost *minus* the $400,000 decline in the February fair value since October 1, 2001. (Note that GAAP measures this fair value decline using the October 1 $0.95 *futures* contract price as the benchmark. The October 1 *spot* price of $0.90 does not enter into the GAAP calculation of the fair value decline.)

In the first entry, the derivative is marked-to-market and a gain on the hedging instrument is recorded to income. But the gain from the futures contracts is fully offset by Rombaurer's loss on copper inventory in the second entry. (In practice, only one "Gain or loss on hedge activity" account is used to record the gain and the loss.) These offsetting gains and losses eliminate earnings volatility.

On February 26, 2002, Rombaurer sells the copper on the spot market for $0.94 a pound and cancels the futures contracts. Rombaurer makes three journal entries at this time. The first entry records the fair value change for the hedging instrument ($0.91 minus $0.94, a $0.03 loss, multiplied by 10 million pounds), the cash returned from the broker, and eliminates the broker receivable:

DR	Cash	$380,000	
DR	Loss on hedge activity (to income)	300,000	
	CR Amount due from broker		$680,000

February copper prices have increased $0.03 a pound since December and the futures contracts are now worth only $100,000 ($0.95 minus $0.94, multiplied by 10 million pounds). Rombaurer receives $380,000 from the broker. This amount is the sum of the returned margin deposit ($280,000) and the settlement value of the contracts ($100,000).

The second entry adjusts the carrying value of the hedged copper inventory for the fair value change ($0.94 minus $0.91, multiplied by 10 million pounds):

DR	Copper inventory	$300,000	
	CR Gain on hedge activity (to income)		$300,000

In this case, the loss from the futures contracts (the first entry) is offset by a gain on copper inventory (the second entry). The final entry records the credit sale of copper inventory at the spot market price:

DR	Accounts receivable	$9,400,000	
DR	Cost of goods sold	6,400,000	
	CR Sales revenue		$9,400,000
	CR Copper inventory		6,400,000

The $6.4 million adjusted carrying value ($0.64 per pound) is determined as:

10/1/01	cost at $0.65 per pound	$6.5 million
12/31/01	adjustment for $0.04 decline	(0.4) million
2/26/02	adjustment for $0.03 increase	0.3 million
2/26/02	adjusted carrying value	$6.4 million

Rombaurer's gross profit from selling copper is $3 million (the $9.4 million selling price minus the $6.4 million adjusted carrying value of the inventory sold). This is exactly the gross profit Rombaurer would have reported if the inventory—originally carried on the books at $6.5 million—had been sold at the anticipated February price of $0.95 a pound, or $9.5 million. By selling futures contracts, Rombaurer "locked in" the February price of $0.95 a pound and eliminated its exposure to commodity price risk. That's the economics behind Rombaurer's hedging activities and that's what the accounting statements report.

Exhibit 11.2 illustrates the accounting for a **cash flow hedge.** Chalk Hill Inc. issues a $10 million three-year floating rate note with interest equal to the LIBOR rate, reset annually. To hedge its exposure to cash flow variability from changes in the LIBOR, Chalk Hill enters into an interest-rate swap with a bank. The bank agrees to make the required floating rate interest payments and Chalk Hill agrees to pay the bank 7.5% fixed rate interest annually for the entire three years. The interest-rate swap allows Chalk Hill to "lock in" the 7.5% fixed rate cash payment for interest even though the actual interest rate charged on the note will rise or fall with changes in the LIBOR rate.

What if Rombaurer did not (or could not) use hedge accounting rules for the copper futures contracts? In that case, *EIC-128* and U.S. GAAP generally require the derivative security to be marked-to-market. So Rombaurer would record a $400,000 gain on December 31, 2001, followed by a $300,000 loss on February 26, 2002—the change in fair value of the futures contracts. But GAAP would not allow an offsetting loss (on December 31, 2001) or gain (on February 26, 2002) to be recorded on the copper inventory itself. Instead, the inventory would continue to be carried at its historical cost of $6,500,000 until sold. The net result is increased earnings volatility: net income for 2001 would include a $400,000 gain, while net income for 2002 would include a $300,000 loss and a $100,000 gross margin reduction due to the higher carrying value of inventory ($0.65 per pound original cost rather than $0.64 per pound adjusted carrying value).

Exhibit 11.2 CHALK HILL'S CASH FLOW HEDGE

Using an Interest-Rate Swap to Hedge Variable Rate Debt

On January 1, 2001, Chalk Hill borrows $10 million, signing a three-year note with interest equal to the LIBOR (currently at 7.5%), reset annually on December 31. To hedge its exposure to the variability in cash flows associated with the floating rate note, Chalk Hill enters into a three-year interest-rate swap with Beringer Bank. Under the swap contract, Chalk Hill pays interest to the bank at a fixed rate of 7.5% and receives interest payments from the bank at a variable rate equal to the LIBOR, based on a notional amount of $10 million. Both the note and swap require that payments be made or received annually on December 31 of each year.

Chalk Hill designates the swap (hedging instrument) as a *cash flow hedge* of its exposure to variability in the cash flows of the floating rate note (hedged item), with the specific risk being changes in cash flows due to changes in the LIBOR rate. This hedge is fully effective because the key terms of the note and swap are identical. The LIBOR rates, cash payments made and received, and the fair value of the swap contract (based on dealer quotes) are:

| | | Gross Cash Flow | | | Swap Fair Value |
	LIBOR Rate	To Beringer Bank	From Beringer Bank	Net Cash Flow	Asset (Liability) from Dealer Quotes
January 1, 2001	7.50%	$750,000	$750,000	—	—
December 31, 2001	8.50	750,000	850,000	$100,000	$323,000
December 31, 2002	7.00	750,000	700,000	(50,000)	(55,000)

Swap contracts are not traded in an organized exchange (like the New York Mercantile Exchange where copper futures contracts are traded), so contract fair values can be difficult to determine. Chalk Hill's fair value estimates ("quotes") are from knowledgeable "dealers" (usually investment bankers) who are actively involved in structuring swap transactions. Chalk Hill makes the following entries over the life of the swap contract and note:

January 1, 2001:

DR Cash	$10,000,000	
CR Note payable		$10,000,000

(To record the initial borrowing by the company. There is no entry for the swap contract because it has no initial value—the "pay" and "receive" rates for both parties are the same, 7.5% times $10 million.)

December 31, 2001:

DR Interest expense	$750,000	
CR Interest payable		$750,000

(To accrue annual interest at a variable rate of 7.5%—the LIBOR rate on January 1, 2001.)

DR Interest payable	$750,000	
CR Cash		$750,000

(To record the annual interest payment on the note. There is no entry for the swap settlement this year because the "pay" and "receive" amounts are the same, $750,000.)

DR Swap contract	$323,000	
CR Deferred gain, or (in the U.S.) Other comprehensive income		$323,000

(To record the change in fair value of the swap based on dealer quotes.)

December 31, 2002:

DR Interest expense	$850,000	
CR Interest payable		$850,000

(To accrue annual interest at a variable rate of 8.5%—the LIBOR rate on December 31, 2001.)

DR Interest payable	$850,000	
CR Cash		$850,000

(To record the annual interest payment on the note.)

Exhibit 11.2 (CONTINUED)

DR Cash $100,000
    CR Interest expense $100,000
(To record the swap settlement net receipt from Beringer Bank.)

DR Deferred gain (or in the U.S.
    Other comprehensive income) $378,000
    CR Swap contract $378,000
(To record the change in fair value of the swap based on dealer quotes. The swap contract account now has a $55,000 credit balance.)

December 31, 2003:

DR Interest expense $700,000
    CR Interest payable $700,000
(To accrue annual interest at a variable rate of 7.0%—the LIBOR rate on December 31, 2002.)

DR Interest payable $700,000
    CR Cash $700,000
(To record the annual interest payment on the note.)

DR Interest expense $50,000
CR Cash $50,000
(To record the swap settlement net payment to Beringer Bank.)

DR Swap contract $55,000
    CR Income $55,000
(To record the change in fair value of the swap. The swap agreement has now been concluded, and the contract has no further value to either party.)

DR Note payable $10,000,000
    CR Cash $10,000,000
(To record payment of the note principal.)

As you work through the journal entries in Exhibit 11.2, notice that the hedging instrument (swap contract) shows up as a balance sheet asset or liability. (If the account has a debit balance, it's an asset; if the balance is a credit, it's a liability.) The carrying value of the swap is its fair value at each balance sheet date. This means that changes in the swap's fair value are recorded when they occur—*but they do not flow directly to the income statement.* Instead, gains and losses on the swap contract flow to "Deferred gains" (or in the U.S., "Other comprehensive income") and shareholders' equity, as indicated in Figure 11.10. What's the reason for this accounting treatment? Changes in the LIBOR rate do not affect the underlying economic value of the floating rate note—as interest rates on a floating rate liability change, the market price of the liability remains constant. So, we are unable to offset fair value changes in the hedging instrument with changes in the fair value of the hedged item. The only way earnings volatility can be avoided is to keep swap gains and losses off the income statement by allowing them to flow to "Deferred gains" (or "Other comprehensive income").

There is one more feature of the Chalk Hill example you should notice. Interest expense is $750,000 each year, or the 7.5% fixed rate of interest multiplied by the $10 million note principal amount. This may at first seem surprising because Chalk Hill makes a floating rate interest payment each year, and the amount paid varies from $700,000 to $850,000 over the three years. But the interest-rate swap insulates

Chalk Hill from this cash flow volatility. For example, in 2002 Chalk Hill pays $850,000 in interest on the note but receives $100,000 from the swap counterparty. The company's net cash payment for interest that year is $750,000, which is also the amount of interest expense reported.

Now let's see how hedge accounting works for a **forecasted transaction.** In this example, Vintage Construction uses lumber options contracts as a cash flow hedge for its projected lumber needs during the year:

Vintage Construction Corporation builds houses in the far northern United States from April through November. No homes are built on speculation. Building begins only after a firm contract is signed. Construction takes four months on average. Since contract prices with home purchases are fixed at the inception of the sale, Vintage is vulnerable to lumber price increases. To protect its margins during the 2001 construction season, Vintage buys 20 lumber futures contracts on April 1, 2001. The expiration dates on these contracts are staggered over the April through November season to approximate the monthly level of construction activity.

Lumber prices rise during the 2001 construction season. Because of these unanticipated higher costs, gross profits from home construction are reduced by $600,000. However, Vintage realized a gain of $580,000 on the futures contracts due to the lumber price increase. How was this gain reflected on the company's financial statements?

Vintage designates the lumber contracts as a *cash flow hedge* of forecasted lumber purchases, with commodity price volatility being the source of market risk. At inception, the futures contracts are recorded as an asset at the purchase price. At each monthly balance sheet date, the contracts are marked-to-market with the change in fair value flowing to "Deferred gains" (or "Other comprehensive income" in the U.S.) and then shareholders' equity. As homes are completed each month, Vintage records the revenues and expenses from the construction business. At the same time, the cumulative gain and loss on the lumber contracts for completed homes is transferred out of "Deferred gains" (or "Other comprehensive income") to the income statement.

This accounting treatment offsets changes in the gross profit from construction due to lumber price fluctuations (the hedged item) with realized gains and losses from lumber futures contracts (the hedging instrument). Earnings volatility is avoided by allowing the futures contracts gains and losses to flow initially to shareholders' equity. These gains and losses eventually flow to earnings, but only when the forecasted transaction is completed *and affects earnings.* For Vintage Construction, that means when the homes are finished and sold—not earlier when lumber is purchased.

Because all of the options contracts were realized in 2001, the $580,000 gain would be included in income and would largely offset the $600,000 gross margin reduction that is reflected in the same period. This income statement result corresponds to the almost perfect hedging strategy followed by Vintage Construction. A "perfect" hedge would have exactly offset the $600,000 margin shortfall.

Few hedges are perfect. When they are not—as here—notice that reported income corresponds to the underlying economics. That is, while Vintage insulated itself from most of the lumber price increase, it did experience a $20,000 earnings reduction. This is precisely the reported income statement effect (i.e., a $580,000 gain on the options and a $600,000 gross margin reduction).

Hedge effectiveness—the derivative's ability to generate offsetting changes in the fair value or cash flows of the hedged item—is a key qualifying criterion for hedge accounting. If critical terms of the hedging instrument and hedged item are the same, changes in the fair value or cash flow of the derivative will completely offset changes in the fair value or cash flow of the hedged item. In this case, the hedge will be "fully

> For interest-rate swaps like the one described in Exhibit 11.2, the critical terms include the notional (i.e., principal) amount, contract term and loan maturity date, "pay" and "receive" rates on the benchmark interest rate, and the interest rate reset dates.

SFAS No. 133 and No. 138 do not provide a bright line that defines "highly effective" and therefore the interpretation of this phrase will often be a matter of judgment. The range of 80% to 125% is becoming an accepted threshold for high effectiveness, but it has not been sanctioned by the FASB. There's one more feature of hedge effectiveness you should know about. Vintage Construction can instead purchase 10 lumber futures contracts and still have a "highly effective" hedge if (1) Vintage designates the contracts as a "partial hedge" of its risk exposure (e.g., 50% of its lumber purchases), and (2) the contracts are "highly effective" in hedging that partial exposure.

In a letter to the FASB, Al Wargo of Eastman Chemical said that hedge accounting could cause his company's quarterly earnings per share (EPS) to fluctuate by roughly 100% in either direction—from a US$0.12 loss to a US$2.24 profit based on Eastman's US$1.12 EPS for the second quarter of 2000. The only way Eastman can eliminate this EPS volatility is to change how it hedges financial risk. But this means replacing a sound economic hedging transaction with a less effective hedge. EPS would then be less volatile but the company may be more exposed to financial risks.[11]

effective." Except for Vintage Construction, all of our examples have involved fully effective hedges.

But what if the hedge is not fully effective? Does that disqualify the derivative from special hedge accounting rules? Not necessarily, because GAAP only require the hedge to be "highly effective" in offsetting changes in those fair values or cash flows that are due to the hedged risk. This requirement must be met both at the inception of the hedge and on an ongoing basis. *SFAS No. 133* provides general guidelines but does not say exactly how effectiveness should be determined.

How effective is "highly effective"? The hedging instrument should offset somewhere between 80% and 125% of the hedged item's fair value or cash flow changes attributable to the hedged risk. For Vintage Construction, this means that the company must purchase enough staggered lumber futures contracts to hedge at least 80% of its exposure to lumber price fluctuations. Purchase less than this amount and the futures contracts are an "ineffective" hedge according to GAAP. On the other hand, if Vintage buys too many contracts, the hedge is also considered ineffective. That's because the futures contracts are excessive and more like a speculative investment than a true hedge of underlying market risk.

The GAAP distinction between *highly effective* and *ineffective* hedges determines when gains and losses on the hedging instrument flow to current income. A highly effective hedge qualifies for special hedge accounting treatment; an ineffective hedge does not. Even if the highly effective test is met, some ineffectiveness may occur. And when it does, the ineffective portion of the hedge must flow directly to income. So, if Vintage Construction buys futures contracts to hedge just 50% of its exposure, all of the gains and losses from this *ineffective* hedge flow directly to current income. That's because the contracts are ineffective and do not qualify for hedge accounting. And if the company buys futures contracts to hedge 110% of its exposure, the gains and losses on the *ineffective* portion of the hedge (the portion over 100% coverage) also flow directly to current income. Gains and losses on the effective portion of the hedge flow to other comprehensive income (to deferred gains in Canada).

Critics of hedge accounting claim that additional income statement and balance sheet volatility is created when the gains and losses on the hedging instrument exceed the losses and gains on the hedged item. *This may force managers to choose between achieving sound economic results—meaning hedges that effectively address real financial risks—or minimizing accounting volatility using risk management approaches that are less efficient or simply not prudent.*

Recap

Derivatives, when used properly, allow companies to stabilize their operating cash flows by eliminating specific sources of volatility such as fluctuations in interest rates, exchange rates, and commodity prices. The GAAP rules for derivatives are detailed and complex, and in Canada are still in a state of flux, but the essential points are simple. Derivative contracts represent balance sheet assets and liabilities that must be marked-to-market at each balance sheet date. The resulting mark-to-market adjustment—the change in fair value—then flows either to current earnings (for fair value hedges, certain foreign currency hedges, and derivatives held for trading and speculation) or to "Deferred gains" (or "Other comprehensive income" in the U.S.) (for cash flow hedges and most other foreign currency hedges). Other aspects of hedge accounting then match gains (or losses) on the derivative with offsetting losses (or gains) on the hedged item. This allows the financial statements to reflect accurately the underlying economics of the hedge.

Canadian GAAP and Financial Instruments

GAAP for financial instruments, both in Canada and elsewhere, is evolving. The current standard, Section 3860 of the *CICA Handbook* ("Financial Instruments—Disclosure and Presentation") does not deal with recognition and measurement issues; a new standard encompassing these issues is expected soon. Some key parts of Section 3860 are shown in Exhibit 11.3, along with a brief commentary.

Exhibit 11.3 CAPSULE COMMENTS ON SELECTED PARTS OF SECTION 3860

Note: Only a small number of selections are given, for illustrative purposes only.

Selection from Section 3860	Comments
Purpose and Scope	These first two paragraphs of Section 3860 set out the rationale for the standard, and point out that it does not deal with recognition and measurement, topics that will be the focus of an Exposure Draft from the CICA's Accounting Standards Board expected soon. However, international accounting bodies seem predisposed towards a comprehensive market-based approach with respect to accounting for financial instruments. For example, in a Discussion Paper (entitled "Accounting for Financial Assets and Financial Liabilities") released in March 1997, the IASC proposed that "An enterprise should recognise a financial asset or financial liability on its balance sheet when it becomes a party to the contractual provisions that comprise the contract" (p. iii) and "An enterprise should measure a financial instrument ... at the fair value of the consideration given or received for it" (p. iv).
.01 The dynamic nature of international financial markets has resulted in the widespread use of a variety of financial instruments ranging from traditional primary instruments such as bonds to various forms of derivative instruments such as interest rate swaps. The purpose of this Section is to enhance financial statement users' understanding of the significance of recognized and unrecognized financial instruments to an entity's financial position, performance and cash flows.	
.02 This Section prescribes certain requirements for presentation of recognized financial instruments and identifies the information that should be disclosed about both recognized and unrecognized financial instruments. The presentation Recommendations deal with the classification of financial instruments between liabilities and equity, the classification of related interest, dividends, losses and gains, and the circumstances in which financial assets and financial liabilities are offset. The disclosure Recommendations deal with information about factors that affect the amount, timing and certainty of an entity's future cash flows relating to financial instruments. In addition, this Section encourages disclosure of information about the nature and extent of an entity's use of financial instruments, the business purposes that they serve, the risks associated with them and management's policies for controlling those risks. This Section does not prescribe the basis on which financial assets and financial liabilities are recognized and measured.	It is important to note that current Canadian GAAP is disclosure- and presentation-oriented, but this is expected to change shortly. Also, it is important to note that this Section deals with presentation and disclosure of financial instruments that an entity has recognized, as well as financial instruments that an entity has not formally recognized, in the accounts. Of course, disclosure is not a substitute for formally capturing information in the accounts, but it is crucial as a means of at least partially fulfilling users' needs described in Section 1000.

Exhibit 11.3 (CONTINUED)

Selection from Section 3860	Comments

Definitions

.05 The following terms are used in this Section with the meanings specified:

(a) A **financial instrument** is any contract that gives rise to both a financial asset of one party and a financial liability or equity instrument of another party.

(b) A **financial asset** is any asset that is: (i) cash; (ii) a contractual right to receive cash or another financial asset from another party; (iii) a contractual right to exchange financial instruments with another party under conditions that are potentially favourable; or (iv) an equity instrument of another entity.

(c) A **financial liability** is any liability that is a contractual obligation: (i) to deliver cash or another financial asset to another party; or (ii) to exchange financial instruments with another party under conditions that are potentially unfavourable.

(d) An **equity instrument** is any contract that evidences a residual interest in the assets of an entity after deducting all of its liabilities.

(e) **Monetary financial assets and financial liabilities** (also referred to as monetary financial instruments) are financial assets and financial liabilities to be received or paid in fixed or determinable amounts of money.

(f) **Fair value** is the amount of the consideration that would be agreed upon in an arm's length transaction between knowledgeable, willing parties who are under no compulsion to act.

(g) **Market value** is the amount obtainable from the sale, or payable on the acquisition, of a financial instrument in an active market.

The definitions in Section 3860 are special cases of Section 1000's definitions. For example, the definition of a "financial liability" in Section 3860 is a special case of the broader definition of "liability" from Section 1000 of the *CICA Handbook*, which defines "liabilities" as follows: "Liabilities are obligations of an entity arising from past transactions or events, the settlement of which may result in the transfer or use of assets, provision of services or other yielding of economic benefits in the future" (para. 1000.32).

The *Handbook* section goes on to provide more detail: "Liabilities have three essential characteristics: (a) they embody a duty or responsibility to others that entails settlement by future transfer or use of assets, provision of services or other yielding of economic benefits, at a specified or determinable date, on occurrence of a specified event, or on demand; (b) the duty or responsibility obligates the entity leaving it little or no discretion to avoid it; and (c) the transaction or event obligating the entity has already occurred (para. 1000.33).

Liabilities do not have to be legally enforceable provided that they otherwise meet the definition of liabilities; they can be based on equitable or constructive obligations. An equitable obligation is a duty based on ethical or moral considerations. A constructive obligation is one that can be inferred from the facts in a particular situation as opposed to a contractually based obligation" (para.1000. 34).

Notice that by defining various categories such as financial assets, financial liabilities, etc., Section 3860 in effect transforms the items that "fit" into these categories into things that can be standardized.

Exhibit 11.3 (CONTINUED)

Selection from Section 3860	Comments
.09 Financial instruments include both primary instruments, such as receivables, payables and equity securities, and derivative instruments, such as financial options, futures and forwards, interest rate swaps and currency swaps. Derivative financial instruments, whether recognized or unrecognized, meet the definition of a financial instrument and, accordingly, are subject to this Section. .10 Derivative financial instruments create rights and obligations that have the effect of transferring between the parties to the instrument one or more of the financial risks inherent in an underlying primary financial instrument. Derivative instruments do not result in a transfer of the underlying primary financial instrument on inception of the contract and such a transfer does not necessarily take place on maturity of the contract.	Paragraph .09 asserts that Section 3860's definition of "financial instrument" is very wide-ranging, covering both everyday accounting items such as receivables and payables and more exotic (but now pervasive) items such as various types of options, forwards, and similar items. Paragraph .10 explains Section 3860's view of what a derivative financial instrument is, and indicates that the key aspects of such a financial instrument, for financial accounting and reporting purposes, are the creation of rights and obligations and the accompanying transfer of risks between the contracting parties. Resolving differing points of view about accounting for such "rights and obligations that have the effect of transferring … the financial risks inherent in an underlying primary instrument" is what has made setting GAAP in this area so difficult. Indeed, before the U.S. FASB issued its 1997 standard in this area, even the Chairman of the U.S. Federal Reserve System lobbied against it! It also probably at least partially explains why the CICA's AcSB delayed the recognition and measurement aspects of financial instrument accounting, and issued Section 3860 as an incomplete standard.

Presentation

Liabilities and equity

.18 *The issuer of a financial instrument should classify the instrument, or its component parts, as a liability or as equity in accordance with the substance of the contractual arrangement on initial recognition and the definitions of a financial liability and an equity instrument.* .19 The substance of a financial instrument, rather than its legal form, governs its classification on the issuer's balance sheet. While substance and legal form are commonly consistent, this is not always the case. For example, some financial instruments take the legal form of equity but are liabilities in substance and others may combine features associated with equity instruments and features associated with financial liabilities. The classification of an instrument is made on the basis of an assessment of its substance when it is first recognized. That classification continues at each subsequent reporting date until the financial instrument is removed from the entity's balance sheet.	Italicized (therefore formal GAAP) para. .18 is a reaffirmation of Section 1000.21 of the *CICA Handbook,* which sets out the "substance over form" qualitative characteristic. In other words, issuers of financial statements which include financial instruments should be wary of words, as should users. Just because a financial instrument is labelled a "liability" doesn't make it so; the proof is in the substance (rights, risks, powers, etc.), not the form. Paragraph .19 (and the paragraphs which follow) are explanatory, and provide useful clarification and examples of the intent of .18. But, of course, the good intentions here might be subverted in any given instance by strong incentives to classify a financial instrument in a way other than its substance (on the basis of the evidence). For example, if an existing debt covenant is in danger of being breached, management may prefer to classify a proposed new financial instrument as equity.

Exhibit 11.3 (CONTINUED)

Selection from Section 3860

Comments

.24 *The issuer of a financial instrument that contains both a liability and an equity element should classify the instrument's component parts separately in accordance with paragraph 3860.18.*

.25 This Recommendation requires the separate presentation on an issuer's balance sheet of liability and equity elements created by a single financial instrument. It is more a matter of form than substance that both liabilities and equity interests are created by a single financial instrument rather than two or more separate instruments. An issuer's financial position is more faithfully represented by separate presentation of the liability and equity components contained in a single instrument according to their nature.

Paragraph .24 is an extension of .18, in the sense that it is also based on the "substance over form" qualitative characteristic. Just because equity and liability features are bound up within a single financial instrument doesn't mean that the debt-like and equity-like portions shouldn't be disaggregated. A clearer picture of debt capacity results, at least according to the framers of this Section. And any portion of periodic payments or other costs attributed to the debt part of the financial instrument would appear on the income statement, while the portion attributed to equity would not, and would be a direct charge to Retained earnings. Paragraph .25 and the following paragraphs are explanatory.

But once the general principle in para. .24 is set out, potentially difficult measurement problems arise (i.e., how to split up the financial instrument into its liability and equity portions). Paragraphs .29 and .30 of Section 3860, as well as the Appendix to the Section, provide some very limited suggestions, but (as para. .29 observes) "This Section does not deal with measurement of financial assets, financial liabilities and equity instruments and does not therefore prescribe any particular method for assigning a carrying amount to liability and equity elements contained in a single instrument."

Exhibit 11.3 (CONTINUED)

Selection from Section 3860	Comments
Disclosure **Terms and conditions** *.52 For each class of financial asset, financial liability and equity instrument, both recognized and unrecognized, an entity should disclose information about the extent and nature of the financial instruments, including significant terms and conditions that may affect the amount, timing and certainty of future cash flows.* **Interest rate risk** *.57 For each class of financial asset and financial liability, both recognized and unrecognized, an entity should disclose information about its exposure to interest rate risk, including: (a) contractual repricing or maturity dates, whichever dates are earlier; and (b) effective interest rates, when applicable.* **Credit risk** *.67 For each class of financial asset, both recognized and unrecognized, an entity should disclose information about its exposure to credit risk, including: (a) the amount that best represents its maximum credit risk exposure at the balance sheet date, without taking account of the fair value of any collateral, in the event other parties fail to perform their obligations under financial instruments; and (b) significant concentrations of credit risk.* **Fair value** *.78 For each class of financial asset and financial liability, both recognized and unrecognized, an entity should disclose information about fair value. When it is not practicable within constraints of timeliness or cost to determine the fair value of a financial asset or financial liability with sufficient reliability, that fact should be disclosed together with information about the principal characteristics of the underlying financial instrument that are pertinent to its fair value.*	Paragraphs .52, .57, .67, and .78 deal with required disclosures. Paragraph .52 requires management to disclose information both about financial instruments it has formally recognized in the accounts and about those it has not recognized in the accounts. Such footnote disclosure for unrecognized financial instruments, when combined with disclosures for those financial instruments that have been booked, are intended—at least in the eyes of the AcSB—to help users gain some insight into "the timing and certainty of future cash flows." But, as may be seen from the wording of this paragraph, considerable scope exists for interpretation (e.g.: What should be included in a "class" of financial liability? What is meant by the "nature" of a financial liability? etc.). But, in spite of some shortcomings, the disclosures required by these four paragraphs are potentially important and therefore useful.
Hedges of Anticipated Future Transactions *.92 When an entity has accounted for a financial instrument as a hedge of risks associated with anticipated future transactions, it should disclose:* *(a) a description of the anticipated transactions, including the period of time until they are expected to occur;* *(b) a description of the hedging instruments; and* *(c) the amount of any deferred or unrecognized gain or loss and the expected timing of recognition as income or expense.*	Management use of financial instruments for hedging purposes has become so pervasive that accounting standards are crucial. Although Section 3860 doesn't deal with many important issues in this area (e.g., When does a hedge-type arrangement qualify for hedge accounting, or deferral of gains and losses?), the disclosures required in this paragraph are important for users' understanding of a company's risk management policies and practices.

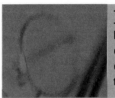

Loss Contingencies

A **loss contingency** occurs when there is an event that raises the possibility of future loss. These contingencies arise from factors like litigation, industrial accidents, debt guarantees, and product warranties. For financial reporting purposes, two questions must be asked: (1) When do such contingencies need to be measured and recognized in the financial statements? and (2) Under what circumstances do these contingencies need to be disclosed in footnotes, even when no liability is recorded on the balance sheet itself?

Measuring and Recognizing Loss Contingencies

The rules for measuring and recognizing loss contingencies in the financial statements are similar to the rules governing revenue recognition. According to GAAP, a loss contingency shall be accrued by a charge to income if *both* of the following conditions are met:

1. It is *likely* that a future event will confirm that an asset has been impaired or a liability has been incurred at the date of the financial statements.
2. The amount of loss can be *reasonably estimated*.[12]

The AcSB has established a range (in Section 3290.06) representing the likelihood of losses occurring, which is depicted in Figure 11.11. Notice that the two loss contingency recognition conditions correspond to the two income recognition conditions—"critical event" and "measurability"—discussed in Chapter 2. Specifically, the critical event for loss recognition is that it is likely a loss has or will occur; similarly, the measurability criterion corresponds closely to how well the loss can be estimated. In this sense, the criteria that trigger income and loss recognition are roughly parallel. For certain categories of events, applying the loss contingency rules has become routine. One example of a routine loss contingency is the expense for **estimated uncollectible receivables** described in Chapter 8. Uncollectibles are a normal cost of business when companies sell goods and services on credit, but the amount of the uncollectible loss is unknown at the time of sale. Since some loss is probable, and since the amount can be estimated, an expense (estimated loss) is recorded in the same period as that in which the sale occurs.

FIGURE 11.11
MEASURE OF UNCERTAINTY FOR LOSS CONTINGENCIES

Note: The AcSB also acknowledges that there may be instances in which it is *not possible* to determine the chance of occurrence of a future event.

In other areas, the issue of whether to recognize a loss contingency is highly subjective and complicated by the fact that recognizing and disclosing the loss could itself cause further harm. Consider a company that is being sued for actions that allegedly harmed others.

> *ABC Corporation manufactures a wide range of chemical food additives sold to numerous food processors throughout the country. Due to a serious production error, a highly toxic batch of a flavour enhancer was produced by ABC and sold in October 2000. Thousands of consumers were made seriously ill; some died. A class action lawsuit seeking $10 billion in damages has been filed.*

The ABC Corporation scenario illustrates a setting in which a straightforward application of the loss contingency rules could prove harmful to the company. Let's say ABC's management was indeed negligent and expects to negotiate an out-of-court settlement that is not less than $2 billion. If ABC accrued a charge for even this minimum expected payout, its negotiating position could be seriously weakened by a disclosure to the plaintiffs that it is prepared to pay at least $2 billion. Because the plaintiffs might be willing to settle for less than $2 billion, candid disclosure of the minimum estimated loss by ABC could raise the ultimate loss payout. Companies like ABC have strong incentives to either (1) accrue a loss that is significantly *smaller* than the real estimated loss or (2) disclose that while a loss may have occurred, its amount is not yet measurable. Consequently, the rules for loss contingencies arising from litigation are difficult to enforce. ***Statement readers must be aware of the potential understatement of litigation losses and liabilities.***

Loss Contingency Disclosures

When a loss contingency has been accrued, companies also frequently disclose separately other information regarding the loss in footnotes to the financial statements. Section 3290 requires this disclosure when a failure to provide additional supplemental data could lead to misleading inferences.

Loss contingency disclosures are also sometimes made even when no loss has been recognized in the income statement itself. For example, if the loss probability is not determinable, no loss accrual needs to be made in the financial statements. ***Nevertheless, footnote disclosure of loss contingencies is necessary.*** Furthermore, even contingencies arising from remote possibilities must be disclosed in certain circumstances, such as when one company guarantees another company's debt—that is, it agrees to repay the loan if the borrower cannot.

Summary

An astounding variety of financial instruments, derivatives, and nontraditional financing arrangements are now used to fund corporate activities and to manage risk. Statement readers face a daunting task when trying to fully grasp the economic implications of some financial innovations. Off-balance-sheet obligations and loss contingencies are difficult to evaluate because the information needed is often not disclosed. Derivatives—whether used for hedging or speculation—are problematic because of both their complexity and the evolving nature of GAAP.

For many companies, however, the single most important long-term obligation is still traditional debt financing. GAAP in this area are quite clear. Noncurrent monetary liabilities are initially recorded at the discounted present value of the contractual cash flows—that is, the issue price. The effective interest method or the straight-line method is then used to compute interest expense and net carrying value each period. Interest rate changes in the market occurring after the debt has been issued are ignored.

GAAP accounting for long-term debt makes it possible to "manage" reported income statement and balance sheet numbers. The opportunity to do so comes from the difference between debt book value and market value when interest rates have changed. The incentives for "managing" income statement and balance sheet numbers may be related to debt covenants, compensation, regulation, or just the desire to paint a favourable picture of a company's performance and health.

Extinguishment gains and losses from early debt retirement and swaps—and those generated by similar transactions—require careful scrutiny. Statement readers need to know whether real economic benefits for the company and its shareholders are produced or if such gains or losses are just window dressing.

Self-Study Problem: Mallard Corporation

Mallard Corporation constructs and operates private waterfowl hunting facilities throughout Western Canada. On July 1, 2002, the company issued $5 million of par value ten-year bonds to finance construction of a guest lodge and shelters at its newest site. The bonds pay interest semiannually (on December 31 and June 30) at an annual rate of 8% and are callable by Mallard at 102% of par value. The bonds were issued at a price that yields 10% annually to maturity.

1. Compute the issue price of the bonds.

The bond cash flows include a semiannual interest payment of $200,000 (or $5 million at 4%) plus the principal payment of $5 million at maturity. With an effective (market) interest rate of 5% for each six-month interval, the present value factors are:

20-period ordinary annuity at 5% = 12.46221

20-period single payment = 0.37689

Multiplying each factor by the corresponding cash flow gives the issue price as:

$$\begin{aligned} \$\ \ 200,000 \times 12.46221 &= \$2,492,442 \\ + \$5,000,000 \times \ \ 0.37689 &= \underline{1,884,450} \\ &\ \ \ \$4,376,892 \end{aligned}$$

The bond was thus issued at a discount of $623,108 (or $5,000,000 − $4,376,892).

2. Compute the amount of interest expense on the bonds for 2002. Mallard Corporation uses the effective interest method for amortizing bond discounts and premiums.

Because the bond was issued on July 1, 2002, only six months of interest needs to be recorded for the year. Interest expense is computed at the effective interest rate of 5%. This rate is multiplied by the amount borrowed (opening book value) to get interest expense:

$$\$4,376,892 \times 5\% = \$218,845 \text{ (rounded)}$$

Computed interest expense is more than the required cash payment of $200,000. The $18,845 difference represents amortization of the bond discount—that is, an increase to the book value of the bond. The year-end financial statements of Mallard Corporation would show the bond at $4,395,737 ($4,376,892 + $18,845).

3. Mallard uses the indirect method of computing cash flows from operations on its cash flow statement. Indicate how much will be added to (or subtracted from) the 2002 accrual basis net income figure that is related to the bonds to obtain cash flows from operations.

The accrual income figure contains interest expense of $218,845, but the cash interest payment is only $200,000. The additional interest expense of $18,845 does not represent an operating cash outflow for the year, and so it is added back to net income to arrive at cash flows from operations. Notice that this amount equals the discount amortization for the year.

4. Assume that the market yield on the bonds had fallen to 9% by July 1, 2004, and that Mallard decided to retire the debt on that date either by purchasing the bonds on the open market or by exercising its 102% call option. Which method of debt retirement is the least expensive for Mallard?

Under the terms of the call option, Mallard can retire the debt by paying bondholders 102% of par value or:

$$\$5,000,000 \times 102\% = \$5,100,000$$

However, the current market value of the bonds at an annual yield of 9% is:

$$\$\ 200,000 \times 11.23402 = \$2,246,804$$
$$+ \$5,000,000 \times\ 0.49447 = \underline{\$2,472,350}$$
$$\underline{\underline{\$4,719,154}}$$

The open-market purchase is the less expensive way for Mallard to retire its debt. (Notice that the present value factors used to compute the current market price are based on a 4.5% semiannual yield and 16 six-month periods to July 1, 2012.)

5. **Produce the journal entry that Mallard Corporation would record on July 1, 2004 when it retired the bonds through an open market purchase.**

Assume that all interest expense and cash interest payments have been recorded. Then the book value of the bonds on July 1, 2004, would be $4,458,115, as shown in the following amortization table:

	Period (Six-Month Interval)	Liability at Start of Period (1)	Effective Interest: 5% per Period (2)	Coupon Rate: 4% of Par (3)	Increase in Recorded Book Value (4)	Liability at End of Period (5)
7/1/02	0					$4,376,892
1/1/03	1	$4,376,892	$218,845	$200,000	$18,845	$4,395,737
7/1/03	2	$4,395,737	$219,787	$200,000	$19,787	$4,415,524
1/1/04	3	$4,415,524	$220,776	$200,000	$20,776	$4,436,300
7/1/04	4	$4,436,300	$221,815	$200,000	$21,815	$4,458,115

In the light of our previous calculation, we find that Mallard would pay $4,719,154 to retire the bonds on that date, so the entry would be:

DR	Bonds payable	$5,000,000	
DR	Loss on retirement	261,039	
CR	Discount on bonds		$ 541,885
CR	Cash		4,719,154

where $541,885 represents the remaining (unamortized) balance of the original issue discount ($5,000,000 face value minus $4,458,115 book value).

For more Exercises, Problems/Discussion Questions, and Cases, visit the Companion Website for this textbook at **www.pearsoned.ca/revsine**.

Exercises

E11-1 Debt-for-equity swap

On January 1, 2001, Tusk Corporation issued $100 million of 10% coupon bonds at par value. Interest is paid semiannually on June 30 and December 31 of each year. The bonds mature in ten years. On January 1, 2004, the market yield on Tusk bonds is 14%.

Required:

1. What is the market value of the bonds on January 1, 2004?
2. Suppose Tusk retired the bonds on January 1, 2004, by exchanging common shares of equal value with bondholders. What journal entry would Tusk record to retire the bonds?

E11-2 Zero coupon bonds

Zero coupon bonds pay no interest—the only cash investors receive is the lump-sum principal payment at maturity. On January 1, 2002, The Ledge Inc. issued $250 million of zero coupon bonds at a market yield rate of 12%. The bonds mature in 20 years.

Required:

1. What was the January 1, 2002, issue price of these zero coupon bonds?
2. How much interest expense will The Ledge record on these bonds in 2002?

E11-3 Floating rate debt

On January 1, 2002, 3Way Energy issued $200 million of 15-year floating rate debentures at par value. The debentures pay interest on June 30 and December 31 of each year. The floating interest rate is set equal to "LIBOR plus 6%" on January 1 of each year. The LIBOR was 6% when the bonds were issued and 8% on January 1, 2003.

Required:

1. How much cash interest did 3Way Energy pay on the debentures in 2002? How much will it pay in 2003?
2. How much interest expense did the company record on the debentures in 2002? How much will it record in 2003?

E11-4 Incentives for early debt retirement

On January 1, 2002, Roland Inc. issued $125 million of 8% coupon bonds at par. The bonds pay interest semiannually on June 30 and December 31 of each year, and they mature in 15 years. On December 31, 2003 (just before the next interest payment is made), the bonds are trading at a market yield of 12% plus accrued interest.

Required:

1. Suppose Roland Inc. repurchased the entire $125 million bonds for cash at the market price on December 31, 2003. Using a 40% corporate tax rate, how much of a gain or loss would the company record on this transaction?
2. Why might the company want to retire the debt early?

E11-5 Off-balance-sheet debt

Wood Company and Willie Inc. form a joint venture—Woodly Partners—to manufacture and distribute agricultural pesticides. Wood and Willie each contribute $20 million cash and receive 50% of Woodly's common shares. Woodly then borrows $200 million from a consortium of banks and uses the money to build its manufacturing and distribution facilities. The loan is made on December 31, 2002, and is fully guaranteed by both Wood and Willie.

Required:

Wood Company's accountant suggests that since the $200 million was borrowed by Woodly and *not* Wood, none of it should be shown on Wood's balance sheet. What is your opinion?

E11-6 Non-interest-bearing loan

McClelland Corporation agreed to purchase some landscaping equipment from Agri-Products for a cash price of $500,000. Before accepting delivery of the equipment, McClelland learned that the same equipment could be purchased from another dealer for $460,000. To avoid losing the sale, Agri-Products has offered McClelland a "no interest" payment plan—McClelland would pay $100,000 at delivery, $200,000 one year later, and the final $200,000 in two years.

Required:

1. McClelland would usually pay annual interest of 9% on a loan of this type. What is the present value of the Agri-Products loan at the delivery date?
2. What journal entry would McClelland make if it accepts the deal and buys from Agri-Products?
3. What should McClelland do?

E11-7 Understanding GAAP hedges

Required:

1. Which of the following qualifies as a hedged item?
   a. A company's work-in-process inventory of unfinished washers, dryers, and refrigerators.
   b. Credit card receivables at Sears Canada Inc.
   c. Bushels of corn owned by the Farmers' Cooperative.
   d. Salaries payable to employees of Ford Canada.
   e. A three-year note issued by General Motors Canada and payable in Canadian dollars.
   f. A three-year note issued by DaimlerChrysler Canada and payable in Euros.

2. Which of the following qualifies as a hedging instrument?

   a. An electricity futures contract purchased by Alliant Energy, an electric power company.
   b. A crop insurance contract purchased by Farmers' Cooperative that pays co-op for crop losses from drought or flood.
   c. An option to buy shares of common stock in Ford Canada.
   d. An option to sell shares of common stock in General Motors Canada.
   e. A four-year lease for office space in downtown Toronto.

3. Which of the following qualifies as an eligible risk for hedge accounting?

   a. Alliant Energy's risk that summer demand for electricity may exceed the company's power generating capacity.

   b. Ford Canada's risk that not enough steel will be available in six months when the company must purchase steel to produce a new sports utility vehicle.

   c. The risk to American Express that its members won't pay their credit card bills.

   d. The risk to Farmers' Cooperative that corn mold will destroy its inventory of corn held in silos for sale next year.

   e. The possibility of changes in the exchange rate of U.S. dollars for Mexican pesos for the Coca-Cola Company, which has a major foreign investment in Mexico.

Problems/Discussion Questions

P11-1 Put options as investments

On March 1, 2001, Kenton Company bought put option contracts for 500 shares of Rugolo Manufacturing common stock. The contracts cost $300, expire in 90 days, and have an exercise price of $50 per share. The market price of Rugolo's stock that day was also $50 a share. On March 31, 2001, Rugolo shares were trading at $52 a share and the fair value of the option contracts was $200—meaning that Kenton could buy the identical $50 strike price contracts on March 31 for $200. On April 30, 2001, the market price of Rugolo stock was $46 a share and the fair value of the options contracts was $2,100.

Required:

1. Prepare the journal entry to record Kenton's purchase of put option contracts on March 1, 2001.

2. Prepare the journal entry to record the change in fair value of the option contracts on March 31, 2001.

3. Prepare the journal entry to record the change in fair value of the option contracts on April 30, 2001.

4. Why are the option contracts worth so much more on April 30 ($2,100) than they were worth on March 31 ($200)?

5. What entry would Kenton make to record exercising the options on May 15, 2001, when Rugolo's shares were trading at $42?

6. Suppose instead that Kenton allowed the option contracts to expire on May 15, 2001, without exercising them. What entry would Kenton then make?

P11-2 Hedging

The following excerpts were taken from the 1996 annual report of Quaker Oats Company (an American corporation):

> **Balance Sheet Hedges.** The Company utilizes net investment hedges and foreign currency swaps to offset foreign currency gains and losses which are recognized in the balance sheet.

> **Net Investment Hedges.** The Company's significant net hedges and the related foreign currency net investments and net exposures as of December 31, 1996 were as follows:

QUAKER OATS
COMPANY
www.quakeroats.
com

(US$ in millions)	Net Investment	Net Hedge	Net Exposure
Currency:			
British pound	$23.2	$ 5.2	$18.0
Canadian dollar	$26.5	$ 9.5	$17.0
Dutch guilder	$19.8	$18.5	$ 1.3
German mark	$20.1	$16.3	$ 3.8
Italian lira	$24.5	$ 4.4	$20.1

The Company actively monitors its net exposures and adjusts the hedge amounts as appropriate. The net hedges are stated above on an after-tax basis. The net exposures are subject to gain or loss if foreign currency exchange rates fluctuate.

Foreign Currency Swaps. In 1988 the Company swapped [US]$15.0 million of long-term debt for 27.9 million in deutsche mark (DM) denominated long-term debt, effectively hedging part of the German net investment.... Due to the sale of the European pet food business in 1995, the net investment in Germany was reduced to the point where the DM swap was no longer effective as a net investment hedge, requiring any subsequent revaluation adjustments to be charged or credited to the consolidated income statement. To offset this charge or credit, the Company entered into a foreign exchange forward contract and the net effect on the consolidated income statements for 1996 and 1995 was not material....

Income Statement Hedges. The Company uses foreign currency options and forwards, commodity options and futures, and interest rate hedges to offset gains and losses which are recognized in the income statement.

Commodity Options and Futures. The Company uses commodity options and futures contracts to reduce its exposure to commodity price changes. The Company regularly hedges purchases of oats, corn, corn sweetener, wheat, coffee beans, and orange juice concentrate. Of the [US]$2.81 billion in cost of goods sold, approximately [US]$275 million to [US]$325 million is in commodities that may be hedged. The Company's strategy is typically to hedge certain production requirements for various periods up to 12 months. As of December 31, 1996 and 1995, approximately 32% and 54%, respectively, of hedgeable production requirements for the next 12 months were hedged. ...

Interest Rate Hedges. The Company actively monitors its interest rate exposure. In 1995 the Company entered into interest rate swap agreements with a notional value of [US]$150.0 million. The swap agreements were used to hedge fixed interest rate risk related to anticipated issuance of long-term debt. The swap agreements were subsequently terminated at a cost of [US]$11.9 million as long-term debt was issued. Included in the consolidated balance sheets as of December 31, 1996 and 1995 were [US]$8.9 million and [US]$10.8 million, respectively, of prepaid interest expense as settlement of all the interest rate swap agreements. Prepaid interest expense is recognized in the consolidated income statements on a straight-line basis over the original term of the swap agreements.... In 1994 the Company entered into interest rate cap agreements with a notional value of [US]$600.0 million to hedge floating interest rate risk. ...

Required:

1. What is a foreign exchange forward contract, and how can it be used to hedge a company's foreign currency exposure?
2. Why does Quaker hedge only 22% of its exposure to the British pound while hedging 93% of its exposure to the Dutch guilder?
3. What did Quaker accomplish by swapping US$15.0 million of its long-term debt for 27.9 million in deutsche mark (DM) denominated long-term debt?
4. Why was the DM swap "no longer effective" after Quaker sold its European pet food business?

5. What are commodity options and futures contracts, and how do they reduce Quaker's exposure to commodity price changes?

6. What is an interest rate swap, and how can it reduce a company's exposure to interest rate risk?

7. How does "prepaid interest" arise on a swap transaction, and why does Quaker Oats amortize it on a straight-line basis over the life of the swap?

8. What is an interest rate cap, and how is it used to reduce a company's exposure to interest rate changes?

P11-3 Working backward from an amortization table

Clovis Company recently issued $500,000 (face value) bonds to finance a new construction project. The company's chief accountant prepared the following bond amortization schedule:

Date	Interest Expense	Semiannual Payment	Premium Amortization	Net Liability
7/1/03				$540,554
12/31/03	$21,622	$25,000	($3,378)	537,176
6/30/04	21,487	25,000	(3,513)	533,663
12/31/04	21,347	25,000	(3,653)	530,010
6/30/05	21,200	25,000	(3,800)	526,210
12/31/05	21,048	25,000	(3,952)	522,258
6/30/06	20,890	25,000	(4,110)	518,148
12/31/06	20,726	25,000	(4,274)	513,874
6/30/07	20,555	25,000	(4,445)	509,429
12/31/07	20,377	25,000	(4,623)	504,806
6/30/08	20,194	25,000	(4,806)	500,000

Required:

1. Compute the discount or premium on the sale of the bonds, the semiannual coupon interest rate, and the semiannual effective interest rate.

2. The company's vice-president of finance wants any discount (or premium) at issuance of the bonds to be recorded immediately as a loss (or gain) at the issue date. Do you agree with this approach? Why or why not?

3. On December 31, 2005, the net carrying value of the bonds is $522,258. In present value terms, what does this amount represent?

4. Suppose market interest rates were 6% semiannually on January 1, 2006, or 12.36% annually. What is the market price of the bond on that date? Is the company better off or worse off because of the interest rate change? Explain.

P11-4 Zero coupon bonds

The following information was taken from the financial statements of ALZA Corporation.

ALZA CORPORATION
www.alza.com

Note 2: Debt Obligations and Other Liabilities

In December 1990, ALZA completed a public offering of zero coupon convertible subordinated debentures. The 20-year debentures, due December 2010, will have a principal amount at maturity of [US]$862.5 million. The debentures were issued at a price of [US]$229.34 per $1,000 principal amount at maturity, resulting in an initial obligation to ALZA of [US]$197.806 million. The yield to maturity is 7% per annum, computed on a semiannual basis, and the notes have no periodic interest payments. Each debenture is convertible, at the option of the holder, into 4.326 shares of ALZA Class A Common Stock. The debentures will be purchased by ALZA, at the option of the holder, on December 21, 1995, December 21, 2000, or December 21, 2005, at purchase prices equal to the issue price plus accreted original issue discount to such purchase date. ALZA, at its option, may elect to deliver either stock or cash in the event of any conversion or purchase of the debentures. The debentures are listed for trading on the American Stock Exchange. In connection with the offering, ALZA incurred underwriting fees and other costs of [US]$5.934 million, which are included in other assets and are being amortized over the term of the debentures.

Required:

1. ALZA issued zero coupon debentures with a total maturity value of US$862.5 million at a total price of US$197.806 million. The company had debt issuance costs of US$5.934 million. Show how the issue price was calculated.
2. If you purchased these debentures at the issue date, what is your annualized expected return?
3. Reproduce the journal entries on ALZA's book, for these debentures over the 1990–93 period. For each **cash entry**, identify whether the cash increase or decrease represents an operating, investing, or financing activity. Do you agree with ALZA's classification of these cash entries in the cash flow statement shown below?
4. ALZA had debt issuance costs of US$5.934 million dollars. According to FASB *Concept Statement No. 6* ("Elements of Financial Statements"), "[d]ebt issuance cost in effect reduces the proceeds of borrowing and increases the effective interest rate and thus may be accounted for the same as debt discount" (para. 237). Does the way in which ALZA accounts for debt issue costs achieve this result?

ALZA Corporation				
Consolidated Statement of Cash Flows Years Ended December 31				
(US$ in thousands)	1993	1992	1991	1990
Cash flows from operating activities				
Net income (loss)	$ 45,612	$72,170	$(62,076)	$ 24,654
Noncash adjustments				
Depreciation and amortization		(Amounts not reproduced)		
Interest on 7½% zero coupon convertible subordinated debentures	14,912	15,746	15,002	412
...				
Total adjustments	30,623	24,395	81,667	(1,395)
Net cash provided by operating activities	76,235	96,565	19,591	23,259
Cash flows from financing activities				
Redemption of 7½% zero coupon convertible subordinated debentures	(243,878)	—	—	$191,872

P11-5 Hedging a Planned Sale (TL)

Newton Grains plans to sell 100,000 bushels of corn from its current inventory in March 2002. The company paid $1 million for the corn during the fall 2001 harvest season. On October 1, 2001, Newton writes a forward contract to sell 100,000 bushels of corn on March 15, 2002, for $1,100,000. The forward contract has zero value at inception. On December 31, 2001, the March forward price for corn is $1,050,000 and the forward contract has a fair value of $95,000. On March 15, 2002, Newton sells the corn for $1,075,000 and settles the forward contract (now valued at $25,000).

Required:

1. Why did Newton hedge its planned sale of corn? Was it a good idea to do so?
2. Newton designates the forward contract as a cash flow hedge of its exposure to corn price fluctuations. What journal entries are made when the forward contract is signed on October 1, 2001?
3. What journal entries are made on December 31, 2001?
4. What journal entries are made on March 15, 2002, when the forward contract is settled and Newton sells the corn?
5. How would your original journal entries change if the forward contract covered only 50,000 bushels of corn? (Contract fair values would then have been $47,500 on December 31, 2001, and $12,500 on March 15, 2002.)

P11-6 Hedge effectiveness

Recall the Rombaurer Metals example described in the chapter: On October 5, 2001, Rombaurer has 10 million pounds of copper inventory on hand at an average cost of $0.65 a pound. The spot price for copper is $0.90 a pound. Instead of selling copper now, Rombaurer decides to hold on to the inventory until February 2002 when management believes the price will return to a normal level of $0.95 a pound. To hedge its position, Rombaurer sells futures contracts at $0.95 for February delivery. Spot and futures prices over the next several months are as follows:

COMEX Copper Prices

	Spot Price	February 2002 Futures Price
October 5, 2001	$0.90	$0.95
December 31, 2001	0.85	0.91
February 26, 2002	0.94	0.94

On February 26, 2002, Rombaurer sells its copper on the spot market for $0.94 a pound and cancels the futures contracts.

The chapter described how "hedge accounting" rules are used when Rombaurer hedges its entire 10 million pounds of copper inventory.

Required:

1. Suppose Rombaurer sells futures contracts for only 5 million pounds of copper. (Management had decided that it is prudent to only hedge half of the company's economic exposure.) The margin requirement on these contracts is $140,000. Because the futures contracts are now "ineffective" in hedging the company's entire fair value exposure to copper price fluctuations, Rombaurer cannot use "hedge accounting." Prepare all journal entries needed to account for the futures contracts and sale of copper from October 5, 2001, through February 26, 2002.

2. Now assume that Rombaurer designates these futures contracts as a "fully effective" hedge of its risk exposure for 5 million pounds of copper inventory. (The remaining 5 million pounds of inventory is not being hedged.) Rombaurer can now use "hedge accounting" for the futures contracts. Prepare all journal entries needed to account for the futures contracts and sale of copper from October 5, 2001, through February 26, 2002.

3. What impact does changing the definition of the hedged item (10 million pounds of copper inventory versus 5 million pounds) have on the company's financial statements for 2001 and 2002?

Cases

C11-1 When the counterparty won't: Accounting for the Royal Bank's Enron/Rabobank swap

On June 23, 2002, the Royal Bank of Canada issued the following news release:

Royal Bank of Canada today issued the following statement in connection with a financial transaction involving the Dutch bank, Cooperatieve Centrale Raiffeisen-Boerenleenbank B.A. (Rabobank).

Late on the afternoon of June 21, we learned that Rabobank had initiated legal proceedings against Royal Bank of Canada in state court in New York. The "complaint" document filed by Rabobank refers to a January 2001 total return swap transaction—a sophisticated derivative frequently used by large international banks to hedge credit risk.

Under the total return swap, Rabobank in effect assumed responsibility for making all payments owed to RBC by Heracles Trust under a US$517 million loan agreement. Heracles Trust owns an interest in Aeneas LLC, a company affiliated with Enron Corporation. Rabobank was actively involved in the negotiation and structuring of the transaction.

Until last Friday, Rabobank had fulfilled its contractual obligations related to the transaction and we expected that Rabobank would continue to act in good faith with respect to the terms of the transaction which include a full and final payment from Rabobank to RBC of US$517 million on June 28, 2002.

We have reviewed the document filed with the New York court with our lawyers and believe the claim to be without merit. It consists of nothing more than innuendo and baseless speculation that inaccurately attempts to portray Rabobank, a large sophisticated international bank with a highly experienced team of derivative specialists and lawyers, as an unwitting victim of circumstance. We find this to be particularly astonishing given Rabobank's involvement in at least one other Enron related off-balance sheet transaction.

The claims also represent a highly irresponsible and unwarranted attack on the reputation of RBC in an attempt to avoid meeting a clear financial obligation. We intend to vigorously defend against Rabobank's claims and to take action against this spurious and totally unfounded attack on our reputation. We will seek through the courts to require Rabobank to meet its financial obligation to Royal Bank of Canada.

Source: Canada NewsWire, June 23, 2002. © RBC Financial Group.

The *Toronto Star* reported the incident described in the bank's news release, claiming that the bank looked "ridiculous."

Outrage premature at Royal Bank, by David Olive

IF CANADA'S biggest bank had kept a lid on its righteous indignation for just a few days last week, it would not look so ridiculous now.

Early this week, it was revealed that a top Dutch lender, Rabobank, had balked at honouring a commitment to pay Royal Bank of Canada the tidy sum of $517 million (U.S.) due last Friday.

That sum originated as an RBC loan in November, 2000, to one of the notorious offshore trusts of Enron Corp., the now collapsed Houston energy trader. Hedging its bet, RBC had promptly traded it in a so-called swap transaction with Rabobank.

Rabobank has claimed that it should not have to pay the money because RBC failed to disclose to the Dutch its knowledge that Enron's management was "corrupt" and was "looting Enron for personal benefit and that Enron's reported financial results were a house of cards waiting to collapse."

Rabobank figures RBC must have gleaned this knowledge from three of its own employees, a trio of hotshot British investment bankers hired by RBC in the spring of 2000. Rabobank claimed this week that those dealmakers had participated in "corrupt insider transactions" with Enron at their previous employer, Britain's National Westminster Bank.

As it happens, Gary Mulgrew, Giles Darby and David Bermingham structured the complicated swap now in dispute between RBC and Rabobank. Then, last November, less than two years after they were hired at RBC, Mulgrew & Co. quietly left the bank just as Enron was filing for deadbeat status as the biggest bankruptcy in history. At the time, a coy RBC said only that the trio was leaving for the usual reason of pursuing other career interests. This week, an anonymous source was feeding the Toronto media a story about how the Brits had been fine upstanding gentlemen who made RBC gobs of money, but the optics of the Enron implosion made their continued employment on these shores untenable.

RBC lost no time last Monday in dismissing Rabobank's allegations as a load of horse poop from a sore loser, calling the Dutch bank a "sophisticated" player in no position to depict itself as a "duped party."

"We were particularly surprised at the hyperbole" in Rabobank's accusations, Chuck Winograd said on Monday. The highly regarded CEO of RBC Dominion Securities Inc., an arm of Royal Bank, managed to sound both hurt and outraged.

"We were surprised at being tarred with the Enron brush," said Winograd. "There was absolutely no reason to have that happen."

On the face of it, there's every reason for it, since RBC and Rabobank, directly or otherwise, were among the many enablers of Enron within the banking fraternity. U.S. federal prosecutors, who are widening their investigation of Enron by leaps and bounds, have said this week that they are now probing the activities of individual bankers at Barclays PLC, J.P. Morgan Chase & Co. and other banks to determine if they illegally gained from their deals with Enron.

Had Winograd only held his tongue until last Thursday, he might not have been in such a rush to claim the high moral ground. Because on that day, the U.S. justice department appeared to confirm at least part of Rabobank's story when it filed a criminal complaint against Mulgrew & Co., accusing them of defrauding NatWest of $7.3 million (U.S.) in Enron-related deals before they decamped for their short stint at RBC.

The feds' evidence includes an e-mail message in which Bermingham describes the trio's effort to lure Enron's then chief financial officer, Andy Fastow, into a deal that would improperly enrich all four men. "I will be the first to be delighted if [Fastow] has found a way to lock it in and steal a large portion himself," wrote Bermingham. "We should be able to appeal to his greed."

So what did RBC know about its drive-by dealmakers? Or more to the point, what did it go to the trouble of knowing? At Drexel Burnham Lambert Inc., General Electric Co., Barings PLC and most recently Allied Irish Banks, all that was known of the poorly supervised Mike Milken, Joseph Lett, Nick Leeson and John Rusnak, respectively, was that they were making a pile of money for their employers, until they weren't.

Even if financial institutions choose to waive the usual due diligence and drug tests for star performers, inviting suspicions that they occasionally defer to some kind of temp agency for go-getters with bent morals, the conduct of Mulgrew & Co. would still appear to be the responsibility of RBC for the duration of their employment.

With that in mind, RBC might have informed itself of the trio's close ties to Fastow, the prime contractor of Enron's thousands of off-the-books projects. In the process, RBC might have also made itself aware that the trio accepted holiday junkets from Enron and in turn hosted Enronites at Treasures, a Houston-area strip club. On grounds of conflict of interest if not bad taste, Mulgrew & Co. certainly bore watching.

We've been treated lately to sermons on the need for a moral rethink by bankers in both Canada and the United States—a sentiment that Winograd traded on last Monday by suggesting that he was simply offended that his company or any Canadians could be mixed up in the odious Enron machinations.

In April, John Hunkin said the greed mentality of the lamented stock market boom was "pretty well everything you need to encourage aggressive, and sometimes unethical, behaviour by a company's management."

Tell us about it, John. Hunkin's firm, Canadian Imperial Bank of Commerce, helped Enron along by investing $115.2 million (U.S.) in an Enron online video distribution scheme with Blockbuster that never flew, but that enabled Enron's then-CEO Jeff Skilling to report a "profit" that consisted almost entirely of CIBC's grubstake.

And it was CIBC that got the unlucky Global Crossing Ltd. off the ground, and milked it for millions of dollars in underwriting and other fees. In its many, possibly conflicting roles, CIBC also took a sizeable equity stake in the fledgling company, on which it booked a staggering $2.6 billion (Canadian) profit. Less happily, it also lent money to the firm, which it can only hope to recover now that the scandal-ridden Global Crossing has come thudding back to earth.

The blame game is well underway, with accounting firms, corporate lawyers, regulators, bankers and securities analysts all pointing at each other, and at ethically deficient CEOs with whom they collaborated, as the prime suspects in the biggest failure of capitalism since 1929.

Given that many revelations are yet to come, it would perhaps be wise for players in this drama to keep silent until spoken to by someone wielding a subpoena.

Source: Toronto Star, June 29, 2002. Reprinted with permission of Torstar Syndication Services.

Required:

ROYAL BANK OF
CANADA
www.royalbank.
com

Using the Royal Bank of Canada's 2001 audited financial statements, any recent financial releases involving this incident, *AcG-13*, and *EIC-128*, answer the following questions:

1. How did the Royal Bank account for the Rabobank total return swap transaction?
2. If *AcG-13* and *EIC-128* had been in effect at the time of the original swap arrangement, would the bank have accounted differently?
3. Was the swap transaction with Rabobank a "hedge"? Explain.
4. What, in your opinion, are the bank's financial reporting responsibilities as of June 21, 2002?
5. Critically evaluate the bank's news release.

C11-2 Enron accounting magic: How to create operating cash flow and cause debt to disappear in a series of incredibly egregious transactions!

On July 23, 2002, the U.S. Senate Permanent Subcommittee on Investigations held the first of two hearings on "The Role of the Financial Institutions in Enron's Collapse." Various materials from that hearing, as listed below, are located at the Companion Website for this textbook at **www.pearsoned.ca/revsine**:

- Statement of Senator Carl Levin
- Statement of Senator Susan M. Collins
- Testimony of Chief Investigator Robert Roach (including Appendices A to E)

The main focus of these hearings was a type of transaction that Enron and major financial institutions entered into called a "prepay," and which Senator Levin characterized as "an accounting sham" intended "to disguise debt."

Required:

Review the material provided on the Companion Website, and answer the following questions.

1. Explain in your own words the concepts of *substance over form* and *representational faithfulness* (see Section 1000 of the *CICA Handbook*).
2. Explain why the investigators concluded that Mahonia and Delta were not independent entities. Why was this important?
3. Explain why it was necessary for accounting purposes for Mahonia and the other entities to be independent in order for the cash flows to be classified as 'operating' from Enron's perspective.
4. Since Enron's total cash flow in each year was apparently unaffected by the accounting, what was the issue?
5. Explain how "hedging" was involved, if at all.
6. Explain how the "Chase" and the "Citibank" deals differed.
7. Explain the economic motivation for Enron to arrange their version of "prepays."
8. Explain the incentives for the financial institutions to support what the investigator's report calls "Enron's Accounting Deceptions."
9. Explain each of the four steps in the Mahonia prepays.
10. Why, in your opinion, was a "financially settled commodity swap" a necessary part of the Mahonia prepays?
11. Explain each step of the Delta/Yosemite Trust prepays.
12. Assume the role of an Enron accountant, and write a memo to the investigative committee justifying Enron's accounting, including its treatment of debt.
13. Outline the ethical issues involved in the prepays, from the perspective of various stakeholders.
14. Was Enron just a giant, complex, financial accounting machine, insofar as the prepays were concerned? Discuss.

 Integrative Running Case Study
Bombardier on the Web

Access the Bombardier Inc. annual report on the Companion Website (**www.pearsoned. ca/revsine**).

Required:

1. Given the footnote information in the audited financial statements, estimate debt payments that the company must make over the next five years ending January 31, 2007.
2. Examine note 23 on pages 98–100 of the annual report. Prepare a 500-word memo to the board of directors explaining the significance of this note.

Endnotes

1. "Financial Statement Concepts," *CICA Handbook*, Section 1000.

2. "Reporting Gains and Losses from Extinguishment of Debt," *Statement of Financial Accounting Standards (SFAS) No. 4* (Stamford, CT: FASB, 1975). From Chapter 2, remember that for an event to qualify as an extraordinary item, the event must be both *unusual and infrequent*; but debt extinguishment is neither unusual nor infrequent.

3. J. R. Dietrich and J. W. Deitrick, "Bond Exchanges in the Airline Industry: Analyzing Public Disclosures," *The Accounting Review*, January 1985, pp. 109–26.

4. See J. R. Dietrich, "Effects of Early Bond Refundings: An Empirical Investigation of Security Returns," *Journal of Accounting and Economics*, April 1984, pp. 67–96; and W. B. Johnson, "Debt Refunding and Shareholder Wealth: The Price Effects of Debt-for-Debt Exchange Offer Announcements," *The Financial Review*, February 1988, pp. 1–23.

5. See R. Masulis, "The Impact of Capital Structure Changes on Firm Value: Some Estimates," *Journal of Finance*, March 1983, pp. 107–26. Interestingly, this same study found that share prices increase by 14% (on average) when firms announce their willingness to retire common shares in exchange for new debt.

6. J.R. Hand, "Did Firms Undertake Debt-Equity Swaps for an Accounting Paper Profit or True Financial Gain?" *Accounting Review*, October 1989, pp. 587–623.

7. We gratefully acknowledge the substantial contribution of Professor Thomas Linsmeier to the material in this section.

8. For an overview of the characteristics and uses of derivative securities, see S. A. Ross, R.W. Westerfield, and B. D. Jordan, *Fundamentals of Corporate Finance*, 2nd ed. (Homewood, IL: Irwin, 1993), Ch. 24; and C. W. Smithson, C. W. Smith, and D.S. Wilford, *Managing Financial Risk* (Homewood, IL: Irwin, 1995).

9. An interest rate "collar" may be part of the swap agreement as well—for example, the two parties could agree that the swap remains in force as long as the Bank of Canada rate is less than 8.5% and greater than 6%.

10. See *AcG–13* and the U.S.'s "Accounting for Derivative Instruments and Hedging Activities," *SFAS No. 133* (Norwalk, CT: FASB, 1998); "Accounting for Certain Derivative Instruments and Certain Hedging Activities," *SFAS No. 138* (Norwalk, CT: FASB, 2000). These statements are summarized and interpreted in the 540-page implementation guide *Accounting for Derivative Instruments and Hedging Activities* (Norwalk, CT: FASB, 2000).

11. See P.A. McKay and J. Niedzielski, "New Accounting Standard Gets Mixed Reviews," *Wall Street Journal*, October 23, 2000.

12. "Contingencies," *CICA Handbook*, Section 3290.

12

Financial Reporting for Leases

LEARNING OBJECTIVES
After studying this chapter, you should be able to:

1. Understand and explain the difference between capital and operating leases

2. Describe the incentives lessees have to keep leases off the balance sheet

3. Identify the criteria used to classify leases on the books of the lessee

4. Describe the treatment of executory costs, residual values, and other aspects of lease contracts

5. Describe the effects of capital versus operating lease treatment on lessees' financial statements.

6. Understand how analysts can adjust for distortions that arise from off-balance-sheet leases when comparing firms

7. Know that lessors also classify leases as capital or operating leases but that their reporting incentives are very different from lessees' reporting incentives

8. Understand the difference between sales-type, direct financing, and operating lease treatment by lessors and the criteria for choosing the accounting treatment

9. Show how the different lessor accounting treatments can affect income and net asset balances

10. Describe sale and leaseback arrangements and other special leasing situations

11. Understand how to use footnote disclosures to estimate the increase in assets and liabilities that would ensue if operating leases had been capitalized instead

A lease is a contract in which the owner of an asset (the **lessor**) conveys to another party (the **lessee**) the right to use a tangible asset. This right is granted in exchange for a fee (the **lease payment**) that is usually paid in installments. Legal title to the asset remains with the lessor. The duration of a lease may be short (e.g., a one-week car rental agreement) or long (a 20-year lease for a retail space in a shopping centre).

At its inception, a lease is called a **mutually unperformed contract.** This means that neither party to the lease arrangement has yet performed all of the duties called for in the contract. For example, the lessor has an obligation to provide the lessee with the right to use the asset for the entire duration of the lease; in exchange, the lessee has an obligation to pay the stipulated periodic fee to the lessor during the lease term.

Evolution of Lease Accounting

Section 3065 of the *CICA Handbook* spells out the current GAAP for leases. Before they were issued in the late 1970s, virtually all leases were accounted for using what is called the **operating lease approach.** Here, the accounting conforms to the legal structure of lease arrangements. Since lease contracts typically do not convey title, the asset remains on the books of the lessor. Furthermore, under the operating lease approach, the lessee did not immediately record as a liability the stream of future payments called for in the contract. No liability was recorded because the lessee was not legally obligated to make the payments until the lessor performed the duties specified in the contract. Because these were mutually unperformed (sometimes called **executory**) contracts, accounting entries were made over time in piecemeal fashion only as partial performance under the contract took place. *As each party performed its respective duties, that portion of the contract that had been performed was no longer considered executory and was accordingly recognized in the financial records.*

The following example illustrates the operating lease approach.

Crest Company owns a building with a book value of $200,000. This building is leased to Iris Company under a five-year lease for a monthly rental of $2,000, which is to be paid at the end of each month.

Upon signing the lease, Iris Company (the lessee) would make no entry on its books. Each month, as Crest performed its part of the agreement by making the premises available to Iris Company, Iris would accrue a liability, as follows:

DR	Rent expense	$2,000
	CR Lease liability	$2,000

Upon payment of the stipulated rental at the end of the month, Iris would make the following entry:[1]

DR	Lease liability	$2,000
	CR Cash	$2,000

Iris does not record any liability on its books for *future* rental payments—neither at the time of signing the lease nor afterwards. The reason is that these future rental payments are contingent upon future performance by Crest, the lessor. The stipulated payments do not become a liability to Iris under the operating lease approach until time passes and performance takes place. As each party to the mutually unperformed contract performs its duties specified in the contract, the "performed" portion is no longer considered executory. The stipulated rental for the period over which performance took place is accrued as a liability; the liability is reduced when payment is made.

Similarly, no entry would be made on the books of Crest, the lessor, at the time this operating lease was signed. However, as piecemeal performance takes place, the following entry would be made on Crest's books:

DR	Cash	$2,000
	CR Rental revenue	$2,000

Since the building remains an asset on the books of Crest Company, periodic amortization would also be recorded, as follows:

DR	Amortization expense—leased building	$XXX
	CR Accumulated amortization—leased building	$XXX

Recap
The operating lease approach conforms to the legal structure of lease arrangements. Journal entries are made in piecemeal fashion over time as partial performance takes place.

Popularity of the Operating Lease Method

Lessees like the operating lease method for lease accounting. One obvious reason is that the operating lease method never reflects the cumulative liability for all future lease payments on the balance sheet of the lessee. Instead, only the next period's portion of the obligation gets accrued piecemeal as partial performance takes place under the lease. The phrase **off-balance-sheet financing** reflects the fact that the lessee has financed the acquisition of asset services without recognizing a liability on the financial statement.

As we will see, GAAP require *footnote* disclosure of the future cash outflows arising from operating leases. And because reasonably informed financial decision makers do read statement footnotes, the liability isn't really "hidden." Nevertheless, it is easy to envision circumstances in which lessees will be made better off by using the operating lease method. To see how, recall that many contracts are linked to financial statement numbers. One example is bank lending agreements that contain covenants—safety measures to protect banks against financial deterioration of the borrower. Since most covenants are based on financial statement numbers—not on footnote numbers—keeping liabilities off the balance sheet may convey benefits to borrowers even if the liabilities are not hidden in a real sense. For example, the numerator of the lessee's debt-to-equity ratio is unaffected at the inception of an operating lease, since no liability is recorded on signing. Keeping the liability off the balance sheet strengthens the debt-to-equity ratio. The off-balance-sheet liability reduces the likelihood that the lessee–borrower will violate a debt-to-equity loan covenant.

Furthermore, some lessees believe that omitting the lease liability improves their ability to obtain *future* credit. Here's why. Lenders use leverage ratios as a rule of thumb in assessing borrowing capacity. Keeping the lease liability off the books lowers reported leverage. The lower the firm's reported leverage, the greater that firm's perceived borrowing capacity. (But again, if lenders read footnotes, the off-balance-sheet liabilities are disclosed and this perception by lessees may be incorrect.)

Lessees also like the operating lease accounting method because it keeps the leased *asset* off the balance sheet. Certain long-term leases give lessees the *exclusive* right to use assets for the preponderance of their economic life. Nevertheless, despite the "ownership-like" property rights conveyed to the lessee, operating leases record no balance sheet asset.

Keeping leased assets off the books produces a favourable impact on lessees' financial statements that is just as substantial as the benefit that arises from omitting lease liabilities. Consider an airline that leases a portion of its aircraft fleet and accounts for the leases using the operating lease method. The leased aircraft generate gross revenues and net profits just as the owned aircraft do. However, not reporting the leased aircraft as assets under the operating lease approach raises the rate of return on assets (ROA) ratio:

$$\text{ROA} = \frac{\text{NOPAT}}{\text{Average assets}}$$

Income generated by the leased assets will appear in the numerator, net operating profit after taxes (NOPAT); however, the leased assets will not appear in the denominator. The net effect increases the return on reported average assets.

Investors and others may use ratios like return on assets to evaluate a firm's performance. The operating lease method makes the ROA for companies that lease a significant portion of their assets *appear* to be higher than the corresponding return for companies that own their assets outright. (An example is illustrated in Appendix 12A to this chapter.)

While lessees have been reluctant to treat leases as a transfer of ownership interest, lessors have not. When a lease is treated as a transfer of ownership interest on the books of the lessor, the timing of the recognition of leasing income is accelerated—thus creating favourable financial statement effects for the lessor, as we'll show later in the chapter.

Rise of Leasing Creates Need for Accounting Principles

When managers and their advisors create new types of transactions and business relationships, new accounting standards are often required to account fairly for these innovations. However, there is often a lag between the appearance of the innovations and the relevant accounting for them. This is illustrated vividly in the case of leasing, which became extremely popular as a means of acquiring capital assets in Canada after the Second World War. Ross Skinner writes:

> *Several factors have contributed to this growth. As a substitute for ownership, a lease generally provides all of the financing for an asset. Thus, a lessee can conserve its equity .... A lessor often has a stronger credit rating than a lessee and may be willing to share the benefits of lower financing costs. A lessor may also be able to utilize tax benefits in connection with the property leased, whereas a lessee may not have enough taxable income to do so immediately, or may be a nontaxable entity. Finally, to the extent that lease financing is "off balance sheet," lessees have felt their financial position appears stronger, with consequent favourable impact on their credit rating and cost of capital.*"[2]

So, by the 1970s, with the frequent use of long-term lease arrangements and little in the way of authoritative accounting rules, the demand for lease accounting GAAP became irresistible, and *CICA Handbook* Section 3065 was issued, which sets standards for both lessees and lessors.

Lessee Accounting

Section 3065 is based on the key idea that "a lease that transfers substantially all of the benefits and risks of ownership to the lessee is in substance an acquisition of an asset and an incurrence of an obligation by the lessee. ..."[3] Leases that meet certain specified criteria *must* be capitalized by the lessee. These types of leases are called **capital leases.** Leases that do not meet the Section 3065 criteria *cannot* be capitalized. Noncapitalized leases are called **operating leases** and are accounted for using the procedures illustrated previously.

Criteria for Capital Lease Treatment

If at its inception a lease satisfies *any one or more* of the following criteria, it must be treated as a capital lease on the books of the lessee:

1. The lease transfers ownership of the asset to the lessee by the end of the lease term.
2. The lease contains a bargain purchase option.
3. The noncancellable lease term is a major portion of the estimated economic life of the leased asset.
4. The present value of the minimum lease payments equals substantially all of the fair value of the leased asset, where "substantially all" usually means 90% or more.

Each criterion represents a condition under which property rights in the leased asset have been transferred to the lessee. This property rights transfer is easily seen in criterion 1. If a lease transfers ownership, title to the asset will eventually pass to the lessee, and the Accounting Standards Board (AcSB) requires that the accounting method conform to the substance of the transaction (an installment purchase) rather than to its form (a long-term lease). Similarly, in lease arrangements in which a bargain purchase option exists—criterion 2—there is a strong probability the lessee will exercise the option and obtain ownership. These two criteria represent instances in which ownership will likely transfer, thus conveying significant property rights in the leased asset. This is the reason Section 3065 requires that such leases be treated as capital leases.

The philosophy underlying the third—economic life—criterion is different, since legal ownership of the asset does not pass to the lessee, but the lessee is expected to receive substantially all of the economic benefits of the leased assets over its expected life. The reason is that the *right to use* a leased asset over substantially all of an asset's expected economic life is *itself* an asset—a valuable property right representing an exclusive claim to the asset's services for the preponderance of its benefit period. Section 3065.06(b) suggests that lease terms equal to or greater than 75% of the expected economic life of the leased asset would usually satisfy this criterion. Note that Section 3065 specifies that the base term includes "all periods covered by bargain renewal options" (3065.03[o][i]).

Criterion 4, sometimes called the **recovery of investment criterion,** is the most technically complicated, but it is still easy to understand in principle. A good indication that the lessor is recovering virtually all of the investment in the asset occurs when the present value of the minimum lease payments is equal to or greater than 90% of the fair market value of the asset itself. The relative magnitude of the payment schedule and the willingness of the lessee to engage in the transaction are both considered evidence that substantial property rights have been transferred to the lessee.

These four criteria for capital leases suggest the AcSB has moved part of the way towards the property rights approach. But it's not a "pure" property rights approach, since these criteria do not consider *all* leases to convey property rights. Only leases that satisfy certain conditions qualify. Thus, Section 3065 is a compromise between the operating lease approach, where *no* leases appear on the lessee's balance sheet, and a strict property rights approach, where the property rights in *all* leases would be shown as assets and liabilities (except, perhaps, for very-short-term leases).

Leases that satisfy at least one of the four criteria are treated as capital leases, and the following entry is made on the books of the lessee at the inception of the lease:[4]

```
DR   Leased equipment—capital lease            $XXX
     CR   Obligation under capital lease                        $XXX
```

Leases that do not satisfy *any* of the previously discussed criteria must be accounted for as operating leases.

Capital Lease Treatment Illustrated

To illustrate the accounting for leases that qualify as capital leases, consider the following example.

The Lessee Company signs a five-year noncancellable lease with the Lessor Company on January 1, 2001, when the lease begins. Other facts pertaining to the lease are:

1. The lease calls for five payments of $79,139.18 to be made at the end of each year.
2. The leased asset has a fair market value of $315,000 on January 1, 2001.
3. The lease has no renewal option and possession of the asset reverts to the lessor on January 1, 2006.
4. Lessee Company regularly uses the straight-line method to amortize owned assets of this type.
5. The leased asset has an expected economic life of six years.

Since the lease term covers more than 75% of the expected economic life of the asset (5/6 = 83.3%), we assume (unless there is evidence to the contrary) that this lease must be treated as a capital lease, following criterion 3. That means the Lessee Company must recognize both an asset and a liability on its books.

But what is the asset and liability dollar amount that should be recorded? Section 3065 requires that the dollar amount be equal to the discounted present value of the **minimum lease payments** specified in the lease. Contingent payments are ignored. The discount rate that is used to determine the present value is the *lower* of the lessee's incremental borrowing rate[5] or the lessor's rate of return that is implicit to the lease.[6]

Assume the Lessee Company's incremental borrowing rate of 10% is lower than the lessor's implicit rate of return on the lease. The discount rate is accordingly 10%, and the present value of the minimum lease payments is:

Present value of minimum lease payments		Minimum lease payment		Present value factor for an ordinary annuity for five years at 10%
	=		×	
$300,000		= $79,139.18 × 3.79079 (from Table 2 of the Appendix)		

Lessee Company would make the following entry on January 1, 2001, at the inception of the lease:

```
DR   Leased equipment—capital lease            $300,000
     CR   Obligation under capital lease                        $300,000
```

It is important to understand that the amount shown for the asset and the amount shown for the related liability ($300,000) are equal only at the inception of the lease. Thereafter, as the term of the lease progresses, the amount in the asset account will equal the amount in the liability account only by sheer coincidence. The reason is that the asset account is reduced in accordance with the Lessee Company's amortization schedule for assets of this type, whereas the liability account is reduced in accordance

Minimum lease payments are defined as follows: If the payment schedule called for a fixed fee of $79,139.18 per year plus an additional fee of 5 cents per unit for each unit manufactured using the leased asset, only the $79,139.18 would be included in the computation of minimum lease payments. The 5 cents per unit for each unit manufactured is *the contingency that is ignored in the calculation.* In more complicated leases, the minimum lease payments also include the amount of any **residual value guarantee** by the lessee (as discussed later), the amount of any bargain purchase option, and any penalties that must be paid if the lessee chooses not to renew the lease.

with the payment schedule contained in the lease. The asset and liability accounts are reduced at independent—and usually different—rates over the life of the lease. These differences are illustrated in Appendix 12A to this chapter.

Each lease payment of $79,139.18 comprises two elements. One represents interest on the amount of the obligation that was outstanding during the year. The other represents a repayment of a portion of the principal amount of the obligation. Section 3065 requires that the interest portion and principal repayment of each $79,139.18 outflow be measured using the effective interest method.

The amortization schedule in Table 12.1 shows this breakdown in columns (b) and (c).

On December 31, 2001, Lessee Company will record both the cash payment of $79,139.18 (column [a]) and the amortization of the capitalized leased asset (column [e]). On the basis of the figures in Table 12.1, the entries are:

DR	Obligation under capital lease	$49,139.18	
DR	Interest expense	30,000.00	
	CR Cash		$79,139.18
DR	Amortization expense—asset under capital lease	$60,000.00	
	CR Accumulated amortization—capital lease		$60,000.00

The amount of interest expense recognized each year is equal to 10% (the discount rate) times the principal amount of the obligation outstanding at the start of the year. Since the principal amount at the start of the lease on January 1, 2001, was $300,000 (column [d]), the interest expense for 2001 is $300,000 times 10%, or $30,000. The difference between the cash payment of $79,139.18 and the interest expense of $30,000 represents repayment of principal. This 2001 difference—$49,139.18—reduces the remaining principal balance at December 31, 2001, to $250,860.82 ($300,000 − $49,139.18). Interest expense for 2002 would then be $250,860.82 times 10%, or $25,086.08.

TABLE 12.1 LESSEE COMPANY

Amortization Schedule—Effective Interest Method

Date	(a) Total Payment	(b) Interest Expense[1]	(c) Principal Payment[2]	(d) Lease Obligation Balance	(e) Amortization of Asset	(f) Total Annual Capital Lease Expense (Col. [b] + Col. [e])
1/1/2001				$300,000.00		
12/31/2001	$ 79,139.18	$30,000.00	$ 49,139.18	250,860.82	$ 60,000.00	$ 90,000.00
12/31/2002	79,139.18	25,086.08	54,053.10	196,807.72	60,000.00	85,086.08
12/31/2003	79,139.18	19,680.77	59,458.41	137,349.31	60,000.00	79,680.77
12/31/2004	79,139.18	13,734.93	65,404.25	71,945.06	60,000.00	73,734.93
12/31/2005	79,139.18	7,194.12[3]	71,945.06	—	60,000.00	67,194.12
	$395,695.90	$95,695.90	$300,000.00		$300,000.00	$395,695.90

[1]Column (d) for preceding year times 10%.

[2]Column (a) minus column (b).

[3]Rounded.

The 2002 journal entry for the cash payment would be:

DR	Obligation under capital lease	$54,053.10	
DR	Interest expense	25,086.08	
	CR Cash		$79,139.18

Notice that the entry to record amortization expense would be the same in all years of the lease, since the Lessee Company uses the straight-line capital asset amortization method.

Executory Costs

Executory costs represent certain incidental costs of using assets, such as maintenance, taxes, and insurance. Often, these costs are paid directly by the lessee. Sometimes they are paid by the lessor and passed along to the lessee as an additional lease payment. For example, if executory costs paid by the Lessor Company total $2,000 per year, the Lessor Company would include an added yearly charge of $2,000 in the lease, in addition to the basic $79,139.18 rental fee.

Since executory costs represent a cost of *using* assets—rather than a cost of the assets themselves—these costs are omitted when determining minimum lease payments, and thus they are not a component of the capitalized amount shown in the "Leased equipment—capital leases" account. Consider this illustration. If the Lessee Company's annual rental fee was $81,139.18—including $2,000 of executory costs—the minimum lease payments to be capitalized would be $79,139.18 (i.e., $81,139.18 − $2,000). Under this assumption, the capitalized amount would still total $300,000 and the amortization schedule would be identical to Table 12.1. The $2,000 of executory costs would be treated as a period cost by the Lessee Company and charged to expense when paid. For example, the payment of $81,139.18 on December 31, 2001, would generate the following accounting entry:

DR	Obligation under capital lease	$49,139.18	
DR	Interest expense	30,000.00	
DR	Miscellaneous lease expense	2,000.00	
	CR Cash		$81,139.18

Residual Value Guarantees

Lease contracts sometimes contain a provision under which the lessee guarantees the lessor that the leased asset will have a certain value at the end of the lease when the lessor retakes possession of the asset. If the actual market value of the asset is less than this **residual value guarantee,** the lessee must pay the difference to the lessor. Let's now assume that the lease required the Lessee Company to guarantee that the asset's residual value would be no lower than $20,000 when the lease ends on January 1, 2006. If the asset's fair market value on that date were $20,000 or higher, Lessee Company would simply return it to the lessor, since the residual value guarantee was satisfied. But if the fair market value were only $15,000 on January 1, 2006, Lessee Company would return the asset and pay $5,000 cash to Lessor Company.

Leased assets often revert to the lessor at the end of the lease term. Residual value guarantees protect the lessor against several types of losses. Unforeseen technological or marketplace changes erode residual value; the residual value guarantee insulates the lessor from these unanticipated changes. Similarly, the lessor is vulnerable to losses if the lessee does not take proper care of the asset over the lease period. The residual value guarantee affords lessors protection against lessees who abuse leased assets, and provides an incentive for lessees to care for such assets.

The lessee must include the amount specified as the residual value guarantee in the computation of minimum lease payments. The reason is that the lessee potentially owes the full amount of the guarantee to the lessor. To illustrate the accounting, let's return to the Lessee Company data on page 544 and now assume there is a $20,000 residual value guarantee. The present value of the minimum lease payments is computed as follows:

$$\text{Present value of minimum lease payments} = \text{Minimum lease payment} \times \text{Present value factor at 10\%}$$

$300,000.00 = $79,139.18 × 3.79079 (Present value factor for five-year ordinary annuity)

$\underline{12,418.40}$ = $20,000.00 × 0.62092 (Present value factor for $1 due in five years)

$\underline{\$312,418.40}$

With the residual value guarantee, Lessee Company would make the following entry on January 1, 2001, at the inception of the lease:

DR	Leased equipment—capital lease	$312,418.40
CR	Obligation under capital lease		$312,418.40

Table 12.2 shows the amortization schedule that Lessee Company would use when this residual value guarantee was included in the lease. Notice that after making the December 31, 2005, cash payment of $79,139.18, the lease obligation balance (column [d]) and the lease asset balance (column [f]) both are $20,000. We're assuming that the asset's value at the end of the lease on January 1, 2006, equals or exceeds $20,000—the amount of the residual value guarantee. When Lessee

TABLE 12.2 LESSEE COMPANY

Amortization Schedule—Effective Interest Method with Guaranteed Residual Value

Date	(a) Total Cash Payment	(b) Interest Expense[1]	(c) Principal Payment[2]	(d) Lease Obligation Balance	(e) Amortization of Asset and Residual Value Return	(f) Lease Asset Balance	(g) Total Annual Capital Lease Expense (b) + (e)
1/1/2001	—	—	—	$312,418.40	—	$312,418.40	—
12/31/2001	$ 79,139.18	$ 31,241.84	$ 47,897.34	264,521.06	$ 58,483.68	253,934.72	$ 89,725.52
12/31/2002	79,139.18	26,452.11	52,687.07	211,834.00	58,483.68	195,451.04	84,935.79
12/31/2003	79,139.18	21,183.40	57,955.78	153,878.22	58,483.68	136,967.36	79,667.08
12/31/2004	79,139.18	15,387.82	63,751.36	90,126.86	58,483.68	78,483.68	73,871.50
12/31/2005	79,139.18	9,012.33[3]	70,126.85	20,000.00	58,483.68	20,000.00	67,496.01
1/1/2006[4]			20,000.00	—	20,000.00	—	
	$395,695.90	$103,277.50	$312,418.40	$ –0–	$312,418.40	$ –0–	$395,695.90

[1]Column (d) for preceding year times 10%.

[2]Column (a) minus column (b).

[3]Rounded by 36 cents.

[4]Asset returned.

Company returns the asset on that date, its obligation to Lessor Company is satisfied and the following entry would be made:

DR	Obligation under capital lease	$20,000.00	
	CR Leased equipment—capital lease		$20,000.00

Now let's alter the example and assume that the asset has a fair market value of only $15,000 at December 31, 2005. Lessee Company would have to pay $5,000 in addition to relinquishing the asset. The entry would be:

DR	Obligation under capital lease	$20,000.00	
DR	Loss on residual value guarantee	5,000.00	
	CR Leased equipment—capital lease		$20,000.00
	CR Cash		5,000.00

Payments in Advance

When lease payments are due at the start of each lease period, the journal entries and amortization tables differ slightly. We'll use the original Lessee Company example to illustrate this. Assume that the annual payment is due at the start of each year and, because the payments are received earlier, the lessor lowers the required annual payment to $71,945. Under these slightly altered conditions, the present value of the minimum lease payments is:

Present value of minimum lease payments	=	Minimum lease payment	×	Present value factor for an annuity in advance for five years at 10%
$300,000	=	$71,945	×	4.16987 (from Table 3 of the Appendix)

Table 12.3 shows the amortization schedule for this lease with up-front payments. Lessee Company records the following two entries on January 1, 2001, upon signing the lease and making the required lease payment:

DR	Leased asset—capital lease	$300,000	
	CR Obligation under capital lease		$300,000
DR	Obligation under capital lease	$ 71,945	
	CR Cash		$ 71,945

Notice from both the second journal entry and from Table 12.3 that no portion of the January 1, 2001, payment represents interest expense; instead, all of the $71,945 payment reduces the principal balance. The reason is that interest expense ensues only as time passes, not at the inception of the lease.

TABLE 12.3 LESSEE COMPANY

Amortization Schedule—Effective Interest Method With Payments at the Start of Each Period

Date	(a) Total Payment	(b) Interest Expense[1]	(c) Principal Payment[2]	(d) Lease Obligation Balance	(e) Amortization of Asset	(f) Total Annual Capital Lease Expense (b) + (e)
1/1/01				$300,000.00		
1/1/01	$ 71,945.00	—	$ 71,945.00	228,055.00	$ 60,000.00	$ 60,000.00
1/1/02	71,945.00	$22,805.50	49,139.50	178,915.50	60,000.00	82,805.50
1/1/03	71,945.00	17,891.55	54,053.45	124,862.05	60,000.00	77,891.55
1/1/04	71,945.00	12,486.21	59,458.79	65,403.26	60,000.00	72,486.21
1/1/05	71,945.00	6,541.74[3]	65,403.26	—	60,000.00	66,541.74
	$359,725.00	$59,725.00	$300,000.00	$ -0-	$300,00.00	$359,725.00

[1]Column (d) for preceding year times 10%

[2]Column (a) minus column (b).

[3]Rounded.

Financial Statement Effects of Capital Versus Operating Lease Treatment

To understand the financial statement effects of lease capitalization, we need to compare the numbers that result from the capital lease approach with the numbers that would have resulted had the operating lease method been used instead.

Let's return to the beginning of the Lessee Company example where we assumed that executory costs were zero and that there was no residual value guarantee. (This is equivalent to assuming that the executory costs are paid directly by the lessee and are not included in the payments due to the lessor.) If that lease had been accounted for as an operating lease, the following journal entry would have been made in each of the five years of the lease:

DR	Lease expense	$79,139.18
	CR Cash	$79,139.18

Under the operating lease method, the total lease expense over the life of the lease is equal to the total cash outflow. This total expense number under the operating lease method is $395,695.90 and is shown at the bottom of column (a) of Table 12.1.

Under the capital lease method, the total lease expense over the life of the lease comprises both (1) the interest payments and (2) the amortization of the capitalized asset amount. The sum of these two elements is shown at the bottom of column (f) of the amortization schedule in Table 12.1. This total is also $395,695.90.

A comparison of the Table 12.1 column (a) total (lifetime expense under the operating lease method) and the column (f) total (lifetime expense under the capital lease method) demonstrates that *the two methods give rise to identical cumulative total lifetime charges to expense.* Over the life of the lease, total income is unaffected by the choice of lease accounting method. However, a comparison of the year-by-year numbers in columns (a) and (f) demonstrates that the *timing* of the expense charge differs between the two methods. The capital lease approach leads to higher expense in the

FIGURE 12.1
LESSEE
COMPANY

Pattern of
expense
recognition:
capital versus
operating lease

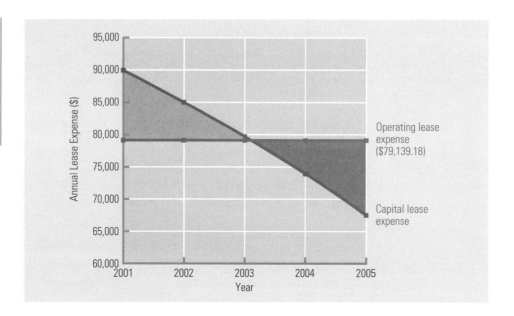

earlier years of the lease and lower lease expense in the later years, as shown in Figure 12.1. From the graphical representation, you can see that in the early lease years, expenses under the capital lease approach exceed lease expenses that would be recognized under the operating lease approach. Ultimately, capital lease expenses drop below operating lease expenses.

This accelerated recognition of lease expenses under the capital lease approach provides yet another reason why many lessees might prefer the operating lease method. Consider the incentives of a manager whose performance evaluations and bonuses are tied to financial numbers. A lease accounting method that front-end loads expenses lowers near-term income and thus also reduces the discounted present value of expected bonuses. Worse yet, if managers' accomplishments are evaluated "strictly by the numbers," the higher expenses and lower profitability may jeopardize their continuing employment and advancement. So managers have a strong incentive to structure lease contracts in ways that circumvent the capitalization rules in some circumstances.

The relative proportion of capital versus operating leases that a particular lessee takes on may provide some insight into the interplay between accounting decisions (in this case, arranging a lease agreement so that it falls on one side or the other of the "operating lease/capital lease" boundary) and the financial circumstances of the particular company. For example, in its Canadian GAAP-basis financial statements for the year ended December 31, 2001,[7] Canadian National Railway (CN) reports total scheduled operating lease payments of $1,253 million, and total scheduled capital lease payments of $1,449 million, a ratio of 0.86 to 1. CN's ratio of reported long-term debt (including capital leases) to shareholders' equity is $5,764 million/$6,361 million, or 0.91. In contrast, Rogers Communications Inc. reported $519 million in scheduled operating lease payments and no capital lease payments in its financial statements for the year ended December 31, 2001. Rogers has long-term debt of $4,990 million and shareholders' equity of $2,416 million.

A possible explanation for the different ratio of scheduled operating-to-capital lease payments between these two companies might be that CN is generally profitable, and indeed was able to issue considerable new debt in 2001, and so there is not much pressure to push lease agreements towards the operating category. On the other

CANADIAN NATIONAL
RAILWAY
www.cn.ca

ROGERS
COMMUNICATIONS
INC.
www.rogers.ca

hand, Rogers has an astronomical amount of debt, relatively speaking, and has only reported a positive net income three times in its last ten years. So there might be pressure to write lease agreements so that they do not meet the capital lease requirements in *CICA Handbook* Section 3065.

Of course, these observations are merely suggestive, but they alert us to the possibility that accounting policy decisions, the way business transactions are arranged, and the incentives existing in the company may all be related.

Recap

Lessees have incentives to keep leases off the balance sheet. Criteria exist for identifying capital leases. However, carefully designing the terms of a lease may permit evasion of these criteria.

Lessees' Footnote Disclosures

Operating leases are much more common than capital leases, probably because operating leases are "off balance sheet." However, capital leases *do* exist, and their frequency does differ across companies, even within the same industry. For this reason, analysts try to adjust financial statements to include the effects of off-balance-sheet operating leases in order to enhance comparisons between firms in an industry. The footnote disclosures required by Section 3065 make these adjustments possible.[8] Exhibit 12.1 shows portions of the leases footnote from WestJet Airlines Ltd.'s 2001 annual report.

Exhibit 12.1 contains the disclosures required of all lessees. Notice that a schedule of future minimum lease payments must be disclosed for both capital leases and operating leases. Payments for each of the ensuing five years must be separately disclosed, as WestJet has done for 2002 through 2006. Minimum lease payments for all later years may be aggregated (e.g., $2,934,000 for capital leases and $197,305,000 for operating leases). *These scheduled payments on operating leases make it possible for analysts to estimate the discounted present value of the off-balance-sheet leases.* Once the present values are determined, they can be used for adjusting ratios needed to enhance comparisons among firms.

WESTJET AIRLINES
www.westjet.com

Adjusting Income

If one company has structured its lease contracts to keep these commitments off the balance sheet while a competitor has not, how do analysts make the two companies' income numbers comparable? It is not difficult to make such adjustments for companies whose average lease is approximately 50% expired.[9] Figure 12.1 shows that halfway through the life of the lease (December 31, 2003), Lessee Company's lease expense under the operating lease approach will be very close to the lease expense under the capital lease approach. Table 12.1 indicates that operating lease expense in year 2003 is $79,139.18 while capital lease expense is virtually the same—$79,680.77.

For mature companies, new leases are being written as old ones expire; thus, the company's lease contracts are, on average, close to halfway through their lives.

We can extend this intuition to comparisons between companies. Assume that two competitors in the same industry have capitalized different percentages of their leases and that both companies have a stable portfolio of leases. Then, despite these different capitalization policies, the two firms will, nevertheless, have comparable lease expense numbers. *For mature firms, the income statement effects of capital versus operating lease treatment will often not be significantly different.*

We will show in the next subsection that this is not true for balance sheet effects. On the contrary, capital versus operating lease treatment can significantly alter balance sheet numbers and resulting ratios.

Balance Sheet and Ratio Effects

Accounting for leases using the capital lease approach invariably worsens certain key ratios on the lessee's balance sheet—thus providing yet another explanation for lessees' resistance to lease capitalization.

One ratio that deteriorates under capital lease accounting is the current ratio. Using numbers in the Lessee Company example from Table 12.1, we will demonstrate that the current ratio over the term of the lease will be lower under the capital lease approach than it would be under the operating lease approach. To see this, assume the Lessee Company is preparing a balance sheet on January 1, 2001, immediately after signing the lease. Under the operating lease approach, the first cash payment of $79,139.18 due on December 31, 2001, is not considered to be a liability; it will become a liability only as time passes and as the lessor performs its duties under the lease. Since no part of the year-end 2001 payment of $79,139.18 is recognized as a liability at January 1, 2001, under the operating lease approach, the current ratio would be unaffected if Lessee Company were somehow able to avoid capitalization and were allowed to treat this as an operating lease.

By contrast, at the inception of the lease, the capital lease approach *does* recognize a liability—called "Obligation under capital lease." As shown in Table 12.1, the balance in this liability account at January 1, 2001, is $300,000.00. Furthermore, Section 3065 requires that a portion of this $300,000.00 balance be classified as a current liability. The current portion of the "Obligation under capital lease" is the reduction in the principal balance that will take place over the ensuing 12 months of 2001. Table 12.1 shows the current portion to be $49,139.18, since this is the expected 2001 reduction in the principal balance. Thus, treating the lease as a capital lease rather than as an operating lease will increase Lessee Company's current liabilities by $49,139.18 and thereby lower its January 1, 2001, current ratio. Table 12.1 illustrates that this negative effect on the current ratio *increases* as the lease grows older, since the portion of each $79,139.18 cash outflow that represents principal repayment grows over time.[10]

To protect the lender, many loan agreements require borrowers to maintain a certain prespecified current ratio level. It is not surprising, therefore, that lessees resist lease capitalization. As the preceding discussion illustrates, treating a lease as a capital lease lowers the current ratio; therefore, capitalization could push financially struggling lessees into technical violation of their existing loan agreements by lowering their current ratio below the prespecified limit.

Two far more obvious cases of ratio deterioration under capital lease accounting relate to the leverage ratio and the return-on-gross-assets ratio. These effects were discussed at the start of the chapter and will not be repeated here.

There are also cash flow statement implications arising from lease treatment. To see this, refer back to Table 12.1, which shows the amortization schedule for a capital lease. On the cash flow statement, the interest expense component—column (b)—of each yearly payment would be classified as an *operating* cash flow while the principal payment component—column (c)—would be classified as a *financing* cash flow. By way of contrast, if the lease had been treated as an operating lease, the entire annual payment of $79,139.18 would be classified as an operating cash flow. So when lessees successfully keep leases off the balance sheet, reported cash flow from operations is lowered.

Recap
We have seen that lease capitalization affects balance sheet ratios and that the Section 3065 capitalization criteria can be circumvented. Since different firms can conceivably treat virtually identical leases dissimilarly, financial statements may not be immediately comparable across firms. To make comparisons, statement users need to adjust for these differences. Appendix 12A to this chapter outlines procedures for capitalizing off-balance-sheet (operating leases) and thereby increasing interfirm statement comparability.

Lessor Accounting

In addition to outlining rules for lessees, Section 3065 specifies the treatment of leases on the books of lessors.

Sales-Type and Direct Financing Leases

From the perspective of the lessor, if a lease arrangement (1) transfers substantially all the benefits and risks of ownership in the leased asset to the lessee *and* (2) allows reasonably accurate estimates regarding the amount and collectibility of the eventual net cash flows to the lessor,[11] the lease is treated as a sort of sale by the lessor in which case the leased asset is considered to be "sold" and is removed from the lessor's books. For lessors, there are two types of such nonoperating leases:

1. a **sales-type lease**, which exists when the lessor is a manufacturer or dealer
2. a **direct financing lease**, which exists when the lessor is a financial institution (e.g., an insurance firm, bank, or financing company), serving the economic function of a financial intermediary between a manufacturer or dealer and the lessee

When both conditions—the transfer of property rights *and* reasonably accurate estimates of net cash flows—are *not simultaneously* met, the lease must be treated as an operating lease.

Figure 12.2 diagrams the various possibilities for lessor accounting, which we are about to explain in detail.

Sales-Type Leases Leases can serve as a marketing vehicle since leasing arrangements generate "sales" from potential customers who are unwilling or unable to buy the assets outright for cash. For example, DaimlerChrysler Canada manufactures vehicles for sale and also leases such equipment through its subsidiary, Chrysler Financial Canada Ltd. A lessor who uses leasing as a means for marketing products earns a profit from two sources:

DAIMLERCHRYSLER
CANADA
**www.
daimlerchrysler.ca**

1. One component of the total return on the lease is called the ***manufacturer's or dealer's profit***—the difference between the fair market value (*cash* sales price) of the asset and its cost to the manufacturer or dealer.

FIGURE 12.2
DECISION TREE FOR LESSOR'S TREATMENT OF LEASES

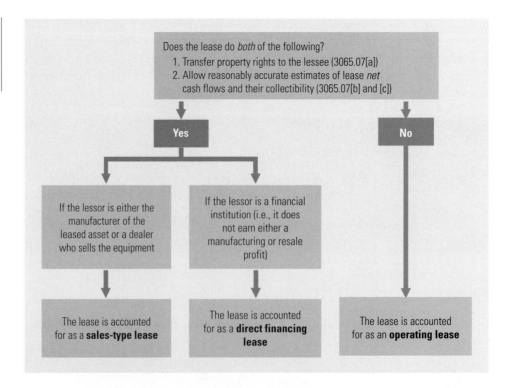

2. Another component of the lessor's return is called **financing profit**—the difference between the total (undiscounted) minimum lease payments plus unguaranteed residual value and the fair market value of the leased asset.

The following sales-type lease example illustrates these components.

ABC Company manufactures tractors. Each tractor has a total production cost of $36,000 and a cash sales price of $50,000. ABC Company "sells" some of these tractors under five-year sales-type leases, which call for annual lease payments of $15,000. At the end of the fifth year, legal ownership of the tractor transfers to the lessee.

ABC Company's total profit over the five years of the lease is $39,000—that is, the lessee's payments of $75,000 ($15,000 per year times five years) minus the production cost of $36,000. This total profit has two components:

Manufacturer's profit: Cash sales price of $50,000 minus production cost of $36,000	$14,000
Financing profit: The difference between the cash sales price of the tractor ($50,000) and the gross inflows from the lessee ($15,000 × 5 years = $75,000)	25,000
Total profit	$39,000

Direct Financing Leases

Some lessors are not manufacturers or dealers; instead, they are organizations like banks, insurance firms, or financing companies that provide lessees with a means for financing asset acquisitions. These organizations acquire assets from manufacturers by paying the fair market value and then leasing the asset to lessees. Lessors who are neither manufacturers nor dealers earn their profit from a single source—the finance fee that they charge the lessee for financing the asset acquisition. The following direct financing lease example illustrates this single profit dimension.

The Pleasant City National Bank leases tractors to local farmers. Tractors are purchased by the bank from ABC Company, the manufacturer, at their fair market value of $50,000. The tractors are then leased to farmers under five-year direct financing leases, which call for annual lease payments of $15,000. At the end of the fifth year, legal ownership of the tractor transfers to the lessee.

The bank's total cumulative profit on this lease is $25,000, which represents the difference between the cost of the tractor to the bank ($50,000) and the gross inflows from the lessee ($75,000).

Lessors' Operating Leases

Some lease arrangements do not transfer property rights in the asset to the lessee; or, if they do transfer property rights, there may be great uncertainty about the ultimate profit or its collectibility. In either case, the leased asset is not considered to be "sold" and remains on the books of the lessor. Such leases are called operating leases.

Distinguishing Between Capital and Operating Leases

Section 3065 identifies two categories of characteristics that must be met for a lease to be treated as either a sales-type or a direct financing lease on the books of the lessor. For ease of reference, these are called Type I and Type II characteristics. A lease meeting *at least one* of the Type I characteristics and *both* of the Type II characteristics is a capital lease. The Type I characteristics are identical to the lessee's criteria for capital lease treatment.

Type I Characteristics

1. The lease transfers ownership of the asset to the lessee by the end of the lease term.
2. The lease contains a bargain purchase option.
3. The noncancellable lease term is a substantial portion of the estimated economic life of the leased asset. A guideline of 75% or more is mentioned in Section 3065.
4. The present value of the minimum lease payments assures that the lessor recovers its investment in the fair market value of the leased asset. A guideline of 90% or more is mentioned in Section 3065.

Type II Characteristics

1. The collectibility of the minimum lease payments is reasonably predictable.
2. There are no important uncertainties surrounding the amount of unreimbursable costs yet to be incurred by the lessor under the lease.

The purpose of these characteristics is to establish the appropriate time for recognizing income on the lessor's books. We already know from Chapter 2 that revenue should be recognized when both of the following conditions exist:

1. The "critical event" in the process of earning the revenue has taken place.
2. The amount of the revenue that has been earned is measurable with a reasonable degree of assurance.

Accounting rules for the lessor in Section 3065 are directly linked to these two criteria. The Type I characteristics dealing with transfer of property rights identify the critical event in determining whether a lease is in substance a "sale of assets." The Type II characteristics in Section 3065 relate to the riskiness of cash flows and thus to the measurability of revenue.

When at least one of the Type I characteristics and both of the Type II characteristics are satisfied by a lease, then the criteria for revenue recognition are met. This means that manufacturers or dealers can immediately recognize the sale, match costs, and reflect manufacturer's or dealer's profit. (By contrast, under the operating lease treatment, this profit recognition occurs over the life of the lease as each party performs its duties.) Furthermore, lessors can begin to recognize financing profit as a function of time when the Type I and Type II characteristics exist in a lease. (Under the operating lease treatment, the recognition of financing profit is related to performance. As we will see, the recognition of financing profit is accelerated when it is recognized as a pure function of time rather than as a function of performance.)

When a lease does not meet any of the Type I characteristics, or when it meets at least one of the Type I characteristics but not *both* of the Type II characteristics, then that lease must be accounted for as an operating lease on the lessor's books. Under the operating lease approach, the lessor's recognition of income takes place piecemeal as contractual performance by the lessor and the lessee progresses.

Section 3065 tries to establish symmetry in the accounting for leases by lessors and lessees. If a lease qualifies as a "sale" from the perspective of the lessor, then the property rights inherent in the lease require asset recognition by the lessee. Of course, this symmetry is not perfect, since a particular lease may meet at least one of the Type I characteristics but not both of the Type II characteristics. In such cases, the asset would appear on *both* the lessor's and the lessee's books. Another factor which inhibits symmetry is that the discount rates used by the lessor and the lessee may differ. The lessor is required to use the rate of return that is implicit to the lease. If this rate is *higher* than the lessee's incremental borrowing rate, then the lessor and the lessee will use different discount rates when accounting for the lease.

Direct Financing Lease Treatment Illustrated

To illustrate the accounting for leases that qualify as direct financing leases, we will use a variation of our earlier lease example. Assume that the Lessee Company signs a noncancellable five-year lease on January 1, 2001, with the Lessor Company. The lease begins on January 1, 2001, and has the following terms:

1. The lease calls for five payments of $79,139.18 to be made at the end of each year.
2. The leased asset has a fair market value of $304,359.49 on January 1, 2001.[12]
3. The lease has no renewal option and possession of the asset reverts to the Lessor Company on January 1, 2006.
4. The leased asset has an expected economic life of six years.
5. The collectibility of the lease payments is reasonably predictable.
6. There are no important uncertainties regarding unreimbursable costs yet to be incurred by Lessor Company.
7. The lease contract requires the lessee to guarantee a residual value of $20,000 at the end of the fifth year of the lease.

These lease terms satisfy both the third and the fourth Type I characteristics. We'll assume the lease satisfies both Type II characteristics. Therefore, this is a not an operating lease. Assume Lessor Company is not a manufacturer or dealer, so this lease is a direct financing lease. Table 12.4 shows that the rate of return implicit to this lease from the perspective of the Lessor Company is 11%.[13] Therefore, the Lessor Company must use an 11% interest factor in accounting for this lease.

The Lessor Company's amortization schedule for this lease is shown in Table 12.5.

At the inception of the lease, Lessor Company puts on its books an account called "Gross investment in leased asset"—the sum of the minimum lease payments plus the guaranteed residual value of the asset at the end of the lease term:

Minimum lease payments over the life of the lease ($79,139.18 × 5)	$395,695.90
Guaranteed residual value at 12/31/05	20,000.00
Gross investment in leased asset	$415,695.90

The journal entry on January 1, 2001, would be:

DR	Gross investment in leased asset	$415,695.90	
	CR Equipment		$304,359.49
	CR Unearned financing income—leases		111,336.41

The unearned financing income is the difference between the gross investment in leased asset and the previous book value of the asset itself. "Unearned financing

TABLE 12.4 LESSOR COMPANY

Computation of Implicit Rate of Return on Lease

Rate of return implicit to the lease is the rate that equates the present value of lease inflows and outflows.

Present value of outflows at 1/1/01

    Fair market value of the leased asset $304,359.49

Present value of inflows at 1/1/01

    Five annual payments times 11% ordinary
      annuity factor:

$$\$79,139.18 \times 3.69590^* = \$292,490.49$$

    Guaranteed residual times 11% five-year single
      payment factor:

$$\$20,000.00 \times 0.59345^\dagger = \$\ 11,869.00$$

                            $304,359.49

Present value of inflows exactly equals present value of outflows at a discount rate of 11%. Hence, Lessor Company's rate of return is 11%.

---

*Present value factor for a five-year ordinary annuity at 11%.

†Present value factor for $1 due in five years at 11%.

income," a contra account to "Gross investment in leased asset," is used to arrive at "Net investment in leased asset." The effect of this entry is to remove the asset account representing the equipment being leased and to replace it with two accounts which together reflect the net investment in the lease. The dollar amount for the asset removed ($304,359.49) is equal to the dollar amount for the net investment in leased asset ($415,695.90 − $111,336.41).

TABLE 12.5 LESSOR COMPANY

Amortization Schedule—Effective Interest Method

Date	(a) Total Receipts	(b) Interest Income[1]	(c) Principal Reduction[2]	(d) Remaining Principal Amount
1/1/01				$304,359.49
12/31/01	$ 79,139.18	$ 33,479.54	$ 45,659.64	258,699.85
12/31/02	79,139.18	28,456.98	50,682.20	208,017.65
12/31/03	79,139.18	22,881.94	56,257.24	151,760.41
12/31/04	79,139.18	16,693.65	62,445.53	89,314.88
12/31/05	79,139.18	9,824.30[3]	69,314.88	20,000.00
	$395,695.90	$111,336.41	$284,359.49	

[1]Column (d) for preceding year times 11%.

[2]Column (a) minus column (b).

[3]Rounded.

At December 31, 2001, Lessor Company would make the following journal entries:

DR	Cash	$79,139.18	
	CR Gross investment in leased asset		$79,139.18
DR	Unearned financing income—leases	$33,479.54	
	CR Financing income—leases		$33,479.54

The amount of financing income recognized in each subsequent year would be equal to the amounts shown in column (b) of Table 12.5, the Lessor Company's amortization schedule. Lessor Company records no amortization since the equipment itself is not being carried on its books.

After the last payment is received at the end of the lease term on December 31, 2005, the balance in the "Gross investment in leased asset" account will be $20,000.00, shown in column (d) of the amortization schedule. This amount represents the guaranteed residual value of the asset on the date that possession of the asset reverts to the Lessor Company. Assume that the fair market value of the asset equals or exceeds $20,000; then the following entry would be made on December 31, 2005, to reflect the end of the lease and physical repossession of the asset.

DR	Equipment—residual value	$20,000.00	
	CR Gross investment in leased asset		$20,000.00

Financial Statement Effects of Direct Financing Versus Operating Leases

Comparing the financial statement effects of direct financing versus operating lease treatment allows a more complete understanding of lessor accounting.

Had the previous lease been accounted for by Lessor Company as an operating lease, the following journal entry would have been made each year:

DR	Cash	$79,139.18	
	CR Rental revenue		$79,139.18

Since the leased asset remains on the lessor's books under the operating method, annual amortization must be recognized. Assume the asset is amortized down to a $20,000 residual value on a straight-line basis; then the annual amortization expense is $56,871.90 ([$304,359.49 – $20,000.00] ÷ 5), and the entry would be:

DR	Amortization expense	$56,871.90	
	CR Accumulated amortization		$56,871.90

Table 12.6 shows operating method amounts in columns (a)–(c) and (f) and contrasts these numbers with direct financing amounts. Income on the operating method totals $111,336.41 over the life of the lease, as shown in column (c) of Table 12.6. This total is identical to the income recognized under the direct financing method, as the total in Table 12.6 column (d) reflects. So income over the life of the lease is unaffected by which accounting method is used. However, the *timing* of income does differ between the two methods, as indicated in column (e) of Table 12.6. The direct financing method recognizes income sooner. Notice that the income timing difference would widen if an accelerated amortization method were used in conjunction with the operating method, as opposed to the straight-line method employed in the example.

TABLE 12.6 LESSOR COMPANY

Operating Method Versus Direct Financing Method Income and Asset Balance Comparison

	Operating Method					Net Asset Balance at End of Year		
Year	(a) Lease Payment Received	(b) Amortization	(c) Operating Method Income[1]	(d) Direct Financing Method Income[2]	(e) Income Difference Between Methods	(f) Operating Method[3]	(g) Direct Financing Method[4]	(h) Asset Balance Difference Between Methods
2001	$ 79,139.18	$ 56,871.90	$ 22,267.28	$ 33,479.54	+$11,212.26	$247,487.59	$258,699.85	+$11,212.26
2002	79,139.18	56,871.90	22,267.28	28,456.98	+ 6,189.70	190,615.69	208,017.65	+ 17,401.96
2003	79,139.18	56,871.90	22,267.28	22,881.94	+ 614.66	133,743.79	151,760.41	+ 18,016.62
2004	79,139.18	56,871.90	22,267.28	16,693.65	− 5,573.63	76,871.89	89,314.88	+ 12,442.99
2005	79,139.18	56,871.89	22,267.29	9,824.30	− 12,442.99	$ 20,000.00	$ 20,000.00	$ −0−
	$395,695.90	$284,359.49	$111,336.41	$111,336.41	$ −0−			

[1]Column (a) minus column (b).

[2]From column (b) of Table 12.5.

[3]$304,359.49 minus the period-to-date cumulative amount from column (b).

[4]From column (d) of Table 12.5.

The "front-ending" of income under the direct financing method may explain why lessors—unlike lessees—have never seriously opposed the property rights approach to lease accounting. Furthermore, the direct financing method results in other favourable financial statement effects. For example, the lessor's rate of return on assets ratio is usually improved under the direct financing method in the early years of a particular lease. Columns (e) and (h) in Table 12.6 illustrate this effect. Income and the end-of-year asset balance are both $11,212.26 higher under the direct financing method in 2001. An equal dollar increase in the numerator and denominator of a ratio will increase the ratio value as long as the initial value of the ratio is under 100%. Since reported rates of return on assets are almost always far less than 100%, the adoption of the direct financing method will almost always increase the lessor's reported rate of return in the early years of the lease.

Of course, Table 12.6 also illustrates that this effect reverses as the lease grows older. In 2005, for example, income is $12,442.99 lower under the direct financing method while the end-of-year asset value is equal to what it would have been under the operating lease treatment. This would make the 2005 return on the direct financing method lower than the return that would have been reported on the operating lease approach.[14]

The current ratio of a lessor who uses the direct financing method will also be improved. Consider the current ratio at December 31, 2001. Under the operating lease method, the 2002 lease cash receipt of $79,139.18 would not be shown as an asset on Lessor Company's books on December 31, 2001, since performance under the lease contract has not yet taken place and will not take place until 2002. Under the direct financing method, however, the 2002 lease payment would be included as a component of the "Net investment in leased assets" account. Returning to Table 12.5, look at the December 31, 2001, balance in this account which is $258,699.85; of this amount, $50,682.20 (the principal reduction in the next 12 months) is classified as a current asset. This amount is shown in column (c) of Table 12.5 and represents the difference between the gross 2002 cash receipt of $79,139.18 from the lessee and the interest income of $28,456.98 that will be recognized in 2002. Thus, current assets on the direct financing basis would be higher than they would have been under the operating lease approach—and the current ratio is accordingly improved.

Sales-Type Lease Treatment Illustrated

Accounting for sales-type leases is a simple extension of the direct financing method. A sales-type lease includes a manufacturer's or dealer's profit *in addition to* financing profit; a direct financing lease doesn't.

To illustrate the accounting for sales-type leases, let's assume that the Lessor Company is the manufacturer of the leased equipment. Prior to the start of the lease on January 1, 2001, the equipment was carried on Lessor Company's books at its manufacturing cost of $240,000. All other facts in the original example remain unchanged.

Lessor Company would record the transaction on January 1, 2001, as follows:

DR	Gross investment in leased asset	$415,695.90	
	CR Sales revenues		$304,359.49
	CR Unearned financing income—leases		111,336.41
DR	Cost of goods sold	$240,000.00	
	CR Inventory		$240,000.00

The net effect of these entries is to recognize $64,359.49 of manufacturing profit ($304,359.49 – $240,000.00) immediately. The $111,336.41 of financing profit will be recognized over the life of the lease, as shown in column (b) of the amortization schedule in Table 12.5. The entries for recording this financing profit are absolutely identical to the entries for the direct financing method on page 559.

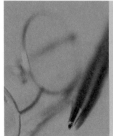

Recap
The capital lease/operating lease dichotomy also exists for lessors. The criteria for classifying these leases include the same four criteria that apply to lessees plus two additional criteria. Lessors' incentives regarding how to classify leases are very different from those of lessees, since capital lease treatment accelerates the timing of income recognition for lessors. In addition, capital lease treatment improves many ratios for lessors in contrast to operating lease treatment.

Additional Leasing Aspects
Sale and Leaseback

A sale and leaseback condition exists when one company sells an asset to another company and immediately leases it back. This is one way of financing asset acquisitions and/or for tax reasons. For example, First Company sells a manufacturing plant (excluding land) with a book value of $800,000 to Second Company for $1,000,000. First Company immediately leases the plant from Second Company for 20 years at an annual rental of $120,000.

First Company may be able to treat the entire annual rental of $120,000 as a deductible expense for tax purposes; if it had continued to own the asset, it could deduct capital cost allowance only for the building itself but not for the land on which the building is located. Thus, total tax deductions may be higher under sale and leaseback arrangements. Also, the cash infusion of $1,000,000 may help meet cash flow needs.

No new lease accounting issues arise in sale and leaseback transactions. If the lease satisfies any of the four lessees' criteria on page 543, First Company must account for the lease as a capital lease; if none of the criteria are met, it is treated as an operating lease. If the lease satisfies at least one of the lessors' Type I characteristics and both of the Type II characteristics (page 556), Second Company treats the lease as a direct financing lease; otherwise, it is an operating lease on Second Company's books.

The only complication in sale and leaseback arrangements is the treatment of the difference between the sale price of $1,000,000 and the $800,000 carrying value of the manufacturing plant on First Company's books. Typically, when assets are sold, this $200,000 would be recognized immediately on First Company's books as a gain on sale.

But this is not the way gains are treated in sale and leaseback transactions.[15] Instead, First Company must record the $200,000 as a balance sheet credit, called a **deferred gain.** If the lease is a capital lease to First Company, this gain is then amortized into income using the same rate and life used to amortize the asset itself. If the lease is an operating lease to First Company, the gain is amortized in proportion to the rental payment.

Assume that the lease qualifies as a capital lease; then First Company's entries would initially be:

DR	Cash (or receivable)	$1,000,000	
	CR Property		$ 800,000
	CR Deferred gain		200,000
DR	Leased equipment—capital lease	$1,000,000	
	CR Obligation under capital lease		$1,000,000

(This assumes that the discounted present value of the minimum lease payment is equal to $1,000,000.)

The rationale for deferring the gain is simple. Notice that at the time of "sale," the sales price of $1,000,000 and the annual lease payment schedule of $120,000 are simultaneously set, and the transaction is not complete. It may be that the property is only "worth" $800,000 and that Second Company is effectively advancing $200,000 to First Company, which will be recovered over time through the $120,000 annual payments on the lease. Recognizing a gain in such circumstances would allow First Company to initially overstate its income by $200,000; this would be offset in later years by overstating its expenses by an identical amount. Thus, the GAAP requirement of deferring the gain protects against income manipulation possibilities. However, the conservatism inherent to GAAP requires that losses in sale and lease-back transactions be recognized immediately on the seller's books.

Other Special Lease Accounting Issues

Real estate leases, leveraged leases (i.e., leases in which the lessor borrows to finance a specific lease transaction), and synthetic lease transactions are examples of special lease accounting issues. The Emerging Issues Committee (EIC) has issued ten *Abstracts* over the years dealing with a variety of lease accounting issues, thus proving the potential complexity of leasing.

The synthetic lease arrangement, for example, is a type of off-balance-sheet financing, the goal of which is to provide the lessee with the "accounting benefits" of treating the asset under the operating lease method while at the same time the lessee treats the asset as if it were owned for income tax filing purposes, thus enjoying deductions on its tax return. In essence, a synthetic lease is structured to achieve the best of both worlds for the lessee: operating lease treatment in the financial statements and capital lease treatment on the tax return. The parties to the synthetic lease arrangement include: the lessee, a lender, outside investors, and a special purpose entity.

Lessors' Disclosures

Exhibit 12.2, taken from various notes of Bombardier Inc.'s financial statements for the year ended January 31, 2002, illustrates Section 3065 disclosure for lessors. Notice that information about minimum lease payments to be received is provided only for the company's nonoperating leases; Section 3065 recommends but does not require that lessors disclose such information for their operating leases. The cost of assets under operating leases must be disclosed, however (3065.58).

BOMBARDIER INC.
www.bombardier.com

Summary

Section 3065 is an attempt to implement the representational faithfulness qualitative characteristic mentioned in Chapter 1. It establishes the general principle that for lease arrangements, in which the legal ownership of an asset resides in one accounting entity (the lessor) and use of the asset resides with another accounting entity (the lessee), there are circumstances in which the transaction is so close to a sale that it should be accounted for virtually as such. Determining the point at which those circumstances occur is the subject of paras. 3065.06 (for lessees) and 3065.07 (for lessors). Notice that the specific cutoffs in these paragraphs (i.e., the 75% and 90%) are guidelines.[16] There may be economic incentives for lessees to arrange lease contracts so that they are not captured by the lease capitalization requirements. Conversely, there may be economic incentives for lessors to write direct financing or sales-type leases rather than operating leases. All this points to the crucial importance of disclosure in lease footnotes.

Exhibit 12.2 BOMBARDIER INC.

January 31, 2002
Illustration of Lessor's Disclosure

4. Finance Receivables (cont'd)

Production Description—BC

...

[v] Lease receivables

Lease receivables consist of the following:

	2002	2001
Total minimum lease payments	$ 955.2	$1,072.2
Unearned income	(144.3)	(176.8)
Unguaranteed residual value	34.8	57.5
	$ 845.7	$ 952.9

The minimum lease payments for the next five years are as follows: 2003 – $473.3 million; 2004 – $160.6 million; 2005 – $98.5 million; 2006 – $58.1 million and 2007 – $52.4 million.

...

5. Assets Under Operating Leases

BC's assets under operating leases were as follows:

	2002	2001
Aircraft		
– Business	$1,133.0	$1,032.2
– Commercial	645.2	521.8
Freight cars—Assets held for resale	81.0	184.0
Industrial equipment	61.7	25.2
Discontinued portfolios (note 4)	88.7	94.4
	2,009.6	1,857.6
Accumulated depreciation	(178.4)	(89.5)
	$1,831.2	$1,768.1

Freight cars held temporarily, pending their financing through sale and leaseback transactions, are presented as assets held for resale. For the purpose of establishing the assets under management, the portfolio of off-balance sheet freight cars amounted to $1,067.9 million as at January 31, 2002 ($917.8 million as at January 31, 2001) which represents the net present value of the minimum lease payments of $1,974.4 million as at January 31, 2002 ($1,737.7 million as at January 31, 2001), pursuant to sale and leaseback transactions disclosed in note 25 [B].

The weighted average maturity of the operating leases was 52 months as at January 31, 2002 (53 months as at January 31, 2001).

Depreciation of assets under operating leases was $132.4 million for the year ended January 31, 2002 ($81.8 million for the year ended January 31, 1001) and is included in depreciation and amortization.

Appendix 12A

Making Balance Sheet Data Comparable by Adjusting for Off-Balance-Sheet Leases

Some lessee companies may deliberately structure leases to evade capital lease criteria, thereby keeping most of their leases off the balance sheet. Other companies are less aggressive and have a larger proportion of capital leases. This complicates comparisons between any two companies, because the companies may have similar lease contract terms but very dissimilar lease balance sheet numbers.

The most straightforward method for making lessees' balance sheet data comparable is to treat *all* leases as if they were capital leases. That is, analysts should use the disclosed minimum *operating* lease payment schedule as a basis for approximating what the balance sheet numbers would have been had those operating leases been treated instead as capital leases. This is called **constructive capitalization.** We use data from Sears, Roebuck and Company to illustrate how this is done.

The liability that would appear on the balance sheet if these operating leases were instead treated as capital leases is the *discounted present value* of the stream of minimum operating lease payments. This payment stream totals $2,419. Two items must be estimated in order to compute this present value. First, a discount rate must be selected. Second, each year's payments beyond 2004 must be estimated, since lease payments for all years after 2004 are aggregated.

SEARS, ROEBUCK AND COMANY
www.sears.com

SEARS, ROEBUCK AND COMPANY

Operating Lease Payments from Lease Footnote

January 1, 2000 Annual Report

(US$ in millions)

Fiscal Year	Minimum Operating Lease Payments
2000	$ 352
2001	303
2002	253
2003	224
2004	195
After 2004	1,092
Total minimum lease payments	$2,419

Selecting a Discount Rate In some cases, a company will disclose in its lease footnote the weighted average discount rate used for all its capital lease commitments. This rate would be appropriate to use for capitalizing operating leases. Alternatively, an estimate of the discount rate can be derived from the lessee's financial statement footnote for long-term debt. The interest rate paid on each debt issue is disclosed in this footnote. The weighted average rate on outstanding long-term debt provides a reasonable estimate of the lease discount rate. Another way to estimate the average long-term debt rate is to compute the ratio of interest expense to average debt outstanding. Doing this using data from Sears' debt footnote yields an estimated rate of 8%.

Estimating Payments Beyond Five Years Procedures for estimating annual operating lease payments for periods after 2004 can also be developed. One approach is as follows. Notice that the annual *decline* in minimum operating lease

Sears discloses interest paid in 1999 was US$1.2 billion. Long-term debt at the beginning of 1999 was US$15.045 billion and at the end of 1999 was US$15.049 billion. So a simple estimate of average debt outstanding is US$15.047 billion. The estimate of the long-term debt rate is:

$$\frac{\$1.2 \text{ billion}}{\$15.047 \text{ billion}} \cong 8\%$$

payments between 2002 and 2004 is US$29 million per year. This suggests that the undisclosed minimum operating lease payment for 2005 is probably in the vicinity of US$166 million—the US$195 million 2004 payment minus approximately US$29 million of estimated yearly decline. The simplest approach for estimating a schedule of annual payments for 2005 and beyond is to assume that all subsequent payments are also somewhere near US$166 million per year. Dividing the total later years' minimum operating lease payments (US$1,092 million, the highlighted figure) by US$166 million yields an initial estimate of how many years beyond 2004 the existing operating leases run. The computation is:

$$\frac{\text{Minimum operating lease payments for years after 2004}}{\text{Estimated yearly lease payment (assumed to be the same for all years)}} = \frac{\$1,092 \text{ million}}{\$166 \text{ million per year}} = 6.578 \text{ years}$$

The initial estimate is 6.578 years, which we round to 7 years. Based on this estimate, the net minimum lease payments will be discounted over a 12-year period—that is, 2000 through 2004 (5 years) plus the estimated 7 years we just computed.

Our estimate of the amount of additional liability that would appear on Sears' balance sheet at January 1, 2000, if all operating leases were capitalized is the highlighted amount shown in Table 12.7. This number is an additional liability of approximately US$1,672.0 million. A small portion (US$218.2 million) would be a current liability and US$1,672 million – US$218.2 million, or US$1,453.8 million, would be a long-term liability.

Once the capitalized operating lease liability has been estimated, the next task is to estimate the capitalized operating lease *asset* amount. One approach is to assume that the amount of the asset equals the amount of the computed operating lease liability. Since the asset and liability amounts are equal at the inception of a capital lease, this approach assumes that this initial equality is maintained over the entire life of the lease. But a more precise estimate can easily be made, as shown in Figure 12.3.

> The current liability of US$218.2 million is determined as follows. Interest expense in fiscal year 2000 on these capitalized operating leases would approximate US$1,672.0 × 8%, or US$133.8 million. The 2000 minimum operating lease payment is US$352 million in Table 12.7. Since interest is a liability that accrues over time, only the difference between the total 2000 payment of US$352 million and the as-yet unaccrued interest of US$133.8 million (i.e., US$218.2 million) is a current liability as of January 1, 2000.

TABLE 12.7 SEARS, ROEBUCK AND COMPANY

Estimate of Capitalized Operating Lease Liability as of January 1, 2000

(US$ in millions) Fiscal Year	Minimum Operating Lease Payment	Present Value Factor at 8%	Discounted Present Value
2000	$352	.92593	$ 325.9
2001	303	.85734	259.8
2002	253	.79383	200.8
2003	224	.73503	164.6
2004	195	.68058	132.7
2005 } 2011 }	166	3.54337[1]	588.2
Total			$1,672.0

[1]Present value of an ordinary annuity for 12 years at 8% minus present value of an ordinary annuity for 5 years at 8%, or 7.53608 minus 3.99271.

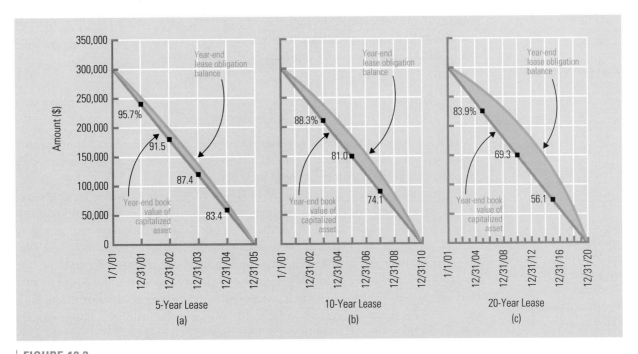

FIGURE 12.3

LESSEE COMPANY

General relationship between capital lease asset and liability when payments are at end of period: (a) five-year lease; (b) ten-year lease; (c) twenty-year lease

Figure 12.3(a) graphically represents the data in Table 12.1 (the Lessee Company) where lease payments are due at the end of each period. The year-end book value of the capitalized asset (the dark straight line in the graph) starts at $300,000 and declines yearly by $60,000—the straight-line amortization amount from column (e) in Table 12.1—until it reaches zero at the end of 2005. The light curved line depicts the year-end lease obligation balance from column (d) in Table 12.1. While the two balances are obviously equal at the beginning and end of the lease, *for all intermediate periods, the asset amount is lower than the liability.* This relationship holds in general, since early-year payments do not reduce the liability by as much as later-year payments do (compare columns [c] and [e] of Table 12.1). Notice that Figure 12.3(a) includes the percentage relationship between the capitalized asset and liability balances for all intermediate lease years. For example, at December 31, 2001, the asset balance is 95.7% of the obligation balance for the five-year lease.

Parts (b) and (c) in the figure show the relationship between the lease asset and lease liability balances for the same basic facts as in (a), but here the lease period is for 10 years and 20 years, respectively. The *difference* between the asset and liability balances *increases* the longer the life of the lease. The reason is that the lease liability balance decreases at a lower rate when lease payments are spread over longer periods—that is, a greater portion of each early lease payment is for interest and a correspondingly smaller portion goes toward reducing the lease obligation the longer the term of the lease.

Lease Payments in Advance
Leases frequently require the lessee to make an up-front payment when the lease is signed. Advance payments in a capital lease mean that at the inception of the lease the amount of the recorded asset will exceed the

liability. Using the example in Table 12.3 (page 549), we assume a 10% discount rate and that Lessee Company makes its five annual payments in advance. Each payment is $71,945. The journal entry on January 1, 2001, is:

DR	Capital lease asset	$300,000.00	
	CR Cash		$ 71,945
	CR Obligation under capital lease		228,055

Figure 12.4 depicts the general relationship between the lease asset and lease liability for a five-, ten-, and twenty-year lease at a 10% discount rate where the contract calls for payments at the beginning of each lease period.

In contrast to the situation depicted in Figure 12.3 where payments are at the end of each lease period, the up-front payment means that the asset carrying amount initially *exceeds* the liability amount, as shown in both the journal entry and in Figure 12.4. With payments in advance, in periods subsequent to the lease signing, the relationship between the leased asset and liability carrying amounts depends on the length of the lease term. With five- and ten-year leases and a 10% discount rate, the carrying value of the lease liability is always less than the asset book value throughout the lease term. However, as shown for a 20-year lease, the liability amount quickly exceeds the asset amount, and this relationship is maintained until the last two years of the lease. This excess is the dark shaded area in Figure 12.4(c). The liability quickly "overtakes" the asset because early year payments on an amortization schedule do not reduce the liability by as much as later year payments do. For a given lease length, the higher the interest rate, the quicker the liability exceeds the asset.

With a $300,000 present value at 10%, the annual payments for a 5-year, 10-year, and 20-year lease are $71,945.00, $44,385.11, and $32,034.44, respectively. The vertical distance between the lease asset and obligation lines on 1/1/01 represent these initial payments.

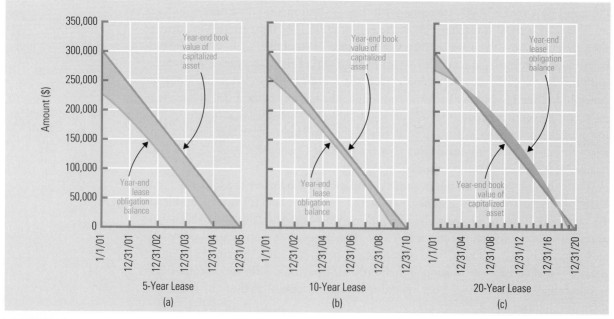

FIGURE 12.4

LESSEE COMPANY

General relationship between capital lease asset and liability when up-front payments are made for a (a) 5-year lease; (b) 10-year lease; (c) 20-year lease.

Most companies have a portfolio of operating leases with different ages, interest rates, and payment timing. Therefore, on average across the entire portfolio, many companies' asset-to-liability ratios will be somewhere in the dark shaded area of Figure 12.4(c). *The capital lease liability will often exceed the asset as illustrated in both Figures 12.3 and 12.4(c).* However, there are exceptions. When most of a firm's leases have up-front payments, the interest rate is low, and/or the life of the average lease is relatively short, then the asset amount *can* exceed the liability amount. As you will see, this is true for Sears at January 1, 2000.

The percentage relationship between the asset and the liability is a function of payment timing, the interest rate, and the length of the lease.[17] Furthermore, the precise relationship *at any specific date* depends upon the average age of existing leases. Rather than attempting to estimate the percentage relationship between the asset and liability for capitalized operating leases, we can use the disclosure the company makes for capital leases. For example, at January 1, 2000, Sears disclosed that its net capital lease assets totalled US$496 million and its net capital lease obligations were US$417 million. This results in an asset-to-liability ratio for capital leases of 119%. It may be reasonable to use this same percentage to estimate the operating lease asset to be capitalized. Our estimate of the balance sheet asset that would arise from capitalized operating leases is therefore the computed liability from Table 12.7—US$1,672.0 million—times 119%, or US$1,989.7 million.

Table 12.8 illustrates the estimated ratio effects for fiscal year 1999 that result from capitalizing operating leases for Sears. Table 12.8(a) column (1) shows financial statement numbers as reported in Sears' 1999 statements. Column (2) shows the adjustments for operating lease capitalization. Notice, in addition to the capital lease asset and liability adjustments, there is a "net credit to balance" of US$318 million—simply the difference between the US$1,990 million estimated asset amount minus the US$1,672 million liability amount. The credit of US$318 million is the net of two items, (1) a debit to a deferred tax asset and (2) a credit to owners' equity.

A deferred tax asset arises because capitalization accelerates expense recognition. Accordingly, capitalizing these leases means that expenses are recognized earlier on the books than on the tax return and a deferred tax asset consequently results. The amount of the deferred tax asset is determined by the cumulative capital versus operating lease expense difference. Unfortunately, this cumulative difference cannot be estimated easily or accurately. As a result, we cannot subdivide the US$318 million between the deferred tax asset and the owners' equity credit.

As discussed in the chapter, the income statement effects of capital lease treatment versus operating lease treatment often will not be significantly different for mature firms. Consequently, we do not adjust income in Table 12.8(a).

Of course, this is only a rough approximation. The higher the proportion of leases with up-front payments, the shorter the lease life, and/or the lower the interest rate, the higher the asset-to-liability ratio. So, if operating leases differ along these dimensions from capital leases, using the disclosed capital leases asset-to-liability ratio will tend to misstate the asset carrying value after capitalizing operating leases.

This paragraph assumes you are comfortable with deferred, or future, tax concepts. If you are not, you can safely skip this paragraph and return to Table 12.8 after reading Chapter 13.

TABLE 12.8 SEARS, ROEBUCK AND COMPANY

Effect on Selected Ratios of Capitalizing Operating Leases
January 1, 2000

	(a) Financial Statement Data			
(US$ in millions) **Statement Item**	**(1)** **January 1, 2000** **Financial** **Statements**	**(2)** **Adjustments** **for Capitalization**		**(3)** **Total After** **Capitalization**
Total assets	$36,954	Capital lease asset	+$1,990	$38,944
		Current portion lease obligation	+ 218	218
Total long-term obligations	16,414	Long-term lease obligation	+ 1,454	17,868
Owners' equity	6,839	Net credit to balance	+318	7,157
Operating income before taxes and other charges	2,413		0	$ 2,413

	(b) Adjusted Ratios After Capitalization	
Ratio	**(1)** **As Reported in** **1/01/00 Financial Statements**	**(2)** **Ratio After** **Capitalization**
Total long-term obligations-to-equity ratio	2.40	2.50[#]
Pre-tax return on total assets	6.530	6.196*

[#]Computed by adding $1,454 to column (1) obligations and $318 to column (1) equity. This ignores the unknown deferred tax effect and distorts the adjusted column (3) ratio slightly.

*Computed by adding $1,990 to column (1) total assets. This ignores the unknown deferred tax effect and distorts the adjusted column (3) ratio slightly.

The adjusted ratios after capitalization are shown in Table 12.8(b). Notice that the adjustments from capitalizing operating leases do not change Sears' ratios significantly. Pre-tax return on assets is lowered by approximately 5.1% and the total long-term obligations-to-equity ratio is increased by approximately 4.2%. Nevertheless, it is important to make adjustments like these if you're making financial comparisons *across* firms. While the effect on Sears is small, some of Sears' competitors may be more aggressive in keeping leases off the balance sheet. So interfirm comparisons may be misleading unless adjustments are also made to the competitors' statements. The underlying real economic differences appear only when the adjusted statements for all firms are compared. The easiest way to overcome these capitalization differences between firms is to treat all leases that convey significant property rights as though they were capital leases.

A movement to do this in the financial statements themselves is emerging internationally. The FASB recently published a special report formulated by a working group comprising standard-setters from Austria, Canada, the International Accounting Standards Committee (IASC), New Zealand, the United Kingdom, and the United States. This report proposed that many leases that are now treated as operating leases should be treated as capital leases.[18]

Exercises

E12-1 Lessee and lessor accounting

Fox Company, a dealer in machinery and equipment, leased equipment to Tiger Inc. on July 1, 2002. The lease is appropriately accounted for as a sale by Fox and as a purchase by Tiger. The lease is for a ten-year period (the useful life of the asset), expiring June 30, 2012. The first of ten equal payments of $500,000 was made on July 1, 2002. Fox had purchased the equipment for $2,675,000 on January 1, 2002 and established a list selling price of $3,375,000 on the equipment. Assume that the present value at July 1, 2002 of the rent payments over the lease term discounted at 12% (the appropriate interest rate) was $3,165,000.

Required:

1. What is the amount of profit on the sale and the amount of interest income that Fox should record for the year ended December 31, 2002? How much interest income should Fox record in 2003?
2. Assume that Tiger uses straight-line amortization and a 12% discount rate. What amount of amortization and interest expense should Tiger record for the year ended December 31, 2002 and for the year ended December 31, 2003?

E12-2 Lessee accounting

CICA adapted

On September 1, 2001, P Ltd. entered into a lease for equipment with a fair market value of $70,000, for a noncancellable period of eight years. The minimum annual lease payment is $12,000, payable at the end of each year of the lease. Both P Ltd. and the lessor company agree that the expected economic life of the equipment is about twelve years, although during the last third of its expected economic life the equipment was not expected to be very efficient.

At the inception of the lease, the prime rate was 10%, P Ltd.'s incremental borrowing rate was 11%, and the rate implicit in the lease was 12%.

Required:

1. From the perspective of the lessee, is this an operating or a capital lease?
2. Is a journal entry required on P's books as of September 1, 2001? If yes, prepare it.
3. *Assume* that the lease is a capital lease (in spite of any possible evidence to the contrary). Prepare P's journal entries in respect to the lease over the complete lease term.

E12-3 Lessee accounting

CICA adapted

Assume the lease described in E12-2 has the following additional contractual requirement: "P Ltd. must make an additional lease payment of $100 for each percentage point of the prime rate in effect on the date on which each of the annual lease payments become due."

Required:

Will your answers to Questions 1 and 2 of E12-2 change because of this additional information?

E12-4 Lessor accounting
CICA adapted

On January 1, 2001, Digitex and Marconex signed an agreement to lease equipment by which substantially all the benefits and risks of ownership were transferred from Marconex to Digitex. The lessee assumed all the costs to insure and maintain the equipment. Digitex's incremental borrowing rate is estimated to be 7%, while the return required by the lessor (on a before-tax basis) is 8%. The lessee does not know the interest rate implicit in the lease. The lease contract includes the following information:

Annual rental payable at the beginning of the year	$20,000
Lease term	5 years
Fair value of the equipment as at January 1, 2001	$95,000
Unguaranteed residual value, December 31, 2005	$12,941

Required:

Compute the amount that should appear on the balance sheet of the lessor as the net investment in a direct financing lease, immediately after the agreement is signed. Assume that the lessor must comply with GAAP.

E12-5 Lessee accounting
CICA adapted
Required:

1. For the lease arrangement described in E12-4, what amortization expense in respect to the leased equipment should the lessee record in its books for the year ended December 31, 2001? Assume GAAP are followed and the leased asset is amortized on a straight-line basis.
2. Prepare all the journal entries that the lessee must prepare under GAAP over the life of the lease agreement.

E12-6 Lessee accounting: Purchase option

East Company leased a new machine from North Company on May 1, 2002 under a lease with the following information:

Lease term	10 years
Annual rental payable at beginning of each lease year	$40,000
Useful life of machine	12 years
Implicit interest rate	14%
Present value of an annuity of $1 paid at the beginning of each of 10 periods at 14%	5.95
Present value of $1 due at the end of 10 periods at 14%	0.27

East has the option to purchase the machine on May 1, 2012, by paying $50,000, which approximates the expected fair market value of the machine on the option exercise date.

Required:

What is the amount of the capitalized leased asset on May 1, 2002?

E12-7 Lessee accounting and classification

On December 31, 2002, Ball Company leased a machine from Cook for a ten-year period, expiring December 31, 2012. Annual payments of $100,000 are due on December 31. The first payment was made on December 31, 2003, and the second payment was made on December 31, 2004. The present value at the inception of the lease for the ten lease payments discounted at 10% was $676,000. The lease is appropriately accounted for as a capital lease by Ball.

Required:

1. Compute the December 31, 2003, amount that Ball should report as lease liability.
2. What portion of this total liability should be classified as a current liability?

Problems/Discussion Questions

P12-1 Lessees' accounting for capital leases including executory costs and residual value guarantee

On January 1, 2001, Bare Trees Company signed a three-year noncancellable lease with Dreams Inc. The lease calls for three payments of $62,258.09, to be made at the end of each year. The lease payments include $3,000 of executory costs. The lease is nonrenewable, and there is no bargain purchase option. The leased asset reverts to Dreams at the end of the lease period, at which time Bare Trees has guaranteed that the leased asset will be worth at least $15,000. The leased asset has an expected useful life of four years, and Bare Trees uses straight-line amortization for financial reporting purposes. Bare Trees' incremental borrowing rate is 9%, which is less than Dreams' implicit rate of return on the lease.

Required:

1. Prepare a schedule for the amortization of the lease liability. Round the amount of the initial lease liability at January 1, 2001 to the nearest dollar. Round all amounts in the amortization table to the nearest cent.
2. Make the journal entry to record (a) the lease on January 1, 2001, (b) the lease payments on December 31, 2001 and 2002, and (c) the amortization of the leased asset in 2001 and 2002.
3. Assume that at the end of the lease term the leased asset is worth $16,000. Make the journal entry to account for the residual value guarantee.
4. Repeat Question 3, but assume that the leased asset is worth only $12,000 at the end of the lease term.

P12-2 Capital lease effects on ratios and income

On December 31, 2000, Thomas Henley, financial vice-president of Kingston Corporation, signed a noncancellable three-year lease for an item of manufacturing equipment. The lease called for annual payments of $41,635 per year, due at the *end* of each of the next three years. The expected economic life of the leased equipment was four years. No cash changed hands since the first payment wasn't due until December 31, 2001.

Mr. Henley was talking with his auditor that afternoon and was surprised to learn that the lease qualified as a capital lease and would have to be put on the balance sheet. Although his intuition told him that capitalization adversely affected certain ratios, the size of these adverse effects was unclear to him. Because similar leases on other equipment were up for renewal in 2001, he wanted a precise measure of the ratio deterioration. "If these effects are excessive," he said, "I'll try to get similar leases on the other machinery to qualify as operating leases when they come up for renewal next year."

Assume that the appropriate rate for discounting the minimum lease payments is 12%. (The present value of an ordinary annuity of $1 per period for three periods at 12% is 2.40183.) Also assume that the asset "Leased equipment under capital leases" will be amortized on a straight-line basis.

Required:

1. Prepare an amortization schedule for the lease.
2. The effect of lease capitalization on the current ratio worried Mr. Henley. *Before factoring in the capital lease signed on December 31, 2000,* Kingston Corporation's current ratio at December 31, 2000 was:

$$\frac{\text{Current assets}}{\text{Current liabilities}} = \frac{\$500,000}{\$294,118} = 1.7$$

   Calculate the revised ratio if the lease is treated as a capital lease.
3. Mr. Henley was also concerned about the effect that lease capitalization would have on net income. He estimated that if the lease previously described were treated as an *operating* lease, 2001 pre-tax income would be $225,000. Determine the 2001 pre-tax income if this lease were treated as a capital lease and if the leased equipment were amortized on a straight-line basis over the life of the lease.

P12-3 Lessors' direct financing lease

Rankin Corporation, a lessor of office machines, purchased a new machine for $725,000 on December 31, 2002, which was delivered the same day (by prior arrangement) to Liska Company, the lessee. The following information relating to the lease transaction is available:

- The leased asset has an estimated useful life of five years, which coincides with the lease term.
- At the end of the lease term, the machine will revert to Rankin, at which time it is expected to have a salvage value of $60,000 (which is not guaranteed by Liska).
- Rankin's implicit rate of return on its net lease investment is 8%, which is known by Liska.
- Liska's incremental borrowing rate is 12% at December 31, 2002.
- Lease rentals consist of five equal annual payments, the first of which was paid on December 31, 2002.
- The lease is appropriately accounted for as a direct financing lease by Rankin and as a capital lease by Liska. Both lessor and lessee are calendar-year corporations and amortize all fixed assets on a straight-line basis.

Required:

Round all amounts to the nearest dollar.

1. Compute the annual rental under the lease.
2. Compute the amounts of the gross rentals receivable and the unearned interest revenue that Rankin should disclose at the inception of the lease on December 31, 2002.
3. What expense should Liska record for the year ended December 31, 2003?

P12-4 Lessor accounting for sales-type leases

On January 1, 2001, ABC Builders Inc. (the lessor) entered into a lease with Winged Foot Company (the lessee) for an asset that ABC Builders had manufactured at a cost of $15,000,000. The fair market value of the asset on January 1, 2001, is $19,354,730. The lease calls for six annual payments of $5,000,000, to be made at the end of each year. The asset has a useful life of six years. The lease contains no renewal or bargain purchase option, and possession of the asset reverts to ABC Builders at the end of the lease. The lease requires that Winged Foot Company guarantee that the residual value of the asset will be at least $1,000,000 at the end of the lease. The collectibility of the payments is reasonably certain, and there are no important uncertainties regarding unreimbursable costs to be incurred by the lessor. ABC Builders has structured the lease so as to earn a rate of return of 15.0%.

Required:

1. Why must ABC Builders account for the lease as a sales-type lease?
2. Prepare an amortization schedule for the lease for ABC Builders. (Round all amounts to the nearest cent.)
3. Make the journal entries for ABC Builders at the inception of the lease and for the payments received in 2001 and 2002.
4. Make the journal entry for ABC Builders at the expiration of the lease. Assume the leased asset's residual value is $0.

P12-5 Financial statement effects for lessees: Capital versus operating leases

Assume that on January 1, 2001, Trans Global Airlines leases two used Boeing 727s from Aircraft Lessors Inc. The eight-year lease calls for payments of $10,000,000 at the end of each year. On January 1, 2001, the Boeing 727s have a total fair market value of $55,000,000 and a remaining useful life of ten years. Assume that Trans Global's incremental borrowing rate is 12% and that it uses straight-line amortization for financial reporting purposes. The lease is noncancellable, cannot be renewed by Trans Global, has no bargain purchase option, and the leased asset reverts to Aircraft Lessors at the end of the lease. Aircraft Lessors' implicit rate of return on the lease is unknown.

Required:

1. Should Trans Global account for the lease as a capital or an operating lease? Why?
2. On the basis of your answer to Question 1, make all the journal entries that Trans Global would make related to the lease for 2001, 2002, 2003, and 2008. Round all amounts to the nearest cent.
3. Make all journal entries related to the lease for 2001, 2002, 2003, and 2008. Assume that Trans Global accounts for the lease using whichever method (capital or operating) that you did not select in Question 1.
4. Prepare a schedule of the year-to-year and total (before-tax) income differences that would result from accounting for the lease as a capital lease versus an operating lease. Round all amounts to the nearest cent.
5. Why might Trans Global's managers prefer the lease to be accounted for as an operating lease rather than as a capital lease?

P12-6 Asset acquisition: Cash purchase versus lease versus note payable

On January 1, 2002, the Corporal Motors Corporation needs to acquire a vehicle painting machine. The company is considering three alternative methods for acquiring the machine.

1. *Option I.* Issue a $125,000 non-interest-bearing note to the seller on January 1, 2002 (due date: December 31, 2006).
2. *Option II.* Lease the machine from the seller. The lease would require five equal annual payments of $22,000 to be made on December 31 each year from 2002 to 2006.
3. *Option III.* Purchase the machine outright by paying $90,000 in cash on January 1, 2002.

Other Information:

- Corporal Motors uses straight-line amortization for financial reporting purposes.
- The machine has a five-year useful life with no salvage value.
- Round all amounts to the nearest whole dollar.
- Corporal Motors' incremental borrowing rate is 8% (compounded annually).
- Corporal Motors reports on a calendar-year basis.

Required:

1. Which of the three alternatives should be selected and why?
2. What will be the total expense (and components making up the total expense) for the first year if Option I is adopted?
3. What will be the total expense (and components making up the total expense) for all five years together if Option I is adopted?
4. What will be the total expense (and components making up the total expense) for the first year if Option II is adopted and if the lease is accounted for as an operating lease?
5. What will be the total expense (and components making up the total expense) for all five years together if Option II is adopted and if the lease is accounted for as an operating lease?
6. What will be the total expense (and components making up the total expense) for the first year if Option II is adopted and if the lease is accounted for as a capital lease?
7. What will be the total expense (and components making up the total expense) for all five years together if Option II is adopted and if the lease is accounted for as a capital lease?
8. What will be the total expense (and components making up the total expense) for the first year if Option III is adopted?
9. What will be the total expense (and components making up the total expense) for all five years together if Option III is adopted?

P12-7 Constructive capitalization of operating leases

The following lease footnote disclosure is provided by Penguin Corporation:

5. Lease Commitments

The Company leases certain of its facilities and equipment under various operating and capital leases. The lease agreements frequently include renewal and purchase provisions and require the Company to pay taxes, insurance, and maintenance costs.

Total rental expense under operating leases was $11,243,000, $9,985,000, and $8,853,000 in 1997, 1996, and 1995, respectively.

The following is a schedule of future minimum lease payments under capital leases and rental payments required under long-term operating leases at the end of the 1997 fiscal year ($ thousands):

Fiscal Years	Operating Leases	Capital Leases
1998	$ 8,494	$77
1999	6,835	—
2000	4,952	—
2001	4,740	—
2002	4,023	—
Later years	12,979	—
Total	$42,023	$77
Less amount representing interest		(7)
Present value of minimum lease payments		$70

Assume that all lease payments are made at the end of the year.

Required:

1. Estimate the interest rate implicit in the firm's capital lease obligation.
2. Based on the rate in Question 1, make the journal entry to record the 1998 capital lease payment.
3. Use the interest rate in Question 1 to estimate the present value of the operating leases as of the end of the 1997 fiscal year. When doing so, assume that the payments due after 2002 are equal and will be made over a four-year period.
4. Prepare a 1997 end-of-year journal entry that would capitalize (i.e., convert from operating to capital) the present value of Penguin's 1997 end-of-year operating leases computed in Question 3.
5. Make the journal entry for the 1998 operating lease payment. Assume that the operating leases are being accounted for as capital leases.
6. Describe the impact on the firm's interest coverage ratio in the 1998 fiscal year if the operating leases were instead accounted for as capital leases at the end of 1997.
7. Describe the impact on the firm's leverage ratios (e.g., total debt to shareholders' equity and long-term debt to shareholders' equity) at the end of 1997 if the operating leases were instead being accounted for as capital leases.
8. If the operating leases were instead being accounted for as capital leases, how would the 1998 payment affect the firm's 1998 cash flow statement?
9. Is the answer to Question 8 the same as or different from what the effect on the cash flow statement would be if the leases were to be accounted for as operating leases?

10. Describe the rationale for treating some leases as capital leases and others as operating leases.

Cases

C12-1 May Department Stores (CW): Constructive capitalization of operating leases

THE MAY
DEPARTMENT STORES
COMPANY
www2.mayco.com

May Department Stores operates department stores in 34 states and the District of Columbia. The company's department stores operate under the following names: Lord & Taylor, Hecht's, Strawbridge's, Foley's, Robinsons-May, Filene's, Kaufmann's, Famous-Barr, L. S. Ayres, The Jones Store, Meier & Frank, ZCMI, and David's Bridal.

The following information is taken from a recent annual report of the company.

Lease Obligations

The company owns approximately 77% of its stores. Rental expense for the company's operating leases consisted of:

(US$ in millions)	1999	1998	1997
Minimum rentals	$48	$49	$47
Contingent rentals based on sales	18	18	17
Real property rentals	66	67	64
Equipment rentals	3	3	4
Total	$69	$70	$68

Future minimum lease payments at January 29, 2000, were as follows:

(US$ in millions)	Capital Leases	Operating Leases	Total
2000	$ 7	$ 51	$ 58
2001	7	46	53
2002	7	43	50
2003	7	40	47
2004	7	38	45
After 2004	93	264	357
Minimum lease payments	$128	$482	$610
Less: imputed interest component	71		
Present value of net minimum lease payments, of which $1 million is included in current liabilities	$ 57		

The present value of operating leases was [US]$291 million at January 29, 2000.

Other Information/Assumptions:

- Assume that the amount of May's operating lease payments due each year after 2004 are equal and that these leases all terminate in the year 2014.
- Excerpted balance sheet data (in U.S. dollars)

	January 29, 2000	January 30, 1999
Long-term debt	$3,560	$3,825
Total shareholders' equity	4,077	3,836

- Assume that all operating lease payments are made at the end of May Department Stores' fiscal year.

1. Make the journal entry to record May's operating leases as if they were being treated as capital leases as of January 29, 2000.
2. Calculate May's ratio of long-term debt to stockholders' equity as of January 29, 2000, using the information reported in the balance sheet. Ignore income tax effects.
3. Repeat Question 2 after capitalizing the firm's operating leases as in Question 1. Comment on the difference between the two ratio results.
4. Demonstrate that the rate of return implicit in the present value of May's operating leases at January 29, 2000, is closer to 8% than to 9%.
5. Assume that the interest rate implicit in the present value of May's operating leases is 8%. Make the journal entry for the operating lease payment of US$51 million in 2000 assuming that the leases had been treated as capital leases rather than as operating leases.
6. Repeat Questions 1 through 3 using data from May Department Stores' most recent financial statements.

C12-2 Sears Canada Inc. and Hudson's Bay Company: Comparison of two lessees in the retail business

Selected information from the audited financial statements, including notes, of the Hudson's Bay Company and Sears Canada Inc. is provided below. Sears' year-end is January 2, 1999, and Hudson's Bay year-end is January 31, 1999.

HUDSON'S BAY COMPANY
www.hbc.ca

SEARS CANADA INC.
www.sears.ca

Required:

1. On the basis of the information provided, constructively capitalize both companies' operating leases. State any assumptions that you find necessary. If you have made assumptions, how sensitive are your results to them?
2. Compare the two companies before and after your constructive leases capitalization estimates.

Hudson's Bay Company

Consolidated Statements of Earnings

(in $000s)	Notes	Years Ended January 31, 1999	1998
Sales and Revenue			
The Bay		**2,485,200**	2,533,397
Zellers		**4,498,113**	3,808,743
Other		**91,665**	104,512
		7,074,978	6,446,652
Earnings Before Interest Expense, Unusual Items and Income Taxes			
The Bay		**52,062**	127,399
Zellers		**133,839**	72,472
Other		**1,308**	37
		187,209	199,908
Interest Expense	4	**(97,171)**	(88,315)
Unusual Items	5	**—**	(243,000)
Earnings (Loss) Before Income Taxes		**90,038**	(131,407)
Income Taxes	6	**(50,361)**	41,674
Net Earnings (Loss)		**39,677**	(89,733)
Earnings (Loss) per Share	7	**$0.55**	($1.47)

Hudson's Bay Company

Consolidated Balance Sheets

(in $000s)	Notes	January 31, 1999	1998
Current Assets			
Cash		8,045	6,912
Short-term deposits		13,919	25,495
Credit card receivables	8	718,686	644,963
Other accounts receivable		169,738	181,873
Income taxes recoverable		61,742	40,108
Merchandise inventories		1,655,618	1,416,595
Prepaid expenses		60,320	54,058
		2,688,068	2,370,004
Secured Receivables	9	37,918	20,644
Investments		59,378	46,642
Fixed Assets	10	1,248,495	1,056,879
Goodwill	11	202,023	71,082
Pensions	12	236,176	216,258
Other Assets	13	132,004	98,684
		4,604,062	3,880,193
Current Liabilities			
Short-term borrowings	14	190,456	82,394
Trade accounts payable		319,808	287,360
Other accounts payable and accrued expenses		608,542	498,326
Long-term debt due within one year	14	112,096	959
		1,230,902	869,039
Long-Term Debt	14	1,289,525	1,224,493
Deferred Income Taxes		25,359	76,498
Contingencies	20		
Shareholders' Equity			
Capital stock	15	1,512,882	1,151,747
Contributed surplus	15	18,422	17,657
Retained earnings		526,972	540,759
		2,058,276	1,710,163
		4,604,062	3,880,193

Hudson's Bay Company

Excerpts from Notes to Financial Statements

4. Interest Expense

Interest expense arises from the following:

(in $000s)	Year Ended January 31, 1999	1998
Long-term debt	97,210	85,334
Net short-term borrowings	2,800	4,125
	100,010	89,459
Less amounts capitalized	(2,839)	(1,144)
	97,171	88,315

...

10. Fixed Assets

Fixed assets comprise the following:

(in $000s)	January 31, 1999	1998
Cost:		
Land	101,790	86,093
Buildings	413,688	354,656
Equipment	1,255,909	1,119,392
Equipment held under capital leases	9,529	7,093
Leasehold improvements	409,510	337,357
Property for sale or development	8,286	21,081
	2,198,712	1,925,672
Accumulated amortization:		
Buildings	(169,771)	(155,419)
Equipment	(654,564)	(606,989)
Equipment held under capital leases	(6,331)	(5,055)
Leasehold improvements	(119,551)	(101,330)
	(950,217)	(868,793)
	1,248,495	1,056,879

...

18. Leases

a) As lessee

The Company conducts a substantial part of its operations from leased stores in shopping centres. All shopping centre leases have been accounted for as operating leases.

Rental expenses related to operating leases charged to earnings in the years ended January 31, 1999 and January 31, 1998 were $200,000,000 and $175,000,000, respectively.

The future minimum rental payments required under leases having initial or remaining lease terms in excess of one year are summarized as follows:

(in $000s)	Operating Leases	Capital Leases
Year ending January 31,		
2000	189,800	2,100
2001	182,300	1,100
2002	172,800	—
2003	163,800	—
2004	153,000	—
Subsequent periods	1,166,600	—
	2,028,300	3,200

In addition to these rental payments (and, in a few cases, relatively minor contingent rentals), the leases generally provide for the payment by the Company of real estate taxes and other related expenses.

b) As lessor

Fixed assets in the Consolidated Balance Sheets at January 31, 1999 and January 31, 1998 include an office tower partially leased to others under operating leases, with a cost of $22,100,000 at January 31, 1999 and January 31, 1998 and related accumulated amortization of $9,300,000 and $8,900,000, respectively. Sales and revenue for the years ended January 31, 1999 and January 31, 1998 include third party rental revenue arising from this property of $3,500,000 and $3,300,000, respectively.

Sears Canada Inc.

Consolidated Statements of Financial Position
As at January 2, 1999 and January 3, 1998

(in millions)	1998	1997
ASSETS		
Current Assets		
Cash and short-term investments	$190.4	68.3
Charge account receivables (Note 2)	595.0	690.1
Other receivables (Note 3)	505.4	534.5
Inventories	738.7	640.3
Prepaid expenses and other assets	57.4	48.9
Future income tax assets (Note 4)	61.6	41.9
	2,148.5	2,024.0
Investments and Other Assets (Note 5)	50.9	22.8
Net Capital Assets (Note 6)	867.6	825.1
Deferred Charges (Note 7)	131.0	135.4
	$3,198.0	$3,007.3

LIABILITIES

Current Liabilities

Accounts payable	**$683.4**	560.2
Accrued liabilities	**312.4**	318.4
Income and other taxes payable	**90.8**	162.7
Principal payments on long-term obligations due within one year (Note 9)	**163.4**	11.6
	1,250.0	1,052.9
Long-Term Obligations (Note 9)	**680.5**	836.1
Future Income Tax Liabilities (Note 4)	**103.2**	75.9
	2,033.7	1,964.9

SHAREHOLDERS' EQUITY

Capital Stock (Note 10)	**451.8**	450.9
Retained Earnings	**712.5**	591.5
	1,164.3	1,042.4
	$3,198.0	$3,007.3

Sears Canada Inc.

Consolidated Statements of Earnings

(in millions, except per-share amounts)	For the 52 Weeks Ended January 2, 1999	For the 53 Weeks Ended January 2, 1998
Total revenues	**$4,966.6**	$4,583.5
Deduct:		
Cost of merchandise sold, operating, administrative and selling expenses	**4,516.8**	4,204.1
Depreciation	**95.5**	78.1
Interest	**85.6**	86.1
	4,697.9	4,368.3
Earnings before income taxes	**268.7**	215.2
Income taxes (Note 4):		
Current	**114.7**	105.0
Future	**7.6**	(6.3)
	122.3	98.7
Net earnings	**$ 146.4**	$ 116.5
Earnings per share	**$ 1.38**	$ 1.10

Sears Canada Inc.

Excerpts from Notes to Consolidated Financial Statements

6. Net Capital Assets

Capital assets are summarized as follows:

(in millions)	1998	1997
Land	$ 64.3	$ 68.1
Buildings and improvements	592.7	561.3
Held by joint ventures	274.9	266.6
Equipment and fixtures	788.5	694.7
Gross capital assets	1,720.4	1,590.7
Accumulated depreciation		
Buildings and improvements	301.7	276.6
Held by joint ventures	47.9	41.5
Equipment and fixtures	503.2	447.5
Total accumulated depreciation	852.8	765.6
Net capital assets	$ 867.6	$ 825.1

The carrying values of land and buildings are evaluated by management on an on-going basis as to their net recoverable amounts. This is a function of their average remaining useful lives, market valuations, cash flows, and capitalization rate models. Situations giving rise to a shortfall in the net recoverable amounts are assessed as either temporary or permanent declines in the carrying values; permanent declines are adjusted. Management does not foresee adjustments in the near term. ...

9. Long-Term Obligations

(in millions)	1998	1997
Unsecured debentures:		
11.00% due May 18, 1999	$150.0	$150.0
11.70% due July 10, 2000	100.0	100.0
8.25% due December 11, 2000	125.0	125.0
7.80% due March 1, 2001	100.0	100.0
6.55% due November 5, 2007	125.0	125.0
Proportionate share of long-term debt of joint ventures with a weighted average interest rate of 9.1% due 1999 to 2013	227.1	229.8
Capital lease obligations:		
Interest rates from 8.0% to 17.0%	16.8	17.9
	843.9	847.7
Less principal payments due within one year included in current liabilities	163.4	11.6
Total long-term obligations	$680.5	$836.1

The Company's proportionate share of the long-term debt of joint ventures is secured by the shopping malls owned by the joint ventures and, in some cases, guaranteed by the Company.

The Company's total principal payments due within one year include $12.4 million ($10.5 million—1997) of the proportionate share of the current debt obligations of joint ventures.

Interest on long-term debt amounted to $78.6 million ($74.5 million—1997).

Principal Payments

For fiscal years subsequent to the fiscal year ended January 2, 1999, principal payments required on the Company's total long-term obligations are as follows:

(in millions)	
1999	$163.4
2000	253.1
2001	134.2
2002	33.3
2003	6.8
Subsequent years	253.1
Total debt outstanding	$843.9

Significant Financing Transactions

On February 26, 1997, the outstanding 9.25% unsecured debentures of Sears Canada Inc. in the amount of $100.0 million matured.

On November 5, 1997, Sears Canada Inc. issued $125.0 million of 6.55% unsecured debentures, due November 5, 2007.

During 1997, long-term financing for new capital projects of real estate joint ventures was obtained in the amount of $9.9 million. In addition, $81.8 million of joint venture debt matured in 1997, of which $78.5 million was refinanced.

On December 23, 1998, Sears filed a shelf prospectus with securities commissions in Canada that qualifies the issuance of up to $500 million in medium-term notes (debt with a term to maturity in excess of one year) over the next two years.

During 1998, long-term financing for new capital projects of real estate joint ventures was obtained in the amount of $3.4 million. In addition, $15.5 million of joint venture debt matured in 1998, of which $9.4 million was refinanced. ...

12. Commitments

Minimum capital and operating lease payments, exclusive of property taxes, insurance and other expenses payable directly by the Company having an initial term of more than one year as at January 2, 1999 are as follows:

(in millions)	Capital Leases	Operating Leases
1999	$ 2.7	$ 69.9
2000	2.7	66.3
2001	2.7	61.1
2002	2.7	56.9
2003	2.7	53.0
Subsequent years	14.3	453.9
Minimum lease payments	$27.8	$761.1
Less imputed interest	11.0	
Total capital lease obligations	$16.8	

Total rentals charged to earnings under all operating leases for the year ended January 2, 1999 amounted to $80.8 million ($79.4 million—1997).

Integrative Running Case Study
Bombardier on the Web

Refer to Bombardier Inc.'s 2002 annual report posted on the Companion Website for this text at **www.pearsoned.ca/revsine**. Note 25 to the audited financial statements includes information (on pages 102–4 of the annual report) about various sale and leaseback transactions and other lease transactions in which Bombardier has engaged.

Required:

1. Who are the parties involved in the transactions described in the sale and leaseback portion of note 25?
2. Is Bombardier's disclosure in note 25(c) in accordance with GAAP?
3. In your opinion, what is the economic motivation for Bombardier to first sell, then lease back, aircraft and freight cars, and then lease these assets to operators?
4. How is Bombardier accounting for these sale and leaseback transactions? How does the fact that most of this equipment was "simultaneously leased to operators" affect Bombardier's accounting for the sale and leaseback transactions, if at all?
5. Section 3065 requires that sale-leaseback transactions should generally result in the deferral of any profit or loss arising from the transaction. Has Bombardier done this?

Endnotes

1. In practice, the accrual for the lease liability is seldom made. Instead, only one entry is made—at the time of cash payment:

    DR Rent expense $2,000
        CR Cash $2,000

2. Ross M. Skinner, *Accounting Standards in Evolution* (Toronto: Holt, Rinehart and Winston of Canada, Limited, 1987), p. 76.

3. "Leases," *CICA Handbook*, Section 3065, para. .05.

4. Section 3065 says: "The lessee should account for a capital lease as an asset and an obligation" (para. 15).

5. The AcSB defines the **lessee's incremental borrowing rate** as the interest rate that, at the inception of the lease, the lessee "would have incurred to borrow, over a similar term and with similar security for the borrowing, the funds necessary to purchase the leased asset" (*CICA Handbook*, Section 3065, para. 03 [p]).

6. The **lessor's rate of return** is the pre-tax internal yield on the lease contract (i.e., that rate which equates the fair value of the asset and the present value of the payments accruing to the lessor).

7. CN publishes two sets of audited financial statements, one based on U.S. GAAP and one based on Canadian GAAP.

8. Similar disclosures are required by the American standard, "Accounting for Leases," *SFAS No. 13* (Stanford, CT: FASB), 1976.

9. See E. A. Imhoff, Jr., R. C. Lipe, and D. W. Wright, "Operating Leases: Impact of Constructive Capitalization," *Accounting Horizons*, March 1991, pp. 51–63.

10. When lease payments must be paid in *advance*, there is also a current ratio numerator effect.

11. Section 3065, para..07(b) and (c) says that the credit risk in the lease must be "normal" and "any unreimbursable costs that are likely to be incurred by the lessor … can be reasonably estimated."

12. This unusual amount was chosen to arrive at a round number (exactly 11%) for the rate of return implicit to the lease. In the previous residual value guarantee example on pages 546–548, Lessee Company capitalized $312,418.40 using a discount rate of 10%. Here in this altered example, we see that the market value of the asset is only $304,359.49. If this market value also applied to the previous example, Lessee Company would only capitalize $304,359.49 and use an 11% amortization rate.

13. Table 12.4 merely demonstrates that the internal rate of return on this lease is 11%. When the rate is unknown and must be determined, standard procedures for computing the internal rate of return on an investment project must be used.

14. The ratio effect described here holds for each lease in isolation. However, most lessors have many leases of various ages outstanding. In these situations, the number of leases outstanding over time determines the effect on the return ratio. Assume Lessor Company's total number of leases is constant over time. Initially, when the Lessor Company switches to the direct financing method for new leases, its reported rate of return will increase. However, with a constant volume of leases, the

average age of the leases accounted for on the direct financing method will eventually stabilize. When this happens, the return-on-assets ratio under the direct financing method will essentially be equal to what it would have been under the operating approach. If the Lessor Company's leasing business is expanding over time, then there will be a constant infusion of new leases, and the average age of the leases in place will be falling. When this situation exists, the rate of return on assets will be higher under the direct financing method.

15. *CICA Handbook,* Section 3065.68–.70.

16. In the United States, *SFAS No. 13* uses these numbers as required cutoff points. Thus, an American lessee desiring to avoid having a lease categorized as a capital lease may ensure that the lease term is just below 75% of the leased asset's expected economic life.

17. See Imhoff, Lipe, and Wright, op. cit., pp. 51–63. A table in this article computes the asset-to-liability ratio for leases of various duration and interest rates. The table presumes that lease payments are made at the *end* of each period.

18. See W. McGregor (Principal Author*), Accounting for Leases: A New Approach*, Financial Accounting Series, Special Report No. 163–A (Norwalk, CT: FASB, 1996).

13

Financial Reporting for Corporate Income Taxes

LEARNING OBJECTIVES

After studying this chapter, you should be able to:

1. List the different goals underlying income determination for financial reporting (book) purposes versus tax-filing purposes

2. Explain the distinction between a temporary (timing) and a permanent difference between book income and taxable income and the items that give rise to each of these differences

3. Identify the distortions that are created if the future tax effects of temporary differences are ignored

4. Outline how tax expense is determined with interperiod tax allocation

5. Describe how the effects of changes in tax rates are measured and recorded

6. Identify the special reporting rules for net operating loss carrybacks and carryforwards

7. Interpret tax footnote disclosures and understand how these footnotes can be used to enhance interfirm comparability

8. Describe how tax footnotes can be used to evaluate the degree of conservatism in firms' book (GAAP) accounting choices

For the 52-week period ended December 29, 2001, Sears Canada Inc. reported earnings before income taxes of $177.5 million. If we multiply this amount by the company's average statutory income tax rate for that year (i.e., 41.92%), we obtain an income tax expense of $74.4 million. But, in its audited financial statements, Sears Canada reported income tax expense of $83.4 million. Why the difference? Why isn't the world of income tax accounting simple and straightforward? Why is there a significant difference between what we intuitively think income tax expense should be and what GAAP financial statements report it to be? The main purpose of this chapter is to provide answers to these questions, and to explain how considerable analytical insight into a company and its quality of earnings can be obtained from an understanding of its income tax reporting.

In Canada and in many other countries, the GAAP principles and rules for computing income for financial reporting purposes (more commonly known as **net income before income tax,** but also known by several other names, including **book income**) are not always the same as the *Income Tax Act* rules for computing income for taxation purposes (referred to as **taxable income**). This divergence makes sense because of the different objectives underlying book income and taxable income.

SEARS CANADA INC
www.sears.ca

Countries where the rules for determining accounting (book) income and taxable income are essentially the same include Germany, Japan, and Switzerland.

Book income, derived according to accounting and GAAP, is intended to reflect increases in a firm's "well-offness." This type of income includes all increases in net assets that meet the GAAP criteria for revenue recognition (measurable and earned) and for costs that have expired according to the expense matching principle (outlined in Chapter 2). Book income also includes all earned inflows of net assets, even inflows not immediately convertible into cash, and reflects expenses as they accrue, as opposed to when they are paid. Even with all its deficiencies, GAAP net income before income tax does indeed have the overall normative goal of measuring a company's financial performance (see, for example, Section 1000 of the *CICA Handbook* for an example of one accounting professional organization's assertions about the objectives of financial reporting).

Determining income for tax-filing purposes under the *Income Tax Act*, its regulations, and the various publications of the Canada Customs and Revenue Agency (the federal government agency that administers Canadian income tax assessment and collection; abbreviated CCRA) does not always focus on changes in a company's well-offness. Instead, taxable income derivation is often governed by the "constructive receipt/ability to pay" doctrine. This means the timing of taxation usually (but not always) follows the inflow of cash or cash equivalents; when liquid assets enter the company, they are frequently taxed, since it is easiest to collect money at that time. For example, rent received in advance may be taxed when received by the CCRA even though it is not yet earned from an accounting standpoint. Similarly, tax deductions generally are allowed only when an actual expenditure is made or when a loss occurs. *Because of different underlying objectives, the rules for determining book income (net income before income tax according to GAAP) diverge from the rules for determining taxable income (according to CCRA administration of the Income Tax Act). This divergence complicates the way that income taxes are accounted for and reported in financial statements.*

This chapter describes the major differences between *net income before income tax* and *taxable income*, and the complexities that arise in reporting tax expense and tax obligations due to these differences. First we outline the major categories of differences between book income and taxable income, and then we illustrate the kinds of distortions that would result on GAAP income statements if tax expense were to be set equal to taxes owed the government. Next, we explain and illustrate the GAAP solution for avoiding these distortions—referred to as **interperiod tax allocation**. We also explore what happens from an accounting standpoint when income tax rates are changed by Parliament, and we discuss how the accounting works for special tax laws that apply to unprofitable firms.

The second part of the chapter focuses more on analysis and takes the reader through typical income tax footnote disclosures. Our purpose is to explain the wealth of information that can be extracted from these disclosures. We demonstrate how analysts can utilize tax footnotes to ferret out information that is not provided elsewhere in the financial statements in order to better understand a company's performance, quality of earnings, and future prospects.

Understanding Income Tax Reporting

In Table 13.1, we compare the financial accounting (GAAP) system with the income tax filing system, as far as income measurement is concerned. As you can see from the table, the financial accounting system has far different objectives and measurement criteria and rules than does the income tax filing system.

Interperiod tax allocation refers to the allocation of income tax expense across periods when book and tax income differ. **Intraperiod income tax allocation**, introduced in Chapter 2, refers to the allocation of the tax cost (benefit) across various components of book income within a given period. For example, the current tax provision (expense) is related to (pre-tax) income from continuing operations, while extraordinary items and cumulative effects of accounting changes are reported *net of tax* on the income statement.

TABLE 13.1 CONTRASTING TWO SYSTEMS FOR MEASURING INCOME

	Financial Accounting System	Income Tax System
Objectives	*CICA Handbook* Section 1000 provides a commonly accepted statement of objectives, including the assertion that financial statements should "provide information about … the economic performance of the entity" (para. .15).	To raise revenues for the operation of government and the common good; to provide incentives to particular industries and activities (such as investing in certain depressed regions) that are deemed worthy of support by Parliament and government.
Governed by:	GAAP.[1]	*Income Tax Act* and other, similar legislation, regulations, and administrative interpretations.
Output	Net income before tax per GAAP, or NIBT.	Taxable income, or TI.

Because of the differences, it's not surprising that, for a given company in a particular year, the following inequality holds:

Net income before tax (per GAAP) for the year ≠ Taxable income for the year

Let's examine this inequality more closely, keeping in mind that it always stands for a *particular* company in a *particular* year. Differences between NIBT (our abbreviation for net income before income tax according to GAAP) and taxable income (or, TI) fall into two categories, *permanent differences* and *timing differences.*

Permanent differences (PD) involve revenues, gains, expenses, expenditure, and losses (or portions of revenues, gains, expenses, and so on) that are included in *either* the financial accounting system *or* the income tax filing system but not in both. For example, suppose that a company paid its income tax installments late, and was fined $10,000 by the CCRA. This penalty, although accounted for as an expense in the financial statements, is not permitted as a tax deduction when the company files its income tax return (after all, the government wants to discourage late tax payments!). Such permanent differences include:

- Items that are revenues for financial accounting, such as dividends that an investor company receives from a qualified investee company, that are never taxable in the hands of the investor company. Another example is the proceeds on life insurance policies on key corporate employees.

- Items that are expenses for financial accounting, such as the late tax installment fine above, but which are never permitted as a tax deduction. Other, similar expenses include nondeductible expenses such as social club dues and expenses incurred to earn nontaxable revenue.

- Items that are deductions for income tax, but which have no financial accounting counterpart, such as depletion allowance of natural resources in excess of the natural resources.

Timing differences (TD) include revenues, gains, expenses, expenditures, and losses that are included in both the financial accounting system's computation of NIBT and the income tax system's computation of TI, *but not in the same reporting period.* Some examples of timing differences between the two systems are shown in Table 13.2.

TABLE 13.2 EXAMPLES OF TIMING BETWEEN NIBT AND TI

Amortization

Capital cost allowance (Canadian tax amortization, often abbreviated as CCA) used for income tax purposes often results in faster writeoffs than amortization used for financial reporting purposes, since accelerated methods may be used for CCA. Therefore, in the early part of capital asset lives, the CCA deduction is greater than the financial-accounting-basis amortization expense. This timing difference reverses over the life of the capital asset, since CCA will be less than amortization later on.

Bad Debts

Bad debts are accrued and recognized under the allowance method for financial accounting purposes, but for income tax the direct writeoff method is required.

Warranties

Warranty expenses are accrued and recorded in the year the product is sold for book purposes, but for tax purposes the deduction is allowed when the actual warranty expenditures are made.

Prepaid Expenses

Some business expenditures, like insurance premiums and rent, are paid in advance. For book purposes these expenditures are initially recorded as assets—prepaid insurance, prepaid rent—but later they are expensed over the periods when the benefits are received. Tax rules allow the deduction generally in the period in which the payment is made. Over time, this temporary difference reverses itself.

Installment Sales

Sales are generally recognized for book purposes when the goods are delivered to the customer regardless of how collections are made. If collections are made over an extended period of time, tax rules may permit revenue to be reported at the time payments are received. So there is a timing difference between the financial accounting basis of the sales revenue and the (lower) tax basis, in the year of the sale and future years until the installment sale is entirely collected.

Revenue Received in Advance

Revenues received in advance (e.g., rent revenue or subscription revenue) are initially recorded as a liability ("Unearned revenue") for book purposes and are transferred to income as those revenues are "earned." For tax purposes, these amounts may be taxed when received.

The relationship between NIBT and TI, after taking into consideration both permanent differences and timing differences, is:

$$\text{NIBT, adjusted for both PDs and TDs} = \text{TI}$$

So, if we begin with the NIBT for a given company for a given year, then make adjustments for all the PDs and all the TDs, we wind up with that year's TI for the company. This equation is the basis for computing a company's taxable income; in other words, companies usually derive their taxable income in a reconciliation format, starting with NIBT, and reconciling this number to TI.

For example, suppose that ABC Company's year 2003 NIBT per GAAP was $525,000. For income tax-filing purposes, capital cost allowance (CCA) claimed on the company's corporate income tax return for the year was $300,000, while capital asset amortization expensed on the income statement was $200,000, and the company had paid a $25,000 social club membership fee (which is never deductible for income tax-filing purposes). The reconciliation format for calculating ABC Company's year 2003 taxable income is:

Net income before tax, per GAAP	$ 525,000
Adjust for permanent differences:	
Add back social club membership fee (expensed, but never deductible)	25,000
Adjust for timing differences:	
Add back amortization expense recorded	200,000
Deduct the CCA	(300,000)
Taxable income	$ 450,000

And if the year 2003 income tax rate was 40%, income tax payable would $0.40 \times 450,000$, or $180,000.

The corresponding journal entry would be:

DR	Current income tax expense	$180,000
	CR Income tax payable	$180,000

Since the obligation to pay income tax is a short-term legally enforceable obligation, the account "Income tax payable" is classified as a current liability on the company's balance sheet. The account "Current income tax expense" is an income statement account—we shall say more about this account later in this chapter.

If a company just used its computed "Income tax payable," as derived for ABC Company above, as the measure of its income tax expense (that is, if it ignored the remainder of this chapter and GAAP!), then it is said to be using the "taxes payable" or "flow through" method of accounting for corporate income taxes. Thus, under the taxes payable method, ABC Company's total 2003 income tax expense would be $180,000. But, as the next section shows, this simple method leads to serious income measurement problems when there are timing differences and is therefore not acceptable under GAAP.

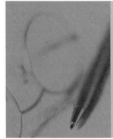

Recap

Timing differences occur when a revenue (gain) or expense (loss) enters into the determination of book (GAAP) income and taxable income in different periods. Timing differences that will cause taxable income to be higher (lower) than book income in future periods give rise to a deferred or future tax liability (asset). Permanent differences are revenue or expense items recognized as part of book income but never recognized as part of taxable income, or vice versa. Permanent differences do not give rise to tax assets or liabilities.

Problems Caused by So-Called Temporary or Timing Differences

To illustrate the issues related to interperiod tax allocation, consider the most prevalent temporary book/tax timing difference: the difference between amortization expense for accounting purposes versus CCA for income tax-filing purposes. For tax-filing purposes, profit-maximizing firms try to *minimize* the discounted present value of their future tax payments. Each dollar of tax deduction today is more valuable than a dollar of tax deduction in the future. This time-value-of-money principle is why most firms use accelerated amortization methods for tax purposes (depending upon the particular year's *Income Tax Act Regulations* specifying what the company may deduct). But many of these same firms use straight-line amortization for financial reporting purposes. This creates a temporary difference between book income and taxable income.

Consider this illustration. Assume Mitchell Corporation buys a new asset for $10,000 on January 1, 2003. The asset has a five-year life and no salvage value. It will be amortized using the straight-line method for book purposes, but for tax-filing purposes the sum-of-the-years'-digits (SYD) method will be used.[2] Table 13.3 and Figure 13.1(a) show the two schedules.

TABLE 13.3 MITCHELL CORPORATION

Book Versus Tax Amortization

Year	(a) Book Amortization	(b) Tax Return Amortization (CCA)	(c) Excess of Tax over Book Amortization	
2003	$ 2,000	$ 3,333	$1,333	Originating timing
2004	2,000	2,667	667	differences
2005	2,000	2,000	—	
2006	2,000	1,333	(667)	Reversing timing
2007	2,000	667	($1,333)	differences
	$10,000	$10,000	–0–	

Let's assume for Mitchell Corporation that amortization constitutes the only book versus tax difference; income before amortization is expected to be $22,000 each year over the next five years; and the statutory income tax rate is 35%. Pre-tax book income, taxable income per the company's income tax return, and taxes payable are shown in Table 13.4. Figure 13.1(b) displays graphically the relation between taxable income and pre-tax book income over the five-year period.

TABLE 13.4 MITCHELL CORPORATION

Income and Income Tax Payable

Year	(a) Pre-tax Book Income ($22,000 – Book Amortization)	(b) Taxable Income per Tax Return ($22,000 – CCA)	(c) Income Tax Payable (35% of Col. b)
2003	$20,000	$18,667	$ 6,533
2004	20,000	19,333	6,767
2005	20,000	20,000	7,000
2006	20,000	20,667	7,233
2007	20,000	21,333	7,467
Total			$35,000

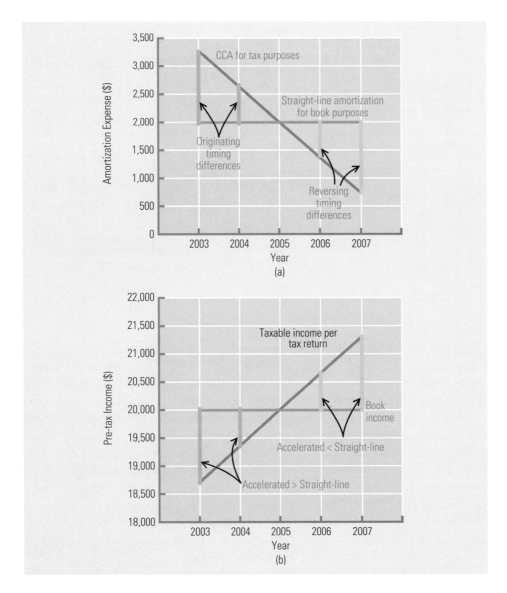

FIGURE 13.1
MITCHELL
CORPORATION

Comparison of:
(a) amortization
expense: book
versus tax,
(b) pre-tax book
income and
taxable income

The easiest way to account for book income tax expense here would be to simply treat the actual taxes payable each year (column (c) of Table 13.4) as the reported book income tax expense. Table 13.5 and Figure 13.2 show what would happen if this were done.

TABLE 13.5 MITCHELL CORPORATION

Result from Treating Actual Taxes Paid as Income Tax Expense

Year	(a) Pre-tax Book Income	(b) Tax Expense = Income Tax Payable	(c) Reported Tax Rate (b ÷ a)	(d) After-Tax Book Income
2003	$20,000	$6,533	32.7%	$13,467
2004	20,000	6,767	33.8	13,233
2005	20,000	7,000	35.0	13,000
2006	20,000	7,233	36.2	12,767
2007	20,000	7,467	37.3	12,533

FIGURE 13.2

MITCHELL
CORPORATION

Tax expense
without
interperiod tax
allocation

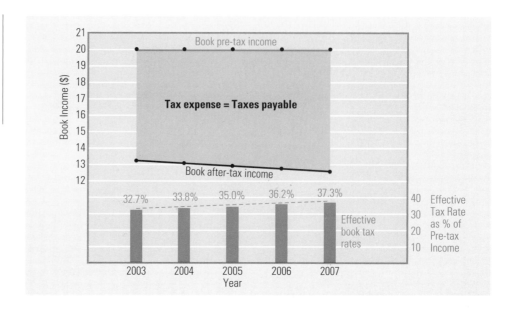

As you can readily see from the tables and figures, this approach *mismatches* tax expense with pre-tax book income, resulting in an increasing effective (book) income tax rate even though the pre-tax book income and the statutory tax rate are stable over the five-year period at $20,000 and 35%, respectively. Treating actual cash taxes payable/paid as income tax expense would *not* reflect what seems to be happening in this situation, if we believe that the matching principle should be followed. Without adjusting tax expense for the temporary differences between book expense and CCA, the results show an *increasing* effective (book) tax rate—and *declining* after-tax income—over the five-year period, as shown both in columns (c) and (d) of Table 13.5 and in Figure 13.2. The effective (book) tax rate would range from 32.7% in 2003 to 37.3% in 2007, and the after-tax earnings would decline from $13,467 in 2003 to $12,533 in 2007. Clearly, this approach leads to an inappropriate matching between pre-tax book income and income tax expense.

Besides leading to a mismatch on the income statement, treating actual cash taxes payable/paid as income tax expense introduces a reporting distortion on the balance sheet. This distortion occurs because total tax amortization (i.e., CCA) deductions on an asset cannot exceed the asset's cost. Accordingly, "extra" tax depreciation or amortization in early years will be offset by lower allowable tax depreciation or amortization in later years. As shown in column (c) of Table 13.3, during 2003 CCA ($3,333) exceeds book amortization ($2,000). The "extra" tax depreciation or CCA of $1,333 means that future years' tax amortization must be $1,333 lower than future years' *book* amortization. Thus, the extra tax return deduction (in relation to what has been recorded as amortization expense in the books of account of the company) amortization taken in 2003 generates a potential liability for future taxes of $1,333 times 35%, or $467.

There is another way to visualize how the extra tax return amortization creates a potential liability for future taxes. The Accounting Standards Board (AcSB) states that an assumption inherent in GAAP is that "an asset will be realized for at least its carrying amount" and, based on that assumption, a difference between the tax return measurement basis of an asset and its reported GAAP amount will result in taxable amounts when the reported amounts are recovered.[3]

> The effective (book) tax rate is the tax expense divided by pre-tax income that is reported on the GAAP income statement.

In our example, at the end of 2003, the reported (book) amount of the asset is $8,000 (i.e., $10,000 minus book amortization of $2,000), while the tax return basis is $6,667 (i.e., $10,000 minus tax amortization of $3,333). Notice that if the asset were sold for its net book value of $8,000, a taxable gain of $1,333 would have resulted, measured as the difference between the $8,000 cash received and the asset's $6,667 *tax* basis. Thus, given the GAAP assumption that reported amounts of assets will be recovered, the extra amortization in 2003 would generate a liability for future taxes of $1,333 times 35%, or $467.

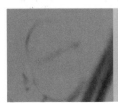

Recap

Setting tax expense equal to current taxes payable ignores the future tax liability that results from temporary differences between book and taxable income, and it results in a mismatching of tax expense with the related revenue and expense items reported on the GAAP income statement.

The Section 3465 Approach to Accounting for Income Taxes: Temporary Differences Between the GAAP Basis and the Tax Basis of Assets and Liabilities

In September 1997, when the CICA's AcSB approved *CICA Handbook* Section 3465 ("Income Taxes"), there was a substantial revision made to the then existing Section 3470 ("Corporate Income Taxes") and Section 3471 ("Corporate Income Taxes— Additional Areas"). The process of crafting Section 3465 was long and arduous: a 1988 exposure draft failed to achieve consensus and was shelved in 1989, and it was only in 1994 (after the U.S. FASB had issued *SFAS No. 96* and *SFAS No. 109*, and the IASC had issued its *IAS 12*) that the AcSB again took up the project of reforming Canadian GAAP for accounting for income taxes. The Canadian standard is very similar to the U.S. *SFAS No. 109.*

Partly because the new standard was such a significant change from Section 3470, the AcSB permitted an extended period of transition during which *both* Section 3470 and the new Section 3465 were GAAP in Canada. The new section became effective for all enterprises (other than rate-regulated enterprises) for fiscal years beginning on or after January 1, 2000, but the AcSB encouraged earlier adoption. Indeed, many Canadian companies adopted the new standard in 1997 and 1998. The *timing* of the adoption of the new standard, and the *method* of accounting for the change, are worthy of examination, since differences between companies in timing and method may reveal differences in corporate financial reporting strategies. We will examine this issue later in the chapter.

Section 3465 adopted the "asset and liability method" of accounting for income taxes (this method is also referred to as the "liability method"), and focused attention on the balance sheet. Old Section 3470 used the "deferral method," and focused on the income statement.

The Canadian standard of accounting for income taxes requires that companies account for *temporary differences* between the GAAP measurement basis of accounting for an asset or liability, and the tax measurement basis of that asset or liability (i.e., the money amount of the asset or liability as determined by the *Income Tax Act*, and associated legislation and administrative rules). For example:

- An asset with a GAAP or accounting basis (also referred to as *carrying amount*, or *book value*) of $2,000 has a tax basis of $1,200. If the asset is realized at its carrying amount of $2,000, a taxable income of $800 will create a future income tax liability, and Section 3465 requires that this "Future income tax liability" be accounted for.

- An accrued pension liability has a book value of $3,000, but is only deductible for income tax purposes when the company actually makes a payment. Therefore, the $3,000 temporary difference between the carrying value of the liability (i.e., $3,000) and its tax basis (i.e., zero), will result in a future deduction when paid, and therefore the AcSB requires, in Section 3465, that the resulting "Future income tax asset" be accounted for.

Thus, a key concept under this accounting standard is that of temporary differences, which are defined in Section 3465's para. .09 (c) as follows:

Temporary differences are differences between the tax basis of an asset or liability and its carrying amount in the balance sheet. Temporary differences may be either:

(i) **Deductible temporary differences**, which are temporary differences that will result in deductible amounts in determining taxable income of future periods when the carrying amount of the asset or liability is recovered or settled;

(ii) **Taxable temporary differences**, which are temporary differences that will result in taxable amounts in determining taxable income of future periods when the carrying amount of the asset or liability is recovered or settled.

GAAP and tax laws may treat the recognition and measurement of various assets, liabilities, revenues, expenses, gains, and losses differently. These different treatments are due, at least partly, to the different objectives of GAAP and tax laws.

Accounting for Future Income Tax Assets and Liabilities: Interperiod Tax Allocation

To avoid the drawbacks illustrated previously with the Mitchell Corporation example, income tax accounting according to Canadian GAAP does not simply equate tax expense and current taxes payable. Instead, the journal entry for income taxes records both taxes currently due as well as any liability for future taxes arising from current period book-versus-tax legislation temporary differences that will reverse in later periods. The GAAP rules are specified in *CICA Handbook* Section 3465.[4] To illustrate them, we continue the Mitchell Corporation example in Table 13.6.

Column (c) shows that for 2003 the *change* in the liability for future taxes is an increase of $467 (35% tax rate × $1,333 amortization temporary difference). Income tax currently payable is 35% of tax return income of $18,667, or $6,533. Under *CICA Handbook* Section 3465, income tax expense equals the total of the current taxes owed and the *change* in the future tax liability. The computation is:

TABLE 13.6 MITCHELL CORPORATION

Computation of Income Tax Expense *with* Interperiod Tax Allocation

Year	(a) Current Income Tax Payable (Table 13.4, Col. c)	(b) Excess (Deficiency) of CCA Relative to Book Amortization (Table 13.3, Col. c)	(c) Increase (Decrease) in Future Income Tax Liability (Col. b × 35%)	(d) Total Income Tax Expense (Col. a + Col. c)	(e) Cumulative Balance in Future Income Tax Liability at Year-End
2003	$ 6,533	$1,333	$467	$ 7,000	$467
2004	6,767	667	233	7,000	700
2005	7,000	—	—	7,000	700
2006	7,233	(667)	(233)	7,000	467
2007	7,467	(1,333)	(467)	7,000	–0–
	$35,000	–0–	–0–	$35,000	

Computation of Income Tax Expense for 2003

1. Current income tax payable (35% × $18,667) $6,533 [this is the current income tax expense]

   plus

2. Increase in liability for future taxes arising during the year ($1,333 × 35%)   467 [this is the future income tax expense]

   Total income tax expense for 2003 = sum of steps 1 and 2 $7,000

The accounting for 2003 income taxes would consist of two parts:
The first part is a journal entry that records the *current income tax expense*:

DR	Current income tax expense	$6,533	
	CR Income tax payable		$6,533

The second part is a journal entry that records what the *CICA Handbook* calls *future income tax expense*.

DR	Future income tax expense	$467	
	CR Future income tax liability		$467

The total income tax expense for the year is the sum of the current income tax expense plus the future income tax expense. Notice that if Mitchell's CCA in 2003 had been *less than* the accounting amortization, a future income tax asset would have resulted.

When tax rates do not change from year to year (this is an important condition—we will relax it later), these entries overcome both of the drawbacks that would exist if we simply measured tax expense as cash taxes payable/paid—the liability for future taxes is explicitly recognized, and the reported tax expense is exactly 35% of pre-tax book income of $20,000 (i.e., $7,000/$20,000 equals 35%). Thus, income tax expense is also "matched" with book income. (This is true provided there are no permanent book/tax differences. When there are permanent differences between book and taxable incomes, then tax expense will *not* equal the tax rate times the pre-tax book income—a point demonstrated later in the chapter.)

In any year that Parliament changes tax rates, this matching disappears under Section 3465. The reason is that Section 3465 focuses on the liability for future taxes, which changes as tax rates change.

Let's combine the previous two journal entries into one "combined" entry for the next bit of our discussion:

DR	Income tax expense	$7,000	
	CR Income tax payable		$6,533
	CR Future income taxes		467

You can readily see what this entry simultaneously accomplishes by carefully analyzing how each of the debits and credits of the entry are computed:

DR Income tax expense $7,000
(A computed or derived or "plug" number
which equals the sum of the current income
tax payable plus the change in the future
income tax liability, in this case. However,
when tax rates are constant and there are
no permanent book/tax differences, this debit
will equal the tax rate [e.g., 35%] times pre-tax
book income [e.g., $20,000].)

   CR Income tax payable $6,533
      (35% times taxable income per tax return
      of $18,667)

   CR Future income tax liability   467
      (35% times the amortization temporary
      difference of $1,333 in 2003—i.e., Table 13.6,
      column (b) "excess" amortization)

> Sometimes the originating temporary differences generate future income tax assets because taxable income will be lower than book income in future periods when those differences reverse. In that circumstance the debit to income tax expense is a computed or derived figure representing the sum of current taxes payable plus the decrease (minus the increase) in the future tax asset account for the period.

As illustrated here, the debit to income tax expense is a computed number that represents the combination of current taxes payable and any *change* in the future tax balance (in this case, a future tax liability) that arises from temporary differences during the year. When the future income tax liability increases, the increase is *added* to current income tax payable to arrive at income tax expense. When the future income tax liability decreases, the decrease is *subtracted* from current income tax payable in order to determine income tax expense. This relation is summarized in Figure 13.3. Even though the debit is a plug number, in any year that the tax rate remains constant (say, at 35%) and there are no permanent book/tax differences, the debit to tax expense will automatically equal pre-tax book income times the 35% tax rate.

Column (b) of Table 13.6 shows that the *original* book-versus-tax amortization differences—labelled "originating timing differences" in Figure 13.1(a)—increase the liability for future taxes (the future tax liability) in 2003 and 2004 (column (c) of Table 13.6). But all originating differences ultimately reverse. This reversal occurs in

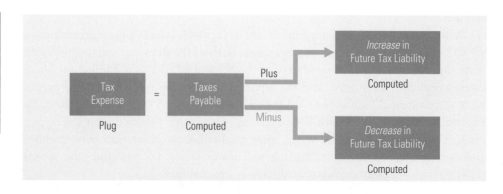

FIGURE 13.3
RELATION
BETWEEN TAX
EXPENSE, TAXES
PAYABLE, AND
CHANGES IN
FUTURE TAX
LIABILITIES

the Mitchell Corporation illustration when tax amortization or CCA drops below book amortization in years 2006 and 2007. The reversals of originating differences are called "reversing timing differences" as labelled in Figure 13.1(a).

To show what happens when book-versus-tax temporary differences reverse, let's consider the income tax entry in year 2006. As we see in Figure 13.3, the formula for computing income tax expense is:

1. Current income tax payable

   minus

2. *Decrease* in liability for future taxes arising during the year
   = Income tax expense

Since book amortization exceeds tax CCA in 2006 by $667, the liability for future taxes *decreases* by $667 times 35%, or $233. Therefore, tax expense for 2006 is:

Computation of Income Tax Expense for 2006

1. Current income tax payable:

   $20,667 × 35% $7,233

   minus

2. *Decrease* in liability for future taxes:

   $667 × 35%   (233)

Total income tax expense for 2006   **$7,000**

The journal entry for year 2006 taxes is:

DR	Income tax expense	$7,000	
DR	Future income tax liability	233	
	CR Income tax payable		$7,233

A more complete journal entry would be:

DR	Current income tax expense	$7,233	
DR	Future income tax liability	233	
	CR Future income tax recovery		$ 233
	CR Income tax payable		7,233

Column (d) of Table 13.6 and Figure 13.4 show the computation of income tax expense for Mitchell Corporation for the entire five-year period (2003–2007) using interperiod tax allocation. Notice that in 2003 and 2004 the future tax liability *increases*, and these increases are *added* to taxes payable to arrive at the tax expense reported on the income statement for those years. In 2006 and 2007, the amortization timing differences reverse, resulting in *decreases* in the future tax liability (since the additional taxes are now being paid), and these decreases are *subtracted* from the taxes payable to arrive at tax expense for those years. By the end of 2007, the amortization book-versus-tax timing differences have totally reversed, and the balance in future income tax liability is zero. With constant tax rates of 35% over the entire period, income tax expense (column [d]) is always 35% times pre-tax book income of $20,000, and the pattern of tax expense matches the pattern of pre-tax book income.

FIGURE 13.4
MITCHELL
CORPORATION

Tax expense with
interperiod tax
allocation

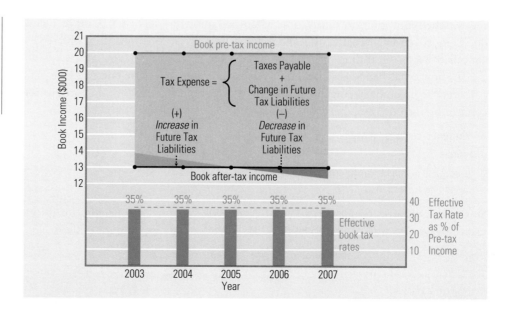

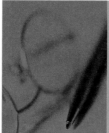

Recap

With interperiod tax allocation, tax expense equals current taxes payable plus (minus) the increase (decrease) in future tax liabilities. This results in a tax expense number matched with the revenue and expense amounts recognized for book purposes. *Note:* In the United States, *under SFAS No. 109* ("Accounting for Income Taxes"), "future income tax assets" and "future income tax liabilities" are called "deferred income tax assets" and "deferred income tax liabilities."

Interperiod Income Tax Accounting When Tax Rates Change

Tax rates periodically get changed by Parliament and at the provincial level as well. When that happens, the tax effects of the reversals of temporary differences change also. To measure future income taxes, Section 3465 adopts the so-called **liability approach**—in any year that tax rates are changed, the income tax expense number absorbs the full effect of the change, and the relationship between that year's tax expense and book income is destroyed.

Returning to the Mitchell Corporation example, let's assume that on December 31, 2005, a new income tax law raises the income tax rate from 35% to 38% beginning January 1, 2006. Reference to column (e) of Table 13.6 shows that just prior to the tax law change on December 31, 2005, the amount of future income tax liability for Mitchell was $700. That number represents the cumulative excess of tax CCA over book amortization or depreciation in 2003 and 2004 (the dollar amount of temporary amortization differences = $1,333 + $667, or $2000) times the initial tax rate of 35%. But because future tax rates have been increased, the liability for future taxes is actually larger than the $700 amount currently reported. At the new, higher income tax rate that will be in effect in 2006 and 2007, the liability for future taxes becomes $760, not $700. This future liability represents the cumulative excess of tax CCA over book amortization ($2,000) multiplied by the new 38% tax rate that will be in effect beginning January 1, 2006.

Under the liability approach of Section 3465, the full change in the amount of future liability for income taxes (in this case, $60) is recognized as an increase in income tax expense in the year that the tax rate change becomes known. Accordingly, income tax expense for 2005 is computed as follows:

1. Current 2005 income tax payable (35% × $20,000 [see Table 13.4]) $7,000

   plus

2. *Increase* in the liability for future taxes arising during 2005
   ($1,333 + $667) × (0.38 − 0.35)   60

   Total income tax expense for 2005   **$7,060**

The accounting entry for 2005 income taxes is:

DR	Current income tax expense	$7,000	
DR	Future income tax expense	60	
	CR Income tax payable		$7,000
	CR Future income tax liability		60

After this entry is made, the balance in future income tax liability will total $760, which is the potential liability for future taxes at the new 38% rate. Also, because tax rates for future years were changed in 2005, the total debits to income tax expense does not equal the $20,000 pre-tax book income times the 2005 tax rate of 35%.

Table 13.7 shows the revised computation of income tax expense and future tax liability for Mitchell Corporation for 2005 through 2007 after reflecting the income tax rate increase.

The journal entry for income taxes in year 2006 would be:

DR	Income tax expense	$7,853	
DR	Future income tax liability	253	
	CR Income tax payable		$7,853
	CR Future income tax expense		253

TABLE 13.7 MITCHELL CORPORATION

Revised Computation of Income Tax Expense

Year	(a) Taxable Income (Table 13.4, Col. b)	(b) Current Income Tax Payable = 38% of Col. a	(c) Difference Between Tax CCA and Book Amortization (Table 13.3, Col. c)	(d) Increase (Decrease) in Liability for Future Taxes = Col. c × 38%	(e) Total Income Tax Expense = Col. b + Col. d	(f) Cumulative Balance in Future Income Tax Liability at Year-End
2005	$20,000	$7,000*	—	$ 60**	$7,060	$760
2006	20,667	7,853	($ 667)	($253)	$7,600	$507
2007	21,333	8,107	($1,333)	($507)	$7,600	$–0–

*Tax rate is still 35% in 2005 so this is $20,000 × 35%.
**This is the increase that arose in 2005 as the rate went from 35% to 38%, i.e., 3% × $2,000 cumulative temporary differences in column (b) of Table 13.6.

Similarly, the year 2007 entry is:

DR	Current income tax expense	$8,107	
DR	Future income tax liability	507	
	CR Income tax payable		$8,107
	CR Future income tax expense		507

As shown in column (f) of Table 13.7, the balance in the future income tax liability account will be zero after the year 2007 entry is made. (This nice, neat result occurs since we [arbitrarily and artificially] chose to use the SYD method to illustrate the CCA deductions, and since SYD fully writes off the asset's cost, there is no difference between the income tax filing system measure of the asset and the GAAP measure of the asset by the end of 2007.)

In determining which tax rate to use, consider that Section 3465 requires that the tax rate be the one expected to apply in the periods in which the future income tax liability or asset is expected to be settled or realized. Usually, this will be the rate in effect at the balance sheet date. However, when there are legislative proposals regarding tax rate changes having the substantive effect of actual enactment, the *proposed* rates should be used where there is persuasive evidence that they will become law. Such evidence may include the fact that the government is able and committed to enacting the proposed legislation in the near future. If the government had a majority, it would probably meet this test. Section 3465 differs from the FASB *SFAS No. 109* on this point: the American standard requires the use of enacted rates only and does not permit the use of anticipated rate changes, since in the American political system executive vetoes may derail such proposals for tax changes.

Because of the oblique way accounting rules recognize the effects of tax rate changes—through an adjustment to the tax expense number—analysts must be alert to recognize how these tax changes can inject one-shot (transitory) adjustments to earnings in the year Parliament passes the new tax rates. Moreover, it is important to recognize that the effect of a tax rate change on bottom-line earnings can vary considerably across companies depending on three factors. These factors are:

1. whether the tax rates are increased or decreased
2. whether the firm has net future tax assets or net future tax liabilities
3. the magnitude of the future tax balance

Consider how differently a tax rate change can affect different companies' bottom-line earnings: Suppose Parliament passes a new tax law in year 2003, one that raises the marginal corporate tax rate from 35% to 45% effective in year 2004. Further assume that Companies A, B, and C have the following net future tax asset (liability) balances on their books when the new tax law is passed:

($ in millions)	Company A	Company B	Company C
Net future tax asset (liability) balance end of year 2003	$100	$0	($100)

Table 13.8 shows how the change in tax rate will affect the after-tax earnings of these three companies in year 2003—the year the new tax rate is passed. We first divide the net future tax asset (liability) balance by the old marginal tax rate to get the dollar magnitude of the temporary differences that gave rise to the balances in these accounts. (Recall that the balances in the future tax asset [liability] accounts equal the cumulative dollar amount of the temporary differences giving rise to future deductible [taxable] amounts times the marginal corporate tax rate when those tem-

($ in millions)	Company A	Company B	Company C
Net future tax asset (liability) balance—year 2003	$ 100	$0	($ 100)
Divide by old marginal tax rate	÷ 35%	÷ 35%	÷ 35%
Dollar amount of timing difference	$285.71 ← Future Deductible Amount	$0	($285.71) ← Future Taxable Amount
Multiply by difference between old and new tax rates (45% – 35%)	× 10%	× 10%	× 10%
Increase (decrease) to after-tax earnings in year of rate change	$28.571	$0	($28.571)

porary differences originated. Therefore, to derive the dollar amount of the temporary differences, we simply divide the future tax asset or liability balance by the relevant tax rate.)

Company A has $285.71 ($100/0.35) million of future *deductible* amounts, Company C has $285.71 million of future *taxable* amounts, and Company B has neither future deductible nor taxable amounts. These temporary differences are then multiplied by the *difference* between the new tax rate and the old tax rate (i.e., 10%) to obtain the increase in the future tax asset (liability) balance and the corresponding increase (decrease) in reported after-tax earnings.

As shown, Company A's year 2003 earnings will *increase* by $28.571 million. This is because each dollar of future deductible amounts will yield an additional $0.10 in tax savings under the newly enacted tax rates (i.e., when these temporary differences reverse). Company C, on the other hand, will report a $28.571 million *decrease* to its after-tax earnings number, since each dollar of future taxable amounts will generate $0.10 of additional taxes as these temporary differences reverse in future years (i.e., when the tax rates will be higher). Company B's year 2003 after-tax earnings are unaffected by the tax rate change because there are no temporary differences.

If the tax rates had been reduced from 35% to 25%, the earnings impacts reported above for Companies A and C would be reversed. As this example demonstrates, tax rate changes can have very different effects on firms' reported earnings, depending on their future tax status and the direction of the tax rate change.

As a final postcript to this section of the chapter, it should be noted that the old GAAP standard that followed the deferral approach to income tax accounting did not take into account changes in income tax rates. And also the income tax rates used were the rates in effect in the year in which a temporary difference *originated*, not when it was expected to *reverse*. This led some critics to argue, with justification, that the old standard was too historic cost based, and ignored current and future information.

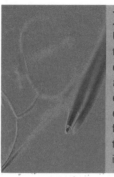
Future Income Tax Assets

The Mitchell Corporation example illustrated a situation in which pre-tax book income initially exceeded taxable income, creating a future income tax liability. Because this temporary difference later reverses, the liability is ultimately eliminated. But as we mentioned earlier in this chapter, temporary differences can go in the opposite direction as well. In certain circumstances, taxable income can initially exceed pre-tax book income, thereby giving rise to future income tax assets.

To illustrate how a future income tax asset comes about, let's assume that in December 2003 Paul Corporation owns an office building, which it leases to another company for $100,000. The lease covers all of 2004 and specifies that the tenant pays the $100,000 to Paul Corporation immediately on signing the lease in 2003. On an accrual basis, rental income will be earned only in 2004. Accordingly, Paul Corporation makes the following entry on receiving the cash:

DR Cash	$100,000	
CR Rent received in advance		$100,000

The account "Rent received in advance" is a liability account that will be reduced monthly by $8,333 (with an offsetting credit to the "Earned lease revenue" account) in 2004 as Paul provides the tenant with the use of the facility and earns the lease revenue. For income tax filing purposes, assume the entire $100,000 rent prepayment by the tenant is included in Paul Corporation's taxable income in 2003 when it is received. Further assume that the lease receipt represents the only book/tax temporary difference for Paul and that 2003 pre-tax book income totals $1,500,000. Taxable income in the tax return will accordingly total $1,600,000 in 2003—$1,500,000 plus the immediately taxable advance rental payment of $100,000. If book income is also $1,500,000 in 2004, then book income will exceed taxable income by $100,000 in 2004 when this temporary difference reverses. These relationships are summarized in Table 13.9.

Table 13.10 shows that when the rent is earned in 2004 for book purposes, accounting income will exceed taxable income by $100,000—but no tax will be due on this difference because the tax has already been paid in 2003. Thus, the temporary difference that *originates* in 2003 because of book/tax differences in lease revenue represents a future income tax asset at the end of 2003. If we assume the income tax rate is 35%, then the computation of 2003 income tax expense is the current taxes payable *minus* the increase in the future tax asset account computed as follows:

TABLE 13.9 PAUL CORPORATION

Book Versus Tax Temporary Differences That Give Rise to a Future Tax Asset

	Book Income	2003 Lease Receipt of $100,000		Tax Return Income
		Included in Book Income?	Included in Tax Return Income?	
2003	$1,500,000	No	Yes	$1,600,000
2004	1,500,000	Yes	No	1,400,000

TABLE 13.10 PAUL CORPORATION

Computation of Tax Expense *with* Interperiod Tax Allocation

Year	(a) Taxable Income per Tax Return	(b) Book Income	(c) Excess (Deficiency) of Tax Lease Revenue over Book Lease Revenue	(d) Taxes Payable (35% of Col. a)	(e) Increase (Decrease) in Future Tax Asset (Col. c × 35%)	(f) Total Income Tax Expense (Col. d – Col. e)
2003	$1,600,000	$1,500,000	$100,000	$560,000	$35,000	$525,000
2004	1,400,000	1,500,000	(100,000)	490,000	(35,000)	525,000

Computation of Income Tax Expense for 2003

1. Current income tax payable

   (Taxable income × 35% =

   $1,600,000 × 35%) $560,000

   minus

2. *Increase* in future tax asset

   ($100,000 × 35%)   (35,000)

   Total income tax expense for 2003 $525,000

Paul Corporation will make the following 2003 entry for income taxes:

DR	Current income tax expense	$560,000	
DR	Future income tax asset	35,000	
CR	Income tax payable		$560,000
CR	Future income tax expense		35,000

In column (b) of Table 13.10, book income is $1,500,000 in 2004 after the $100,000 of rent revenue *earned* during the year is included. If we assume that there are no other book/tax temporary differences, then taxable income in the tax return will be $1,400,000, since the $100,000 advance rental receipt was included in taxable income in 2003—the previous year—when the rent revenue was *collected*. The $100,000 temporary difference in lease revenue that *originated* in 2003 reverses in 2004. The related future tax asset of $35,000 that was created in 2003 (column [e]) is decreased and eliminated in 2004. As shown in column (f), the decrease in the future tax asset of $35,000 is added to the taxes payable for that year to arrive at the tax expense (plug) number of $525,000. Paul will record the following income tax expense entry in 2004 when the timing difference reverses.

DR	Current income tax expense	$490,000	
DR	Future income tax expense	35,000	
	CR Future income tax asset		$ 35,000
	CR Income tax payable		490,000

Figure 13.5 depicts the relationships for computing Section 3465 income tax expense by adjusting taxes payable for changes in future income tax assets and liabilities.

Even though the existing CICA standard for income tax accounting, Section 3465, does not use the old deferral approach, some Canadian companies, for example, Canadian National Railway, refer to their future tax assets and future tax liabilities as deferred tax assets and deferred tax liabilities. The U.S. GAAP in this area, while using the asset/liability approach consistent with *CICA Handbook* Section 3465, still employ the "deferral" terminology. So, as for all areas in financial accounting, beware of words, and examine the underlying meaning!

FIGURE 13.5

RELATION BETWEEN TAX EXPENSE, TAXES PAYABLE, AND CHANGES IN FUTURE TAX ASSETS AND LIABILITIES

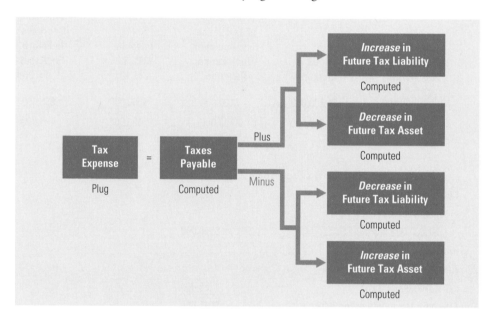

GAAP for Income Taxes in Action: Understanding a More Complex Illustration

Case C13–2 (Tellier Company), at the end of this chapter, provides a more complex illustration of the asset/liability approach. It might be useful to attempt it at this point.

Future Income Tax Asset Valuation

If Paul Corporation had experienced business adversity in 2004 and had no taxable income in that year, the $35,000 future income tax asset would generate no benefit—that is, if 2004 taxes were zero, the "benefits" arising from the $35,000 tax payment on the 2003 advance rental receipt would be lost. Thus, it is always possible that a company that has recognized future income tax assets on its balance sheet may not receive tax payment reductions in future years. For this reason, Section 3465 requires companies with future income tax assets to assess the likelihood that these assets may not be fully realized in future periods.

The realization of tax benefits from existing future income tax assets depends on whether or not the company has future taxable income. According to Section 3465, if the company's management plausibly believes that the probability of future taxable income is greater than 50% (and presumably can convince the company's external auditor, as well!), then future income tax assets can be recognized (without adjustment) in their entirety. However, if management's assessment indicates that *it is more likely than not* that some portion of the benefit will not be realized in its entirety, a **future tax asset valuation allowance** is required. The AcSB states that this valuation allowance *should be sufficient to reduce the future income tax asset to the amount that is more likely than not to be realized.*[5]

To illustrate the procedure for establishing a valuation allowance for future tax assets, let us assume that for book purposes (1) Norman Corporation accrued $900,000 of estimated warranty expenses associated with product sales in 2003 and (2) the actual warranty parts and services from these sales are provided in year 2004 and beyond. Since the *Income Tax Act* only permits companies to deduct warranty costs when the warranty services are provided, this temporary difference gives rise to a future tax asset of $315,000 (35% tax rate × $900,000 temporary difference) that would be recorded in 2003. If we assume Norman's pre-tax book income is $600,000, the 2003 entry for tax expense would be (combining the current and future income tax expense components together):

DR	Income tax expense		
	($600,000 × 0.35)	$210,000	
DR	Future income tax asset		
	($900,000 × 0.35)	315,000	
	CR Income tax payable		
	($1,500,000 × 0.35)		$525,000

Now assume that early in the year 2004 Norman Corporation determines that it is unlikely to earn enough taxable income in future years to realize more than $200,000 of the future tax asset. The following entry would be made in 2004:

DR	Income tax expense		
	($315,000 − $200,000)	$115,000	
	CR Allowance to reduce future tax asset to		
	expected realizable value		$115,000

The credit to the allowance account reduces the net carrying amount of the future tax asset to $200,000—its estimated realizable value. The allowance account would be shown on the balance sheet as a contra account to the future tax asset. Notice that income tax expense is increased in the year during which it is determined that a portion of the income tax asset is unlikely to be recovered. Accordingly, income tax expense will exceed pre-tax book income multiplied by the tax rate in years when allowance accounts are established or increased. If Norman Corporation's prospects improve and if in 2005 it is determined that an allowance account is no longer needed, a credit to income tax expense is made in order to offset the reduction of the allowance account.

This allowance approach (also called an "impairment" approach), under which all future income tax assets are recognized, but are then reduced by a valuation allowance or provision for impairment, although acceptable under the new Canadian standard's para. .30 (and required under the corresponding U.S. standard *SFAS No. 109*), is permitted as an alternative to the so-called "affirmative judgement" approach to measuring future income tax assets. Under this approach, at each balance sheet date, future income tax assets are recognized for all deductible temporary differences, but the "amount recognized should be limited to the amount that is more likely than not to be realized." (para. .24). Both the allowance (or impairment) approach and the affirmative judgment approach result in the same net assets being recorded on the balance sheet.

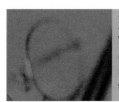

Recap

When circumstances indicate that it is "more likely than not" that some portion of the future tax benefit from a future tax asset will not be realized, then management must reduce the future tax asset book value to the amount expected to be realized.

Net Operating Losses: Carrybacks and Carryforwards

Since firms pay taxes during profitable years, it would be inequitable from the perspective of public policy to deny them some form of tax relief in unprofitable years. Therefore, the *Income Tax Act* provides an opportunity for firms reporting operating losses to offset those losses against either past or future tax payments—that is, when an operating loss occurs (e.g., when deductible expenses exceed taxable revenues), firms can elect to carry back and carry forward incurred losses. In this way, the tax law permits companies that have incurred a tax loss in the current year to recover taxes previously paid, or to reduce future income taxes. This feature of the *Income Tax Act* system creates the need for GAAP to account for these loss carryovers.

Carryback and Carryforward Assume that Unfortunato Corporation experienced a $2,000,000 negative taxable income in 2003. Under tax law, Unfortunato can elect to carry back the operating loss and offset it against taxable income in the previous three years—2000 to 2002. The loss must be offset against the earliest year first—in this case, 2000. If the loss exceeds the total taxable income for the 2000–2002 period, then the remaining portion of the loss can be carried forward and offset against *future* taxable income in the ensuing seven years—2004 through 2010—as shown in Figure 13.6.

FIGURE 13.6
ILLUSTRATION OF
TAX LOSS
CARRYBACK/
CARRYFORWARD
PROVISION

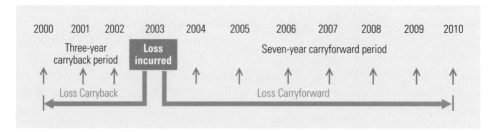

To illustrate how this loss carryover system works, let's assume that the tax rate in effect from 2000 through 2003 was 35% and that Unfortunato had the following taxable income in those years:

Year	Taxable Income (Loss)	Tax (@ 35%)
2000	300,000	$105,000
2001	400,000	140,000
2002	350,000	122,500
2003	($2,000,000)	—

If Unfortunato Corporation elects to carry back the year 2003 tax loss of $2,000,000, losses must first be offset against 2000 taxable income ($300,000), the earliest year in the three-year carryback time frame, and then against 2001 taxable income ($400,000) and 2002 taxable income ($350,000). This offsets $1,050,000 of the 2003 loss and generates a tax refund of $367,500 ($105,000 + $140,000 + $122,500). Unfortunato would make the following entry in 2003 in order to record the refund due from the CCRA:

(a) DR Income tax refund receivable $367,500
         CR Current income tax expense $367,500
         (To record the carryback benefit.)

Note that the account "Income tax refund receivable" is a current asset.

The year 2003 tax loss in excess of the combined prior three years' taxable incomes ($2,000,000 − $300,000 − $400,000 − $350,000 = $950,000) will result in future tax benefits—if Unfortunato becomes profitable again before 2010. If we assume that future tax rates will remain at 35%, these potential future benefits would total $332,500 ($950,000 × 35%). If Unfortunato expects that pre-tax income in the ensuing seven years will exceed $950,000, then the following additional entry would be made in 2003:

(b) DR Future income tax asset $332,500
         CR Future income tax expense $332,500
         (To record the carryforward benefit.)

But entry (b) requires close scrutiny. The previous entry (a), recognizing the benefit in the tax loss year (2003) of the *carryback*, is easily supported by the strong evidence that the receivable from the government exists (indeed, it is almost always a **current** asset), but the entry recording the future income tax asset of $332,500 from the carryforward of the $950,000 is much more uncertain. The AcSB's Section 3465, in para. 24, writes "At each balance sheet date … a future income tax asset should be recognized for all … unused tax losses. … The amount recognized should be limited to the amount that is more likely than not to be realized."

Therefore, if Unfortunato Corporation's management decides that the $950,000 unused portion of the year 2003 tax loss (i.e., the portion remaining after carrying the $1,050,000 back to years 2000 to 2002) will be able to generate future economic benefits by being carried forward and applied to reduce income taxes otherwise payable during the seven-year carryforward period, entry (b) may be recorded. Otherwise, it should not be. If a portion of the $950,000 remaining tax loss is more likely than not to be usable, then only the tax benefit of this portion should be recorded. In effect, Section 3465 requires that management assess whether or not carryforward losses have asset status. This is a much weaker criterion than that which existed under old

Section 3470, which required "virtual certainty" of future realization before a journal entry like (b) could be recorded.

The "Income tax refund receivable" asset account would be shown among current assets on the balance sheet, and the future income tax asset would be apportioned between current and noncurrent categories in accordance with the expected timing of the future income. If we were to assume that the pre-tax book loss equalled the taxable loss, then the credits would be shown on the accompanying income statement for 2003 as follows:

Pre-tax operating loss	($2,000,000)
Current income tax (expense) benefit due to tax loss carryback	367,500
Future income tax (expense) benefit due to tax loss carryforward	332,500
After-tax operating loss	($1,300,000)

Future income tax assets that result from operating loss carryforwards will generate future benefits only if the firm earns profits in the ensuing seven years (seven years being the current legal loss carryforward limit in Canada—it could change, and is different in other countries). Because future profits are never assured, the probability of realizing future income tax assets arising from tax loss carryforwards must be carefully evaluated. The criterion here for deciding whether a valuation allowance is needed is identical to the criterion applied to future tax assets arising from book-versus-tax-timing differences—if *it is more likely than not* that the benefit will not be realized in its entirety, a valuation allowance is required. This allowance should reduce the asset to a net amount that is more likely than not to be realized.

Recap
Tax rules allow firms to offset tax losses against taxable income. Firms can elect to carry back losses up to three years, with any unused loss carried forward up to seven years. The tax benefit associated with the loss carryback or carryforward is recorded as an adjustment to tax expense in the year of the loss.

Caveat Emptor: Monitoring a Firm's Accounting for Valuation Allowances and Loss Carryforwards

Section 3465 represented a major change in accounting for corporate income tax effects, and the accounting for loss carryforwards is no exception. Companies with tax loss carryforwards are required to do the following:

- If the future income tax asset related to the tax loss carryforward has been recorded in the accounts because its benefit was more likely than not to be realized, as judged by management (and presumably agreed to by the auditors), then at each succeeding reporting date, management must reevaluate the future income tax asset to ensure that it is recorded at an amount no greater than its realizable value (*CICA Handbook*, 3465.31[a]).

- If a future income tax asset related to a loss carryforward was not recorded in the accounts (because its realization was not more likely than not), but as time unfolds and the situation changes (with improved prospects of future taxable profits), a future income tax asset and its associated tax benefit should be recorded (3465.31[b]).

It seems that Section 3465 opens up the potential for income manipulation, and thus imposes a greater responsibility on users to monitor management's actions with respect to accounting for loss carryforwards, and for future income tax assets in general. Let's look at some questions that might be raised when a company changes its valuation allowance for future income tax assets.

Exhibit 13.1 contains an excerpt from a news release issued by Air Canada about two and a half months after the terrible events of September 11, 2001. The airline industry was, as we know, impacted significantly by these events, and Air Canada was no exception. In fact, Air Canada had not been doing well even before then. The news release raises questions regarding the recoverability of the future income tax asset. In this excerpt, the company discusses the need for a valuation allowance and explains very generally how the size of the allowance was derived. Notice that this disclosure

AIR CANADA INC.
www.aircanada.ca

Exhibit 13.1 AIR CANADA

Excerpt from News Release

[All dollar amounts are in Canadian dollars.]

Air Canada Writes Down $410 Million Intangible Tax Asset; Reports Final Third Quarter 2001 Results

OVERVIEW

- Intangible tax asset writedown of $410 million; review required other adjustments
- Writedown does not impact cash position
- Cash balance approximately $900 million as of November 26, 2001—essentially unchanged from November 2, 2001 cash balance

MONTREAL, Nov. 26/CNW/—Air Canada reported preliminary third quarter results on November 2, 2001. At that time, the company advised that it was completing a review of the carrying value of its intangible assets in view of the events of September 11, 2001, and the increased economic uncertainty. The company reported that the review would likely require significant downward adjustments to existing intangible asset values such as future income taxes, goodwill and other intangible assets. The review has now been completed, and as stated on November 2, 2001, the adjustments have no impact on Air Canada's cash position.

For the quarter ended September 30, 2001, Air Canada reported an operating loss of $57 million and a pre-tax loss of $160 million and these figures remain unchanged in this final results release. The operating loss was the best result, pre-government assistance, of any major international carrier in North America. A detailed analysis of the pre-tax loss can be found in the Management Discussion and Analysis of Results released on November 2, 2001.

The results reported today reflect the outcome of the intangible asset review announced on November 2, 2001. Air Canada has recorded a $410 million valuation allowance against the value of the $812 million non-cash future income tax asset. The valuation allowance, combined with Air Canada's decision to report results of operations without tax affecting losses in the third quarter 2001, results in an unrecognized off balance sheet income tax benefit of $455 million as at September 30, 2001. No other adjustments to the carrying value of the Corporation's intangible assets were considered necessary as a result of this review which reflects the changing operating environment.

"The accounting standard that relates to income tax assets requires the valuation decision to be based primarily on the results of the recent past and current conditions," said Rob Peterson, Executive Vice-President and Chief Financial Officer. "As a consequence of this relatively conservative approach we have retained the tax asset off balance sheet. The $455 million off balance sheet tax benefit remains available for use, with substantially an indefinite life. While the review has resulted in an adjustment to the carrying value of the tax asset, it has also reaffirmed the carrying value of all the other intangible assets of the Corporation and there is no impact on our liquidity position," concluded Mr. Peterson.

Source: Canada NewsWire, Montreal, November 26, 2001.

provides information regarding expected future earnings. Consequently, it can be used by analysts to develop or refine estimates of the company's future performance.

The determination of whether a valuation allowance is necessary requires subjective assessments. Similarly, the amount of the allowance is also not based on readily observable criteria. When a valuation allowance is established, the offsetting debit is to income tax expense, which thus reduces income; similarly, when a previously existing allowance is lowered, the offsetting credit to income tax expense increases income. Because of the subjective judgments used when determining the need for (and the amount of) valuation allowances, the possibility of income manipulation exists. Specifically, valuation allowances could conceivably be used to smooth year-to-year earnings fluctuations. For example, in a "good" earnings year management might decide to establish an allowance account, assuming the offsetting charge to earnings is relatively small.

Once the allowance is established, it can be diminished or even eliminated in subsequent "bad" earnings years. The credit arising from an allowance reversal increases reported income, thereby partially offsetting the bad earnings. The result is that income fluctuations are smoothed across years. One recent study investigated whether managers use the valuation allowance to manage earnings.[6] Two types of earnings management are considered: (1) income smoothing (as just described) and (2) "big bath" charge-offs in bad years. While there is anecdotal evidence that the valuation allowance may be used by some firms to manage earnings, the general conclusion is that this is not a pervasive practice. Nevertheless, statement readers must be careful to analyze whether reported changes in valuation allowance amounts seem reasonable in the context of the firm's known prospects. Such close attention to changes in valuation allowances might provide some insight into a company's quality of earnings.

Using Footnote Disclosures to Improve Financial Analysis
Understanding Footnote Disclosures

The disclosures contained in a typical income tax footnote provide financial statement users with a wealth of data. Understanding the nature of these disclosures will enable you to extract useful insights about a firm's performance and prospects.

MAGNA
INTERNATIONAL
www.magna.ca

To illustrate the process, let's look at the income tax footnote for Magna International, as published in the company's audited financial statements for the year ended December 31, 2001. Magna reported in its income statement that income tax expense for the year ended December 2001 was US$290 million. Also, keep in mind that Magna is one of the many Canadian companies that reports in U.S. dollars.

The company's financial statement note for income taxes reads as follows:

Notes to Consolidated Financial Statements
Magna International Inc.

[All dollar amounts are in U.S. dollars.]

12. Income Taxes

(a) The provision for income taxes differs from the expense that would be obtained by applying Canadian statutory rates as a result of the following:

	Years ended December 31,		
	2001	**2000**	**1999**
Canadian statutory income tax rate	41.7%	44.0%	44.6%
Manufacturing and processing profits deduction	(4.8)	(4.5)	(5.8)
Foreign rate differentials	(3.8)	(4.9)	(5.5)
Losses not benefited	1.4	1.9	0.9
Earnings of equity investees	(0.7)	(0.6)	(1.1)
Gains on sales and issues of shares by subsidiaries	(2.1)	(1.1)	—
Reduction in enacted tax rates	(1.3)	—	—
Other	1.1	1.0	1.2
Effective income tax rate	31.5%	35.8%	34.3%

(b) The details of income before income taxes and minority interest by jurisdiction are as follows:

	Years ended December 31,		
	2001	**2000**	**1999**
Canadian	$610	$645	$499
Foreign	308	327	168
	$918	$972	$667

(c) The details of the income tax provision are as follows:

	Years ended December 31,		
	2001	**2000**	**1999**
Current provision			
Canadian federal taxes	$118	$132	$103
Provincial taxes	64	76	62
Foreign taxes	88	113	80
	270	321	245
Future provision			
Canadian federal taxes	(5)	12	11
Provincial taxes	(2)	7	7
Foreign taxes	27	8	(34)
	20	27	(16)
	$290	$348	$229

(d) Future income taxes have been provided on temporary differences which consist of the following:

	Years ended December 31,		
	2001	2000	1999
Tax depreciation in excess of book depreciation	$48	$28	$17
Reduction in enacted tax rates	(12)	—	—
Tax losses benefited	(18)	(7)	(27)
Other	2	6	(6)
	$20	$27	$(16)

(e) Future tax assets and liabilities consist of the following temporary differences:

	2001	2000
Assets		
Tax benefit of loss carryforwards		
Pre-acquisition	$20	$24
Post acquisition	148	111
Share and convertible subordinated debenture issue costs	3	3
	171	138
Valuation allowance against tax benefit of loss carryforwards		
Pre-acquisition	(18)	(18)
Post acquisition	(39)	(24)
	114	96
Liabilities		
Tax depreciation in excess of book depreciation	184	177
Other assets book value in excess of tax value	63	37
Other	29	10
	276	224
Net future tax liability	$162	$128

(f) Income taxes paid in cash were $252 million for the year ended December 31, 2001 (2000 – $267 million; 1999 – $192 million).

(g) At December 31, 2001, the Company has income tax loss carryforwards of approximately $157 million which relate to certain foreign subsidiaries, including $49 million of losses obtained on acquisitions, the tax benefits of which have not been recognized in the consolidated financial statements. Of the total losses, $73 million expire between 2002 and 2008 and the remainder have no expiry date.

(h) Consolidated retained earnings include approximately $1.0 billion at December 31, 2001 of undistributed earnings of foreign subsidiaries that may be subject to tax if remittted to the Canadian parent company. No provision has been made for such taxes as these earnings are considered to be reinvested for the foreseeable future.

Part (a) of the note shows why the provision for income taxes (which we mentioned above was $290 million; this amount also appears as the "bottom line" in part [c] of the note) differs from multiplying the 2001 Canadian statutory income tax rate of 41.7% times the company's fiscal 2001 income before taxes and minority interest of US$918 million, or US$382.8 million. The 2001 "Effective income tax rate" of 31.5%, times the 2001 income before income taxes and minority interest of US$918 million, gives the reported US$290 million (actually, it gives US$289.2, so Magna must have done some rounding). The differences between Magna's expected and effective income tax rates, as revealed in part (a) of the note, are due to several factors, some of which are:

- Since Magna is a manufacturer, it can take advantage of the manufacturing and processing profits deduction on its corporate income tax return. This reduced Magna's income tax rate by 4.8 percentage points in 2001.

- Since Magna operates in foreign jurisdictions as well as domestically, the portion of its income earned in those foreign jurisdictions is subject to foreign tax authorities, the tax rates of which may be higher or lower than domestic rates. In 2001, the foreign rates happened to be 3.8 percentage points lower, but notice the variability in this line item over time. Back in 1999, it was 5.5 points lower.

- There is a 1.4 percentage point *increase* from the statutory rate in 2001 due to something that Magna calls "Losses not benefited." Let's leave the explanation for this until after we deal with parts (d) and (e) of the tax note, below.

- There is a 0.7 percentage point reduction due to the fact that a portion of Magna's income before taxes and minority interest in 2001 was Magna's share of the earnings of companies in which Magna had a less-than-controlling but significant influence. Accounting in this type of situation is explained in Chapter 16; for purposes of our present discussion, Magna's share of these other companies' earnings is not taxable, so the effective income tax rate is less than the expected rate.

- In 2001, there was a 2.1 percentage point reduction from the expected rate because accounting gains reported by Magna when it sold shares in subsidiaries, or when its subsidiaries issued shares, were not taxable.

An important question for analysts of financial statements is: How sustainable are these reductions from the expected corporate income tax rate? The answer to this question relates to government public policy and also the specific activities of the company being analyzed. Canadian federal and provincial governments might change, or even eliminate, special incentives such as the manufacturing and processing profits deduction, as a matter of public policy, thus causing the expected rate itself to change. Also, the tax status of gains on subsidiary share transactions might change. Such policy factors are difficult to forecast, but any probable changes which are in, say, draft legislation form, should be taken into account by financial analysts as they attempt to forecast future corporate net income for use in valuation models and other purposes. At the company-specific level, if Magna decided to shift a greater proportion of its operations to lower income tax foreign jurisdictions, this would impact judgments about both the sustainability and magnitude of such reductions from the expected corporate income tax rate.

Part (c) of Magna's income tax note shows the details of the US$290 million 2001 income tax expense divided up in two ways: jurisdiction and current/future. We can reconstruct an estimated journal entry recording 2001 income taxes from this part of the note, as follows:

DR	Income tax expense	290	
	CR Income tax payable		270
	CR Future income tax liability		20

This entry indicates that, on the basis of Magna's tax return, cash payments owed to the government in respect of income taxes in fiscal 2001 were US$270 million. However, the company actually paid US$252 million in fiscal 2001, according to part (f) of the note. Such lags between payables and cash outflows are, of course, not unusual.

The debit to "Income tax expense" is made up of two quite different components, in accordance with Section 3465 of the *CICA Handbook*. The US$270 million represents an actual cash outflow (which may have already been completely disbursed, or—as in the case of Magna—almost completely). The US$20 million portion of the expense debit is caused by the *increase* in Magna's future income tax liabilities, on a net basis (the "Foreign taxes" portion has increased by US$27 million in fiscal 2001 while the sum of the Canadian federal and provincial portion has declined by a total of US$7 million according to part [c]), as required by the rules in Section 3465. These rules require that companies account for the year's changes in the temporary differences between the tax and GAAP bases of the company's assets and liabilities, and Magna discloses the major components of these changes in part (d) of the note. In 2001, the company deducted CCA on its tax return in excess of amortization on capital assets expensed in the accounts, creating additional future income tax liabilities of US$48 million. This CCA/book amortization difference increased significantly in 2001 over the two comparative years.

Part (d) of the note also informs us that "Reduction in enacted tax rates" and "Tax losses benefited" each caused a significant offset to the CCA/amortization increase of US$48 million. Section 3465 requires that companies adjust their future income tax assets and income tax liabilities when enacted or substantially enacted income tax rates change, and Magna has done just that, thereby reducing its 2001 income tax expense by US$12 million. The US$18 million reduction (disclosed in part (d) of the note) in 2001 income tax expense due to "Tax losses benefited" is explained in part (e) of the note, which discloses details supporting the various balance sheet numbers concerning future income taxes. On December 31, 2001, Magna reported future income tax assets due to "Tax benefits of loss carryforwards" of US$168 million (this amount was disclosed as being made up of two categories by Magna: US$20 million which was due to operations before companies were acquired by Magna, and US$148 million due to post acquisition). But the company has reduced this US$168 million by a valuation allowance against the loss carryforwards of US$57 million (US$18 million plus US$39 million), resulting in a net amount for loss carryforward future tax assets of US$168 million minus US$57 million, or US$111 million as of December 31, 2001. The corresponding number for the comparative year, December 31, 2000, is US$93 million, and so the net change in this category of future income tax assets is an *increase* of $18 million. This appears to be the $18 million that we need to "explain" the $18 million "Tax losses benefited" disclosed in part (d), which reduced the future portion of the company's 2001 income tax expense. To make this a bit clearer, the part of the 2001 income tax journal entry due to this factor would be:

DR	Future income tax asset due to loss carryforwards (net)	33 (see part [e] of Magna's income tax note: 20 + 148 − 24 − 111)
CR	Valuation allowance against tax benefit of loss carryforwards (net)	15 (see part [e]: 18 + 39 − 18 − 24)
CR	Future income tax expense	18

The future tax asset due to loss carryforwards, $168 million as of December 31, 2001, has been reduced by $57 million, signalling that the company expects to actually realize only about $111 million in reduction of future income taxes otherwise payable. Some explanation for the large size of this valuation allowance is provided in part (g) of the income tax note, which indicates that pre-tax loss carryforwards of $73 million expire between 2002 and 2008.

Remember that we said that we could get back to the line item in part (a) of the note, "Losses not benefited"? This was the 1.4 percentage point increase in Magna's effective corporate income tax rate for 2001 compared to the Canadian statutory rate. The information on loss carryforwards in parts (d) and (e) of Magna's income tax note deals only with those future income tax assets that Magna has recorded. It must have been the case that, within the overall profits that Magna reported in 2001, there were some jurisdictions in which the company reported losses for income tax purposes. This seems reasonable since Magna increased its tax benefit of loss carryforwards in 2001 (part [e]). But not all the losses were accounted for by Magna, since Section 3465 does require some degree of assurance that the losses will result in future tax benefits to the company. It is these *unrecorded* 2001 loss carryforwards that caused the effective income tax rate to be 1.4 percentage points higher than the statutory rate.

Using Income Tax Footnotes to Help Assess Quality of Earnings

We know that if a company lengthens the estimated useful lives of its capital (fixed) assets, book depreciation will be lowered and the excess of book income over taxable income will probably be widened, causing an increase in future income tax liabilities, if all other things are equal. Other explanations for the increase in the future tax liability that are related to depreciation/amortization and CCA temporary differences include growth in capital expenditures and tax law changes which permit more accelerated CCA for income tax filing purposes. If investigation reveals that the future income tax liability increased without either a corresponding increase in capital expenditures or a change in tax CCA schedules, then the analyst should try to determine whether an undisclosed change in useful lives has been made to raise the company's income. Similar investigations should be undertaken for other sudden increases in other types of future income tax liabilities, or future income tax assets. Such an investigation might therefore provide evidence for concluding that earnings quality was less than desirable.

We will use warranty expense as an example to illustrate that sudden decreases in future income tax assets, for example, might be a sign of possible deteriorating earnings quality.

We saw earlier that accruals for product warranties generate future tax assets. The reason is that GAAP require warranty expenses to be matched against the revenues of the products to which the warranty applies. But income tax rules do not allow deductions for warranty expenses until the costs of providing the warranty services are actually incurred. This is often later than the period in which the revenues have been recognized. Accordingly, for growing companies, GAAP warranty expenses exceed tax return warranty expenses, giving rise to a future tax asset.

Assume that on January 1, 2003, Carson Company begins offering a one-year warranty on all sales. Its 2003 sales were $20,000,000, and Carson estimates that warranty expenses will be 1% of sales; therefore, $200,000 of warranty expense is deducted on Carson's books in 2003.

Assume that **tax deductions** for warranties in 2003 were zero. If tax rates in 2003 are 35%, Carson will have a future tax asset of $70,000 for warranties at December 31, 2003—the $200,000 book-versus-tax-warranty difference times 35%. If the *actual* warranty costs incurred in year 2004 that are associated with 2003 sales were precisely $200,000, this would indicate that Carson's warranty estimate was accurate and should be maintained in year 2004.

Table 13.11(a) shows what will happen if Carson Company uses the same warranty expense estimate of 1% of sales in year 2004. Here it is assumed that sales in year 2004 are again $20,000,000 and that actual warranty costs on year 2004 sales are not incurred until 2005. Using these assumptions, notice that Carson's December 31, 2004 future tax asset balance will still be $70,000. That is, the 2003 book versus tax timing difference reversed in year 2004, but a new $200,000 timing difference on warranties associated with year 2004 sales originated. The example in Table 13.11(a) is designed to demonstrate that the future income tax asset balance will remain stable if the warranty estimate is accurate and if sales volume is unchanged.

To illustrate why it is also important to scrutinize future tax asset balances as one means to help assess the quality of earnings, let us now assume that instead of maintaining the warranty expense estimate at 1% of sales, Carson lowers the estimate to 0.5% of sales in year 2004. Carson does this because its managers wish to increase year 2004 income despite the fact that the 1% estimate reflects actual warranty experience. Notice that since the 1% estimate accurately reflected warranty experience in 2003, this change of an accounting estimate in year 2004 represents a deterioration in earnings quality.

TABLE 13.11(a) CARSON COMPANY

Illustration of Decline in Future Tax Assets

Warranty Percentage Unchanged

	2004	2003
Sales revenues	$20,000,000	$20,000,000
Estimated warranty cost percentage	0.01	0.01
Warranty expense per books	$ 200,000	$ 200,000
Warranty expense per tax return:		
Attributable to year 2003 sales	$ 200,000	—
Attributable to year 2004 sales	—	—
Book versus tax difference:		
Arising from year 2003 sales	—	$ 200,000
Arising from year 2004 sales	$ 200,000	—
Tax rate	0.35	0.35
December 31 future tax asset balance	$ 70,000	$ 70,000

Table 13.11(b) shows that the future tax asset balance will decrease from $70,000 to $35,000 under these circumstances. The reason for the decrease in the future income tax asset balance is that the book versus tax difference narrowed from $200,000 in 2003 to $100,000 in 2004 as a consequence of the reduction in estimated warranty expense from 1% to 0.5% of sales.

TABLE 13.11(b) CARSON COMPANY

Illustration of Decline in Future Tax Assets

Warranty Percentage Lowered in 2004

	2004	2003
Sales revenues	$20,000,000	$20,000,000
Estimated warranty cost percentage	0.005	0.01
Warranty expense per books	$ 100,000	$ 200,000
Warranty expense per tax return:		
Attributable to year 2003 sales	$ 200,000	—
Attributable to year 2004 sales	—	—
Book versus tax difference:		
Arising from year 2003 sales	—	$ 200,000
Arising from year 2004 sales	$ 100,000	—
Tax rate	0.35	0.35
December 31 future tax asset balance	$ 35,000	$ 70,000

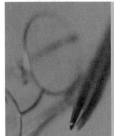

Recap

This example demonstrates why shrinkage in a future tax asset balance should be investigated. Year-to-year changes in warranty expense estimates are just like other changes in accounting estimates in that they need to be disclosed only if they are material. Since materiality guidelines are subjective, companies can conceivably use undisclosed estimate changes as a way to artificially increase earnings. Decreases in future tax asset balances can provide clues of such possibilities to statement readers.[7]

Using Tax Footnotes to Improve Intercompany Comparability

The future or deferred tax portion of the income tax footnote can be used to undo differences in financial reporting choices across firms and thus to improve intercompany comparisons.

Here's a specific illustration. Lubrizol and Cambrex are both classified in the same Standard Industrial Classification (SIC) code and compete in many product categories. But each uses different depreciation methods. Lubrizol's 1999 10-K states the following:

Accelerated depreciation methods are used in computing depreciation on certain machinery and equipment, which comprise approximately 21% of the depreciable assets. The remaining assets are depreciated using the straight-line method. The estimated useful lives are 10 to 40 years for buildings and land improvements and range from 3 to 20 years for machinery and equipment.

In the United States, SIC is a system maintained by the Office of Federal Statistical Policy and Standards in the Department of Commerce to classify firms by the nature of their operations. Lubrizol and Cambrex are both in SIC Code 2860—Industrial Organic Chemicals.

So Lubrizol is using accelerated depreciation for some of its assets. By contrast, Cambrex's 1999 report says:

> Property, plant and equipment is stated at cost, net of accumulated depreciation. Plant and equipment are depreciated on a straight-line basis over the estimated useful lives for each applicable asset group as follows:
>
> | | |
> |---|---|
> | Buildings and improvements | 15 to 20 years |
> | Machinery and equipment | 5 to 10 years |
> | Furniture and fixtures | 3 to 5 years |

Table 13.12 gives several key financial statement figures for each company from their respective 1999 10-Ks and excerpts from their income tax footnotes. It's possible that the different depreciation choices of each firm conform perfectly to differences in the service potential of each firm's assets. But what if they don't? How can an analyst adjust the numbers to improve interfirm comparisons?

Let's begin by looking at Table 13.12(a), which shows the balances in the subcomponents of the deferred tax liability account for Lubrizol. The highlighted depre-

TABLE 13.12 SELECTED FINANCIAL STATEMENT DISCLOSURES FROM THE 1999 10-K REPORTS OF LUBRIZOL AND CAMBREX

(a)

	December 31	
Lubrizol (US$ in thousands)	1999	1998
Book depreciation	$ 88,300	$ 79,700
Income before income taxes	195,350	118,814
Property, plant & equipment, net of accumulated depreciation (at year-end)	670,512	718,850
Significant deferred tax liabilities	**1999**	**1998**
Depreciation and other basis differences	$ 99,938	$101,658
Undistributed foreign equity income	5,566	3,894
Inventory basis difference	1,497	3,706
Other	3,977	2,986

(b)

	December 31	
Cambrex (US$ in thousands)	1999	1998
Book depreciation	$ 33,118	$ 30,547
Income before income taxes	58,901	61,695
Property, plant & equipment, net of accumulated depreciation (at year-end)	280,163	255,016
Significant deferred tax liabilities	**1999**	**1998**
Depreciation	$ 30,967	$ 29,591
Environmental reserves	796	—
Intangibles	14,963	14,839
Italian intangibles	4,581	6,086
Other benefits	2,143	—
Other	1,722	1,667

ciation item reflects the US$99.9 million cumulative deferred tax liability arising from book versus tax depreciation expense at December 31, 1999.

Companies like Lubrizol have an incentive to use the most accelerated depreciation method that the tax law allows and to depreciate the assets over the shortest allowable tax life. This minimizes the discounted present value of their tax liability by accelerating deductions to the fullest legal extent. These *tax* depreciation rate and useful life deductions exceed the *book* accelerated method and useful lives chosen by Lubrizol, so a deferred liability results. The liability declined by US$1.7 million during 1999 (US$99.9 million minus US$101.6 million).

The change in the deferred income tax liability arising from depreciation is:

$$\text{Change} = (\text{Tax depreciation} - \text{Book depreciation}) \times \text{Statutory tax rate}$$

Lubrizol's statutory tax rate is 35%, and the depreciation deferred tax *change* was –US$1.7 million (a decrease), as shown in Table 13.12(a). Substituting these values into the preceding equation, we get:

$$-\$1.7 \text{ million} = (\text{Tax depreciation} - \text{Book depreciation}) \times 0.35$$

Dividing both sides by 0.35 yields:

$$-\$4.9 \text{ million} = (\text{Tax depreciation} - \text{Book depreciation})$$

Since Table 13.12(a) shows that Lubrizol's book depreciation was US$88.3 million, tax depreciation must have been $88.3 million – $4.9 million = $83.4 million, which was 5.5% lower.

We can now perform the same analysis on Cambrex and determine what its tax depreciation was in 1999. The highlighted portion of Table 13.12(b) shows that Cambrex's depreciation-related deferred income tax liability was slightly less than US$31.0 million in 1999—an increase of US$1.4 million over the previous year. Repeating the analytical approach we used for Lubrizol yields:

$$\text{Change} = (\text{Tax depreciation} - \text{Book depreciation}) \times \text{Statutory tax rate}$$

or:

$$\$1.4 \text{ million} = (\text{Tax depreciation} - \text{Book depreciation}) \times 0.35$$

or:

$$\$4 \text{ million} = (\text{Tax depreciation} - \text{Book depreciation})$$

Cambrex's book depreciation was US$33.1 million (Table 13.12[b]), so tax depreciation must have been $33.1 million + $4 million = $37.1 million, an increase of 12.1%.

We have now approximated the tax return depreciation taken by each firm and established a "common denominator" for interfirm analysis. While we do not have enough information to put Cambrex on Lubrizol's book depreciation basis, we do have enough information to put each firm on an identical tax depreciation basis, thereby facilitating comparisons.

Adjusting each firm's financial reporting to the same rate as well as the useful lives used for tax purposes increases Lubrizol's pre-tax income by 2.5% ($4.9 million ÷ $195.4 million). Cambrex's pre-tax income is lowered by 6.8% ($4 million ÷ $58.9 million). In any setting, the difference may—or may not—be significant. But mak-

A reduction in the deferred tax liability related to depreciation timing differences probably arises because either: (1) accelerated methods used for books gives higher depreciation than allowed for tax purposes, or (2) assets for which Lubrizol uses straight-line depreciation for books have reached a point in their useful lives where the straight-line depreciation exceeds the accelerated depreciation per tax return (see again Figure 13.1).

ing interfirm comparisons using comparable data is better than basing the analysis on diverse financial reporting choices.

The preceding analysis works only in those situations where firms have not had major asset disposals during the year. When depreciable assets are sold, the deferred tax amounts for these assets are eliminated from the deferred tax liability account. Moreover, the amount eliminated due to asset sales is rarely disclosed. So the year-to-year change in the deferred tax liability balance for depreciation no longer reflects only current period book versus tax depreciation differences. We can determine if the firm sold assets during the period by looking in the "Investing activity" section of the cash flow statement to see if cash was generated from asset sales. In this illustration, neither Lubrizol nor Cambrex reported major asset sales in their 1999 cash flow statements.

Using Income Tax Footnotes to Assess the Degree of Conservatism in Firms' Accounting Choices

Determining the degree of conservatism in a firm's set of accounting choices is an important part of assessing the earnings quality for that company. Conservative choices, like accelerated depreciation, decrease earnings and asset values relative to more liberal techniques, like straight-line depreciation. *Ceteris paribus*, the more conservative the set of accounting choices, the higher the quality of earnings.

To assess the degree of conservatism in a firm's portfolio of accounting choices, compare the ratio of pre-tax book income to taxable income in the income tax footnote. While this is a relatively coarse assessment of accounting conservatism, it can be useful in selected settings. The ratio is computed as:

$$EC = \frac{\text{Pre-tax book income (adjusted for permanent differences)}}{\text{Taxable income per tax return}}$$

where EC is the current period's **earnings conservatism** ratio.

Consider the denominator, "Taxable income per tax return." In most instances, firms seek to minimize tax return income.[8] Because of this income minimization incentive, the denominator represents a very conservative income benchmark. In most cases, it is the lowest permissible—meaning "legal"—taxable income number for the period.

The numerator—GAAP income—incorporates the latitude available to firms in selecting accounting method choices, accounting estimates for things like bad debts expense and asset useful lives, and discretionary expenses such as advertising and research and development (R&D) that we have outlined elsewhere in the book. Consequently, the numerator can range from a highly aggressive (income increasing) number to a highly conservative (income decreasing) number.

To illustrate how this ratio is used, we will compute the EC ratio for Sample Corporation, whose 2001 income before income taxes is $3,965 million. This is the numerator of EC. Since most companies do not disclose details of their income tax returns, we need to estimate the denominator, "Taxable income per tax return." This is easily done. If income taxes currently payable in 2001 totalled $1,109 million, taxable income can then be computed as (assuming an effective tax rate of 28.5%):

In a computation of the EC ratio, permanent differences should be removed from the numerator—that is, including items like nondeductible goodwill amortization injects an element into EC that is unrelated to quality-of-earnings choices.

$$\begin{array}{c}\text{Income taxes} \\ \text{currently} \\ \text{payable}\end{array} = \begin{array}{c}\text{Taxable income} \\ \text{per tax return}\end{array} \times \begin{array}{c}\text{Effective} \\ \text{tax rate}\end{array}$$

Substituting the two pieces of data, we get:

$$\begin{array}{c}\text{Income taxes} \\ \text{currently} \\ \text{payable}\end{array} = \begin{array}{c}\text{Taxable income} \\ \text{per tax return}\end{array} \times \begin{array}{c}\text{Effective} \\ \text{tax rate}\end{array}$$

$$\$1{,}109 \text{ million} = \qquad ? \qquad \times \quad 0.285$$

Rearranging, in order to isolate the unknown taxable income per tax return on the left side, we get:

$$\begin{array}{c}\text{Taxable} \\ \text{income}\end{array} = \$1{,}109 \text{ million} \div 0.285$$

or:

$$\begin{array}{c}\text{Taxable} \\ \text{income}\end{array} = \$3{,}891 \text{ million}$$

Thus, EC for Sample is:

$$EC = \frac{\text{Pre-tax book income}}{\text{Taxable income}}$$

$$EC = \frac{\$3{,}965}{\$3{,}891}$$

$$EC = 1.02$$

In general, an EC ratio close to 1.0 indicates relatively conservative financial reporting choices. (Remember, companies have an incentive to minimize the denominator, "Taxable income per tax return." When the numerator, pre-tax book income, is even smaller, this suggests that earnings conservatism is high.)

Analysts can also compare EC ratios for a single company over time to monitor overall earnings conservatism. For example, suppose we have the following data for Sample Corporation for 2000:

$$\begin{array}{c}2000 \\ \text{taxable} \\ \text{income}\end{array} = \begin{array}{c}2000 \text{ income} \\ \text{taxes currently} \\ \text{payable}\end{array} \div \begin{array}{c}2000 \\ \text{effective} \\ \text{tax rate}\end{array}$$

$$\begin{array}{c}2000 \\ \text{taxable} \\ \text{income}\end{array} = \$837 \text{ million} \div 0.225$$

$$\begin{array}{c}2000 \\ \text{taxable} \\ \text{income}\end{array} = \$3{,}720 \text{ million}$$

EC is accordingly:

$$EC = \frac{2000 \text{ pre-tax book income}}{2000 \text{ taxable income}}$$

$$EC = \frac{\$2{,}404}{\$3{,}720}, \text{ assuming pre-tax book income of } \$2{,}404$$

$$EC = 0.646$$

The increase from 0.646 to 1.02 suggests that Sample may have been somewhat more aggressive in its financial reporting choices for 2001 relative to 2000. However, year-to-year changes in EC ratios must be interpreted with caution when the effective tax rates—used to solve for the unknown taxable income number—change dramatically as they did for Sample (0.225 versus 0.285).

Effective tax rates are influenced by permanent difference items that do not necessarily indicate a change in a firm's reporting aggressiveness. For example, if the amount of income derived from investments in subsidiary companies—which is non-taxable—decreases from year to year, the firm's effective tax rate will be increased. This, in turn, will *decrease* the imputed taxable income number and *increase* the EC ratio even though the firm's financial reporting choices have remained unchanged. The point here is that the analyst must be careful to scrutinize the tax footnotes to determine the reasons behind changes in effective tax rates when comparing EC ratios over time.

The earnings conservatism ratio can also be used to compare reporting choices across companies. For example, Sample's EC might be compared with the EC ratio of a competitor to assess whether each has similar earnings conservatism.

Having introduced the EC ratio, we now need to emphasize its primary limitations.

1. EC ratio comparisons for a single company over time can be misleading if the tax law has changed over the period of comparison. For example, if the taxation authority allows more accelerated tax depreciation schedules, this will cause the EC ratio to rise (i.e., showing *lower* earnings conservatism) even though the firm's real earnings conservatism has remained constant.
2. Comparisons across companies in different industries should be made cautiously. Specifically, the impact of tax burdens can vary because of differences in capital intensity or specific tax rules which affect only certain industries.

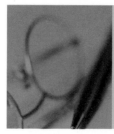

Recap

Tax footnotes provide information that allows the analyst to estimate firms' taxable income. By comparing pre-tax accounting income with the estimate of taxable income, analysts can develop a rough index (subject to the limitations noted above) of the overall degree of conservatism in a firm's set of GAAP accounting choices. The degree of conservatism in a firm's set of accounting choices is an important part of assessing the earnings quality of that company.

Summary of Financial Reporting for Corporate Income Taxes and Quality of Earnings Links

As this chapter has shown, a close, careful reading of the corporate income tax information provided by a company in its financial statements may be helpful in forming judgments about quality of earnings (QOE). The following table brings these ideas together and serves as a summary and an extension:

Feature of corporate income tax reporting	QOE issues
Information reconciling statutory tax rate to effective tax rate	Indication of one-time-only reductions; sustainability of reductions going forward; special reductions due to geographic location of taxable income might signal questionable sourcing decisions or transfer prices
Changes to future income tax asset valuation account	Hard to evaluate whether justified or not, therefore full disclosure imperative
Changes in future income tax assets and/or future income tax liabilities	Significant, sudden, changes might suggest inappropriate changes in accruals, capital asset depreciation/amortization methods or asset lives
Earnings conservatism ratio	Useful in limited circumstances, and must be used with caution
Disclosure—compliance with GAAP is a minimum; use "Other" category?; strategic disclosures?	A complete understanding of how a company implements GAAP for reporting corporate income taxes requires more than just a "minimum compliance" approach. Also, watch for the "hiding" of bad information by packaging it with other information.

Summary

- Interperiod income tax allocation accounting is used whenever temporary or timing differences exist between book and taxable incomes.
- The method specified in Section 3465 for income tax accounting is called the "asset and liability method." This method takes a balance sheet approach to determine future tax amounts, and it focuses on temporary differences that result in future tax liabilities (termed "future taxable amounts") and temporary differences that result in future tax assets (termed "future deductible amounts").
- When existing tax rates change (or are substantially enacted), the amounts of future tax assets or liabilities are adjusted to reflect the new rates.
- If previously profitable firms suffer losses, tax law provides for tax recovery through net operating loss carrybacks and carryforwards.
- Remeasuring or valuation allowances are required for future tax assets if "it is more likely than not" that some portion of the asset will not be realized.
- The income tax footnote provides useful information for assessing a company's earnings quality. To glean this information from footnotes, analysts should monitor changes in future tax balances and investigate unusual sudden increases or decreases.
- The relationship between pre-tax book income and taxable income can serve as a rough indicator of the degree of conservatism with respect to a firm's portfolio of accounting choices.

A Comprehensive Interperiod Tax Allocation Problem

The following example involving Mulray Corporation combines the various aspects of accounting for income taxes discussed in this chapter to demonstrate the interrelation between pre-tax accounting income, taxable income, taxes payable, future income taxes, and tax expense. Working through this example will demonstrate the following points:

1. how to convert a pre-tax accounting income number to a taxable income number
2. how taxes payable are determined
3. how the changes in future tax assets and future tax liabilities are determined
4. how current income tax expense and future income tax expense are determined
5. how to reconcile the total tax costs (benefits) reported in the income statement with the total taxes payable according to the tax return for the period

Here's the example:

Mulray Corporation (MC), a public company founded many years ago, began fiscal 2001 with the following items on its balance sheet:

Future income tax asset:	$14,000 [due to loss carryforward, at a tax rate of 40%]
Future income tax liability:	$nil

No other future tax information appears on the company's balance sheet.

The current year (2001) income tax rate is 40%, but recently enacted legislation specifies that for the years 2002 and 2003 the rate will be 35% for each of these years, and thereafter 30%.

MC's net income before income tax (NIBT) according to GAAP is $500,000. The following additional information is available:

- NIBT includes $12,000 of nontaxable dividend income.

- Year 2001 depreciation was $100,000, and will be over the remaining four years of MC's capital assets' average expected lives. CCA in 2001 was $140,000, and is expected to be $120,000 in 2002, $100,000 in 2003, and below $100,000 thereafter.

- On December 31, 2001, the last day of its fiscal year, MC collected $60,000 in rent on a warehouse that it had just agreed to lease. The lease term runs for one year beginning March 31, 2002. MC collected the entire agreed-upon payment in advance. The company's CEO resented strongly that the amount was taxable in the period received.

- While MC expended $35,000 in warranty payments in 2001, it recorded the following journal entry:

DR Warranty expense	$50,000	
CR Estimated warranty costs		$50,000

MC sells its products under a two-year warranty. Warranty costs are deductible when incurred for tax return purposes.

- Bad debts written off in 2001 totalled $20,000. This amount was deducted on MC's income tax return. However, the provision for bad debts under the allowance method, as recorded in the company's books, was $15,000.

- NIBT contains a $17,000 expense for non-tax-deductible life insurance premiums on MC's executives.

- In 2001, MC collected $80,000 as the first installment on a sale of land that closed on June 30, 2001. The cost of the land was $300,000, and the selling price was $400,000, to be received by MC in five equal installments beginning December 30, 2001. For tax return purposes, any profits are reported in proportion to cash receipts, i.e., on an installment basis.

- MC has $35,000 of unused loss carryforward as of the start of 2001.

Required:

(a) Prepare all journal entries to record MC's 2001 income tax. Show supporting calculations, and indicate whether balance sheet items are current or noncurrent. Follow Canadian GAAP.

(b) Show the bottom portion of MC's 2001 income statement beginning with "Net income before income taxes."

A solution guide for Mulray's income tax accounting follows:

(a) Journal entries:

Computation of taxable income for 2001:

NIBT	$500,000
Dividend income	(12,000)
CCA > Depreciation	(40,000)
Rent in advance	60,000
Warranty expense exceeds warranty paid by	15,000
Bad debt writeoff exceeds expense by	(5,000)
Insurance expense	17,000
Deferred land profit	(80,000)[1]
Loss carryforward	(35,000)
Taxable income	$420,000

[1] If you assume that the income tax treatment and the book treatment were the same, there would be no temporary difference with respect to the land sale. But this is highly unlikely, since the GAAP treatment for the gross profit for this transaction would likely be to record it on the closing of the real estate sale (i.e., in the current year).

Therefore, current income tax = $420,000 × 40% = $168,000
The journal entry for the current income tax expense is:

DR	Current income tax expense	$168,000	
	CR Income tax payable		$168,000

[The "Income tax payable" account is classified as a current liability on the balance sheet.]

Temporary differences:

ADDITIONAL INFORMATION ITEM	TREATMENT AS TEMPORARY DIFFERENCE					
Nontaxable dividend income: Permanent difference	Not applicable					
Depreciation/CCA: Temporary difference; since there is no FTA or future tax liability (FTL) at the start of fiscal 2001 other than that due to LCF, there is no opening temporary difference due to depreciation/CCA.	The 2001 difference is an originating difference that will reverse in the future as follows:					
	Year	**Depreciation**	**CCA**	**Tax Rate**	**Difference**	**After Tax**
	2002	$100,000	$120,000	35%	$20,000	$7,000
	2003	100,000	100,000	35%	—	—
	All future years	200,000	140,000 [plug]	30%	(60,000)	(18,000)
	Total	**$400,000**	**$360,000**			**$(11,000)**
	Therefore, the 2001 temporary difference of $40,000 leads to a future tax liability (FTL) of $11,000.					
Rent received in advance: Creates a future tax assessment (FTA)	FTA = 35% × $60,000 = $21,000					
Warranty: Creates FTA	FTA = 35% × $15,000 = $5,250					
Bad debts: Creates FTL	FTL = 35% × $5,000 = $1,750					
Life insurance premiums: Permanent difference	Not applicable					
Land sale: Creates FTL	Total profit = $400,000 − $300,000 = $100,000; Deferred profit = $80,000 FTL = ($20,000 × 2 × 35%) + ($20,000 × 2 × 30%) = $26,000					
Opening FTA due to recorded a loss carryforward (LCF): The LCF of $35,000 was applied to reduce 2001 taxable income.	The opening FTA due to LCF was reduced to zero, and so was credited.					

Therefore, the future portion of the 2001 income tax journal entry is:

DR	Future income tax expense [plug]	$26,500	
DR	FTA due to rent in advance	21,000	Current item
DR	FTA due to warranty	5,250	Current item
	CR FTL due to CCA/Depreciation	$11,000	Noncurrent item
	CR FTL due to bad debts	1,750	Current item
	CR FTL due to land sale	26,000	Noncurrent item
	CR FTA due to LCF reduced	14,000	Reduced to zero

(b) Bottom portion of income statement:

Net income before income tax		$500,000
Income taxes:		
Current	$200,000	
Future	26,500	
		226,500
Net income		$273,500

For more Exercises, Problems/Discussion Questions, and Cases, visit the Companion Website for this textbook at **www.pearsoned.ca/revsine**.

Exercises

E13-1 Determining future tax liability

Huff Corporation began operations on January 1, 2003. Huff recognizes revenues from all sales under the accrual method for financial reporting purposes and appropriately uses the installment method for income tax-filing purposes. Huff's gross margin on installment sales under each method was as follows:

Year	Accrual Method	Installment Method
2003	$ 800,000	$300,000
2004	1,300,000	700,000

Enacted income tax rates are 30% for 2004 and 25% thereafter. There are no other temporary differences.

Required:

In Huff's December 31, 2004, balance sheet, how much should the future income tax liability be?

E13-2 Future tax effects on balance sheet

As a result of differences between amortization for financial reporting purposes and tax purposes, the financial reporting basis of Noor Company's sole amortizable asset, acquired in 2003, exceeded its tax basis by $250,000 at December 31, 2003. This difference will reverse in future years. The enacted tax rate is 30% for 2003, and 40% for future years. Noor has no other temporary differences.

Required:

In its December 31, 2003, balance sheet, how much should Noor report as the future tax effect of this difference? Indicate the amount and whether it is an asset or a liability.

E13-3 Determining future tax liability and current portion of tax expense

Kent Inc.'s reconciliation between financial statement and taxable income for 2001 follows:

Pre-tax financial income	$150,000
Permanent difference	(12,000)
	138,000
Temporary difference—amortization	(9,000)
Taxable income	$129,000

Additional Information:

	At December 31,	
	2000	2001
Cumulative temporary difference (future taxable amounts)	$11,000	$20,000

The enacted tax rate was 34% for 2000 and 40% for 2001 and years thereafter.

Required:

1. In its December 31, 2001, balance sheet, what amount should Kent report as its future income tax liability?
2. In its 2001 income statement, what amount should Kent report as the current portion of income tax expense?

E13-4 Determining future tax asset amounts

West Corporation leased a building and received the $36,000 annual rental payment on June 15, 2003. The beginning of the lease was July 1, 2003. Rental income is taxable when received. West's tax rates are 30% for 2003 and 40% thereafter. West had no other permanent or temporary differences.

Required:

What amount of future tax asset should West report in its December 31, 2003, balance sheet?

E13-5 Loss carrybacks and carryforwards

Town, a calendar-year corporation that was incorporated in January 2002, experienced a $600,000 net operating loss (NOL) in 2004. For the years 2002 and 2003, Town reported taxable income in each year and a total of $450,000 for the two years combined. Assume that (1) there are no differences between pre-tax book income and taxable income for all years; (2) the income tax rate is 40% for all years; (3) the NOL will be carried back to the profit years (2002–2003) to the extent of $450,000, and $150,000 will be carried forward to future periods; and (4) Town expects to report taxable income for the foreseeable future.

Required:

1. What amounts should Town report as "tax benefit due to NOL carryback and carryforward" in its 2004 income statement?
2. How much will Town report as a future tax asset on its December 31, 2004, balance sheet?

E13-6 Future tax asset and valuation allowance

In Figland Company's first year of operations (2003), the company had pre-tax book income of $500,000 and taxable income of $800,000 at the December year-end. Figland expected to maintain this level of taxable income in future years. Figland's only temporary difference is for accrued product warranty costs, which are expected to be paid as follows over the next two years:

| 2004 | $100,000 |
| 2005 | $200,000 |

The enacted income tax rate for these years is 30%. Figland believes there is a high likelihood that one-third of the tax benefit associated with this future deductible amount will not be realized.

Required:

Compute the amount of future tax asset that would be reported in Figland's 2003 tax footnote.

E13-7 Determining tax expense, taxes payable, and future taxes

The following information is provided for Lally Corporation for 2003 and 2004:

	2003	2004
Book income before income taxes	$4,000,000	$5,000,000
Dividend income included above that was not subject to income taxes	100,000	100,000

- Income before income taxes in 2003 included accrued rent revenue of $80,000 that was not subject to income taxes until its receipt in 2004.
- Lally was subject to an income tax rate of 40% in 2003 and 2004.

Required:

1. What was Lally's taxable income for 2003?
2. Lally Corporation's taxes payable for 2003 was how much?
3. What was the change in Lally's future tax asset (liability) balance for 2003?
4. What amount of income tax expense would Lally report on its 2003 income statement?
5. Repeat Questions 1 through 4 for 2004.

Problems/Discussion Questions

P13-1 Future tax amounts with different tax rates

Moss Inc. uses the accrual method of accounting for financial reporting purposes and appropriately uses the installment method of accounting for income tax purposes. Installment income of $250,000 will be collected in the following years when the enacted tax rates are as indicated.

	Collection of Income	Enacted Tax Rates
2001	$ 25,000	35%
2002	50,000	30
2003	75,000	30
2004	100,000	25

The installment income is Moss's only temporary difference.

Required:

What amount should be included as the future income tax liability in Moss's December 31, 2001, balance sheet?

P13-2 Tax expense and future tax calculations

Nelson Inc. purchased machinery at the beginning of 2004 for $90,000. Management used the straight-line method to amortize the cost for financial reporting purposes and the sum-of-the-years'-digits method to amortize the cost for tax purposes. The life of the machinery was estimated to be two years, and the salvage value was estimated at zero. Revenues less expenses other than amortization expense and amortization of goodwill equalled $500,000 for 2004 and 2005. Nelson pays income tax at the rate of 20% of taxable income. The amortization of goodwill equalled $50,000 for 2004 and 2005.

1. Compute the taxable income and the financial reporting income (before tax) for the years 2004 and 2005.
2. What are the permanent and temporary differences? Give an example of each for Nelson Inc.
3. Complete the following table based on your answer to part 1.

Year	Ending Balance in Tax Liability	Tax Expense	Ending Balance in Future Income Taxes
2004			
2005			

Note: Be sure to identify whether it is a debit or credit balance for future income taxes.

4. Assume that the tax rate was changed by the federal government to 30% at the beginning of 2005. Compute the following:

   Increase/decrease in future income taxes
   Income tax liability for 2005
   Income tax expense for 2005

P13-3 Various income tax accounting items

The accountant for Zigoma Limited (ZL) collected the following information:

(i) At its December 31, 2005, fiscal year-end, ZL has $160,000 of temporary differences (for the first time) due to amortizable capital assets: over the period 2006 to 2010, the following taxable amounts are expected due to these temporary differences:

2006	$10,000
2007	20,000
2008	30,000
2009	40,000
2010	20,000

(ii) As of December 31, 2005, ZL had accrued $100,000 in warranty liabilities. The company had just started to sell its products under warranty in the year 2005, and had not actually expended any cash on warranty claims. Payments were expected to be made as follows:

2006	$10,000
2007	20,000
2008	70,000

(iii) ZL had an unused loss carryforward of $30,000 as of December 31, 2004. The tax benefit of this loss was not recorded in the accounts in prior years, but in 2005 management expected that its complete realization was more likely than not during the remaining carryforward period.

(iv) Tax rates enacted as at December 31, 2003, were as follows: 60% in 2005, 50% in 2006, 40% in 2007, and 60% thereafter.

(v) Taxable income for 2005 was $310,000.

(vi) The company paid $20,000 in life insurance premiums for key officers in 2005.

Required:

1. Compute ZL's net income before taxes for the year 2005.
2. Prepare journal entries to record both the current and future portions of 2005's income tax expense.

3. Prepare a partial income statement, starting with net income before income taxes for 2005.
4. What evidence justifies management's expectation that the unused loss carryforward of $30,000 was now (in 2005) more likely than not to be realized? Assume that ZL manufactures computer zip drives.

P13-4 Entries for loss carrybacks and carryforwards

Smith Corporation started doing business in 2004. The following table summarizes the taxable income (loss) of the company over the 2004–2016 period, along with the statutory tax rate effective in each of the years:

Year	Taxable Income (Loss)	Enacted Tax Rate
2004	$ 100,000	40%
2005	200,000	40
2006	250,000	35
2007	400,000	32
2008	(350,000)	30
2009	(275,000)	30
2010	125,000	30
2011	175,000	30
2012	275,000	30
2013	300,000	35
2014	(800,000)	35
2015	(250,000)	35
2016	150,000	35

Since the company had no permanent or temporary differences during this period, its pre-tax financial reporting income was identical to its taxable income in each of these years. During the 2013–2016 period, the company expected the current and future tax rates to be 35%. Whenever possible, the company took advantage of the loss carryback provision of the tax law. When recording the tax benefits of the loss carryforward provision, the company felt it was more likely than not that the tax benefits would be fully realized.

Required:

1. Provide journal entries to record income tax expense for the years 2008, 2009, 2014, 2015, and 2016.
2. You can assume that during 2014 and 2015, Smith Corporation felt it was more likely than not that only 40% of the tax benefits would be realized through a loss carryforward. However, during 2016 the company revised its expectation and felt that it was more likely than not that 100% of the tax benefits would be fully realized through a loss carryforward. Provide journal entries to record income tax expense for the years 2014, 2015, and 2016. Also show how the future tax asset will be reported as of the end of 2014, 2015, and 2016.

P13-5 Analytical insights from deferred (or future) tax account

Weber Manufacturing Company started doing business on January 1, 2003. The company's current business plan predicts significant growth in sales over the next several years. To respond to this predicted growth, Weber is planning to buy new factory equipment annually at a cost of $60,000 during the first six years of its operations (2003 through 2008). The first piece of equipment was purchased on January 1, 2003. The company plans to use the straight-line method to amortize the equipment cost for financial reporting purposes. Assume that the sum-of-the-years'-digits method can be used for tax purposes. The useful life of the factory equipment was estimated to be three years, with no salvage value for both tax and financial reporting purposes. Weber expects to pay income taxes at the rate of 35% of its taxable income. Apart from the amortization expense, Weber expects no other temporary differences.

Required:

1. Calculate the balance in the future income tax liability account as of the end of years 2003 through 2008.
2. Assume that Weber purchased the factory equipment at the beginning of each year (starting from 2003) for six years. However, the equipment costs $60,000 in 2003, which is expected to increase by $6,000 each year over the following five years ($66,000 in 2004, $72,000 in 2005, and so on). Calculate the balance in the future income tax liability account as of the end of the years 2003 through 2008.
3. Consider the facts in Question 2. Due to expected changes in business technology, the company expects the demand for its current products to start falling beginning in the year 2009. Consequently, it plans to cut its production down substantially after 2009. In fact, Weber expects to purchase no more machinery after 2008. With this new information, compute the balance in the future income tax liability account for the years 2009 and 2010.
4. Considering your answers to Questions 1 through 3, and changes in its future tax liability account, what conclusions might you draw about the financial condition of Weber?

P13-6 Comprehensive tax allocation problem

Bush Inc. started its retail business on January 1, 2003. The following information is extracted from the financial reporting income statements of the company for the years 2003 and 2004.

Bush Inc.		
Income Statements for the Years Ended December 31		
	2003	2004
Sales revenue	$1,000,000	$1,200,000
Dividends:	60,000	75,000
Cost of goods sold	(400,000)	(504,000)
Amortization expense	?	?
Warranty expense	(100,000)	(110,000)
Provision for uncollectibles	?	?
Life insurance premium for senior executives	(30,000)	(30,000)
Other operating expenses	(300,000)	(350,000)
Income before income taxes	?	?
Income tax expense	?	?
Net income	?	?

Required:

1. Using the following additional information, complete the income statements for the years 2003 and 2004:

    (a) The company purchased a piece of computer equipment on January 1, 2003, for $330,000. The equipment has a useful life of five years and an estimated salvage value of nil. The company uses the straight-line method of amortization for financial reporting purposes. This was the company's only amortizable asset.

    (b) The company estimates bad debt expense (or provision for uncollectibles) at 8% of sales revenue.

    (c) Bush Inc. is the beneficiary of the life insurance policies of its senior executives.

    (d) The income tax rate is 35%.

2. Using the following additional information, calculate taxable income and the income tax liability for the years 2003 and 2004:

    (a) The company writes off the computer equipment over two years straight-line for tax purposes.

    (b) The warranty liability account had balances of $15,000 and $25,000 at the end of the years 2003 and 2004, respectively.

    (c) The allowance for uncollectibles had balances of $50,000 and $21,000 at the end of the years 2003 and 2004, respectively.

3. Provide a schedule showing why the effective tax rates for the company during 2003 and 2004 are different from the statutory tax rate of 35%.

4. Calculate the balances in the future tax accounts at the end of 2003 and 2004.

5. Provide a schedule reconciling the income tax expense with the income tax liability for each of the years 2003 and 2004.

6. Provide journal entries to record income tax expense for the years 2003 and 2004.

P13-7 Leasing and future taxes

The following information pertains to Crum International Corporation.

The company entered into the following lease agreement with Capital Leases Inc. as of January 1, 2003. In accordance with the agreement, Crum leased a piece of computer equipment with a fair market value of $24,869 for its entire useful life of three years. In return, Crum promised to pay $10,000 per year *payable at the end of each year*, with the first payment to be made on December 31, 2003. At the end of the lease agreement, the estimated salvage value of the asset is zero.

For both tax and financial reporting purposes, Crum has *annual* income of $100,000 before taxes and before recording any expense on this lease transaction during each of the years 2003, 2004, and 2005. The tax rate is 40%.

Required:

1. Assuming that Crum treats the lease transaction as an *operating lease for tax purposes*, compute the taxable income for the years 2003–2005. Also calculate the amount of tax liability in each of the three years.

2. Assume Crum treats the lease transaction as a *capital lease for financial reporting purposes.* (The implicit interest rate in the lease contract is 10%.) Prepare a lease amortization schedule allocating the annual payments between interest expense

and repayment of lease obligation. Clearly indicate the outstanding lease liability at the end of each period. Assuming further that Crum uses the straight-line method of amortization for financial reporting purposes, prepare *income statements for financial reporting purposes,* clearly indicating the amount of tax expense for each of the three years.

3. Using all the assumptions up to this point, prepare journal entries to record the tax expense for each of the three years.

Cases

C13-1 CN adopts new *Handbook* section on reporting income taxes

CANADIAN NATIONAL
RAILWAY
www.cn.ca

Answer the questions below with respect to the Canadian National Railway Company's (CN) 1997 annual report excerpts, which appear on pages 639–644:

(a) Reconstruct CN's 1997 continuing operations journal entry accounting for income taxes.

(b) Describe how CN accounted for the change in note 2. Specifically, what accounts were affected, and how was the change reported in the financial statements? In its 1996 annual report, CN's 1996 "Income from continuing operations" was $124,000,000 after income tax expense of $11,000,000.

(c) In your opinion, is CN's balance sheet disclosure consistent with Section 3465? To answer this question, carefully read the disclosure requirements of Section 3465, and compare CN's disclosure to them.

(d) In your opinion, is the asset/liability method of accounting for income taxes an improvement over the deferral method?

(e) What is there about the changes in the magnitudes of the components of CN's deferred income tax assets and liabilities in note 13 that in your opinion is significant? Please explain.

(f) Paragraph 105 of Section 3465 reads: *"The Recommendations of this Section should be applied for fiscal years beginning on or after January 1, 2000. Earlier adoption is encouraged."* CN, in its 1997 audited financial statements, retroactively adopted Section 3465 for its comparative (1996) financial statements. Magna International Inc., an Aurora, Ontario global supplier of automotive systems with fiscal 1998 revenues of $9.2 billion, adopted the new standard in 1998, without restated prior years. Up until January 1, 2000, both Section 3465 and Section 3470 were GAAP in Canada, and companies could choose the timing of their adoption of the new standard within a two-year window. Suggest some plausible reasons why CN and Magna made different choices.

(g) What comments do you have about CN's quality of earnings, on the basis of your analysis above?

Canadian National Railway Company

Excerpts from 1997 Annual Report

Canadian National Railway Company (CN) is Canada's largest railway system, with more than 14,500 route miles of track in Canada and approximately 750 route miles of track in the United States.

CN's rail network serves all five of Canada's major ports: Halifax, Montreal, Thunder Bay, Prince Rupert and Vancouver, and includes strategic connections to the United States through the Chicago gateway, Detroit and other major cities.

Financial and Statistical Five-Year Summary

($ in millions, except per share data, or unless otherwise indicated)	1997	1996	1995	1994	1993
Financial results					
Revenues	$4,352	$3,995	$3,954	$4,165	$3,829
Operating expenses excluding special charges	3,545	3,385	3,514	3,708	3,627
Special charges	—	381	1,453	—	49
Operating income (loss)	807	229	(1,013)	457	153
Operating income excluding special charges	807	610	440	457	202
Interest expense—net	118	114	198	196	198
Other income	57	27	100	36	12
Income (loss) from continuing operations	421	836	(1,092)	269	(59)
Income (loss) from continuing operations excluding special charges	421	1,217	361	269	(10)
Capital expenditures	577	496	326	539	442
Earnings (loss) per share from continuing operations	4.95	9.85	(13.57)	3.36	(0.74)
Earnings (loss) per share from continuing operations excluding special charges	4.95	12.39	4.49	3.36	(0.13)
Other statistical highlights					
Rail operating ratio excluding special charges (%)	81.5	84.7	88.9	89.0	94.7
Route miles (includes Canada and U.S.)	15,292	17,124	17,918	18,414	18,851
Carloads (thousands)	2,547	2,315	2,295	2,354	2,182
Gross ton miles (millions)	228,353	208,328	204,143	211,805	193,797
Revenue ton miles (millions)	119,534	107,470	105,487	109,004	98,650
Rail employees (average for the year)	22,800	24,064	26,951	29,884	31,385
Diesel fuel consumed (Canadian gallons in millions)	272	259	256	266	250
Average price per Canadian gallon (dollars)	$ 1.23	$ 1.22	$ 1.08	$ 1.03	$ 1.04

Consolidated Statement of Income

(in millions)	1997	Year Ended December 31, 1996 (restated)	1995 (restated)
Revenues:			
Industrial products	$ 893	$ 851	$ 838
Forest products	824	787	771
Grain and grain products	692	564	600
Coal, sulphur, and fertilizers	635	618	601
Intermodal	776	677	635
Automotive	435	389	399
Other items	97	109	110
Total revenues	4,352	3,995	3,954
Operating expenses:			
Labour and fringe benefits	1,431	1,381	1,477
Material	316	297	318
Fuel	335	314	277
Depreciation and amortization	200	194	231
Operating taxes	186	171	192
Equipment rental	219	216	194
Net car hire	116	108	117
Purchased services	363	348	354
Casualty and insurance	103	85	52
Other	276	271	302
Special charges (Note 10)	—	381	1,453
Total operating expenses	3,545	3,766	4,967
Operating income (loss)	807	229	(1,013)
Interest expense (Note 11)	(118)	(114)	(198)
Other income (Note 2)	57	27	100
Income (loss) from continuing operations before income taxes	746	142	(1,111)
Income tax (expense) recovery from continuing operations (Note 13)	(325)	694	19
Income (loss) from continuing operations	421	836	(1,092)
Discontinued operations (net of applicable income taxes) (Note 14)	(18)	14	7
Net income (loss)	$ 403	$ 850	$(1,085)

Consolidated Balance Sheet

	December 31,	
(in millions)	1997	1996 (restated)
Assets		
Current assets:		
Cash and cash equivalents	$ 365	$ 106
Accounts receivable (Note 3)	681	694
Material and supplies	150	158
Deferred income taxes	241	186
Other	112	99
	1,549	1,243
Properties (Note 4)	5,122	4,889
Deferred income taxes (Note 13)	164	522
Other assets and deferred charges	240	206
Total assets	$7,075	$6,840
Liabilities and shareholders' equity		
Current liabilities:		
Accounts payable and accrued charges	$1,066	$1,085
Current portion of long-term debt (Note 6)	43	27
Other	96	121
	1,205	1,233
Other liabilities and deferred credits (Note 7)	813	1,020
Long-term debt (Note 8)	1,640	1,499
Shareholders' equity (Note 9):		
Capital stock	2,016	2,012
Contributed surplus	190	190
Retained earnings	1,211	886
	3,417	3,088
Total liabilities and shareholders' equity	$7,075	$6,840

Consolidated Statement of Changes in Financial Position

(in millions)	1997	1996 (restated)	1995 (restated)
Operating activities			
Income (loss) from continuing operations	$ 421	$ 836	$(1,092)
Non-cash items in income (loss):			
Depreciation and amortization (Note 15(C))	202	196	234
Deferred income taxes (Note 13)	315	(705)	—
Special charges	—	365	1,415
Gain on disposal of rail subsidiary's operating assets	—	—	(39)
Gain on sale of interest in joint venture	(21)	—	(5)
Changes in:			
Accounts receivable	5	59	(127)
Material and supplies	7	16	20
Accounts payable and accrued charges	19	142	(133)
Other net current assets and liabilities	(44)	(49)	23
Payments for workforce reduction	(197)	(307)	(245)
Other	(45)	4	(18)
Cash provided from continuing operations	662	557	33
Investing activities			
Additions to properties (Note 15(C))	(577)	(496)	(326)
Net proceeds from disposal of properties	122	64	82
Net proceeds from disposal of rail subsidiary's operating assets	—	—	50
Net proceeds from sale of interest in joint venture	23	—	10
Other	8	1	(4)
Cash used by investing activities	(424)	(431)	(188)
Dividends paid to shareholders	(78)	(68)	—
Financial activities			
Issuance of long-term debt	213	213	3
Reduction of long-term debt	(98)	(294)	(814)
Redemption of auction preferred stock	—	—	(271)
Issuance of capital stock (Note 9)	4	—	1,033
Costs related to the sale of shares	—	—	(33)
Cash provided from (used by) financing activities	119	(81)	(82)
Cash (used by) provided from discontinued operations (Note 14)	(20)	10	101
Net increase (decrease) in cash	259	(13)	(136)
Cash and cash equivalents, beginning of year	106	119	255
Cash and cash equivalents, end of year	$ 365	$ 106	$ 119

Excerpts from Footnotes

1. Income taxes

The Company follows the asset and liability method for accounting for income taxes. Under the asset and liability method, the change in the net deferred tax asset or liability is to be included in income. Deferred tax assets and liabilities are measured using enacted tax rates expected to apply to taxable income in the years in which temporary differences are expected to be recovered or settled. ...

2. Adoption of new accounting standard

Income taxes

Effective with the fourth quarter of 1997, the Company adopted the new Canadian Institute of Chartered Accountants' (CICA) recommendations for the accounting for income taxes. The new standard requires the use of the asset and liability method for accounting for income taxes. Under the asset and liability method, deferred income taxes are recognized for the future income tax consequences attributable to differences between the financial statement carrying values and their respective income tax basis (temporary differences). Deferred income tax assets and liabilities are measured using enacted income tax rates expected to apply to taxable income in the years in which temporary differences are expected to be recovered or settled. The effect on deferred income tax assets and liabilities of a change in tax rates is included in income in the period that includes the enactment date. Deferred income tax assets are evaluated and if realization is not considered "more likely than not," a valuation allowance is provided.

Previously, the Company followed the deferral method of accounting for income taxes which related the provision for income taxes to the accounting income for the period. Under the deferral method, the amount by which the income tax provision differed from the amount of income taxes currently payable was considered to represent the deferring to future periods of benefits obtained or expenditures incurred in the current period and accordingly was computed at current income tax rates. The accumulated income tax allocation debit or credit balance was not adjusted to reflect subsequent changes in income tax rates. Also, under the deferral method, tax benefits, related to accounting losses, could only be recognized in the period the loss was incurred if there was virtual certainty of realizing these benefits.

As a result of the change in accounting policy, an income tax recovery (including discontinued operations) of $708 million, or $8.34 per share, was recorded in 1996 for income tax benefits related to years prior in 1997. In 1997, income tax expense of $303 million, or $3.56 per share, related to income before tax was recorded. There was no effect on the comparative figures prior to 1996. ...

13. Income taxes

The Company's income tax (expense) recovery from continuing operations is as follows:

(in millions)	Year Ended December 31,		
	1997	1996	1995
Combined basic Canadian federal and provincial tax rate (combined basic tax rate)	44.4%	44.4%	41.9%
Income tax (expense) recovery from continuing operations based on the combined basic tax rate	$(331)	$ (63)	$466
Income tax (expense) recovery resulting from:			
Federal large corporations tax and other cash taxes	(10)	(11)	(13)
Gain on disposal of properties	4	5	6
Other	12	(5)	(9)
Recognition of income tax benefits related to prior years	—	768	—
Losses for which an income tax benefit has not been recognized	—	—	(431)
Income tax (expense) recovery from continuing operations	$(325)	$694	$ 19
Income tax (expense) recovery from continuing operations is represented by:			
Current	$ (10)	$ (11)	$ (13)
Deferred	(315)	705	—
Income related to dividend in kind and other	—	—	32
	$(325)	$694	$ 19
Income tax recovery (expense) related to discontinued operations	$ 12	$ (3)	$ (4)
Cash payments for income taxes	$ 10	$ 11	$ 13

Significant components of deferred income tax assets and liabilities are as follows:

(in millions)	December 31,	
	1997	1996
Assets		
Loss carryforwards	$165	$264
Workforce reduction provisions	178	249
Accruals and other reserves	42	55
Post-retirement benefits	45	42
Properties	—	98
	430	708
Liabilities		
Properties	25	—
Total net deferred income tax asset	405	708
Less: current portion	241	186
Total long-term portion of net deferred income tax asset	$164	$522

C13-2 Tellier Company

Tellier Company, a public company which began business in January 2000, manufactures innovative and highly efficient locomotive engines on a contract basis for various North American railroad companies. With deregulation in the railway industry and in transportation generally, and the maturity of the North American Free Trade Agreement, the demand for Tellier's products has increased significantly, so the outlook for the company was especially positive.

The Year 2000: Tellier Begins Operations

Tellier Company has chosen a December 31 year-end. The enacted combined provincial and federal corporate income tax rate for 2000 is 42%, and management has decided that the enacted or substantially enacted income tax rates for all future years up to 2003 are expected to be equal to 35%, and 30% thereafter.

Revenues: Tellier began and completed three contracts during the year. The details of each contract were as follows:

Contract Number	Total Contract Amount	Payment Arrangements
1	$3,000,000	Three equal annual installments, beginning Dec 31, 2000
2	$2,500,000	Two equal annual installments, beginning Dec 31, 2001
3	$6,000,000	Two equal annual installments, beginning Dec 31, 2000

Usually, Tellier prices its contracts so that they earn a gross profit equal to 40% of the contract price, except the gross profit of the first contract was only 30% since Tellier was "the new kid on the block." In preparing its corporate income tax return, the company reports gross profit on the installment basis; for financial reporting, gross profit is reported on contract completion. The company also recorded $5,000,000 in other revenues, all for repair work, and all of which had been collected by December 31, 2000.

The GAAP-basis and tax-basis measures of the assets created by the company's sales operations are as follows:

Contract 1: The debit to "Installment sales receivable" for this contract is $3,000,000 less the December 31, 2000, payment received of $1,000,000, or $2,000,000. The gross profit recorded in 2000 was 30% of $3,000,000, or $900,000. For tax return purposes, only one-third of the total gross profit of $900,000 is reported in 2000, with the remaining $600,000 deferred, so the "Installment sales receivable" tax measure generated by this contract as at December 31, 2000, is only $2,000,000 – $600,000 = $1,400,000. So, there is a temporary difference of $600,000 due to this contract, and it is a *taxable* temporary difference. The summary for all three contracts as at December 31, 2000, is as follows:

	GAAP-Basis	Tax Basis	
Future Year	Installment Sales Receivable	Gross Profit Deferred	Installment Sales Receivable (net)
2000	$7,500,000	($2,800,000)	$4,700,000
2001	$2,250,000	($800,000)	$1,450,000
2002	—	—	—

Depreciable capital assets: When the company started up operations, it purchased depreciable capital assets at a total cost of $15,000,000. Assume that Tellier amortizes these assets on a straight-line basis over five years, with no salvage value (for simplicity, we are assuming all capital assets have the same service life), and CCA is at 30% declining balance, with the half-year rule in effect. For GAAP and tax return purposes, Tellier's capital assets are therefore as follows:

	GAAP-Basis		Tax Basis	
Year	Amortization	Carrying Value	CCA	UCC
2000	$ 3,000,000	$12,000,000	$ 2,250,000*	$12,750,000
2001	$ 3,000,000	$ 9,000,000	$ 3,825,000	$ 8,925,000
2002	$ 3,000,000	$ 6,000,000	$ 2,677,500	$ 6,247,500
2003	$ 3,000,000	$ 3,000,000	$ 1,874,250	$ 4,373,250
2004	$ 3,000,000	—	$ 1,311,975	$ 3,061,275
2005 and future	—	—	$ 3,061,275	Various amounts
Total	**$15,000,000**		**$15,000,000**	

*Note: The half-year rule is used.

Various other items: For fiscal 2000, Tellier reported net income before income taxes of $3,200,000, which included nontaxable dividend income of $30,000, nondeductible penalties and fines of $50,000, and warranty expense of $300,000 (of which $75,000 was expended in 2000, and the remainder is expected by management to be expended evenly over the years 2001 and 2002).

The year 2000 income tax return: The company's 2000 income tax return is the source of several important items for the 2000 financial statements. These items, based upon *CICA Handbook* Section 3465, are "taxable income," "income tax payable," and "current income tax expense." A reconciliation format for the calculation of taxable income, beginning with the company's year 2000 net income before income tax (computed according to GAAP), is as follows:

Net income before income per GAAP	$3,200,000
Deferred installment sales profits	(2,800,000)
Difference between amortization and CCA	750,000
Difference between warranty expense and payments	225,000
Nontaxable dividend income	(30,000)
Nondeductible penalties and fines	50,000
Taxable income	$1,395,000

Tellier's 2000 income tax payable is therefore equal to the year 2000 taxable income of $1,395,000 multiplied by the year 2000 income tax rate of 42%, or $585,900. This leads to the first part of the 2000 income tax journal entry:

DR	Current income tax expense	$585,900	
	CR	Income tax payable	$585,900

Year 2000 future income tax assets, future income tax liabilities, and future income tax expense: Section 3465 of the *CICA Handbook* requires that a "future income tax expense" be recorded as part of a company's income tax expense (the other part being the "current income tax expense"). This "future income tax expense" for any given period equals the net change in the future income tax assets and liabilities for that period. Since Tellier Company began operations in 2000, we know that the opening balances for future income tax assets and liabilities must be zero, so all we must compute are the closing balances as at December 31, 2000. The computations are as follows:

Balance Sheet Asset or Liability	GAAP-Basis measure	Tax-Basis Measure	Taxable or (Deductible) Temporary Difference
Installment sales receivables	$ 7,500,000	$ 4,700,000	$2,800,000
Capital assets	$12,000,000	$12,750,000	(750,000)
Warranty liability	$ 225,000	—	(225,000)
Net taxable temporary differences			$1,825,000

The $2,800,000 taxable temporary difference existing as of December 31, 2000, due to the installment sales, will completely reverse over the years 2001 and 2002, during which time the enacted or substantially enacted income tax rate will be 35%. This rate is used to compute the "future income tax liability" arising from the temporary difference source (i.e., $2,800,000 × 35% = $980,000). The deductible temporary difference of $225,000 due to the warranty is expected to completely reverse by 2002 also, so the 35% rate is used to compute the "future income tax asset" arising from this temporary difference source: $225,000 × 35% = $78,750.

The temporary difference created in 2000 by the CCA/amortization difference is a bit more complicated, since it is expected to reverse during a time interval in which two income tax rates are expected to be relevant. For the interval 2001 to 2003, the rate is 35%, and for 2004 onward it is 30%. So the $750,000 deductible temporary difference created in 2000 reverses as follows:

Year	GAAP-Basis Amortization	Tax-Basis CCA		Tax Rate	After Tax
2001	$3,000,000	$3,825,000	$ 825,000	35%	$ 288,750.00
2002	$3,000,000	$2,677,500	$ (322,500)	35%	$(112,875.00)
2003	$3,000,000	$1,874,250	$(1,125,750)	35%	$(394,012.50)
2004	$3,000,000	$1,311,975	$(1,688,025)	30%	$(506,407.50)
2005 and future	—	$3,061,275	$ 3,061,275	30%	$ 918,382.50
Total			$ 750,000		$ 193,837.50

So the "future income tax asset" that results from the capital asset UCC/NBV temporary difference of $750,000 in 2000 is $193,837.50.

Now, the 2000 "future income tax expense" must be computed:

Temporary Difference Item	Closing Balance, December 31, 2000	Opening Balance, January 1, 2000	Change in 2000
Future income tax liability due to installment sales receivables	$(980,000)	—	$(980,000)
Future income tax asset due to capital assets	$ 193,837.50	—	$ 193,837.50
Future income tax asset due to warranty liability	$ 78,750	—	$ 78,750
Totals	$(707,412.50)	—	$(707,412.50)

Here is the corresponding year 2000 income tax journal entry :

DR	Future income tax expense	$707,412.50	
DR	Future income tax asset: current	78,750	
DR	Future income tax asset: noncurrent	193,837.50	
	CR	Future income tax liability: current	$980,000

Both the $193,837.50 future income tax asset and the $980,000 income tax liability should be allocated between current and long-term portions; we haven't done this here for simplicity.

Notice that the total 2000 income tax expense is $1,293,312.50, as reported on the bottom of Tellier Company's 2000 income statement

Net income before income taxes		$3,200,000.00
Current income tax expense	585,900.00	
Future income tax expense	707,412.50	
		1,293,312.50
Net income		$1,906,687.50

Required:

1. Assume that you have been engaged by Tellier to evaluate the company's accounting for its corporate income taxes. Prepare an appropriate report for senior management.
2. Assume that you have been engaged to advise the compensation committee of the company's board of directors whether the bonus component of the top executives' compensation plan should be based upon income before or after income tax. Prepare a report outlining your advice.

Integrative Running Case Study
Bombardier on the Web

Refer to Bombardier Inc.'s annual report on the Companion Website for this text, **www.pearsoned.ca/revsine**, for the year ended January 31, 2002. Bombardier's accounting policy with respect to income taxes is on page 74, and its tax note is on pages 96–97.

Required:

1. Attempt to reconstruct the company's income tax journal entry for the year ended January 31, 2002. Is Bombardier following Section 3465?
2. Reconcile the opening and closing balance sheet amounts for "Deferred income taxes" for the year ended January 31, 2002.
3. Would a financial analyst be interested in the reasons for the difference between Bombardier's income taxes calculated at statutory rates of $214.0 million and its income tax expense of $167.0 million? Explain.
4. Critically evaluate Bombardier's income tax disclosure.
5. Suggest reasons for the change in Bombardier's deferred income taxes for the year ended January 31, 2002, given the nature of the company's business activities.

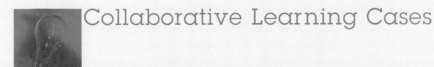
Collaborative Learning Cases

CL13-1 Waste Management: Analysis of tax footnotes

Waste Management is one of the largest trash haulers in the United States. In the late 1980s, the firm was widely viewed as a growth company. In an article about the company written 10 years later, *Fortune* stated that Waste Management "used improper, overly aggressive accounting tactics in an effort to boost sagging earnings … to retain its status as a Wall Street highflier …."[9] In early 1998, the firm announced it would take a US$3.54 billion pre-tax charge to correct these "accounting irregularities." The two largest charge-offs resulted from aggressive extensions of the expected depreciable lives of trucks and dumpsters and understated revenues for federal environmental liabilities. One magazine article reported that the earnings "hit" taken by Waste management "stunned the investment community." Reproduced below are selected excerpts from Waste Management's financial statements over the period 1993–1996. Using your understanding of financial reporting and your ability to make inferences from these pre-1998 disclosures, should knowledgeable investors have been "stunned" by the early 1998 writeoff? More explicit questions to guide your analysis follow the statement excerpts.

WASTE MANAGEMENT				
Consolidated Condensed Income Statement Data (Before Correction)				
	Years Ended December 31			
(US$ in thousands)	1993	1994	1995	1996
Revenue	$7,827,280	$8,482,718	$9,053,018	$9,186,970
Costs and expenses	6,361,233	6,824,806	7,225,747	7,352,037
Special charges	550,000	—	335,193	471,635
Gains from stock transactions of subsidiaries and exchange of Exchangeable LYONS	(15,109)	—	—	—
Other expense	193,272	363,000	390,165	320,460
Income from continuing operations before income taxes	737,884	1,294,912	1,101,913	1,042,838
Provision for income taxes	319,798	552,606	483,670	565,047
Income from continuing operations	418,086	742,306	618,243	477,791
Income (loss) from discontinued operations	34,690	42,075	(14,344)	(285,706)
Net income	$ 452,776	$ 784,381	$ 603,899	$ 192,085

Consolidated Condensed Balance Sheets (Before Correction)-*continued*

(US$ in thousands)	As of December 31,			
	1993	1994	1995	1996
Total Current Assets	$ 2,777,520	$ 3,088,844	$ 2,608,085	$ 3,093,224
Property and Equipment, at cost				
Land, primarily disposal sites	3,625,412	4,162,418	4,553,717	5,019,065
Buildings	1,223,139	1,372,782	1,532,305	1,495,252
Vehicles and equipment	6,856,044	7,162,217	7,164,767	7,520,902
Leasehold improvements	100,262	91,554	84,587	85,998
	11,804,857	12,788,971	13,335,376	14,121,217
Less-Accumulated depreciation and amortization	(3,035,398)	(3,503,219)	(3,829,658)	(4,399,508)
Total Property and Equipment, Net	8,769,459	9,285,752	9,505,718	9,721,709
Total Other Assets	4,717,497	5,164,318	6,250,471	5,551,659
Total Assets	16,264,476	17,538,914	18,364,274	18,366,592
Total Current Liabilities	$ 2,677,562	$ 3,179,731	$ 3,192,484	$ 3,038,708
Total Deferred Items	1,933,319	1,985,298	2,192,150	2,197,234
Long-Term Debt, less portion payable within one year	6,145,584	6,044,411	6,390,041	6,971,607
Minority Interest in Subsidiaries	1,348,559	1,536,165	1,385,301	1,186,955
Put Options	—	252,328	261,959	95,789
Total Stockholders' Equity	4,159,452	4,540,981	4,942,339	4,876,299
Total Liabilities and Stockholders' Equity	$16,264,476	$17,538,914	$18,364,274	$18,366,592

Additional Financial Disclosures (Before Correction)

(US$ in thousands)	1993	1994	1995	1996
From the Consolidated Statement of Cash Flows:				
Depreciation and amortization	$796,691	$880,466	$885,384	$920,685

From Management's Discussion and Analysis*: (Before Correction)

Acquisitions and Capital Expenditures Capital expenditures, including [US$443.5 million,] US$56.8 million, US$154.1 million, and US$91.8 million for property and equipment of purchased businesses in [1993], 1994, 1995, and 1996, respectively, are shown in the following table:

(US$ in millions)	1993	1994	1995	1996
Land (primarily disposal sites)	$ 660.2	$ 582.3	$ 517.2	$ 467.7
Buildings and leasehold improvements	195.5	141.2	148.8	109.3
Vehicles	373.0	226.0	345.8	204.9
Containers	231.6	167.9	181.2	115.8
Other equipment	702.4	395.0	348.1	319.2
Total	$2,162.7	$1,512.4	$1,541.1	$1,216.9

*The text is from the 1996 Annual Report and is edited to include 1993 data.

From the summary of Accounting Policies Footnote: (Before Correction)

Property and Equipment Property and equipment (including major repairs and improvements) are capitalized and stated at cost. Items of an ordinary maintenance or repair nature are charged directly to operations. Disposal sites are carried at cost and to the extent this exceeds end use realizable value, such excess is amortized over the estimated life of the disposal site. Disposal site improvement costs are capitalized and charged to operations over the shorter of the estimated usable life of the site or the improvement.

...

Depreciation and Amortization The cost, less estimated salvage value, of property and equipment is depreciated over the estimated useful lives on the straight-line method as follows: buildings—10 to 40 years; vehicles and equipment—3 to 20 years; leasehold improvements—over the life of the applicable lease.

Annual Report Condensed Note on Income Taxes (Before Correction)*				
(US$ in thousands)	1993	1994	1995	1996
Deferred tax assets				
Reserves not deductible until paid	($ 538,062)	($ 494,549)	($ 503,074)	($ 495,940)
Deferred revenue	(27,714)	(25,708)	(37,284)	(16,158)
Net operating losses and tax credit carryforwards	(43,028)	(110,073)	(266,916)	(233,008)
Other	(104,059)	(70,281)	(78,474)	(73,229)
Subtotal	($ 712,863)	($ 700,611)	($ 885,748)	($ 818,335)
Deferred tax liabilities				
Depreciation and amortization	$ 948,024	$1,106,155	$1,335,559	$1,384,164
Other	183,655	233,178	374,084	359,035
Subtotal	1,131,679	1,339,333	1,709,643	1,743,199
Valuation allowance	29,890	26,955	98,605	86,729
Net deferred tax liabilities	$ 448,706	$ 665,677	$ 922,500	$1,011,593

Note: In the notes accompanying its pre-correction 1996 Annual Report, the Company says: "Certain amounts in previously issued financial statements have been restated to conform to 1996 classifications." Similar statements were made in the 1994 and 1995 annual reports relating to those reporting years. Since only two years of comparative data were given in each report, the 1994 data are not strictly classified in conformity with the 1996 classifications. The differences from year to year appear to be minor. However, the reader should be aware that adjacent years' data are not always perfectly comparable.

Annual Report Note on Environmental Costs and Liabilities (Text from 1996 Annual Report, Before Correction)

The continuing business in which the Company is engaged is intrinsically connected with the protection of the environment. As such, a significant portion of the Company's operating costs and capital expenditures could be characterized as costs of environmental protection …

Estimates of the extent of the Company's degree of responsibility for remediation of a particular site and the method and ultimate cost of remediation require a number of assumptions and are inherently difficult, and the ultimate outcome may differ from current estimates. However, the Company believes that its extensive experience in the environmental services business, as well as its involvement with a large number of sites, provides a reasonable basis for estimating its aggregate liability. As additional information becomes available, estimates are adjusted as necessary. While the Company does not anticipate that any such adjustment would be material to its financial statements, it is reasonably possible that technological, regulatory, or enforcement developments, the results of environmental studies, or other factors could necessitate the recording of additional liabilities, which could be material.

Where the Company believes that both the amount of a particular environmental liability and the timing of the payments are reliably determinable, the cost in current dollars is inflated at 3% until expected time of payment and then discounted to present value at 7%. Had the Company not discounted any portion of its liability, the amount recorded would have been increased by approximately $160 million at December 31, 1996.

The Company's active landfill sites have estimated remaining lives ranging from 1 to over 100 years based upon current site plans and annual volumes of waste. During this remaining site life, the Company will provide for an additional $1.03 billion of closure and post-closure costs, including accretion for the discount recognized to date.

As of December 31, the Company's liabilities for closure, post-closure monitoring and environmental remediation costs were as follows:

(US$ in thousands)	1993	1994	1995	1996
Current portion, included in accrued expenses	$ 130,863	$ 108,750	$ 138,533	$ 122,209
Non-current portion	745,637	704,015	621,186	543,723
Total recorded	876,500	812,765	759,719	665,932
Amount to be provided over remaining life of active sites,				
• including discount of $154 million in 1993 and $169 million in 1994	987,000	1,149,617		
• including discount of $171 million in 1995 and $160 million in 1996			1,118,739	1,028,437
Expected aggregate undiscounted environmental liabilities	$1,863,500	$1,962,382	$1,878,458	$1,694,369

Anticipated payments of environmental liabilities at December 31, 1996, are as follows:

(US$ in thousands)	
1997	$ 122,209
1998	56,000
1999	47,450
2000	33,571
2001	38,429
Thereafter	1,396,710
	$1,694,369

Required:

What elements in the Waste Management financial data and footnote excerpts included in the case might have given analysts an inkling of the excessive depreciable lives estimates and understated environment reserves? (*Hints:* (1) Explain why the deferred tax liability for depreciation and amortization is increasing. Is this increasing CR balance consistent with year-to-year capital expenditure patterns? (2) Carefully compare recorded environmental liabilities with asset amounts.)

Endnotes:

1. Of course, GAAP govern only that portion of financial accounting which must be audited to ensure compliance with GAAP. Our emphasis in this chapter is on the differences between GAAP measures of income and tax legislation-based measures of income.

2. We use Sum of Years Digits here as a hypothetical example of an accelerated CCA method to simplify the illustration of temporary differences. This simplification results since SYD leaves no undepreciated residual at the end of the asset's life. Actual Canadian income tax rules require different methods for different categories of assets, with declining balance methods being quite common.

3. "Income Taxes," *CICA Handbook*, Section 3465, para. .02.

4. Ibid.

5. Ibid., para. .30.

6. G. Miller and D. J. Skinner, "Determinants of the Valuation Allowance for Deferred Tax Assets Under SFAS-109," *The Accounting Review*, April 1998, pp. 213–234.

7. Changes in future income tax asset or liability balances can also provide evidence regarding aggressive tax behaviour that could result in subsequent additional assessments.

8. The only exceptions will arise where firms either (1) have unused operating loss carryforwards that are about to expire or (2) expect future tax rates to rise sharply.

9. Peter Elkind, "Garbage In: Garbage Out," *Fortune*, May 25, 1998.

14
Reporting Employee Future Benefits

LEARNING OBJECTIVES
After studying this chapter, you should be able to:

1. Identify the difference between defined contribution and defined benefit pension plans

2. Describe the components of pension expense and their relation to the pension liability

3. Explain the requirements for funding pension plans, compute the return on plan assets, and describe the role of the plan trustee

4. Tell how GAAP smooth the volatility inherent in pension estimates and forecasts

5. List the determinants of the pension funding decision

6. Analyze the funded status footnote and use this information

7. Explain the financial reporting rules for other postretirement benefits

8. Explain the usefulness, through research, of the detailed pension and other postretirement benefits disclosures

Companies typically provide their employees with a variety of **future benefits**, in addition to current-period salary, wages, bonuses, and other current-year benefits. These future benefits can be classified as follows:

- **future benefits that accumulate over time**, including (a) postretirement pensions and (b) preretirement benefits, such as post-employment benefits (long- and short-term disability, salary continuance, job training, severance) and compensated absences (such as vesting sick days, sabbaticals)

- **future benefits that are not a function of time** (i.e., the benefit is the same regardless of the number of years of service by the employee); included in this category are benefits such as preretirement compensated parental leave, and preretirement post-employment nonservice-related disability.

The services enjoyed by the accounting entity occur (usually) many years before the employee receives the particular future benefit, so accounting for employee future benefits—like most other forms of accrual accounting over many periods—presents a host of conceptual and measurement problems. And the numbers involved are often very big, so how a company accounts for, and discloses information about, its employee future benefits has a significant impact on the company's quality of earnings.

Before we look at the technical and conceptual sides of accounting for employee future benefits, we'll provide some flavour of the issues and controversies involved. In Exhibit 14.1, we refer to some views on pension accounting by commentator

Al Rosen; as well, we look at how major Canadian banks' pension accounting numbers shape up. Even though you will probably not quite yet understand all the details of the concepts in the exhibit, it serves to illustrate vividly the potentially material impact that accounting for future employee benefits, and pension accounting in particular, can have on quality of earnings.

The numbers in Exhibit 14.1 are for the year 2002, but when we look back to fiscal year 2001, we find equally large disparities between the *expected* gain in pension fund assets (which, as the article points out, is the number used in computing pension expense), and the *actual* gain in pension fund assets. Some examples:

Company	Expected Gain in Pension Fund Assets for 2001	Actual Gain in Pension Fund Assets for 2001
Bombardier Inc. (for the year ended Jan. 31, 2002)	a *gain* of $281.8 million	a *loss* of $335.9 million
Royal Bank of Canada	a *gain* of $123 million	a *gain* of $306 million
General Electric Company	a *gain* of US$4.3 billion	a *loss* of US$2.9 billion

We included the American company General Electric (GE) for two reasons. First, Canadian and U.S. GAAP in this area are essentially identical, and second, the numbers in the GE case are especially astounding, as we will now show.

In 2001, GE reported net income before income taxes of US$19.7 billion. An important part of this net income was US$2.1 billion *income* (not expense!) from the company's pension plans that are provided as a future employee benefit. This pension income was crafted by using an expected return on pension plan assets of US$4.3 billion in 2001, and not the actual *loss* on pension plan assets of US$2.9 billion. This US$7.2-billion variance between the expected and actual certainly had a materially favourable impact on GE's 2001 bottom line. This accounting meets GAAP criteria. So, accounting for future employee benefits is a very sensitive area. But, to be fair, let's examine this variance in GE's case over a three-year period in which the financial instruments invested in the pension fund went from performing well (a bull market) to poorly (a bear market):

Year	Expected Gain in Pension Fund Assets (used by GE in computing its pension expense)	Actual Gain in Pension Fund Assets	Variance
2001	US$4.3 billion gain	US$2.9 billion loss	US$7.2 billion, favourable to GE's net income before income taxes
2000	US$3.8 billion gain	US$1.3 billion gain	US$2.5 billion, favourable to GE's net income before income taxes
1999	US$3.4 billion gain	US$8.5 billion gain	US$5.1 billion, unfavourable to GE's net income before income taxes

Source: GE audited financial statements, 2001 and 2000

We can see from this chart that the method of GAAP pension accounting—the method to which Al Rosen alerts us—in effect *smooths* the impact of pension plan asset returns over time. The huge boost to GE's 2001 bottom line was "offset" by the US$5.1 unfavourable impact in 1999. We'll discuss this smoothing effect later, but now we will describe the details behind accounting for future employee benefits, focusing on pension accounting in particular.

GENERAL ELECTRIC COMPANY www.ge.com

Exhibit 14.1 FALLING PENSION INVESTMENTS, REPORTING PENSION EXPENSE, AND THE FINANCIAL COMMENTATOR

Pension expense is often disclosed in audited financial statement notes, as we will see later in this chapter. For pensions that promise, or guarantee, some sort of pension to retirees (a so-called "defined benefit" pension plan), pension expense is made up of several components. The main components are: current service cost; plus the interest cost on the pension liability; plus various amortizations; minus the expected return on the pension plan's assets. The total of these numbers is, as we explain later in the chapter, "pension expense." As well-known financial commentator Al Rosen writes in his column in *Canadian Business* ("Pension Ploys," February 18, 2002, p. 53): "The item of immense concern to investors is the subtraction from the pension expense of management's expected rates of gain on pension plan assets. In essence, pension expense can be reduced significantly by a management estimate."

Because of this GAAP requirement for making such a management estimate, the stock market decline over the past couple of years or so has had an interesting, perhaps even bizarre, side effect when it comes to accounting for and reporting pension expense. This side effect is due to the fact that Canadian GAAP requires companies to make a deduction of the *expected*, not the *actual*, gains on the assets invested in their pension plans when they figure out their pension expense, as Rosen mentions above. As an example, the magnitude of using expected instead of actual numbers on Canadian banks' reported pension expense is considerable, as shown by the information on the major Canadian banks, below. For instance, the $316 million difference for the Bank of Nova Scotia was so great that it turned what would have otherwise been an overall pension expense into pension *income* for the bank; the bank reported pension income of $14 million for 2002. This also happened in the previous year as well—the Bank of Nova Scotia reported $4 million in 2001.

Rosen claims that companies may use the estimates that GAAP requires in pension accounting (and determining the expected return on pension plan assets is only one of many estimates in pension accounting, as you will see) as "aggressive shenanigans" that users of financial statements should be on the lookout for.

Accounting for the Effect of Pension Investments on Canadian Banks Pension Expense, Year Ended October 31, 2002

Bank	Expected annual gain on pension assets (%) (A)	Reduction in pension expense for expected gain ($ mil) (B)	What did the pension assets actually gain? ($mil) (C)	Deviation between actual and expected [C-B] (D)
Toronto-Dominion	6.75	81	55	26
Bank of Nova Scotia	7.5	275	41 loss	316
Bank of Montreal	7.5	235	188 loss	423
CIBC	7.5	199	106	93
Royal Bank	7.0	300	133 loss	433

Accounting for Pension Plans

A **pension plan** is an agreement by an organization to provide a series of payments—called a pension—to employees when they retire. In most instances, these company pension payments supplement payments from government-sponsored pension plans in Canada—such as the Canada Pension Plan, or CPP. A pension plan represents a valuable benefit to employees. Employers create these plans as a way of attracting and retaining a qualified workforce. Firms also derive benefits from pension plans, since they help them retain a more capable workforce with higher morale. For this reason, the cost of a worker's pension plan is treated as an expense over that worker's period of employment.

Pension plans can be divided into two categories—**defined contribution** plans and **defined benefit** plans—on the basis of the nature of the promise embedded in the plan.

Defined contribution plans specify the amount of cash that the employer puts *into* the plan for the benefit of the employee. In a defined contribution plan, no explicit promise is made about the size of the periodic payments the employee will receive on retirement. The amount that will ultimately be paid out to the employee is determined by the accumulated value at retirement of the amounts contributed to the plan over the period of employment. In defined contribution plans, the employee bears the risk that the ultimate pension payments will be large enough to sustain a comfortable retirement income. Accounting for such plans is straightforward. Pension expense in any period is equal to the amount of cash contributed to the plan by the employer. The entry is:

DR Pension expense	XXX	
CR Cash		XXX

A defined benefit plan is quite different. These agreements specify the formula for determining the amount that will be paid *out* to the employee after retirement rather than the amount that will be put into the plan. To illustrate the difference:

- *Defined benefit plan.* ABC Company sponsors a pension plan in which employees qualify for a pension equal to 3% of their salary at retirement for each year of service. Thus, an employee with 25 years of service and with an annual salary at retirement of $60,000 would receive an annual pension of $45,000 (25 years of service times 3% for each year—75%—multiplied by the ending salary of $60,000).

- *Defined contribution plan.* XYZ Company sponsors a pension plan under which it makes an annual contribution of 10% of the employee's salary into a fund whose accumulated proceeds will be paid to the employee at retirement. The employee's salary in 2003 is $40,000 and in 2004 is $42,000. Accordingly, the contributions to the plan are $4,000 in 2003 and $4,200 in 2004.

A defined contribution plan specifies the initial level of pay*in* to the plan. A defined benefit plan specifies the formula for determining pension pay*outs*.

> In defined contribution pension plans, the employee is sometimes also required to contribute to the plan. For example, a plan might specify that the employer is to contribute 10% of the employee's salary to the plan and that the employee is to contribute 5%, for a total of 15%. The employee's 5% contribution is typically deducted from the employee's paycheque and directly transferred to the plan trustee, whose role is discussed later.

As the following paragraph points out, changing economic times lead to shifts in the proportion of defined benefit versus defined contribution pension plans.

Defined contribution (DC) pension plans have increased in number relative to defined benefit (DB) plans over the past decade or so in Canada, and the reasons are not hard to understand. The employee members of pension plans wanted more control and higher rates of return on their pension investments (they saw what the stock market was doing in the late 1990s), and employers wanted to avoid some of the costs and requirements associated with DB plans. Employers may have felt constrained, for example, by the obligation to guarantee a certain level of pension under DB plans, even when their business wasn't doing so well. David Burke and Anne Cowling, in an article published in *Benefits Canada* ("A DB revival," v. 26(4), April 2002, pp. 34–35) mention that a recent survey indicated that 42% of the 603 Canadian companies examined had DC plans, but only 28% had DB plans (13% had a combination of DC and DB plans). However, recent significant changes in the economic climate may alter this picture, as Burke and Cowling write: "But times change. And so may have employees' preference for DC plans. In the midst of economic uncertainty, the security of DB plans is attractive again. ..."

So, a significant proportion of the Canadian workforce is covered by defined benefit pension plans, and, although there has been a significant shift towards defined contribution plans, the above paragraph indicates that the trend might be reversed. A defined benefit pension plan raises many financial reporting complications. The main complication is how much should be charged to pension expense in each year during which employees covered under the plan work. This is not an issue under defined contribution plans, where pension expense in any period is equal to the specified *pay-in* by the employer.

Financial reporting for defined benefit plans is complicated because only the *pay-out formula* is specified, not the payout *amount*. In the ABC Company example, at the time the plan was adopted it was known that retiring employees with 25 years of service would receive a pension equal to 75% of their annual salary at the time of retirement. However, to determine the periodic pension expense (from the viewpoint of the employer's accounting entity) over the span of the employees' working careers, first estimate the following factors:

1. What proportion of the workforce will remain with the company long enough to qualify for benefits under the plan? Qualifying for benefits is called **vesting**. A forecast of the length of employee service requires actuarial assumptions regarding expected personnel turnover, mortality rates, and disability.
2. At what rate will salaries rise over the period until eventual retirement?
3. What is the anticipated life span of covered employees after retirement—that is, over what length of time will the pension benefits be paid?
4. What rate of return will be earned on the investments made with the cash contributed by the employer to fund the plan?
5. What is the appropriate discount rate that should be used to reflect the present value of the future benefits earned by employees in the current period?

CICA Handbook Section 3461 ("Employee Future Benefits"), which was issued in March 1999, mandated new accounting and disclosure rules for pensions.[1] Both Sections 3460 (the previous section) and 3461 were designed to avoid volatility in pension expense. This objective was achieved by using numerous smoothing devices and deferrals in computing pension expense. The result is arguably the most technically complicated financial reporting pronouncement ever issued. Consequently, analysts and other external users have experienced considerable difficulty in comprehending the concepts underlying the reported numbers. We try to clarify the topic by providing an intuitive overview of the financial reporting rules for employers' pension plans.[2]

Financial Reporting for Defined Benefit Pensions

Under current GAAP, pension expense for defined benefit pension plans comprises six major components.[3] These components are (+ indicates increase in expense and – indicates decrease in expense):

1. service cost (+)
2. interest cost (+)
3. expected return on plan assets (–)
4. recognized gains or losses (– or +)
5. amortization of unrecognized transition asset or obligation (– or +)
6. recognized prior service cost (– or +)

We use a simple example to illustrate how pension expense is computed under current GAAP rules. The example assumes an environment characterized by *complete certainty*. This assumption simplifies the setting and clarifies the relationship among the various pension expense components. The complete certainty assumption makes it easy to see that there would be no need for components 4–6 in an environment with no surprises. Later, we will show how components 4–6 come into play in a world of uncertainty, one where expectations are frequently not realized and where changes in assumptions frequently occur.

A Simple Example in a Certainty Setting

Consider the following example.[4]

On January 1, 2003, Wildcat Corporation decides to provide a $20,000 lump-sum pension to its sole employee, Ed Cate. No previous pension plan existed. Wildcat expects Cate to retire on December 31, 2004, and desires to pay the pension in one lump sum on December 31, 2005. Assume that the pension vests at the end of each year—that is, Cate is assured of at least a $10,000 pension if he works through December 31, 2003, and a $20,000 pension if he stays with Wildcat until his retirement on December 31, 2004.

Further assume that interest rates are known with certainty. Wildcat's discount rate is 7%, and the pension assets will also earn exactly 7% on all contributions to the pension fund, which are funded fully as soon as they vest.

Component 1—Service Cost
In a typical defined benefit pension plan, the pension payout increases for each additional year of service. This increase in the expected payout results in an increase in the discounted present value of the liability.

This increase is the **service cost**. Stated more rigorously, *service cost is the increase in the discounted present value of the pension benefits ultimately payable that is attributable to an additional year's employment.* The matching concept justifies this being accounted for as an expense of the employer.

In the simplified example, Cate worked throughout 2003 and as a consequence became eligible for a $10,000 pension payable on December 31, 2005. The discounted present value of this obligation on December 31, 2003 (at a 7% discount rate) is $8,734. Because no obligation existed at the start of the year, the *increase* in the discounted present value of the obligation during the year is $8,734—this is the service cost element of pension expense on Wildcat's books for 2003. Because Wildcat fully funds the pension expense, the status of the pension at December 31, 2003, is:

Pension Expense	**Pension Fund Assets and Liabilities**
$\frac{\$10,000}{(1.07)^2} = \$8,734$ service cost	$8,734

Ed Cate's continued employment throughout 2004 qualifies him for a $20,000 pension payable on December 31, 2005. The service cost element of pension expense for the year 2004 is the increase in the present value of the amount ultimately payable that is attributable to an additional year's employment. Table 14.1 shows the computation.

TABLE 14.1 WILDCAT CORPORATION

Computation of Service Cost for 2004

Pension payout to Cate with two years of service (2003 and 2004)		$20,000
Less: Pension payout to Cate with one year of service (2003)	−	10,000
Undiscounted increase attributable to 2004 service	=	10,000
Discount factor at 7% for one year (this increase is discounted since the additional payout is one year away)	×	0.9346
Service cost for 2004	=	$ 9,346

The ultimate pension payout has grown by $10,000, since Cate earned additional benefits by working in 2004. As shown in Table 14.1, the discounted present value of this increase is $10,000 × 0.9346—or $9,346. By definition, this amount is service cost.

In addition to service cost, 2004 *total* pension expense for Wildcat Corporation includes two other items—interest cost and return on plan assets.

Component 2—Interest Cost

Service cost for 2003 was initially recorded at $8,734, the discounted present value of the pension payment due on December 31, 2005. Because the payment of this liability drew one year closer by the end of 2004, its present value has increased by $611 ($8,734 × 7%). Therefore, in addition to service cost, there is interest cost in 2004. The **interest cost** component of pension expense (and the increase in the liability) arises from the passage of time. (By contrast, the service cost element arises because the pension liability grows as workers accumulate additional years of service.) Interest cost is computed by taking the pension liability at the beginning of the period ($8,734) and multiplying it by the 7% interest rate factor.

Most pension plans create a trust—a legal entity that takes custody of assets contributed by the employer and manages them for the benefit of the employees. Contributing assets to the plan is termed **funding**. When the employer *funds* the plan, these assets are transferred to the trustee.

Component 3—Expected Return on Plan Assets

At December 31, 2003, the pension fund assets (held by the trustee) also had a balance of $8,734. During 2004, these assets earned a return of $611 ($8,734 × 7%). (Because our example is set in a world of complete certainty, the expected return and the actual return on plan assets are equal.) The **expected return on plan assets** reduces pension expense. As a consequence of all of these events, total pension expense for 2004 is $9,346 ($9,346 + $611 – $611). Table 14.2 gives the 2004 pension expense components and pension fund asset balance at December 31, 2004.

If Cate retires at the end of 2004, there will be no service cost component of pension expense in 2005. Table 14.3 shows that 2005 pension expense is zero and that the December 31, 2005, accumulated asset balance of $20,000 is exactly equal to the required pension payment.

In this example, perfect certainty meant:

1. The exact *date of retirement was known* at the time the plan was initiated. In technical terms, the precise service life of employees was known with certainty.

TABLE 14.2 WILDCAT CORPORATION

Pension Expense and Assets for 2004

Pension Expense

Service cost ($10,000)/1.07	=	$ 9,346
Interest cost ($8,734 × 7%)	=	611
Expected return on plan assets ($8,734 × 7%)	=	(611)
2004 pension expense	=	$ 9,346

Pension Fund Assets

Accumulated balance of 12/31/03 amount as of 12/31/04 ($8,734 × 1.07)	=	$ 9,346*
Service cost and funding at 12/31/04	=	$ 9,346
Balance at 12/31/04	=	$18,692

*Rounded.

TABLE 14.3 WILDCAT CORPORATION

Pension Expense and Assets for 2005

Pension Expense

Interest cost ($18,692 × 7%)	=	$ 1,308
Expected return on plan assets ($18,692 × 7%)	=	$ (1,308)
2005 pension expense	=	–0–

Pension Fund Assets

Accumulated balance of 12/31/04 fund assets ($18,692 × 1.07)	=	$20,000
12/31/05 payment to Cate	=	(20,000)
Balance at 12/31/05	=	–0–

2. The ultimate *amount of the pension was also known in advance.* No unexpected salary increases raised the amount of the final payment, nor were there unforeseen actuarial events such as turnover or death.

3. *Discount rates and earnings rates were equal and could be perfectly forecast over the entire period.*

With these simple (but unrealistic) circumstances, pension expense is equal to service cost in every period over which the pension plan is in effect, as shown next:

Year	Service Cost	Total Pension Expense
2003	$8,734	$8,734
2004	$9,346	$9,346
2005	–0–	–0–

Pension expense equals service cost when there is complete certainty because interest cost is exactly offset by the return on plan assets. This also means that the accumulated amount of pension assets is exactly sufficient to pay the liability. Relaxing these certainty assumptions complicates pension financial reporting considerably.

We use perfect certainty in this example to help you see the relationship between the components comprising pension expense. There is no perfect certainty in the real pension world. On the contrary, unforeseen pension events arise continually, for example higher or lower than anticipated employee turnover and unusually high or low preretirement mortality. In addition, the return earned on pension plan assets could differ significantly from expectations, as we saw with the examples at the start of this chapter. Furthermore, changes in social and economic conditions may prompt companies to retroactively alter the level of benefits promised upon retirement or to alter the discount rate assumptions.

All these factors explain why there is no simple equality between plan assets and liabilities and why pension expense does not equal service cost in the real world. Depending on the age distribution of the workforce and the amount of retroactive plan alterations, interest cost—not service cost—could be the dominant part of pension expense.

Our example does capture one real-world characteristic of pension plans. Wildcat Corporation (the plan sponsor) recognized on its books only the pension expense and the cash payout when funding the pension. The assets and liabilities of the pension plan are not included in Wildcat's financial statements. Instead, the assets and liabilities are reflected on the statements of the **plan trustee**. The plan trustee receives the payments and disburses pension benefits. The relationship between the firm that establishes the pension plan (the plan sponsor), the plan trustee, and the plan beneficiaries (the eventual retirees) is shown in Figure 14.1.

> Among other reasons, pension expense does not equal service cost because when unexpected events occur, past funding (which was based on the original actuarial and earnings assumptions) generates returns that are larger or smaller than interest cost (which is based on the revised actuarial and earnings assumptions).

Recap

If the future were known with certainty, pension expense would always equal service cost and pension plan assets would always equal plan liabilities. Starting with this simple setting will help you understand better the complications that uncertainty introduces.

FIGURE 14.1
PENSION PLAN
ENTITIES AND
RELATIONSHIPS

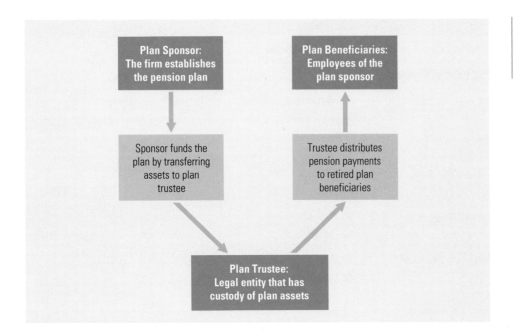

Uncertainty Introduces Deferrals and Amortizations in Existing GAAP-Based Defined Benefit Pension Accounting

Uncertainty requires estimates of future discount rates, the return on plan assets, and numerous other future events like employee turnover and longevity beyond retirement. GAAP require that the same rate be used for computing both the service cost *and* the interest cost components of pension expense. However, companies are free to choose some other rate for computing the *expected* rate of return on pension plan assets and many do.

The simplified complete certainty example suggests that the higher the interest rate initially chosen for computing service cost, the lower the reported service cost component of pension expense. This reduction in service cost is offset by an increase in the interest cost component of pension expense, which is due to the higher interest rate. In our example, if the same higher rate is *also* used for computing the expected return on plan assets, then pension expense is reduced. Table 14.4 illustrates the decrease in pension expense that results from using an 8% rate rather than 7% in the Wildcat Corporation example.

If the assumed 8% interest rate is not actually *earned* on plan assets, the accumulated pension fund assets will be too small to fund Cate's pension. But generalizing from Table 14.4, we see that companies can temporarily (and significantly: recall the GE example at the beginning of the chapter) alter pension expense by choosing higher or lower discount rates and expected rates of return on plan assets.

TABLE 14.4 WILDCAT CORPORATION

Pension Expense at Two Different Interest Rates

2003 Pension Expense			@ 8%	@ 7%
2003 service cost	$10,000/(1.08)^2$	=	$8,573	
	$10,000/(1.07)^2$	=		$8,734
2004 Pension Expense				
2004 service cost	($20,000 – $10,000)/1.08	=	$9,259	
	($20,000 – $10,000)/1.07	=		$9,346
Interest cost	$8,573 × 8%	=	686	
	$8,734 × 7%	=		611
Return on plan assets	$8,573 × 8%	=	(686)	
	$8,734 × 7%	=		(611)
			$9,259	$9,346

Let's look at some rates that affect defined benefit pension plan accounting under GAAP from a sample of companies for the year 2001 (rates for 2000 are in parentheses for comparison):

Company	Discount Rate for Pension Obligation 2001 (2000)	Expected Return on Pension Plan Assets	Expected Rate of Compensation Increase
Agrium Inc.	7% (7%)*	8% (8%)	5% (5%)
Alberta Energy Company Ltd.	6.7% (6.9%)	6.9% (6.9%)	5.0% (5.0%)
BCE Inc.	6.5% (7.0%)	8.8% (8.5%)	3.5% (3.9%)
BC Gas Inc.	6.81% (7.19%)	7.15% (7.16%)	3.21% (3.29%)
Bombardier Inc.**	6.10% (6.70%)	8.00% (8.00%)	3.78% (4.25%)
Canadian National Railway	6.50% (6.50%)	9.00% (9.00%)	4.00% (4.25%)
Canadian Pacific Railway Limited	6.75% (6.75%)	8.00% (8.00%)	3.00% (3.00%)
Noranda Inc.***	6.90% (6.98%)	7.07% (7.14%)	3.71% (4.12%)
Potash Corporation of Saskatchewan Inc.	7.25% (7.50%)	9.00% (9.00%)	4.50% (5.00%)
Rogers Communications Inc.	7.00% (7.00%)	8.25% (8.25%)	5.00% (5.00%)
Royal Bank of Canada	7.00% (7.25%)	7.00% (7.00%)	4.4% (4.4%)
The Thomson Corporation	6.8% (7.2%)	8.9% (9.0%)	4.9% (4.8%)
Highest rate	7.25% (7.50%)	9.00% (9.00%)	5.00% (5.00%)
Lowest rate	6.10% (6.50%)	6.9% (6.9%)	3.00% (3.00%)

*Agrium reports its rates as a single digit.

**Bombardier reports as of January 31 of 2002.

***For Noranda and its wholly owned subsidiaries.

Keeping in mind that even small differences in rates result in significant differences in components of defined benefit pension plan expense, notice the following features about this data:

- Even similar companies have different rates (Canadian National versus Canadian Pacific).
- The rates for most companies changed from 2000 to 2001, but not for some companies such as Rogers Communications.
- The range between the highest and lowest rates for each of the three categories is quite significant.

Section 3461 provides criteria that companies with defined benefit pension plans must use in order to estimate the discount rate used to compute the present value of the pension obligation (called the "accrued benefit obligation" in Section 3461). These criteria are necessary, since even small changes in the discount rate may result in large changes in pension expense; users of financial statements must monitor these rates carefully. Paragraph 3461.050 says:

For a defined benefit plan, the discount rate used to determine the accrued benefit obligation should be an interest rate determined by reference to:

(a) market interest rates at the measurement date on high-quality debt instruments with cash flows that match the timing and amount of expected benefit payments; or

(b) the interest rate inherent in the amount at which the accrued benefit obligation could be settled.

Paragraph 3461.050 is the formal GAAP. Paragraphs 3461.051 to 3461.055 provide elaboration.

Under old Section 3460, companies had to choose discount rates by making what the section called "best estimates," resulting in a fair bit of variation among companies. Of course, this variation could have been justified by differences in circumstances, but it was virtually impossible for an external user of financial statements to know. Even though Section 3461 has more detailed guidelines, tracking changes in the discount rates chosen by companies is still important.

Components 4 Through 6—Smoothing Devices

Uncertainty not only complicates the measurement of service cost and interest cost; it also means realizations will likely differ from expectations. For example, the actual return on pension plan assets will differ from the expected return, and the actual turnover and pay increase experience will differ from actuarial assumptions. These deviations between expected and actual events—if recognized immediately—would inject volatility into the periodic measure of pension expense. Components 4 through 6 of the annual pension expense calculation are designed to smooth this volatility over future years.

Our discussion now turns to each of these components of pension expense.

Component 4—Recognized Gains or Losses In an uncertain environment, the actual return on pension plan assets can differ markedly from the expected return in any year. Volatility in asset returns—without smoothing—would translate directly into net income volatility since the return on plan assets reduces pension expense.

To illustrate this volatility, let's assume Anna Corporation's service cost and interest cost components of pension expense in 2003 and 2004 were:

	2003	2004
Service cost	$1,000	$1,050
Interest cost	1,000	1,050

In addition, assume that the *actual* return on plan assets in 2003 was $1,500 but (because of adverse market conditions) was only $100 in 2004. If no smoothing were permitted, Anna's pension expense in the two years would be:

	2003	2004
Service cost	$ 1,000	$1,050
Interest cost	1,000	1,050
Less: Actual return on plan assets	(1,500)	(100)
Pension expense	$ 500	$2,000

The extreme change in year-to-year pension expense would cause year-to-year volatility in the firm's earnings.

Section 3461 makes it possible to avert this volatility by allowing firms to reduce pension expense by the *expected* return on plan assets rather than by the actual return. This result is accomplished using a two-stage process. First, firms select a target return that they expect to earn on plan assets in the long run. (We saw with our sample of companies that the range of expected returns can be fairly wide—in our sample, the range was 6.9% to 9.0% for 2001.) Second, any difference between this expected return and the actual return that is earned in a given year is kept track of "off the balance sheet" and the cumulative balance of these unrecognized gains (losses) is monitored over time.

To show how the smoothing works, assume that Anna's pension plan assets were $10,000 and $11,500 at the start of 2003 and 2004, respectively. Further assume that given the riskiness of the investment strategy selected, Anna expects to earn a return of 9% on average each year. Under the Section 3461 smoothing approach, Anna's pension expense would be reduced by the *expected* return in each year—$900 in 2003 ($10,000 × 9%) and $1,035 in 2004 ($11,500 × 9%). This is component 3, discussed earlier. The difference between the expected and actual returns in each year is deferred using an off-balance-sheet smoothing device called the **unrecognized gain or loss**. Specifically:

	2003		2004	
Service cost		$1,000		$1,050
Interest cost		1,000		1,050
Less:				
Actual return on plan assets	($1,500)		($100)	
Unrecognized gain (loss)	600		(935)	
Expected return on plan assets		(900)		(1,035)
Pension expense		$1,100		$1,065

In years like 2003 when the actual return ($1,500) exceeds the expected return ($900), there is an unrecognized gain. In years like 2004, there is an unrecognized loss of $935 since the actual return ($100) was less than the expected return ($1,035). By using the expected return to compute pension expense and deferring the unrecognized gain or loss, the year-to-year change in Anna Corporation's pension expense was only $35 ($1,100 − $1,065), much smaller than the year-to-year change in *actual* return on plan assets of $1,400 ($1,500 − $100).

FIGURE 14.2
GENERAL
ELECTRIC
COMPANY
COMPARISON OF
ACTUAL AND
EXPECTED
RETURN ON
PENSION PLAN
ASSETS

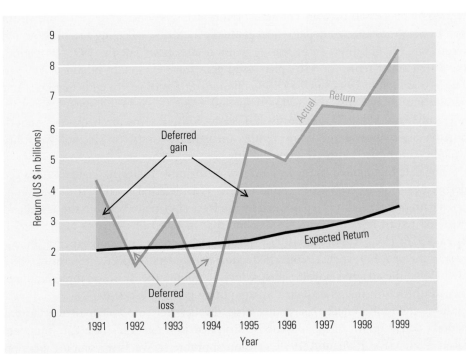

Excerpts from General Electric Company Footnotes Underlying Figure 14.2 Data

(US$ in billions)	1991	1992	1993	1994	1995	1996	1997	1998	1999
Actual dollar return on pension plan assets	$ 4.331	$ 1.562	$ 3.221	$ 0.316	$ 5.439	$ 4.916	$ 6.587	$ 6.363	$ 8.472
Market value of plan assets[1]	$22.933	$26.133	$26.466	$27.193	$26.166	$30.200	$33.686	$38.742	$43.447
Actual return on plan assets	18.9%	6.0%	12.2%	1.2%	20.8%	16.3%	19.6%	16.4%	19.5%
Long-run expected return	9.5%	9.5%	9.5%	9.5%	9.5%	9.5%	9.5%	9.5%	9.5%
Expected dollar return on plan assets[2]	$ 2.059	$ 2.146	$ 2.155	$ 2.267	$ 2.352	$ 2.587	$ 2.721	$ 3.024	$ 3.407
Unrecognized gains or losses (actual minus expected return)	$ 2.272	($ 0.584)	$ 1.066	($ 1.951)	$ 3.087	$ 2.329	$ 3.866	$ 3.339	$ 5.065

[1]This is the value of the plan assets at the *start* of each year.

[2]You may notice that the expected dollar return for any year is not equal to the beginning market value of plan assets times the expected return rate. To illustrate using 1999, we get:

Market value of plan assets ($43.477) × expected return (.095) = $4.127 Expected dollar return

[This amount differs from the $3.407 reported by GE. Why? The reason is that firms are allowed to compute the expected return on a moving-average of the market value of plan assets over a period not exceeding the preceding five years. GE apparently did this, so the 9.5% expected return was applied to some measure of late 1990s average plan assets. We do not have enough information to compute the $3.407 directly.]

Source: General Electric Company Annual Reports, 1991–99.

Figure 14.2 graphically shows how large the differences between the actual and expected returns on pension plan assets can be. The graph in Figure 14.2 is based on data that can be found in the pension footnotes for General Electric Company (GE) for the years 1991 through 1999. We include excerpts from these footnotes that show this underlying data. While GE's long-run expected rate of return on plan assets was 9.5% over the entire period, the actual rate of return ranged from a high of 20.8% in 1995 to a low of 1.2% in 1994. Figure 14.2 depicts the actual and expected dollar

GENERAL ELECTRIC
COMPANY
www.ge.com

returns on plan assets by year. The actual return displays considerable variability from year to year; the expected dollar return gradually increases, reflecting a stable expected return rate (9.5%) times an increasing pension asset base. For the 1993–95 period, the actual dollar return on GE's plan assets goes from US$3.221 billion in 1993 to US$316 million in 1994 to US$5.439 billion in 1995. GE's earnings before taxes and accounting charges for the 1993–95 period were (US$ in billions) US$6.136, US$8.661, and US$9.737, respectively. Clearly, without some mechanism to smooth out the big swings in the yearly returns on pension assets, considerable volatility would be introduced into GE's bottom line.

The data highlighted in the bottom row of the table following Figure 14.2 is the deferred portion of each year's actual return. This deferred portion is the unrecognized gain or loss, and it is represented by the vertical distance between the actual and expected return lines in Figure 14.2. Note that in seven of the years (1991, 1993, 1995, 1996, 1997, 1998, and 1999), this deferral increases pension expense since it *reduces* the pension expense return deduction *down* to the expected return. In 1992 and 1994, the deferral adjustments reduce pension expense since these amounts *increase* the return that is deducted in computing pension expense.

The smoothing effect that results from the deferral component of the current period's actual return on plan assets is illustrated in Table 14.5 (the data there are taken from GE's 1994 and 1995 pension footnotes). We first compute pension expense without deferring the unexpected return, then we calculate pension expense with adjustment for the deferral.

TABLE 14.5 GENERAL ELECTRIC COMPANY

Smoothing Effect of Deferring Unexpected Gains or Losses

(US$ in millions)		1994		1995
Without Deferral				
Component 1: Service cost		$ 496		$ 469
Component 2: Interest cost		1,491		1,580
Component 3: Actual return on plan assets		(316)		(5,439)
Pension expense *without deferral* of unexpected gain or loss		$1,671 **DR**		($3,390) **CR**

Year-to-year "swing" of $5,061

With Deferral				
Component 1: Service cost		$ 496		$ 469
Component 2: Interest cost		1,491		1,580
Actual return on plan assets	(316)		(5,439)	
Deferral of unexpected gain (or loss)	(1,951)		3,087	
Component 3: Expected return on plan assets		(2,267)		(2,352)
Pension expense *with deferral* of unexpected return		$ (280) **CR**		($ 303) **CR**

Year-to-year "swing" of $23

Looking at the data following Figure 14.2, in 1994 the actual return on plan assets was US$316 million, which was US$1.951 billion *below* the expected return of US$2.267 billion. In 1995, the actual return was US$5.439 billion, which was US$3.087 billion *higher* than the expected return of US$2.352 billion. As these two years illustrate, the deferred portion of the current period's return can either increase or decrease pension expense. Without deferral, GE's pension expense would have gone from a US$1.671 billion *debit* in 1994 to a US$3.390 billion *credit* in 1995, a swing of US$5.061 billion.[5] By deferring the unexpected gain or loss, the year-to-year change is reduced to only US$23 million, as shown in Table 14.5.

Companies are free to use a rate for computing the *expected* return on plan assets that differs from the discount rate used for service and interest costs. That makes it possible to lower pension expense in the short-run by using an expected asset return rate that is higher than the discount rate. Large disparities between the two rates affect the pension expense calculation.

How Component 4 Is Measured If gains and losses do not offset one another over time, the cumulative off-balance-sheet deferred amounts continue to grow. When this happens, some adjustment is needed to correct for the past smoothing. This is the role of component 4—recognized gains or losses.

Cumulative off-balance-sheet net gains or losses can arise as a result of any of the following:

1. the accumulation of differences between actual and expected returns on pension plan assets—as illustrated previously
2. the accumulation of differences between actuarial assumptions and actual experience—for example, employee turnover, pay increases, and longevity beyond retirement
3. changes in assumptions, for example, a change in the discount rate used for computing current service cost and interest cost

Because pension accounting requires numerous estimates of future events, differences between forecasted amounts and subsequent occurrences should be expected. These differences mean that *past* measures of pension expense were misstated:

- Cumulative asset return differences mean that the difference between actual return on plan assets and expected return on plan assets did not offset one another over time.

- Cumulative actuarial assumption differences mean that service cost (component 1) was either over- or understated.

- Finally, changes in the assumed discount rate mean that both service cost (component 1) and interest cost (component 2) were misstated in some previous years.

These misstatements of *past* pension expense exist because the CICA's Accounting Standards Board (AcSB) and the Financial Accounting Standards Board (FASB) in the United States responded to corporate managers' dislike for income volatility and opted to smooth period-to-period fluctuations. Section 3461 does not require each year's results to correspond perfectly to market returns or actuarial experience. However, if the smoothing adjustments do not offset one another over time, the periodic differences will ultimately accumulate and exceed some threshold level. The AcSB believes that these past errors must be corrected once this threshold is exceeded. Rather than requiring that the total correction be made at one time, the AcSB again opted for a smoothing approach and allowed the correction for cumulative *past* errors to be spread over a series of *future* years.

Here's how the component 4 adjustment mechanism works. At the *start* of each reporting year, the cumulative unrecognized off-balance-sheet gain (or loss) is computed. A portion of this cumulative gain or loss will be amortized over current and future years if it exceeds a certain materiality threshold defined as 10% of the *larger* of the following two numbers, which are measured at the *beginning* of the year: (1) the present value of pension obligations based on assumed future compensation levels (called the **accrued benefit obligation**) and (2) the **market-related value** of pension plan assets. If the 10% threshold is exceeded, the excess cumulative gain or loss is amortized straight-line over the estimated **average remaining service period** of active employees.

To illustrate, suppose that on January 1, 2003, Dore Corporation had a cumulative unrecognized gain of $1,600,000 arising from (1) differences between actual and expected returns on plan assets, (2) differences between actuarial assumptions and actual experience, and (3) changes in interest rate assumptions. The market-related value of pension plan assets on that date was $10,000,000, and the accrued benefit obligation was $8,500,000. The estimated average remaining service period of active employees is 15 years.

The 10% threshold is $1,000,000, which is 10% of $10,000,000 (the larger of the $8,500,000 obligation and the $10,000,000 asset totals). Because the cumulative unrecognized gain of $1,600,000 is larger than the $1,000,000 threshold, component 4 is triggered. The $600,000 amount in excess of the threshold will be amortized over 15 years. This means that pension expense component 4 will be *credited* for $40,000 of the unrecognized gain ($600,000 ÷ 15), thereby *reducing* pension expense. ($40,000 is the minimum gain that must be recognized. A systematic method consistently applied to both gains and losses that results in a larger amount is permissible.)

If there were no future misestimates, the unamortized excess—$600,000 minus the $40,000 of 2003 amortization—would be totally taken into income over the ensuing 14 years. Realistically, pension accounting requires many estimates of uncertain future events. Uncertainty means that further misestimates are likely. Consequently, Section 3461 requires that the computation illustrated in the example be redone at the start of each subsequent year to determine the amount of that year's pension expense component 4.

It is easy to understand why the AcSB chose the accrued benefit obligation and the market-related value of pension plan assets as the two benchmarks that potentially trigger the component 4 amortization. Measures of accrued benefit obligations and plan assets constitute the "critical 10% corridor" because the factors giving rise to the cumulative gain or loss represent misestimates of the "real" obligations and assets.

In other words, **cumulative asset gains or losses** occur because the rate chosen for the expected return on plan assets in the computation of pension expense either understated or overstated the actual increase in pension assets. Similarly, **cumulative obligation gains or losses** occur because the amount of service cost included in pension expense either understated or overstated the actual increase in pension obligations. Thus, obligations and assets constitute the appropriate benchmarks for assessing when the cumulative error is "excessive." The 10% threshold is simply an arbitrary measure of this "excessiveness."

Component 5—Amortization of Unrecognized Transition Asset or Obligation

Even before accounting standards for pensions were issued, there was usually a disparity between the value of pension plan assets and the present value of the pension obligation. Some plans were overfunded (i.e., assets exceeded obligations), while others were underfunded (obligations exceeded assets). The AcSB sought to reduce future periods' pension expense charges for overfunded plans and to increase future pension expense for underfunded plans when a company first adopts pension accounting GAAP.

The following example illustrates the approach. Rett Corporation adopted old Section 3460 (the section that Section 3461 replaced) on January 1, 1987. On that date, the fair value of the pension plan assets was $238,000,000, and the pension liability was $202,000,000. The actuarial estimate of the average remaining service period of employees who are expected to receive benefits under the plan was 18 years.

The AcSB required that the amount of overfunding or underfunding be computed at the time old Section 3460 was first adopted. To determine the funding status, a firm must compare the amount of the pension liability and the pension plan assets. The difference—the **transition asset or liability**—is to be amortized over the average remaining service period of employees who are expected to receive benefits under the plan. Rett's $202,000,000 **accrued benefit obligation (ABO)** is the discounted present value of the expected pension payments, which takes into account expected pay raises over future years. This ABO is then compared to the fair value of plan assets—here $238,000,000. The funded status of the plan at adoption was an *overfunding* of $36,000,000. This transition asset amount will be amortized as component 5 over 18 years on a straight-line basis. Therefore, component 5 for Rett Corporation will be a $2,000,000 *credit* (reduction) to pension expense for each of the years 1987 through 2004. (Amortization of a transition liability results in a debit—addition—to pension expense.)

Components 5 and 4 both represent a smoothing approach for correcting *past* errors in the computation of pension expense. In the case of component 5, the pension expense errors arose prior to the adoption of old Section 3460 (or new Section 3461, if the company was not previously subject to GAAP)—that is, a plan that was overfunded at transition presumably used asset earnings rate assumptions that were too low, or service cost estimates that were too high, or both. In the case of component 4, similar errors arose *after* the adoption of GAAP. In either case, the effect is the same: past errors in computing pension expense are corrected in a smoothed fashion over current and *future* years.

Component 6—Recognized Prior or Past Service Cost Pension plans are frequently amended to provide increased benefits to employees. A firm may do this because increases in retirees' living costs warrant an increase in pension benefits. When a firm retroactively enhances the benefits provided by its pension plan, it means past pension expense and pension funding—which were both based on the "old" pension plan terms—were too low. This also means that when a firm enhances its pension plan, it immediately increases its accrued benefit obligation under the plan. The dollar amount of the increase in the obligation due to plan enhancements is called **past service cost.** Of course, the opposite situation also sometimes occurs—when pension plans are changed to *reduce* benefits. This might occur when a union "gives back" previously obtained pension enhancements to help the employer avoid bankruptcy.

The following example shows how past service cost arises. Schiller Corporation's pension plan granted employees a pension of 2% of ending salary at retirement for each year of service to a maximum of 30 years. Therefore, an employee with 30 years of service at Schiller could retire with a pension equal to 60% of his or her salary at retirement.

Management at Schiller Corporation now believes that the 60% pension maximum is inadequate given existing general economic conditions. The pension plan is retroactively changed on January 1, 2000. Under the revised plan, employees qualify for a pension of 2.25% of ending salary at retirement for each year of service, again to a maximum of 30 years. Under the revised plan, the maximum pension is 67.5% of the employee's salary at retirement (2.25% × 30 years).

Firms retroactively enhance—or "sweeten"—pension plans for various reasons. One is to generate employee goodwill and loyalty to the organization; firms do this to retain a quality workforce. Another reason for retroactive pension enhancement arises as a result of union demands in labour negotiations.

The traditional accounting argument has long been that even though these sweeteners are computed on the basis of services rendered in prior periods, the benefits to the firm will be realized in future periods. The benefits of retroactive plan enhancements are realized by the firm in future periods because of decreased employee turnover or better labour relations. Accordingly, Section 3461 allows these prior service costs to be amortized into pension expense on a straight-line basis over the expected service lives of employees who are expected to receive benefits under the plan, "by assigning an equal amount to each remaining service period up to the full eligibility date of each employee active at the date of the plan... amendment..." (Section 3461.079). If Schiller's plan enhancement increased the benefit obligation by $14,000,000 and if the average remaining service period of employees expected to receive benefits under the plan is 10 years, then $1,400,000 would be added to pension expense over each of the next 10 years. This is the role of component 6.

Practice with GAAP

At this point, please review "Situation 1" in Appendix A of Section 3461 of the *CICA Handbook*, in order to ensure that you have a general understanding of GAAP for defined benefit pension plans. We recommend that you work through this example in detail, in order to understand the variety of assumptions and arbitrary decisions under GAAP in this area.

Relative Magnitude of Pension Expense Components

Figure 14.3 shows the relative magnitude of the various components of pension expense for a sample of U.S. firms over the 1987–90 period.[6] The bars above the zero line represent debits that *increased* pension expense; the bars below the line depict credits that *decreased* pension expense. The bar labelled PENX (NET) at the end of each year's data represents that portion of the total charges to pension expense that remain after offsetting the credit items against the debit items (the **net pension expense** reported on the income statement).

Three items represented in Figure 14.3 are noteworthy. First, for the average firm, the service cost and interest cost components are fairly stable through time. The interest component is more than twice as large as the service cost component (an average of US$0.69 per share versus US$0.28 per share, respectively, over the four years), which means the cumulative pension obligation from past years of service far exceeds the obligation that arises from the current period employee service. One potential explanation for this is the prevalence of retroactive plan enhancements; another is an ageing workforce.

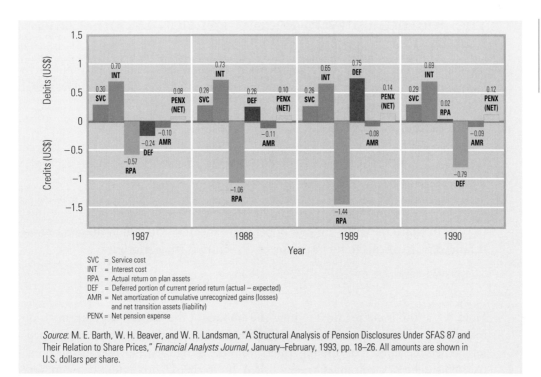

FIGURE 14.3
PENSION
EXPENSE
COMPONENTS
(1987–90)

SVC = Service cost
INT = Interest cost
RPA = Actual return on plan assets
DEF = Deferred portion of current period return (actual − expected)
AMR = Net amortization of cumulative unrecognized gains (losses)
and net transition assets (liability)
PENX = Net pension expense

Source: M. E. Barth, W. H. Beaver, and W. R. Landsman, "A Structural Analysis of Pension Disclosures Under SFAS 87 and Their Relation to Share Prices," *Financial Analysts Journal,* January–February, 1993, pp. 18–26. All amounts are shown in U.S. dollars per share.

Second, in contrast to the stable service and interest cost components, the actual return on plan assets varies considerably over this four-year period, ranging from a high of US$1.44 per share in 1989 to a low of –US$0.02 per share in 1990. This variability reflects the general fortunes of stocks during this period, which make up a major portion of many pension fund portfolios. Without the smoothing effects that result from deferring the unexpected return on plan assets, pension expense would have been quite volatile over this period. With the deferral of unrecognized gains or losses (note in some years this increases pension expense while in other years it decreases pension expense), the volatility in actual return is diminished, leaving a relatively stable credit adjustment to pension expense for the *expected* return on plan assets.

Third, the net amortization of components 4 through 6 is a credit to pension expense of roughly US$0.09 per share. This suggests that the average firm's pension plan was overfunded at transition and/or that there are cumulative unrecognized gains being amortized as a reduction to pension expense.

The net effect of the various smoothing procedures allowed under GAAP is apparent in the pattern of *net* pension expense amounts—the PENX (NET) bar—in Figure 14.3. Although individual components of pension expense are relatively large and actual return on plan assets is quite volatile, the net pension expense amount is relatively stable, averaging about US$0.11 per share over the period.

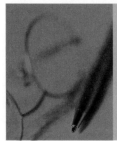

Recap

Estimates pervade pension accounting. When these estimates need to be adjusted, the adjustments could conceivably be recorded all at once. Doing this would make pension expense volatile from year to year. The CICA's AcSB (and the U.S. FASB) chose a different approach, based upon "smoothing," for adjusting pension estimates and plan changes. Components 4 through 6 are designed to be smoothing devices. When an adjustment is made, its effect is initially deferred and brought into pension expense slowly over a series of future years.

The Journal Entry to Record Pension Expense and Funding

To illustrate the journal entry for pension expense, let's assume that Northern Corporation disclosed the following components in its pension footnote at December 31, 2003:

Service cost	$23,000
Interest cost	42,500
Expected return on plan assets	(38,250)
Components 4–6	22,750
2003 pension expense	$50,000

In years in which the entire amount of pension expense—$50,000 in this example—is funded by payments to the plan trustee, the entry is straightforward:

DR Pension expense	$50,000	
CR Cash		$50,000

However, a firm is not required to fund the amount of the pension expense provision each period. (Factors that affect firms' funding policies are discussed later in the chapter.) When the amount of funding differs from the recognized expense, an additional balancing debit or credit must be established. If Northern Corporation chose to fund $53,000 in 2003, the entry would be:

DR Pension expense	$50,000	
DR Accrued benefit asset	3,000	
CR Cash		$53,000

The "Accrued benefit asset" account would be shown as an asset on the December 31, 2003 balance sheet.

If Northern had chosen to make a funding payment of only $44,000 in 2003, the entry would be:

DR Pension expense	$50,000	
CR Cash		$44,000
CR Accrued benefit liability		6,000

The "Accrued benefit liability" account in this entry would appear on the balance sheet as a liability. (Note that in practice other titles might be used for these accounts.)

Terminology alert: Section 3461 distinguishes between an "accrued benefit liability" and an "accrued benefit obligation." The distinction is as follows, based upon definitions in para. 24 of the section:

"Accrued benefit liability" is the amount of any liability recognized on an entity's balance sheet in respect of employee future benefits. It is the sum of the current and prior years' benefit expenses less the entity's accumulated cash contributions.

"Accrued benefit obligation" is the actuarial present value of benefits attributed to employee services rendered to a particular date. Under Section 3460, which preceded the current Section 3461, it was known as the "projected benefit obligation," a term still used in the U.S.

Defined Benefit Pension Accounting Spreadsheet

Exhibit 14.2 shows a spreadsheet that will serve as the basis for collecting—in a systematic fashion—the information necessary for preparing journal entries based on

Exhibit 14.2 DEFINED BENEFIT PENSION SPREADSHEET

	Item	Expense	Cash Flow	ABL/A	ABO	PA	UPSC	UEG/L
1	1/1/2003				−440,000	440,000		
2	Annual service cost	34,000			−34,000			
3	Interest cost	44,000			−44,000			
4	Expected return	−44,000				44,000		
5	Asset loss					−6,000		6,000
6	Funding		−34,000			34,000		
7	Payments				28,000	−28,000		
8	12/31/03	34,000	−34,000		−490,000	484,000		6,000
9	Plan amended				−330,000		330,000	
10					−820,000			
11	Annual service cost	40,000			−40,000			
12	Amortize UEG/L	−0−						−0−
13	Interest cost	82,000			−82,000			
14	Expected return	−48,400				48,400		
15	Amortize UPSC	33,000					−33,000	
16	Funding		−43,000			43,000		
17	Payments				32,800	−32,800		
18	12/31/04	106,600	−43,000	−63,600	−909,200	542,600	297,000	6,000
19	Annual service cost	56,000			−56,000			
20	Interest cost	90,920			−90,920			
21	Expected return	−54,260				54,260		
22	Asset loss					−4,260		4,260
23	Amortize UPSC	33,000					−33,000	
24	Funding		−100,000			100,000		
25	Payments				41,000	−41,000		
26	PBO revaluation				−14,880			14,880
27	12/31/05	125,660	−100,000	−25,660	−1,030,000	651,600	264,000	25,140	−89,260
				−89,260				

Note: Minus signs indicate credit.

GAAP for defined benefit pension plans. And, as we'll see later, this spreadsheet technique also serves as a useful analytical device to help external users of financial statements understand a company's defined benefit pension footnote information. The following hypothetical information about a company's defined benefit pension will be used in the illustration.

Whynot Inc., a company with a December 31 year-end, establishes a defined benefit pension plan for eligible employees on January 1, 2003, at which time the plan's accrued benefit obligation (ABO) is estimated by an actuary to be $440,000. Whynot Inc. immediately fully funds the new plan by transferring $440,000 to a trustee. Over the next three years, the plan has the following history:

	Year-End December 31,		
	2003	**2004**	**2005**
Annual service cost	34,000	40,000	56,000
Interest rate for ABO	10%	10%	10%
Expected return on assets	10%	10%	10%
Actual return on assets	38,000	48,400	50,000
Payments to trustee	34,000	43,000	100,000
Payments to retirees	28,000	32,800	41,000

All amortization periods are ten years. Effective January 1, 2004, the pension plan was amended with a resulting past service cost of $330,000. An actuarial valuation of the plan's ABO was conducted as of December 31, 2005, at which time the ABO was estimated to be $1,030,000.

A spreadsheet capturing the above information is shown as Exhibit 14.2. The column headed "Expense" keeps track of the various components of pension expense, and the column headed "Cash Flow" does the same for the actual cash outflows from Whynot Inc. to the trustee of the defined benefit pension plan. The column headed ABL/A, for "Accrued Benefit Liability or Asset," refers to the balancing account. These three columns represent actual general ledger accounts for the company. The remaining four columns represent information that is disclosed in the company's pension footnote, as required by Section 3461. The abbreviations stand for the following:

- "ABO" is accrued benefit obligation
- "PA" is plan assets
- "UPSC" is unrecognized past service cost
- "UEG/L" is unrecognized experience gain or loss

Now let's go through the spreadsheet. In row 1, the opening balances of the ABO and PA are entered. Since both are $440,000, the pension plan is neither over- nor underfunded at this point. Notice that neither the ABO nor the PA is entered into Whynot Inc.'s formal general ledger accounts. We pick up the story in the following table:

Row	Comments
2	The $34,000 current annual service cost for the year 2003 increases the pension expense for that year, as well as increasing the ABO.
3	Interest cost on the ABO is accrued, at 10%. This also increases pension expense.
4	Since Whynot's management expects that the pension plan's assets will earn a 10% return, this amount (10% of the opening PA for the year 2003) is added to the PA and reduces the year's pension expense.
5	Since the actual return in the year 2003 was only $38,000, a $6,000 asset loss ($44,000 – $38,000) resulted. GAAP permit this type of accounting item to be deferred, with any required amortization beginning the following year if the cumulative balance in the UEG/L column is greater than 10% of the year's opening balance for the larger of the ABO or PA.
6	$34,000 was paid by Whynot to the trustee. This was a cash outflow from Whynot and an increase in PA.
7	$28,000 was paid by the trustee. This payment reduced the plan's obligation to the retirees (i.e., reduced ABO), and also the plan's assets (PA).

8   The formal pension entry for 2003 is:

DR Pension expense   34,000
     CR Cash   34,000

The ABO of $490,000, the PA of $484,000, and the Unrecognized Experience Loss of $6,000 are disclosed in Whynot's pension footnote.

9   The plan was amended, with the result that the ABO increased immediately by $330,000. Perhaps Whynot's union successfully negotiated a much better defined benefit plan. GAAP permit the past service cost of $330,000 to be amortized over the future.

10 The new ABO is $820,000.

11 In the year 2004, the current annual service cost is $40,000, so both pension expense and ABO are increased by this amount.

12 Since the balance in the UEG/L column is less than 10% of the greater of ABO or PA, no amortization is required.

13 The 10% interest cost is accrued, thus increasing both pension expense and ABO in 2004.

14 The opening balance of PA in the year 2004 is $484,000, so the expected return in this year at 10% is $48,400, and this amount is added to PA and deducted from the year's pension expense. Also, notice that since the expected return is equal to this year's actual return, there is no addition to the UEG/L column.

15 The previously unrecognized (in the formal general ledger accounts, that is) past service cost due to the pension plan improvement starts to be amortized, over ten years in our example. So $33,000 is added to pension expense this year, and the UPSC column is reduced by the same amount.

16 The $43,000 paid by Whynot to the trustee reduces Whynot's cash and increases PA.

17 The $32,800 paid by the trustee out of PA to the retirees has no effect on Whynot's formal accounting records, but reduces both PA and ABO.

18 The journal entry for the year ended December 31, 2004, is:

DR Pension expense   106,600
     CR Cash   43,000
     CR Accrued benefit liability   63,600

This last account item, "Accrued benefit liability" (symbolized as "ABL/A" on the spreadsheet), is equal to the year's change in the net balance of all the off-balance-sheet accounts (the ABO, the PA, the UPSC, and the UEG/L). It is sort of a "link" between the formal general ledger records of the company, and the footnote-only disclosed details of the defined benefit pension plan. There was no ABL/A last year, since the net balance of these off-balance-sheet accounts was zero.

19 to 27 These rows explain, in a way similar to the above, the "story" in the remaining time period up to the end of 2005.

The Pension Funding Decision

Legislation, income tax rules, and the company's general cash budgeting have a strong influence on pension plan funding.

When companies establish defined benefit pension plans, they must follow legal requirements for funding such plans. Also, the tax deductibility of company contributions to such plans, as well as the (usually) tax-free status of plan earnings, influence plan-funding decisions.

Finally, firms with pension plans have a wide range of other uses for cash flows generated by operating activities. Examples include plant expansions, corporate acquisitions, debt retirement, and dividend increases. So firms sometimes reduce or even forgo funding of the current period's pension expense—provided minimum legal funding requirements are satisfied—to meet competing investment or financing cash needs.

The longer-term pension funding strategy that a firm chooses to follow is determined not only by its internal cash flow needs but also by many complex economic forces. Two studies have sought to explain variation in firms' funding strategies by examining the relationship between *funding ratios*—plan assets divided by accrued pension obligations—and a variety of variables that represent the economic incentives (and costs) associated with pension funding.[7] These economic incentives can be broadly classified as: (1) tax incentives, (2) finance incentives, (3) labour incentives, and (4) contracting/political cost incentives.[8]

The findings included the following:

- Firms with high effective marginal tax rates tended to have higher funding ratios—higher marginal tax rates provide an incentive to overfund.

- Funding ratios were positively associated with capital availability (finance incentives) and with unionization (labour incentives)—that is, firms with less stringent capital constraints and larger union membership had higher funding ratios.

- Funding ratios were negatively associated with debt-to-equity ratios (contracting incentives) which measure how close firms are to violating debt covenant restrictions. This means that firms with more "precarious" debt/equity ratios tend to fund a lower proportion of their pension obligations.

In general, variables designed to measure political costs were not found to be significant determinants of pension funding ratios.

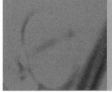

Recap
While economic incentives appear to influence long-run corporate pension funding strategies, our understanding of this complex multidimensional decision is far from complete. More work remains to be done on this important issue by researchers and others.

The Pension Footnote

CANADIAN NATIONAL
RAILWAY
www.cn.ca

Exhibit 14.3 reproduces the pension footnote (as amended) from the 2001 annual report of the Canadian National Railway Company. The information in the footnote is used to construct the spreadsheet shown as Exhibit 14.4 on page 682. In effect, we are adopting the role of an external financial analyst, using the spreadsheet to assist us in interpreting the disclosures in the company's pension footnote.

Exhibit 14.3 CANADIAN NATIONAL RAILWAY COMPANY

Pension Footnote from 2001 Audited Financial Statements

13 Pensions

The Company has retirement benefit plans under which substantially all employees are entitled to benefits at retirement age, generally based on compensation and length of service and/or contributions. The tables that follow pertain to all such plans. However, the following descriptions relate solely to the Company's main pension plan, the CN Pension Plan (the Pension Plan). The Company's other pension plans are not significant.

Description of plan

The Pension Plan is a contributory defined benefit pension plan that covers substantially all CN employees. It provides for pensions based mainly on years of service and final average pensionable earnings and is generally applicable from the first day of employment. Indexation of pensions is provided after retirement through a gain (loss) sharing mechanism, subject to guaranteed minimum increases. An independent trust company is the Trustee of the Canadian National Railways Pension Trust Funds (CN Pension Trust Funds). As Trustee, the trust company performs certain duties which include holding legal title to the assets of the CN Pension Funds and ensuring that the Company, as Administrator, complies with the provisions of the Pension Plan and the related legislation.

Funding policy

Employee contributions to the Pension Plan are determined by the plan rules. Company contributions are in accordance with the requirements of the Government of Canada legislation, The Pension Benefits Standards Act, 1985, and are determined by actuarial valuations conducted at least on a triennial basis. These valuations are made in accordance with legislative requirements and with the recommendations of the Canadian Institute of Actuaries for the valuation of pension plans.

Description of fund assets

The assets of the Pension Plan are accounted for separately in the CN Pension Trust Funds and consist of cash and short-term investments, bonds, mortgages, Canadian and foreign equities, real estate, and oil and gas assets.

(a) Change in benefit obligation

In millions Year ended December 31,	2001	2000
Benefit obligation at beginning of year	$10,855	$9,935
Interest cost	701	690
Actuarial loss	94	730
Service cost	92	70
Plan participants' contributions	73	74
Foreign currency changes	6	3
Benefit payments and transfers	(665)	(647)
Benefit obligation at end of year	$11,156	$10,855

(b) Change in plan assets

In millions Year ended December 31,	2001	2000
Fair value of plan assets at beginning of year	$12,455	$11,768
Employer contributions	69	59
Plan participants' contributions	73	74
Foreign currency changes	6	3
Actual return on plan assets	(175)	1,198
Benefit payments and transfers	(665)	(647)
Fair value of plan assets at end of year	$11,763	$12,455

(c) Funded status

In millions December 31,	2001	2000
Excess of fair value of plan assets over benefit obligation at end of year [1]	$607	$1,600
Unrecognized net actuarial gain[1]	(537)	(1,652)
Unrecognized net transition obligation	39	59
Unrecognized prior service cost	133	153
Net amount recognized	$242	$160

(1) Subject to future reduction for gain sharing under the terms of the plan.

(d) Amount recognized in the Consolidated Balance Sheet

In millions December 31,	2001	2000
Prepaid benefit cost (Note 6)	$251	$166
Accrued benefit cost	(9)	(6)
Net amount recognized	$242	$160

(e) Components of net periodic benefit cost

In millions Year ended December 31,	2001	2000	1999
Interest cost	$701	$690	$632
Service cost	92	70	95
Amortization of net transition obligation	20	19	19
Amortization of prior service cost	20	19	20
Expected return on plan assets	(846)	(792)	(732)
Recognized net actuarial loss	—	—	23
Net periodic benefit cost (income)	$(13)	$6	$57

(f) Weighted-average assumptions

December 31,	2001	2000	1999
Discount rate	6.50%	6.50%	7.00%
Rate of compensation increase	4.00%	4.25%	4.25%
Expected return on plan assets for year ending December 31	9.00%	9.00%	9.00%

Before we look at the spreadsheet that we have constructed from CN's pension footnote, we'll examine the note itself.

The first four paragraphs generally describe the main CN plan. We learn that:

- the plan is a contributory plan;
- it's a defined benefit pension plan;
- the pension benefit is based upon years of service and final average pensionable earnings; and
- it apparently vests immediately on employment.

Part (a), "Change in benefit obligation," shows how the ABO (notice that CN calls this the "benefit obligation") changes over the two years presented, 2001 and the comparative year 2000. Part (b), "Change in plan assets," shows how the plan assets—which CN measures at their fair value—have changed over the two years. Notice that "Benefits payments and transfers" in this part are $665 million, the same as in part (a). This makes sense since the $665 million was paid out *from* the plan assets *to* the pensioners. Also notice that the degree to which the plan is overfunded has changed over the three year-ends presented, as follows (all amounts in $ millions):

Date	Fair Value of Plan Assets	Benefit Obligation	Overfunded/Underfunded	Ratio of Plan Assets to Benefit Obligation
December 31, 1999	$11,768	$9,935	$1,833 overfunded	1.18
December 31, 2000	$12,445	$10,855	$1,590 overfunded	1.15
December 31, 2001	$11,763	$11,156	$607 overfunded	1.05

Therefore, the plan seems relatively less well-funded since the ratio of the fair value of plan assets to benefit obligation has steadily decreased from 1.18 to 1.05 over the three years.

Part (c), "Funded status," reconciles the $607 million overfunding as of December 31, 2001, that we just derived in the above table, to the $242 million amount that CN has recorded on its balance sheet. The reconciling items include an unrecognized net actuarial gain of $537 million, an unrecognized net transition obligation of $39 million, and an unrecognized prior service cost of $133 million. CN tells us that it "breaks" the $242 million into two parts on its balance sheet: a $251 million "Prepaid benefit cost" (which, according to Section 3461's terminology, is an "accrued benefit asset"), and a $9 million "Accrued benefit cost" (called an "accrued benefit liability," according to Section 3461).

Part (e) of the pension note discloses the components of CN's annual pension expense. In 2001, this was a *credit* of $13 million, while in 2000 this expense was a *debit* of $6 million and in 1999 it was an expense (debit) of $57 million. Let's compare the expected and actual returns on plan assets for 2001 and 2000 to see how this smoothing component affected CN's pension expense ($ millions):

Year	Expected Return on Plan Assets (from part [e] of the note)	Actual Return on Plan Assets (from part [b] of note)	Variance
2001	$846 gain	$175 loss	$1,021 favourable to CN's earnings
2000	$792 gain	$1,198 gain	$406 unfavourable to CN's earnings

So the 2001 pension *income* of $13 million was driven by the $1,021 million favourable variance between the actual pension asset loss for the year and the expected gain; this sort of result is what irritates critics of the built-in smoothing effects of GAAP pension accounting, as we saw at the beginning of this chapter.

Part (f), "Weighted average assumptions," discloses CN's various rate assumptions. We can see that the expected return on plan assets has remained constant over the three years at 9.00%. Clearly, as CN's own experience has shown (with a loss of $175 million on the pension asset portfolio in 2001), this assumption does not reflect current experience. But keep in mind this is supposed to be a long-term expected rate of return (Section 3461, para. 76). The question is, though, how susceptible to income smoothing is such a choice in the hands of management, even when attested to by an external auditor? Hard to tell, especially in a volatile market; the implications for quality of earnings are serious.

Now, let's examine a spreadsheet (in Exhibit 14.4) for CN's defined benefit pension plan information, similar to the one we introduced previously with the hypothetical Whynot Inc. example in Exhibit 14.2 ($ millions).

The rows in the spreadsheet are numbered from 1 to 13 for reference. We've taken the information from CN's pension footnote and inserted it into the appropriate columns and rows of the spreadsheet, ensuring that the final totals in row 13 add to the amounts given in the note. Along the way, we've learned a few things about CN's defined benefit pension accounting:

- CN contributed only $69 million to the pension plan trustee. This seems rather low, especially during a year in which the plan assets incurred a loss and the accrued benefit obligation rose. Is CN conserving cash for some reason? Perhaps an examination of CN's cash flow statement and the accompanying footnotes would reveal if this is the case.

- Therefore, the journal entry that CN recorded in its books must have been:

DR	Accrued benefits liability/asset (which, recall, CN calls by other names)	$82 million	
	CR Pension income		$13 million
	CR Cash		69 million

- There was no amortization of the opening balance of $1,652 million (a credit) in "Unrecognized net actuarial gain." Of course, the huge unfavourable variance of $1,021 million due to the difference between the pension plan's actual and expected returns reduced this amount over the year, so that by the end of the year it was below the 10% corridor level. But Section 3461, para. 88 requires that the corridor test be made "as of the beginning of the period."

Funded Status Reconciliation

We explained earlier that neither pension plan assets nor liabilities appear on the balance sheet of the plan sponsor but are instead shown on the separate statements of the plan trustee. The Wildcat Corporation example (Tables 14.1 through 14.4) showed that when the future was known with certainty the (off-balance-sheet) pension assets are exactly equal to the (off-balance-sheet) pension liability for funded plans. In the not-so-simple real world, where, as we have seen, future events are uncertain and changes in pension assumptions occur, *the off-balance-sheet pension assets and liabilities will usually differ*. When pension assets exceed liabilities, a plan is

Exhibit 14.4 CANADIAN NATIONAL RAILWAY COMPANY

Pension Spreadsheet for 2001

	Expense	Cash Flow	Accrued Benefit Liability/ Asset	Accrued Benefit Obligations (CN calls this the "benefit obligation")	Plan Assets	Unrecognized Net Actuarial Gain	Unrecognized Net Transition Obligation	Unrecognized Prior Service Cost
1 (31/12/2000)			160	-10,855	12,455	-1,652	59	153
2 Annual service cost	92			-92				
3 Interest cost	701			-701				
4 Amortization of net transition obligation	20						-20	
5 Amortization of prior service cost	20							-20
6 Return on plan assets	-846				-175	1,021		
7 Actuarial loss on benefit obligation				-94		94		
8 Plan participants' contributions				-73	73			
9 Foreign currency changes				-6	6			
10 Benefit payments and transfers				665	-665			
11 Employer contributions		-69			69			
12 Plug to accrued benefit liability/asset			82					
13 (31/12/2001)	-13	-69	242	-11,156	11,763	-537	39	133

[Minus signs signify credits.]

overfunded. If pension liabilities exceed plan assets, a plan is **underfunded.** Since both the pension plan assets and liabilities are off the plan sponsor's balance sheet, the **funded status** of the plan can only be determined from footnote disclosures. This disclosure is important to statement readers, since the plan sponsor—the reporting entity—is ultimately responsible for underfunded pension plans. In this subsection, we illustrate and interpret the funded status footnote disclosure.

To understand the funded status of a plan, we must understand what factors cause the pension plan assets and liabilities to change over time. Figure 14.4 displays the most common causes for increases and decreases in plan assets. As disclosure practice improves over time, the availability of this information in published footnotes will increase.

- Item A represents the beginning-of-period market value of the pension plan assets.

- The dollar value of plan assets is increased by item B, the actual return on plan assets. In very bad investment years, item B can be negative, thereby reducing plan assets.

- Plan assets are further increased by item C, the amount that the plan sponsor funds during the period, and by any contributions by plan participants (if applicable).

- Retirees receive benefits during the period; these benefits are disbursed by the plan trustee and reduce plan assets, as indicated by item D.

- The end-of-period market value of plan assets is item E.

Figure 14.5 shows changes in the pension plan liabilities—the ABO.

- Item F is the start-of-period present value of expected future benefits that will ultimately be paid both to active and already retired employees.

- Item G represents the increase in benefits that active employees continue to earn from additional years of work. This increase in the accrued benefit obligation is service cost.

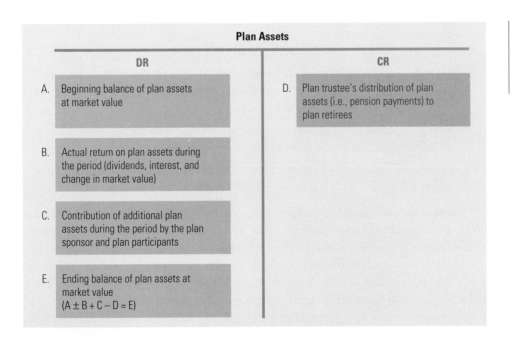

Plan Assets

DR	CR
A. Beginning balance of plan assets at market value	D. Plan trustee's distribution of plan assets (i.e., pension payments) to plan retirees
B. Actual return on plan assets during the period (dividends, interest, and change in market value)	
C. Contribution of additional plan assets during the period by the plan sponsor and plan participants	
E. Ending balance of plan assets at market value ($A \pm B + C - D = E$)	

FIGURE 14.4
CAUSES OF INCREASES AND DECREASES IN PLAN ASSETS

FIGURE 14.5
CAUSES OF
INCREASES AND
DECREASES IN
BENEFIT
OBLIGATION

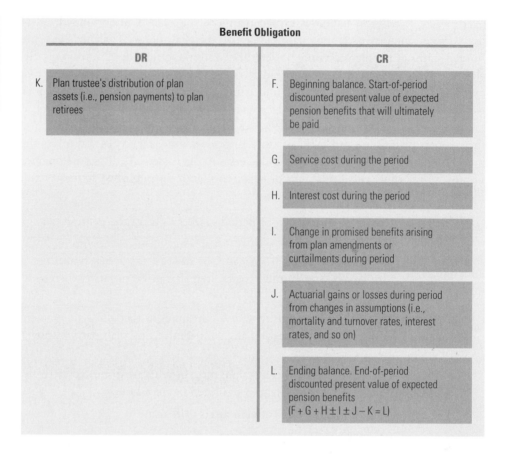

Benefit Obligation

DR	CR
K. Plan trustee's distribution of plan assets (i.e., pension payments) to plan retirees	F. Beginning balance. Start-of-period discounted present value of expected pension benefits that will ultimately be paid
	G. Service cost during the period
	H. Interest cost during the period
	I. Change in promised benefits arising from plan amendments or curtailments during period
	J. Actuarial gains or losses during period from changes in assumptions (i.e., mortality and turnover rates, interest rates, and so on)
	L. Ending balance. End-of-period discounted present value of expected pension benefits $(F + G + H \pm I \pm J - K = L)$

- As time passes, the present value of future pension benefit payouts becomes larger because the number of discount periods is getting smaller. This increase in the discounted present value of the liability represents interest cost, which increases the ABO (as shown in item H).

- Changes in economic and other social conditions cause firms to adjust promised benefits, as indicated by item I. These prior service cost adjustments either raise the ABO (when the plan is sweetened) or reduce the ABO (when benefits are curtailed).

- The assumptions used in estimating the pension liability lead to gains or losses due to changing medical, lifestyle, and economic conditions. Denoted by item J, these increases (or decreases) in the ABO can also arise from revised interest rate assumptions.

- Item K represents the payout of retirement benefits to participants. This is the offsetting debit to the item D credit in Figure 14.4.

- Finally, the ending ABO balance (item L) is the net result of each of the preceding items $(L = F + G + H \pm I \pm J - K)$.

Because the pension assets and liabilities do not appear on the sponsor's balance sheet and because the plan can be either over- or underfunded, disclosure of the funded status of the plan is required under GAAP.

The smoothing objective that pervades Section 3461 keeps numerous gains and losses that have already occurred off the balance sheet and income statement. These deferred gains and losses are brought into income slowly over current and future years through components 4–6. Until these past gains and losses are totally amortized, the balance sheet will not reflect the current *economic status* of the pension plan. The current economic status of a pension plan at a given date is the difference between the fair value of the plan assets at that date and the discounted present value of the expected liability. This liability should be computed using projected future compensation levels—this is the projected benefit obligation that results in the ABO.

The AcSB believes the current economic status of the pension plan at the balance sheet date constitutes the benchmark against which companies' balance sheet pension accounts ought to be compared. For this reason, companies provide footnote disclosure that reconciles (i.e., explains the difference between) the *current* economic status of the pension plan and the *recorded* balance sheet amounts. Part (c), "Funded status," of CN's pension footnote described and analyzed above, is an example of such disclosure.

When the economic status of the plan becomes the focus, the funded status portion of the pension footnote overcomes some of the confusing smoothing-driven complexities that pervade pension accounting. The footnote reconciliation directs attention to the *current* status of the plan rather than to *past* funding decisions.

A plan's current funding status can give clues regarding future funding. Companies with greatly overfunded plans can suspend funding and use the cash for other operating purposes. On the other hand, underfunded plans may be an indicator of past and continuing cash flow difficulties. Recall that we had a question about CN's cash flow viability since its plan was becoming relatively less overfunded.

Because pension funding status is important for assessing current and future cash flows of a firm, we need to stress how sensitive the component asset and liability measures are to changes in interest rates. A 1% decrease in the discount rate will typically boost the estimated pension obligation (either accumulated benefit obligation or projected benefit obligation) by 10% to 15%.[9] For firms with a relatively young workforce where the pension commitments will be paid 20 to 30 years in the future, small changes in interest (settlement) rate assumptions can cause large increases in the present value of these estimated obligations. Why is there this relatively large multiplier effect from small changes in interest rates? This effect is due to the impact of duration—the further into the future the cash flows are to be paid out, the greater the impact of a change in interest rates on the present value of those cash flows.

The effect of a 1% change in interest rates on the asset side is typically much smaller since fixed income investments generally represent only a fraction of the pension asset portfolio and the maturity of those investments is typically much shorter. Therefore, even modest declines in interest rates can easily shift firms from being in an overfunded position in one year to an underfunded position in the next year.

Recap
The pension footnote provides important information about the current economic status of the pension plan. This allows readers to gain insight regarding expected future pension-related cash flows.

The Structure of Section 3461 and Accounting for Employee Future Benefits (EFBs)

With all its controversial aspects, Section 3461 is still a major advance in accounting for employee future benefits. We will provide an overview of the section, highlighting some of its important features in addition to the items that we have already mentioned in describing GAAP for defined benefit pension plans.

Objective and Basic Principles of Section 3461 The first two paragraphs of the section read as follows:

PURPOSE

.001 This Section establishes standards for the recognition, measurement, and disclosure of the cost of employee future benefits. It requires an entity to recognize the cost of retirement benefits and certain post-employment benefits over the periods in which employees render services to the entity in return for the benefits. Other post-employment benefits are recognized when the event that obligates the entity occurs.

OBJECTIVE AND BASIC PRINCIPLES

.002 The objective of accounting for the cost of employee future benefits is to recognize a liability and an expense in the reporting period in which an employee has provided the service that gives rise to the benefits. Benefit plans are considered part of an employee's compensation arrangement. Certain benefit plans oblige an entity to provide benefits to an employee in future periods for service provided by the employee in the current period. The cost of providing future benefits under such plans is recognized in the period in which benefits are earned by the employee because the obligation to provide benefits arises as the employee renders the service.

These two paragraphs set accounting for employee future benefits in Canada along the course of full accrual accounting, which is similar to the situation in the U.S. The oft-cited concept of "matching" underpins these paragraphs, which in turn set the general policy for accounting for employee future benefits. As we saw with accounting for defined benefit pension plans, though, the section makes many compromises along the way, so that the normative goals set out in these first two paragraphs, and the matching principle which provides their foundation, are only partly achieved.

In paragraph 3, the section reminds readers of the definition of a liability which is set out in Section 1000, "Financial Statement Concepts," and then argues that "[a]n obligation for employee future benefits possesses these characteristics," thus reinforcing the adoption of a full accrual approach to such obligations. Paragraph 4 points out that employee future benefits can be provided in two ways—as part of a defined contribution plan or as part of a defined benefit plan—and that the latter "involves an actuarial valuation and an attribution method," where "attribution method" is the method for allocating the costs of a defined benefit plan to accounting periods.

The scope of the section may be summarized by the following (recall that this is how we introduced the chapter):

Companies typically provide their employees with a variety of **future benefits,** in addition to current-period salary, wages, bonuses, and other current-year benefits. These future benefits can be classified as follows:

- **future benefits that accumulate over time,** including (a) postretirement pensions, and other postretirement benefits such as health care and life insurance; and (b) preretirement benefits, such as post-employment benefits (long- and short-term disability, salary continuance, job training, severance) and compensated absences (such as vesting sick days, sabbaticals)

- **future benefits that are not a function of time** (i.e., the benefit is the same regardless of the number of years of service by the employee); included in this category are benefits such as preretirement compensated parental leave, preretirement post-employment non-service related disability, and termination benefits such as severance pay

The section sets out several definitions of key terms that "have been adopted for the purpose of this Section" (paragraph 9), and additional technical terms are defined throughout the section. The section includes a "Glossary of Defined Terms" following paragraph 172. Perhaps unfortunately, many companies that comply with the accounting standards set out in this section do not fully adopt the terminology—we saw this when we analyzed the Canadian National Railway Company's defined benefit pension footnote. This presents an additional challenge to those who wish to understand financial statements in this area, and reinforces the notion that close reading for meaning is crucial.

Defined contribution versus defined benefit plans: substance over form: All employee future benefits (EFBs) are provided by the employer under one of two general typologies: defined contribution (DC) plans or defined benefit (DB) plans (paragraphs 10 to 13). These paragraphs make several important points:

- Employees bear more risk under DC plans than under DB plans; the opposite case pertains to employers.
- The "economic substance of the plan established by its terms and conditions" determines whether a plan is DC or DB. This classification, based on substance over form and representational faithfulness, is crucial in accounting for EFBs, since the accounting for DC plans is radically different from the accounting for DB plans as we saw earlier in this chapter.
- Some plans may contain both DC and DB components, and these should be "accounted for separately according to their substance." Again, substance over form is intended to be the basic principle in this section.

Defined contribution EFBs: Paragraphs 14 to 23 set out Canadian GAAP for DC plans. Notice that even though there are some complications with respect to how the particular plan's defined contributions for a period are determined (i.e., defining the contribution might, in any given instance, be a bit tricky and require some close attention), these paragraphs basically require that the contribution amounts for a period be expensed in the period they are incurred. The only complications involve deferrals and accruals in order to determine the amount of *input* that the employer is responsible for in a period.

Defined benefit EFBs: Paragraphs 24 to 134, the bulk of the section, are devoted to DB plans. We examined important features of these paragraphs when we discussed and explained defined benefit pension plans earlier in the chapter. In this part of the chapter, we will briefly refer to some additional aspects of DB plans covered in these paragraphs. In the next part of the chapter, we will describe some aspects of nonpension defined plans, such as postretirement health plans.

One key thing to notice in these paragraphs is that *funding* and *accounting for a DB plan's costs and obligations* are two separate (although related) processes. In other words, costs and liabilities must be accounted for when a DB plan exists, even though no cash has left the employer accounting entity. Before the mid-1980s, when Section 3461's predecessor Section 3460 was promulgated, there was a tendency to use an almost cash-basis approach to accounting for DB plans. No costs/expenses were accrued for (most) DB pension plans (although some disclosure was required in many cases), and postretirement defined benefits such as health care were not accrued at all.

Paragraph 27 provides a sort of "ten-step" overview guide to accounting for DB plans.

Paragraphs 29 to 33 discuss recognition, i.e., the point in time when DB plan expenses/costs and liabilities should be recorded in the accounts of the employer. The key here is again substance over form, in combination with Section 1000's definition of a liability, which is broader than a strictly legal obligation. The examples given in paragraph 33 are worth reviewing, since they help us understand the types of "triggering events" that would require recognition of DB plan expenses/costs and liabilities.

Paragraphs 34 to 95 set out accounting measurement rules for DB plans, from the employer's perspective. We have already described many aspects of these paragraphs, so we will just highlight some additional worthy issues:

- Paragraph 34 requires that the accrued benefit obligation (ABO) should be determined by taking into consideration "future salary levels or cost escalation." In other words, a career perspective is adopted for the employees covered by a particular DB plan (see also paragraphs 56 to 65).

- Paragraphs 38 to 41 deal with "attribution," which is the process of determining the number of accounting periods over which the DB plan costs should be expensed. Looking at just one of the examples provided in paragraph 40 will serve to show some of the possible complexities involved. The fact that determining the attribution period requires judgment in some cases and could be susceptible to manipulation has implications for the quality of earnings.

- Paragraph 94 requires that "*[f]or a defined benefit plan, the effect of any temporary deviation from the plan should be recognized in income immediately.*" For example, a company might decide to make up a shortfall in a DB health plan for retirees (paragraph 95), and therefore the amount of the shortfall provided by the company should be expensed in the period in which the company's contribution is made.

Other Accounting Aspects of Defined Benefit Pension Plans

In this part of the chapter, we briefly describe additional aspects of Section 3461's accounting for defined benefit pension plans.

- Paragraph 3461.102 sets an upper limit on the amount that a company may include in an accrued benefit asset. An accrued benefit asset is created under the rules of Section 3461 when the accumulated cash payments to the plan's trustee exceed the pension expenses recognized since the beginning of the plan. As we saw above, this amount is equal to the excess of the PA over the ABO (the plan surplus), "net of all unamortized balances for past service costs, actuarial gains and losses and transitional asset or transitional obligation" (Section 3461.103). If the company is not fully entitled to the plan surplus because of legal or other restrictions, Section 3461 requires that the company reduce the accrued benefit asset by a valuation allowance so that the remaining accrued benefit asset is equal to the amount that can be realized in the future.

- Plan settlements and curtailments are described by Section 3461 as follows: "A curtailment is an event that, under a defined benefit plan, results in: (i) a significant reduction of the expected years of future service of active employees; or (ii) the elimination, for a significant number of active employees, of the right to earn defined benefits for some, or all, of their future services," 3461.111(a), and a "settlement is a transaction in which an entity substantially discharges or settles all, or part, of an accrued benefit obligation ... [such as] (i) making lump-sum cash payments to employees in exchange for their rights to receive specified benefits; and (ii) purchasing non-participating insurance contracts," 3461.111(c). Under a settlement, the employees continue to earn benefits by providing services to the company, but the company has shifted its actuarial and investment risks onto a third party. Under a curtailment, employees no longer earn benefits, but the company's actuarial and investment risks are not eliminated. Section 3461 requires that the company recognize the "gain or loss resulting from remeasuring the accrued benefit obligation and plan assets at the date of settlement together with the related unamortized actuarial gain or loss ... [but] unrecognized past service costs are not recognized at the date of settlement since employees will continue to provide services in the future" (3461.112). In contrast, "a curtailment is accounted for by recognizing as a loss the unamortized past service costs attributable to the employees whose ability to earn benefits has been curtailed, together with the gain or loss from remeasuring the related accrued benefit obligation to the extent this gain or loss does not represent a reversal of unamortized actuarial gains or losses or previous years' service costs ..." (3461.112). With many companies striving to move their employees off defined benefit plans, accounting for settlements and curtailments is becoming very important.

Employee Future Benefits Other Than Pensions

Many companies promise to provide health care and life insurance to employees and their spouses after retirement. Analyzing these promises indicates that—like pensions—the intent of these benefits is to attract and retain a highly qualified workforce. Under a strict interpretation of accrual accounting, an expense should be recognized over the period of employment as employees qualify for these postretirement benefits. However, up until the advent of Section 3461, few companies with postretirement benefit plans made such expense accruals. Instead, "pay-as-you-go" accounting was employed—that is, as cash payments were made to provide the health-care benefit coverage to retired employees, the amount of the cash outflow was charged to expense. No liability appeared on the books. Worse yet, few companies funded the plans as benefits were earned. As a result of these circumstances, by the mid-1990s significant unrecorded (off-balance-sheet) liabilities for postretirement benefits existed, but periodic income did not reflect their continued growth.

To correct this situation, the AcSB required in 1999 that such arrangements be accounted for in a way similar to defined benefit pension plans. An example of accounting for postretirement benefits other than pensions is provided by the Canadian National Railway Company in Exhibit 14.5. In the United States, accrual accounting for these benefits was required earlier than in Canada, in 1993.[10]

Exhibit 14.5 CANADIAN NATIONAL RAILWAY COMPANY

Employee Future Benefits Other Than Pensions

Notes to Consolidated Financial Statements

9 Other liabilities and deferred credits

In millions December 31,	2001	2000
Personal injury and other claims	$ 379	$ 373
Workforce reduction provisions, net of current portion *(A)*	340	376
Accrual for postretirement benefits other than pensions *(B)*	258	231
Environmental reserve, net of current portion	73	64
Deferred credits and other	246	149
	$1,296	$1,193

A. Workforce reduction provisions

The workforce reduction provisions, which cover employees in both Canada and the United States, are mainly comprised of severance payments, the majority of which will be disbursed within the next five years. Other elements of the provisions mainly include early retirement incentives and bridging to early retirement. Payments for severance and other elements of the provisions have reduced the provisions by $169 million for the year ended December 31, 2001 ($189 million for the year ended December 31, 2000). The aggregate provisions amount to $491 million at December 31, 2001.

B. Post-retirement benefits other than pensions

(i) Change in benefit obligation

In millions Year ended December 31,	2001	2000
Benefit obligation at beginning of year	$242	$230
Amendments	25	—
Actuarial loss	20	3
Interest cost	19	15
Service cost	11	8
Foreign currency changes	6	3
Transfer from other plans	5	—
Benefits paid	(19)	(17)
Benefit obligation at end of year	$309	$242

(ii) Funded status

In millions December 31,	2001	2000
Unfunded benefit obligation at end of year	$309	$242
Unrecognized net actuarial loss	(26)	(8)
Unrecognized prior service cost	(25)	(3)
Accrued benefit cost for postretirement benefits other than pensions	$258	$231

(iii) Components of net periodic benefit cost

In millions Year ended December 31,	2001	2000	1999
Interest cost	$19	$15	$15
Service cost	11	8	8
Amortization of prior service cost	3	1	1
Recognized net actuarial loss	2	1	2
Net periodic benefit cost	$35	$25	$26

(iv) Weighted-average assumptions

December 31,	2001	2000	1999
Discount rate	6.97%	6.95%	7.39%
Rate of compensation increase	4.00%	4.25%	4.25%

For measurement purposes, increases in the per capita cost of covered health care benefits were assumed to be 8% for 2002 and 6% for 2001. It is assumed the rate will decrease gradually to an ultimate rate of 6% for 2004 and remain at that level thereafter.

A one-percentage-point change in the health care trend rate would not cause a material change in the Company's net periodic benefit cost nor the postretirement benefit obligation.

The computations for postretirement benefits expense and measures of the liability generally parallel the format for pension expense and liability. Notice in Exhibit 14.5 that the net postretirement benefit cost of $35 million for 2001 does not include a reduction for return on plan assets in CN's case since—given the absence of disclosures about plan assets—the footnote indicates that the plan is unfunded. This is a common difference from DB pension plans, which are usually funded because of legal requirements.

Both Section 3461 and the U.S. *SFAS No. 106* incorporate smoothing devices that are virtually identical to components 4–6 in pension accounting. Specifically, when plans are funded, postretirement benefit expense is reduced by the *expected* return on plan assets; to accomplish this, asset gains or losses are deferred off balance sheet. Similarly, these gains and losses are accumulated and amortized as component 4 if they exceed a 10% corridor, just as in pension accounting. Pension component 5—amortization of transition liability—also exists in postretirement benefits accounting. Finally, a counterpart to pension component 6—amortization of prior service costs—exists as well in instances in which firms enhance or reduce the level of postretirement benefits.

One difference between accounting for pensions and accounting for postretirement benefits is that postretirement benefits are rarely tied to salary at retirement. The typical postretirement benefit plan promises employees full coverage (e.g., comprehensive postretirement health insurance) after a certain period of employment—say ten years. In such circumstances, the actuarially determined service cost of the plan will also be accrued over ten years.

Terminology alert: Employee future benefits other than pensions are often called **other post-employment benefits,** or OPEB.

> The actuarial and other assumptions that are required encompass factors such as (1) what proportion of employees will work for at least ten years and thereby qualify for benefits, (2) how long after retirement will the employee live to receive benefits, and (3) what will be the annual cost of providing the benefit over the retirement years.

Recap

The financial reporting and disclosures for postretirement benefit plans are similar to pension reporting and disclosures. However, most postretirement benefit plans are unfunded. Consequently, statement readers must be mindful of future cash outflows that these unfunded plans might precipitate.

Are Pension and Other Postemployment Benefits (OPEB) Disclosures Useful? The Research Evidence

Pension and other postretirement benefits disclosures and measurement rules are not simple. Detailed breakdowns of expense components abound (service cost, interest cost, etc.). But are the detailed components of pension and postretirement benefits expense, and footnote disclosures of asset and liability amounts, useful to statement readers in equity valuation? This section describes the research evidence on this question, which, though U.S.-based, is relevant to the Canadian financial reporting scene.

Do the Components of Net Periodic Pension Cost Have Different Equity Pricing Implications?

The decision of standard setters to require separate disclosure of the various components of net periodic pension expense, as detailed earlier in this chapter, raises an interesting question: Is the distinction between these pension expense components important to investors and other statement users? In valuing a company's stock, does the market assign different multiples to the various components of net periodic pension cost? For example, does a dollar of service cost have the same impact on share price as a dollar of amortization of unrecognized transition asset or obligation? If not, why not?

These questions are addressed in a research study that used Chapter 6's simple earnings capitalization equity valuation model, which expresses the market value of equity as the capitalized value of a firm's "permanent" or sustainable earnings.[11] The study conjectures that the various components of net periodic pension expense (service cost, interest cost, expected return on plan assets, and so on) convey different information regarding the firm's permanent earnings potential, and, therefore, each will have a different multiple applied to it. Specifically, service cost, interest cost, and *expected* return on plan assets are relatively permanent components of earnings that are likely to persist into the future. Consequently, these components are expected to have multiples approximating $1/r$, where r is the firm's cost of equity capital. Thus, if r is 8%, the multiple applied to these earnings components would be 1/0.08, or 12.5—that is, each dollar of these expenses would lower permanent earnings and thus lower market value by $12.50, while each dollar of expected return would raise market value by $12.50.

Other components of pension expense are viewed as more transitory, and, therefore, they are expected to have a lower multiple. This lower multiple reflects the presumably less sustainable nature of these items. For example, a lower multiple would be expected for the deferred portion of the current period's actual return on plan assets. The deferred portion reflects the difference between the actual and expected returns in the current period (the unexpected return), **which is expected to net to zero in the long run.** Because the unexpected gain or loss in a given year is *not* expected to recur, the multiple for this component period's pension expense is expected to be approximately 1. A multiple of 1—which is far below 12.5—would reflect the one-time transitory effect of this item on the market value of equity.

The researchers hypothesize that components 4, 5, and 6 provide no incremental information about future permanent earnings that is not already reflected in other pension expense components. For example, the recognition of total net deferrals of gains and losses from previous periods (component 4) and the amortization of the net transition assets or liability (component 5) are viewed as "stale" numbers, since they derive from past gains and losses. Accordingly, these components of pension expense are viewed as price-irrelevant, and so the multiple applied to these amounts is expected to be zero.

To see whether different multiples are applied to different components of pension cost in the determination of security prices, the researchers expressed market value of equity as a function of various nonpension- and pension-related components of net income, as depicted in Figure 14.6. Overall, the variables depicted in the figure (including the nonpension variables) explain roughly 55% to 65% of the variation in

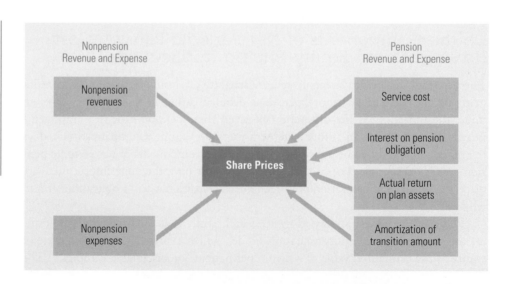

FIGURE 14.6
RESEARCH FINDINGS ON THE RELATIONSHIP BETWEEN SHARE PRICES AND COMPONENTS OF PENSION EXPENSE

year-end share prices across firms in the sample. The study found that the multiples applied to the pension variables in Figure 14.6 are *significantly different from one another*. This difference in multiples implies that the various components of pension expense affect share price differently. In particular, the multiple on the amortization of the transition amount (component 5) is essentially zero, thus suggesting that this item is viewed by the market as a low-quality component of earnings that is price-irrelevant. This finding is noteworthy because many of the firms that adopted U.S. standard *SFAS No. 87* early (in 1986) were in large overfunded positions—the fair market value of plan assets exceeded the projected benefit obligation. This overfunding resulted in a large and significant reduction in reported pension expense in the adoption year and in subsequent periods (as this transition asset was amortized). The study suggests that the market views this earnings boost to be largely transitory and not a significant determinant of equity prices. The study further shows that the multiples applied to the service cost, interest, and return on plan assets components of pension expense generally have the predicted sign and magnitude.

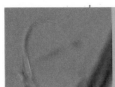

Recap

Research results suggest that the breakdown of the components of pension expense is useful to investors, since these components appear to have different share-price implications.

Equity Pricing Implications of Pension Cost: An Alternative View

The research just described tells us how the stock market appears to use pension disclosures in valuing firms. More recent articles have argued for a different approach.[12]

During the "bull market" of the late 1990s, "pension expense" gradually became "pension income" for some firms with greatly overfunded pension plans. This happened because rising equity values raised the base on which the expected return on plan assets is computed.[13] Consequently, the expected return—*which lowers pension expense*—ultimately exceeded charges to pension expense like service cost and interest cost. For example, in 1999 GE had pension *income* of US$1,380 million. Pension income grew so large that, for many firms, it had a discernible positive effect on operating income. Table 14.6 shows pension income as a percentage of pre-tax operating income in 1998 for several firms with a very high ratio of pension income to operating income.

Some analysts and financial writers have argued that deducting pension expense or adding pension income in the operating section of the income statement misstates *operating* income. They maintain that only service cost is a true current period *operating* item since service cost represents the present value of the increased pension payout arising from current services. Interest cost (component 2 of pension expense) is thought to be a financing cost and not an element of operating income. Similarly, these critics feel that the expected return on plan assets (component 3) should be shown in other income, just like the return on investment securities firms may hold.[14] Consistent with the research result in the previous section, amortization components 4 through 6 are considered valuation irrelevant. In these critics' view, only service cost is related to core operations and, accordingly, should receive a different valuation multiple than interest cost and return on plan assets.

These proponents further contend that OPEB items—other than service cost—also should not be included in operating income. Since OPEB obligations are seldom funded, return on assets is not a significant issue here; only interest cost is. Consequently, critics contend that the OPEB effect in isolation tends to *understate* operating income.

TABLE 14.6 RATIO OF 1998 PENSION INCOME TO 1998 PRE-TAX OPERATING INCOME FOR SELECTED FIRMS

Firm	Ratio
Boeing Company	8%
Crown Cork & Seal Company	12
Eaton Corporation	10
General Electric Company	7
GTE Corporation	8
International Business Machines Corporation	6
International Paper Company	8
Lucent Technologies Incorporated	15
Nicor Incorporated	10
PG&E Corporation	11
Tenneco Incorporated	10
Unocal Corporation	38

Source: Bear Stearns *Accounting Issues*, September 17, 1999.

Table 14.7 shows how the adjustments just described for pensions and OPEB would alter the year-to-year percentage decline in Bethlehem Steel's 1997 and 1998 operating income. Rather than a 6% decline in continuing, core operating income, the adjusted decline is 16%.

This view of pension/OPEB expense (income) as comprising of several nonoperating elements is controversial. Here's why. At the start of this chapter, we showed that in a world of certainty the return on plan assets would exactly offset interest cost. Pension expense would consist exclusively of service cost. In the real world, this offset won't be precise. Sometimes there will be a return shortfall. If this persists, pension expense will grow. In other words, this growing charge to pension expense means the firm will have to make up the shortfall by expending cash in later periods to adequately fund pension payouts. In this scenario, it seems that the entirety of pension expense (i.e., service cost, interest cost, and the reduction for return on plan assets)

TABLE 14.7 BETHLEHEM STEEL'S GROWTH RATE COMPARISON

(US$ in millions)	1998	1997	Year-over-Year Growth Rate
Reported operating income	$190	$374	
Add (deduct) loss (gain) on exiting a business	35	(135)	
Recurring *reported* operating income	225	239	–6%
Add back:			
Net pension cost	85	155	
Net other retirement benefit cost	165	150	
Deduct:			
Service cost—pensions	(55)	(48)	
Service cost—other retirement benefits	(9)	(7)	
Recurring *adjusted* operating income	$411	$489	–16%

Source: Bear Stearns *Accounting Issues*, September 17, 1999.

should be included as an expense in determining operating income. A growing year-to-year charge to pension expense means that events of the current and recent past periods point to the need for increased *future* pension funding to deliver the promised benefits.

At the other extreme, sometimes return on plan assets will exceed interest. When this persists, pension expense may reverse and become pension income and even grow over time, as happened in the late 1990s for some firms. This growing excess means that the firm's need to use additional resources in the future to fund benefits currently earned is shrinking. Again, in this scenario of rising returns, it seems appropriate to treat the entirety of pension income as an increase in operating income.

How to treat interest cost and return on pension plan assets in equity valuations is an unsettled issue. We expect continuing debate among financial observers.

Summary

Accounting for and reporting employee future benefits has moved closer to an accrual model, but several compromises have been made and the resulting GAAP are very controversial. Under Section 3461, pension expense consists of service cost, interest cost, expected return on plan assets, and three other components. The three latter components are smoothing mechanisms that avoid year-to-year volatility in pension expense but make pension accounting exceedingly complex, since many pension-related items are "off balance sheet."

Because some pension items are "off balance sheet," the AcSB requires firms to disclose the funded status of the plan—the difference between the market value of plan assets and the accrued benefit obligation—and to reconcile funded status to reported balance sheet amounts. An understanding of the funded status provides readers with an improved basis for assessing future operating cash flow.

The reporting rules for nonpension future employee benefit plans closely parallel the pension accounting rules. Prior to the issuance of Section 3461, few companies funded postretirement benefits other than pensions. Consequently, significant amounts of off-balance-sheet liabilities exist for many firms. Careful scrutiny of the footnote disclosures will provide analysts with an improved basis for assessing the future cash outflows that are associated with existing promises to provide postretirement benefits.

For more Exercises, Problems/Discussion Questions, and Cases, visit the Companion Website for this textbook at **www.pearsoned.ca/revsine**.

Exercises

E14-1 Determining benefit obligation

The following information pertains to Major Company's pension plan:

Actuarial estimate of accrued benefit obligation at 1/1/2003	$92,000
Assumed discount rate	10%
Service costs for 2003	$18,000
Pension benefits paid during 2003	$15,000

Required:

If *no* change in actuarial estimates occurred during 2003, Major's accrued benefit obligation at December 31, 2003, would be how much?

E14-2 Pension "liability" on balance sheet

At December 31, 2001, the following information was provided by Colonel Corporation's pension plan administrator:

Fair value of plan assets	$3,450,000
Accrued benefit liability	2,250,000
Accrued benefit obligation	5,700,000

Required:

What is the amount related to the pension that should be shown on Colonel's December 31, 2001, balance sheet?

E14-3 Determining accrued benefit asset or liability

On January 2, 2002, Loch Company established a noncontributory defined benefit plan covering all employees, and it contributed $1,000,000 to the plan. At December 31, 2002, Loch determined that the 2002 service and interest costs on the plan were $620,000. The expected and the actual rates of return on plan assets for 2002 were 10%. There are no other components of Loch's pension expense.

Required:

What amount should Loch report in its December 31, 2002, balance sheet as an accrued benefit asset or liability?

E14-4 Determining employer's pension contribution

Webb Company implemented a defined benefit pension plan for its employees on January 1, 2000. During 2000 and 2001, Webb's contributions fully funded the plan. The following data are provided for 2002 and 2003:

	2003 Estimated	2002 Actual
Accrued benefit obligation, December 31	$750,000	$700,000
Plan assets at fair value, December 31	675,000	600,000
Accrued benefit obligation in excess of plan assets	75,000	100,000
Pension expense	90,000	75,000
Employer's contribution	?	50,000

Required:

What amount should Webb contribute in order to report an accrued pension liability of $15,000 in its December 31, 2003, balance sheet?

E14-5 Computing pension expense

Nu Company established a noncontributory defined contribution pension plan as of January 1, 2001. According to the collective bargaining agreement between Nu Company and its union, 5% of total employee compensation (exclusive of pensions) is to be transferred to a trustee each year as the company's required defined contribution under the pension plan. In the fiscal year ended December 31, 2001, total employee compensation for purposes of determining Nu Company's 2001 payment to the trustee was $17,500,000. Unfortunately, the company was only able to contribute $500,000 in 2001.

Required:

Prepare a journal entry to record Nu Company's pension expense for fiscal 2001.

E14-6 Determining actual return on plan assets

The following information pertains to Sarge Company's defined benefit pension plan for 2002:

Fair value of plan assets, beginning of year	$500,000
Fair value of plan assets, end of year	725,000
Employer contributions	110,000
Benefits paid	85,000

Required:

What was the actual return on plan assets?

E14-7 Determining accrued benefit liability on balance sheet

The following information pertains to Kane Company's defined benefit pension plan:

Prepaid pension cost (accrued pension asset), 1/1/02	$ 2,000
Service cost	19,000
Interest cost	38,000
Expected return on plan assets	22,000
Amortization of unrecognized prior service cost	52,000
Employer contributions	40,000

Required:

In its December 31, 2002, balance sheet, what amount should Kane report as accrued pension cost or liability?

Problems/Discussion Questions

P14-1 Effect of funding and discount rate assumption on pension expense

On January 1, 2002, Magee Corporation started doing business by hiring G. Barnett as an employee at an annual salary of $50,000, with an annual salary increment of $10,000. Because of his current age and the company's retirement program, Mr. Barnett is required to retire at the end of the year in 2005. However, at his option, Mr. Barnett could retire any time after completing one full year of service. Regardless of when he retires, the company will pay a lump-sum pension at the end of the year in 2006. The lump-sum payment is calculated to be 25% of the cumulative lifetime salary earned by Mr. Barnett. Magee's annual discount rate is 10%. Assume that Mr. Barnett retires at the end of the year in 2005.

Required:

1. Assuming that Magee Corporation does not fund its pension expense, calculate the pension expense for the years 2002–2005. Clearly identify the service and interest cost components. On the basis of your calculations, provide journal entries both to record the pension expense during the 2002–2005 period and to record the lump-sum payment of Mr. Barnett's pension at the end of the year in 2006.

2. Assume that Magee Corporation fully funds its pension cost as soon as it vests and that the contributions to the pension fund earn exactly a 10% rate of return annually. With these revised assumptions, redo Question 1.

3. Explain why the total pension expense in question 1 is different from that in Question 2.

4. Assume that Magee Corporation does not fund its pension expense. Discuss how different assumptions regarding the discount rate affect the pension expense. You may compare the pension expense with discount rates of 5%, 10%, and 15%.

P14-2 Determining effect of discount rate assumption on pension expense and ABO

Use the same set of facts as in P14-1. In addition, assume that, on its actuary's advice, Magee Corporation decides to contribute the following amounts to the pension fund:

	2002	2003	2004	2005
Contributions	$8,475	$11,000	$15,000	$18,000

Magee Corporation intends to fund the pension plan only to the extent required by the actuary. Assume that the contributions to the pension fund earn exactly a 10% rate of return annually.

Required:

1. The CEO of the company, Mr. R. Magee, is considering three possible discount rates (8%, 10%, and 12%) for calculating the annual pension expense. Provide schedules showing how much pension expense will be reported under each of the three scenarios during the 2002–05 period.

2. Provide schedules showing the funding status of the pension plan during the 2002–05 period.

3. Mr. Magee is wondering which of the three discount rate assumptions would be considered the most and the least conservative for purposes of determining net income. Moreover, the CEO is also puzzled by how the total pension expense compares across the three discount rate assumptions. Explain.

P14-3 Components of pension liability and pension expense

The following is the funding status of the pension plan of Saddington Inc. as of December 31, 2002:

	End of Year 2002
Accrued benefit obligation	($1,000,000)
Fair value of plan assets	1,000,000
Fair value in excess of ABO	—
Unrecognized gain	—
Accrued pension liability	—

The following information is provided for the years 2003–2006:

	2003	2004	2005	2006
Actual rate of return on plan assets	22%	20%	12%	10%
Contribution to pension fund	$220,000	$260,000	$300,000	$340,000
Pension payments	$200,000	$260,000	$320,000	$380,000
Service cost	$300,000	$350,000	$400,000	$450,000
Average remaining service period of active employees (in years)	10	10	10	10

The "Contribution to pension fund" component represents the cash flows from the company to the pension fund. The "Pension payments" component represents the payments made by the pension fund to the retired employees. The income earned by the pension fund in a given year is found by multiplying the fair value of the plan assets at the beginning of the year by the actual rate of return on plan assets for that year. The discount rate is 10% and the expected rate of return is 12% during each year from 2003 to 2006.

Required:

1. Prepare schedules showing the changes in the following components of the pension liability over the 2003–2006 period:
   (a) accrued benefit obligation
   (b) fair value of plan assets
   (c) unrecognized gain

2. Using your answer to Question 1, show the funded status of the plan at the end of years 2003 through 2006.

3. Calculate the pension expense for the years 2003 through 2006 and provide the breakdowns for service cost, interest cost, actual return on plan assets, unrecognized portion of return, and gain or loss amounts recognized.

4. Prepare all necessary journal entries pertaining to the accrued benefit liability for the years 2003–2006. On the basis of the journal entries, construct the T-account for accrued benefit liability over the same period.

P14-4 Effect of actual versus expected return on pension funding status and pension expense

On December 31, 2002, Muller Corporation eliminated its employee pension plan. The company has currently funded its pension plan for $100,000 (which is the value of the pension plan assets and ABO as of December 31, 2002). The expected return on plan assets and the settlement rate are both 10%. As part of the agreement with the current employees, the company expects to pay a lump sum of $133,100 on January 1, 2006, for pension obligations existing under the cancelled pension plan. While the annual expected rate of return is 10%, the realized rates of return on pension assets depend on the nature of the economy over the next three years. Assume that depending on whether the economy is stable, growing, or declining, the pension assets earn the following rates of return over the next three years:

State of the Economy	Actual Rates of Return For:		
	2003	2004	2005
Scenario 1: Stable economy	10.00%	10.00%	10.00%
Scenario 2: Growth	5.00%	10.00%	15.24%
Scenario 3: Decline	15.00%	10.00%	5.22%

Required:

1. Show for each state of the economy over the next three years that the pension plan will have sufficient funds to meet the pension obligation at the end of year 2005. Indicate the value of the pension plan assets at the end of the years 2003–2005. Over the three-year period, what is the difference between the actual and expected annual rates of return under each state of the economy?
2. Ignoring pension expense component 4, calculate the pension expense of Muller Corporation over the next three years under each of the three states of the economy.
3. Recalculate the pension expense of Muller Corporation over the next three years under each of the three states of the economy after incorporating pension expense component 4. Also show the funded status of the pension plan at the end of 2003, 2004, and 2005.
4. Keeping in mind your answers so far, discuss the potential benefit of including recognized gains or losses in the calculation of pension expense.

P14-5 Pension expense and funded status

The following is the funded status of the pension plan of McKeown Consulting Company at December 31, 2002:

	2002
Accrued benefit obligation	$ (900,000)
Fair value of plan assets	1,000,000
Fair value in excess of ABO	100,000
Unrecognized prior service cost	—
Unrecognized (gain) loss	—
Accrued pension asset (liability)	$ 100,000

The following information is available for the years 2003 and 2004:

| | For the Years Ended December 31, | |
	2003	2004
Discount rate	10%	10%
Expected rate of return on plan assets	9%	11%

The service costs for 2003 and 2004 are $125,000 and $145,000, respectively. The interest cost for a given year is estimated by multiplying the ABO at the beginning of the year by the discount rate for the year. Similarly, the expected return on plan assets is computed by multiplying the fair value of plan assets at the beginning of the year by the assumed expected rate of return for the year. During the years 2003 and 2004, the pension fund's actual earnings are $100,000 and $64,740, respectively.

At the end of 2003, McKeown Consulting Company retroactively enhanced the benefits provided under its pension plan, and this increased the accrued benefit obligation by $110,000. The average remaining service period of employees expected to receive these retroactive benefits under the plan was ten years.

During 2003 and 2004, the company made contributions of $99,000 and $123,000, respectively, to the pension fund. In turn, the pension fund made payments of $120,000 and $85,000 to the retired employees during the same periods.

Required:

1. Compute the pension expense for the years 2003 and 2004. Show the funded status of the pension plan and the funded status reconciliation as of the end of the same years. (*Hint*: You will need to calculate the ending balances for ABO, fair value of plan assets, unrecognized prior service costs, and the unrecognized gain [loss] at the end of the year.)

2. Provide necessary journal entries in the books of McKeown Consulting Company for the years 2003 and 2004 to record all transactions relating to its pension plan. Also, explain the changes in the accrued pension asset (liability) over the same period.

3. Explain how the economic status of the pension plan differs from the reported status as of the end of the years 2002 through 2004.

P14-6 Components of OPEB and journal entries

UNICOM
CORPORATION
www.unicomcorp.
com

Excerpts from Unicom Corporation's footnotes for the year ended December 31, 1999, follow:

ComEd and certain of Unicom's subsidiaries provide certain postretirement medical, dental and vision care, and life insurance for retirees and their dependents and for the surviving dependants of eligible employees and retirees. Generally, the employees become eligible for postretirement benefits if they retire no earlier than age 55 with ten years of service. The liability for postretirement benefits is funded through trust funds based upon actuarially determined contributions that take into account the amount deductible for income tax purposes. The health care plans are contributory, funded jointly by the companies and the participating retirees. The December 31, 1999 and 1998 postretirement benefit liabilities and related data were determined using the January 1, 1999 actuarial valuations.

Reconciliation of the beginning and ending balances of the accumulated postretirement benefit obligation, and the funded status of the plan for the years 1999 and 1998 follows:

	Year ended December 31	
(US$ in thousands)	1999	1998
Change in benefit obligation		
Benefit obligation at beginning of period	$1,236,000	$1,139,000
Service cost	41,000	38,000
Interest cost	82,000	78,000
Plan participants' contributions	4,000	3,000
Actuarial loss (gain)	(188,000)	25,000
Benefits paid	(51,000)	(47,000)
Special termination benefits	27,000	—
Benefit obligation at end of period	1,151,000	1,236,000
Change in plan assets		
Fair value of plan assets at beginning of period	865,000	767,000
Actual return on plan assets	105,000	122,000
Employer contributions	24,000	20,000
Plan participants' contributions	4,000	3,000
Benefits paid	(51,000)	(47,000)
Fair value of plan assets at end of period	947,000	865,000
Plan assets less than benefit obligations	(204,000)	(371,000)
Unrecognized net actuarial gain	(555,000)	(371,000)
Unrecognized prior service cost	41,000	48,000
Unrecognized transition obligation	276,000	323,000
Accrued liability for benefits	($ 442,000)	($ 371,000)

The assumed discount rate used to determine the benefit obligation as of December 31, 1999 and 1998 was 7.75% and 6.75%, respectively. The fair value of plan assets excludes $9 million and $7 million held in a grantor trust as of December 31, 1999 and 1998, respectively, for the payment of postretirement medical benefits.

The components of other postretirement benefit costs, portions of which were recorded as components of construction costs for the years 1999, 1998 and 1997 were as follows:

(US$ in thousands)	1999	1998	1997
Service cost	$?	$?	$34,000
Interest cost on accumulated benefit obligation	?	?	76,000
Expected return on plan assets	?	?	(61,000)
Amortization of transition obligation	22,000	22,000	22,000
Amortization of prior service costs	4,000	4,000	4,000
Recognized gain	(14,000)	(14,000)	(13,000)
Severance plan costs	1,000	6,000	8,000
Curtailment loss	35,000	–0–	–0–
Net periodic benefit cost	$?	$?	$70,000

The other postretirement benefit curtailment losses in December 1999 represent the recognition of prior service costs and transition obligations, and an increase in the benefit obligations resulting from special termination benefits, related to the reduction in the number of employees due to ComEd's sale of the fossil stations.

The health care cost trend rates used to measure the expected cost of the postretirement medical benefits are assumed to be 8.0% for pre-Medicare recipients and 6.0% for Medicare recipients for 1999. Those rates are assumed to decrease in 0.5% annual increments to 5% for the years 2005 and 2001, respectively, and to remain level thereafter. The health-care cost trend rates, used to measure the expected cost of postretirement dental and vision benefits, are a level 3.5% and 2.0% per year, respectively. Assumed health care cost trend rates have a significant effect on the amounts reported for the health care plans. A one-percentage point change in the assumed health care cost trend rates would have the following effects:

(US$ in thousands)	1 Percentage Point	
	Increase	Decrease
Effect on total 1999 service and interest cost components	$ 26,000	($ 20,000)
Effect on postretirement benefit obligation as of 12/31/1999	190,000	151,000

Required:

1. Assuming an expected rate of return on plan assets for 1999 and 1998 of 8.8% and 9%, compute the missing amounts in the above table and determine the "Net periodic benefit cost" for years 1999 and 1998. (Round amounts to nearest million.)

2. Assuming that the US$4,000,000 of participant contributions were submitted directly to the trustee by the employees, show the journal entry that Unicom would make to record the 1999 company (employer) contribution and its related "Net periodic benefit cost."

3. What amount (if any) would appear on Unicom's 1999 balance sheet relating to its OPEB plans and how would it be classified?

Cases

C14-1 Inco Limited: Interpreting postretirement benefit disclosures

INCO LIMITED
www.inco.com

Although Section 3461 requiring an accrual accounting approach for postretirement benefits was only issued in 1999, some Canadian companies adopted accrual accounting for these costs much earlier. Inco Limited was one such company. The 1998 postretirement benefits footnote (covering both pensions and other benefits) is shown on pp. 705–707, along with Inco's 1998 income statement.

Required:

1. Prepare spreadsheets tracking both pension and postretirement benefits other than pensions, over the three-year period disclosed in the footnote. List any assumptions you had to make.

2. Do you have any comments on the impact of these various plans, and how they were accounted for, on Inco's quality of earnings?

Note 8. Post-retirement Benefits

The Company has defined pension plans covering essentially all employees and provides certain health care and life insurance benefits for retired employees.

The change in the funded status of the Company's post-retirement benefit plans was as follows:

Year Ended December 31	Pension Benefits			Post-retirement Benefits Other Than Pensions		
	1998	1997	1996	1998	1997	1996
Change in post-retirement Benefits obligation						
Obligation at beginning of year	$1,823	$1,768	$1,683	$645	$607	$609
Service cost	28	32	30	8	8	9
Interest cost	140	144	136	48	48	50
Plan amendments	—	53	6	—	—	—
Changes in assumptions	204	—	(2)	48	30	—
Actuarial losses (gains)	65	74	39	—	9	(43)
Benefits paid	(126)	(136)	(138)	(27)	(32)	(27)
Sale of discontinued operations	(254)	(48)	—	(164)	(8)	—
Currency translation adjustments	(95)	(64)	14	(32)	(17)	9
Obligation at end of year	$1,785	$1,823	$1,768	$526	$645	$607
Change in pension plan assets						
Fair value of plan assets at beginning of year	$1,877	$1,723	$1,547			
Actual return on plan assets	126	323	222			
Employer contributions	70	71	64			
Benefits paid	(123)	(122)	(123)			
Sale of discontinued operations	(287)	(55)	—			
Currency translation adjustments	(94)	(63)	13			
Fair value of plan assets at end of year	$1,569	$1,877	$1,723			
Funded (unfunded) status of plans at end of year	$(216)	$ 54	$ (45)	$(526)	$(645)	$(607)
Unrecognized balance of January 1, 1986 net asset	—	(11)	(26)	—	—	—
Unrecognized actuarial and investment losses (gains)	205	(137)	(96)	52	5	(26)
Unrecognized prior service costs	81	131	164	—	—	—
Net post-retirement benefits asset (liability) at end of year	$ 70	$ 37	$ (3)	$(474)	$(640)	$(633)

The net post-retirement benefits asset (liability) is reflected in the consolidated balance sheet as follows:

	Pension Benefits			Post-retirement Benefits Other Than Pensions		
December 31	1998	1997	1996	1998	1997	1996
Deferred charges	$82	$52	$12	$ —	$ —	$ —
Accrued payrolls and benefits	(12)	(15)	(15)	(19)	(26)	(26)
Post-retirement benefits	—	—	—	(455)	(614)	(607)
Net post-retirement benefits asset (liability)	$70	$37	$(3)	$(474)	$(640)	$(633)

Post-retirement benefits expense included the following components:

	Pension Benefits			Post-retirement Benefits Other Than Pensions		
Year Ended December 31	1998	1997	1996	1998	1997	1996
Service cost	$ 28	$ 32	$ 30	$ 8	$ 8	$ 9
Interest cost	140	144	136	48	48	50
Expected return on plan assets	(137)	(134)	(127)	—	—	—
Amortization of net asset at January 1, 1986	(11)	(15)	(18)	—	—	—
Amortization of actuarial and investment losses (gains)	(14)	(6)	(2)	1	(2)	—
Amortization of unrecognized prior service costs	24	25	25	—	—	—
Settlement cost	6	—	—	—	—	—
Defined benefit pension and post-retirement benefits other than pensions expense	36	46	44	57	54	59
Defined contribution pension expense	5	7	8	—	—	—
Post-retirement benefits expense	$41	$53	$52	$57	$54	$59

Post-retirement benefits expense shown above includes pension income of $3 million in 1998 (1997—$1 million expense; 1996—$1 million expense) and post-retirement benefits other than pension expense of $8 million in 1998 (1997—$11 million; 1996—$2 million) in respect of the Company's discontinued operations.

The weighted average assumptions used in the determination of the post-retirement benefits obligations at year-end were as follows:

	Pension Benefits			Post-retirement Benefits Other Than Pensions		
December 31	1998	1997	1996	1998	1997	1996
Discount rate:						
Canada	7.0%	8.5%	8.5%	7.0%	8.5%	8.5%
United States	7.0%	7.5%	7.5%	7.0%	7.5%	7.5%
United Kingdom	7.0%	8.5%	8.5%			
Expected return on plan assets	9.0%	9.0%	9.0%			
Rate of compensation increase	4.0%	5.0%	4.8%			

The composite health care cost trend rate used in measuring post-retirement benefits other than pensions was assumed to begin at eight per cent, gradually declining to five per cent by 2005 and remaining at those levels thereafter.

The projected pension benefits obligation and fair value of plan assets for pension plans with accumulated benefits obligations in excess of plan assets were as follows:

December 31	Pension Benefits		
	1998	1997	1996
Projected benefits obligation	$1,637	$ 175	$1,143
Fair value of plan assets	1,394	68	1,006
Unfunded status	$ (243)	$(107)	$ (137)

A one per cent increase (decrease) in the assumed composite health care cost trend rate for each year would increase (decrease) the accumulated post-retirement benefits other than pensions obligation at December 31, 1998 and net periodic post-retirement benefits other than pensions expense by approximately $67 million ($54 million) and $7 million ($6 million), respectively.

Inco Limited
Consolidated Statement of Earnings

(in millions of United States dollars except per share amounts)	Year Ended December 31,		
	1998	1997	1996
Net sales	$1,766	$2,367	$2,460
Costs and expenses			
Cost of sales and operating expenses	1,735	2,051	1,912
Selling, general and administrative	96	109	111
Research and development	18	28	23
Exploration	29	38	40
Interest	86	81	85
	1,964	2,307	2,171
Earnings (loss) before income and mining taxes and minority interest	(198)	60	289
Income and mining taxes (Note 3)	(94)	30	107
Earnings (loss) before minority interest	(104)	30	182
Minority interest	8	13	34
Earnings (loss) from continuing operations	(112)	17	148
Earnings from discontinued operations (Note 4)	36	58	31
Net earnings (loss)	(76)	75	179
Dividends on preferred and class VBN shares (Note 11)	(28)	(34)	(22)
Net earnings (loss) applicable to common shares	$ (104)	$ 41	$ 157
Net earnings (loss) per common share (Notes 1 and 4):			
Basic:			
Continuing operations	$ (0.85)	$ (0.10)	$ 0.94
Discontinued operations	0.22	0.35	0.23
	$ (0.63)	$ 0.25	$ 1.17
Fully diluted:			
Continuing operations	(0.85)	(0.10)	$ 0.86
Discontinued operations	0.22	0.35	0.23
	$ (0.63)	$ 0.25	$ 1.09

C14-2 Potash's future employee benefit disclosure

Required:

Access the SEDAR website from this text's Companion Website at **www.pearsoned.ca/ revsine**, and look at the audited financial statements for Potash Corporation of Saskatchewan Inc.

1. Examine note 14, "Postretirement/Post-Employment Benefits" for Potash. Are there any interesting features or questions? Reconstruct Potash's 2000 journal entries for both pension plans and other postretirement plans.
2. What was Potash's 2000 expected return on plan assets for its pensions? For its other postretirement/postemployment plans?
3. Potash discloses that the long-term rate of return on assets that it used in 2000 was 9.0%. Verify that this rate was used in computing Potash's year 2000 net pension expense of $18.2 million.

Integrative Running Case Study
Bombardier on the Web

Refer to Bombardier Inc.'s annual report for the year ended January 31, 2002, located on the Companion Website for this text (**www.pearsoned.ca/revsine**). The company describes its accounting policy with respect to "Employee future benefits" on page 75; the pension note is on pages 100–2. An item termed "Accrued benefit liability" is disclosed as part of "Other Liabilities" in note 13.

Required:

1. On the basis of the information provided in Bombardier's annual report, reconstruct the company's pension journal entry and other benefits entry.
2. James Daw, who writes the "Money Talk" column in the *Toronto Star*, reports that pension experts anticipate that Section 3461's rules regarding other postemployment benefits might induce employers to cut back on such plans ("New Accounting Rules May Hit Benefits," *Toronto Star*, September 30, 1999, p. D4). Is there any evidence that Bombardier has done so?

Endnotes

1. Section 3461 replaced Section 3460 ("Pension Costs and Obligations"), which was issued in 1986. Section 3461 is more comprehensive, covering in addition to pensions other future employee benefits.

2. Most of the material on pp. 679–682 and 659–671 is adapted from L. Revsine, "Understanding Financial Accounting Standard 87," *Financial Analysts Journal,* January–February 1989, pp. 61–8, and is presented here by permission from the publisher.

3. If a company either (1) curtails a plan or (2) settles a plan's liabilities by purchasing an annuity contract and generates a gain or loss from either event, that gain or loss would also be included in pension expense as a seventh element. Measuring the gain or loss on plan settlements or curtailments is outlined in paras. 111 to 134 of Section 3461. There are some other possible components of pension expense as well—see Section 3461, para. 070.

4. This example is adapted from an illustration that was prepared by Professor Norman Bartczak.

5. These numbers ignore any additional amortizations due to components 4, 5, or 6. GE's earnings before taxes and accounting changes were US$8.661 billion and US$9.737 billion in 1994 and 1995, respectively. So reducing the pension expense "swing" by US$5.038 billion (i.e., US$5.061 billion versus US$23 million) is significant in relation to pre-tax earnings.

6. The average values for the 1987–90 period are based on a sample of 300 firms representing a broad cross-section of industries. See M. E. Barth, W. H. Beaver, and W. R. Landsman, "A Structural Analysis of Pension Disclosures Under SFAS 87 and Their Relation to Share Prices," *Financial Analysts Journal,* January–February, 1993, pp. 18–26. The American accounting standard, *Statement of Financial Accounting Standards No. 87,* is very similar to Section 3461.

7. See J. R. Francis and S. A. Reiter, "Determinants of Corporate Pension Funding Strategy," *Journal of Accounting and Economics,* April 1987, pp. 35–60; and J. K. Thomas, "Corporate Taxes and Defined Benefit Pension Plans," *Journal of Accounting and Economics,* July 1988, pp. 199–238.

8. The reader is referred to the articles cited in footnote 7 for a more complete discussion of each of these incentives and their hypothesized effect on firms' pension funding strategy.

9. See the articles by L. Jeresky, "Tapping the Golden Pool," *Forbes,* April 21, 1986, pp. 35–6 and "The Surplus Vanishes," *Forbes,* November 17, 1986, p. 94.

10. "Employers' Accounting for Postretirement Benefits Other Than Pensions," *SFAS No. 106* (Norwalk, CT: FASB, 1990).

11. M. E. Barth, W. H. Beaver, and W. R. Landsman, "The Market Valuation Implications of Net Periodic Pension Cost Components," *Journal of Accounting and Economics,* March 1992, pp. 27–62.

12. For example, see R. McGough and E. E. Schultz, "How Pension Surpluses Lift Profits," *Wall Street Journal,* September 20, 1999, and G. Morgenson, "What's Hiding in Big Blue's Small Print," *New York Times,* June 4, 2000.

13. Recall this pension plan asset base is termed the market-related asset value. Firms can compute this in either of two ways. One is to use the fair market value (FMV) of the plan assets at the start of the reporting period. The other is to use some sort of moving average (not to exceed five years) which smooths out the year-to-year volatility inherent in a point estimate like FMV on a specific date.

14. See Bear Stearns, "Retirement Benefits Impact Operating Income," *Accounting Issues* (Bear, Stearns & Co. Inc.: September 17, 1999) for a thorough exposition of this position.

15
Financial Reporting for Owners' Equity

LEARNING OBJECTIVES

After studying this chapter, you should be able to:

1. Understand why some financial transactions—like debt repurchases—generate reported gains and losses, while other financial transactions—like share repurchases—do not

2. Understand why companies buy back their shares and how they do it

3. Examine why some preferred shares look a lot like debt, and know how to report such items

4. Tell how and when retained earnings limits a company's distributions to common shareholders

5. Calculate basic and diluted earnings per share (EPS), and determine whether EPS is a meaningful number

6. Know what GAAP say about employee share options, and understand why this accounting treatment has been so controversial

7. Determine whether GAAP understate the true cost of convertible debt, and then deal with this understatement

8. Understand why employee stock ownership plans (ESOPs) have become so popular, and what they mean for statement readers

Statement readers must understand the accounting procedures and reporting conventions for owners' equity for these reasons:

1. *Appropriate income measurement.* Differentiating between owners' equity changes that do increase or decrease income and changes that do not will help answer questions like "Why are bond interest payments an expense that reduces income, while dividend payments on common and preferred shares are not?" "Why do certain financing transactions—like early debt retirements—generate accounting gains and losses while others—like share repurchases—do not?"

2. *Compliance with contract terms and restrictions.* Within the past decade many "exotic" securities having characteristics of both debt and equity have been invented. How should these hybrid securities be classified for purposes of monitoring compliance with contractual restrictions (like maximum allowable debt-to-equity ratios)?

3. *Legality of corporate distributions to owners.* Owners' equity is generally regarded as a financial "cushion" that protects corporate creditors. Cash distributions to shareholders—dividends and share repurchases—reduce this safety net. How much of this cushion can legally be distributed in the form

of dividends? In case of corporate liquidation, in what order can cash payouts be made to various claimants?

4. *Linkage to equity valuation and earnings per share.* Analyzing the worth of equity shares requires an understanding of the amount of earnings that accrue to each share. Equity valuation thus depends on how a company's options, warrants, and convertible instruments affect its earnings per share. After discussing each of these issues, we will look at existing GAAP for share options granted to employees and the controversy surrounding current reporting practice.

Appropriate Income Measurement

Whose Company Is It? Entity Versus Proprietary Views

Some increases (decreases) in owners' equity are considered in accounting to be income (loss), while other increases are not considered income. To see why, we must understand the modern GAAP definition of the "firm," which we can do by recalling the basic accounting equation:

Entity view of the firm:

$$\underbrace{\text{Assets}}_{\text{Capital deployed}} = \underbrace{\text{Liabilities} + \text{Shareholders' or Owners' equity}}_{\text{Capital sources}}$$

Expressed in this way, the equation lumps debt and shareholder financing together. According to this perspective—called the **entity view** of the company—the assets of the company are what's important. The company's assets are considered to drive economic performance, so the company *is* its assets. Who provided those assets (creditors versus shareholders) is of secondary importance.

Prevailing GAAP are based on a different perspective—called the **proprietary view** of the firm—which looks at the basic accounting equation from the viewpoint of owners' equity and sharply differentiates between capital provided by shareholders and capital provided by creditors.

Proprietary view of the firm:

$$\underbrace{\text{Assets} - \text{Liabilities}}_{\text{Net capital deployed}} = \underbrace{\text{Shareholders' or Owners' equity}}_{\text{Owners' capital}}$$

The prevalence of the proprietary view in GAAP greatly influences income measurement. To illustrate why, consider the basic accounting principle that income can be earned (or expenses incurred) *only* through transactions between the firm and "outsiders." But who is "inside" the firm and who are the outsiders? *Under the proprietary view, the firm and its owners are regarded as the same.* Consequently, no income (or loss) can arise from transactions between the firm and its owners, because owners are not outsiders. This perspective explains why interest payments to banks or bondholders are expenses that reduce income, while dividend payments to common and preferred shareholders are *not* expenses that reduce income. Banks and bondholders are outsiders—hence, interest costs are expenses. Shareholders are not outsiders—thus, dividends are a *distribution* of earnings to owners, not an expense of the company.

The proprietary view helps us understand why certain financing transactions generate income (or losses), while other transactions do not.

Terminology: The Word "Capital"

When accountants use the word "capital," they are usually referring to shareholders' equity. But this word has other, closely related meanings as well. For example, in the field of corporate law a company's *capital* is the part of shareholders' equity that, by legal statute, is required to be kept in the business in order to protect the company's creditors. Thus, a company's *legal* or *stated* capital is quantitatively equal to the amount of money that the company received for shares it issued,[1] according to the *Canada Business Corporations Act* (CBCA) and most provincial acts, although in some jurisdictions (including the United States) legal capital may be equal to so-called *par value*.

While companies incorporated under the authority of the CBCA must issue shares without par value, previously companies could choose an arbitrary amount per share and call it "par value," and that became the legal capital of the company. Any amount received for the issued shares in excess of the par value amount was credited to an owners' equity account labelled "Contributed capital in excess of par" or a similarly descriptive title. Par value is a rather arbitrary number, has little relationship with a share's market value, and has become of historical interest in Canada because of the CBCA requirements to credit all monies received from a corporation's share issue to the share capital account.

Financing Transactions

One way corporations raise capital is by selling equity shares to investors. Called **common shares,** these provide the opportunity for purchasers to participate in the company's future profitability. In addition to conveying ownership rights, common shares have **limited liability.** The shareholder's potential future loss is limited to the original purchase price of the common share. Limited liability makes investing in common shares attractive because although potential gains from ownership are unlimited, downside risk of loss is limited to the share purchase price.

By contrast, purchasers of debt instruments such as bonds gain only a specified fixed (or variable) rate of return—for example, "7% interest per annum," or in the case of variable rate debt, "prime plus $\frac{1}{2}$%."

Let us illustrate financial reporting for common shares. Assume that at its creation Nahigian Corporation sells 5,000 common shares at $50 per share. Nahigian would record the share issuance as:

DR	Cash	$250,000	
	CR Common shares		$250,000

"Common shares" may go by other names, such as "Capital stock" or "Share capital."

Suppose that several years later, Nahigian Corporation reacquires 200 of these shares at a cost of $48 each. When a corporation buys back its own shares, the repurchased stock is called **treasury shares** or **treasury stock** because the shares are held in the corporate treasury for later use. The accounting entry is:

DR	Treasury shares	$9,600	
	CR Cash		$9,600

Notice that no gain or loss is recorded for the difference between the $50-per-share price at which the shares were first issued and the $48 repurchase price. *The reason share repurchases do not involve accounting gains and losses is that they are transactions between the company and its owners.* This is the proprietary view of the firm in action!

Although some Canadian provinces and countries such as the United States permit treasury share transactions, the *Canada Business Corporations Act* generally requires companies that acquire their own shares to cancel them (or, if the company's incorporating documents limit the number of authorized shares, the acquired shares are to become authorized but unissued). Therefore, one is unlikely to come across treasury shares for Canadian companies incorporated under the CBCA. Treasury shares do exist in Canadian financial statements, however; for example, Canadian Tire Corporation.

When treasury shares are acquired, they are not considered a corporate asset. Treasury shares are debited, as shown earlier, and treated as a **contra-equity** account on the balance sheet, i.e., as a deduction from shareholders' equity.[2]

Nahigian Corporation	
Shareholders' Equity	
Common stock, 5,000 shares issued	$250,000
Retained earnings (assumed for illustration)	700,000
Total paid-in capital and retained earnings	$950,000
Less: Treasury shares (at cost)	(9,600)
Total shareholders' equity	$940,400

Now let's say Nahigian decides to raise more equity capital by reselling all 200 treasury shares several months later at $53 per share. The entry would be:

DR	Cash		$10,600	
	CR	Treasury shares		$9,600
	CR	Contributed surplus		1,000

This entry eliminates the contra-equity account called "Treasury shares." The per-share selling price of $53 is $5 per share higher than the $48 paid to reacquire the shares. Despite this "excess," *no income is recognized on the transaction.* Instead, the difference of $1,000 (200 shares × [$53 – $48]) is added to the "Contributed surplus" account.[3]

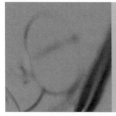

Recap

No income (or expense) arises from treasury share transactions—not in the proprietary view, which equates the firm with its owners. Since treasury share transactions are between the company and its shareholders (owners) and not outsiders, no income is recognized—not even when the successive share transactions are favourable, like those in the Nahigian Corporation illustration.

But if Nahigian had reacquired outstanding *debt* at a price lower than its book value, then a gain *would* be recorded, as described in Chapter 11. Debt repurchases generate gains (and losses) while share repurchases do not, because debtholders are outsiders under the GAAP proprietary view while shareholders are insiders.

Appendix 15A to this chapter includes comprehensive examples of equity journal entries, for both no par value and par value situations.

Why Companies Repurchase Their Shares

Firms reacquire their own common shares for many reasons. Sometimes a company needs a supply of shares to have available for employee stock options. Sometimes management may conclude that the company's shares are undervalued at the existing market price and that the best use of corporate funds is to invest in the firm's own shares. Other times, perhaps management just wants to distribute surplus cash to shareholders rather than to keep it inside the company, when satisfactory projects are not available.

A company's *surplus* cash—the amount over and above what is needed for day-to-day operating activities—can be a problem for management and for shareholders. Management worries that another company or investor group might launch a hostile takeover of the business, using the company's own cash surplus to partially finance the takeover. If such a takeover is successful, some managers will inevitably lose their jobs. Shareholders on the other hand worry that management might spend the company's surplus cash on unprofitable—negative net present value—projects and lavish "perks" such as corporate speedboats or racecars. It is better to give the money to shareholders —after all, it is their money.

Share repurchases have one other advantage: shareholders who take the cash may be taxed at capital gain rates. If the cash is paid out as dividends, shareholders would be taxed at dividend rates, which are usually higher than capital gains rates.

The popularity of share repurchases has varied over time as a result of changes in the economic climate, share market price levels, and the availability of surplus corporate cash.

There are a number of ways a company can repurchase its shares. At one time, the most common was the **fixed price** offer, one in which the company announces both the number of shares it wants to repurchase and the price it will pay for those shares.

In the 1980s, a technique called the **Dutch auction** became popular. Here, the company announces the total number of shares it will repurchase and sets a range of prices within which it is willing to buy back shares. Shareholders responding to the offer must specify how many shares they are willing to sell and at what price within the range. The company then determines the lowest offered price that allows it to repurchase the number of shares it seeks. All the shares are purchased at this single price.[4]

The Dutch auction looks like the most satisfactory way in which to treat shareholders fairly. If a shareholder names too high a price, that shareholder may have no shares accepted. Naming too low a price simply increases the likelihood that the price paid will be low. Consequently, this approach encourages shareholders to be truthful and to name a price that reflects their personal valuation of the shares.

The typical share repurchase is at a price about 23% greater than the share's market value just before the repurchase offer is announced.[5] Those shareholders who sell their shares back to the company capture this price premium. But what about the shareholders who don't sell? According to perhaps the best known study on the subject, the shares of the average corporation that repurchases its shares outperform the rest of the market by 13% over the four years following the announcement of the repurchase program. Even better, high book-to-market price shares that are repurchased beat the market by 45% over the subsequent four years.[6]

But not all buybacks are created equal. While share repurchases as a whole help to boost returns to share market investors, companies don't always use them just to demonstrate that their shares are undervalued or to distribute excess cash to shareholders, skeptics say. It has become increasingly important for prudent investors and analysts to sort through the individual share repurchase plans and to determine the reasons behind the buyback. Only then can they figure out whether a repurchase plan is a sign to buy—or to avoid the shares.

Here's what Microsoft says about its share repurchase program:

Management believes existing cash and short-term investments together with funds generated from operations will be sufficient to meet operating requirements for the next twelve months. Microsoft's cash and short-term investments are available for strategic investments, mergers and acquisitions, other potential large-scale cash needs that may arise, and to fund an increased share buyback program over historical levels to reduce the dilutive impact of the Company's employee share option and purchase programs. Despite recent increases in share repurchases, the buyback program has not kept pace with employee share option grants or exercises. *Beginning in fiscal 1990, Microsoft has repurchased 134 million common shares for [US]$4.2 billion while 336 million shares were issued under the Company's employee share option and purchase plans. The market value of all outstanding share options was [US]$21.8 billion as of December 31, 1996.*[7]

MICROSOFT
www.microsoft.com

Microsoft's buyback program partially offsets share dilution caused by the company's share option and purchase plans. But what is gained if a company is buying back its shares with one hand but is issuing shares through options with the other hand? Some analysts answer: not much. While an employee usually buys shares for less than the market price under option programs, the company pays the market price to buy them back. In dollar terms, the number of shares outstanding may seem to be shrinking, because the company has spent more to buy back shares than employees have spent to acquire them. But in fact, the number of shares could remain unchanged or even grow.

Intel's experience highlights the issue. Every year since 1992 the semiconductor manufacturer has bought back shares. But in 1999, for example, while it issued only US$543 million of shares and bought back a whopping US$4.6 billion under its repurchase plan, its *common shares outstanding actually grew* to 3,334 million from 3,315 million. What is the reason? The company paid US$64.95 a share for the shares it repurchased—but it received only US$9.70 for each share issued through options. (Intel also issued 34 million shares in connection with an acquisition.)

INTEL
www.intel.com

Another factor of concern to analysts is that many companies borrow to finance their share repurchase programs. While such moves might have tax or other advantages, they simply replace equity with debt, so shareholders get the buyback's benefits only at the expense of owning a more leveraged company. They also face the risk that an economic downturn could make it harder to service debt.

Even more worrisome is that **some stock buybacks are motivated solely by a desire to boost earnings per share (EPS).** Consider Rocket Software. The company just completed a successful third quarter with earnings of $220,000 and EPS of $1.00. This is the ninth consecutive quarter that Rocket Software's EPS has grown by 10% or more. But it looks like this string of EPS increases is about to be broken—fourth quarter earnings are projected to be only $220,000, unchanged from the third quarter.

How can the company keep its EPS record intact? Management could increase earnings (as well as EPS) by finding ways to grow sales revenues or reduce expenses. Or, Rocket Software could buy back some of its common stock:

	Without Buyback	With Buyback
Projected fourth quarter earnings	$220,000	$220,000
÷ Common shares outstanding	220,000	200,000
Projected EPS	$ 1.00	$ 1.10

If the buyback reduces total shares outstanding from 220,000 to 200,000, fourth quarter EPS will be $1.10 and the company can claim another quarter of 10% EPS growth.

Sounds simple, but it's not—there is a hidden assumption. Stock buybacks consume cash. Where did Rocket Software get the cash needed for its buyback? Suppose the company had to borrow the cash. The (after-tax) interest expense on the loan—let's say it's $5,500—would reduce projected fourth quarter earnings to $214,500. The company would then have to buy back 25,000 shares—or 5,000 more than originally anticipated—to reach its $1.10 EPS goal ($1.10 EPS = $214,500/195,000 shares outstanding after the expanded buyback). Instead of borrowing the cash, Rocket Software could sell some of its marketable securities, investments, or other productive assets. But asset sales may also have a dampening effect on future earnings.

As long as earnings fall by less (in percentage terms) than the buyback percentage reduction in shares outstanding, EPS will indeed go up! But this EPS increase may actually mask deteriorating business fundamentals. When it comes to stock buybacks and EPS growth, it pays to look behind the numbers.

Recap
Share repurchases don't produce accounting gains or losses, but they can produce above-market returns for investors. Still, it's important to look behind the numbers and determine why a company is buying back its shares and how.

Compliance with Contract Terms

Owners' equity is specified in many contracts with lenders, suppliers, and others (Chapter 7). For example, lending agreements usually include covenants that restrict maximum allowable debt-to-equity levels, where equity refers to the book value amount disclosed on the company's balance sheet. Firms have incentives to use financial reporting latitude to circumvent these constraints. Consequently, financial statement analysts must understand how owners' equity is reported to determine whether companies are in compliance with their contractual terms.

IPSCO INC.
www.ipsco.com

For example, the 2001 audited financial statements of IPSCO Inc., a major mini-mill producer of steel and steel products, contained the following footnote (amounts in thousands of U.S. dollars):

> ### 13. Dividends
> The most restrictive covenant pertaining to dividend payments in the company's financing agreements requires consolidated shareholders' equity, excluding the balance of outstanding subordinated notes, to be maintained at a minimum of [US]$570,000 plus 50% of net income earned after 31 December 1998. At 31 December 2001, the company's shareholders' equity exceeded this requirement by [US]$225.046.

In this case, providers of financing to IPSCO are using an owners' equity accounting item—the total dollar amount credited to consolidated shareholders' equity excluding outstanding subordinated notes—to restrict the ability of IPSCO to declare and pay dividends. This restriction is intended to ensure that IPSCO maintains a cash cushion for repayment of its debt principal and interest. Monitoring compliance with the form and substance of this restriction requires an understanding of accounting for shareholders' equity.

Preferred shares do not ordinarily carry voting rights. **Participating** preferred shares entitle their holders to share in profits above and beyond the declared dividend, along with common shareholders. Most preferred shares are **nonparticipating** insofar as holders are only entitled to receive the stipulated dividends.

Some financial experts suggest that certain equity instruments, such as **preferred shares,** are popular because they can be used to avoid various contractual constraints. Preferred shares get their name because relative to common shares, they confer to investors certain preferences to dividend payments and the distribution of corporate assets. Preferred shareholders must be paid their dividends in full before *any* cash distribution can be made to common shareholders; and if the company is liquidated, preferred shareholders must receive cash or other assets at least equal to the **stated value** of their shares before any assets are distributed to common shareholders.

The stated value of preferred shares is typically $100 per share. The dividend is often expressed as a percentage of the stated value. For example, a typical 8% preferred issue would promise a dividend of $8 per share ($100 stated value × 8%). Unlike bond interest expense, however, preferred share dividends are not a contractual obligation, which, if unpaid, could precipitate bankruptcy proceedings. Instead, preferred dividends are declared quarterly by the company's board of directors and can be omitted even in profitable years.

However, preferred shares are usually *cumulative*. This means that if for any reason a particular quarter's preferred dividend is not paid, then no dividends on common shares can be paid until all unpaid past and current preferred dividends are paid. This feature protects purchasers of preferred shares from excessive cash distributions to common shareholders. Also, because it's okay to "skip" a preferred dividend, preferred shares are less risky than debt to issuing corporations.

The widespread use of preferred shares by companies is an interesting phenomenon. Preferred dividends—unlike bond interest expense—are not a deductible expense for tax purposes. Why do companies choose to raise capital this way rather than through debt where tax-deductible interest payments reduce financing costs relative to preferred share issues?

Corporations who *issue* preferred shares do so because of one or more of the following reasons:

1. Financially weak corporations may consider preferred shares to be less risky than debt, since missing a preferred dividend payment, unlike missing an interest payment, will not precipitate bankruptcy.
2. Companies with a history of operating losses usually don't pay income taxes as a result of their operating loss carryforwards. For these companies, debt no longer has a tax advantage, and thus preferred shares become more attractive.
3. Preferred shares are treated as equity rather than debt on financial statements. Companies precluded from issuing additional debt because of covenant restrictions can issue preferred shares instead and evade these restrictions.

The distinction between preferred shares and debt is often murky, since preferred shares (like debt) usually do not grant holders voting rights, and preferred shareholders have no direct control over the affairs of the company. The distinction between debt and preferred shares has been further blurred as companies began issuing **mandatorily redeemable preferred shares.** Although called preferred *shares*, these financial instruments require the issuing company to retire them (just like debt) at some future date—commonly in five or ten years. This kind of preferred share represents what many consider to be debt "disguised" as equity, and raises the general issue of whether these and similar securities should be classified on the balance sheet as debt or owners' equity.

For example, *CICA Handbook* Section 3860, "Financial Instruments—Disclosure and Presentation," requires companies to classify financial instruments on the basis of their economic substance rather than the legal form of the instrument, so even if a financial security is called preferred *shares*, its substance may indicate that it should be accounted for as debt. As an illustration, the American company L. A. Gear, Inc. issued mandatorily redeemable shares in the early 1990s, in which "[t]he Company is required to redeem 350,000 shares of the original issue on August 31, 1996, and 162,500 shares on August 31 thereafter until all remaining shares of Series A Preferred Stock have been redeemed" (L. A. Gear, Inc., 1994 annual report), and the SEC in the United States made the company account for these securities *outside of* share-

An alternative to the 8% fixed-rate preferred shares in this example is an **adjustable-rate** preferred, which pays a dividend that is adjusted, usually quarterly, based on money market or other rates.

L. A. GEAR
www.lagear.com

holders' equity on its balance sheet. By contrast, in its 1997 audited financial statements, MacMillan Bloedel Limited, a major Canadian forest products company until its recent takeover, classified its Series 8 preferred shares as part of shareholders' equity in spite of the fact that it is required "to make all reasonable efforts to purchase 18,998 Series 8 shares quarterly at a price not exceeding $25.00 per share." MacMillan Bloedel classified its shares in this way presumably because there was no compulsion to redeem them, only a requirement to make "all reasonable efforts."

So classification of preferred share-like securities requires that users and other analysts of a company's financial statements attempt to garner as much information as possible to ensure that they are comfortable with the company's classification. After all, classifying a financial instrument as equity rather than debt, or vice versa, has significant implications for income measurement and financial position measurement. For instance, Agrium Inc. issued an innovative type of financial instrument in 1998 called Canadian Originated Preferred Securities (or COPrS), and included the US$171 million credit amount as part of shareholders' equity. Note 15 (entitled "Preferred Securities") of the company's 1998 audited financial statements described these securities as follows:

AGRIUM INC.
www.agrium.com

> *In April 1998, the Corporation issued [US]$175 million 8% unsecured Canadian Originated Preferred Securities ("COPrS") due June 30, 2047, accruing charges from the date of issuance and payable quarterly commencing June 30, 1998. The Corporation also has the ability to defer the charges for up to 20 consecutive periods, subject to certain restrictions. The COPrS are redeemable at the option of the Corporation, in whole or in part, on or after April 22, 2003 at the principal amount plus accrued and unpaid charges (the "Redemption price") to the date of redemption. The Corporation may, at its option, pay the Redemption Price or any quarterly charges in cash or by delivering common shares to a trustee for subsequent sale, in which event the holder of the COPrS shall be entitled to receive a cash payment equal to the Redemption Price or any quarterly charges from proceeds from the sale of common shares on behalf of the holder. Holders of the COPrS will not be entitled to receive any common shares in satisfaction of the obligation to pay the Redemption Price.*
>
> *The principal amount of the COPrS, net of after-tax issue costs of [US]$4 million, is classified as preferred securities in Shareholders' Equity. Preferred securities charges are recorded, after current tax (1998—[US]$4 million), against retained earnings.*

In addition, the prospectus that Agrium issued (April 15, 1998) in connection with the COPrS securities indicated that:

- "The Securities will be issued as unsecured junior subordinated debt of the Corporation" (p. 7)
- "There are no terms in the Securities that limit the ability of the Corporation or its subsidiaries to incur additional indebtedness"(p. 7)
- The maturity date of the securities is June 30, 2047, and the company may not extend any interest payment extensions beyond the maturity date (p. 7)
- "Except in limited circumstances described herein, the Corporation shall not pay or declare dividends on any of its capital stock (except by way of stock dividend) at any time when interest on the Securities is either in default or is being deferred"(p. 7)
- No assets are being set aside in a sinking fund to satisfy the COPrS (p. 8)

- "The net proceeds from the sale of the Securities offered hereby will be used to finance share repurchases with any balance to be used for general corporate purposes" (p. 8)

Are these so-called COPrS really preferred stock and thus part of shareholders' equity—as Agrium has accounted for them—or are they better classified as debt? They seem to contain characteristics of both. For example, the existence of a maturity date (June 30, 2047) strongly signals a debt-like financial instrument (and probably debt classification in the United States—see the L. A. Gear example above). But the ability to defer "interest" payments seems at least a bit equity-like, at least in the short run.

Recap

Is it equity or is it debt? When it comes to mandatorily redeemable preferred shares, the answer isn't obvious. That's why it is important for analysts to examine carefully the *substance* of such financial instruments.

Legality of Corporate Distributions

Corporate distributions to shareholders are governed by laws that vary from one jurisdiction to another. The intent of these laws is to prohibit companies from distributing "excessive" assets to owners and thereby making themselves insolvent—that is, incapable of repaying creditor claims. These laws were designed to protect creditors by ensuring that only solvent companies distribute cash to owners.

Whether or not dividends are legally able to be declared and paid by a corporation requires that management examine the particular legislation under which the company was incorporated. Historically, many jurisdictions prohibited dividends if the balance in the retained earnings account, and perhaps other sections of shareholders' equity, became negative as a result of the dividend. But more modern legislation tends to adopt an approach towards assessing the legality of dividends based on the ability of the company to continue as a going concern and not on historical cost-based accounting requirements. For example, the CBCA proscribes the declaration or payment of a dividend if as a result it is reasonable to believe that such an action would result in insolvency such that:

- the company would be unable to pay its liabilities as they become due; or
- the sum of the company's liabilities plus its legal capital would be less than the realizable value of its assets

This last test is very similar to that in the 1984 *Revised Model Business Corporation Act* in the United States, which said that as long as the *fair value of assets* exceeds the *fair value of liabilities* after the dividend transaction, the company is considered to be solvent. *The point is that the book value of shareholders' equity may not give an accurate picture of potentially legal distributions in jurisdictions that focus on insolvency tests rather than tests based on recorded shareholders' equity.* For example, Rogers Communications Inc. paid dividends in 1998 on its preferred shares even though it had a deficit of $854,134,000 and an overall shareholders' equity deficiency of $41,525,000 as at its year-end of December 31, 1998.

Existing disclosure rules for owners' equity *emphasize the source of capital, but ignore the ability of the corporation to make distributions to shareholders*. To ascertain the amount of potential distributions, statement analysts would need to know

Remember the **repayment problem** described in Chapter 7? Managers have incentives to borrow money and then pay all the cash out to shareholders, leaving the company insolvent and the bank with a loan receivable that will never be repaid.

ROGERS
COMMUNICATIONS
INC.
www.rogers.ca

two things: (1) the distribution law in the jurisdiction where the firm is incorporated and (2) fair value information if the law permits distributions based on the excess fair value of net assets. Unfortunately, this fair value information may be difficult to obtain, since GAAP do not require its disclosure except for marketable securities and certain investments (Chapter 16) and limited other items.

Recap

GAAP reporting rules are often sufficient to allow analysts and others to ascertain the maximum legal distribution available to common shareholders. Analysts must be aware that other data may have to be gathered to ascertain the dollar amount that can be distributed.

Illustration of the Shareholders' Equity Section of a Balance Sheet

The Shareholders' Equity section of Agrium Inc.'s 1998 consolidated balance sheet is shown in Exhibit 15.1. Notice that it contains four broad subdivisions; the changes over time in these subdivisions of Agrium's shareholders' equity are tracked in the company's Consolidated Statement of Changes in Shareholders' Equity shown in Exhibit 15.2 on page 722, a financial statement that some companies publish (Agrium stopped doing so in 2000). We will use this statement to reconstruct the journal entries accounting for changes in Agrium's shareholders' equity over the first year of the three-year period shown, from January 1, 1996, to December 31, 1996, and let you complete the reconstruction of journal entries from January 1, 1997, to December 31, 1998. In this way, we illustrate some of the complexities of GAAP-basis accounting for shareholders' equity, and how some useful information may be extracted.

Exhibit 15.1 AGRIUM INC.

Consolidated Balance Sheets—Excerpt

	As at December 31,	
(millions of US$)	1998	1997
Shareholders' Equity		
Preferred securities	171	—
Common shares	359	389
Retained earnings	243	258
Cumulative translation adjustment	(50)	(16)
	$723	$631

Let's begin with the first change to the opening 1996 balance. According to Exhibit 15.2, 1 million common shares were repurchased for cash (all amounts are rounded to the nearest million in Agrium's published statement; also notice that Agrium reports in U.S. dollars, a not-uncommon practice of many Canadian companies with a debit of US$3 million to "Common shares" and US$10 million to "Retained earnings." The journal entry was therefore:

DR	Common shares	$ 3 million	
DR	Retained earnings	10 million	
	CR Cash		$13 million

Since no "Treasury shares" account was used, it seems that these 1 million common shares were cancelled. If they were, Section 3240 of the *CICA Handbook* requires that the cost of reacquiring the shares should be debited "[t]o share capital, in an amount equal to the par, stated or assigned value of the shares … [and] … [a]ny excess, to retained earnings" (Section 3240, para. 15). So therefore we can deduce that the sum of the debits to the "Common shares" and "Retained earnings" accounts must have equalled the credit to "Cash," as in the above reconstructed journal entry.

The next line in the financial statement in Exhibit 15.2, "Issued on exercise of stock options," seems to have resulted in this journal entry:

DR	Cash	$15 million	
	CR Common shares		$15 million

And the next line, "Issued on employee incentive plans," suggests that common shares should be credited for US$5 million. But, according to the financial statement in Exhibit 15.2, no actual shares were issued, so how can we deduce the debit side of this journal entry? The answer is that we cannot from the information in the financial statement given in Exhibit 15.2, but if we look back at Agrium's 1996 audited financial statements, we find that note 12 of that year discloses that 425,265 common shares were issued for US$4,631,000 with respect to employee incentives. The actual journal entry is then:

DR	Cash	$4,631,000	
	CR Common shares		$4,631,000

So the rounding to the nearest million dollars and million shares in Agrium's 1998 Consolidated Statements of Changes in Shareholders' Equity was very misleading.

The next line item, "Conversion of preferred shares to common shares," is straightforward, resulting in the following entry:

DR	Preferred shares	$31 million	
	CR Common shares		$31 million

"Share issue costs" which result in a debit of US$3 million to "Common shares," are explained by the reconstructed entry:

DR	Common shares	$3 million	
	CR Cash		$3 million

The account "Cash" was credited in our reconstructed entry, even though other resources in addition to cash might have been used, although this is unlikely. Notice that the debit side of this entry goes to shareholders' equity and not net income since it is a capital transaction, and Section 3610 says that "*Capital transactions should be excluded from the determination of net income …*" (para. .01).

The next line item, "Distribution to shareholders of discontinued operations," is partly explained by examining note 6 to Agrium's 1998 audited financial statements, which says, "On June 26, 1996, the Corporation transferred cash [and other assets] to a new wholly-owned subsidiary. The book value of net assets of the subsidiary were subsequently distributed to the Corporation's shareholders for [US]$248 million, including cash of [US]$137 million." The reconstructed entry is then:

DR	Common shares	$183 million	
DR	Retained earnings	65 million	
	CR Various assets of discontinued business		$248 million

Exhibit 15.2 AGRIUM INC.
Consolidated Statements of Changes in Shareholders' Equity

| | Capital | | | | | | | |
| | Preferred | | Common | | | | Cumulative | |
(millions of US$ and millions of shares)	Shares/ Securities	Amount	Shares	Amount	Contributed Surplus	Retained Earnings	Translation Adjustment	Total
1996								
Balance as at January 1, 1996	1	$ 31	134	$569	$51	$196	$17	$864
Repurchased for cash	—	—	(1)	(3)	—	(10)	—	(13)
Issued on exercise of stock options	—	—	3	15	—	—	—	15
Issued on employee incentive plans	—	—	—	5	—	—	—	5
Conversion of preferred shares to common shares	(1)	(31)	4	31	—	—	—	—
Share issue costs	—	—	—	(3)	—	—	—	(3)
Distribution to shareholders of discontinued operations (Note 6)	—	—	—	(183)	—	(65)	—	(248)
Net earnings	—	—	—	—	—	151	—	151
Dividends declared	—	—	—	—	—	(62)	—	(62)
Business combination costs (Note 5)	—	—	—	—	—	(6)	—	(6)
Translation adjustment	—	—	—	—	—	—	(2)	(2)
Balance as at December 31, 1996	—	—	140	431	51	204	15	701
1997								
Repurchased for cash	—	—	(15)	(46)	(51)	(116)	—	(213)
Issued on exercise of stock options	—	—	1	4	—	—	—	4
Net earnings	—	—	—	—	—	185	—	185
Dividends declared	—	—	—	—	—	(15)	—	(15)
Translation adjustment	—	—	—	—	—	—	(31)	(31)
Balance as at December 31, 1997	—	—	126	389	—	258	(16)	631
1998								
Issued for cash—Canadian Originated Preferred Securities ("COPrS")	7	175	—	—	—	—	—	175
COPrS issue costs	—	(4)	—	—	—	—	—	(4)
Repurchased for cash	—	—	(12)	(35)	—	(117)	—	(152)
Issued on exercise of stock options	—	—	1	5	—	—	—	5
Net earnings	—	—	—	—	—	121	—	121
Common share dividends declared	—	—	—	—	—	(13)	—	(13)
Preferred securities charges	—	—	—	—	—	(6)	—	(6)
Translation adjustment	—	—	—	—	—	—	(34)	(34)
Balance as at December 31, 1998	7	$171	115	$359	$—	$243	$(50)	$723

The line "Net earnings" results in:

DR   Various income accounts closed out $151 million
      CR   Retained earnings $151 million

"Dividends declared" is captured by the following journal entry:

DR   Retained earnings $62 million
      CR   Dividends payable, or Cash $62 million

The next line item, "Business combination costs," refers the reader to note 5 of the 1998 audited financial statements, which describes a business combination between Agrium and a company called Viridian Inc. The combination was carried out by means of the two companies exchanging shares, and accounted for as a "pooling of interests" since neither company could be identified as the acquirer for accounting purposes. Such business combinations are described in Chapter 16. For our purposes here, all we need to know is that in 1998, Section 3610 of the *CICA Handbook*, "Capital Transactions," explicitly identified "expenses directly incurred in effecting a business combination accounted for as a pooling of interests" (para. .02) as part of the category of capital transactions that must be excluded from income, as Agrium has done. So the entry is:

DR   Retained earnings $6 million
      CR   Cash, or other assets $6 million

The final line item for 1996 is something called "Translation adjustment," and it is a debit to a shareholders' equity account labelled "Cumulative translation adjustment." This account is created because Agrium does a considerable amount of its business in money units other than the units in which it prepares its financial statements. Keep in mind that while Agrium is a Canadian company, and follows Canadian GAAP, it uses the U.S. dollar as its reporting currency since, according to its 1998 accounting policy note, the "U.S. dollar is the unit of measurement for the majority of the Corporation's business transactions." So any Canadian-denominated (or other non–U.S. dollar) transactions that it engages in, or Canadian-denominated (or other non–U.S. dollar) financial statements that any of the company's subsidiaries prepare, must be translated into U.S. dollars for purposes of preparing Agrium's (Canadian-GAAP!) financial statements that it reports to its shareholders and others. Canadian GAAP require that any translation gains or losses due to this process of translating financial statements from one money unit to another be deferred as a separate component of shareholders' equity (unless there is a realized reduction in the net investment). The reconstructed journal entry is then:

DR   Cumulative translation adjustment $2 million
      CR   Various assets and liabilities $2 million

Notice that the 1998 change in the account "Cumulative translation adjustment" is a debit, while the opening balance at the start of 1996 was a US$17 million credit. In fact, there's a debit to this account of US$31 million in 1997 and US$34 million in 1998 (see Exhibit 15.2). This all makes some sense when we recall that the U.S. dollar has strengthened against the Canadian dollar during the period 1997–98, so we might expect that Canadian dollars would equal fewer U.S. dollars, and a translation "loss," or debit would result.

Earnings per Share

Many people believe that the amounts of future income and cash flow that a company is expected to generate are major determinants of firm value (Chapter 6). Valuing the firm *as a whole* is crucial during merger negotiations, during buyouts, and in similar settings—relatively rare events in the ongoing life of a company. For day-to-day valuations, many analysts prefer to focus on the value of *individual* common shares. For this purpose it is helpful to know how much of the company's total earnings accrue to each share. This is why **earnings per share (EPS)** is computed.

Computing EPS is straightforward when the company has a simple capital structure. We first describe these procedures, and then we extend the analysis to situations involving more complicated capital structures.

Simple Capital Structure

A simple capital structure exists when a company has no convertible securities (either convertible debt or convertible preferred shares) and no options or warrants outstanding. In these circumstances, the following straightforward formula is used to compute what is called **basic earnings per common share** (EPS).[8] This is computed as follows:

$$\text{Basic EPS} = \frac{\text{Net income} - \text{Preferred dividends}}{\text{Weighted average number of common shares outstanding}}$$

To illustrate, let us assume Solomon Corporation had the following capital structure in the year 2003:

	January 1	December 31
Preferred shares, $100 stated value, 7%,		
10,000 shares issued and outstanding	$ 1,000,000	$ 1,000,000
Common shares,		
160,000 shares issued and outstanding	12,160,000	
200,000 shares issued and outstanding		16,200,000
Retained earnings	1,100,000	1,800,000
Total shareholders' equity	$14,260,000	$19,000,000

The 40,000 additional common shares were issued on September 1 and thus were outstanding for the last third of the year. The following factors explain the change in retained earnings during 2003:

Retained earnings, January 1	$1,100,000
Net income for the year	1,257,331
Preferred share dividends	(70,000)
Common share dividends	(487,331)
Retained earnings, December 31	$1,800,000

The denominator of the basic EPS formula uses the **weighted average** number of common shares outstanding over the accounting period. Since additional shares were issued during the year, this weighted average number of outstanding shares must be computed as follows:

Time Span	(a) Shares Outstanding	(b) Portion of Year	(c) Weighted Shares (Col. a × Col. b)
January 1–August 31	160,000	⅔	106,667
September 1–December 31	200,000	⅓	66,667
			173,334

Solomon Corporation's basic EPS for the year 2003 is:

$$\text{Basic EPS} = \frac{\text{Net income} - \text{Preferred dividends}}{\text{Weighted average number of common shares outstanding}}$$

$$= \frac{\$1,257,331 - \$70,000}{173,334 \text{ shares}} = \$6.85 \text{ per share}$$

Complex Capital Structure

A firm has a **complex capital structure** when its financing includes either securities that are convertible into common stock, or options and warrants that entitle holders to obtain common stock under specified conditions. These financial instruments increase the likelihood that additional common shares will be issued in the future. This possible increase in the number of shares is called potential **dilution.**

Suppose Jackson Products Company has 30,000 shares of common stock outstanding along with $100,000 of convertible debentures—that is, bonds that can be converted into common stock. According to the terms of the debenture agreement, each $1,000 face value bond can be exchanged for 300 common shares or common stock. If all debentures were exchanged, bondholders would receive 30,000 new shares of common stock. The effect on current common shareholders would be to *dilute* their claim to earnings from 100%—when they own all the common stock—to 50%—when they own only half of all outstanding shares.

Computed basic EPS ignores this potential dilution of current shareholders' ownership interest in the company. To recognize the increase in outstanding shares that would ensue from conversion or options exercise, Section 3500 and the U.S. *SFAS No. 128* requires companies with complex capital structures to compute another measure, one called **diluted EPS.**

The diluted EPS figure is a conservative measure of the earnings flow to each share of stock. It's conservative because the diluted EPS measure presumes the *maximum* possible new share creation—and thus the *minimum* earnings flow to each share. The computation of diluted EPS is based upon some reasonable assumptions. For example, consider the potential conversion of convertible debentures into common shares. Obviously, once the bonds are converted to common stock, the company does not need to make further debt principal and interest payments. Consequently, the diluted EPS computation recognizes (1) the new shares issued upon conversion (a denominator effect), and (2) the increase in after-tax net income that follows from the elimination of debt interest payments after conversion (a numerator effect).

You must also make assumptions for options or warrants when computing diluted EPS. When holders of options or warrants exercise them, they receive common shares; but at the same time, the company receives cash in an amount representing the exercise price of the options or warrants. In the

Convertibles are corporate securities—usually preferred shares or bonds—that are exchangeable for a set number of other securities—usually common shares—at a prestated price. From the issuer's standpoint, the convertible feature "sweetens" the marketability of the bond or preferred stock. A **call option** gives the holder the right to buy shares (typically 100) of the underlying stock at a fixed price before a specified date in the future—usually three, six, or nine months. **Employee stock options** are often of three to five years in duration. If the stock option is not exercised, the right to buy common shares expires. A **subscription warrant** is a security usually issued together with a bond or preferred stock that entitles the holder to buy a proportionate amount of common stock at a specified price—usually higher than market price at the time of issuance—for a period of years or in perpetuity.

Remember Microsoft's stock repurchase program cited earlier? Between 1990 and 1996, the company bought back 134 million shares of common stock for [US]$4.2 billion, while 336 million shares were issued under the company's employee stock option and purchases plan. But there's more! At the end of 1996, Microsoft employees owned stock options worth [US]$21.8 billion, so the potential future dilution was even greater.

computation of diluted EPS, this cash is assumed to be used to acquire already outstanding common shares in the market. Because of adjustments like these, the diluted EPS formula is slightly more complicated, as shown here:

Diluted earnings per share:

$$\text{Diluted EPS} = \frac{\text{Net income} - \text{Preferred dividends} + \begin{array}{c}\text{Income adjustments} \\ \text{due to dilutive} \\ \text{financial instruments}\end{array}}{\begin{array}{c}\text{Weighted average number of} \\ \text{common shares outstanding}\end{array} + \begin{array}{c}\text{Newly issuable shares} \\ \text{due to dilutive} \\ \text{financial instruments}\end{array}}$$

To illustrate how the diluted EPS computation works, we will extend the Solomon Corporation example. Assume that as of January 1, 2003, Solomon also had the following financial instruments outstanding:

- $1,000,000 of 5% convertible debenture bonds due in 15 years, which were sold at par ($1,000 per bond). Each $1,000 bond pays interest of $50 per year and is convertible into 10 shares of common stock.

- Options to buy 20,000 common shares at $100 per share. These options were issued on February 9, 2001, and expire on February 9, 2004.

Let's say the tax rate is 35% and Solomon stock sold for an average market price of $114 during 2003. Each financial instrument is potentially dilutive and must be incorporated into the diluted EPS computation as shown on the next page.

The convertible debentures are included in diluted EPS by assuming conversion on the first day of the reporting period (here, January 1, 2003). The after-tax effect of interest payments on the debt is *added back* in the EPS numerator, and the additional shares that would be issued on conversion are added to the denominator. Section 3500 calls this the **"if-converted" method.** We now illustrate the computation of diluted EPS in the presence of convertible debt.

The convertible debentures are presumed to have been converted into 10,000 additional shares of stock at the beginning of the year (January 1, 2003). Accordingly, 10,000 new common shares are added to the EPS denominator. Under the if-converted method, no interest would have been paid on the debentures this year because all bonds are assumed to be converted as of January 1. This means that interest of $50,000 would not have been paid on the presumptively converted bonds. With a 35% tax rate, net income would increase by $32,500 (i.e., $50,000 × [1 − 0.35]), and this amount is added to the diluted EPS numerator.

There were 1,000 bonds outstanding ($1,000,000 ÷ $1,000 par = 1,000 bonds), each convertible into 10 shares of common stock. Conversion of all bonds results in 1,000 bonds × 10 shares per bond = 10,000 new shares.

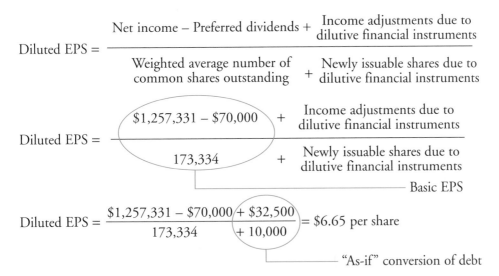

$$\text{Diluted EPS} = \frac{\text{Net income} - \text{Preferred dividends} + \begin{array}{c}\text{Income adjustments due to}\\\text{dilutive financial instruments}\end{array}}{\begin{array}{c}\text{Weighted average number of}\\\text{common shares outstanding}\end{array} + \begin{array}{c}\text{Newly issuable shares due to}\\\text{dilutive financial instruments}\end{array}}$$

$$\text{Diluted EPS} = \frac{\$1{,}257{,}331 - \$70{,}000 + \begin{array}{c}\text{Income adjustments due to}\\\text{dilutive financial instruments}\end{array}}{173{,}334 + \begin{array}{c}\text{Newly issuable shares due to}\\\text{dilutive financial instruments}\end{array}}$$

Basic EPS

$$\text{Diluted EPS} = \frac{\$1{,}257{,}331 - \$70{,}000 + \$32{,}500}{173{,}334 + 10{,}000} = \$6.65 \text{ per share}$$

"As-if" conversion of debt

In our example, the outstanding stock options will affect only the denominator of the diluted EPS computation. This adjustment reflects the difference between the option **exercise price** ($100 per common share) and the **average market price** ($114 per common share) during the period. Section 3500 assumes that any proceeds received on exercise of the options ($100 per share) are used to buy back already outstanding common shares at the average market price for the period. This is called the **treasury stock method.** We now illustrate the adjustment to compute diluted EPS under the treasury stock method.

Stock options are dilutive when they are "in the money"—that is, when the average market price ($114) exceeds the option price ($100). Using the treasury stock method, we assume that the $2,000,000 proceeds to the company from the presumptive exercise of the options (i.e., 20,000 shares at $100 per share) are used to repurchase previously issued common shares at the $114 average market price. The cash from the options is sufficient to acquire 17,544 shares (i.e., $2,000,000 ÷ $114 per share = 17,544 shares). Since 20,000 shares are presumed issued and 17,544 are presumed acquired, the difference (2,456 net new common shares) is added to the diluted EPS denominator:

In-the-money options are dilutive because the number of shares that can be repurchased with the proceeds from the options is smaller than the number of new shares issued on exercise of the options.

$$\text{Diluted EPS} = \frac{\$1{,}257{,}331 - \$70{,}000 + \$32{,}500}{173{,}334 + 10{,}000 + 2{,}456} = \$6.57 \text{ per share}$$

Treasury stock conversion of options

Notice that diluted EPS equals $6.57, an amount lower than the basic EPS number of $6.85. It is this potential decrease in the computed earnings flow to each common share that motivates the diluted EPS computation.

Is Earnings per Share a Meaningful Number?

EPS data are reported in the financial news and are prominent in corporate annual reports even though EPS suffers as a financial performance measure.

EPS ignores the amount of *capital* required to generate the reported earnings. This is easy to show with the following example that contrasts the 2003 financial performance of two companies:

	Company A	Company B
Net income available to common shareholders	$ 1,000,000	$ 1,000,000
Weighted average common shares outstanding	100,000	100,000
Basic earnings per share	$ 10	$ 10
Gross assets	$20,000,000	$30,000,000
Liabilities	$10,000,000	$10,000,000
Equity capital (assets – liabilities)	$10,000,000	$20,000,000
Return on equity	10%	5%

Both Company A and Company B report identical basic EPS of $10. But Company B needed twice as much equity capital and 50% more gross assets to attain the $1,000,000 net income. Even though the two companies report the same *level* of net income and EPS, Company B has a return on equity of only 5%, while Company A's figure is 10%. Company A generates more earnings from existing resources—that is, equity capital.

Because EPS ignores capital commitments, problems can arise when trying to interpret it. The narrow focus of the EPS ratio clouds comparisons between companies as well as year-to-year EPS changes for a single company. For example, even if year-to-year earnings' levels are the same, a company can "improve" its reported EPS by simply repurchasing some previously outstanding common shares. In addition, the numerator of the EPS ratio is largely based upon GAAP net income, a number that as we know has significant shortcomings.

Perhaps these shortcomings were made most vivid in the case of Enron. In the company's 2000 annual report (the last annual report issued before its late 2001 bankruptcy), Enron's two most senior managers, Kenneth Lay and Jeffrey Skilling, wrote in the shareholders' letter, "Enron is laser-focused on earnings per share …."

It is unnerving to observe an organization proclaim publicly that it (or its leadership cohort) "is laser-focused" on anything. This metaphor connotes an almost irrational tunnel vision and single-mindedness. Surely there are other goals, or targets, that also deserve management's attention? To be "laser-focused on earnings per share" is especially troubling. It suggests that "earnings per share" is a target, to be conquered or destroyed, rather than to be regarded as a measure by which success is partially assessed. Even if earnings per share is not a target, then it might bias managers' behaviour. After all, earnings per share is a measure with fundamental flaws. For example, the numerator is past-oriented, historic-cost based and subject to innumerable arbitrary allocations of revenues and expenses (both inter- and intra-temporally). The denominator may also be manipulated via, for example, share buybacks. Therefore, EPS should serve as the object of "laser-focused" attention only if management is terribly ill-informed … or perhaps worse, it is terribly knowledgeable about the capacity for earnings per share to be manipulated with abandon.

So, to answer the question "Is earnings per share a meaningful number?", we would suggest that earnings per share becomes meaningful in those corporate settings in which it is a target for executive compensation or other corporate goals (with Enron being an extreme example … in essence, Enron seemed to be a giant EPS machine!), meaningful to the people who must operate under its dominance. And therefore, it becomes meaningful for all those who have an interest in the corporation since managers whose compensation is affected by EPS will make decisions at least partly with EPS in mind. But, is it "meaningful" in the sense of fairly presenting the portion of an entity's earnings that accrue to each share? This question is difficult to answer, but we think the answer would have to be "no." EPS is a very dangerous number, and so deserves close scrutiny.

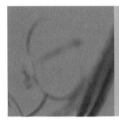

Recap

Earnings per share (EPS) is a popular but perhaps less-than-useful summary measure of a company's profit performance. Its fully diluted version tells you how much profit (or loss) each common share has earned after adjustments for potential dilution from options, warrants, and convertible securities are factored in. But EPS has its limitations.

Accounting for Stock-Based Compensation

Many companies compensate managers and other salaried employees with a combination of cash and share options—that is, options to purchase equity shares in the company. A typical employee share option gives the employee the right to purchase a specified number of common shares at a specified price over some specified time period. The specified price—called the **exercise price**—is usually equal to or higher than the market price of the underlying shares at the time the options are issued. An option to buy 100 shares at $50 per share at any time within the next five years might be issued when the shares themselves are selling for $30. When the exercise price exceeds the current price, the share option is "out of the money." An option to purchase common shares at $50 is valuable even though the shares are currently selling for only $30 because there's a chance the price will climb above $50 sometime during the ensuing five years.

Companies use share options to augment cash compensation for several reasons. First, options might help align employees' interests with those of owners (shareholders). Employees with share options as a significant portion of their compensation have a strong incentive to make decisions that ultimately cause the share price to exceed the option exercise price.

Second, many "startup" high-growth companies are "cash-starved" and cannot afford to pay competitive cash salaries. Share options provide a way for them to attract talented employees while conserving cash.

Third, generally this compensation is not taxable to the employee until the option is exercised. This is an attractive feature, because it allows employees to accumulate wealth while postponing taxes.

Fourth, GAAP permitted companies to avoid recording a compensation expense when stock options were part of a remuneration package for executives. In many cases, this was alleged to have had a materially positive impact on the company's bottom line. But, as of early 2003, the AcSB is considering requiring companies to record such expenses.

Canadian accounting standards for stock-based compensation were until recently quite limited, and focused on disclosure of the commitments to issue shares under the options, and the details of actual share transactions during the reporting periods (Section 3240.04 and .05). Further, the AcSB issued new Canadian GAAP (Section 3870, "Stock-Based Compensation and Other Stock-Based Payments"), effective on or after January 1, 2002. This GAAP is essentially the same as existing U.S. GAAP. Some Canadian companies have provided early disclosure with respect to this standard. An example is shown in Exhibit 15.3, which reproduces the pertinent portions of Canadian Tire Corporation's note 8 ("Stock-Based Compensation Plans") to its audited financial statements for the period ended December 29, 2001.

As we can see from the exhibit, Canadian Tire has five types of stock-based compensation plans; our concern here is the "Stock options" plan. The new information

CANADIAN TIRE
CORPORATION
**www.canadiantire.
ca**

EXHIBIT 15.3 CANADIAN TIRE CORPORATION

Excerpt from 2001 Audited Financial Statements

8. STOCK-BASED COMPENSATION PLANS

The Corporation has five stock-based compensation plans, which are described below.

Employee Profit Sharing Plans

The Corporation offers its employees a Deferred Profit Sharing Plan ("DPSP") and previously offered an Employee Profit Sharing Plan ("EPSP"). The amount of the award is contingent on the Corporation's profitability. The maximum amount available is based on 6.75 percent of pre-tax profits, after certain adjustments. The maximum amount of the contribution to the DPSP per employee per year is subject to maximum limits as set by Canada Customs and Revenue Agency. The DPSP is required to invest and maintain 10 percent of its holdings in the Corporation's Class A Non-Voting Shares. The participants of the former EPSP elected to terminate the Plan and accordingly, the assets were distributed to the participants in February 2001. This had no impact on the Corporation's earnings for the year.

In 2001, the Corporation contributed $12.4 million (2000 – $16.1 million) under terms of the DPSP and the EPSP, towards the Trustee-managed investment portfolio. As of December 29, 2001, the DPSP held 419,280 Common Shares (2000 – 419,280) and 3,312,715 Class A Non-Voting Shares (2000 – 3,794,914) of the Corporation.

Employee Stock Purchase Plan

The Corporation offers an Employee Stock Purchase Plan ("ESPP") to its employees, whereby employees can choose to have up to 10 percent of their annual base earnings withheld to purchase Class A Non-Voting Shares of the Corporation. The purchase price of the shares is calculated monthly and is equal to the weighted average share price at which Class A Non-Voting Shares of the Corporation trade on the Toronto Stock Exchange for a given month. The Corporation may elect to match up to 50 percent of employee contributions to the ESPP.

The Corporation contributed $8.1 million in 2001 (2000 – $7.9 million), under the terms of the ESPP, towards the purchase of Class A Non-Voting Shares. These shares were purchased on the Toronto Stock Exchange. Under the Plan, the Corporation issued from treasury 740,479 Class A Non-Voting Shares in 2001 (2000 – 817,673) to employees.

Deferred Share Unit Plan

The Corporation offers a Deferred Share Unit Plan ("DSUP") for members of the Board of Directors. Under the DSUP each director may elect to receive all or a percentage of his or her annual compensation in the form of notional Class A Non-Voting Shares of the Corporation called deferred share units ("DSUs"). The issue price of each DSU is equal to the weighted average share price at which Class A Non-Voting Shares of the Corporation trade on the Toronto Stock Exchange during the 10-day period prior to the last day of the quarter in which the DSU is issued. A director must elect to participate or change his or her participation in the DSUP prior to the beginning of a fiscal quarter. The DSU account of each director includes the value of dividends, if any, as if reinvested in additional DSUs. The director is not permitted to convert DSUs into cash until retirement from the Board. The value of the DSUs, when converted to cash, will be equivalent to the market value of the Class A Non-Voting Shares at the time the conversion takes place. The value of the outstanding DSUs as at December 29, 2001 was $833,000 (2000 – $331,000).

Restricted Share Units

The Corporation has granted restricted share units ("RSUs") to certain employees which entitle the participant to receive a cash payment in an amount equal to the weighted average closing price of Class A Non-Voting Shares traded on the Toronto Stock Exchange for the 20-day period prior to and including the last day of the restriction period, multiplied by an applicable multiplier if specific performance-based criteria are met. The restriction period is a maximum of three years less 30 days from the date of grant. Compensation expense related to the RSUs is accrued over the term of the RSU based on the expected total compensation to be paid out at the end of the restriction period, factoring in the probability of any performance-based criteria being met during that period. The end of the restriction period is October 3, 2003. The compensation expense recorded for the year ended December 29, 2001, in respect of this plan was $5,786,000 (2000 – $631,000).

Stock Options

The Corporation has granted options to certain employees for the purchase of Class A Non-Voting Shares, with vesting occurring on a graduated basis over a four-year period. The exercise price of each option equals the weighted average closing price of Class A Non-Voting shares on the Toronto Stock Exchange for the 10-day period preceding the date of grant. Options may be exercisable over a term of 10 years. The Corporation is authorized to grant options to its employees in respect of up to 8.4 million Class A Non-Voting Shares.

The Corporation attributes no compensation expense at the grant date. When the options are exercised, the proceeds received are credited to share capital. The outstanding options as at December 29, 2001 were granted at prices between $11.06 and $40.82 and expire between May 2002 and November 2011.

Stock option transactions during 2001 and 2000 were as follows:

| | 2001 | | 2000 | |
	Number of Shares	Weighted Average Exercise Price	Number of Shares	Weighted Average Exercise Price
Outstanding at beginning of year	3,882,129	$24.79	2,068,877	$28.70
Granted	791,500	21.36	2,213,000	21.53
Exercised	(210,246)	15.77	(63,834)	14.25
Forfeited and expired	(321,703)	27.32	(335,914)	29.35
Outstanding at end of year	4,141,680	$24.46	3,882,129	$24.79

The following table summarizes information about stock options outstanding at December 29, 2001:

| | Options Outstanding | | | Options Exercisable | |
Range of Exercise Prices	Number of Outstanding Shares	Weighted Average Remaining Contractual Life	Weighted Average Exercise Price	Number Exercisable at December 29, 2001	Weighted Average Exercise Prices
$27.53 to 40.82	997,601	6.79	$36.00	611,201	$35.01
24.96 to 26.81	1,057,002	7.63	26.38	400,102	25.90
16.61 to 23.87	895,213	8.43	19.56	103,025	18.40
11.06 to 16.47	1,191,864	7.66	15.94	462,239	15.11
$11.06 to 40.82	4,141,680	7.67	$24.46	1,576,567	$25.78

Pro-Forma Disclosure

In November 2001, The Canadian Institute of Chartered Accountants issued handbook section 3870, "Stock-based compensation and other stock-based payments," which will be effective for fiscal years beginning on or after January 1, 2002. This new standard requires pro-forma disclosures of the impact of stock option grants on net earnings and earnings per share as if the fair-value based method had been used to account for stock-based compensation cost. The Corporation will apply the provisions of this new standard in 2002. Provided below, however, is the pro-forma disclosure for 2001 that would have been required for stock options granted during 2001 if the new standard had been in effect for 2001.

The weighted-average grant-date fair value of options granted in 2001 has been estimated at $7.56 using the Black–Scholes model for pricing options. The pricing model assumes weighted-average expected dividend yields of 1.47 percent annually, weighted-average risk free interest rate of 5.3 percent, weighted-average expected common stock price volatility of 35.2 percent and a weighted-average expected life of 4.5 years.

Had the fair-value based method been used for stock option awards granted in 2001, the Corporation's net earnings in 2001 would have decreased by $1.2 million and basic and diluted earnings per share reduced by $0.02. These impacts on net earnings and basic and diluted earnings per share omit the effect of awards granted before December 31, 2000.

to be disclosed under Section 3870 is shown in the "Pro-Forma Disclosure," the technical details of which we will explain later in this chapter. The note tells us that "[h]ad the fair-value based method been used for stock option awards granted in 2001, the Corporation's net earnings in 2001 would have decreased by $1.2 million ...." Since Canadian Tire reported $177 million of earnings in 2001, this is an immaterial amount. But these stock option expense magnitudes can be material; this may be illustrated by referring to two examples of Canadian companies that even some years ago (in 1998) provided statement readers with disclosures similar to what Section 3870 will require, since these companies followed the U.S. GAAP in this area, *SFAS No. 123*, "Accounting for Stock-Based Compensation":

| | 1998 | |
Company	Net Income as Reported (US$ millions)	SFAS No. 123 Disclosure of Stock-Based Compensation (US$ millions)
Jet Form Corporation	11	5
IPSCO Inc.	113	17

The development of U.S. *SFAS No. 123* was very controversial. Since the Canadian Section 3870 is very similar, it is instructive to look at the U.S. history a bit.

Historical Perspective: What Happened in the United States

Suppose an employee agrees to work this year in exchange for a small current salary and the promise of additional cash compensation five years later. No one disputes the notion that the employee's salary should be recorded on the company's books as an expense of the current year. But what about promised compensation? Should it be recorded as a current year expense, or should the expense be postponed five years until the employee actually receives the cash? This question is at the heart of the employee share options debate, at least from an accounting theory perspective.

Before *SFAS No. 123* was adopted in the United States in 1995, accounting for share-based compensation was governed by *Accounting Principles Board (APB) No. 25*.[9] This pronouncement was issued in 1972, one year prior to publication of what is now the universally accepted approach for valuing traditional stock (share) options—the Black–Scholes method.[10] Because *APB No. 25* preceded modern option pricing theory, it offered no mechanisms for establishing the value of stock options granted as compensation to employees. Options issued with an exercise price equal to or above the market price of the underlying common shares *were assumed to have no value* for compensation expense purposes. Under *APB No. 25*, if Ramos Corporation issued on June 28, 1972, ten-year options to employees that entitled each one of them to buy 100 shares at $10 per share when the existing share price was also $10, *no compensation expense would be recognized because these options were deemed to be valueless.*

Obviously, options with terms like those in the Ramos Corporation example are valuable; the price of the company's common share could easily rise above the $10 exercise price sometime during the ten-year life of the option. Over the 1970s and early 1980s, option pricing *theory* evolved into option pricing *practice* using the Black–Scholes model as the standard device for valuing traded options. Despite this post–*APB No. 25* breakthrough, options issued as compensation were generally treated as being valueless at the grant date. Compensation expense *was* recognized in rare instances.

During the 1980s companies increasingly adopted employee compensation packages designed to link employee pay to company performance, thus causing stock option plans to proliferate as an element of employee compensation. Many auditors and other financial experts considered the *APB No. 25* presumption that options were valueless to be simply incorrect. Because these beliefs were widespread, the U.S. FASB began reconsidering the accounting for share options in 1984.

Sentiment in the business community soon shifted considerably. Strong and widespread opposition to the FASB initiative surfaced as it became clear that the new proposal would result in expenses, at times material, being recognized on the income statement when share options were granted. Those opposed to the FASB's proposal raised arguments against expense recognition that roughly parallel the themes of this chapter. Their criticisms cited four issues: (1) appropriate income measurement, (2) compliance with contract terms and restrictions, (3) legality of corporate distributions to owners, and (4) linkage to equity valuation.

In the next subsection, we briefly survey these objections to the FASB's share options approach. Understanding these objections is important from a Canadian perspective, since many Canadian companies comply with the U.S. accounting standard that ultimately resulted.

Opposition to the FASB

Some opponents of the FASB's proposal questioned whether providing share options to employees constituted an accounting expense. These opponents contended that treating share options as an expense would violate **appropriate income measurement** because share options do not involve a cash outflow. On the contrary, they argued, when—and if—the options were eventually exercised, cash would flow *into* the company, not *out*. Supporters of the FASB counterargued that cash was not the issue. Expenses often arise independently of cash outflows. One prominent advocate of this position was Warren Buffett, CEO of Berkshire Hathaway, Inc., who said:

> *[Some contend] that options should not be viewed as a cost because they "aren't dollars out of a company's coffers." I see this line of reasoning as offering exciting possibilities to American corporations for instantly improving their reported profits. For example, they could eliminate the cost of insurance by paying for it with options. So if you're a CEO and subscribe to this "no cash–no cost" theory of accounting, I'll make you an offer you can't refuse: Give us a call at Berkshire and we will happily sell you insurance in exchange for a bundle of long-term options on your company's stock.*
>
> *Shareholders should understand that companies incur costs when they deliver something of value to another party and not just when cash changes hands.*[11]

Buffett's position that expenses arise when stock options are issued is consistent with the proprietary view of financial reporting—the idea that the firm and its owners are the same. Shareholders are giving up a portion of their ownership interest by having the company issue additional shares—or options for shares—to employees. From this perspective, issuing stock options to employees represents an expense to the company.

Another argument raised by opponents to the FASB's proposal was that treating employee stock options as an expense could jeopardize **compliance with contract terms and conditions.** Companies with large employee share option awards might, under the FASB's proposal, violate loan covenants tied to reported earnings. For example, the "times-interest-earned" ratio would deteriorate if these option grants were expensed.

Impartial observers who understand contracting incentives can see why companies with significant employee options would raise this objection. Their interests would be harmed by the FASB proposal, and economic intuition tells us that companies would strongly resist such initiatives. On the other hand, one can appreciate the FASB's mission to "do the right thing"—to draft rules that closely mirror underlying economic circumstances. If a particular accounting proposal correctly captures these economic effects, it presumably should be issued even though it may harm some companies. Furthermore, many of the FASB's most vocal opponents were companies whose employee share options—if expensed—would have decreased earnings by a trivial amount. Since the potential impact of the FASB proposal on these firms' covenants and other contracts was insignificant, what was really motivating their opposition?

The compensation paid to top corporate executives was under intense scrutiny in the early 1990s. Corporate restructurings and layoffs were widespread, a recession was in progress, and many companies demonstrated lacklustre financial performance. In this climate, some critics questioned whether top corporate executives should continue to enjoy increasingly large salaries and bonuses while their employees were experiencing financial hardship. The issue quickly became political.

In 1993, the U.S. Congress limited the tax deductibility of executive compensation to $1,000,000 per employee—any excess could not be claimed as a deduction on the corporate tax return except when compensation **was tied to the achievement of explicit and preset performance goals.** The passage of this law clearly illustrates public sentiment on this issue. Corporate leaders, sensitive to the growing scrutiny of executive compensation levels, may have felt that the FASB's plan would draw unwanted attention to executive pay.

The **legality of corporate distributions to owners** was never at issue regarding executive compensation. Political considerations aside, companies are free under the law to pay corporate executives whatever amounts are deemed appropriate by their board of directors. However, an issue did arise—whether large executive salaries were *proper*. Some companies were perceived to oppose the FASB's proposal because it would add the value of options to cash compensation and thus make it easier for critics of "excessive" pay to spotlight certain companies and executives.

Opponents to the FASB's proposal also invoked an argument based on the **linkage to equity valuation.** They believed that a simple "price-earnings multiple" relationship exists between reported earnings and common share values. Under the FASB's plan, they argued, employee share option grants would increase compensation expense and lower earnings—and thus lower share price. (Our discussion of the earnings capitalization model in Chapter 6 suggests that the relationship between earnings and share price is more complicated than this.) They argued that as share prices fell, small companies who were heavy users of share options would have difficulty raising new equity capital. This position was clearly articulated by U.S. Senator Feinstein (Democrat, California) when she introduced legislation designed to block the FASB's plan. She said:

[The Bill] will also require the Financial Accounting Standards Board (FASB) to reexamine [its] recent decision to impose huge new accounting charges on the use of employee share options. I am seriously concerned that if FASB's rule is adopted, tens of thousands of desperately needed jobs in California and the Nation will never be created.[12]

Senator Feinstein believed that the FASB plan would make it more difficult for high-technology companies to raise new equity capital, thereby inhibiting expansion and job creation.

Despite growing business opposition, the FASB persisted and continued to move toward expense treatment of share-based compensation. Congress later initiated legislation which would have eliminated the FASB's independence by requiring the SEC to approve of all new FASB standards.[13] Faced with this threat, the FASB was compelled to abandon its proposal and implement a compromise treatment.

The Compromise—*SFAS No. 123*

The widespread, powerful opposition to recognizing share-based compensation as an expense caused the FASB to allow a choice of accounting methods:

1. Companies in the United States could choose to continue using the *APB No. 25* approach, under which compensation expense was rarely recognized.
2. Alternatively, companies could measure the **fair value** of the share option and charge this amount to expense.

The AcSB adopted the same compromise in Section 3870; however, consideration is being given (as of early 2003) to making the fair value/expensing treatment compulsory.

The fair value of a share option is measured using standard option pricing models, with adjustments for the unique factors of the option. The FASB encouraged companies to adopt the fair value approach rather than to continue using *APB No. 25*, since it considered the fair value approach to be preferable. Companies that chose to continue using *APB No. 25* accounting were also required to disclose in a footnote what net income would have been had compensation expense been recognized under the fair value approach, and this is the choice that our small sample of Canadian companies, discussed previously, made. The share option reporting alternatives are represented graphically in Figure 15.1.

Implementing the fair value approach of Section 3870 and *SFAS No. 123* is not, in principle, difficult. The standards contain many detailed guidelines for measuring compensation expense. We describe these procedures tersely using a "big-picture" approach—that's all you need to grasp the overall impact on financial numbers.

Assume that Guyton Corporation grants 100 common share options to each of its top 300 managers on January 1, 2000. At that date, both the exercise price of the options and the market price of Guyton's shares is $30. To provide managers with an incentive to remain at Guyton, the options cannot be exercised before January 1, 2003. This time span between the grant date and the first available exercise date is called the **vesting period.** Guyton's options do not expire until January 1, 2010, giving the options a ten-year legal life. But Section 3870 and *SFAS No. 123* require that we estimate the **expected life of the options**—meaning we must forecast when the options are likely to be exercised by employees. Factors to consider in estimating the expected life include the average length of time similar grants have remained outstanding in the past and the expected volatility of the company's common share price. Let's assume Guyton's options have an expected life of five years.

FIGURE 15.1
EMPLOYEE
STOCK OPTION
REPORTING
ALTERNATIVES
UNDER *SFAS
NO. 123*

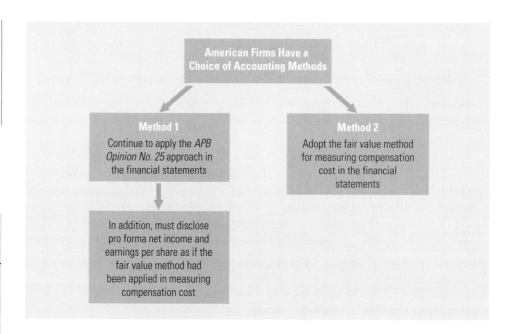

Volatility in option pricing models is measured using a benchmark of one standard deviation of the continuously compounded rate of return on the stock over a specified time period. Assume Guyton shares have experienced a continuously compounded rate of return of 10%. Since one standard deviation encompasses roughly 66% of a normal distribution, the 20% expected volatility means there is a 66% probability that the rate of return on Guyton's shares will be 10% ± 20% in any one year—that is, there is a two-thirds chance that the return in any year will range between a low of –10% and a high of +30%.

Both Section 3870 (para. 44) and *SFAS No. 123* (para. 28) require firms to estimate what proportion of the options originally granted will never vest due to employee turnover. Compensation expense includes only those options that are not forfeited. For example, if Guyton Corporation estimated that only 29,000 options would ultimately vest, compensation cost would be $291,450 (i.e., $10.05 × 29,000) rather than $301,500.

Section 3870 and *SFAS No. 123* specify that the fair value of the share options is to be measured at the **grant date**—the date when both the terms are mutually agreed upon and the share options are awarded to individual employees. The following approach should be used in determining the fair value of share options, according to the standards.

The fair value of a share option should be estimated using an option-pricing model (for example, the Black–Scholes or a binomial model) that takes into account, as of the grant date, the exercise price and expected life of the option, the current price of the underlying stock and its expected volatility, expected dividends on the stock and the risk-free interest rate for the expected term of the option.

It is not necessary to understand the theory behind option pricing models to understand the financial reporting for employee share options. As the preceding paragraph indicates, the measurement of fair value requires estimates of several other variables that we have not yet specified in the Guyton example. We will assume that the risk-free interest rate is 7%, that no dividends are forecasted for the company's common shares, and that the expected volatility of Guyton's common shares is 20%. These facts are summarized in Table 15.1.

Inserting the numbers in Table 15.1 into the Black–Scholes option pricing model indicates that each option has a fair value of $10.05 at the grant date.[14] The total compensation cost of all employee share option awards is $301,500 ($10.05 × 30,000 options). Let's assume that all 300 managers will meet the vesting requirements and ultimately exercise all 30,000 options.

Stock-based compensation is intended to increase the employees' stake in the firm, creating an incentive for employees to work in the best interests of all the other owners. The vesting requirements provide an extra incentive to stay with the company long enough to benefit from the anticipated value of the options. For these reasons, total compensation cost of $301,500 is charged to expense on a *straight-line basis over the vesting period*. Guyton

TABLE 15.1 GUYTON CORPORATION

Relevant Variables for Determining the Value of Employee Stock Options

Options granted (100 shares × 300 employees)	30,000
Exercise price (E)	$30
Share price at grant date (S)	$30
Expected life of options (t)	5 years
Risk-free interest rate (r)	7%
Expected volatility of common shares (σ)	20%
Expected dividends on common shares	–0–

Black–Scholes Option Valuation (V) Formula

$$V = SN(d_1) - Ee^{-rt}N(d_2)$$

where $N(d)$ is the value of the cumulative standard normal function,

$$d_1 = [\log(S/E) + (r + 0.5\sigma^2)t]/\sigma t^{1/2} \text{ and}$$
$$d_2 = d_1 - \sigma t^{1/2}$$

The fair market value of each Guyton option is estimated to be $10.05 at the grant date.

Corporation would recognize $100,500 ($301,500 ÷ 3) as compensation expense in each of the years 2000 through 2002.

DR Compensation expense	$100,500	
CR Paid-in capital—share options		$100,500

This same entry is made each year even though the market value of the company's shares—and therefore the value of outstanding employee share options—will undoubtedly change over time. *Compensation cost—option fair value—is measured only once (i.e., at the grant date).*

Let's say that Guyton's share price rises above the $30 exercise price after the vesting period and that all 30,000 options are exercised by managers on the same day. The entry to record the exercise of employee share options is (assuming $20 par value shares):

DR Cash (30,000 × $30)	$900,000	
DR Paid-in capital—share options		
($100,500 × 3 years)	301,500	
CR Common shares—par ($20 × 30,000)		$600,000
CR Paid-in capital in excess of par		601,500

In evaluating the financial statement effect of these two entries, notice that: (1) compensation expense is recognized in the same amount each year over the vesting period; and (2) if the options are exercised, the total amount added to the common shares and capital in excess of par is $1,201,500—the sum of the cash received by the company when the options are exercised plus the calculated fair value of the options at the grant date.

If we assume that Guyton's share price never rises above the exercise price, then the options will never be exercised. No cash will flow in. The offset to cumulative three-year compensation expense ($301,500) will remain in the "Paid-in capital—

> We ignore future income tax considerations (discussed in Chapter 13) for simplicity. Future income taxes arise because compensation expense is recognized in the financial statements and for income tax purposes at different amounts and in different periods.

share options" account. This dollar figure represents the estimated value of enhanced employee productivity (measured at the option grant date) that in effect was "donated" to the company without any corresponding ownership claim being given up to Guyton's employees.

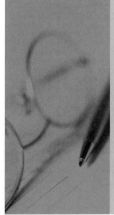

Recap

SFAS No. 123 represented a political compromise in the United States when it was issued in 1995. Section 3870 represented a Canadian attempt to "harmonize" Canadian GAAP with U.S. GAAP in this area. The FASB was unanimous in its belief that expenses are incurred when companies grant stock options to employees as a part of a compensation package. Nevertheless, American companies were not required to record this expense in the financial statements. Instead, the compromise allowed firms to disclose the fair value amount of stock-based compensation in a footnote to the financial statements. As we shall see immediately below, Canadian standard-setters were quite vocal in their opposition to what they felt was a bad compromise. And, as the fallout from Enron and other accounting scandals proceeded in 2002, pressure mounted to make stock option expensing compulsory.

A Herd Instinct? The Rush to Expense Stock Options

In late 2001, just before the AcSB promulgated its new standard on stock options, the AcSB chair, Paul Cherry, isssued a statement, an excerpt of which follows:

Excerpt from FYI (Activities of the CICA Accounting Standards Board and Staff)

Message from the Chair

Recent academic research has shown that "more than 80% of shares reserved for conversion and exercise by US firms relate to stock options." It is indisputable that stock options can have value and that their value can, at times, be very significant and a major component of employee compensation. The new Standard on *Stock-based Compensation and Other Stock-based Payments*, approved by the Accounting Standards Board in September requires the recognition of the true economic cost of most stock-based compensation schemes. Ironically, it falls short in the most straight-forward scenario—where the option can be settled only by issuing equity shares—giving a choice between fair value based accounting and providing disclosure of pro forma adjusted net income and earnings per share. It is well accepted that disclosure does not compensate for inadequate accounting. However, experience indicates that many enterprises will choose the pro forma disclosure alternative.

Why allow the disclosure alternative? The Board decided to do so only reluctantly and, hopefully, for a brief period of time. The Board balanced the competing needs for quick action and rigorous due process. Also, imposing fair value based measurements in all cases would go further than the current US rules. But the books are not closed on this one. Harmonization with US GAAP is important, but not at the price of producing inadequate standards.

Accounting for share-based payments is also a 'high priority' item on the IASB agenda and the AcSB will work closely and vigorously with the IASB and our partner bodies in that organization for timely completion of a high quality standard. The early indications are encouraging for international convergence based on a requirement for fair value based measurements in all stock-based transactions. The deciding factor may well be the willingness of institutional and individual investors, analysts, regulators and other users of financial statements to stand up and be counted. It will then remain for our American colleagues to come onside, establishing definitively the worth of global harmonization.

Source: Paul Cherry, "FYI (Activities of the CICA Accounting Standards Board and Staff)," October 2001.

Clearly, Canadian standard-setters did not agree with the FASB *SFAS No. 123* compromise, but felt compelled to comply with it by adopting the new Section 3870. Events in 2002, mainly related to the Enron and other accounting scandals, stimulated many commentators on accounting to urge strongly that, as part of an overall accounting reform, stock option compensation be recorded as a formal expense. For example, an editorial in the *Toronto Star* asserted the following:

Investors no longer know what to make of reported corporate numbers

While the crisis in confidence was brought to a head by revelations of accounting fraud at Enron and WorldCom, it reflects a far more pervasive problem—the propensity of corporations to resort to questionable, if perfectly legal, accounting practices.

Most companies, for example, do not treat the stock options they give to their executives as a normal business expense. As a result, costs tend to be understated and profits overstated.

As investors learned more about such dubious practices in the wake of the big scandals, they began to lose faith in the reporting of corporate numbers in general.

Source: Toronto Star, July 12, 2002, p. A22. Reprinted with permission of Torstar Syndication Services.

THE TORONTO STAR
www.thestar.com

Stimulated more by, perhaps, the need to be seen as "good corporate accounting citizens" than any conversion to leadership in good reporting, several large companies in the United States and Canada announced that they would elect to expense their stock option costs. Included were the following companies, among others: Sun Life Financial Services Canada, General Electric Co., Toronto-Dominion Bank, Bank of Montreal, Coca-Cola, and Amazon.com. Accounting standard-setters such as the AcSB's Paul Cherry, were encouraged by the trend. For example, the following news article reported Paul Cherry's reaction:

Accounting board to tackle expensing options: Rule could give Canadian firms competitive lead

The growing wave of companies cleaning up their books by treating stock options as an expense could lead to the practice being required under Canadian accounting rules sooner rather than later.

"The momentum is clearly building," Paul Cherry, chairman of the Canadian Accounting Standards Board, said yesterday, a day after Sun Life Financial Services Canada and General Electric Co. joined the voluntary movement.

"The question now is how quickly do we put everybody on the same track?"

The board, which sets accounting standards in Canada, next meets in September and Cherry said the issue will be high on the discussion list and it could come as early as next year.

Some companies have fought the push to account for stock options as expenses because it reduces net profits or enlarges losses, which makes a company look less successful to investors. It can also drive down stock prices.

But proponents of the idea say it gives a clearer view of a company's financial picture, a factor that has become paramount since the accounting scandals at Enron Corp., WorldCom Inc. and auditing firm Arthur Andersen LLP spooked the investment world.

The scandals were in part spurred by efforts to boost stock prices, so executives cashing in stock options could rake in even more money.

Here's how options work: An executive is given the right to purchase large numbers of shares at a pre-set price, say $20 each. If the share price on stock markets rises to $30, the executive has a pre-tax gain of $10 per share, a gross return of 30 per cent, even if the share price later falls.

Retired Nortel Networks chief executive John Roth walked away with more than $100 million. Nortel shares, once worth $124.50, can now be bought for less than $2. Enron chairman Kenneth Lay exercised $123.4 million (U.S.) in stock options in 2000. The energy company's shares are now virtually worthless.

High-tech companies, including Microsoft Corp., have balked at expensing options because options have typically been a larger portion of the pay package. In Microsoft's case, profits for the 12 months ending June 30 would have been $5.36 billion if options had been expensed, instead of the $7.83 billion reported.

At the height of the dot-com boom, some U.S. tech companies were granting as much as 40 per cent of their shares as options, when a 10 per cent figure would be more reasonable, said Ian Ainsworth, managing director of equities at Altamira Financial Services Ltd.

"Most of the dot-coms wouldn't have made money even without expensing options."

Until recently, the concern in Canadian accounting circles has been whether companies would be at a disadvantage or suffer "competitive harm" by expensing stock options if the United States did not require the move as well, said Cherry.

"Now some people are saying maybe that's too cautious."

The view is now changing to the point that moving in front of the U.S. on this issue could become a competitive advantage for Canadian companies and financial markets.

"There could be a benefit of being perceived as a better financial reporting system," Cherry said. "That's the big debate. Many important players are re-thinking their positions."

The United States missed its chance this week as President George W. Bush signed a new law amid great fanfare to tighten the regulation of corporate financial reporting—including the requirement that chief executives personally vouch for their company's financial results—and provide for oversight of independent auditors going through corporate books. The law did not include a requirement that stock options be treated as an expense.

"I think we could move quickly once we sort out the competitive harm issue," Cherry said, noting that the London-based International Accounting Standards Board has agreed to a plan on standards for expensing stock options. It will be made public in October.

"That's the sort of signal we all need."

There is still hope that the U.S. could be persuaded to make the change because of the large number of well-known companies—including Toronto-Dominion Bank, Bank of Montreal, Coca-Cola and Amazon.com—that have decided to do it, Cherry said.

"It's amazing how much things have changed in the last couple of months.... The chances of getting the U.S. to change their rules are much better."

Accounting rules in the U.S. and Canada already require companies to state the impact on earnings if stock options have been expensed.

Source: Rob Ferguson, *Toronto Star,* August 2, 2002, pp. E1 and E9. Reprinted with permission of Torstar Syndication Services.

BUSINESS WEEK
**www.businessweek.
com**

But is this how accounting standards should be adopted by companies, let alone set by standard-setters … that is, as part of the "herd effect"? Some observers of the adoption of *SFAS No. 123* and Section 3870 urge caution; for example, *Business Week* gave both the Black–Scholes and binomial option-pricing models "thumbs down" as ways of valuing options for purposes of determining stock option expense.[15] Financial models, such as the Black–Scholes model, should be used with care since small changes in the assumptions may lead to large changes in accounting numbers, and thereby lower the quality of earnings if the changes are not justifiable.

To see how sensitive fair value accounting under Section 3870 is, we will examine Illustration BVII in Appendix B of this section of the *CICA Handbook.*

First, read through the illustration, which is reproduced here:

Financial Reporting and Analysis

ILLUSTRATIVE COMPUTATIONS OF STOCK-BASED EMPLOYEE COMPENSATION

Illustration BVII—Fixed stock option (from *CICA Handbook,* Section 3870)

B6 Company S., a public enterprise, grants options with a maximum term of 10 years to its employees. The exercise price of each option equals the market price of its stock on the grant date. All options vest at the end of three years (cliff vesting). No account is taken of the impact of income taxes, if any.

B7 The following table shows assumptions and information about options granted on January 1, 20Y2.

Options granted	900,000
Employees granted options	3,000
Expected forfeitures per year	3%
Stock price	$50
Expected life of options	6 years
Risk-free interest rate	7.5%
Expected volatility	30%
Expected dividend yield	2.5%

B8 Using as inputs the last six items from the table above, the Black–Scholes option pricing model modified for dividends determines a fair value of $17.15 for each option....

B9 Total compensation cost recognized over the vesting period will be the fair value of all options that actually vest, determined based on the stock price at the grant date.... This example assumes that Company S estimates at the grant date the number of options that will vest and subsequently adjusts compensation cost for changes in the assumed rate of forfeitures and differences between expectations and actual experience.

...

B10 The estimate of the expected number of forfeitures considers historical employee turnover rates and expectations about the future. Company S has experienced historical turnover rates of approximately three percent per year for employees at the grantees' level having non-vested options, and it expects that rate to continue. Therefore, Company S estimates the total value of the award at the grant date based on an expected forfeiture rate of three percent per year. Actual forfeitures are five percent in 20Y2, but no adjustments to cost are recognized in 20Y2 because Company S still expects actual forfeitures to average three percent per year over the three-year vesting period. During 20Y3, however, management decides that the rate of forfeitures is likely to continue to increase through 20Y4, and the assumed forfeiture rate for the entire award is changed to six percent per year. Adjustments to cumulative cost to reflect the higher forfeiture rate are made at the end of 20Y3. At the end of 20Y4 when the award becomes vested, actual forfeitures have averaged six percent per year, and no further adjustment is necessary.

...

B11 The ... calculation ... illustrates the accounting for the award of options on January 1, 20Y2, assuming that the entire award vests at the end of three years, that is, the award provides for cliff vesting rather than graded vesting.... The number of options expected to vest is estimated at the grant date to be 821,406 (900,000 × 0.97 × 0.97 × 0.97). Thus, as shown in Exhibit B12A, the estimated value of the award at January 1, 20Y2 is $14,087,113 (821,406 × $17.15), and the compensation cost to be recognized during each year of the three-year vesting period if $4,695,704 ($14,087,113 ÷ 3). The journal entries to recognize compensation cost follow.

For 20Y2:

Compensation cost	4,695,704	
Contributed surplus		4,695,704
To recognize compensation cost.		

B12 In the absence of a change in estimate or experience different from that initially assumed, the same journal entry would be made to recognize compensation cost for 20Y3 and 20Y4. However, at the end of 20Y3, management changes its estimated employee forfeiture rate from three percent to six percent per year. The revised number of options expected to vest is 747,526 ($900,000 \times 0.94 \times 0.94 \times 0.94$). Accordingly, the revised total compensation cost to be recognized by the end of 20Y4 is $12,820,071 ($747,526 \times \$17.15$). The cumulative adjustment to reflect the effect of adjusting the forfeiture rate is the difference between two-thirds of the revised cost of the award and the cost already recognized for 20Y2 and 20Y3. The related journal entry and the computations follow:

At December 31, 20Y3 to adjust for new forfeiture rate:

Revised total compensation cost	$12,820,071
Revised cumulative cost as of 12/31/Y3 ($12,820,071 × 2/3)	$ 8,546,714
Cost already recognized in 20Y2 and 20Y3 ($4,695,704 × 2)	9,391,408
Adjustment to cost at 12/31/Y3	$ (844,694)

The related journal entry is:

Contributed surplus	844,694	
Compensation cost		844,694

For 20Y4:

Compensation cost	4,273,357	
Contributed surplus		4,273,357
To recognize compensation cost	($12,820,071 ÷ 3 = $4,273,357).	

At December 31, 20Y4, the enterprise would examine its actual forfeitures and make any necessary adjustments to reflect compensation cost for the number of shares that actually vested.

EXHIBIT B12A—FIXED STOCK OPTION—CLIFF VESTING

Year	Total value of award	Pre-tax cost for year	Cumulative pre-tax cost
20Y3	$14,087,113	$4,695,704	$ 4,695,704
	(821,406 × $17.15)	($14,087,113 ÷ 3)	
20Y3	$12,820,071	$3,851,010	$ 8,546,714
	(747,526 × $17.15)	[($12,820,071 × 2/3) − $4,695,704]	
20Y4	$12,820,071	$4,273,357	$12,820,071
	(747,526 × $17.15)	($12,820,071 ÷ 3)	

B13 For simplicity, the illustration assumes that all of the options are exercised on the same day. The amount credited to shareholders' equity for the exercise of the options is the sum of (a) the cash proceeds received and (b) the amounts credited to contributed surplus for services received earlier that were charged to compensation cost. At exercise, the stock price is assumed to be $70.

At exercise:

Cash (747,526 × $50)	37,376,300	
Contributed surplus	12,820,071	
Common stock		50,196,371
To recognize the issuance of stock upon exercise of options.		

Paragraph B8 of the *CICA Handbook*'s Section 3870's Appendix (as above) tells us that:

B8 Using as inputs the last six items from the table above, the Black–Scholes option pricing model modified for dividends determines a fair value of $17.15 for each option ....

The key input to the accounting is this $17.15 per option number. Using the Black–Scholes formula adopted by the AcSB, which is shown in this example, we prepared a spreadsheet to test the sensitivity of the formula in this case. If we vary just two of the parameters, changing volatility to 0.2 from 0.3 and expected option life to 4 years from 5, the per option price becomes $11.41, a 34% decrease from $17.15, with all the accounting expense numbers changing accordingly. So, caveat emptor, when it comes to the option compensation expense numbers that Canadian companies now at least must disclose or, for an increasing number, will elect to record in the formal financial statements. Events are moving rapidly in this area: as of early 2003, the AcSB is still considering whether or not to make stock option compensation expensing mandatory.

Convertible Debt

On September 7, 1999, VerticalNet offered investors the opportunity to purchase up to US$100 million of convertible subordinate debentures. These bonds paid a stated interest rate of 5.25% annually, matured in 5 years, and could be exchanged at any time for VerticalNet shares at a conversion price of US$20 per common share. Because the debentures were issued in units of US$1,000 face value, the conversion price meant investors could exchange each bond for 50 shares ($1,000 ÷ $20 = 50 shares).

VERTICALNET
www.verticalnet.com

What price do you suppose VerticalNet received for each US$1,000 face value debenture?

To put this question in context, the yield to maturity—the effective interest rate—on risk-free U.S. government bonds of a similar duration was 5.9% in September 1999, and the average yield on newly issued high-grade industrial debt that month was about 8%. Given the economic climate of the time, it may surprise you to learn that VerticalNet was able to sell its 5.25% bonds at a price of 100%, receiving US$1,000 in cash for each US$1,000 face value issued. By contrast, the promised cash flows associated with each bond—US$52.50 each year plus another US$1,000 at maturity in the year 2004—have a discounted present value at 8% of only US$890.20. *Investors were willing to pay US$109.80 more than the present value of a VerticalNet bond because of the conversion feature attached to the debt.*

We now explain the financial reporting for convertible debt and its implications for those who use financial statements.

Background

The VerticalNet example illustrates that convertible bonds give investors the opportunity to exchange a company's debt for common shares in accordance with terms in the bond indenture. The **conversion price**—the dollar value at which the debt can be converted into common shares—is typically above the prevailing market price of the company's common shares at the time the debt is issued. The option to convert is solely at the discretion of the investor, and it will only be exercised when and if the investor finds the exchange desirable. Shares of VerticalNet were trading around US$16 in September 1999—or about US$4 below the conversion price. Investors had little incentive to exchange their bonds for shares immediately. The real value of the conversion feature to investors was the possibility that the share price might climb above US$20 sometime over the next 5 years.

To illustrate, suppose that VerticalNet's share price reached US$25 per share in 2000. Each US$1,000 par-value convertible bond would then represent a claim to US$1,250 in common shares (50 shares × $25 per share). Suppose that VerticalNet's bonds were callable at a price of US$1,027.50 in cash. The company could force conversion by "calling" the debt—investors would take the more valuable common shares rather than the less valuable cash payment.

Convertible bonds are typically **subordinated debentures.** This means that in the event of insolvency or bankruptcy the claims of "senior" creditors must be settled in full before any payment will be made to holders of subordinated debentures. Senior creditors typically encompass all other long-term debt issues and bank loans. However, subordinated debentures do have priority over common and preferred shares.

Convertible bonds are also usually **callable,** or redeemable, by the issuer at a specified price before maturity. When convertible bonds are called, investors must either convert them or have the debt redeemed for a cash price that is generally less than the value of the common shares into which the debt can be converted. Call provisions protect the company against extreme price increases by forcing investor action. Otherwise, investors would simply continue holding the debt in anticipation of further share price increases.

Financial Reporting Issues

Convertible debt poses this financial reporting dilemma: Should a value be assigned to the debt's conversion feature? Clearly, conversion features are valuable to both the issuing company and investors. The convertibility option enabled VerticalNet to borrow US$100 million at 5.25% interest when other companies were paying 8% interest. Moreover, the availability of Black–Scholes and other option pricing models means that we now have well-established (although controversial) methods for assigning values to option features—in this example, the option is a conversion privilege.

CICA Handbook Section 3860 contains the following two important requirements:

> *The issuer of a financial instrument should classify the instrument, or its component parts, as a liability or as equity in accordance with the substance of the contractual arrangement on initial recognition and the definitions of a financial liability and an equity instrument. (3860.18)*
>
> …
>
> *The issuer of a financial instrument that contains both a liability and an equity element should classify the instrument's component parts separately in accordance with paragraph 3860.18. (3860.24)*

These paragraphs clearly mandate that companies reporting under Canadian GAAP must examine the *substance* of the financial instruments that they issue, and classify and account for those issues accordingly. Therefore, convertible debt may be "debt" in name only, and might—depending on the facts of the issue in question—be accounted for as part debt and part equity, or even as entirely equity. For example, O & Y Properties Corporation has divided its debentures, notes, and preferred shares into a liability component and a shareholders' equity component, as shown in the company's balance sheet and the related note in Exhibit 15.4. Notice as at January 31, 1999, that the "Convertible unsecured subordinated debentures" have a liability component of $22,426,000 and an equity component of $76,285,000. The need, under Canadian GAAP, to allocate the balance sheet presentation of these convertible securities into these two categories arises because these securities are neither strictly debt nor strictly equity, but a combination of the two.

O & Y PROPERTIES
CORPORATION
www.oyp.com

In the United States, GAAP for convertible debt is outlined in *APB No. 14*, which predates the development of modern option pricing theory.[16]

APB No. 14 specifies that convertible bonds must be recorded as *debt only*, with

Exhibit 15.4 O & Y PROPERTIES CORPORATION

Consolidated Balance Sheet and Related Note

(in thousands of CDN$)	Notes	As at January 31, 1999	As at January 31, 1998
Assets			
Rental properties	3,4,5	$658,588	$490,942
Land held for development	5	21,099	8,383
Real estate services contracts	3	31,223	11,627
Amounts receivable		11,362	8,824
Deferred costs and other assets		4,444	2,480
Cash and short-term investments	6	48,352	54,479
		$775,068	576,735
Liabilities			
Secured debt	8	$301,195	263,974
Accounts payable and accrued liabilities		33,901	32,049
Debentures, notes and preferred shares, liability component	9	39,190	17,505
		374,286	313,528
Shareholders' equity			
Debentures, notes and preferred shares, equity component	9	95,506	18,191
Common shares	10	244,535	214,979
Retained earnings		60,741	30,037
		400,782	263,207
Commitments and contingencies	14		
		$775,068	$576,735

See accompanying notes to financial statements.

9. Debentures, notes and preferred shares

January 31, 1999	Liability	Equity	Total
Convertible unsecured subordinated debentures	$22,426	76,285	$ 98,711
Series 1 convertible preferred shares	4,362	10,857	15,219
Exchangeable notes of a subsidiary	3,324	5,790	9,114
Series A convertible debentures	1,478	2,574	4,052
Series 1 redeemable preferred shares of a subsidiary	6,000	—	6,000
Series 2 redeemable preferred shares of a subsidiary	1,600	—	1,600
	$39,190	95,506	$134,696

January 31, 1998	Liability	Equity	Total
Series 1 convertible preferred shares	$ 4,729	10,325	15,054
Exchangeable notes of a subsidiary	5,176	7,866	13,042
Series 1 redeemable preferred shares of a subsidiary	6,000	—	6,000
Series 2 redeemable preferred shares of a subsidiary	1,600	—	1,600
	$17,505	18,191	$35,696

The Company is authorized to issue an unlimited number of preferred shares. The preferred shares are non-voting, issuable in series, each series ranking equally, and are senior to the common shares.

On June 30, 1998, the Company issued $100 million of 5.9% convertible unsecured subordinated debentures (the "Subordinated Debentures") due June 30, 2008. The Subordinated Debentures are convertible into common shares at $11.50 per common share, are redeemable at the option of the Company in cash or shares on or after June 30, 2003 and are also redeemable at the option of the Company under certain circumstances during the prior year.

The aggregate face amount of the 4.44% Series 1 convertible preferred shares (the "Preferred Shares") is $15 million (600,000 shares). The Preferred Shares are required to be redeemed on September 25, 2007, convertible into common shares of the Company at $8.25 at the option of the holder and redeemable under certain conditions at the option of the Company after September 25, 2002 (or after September 25, 2000 if the market price of the Company's common shares exceeds $10.31) in cash or common shares.

The aggregate original principal amount of the notes of a subsidiary (which are exchangeable into 6% convertible debentures or common shares of the Company) (the "Notes") was $13 million. During the year, $4 million of these Notes were converted into $4 million of Series A convertible debentures (the "Convertible Debentures") of the Company. The Notes and Convertible Debentures are redeemable and convertible on substantially the same terms as the Preferred Shares.

The Preferred Shares, Notes, Convertible Debentures and Subordinated Debentures (the "Financial Instruments") may be settled at the issuer's option in cash or its own equity instruments. Accordingly, the obligation to make cash payments on account of interest is reflected as a liability (at the net original present value of such payments) with the remaining amount, being the present value of the principal portion of the security, reflected as equity.

The liability component of the Financial Instruments is calculated as the present value of the future Interest payments and is increased for the accretion of the discount each year to reflect the time value of money and reduced by cash payments of interest. The accretion is reflected as financing expense in the consolidated statement of earnings and retained earnings. The ongoing accretion of the equity component, which will increase this component from its initial carrying amount to the stated principal amount of the Financial Instruments, is reflected as a charge to retained earnings, net of income taxes. In computing earnings per common share, these charges to retained earnings are deducted from earnings available to common shareholders.

The 1,000,000 outstanding Series 1 redeemable preferred shares of a subsidiary are non-dividend bearing and are redeemable at the option of the Company or the holder. The 1,600 outstanding Series 2 redeemable preferred shares of a subsidiary are non-dividend bearing and are redeemable at the option of the Company at any time and at the option of the holder on or after March 25, 2005.

no value assigned to the conversion privilege. The APB cited two reasons for this treatment: (1) the inseparability of the conversion feature from the debt component of the convertible security; and (2) the practical problems of determining separate values for the debt and the conversion option in the absence of separability.

On this last point, the APB concluded:

In the absence of separate transferability, values are not established in the marketplace, and accordingly, the value assigned to each feature is necessarily subjective. A determination of the value of the conversion feature poses problems because of the uncertain duration of the right to obtain the share and the uncertainty as to the future value of the share obtainable upon conversion. Furthermore, issuers often claim that a subjective valuation of a debt security without the conversion option but with identical other terms ... is difficult because such a security could not be sold at a price which the issuer would regard as producing an acceptable cost of financing. (APB No. 14, para. 8)

Given modern option pricing methods, it is unlikely that accounting standard setters would reach the same conclusion today. Nevertheless, APB No. 14 *continues to be GAAP for convertible debt in the United States.*

The following entry illustrates how VerticalNet would record the issuance of all US$100 million of its convertible subordinate debentures at par value:

DR Cash	$100,000,000	
CR Convertible subordinated debentures		$100,000,000

This entry assigns the entire US$100 million to the convertible debt liability. One year later, VerticalNet would record an interest payment of US$5,250,000 (or 5.25% times $100 million):

DR Interest expense	$5,250,000	
CR Cash		$5,250,000

(This entry ignores the real-world complication that arises when companies accrue interest throughout the year.)

Thus far, the accounting for convertible debt parallels that for the straight-debt securities described in Chapter 11. VerticalNet will continue to record interest expense at the rate of 5.25% annually until the debt is retired or converted. Let's move forward to see what happens at conversion.

Suppose it is 2001, and some (but not all) investors have chosen to exercise their conversion privilege by exchanging US$50 million of the debentures. Furthermore, the company's stock has a current market value of US$30 per share, which is above the US$20 conversion price. This means that investors will surrender bonds with a face value (and book value) of US$50 million in exchange for common shares with a market value of US$75 million. *APB No. 14* permits companies to record debt conversion in either of two ways (we assume that VerticalNet, a U.S. firm, has common shares of $1 par value):

> At the stated conversion price, investors will receive 2,500,000 common shares for their US$50 million of debentures (US$50 million divided by US$20 price per share). Since each share has a market value of US$30, investors receive stock worth US$75 million.

1. The **book value method** records the newly issued shares at the book value of debt retired.

DR Convertible subordinated debentures	$50,000,000	
CR Common shares ($1 par)		$ 2,500,000
CR Paid-in capital in excess of par		47,500,000

2. The **market value method** records the newly issued shares at their current market value. Any difference between that market value and the conversion price is recognized as a loss (or gain) on conversion.

DR Convertible subordinated debentures	$50,000,000	
DR Loss on debt conversion	25,000,000	
CR Common shares ($1 par)		$ 2,500,000
CR Paid-in capital in excess of par		47,500,000

The conversion loss is not classified as an extraordinary item because it was initiated by investors. Of course, VerticalNet would continue to record interest expense on the remaining $50 million of outstanding convertible debentures.

Under the book value approach, no accounting gain or loss is recognized at retirement, because the debt book value is just transferred to the common shares account. Under the market value approach, however, common shares are credited at full market value *as if* the shares issued were sold for cash on the conversion date. It is easy to see why the book value method is more popular. Almost all debt conversions occur when the company's share price is above the conversion price, and this situation triggers recognition of an accounting loss under the market value method. Managers can avoid recording this loss by instead selecting the book value approach.

Implications for Analysis

There are two messages in this discussion of convertible debt for financial statement readers.

First, *estimating the future cash flow implications of convertible debt is difficult.* This is because it is necessary to consider both the scheduled interest and principal payments for the debt, as well as the likelihood of conversion prior to maturity. Option pricing methods can be used to evaluate the probability of conversion over long time intervals. For near-term projections, however, a simple comparison of the conversion price with the current market price of common shares can prove informative—that is, if the exercise price is considerably above the current share price and the options are close to expiration, it is unlikely they will be exercised. The bond indenture agreement should also be examined for call provision details.

Second, for American companies *recorded interest expense may seriously understate the true cost of debt financing for companies that issue convertible bonds or notes.* Few people would argue that VerticalNet is more creditworthy than the U.S. government. Yet the company borrowed money at 5.25% when investors were charging the federal government more than 5.9% for loans of similar duration. By ignoring the value of conversion features, current U.S. GAAP understate interest expense.

Recap
Convertible debt gives investors the upside potential of common shares and the safety net of debt. That's why the interest rate on convertible debt is so low—the option value of the conversion feature compensates for the lower interest paid to investors. Because U.S. GAAP ignores the conversion option, interest expense may be understated and cash flow forecasting may be impeded. Canadian GAAP require companies to account for the debt and equity features separately.

Summary

Many aspects of financial reporting for shareholders' equity transactions are built on highly technical rules and procedures that have evolved over time. Some aspects of owners' equity accounting have not changed despite changing economic and legal environments. Still other aspects of owners' equity accounting involve complicated pronouncements that reflect political compromise. Financial statement readers must recognize these influences and avoid unwarranted inferences based on the reported figures.

Here's some of what we've learned. Share buybacks don't produce accounting gains and losses, but they can boost the returns to stock market investors. Preferred shares look a lot like debt when they have a mandatory redemption feature. Some companies can pay dividends in excess of their retained earnings' balance, but their ability to do so depends on the particular law in effect. Earnings-per-share (EPS) numbers are adjusted for potential dilution from stock options, warrants, and convertible securities, but GAAP do not require companies to record compensation expense when stock options are given to employees. But GAAP do not ignore the option value in convertible debt, at least in Canada.

While some rules for owners' equity accounting may seem arbitrary—and therefore insignificant—you must remember that these financial statement items have a profound impact on lending agreements, regulation, and cost of equity capital. Furthermore, managers have strong incentives to use the financial reporting latitude described in this chapter to achieve various economic goals.

Appendix 15A

Accounting for Shares

In this appendix, we illustrate the journal entries that would be required in a variety of situations involving accounting for shares, for shares both with and without par value. As mentioned in the body of the chapter, even though par value shares are becoming rare in Canada, they are still used in some jurisdictions, and especially the United States. In the following examples, we assume that the par value of the shares is $1.

Situation	Shares Without Par Value	Shares With Par Value of $1

Alpha Corporation issues 1,000 common shares for $10 in cash per share.	**DR** Cash 10,000
	    CR Common shares 10,000
		DR Cash 10,000
		    CR Common shares 1,000
		    CR Contributed surplus
		         in excess of par* 9,000

Alpha Corporation sells its shares, not for cash, but on a *subscription* or *installment* basis, in which the full price is not received immediately. Actual common shares are not issued until the shares are fully paid. Suppose that Alpha sells its shares for 40% down and 60% to be received in three months.	**At the date the original subscriptions for the shares are received:**
	
	DR Cash 4,000
	DR Subscriptions
	     receivable 6,000
	    CR Common shares
	         subscribed 10,000
	
	("Common shares subscribed" and "Subscriptions receivable" are shown in the shareholders' equity portion of the balance sheet.)
	
	Three months later:
	
	DR Cash 6,000
	    CR Subscriptions
	         receivable 6,000
	DR Common shares
	     subscribed 10,000
	    CR Common shares 10,000
		At the date the original subscriptions for the shares are received:
		
		DR Cash 4,000
		DR Subscriptions
		     receivable 6,000
		    CR Common shares
		         subscribed 1,000
		    CR Contributed surplus
		         in excess of par 9,000
		
		Three months later:
		
		DR Cash 6,000
		    CR Subscriptions
		         receivable 6,000
		
		DR Common shares
		     subscribed 1,000
		    CR Common shares 1,000

Alpha Corporation purchases and cancels 300 of the previously issued common shares. Alpha pays $9 per share.	**DR** Common shares 3,000
	    CR Cash 2,100
	    CR Contributed surplus 900
	
	(Section 3240, para. 15 says that the debit to the common shares account is based upon an assigned value equal to the average per-share amount for shares of the class purchased and cancelled. In Alpha's case, this is $10,000/1,000, or $10. If Alpha had paid *more than* the assigned value of $10 per share, then more complex rules set out in Section 3240 would come into play [Section 3240, paras. 15 and 18].)
		DR Common shares 300
		DR Contributed surplus in
		     excess of par 1,800
		    CR Cash 2,100
		
		(The $1,800 debit to the account "Contributed surplus in excess of par" is computed using the rule in Section 3240, para. 15 (c), which says that the maximum debit in this case is the pro rata share of the cancelled shares' original excess above par—that is, (300 shares/1,000 shares) × $9,000, or $2,700. All we need is $1,800 in this case.)

*Various account names are used in practice; another is "Premium on common shares."

For more Exercises, Problems/Discussion Questions, and Cases, visit the Companion Website for this textbook at **www.pearsoned.ca/revsine**.

Exercises

E15-1 Earnings per share

CICA adapted

Which of the following per-share measurements for a company would be the best predictor of next year's EPS? Why?
  (a) basic earnings per common share
  (b) diluted earnings per share
  (c) diluted earnings per share before extraordinary items
  (d) dividends per share

E15-2 Entity and proprietary views

ForeEver Yours Inc., a manufacturer of wedding rings, issued two financial instruments at the beginning of 2003: a $10 million, 40-year bond that pays interest at the rate of 11% annually, and 10,000 shares of $100 preferred stock that pays a dividend of 7.5% annually. The preferred share has a mandatory redemption feature that requires the company to repurchase all outstanding shares at par ($100 per share) in 40 years.

Required:

  1. Describe how each financial instrument will affect the company's balance sheet and income statement in 2003.
  2. Do GAAP treat preferred shares differently from the 40-year bond?

E15-3 Employee share options

On July 1, 2002, Trudeau Company granted Harry Ross, an employee, an option to buy 500 Trudeau common shares at $30 per share. The option was exercisable for five years from the date of the grant. Ross exercised his option on October 1, 2002, and sold his shares on December 2, 2002. The quoted market prices for Trudeau common shares during the year were:

July 1	$30 per share
October 1	$35 per share
December 2	$37 per share

Required:

  1. How much compensation expense should Trudeau recognize in 2002 as a result of the option granted to Ross?
  2. Suppose Trudeau was an American company. How would your answer to Question 1 differ?

E15-4 Earnings per share

Information concerning the capital structure of the Petrock Corporation is as follows:

| | December 31, | |
	2002	2003
Common shares	90,000 shares	90,000 shares
Convertible preferred shares	10,000 shares	10,000 shares
8% convertible bonds	$1,000,000	$1,000,000

During 2003, Petrock paid dividends of $1 per share on its common shares and $2.40 per share on its preferred shares. The preferred stock is convertible into 20,000 common shares. The 8% convertible bonds are convertible into 30,000 common shares. The net income for the year ending December 31, 2003, was $285,000, and the company's income tax rate was 40%.

Required:

1. What was basic EPS for 2003, rounded to the nearest penny?
2. What was diluted EPS for 2003, rounded to the nearest penny?

E15-5 Incentives for share repurchases

Keystone Enterprises just announced record 2001 EPS of $5, up $0.25 from last year. This makes the tenth consecutive year the company has increased its EPS, an enviable record to be sure. Unfortunately, it looks to management like this string of EPS increases is about to be broken. Keystone is forecasting net income for 2002 and 2003 at $10 million each year, the same level earned in 2001. The company has 2,000,000 shares of common stock outstanding, no preferred stock, and no convertible debt.

Required:

1. How many common shares does Keystone need to buy back at the beginning of 2002 *and* in 2003 to maintain EPS growth of $0.25 per share each year?
2. Explain why your answer to Question 1 would change if the buybacks were to occur in the middle of each year.
3. Why do you think Keystone's management would be concerned about maintaining the company's record of EPS growth?

Problems/Discussion Questions

P15-1 EPS computations

The shareholders' equity section of the balance sheet for Holiday Roads Company shows:

	January 1, 2001	December 31, 2001
Preferred shares, $200 par value, 5% dividend, 20,000 issued and outstanding	$ 4,000,000	$ 4,000,000
Common shares, 200,000 issued and outstanding at December 31	20,000,000	27,320,000
Retained earnings	3,000,000	4,000,000
Total shareholders' equity	$27,000,000	$35,320,000

Net income for 2001 was $1,700,000, preferred share dividends were $200,000, and common share dividends were $500,000. The company issued 60,000 common shares on July 1, 2001.

Required:

1. What is the company's basic EPS for 2001?
2. Suppose Holiday Roads also had $500,000 of 10% convertible subordinated debentures outstanding at the beginning and end of 2001. Each $1,000 bond is convertible into 100 common shares, and the company's income tax rate is 40%. What is the company's diluted EPS for 2001?
3. What other types of securities—in addition to convertible debt—can affect the calculation of diluted EPS?

P15-2 Shareholders' equity disclosure

BCE Inc. is one of Canada's largest and best-known companies. BCE's consolidated balance sheet as at December 31, 1998, and income and retained earnings statements for the year then ended, as well as notes 16 and 17, are shown on pages 754–758.

BCE INC.
www.bce.ca

Required:

1. Assume the role of BCE's chief financial officer. During a meeting of the company's board of directors, you have been asked to explain BCE's balance sheet presentation of preferred and common shares. Specifically, a board member has asked you if the company's "preferred shares are really debt, and if so how would they and their associated dividends be treated for purposes of calculating key financial ratios?" Prepare a brief, to-the-point response to be distributed at the next board meeting, drawing upon note 16 and any other relevant information.
2. On the basis of a careful reading of note 17, describe the financial reporting implications, if any, of the DRP, the ESP, and the stock options.

BCE Inc.

Consolidated Statement of Operations

($ millions, except per share amounts)	Notes	For the Years Ended December 31, 1998	1997
Revenues	(3)	27,454	34,517
Operating expenses		21,734	26,989
Research and development expense		2,232	2,911
Purchased in-process research and development expense		688	—
Restructuring and other charges	(5)	654	132
Operating profit		2,146	4,485
Gain on reduction of ownership in subsidiary and associated companies	(6)	4,146	257
Other income	(7)	994	108
Operating earnings		7,286	4,850
Interest expense:			
Long-term debt		1,022	1,111
Other debt		259	121
Total interest expense		1,281	1,232
Earnings before income taxes, non-controlling interest and extraordinary item		6,005	3,618
Income taxes	(8)	(1,548)	(1,522)
Non-controlling interest		141	(682)
Net earnings before extraordinary item		4,598	1,414
Extraordinary item	(2)	—	(2,950)
Net earnings (loss)		4,598	(1,536)
Dividends on preferred shares		(93)	(74)
Net earnings (loss) applicable to common shares		4,505	(1,610)
Earnings (loss) per common share:			
Net earnings before extraordinary item		7.07	2.11
Extraordinary item		—	(4.64)
Net earnings (loss)		7.07	(2.53)
Dividends per common share		1.36	1.36
Average number of common shares outstanding (millions)		637.6	636.0

BCE Inc.

Consolidated Statement of Retained Earnings

($ millions)	Notes	For the Years Ended December 31, 1998	1997
Balance at beginning of year		596	3,173
Net earnings (loss)		4,598	(1,536)
		5,194	1,637
Deduct:			
Dividends:			
Preferred shares		93	74
Common shares		868	865
		961	939
Purchase of common shares for cancellation	(17)	24	93
Costs related to issuance and redemption of share capital of BCE Inc. and of subsidiaries		2	9
		987	1,041
Balance at end of year		4,207	596

Consolidated Balance Sheet

($ millions)	Notes	At December 31, 1998	1997
Assets			
Current assets			
Cash and short-term investments, at cost (approximates market value)		370	2,249
Accounts receivable	(9)	1,922	8,625
Inventories	(9)	176	2,726
Other current assets		312	985
Total current assets		2,780	14,585
Investments in associated and other companies	(11)	9,536	2,929
Capital assets, net	(12)	16,745	18,555
Long-term notes and other receivables		72	553
Deferred charges	(9)	2,159	2,088
Goodwill		780	1,588
Total assets		32,072	40,298
Liabilities			
Current liabilities			
Accounts payable and accrued liabilities		3,255	8,955
Income and other taxes payable		472	372
Debt due within one year	(9)	2,075	2,402
Total current liabilities		5,802	11,729
Long-term debt	(13)	9,260	11,155
Deferred income taxes		639	454
Other long-term liabilities		1,368	1,540
Total liabilities		17,069	24,878

BCE Inc.

Consolidated Balance Sheet (cont.)

($ millions)	Notes	At December 31, 1998	1997
Non-controlling interest	(15)	1,358	5,611
Preferred shares	(16)	1,700	1,700
Common Shareholders' Equity			
Common shares	(17)	6,559	6,316
Contributed surplus		997	998
Retained earnings		4,207	596
Currency translation adjustment		182	199
Total common shareholders' equity		11,945	8,109
Commitments and contingent liabilities	(19)		
Total liabilities and shareholders' equity		32,072	40,298

BCE Inc.

Excerpts from Notes to Consolidated Financial Statements

16. Preferred Shares

Authorized

The articles of incorporation of the Corporation provide for an unlimited number of First Preferred Shares and Second Preferred Shares. The articles authorize the Directors to issue such shares in one or more series and to fix the number of shares of each series, and the conditions attaching to them.

Authorized and outstanding

The following provides a summary of the principal terms and conditions relating to the Corporation's authorized and outstanding series of First Preferred Shares. The detailed terms and conditions of shares are set forth in the Corporation's articles of incorporation.

Cumulative Redeemable First Preferred Shares

Series	Annual Dividend Rate		Convertible Date (on or after)	Convertible Into:	Redemption Date	Redemption Price		Authorized Number of shares		Outstanding At December 31 Stated Capital 1998	1997
P	$1.600		July 15, 2002 (a)	Common shares	April 15, 2002	$25		16,000,000	(h)	400	400
Q	$1.725	(b)	December 1, 2000	Series R	December 1, 2000	$25	(c)	8,000,000	(h)	200	200
R		(g)	December 1, 2005	Series Q	December 1, 2005	$25		8,000,000		—	—
S	$1.320	(b)	November 1, 2001	Series T	November 1, 2001	$25	(c)	8,000,000	(h)	200	200
T		(g)	November 1, 2006	Series S	November 1, 2006	$25		8,000,000		—	—
U(d)	$1.385	(e)	March 1, 2007	Series V	March 1, 2007	$25	(f)	22,000,000	(h)	350	350
V		(g)	March 1, 2012	Series U	March 1, 2012	$25		22,000,000		—	—
W(d)	$1.363	(e)	September 1, 2007	Series X	September 1, 2007	$25	(f)	20,000,000	(h)	300	300
X		(g)	September 1, 2012	Series W	September 1, 2012	$25		20,000,000		—	—
Y	$1.150	(b)	December 1, 2002	Series Z	December 1, 2002	$25	(c)	10,000,000	(h)	250	250
Z		(g)	December 1, 2007	Series Y	December 1, 2007	$25		10,000,000		—	—
										1,700	1,700

All series outstanding as at December 31, 1998 are non-voting except under certain circumstances when the holders are entitled to one vote per share and are convertible at the holder's option.

(a) The Corporation may, at any time, elect to create a further series of preferred shares into which the Series P shares will be convertible on a share-for-share basis at the option of the holder. The Series P shares are, subject to the approval of certain stock exchanges, also convertible into common shares at the Corporation's option.

(b) Holders of Series Q, Series S and Series Y shares will be entitled to floating adjustable cumulative dividends commencing with the month of January 2001, December 2001 and January 2003, respectively.

(c) The Corporation may redeem Series Q, Series S and Series Y shares at any time after December 1, 2000, November 1, 2001 and December 1, 2002, respectively, for $25.50 per share.

(d) The Corporation has entered into interest rate swap agreements until 2007 to effectively convert the Series U and W fixed dividends to floating rate dividends equal to the 90-day Bankers' Acceptance Rate less 0.675% and 0.594%, respectively.

(e) Holders of Series U and Series W shares will be entitled to floating cumulative dividends commencing with the month of April 2007 and October 2007, respectively.

(f) The Corporation may redeem the Series U and Series W shares on and after March 1, 2007 and September 1, 2007, respectively. However, if these Series are listed on the Montreal or Toronto stock exchange, the redemption price after these dates shall be $25.50 per share.

(g) Authorized but not issued.

(h) Authorized and outstanding, except that only 14,000,000 Series U shares and 12,000,000 Series W shares are outstanding.

17. Common Shares

All references to number of common shares, stock options and per share amounts have been restated to reflect the subdivision of common shares on a two-for-one basis on May 14, 1997.

Authorized: an unlimited number of common shares.

| | At December 31, | | | |
| | 1998 | | 1997 | |
	Number of Shares	Stated Capital	Number of Shares	Stated Capital
Outstanding	640,131,136	6,559	635,949,923	6,316
Changes in the number of common shares outstanding during the last two years:				
Shares issued:				
For cash:				
Shareholder Dividend Reinvestment and Stock Purchase Plan	2,017,882	106	3,054,189	113
Employees' Savings Plan	1,338,311	75	—	—
Exercise of stock options	603,375	15	525,313	12
Exercise of put options by CGI shareholders (see Note 4)	878,045	54	—	—
Shares purchased for cancellation	(656,400)	(7)	(3,560,303)	(35)
	4,181,213	243	19,199	90

During the year ended December 31, 1998, the Corporation purchased 656,400 of its common shares (3,560,303 in 1997), under a normal course issuer bid, for an aggregate price of $32 million ($134 million in 1997), of which $1 million was charged to contributed surplus ($6 million in 1997) and $24 million was charged to retained earnings ($93 million in 1997).

Shareholder Dividend Reinvestment and Stock Purchase Plan (DRP)

The Corporation's DRP allows holders of its common shares to invest cash dividends and optional cash payments in newly issued common shares of the Corporation. Participants may purchase shares quarterly with common share cash dividends; in addition, participants may purchase shares monthly with optional cash payments up to an aggregate sum of $20,000 in each 12-month period ending October 15. Optional cash payments amounted to $20 million in 1998 and $29 million in 1997.

The issue price of DRP shares is the average of the closing prices for a board lot trade of the common shares of the Corporation on the Montreal and Toronto stock exchanges on the five trading days immediately preceding the investment date. No price discount is offered to participants. Eight percent of the number of outstanding common shares were enrolled in the DRP as at December 31, 1998 (ten percent as at December 31, 1997).

At December 31, 1998, 1,468,979 common shares were reserved for issuance under the DRP.

Employees' Savings Plan (ESP)

The ESP enables employees of the Corporation and its participating subsidiaries to acquire BCE Inc. common shares through regular payroll deductions plus employer contributions, if applicable. The purpose of the ESP is to encourage employees to own shares of the Corporation. Participation at December 31,1998, was 34,793 employees (39,825 employees in 1997).

Common shares of the Corporation are purchased by the ESP Trustee on behalf of the participants on the open market, by private purchase or from BCE Inc., as determined from time to time by BCE Inc. The total number of ESP shares purchased on behalf of employees, including purchases from the Corporation shown in the table above, was 3,004,844 during 1998 and 4,723,677 in 1997.

At December 31, 1998, 9,500,215 common shares were reserved for issuance under the ESP.

Stock Options

Under the Long-Term Incentive (Stock Option) Program (1985), options may be granted to officers and other key employees of the Corporation and of its subsidiaries to purchase common shares of the Corporation at a subscription price of 100% of market value on the last trading day prior to the effective date of the grant. The options are exercisable during a period not to exceed ten years. The right to exercise options generally accrues over a period of four years of continuous employment. Options are not generally exercisable during the first 12 months after the date of the grant. At December 31, 1998, a total of 2,820,295 options were outstanding (2,329,629 in 1997) at prices ranging between $20.0625 and $63.5250 ($18.4062 and $42.25 in 1997), of which 733,789 options were exercisable (738,875 in 1997) at prices ranging between $20.0625 and $42.250 ($18.4062 and $33.50 in 1997). At December 31, 1998, a total of 6,873,202 common shares remained authorized for issuance under this Program. Shares covered by options granted with respect to any year may not exceed 0.5% of the outstanding common shares of the Corporation at the end of the immediately preceding year.

Simultaneously with the grant of an option, the employee may also be granted the right to a special compensation payment (SCP). The amount of any SCP is equal to the increase in market value of the number of the BCE Inc. shares covered by the SCP (which may not exceed the number of shares covered by the option to which it is related) from the date of grant of the SCP to the date of exercise of the option to which the SCP is related. SCPs have been granted as follows: 1,421,650 in 1998 and 861,900 in 1997. At December 31, 1998, 2,638,107 SCPs covering the same number of shares as the options to which they are related are outstanding.

P15-3 Equity management

Abbott Stores must raise $100 million on January 1, 2002, to finance its expansion into a lucrative metropolitan market. The money will be used to finance construction of five retail stores and a distribution centre. The stores are expected to open later that year. Three alternatives for raising the money are being considered:

1. Issue $100 million of 8% nonconvertible debt due in 20 years.
2. Issue $100 million of 6% nonconvertible preferred shares (100,000).
3. Issue $100 million of common shares (1 million).

The company's internal projections indicate the following 2002 year-end amounts (before the impact of the $100 million of new financing is considered):

($ in mllions)	
Total debt	$425
Total shareholders' equity	$250
Net income for the year	$10

Abbott has no preferred shares outstanding. There are 10 million common shares outstanding, and EPS has been declining for the past several years. Earnings in 2001 were $1 per share, down from $1.10 the year before, and management wants to avoid another decline this year. One of the company's existing loan agreements requires its debt-to-equity ratio to be less than 2. Abbott pays taxes at a 40% rate.

Required:

1. Assess the impact of each financing alternative on 2002 EPS and the year-end debt-to-equity ratio.
2. Which financing alternative would you recommend? Why? Respond by considering a variety of pros and cons for each alternative, from different parties' perspectives.

P15-4 Stock buyback incentives

Hershey Foods Corporation is an American company that manufactures, sells, and distributes consumer food products including chocolate bars, chocolate drink mixes, refrigerated puddings, beverages, pasta, cough drops, and jellybeans. In August 1995 the company repurchased 9,049,773 common shares from a single shareholder—Milton Hershey School Trust—for US$500 million. This buyback, plus other repurchases that year, reduced shareholders' equity by 25%.

Excerpts from Hershey Foods' 1995 annual report follow. (All dollar amounts are in U.S. dollars.)

As of December 31, 1995, the Corporation had 530,000,000 authorized shares of capital stock. Of this total, 450,000,000 shares were designated as Common Stock, 75,000,000 shares as Class B Common Stock (Class B Stock), and 5,000,000 shares as Preferred Stock, each class having a par value of one dollar per share. As of December 31, 1995, a combined total of 89,975,436 shares of both classes of common stock had been issued, of which 77,265,883 shares were outstanding. No shares of the Preferred Stock were issued or outstanding during the three-year period ended December 31, 1995.

Holders of the Common Stock and the Class B Stock generally vote together without regard to class on matters submitted to shareholders, including the election of directors, with the Common Stock having one vote per share and the Class B stock having ten votes per share. However, the Common Stock, voting separately as a class, is entitled to elect one-sixth of the Board of Directors. With respect to dividend rights, the Common Stock is entitled to cash dividends 10% higher than those declared and paid on the Class B Stock. . . . Class B Stock can be converted into Common Stock on a share-for-share basis at any time.

Hershey Trust Company, as Trustee for the benefit of Milton Hershey School . . . and as direct owner of investment shares . . . was entitled to cast approximately 76% of the total votes of both classes of the Corporation's common stock [as of December 31, 1995]. The Milton Hershey School Trust must approve the issuance of shares of Common Stock or any other action which would result in the Milton Hershey School Trust not continuing to have voting control of the Corporation.

In August 1995, the Corporation purchased an additional 9,049,773 shares of its Common Stock to be held as Treasury Stock from the Milton Hershey School Trust for $500.0 million. In connection with the share repurchase program begun in 1993, a total of 2,000,000 shares were also acquired from the Milton Hershey School Trust in 1993 for approximately $103.1 million.

(US$ in thousands)	Year Ended December 31,	
	1995	1994
Cash flows from operating activities	$494,929	$337,306
Common share book value	$137,707	$139,802
Treasury share book value	$685,076	$158,711
Common shares outstanding	74,733.9	74,679.4
Class B shares outstanding	15,241.4	15,242.9
	89,975.3	89,922.3
Treasury shares held	12,709.5	3,187.1

Required:

1. Why has Hershey Foods Corporation issued two classes of common shares? Both types have a [US]$1 par value. Do they have the same market price?
2. On the basis of the 1995 year-end balance sheet amounts, compute the average price per share that Hershey Foods received for its common and Class B shares.
3. Compute the average price Hershey Foods paid for treasury shares held at the end of 1994. How does this price compare to the average price paid for treasury shares held at the end of 1995?
4. What was the per-share price Hershey Foods paid for the shares it bought back from Milton Hershey School Trust in 1995 and in 1993?
5. Why did the company buy back its shares? What are some other reasons companies repurchase their common shares?
6. As a credit analyst, how would you react to the company's announcement of its 1995 buyback?

P15-5 Comprehensive EPS calculations

Access Example 1 ("Comprehensive example on computation and presentation of basic and diluted earnings per share") in Appendix B of Section 3500 of the *CICA Handbook*. Review the example in detail, ensuring that you understand the technical details.

Required:

1. As you review the example, list all the assumptions that the calculations require. What opinions do you have regarding these assumptions?
2. Explain the rationale behind the computation of diluted EPS.
3. Explain the rationale behind the if-converted method.
4. Explain the rationale behind the treasury stock method. Explain how it is different from the if-converted method.
5. Critically evaluate the treasury stock method. Previously, Canadian GAAP regarding EPS required companies to estimate what imputed income would be in calculating the dilutive effects of options, warrants, and equivalents.
6. Should basic EPS or diluted EPS be used in valuation models (Chapter 6)? Explain.

P15-6 Valuing stock option grants

Texas Instruments manufactures and sells electrical and electronic products, including semiconductor integrated circuits and subassemblies, electronic control devices, notebook computers, electronic calculators, and learning aids. The company also manufactures metallurgical materials. Two types of share option plans are used at Texas Instruments:

TEXAS INSTRUMENTS
www.ti.com

- *Long-term incentive plans.* Options granted under this plan have a ten-year term and cannot be exercised for eight years, although exercisability may be accelerated to the extent that EPS goals are achieved. The exercise price per share cannot be less than 100% of the fair market value of common shares on the date of grant.
- *Employee share option purchase plan.* This plan provides for options to be offered to all eligible employees in amounts based on a percentage of the employee's prior year's compensation. These options become exercisable in 14 months—and expire not more than 27 months—from the date of grant.

The footnote on the next page appeared in the company's 1996 annual report. (All dollar amounts in U.S. dollars.)

In accordance with the terms of APB No. 25, the company records no compensation expense of its stock option awards. As required by SFAS No. 123, the company provides the following disclosure of hypothetical values for these awards. The weighted-average grant-date value of options granted during 1996 was estimated to be $18.47 under the Long-Term Incentive Plans and $12.10 under the Employee Stock Option Purchase Plan. These values were estimated using the Black–Scholes option pricing model with the following weighted-average assumptions: expected dividend yield of 1.48% (Long-Term Plans) and 1.21% (Employees' Plan), expected volatility of 39%, risk-free interest rates of 5.42% (Long-Term Plans), and 6.15% (Employees' Plan), and expected lives of 6 years (Long-Term Plans) and 1.5 years (Employees' Plan).

Had compensation expense been recorded based on these hypothetical values, the company's 1996 net income would have been $40 million, or $0.21 per share. A similar computation for 1995 would have resulted in net income of $1,078 million, or $5.57 per share. Because options vest over several years and additional option grants are expected, the effects of these hypothetical calculations are not likely to be representative of similar future calculations.

	Number of Shares	Weighted Average Exercise Price
Long-term incentive plans		
Outstanding 12/31/95	7,882,572	$29.24
Granted	2,663,375	45.84
Exercised	(434,660)	25.80
Lapsed or canceled	(198,739)	26.16
Outstanding 12/31/96	9,912,548	33.91
Employees' stock option plan		
Outstanding 12/31/95	1,133,709	56.13
Granted	848,546	56.25
Exercised	(386,162)	50.86
Lapsed or canceled	(399,909)	58.43
Outstanding 12/31/96	1,196,184	57.31

The company reported net income of US$63 million in 1996 and US$1,088 million in 1995.

Required:

1. Why does the company use a higher risk-free rate for its long-term incentive plans than it does for its employees' plan?
2. Using the Black–Scholes option pricing model and the company's weighted average assumptions, verify the US$18.47 valuation for long-term incentive plans and the US$12.10 valuation for the employees' plan. Assume all options granted had an exercise price equal to the fair value of the shares at the grant date.
3. Using the Black–Scholes option pricing model, compute per-share valuations for long-term incentive plans and the employees' plan using the following weighted average assumptions:

		Long-Term Incentive Plans	Employees' Plans	All Other Black–Scholes Variables
1.	Expected dividend yield	0%	0%	Use the company's original estimates
2.	Expected dividend yield	5	5	Use the company's original estimates
3.	Expected volatility	29	29	Use the company's original estimates
4.	Expected volatility	49	49	Use the company's original estimates
5.	Risk-free interest rate	4.92	5.65	Use the company's original estimates
6.	Risk-free interest rate	5.92	6.65	Use the company's original estimates
7.	Expected life	4 years	0.5 years	Use the company's original estimates
8.	Expected life	8 years	2.5 years	Use the company's original estimates

Assume all options granted had an exercise price equal to the fair value of the shares at the grant date. You will be computing eight valuation estimates for each share option plan.

4. Which variable—dividend yield, expected volatility, risk-free interest rate, or expected life—has the greatest impact on the option valuation estimates?

5. Using the valuation estimates from part 3, compute the maximum and minimum compensation expense for Texas Instruments' 1996 share option grants. Assume that long-term options vest over eight years and that employee-plan options vest over two years.

Cases

C15-1 Shaw Communications Inc.'s September 1997 financings

In September 1997, Shaw Communications Inc. made a public offering of two financial securities: US$142,500,000 8.45% Series A Canadian Originated Preferred Securities ("COPrS"; US$25 principal amount per security), and CDN$100,000,000 8.54% Series B Capital Securities (CDN$1,000 principal amount per security). Shaw is a diversified Calgary-based entertainment, information, and communications company, with interests in cable television and Internet access services, media programming, radio, and telecommunications. Revenues for the year ended August 31, 1996, were $611 million. Selected excerpts from the prospectus dated September 25, 1997, are shown on pages 764–767.

SHAW
COMMUNICATIONS
INC.
www.shaw.ca

Required:

1. How should these two securities be accounted for?
2. How has Shaw proposed to account for these securities?

The Offering

Issues U.S.$142,500,000 of 8.45% Series A Canadian Originated Preferred Securities ("COPrS")^{SM} ("Series A Securities").

Cdn.$100,000,000 of 8.54% Series B Capital Securities ("Series B Securities").

Interest Payment Dates

Series A Securities March 31, June 30, September 30 and December 31 of each year, commencing December 31, 1997.

Series B Securities March 31 and September 30 of each year, commencing March 31, 1998.

Maturity

Series A Securities September 30, 2046.

Series B Securities September 30, 2027.

Ranking The Securities will be issued as unsecured junior subordinated debt of Shaw. The Series A Securities and Series B Securities will rank *pari passu* with each other.

Additional Amounts Any payments with respect to the Securities made by Shaw will be made without withholding or deduction for Canadian taxes, unless required by law or the interpretation or administration thereof, in which case Shaw will pay such additional amounts as may be necessary so that the net amount received by holders of the Securities (other than certain excluded holders) after such withholding or deduction will not be less than the amount that would have been received in the absence of such withholding or deduction. See "Description of the Securities—Canadian Withholding Taxes."

Optional Redemption

Series A Securities The Series A Securities are redeemable by Shaw, in whole or in part, at any time and from time to time on or after September 30, 2002 at a redemption price equal to 100% of the principal amount of the Series A Securities to be redeemed plus accrued and unpaid interest thereon to the date of such redemption. In addition, the Series A Securities are redeemable by Shaw, in whole but not in part, at any time upon the occurrence of a Redemption Tax Event at a redemption price equal to 100% of the principal amount thereof plus any accrued and unpaid interest to the date of redemption. See "Description of the Securities—Optional Redemption—Series A Securities" and "—Redemption for Changes in Canadian Tax Law."

Series B Securities The Series B Securities are redeemable by Shaw, in whole or in part, at any time and from time to time on or after September 30, 2007 at the redemption prices set forth herein plus accrued and unpaid interest thereon to the date of such redemption. The Series B Securities are also redeemable by Shaw, in whole but not in part, at any time upon the occurrence of a Redemption Tax Event at a redemption price equal to (i) if redeemed prior to September 30, 2007, the Make-Whole Amount plus accrued and unpaid interest on the principal amount of the Series B Securities to the date of such redemption or (ii) if redeemed on or after September 30, 2007, 100% of the principal amount thereof plus accrued and unpaid interest to the date of such redemption. See "Description of the Securities—Optional Redemption—Series A Securities" and "—Redemption for Changes in Canadian Tax Law."

Interest Deferral	Shaw has the right to defer, at any time and from time to time, subject to certain conditions, payments of interest on the Securities by extending the interest payment period on the Securities for a period (each such period, an "Extension Period") of up to 20 consecutive quarterly periods.
	Except in certain limited circumstances described herein, Shaw shall not pay or declare dividends to holders of its common or preferred shares (except by way of stock dividend) at any time when any outstanding interest on the Securities is either in default or is being deferred as contemplated above. There may be multiple Extension Periods of varying lengths, each of up to 20 consecutive quarterly periods throughout the term of either series of Securities. During an Extension Period, interest will accrue but will not compound. Shaw may satisfy its obligation to pay Deferred Interest (as defined herein) on any applicable Interest Payment Date by delivering to the Trustee Class B Shares, in which event the holder of a Security shall be entitled to receive cash payments equal to the Deferred Interest from proceeds of the sale of the requisite Class B Shares by the Trustee. See "Description of the Securities—Option to Extend Interest Payment Periods" and "—Class B Shares Payment Election."
Currency of Payment	
Series A Securities	The Series A Securities are denominated in U.S. dollars.
Series B Securities	The Series B Securities are denominated in Canadian dollars and all payments on the Series B Securities are payable by Shaw in Canadian dollars. However, in accordance with the provisions described herein, unless beneficial holders of the Series B Securities who hold their Securities through DTC elect to receive Canadian dollars, the principal of and interest on the Series B Securities will be paid to such holders in U.S. dollars. All currency exchange costs will be borne by such holders receiving payments in U.S. dollars. For information as to changes in the relative value of the U.S. dollar and the Canadian dollar and certain financial and tax consequences to holders of the Series B Securities, see "Exchange Rate Data" and "Risk Factors—Foreign Exchange Risks to Investors." Purchasers of the Series B Securities will be required to pay for the Series B Securities in Canadian dollars. See "Underwriting."
Sinking Fund	None.
Use of Proceeds	The net proceeds from the sale of the Securities offered hereby, after payment of expenses of the offering and underwriting commission, are estimated to be U.S.$209.0 million (Cdn. $289.3 million) based on the Noon Buying Rate on September 25, 1997. The net proceeds will be used for general corporate purposes, including to fund working capital requirements, capital expenditures, debt repayments and acquisitions. Pending any specific application, such net proceeds will be invested in short-term securities or used to temporarily reduce amounts outstanding under Shaw's revolving credit facility. See "Use of Proceeds."
Governing Law	The Indenture and the Securities will be governed by the laws of the State of New York.
Stock Exchange Listing	
Series A Securities	The Series A Securities have been approved for listing on the NYSE, subject to notice of issuance, under the trading symbol "STV."
Series B Securities	The Series B Securities will not be listed on any exchange.

Holding Company Structure

Substantially all of Shaw's business activities are operated by its subsidiaries. As a holding company, Shaw's ability to meet its financial obligations is dependent primarily upon the receipt of interest and principal payments on intercompany advances, management fees, cash dividends and other payments from its subsidiaries together with proceeds raised by Shaw through the issuance of equity and debt and from the proceeds from the sale of assets. Shaw's subsidiaries are distinct legal entities and have no obligation, contingent or otherwise, to pay any amount due pursuant to the Securities or to make any funds available therefor, whether by dividends, interest, loans, advances or other payments. In addition, the payment of dividends and the making of loans, advances and other payments to Shaw by its subsidiaries may be subject to statutory or contractual restrictions, are contingent upon the earnings of those subsidiaries and are subject to various business and other considerations.

In addition, because Shaw is a holding company, the Securities are effectively subordinated to all existing and future liabilities, including trade payables and other indebtedness, of Shaw's subsidiaries, except to the extent Shaw is a creditor of such subsidiaries. Should any of Shaw's subsidiaries be liquidated, restructured or become insolvent, Shaw's ability to meet its financial obligations, including its obligations under the Securities, would be affected to the extent that such subsidiaries could no longer make payments to Shaw. In addition, any right of Shaw as an equity holder to participate in any distribution of the assets of any of Shaw's subsidiaries upon the liquidation, organization or insolvency of any such subsidiaries (and the consequent right of the holders of the Securities to participate in such distributions) will be subject to the claims of the creditors (including trade creditors) and any preferred shareholders of such subsidiaries. As at May 31, 1997, indebtedness and other liabilities of Shaw's subsidiaries totaled approximately $124 million.

Adverse Consequences of Financial Leverage

As of May 31, 1997 Shaw's outstanding Senior Indebtedness aggregated approximately $1.4 billion and Shaw had the capacity to additionally incur approximately $400 million under its existing bank credit facilities.

The ability of Shaw to meet its debt service obligations will depend on the future performance of Shaw, which will be subject to prevailing economic conditions and to financial, business and other factors beyond the control of Shaw. While Shaw is in compliance with all of its financial and operating covenants, the existence of such financial leverage could have important consequences to holders of the Securities, including: (i) Shaw's ability to obtain additional financing for working capital, capital expenditures, acquisitions, general corporate purposes or other purposes may be impaired and (ii) a substantial portion of Shaw's cash flow from operations will be dedicated to the payment of principal and interest on its outstanding indebtedness, thereby reducing the funds available to Shaw for its existing operations and any future business opportunities. ...

Subordination of Securities

Shaw's obligations under the Securities are subordinate and junior in right of payment to all present and future Senior Indebtedness of Shaw. Such obligations are also effectively subordinate to claims of creditors of Shaw's subsidiaries, except to the extent Shaw is a creditor of such subsidiaries ranking at least *pari passu* with other creditors. As of May 31, 1997, Shaw had approximately $1.4 billion of Senior Indebtedness and the subsidiaries of Shaw had approximately $124 million of indebtedness and other liabilities. There are no terms of the Securities that limit the ability of Shaw or its subsidiaries to incur additional indebtedness, including indebtedness that ranks senior to the Securities. See "Description of the Securities—Subordination." ...

Capitalization

The following table summarizes the consolidated capitalization of Shaw at May 31, 1997, both actual and as adjusted to give effect to the issuance of the Securities after deduction of the underwriting commission and the expenses of the offering. The information presented below should be read in conjunction with Shaw's unaudited consolidated financial statements and audited consolidated financial statements included elsewhere and incorporated by reference in this Prospectus.

(in thousands of dollars)	May 31, 1997(1) Actual	As Adjusted
Cash	$ —	$ 289,285
Long-term debt (2):		
Mortgages	2,056	2,056
Debentures:		
Series B, due July 29, 1999 (3)	60,000	60,000
1998 Series, due April 8, 1998	35,000	35,000
2003 Series, due January 8, 2003	24,000	24,000
2003 (US) Series, due February 4, 2003	70,000	70,000
2005 Series, due November 30, 2005	156,299	156,299
2007 (US) Series, due March 19, 2007	284,200	284,200
2007 Series, due March 19, 2007	45,000	45,000
2008 Series, due January 8, 2008	42,000	42,000
Bank loans (4)	614,205	614,205
Notes payable in annual installments of $19,546 on July 31	78,184	78,184
Mandatorily redeemable preferred shares	15,571	15,571
Total long-term debt	1,426,515	1,426,515
Minority interest (5)	984	984
Shareholders' equity:		
Securities offered hereby (6)	—	289,285
Share capital (7)	5,631	5,631
Contributed surplus	362,299	362,299
Retained earnings	209,809	209,809
Total shareholders' equity	577,739	867,024
Total capitalization	$2,005,238	$2,294,523

...

(6) The "As Adjusted" amount gives effect to the proposed issuance of the Securities net of expenses of the offering. Under U.S. GAAP, none of the proposed issuance of the Securities would be included in shareholders' equity. Solely for the convenience of the reader, the Series A Securities have been converted to Canadian dollars based upon the Noon Buying Rate on September 25, 1997 of U.S.$1.00 = Cdn.$1.3842.

C15-2 An influential business columnist urges accounting reform on stock options

On July 16, 2002, David Crane, one of the preeminent business writers in Canada, wrote about stock option accounting in the article on the next page.

Required:

1. Do you agree with David Crane about the importance of stock option accounting? Explain.
2. In Crane's view, is accounting standard-setting political?
3. What are the costs and benefits of setting Canadian accounting standards—specifically the stock option standard—that differ from the American standard?

4. What assumptions about accounting measurement and disclosure seem to be implicit in Crane's column?
5. Assume the role of a newly hired member of a company's accounting group. Prepare a 500-word memo to the audit committee of your company's board of directors outlining the pros and cons of expensing stock options. Your company includes stock options as part of the total compensation incentive package for senior corporate and divisional managers.

Rules on stock options must be changed

For all the tough talk about corporate reform in the United States, it appears business lobbyists have won the day again, using the power of campaign contributions to keep U.S. politicians in line.

Last week, a U.S. Senate vote defeated a proposal by Senator John McCain that would have forced companies to treat the value of stock options issued to senior executives as a business expense, thus providing shareholders with a more accurate account of corporate performance.

Yet the treatment of stock options is the underlying cause of widespread greed and even corruption in the business world, not just in the United States but Canada as well.

Unfortunately, the Canadian Institute of Chartered Accountants has indicated it will not require the expensing of stock options unless the United States does as well. That means we are allowing U.S. "crony capitalism" to set policy in Canada. Yet surely the Canadian accounting profession should have the interests of honest disclosure as its highest priority, something that's lacking with the current treatment of stock options.

The Canadian Council of Chief Executives (formerly the Business Council on National Issues) has announced it will unveil new standards of corporate governance this fall. But unless it contains a commitment to treat stock options as an expense, the exercise will be a waste of time. Even then, the voluntary standards will be of limited value since they will not be enforceable and will not apply to the large number of public companies that are not members of the group.

Stock options became increasingly popular, starting in the 1980s but much more so in the 1990s, supposedly as an incentive to encourage senior executives to work hard to boost the value of their company's shares by building the business.

In stock option plans, executives were given the right to purchase large numbers of their company's shares in the future at the price that existed when the option was issued. Their profit would be the difference between the option price and the price of the shares when the options were exercised. Many executives made huge profits, cashing out and keeping their winnings, even when share prices in their companies subsequently tanked. John Roth, former CEO of Nortel Networks Corp., walked away with more than $100 million, for example.

Stock options soon became a flawed incentive. Instead of encouraging executives to build strong businesses, options encouraged too many executives to resort to dubious accounting practices and short-term business decisions to temporarily inflate stock prices and cash out with huge capital gains. This is at the root of the crisis of trust in business today. While executives have used stock options to enrich themselves, ordinary shareholders have in some instances seen their life savings evaporate or their pensions sharply reduced in value. Enron Corp. chairman Kenneth Lay exercised $123.4 million (U.S.) in stock options in 2000 alone; the company today is almost worthless.

The failure to treat stock options as an expense is a systemic flaw in the financial system. Indeed, there are good arguments for abolishing them.

Among those campaigning for the expensing of stock options is Alan Greenspan, chairman of the U.S. Federal Reserve Board, who contends their current treatment distorts true earnings; he says changing the system to expense stock options is the most important reform he would like to see in the aftermath of the Enron collapse.

But as the *Wall Street Journal* reported in March, when the issue resurfaced this year, lobbyists of 30 of the largest U.S. companies met in the offices of Oracle Corp., with another 30 connected by telephone conference call, to map out a strategy to defeat corporate reform.

To be sure, some firms do expense options, with Boeing Inc. a top example. Now, Coca-Cola Co. says it will do the same. And in Canada, Manulife Financial Corp. has indicated it will.

But in the apparent absence of serious reform in the United States, we should still go ahead in Canada with regulatory change:

Stock options should be reported as expenses in company financial statements.

Senior executives should be allowed to exercise options while holding their job but not sell the acquired shares until after they leave.

Annual meetings should include a discussion and vote on executive compensation, including stock options

If serious reform is unlikely in the United States, that's no excuse for inaction in Canada. We could be a leader in business reform.

Source: David Crane, *Toronto Star*, July 16, 2002. Reprinted with permission of Torstar Syndication Services.

Integrative Running Case Study
Bombardier on the Web

This case draws upon information in Bombardier Inc.'s audited financial statements for the year ended January 31, 2002, as published in the company's annual report. You can find this report on the Companion Website for this text (**www.pearsoned.ca/revsine**).

Required:

1. Refer to the Consolidated Statements of Shareholders' Equity, on page 70 of the annual report. Reconstruct journal entries to account for the changes in the various shareholders' equity accounts from the start to the end of the year ended January 31, 2002.
2. Carefully read notes 14 ("Share Capital") and 15 ("Share-Based Plans").
   (a) In your opinion, has the company complied with GAAP in these notes?
   (b) Explain how information contained in these notes might have an important bearing on an assessment of the company's quality of earnings.

Collaborative Learning Cases
CL15-1 Time Warner Inc.:
Is it equity or debt?

Your boss, Barbara Wallace, has asked you to review the "Time Warner situation." It's only your second day on the job as a credit analyst at the bank, and Time Warner is your first real assignment.

TIME WARNER INC.
www.timewarner.com

"What do you mean, the Time Warner *situation*?" you ask. Wallace explains that the bank has a US$200 million credit facility with Time Warner that is undergoing a renewal review. The loan agreement states that Time Warner must maintain a long-term debt-to-total-equity ratio of no more than 2.0; otherwise the interest rate on the facility gets increased by 25 basis points (0.25%). The company must also maintain a times-interest-earned ratio of at least 1.0 or the interest rate is raised another 25 basis points. The loan agreement specifies both that total equity includes the book value of any preferred shares issued and outstanding, and that preferred dividends are not counted in the computation of the times-interest-earned ratio.

Wallace goes on to clarify your task. "The situation is this—Time Warner now has about [US]$2.6 billion of preferred shares, far more than we thought possible when we negotiated the credit facility; and although it's called preferred shares, it looks a lot like debt. I want you to dig into the details of the company's preferred shares and decide how it should be classified—as debt or equity?—from the bank's perspective. Then see if the company is still in compliance with its covenants. I'll need a memo outlining your reasoning for debt or equity treatment of each type of preferred. I'd also like you to suggest some new covenant language so that we can avoid situations like this in the future."

Time Warner Inc. is a holding company with subsidiaries which produce and distribute theatrical motion pictures, cartoons, television series, films, and recorded music. The company also operates a television network and theme parks. Its retail stores feature consumer products based on the company's characters and brands.

During 1995 and 1996, the company issued several types of preferred shares as part of the company's debt reduction program. This program was described in the company's 1996 annual report to shareholders as follows:

TWE is Time Warner Entertainment, a subsidiary of Time Warner Inc. The parent company has a substantial investment in the common share of Hasbro, a toy manufacturer. Time Warner Inc. goes on to describe its financial condition and its preferred shares as follows. (All dollar amounts in U.S. dollars.)

1996 Financial Condition

At December 31, 1996, Time Warner had $12.7 billion of debt, $452 million of available cash and equivalents (net debt of $12.2 billion), $488 million of borrowings against future stock option proceeds, $949 million of mandatorily redeemable preferred securities of subsidiaries, $1.7 billion of Series M Preferred Stock, and $9.5 billion of shareholders' equity, compared to $9.9 billion of debt, $1.2 billion of available cash and equivalents (net debt of $8.7 billion), $949 million of mandatorily redeemable preferred securities of subsidiaries, and $3.7 billion of shareholders' equity at December 31, 1995. At December 31, 1996, Time Warner also had $62 million of noncurrent cash and equivalents held in escrow for purposes of funding certain preferred dividend requirements.

The increase in net debt principally reflects the assumption or incurrence of approximately $4.8 billion of debt related to the TBS [Turner Broadcasting System] Transaction and the CVI Acquisition, offset in part by the use of approximately $1.55 billion of net proceeds from the issuance of the Series M Preferred Stock for debt reduction. The increase in shareholders' equity principally reflects the issuance in 1996 of approximately 173.4 million shares of common stock in connection with the TBS Transaction and approximately 2.9 million shares of common stock and 6.3 million shares of preferred stock in connection with the CVI Acquisition. The effect from such issuances was offset in part by an increase in dividend requirements and the repurchase of approximately 11.4 million shares of Time Warner common stock at an aggregate cost of $456 million.

9. Mandatorily Redeemable Preferred Securities

In August 1995, Time Warner issued approximately 12.1 million Company-obligated mandatorily redeemable preferred securities of a wholly owned subsidiary ("PERCS") for aggregate gross proceeds of $374 million. The sole assets of the subsidiary that is the obligor on the PERCS are $385 million principal amount of 4% subordinated notes of Old Time Warner [the predecessor company] due December 23, 1997. Cumulative cash distributions are payable on the PERCS at an annual rate of 4%. The PERCS are mandatorily redeemable on December 23, 1997, for an amount per PERCS equal to the lesser of $54.41, and the market value of 1.5 shares of common stock of Hasbro on December 17, 1997 (as adjusted for the Hasbro Stock Split), payable in cash or, at Time Warner's option, Hasbro common stock. Time Warner has the right to redeem the PERCS at any time prior to December 23, 1997, at an amount per PERCS equal to $54.41 (or in certain limited circumstances the lesser of such amount and the market value of 1.5 shares of Hasbro common stock at the time of redemption) plus accrued and unpaid distributions thereon and a declining premium, payable in cash or, at Time Warner's option, Hasbro common stock.

In December 1995, Time Warner issued approximately 23 million Company-obligated mandatorily redeemable preferred securities of a wholly owned subsidiary ("Preferred Trust Securities") for aggregate gross proceeds of $575 million. The sole assets of the subsidiary that is the obligor on the Preferred Trust Securities are $592 million principal amount of 8-7/8% subordinated debentures of Old Time Warner due December 31, 2025. Cumulative cash distributions are payable on the Preferred Trust Securities at an annual rate of 8-7/8%. The Preferred Trust Securities are mandatorily redeemable for cash on December 31, 2025, and Time Warner has the right to redeem the Preferred Trust Securities, in whole or in part, on or after December 31, 2000, or in other certain circumstances, in each case at an amount per Preferred Trust Security equal to $25 plus accrued and unpaid distributions thereon.

10. Series M Exchangeable Preferred Stock

In April 1996, Time Warner raised approximately $1.55 billion of net proceeds in a private placement of 1.6 million shares of 10-1/4% exchangeable preferred stock. This issuance allowed the Company to realize cash proceeds through a security whose payment terms are principally linked (until a reorganization of TWE occurs, if any) to a portion of Time Warner's currently noncash-generating interest in the Series B Capital of TWE. The proceeds raised from this transaction were used by Time Warner to reduce debt. As part of the TBS Transaction, these preferred shares were converted into registered shares of Series M exchangeable preferred stock with substantially identical terms ("Series M Preferred Stock").

Each share of Series M Preferred Stock is entitled to a liquidation preference of $1,000 and entitles the holder thereof to receive cumulative dividends at the rate of 10-1/4% per annum, payable quarterly (1) in cash, to the extent of an amount equal to the Pro Rata Percentage (as defined below) multiplied by the amount of cash distributions received by Time Warner from TWE with respect to its interests in the Series B Capital and Residual Capital of TWE, excluding stock option related distributions and certain tax related distributions (collectively, "Eligible TWE Cash Distributions"), or (2) to the extent of any balance, at Time Warner's option, (i) in cash or (ii) in-kind, through the issuance of additional shares of Series M Preferred Stock with an aggregate liquidation preference equal to the amount of such dividends. The "Pro Rata Percentage" is equal to the ratio of (1) the aggregate liquidation preference of the outstanding shares of Series M Preferred Stock, including any accumulated and unpaid dividends

thereon, to (2) Time Warner's total interest in the Series B Capital of TWE, including any undistributed priority capital return thereon. Because cash distributions to Time Warner with respect to its interests in the Series B Capital and Residual Capital of TWE are generally restricted until June 30, 1998 and are subject to additional limitations thereafter under the TWE partnership agreement, Time Warner does not expect to pay cash dividends in the foreseeable future.

The Series M Preferred Stock may be redeemed at the option of Time Warner, in whole or in part, on or after July 1, 2006, subject to certain conditions, at an amount per share equal to its liquidation preference plus accumulated and accrued and unpaid dividends thereon, and a declining premium through July 1, 2010 (the "Optional Redemption Price"). Time Warner is required to redeem shares of Series M Preferred Stock representing up to 20%, 25%, 33-1/3%, and 50% of the then-outstanding liquidation preference of the Series M Preferred Stock on July 1 of 2012, 2013, 2014, and 2015, respectively, at an amount equal to the aggregate liquidation preference of the number of shares to be redeemed plus accumulated and accrued and unpaid dividends thereon (the "Mandatory Redemption Price"). Total payments in respect of such mandatory redemption obligations on any redemption date are limited to an amount equal to the Pro Rata Percentage of any cash distributions received by Time Warner from TWE in the preceding year in connection with the redemption of Time Warner's interest in the Series B Capital of TWE and in connection with certain cash distributions related to Time Warner's interest in the Residual Capital of TWE. The redemption of the Series B Capital of TWE is scheduled to occur ratably over a five-year period commencing on June 30, 2011. Time Warner is required to redeem any remaining outstanding shares of Series M Preferred Stock on July 1, 2016 at the Mandatory Redemption Price; however, in the event that Time Warner's interest in the Series B Capital of TWE has not been redeemed in full prior to such final mandatory redemption date, payments in respect of the final mandatory redemption obligation of the Series M Preferred Stock in 2016 will be limited to an amount equal to the lesser of the Mandatory Redemption Price and an amount equal to the Pro Rata Percentage of the fair market value of TWE (net of taxes) attributable to Time Warner's interests in the Series B Capital and Residual Capital of TWE.

Upon a reorganization of TWE, as defined in the related certificate of designation, Time Warner must elect either to (1) exchange each outstanding share of Series M Preferred Stock for shares of a new series of 10-1/4% exchangeable preferred stock ("Series L

Preferred Stock") or (2) subject to certain conditions, redeem the outstanding shares of Series M Preferred Stock at an amount per share equal to 110% of the liquidation preference thereof, plus accumulated and accrued and unpaid dividends thereon or, after July 1, 2006, at the Optional Redemption Price. The Series L Preferred Stock has terms similar to those of the Series M Preferred Stock, except that (i) Time Warner may only pay dividends in-kind until June 30, 2006, (ii) Time Warner is required to redeem the outstanding shares of Series L Preferred Stock on July 1, 2011 at an amount per share equal to the liquidation preference thereof, plus accumulated and accrued and unpaid dividends thereon and (iii) Time Warner has the option to exchange, in whole but not in part, subject to certain conditions, the outstanding shares of Series L Preferred Stock for Time Warner 10-1/4% Senior Subordinated Debentures due July 1, 2011 (the "Senior Subordinated Debentures") having a principal amount equal to the liquidation preference of the Series L Preferred Stock plus accrued and unpaid dividends thereon. Interest on the Senior Subordinated Debentures is payable in cash or, at Time Warner's option through June 30, 2006, in-kind through the issuance of additional Senior Subordinated Debentures with a principal amount equal to such interest. The Senior Subordinated Debentures may be redeemed at the option of Time Warner, in whole or in part, on or after July 1, 2006, subject to certain conditions, at an amount per debenture equal to its principal amount plus accrued and unpaid interest, and a declining premium through July 1, 2010.

Source: Time Warner Inc. 1996 annual report.

Information taken from Time Warner's 1996 annual report to shareholders follows:

(US$ in millions)	December 31, 1996	December 31, 1995
Long-term debt	$13,201	$9,907
Preferred shares	$ 2,625	$ 979
Common shareholders' equity	$ 9,498	$3,637
Total shareholders' equity	$12,123	$4,616
Net income before interest and taxes	$ 1,178	$ 879
Interest expense	$ 1,174	$ 877
Long-term debt/total equity	1.09	2.15
Times interest earned	1.00	1.00

Required:

1. From the bank's perspective, should Time Warner's preferred shares be classified as debt or equity? Draft a brief memo outlining your reasoning.
2. Based on your classification of the company's preferred shares, would you say that Time Warner is still in compliance with its debt covenants?
3. What new covenant language would you suggest the bank add to its loan agreement?

CL15-2 Celestica Inc. and financial reporting for owners' equity

CELESTICA INC.
www.celestica.
com

Excerpts from a recent regulatory filing by Celestica Inc. follows.

Required:

1. Assume the role of an assistant to the CFO of Celestica. A major American institutional investor interested in Celestica's shares has inquired about how the company accounts for the company's Liquid Yield Option^{TM} Notes (LYONs).

Prepare a 500-word memo responding to the inquiry comparing the company's practice to U.S. practice. Which accounting treatment—Canadian or American—is "better"?

2. Reconstruct all journal entries related to the LYONs from August 2000 to the end of 2001. What assumptions and estimates did you have to make?

3. Based upon information in Celestica's Consolidated Statements of Shareholders' Equity, and any other relevant information provided, prepare journal entries tracking the changes in shareholders' equity from December 31, 1998 to December 31, 2001.

4. What, if any, impact does Celestica's accounting for the LYONs have on its cash flow statement?

5. Explain in detail, avoiding technical jargon, how Celestica constructed its EPS numbers for 2001, 2000, and 1999, based upon the information in note 12, and any other relevant information provided.

6. In April 2002, the AcSB issued an exposure draft entitled "Cash Flow and Other Per Share Information," which proposed to severely restrict the disclosure of cash flow per share amounts in the financial statements. Assume the role (again!) of an assistant to the CFO of Celestica, and prepare a 500-word memo as a submission to the AcSB regarding the exposure draft, arguing that "cash flow from operations per share" *should* be included in financial statements.

Item 4. Information on the Company

A. History and Development of the Company

Celestica was incorporated in Ontario, Canada under the name Celestica International Holdings Inc. on September 27, 1996. Since that date, we have amended our articles of incorporation on various occasions principally to modify our corporate name and our share capital. Our legal name and commercial name is Celestica Inc. We are a corporation domiciled in the Province of Ontario, Canada and operate under the Ontario Business Corporations Act. Our principal executive offices are located at 12 Concorde Place, Toronto, Ontario, Canada M3C 3R8 and our telephone number is (416) 448-5800. Our web site is www.celestica.com. Information on our web site is not incorporated by reference in this Annual Report.

We are a leading provider of electronics manufacturing services to OEMs worldwide, with revenue for the year ended December 31, 2001 in excess of [US]$10.0 billion. We provide a wide variety of products and services to our customers, including the high-volume manufacture of complex PCAs and the full system assembly of final products. In addition, we are a leading-edge provider of design, repair and engineering services, supply chain management and power products. We operate facilities in North America, Europe, Asia and Latin America.

As an important IBM manufacturing unit, Celestica provided manufacturing services to IBM for more than 75 years. In 1993, we began providing EMS services to non-IBM customers. In October 1996, Celestica was purchased from IBM by an investor group, led by Onex, which included our management.

...

CELESTICA INC.
CONSOLIDATED BALANCE SHEETS
(in millions of U.S. dollars)

	As at December 31	
	2000	2001
Assets		
Current assets:		
Cash and short-term investments	$ 883.8	$1,342.8
Accounts receivable (note 4)	1,785.7	1,054.1
Inventories (note 5)	1,664.3	1,372.7
Prepaid and other assets	138.8	177.3
Deferred income taxes	48.4	49.7
	4,521.0	3,996.6
Capital assets (note 6)	633.4	915.1
Intangible assets (note 7)	578.3	1,556.0
Other assets (note 8)	205.3	165.2
	$5,938.0	$6,632.9
Liabilities and Shareholders' Equity		
Current liabilities:		
Accounts payable	$1,730.4	$1,198.3
Accrued liabilities	466.3	405.7
Income taxes payable	52.6	21.0
Deferred income taxes	7.7	21.8
Current portion of long-term debt (note 9)	1.4	10.0
	2,258.4	1,656.8
Long-term debt (note 9)	130.6	137.4
Accrued post-retirement benefits (note 16)	38.1	47.3
Deferred income taxes	38.6	41.5
Other long-term liabilities	3.0	4.3
	2,468.7	1,887.3
Shareholders' equity	3,469.3	4,745.6
	$5,938.0	$6,632.9

Commitments and contingencies (note 18)

Subsequent event (note 21)

Canadian and United States accounting policy differences (note 22)

See accompanying notes to consolidated financial statements.

CELESTICA INC.
CONSOLIDATED STATEMENTS OF EARNINGS (LOSS)
(in millions of U.S. dollars, except per share amounts)

	Year ended December 31		
	1999	2000	2001
Revenue	$5,297.2	$9,752.1	$10,004.4
Cost of sales	4,914.7	9,064.1	9,291.9
Gross profit	382.5	688.0	712.5
Selling, general and administrative expenses	202.2	326.1	341.4
Amortization of intangible assets (note 7)	55.6	88.9	125.0
Integration costs related to acquisitions (note 3)	9.6	16.1	22.8
Other charges (note 13)	—	—	273.1
	267.4	431.1	762.3
Operating income (loss)	115.1	256.9	(49.8)
Interest on long-term debt	17.3	17.8	19.8
Interest income, net	(6.6)	(36.8)	(27.7)
Earnings (loss) before income taxes	104.4	275.9	(41.9)
Income taxes (note 14):			
Current	30.7	80.1	25.8
Deferred (recovery)	5.3	(10.9)	(27.9)
	36.0	69.2	(2.1)
Net earnings (loss)	$ 68.4	$ 206.7	$ (39.8)
Basic earnings (loss) per share (note 12)	$ 0.41	$ 1.01	$ (0.26)
Diluted earnings (loss) per share (notes 2, 12)	$ 0.40	$ 0.98	$ (0.26)
Weighted average number of shares outstanding (note 12)			
Basic (in millions)	167.2	199.8	213.9
Diluted (in millions) (note 2)	171.2	211.8	213.9
Net earnings (loss) in accordance with U.S. GAAP (note 22)	$ 66.5	$ 197.4	$ (51.3)
Basic earnings (loss) per share, in accordance with U.S. GAAP (note 22)	$ 0.40	$ 0.99	$ (0.24)
Diluted earnings (loss) per share, in accordance with U.S. GAAP (note 22)	$ 0.39	$ 0.96	$ (0.24)

See accompanying notes to consolidated financial statements.

CELESTICA INC.
CONSOLIDATED STATEMENTS OF SHAREHOLDERS' EQUITY
(in millions of U.S. dollars)

	Convertible Debt (note 10)	Capital Stock (note 11)	Retained Earnings (Deficit)	Foreign Currency Translation Adjustment	Total Shareholders' Equity
Balance—December 31, 1998	$ —	$ 912.1	$ (52.2)	$(0.6)	$ 859.3
Shares issued, net	—	734.0	—	—	734.0
Currency translation	—	—	—	(3.5)	(3.5)
Net earnings for the year	—	—	68.4	—	68.4
Balance—December 31, 1999	—	1,646.1	16.2	(4.1)	1,658.2
Convertible debt issued, net	850.4	—	—	—	850.4
Convertible debt accretion, net of tax	10.1	—	(5.4)	—	4.7
Shares issued, net	—	749.3	—	—	749.3
Net earnings for the year	—	—	206.7	—	206.7
Balance—December 31, 2000	860.5	2,395.4	217.5	(4.1)	3,469.3
Convertible debt accretion, net of tax	26.3	—	(15.0)	—	11.3
Shares issued, net	—	1,303.6	—	—	1,303.6
Currency translation	—	—	—	1.2	1.2
Net loss for the year	—	—	(39.8)	—	(39.8)
Balance—December 31, 2001	$886.8	$3,699.0	$162.7	$(2.9)	$4,745.6

See accompanying notes to consolidated financial statements.

CELESTICA INC.
CONSOLIDATED STATEMENTS OF CASH FLOWS
(in millions of U.S. dollars)

| | Year ended December 31 | | |
	1999	2000	2001
Cash provided by (used in):			
Operations:			
Net earnings (loss)	$ 68.4	$ 206.7	$ (39.8)
Items not affecting cash:			
Depreciation and amortization	126.5	212.5	319.5
Deferred income taxes	5.3	(10.9)	(27.9)
Other charges (note 13)	—	—	134.7
Other	(2.9)	(4.4)	1.7
Cash from earnings	197.3	403.9	388.2
Changes in non-cash working capital items:			
Accounts receivable	(227.7)	(995.3)	887.2
Inventories	(265.0)	(656.7)	822.5
Other assets	1.7	(94.7)	45.7
Accounts payable and accrued liabilities	194.6	1,230.4	(854.0)
Income taxes payable	4.7	27.3	0.9
Non-cash working capital changes	(291.7)	(489.0)	902.3
Cash provided by (used in) operations	(94.4)	(85.1)	1,290.5
Investing:			
Acquisitions, net of cash acquired	(64.8)	(634.7)	(1,299.7)
Purchase of capital assets	(211.8)	(282.8)	(199.3)
Other	(0.6)	(59.5)	1.4
Cash used in investing activities	(277.2)	(977.0)	(1,497.6)
Financing:			
Bank indebtedness	—	(8.6)	(2.8)
Repayments of long-term debt	(10.0)	(2.2)	(56.0)
Deferred financing costs	(1.5)	(0.1)	(3.9)
Issuance of convertible debt	—	862.9	—
Convertible debt issue costs, pre-tax	—	(19.4)	—
Issuance of share capital	758.2	766.6	737.7
Share issue costs, pre-tax	(34.3)	(26.8)	(10.0)
Other	(1.0)	2.0	1.1
Cash provided by financing activities	711.4	1,574.4	666.1
Increase in cash	339.8	512.3	459.0
Cash, beginning of year	31.7	371.5	883.8
Cash, end of year	$ 371.5	$ 883.8	$1,342.8
Supplemental information			
Paid during the year:			
Interest	$ 17.2	$ 15.9	$ 20.7
Taxes	$ 26.1	$ 55.0	$ 89.0
Non-cash financing activities:			
Convertible debt accretion, net of tax (note 10)	$ —	$ 5.4	$ 15.0
Shares issued for acquisitions	$ —	$ —	$ 567.0

Cash is comprised of cash and short-term investments.

See accompanying notes to consolidated financial statements.

CELESTICA INC.
NOTES TO CONSOLIDATED FINANCIAL STATEMENTS (Continued)
(in millions of U.S. dollars, except per share amounts)

...

9. Long-term debt:

	2000	2001
Global, unsecured, revolving credit facility due 2003 (a)	$ —	$ —
Global, unsecured, revolving credit facility due 2004 (b)	—	—
Unsecured revolving credit facility due 2005 (c)	—	—
Senior Subordinated Notes due 2006 (d)	130.0	130.0
Other (e)	2.0	17.4
	132.0	147.4
Less current portion	1.4	10.0
	$ 130.6	$ 137.4

(a) Concurrently with the initial public offering on July 7, 1998, the Company entered into a global, unsecured, revolving credit facility providing up to $250.0 of borrowings. The credit facility permits the Company and certain designated subsidiaries to borrow funds for general corporate purposes (including acquisitions). Borrowings under the facility bear interest at LIBOR plus a margin and are repayable in July 2003. There were no borrowings on this facility during 2000 and 2001. Commitment fees in 2001 were $0.4.

(b) In February 2000, the Company renewed its second global, unsecured, revolving credit facility providing up to $250.0 of borrowings including a swing line facility that provides for short-term borrowings up to a maximum of seven days. The credit facility permits the Company and certain designated subsidiaries to borrow funds for general corporate purposes (including acquisitions). The revolving facility is repayable in April 2004. Borrowings under the facility bear interest at LIBOR plus a margin except that borrowings under the swing line facility bear interest at a base rate. There were no borrowings on this facility during 2000 and 2001. Commitment fees in 2001 were $0.6.

(c) In July 2001, the Company entered into an unsecured, revolving credit facility providing up to $500.0 of borrowings including a swing line facility that provides for short-term borrowings up to a maximum of seven days. The credit facility permits the Company and certain designated subsidiaries to borrow funds for general corporate purposes (including acquisitions). The revolving facility is repayable in July 2005. Borrowings under the facility bear interest at LIBOR plus a margin except that borrowings under the swing line facility bear interest at a base rate. There were no borrowings on this facility in 2001. Commitment fees in 2001 were $0.5.

(d) The Senior Subordinated Notes bear interest at 10.5%, are unsecured and are subordinated to the payment of all senior debt of the Company. The Senior Subordinated Notes may be redeemed at various premiums above face value.

(e) Other long-term debt includes secured loan facilities of one of the Company's subsidiaries of which $13.0 is outstanding at December 31, 2001. The weighted average interest rate on these facilities in 2001 was 4.4%. The loans are denominated in Singapore Dollars and are repayable through quarterly payments. There were no commitment fees for 2001.

As at December 31, 2001, principal repayments due within each of the next five years on all long-term debt are as follows:

2002	$ 10.0
2003	4.5
2004	1.3
2005	0.7
2006	130.6
Thereafter	0.3

The unsecured, revolving credit facilities have restrictive covenants relating to debt incurrence and sale of assets and also contain financial covenants that indirectly restrict the Company's ability to pay dividends. A change of control is an event of default. The Company's Senior Subordinated Notes due 2006 include a covenant restricting the Company's ability to pay dividends.

10. Convertible debt:

In August 2000, Celestica issued Liquid Yield Option Notes (LYONs) with a principal amount at maturity of $1,813.6, payable August 1, 2020. The Company received gross proceeds of $862.9 and incurred $12.5 in underwriting commissions, net of tax of $6.9. No interest is payable on the LYONs and the issue price of the LYONs represents a yield to maturity of 3.75%. The LYONs are subordinated in right of payment to all existing and future senior indebtedness of the Company.

The LYONs are convertible at any time at the option of the holder, unless previously redeemed or repurchased, into 5.6748 subordinate voting shares for each one thousand dollars principal amount at maturity. Holders may require the Company to repurchase all or a portion of their LYONs on August 2, 2005, August 1, 2010 and August 1, 2015 and the Company may redeem the LYONs at any time on or after August 1, 2005 (and, under certain circumstances, before that date). The Company is required to offer to repurchase the LYONs if there is a change in control or a delisting event. Generally, the redemption or repurchase price is equal to the accreted value of the LYONs. The Company may elect to pay the principal amount at maturity of the LYONs or the repurchase price that is payable in certain circumstances, in cash or subordinate voting shares or any combination thereof.

Pursuant to Canadian generally accepted accounting principles, the LYONs are recorded as an equity instrument and bifurcated into a principal equity component (representing the present value of the notes) and an option component (representing the value of the conversion features of the notes). The principal equity component is accreted over the 20-year term through periodic charges to retained earnings.

11. Capital stock:

(a) Authorized:

An unlimited number of subordinate voting shares, which entitle the holder to one vote per share, and an unlimited number of multiple voting shares, which entitle the holder to twenty-five votes per share. Except as otherwise required by law, the subordinate voting shares and multiple voting shares vote together as a single class on all matters submitted to a vote of shareholders, including the election of directors. The holders of the subordinate voting shares and multiple voting shares are entitled to share ratably, as a single class, in any dividends declared subject to any preferential rights of any outstanding preferred shares in respect of the payment of dividends. Each multiple voting share is convertible at any time at the option of the holder thereof into one subordinate voting share. The Company is also authorized to issue an unlimited number of preferred shares, issuable in series.

(b) Issued and outstanding:

Number of Shares (in millions)	Subordinate Voting Shares	Multiple Voting Shares	Total Subordinate and Multiple Voting Shares Outstanding	Shares to be issued
Balance December 31, 1999	146.3	39.1	185.4	0.5
Equity offering (i)	16.6	—	16.6	—
Other share issuances (ii)	1.3	—	1.3	—
Issued as consideration for acquisitions (iii)	0.1	—	0.1	(0.1)
Balance December 31, 2000	164.3	39.1	203.4	0.4
Equity offering (iv)	12.0	—	12.0	—
Other share issuances (v)	1.1	—	1.1	—
Issued as consideration for acquisitions (vi)	13.2	—	13.2	0.1
Balance December 31, 2001	190.6	39.1	229.7	0.5

Amount	Subordinate Voting Shares	Multiple Voting Shares	Shares to be issued	Total Amount
Balance December 31, 1999	$1,504.5	$138.8	$2.8	$1,646.1
Equity offering, net of issue costs (i)	740.1	—	—	740.1
Other share issuances (ii)	9.2	—	—	9.2
Issued as consideration for acquisitions (iii)	1.1	—	(1.1)	—
Balance December 31, 2000	2,254.9	138.8	1.7	2,395.4
Equity offering, net of issue costs (iv)	707.4	—	—	707.4
Other share issuances (v)	29.2	—	—	29.2
Issued as consideration for acquisitions (vi)	562.8	—	4.2	567.0
Balance December 31, 2001	$3,554.3	$138.8	$5.9	$3,699.0

2000 Capital Transactions:
(i)   In March 2000, the Company issued 16.6 million subordinate voting shares for gross cash proceeds of $757.4 and incurred $17.3 in share issue costs, net of tax of $9.5.
(ii) During 2000, pursuant to employee share purchase and option plans and LTIP awards, the Company issued 1.3 million subordinate voting shares as a result of the exercise of options for cash of $9.2.
(iii) During 2000, the Company issued 0.1 million of reserved shares at an ascribed value of $1.1 for $0.2 cash. As at December 31, 2000, 0.4 million subordinate voting shares remain reserved for issuance at an ascribed value of $1.7.

2001 Capital Transactions:
(iv) In May 2001, the Company issued 12.0 million subordinate voting shares for gross cash proceeds of $714.0 and incurred $6.6 in share issuance costs, net of tax of $3.4.
(v)   During 2001, pursuant to employee share purchase and option plans and LTIP awards, the Company issued 1.1 million subordinate voting shares as a result of the exercise of options for cash of $23.7 and recorded a tax benefit of $5.5.
(vi) In 2001, the Company issued 12.7 million subordinate voting shares, as consideration for acquisitions, for an ascribed value of $558.5 and reserved 0.6 million shares at an ascribed value of $8.5. During 2001, the Company issued 0.5 million of reserved shares at an ascribed value of $4.3. As at December 31, 2001, 0.5 million subordinate voting shares remain reserved for issuance at an ascribed value of $5.9.

(c) Stock option plans:

(i) Long-Term Incentive Plan (LTIP)

The Company established the LTIP prior to the closing of its initial public offering. Under this plan, the Company may grant stock options, performance shares, performance share units and stock appreciation rights to directors, permanent employees and consultants ("eligible participants") of the Company, its subsidiaries and other companies or partnerships in which the Company has a significant investment. Under the LTIP, up to 23.0 million subordinate voting shares may be issued from treasury. Options are granted at prices equal to the market value of the day prior to the date of the grant and are exercisable during a period not to exceed ten years from such date.

(ii) Employee Share Purchase and Option Plans (ESPO)

The Company has ESPO plans that were available to certain of its employees and executives. As a result of the establishment of the LTIP, no further options or shares may be issued under the ESPO plans. Pursuant to the ESPO plans, employees and executives of the Company were offered the opportunity to purchase, at prices equal to market value, subordinate voting shares and, in connection with such purchase, receive options to acquire an additional number of subordinate voting shares based on the number of subordinate voting shares acquired by them under the ESPO plans. The exercise price for the options is equal to the price per share paid for the corresponding subordinate voting shares acquired under the ESPO plans.

Stock option transactions were as follows:

Number of options (in millions)	Shares	Weighted Average Exercise Price
Outstanding at December 31, 1998	11.5	$ 5.41
Granted	5.2	$30.05
Exercised	(1.7)	$ 8.25
Cancelled	(0.4)	$ 7.37
Outstanding at December 31, 1999	14.6	$14.84
Granted	4.2	$55.40
Exercised	(1.4)	$ 6.85
Cancelled	(0.2)	$ 7.33
Outstanding at December 31, 2000	17.2	$25.16
Granted/assumed	8.5	$42.54
Exercised	(1.6)	$14.89
Cancelled	(0.2)	$23.36
Outstanding at December 31, 2001	23.9	$31.67
Cash consideration received on options exercised	$23.7	
Shares reserved for issuance upon exercise of stock options or awards (in millions)	28.8	

The following options were outstanding as at December 31, 2001:

Plan	Range of Exercise Prices	Outstanding Options	Weighted Average Exercise Price	Exercisable Options	Weighted Average Exercise Price	Remaining Life
			(in millions)	(in millions)		(years)
ESPO	$ 5.00 – $ 7.50	5.3	$ 5.34	3.9	$ 5.42	6
LTIP	$ 8.75 – $13.69	1.7	$12.16	0.9	$11.96	7
	$24.18 – $24.18	0.8	$24.18	0.4	$24.18	8
	$24.91 – $36.89	0.8	$30.58	—	—	10
	$39.03 – $39.03	2.9	$39.03	1.4	$39.03	8
	$41.89 – $41.89	6.4	$41.89	—	—	10
	$44.23 – $54.15	0.6	$49.46	—	—	9
	$55.40 – $60.06	4.1	$55.96	1.0	$55.96	9
	$73.04 – $74.90	0.1	$73.42	—	—	9
Other	$ 0.93 – $13.31	1.0	$ 5.73	0.9	$ 5.67	5
Other	$29.73 – $72.84	0.2	$46.28	—	—	5
		23.9				

12. Earnings per share:

The following table sets forth the calculation of basic and diluted earnings (loss) per share:

	Year ended December 31		
	1999	2000	2001
Numerator:			
Net earnings (loss)	$ 68.4	$206.7	$(39.8)
Convertible debt accretion, net of tax	—	(5.4)	(15.0)
Earnings (loss) available to common shareholders	$ 68.4	$201.3	$(54.8)
Denominator:			
Weighted average shares—basic (in millions)	167.2	199.8	213.9
Effect of dilutive securities (in millions):			
Employee stock options[1]	4.0	7.8	—
Convertible debt	—	4.2	—
Weighted average shares—diluted (in millions)[2]	171.2	211.8	213.9
Earnings (loss) per share:			
Basic	$ 0.41	$ 1.01	$(0.26)
Diluted	$ 0.40	$ 0.98	$(0.26)

(1) For 1999 and 2000, excludes the effect of 3.4 million and 3.3 million "out of the money" options, respectively, as they are anti-dilutive.

(2) For 2001, excludes the effect of options and convertible debt as they are anti-dilutive due to the loss.

Endnotes

1. Of course, *capital* does not equal the money itself, just the owners' interest *in* the money and assets generated by its use. In other words, credits equal debits.

2. "Share Capital," *CICA Handbook,* Section 3240, para. 11.

3. "Share Capital," *CICA Handbook,* Section 3240, para..20.

4. See D. B. Hausch, D. E. Logue, and J. K. Seward, "Dutch Auction Share Repurchases: Theory and Evidence," *Journal of Applied Corporate Finance,* Spring 1992, pp. 44–9.

5. T. Vermaelen, "Common Stock Repurchases and Market Signaling: An Empirical Study," *Journal of Financial Economics,* June 1981, p. 152.

6. D. Ikenberry and J. Lakonishok, "Market Underreaction to Open Market Share Repurchases," *Journal of Financial Economics,* October 1995, pp. 181–208.

7. Microsoft Corporation, *Quarterly Report to Shareholders* [10-Q filing], March 31, 1997. Emphasis added. Microsoft ended its stock buyback program in 2000.

8. The guidelines for computing EPS are contained in "Earnings per Share," *CICA Handbook,* Section 3500, which has recently been amended.

9. "Accounting for Stock Issued to Employees," *APB No. 25* (New York: American Institute of Certified Public Accountants, 1972).

10. F. Black and M. Scholes, "The Pricing of Options and Corporate Liabilities," *The Journal of Political Economy,* May–June, 1973, pp. 637–54. Corporate finance books explore the derivation of the Black–Scholes model and other option valuation techniques in detail. See, for example, R. A. Brealey and S. C. Meyers, *Principles of Corporate Finance,* 4th ed. (New York: McGraw-Hill, 1991), pp. 483–504.

11. Warren Buffett, "Letter to Shareholders," Berkshire Hathaway, Inc., 1992 annual report.

12. Congressional Record, Senate, June 29, 1993, S8252.

13. This bill, called the *Accounting Standards Reform Act of 1994,* was introduced by Senator Lieberman (Democrat, Connecticut). Congressional Record, Senate, October 6, 1994, S14510.

14. The Black–Scholes formula in Table 15.1 can be used only when there are no dividends being paid on the common shares. If the shares pay dividends, a modified version of the Black–Scholes option valuation model should be used where the current share price (S) is replaced with the price adjusted for continuous dividends. To illustrate, suppose the common shares described in Table 15.1 will pay a $1 quarterly dividend in 90 days (and every subsequent quarter). This implies a continuous dividend rate of 13.75%. So we replace the current price (S = $30) with the price adjusted for the continuous dividend ($Se^{-\delta t}$ = $30e^{-13.75\% \times 5 \text{ years}}$) and solve the Black–Scholes formula.

15. *Business Week,* July 19, 2002.

16. "Accounting for Convertible Debt and Debt Issued with Stock Purchase Warrants," *APB No. 14* (New York: AICPA, 1969). This opinion was effective for fiscal periods beginning after December 31, 1966.

16
Intercorporate Equity Investments, Consolidated Financial Statements, and Special Purpose Entities

LEARNING OBJECTIVES
After studying this chapter, you should be able to:

1. Understand how a company can benefit from owning another company's common shares

2. Comprehend how an investor's ownership share, and more generally, *control* is used to determine the accounting treatment of equity investments

3. Distinguish between the accounting for short-term investments and the accounting for long-term investments

4. Understand the equity method and apply it

5. Understand consolidated financial statements, and their compilation

6. Describe and analyze accounting goodwill on financial statements

7. Record business acquisitions and mergers and understand why the recording method matters to financial statement readers

8. Know how to treat foreign subsidiaries when preparing financial statements in dollars

9. Account for special purpose entities (SPEs)

Throughout this book, we have seen that there is continual tension between making accounting rules too technical and narrow, and setting broad accounting standards that rely upon professional judgment and a system that encourages responsible, transparent, and fair financial reporting. While Canada has in the past tended to adopt broader standards than the more rule-based American approach, there seemed to be a movement in Canadian standard-setting towards more detailed rules ... at least until Enron! Enron[1] seems to intrude everywhere, even in a chapter on "Intercorporate Equity Investments, Consolidated Financial Statements, and Special Purpose Entities."

The Enron connection in this chapter has to do with how we should determine the *scope* of the accounting entity; that is, what assets and liabilities should be included within an accounting entity's financial statements. Recall from Chapter 8 that special purpose entities (SPEs) are routinely used by companies to hive off accounts receivable (and also other asset clusters) in order to reduce financing costs. Also recall from Chapter 11 that Enron and some major financial institutions apparently obscured Enron's debt and operating cash flow reporting by using SPEs (at least according to an investigative committee of the U.S. Senate). So a crucial accounting policy issue for companies is to decide how inclusive their financial statements should be. And related to this issue is the appropriate disclosure of SPEs or other asset/liability structures that the reporting entity has not included in its financial statements.

The CICA's Accounting Standards Board (AcSB) was so concerned (appropriately so!) about these issues that, when it announced its intention to establish new guidance in these areas, it placed the following notice in the August 2002 *CA Magazine* (p. 22):

Overview

The Accounting Standards Board (AcSB) proposes, subject to comments received following exposure, to issue two new Accounting Guidelines as part of its program of improving Canadian GAAP in light of the lessons learned from the failure of Enron Corp.

The proposed Accounting Guideline, *Consolidation of Special-Purpose Entities*, provides guidance for applying the consolidation principles in SUBSIDIARIES, Section 1590, to certain special-purpose entities (SPEs). Some SPEs rely on the financial support of another entity that is the primary beneficiary of the SPE's activities. The relationship between the SPE and the primary beneficiary is such that control over the SPE rests with the primary beneficiary, rather than with the nominal owner of the SPE. In such circumstances, the primary beneficiary would consolidate the SPE. These proposals would become effective for annual and interim fiscal periods beginning on or after April 1, 2003, although certain requirements would become effective upon issuance of the Guideline.

The proposed Accounting Guideline, *Disclosure of Guarantees*, would require entities to disclose key information about certain types of guarantee contracts that require payments contingent on specified types of future events. Disclosures would include the nature of the guarantee, how it arose, the events or circumstances that would trigger performance under the guarantee, the maximum potential future payments under the guarantee, the carrying amount of the related liability, and information about recourse or collateral. The proposed Guideline would become effective for annual and interim fiscal periods ending on or after December 31, 2002.

So, even though "Enron" is thought mainly to be an American phenomenon, it clearly has international importance in terms of financial reporting reform, and, specifically in our case, Canadian importance.

We will build up to understanding the Enron-stimulated AcSB suggested reforms regarding SPEs and disclosure of guarantees by first looking at some fairly traditional topics in accounting for intercorporate equity investments and consolidated financial statements. But even as far as these topics are concerned, there has been a lot happening in accounting, with new accounting standards introducing significant changes, and all this has important implications for the quality of earnings!

One company will buy equity shares in another company to earn an investment return or to improve its competitive position. When a company buys equity shares for investment purposes, its return comes from share price increases and dividends. But when a company buys shares to improve its competitive position, its return comes from increased operating profits and growth. A company that owns shares in another company that is a supplier or customer gains influence over that company, as well as access to new markets or greater production capacity.

In existing Canadian GAAP, the method of accounting for intercorporate investments depends on the degree of control that the investor corporation has over the investee corporation. Degree of control is often, but not always, determined by percentage ownership.

We first discuss minority ownership—i.e., cases in which the corporate investor usually owns less than 50% of the voting shares of another company. Then we analyze majority (more than 50%) ownership, and we'll look at the special reporting problems created by subsidiaries in foreign countries.

The accounting alternative for equity shares that an investor company (the company owning shares in another company, the investee company) must follow depends upon the relationship between the two companies. For *temporary* investment relationships, Section 3010 of the *CICA Handbook* requires that the financial assets (which could be equity instruments or debt instruments, including common shares, preference shares, bonds, etc.) be classified as current assets on the investor's balance sheet and be carried at the lower of cost and market value (Section 3010.06). In addition, in order to qualify as a temporary investment, securities must be readily marketable and intended by investee management to be converted into cash within one year or the operating cycle, whichever is longer. In the United States, by contrast, such short-term investments are accounted for on a mark-to-market basis, in which the asset is adjusted to market value each balance sheet date, with the offsetting debit or credit going to an income statement account.

For *long-term* investment relationships, Canadian GAAP specify three types of fact situations, based upon the degree of influence that the investor has over the investee's strategic, operating, investing, and financial decisions, with each type of situation requiring a different accounting alternative:

Fact Situation Between Investor and Investee	Required Accounting by Investor
Investor has *no significant influence* over investee; therefore, a *portfolio* investment situation exists	The *cost* method must be used
Investor is able to exert *significant influence* over investee, but does not *control* the investee	The *equity* method must be used
Investor is able to *control* the investee, and therefore the investee is a *subsidiary* of the investor (and the investor company is the *parent* of the subsidiary)[*]	The *consolidation* method must be used

[*]The *CICA Handbook* also recognizes a situation of *joint control*, in which two (or more) organizations (called the *venturers*) have agreed by contract to share control of another entity, the joint venture (Section 3055, "Interests in Joint Ventures"). In such cases, each of the venturers consolidates only its own proportionate share of the joint venture's assets, liabilities, etc.

A key point to keep in mind is that the fact situation between the investor and investee determines the appropriate accounting.

As used above, the terms *significant influence, control, subsidiary, cost method, equity method,* and *consolidation methods* are all technical terms, with specific meanings set by GAAP. These technical meanings are summarized as follows.

Term	Meaning as Set Out in *CICA Handbook*
Significant influence	Section 3050 ("Long-Term Investments") says that *significant influence* is less powerful than *control*, but does indicate some degree of power by the investor over the investee: "Significant influence differs from control and joint control. … An investor may be able to exercise significant influence over … [an] investee … by, for example, representation on the board of directors, participation in policy-making processes, material intercompany transactions, interchange of managerial personnel or provision of technical information. If the investor holds less than 20% of the voting interest in the investee, it is presumed that the investor does not have the ability to exercise significant influence, unless such influence is clearly demonstrated. On the other hand, the holding of 20% or more of the voting interest in the investee does not in itself confirm the ability to exercise significant influence" (3050.04).
Control	Section 1590 ("Subsidiaries") says that "[c]ontrol of an enterprise is the continuing power to determine its strategic operating, investing and financing policies without the co-operation of others" (1590.03). Although owning a majority of an investee's equity most often signals *control*, Section 1590 recognizes that in some situations control might exist even though less than 50% plus one share of equity is owned by the investor; for example, an investor might have the ongoing ability to elect a majority of the investee's board of directors through rights, share options, and other financial instruments that, if exercised, would result in majority ownership (1590.13).
Subsidiary	Section 1590 ("Subsidiaries") says that "[a] subsidiary is an enterprise controlled by another enterprise (the parent) that has the right and ability to obtain future economic benefits from the resources of the enterprise and is exposed to the related risks" (1590.03). The section reinforces the importance of professional judgement in determining whether a particular investee is an investor's subsidiary by asserting that "[t]he existence of control in a particular situation is a question of fact" (1590.09).
Cost method	According to Section 3050, the cost method "is a basis of accounting for long-term investments [by an investor in the shares of an investee] whereby the investment is initially recorded at cost; earnings from such investments are recognized only to the extent received or receivable" (3050.02). So this is a very passive method of accounting by the investor. Investee management controls the amount and timing of its dividends (i.e., the "earnings" to which the investor is entitled), and the investor just records them as "received or receivable." In the United States, by contrast, a long-term investor not able to exert significant influence over the investee is required to use mark-to-market accounting, with any offsetting debit or credit to a special owners' equity account.
Equity method	This accounting method is based upon the active, although not controlling, role that the investor takes in the affairs of the investee, by being able to exert "significant influence" over the investee. The investor records the investment initially at its cost, then accrues its pro rata share of the investee's earnings, in order to acknowledge that it (the investor) is able to "significantly influence" the generation of those earnings. The important technical aspects to this method are explained later in this chapter.
Consolidation methods	The investor and investee, previously two separate accounting entities, are now one by virtue of the fact that the investor controls the investee and so the investee is the investor's subsidiary.

Minority Ownership

Share ownership usually entitles the shareholder (the corporate investor) to vote at the company's shareholder meetings. Shareholders vote to elect company directors and to approve or reject proposals put forth by management or by shareholders. Management will ask shareholders to approve the company's outside auditor, proposed mergers and buyouts, compensation plan changes, and corporate charter amendments. Shareholder proposals often address environmental, social, and political issues such as prohibiting the company from doing business in unfavoured countries.

A "one share, one vote" rule governs shareholder voting procedures in most companies. This means that each shareholder's influence over the company is proportional to the shares (votes) owned. A majority shareholder—one who owns more than 50% of the votes—can often dictate the company's business strategy and its major operating, investment, and financing decisions. A minority investor—one who owns less than 50% of the votes—has less influence over the company but still may be able to elect a corporate director or gain the ear of management.

For financial reporting purposes, minority investments fall into one of two categories: **minority passive** investments, those in which the shareholder has no ability to influence the company; or **minority active** investments, in which the ownership percentage is large enough for shareholder influence. Owning a single share of stock is a minority passive investment, but owning 49.9% of the company's voting shares may be a minority active investment. Deciding where to draw the line between passive and active minority investments can be difficult, as we shall see.

> Each share of **common stock** usually entitles the owner to one vote, while those who own **preferred stock** usually have no voting rights. There are exceptions. Some companies issue dual-class common stock (often denoted Common A and Common B), in which one class has voting rights and the other does not. In addition, some companies do issue voting preferred stock.

Passive and Active Minority Long-Term Investment Relationships, and Substance over Form

Passive long-term intercorporate investments are accounted for by the investor using the so-called cost method, while active long-term minority investments are accounted for by the investor using the so-called equity method.

- **Cost method.** This accounting method reflects the passive relationship by accounting for dividends received (or receivable) by Investor upstream from Investee, as Investor's income. Investor management does not have control over Investee, and so cannot tell Investee management what to do, such as when to declare dividends. The only economic benefit that Investor enjoys from the relationship (aside from any gain or loss when Investor ultimately sells its Investee common shares) is the upstream dividends, the amount and timing over which it has no control. So, by accounting for upstream dividends as Investor's income, the cost method accounts for the substance of the passive relationship. We'll illustrate the details of this method a little later.

- **Equity method.** When Investor is able to exert significant influence over the strategic operating, investing, and financing policies of Investee, upstream dividends are accounted for not as Investor income, but rather as a partial return of Investor's investment in Investee. This reflects the substance of the relationship, since Investor management could significantly influence Investee's declaring of the dividend, and thus inappropriately manipulate its own income if the dividends were accounted for as income. Investor, under the equity method, also accrues its pro rata share of Investee's net income or loss, since it had significant influence in Investee's earning of the income or incurrence of the loss. The details of the equity method are also illustrated later.

The "Cost" Method

The "Cost" Method Suppose that on February 10, 2003, Hallmark Inc. (henceforth HI), a manufacturer of kitchen furniture, acquired 10,000 common shares of FAS Ltd. on the stock exchange, with the intent of including the FAS shares as part of its long-term investment portfolio. HI paid $21 per share, plus a brokerage fee of $10,000, for a total of $220,000 in cash. FAS Ltd. has 900,000 common shares issued and outstanding, so HI's investment, at about 1% of the total, is definitely a passive one, and the cost method is the appropriate method of accounting under GAAP.

The journal entry on HI's books to record this acquisition of a financial asset on February 10 is:

```
DR   Investment in common shares          220,000
     CR   Cash                                         220,000
```

The account "Investment in common shares" is classified as a long-term asset on HI's balance sheet.

HI has a December 31 year-end. In early December 2003, HI's management learned that FAS had declared a cash dividend of $1 per share of common stock, payable to shareholders of record as of November 30, 2003, and on December 20, HI received a cheque for $10,000 from the financial institution that looked after FAS's share-related affairs. The entry on HI's books to record the cash receipt is:

```
DR   Cash                                10,000
     CR   Dividend income                               10,000
```

(Of course, if the cash has not yet been received, the debit is to dividends receivable.)

So, on its income statement for fiscal 2003, HI will show nonoperating investment income of $10,000. This entry accounts for the dividend as an income item from HI's perspective, and under "normal" circumstances this is just what the cost method requires. However, if the $10,000 in dividends were out of FAS's pre-acquisition earnings (in other words, if FAS had recorded a loss this year, during which time HI owned the FAS shares), then the credit side of the entry would go to the balance sheet account "Investment in common shares," as a return *of* (not *on*) the investment.

Minority Active Investments

Deutsche Telekom Will Take Stake in Net Phone Firm

German phone giant Deutsche Telekom AG, in an effort to capitalize on the emerging industry of Internet telephony rather than lose business to it, is expected to announce today that it has agreed to buy a 21.3% stake in Internet phone pioneer VocalTec Communications Ltd.

Deutsche Telekom agreed to buy 2.3 million shares of VocalTec for [US]$48.3 million, according to VocalTec's chairman. ... The German phone company also agreed to buy more than [US]$30 million in goods and services from the tiny Israeli software firm during the next two years.

Various companies are working on Internet-based phone technology, including phone companies that want to ensure they don't miss out on a business that could threaten their own. While Internet-based phone calls don't yet have the reliability or clarity of those placed over the traditional phone system, they are often a fraction of the price because the technology of the global network makes more efficient use of its resources. ... (A)s much as [US]$10 billion in phone-company revenues could be lost

DEUTSCHE TELEKOM AG
www.dtag.de

VOCALTEC
www.vocaltec.com

to Internet telephony in the U.S. between 1997 and 2001, representing almost an 8% decrease in phone traffic over traditional networks.

Source: *Wall Street Journal*, August 28, 1997.

When the ownership percentage exceeds about 20%, GAAP presume the following:

1. A significant ownership position like 20% implies that the investor has the capability to exert significant influence over the investee company. This influence could encompass operating decisions, such as which research and development projects should be undertaken, and financing decisions, such as dividend payouts.
2. A substantial ownership percentage also implies a continuing relationship between the two companies, since investments of this magnitude are usually entered into in order to achieve some long-run strategic objective.

Both elements are present in Deutsche Telekom's ownership stake in VocalTec shares.

Once the ownership percentage becomes large enough for the investor to be able to exercise significant influence, the simple accounting system introduced for long-term passive investments is no longer suitable. To see why, recall that the entry made on a minority passive investor's books when dividends are declared is:

DR	Dividends receivable	$XX
CR	Dividend income	$XX

When the investor can influence the company's dividend policy, the minority passive accounting treatment would allow the investor to augment its own reported income. Suppose Deutsche Telekom wants to increase reported earnings during the period. It owns enough VocalTec stock to influence the company's dividend policy, and it uses that influence to raise VocalTec's dividend. This higher dividend would immediately run through Deutsche Telekom's income statement.

To preclude use of this avenue for income distortion, minority active investments are accounted for using the so-called equity method. Under the **equity method,** Deutsche Telekom would record its initial investment in VocalTec at cost.[2] Subsequently, however, the investment account is increased for the pro rata share of VocalTec's income, and there is a corresponding credit to the investment income account—or, in the case of a loss, Deutsche Telekom's investment account decreases and there's a corresponding debit to the investment loss account.

Since Deutsche Telekom's earnings are increased for its share of VocalTec's earnings each period, it would be inappropriate to record dividend distributions received from VocalTec as income too. This would "double-count" VocalTec's earnings on Deutsche Telekom's books. Under the equity method, dividends from VocalTec are recorded as an increase (debit) to cash—or dividends receivable—and a decrease (credit) to the investment account. ***Thus, the investment account is increased for Deutsche Telekom's share of VocalTec's earnings and decreased when those earnings are received in the form of dividends.***

The following example illustrates the entries under the equity method.

On January 1, 2003, Willis Company purchases 30% of the outstanding common shares of Planet Burbank, Inc. for $9,000,000. The book value and market value of Planet Burbank's net assets (assets minus liabilities) is $30,000,000. During 2003, Planet Burbank earns net profit of $10,000,000, and the company declares a dividend of $500,000 on December 31, 2003. Using the equity method, the entries made by Willis are:

- January 1, 2003.

DR	Investment in Planet Burbank	$9,000,000
CR	Cash	$9,000,000

- December 31, 2003.

DR	Investment in Planet Burbank	$3,000,000
CR	Income from affiliate	$3,000,000

To recognize 30% of Planet Burbank's total reported income of $10,000,000.

- December 31, 2003.

DR	Dividend receivable from affiliate	$150,000
CR	Investment in Planet Burbank	$150,000

To reduce the investment account for dividends declared—30% of $500,000.

The example shows how the equity method reduces possibilities for income distortion. Willis Company's income statement is affected only by its pro rata share of Planet Burbank's income. *The dividend declaration—and subsequent payment—by Planet Burbank has no effect on Willis' income.* Thus, while Willis could conceivably use the influence arising from its 30% ownership share to increase Planet Burbank's dividend declaration, doing so would leave its income unchanged *when the equity method is used.* Under the equity method, the carrying amount in the investment account at any point in time comprises the following items:

Initial investment amount	$ 9,000,000
Plus: Willis' cumulative pro rata share of Planet Burbank's income	3,000,000
Minus: Willis' cumulative pro rata share of dividends declared by Planet Burbank	(150,000)
Investment account carrying amount	$11,850,000

When Cost and Book Value Differ

In contrast to our Planet Burbank example, investors rarely buy shares at a price exactly equal to the book value of those shares, and when the investor's cost differs from book value, a new issue surfaces.

To illustrate, let's return to the Willis Company purchase of Planet Burbank shares. Here book value is $30,000,000, but let's say Willis paid $24,000,000 for its 30% stake. Why would Willis pay $24,000,000 when the book value of the shares purchased is only $9,000,000 (30% of $30,000,000)? Why would an informed buyer pay $15,000,000 ($24,000,000 minus $9,000,000) more than book value?

There are two reasons. First, Planet Burbank's books are prepared using GAAP, which reflect balance sheet items at historical cost rather than at current value. As shown in Exhibit 16.1(a), the fair market value of Planet Burbank's *net* assets is $70,000,000, or $40,000,000 above the $30,000,000 book value. Sellers of Planet Burbank stock presumably know that the company's *net* assets are worth $70,000,000 rather than the lower $30,000,000 book value. On the basis of this knowledge, the asking price for the shares acquired by Willis Company will be higher than book value. But how much higher?

Willis decided to pay $24,000,000, or $15,000,000 more than book value. Exhibit 16.1(b) shows that $12,000,000 of the $15,000,000 excess of cost over book value is explained by the difference between fair value and book value of inventories and fixed assets (see the "Difference" column). This still leaves $3,000,000 of the disparity unexplained. The remaining difference brings us to the second reason why an informed buyer would knowingly pay a premium to acquire influence over another company.

This second potential explanation relates to **goodwill.** Goodwill exists because thriving, successful companies are frequently worth more than the sum of the current values of their assets less liabilities. Planet Burbank has developed a reputation for product quality, prompt service, and fair treatment of both employees and customers. Consequently, employees like to work for the company, and customers actively seek out its products. The result is that Planet Burbank is exceptionally profitable—it earns a very large return on its investment base. The capitalized value of this earning potential is what gives rise to the remaining $3,000,000 difference. This "superior" earnings potential is called goodwill.

A summary of the factors making up the $24,000,000 purchase price for 30% of Planet Burbank is ($ in millions):

Recorded historical book value of the company's net assets ($50 − $20) × 30%	$ 9
Difference between fair value and cost of net assets ($40 × 30%)	12
Amount attributable to goodwill (plug figure)	3
Purchase price	$24

When the cost of the shares exceeds the underlying book value at the acquisition date, the investor is required to amortize any excess that is attributable to (1) inventory and (2) amortizable capital assets. Amortization is recorded as a reduction (debit) to investment income and a reduction (credit) to the investment account. The rationale for amortizing these items is based on the matching principle. Since Willis is picking up its share of Planet Burbank's reported earnings each period as investment income, it follows that Willis should write off any amount paid in excess of Planet Burbank's book value as a cost of gaining access to those earnings. Up until 2001, the goodwill arising under equity accounting was also to be amortized. But revisions to Section 3050 ("Long-term Investments") now specify that equity method goodwill "is not amortized" (Section 3050, para. 12).

Using the equity method, the entries based on the preceding set of facts are:

- January 1, 2003: Initial investment in Planet Burbank.

  DR Investment in Planet Burbank $24,000,000

      CR   Cash $24,000,000

- December 31, 2003: Investor's share of earnings.

  DR Investment in Planet Burbank $3,000,000

      CR   Investment income $3,000,000

  To recognize 30% of Planet Burbank's total reported income of $10,000,000.

- December 31, 2003: Investor's share of dividends declared.

  DR Dividend receivable from Planet Burbank $1,200,000

      CR   Investment in Planet Burbank $1,200,000

  To reduce the investment account for dividend declared—30% of $4,000,000.

- December 31, 2003: Amortization of excess cost over book value attributable to inventory and amortizable assets.

  DR Investment income $3,900,000

      CR   Investment in Planet Burbank $3,900,000

Exhibit 16.1 WILLIS COMPANY

Investment with Goodwill

On January 1, 2003, Willis Company purchases 30% of the outstanding shares of common stock of Planet Burbank for $24,000,000. The book value and fair value of Planet Burbank's net assets on this date are:

($ in millions)	Book Value	Fair Value	Difference	Investor's Share (30%)
Cash and receivables	$10	$10	$ 0	$ 0
Inventories (FIFO cost flow)	15	25	10	3
Amortizable assets (net of amortization)*	25	55	30	9
Total Assets	$50	$90	$40	$12
Minus Liabilities	($20)	($20)	$ 0	$ 0
Net Assets	$30	$70	$40	$12

*Average remaining useful life of 10 years.

During 2003, Planet Burbank reported a net profit of $10,000,000, and the company declared a dividend of $4,000,000 on December 31, 2003.

(a)

Analysis of Willis' investment cost over book value ($ in millions):

Cost of 30% investment	$24
30% of Planet Burbank's net asset book value (30% × $30)	(9)
Excess of cost over book value of Willis' shares	$15

Amount of excess attributable to:

Inventories—30% × ($25 – $15)	$ 3
Amortizable assets—30% × ($55 – $25)	9
Remainder attributable to implicit goodwill (plug figure)	3
	$15

(b)

	Amount	Amortization
Amortization is computed as:		
Attributed to inventory (all sold during the year)	$3,000,000	$3,000,000
Attributed to depreciable assets (over 10 years)	$9,000,000	900,000
		$3,900,000

The excess investment cost over book value attributable to inventory is assigned to inventory items on hand on January 1, 2003, when Willis purchased Planet Burbank's stock. This inventory is presumed to have been sold during 2003 under the FIFO cost flow assumption. The amount attributed to amortizable assets is amortized over the average remaining 10-year life of those assets.

The December 31, 2003, balance in the investment in Planet Burbank's account on Willis Company's balance sheet is $21,900,000 ($24,000,000 + $3,000,000 – $1,200,000 – $3,900,000).

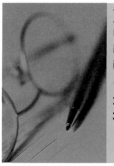

Control Relationships (Usually Signified by a Majority Ownership)

When one company owns more than 50% of the voting shares of another company, the investee is usually controlled by the investor. Under these circumstances, the financial statements of the investee are combined—line by line—with those of the investor using a process called **consolidation**. Section 1590 ("Subsidiaries") is careful *not* to equate ownership of a majority of an investee's voting shares with *control*; rather, such ownership "leads to a presumption regarding control" that may be overcome by other factors (para. 8).

When there is control, the investor corporation—usually called the "parent" company—literally directs the resources, business strategy, and operating decisions of the investee, or "subsidiary" company. Since true control exists, the two companies are really *one* in an economic sense. **Consolidated financial statements** are designed to cut across artificial corporate legal boundaries to portray the overall economic entity directed by the parent. Let's see how this happens using the following example. On December 31, 2002, the balance sheet of Alphonse Corporation was:

Assets:

Current assets	$ 5,000,000
Property, plant, and equipment (PP&E) minus accumulated amortization	20,000,000
Total assets	$25,000,000

Liabilities and shareholders' equity:

Current liabilities	$ 1,000,000
Common shares	24,000,000
Total liabilities and shareholders' equity	$25,000,000

On January 1, 2003, Alphonse issues 8,000,000 additional common shares to new outside investors for $10,000,000 cash. Immediately after the share issue, the balance sheet of Alphonse Corporation is:

Assets:	
Current assets	$15,000,000
PP&E minus accumulated amortization	20,000,000
Total assets	$35,000,000
Liabilities and shareholders' equity	
Current liabilities	$ 1,000,000
Common shares	34,000,000
Total liabilities and shareholders' equity	$35,000,000

Alphonse immediately uses the cash to buy all of the outstanding shares of Gaston Corporation for $10,000,000. Since Alphonse has used its cash to make an investment, after buying Gaston's shares Alphonse's current assets will be $10,000,000 lower than before and an investment account of $10,000,000 will exist. Alphonse's balance sheet after the share purchase, as well as Gaston's, are shown in Exhibit 16.2.

The steps that follow describe the procedures for preparing the consolidated balance sheet for Alphonse and Gaston in Exhibit 16.2. The individual balance sheets of the two companies are *not* simply added together; doing that would result in double-counting, as we'll see.

Step 1. Analysis of the "Investment in Gaston" Account

Alphonse paid $10,000,000 for Gaston, a company whose net assets total only $8,000,000 (assets of $8,500,000 minus $500,000 of liabilities). Why did Alphonse pay more than $8,000,000? There are two reasons why an informed buyer would pay more than book value: (1) the fair market value of Gaston's individual assets is greater than their combined book value (we assume this excess is $1,500,000 here and is attributable to the PP&E); and (2) goodwill, which is the remaining $500,000.

Exhibit 16.2 PREPARATION OF CONSOLIDATED BALANCE SHEET (PURCHASE METHOD)

	After the Acquisition		Adjustments		Consolidated Balance Sheet
	Alphonse	Gaston			
Assets					
Current assets	$ 5,000,000	$2,000,000			$ 7,000,000
PP&E minus accumulated amortization	20,000,000	$6,500,000	1,500,000	B	28,000,000
			(8,000,000)	A	
Investment in Gaston	10,000,000	—	(1,500,000)	B	—
			(500,000)	C	
Goodwill			500,000	C	500,000
	$35,000,000	$8,500,000			$35,500,000
Liabilities and Equity					
Current liabilities	$ 1,000,000	$ 500,000			$ 1,500,000
Common shares	34,000,000	8,000,000	(8,000,000)	D	34,000,000
	$35,000,000	$8,500,000			$35,500,000

The components of the $10,000,000 purchase price for Gaston are:

Recorded book value of Gaston's net assets	$ 8,000,000
Unrecorded difference between fair value and *book value* of Gaston's capital assets ($8,000,000 – $6,500,000)	1,500,000
Unrecorded value of Gaston's goodwill	500,000
Purchase price	$10,000,000

This purchase price breakdown explains why we do not add the two balance sheets together to get the consolidated balance sheet. Adding the two balance sheets together would double-count the $8,000,000 book value of Gaston's net assets. To see why, notice that the full purchase price of $10,000,000 is already on Alphonse's balance sheet (under "Investment in Gaston" in Exhibit 16.2); but as we have just seen, $8,000,000 of this purchase price represents the **book value** of Gaston's net assets. Since this $8,000,000 already appears on Gaston's balance sheet (assets of $8,500,000 minus $500,000 of liabilities), simply adding the two balance sheets together would double-count the $8,000,000. To avoid doing this, we have to remove $8,000,000 from Alphonse's "Investment in Gaston" account, leaving a balance of $2,000,000. Notice that this is done in Exhibit 16.2 in the "Adjustments" column (next to notation A).

Step 2. Eliminate the "Investment in Gaston" Account

The remaining balance in the "Investment in Gaston" account represents the amount of the purchase price that is not reflected in Gaston's balance sheet book values. As shown in the purchase price breakdown, this $2,000,000 remaining balance represents unrecorded PP&E appreciation of $1,500,000 and goodwill of $500,000. These amounts must stay on the consolidated balance sheet, since Alphonse paid for them. However, they must be assigned to the items they actually represent: (1) an increase to PP&E and (2) the recognition of purchased goodwill. This is done in Exhibit 16.2 in the "Adjustments" column (next to the notations B and C). After these adjustments are made, notice that the "Investment in Gaston" account has been eliminated and thus does not appear in the consolidated column of Exhibit 16.2. Also, consolidated PP&E assets have been increased by $1,500,000, and goodwill of $500,000 is separately reported.

Step 3. Analysis of the Common Stock Account

To consolidate both balance sheets, we need to eliminate one more element of potential double-counting. Consider the $34,000,000 common share account on the books of Alphonse. Since Alphonse owns Gaston, Alphonse's common share account shows the ultimate ownership of both companies.

Now consider the $8,000,000 balance in the common share account of Gaston. These shares represent ownership of Gaston by Alphonse. *If the two common share accounts were simply added together, ownership of Gaston would be counted twice—* once as a part of the $34,000,000 on Alphonse's books and once again in the $8,000,000 on Gaston's books.

To avoid this double-counting, the equity of Gaston is eliminated when the consolidated balance sheet is prepared. This is done opposite notation D in the "Adjustments" column in Exhibit 16.2. After this is done, consolidated owners' equity is made up only of Alphonse's common stock, since this alone represents ownership of the entire consolidated entity.

The adjustment process described here can also be expressed in journal entry form.[3] For example, the entry to avoid double-counting both the book value of Gaston's net assets and its owners' equity (adjustment notations A and D in Exhibit 16.2) is:

```
DR   Common shares                        $8,000,000
     CR   Investment in Gaston                           $8,000,000
To avoid double-counting Gaston's net assets (adjustment notation A) and its owners' equity
(adjustment notation D).
```

Similarly, reclassification of the remaining $2,000,000 in the "Investment in Gaston" account can also be expressed in journal entry form:

```
DR   PP&E assets                          $1,500,000
DR   Goodwill                                500,000
     CR   Investment in Gaston                           $2,000,000
Elimination of the remaining investment account balance (adjustment notations B and C).
```

The consolidation accounting procedure outlined above is called **purchase accounting.** Later in the chapter, we describe another method for accounting for consolidations—the **pooling of interests** method. We should note at this point that for all business combinations initiated on or after June 1, 2001, pooling has been banned—purchase consolidation accounting must be used.

Other Consolidation Adjustments
Suppose that several months prior to the Gaston acquisition, Alphonse had borrowed $300,000 from Gaston; this borrowing had not been repaid at the time of the acquisition on January 1, 2003. Under these circumstances, another adjustment is needed to consolidate the financial statements.

This adjustment is necessary because Alphonse and Gaston are now part of the same economic unit. The *Alphonse loan receivable* on Gaston's books and the *Gaston loan payable* on Alphonse's books are not owed to outsiders (i.e., outside of the consolidated group). To include the intercompany receivable and payable in the consolidated balance sheet would overstate assets and overstate liabilities, each by $300,000. That's why the following consolidation adjustment is made in preparing the consolidated statements:

```
DR   Loan payable—Gaston (on Alphonse's books)      $300,000
     CR   Loan receivable—Alphonse (on Gaston's books)         $300,000
To eliminate intercompany loan from Gaston to Alphonse.
```

Another frequently encountered consolidation adjustment arises when Gaston and Alphonse make sales to one another. Suppose Alphonse sold goods to Gaston on March 15, 2003, after the January 1, 2003, acquisition, and then Gaston resold all these goods to outside customers. The facts are:

Intercompany Sale

	Alphonse's Sale to Gaston	Gaston's Resale to "Outsiders"	Total
Selling price	$25,000	$34,000	$59,000
Cost of goods sold	$20,000	$25,000	$45,000
Profit	$ 5,000	$ 9,000	$14,000

If Alphonse's and Gaston's income statements were merely added together to form the consolidated income statement, double-counting would result. This happens because neither Alphonse's $25,000 sale to Gaston nor the $25,000 of cost of goods sold on Gaston's income statement represents a transaction with outsiders. This means that the intercompany sales transaction must be eliminated in preparing the consolidated income statement, as follows:

Eliminating $25,000 Intercompany Sale

| | Income Statement Totals | | | |
	Alphonse	Gaston	Sale Elimination	Consolidated
Sales	$250,000,000	$150,000,000	($25,000)	$399,975,000
Cost of goods sold	$200,000,000	$109,000,000	($25,000)	$308,975,000
Gross margin	$ 50,000,000	$ 41,000,000		$ 91,000,000

After this elimination, all that remains of the intercompany sale and Gaston's subsequent resale of the goods to outsiders is:

	Alphonse's Sale to Gaston	Gaston's Resale to "Outsiders"	Sale Elimination	Net
Selling price	$25,000	$34,000	($25,000)	$34,000
Cost of goods sold	$20,000	$25,000	($25,000)	$20,000
Profit	$ 5,000	$ 9,000		$14,000

Notice that the consolidated income statement now only reflects revenues *realized from outsiders* ($34,000) and costs paid to outsiders ($20,000). The double-counting of the intercompany sales and cost of goods sold has been eliminated.

Recap

Consolidated financial statements portray the parent company and its subsidiaries as a single economic unit. But the individual balance sheets (and income statements) of each subsidiary and the parent are not simply added together. Instead, consolidation adjustments are made to avoid double-counting internal business transactions as well as various balance sheet items.

Pooling of Interests

WEYERHAEUSER
COMPANY
www.weyerhaeuser.
com

Up until 2001, when two companies merged in a business combination and it was not possible to determine which one of the companies was the "acquirer," so-called pooling consolidation accounting was required.[4] Instead of paying cash to acquire another company, mergers were sometimes accomplished using a "stock-for-stock" exchange. For example, the American forest products giant Weyerhaeuser Company announced on June 21, 1999, that it had acquired, by means of a share exchange, MacMillan Bloedel Limited, a major Canadian forest products company. In this type of transaction, one company exchanges equity shares with the shareholders of another company. The accounting for these mergers followed (under certain conditions) a consolidation procedure called **pooling of interests**. Let's see how Alphonse and Gaston would have pooled.

Recall that Alphonse Corporation issued 8,000,000 new shares of stock for $10,000,000 cash and then used the cash to buy all of the outstanding shares of Gaston Corporation. To illustrate how pooling of interests works, let's assume Alphonse does not issue new shares for cash. Instead, on January 1, 2003, Gaston's shareholders agree to relinquish all of their shares in exchange for 8,000,000 newly issued shares of Alphonse stock. After the transaction is completed, Alphonse shareholders own both companies—that is, the merger has been accomplished by an exchange of shares rather than by an outright cash buyout.

In a stock-for-stock exchange, the owners of *both* Alphonse and Gaston continue as equity investors in the newly merged corporation. This continuation of ownership interests in poolings is in sharp contrast to what happens in a cash buyout, one in which the acquired company's shareholders accept cash and—after the buyout—have no further equity interest in the combined enterprise.

GAAP in effect up until 2001 treated pooling of interests as though two formerly independent companies had decided to join resources and "keep house together." Since both original ownership interests survived, *no buyout was considered to have taken place.* In the consolidation of ◄ Alphonse's and Gaston's financial statements, the *book values* of the two entities were combined. As in purchase accounting, however, inter-company transactions and double-counted items must be eliminated, as shown in Exhibit 16.3.

> The entry to record the acquisition on Alphonse's books would use the *book value* of Gaston's net assets ($2,000,000 + $6,500,000 – $500,000) as the carrying amount in the investment account—that is:
>
> DR Investment in Gaston $8,000,000
>   CR Common shares $8,000,000

The only adjustment needed here is the elimination of the potential double-counting of Gaston's net assets and equity. This entry is identical to the purchase accounting (or cash buyout) adjustment illustrated in Exhibit 16.2 (see notations A and D). No other adjustments or reclassifications are needed, since Alphonse's "Investment in Gaston" account equals the net book value shown on Gaston's books. This means that under a pooling of interests there would never be a writeup of assets to a new, higher carrying value. Similarly, there would never be any goodwill recognized.

Even though pooling consolidation accounting is no longer GAAP practice in Canada (or the U.S.), it is still useful to have a general understanding of the practice, since:

- Poolings that occurred prior to the 2001 cutoff date still affect corporate consolidated financial statements going forward.

Exhibit 16.3

Preparation of Consolidated Balance Sheet (Pooling of Interests Method)

| | After the Merger | | Adjustments | Consolidated Balance Sheet |
	Alphonse	Gaston		
Assets				
Current assets	$ 5,000,000	$2,000,000		$ 7,000,000
PP&E assets minus accumulated amortization	20,000,000	6,500,000		26,500,000
Investment in Gaston	8,000,000	—	(8,000,000)	—
	$33,000,000	$8,500,000		$33,500,000
Liabilities and Equity				
Current liabilities	$ 1,000,000	$ 500,000		$ 1,500,000
Common shares	32,000,000	8,000,000	(8,000,000)	32,000,000
	$33,000,000	$8,500,000		$33,500,000

- Some companies adopted pooling up until the "bitter end." For example, when Barrick Gold Corporation of Toronto and Homestake Mining Company of Walnut Creek, California, entered into a business combination in 2001, the registration statement that they filed with the U.S. Securities and Exchange Commission (SEC) specified (on page 89) that both companies would strive to ensure that the merger would be accounted for as a pooling under U.S. GAAP.

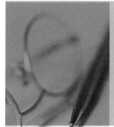

Recap

In poolings of interests, the owners of previously separate companies own the merged organization. No buyout has occurred and therefore no new accounting basis—no asset "writeup" to fair value—is recognized in the consolidated statements. Instead, the book values of the previously separate companies are carried forward to the consolidated financial statements. Pooling is no longer a Canadian (or U.S.) GAAP practice as of 2001.

Purchase, Pooling, and Financial Analysis

The pooling of interests method had been widely criticized. To help understand why, consider Exhibit 16.4, which highlights the differences in consolidated balance sheets that would result for Alphonse & Gaston Company—the combined organization—under purchase accounting versus pooling of interests accounting.

By contrast, under purchase accounting, goodwill was required to be amortized over a period *not longer than* 40 years prior to 2001. Not surprisingly, most companies choose the longest allowable amortization period and write goodwill off over 40 years. With the banning of pooling, both Canadian and U.S. standard-setters attempted to make purchase consolidation accounting more palatable by no longer requiring goodwill amortization; henceforth, an annual "impairment test" was to be applied. (There is more about the impairment test later in this chapter.)

This comparison makes the financial statement differences under purchase versus pooling of interests accounting easy to see. Prior to the acquisition, Gaston had a fair value of $10,000,000—the amount of cash Alphonse was willing to pay to gain control. Purchase accounting brings Gaston into the consolidated statement at its fair value of $10,000,000; under pooling of interests accounting, Gaston is shown in the consolidated statement at its net book value of $8,000,000. The $2,000,000 difference is shown in the "Difference" column in Exhibit 16.4.

Critics argued that pooling permitted acquiring companies to record acquisitions at artificially low amounts. In our example, Gaston is *worth* $10,000,000, and this is presumably the value that the sellers demanded. Therefore, the value of Alphonse shares that Gaston's shareholders received must have been close to $10,000,000. *Despite this economic reality, the transaction is booked at $8,000,000 under the pooling of interests method.* Critics charged that this understatement distorted the balance sheet as well as subsequent income statements. The income in future years would be affected since capital assets are $1,500,000 lower—the unrecorded difference between fair value and book value—under pooling than under purchase accounting, thereby lowering future amortization expense. Similarly, since there is no potential goodwill under pooling, there is no goodwill impairment to reduce future earnings. Both of these effects make income under pooling higher.

Critics further charged that the lower pooling balance sheet numbers for gross assets and equity made rate-of-return ratios appear higher. That's because, under pooling, the denominator of both the return-on-assets and return-on-equity ratios is lower. Some critics went so far as to suggest that these distortions are not accidental. They argued that the *cosmetic* statement effects of pooling explain its popularity among takeover-minded executives. Pooling provided an opportunity—critics contended—to buy companies and then record the acquisition on the books at artificially low numbers, thereby improving the appearance (but not the substance!) of subsequent financial statements.

Exhibit 16.4

Purchase Method Versus Pooling of Interests Method: Comparative Consolidated Balance Sheets for Alphonse & Gaston Company

	Purchase Accounting	Pooling of Interests Accounting	Difference
Assets			
Current assets	$ 7,000,000	$ 7,000,000	—
PP&E assets minus accumulated amortization	28,000,000	26,500,000	$1,500,000
Goodwill	500,000	—	500,000
	$35,500,000	$33,500,000	$2,000,000
Liabilities and Equity			
Current liabilities	$ 1,500,000	$ 1,500,000	—
Common shares	34,000,000	32,000,000	$2,000,000
	$35,500,000	$33,500,000	$2,000,000

Although quite rare in Canada, pooling was still important. For example, when BC Telecom Inc. and Telus Corporation, two of the largest telecommunications companies in the country, announced the details of their merger on December 8, 1998, they indicated that the transaction would be accounted for as a pooling of interests. Indeed, it might have been because of the apparent accounting number advantages in using pooling consolidation that management was perhaps tempted to *arrange* an acquisition transaction so that it qualified as a pooling. Of course, it would not be the first time that a desired accounting outcome became a major motivation for structuring a deal, or even entering into a deal in the first place!

TELUS CORPORATION
www.telus.com

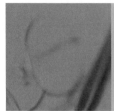

Recap

Pooling permitted companies to record business acquisitions at often artificially low amounts—at book value rather than at fair market value. This made rate-of-return ratios and other financial performance measures appear higher than they should have been. That's why pooling was banned. But its effect continues on into the future.

More Complexities in Consolidation Accounting

Minority Interests

Our description of consolidation accounting has only dealt with fairly simple situations. More advanced financial accounting textbooks deal with complexities such as:

- the existence of a minority shareholding in the subsidiary
- a parent company selling off a portion of its shares in a subsidiary
- indirect, multilayer, and reciprocal share holdings

- accounting for intangible and in-process R&D assets

- etc.

Since it is common to find an account labelled "Minority interest" (thus indicating that there is at least one minority shareholder group owning a portion of one of the reporting parent company's subsidiaries) on published consolidated balance sheets, we will briefly describe how this account operates. Suppose that in the Alphonse and Gaston example illustrating the purchase consolidation method earlier in the chapter, Alphonse purchased just 80% of Gaston's outstanding shares for $8,000,000 (recall that in the original example, Gaston had paid $10,000,000 for 100%). Then the 20% of Gaston's shareholders' equity *not* owned by Alphonse represents an outsider shareholders' group, almost a sort of liability from the viewpoint of the consolidated accounting entity. On January 1, 2003, the date that Alphonse acquired its now-80% majority interest in Gaston, this 20% minority interest has a book value of 20% × $8,000,000, or $1,600,000. The following journal entries show how to account, under Canadian GAAP, for the less-than-100% consolidation. (These entries are modifications of the entries under "Step 3. Analysis of the Common Stock Account" in the 100%-acquisition example shown previously):

DR	Common shares	$8,000,000	
DR	PP&E assets	1,200,000	
DR	Goodwill	400,000	
	CR Investment in Gaston		$8,000,000
	CR Minority interest		1,600,000

(This consolidation entry eliminates Gaston's shareholders' equity, establishes the "Minority interest" account on the consolidated balance sheet, where it is shown *between* shareholders' equity and liabilities, and increases the dollar amount of PP&E assets by 80% of the difference between book value and fair value. It also records the resulting goodwill.)

The calculation of goodwill is as follows:

Recorded book value of 80% of Gaston's net assets	$6,400,000
80% of unrecorded difference between fair value and book value of Gaston's PP&E assets (80% × [$8,000,000 − $6,500,000])	1,200,000
Fair value of 80% of net assets acquired	$7,600,000
But Alphonse paid:	8,000,000
Residual is unrecorded value of Gaston's goodwill	$ 400,000

Notice that on the consolidated balance sheet, Gaston's PP&E assets will be recorded not at their full fair value, but at only 80% of their fair value, a treatment that GAAP require (*CICA Handbook*, Section 1600, para. .15).

Goodwill

Under new Section 3062 ("Goodwill and Other Intangible Assets"), goodwill recognized on consolidation should not be amortized (recall that under previous GAAP it was amortized). Rather, it must be tested each year for "impairment." This testing must be done for a consolidated entity's reporting units (Section 3062, para. 5[d]), using a two-step process, as follows:

1. Compare the fair value of a reporting unit with its carrying amount (including goodwill). If the fair value is greater, then goodwill is not impaired and there is no need to go on to the second step.
2. If the fair value is *less*, then the fair value of the reporting unit's goodwill is compared with its carrying amount. If the carrying amount of the reporting unit's goodwill is greater than the fair value of the goodwill, an impairment loss equal to the excess should be recorded in income (Section 3062, para. 27).

Foreign Subsidiaries

All majority-owned subsidiaries—foreign and domestic—must be consolidated using the methods we've just described. Regrettably, there's an additional complication when consolidating foreign subsidiaries—that is, the financial records of the subsidiary will be expressed in foreign currency units. The subsidiary's numbers must first be *transformed* into the parent's currency units—usually into Canadian dollars, if it's a Canadian parent—before the consolidation process can begin.

The transformation under Canadian GAAP specifies one of two procedures, depending on the operating characteristics of the foreign subsidiary:[5]

1. Foreign subsidiaries that are mere extensions of the parent with no self-sufficiency (i.e., *integrated* operations) are **remeasured** using the **temporal method.** For example, in the case of a European sales subsidiary of a Canadian fertilizer company, the subsidiary sells fertilizer produced by the Canadian parent to European farmers and sends the cash proceeds back to Canada.
2. Foreign subsidiaries that are essentially freestanding units with self-contained (or self-sustaining) foreign operations are **translated** using the **current rate method.** For example, in the case of an American manufacturing and sales subsidiary of a Canadian telecommunications company, the subsidiary buys parts in the United States, assembles the final product, and sells it to American businesses, retaining the cash proceeds for growth and expansion.

What guides this choice is subtle; foreign subsidiaries whose operations are not self-contained are considered to be engaging in a continuing series of **foreign currency transactions.** The consolidation process accordingly treats the financial results of these subsidiaries in the same way foreign currency transactions are treated. To illustrate, we must digress briefly to explain the accounting for foreign currency transactions.

Foreign Currency Transactions

Foreign currency transactions are simply business transactions denominated in units of a foreign currency. Examples include a Canadian company taking out a bank loan denominated in British pounds or purchasing inventory on credit for a price expressed in U.S. dollars. The accounting for foreign currency transactions depends on the type of asset acquired or liability incurred. Let's consider a foreign currency transaction that involves the acquisition of a **monetary asset**—that is, an asset like cash or accounts receivable whose value is derived from the number of monetary units into which it is convertible.

Assume that on January 1, 2003, Cambior Corporation (a Canadian company) sells 100 units of its product to a U.K. customer. The selling price is £10 per unit, or £1,000 total. Payment is due on April 1, 2003. On January 1, 2003, let's say that one British pound is worth $2, and that the per-unit cost of production incurred by Cambior is $8.00. Given this information, we would record the foreign currency transaction on Cambior's books in this way:

DR Accounts receivable	$2,000	
CR Sales revenue		$2,000
To record the receivable of £1,000 at its 1/1/03 dollar equivalent of $2,000.		
DR Cost of goods sold	$800	
CR Inventory		$800

The receivable is denominated in pounds—which is what makes this a foreign currency transaction. Since Cambior keeps its books in Canadian dollars, the receivable must be re-expressed in home-currency units when preparing financial statements. This is done using the exchange rate in effect at the transaction date: £1 = $2. It is important to understand that while the receivable is initially reflected on the books at $2,000, in reality what's owed by the customer is £1,000.

By the end of the quarter, the pound has fallen relative to the dollar, so that on March 31, 2003, the exchange rate is £1 = $1.80. This means that at current exchange rates the receivable is worth only $1,800, and so Cambior would book the following entry when preparing its quarterly statements:

DR Foreign currency transaction loss	$200	
CR Accounts receivable		$200
To reflect the £1,000 receivable at its end-of-quarter dollar equivalent of $1,800.		

Cambior has a loss because it was owed pounds but the pound has fallen in value. This loss is reflected in the income statement of the period in which the loss occurs. Monetary assets (like accounts receivable) that arise from foreign currency transactions are shown in the financial statements at their dollar equivalent using *the exchange rate in effect at the financial statement date*. Monetary liabilities (like accounts or bonds payable) are similarly translated using the exchange rate in effect at the statement date. The statement date exchange rate is referred to as the **current rate**.

Suppose the exchange rate on April 1, 2003, when the receivable is paid, is still £1 = $1.80. The customer remits £1,000, which Cambior then converts into dollars. The entry on Cambior's books is:

DR Cash	$1,800	
CR Accounts receivable		$1,800
To remove the receivable from the books. The initial $2,000 minus the 3/31/03 writedown of $200 equals the carrying amount of $1,800.		

We next illustrate the accounting for a foreign currency transaction that involves a nonmonetary asset. Nonmonetary assets are items like inventory, equipment, land, buildings, and trucks whose value is determined by supply and demand.

Suppose Cambior—because of its growing volume of sales to U.K. customers—decides to purchase a warehouse in London to store inventory awaiting shipment to customers. A building is purchased on June 30, 2003, for £300,000; on that date the exchange rate is £1 = $1.75. The building is recorded on Cambior's books at the dollar equivalent of the foreign currency transaction price at the purchase date:

Most liabilities are monetary since they are expressed in units of currency (e.g., a Japanese yen account payable of ¥9,000,000) and will be settled using foreign currency monetary assets. However, there are a few liabilities that are settled by using *nonmonetary assets*; this small class of liabilities is considered to be nonmonetary. Examples include estimated product warranty liabilities and customer deposits for products to be produced and delivered in future periods.

DR Warehouse building	$525,000	
CR Cash		$525,000

To record the acquisition of the London warehouse at the dollar equivalent of the foreign currency transaction price: £300,000 × 1.75 = $525,000.

The subsequent accounting for nonmonetary assets acquired in a foreign currency transaction is identical to the accounting for nonmonetary assets acquired in the domestic currency. Specifically, the historical cost of the fixed asset in dollars is used as the measurement basis in subsequent financial statements throughout the asset's life. Even if the value of the pound falls to £1 = $1.60 by year-end 2003, the London warehouse would still be shown on Cambior's books at $525,000—that is, at its acquisition cost in dollars (minus amortization, of course). Thus, to reflect the gross carrying amount of nonmonetary assets acquired in a foreign currency transaction, Cambior would use the exchange rate in effect at the time of the transaction. This rate is called the **historical exchange rate**.

Recap

The accounting for assets and liabilities arising from foreign currency transactions depends on the nature of the item—that is:

1. Foreign currency monetary assets and liabilities are remeasured using the current rate of exchange in effect at the balance sheet date.
2. Foreign currency nonmonetary assets (and liabilities) are remeasured using the historical rate of exchange that was in effect at the time the item was acquired or incurred.

Accounting for Non-freestanding or Integrated Subsidiaries

Now that we've outlined the accounting for foreign currency transactions, we can return to our main theme—that is, accounting for foreign subsidiaries. In introducing this topic, we said the method used to transform the foreign currency accounts of foreign subsidiaries depends on the *nature* of the subsidiary. The financial statements of subsidiaries that are not freestanding—that is, subsidiaries whose operations are simply an extension of the parent—are translated into Canadian dollars (or other reporting currency) using the temporal method. We now explain why.

To see what it means when we say a foreign subsidiary is not freestanding, let us consider a Canadian company, Doodle Corporation, with a U.K. subsidiary called Dandy Ltd. The role of Dandy is to serve as the U.K. marketing arm of Doodle. Doodle manufactures a product in Canada using domestic-sourced materials and labour. Some of the production is shipped to the United Kingdom where it is sold to U.K. customers at a price denominated in pounds sterling. The distribution of the product and collection of the receivables are coordinated by two U.K. employees of Dandy Ltd. Upon collection of the receivables, the pounds are remitted to Canada. This cycle is repeated as the pounds are converted into dollars, the dollars are used in Canada to manufacture more inventory, and some portion of the inventory is again shipped to the United Kingdom for sale to customers there. Dandy's only U.K. assets are (1) a small amount of cash to pay expenses, (2) inventory from Doodle that has not yet been shipped to customers, and (3) a building that serves as both a warehouse and an office for the two employees.

The situation described here is a classic illustration of a foreign subsidiary that is merely an extension of the parent. Dandy Ltd. is a marketing arm of Doodle rather than a viable, freestanding company. It is a conduit for administering foreign sales, and it has no independent life.

Under Section 1650, subsidiaries like Dandy Ltd. are treated as if they were invented for the sole purpose of facilitating foreign currency transactions. Because such subsidiaries are a conduit for foreign transactions, upon consolidation they are treated as if the parent company had engaged in the foreign transactions directly. That is, *the numbers included when consolidating a non-freestanding subsidiary are identical to the numbers that would have been included had the subsidiary not existed and instead the parent had engaged in the foreign currency transactions directly.*

To achieve this effect in the financial statements, the so-called temporal method is used to translate the subsidiary's foreign currency statements into dollars. The exchange rates for translating various accounts under the temporal method are shown in Table 16.1.

To illustrate the temporal method, consider this information. Dandy Ltd. has the following transactions during 2003:

1. On January 1, 2003, it received inventory costing $800 from Doodle when £1 = $2, and sold these goods on credit for £1,000.
2. The pound falls to £1 = $1.80 on March 31, 2003. Receivables of £1,000 were collected on April 1, 2003, when £1 = $1.80.
3. The company purchased a building in London for £300,000 on June 30, 2003, when £1 = $1.75.

These transactions are identical to the foreign currency transactions entered into by Cambior Corporation earlier in this section. In Table 16.2, we show the result of using the temporal method to translate Dandy Ltd.'s statements. The results under GAAP for Cambior's foreign currency transactions are displayed in the shaded column for comparison.

Comparing the Dandy statement numbers with those of Cambior in Table 16.2 demonstrates the point of the example. Using the temporal method results in Dandy statements whose dollar figures are equal to those of Cambior. This is no coincidence. *Both Dandy and Cambior are considered to have engaged in identical foreign currency transactions, so the two sets of results should be equal.* Notice how the translation rules under the temporal method help achieve this result.

TABLE 16.1 TRANSLATION EXCHANGE RATES UNDER THE TEMPORAL METHOD

Account Category	Rate Used
Balance Sheet	
Monetary assets and liabilities	Current rate
Nonmonetary assets and liabilities	Historical rate
Income Statement	
All revenue and expense accounts except those listed below	Rate at time of transaction
Cost of goods sold and amortization	Historical rate

| | Temporal Method Translation | | | Foreign Currency Transactions |
	Dandy Ltd. in £	Rate	Dandy Ltd. in $	Cambior Corporation
Income Statement				
Sales	£ 1,000	£1 = $2	$ 2,000	$ 2,000
Cost of sales	400	£1 = $2	800	800
Gross margin	£ 600		$ 1,200	$ 1,200
Loss on receivables*	—		200	200
Gross income	£ 600		$ 1,000	$ 1,000
Selected Balance Sheet Accounts				
At 3/31/03:				
Account receivable	£ 1,000	£1 = $1.80	$ 1,800	$ 1,800
At 4/1/03:				
Cash	£ 1,000	£1 = $1.80	$ 1,800	$ 1,800
At 6/30/03:				
Building	£300,000	£1 = $1.75	$525,000	$525,000

*Computed as:

Monetary asset on acquisition,	£1,000 when £1 = $2.00 =	$2,000
Monetary asset at March 31, 2003,	£1,000 when £1 = $1.80 =	$1,800
Loss on receivable		$ 200

Accounting for Self-Contained or Self-Sustaining Foreign Subsidiaries

When the majority-owned foreign subsidiary and its parent operate independently, the translation of the subsidiary's financial statements into dollars uses the current rate method. To understand why, let us consider a self-sustained subsidiary whose operations do not rely extensively on the parent.

A Canadian food company has a Swiss subsidiary that was formed by a capital infusion from the Canadian parent. Once the equity cushion was in place, the remainder of the Swiss subsidiary's long-term capital was raised using Swiss-franc borrowing. The subsidiary does not engage in any transactions with the parent. Operations are entirely contained in Switzerland, where the company hires employees, buys inventory, manufactures its product line, and sells to Swiss and other European customers. Operating profits are plowed back into the Swiss operation to expand into new product lines and to increase production capacity. While the parent may periodically receive dividends from the subsidiary, its investment will remain until the subsidiary is either sold or liquidated.

For self-sustaining foreign subsidiaries, the effect of exchange rate changes on future dollar cash flows is uncertain. Consider a rise in the Swiss franc. One possible effect of the rise is that it will make the subsidiary's products more expensive to foreign purchasers and could adversely affect profits. On the other hand, the rise in the Swiss franc means that input purchases in other currencies are cheaper, so a favourable profit effect could ensue. The possibilities are many and depend on the individual characteristics of the subsidiary and on the characteristics of the markets in which it operates. These include:

1. Does the subsidiary price its product sales in countries outside Switzerland in Swiss francs or in units of the foreign currencies?
2. Does the subsidiary adjust its Swiss franc selling price when the value of the franc rises or falls?
3. What proportion of the product input is purchased locally in Switzerland in francs?
4. Does the Swiss franc borrowing have a floating rate of interest which would be sensitive to exchange rate changes?

These are only a few of the many possibilities that could influence the magnitude and direction of the effect of the exchange rate change on ultimate dollar cash flows from the subsidiary. *Because the ultimate exchange rate effects on dollar cash flows are uncertain, the AcSB decided that such subsidiaries should be translated using the current rate method and that any debit or credit arising from translation "gains" or "losses" should be put directly into an owners' equity account and not run through the income statement.* Under the current rate method, all balance sheet accounts are translated at the current exchange rate in effect at the balance sheet date and *all* income statement accounts are translated at the weighted average rate of exchange that was in effect over the period covered by the statement.

If *all* accounts in a statement are translated at the *same* rate—which is what happens under the current rate method—then the translated statements have the same proportionality as the untranslated statements expressed in foreign currency units. In other words, the quick ratio of the Swiss subsidiary derived from its pretranslated Swiss-franc statements will be identical to the quick ratio once the statements are translated into dollars using the current rate method. The current rate method provides a practical way to get from foreign currency units to dollars while still maintaining the subsidiary's financial ratios. *Furthermore, by denying income statement recognition to the balancing debit or credit that arises from translation, the uncertain ultimate effect of exchange rate changes is explicitly carried forward.* Figure 16.1 is a diagram of the Section 1650 translation approach.

Figure 16.1 shows that GAAP require firms to categorize their foreign subsidiaries into one of two groups: (1) *non-freestanding subsidiaries*, whose activities are so closely integrated with the parent that they are considered to be engaging in foreign currency transactions on behalf of the parent; or (2) *self-sustaining subsidiaries* with an independent or virtually independent operating existence of their own. For subsidiaries in the first group, exchange rate movements have an immediately determinable effect on dollar cash flows; for this reason, translation gains or losses are run through the income statement. By contrast, subsidiaries in the second group are put into an income "holding pattern," because exchange rate movements have an indeterminate impact on the parent's ultimate dollar cash flows. Consequently, a neutral translation mechanism—the current rate method—is used for these subsidiaries, and the resulting equity debits or credits are simply treated as balancing items rather than as elements of income.

FIGURE 16.1
TRANSLATION
APPROACH USED
IN SECTION 1650

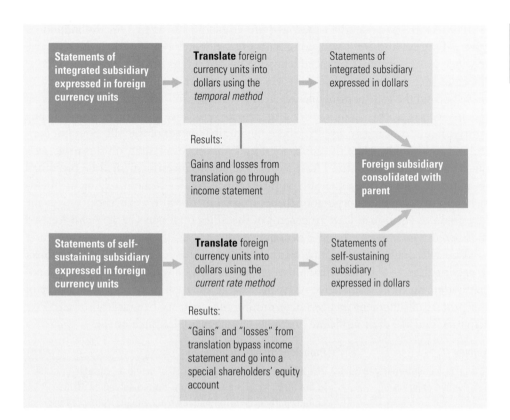

Accounting for Special Purpose Entities

In a submission to the Canadian Senate's Standing Committee on Banking, Trade and Commerce on June 12, 2002, Paul Cherry, the AcSB's chair, made the following statement.

> *Enron made extensive use of structures, known as "special purpose entities," purposefully designed to keep debt and other transactions "off balance sheet." An exacerbating circumstance was that derivatives trading contributed most of Enron's bottom line. Enron needed an investment-grade credit rating to stay in that business. So the ability of Enron to make its debt/equity ratio look better by using SPEs was extremely important, and when doubts about Enron's financial condition surfaced, the whole thing came crashing down like a house of cards.*
>
> > *Enron provides vivid evidence of just how abusive the use of off-balance-sheet structures can be when taken to extremes. The Board is taking immediate action to eliminate the abuses. The intended remedial action is substantially the same as is being proposed in the U.S.: any SPE that lacks sufficient independent economic substance must be consolidated by the entity that is the primary beneficiary. The new rule will not apply to "securitizations," which are a well-established source of low-cost financing for such things as credit card, mortgage and lease portfolios. ... Enron also entered into arrangements to provide financial support to the parties it was doing business with. This often involved guarantees of third party debts incurred by SPEs. The Board's* Handbook *Section 3860 on disclosure and presentation of financial instruments is among the most robust standards in the world and already requires certain disclosures, including the maximum loss that could arise and information about fair value of guarantees given. Nonetheless, the Board intends to expand our disclosure requirements in this area ...."*

The AcSB subsequently issued a draft guideline on SPEs ("Consolidation of Special-Purpose Entities"), with comments due by September 30, 2002, the objective of which was "to improve financial reporting by enterprises involved with ... SPEs ... not to restrict the use of SPEs" (p. i). Essentially, the draft guideline was intended to move beyond the general principles regarding when consolidation is appropriate as set out in Section 1590 ("Subsidiaries") to provide guidance on which entity (if any entity) should consolidate an SPE when the nominal owner of the SPE does not control it. Interestingly, while the corresponding FASB exposure draft on this topic set a quantitative benchmark (the FASB wrote: "An equity investment shall be presumed to be insufficient to allow the SPE to finance its activities without relying on financial support from [the corporation benefiting from the SPE's existence] unless the investment is equal to at least 10 percent of the SPE's total assets"), the AcSB focused more on the *substance* of the SPE situation.

This SPE draft guideline provides a series of comprehensive guidelines, all subject to varying degrees of professional judgment, to determine whether a company should consolidate an SPE, irrespective of its percentage ownership. An essential aspect of this process of judgment involves determining the "primary beneficiary" of an SPE's activities, and the draft guideline provided several examples, such as:

Activity	Probable Primary Beneficiary
Acting as a counterparty to a derivative contract	The enterprise that bears the risk of losing a "variable interest" in the SPE. (In the case of Enron, it often served as its own counterparty in SPE-derivative arrangements, thus creating misleading financial statements when the particular SPE was not consolidated.)

As of this writing (early December 2002), the accounting literature in this area is still in flux. But the general direction seems clear: SPEs should be consolidated if the risks and rewards of their existence are substantially borne by the company for which they were created.

Summary

Financial reporting for long-term intercorporate equity investments depends on whether the investor can exert significant influence or control, and this often depends in turn on the size of the investor's ownership share. Proportionate share size is often used to infer the purpose of the investment.

When the ownership share is less than about 20%, it is presumed that the investor cannot exert significant influence on the decisions of the investee. These **minority passive investments** are shown at cost on the balance sheet. **Minority active investments** may involve between 20% and 50% ownership. Investment at this level presumably conveys both permanency and the ability to influence decisions—and thus, the equity method is used. Full consolidation is required when the investor exerts control, which often happens when ownership exceeds 50%.

Majority-owned foreign subsidiaries also need to be consolidated. Doing so requires that foreign currency amounts be re-expressed in dollars. Foreign subsidiaries that are mere extensions of the Canadian parent and have no self-sufficiency have their financial statements translated by the **temporal method**. The temporal method treats the subsidiaries' business transactions as if they had been undertaken by the parent—but in the foreign currency. Foreign subsidiaries that are self-sustaining economic units are remeasured using the **current rate method**. This method provides an easy way to re-express foreign currency amounts in dollars while still maintaining the subsidiary's financial ratios.

Special purpose entities, which have (usually) legitimate roles to play in facilitating transactions, raising finance, and managing risk, have been subject to abuse, and thus new GAAP are required.

For more Exercises, Problems/Discussion Questions, and Cases, visit the Companion Website for this textbook at **www.pearsoned.ca/revsine**.

Exercises

E16-1 Consolidation in the presence of a minority interest

CICA adapted

A parent company acquires 80% of the shares of a subsidiary for $400,000. The carrying value of the subsidiary's net assets on its individual company financial statements is $350,000. The fair market value of the net assets of the subsidiary is $380,000.

1. According to GAAP, which of the following represents the amount of goodwill that should be recorded at the time of acquisition?
   (a) $16,000
   (b) $20,000
   (c) $96,000
   (d) $120,000
   (e) none of the above

2. Which of the following represents minority interest when the acquisition takes place?
   (a) $70,000
   (b) $76,000
   (c) $80,000
   (d) $100,000
   (e) none of the above

E16-2 Accounting for marketable securities

CICA adapted

During the current year, Roy Incorporated purchased marketable securities that it intended to hold for three months for $100,000. At year-end, the securities had a market value of $95,000.

Required:

At what amount should the marketable securities be shown on the year-end balance sheet? Are there any disclosure implications?

E16-3 Accounting for foreign currency–denominated marketable securities

CICA adapted

During the current year, Roy Incorporated purchased marketable securities that it intended to hold for three months for US$100,000 when the exchange rate was US$1 = CDN$1.25. At year-end, the securities had a market value of US$95,000 and the exchange rate was $1.30. Roy reports in Canadian dollars. Which of the following is the foreign exchange gain or loss on translation into Canadian dollars at year-end?

(a) $1,500 loss
(b) $4,750 gain
(c) $5,000 gain
(d) $6,500 loss
(e) none of the above

E16-4 Consolidation accounting

CICA adapted

On August 31, 2003, Parent acquired 75% of Sub's issued voting shares. On May 31, 2003, Sub sold $40,000 worth of goods to Parent and recorded a 40% gross margin on the sale. Half of the goods purchased were still recorded as inventory in Parent's accounts as at August 31, 2003. At that date, Parent still owed Sub $20,000 on the goods purchased on May 31, 2003. Which one of the following statements best describes the accounting treatment required when preparing the consolidated financial statements according to GAAP *immediately after* the Sub share acquisition by parent?

(a) Eliminate the full $20,000 balance from the intercompany asset and liability accounts.

(b) Eliminate Parent's portion (i.e., 75% of the $20,000) from the intercompany asset and liability accounts.

(c) Eliminate the full $20,000 balance from the intercompany asset and liability accounts, as well as the entire intercompany sales transaction and corresponding gain.

(d) Eliminate the full $20,000 balance from the intercompany asset and liability accounts, as well as 75% of the intercompany sales transaction and corresponding gain.

(e) None of the above. (If you choose this option, please provide the correct answer.)

E16-5 Consolidated net income

CICA adapted

On October 1, 2003, A Ltd. acquired 80% of B Ltd.'s issued voting shares for $5.8 million. A Ltd. accounted for this investment on its own individual-company books using the cost basis, but A's management knew that consolidated financial statements would be required for reporting purposes. As of October 1, 2003, B's shareholder equity accounts totalled $7 million, and the fair value of each of B's identifiable assets and liabilities corresponded to its carrying value, except for a parcel of land the fair value of which exceeded its carrying value by $250,000. There was no goodwill recognized on the purchase.

The net incomes of A and B for the year ended September 30, 2004, are $1.2 million and $400,000, respectively. Each company paid half of its net income in the form of dividends to its shareholders (keep in mind that A uses the cost method for its individual-company statements to account for its investment in B). During the year, B Ltd. sold the parcel of land and recorded a $300,000 gain in income.

Which of the following amounts best represents consolidated net income for the year ended September 30, 2004?

(a) $1,160,000
(b) $1,360,000
(c) $1,520,000
(d) $1,560,000
(e) None of the above. (If you choose this option, please provide the correct answer.)

E16-6 Choosing a translation method

CICA adapted

ABC Co. has a foreign operation (which it controls through a 60% ownership of voting shares), XYZ Co., located in Australia. XYZ Co. sells goods to the local market and in the past has financed its own operations through operating income retention and local borrowing. In fiscal 2001, ABC decided that, in order for XYZ to maximize its profitability,

ABC's management would become actively engaged in the operations, and all financing would be sourced through ABC. Which one of the following approaches should ABC use to report XYZ's results in ABC's consolidated financial statements for fiscal 2001?

(a) The current rate method should be adopted in place of the temporal method, and the change should be accounted for prospectively.

(b) The current rate method should be adopted in place of the temporal method, and the change should be accounted for retroactively.

(c) The temporal method should be adopted in place of the current rate method, and the change should be accounted for prospectively.

(d) The temporal method should be adopted in place of the current rate method, and the change should be accounted for retroactively.

(e) Neither the temporal nor the current rate method should be used, since ABC is not permitted under GAAP to consolidate XYZ.

E16-7 Consolidated capital asset accounting

CICA adapted

On September 1, 2001, MIL acquired 20% of FIL's issued voting shares for $4 million. The investment was accounted for on the equity basis. At that date, the carrying value of FIL's net assets totalled $19 million, and the fair value of each of FIL's identifiable assets and liabilities equalled its carrying value, except for equipment, the fair value of which exceeded its carrying value by $1 million. Its remaining useful life was eight years.

On September 1, 2002, MIL acquired an additional 35% of FIL's issued voting shares for $7.7 million. At that date, the carrying value of FIL's net assets totalled $20.6 million, and the fair value of each of FIL's identifiable assets and liabilities corresponded to its carrying value, except for the equipment mentioned above. Its fair value exceeded its carrying value by $1.4 million, and its remaining useful life was now only seven years.

As at August 31, 2003, the equipment was recorded on FIL's books at cost of $2.5 million, less accumulated amortization of $600,000, calculated according to the straight-line method.

Which of the following best represents the net carrying value of the equipment on MIL's consolidated balance sheet, as at August 31, 2003?

(a) $2,470,000

(b) $2,477,500

(c) $2,535,000

(d) $2,560,000

(e) Another number to be computed by you

Problems/Discussion Questions

P16-1 Intercorporate investments—balance sheet

The balance sheets of Herb Corporation and Aside Chemical Company at December 31, 2001, were:

($ in 000)	Herb	Aside
Assets	$850	$400
Liabilities	$275	$100
Common shares	200	100
Other equity (paid-in capital plus retained earnings)	375	200
	$850	$400

1. Assume that on January 1, 2002, Herb Corporation sold an additional 100,000 shares of its stock to its existing shareholders for $425,000. The entire proceeds of the issue were then used to buy all the shares of Aside. Prepare a consolidated balance sheet after the acquisition.

2. Assume the preceding facts except that Herb acquired only 80% of the shares for a cash payment of $425,000. How would the consolidated balance sheet differ from that in Question 1?

3. Now assume a slightly altered set of initial conditions. While the respective December 31, 2001, balance sheets for the two companies were identical to those shown on the previous page, the 100,000 Herb shares were not sold to existing Herb Corporation shareholders. Instead, assume that these 100,000 shares (which had a January 1, 2002, market value of $425,000) were issued to Aside's shareholders in exchange for all 100,000 of Aside's. Prepare a consolidated balance sheet after the acquisition.

P16-2 Comprehensive intercorporate investments problem

At December 31, 2002, Poe Corporation reported as short-term investments the following marketable securities. All these securities were acquired in 2002.

	Cost	Fair Value
Axe Corporation, 1,000 shares, $2.40 convertible preferred shares	$ 40,000	$ 42,000
Purl, Inc., 6,000 common shares	60,000	66,000
Day Company, 2,000 common shares	55,000	40,000
Total	$155,000	$148,000

On January 2, 2003, Poe purchased 100,000 common shares of Scott Corporation for $1,700,000, representing 30% of Scott's outstanding common shares and an underlying equity of $1,400,000 in Scott's net assets on that date. Poe had no other financial transactions with Scott during 2003. As a result of Poe's 30% ownership of Scott, Poe has the ability to exercise significant influence over Scott's financial and operating policies.

During 2003, Poe disposed of the following securities:

- January 18—sold 2,500 shares of Purl for $13 per share
- June 1—sold 500 shares of Day for $21 per share.

The following 2003 dividend information pertains to stock owned by Poe:

- April 5 and October 5—Axe paid dividends of $1.20 per share on its $2.40 preferred shares to shareholders of record on March 9 and September 9, respectively.
- June 30—Purl paid a $1-per-share dividend on its common shares.
- March 1, June 1, September 1, and December 1—Scott paid quarterly dividends of $0.50 per share on each of these dates. Scott's net income for the year ended December 31, 2003 was $1,200,000.

At December 31, 2003, Poe's management intended to hold Scott's shares on a long-term basis. Market prices per share of Poe's other investment securities were as follows:

	Market Value at December 31, 2003
Axe Corporation—preferred	$56
Purl, Inc.—common	11
Day Company—common	22
Scott Corporation—common	16

Prepare all Poe's journal entries, using the above information, for December 31, 2002, onward.

P16-3 Intercorporate investments—equity method

Consider the following sequence of events:

- On January 1, 2002, Big Time Motors purchases 25% of Cooper Tire Company's common shares (one of its suppliers) for $150 million. The book value of Cooper Tire Company's net assets on this date was $400 million. All of the excess is attributed to goodwill. No other single Cooper shareholder owns more than 20%, and Big Time can exert significant influence.
- Cooper Tire Company earned $25 million in net income for 2002.
- Cooper Tire Company pays total dividends of $15 million during 2002.
- On January 1, 2003, Big Time Motors purchases an additional 15% of Cooper Tire Company common shares for $100 million. The excess of cost over book value is attributed to goodwill.
- Cooper Tire Company had a net loss of $40 million for 2003.
- Cooper Tire Company pays total dividends of $18 million during 2003.

Required:

1. What amount of investment income should Big Time Motors report on its 2002 income statement as a result of its investment in Cooper Tire? At what amount would Big Time Motors report its investment in Cooper Tire Company in its December 31, 2002, balance sheet? Are any assumptions necessary?
2. At what amount should Big Time Motors report its investment in Cooper Tire Company in its December 31, 2003, balance sheet?

P16-4 Business acquisitions and ratio analysis

Company B, an auto parts company, has made several acquisitions with newly issued shares over the past five years, using the purchase method of accounting. In each case, the purchase price exceeded the fair value of the net assets of the acquired company. AutoParts Heaven has not made any acquisitions. Wholesale prices of auto parts have been rising over the last five years. Both Company B and AutoParts Heaven account for inventories using the FIFO method.

Required:

1. Briefly explain why Company B's acquisition history makes it difficult to analyze the *trend* of Company B's financial data and ratios from its published statements.
2. Briefly explain why Company B's acquisition history makes it difficult to compare the *ratios* of Company B with those for AutoParts Heaven.
3. For each of the following financial measures, compare the effect (higher, lower, or no effect) of the purchase method on the financial measure of Company B with the effect of the pooling method. Briefly explain why each effect occurs:
   (a) gross profit margin percentage
   (b) long-term debt-to-equity ratio
   (c) pre-tax earnings

P16-5 Business acquisitions and ratio analysis

The balance sheets of ABD Inc. and C Corporation on December 31, 2001, are given next (unless otherwise noted, all amounts are in millions):

	ABD Inc.	C Corporation
Assets:		
Cash	$200	$ –0–
Accounts receivable	–0–	600
Inventory	300	–0–
Current assets	500	600
Plant and equipment, net	–0–	800
Total	$500	$1,400
Liabilities and shareholders' equity:		
Accounts payable	$250	$ –0–
Long-term debt	–0–	1,050
Total liabilities	$250	$1,050
Common shares	150	200
Retained earnings	100	150
Total	$500	$1,400

1. Immediately following the preparation of the preceding balance sheets, ABD issues 250 common shares and receives $350 in cash proceeds. ABD immediately uses these cash proceeds to purchase 100% of the common shares of C Corporation. Provide the balance sheet for ABD Inc. after these two transactions. (*Note:* On its own individual-company financial statements, ABD accounts for its investment in C Corporation using the equity method.)

2. Provide the *consolidated* balance sheet that ABD Inc. would report immediately following the investment in C Corporation. How do these two methods of reporting the acquisition, in Questions 1 and 2, differ in their description of what ABD bought? What are some key ratios that are affected by the accounting method?

3. For this question only, suppose that C Corporation's "Plant and equipment, net" account had been $5,800 and its "Long-term debt" account had been $6,050. How would your answers to Questions 1 and 2 have changed? (A qualitative answer, rather than a whole balance sheet, will do here.)

4. For this question only, suppose that at the time of the acquisition, ABD owed $20 to C Corporation for services it had provided in the preceding year. How would your answer to Question 2 change? (Again, a qualitative answer will do.)

5. For this question, suppose that ABD Inc. issued 250 common shares, received $400 in proceeds, and used the entire proceeds to purchase 100% of the outstanding common shares of C Corporation. Provide the *consolidated* balance sheet that ABD Inc. would report immediately following the investment in C Corporation.

6. Start with the information in Question 5. Now suppose that ABD only acquired 80% of the outstanding common shares of C Corporation. Provide the *consolidated* balance sheet that ABD Inc. would report immediately following the investment in C Corporation.

7. Start with the information in Question 5. Now suppose that ABD *exchanged* its 250 common shares (which had a market value of $400) for the 200 outstanding common shares of C Corporation. What method would ABD use to account for the acquisition? Provide the *consolidated* balance sheet that ABD Inc. would report immediately following the investment in C Corporation. Why might the management of ABD prefer to structure the acquisition and consolidation in this fashion?

P16-6 A bit of consolidation theory

Assume that you and a fellow student have been assigned a project in which you are to prepare a ten-minute presentation explaining consolidation accounting to the class. Your partner has prepared the draft that follows, and your job is to assess it critically.

Required:

Prepare a written critique of the draft that follows.

> Suppose that there are two corporations, Investor and Investee, and Investor owns all the voting shares of Investee. When Investor can exercise control in virtually all aspects of Investee's strategic operating, investing, and financing decisions, two separate accounting entities no longer exist. We now have, in substance, one *consolidated* accounting entity (in spite of the fact that two legal corporations are involved), and the consolidation accounting method reflects this fact. The consolidated accounting entity has one set of financial statements that it presents to users, in which all transactions between the two companies have been eliminated, since the transactions are now viewed as occurring within the (now-enlarged) accounting entity. The graphic that follows represents the situation:

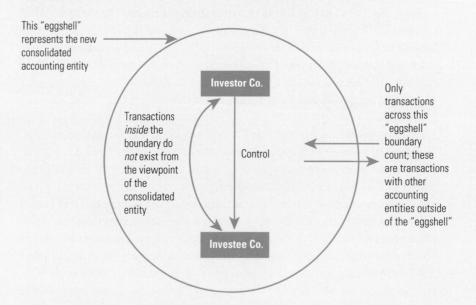

> The "eggshell" represents the boundary between the consolidated accounting entity and the rest of the world. Only transactions that cross this boundary may be accounted for; all transactions between Investor Co. and Investee Co. are inside the boundary, and therefore do not exist as far as the consolidated financial statements are concerned. Suppose Investee sold a parcel of land to Investor for $150,000. The land cost Investee $100,000, and this is the amount that Investee carries it at on its individual-company balance sheet. After the sale,

Investee records a nonoperating gain on its individual-company income statement of $50,000 from the sale of land. Also, Investor now accounts for the land at $150,000 on its individual-company balance sheet. The $50,000 profit has been realized from Investee's individual-company perspective, and the cost of the land from Investor's individual-company perspective is $150,000, so these numbers are recorded in the respective general ledgers of the two companies. But from the perspective of the consolidated entity, no transaction ever took place. So our view of when a transaction takes place changes as we alter the accounting entity.

The historic cost of the land on the consolidated entity's balance sheet is $100,000, and the consolidated entity earned no profit on a land sale, since no transaction took place between it and an accounting entity outside of the eggshell. So when consolidated financial statements are prepared from the two sets of individual company financial statements, such items must be dealt with. The consolidation is performed by means of a spreadsheet, in which the two sets of legal company financial statements are modified for items like the "inside the eggshell" land sale by means of "consolidation worksheet entries." These entries don't appear in either company's books of account, but only on the consolidation spreadsheet. The consolidation worksheet entry for the land sale, for example, would be (ignoring any tax implications for simplicity):

DR	Gain on sale of land	$50,000	
	CR Land		$50,000

So, in a very real sense, consolidation accounting is just an application of the idea of the accounting entity.

P16-7 "Push-down accounting"

Many people have argued that when an investee company is acquired by an investor company, sufficient evidence might exist for the assets and liabilities of the investee to be comprehensively revalued, an accounting approach that has been called "push-down accounting." In fact, *CICA Handbook* Section 1625 ("Comprehensive Revaluation of Assets and Liabilities") says in para. .04 that:

> *The following conditions are required to be satisfied for an enterprise's assets and liabilities to be comprehensively revalued:*
>
> (a) *All or virtually all of the equity interests in the enterprise have been acquired, in one or more transactions between non-related parties, by an acquirer who controls the enterprise after the transaction or transactions; or*
>
> (b) *The enterprise has been subject to a financial reorganization, and the same party does not control the enterprise both before and after the reorganization;*
>
> *and in either situation new costs are reasonably determinable*

"Push-down accounting" is defined in this section as "a technique that attributes revised values to the assets and liabilities reported in the financial statements of an enterprise based on a purchase transaction or transactions of its equity interests. Application of the technique results in the acquirer's cost being assigned to the assets and liabilities of the acquired enterprise" (para. .03).

Required:

1. As explained in this chapter, when an investor company acquires an investee company and is able to exert control over the investee, the investee company becomes a subsidiary and the investor must consolidate it. The assets and liabilities of the investee included in the investor's consolidated financial statements are accounted for on the basis of the investor's pro rata share of their *fair*, not book, values. "Push-down accounting" is an attempt to extend this revaluation

to the investee's financial statements. On the basis of accounting theory, is "push-down accounting" justified?

2. What are the incentives and disincentives that the following groups might have to support "push-down accounting"?

- parent company management
- subsidiary company management
- parent company shareholders
- subsidiary noncontrolling shareholders
- subsidiary employees

Cases

C16-1 BCE Inc. writes down goodwill

BCE INC.
www.bce.ca

BCE issued the press release that follows on July 24, 2002.

Required:

1. The press release states that:

In the second quarter of 2002, an impairment of $8,180 million was charged to opening retained earnings as of January 1, 2002, as required by the transitional provisions of the new *CICA Handbook* section 3062, regarding the accounting for goodwill and other intangible assets, relating to impaired goodwill of reporting units within Teleglobe ($7,516 million), Bell Globemedia ($545 million) and BCE Emergis ($119 million).

Are the transitional provisions of Section 3062 susceptible to "big bath" accounting? Are Teleglobe, Bell Globemedia, and BCE Emergis appropriate "reporting units" for purposes of goodwill impairment?

2. How might Canadian GAAP with respect to goodwill impairment affect the quality of earnings? What is the external auditor's role here? What evidence would be necessary to support goodwill impairment in the case of each of the three reporting units in the BCE press release?

BCE Announces Second Quarter Results—Revenues Up 4%, EBITDA Up 7%; $8.2 Billion Goodwill Write-Down

MONTREAL, July 24—For the second quarter of 2002, BCE Inc. (TSX, NYSE: BCE) reported total revenue of $4.9 billion, EBITDA (1) of $1.9 billion, and net earnings applicable to common shares of $11 million ($0.01 per common share). Net earnings before non-recurring items (2) were $400 million ($0.49 per common share).

"In the face of challenging times within our industry, BCE's results in the second quarter are on plan," said Michael Sabia, President and Chief Executive Officer of BCE Inc. "BCE achieved its solid performance as a result of productivity initiatives and rigorous expense management. During the quarter, BCE completed an extensive balance sheet review of all its operations. The resulting charges which we have announced today will allow us to move forward with a clear balance sheet. And, as we do, all our efforts will focus on leveraging the capabilities of BCE to grow and expand our 24 million customer connections."

OPERATIONAL HIGHLIGHTS (Q2 2002 vs. Q2 2001 unless otherwise indicated)

- High-speed Internet (DSL) net additions in the quarter were 43,000; total subscribers grew by 72% to reach 909,000;
- Postpaid cellular and PCS subscribers net additions in the quarter were 117,000; total cellular and PCS subscribers grew by 20% to reach 3,645,000;
- Bell ExpressVu net activations in the quarter were 31,000; total subscribers grew 39% to reach 1,176,000;
- Bell Globemedia's EBITDA improved 41% to $58 million;
- BCE Emergis' revenues increased by 8% over the first quarter of 2002 to $142 million; and,
- Productivity savings of $225 million achieved in the quarter.

"At Bell Canada, we are pleased with the traction we have achieved on productivity initiatives while maintaining growth in key areas," Mr. Sabia said. "Revenues from our wireless operations increased by 21% while Bell ExpressVu revenues increased by 35%."

"At Bell Globemedia cost-control measures and an increase in revenues due partially to higher demand for advertising have enhanced EBITDA performance," Mr. Sabia concluded. "BCE Emergis' revised business plan and restructuring efforts contributed to returning the company to positive EBITDA."

Total revenue at BCE increased 4% over the second quarter of 2001 mainly as a result of growth from BCE's wireless, DTH (Direct-to-Home) satellite entertainment and data services and increased revenues at Bell Globemedia. EBITDA improved by 7% compared to the same period last year, mainly due to prudent cost management across all areas and higher overall revenue.

BCE completed an extensive review of the carrying value of its assets on its balance sheet and as a result recorded the following after-tax charges in the second quarter of 2002:

- A transitional goodwill impairment charge of $8.2 billion applied to opening retained earnings in accordance with the changes from the Canadian Institute of Chartered Accountants on goodwill accounting. The charge pertains to Teleglobe ($7.5 billion), Bell Globemedia ($545 million), and BCE Emergis ($119 million) (see "Goodwill Note: at the end of this press release);
- A loss from discontinued operations of $295 million, relating to BCE's investments in BCI and Teleglobe;
- Restructuring and other charges totalling $153 million at Bell Canada, mainly relating to accounts receivables write-offs from legacy systems dating back to the early 1990s as part of the modernization of Bell's billing systems, including the introduction of a new billing platform; and,
- A $63 million restructuring and other charge at BCE Emergis.

BCE also recorded net gains on investments of $122 million, mainly the gain on the sale by Bell Canada of an approximate 36% interest in Télébec and Northern Telephone.

OTHER DEVELOPMENTS

Effective in the second quarter, BCE has classified Teleglobe as a discontinued operation. BCI had been classified as a discontinued operation effective in the first quarter of 2002. In addition, BCE deconsolidated Teleglobe and BCI effective in the second quarter.

OUTLOOK

The Company outlined its financial guidance for the third quarter of 2002 and confirmed its financial guidance for the full year 2002, excluding discontinued operations, as follows:

GUIDANCE	Q3 2002	Full Year 2002 Outlook
Revenue (billions)	$4.8 – $5.1	$19.5 – $20.5
EBITDA (billions)	$1.8 – $2.0	$7.5 – $8.0
Net earnings per share (before non-recurring items)	$0.45 – $0.48	$1.80 – $1.90

RESULTS BY BUSINESS GROUP (unaudited)

BCE's operations as at June 30, 2002, included the Bell Canada segment, Bell Globemedia, and BCE Emergis. BCE Ventures consists of BCE's other investments.

	(CDN$ millions, except for share amounts)			
	Second Quarter		Six Months	
For the period ended June 30	2002	2001	2002	2001
Revenue				
Bell Canada	4,368	4,248	8,643	8,355
Bell Globemedia	326	297	638	603
Bell Emergis	142	159	274	302
BCE Ventures	261	261	524	495
Corporate and Other, including Inter-segment eliminations	(157)	(198)	(305)	(346)
Total revenue	4,940	4,767	9,774	9,409
EBITDA				
Bell Canada	1,850	1,719	3,610	3,354
Bell Globemedia	58	41	91	71
BCE Emergis	11	31	(9)	57
BCE Ventures	73	72	150	129
Corporate and Other, including Inter-segment eliminations	(47)	(39)	(85)	(73)
Total EBITDA	1,945	1,824	3,757	3,538
Net earnings (loss)				
Bell Canada	359	330	680	492
Bell Globemedia	11	(40)	12	(73)
BCE Emergis	(62)	(75)	(77)	(166)
BCE Ventures	59	24	83	92
Corporate and Other, including Inter-segment eliminations	(47)	36	(19)	2,979
Earnings from continuing operations	320	275	679	3,324
Discontinued operations	(295)	(253)	(340)	(2,397)
Dividends on preferred shares	(14)	(16)	(27)	(34)
Net earnings applicable to common shares	11	6	312	893
Net earnings per common share	0.01	0.01	0.39	1.11
Impact of non-recurring items on net earnings per common share				
Amortization of goodwill	—	0.31	—	0.62
Other items	0.48	0.14	0.53	(0.86)
Net earnings before non-recurring items	0.49	0.46	0.92	0.87

Second Quarter Review (Q2 2002 vs. Q2 2001, unless otherwise indicated)

BELL CANADA

The Bell Canada segment includes Bell Canada, Aliant, Bell ExpressVu and Bell Canada's interests in other Canadian telcos.

- Total revenue in the second quarter was up 3% to $4.4 billion, driven mainly by growth in wireless, DTH and data revenues.
- Local and access revenues decreased by 4% to $1.5 billion, mainly due to lower network access and carrier access tariff revenues, partially offset by higher consumer terminal sales.
- Long distance revenue remained flat at $645 million. The effect of a 5% increase in Bell's long distance conversation minutes, to 4.7 billion minutes, was offset by lower pricing due to competitive pricing pressures.
- Wireless revenue was up 21% to $542 million due mainly to strong growth in cellular and PCS subscribers.
- Data revenue increased 8% to $947 million, mainly due to higher IP/Broadband and Sympatico ISP revenues.
- Total Internet (DSL and dial-up) subscribers reached 1.9 million as at June 30.
- Bell ExpressVu had net subscriber activations in the quarter of 31,000, bringing the total customer base to almost 1.2 million. Year-over-year, the number of ExpressVu subscribers grew by 39%.
- Bell Canada's EBITDA grew by $131 million or 8% in the second quarter to reach $1.9 billion due mainly to continued productivity improvements and the growth in revenues.

BELL GLOBEMEDIA

Bell Globemedia includes CTV, The Globe and Mail and Bell Globemedia Interactive.

- Total revenue was $326 million in the quarter compared with revenue of $297 million for the same period last year. This increase includes the impact of the acquisitions of CFCF-TV, CKY-TV and ROB TV, which were purchased in the latter part of 2001, as well as organic growth.
- Advertising revenue was $230 million in the quarter, an increase of 8% compared to the second quarter of 2001.
- Subscriber revenues increased by 11% to reach $70 million, reflecting the recognition of revenue from the new digital specialty channels starting in January 2002, a higher penetration of the DTH market, and increased print circulation revenues due mainly to rate increases.
- EBITDA was $58 million in the second quarter compared with $41 million for the same period last year, reflecting the increase in revenues and implemented productivity initiatives.

BCE EMERGIS

- BCE Emergis revenue was $142 million in the quarter, compared with $159 million in revenues for the same period in 2001, due mainly to a decline in non-recurring revenues.
- BCE Emergis' revenue increased by 8% when compared to the first quarter of 2002, primarily due to higher revenues in the eHealth Solutions Group.
- EBITDA decreased by $20 million to $11 million, mainly reflecting the shortfall in revenues.
- Second quarter of 2002 EBITDA compared favourably to the first quarter of 2002 EBITDA shortfall of $20 million. The improvement in sequential quarter over quarter EBITDA was mainly related to lower employment costs and productivity improvements.
- In the quarter, 40% of BCE Emergis' total revenue was from its U.S. operations.
- During the second quarter, BCE Emergis implemented a cost reduction plan and recorded pre-tax restructuring and other charges of $119 million (BCE's share, on an after-tax basis, is $63 million).

BCE VENTURES

BCE Ventures includes the activities of CGI, Telesat and other investments.

- BCE Ventures' revenue was $261 million in the quarter, flat compared with the same period of 2001. Revenues at both CGI and Telesat were higher, offset by lower revenues from other Ventures' businesses.
- EBITDA was $73 million in the quarter compared with $72 million in the second quarter of 2001. Higher EBITDA at CGI and Telesat was partially offset by lower EBITDA from other Ventures' businesses.
- In July 2002, BCI's Plan of Arrangement was approved by its noteholders, its shareholders, and the courts.

BELL CANADA STATUTORY RESULTS

Bell Canada "statutory" includes Bell Canada, Bell Canada's interests in other Canadian telcos, and Bell Canada's 39% interest in Aliant (equity-accounted).

Bell Canada's reported revenue was $3.6 billion in the second quarter compared with $3.5 billion in the same quarter of 2001. The net loss applicable to common shares was $1 billion in the quarter compared with net earnings applicable to common shares of $466 million for the same period last year. One-time charges in the quarter included the write-down of the Bell Canada's 23% interest in Teleglobe as well as the impact of the charge relating to the accounts receivable write-down.

GOODWILL NOTE

The CICA recently issued new *Handbook* Sections 1581, Business Combinations, and 3062, Goodwill and Other Intangible Assets. Effective July 1, 2001, the standards require that all business combinations be accounted for using the purchase method. Additionally, effective January 1, 2002, goodwill and intangible assets with an indefinite life are no longer being amortized to earnings and will be assessed for impairment on an annual basis in accordance with the new standards, including a transitional impairment test whereby any resulting impairment was charged to opening retained earnings. As of June 30, 2002, BCE's management had allocated its existing goodwill and intangible assets with an indefinite life to its reporting units and completed the assessment of the quantitative impact of the transitional impairment test on its financial statements. In the second quarter of 2002, an impairment of $8,180 million was charged to opening retained earnings as of January 1, 2002, as required by the transitional provisions of the new *CICA Handbook* Section 3062, regarding the accounting for goodwill and other intangible assets, relating to impaired goodwill of reporting units within Teleglobe ($7,516 million), Bell Globemedia ($545 million) and BCE Emergis ($119 million).

ABOUT BCE

BCE is Canada's largest communications company. It has 24 million customer connections through the wireline, wireless, data/Internet and satellite services it provides, largely under the Bell brand. BCE leverages those connections with extensive content creation capabilities through Bell Globemedia which features some of the strongest brands in the industry— CTV, Canada's leading private broadcaster, The Globe and Mail, Canada's National Newspaper and Sympatico-Lycos, the leading Canadian Internet portal. As well, BCE has extensive e-commerce capabilities provided under the BCE Emergis brand. BCE shares are listed in Canada, the United States and Europe.

---

(1) EBITDA is defined as operating revenues less operating expenses and therefore reflects earnings before interest, taxes, depreciation and amortization, as well as any non-recurring items. BCE uses EBITDA, amongst other measures, to assess the operating performance of its ongoing businesses. The term EBITDA does not have a standardized meaning prescribed by Canadian generally accepted accounting principles and therefore may not be comparable to similarly titled measures presented by other publicly traded companies. EBITDA should not be construed as the equivalent of net cashflows from operating activities.

(2) Refer to the discussion on after-tax charges and Results of Business Group for a description of non-recurring items.

C16-2 EnCana Corporation: Unaudited pro forma consolidated financial statements

In a regulatory filing required as part of their business combination process to create EnCana Corporation, PanCanadian Energy Corporation and Alberta Energy Company Ltd. submitted the unaudited pro forma consolidated financial statements that follow.

Required:

1. In each pro forma financial statement presented, several pro forma adjustments are included. Explain each adjustment in each statement, line by line in your own words.
2. Are any pro forma adjustments difficult to understand and/or rationalize? Explain.
3. Are any pro forma adjustments "arbitrary"? Explain.
4. EnCana pro forma consolidated basic EPS is reported as $4.46. Is this number unique? Could it be used for valuation purposes?

APPENDIX F

UNAUDITED PRO FORMA CONSOLIDATED FINANCIAL STATEMENTS

ENCANA CORPORATION

(formerly PanCanadian Energy Corporation)

Unaudited Pro Forma Consolidated Financial Statements

Compilation Report

To the Directors of PanCanadian Energy Corporation and Alberta Energy Company Ltd.

We have reviewed, as to compilation only, the accompanying unaudited Pro Forma Consolidated Balance Sheet of EnCana Corporation as at December 31, 2001 and the unaudited Pro Forma Consolidated Statements of Earnings and Cash from Operating Activities for the year ended December 31, 2001, which have been prepared for inclusion in this Joint Information Circular. In our opinion, the unaudited Pro Forma Consolidated Balance Sheet and the unaudited Pro Forma Consolidated Statements of Earnings and Cash from Operating Activities have been properly compiled to give effect to the proposed transaction and the assumptions described in the notes thereto.

PricewaterhouseCoopers LLP
Chartered Accountants
Calgary, Alberta, Canada
February 21, 2002

Comments for United States Readers on Differences Between Canadian and United States Reporting Standards

The above opinion, provided solely pursuant to Canadian requirements, is expressed in accordance with standards of reporting generally accepted in Canada. Such standards contemplate the expression of an opinion with respect to the compilation of Pro Forma Financial Statements. United States standards do not provide for the expression of an opinion on the compilation of Pro Forma Financial Statements. To report in conformity with United States standards on the reasonableness of pro forma adjustments and their application to the Pro Forma Financial Statements would require an examination or review which would be substantially greater in scope than the review as to compilation only that we have conducted. Consequently, under United States standards, we would be unable to express any opinion with respect to the compilation of the accompanying unaudited Pro Forma Consolidated Balance Sheet and the unaudited Pro Forma Consolidated Statements of Earnings and Cash from Operating Activities.

PricewaterhouseCoopers LLP
Chartered Accountants
Calgary, Alberta, Canada
February 21, 2002

ENCANA CORPORATION
PRO FORMA CONSOLIDATED STATEMENTS OF EARNINGS

(Unaudited)
($ millions, except per share amounts)

	PanCanadian Year Ended December 31, 2001	AEC Year Ended December 31, 2001	Pro Forma Adjustments Note 3	Note 4	EnCana Pro Forma Consolidated
Revenues, net of royalties and production taxes					
Upstream	$3,251	$4,519	$(1,158) (c)(i)	$ —	$6,707
			5 (c)(iv)		
			90 (c)(ii)		
Midstream and Marketing	6,801	1,753	123 (a)	—	9,909
			1,158 (c)(i)		
			74 (c)(ii)		
Other	46	—	14 (b)	—	(3)
			6 (c)(iv)		
			(35) (c)(v)		
			(34) (c)(vi)		
	10,098	6,272	243	—	16,613
Expenses					
Transportation and selling	—	301	269 (c)(ii)	—	570
Direct	7,031	—	(7,031) (c)(iii)	—	—
Operating	—	917	673 (c)(iii)	—	1,590
Cost of product purchased	—	2,289	37 (a)	—	8,579
			(105) (c)(ii)		
			6,358 (c)(iii)		
General and administrative	157	80	—	—	237
Interest, net	98	256	(35) (c)(v)	36 (e)	336
			(19) (b)		
Foreign exchange	—	112	51 (b)	—	129
			(34) (c)(vi)		
Provision for doubtful accounts	—	36	11 (c)(iv)	—	47
Depreciation, depletion and amortization	856	1,252	—	—	2,108
Earnings Before the Undernoted	1,956	1,029	68	(36)	3,017
Gain on sale of assets	—	238	—	—	238
Income tax expense (recovery)	652	443	37 (a)	(15) (e)	1,117
Net Earnings	1,304	824	31	(21)	2,138
Distributions on preferred securities, net of tax	4	42	—	(21) (e)	25
Net Earnings Attributable to Common Shareholders	$1,300	$ 782	$ 31	$ —	$2,113
Earnings per Common Share					
Basic	$ 5.09	$ 5.24			$ 4.46
Diluted	$ 5.00	$ 4.98			$ 4.37

ENCANA CORPORATION
PRO FORMA CONSOLIDATED BALANCE SHEET
(Unaudited)
($ millions)

	PanCanadian Year Ended December 31, 2001	AEC Year Ended December 31, 2001	Pro Forma Adjustments Note 3	Pro Forma Adjustments Note 4	EnCan Pro For Consolid
Assets					
Current Assets					
Cash and cash equivalents	$ 963	$ 104	$—	$ —	$ 1,06
Accounts receivable and accrued revenue, net	841	984	—	—	1,82
Risk management assets	414	—	249 (a)	—	66
Inventories	157	321	—	—	47
	2,375	1,409	249	—	4,03
Capital Assets, net	8,171	11,867	—	1,382 (a)	21,42
Investments and Other Assets	313	822	(59) (b)	—	1,07
Goodwill	—	—	—	2,704 (a)	2,70
	$10,859	$14,098	$190	$4,086	$29,23
Liabilities and Shareholders' Equity					
Current Liabilities					
Accounts payable and accrued liabilities	$ 990	$ 1,043	$—	$ 150 (a)	$ 2,18
Income taxes payable	656	242	—	—	89
Risk management liabilities	378	—	163 (a)	—	54
Current portion of other liabilities	40	—	—	—	4
Current portion of long-term debt	160	49	—	—	20
	2,224	1,334	163	150	3,87
Long-Term Debt	2,118	3,658	—	61 (a)	6,28
				449 (e)	
Project Financing Debt	—	584	—	11 (a)	59
Other Liabilities	419	204	—	—	62
Future Income Taxes	2,060	2,361	37 (a)	490 (a)	4,94
	6,821	8,141	200	1,161	16,32
Shareholders' Equity					
Preferred securities	126	859	—	53 (a)	58
				(449) (e)	
Share capital	196	3,052	—	(3,052) (a)	8,66
			—	8,468 (a)	
Paid in surplus	27	—	—		2
Retained earnings	3,689	1,788	49 (a)	(1,837) (a)	3,630
			(59) (b)		
Foreign currency translation adjustment	—	258	—	(258) (a)	—
	4,038	5,957	(10)	2,925	12,91
	$10,859	$14,098	$190	$4,086	$29,23

ENCANA CORPORATION
PRO FORMA CONSOLIDATED STATEMENT OF CASH FROM OPERATING ACTIVITIES

(Unaudited)
($ millions, except per share amounts)

	PanCanadian Year Ended December 31, 2001	AEC Year Ended December 31, 2001	Pro Forma Adjustments Note 3	Pro Forma Adjustments Note 4	EnCana Pro Forma Consolidated
Operating Activities					
Net earnings	$1,304	$ 824	$31	$(21) (e)	$2,138
Depreciation, depletion and amortization	856	1,252		—	2,108
Future income taxes	144	29	37 (a)	—	210
Gain on sale of assets	—	(238)		—	(238)
Cash tax on sale of assets	—	57		—	57
Other	2	99	18 (b)	—	119
Cash Flow	$2,306	$2,023	$86	$(21)	$4,394
Net change in deferred items	(96)	—			(96)
Net change in non-cash working capital	564	477	(86) (a)	150 (a)	1,105
Cash from Operating Activities	$2,774	$2,500	$—	$129	$5,403
Cash Flow per Common Share					
Basic	$ 9.02	$13.55			$ 9.28
Diluted	$ 8.82	$12.57			$ 9.08

ENCANA CORPORATION
(formerly PanCanadian Energy Corporation)
NOTES TO PRO FORMA CONSOLIDATED FINANCIAL STATEMENTS
December 31, 2001
(Unaudited)

1. BASIS OF PRESENTATION

These unaudited Pro Forma Consolidated Financial Statements have been prepared for inclusion in the Joint Information Circular concerning the merger of Alberta Energy Company Ltd. (AEC) and PanCanadian Energy Corporation (PanCanadian).

The unaudited Pro Forma Consolidated Financial Statements have been prepared from:

(a) PanCanadian's audited consolidated financial statements as at and for the year ended December 31, 2001

(b) AEC's audited consolidated financial statements as at and for the year ended December 31, 2001

In the opinion of Management of both PanCanadian and AEC these unaudited Pro Forma Consolidated Financial Statements include all adjustments necessary for fair presentation in accordance with Canadian generally accepted accounting principles. The unaudited Pro Forma Consolidated Balance sheet gives effect to the transaction described in Note 4 as if it had occurred on December 31, 2001. The unaudited Pro Forma Consolidated Statements of Earnings and Cash from Operating Activities give effect to the transaction as if it occurred on January 1, 2001.

These unaudited Pro Forma Consolidated Financial Statements may not be indicative of the results that actually would have occurred if the events reflected therein had been in effect on the dates indicated or of the results that may be obtained in the future.

These unaudited Pro Forma Consolidated Financial Statements should be read in conjunction with the consolidated financial statements of PanCanadian and AEC contained in the Joint Information Circular.

2. PRINCIPLES OF CONSOLIDATION

These unaudited Pro Forma Consolidated Financial Statements have been prepared on the basis that PanCanadian will account for the transaction as a purchase of AEC using the purchase method of accounting. Accordingly, the assets and liabilities of AEC will be recorded at their estimated fair value.

In completing the transaction, PanCanadian will issue 1.472 Common Shares for each issued and outstanding Common Share of AEC.

3. PRO FORMA ACCOUNTING AND PRESENTATION ADJUSTMENTS AND ASSUMPTIONS

PanCanadian and AEC prepare their consolidated financial statements using similar accounting policies and presentation with the exception of the items noted below. The following accounting policy and financial statement presentation adjustments have been made to conform the accounting.

(a) Mark-to-Market Accounting for Midstream and Marketing Activities

PanCanadian accounts for its Midstream and Marketing activities using mark-to-market accounting. Certain of AEC's activities related to Midstream and Marketing, specifically purchased gas marketing and gas storage optimization activities, have been restated to a mark-to-market basis of accounting.

(b) Accounting for Foreign Currency Translation

Effective December 31, 2001, AEC early adopted the amendments to the Canadian accounting standard for foreign currency translation. As required by the standard, all prior periods were restated. PanCanadian's financial statements have been adjusted to reflect the early adoption of this standard.

(c) Financial Statement Presentation Adjustments

(i) To be consistent with PanCanadian's presentation, revenues associated with AEC's purchased gas activity have been reclassified from Upstream revenue.

(ii) To be consistent with AEC's presentation, PanCanadian's Transportation and selling expenses have been reclassified from Upstream and Midstream and Marketing revenues and Cost of product purchased.

(iii) To be consistent with AEC's presentation, PanCanadian's Operating expenses and Cost of product purchased have been reclassified from Direct expenses.

(iv) To be consistent with AEC's presentation, PanCanadian's Provision for doubtful accounts has been reclassified from Upstream revenue ($5 million) and Other revenue ($6 million).

(v) To be consistent with AEC's presentation, PanCanadian's interest revenue has been reclassified from Other revenue.

(vi) To be consistent with AEC's presentation, PanCanadian's net foreign exchange gain has been reclassified from Other revenue.

4. PRO FORMA ACQUISITION ADJUSTMENTS AND ASSUMPTIONS

(a) The purchase of AEC for aggregate consideration of $8,618 million comprising 217.6 million Common Shares of PanCanadian based on the exchange ratio of 1.472 PCE Common Shares for each AEC Common Share.

		$ Million
Calculation and preliminary allocation of purchase price:		
PanCanadian Common Shares issued to AEC shareholders (million)	217.6	
Price of PanCanadian Common Shares ($ per Common Share)	38.43	
Value of PanCanadian Common shares issued		$ 8,364
Fair value of AEC Share Options exchanged for Share Options of EnCana Corporation		104
Transaction costs		150
Total Purchase Price		8,618
Plus: Fair value of liabilities assumed by PanCanadian		
Current liabilities		1,497
Long-term debt		3,719
Project financing debt		595
Preferred securities		423
Capital securities		489
Other non-current liabilities		204
Future income taxes		2,888
Total Purchase Price and Liabilities assumed		$18,433
Fair value of assets acquired:		
Current assets		$ 1,658
Capital assets		13,249
Other non-current assets		822
Goodwill		2,704
Total fair value of assets acquired		$18,433

(b) The number of issued and outstanding AEC Common Shares on the date of the transaction has been assumed to be 147.9 million. This assumes that none of the outstanding options to purchase AEC Common Shares are exercised and converted to AEC Common Shares prior to the date of the transaction.

(c) The number of issued and outstanding options to purchase AEC common shares on the date of the transaction has been assumed to be 9.9 million. The fair value of these options has been included in the calculation of the purchase price. The fair value of these options was estimated using the Black–Scholes option pricing model with the same assumptions as disclosed in Note 13 of the Notes to the AEC 2001 Consolidated Financial Statements. The fair value of these options was calculated to be $104 million.

(d) The total purchase price includes the value of the PanCanadian Common Shares to be issued to the AEC shareholders plus the cash costs of completing the transaction. These costs, estimated to be $150 million, include investment advisor fees, legal and accounting fees, printing and mailing costs and other transaction related costs. These costs have been added to Accounts payable and accrued liabilities on the unaudited Pro Forma Consolidated Balance Sheet.

(e) Included in AEC's Preferred securities are $430 million principal amount of Capital Securities which are convertible, at the option of the holder, into Common Shares of AEC. AEC also has the option to repay both interest and principal through the issuance of Common Shares. These securities are treated as equity for accounting purposes and distributions in respect of these securities, net of income tax, are charged directly to Retained earnings. Immediately prior to the closing of the transaction, AEC will supplement the Trust Indenture covering these securities to remove AEC's option to pay interest and principal through the issuance of Common Shares. With the removal of this option, these securities are treated as Long-Term Debt and distributions are recorded as interest expense in the unaudited Pro Forma Consolidated Financial Statements.

(f) Future income tax expense has been adjusted for the impact of the items noted above that affect current year net earnings.

(g) No adjustment has been made to reflect operating synergies that may be realized as a result of the transaction.

(h) The increase in the carrying value of Capital Assets relates to unproved properties and therefore no adjustment has been made to Depreciation, depletion and amortization.

The purchase price allocation is preliminary and may change as a result of several factors, including:

- changes in the fair values of AEC's assets and liabilities between December 31, 2001 and the closing of the transaction;

- actual number of AEC Common Shares and options to acquire AEC Common Shares outstanding at the date of the closing;

- actual transaction costs incurred.

These changes will not be known until the completion of the transaction. However, Management of PanCanadian and AEC do not believe that the final purchase price allocation will differ materially from that presented in the unaudited Pro Forma Consolidated Financial Statements.

5. GOODWILL

The preliminary purchase price allocation includes approximately $2.7 billion of Goodwill. As required under Canadian generally accepted accounting principles, goodwill will not be amortized into income. However, goodwill will be subject to an annual impairment review and should there be an impairment, that amount would be charged to income.

As stated in Note 4, the allocation of the purchase price presented is preliminary. EnCana will finalize the purchase price allocation after closing the transaction. Prior to that time, Management of PanCanadian and AEC may determine that there are intangible assets acquired in the transaction, separate and apart from goodwill. To the extent that such intangibles, if any, have definite useful lives, the value assigned to them will be amortized into income over those useful lives. Although the amount allocated to such intangibles, if any, will not be known until the closing of the transaction, Management of PanCanadian and AEC do not believe that any such value, or the related amortization expense, would have a material effect on the unaudited Pro Forma Consolidated Financial Statements presented.

C16-3 Rogers Communications and the Blue Jays: Equity accounting

Included in note 6 ("Investments") of Rogers Communications Inc.'s 2001 audited financial statements is the information regarding the Toronto Blue Jays Baseball Club, which follows.

ROGERS COMMUNICATIONS INC.
www.rogers.ca

TORONTO BLUE JAYS
www.bluejays.mlb. com

Required:

1. Rogers acquired an 80% interest in the Blue Jays effective December 31, 2000 for cash of $163,898,000, net. Prepare a plausible journal entry to account for the transaction. Should Rogers consolidate the Blue Jays, as of December 31, 2000?

2. Explain why Rogers stopped consolidating the Blue Jays on April 1, 2001. Is the evidence provided for deconsolidating the Blue Jays as of April 1, 2001, and using the equity method, convincing? Explain.

3. Rogers recorded 100% of the Blue Jays' 2001 operating losses, even though Rogers only owned 80%, and equity accounted for its investment. Explain.

4. Reconstruct all the journal entries that Rogers likely recorded to account for the option to acquire the minority interest.

A. INVESTMENTS ACCOUNTED FOR BY THE EQUITY METHOD

i. Toronto Blue Jays Baseball Club

Effective December 31, 2000, the Company purchased an 80% interest in the Toronto Blue Jays Baseball Club ("Blue Jays") for cash of $163,898,000, net of cash acquired.

Effective April 1, 2001, Rogers Telecommunications Ltd. ("RTL"), a company controlled by the controlling shareholder of the Company, acquired the Class A Preferred shares of the subsidiary of RCI that owns the Blue Jays ("Blue Jays Holdco") for $30,000,000. These Class A Preferred shares are voting, redeemable for cash of $30,000,000 plus any accrued, unpaid dividends, at the option of Blue Jays Holdco at any time after September 14, 2004. Any such redemption requires the consent of a committee of the board of Blue Jays Holdco comprising directors that are not related to RTL, RTL's affiliates or its controlling shareholder and requires the prior written consent of the Board of Directors of the Company. These Class A Preferred shares may be acquired by the Company at its option at any time; however, the Company does not intend to exercise this option in the foreseeable future. The Class A Preferred shares pay cumulative dividends at a rate of 9.167% per annum. For periods up to July 31, 2004, Blue Jays Holdco may satisfy the cumulative dividends on its Class A Preferred shares in kind by transferring to RTL income tax loss carryforwards, having an agreed value equal to the amount of the dividends.

During 2001, the Company contributed $52,300,000 to the Blue Jays to finance a portion of its operating losses. It is the Company's intention to continue to finance cash requirements of the Blue Jays in 2002, which are expected to be approximately $55,000,000.

The Company has the option to acquire the minority interest in the Blue Jays at any time, and the minority interest owner has the right to require the Company to purchase its interest at any time after December 15, 2003, for approximately $45,000,000 (US$28,000,000) plus interest at 9% per annum from December 15, 2000. This obligation has been recorded as a liability by the Company.

As a result of the issuance of the Class A Preferred shares of Blue Jays Holdco to RTL, the Company no longer has voting control of the Blue Jays. Accordingly, effective April 1, 2001, the Company accounts for its investment in the Blue Jays using the equity method and the Blue Jays are no longer consolidated.

The 20% minority interest owner of the Blue Jays is not required to fund operating losses of the Blue Jays and, as a result, as required under GAAP, the Company has recorded 100% of the operating losses of the Blue Jays in 2001. During the period April 1 to December 31, 2001, the Company recorded equity losses of $82,600,000. The results of operations of the Blue Jays for the three months ended March 31, 2001, are consolidated in the statement of income of the Company.

Condensed consolidated financial information of Blue Jays Holdco, after giving pro forma effect to the acquisition adjustments to allocate the cost of the Company's purchase of the Blue Jays, is presented below:

(In thousands of dollars)

Year ended December 31	2001
Revenue	$ 125,086
Operating expenses	(202,018)
	(76,932)
Depreciation and amortization	(19,893)
Interest expense	(1,503)
Loss for the year	$ (98,328)

(In thousands of dollars)

As at December 31	2001
Assets	
Cash and accounts receivable	$ 24,049
Deferred compensation	27,625
Goodwill and other intangible assets	203,442
Other assets	23,950
	$ 279,066
Liabilities and Shareholders' Equity	
Accounts payable and accrued liabilities	$ 21,076
Deferred obligations	50,442
	71,518
Shareholders' equity	207,548
	$ 279,066

Endnotes

1. We use Enron, of course, as a sort of theme or code word for recent financial reporting failures in general.

2. As a German company, Deutsche Telekom is actually prohibited from using the equity method by German GAAP. If it were a Canadian company, Deutsche Telekom would be required to use the equity method. This is one area where German and Canadian GAAP currently differ.

3. But such "consolidation" journal entries do not go through any company's books; they are just used to help construct the consolidated statements.

4. But in the United States, a series of technical rules were used to determine if pooling was appropriate (for example, the business combination had to be accomplished by an exchange of shares). Many U.S. companies strived to comply with the pooling rules, since the resulting consolidated statements usually portrayed a better picture than purchase consolidation accounting.

5. Section 1650, "Foreign Currency Translation." Although our discussion centres on consolidation of a foreign subsidiary, the rules described here must also be used in conjunction with the equity method when the parent owns between about 20% and 50% of a foreign company (i.e., exerts significant influence).

17
Cash Flow Statement

LEARNING OBJECTIVES
After studying this chapter, you should be able to:

1. Identify the major sources and uses of cash reported in the operating, investing, and financing sections of the cash flow statement

2. Understand why accrual net income and operating cash flows differ and the factors that explain this difference

3. Distinguish between the direct and indirect methods of determining cash flows from operations

4. Prepare a cash flow statement from comparative balance sheet data, an income statement, and other financial information

5 Understand why changes in balance sheet accounts over a year may not reconcile to the corresponding account changes included in the cash flow statement

Ode to Cash Flow
Though my bottom line is black, I am flat upon my back,
My cash flows out and my customers pay slow.
The growth of my receivables is almost unbelievable;
The result is certain—unremitting woe!
And I hear the banker utter an ominous low mutter,
"Watch cash flow!" [1]

As the above poem suggests, accrual earnings may not always provide a reliable measure of enterprise performance and financial health. There may be several reasons for this. Accrual accounting is often based upon subjective judgments that can introduce measurement error and uncertainty into the reported earnings number. Examples include estimates of uncollectible receivables, useful lives of assets, and future pension and health-care benefits. One-time writeoffs and restructuring charges require subjective judgments that can adversely affect the quality of the reported earnings number as a reliable indicator of the long-run performance of a company. Moreover, managers can readily manipulate accrual income by postponing discretionary expenditures for research and development or advertising or by purposeful last-in, first-out (LIFO) dipping. And widespread publicity involving Enron, WorldCom, Nortel, and many other companies has made analysts wary of accrual accounting income numbers.

For these reasons, analysts must scrutinize a firm's cash flows—not just its accrual earnings—to evaluate its performance and creditworthiness. A significant difference between accrual earnings and operating cash flow may be a "red flag" that signals distortions of reported profits or impending financial difficulties.

Equity analysts are interested in operating cash flows because they believe a firm's value ultimately depends upon the discounted present value of its expected future cash flows. Recent operating cash flows are sometimes used as a jumping-off point for generating forecasts of expected future operating cash flows. Thus, cash flows can provide useful information for assessing equity values.

Commercial lenders monitor a firm's operating cash flows because they believe such cash flows provide the resources for periodic interest payments and the eventual repayment of principal. Firms experiencing low or negative operating cash flows may be poor credit risks.

Investment bankers scrutinize operating cash flows before deciding whether to underwrite a debt or equity issue. They know that the ultimate purchasers of the securities will assess the attractiveness of the securities based, in part, upon the firms' expected operating cash flows.

Statement Format

> "Funds" is a generic term used to describe liquid assets—those readily convertible into cash or cash equivalents. The two most common definitions of funds are *working capital* and *cash*. A funds flow statement shows the inflows and outflows of funds as defined for that statement.

Some form of **funds flow statement** has been required under GAAP since the early 1970s. The purpose of this statement is to clearly explain why the liquid assets of the company increased or decreased during the reporting period and to explain changes in **working capital**—current assets minus current liabilities. But recent GAAP have mandated that firms provide a **cash flow statement** that explains the sources and uses of cash.[2] Firms are required to disclose cash flows generated (or used) from three distinct types of activities:

1. **Operating cash flows** result from events or transactions that enter into the determination of net income—that is, transactions related to the production and delivery of goods and services to customers. In effect, operating cash flows are the cash-basis revenues and expenses of a company.
2. **Investing cash flows** result from the purchase or sale of productive assets like plant and equipment, from the purchase or sale of marketable securities (government bonds or stocks and bonds issued by other companies), and from the acquisitions and divestitures of other companies.
3. **Financing cash flows** result when a company sells its own shares or bonds, pays dividends or buys back its own shares (treasury shares), or borrows money and repays the amounts borrowed.

Section 1540 allows firms the option of choosing between two alternative formats for presenting cash flows from *operating* activities: (1) the **direct approach** and (2) the **indirect approach** (although the direct approach is encouraged in this section). Each of these alternative formats is illustrated on the following pages.

The Direct Approach

The *CICA Handbook* revision to Section 1540, "Cash Flow Statements," permits either the direct or the indirect approach to presenting cash flows from operating activities. Under the direct approach, the actual cash amounts due to sales activity are disclosed, along with cash payments for various operating expenditures. In contrast, the indirect approach adopts a reconciliation format, in which the income number, prepared according to the procedures of accrual accounting and GAAP, is adjusted for noncash items and thus reconciled to the cash flow from operating activities number. The *Handbook* indicates why the AcSB prefers the direct method:

Enterprises are encouraged to report such cash flows using the direct method. The direct method provides information which may be useful in estimating future cash flows and which is not available under the indirect method. (Section 1540, para. 21)

But the direct method is not currently popular in Canada; in fact, only one of the 200 companies surveyed in *Financial Reporting in Canada*'s 1998 edition has used the direct method in recent years (p. 116): the uranium producer Cameco Corporation, of Saskatoon. In the 2002 edition of *Financial Reporting in Canada*, the only example of a company using the direct method is Pan American Silver Corp. of Vancouver. We will use Cameco's 1997 consolidated cash flow statement to illustrate the direct approach. (Cameco switched to the indirect method in 1998.)

Exhibit 17.1 presents the 1997 cash flow statement for Cameco, which the company calls "Consolidated Statements of Changes in Cash Resources." The standard breakdown into operating, investing, and financing activities is provided. Operating

CAMECO CORPORATION
www.cameco.com

PAN AMERICAN SILVER CORP.
www. panamericansilver. com

Exhibit 17.1 CAMECO CORPORATION

Example of "Direct Approach"

Consolidated Statements of Changes in Cash Resources

(thousands)	For the Year Ended December 31,		
	1997	1996	1995
Operating activities:			
Sale of products and services	$ 642,148	$ 570,808	$ 377,400
Products and services purchased	(396,068)	(331,319)	(202,202)
Administration and R&D	(32,389)	(24,972)	(19,898)
Exploration	(31,006)	(28,872)	(16,561)
Income taxes	(6,425)	(4,802)	(3,586)
Interest	(14,154)	(2,940)	(2,632)
Cash provided by operations (notes 15, 24)	162,106	177,903	132,521
Investing activities:			
Additions to property, plant, and equipment	(126,143)	(168,141)	(175,212)
Additions to long-term receivables and investments	(49,042)	(27,730)	(77,470)
Repayment of additional subordinated loan	—	31,591	—
Acquisition of net business assets	(155,975)	—	—
Proceeds on sale of property, plant, and equipment	6,315	2,227	200
Cash used in investing	(324,845)	(162,053)	(252,482)
Financing activities:			
Increase in debt	150,412	88,415	189,914
Repayment of debt	(63,699)	(84,859)	(55,020)
Issue of shares, net of issue costs	198,188	6,948	5,415
Dividends	(27,043)	(26,393)	(26,166)
Cash provided by (used in) financing	257,858	(15,889)	114,143
Increase (decrease) in cash during the year	95,119	(39)	(5,818)
Cash at beginning of year	14,603	14,642	20,460
Cash at end of year	$ 109,722	$ 14,603	$ 14,642

The specific categories suggested by AcSB in para. .16 of Section 1540 include:
(a) cash collected from customers (including lessees and licensees)
(b) interest and dividends received
(c) other operating cash receipts
(d) cash paid to employees and other suppliers of goods and services
(e) interest paid
(f) income taxes paid
(g) other operating cash payments

activities generated a positive cash flow of $162,106,000. Investing activities resulted in a net cash outflow of $324,845,000, and most of this total was due to capital expenditures for property, plant, and equipment, and to investment in other businesses. The company raised, on a net basis, $257,858,000 in financing, through debt and issue of shares. Thus, Cameco's overall cash position increased by about $95 million in 1997 ($162 − $325 + $258).

In 1997, Cameco followed the direct approach to presenting cash flows from operations. The direct approach requires that firms report major classes of gross cash receipts (cash revenues) and gross cash payments (cash expenses). Note that "Interest" is shown as a component of cash flow from operating activities. This treatment is in accordance with Section 1540. Many financial analysts and other statement users believe that interest paid should be included as part of cash flows from financing activities while interest received should be included with cash flows from investing activities. But GAAP classify items as elements of cash flows from operating activities because cash flows from operating activities should reflect the cash effects of transactions and other events that enter into the determination of net income.

Cameco discloses cash "Sale of products and services" of $642,148,000 on its 1997 cash flow statement. This number differs from the accrual accounting revenue number of $642,945,000, which is reported on Cameco's 1997 income statement and shown in Exhibit 17.2. There are several possible reasons for this difference, including the following:

1. Some 1997 credit sales made late in the year may not have been collected in cash by year-end.
2. Some 1997 credit sales were made to customers who ultimately were unable to pay their balance due.
3. During 1997, cash was received for payment on accounts receivable generated from sales in prior years.

For analogous reasons, the cash "Products and services purchased" of $396,068,000 on Cameco's 1997 cash flow statement (Exhibit 17.1) differs from the sum of "Products and services sold," "Administration," "Exploration," and "Research and Development" reported on the accrual-basis income statement (Exhibit 17.2). Similarly, the other cash flow and income numbers differ.

Overall, Exhibits 17.1 and 17.2 show that Cameco generated positive operating cash flows of $162,106,000 in 1997, while its accrual-basis income was considerably smaller—that is, $81,979,000. What are the major reasons for the rather large discrepancy between Cameco's net income and operating cash flows? The answer is found in the reconciliation of net income to cash from operations, which is reported in note 15 of the company's 1997 financial statements and shown in Exhibit 17.3. This schedule illustrates the determination of operating cash flows under the indirect method.

The Indirect Approach

The indirect approach begins with the accrual-basis net income (before extraordinary items)[3] and adjusts for:

- items *included* in accrual-basis net income that *did not* affect cash in the current period, such as:

    1. noncash revenues or gains (e.g., revenues earned but not received in cash, and gains on disposal of fixed assets)

Exhibit 17.2 CAMECO CORPORATION

Consolidated Statements of Earnings

(thousands)	For the Year Ended December 31,		
	1997	**1996**	**1995**
Revenue from:			
Products and services	$642,945	$590,861	$395,271
Expenses:			
Products and services sold	316,108	298,205	190,210
Depreciation, depletion, and reclamation*	122,676	94,974	67,481
Administration	27,213	23,255	19,617
Exploration	32,023	29,223	16,991
Research and development	1,893	3,334	1,629
Interest (note 13)	(7,962)	(3,396)	(4,412)
	491,951	445,595	291,516
Earnings from operations (note 24)	150,994	145,266	103,755
Other income (expense)	(3,958)	(2,422)	1,858
Earnings before income taxes	147,036	142,844	105,613
Income taxes (note 14)	65,057	5,311	3,528
Net earnings (note 24)	$ 81,979	$137,533	$102,085

*Author's Note: "Reclamation" refers to Cameco's practice, as a mining company, of charging estimates of future mine site decommissioning and reclamation costs against income. Cameco uses the units-of-production method to provide for these future costs.

2. noncash expenses or losses (e.g., depreciation and amortization, expenses accrued but not paid in cash, and losses on disposal of fixed assets)

- items excluded from accrual-basis income that did affect operating cash flows in the current period, such as:

3. cash inflows (revenues) received but not recognized as earned in the current period (e.g., rent received in advance and collections on account)
4. cash outflows (expenses) paid but not recognized for accrual purposes in the current period (e.g., prepaid insurance and payments on account)

The indirect approach is used by the overwhelming majority of public companies, for two reasons:

1. The indirect approach is easier for firms to implement because it relies exclusively on data already available in the accrual accounts.
2. The indirect approach is more familiar to many accountants because this format was widely used in the changes in working capital statement that preceded current GAAP's cash flow statement.

We'll show with Exhibit 17.3 how the indirect approach reconciles accrual accounting net income ($81,979,000 in Exhibit 17.2) with cash flow from operations ($162,106,000 in Exhibit 17.1). Each of the reconciling items is discussed individually.

Exhibit 17.3 CAMECO CORPORATION

Footnote to 1997 Financial Statements

15. Reconciliation of Net Earnings to Cash Provided by Operations

(thousands)	1997	1996	1995
Net earnings	$ 81,979	$137,533	$102,085
Add non-cash items:			
1 * Depreciation, depletion and reclamation	122,676	94,974	67,481
2 Deferred income taxes	58,847	—	—
3 Other	(3,764)	1,251	(2,729)
	259,738	233,758	166,837
Changes in non-cash items relating to operations:			
4 Accounts receivable	(19,669)	(28,844)	(21,247)
5 Long-term receivables	(14,643)	(6,374)	(5,915)
6 Inventories	(114,498)	(1,078)	(26,094)
7 Supplies and prepaid expenses	(8,757)	(4,814)	(1,842)
8 Accounts payable and accrued liabilities	24,362	(761)	22,021
9 Other liabilities	19,136	(12,518)	551
10 Deferred revenue	22,137	2,201	(659)
11 Reclamation	(3,550)	(2,809)	(1,103)
12 Other	(2,150)	(858)	(28)
Cash provided by operations	**$162,106**	**$177,903**	**$132,521**

*Author's Note: The highlighted numbers have been added by the authors for explanatory purposes.

Items 1 through 3 represent amounts included in Cameco's net income figure *that did not have a cash flow effect*—that is, they did not cause cash to increase or decrease during the year. Since they did not have a cash flow effect, the accrual-basis net income must be adjusted for these items to arrive at cash flows from operations.

1 **Depreciation, Depletion and Reclamation** This is the most common example of an indirect method adjustment. During 1997, Cameco made the following entry for depreciation and amortization expense:

DR   Depreciation, depletion, and reclamation $122,676,000
     CR   Accumulated depreciation and amortization
     (and in the case of a mining company like
     Cameco, "Provision for reclamation") $122,676,000

While the debit reduced income, the credit did not represent a cash outflow. Hence, this typical noncash expense causes "Net income" to diverge from "Cash from operating activities." That's why amortization and such similar expense items must be added back to income in the indirect method statement as a reconciling item.

2 **Deferred Income Taxes** Cameco's taxable income was less than its book income in 1997 due to a variety of temporary differences (Chapter 13). As a consequence, the credit balance in the deferred income taxes account increased during the year. When

this happens, the debit to income tax expense exceeds the cash taxes payable and probably paid. Thus, the increase in deferred taxes over the year must be added to the accrual-basis income, since reported income tax expense *overstated* the actual cash outflow for taxes. Also, keep in mind that the "deferred tax" terminology would now refer to "future income tax assets" or "future income tax liabilities" (see Chapter 13).

3 Other Several items are possible. For example, Cameco may have investments in affiliates and these investments are accounted for using the equity method (Chapter 16). If so, Cameco recognized its proportionate share of their income by making the following entry:

| DR | Investments | $3,764,000 | |
| | CR Investment income | | $3,764,000 |

The debit increased net income *but did not increase the consolidated cash account.*

Items **4** through **12** represent amounts that were included in the net income figure for which the *income effect either exceeds or falls below the cash flow effect.* Because the income effect and the cash flow effect differ, some adjustments must appear in the reconciliation, and these adjustments are explained as follows.

4 Change (Increase) in Accounts Receivable During 1997, Cameco's accounts receivable increased by $19,669,000. This means that sales on account (accrual-basis revenue) exceeded cash collections on account (cash-basis revenue). Accordingly, a *subtraction* must be made from accrual-basis income to arrive at the total cash provided by operating activities. Similar logic holds for item **5**, "Long-term receivables."

6 Change (Increase) in Inventories Cameco's inventories increased by $114,498,000 during fiscal 1997. This adjustment may be explained by recalling from introductory financial accounting that:

$$\text{Cost of sales} = \text{Opening inventory} + \text{Purchases} - \text{Closing inventory} \qquad [A]$$

and that:

$$\text{Opening accounts payable} + \text{Purchases} - \text{Payments} = \text{Closing accounts payable} \quad [B]$$

Let ΔI represent the change (increase) in inventory, that is (Closing inventory – Opening inventory), and $\Delta A/P$ represent the change (increase) in accounts payable, that is (Closing accounts payable – Opening accounts payable).

Then [A] becomes (after some rearranging):

$$\Delta I + \text{Cost of sales} = \text{Purchases}$$

[B] becomes (after some rearranging):

$$\Delta A/P + \text{Payments} = \text{Purchases}$$

Therefore:

$$\Delta I + \text{Cost of sales} = \Delta A/P + \text{Payments}$$

and:

$$\text{Payments} = \text{Cost of sales} + \Delta I - \Delta A/P$$

This last equation explains how the cost of sales number, which is an accrual number, is converted to the actual cash outflows, or payments. If inventories increased over the accounting period (that is, if ΔI is greater than zero), this has the effect of making payments exceed the accrual cost of sales number, and helps us understand why, in reconciling item 6 in Exhibit 17.3, an increase in inventory is *deducted* as we go from net income to cash flow from operations.

Also, if Accounts payable increased over the accounting period (that is, if $\Delta A/P$ is greater than zero), actual cash payments will be *less than* Cost of sales—this explains reconciling item 8 (at least part of 8, since Cameco has grouped "Accrued liabilities" in with payables in its Exhibit 17.3 disclosure).

Items 7, 9, 10, 11, and 12 have similar explanations.

Both the direct and indirect approaches for computing net cash provided by operating activities will obviously report the same number—$162,106,000 in Cameco's 1997 annual report. Those who prefer the direct approach claim that this method discloses operating cash flows by category—inflows from customers, outflows to suppliers, etc. They contend that this categorization facilitates cash flow predictions. For example, assume that an analyst expects product selling prices to increase by 6% in the ensuing year. The direct method's disclosure of cash received from customers could then be multiplied by 106% to construct next year's cash forecast. (There is no similarly easy way to incorporate the expectation of a 6% price increase in the indirect method.)

Analysts who prefer the indirect approach do so because the size and direction of the items reconciling income to operating cash flow provide a rough yardstick for evaluating the quality of earnings. When a company reports relatively high accounting income but simultaneously experiences low or negative cash flow from operations, this situation is considered a sign of low-quality earnings that are not sustainable. For example, if the excess of income over cash flow is accompanied by a large buildup in accounts receivable, this increase could indicate that the company is playing revenue recognition games—that is, the receivables buildup may have occurred because the recorded amounts reflect an aggressive policy of shipping unwanted merchandise to distributors or of making sales that may never be collected to customers with marginal creditworthiness.

Firms are required to separately disclose the amount of interest paid. Consequently, those who believe interest expense represents a cash flow from financing activities will always have sufficient information available to reclassify this item out of cash flows from operating activities for firms using the indirect approach.

One additional difficulty confronting analysts using Section 1540 disclosures relates to the treatment of income taxes. Recollect from Chapter 2 that intraperiod income tax allocation is followed in constructing the income statement—that is, the income tax expense associated with income from continuing operations is separately disclosed. Items not included in the computation of income from continuing operations (such as extraordinary items and the cumulative effects of changes in accounting principles) are reflected *net* of their associated income tax effects. This is done to facilitate predictions by statement users. The tax expense associated with the presumably recurring income from continuing operations is reported separately from the tax expense associated with items appearing below income from continuing operations. Section 1540 urges, but does not require, firms to treat *cash* outflows for income taxes in the same way. So the entire amount of taxes paid in cash is included in the "Cash flows from operating activities" computation even though some of the taxes relate, for example, to gains on sales of assets whose gross cash flows are included in the "Cash flows from investing activities" section of the statement. The failure to differentiate tax cash flows by type (those pertaining to income from continuing operations versus other items) complicates forecasts of future cash flows.

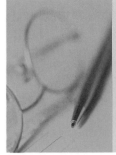

Recap

The cash flow statement provides a summary of a firm's operating, investing, and financing activities that explains its change in cash position for the period. Operating cash flows can be presented using either the direct or indirect approach. The direct approach details major sources of cash receipts and major categories of cash expenditures. The indirect approach begins with accrual earnings and adjusts for (1) items included in accrual-basis income that did not affect cash and (2) items excluded from accrual earnings that did affect operating cash flows.

Other Elements of the Cash Flow Statement

Let's return to Exhibit 17.1. Cameco's cash flow statement illustrates the typical range of items included in the "Investing activities" and "Financing activities" sections of the statement. The items included are relatively straightforward, and there should be no difficulties in interpreting these disclosures. For example, Cameco shows investing cash outflows in 1997 for purchases of property and equipment ($126 million) and investments in business acquisitions ($156 million). Direct cash inflows from investing activities resulted from the sale of property, plant, and equipment ($6 million).

Financing cash inflows resulted from the issuance of debt and of shares. Major financing cash outflows occurred for the repayment of debt ($64 million) and dividends ($27 million).

Investing and financing transactions that do not require the use of cash or cash equivalents are to be excluded from the cash flow statement (Section 1540, para. .46). To illustrate, let's consider a situation in which a company acquired the use of a factory building by signing a long-term capital lease. The accounting entry is:

DR Leased building under capital lease   XXX
    CR Obligation under capital lease   XXX

This transaction results in both an increase in an investment (the property rights in the building) and an increase in a liability to finance the asset. Incurring the obligation means both that *future* cash outflows will take place as the periodic lease payments are made and that the factory building will itself help generate *future* cash inflows. However, cash is initially unaffected by this transaction. Because cash is initially unaffected, Section 1540 does not include either the increase in the investment or the increase in the financing within the cash flow statement. These transactions are excluded to avoid complicating the statement. However, since the ultimate effect of assuming debt to acquire an asset is identical to borrowing cash to buy the asset, the AcSB felt that such transactions must be disclosed in a separate schedule or as a footnote to the cash flow statement.

> Such transactions are typically referred to as simultaneous financing and investing activities.

Preparing the Cash Flow Statement

This section illustrates the procedures for preparing a cash flow statement. Exhibit 17.4 (a) and (b) provides comparative 2001–2002 balance sheet data, a 2002 income statement, and selected additional information for Burris Products Corporation.

Exhibit 17.4 BURRIS PRODUCTS CORPORATION

Comparative Balance Sheets, 2002 Income Statement, and Additional Information

Comparative Balance Sheets	December 31, 2002	2001	Increase or Decrease	
Cash	$ 25,000	$ 33,000	$ 8,000	decrease
Accounts receivable	171,000	180,000	9,000	decrease
Inventory	307,000	295,000	12,000	increase
Land	336,000	250,000	86,000	increase
Buildings and equipment	1,628,000	1,430,000	198,000	increase
Accumulated amortization	(653,000)	(518,000)	135,000	increase
	$ 1,814,000	$ 1,670,000		
Accounts payable	$ 163,000	$ 160,000	$ 3,000	increase
Customer advance deposits	99,000	110,000	11,000	decrease
Bonds payable	500,000	500,000	–0–	
Discount on bonds payable	(66,000)	(70,000)	4,000	decrease
Future income tax	100,000	94,000	6,000	increase
Common shares	850,000	800,000	50,000	increase
Retained earnings	168,000	76,000	92,000	increase
	$ 1,814,000	$ 1,670,000		

(a)

2002 Income Statement

Sales revenues	$ 3,030,000
Cost of goods sold	(2,526,625)
Amortization expense	(158,000)
Sales commissions (all cash)	(34,000)
Interest expense	(44,000)
Gain on sale of equipment	17,000
	$ 284,375
Income tax expense	(102,375)
Net income	$ 182,000

(b)

Additional information:

1. Equipment with a cost of $63,000 and a book value of $40,000 was sold for $57,000.

2. Cash dividends of $90,000 were paid in 2002.

Reviewing the comparative balance sheets in Exhibit 17.4 (a) shows that the cash balance decreased by $8,000 during 2002. The purpose of a cash flow statement is to explain the underlying *causes* for this $8,000 change in the cash balance. Recall that the causes for change arise from operating, investing, and financing activities.

Constructing a cash flow statement requires the gathering of information like that in Exhibit 17.4. Then use a three-step process to build the components of the statement:

Step 1. Identify the journal entry or entries that led to the reported change in each balance sheet account.

Step 2. Determine the net cash flow effect of the journal entry (or entries) identified in Step 1.

Step 3. Compare the financial statement effect of the entry (Step 1) with its cash flow effect (Step 2) to determine what cash flow statement treatment is necessary for each item.

This three-step approach is used to develop Burris' cash flow statement in Exhibit 17.5 using the indirect method of determining cash flow from operations.

Exhibit 17.5 BURRIS PRODUCTS CORPORATION

2002 Cash Flow Statement

Operating Activities		
Net income		$182,000
Adjustments to reconcile net income to cash provided by operating activities:		
1 Amortization	$158,000	
2 Gain on equipment sale	(17,000)	
3 Amortization of bond discount	4,000	
4 Future income taxes increase	6,000	
5 Accounts receivable decrease	9,000	
6 Customer advance deposits decrease	(11,000)	
7 Inventory increase	(12,000)	
8 Accounts payable increase	3,000	
		140,000
Cash Provided by Operating Activities		322,000
Investing Activities		
2 Equipment sale		$ 57,000
9 Land purchase		(86,000)
10 Buildings and equipment purchase		(261,000)
Cash Used for Investing Activities		(290,000)
Financing Activities		
11 Common shares issued		$ 50,000
12 Dividend paid		(90,000)
Cash Used for Financing Activities		(40,000)
Net decrease in cash during 2002		$ (8,000)

Cash Flows from Operations

The operating cash flow section of the statement in Exhibit 17.5 begins with net income of $182,000. Under the indirect approach, net income represents an initial very, very rough approximation of the cash generated by operations. Starting the statement with net income presumes that revenues are ultimately collected in cash and that expenses represent cash outflows. In the long run, this approximation is basically correct. However, in any single period, accrual accounting net income will not equal that same period's cash flow from operations. The reason is that cash flows for some revenue and expense items occur either before or after accrual accounting revenues and expenses are recognized. The adjustments for these differences between the timing of revenue/expense recognition and cash flow impact appear as the eight numbered items below the net income figure in Exhibit 17.5. We now explain each of these items.

1 Amortization The income statement in Exhibit 17.4 indicates that amortization expense recognized during 2002 was $158,000. Use the three-step analytic approach, as follows:

Step 1. The journal entry that generated the account change was:

DR Amortization expense	$158,000	
CR Accumulated amortization		$158,000

Step 2. Neither of the two accounts that appear in the Step 1 journal entry involves cash. Indeed, amortization is unlike most other expenses, since the cash outflow occurred *before* the expense recognition—that is, when the asset was initially purchased.

Step 3. Amortization expense was included as an element in the determination of net income (Step 1) as if it were a cash outflow. But amortization expense does not represent a cash outflow (Step 2). Consequently, amortization expense must be added back to net income.

In short, amortization expense is added back because it was included in the determination of net income even though—unlike many other expenses—it does not represent a cash outflow of the current period.

2 Gain on Equipment Sale The net income number includes a gain on equipment sale of $17,000, as shown in Exhibit 17.4. Using the same three-step approach, we arrive at the following:

Step 1. With the additional information disclosed beneath the income statement in Exhibit 17.4, we can develop the following journal entry for the gain:

DR Accumulated amortization	$23,000	
DR Cash	57,000	
CR Equipment		$63,000
CR Gain on sale		17,000

> Notice that if the equipment originally cost $63,000 and its book value was $40,000, the accumulated amortization must have been $23,000.

Step 2. Scrutiny of the journal entry reveals that the sale resulted in a cash inflow of $57,000. This cash inflow is the result of investment activities.

Step 3. Comparing the accrual accounting effect (Step 1) to the cash flow effect (Step 2) reveals three problems: (1) the recognized accrual gain ($17,000) does not correspond to the cash inflow ($57,000); (2) the $17,000 gain is included in income, and thus would be categorized as an operating cash inflow unless corrective measures are taken; and (3) the $57,000 cash inflow from investing activities must be separately reflected in the statement.

The cash flow statement in Exhibit 17.5 reflects the information uncovered in Step 3. The gain of $17,000 is subtracted from cash flow from operations, and the total cash inflow of $57,000 is correctly categorized and shown in cash flow from investing activities.

3 **Amortization of Bond Discount** Exhibit 17.4 discloses that the discount on bonds payable account diminished by $4,000 during 2002. The three-step approach shows the following:

Step 1. Since the income statement reports interest expense as $44,000, the journal entry that led to the balance sheet change for discount on bonds payable was:

DR Interest expense	$44,000	
CR Discount on bonds payable		$ 4,000
CR Cash		40,000

Step 2. An examination of the journal entry reveals that interest expense of $44,000 was deducted in computing net income, although the cash outflow for the payment of interest in 2002 was only $40,000.

Step 3. Since the accrual accounting income statement charge for interest expense ($44,000) exceeds the cash outflow ($40,000), the difference of $4,000 must be added back to net income in the operating section of the cash flow statement.

4 **Future Income Taxes Increase** Future income taxes increased by $6,000, as shown in Exhibit 17.4. The three-step approach shows the following:

Step 1. Since income tax expense for 2002 was $102,375, the journal entry for taxes in 2002 was:

DR Income tax expense	$102,375	
CR Future income taxes		$ 6,000
CR Cash		96,375

Step 2. Again, there is a disparity between the amount of the expense included in the determination of net income ($102,375) and the cash outflow to pay taxes ($96,375).

Step 3. Because the income statement expense charge is larger than the cash outflow by $6,000, in Exhibit 17.5 this $6,000 must be added back in the operating activities section of the cash flow statement.

5 **Accounts Receivable Decrease** During 2002, Exhibit 17.4 shows that accounts receivable decreased by $9,000. Following the three-step approach:

Step 1. If we assume that all 2002 sales were initially credit sales, the aggregate entry to record these sales would be:

DR Accounts receivable	$3,030,000	
CR Sales revenue		$3,030,000

Since accounts receivable *decreased* by $9,000 during 2002, the entry for 2002 cash collections must have been:

DR Cash	$3,039,000	
CR Accounts receivable		$3,039,000

Step 2. Examination of the entries in Step 1 reveals that when the total in accounts receivable decreased, the amount of cash collections during the year ($3,039,000) exceeded the amount of accrual revenues included in income ($3,030,000).

Step 3. The $9,000 excess of cash collections over accrual revenues must be added back to net income in Exhibit 17.5.

6 Customer Advance Deposits Decrease Burris Products Corporation requires cash payments from customers prior to the sale of certain special order custom merchandise. This advance payment represents a liability on the balance sheet. As the custom products are delivered to customers, the liability is reduced and revenue is recognized. During 2002, the amount of the liability decreased by $11,000, as shown in Exhibit 17.4.

Step 1. The accounting entry that reflects the reduction in the advance payment liability during 2002 was:

DR Customer advance deposits	$11,000	
CR Sales revenues		$11,000

Step 2. Scrutinizing the entry in Step 1 indicates that accrual sales revenues were increased by $11,000. However, there was no corresponding cash flow effect this year since the cash flow originated in 2001 when the liability was initially recorded.

Step 3. Because revenues included in the computation of 2002 net income exceeded 2002 cash inflows by $11,000, this amount must be deducted in the operating section of the cash flow statement.

7 Increase in Inventory When inventory increases during a period, the dollar amount of new inventory purchases exceeds the cost of goods that were sold.

Step 1. If we initially assume that all inventory is purchased for cash (we will relax this assumption in adjustment 8 discussed next), then the accounting entries giving rise to a $12,000 increase in inventory (see Exhibit 17.4) are:

DR Inventory	$2,538,625	
CR Cash		$2,538,625

($2,526,625 cost of goods sold + $307,000 ending inventory − $295,000 beginning inventory)

and:

DR Cost of goods sold	$2,526,625	
CR Inventory		$2,526,625

Notice that the combined result of these two entries increases inventory by $12,000.

Step 2. Comparing the two journal entries in Step 1 indicates that the cost-of-goods-sold number that is deducted in the computation of net income ($2,526,625) is $12,000 *lower* than the cash outflow to buy inventory.

Step 3. Since net income understates the cash outflow to acquire inventory, $12,000 must be deducted from income in Exhibit 17.5.

8 Increase in Accounts Payable Adjustment 7 for the increase in inventory was computed under the assumption that all inventory was purchased for cash.

We assumed this because it makes it easier to see why an increase in inventory must be adjusted for when preparing a cash flow statement. We now relax this assumption since scrutiny of Exhibit 17.4 shows that accounts payable increased by $3,000 during 2002. A $3,000 increase in accounts payable means that $3,000 of the $12,000 inventory increase during the year was not paid for in cash. Therefore, $3,000 is added to net income in the cash flow statement.

Cash Flows from Investment Activities

Turning to the investing activities section of Burris' cash flow statement (Exhibit 17.5), we see that three transactions affected cash—one that resulted in a cash inflow and two that reduced cash.

Recall that there is another way to look at adjustments **7** and **8** that may make it easier for you to understand the accrual to cash adjustment. Together, adjustments **7** and **8** are designed to isolate the difference between accrual accounting's cost-of-goods-sold measure and cash inventory purchases. Specifically:

Accrual accounting cost-of-goods-sold deduction included in determining income	$2,526,625
Adjustment **7** (inventory increase)	12,000
Equals: 2002 *total* inventory purchases	$2,538,625
Adjustment **8** (payables increase)	(3,000)
Equals: 2002 *cash* inventory purchases	$2,535,625

In combination, adjustments **7** and **8** subtract $9,000 from income, an amount which is equal to the difference between cost of goods sold ($2,526,625) and cash purchases ($2,535,625).

2 **Equipment Sale** This transaction was analyzed earlier when we adjusted accrual net income for the gain on sale of equipment. The $57,000 cash received when this equipment was sold represents an investing source of cash.

9 **Land** Exhibit 17.4 indicates that the land account increased by $86,000. The analysis here is straightforward.

Step 1. The journal entry that reflects this increase is:

DR Land	$86,000	
CR Cash		$86,000

Step 2. This transaction represents an outflow of cash of $86,000.

Step 3. The cash outflow should be categorized as an investment outflow of $86,000.

10 **Buildings and Equipment Purchase** The "Buildings and equipment" account increased by $198,000 during 2002 (see Exhibit 17.4). However, in computing the cash outflow that was incurred to acquire these fixed assets, we cannot simply use the $198,000 net account change. The reason is that some equipment was also sold during 2002 (see preceding item **2**). It is therefore necessary to adjust the change in the buildings and equipment account for the cost of the equipment sold in order to deduce the amount of buildings and equipment purchased.

Step 1. When several items affect a particular account, it is useful to begin by reconstructing the account over the period being analyzed.

Buildings and Equipment

12/31/2001 balance	$1,430,000		
"Plug" figure necessary to balance the account	261,000	Reduction in account arising from sale of equipment (see discussion of item **2**)	$63,000
12/31/2002 balance	$1,628,000		

The analysis reveals that the gross increase in buildings and equipment was $261,000 and resulted in the following journal entry:

DR Buildings and equipment $261,000
    CR Cash $261,000

Step 2. This transaction represents a cash outflow of $261,000.

Step 3. The outflow should be categorized as an investing cash outflow of $261,000.

This adjustment illustrates that, when constructing a cash flow statement, the analyst must be careful to look beyond just the net change in the account—he or she must also consider other known items that were added to or subtracted from the account during the period.

Cash Flows from Financing Activities

The financing section of Burris' cash flow statement in Exhibit 17.5 shows two other account changes during the period that had cash flow implications.

11 and **12** **Stock Sale and Dividend Paid** The increase in the common stock account indicates that additional capital was raised when new shares were sold. Furthermore, the additional information lists a cash dividend of $90,000 (see Exhibit 17.5). The analysis of these items is straightforward:

Step 1. The stock sale journal entry was:

DR Cash $50,000
    CR Common stock $50,000

The dividend generated the following entry:

DR Retained earnings $90,000
    CR Cash $90,000

Step 2. The cash effects of these items are unambiguously indicated in the entries—that is, a $50,000 inflow for the new financing and a $90,000 dividend outflow.

Step 3. Both the cash inflow of $50,000 and the cash outflow of $90,000 should be categorized as cash flows from financing activities.

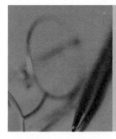

Recap

To prepare a cash flow statement: (1) recreate the accounting entries that explain the changes in all noncash balance sheet accounts, (2) determine the net cash flow effect of the entry and the type of activity that generated or used the cash, and (3) compare the accrual accounting effect of the entry with the cash flow effect to determine what adjustments, if any, are needed to convert accrual earnings to cash flow from operations.

Reconciling Between Statements: Some Complexities

Users of financial statements will frequently encounter situations in which changes in balance sheet accounts over the year will *not* reconcile to the corresponding account changes in the cash flow statement. We'll demonstrate this discrepancy and explain why it happens using data from the H.J. Heinz Company's 2000 annual report. Exhibit 17.6 shows Heinz' consolidated statement of cash flows for the fiscal year ended May 3, 2000 and the previous fiscal year. The operating section of Heinz' consolidated statement of cash flows is prepared using the indirect approach, and starts with fiscal 2000 accrual-basis net income of US$890,553,000. Adjustments to reconcile net income to cash provided by operations are presented next. We'll refer to these as **net accrual adjustments** because these are the items that cause accrual income to differ from operating cash flows. These adjustments total US$347,478,000 (highlighted in Exhibit 17.6), resulting in US$543,075,000 cash provided by operating activities. Notice that Heinz' net accrual adjustments cause net income to exceed cash from operations. We will call these **income-increasing accrual adjustments.**

Exhibit 17.7 compares the working capital accrual adjustments from the statement of cash flows to the changes in noncash working capital accounts taken from Heinz' comparative balance sheets for fiscal years 1999 and 2000. This exhibit shows that *changes in balance sheet working capital account balances are not necessarily equal to the net accrual adjustments in the operating section of the cash flow statement.* We'll explain why shortly.

Column 1 of Exhibit 17.7 shows that Heinz reported income-increasing net working capital accrual adjustments of US$659,300,000 (highlighted). Column 3 shows the corresponding changes in working capital accounts taken directly from Heinz' comparative balance sheets for fiscal 1999–2000 (Exhibit 17.8), which imply income-increasing accrual adjustments of only US$162,701,000. Thus, the change in noncash working capital accounts from the balance sheet understates Heinz' income-increasing accrual adjustments by nearly *half a billion U.S. dollars* ($659,300,000 – $162,701,000 = $496,599,000).

A similar discrepancy exists when trying to reconcile changes in Heinz' property, plant, and equipment balance sheet account with information presented on its cash flow statement. Exhibit 17.8 also shows comparative balance sheet data for Heinz' Property, plant, and equipment account. The year-to-year increase in this account (before accumulated depreciation) is US$273,772,000 (highlighted). However, the "Investing activities" section of Heinz' statement of cash flows (Exhibit 17.6) shows fiscal year 2000 capital expenditures of US$452,444,000—a difference of nearly US$178,672,000. What accounts for these differences in working capital and fixed asset accounts? There are at least four reasons for these differences:

1. Asset writeoffs due to impairment, corporate restructuring, or retirement
2. Translation adjustments on assets and liabilities held by foreign subsidiaries
3. Acquisitions and divestitures of other companies
4. Simultaneous investing and financing activities not directly affecting cash

Discrepancies in Current Accruals

We'll use the Inventory account to illustrate reasons for the discrepancy between working capital components of net accrual adjustments on the cash flow statement and changes in these accounts on the balance sheet. From Exhibit 17.7, the change in inventories from the balance sheet is +US$190,255,000 (column [3]), while the inventory increase reflected in the cash flow statement is +US$217,127,000 (column [1]). Although a precise reconciliation is not possible, the primary factors causing the US$26,872,000 difference arise from the reasons explained next.

Note the US$217,127,000 change in the inventory balance (excluding the effects of acquisitions and divestitures) is *subtracted* from accrual-basis net income to arrive at cash provided by operations. This means that inventory *increased* during the period after adjusting for the effects of acquisitions and divestitures.

Exhibit 17.6 H.J. HEINZ COMPANY AND SUBSIDIARIES

Consolidated Statement of Cash Flows

(US$ in thousands)	Fiscal Year Ended May 3, 2000 (53 Weeks)	April 28, 1999 (52 Weeks)
Operating Activities:		
Net income	$ 890,553	$ 474,341
Adjustments to reconcile net income to cash provided by operating activities:		
Depreciation	219,255	207,852
Amortization	87,228	94,360
Deferred tax provision	28,331	23,564
[1] Gain on sale of Weight Watchers	(464,617)	—
Gain on sale of bakery products unit	—	(5,717)
Gain on sale of Ore-Ida frozen food-service business	—	—
[2] Provision for restructuring	392,720	527,107
Other items, net	48,905	(43,147)
Changes in current assets and liabilities, excluding effects of acquisitions and divestitures:		
Receivables	(123,994)	(88,742)
[3] Inventories	(217,127)	(115,743)
Prepaid expenses and other current assets	(23,296)	2,604
Accounts payable	111,976	3,410
Accrued liabilities	(372,999)	(150,533)
Income taxes	(33,860)	(19,220)
Net accrual adjustments*	(347,478)	435,795
Cash provided by operating activities	543,075	910,136
Investing Activities:		
[4] Capital expenditures	(452,444)	(316,723)
[5] Acquisitions, net of cash acquired	(394,418)	(268,951)
[6] Proceeds from divestitures	726,493	180,400
Purchases of short-term investments	(1,175,538)	(915,596)
Sales and maturities of short-term investments	1,119,809	883,945
Investments in The Hain Celestial Group, Inc.	(99,764)	—
Other items, net	7,188	46,396
Cash (used for) provided by investing activities	(268,674)	(390,529)
Financing Activities:		
Proceeds from long-term debt	834,328	259,593
Payments on long-term debt	(627,498)	(65,744)
Proceeds from (payments on) commercial paper and short term borrowings, net	532,305	74,464
Dividends	(513,782)	(484,847)
Purchase of treasury stock	(511,480)	(410,103)
Exercise of stock options	20,027	77,158
Other items, net	6,937	33,989
Cash used for financing activities	(259,163)	(515,490)
Effect of exchange rate changes on cash and cash equivalents	6,397	15,565
Net increase (decrease) in cash and cash equivalents	21,635	19,682
Cash and cash equivalents at beginning of year	115,982	96,300
Cash and cash equivalents at end of year	$ 137,617	$ 115,982

*This line added by authors for clarity.

Exhibit 17.7 H.J. HEINZ COMPANY

Comparison of Implied Accruals from Change in Balance Sheet
Accounts Versus Actual Accruals from Cash Flow Statement
Fiscal Year Ending May 3, 2000

(US$ in thousands)	(1) Statement of Cash Flows	(2) Actual Effect of Accrual on Income*	(3) Adjustments to Arrive at Cash Flow from Operations Based on Changes in Balance Sheet Accounts	(4) Implied Effect of Balance Sheet Working Capital Changes on Income*
Operating Activities:				
Net income	$ 890,553			
Adjustments to reconcile net income to cash provided by operating activities:				
Depreciation	219,255	−		
Amortization	87,228	−		
Deferred tax provision	28,331	−		
Gain on sale of Weight Watchers	(464,617)	+		
Provision for restructuring	392,720	−		
Other items, net	48,905	−		
	311,822			
Changes in current assets and liabilities:				
Receivables	(123,994)	+	(73,889)	+
Inventories	(217,127)	+	(190,255)	+
Prepaid expenses and other current assets	(23,296)	+	11,981[a]	−
Accounts payable	111,976	−	81,472	−
Accrued liabilities	(372,999)	+	(20,586)[b]	+
Income taxes	(33,860)	+	28,576	−
Working capital accruals	(659,300)	+	(162,701)	+
Cash provided by operating activities	$ 543,075			

*A plus (+) indicates an income-increasing accrual adjustment; a minus (−) indicates an income decreasing accrual adjustment. Remember, income-increasing accrual adjustments are *subtracted* from net income to arrive at cash provided by operating activities.

[a]This amount is the net change in two current asset accounts on Heinz' balance sheet : US$16,980,000 increase in "Prepaid expenses" minus the US$28,961,000 decrease in "Other current assets" (see Exhibit 17.8).

[b]This amount is the net change in three current liability (payable) accounts on Heinz' balance sheet: US$18,751,000 increase in "Accrued marketing" minus the US$25,452,000 decrease in "Salaries and wages" minus the US$13,885,000 decrease in "Other accrued liabilities" (see Exhibit 17.8).

Writeoffs Due to Restructuring

The following excerpt from Heinz' footnote 4 describing its 2000 "Operation Excel" reorganization and restructuring program reveals that a portion of the restructuring charge (highlighted) relates to inventory writeoffs:

Exhibit 17.8 H.J. HEINZ COMPANY AND SUBSIDIARIES

Selected Accounts from Comparative Balance Sheets

(US$ in thousands)	May 3, 2000	April 28, 1999	Changes in Selected Account Balances*	*Implied* Effect on Income
Selected Current Asset Accounts:				
Receivables (net of allowances: 2000—$18,697 and 1999—$21,633	$1,237,804	$1,163,915	$73,889	+
Inventories:				
Finished goods and work-in-process	1,270,329	1,064,015		
Packaging material and ingredients	329,577	345,636		
Total inventories	1,599,906	1,409,651	190,255	+
Prepaid expenses	171,599	154,619	16,980	+
Other current assets	6,511	35,472	(28,961)	−
Selected Current Liability Accounts:				
Accounts payable	1,026,960	945,488	81,472	−
Salaries and wages	48,646	74,098	(25,452)	+
Accrued marketing	200,775	182,024	18,751	−
Accrued restructuring costs	125,704	147,786		
Other accrued liabilities	358,738	372,623	(13,885)	+
Income taxes	188,672	160,096	28,576	−
Property, Plant, and Equipment Accounts:				
Land	45,959	48,649	(2,690)	
Buildings and leasehold improvements	860,873	798,307	62,566	
Equipment, furniture and other	3,440,915	3,227,019	213,896	
	4,347,747	4,073,975	273,772	
Less: Accumulated depreciation	−1,988,994	−1,902,951	−86,043	
Total property, plant, and equipment, net	$2,358,753	$2,171,024	$187,729 ◀—	

*Amounts without parentheses represent increases in accounts from 1999 to 2000, while amounts with parentheses represent decreases in accounts.

> *During Fiscal 2000, the company recognized net restructuring charges and implementation costs totaling [US]$392.7 million pre-tax. ... Non-cash asset write-downs totaled [US]$61.6 million in Fiscal 2000 and related to property, plant and equipment ([US]$48.7 million) and current assets ([US]$12.9 million). ... Current asset write-downs included inventory and packaging material, prepaids and other current assets and were determined based on management's estimate of net realizable value.*

The writeoff resulted in a decrease of an undisclosed amount to the Inventory accounts unrelated to the sales of merchandise. It is part of the US$392.7 million **"Provision for restructuring"** that is added back to accrual-basis net income shown in the "Operating activities" section of Heinz' 2000 statement of cash flows (item 2 in Exhibit 17.6). So this writedown in inventory on the balance sheet is not part of the US$217,127,000 inventory accrual adjustment shown in the consolidated statement of cash flows (item 3 in Exhibit 17.6).

Translation Adjustments

Heinz has numerous foreign subsidiaries whose statements are translated using the current rate approach described in Chapter 16. This method of measuring the increase or decrease in inventories of foreign subsidiaries generates a potential discrepancy between the balance sheet inventory change figure and the statement of cash flows inventory change figure. Here's why. On the cash flow statement, inventory change is computed by comparing purchases with cost of goods sold. If purchases exceed cost of goods sold, an inventory increase is indicated. To determine the direction of the inventory change for *foreign* subsidiaries, *translated* purchases and cost of goods sold are compared. Inventory purchases and cost of goods sold are translated into dollars using the exchange rate in effect at the time of the transaction. In contrast, the inventory change on the balance sheet is computed differently. Foreign subsidiaries' beginning inventories are translated at the beginning-of-period rate of exchange while ending inventories are translated at the end-of-period rate of exchange. The difference corresponds to the different nature of the two statements: the balance sheet reflects an *instant in time* (and thus uses the *exchange rate at that instant*); the cash flow statement uses a *series of exchange rates*. It should not be surprising therefore that the measures of inventory change on the two statements will differ.

For simplicity, the translation may also be done using the weighted-average rate of exchange in effect over the period.

This difference will usually not arise when *all* foreign subsidiaries are accounted for using the temporal method (Chapter 16). The reason is that the method for computing inventory change for temporal method subsidiaries on the cash flow statement translates both beginning and ending inventory at the *historical* rate of exchange. The historical rate is also used on the balance sheet. For firms whose subsidiaries all utilize the temporal approach, inventory change differences between the two statements will usually not arise.

Acquisitions and Divestitures

Another reason why the inventory change on the two statements differs is because of acquisitions and divestitures. Companies bought and sold usually possess inventories. The ending inventory number reported on the consolidated balance sheet includes the inventory of subsidiary companies purchased and excludes the inventories of subsidiaries or divisions sold during the year. But on the statement of cash flows, the inventory of companies acquired is reported as a component of "Acquisitions, net of cash acquired" and the inventory of companies sold is part of the "Proceeds from divestitures" reported in the "Investing activities" section of Exhibit 17.6. **Therefore, the inventory change figure on the cash flow statement is limited to inventory changes for those segments of the firm that were owned at both the start and end of the reporting period.**

Changes in inventories due to acquisitions or divestitures do not create a corresponding accrual adjustment to cost of goods sold on the income statement. Therefore, changes due to these events would *not* be included as part of the inventory adjustment to accrual-basis income (item 3 in Exhibit 17.6) to arrive at operating cash flows.

The same factors will explain discrepancies between changes in other working capital accounts on the balance sheet and accrual adjustments shown on the cash flow statement.

Discrepancies Related to Property, Plant, and Equipment

A portion of the discrepancy between the change in property, plant, and equipment on the balance sheet and capital expenditures on the statement of cash flows can be explained by asset writedowns taken in conjunction with Heinz' "Operation Excel" reorganization and restructuring program described earlier. As shown above in the excerpt from footnote 4 in Heinz' 2000 10-K report, US$48.7 million of the US$61.6 million asset writedown related to property, plant, and equipment, which explains some of the change in this account on the balance sheet. Without this writedown, the year-to-year change in property, plant, and equipment net of depreciation would have been a US$236,429,000 increase [$187,729,000 increase from Exhibit 17.8 (see arrow) + $48,700,000 writedown]—still far short of the US$452,444,000 increase shown for capital expenditures in the "Investing Activities" section on Heinz' consolidated statement of cash flows in Exhibit 17.6.

Three additional events are likely to have contributed to the reported balance sheet change. They are retirements, foreign currency translation adjustment, and acquisitions and divestitures.

Retirements During the year, Heinz may have retired fixed assets (not related to the restructuring) that were not fully depreciated. Recall from Chapter 10 that the entry to record the retirement would take the following form:

DR	Accumulated depreciation—plant and equipment	XXX	
DR	Loss on retirement	XXX	
	CR Plant and equipment (for cost of assets retired)		XXX

Prior to 1995, it was possible to determine the cost of assets retired from Schedule V, Property, Plant and Equipment—a required schedule in firms' 10-K reports filed with the SEC—that reconciled the beginning and ending balances of the property, plant, and equipment account reported in firms' balance sheets. Unfortunately, this schedule is no longer required. Therefore, it is generally not possible for external users to determine the exact dollar amount of the year-to-year change in fixed asset accounts due to retirements.

Foreign Currency Translation Adjustment As noted already, Heinz translates the accounts of most of its foreign subsidiaries using the current rate approach. Accordingly, the property, plant, and equipment accounts of these subsidiaries are translated using the current rate of exchange—at the balance sheet date—between the dollar and the foreign currency. If the dollar falls (rises) in relation to the functional currencies of these subsidiaries, this would result in an increase (decrease) in the balance of property, plant, and equipment account that would not be reflected on the cash flow statement. Again, these adjustments were recorded in Schedule V of the 10-K report prior to 1995 but are no longer disclosed, making it difficult to ascertain the impact of translation adjustments on individual changes in balance sheet accounts.

Acquisitions and Divestitures Heinz acquired and sold companies during the year. These companies all owned property, plant, and equipment. This immediately raises a classification dilemma on Heinz' statement of cash flows: Should that portion of cash flow related to the cost of properties acquired be classified as "Capital expenditure" or should it be included as a part of "Acquisitions, net of cash acquired"? Under the U.S. *SFAS 95* classification criteria, "Capital expenditures" contain only cash outflows made to acquire property directly. Cash outflows for property acquired as part of a business acquisition are classified under "Acquisitions," following *SFAS 95* guidelines. You can see from examining the "Investing activities" section of the consolidated statement of cash flows in Exhibit 17.6 that Heinz paid US$394,418,000 for acquisitions, net of cash acquired (item 🔳). Part of this purchase price would contribute to an increase in property, plant, and equipment because the acquired firms' assets are included in Heinz' consolidated reports if Heinz' ownership exceeds 50%.

The "Investing activities" section of Exhibit 17.6 also shows cash proceeds from divestitures of US$726,493,000 (item 🔳). When business units included as part of a consolidated entity are sold, the Property, plant, and equipment account is reduced by the book value—cost minus accumulated depreciation—of the fixed assets in the business unit sold. Before it was eliminated by the SEC, Schedule V of the 10-K report provided detailed information on increases and decreases in the Property, plant, and equipment account due to acquisitions and divestitures. Now that this schedule is no longer required, analysts and other statement users must rely on fragmented and somewhat incomplete information provided elsewhere in the statements to deduce the book value of assets sold.

To illustrate how this is done, recall from Chapter 10 that the gain or loss on asset disposal is the difference between the sales price and the book value of the assets sold. Heinz' consolidated statement of cash flows (Exhibit 17.6) shows "Proceeds from divestitures" of US$726,493,000 (item **6**) in the "Investing activities" section and a "Gain on sale of Weight Watchers" of US$464,617,000 (item **1**) as a noncash adjustment to income in the "Operating activities" section. Combining these two pieces of information, we can deduce the book value of assets sold or divested in this transaction as follows:

	(US$ in thousands)
Proceeds from divestitures	$ 726,493
Less: Gain on assets sold	(464,617)
Book value of assets sold	$ 261,876

> This calculation assumes that the cash proceeds from divestiture represents the entire sales price of the assets sold. If noncash consideration was received (e.g., a promissory note), then the sales price and the cash proceeds would differ and the amount of the note would need to be considered in calculating the book value of assets sold.

Unfortunately, it is not possible to determine from the information given what portion of this US$261,876,000 book value relates to property, plant, and equipment versus current assets like inventory or receivables held by the business unit that was sold.

Simultaneous Noncash Financing and Investing Activities

Occasionally firms will engage in investing and financing activities that cause changes in balance sheet asset and liability accounts even though they do not affect cash receipts or cash payments. Examples include: (1) purchasing a building by incurring a mortgage to the seller; (2) acquiring an asset by entering into a capital lease; or (3) issuing stock for noncash assets in connection with a business acquisition. *GAAP 95* requires firms to disclose these noncash simultaneous financing and investing activities either in a narrative or in a schedule, which is sometimes included as a separate section of the statement of cash flows. Although there is no evidence in Heinz' 2000 annual report that any of the balance sheet changes in property, plant, and equipment were acquired with noncash consideration, this is fairly common, especially for Internet and start-up companies that are typically short on cash.

Exhibit 17.9 shows Amazon.com's 1999 cash flow statement. Note the supplemental schedule (at the bottom of this statement) summarizing each of the three types of simultaneous financing and investing activities we just discussed. Each of these transactions resulted in increases in fixed asset accounts on Amazon's balance sheet but did not have a direct effect on cash flows. Also note that Amazon received noncash revenues in the form of equity securities of other companies for advertising and promotional services. The latter is a common form of transaction among Internet companies.

AMAZON.COM
www.amazon.com

Exhibit 17.9 AMAZON.COM, INC.

Consolidated Statement of Cash Flows

($ in thousands)	December 31 1999	December 31 1998	December 31 1997
		Fiscal Year Ended	
Operating Activities:			
Net loss	($ 719,968)	($124,546)	($ 31,020)
Adjustments to reconcile net loss to net cash provided (used) in operating activities:			
Depreciation and amortization of fixed assets	36,806	9,421	3,442
Amortization of deferred stock-based compensation	30,618	2,386	1,354
Equity in losses of equity-method investees	76,769	2,905	—
Amortization of goodwill and other intangibles	214,694	42,599	—
Non-cash merger, acquisition, and investment costs	8,072	1,561	—
Non-cash revenue for advertising and promotional services	(5,837)	—	—
Loss on sale of marketable securities	8,688	271	—
Non-cash interest expense	29,171	23,970	64
Changes in operating assets and liabilities, net of effects from acquisitions:			
Inventories	(172,069)	(20,513)	(8,400)
Prepaid expenses and other current assets	(60,628)	(16,758)	(3,055)
Accounts payable	330,166	78,674	30,172
Accrued expenses and other current liabilities	65,121	21,615	5,274
Accrued advertising	42,382	9,617	2,856
Deferred revenue	262	—	—
Interest payable	24,878	(167)	—
Net cash provided (used) in operating activities	(90,875)	31,035	687
Investing Activities:			
Sales and maturities of marketable securities	2,064,101	227,789	5,198
Purchases of marketable securities	(2,359,398)	(504,435)	(20,454)
Purchases of fixed assets	(287,055)	(28,333)	(7,603)
Acquisitions and investments in businesses, net of cash acquired	(369,607)	(19,019)	—
Net cash used in investing activities	(951,959)	(323,998)	(22,859)
Financing Activities:			
Proceeds from issuance of capital stock and exercise of stock options	64,469	14,366	53,358
Proceeds from long-term debt	1,263,639	325,987	75,000
Repayment of long-term debt	(188,886)	(78,108)	(47)
Financing costs	(35,151)	(7,783)	(2,309)
Net cash provided by financing activities	1,104,071	254,462	126,002
Effect of exchange rate changes	489	(35)	—
Net increase (decrease) in cash and cash equivalents	61,726	(38,536)	103,830
Cash and cash equivalents at beginning of period	71,583	110,119	6,289
Cash and cash equivalents at end of period	$ 133,309	$ 71,583	$110,119
Supplemental Cash Flow Information:			
Fixed assets acquired under capital leases	$ 25,850	—	$ 3,463
Fixed assets acquired under financing agreements	5,608	—	1,500
Stock issued in connection with business acquisitions	774,409	$217,241	—
Equity securities of other companies received for non-cash revenue for advertising and promotional services	54,402	—	—
Cash paid for interest, net of amounts capitalized	59,688	26,629	326

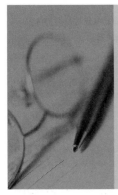

Recap

The year-to-year changes in comparative balance sheet accounts may not coincide with the changes implied from amounts reported on the cash flow statement. The factors contributing to these differences include (1) asset write-downs due to impairment or restructuring, (2) the translation of foreign subsidiary accounts using the year-end current exchange rate between the dollar and the foreign currency, (3) acquisitions and divestitures of other companies, and (4) simultaneous noncash financing and investing transactions. Footnote disclosures, along with information in the income statement and in the operating section of the cash flow statement, are often helpful to reconciling some of these differences.

Summary

The cash flow statement provides information that enables the analyst to assess the ability of a firm to generate sufficient cash to pay operating expenses, to pay for capital improvements, and to meet currently maturing obligations. Firms able to generate consistently strong positive cash flows from operations are considered better credit risks and will benefit from a lower cost of capital.

This chapter outlined the major sections within the cash flow statement—operating, investing, and financing—and the kinds of transactions reported within each of these sections. We compared and contrasted the direct and indirect approaches for presenting cash flow from operations, and we demonstrated how the latter provides a reconciliation of the difference between accrual earnings and operating cash flows. Knowing how to prepare and interpret cash flow statements is critical to those interested in conducting sound credit analysis and making informed lending decisions.

For more Exercises, Problems/Discussion Questions, and Cases, visit the Companion Website for this textbook at **www.pearsoned.ca/revsine**.

Exercises

E17-1 Determining cash flows from operations

Information for ABC Company is as follows ($ in thousands):

Net income	$280
Equity in investee loss	20
Decrease in prepaid expenses	7
Cash paid for new plant equipment	30
Amortization of premium on bonds payable	10
Decrease in accounts payable	2
Increase in inventory	21
Amortization expense	13
Increase in salaries payable	8
Increase in accounts receivable	15
Dividends paid to shareholders	5

Required:

What is the net cash provided by operating activities?

E17-2 Determining a cash flow number

CICA adapted

ST Ltd. wishes to use the direct method to present its cash flow statement. Given the following information, what is the amount that should be reported under "Cash from clients"?

Net income	$165,000
Sales	350,000
Reduction of accounts receivable	10,000
Amortization	20,000

(a) $175,000
(b) $195,000
(c) $340,000
(d) $360,000
(e) none of the above

E17-3 Determining cash flows from operations

Oscar Company's worksheet for the preparation of its 2003 cash flow statement included the following information:

	December 31	January 1
Accounts receivable	$29,000	$23,000
Allowance for uncollectible accounts	1,000	800
Prepaid rent expense	8,200	12,400
Accounts payable	22,400	20,400

Oscar's 2003 net income is $150,000.

What amount should the company report as net cash that is provided by operating activities in the cash flow statement?

E17-4 Cash flows from operations

Cornell Corporation has estimated its activity for December 2003. Selected data from these estimated amounts are as follows:

- Sales $340,000
- Gross profit (based on sales)   40%
- Increase in gross trade accounts receivable during month $10,500
- Change in accounts payable during month   –0–
- Increase in inventory during month $4,000
- Variable selling, general, and administrative (SG&A) expenses includes a charge for uncollectible accounts of 1% of sales; accounts receivable writeoffs were $3,000
- Total SG&A of $35,000 per month plus 15% of sales
- Amortization expense of $20,000 per month is included in fixed SG&A

Required:

1. Calculate net income for December.
2. On the basis of the preceding data, what is the net cash flow provided from operating activities for December?

E17-5 Analysis of changes in balance sheet accounts

Maxall Company is preparing its cash flow statement for the year ended December 31, 2004. It has the following account balances:

	December 31,	
	2003	2004
Machinery	$250,000	$320,000
Accumulated amortization—machinery	102,000	120,000
Loss on sale of machinery		4,000

During 2004, Maxall sold a machine that cost $44,000 for $30,000, and purchased several items of machinery. Only the one machine was sold.

Required:

1. How much was amortization on machinery for 2004? How does this affect cash from operations under the indirect method?
2. What was the amount of machinery purchases for 2004? How does this affect operating, investing, or financing cash flows?

E17-6 Cash flows from investing and financing activities
AICPA adapted

Karr Inc. reported net income of $300,000 for 2004. Changes occurred in several balance sheet accounts as follows:

Equipment	$25,000 increase
Accumulated amortization	40,000 increase
Note payable	30,000 increase

1. During 2004, Karr sold equipment that cost $25,000 and had accumulated amortization of $12,000, for a gain of $5,000.
2. In December 2004, Karr purchased equipment costing $50,000 with $20,000 cash and a 12% note payable of $30,000.
3. Amortization expense for the year was $52,000.

Required:

1. In Karr's 2004 cash flow statement, what should be the net cash from operating activities?
2. In Karr's 2004 cash flow statement, what should be the net cash used in investing and in financing activities?

E17-7 Cash flows from investing activities

Zip Inc. engaged in the following activities during 2004:

- Acquired 2,000 shares of stock in Newman Ltd. for $160,000. The shares are readily marketable, and will be held only for a short time.
- Sold an investment in Al Ltd. for $35,000 when the carrying value was $33,000.
- Acquired a $50,000, four-year certificate of deposit from a bank. (During the year, interest of $3,750 was paid to Zip.)
- Collected dividends of $3,000 on equity investments.

Required:

In Zip's 2004 cash flow statement, at what amount should net cash from investing activities be shown?

Problems/Discussion Questions

P17-1 Comparing direct and indirect methods of determining cash flows from operations

CMA adapted

The Spoke Company, a major retailer of bicycles and accessories, operates several stores and is a publicly traded company. The comparative statement of financial position and income statement for Spoke as of May 31, 2001, follow. The company is preparing its cash flow statement to comply with "Cash Flow Statements," Section 1540 of the *CICA Handbook*.

Spoke Company

Comparative Statement of Financial Position as of May 31, 2001 and May 31, 2000

	May 31,	
	2001	**2000**
Assets		
Cash	$ 43,250	$ 20,000
Accounts receivable	70,000	50,000
Merchandise inventory	210,000	250,000
Prepaid expenses	9,000	7,000
Total current assets	$332,250	$327,000
Capital assets:		
Capital assets	600,000	510,000
Less: Accumulated amortization	(150,000)	(125,000)
Net capital assets	450,000	385,000
Total assets	$782,250	$712,000
Liabilities and Shareholders' Equity		
Accounts payable	$123,000	$115,000
Salaries payable	47,250	72,000
Interest payable	27,000	25,000
Total current liabilities	197,250	212,000
Long-term debt:		
Bonds payable	70,000	100,000
Total liabilities	267,250	312,000
Shareholders' Equity		
Common shares	370,000	280,000
Retained earnings	145,000	120,000
Total shareholders' equity	515,000	400,000
Total liabilities and shareholders' equity	$782,250	$712,000

Spoke Company

Income Statement for the Year Ended May 31, 2001

Sales	$1,255,250
Cost of merchandise sold	712,000
Gross margin	543,250
Expenses:	
Salary expense	252,100
Interest expense	75,000
Other expenses	8,150
Amortization expense	25,000
Total expenses	360,250
Operating income	183,000
Income tax expense	43,000
Net income	$ 140,000

The following is additional information concerning Spoke's transactions during the year ended May 31, 2001:

- All sales during the year were made on account.
- All merchandise was purchased on account, making up the total accounts payable account.
- Capital assets costing $90,000 were purchased by paying $40,000 in cash and by issuing 5,000 shares of stock.
- The "Other expenses" are related to prepaid items.
- All income taxes incurred during the year were paid during the year.
- In order to supplement its cash, Spoke issued 4,000 common shares at $10 per share.
- There were no penalties assessed for the retirement of bonds.
- Cash dividends of $115,000 were declared and paid at the end of the fiscal year.

Required:

1. Prepare a cash flow statement for Spoke Company for the year ended May 31, 2001, using the direct method. Be sure to support the statement with appropriate calculations. (A reconciliation of net income to net cash is not required.)
2. Using the indirect method, calculate only the net cash flow from operating activities for Spoke Company for the year ended May 31, 2001.
3. Compare and contrast the direct method and the indirect method for reporting cash flows from operating activities. What are the advantages and limitations of each approach?

P17-2 Determining amounts reported on the cash flow statement

The following are selected balance sheet accounts of Zach Corporation at December 31, 2001 and 2000, as well as the increases or decreases in each account from 2000 to 2001. Also presented is selected income statement information for the year ended December 31, 2001, as well as additional information.

Selected Balance Sheet Accounts

	2001	2000	Increase (Decrease)
Assets			
Accounts receivable	$ 34,000	$ 24,000	$10,000
Property, plant, and equipment	277,000	247,000	30,000
Accumulated amortization	(178,000)	(167,000)	11,000
Liabilities and Stockholders' Equity			
Bonds payable	49,000	46,000	3,000
Dividends payable	8,000	5,000	3,000
Common shares, $1 par	22,000	19,000	3,000
Additional paid-in capital	9,000	3,000	6,000
Retained earnings	104,000	91,000	13,000

Selected Income Statement Information for the Year Ended December 31, 2001

Sales revenue	$155,000
Amortization	33,000
Gain on sale of equipment	13,000
Net income	28,000

Additional Information:

- Accounts receivable relate to sales of merchandise.
- During 2001, equipment that cost $40,000 was sold for cash.
- During 2001, $20,000 of bonds payable were issued in exchange for property, plant, and equipment. There was no amortization of bond discount or premium.

Required:

Items 1 through 5 that follow represent activities that will be reported in Zach's cash flow statement for the year ended December 31, 2001. For each item, determine both the amount that should be reported in Zach's 2001 cash flow statement and the section (operating, investing, or financing) in which the item will appear.

1. cash collections from customers (direct method)
2. payments for the purchase of property, plant, and equipment
3. proceeds from the sale of equipment
4. cash dividends paid
5. redemption of bonds payable

P17-3 Preparation of the cash flow statement and balance sheet

The following is the cash account of JKI Advertising Agencies for the year ended December 31, 2004:

Cash Account

	DR	CR
Beginning balance as of 1/1/2004	$ 30,000	
Cash collected from clients	215,000	
Cash received from sale of land at book value	150,000	
Rent collected	50,000	
Capital contributions	35,000	
Line of credit borrowing from Town Bank	50,000	
Salaries paid		$130,000
Purchase of office equipment		20,000
Cash paid for insurance		12,000
Building loan repaid		85,000
Cash paid for interest		9,000
Dividends declared and paid		18,000
Cash paid for customer lawsuit		32,000
Cash paid for taxes		31,000
	$530,000	$337,000
Ending balance as of 12/31/2004	$193,000	

Provided next are the income statement for the year ended December 31, 2004, and the balance sheet as of December 31, 2004, of JKI Advertising Agencies.

Assume there are no bad debts and no future or deferred taxes.

JKI Advertising Agencies

Income Statement for the Year Ended December 31, 2004

Advertising revenue	$250,000
Rent revenue	36,000
Salaries expense	(126,000)
Employee incentive bonus	(25,200)
Amortization expense—building	(20,000)
Amortization expense—office equipment	(8,000)
Insurance expense	(12,000)
Interest expense	(10,000)
Income before taxes	84,800
Income tax expense	(33,920)
Net income	$ 50,880

JKI Advertising Agencies

Balance Sheet as of December 31, 2004

Cash	$193,000
Accounts receivable	80,000
Prepaid insurance	3,000
Building	600,000
Less: Accumulated amortization	(380,000)
Office equipment	80,000
Less: Accumulated amortization	(39,000)
Total assets	$537,000
Salaries payable	7,000
Interest payable	3,500
Rent received in advance	14,000
Bonus payable	25,200
Taxes payable	2,920
Borrowing from Town Bank	50,000
Building loan	35,000
Capital stock	135,000
Retained earnings	264,380
Total of liabilities and equities	$537,000

Required:

1. Based on the cash account, prepare a cash flow statement using the direct approach.
2. Complete the balance sheet as of December 31, 2003.
3. Prepare the operating section of the cash flow statement for the year ended December 31, 2004, under the indirect approach.

4. Evaluate the following statements:
   (a) "Since depreciation or amortization is added to net income when calculating cash flow from operations, it is a direct source of operating cash flow."
   (b) "Over the life of a company, its cash flow from operations will equal its net income."
5. JKI has a policy of accruing an employee's incentive bonus at 20% of salary. Instead, if JKI had calculated the bonus at 25% of salary, what would be the revised figure for cash flow from operations under the indirect approach?

P17-4 Preparation of cash flow statement—indirect method

Presented next are the balance sheet accounts of Bergen Corporation as of December 31, 2004 and 2003.

	2004	2003	Increase (Decrease)
Assets			
Current assets:			
Cash	$ 541,000	$ 308,000	$233,000
Accounts receivable, net	585,000	495,000	90,000
Inventories	895,000	780,000	115,000
Total current assets	2,021,000	1,583,000	438,000
Land	350,000	250,000	100,000
Plant and equipment	1,060,000	720,000	340,000
Accumulated amortization	(295,000)	(170,000)	(125,000)
Leased equipment under capital lease	158,000	—	158,000
Marketable investment securities, at cost	—	75,000	(75,000)
Investment in Mason Inc. at cost	180,000	180,000	—
Total assets	$3,474,000	$2,638,000	$836,000
Liabilities and Stockholders' Equity			
Current liabilities:			
Current portion of long-term debt	$ 159,000	$ —	$159,000
Accounts payable and accrued expenses	760,000	823,000	(63,000)
Total current liabilities	919,000	823,000	96,000
Note payable, long-term	300,000	—	300,000
Liability under capital lease	124,000	—	124,000
Bonds payable	500,000	500,000	—
Unamortized bond premium	16,000	18,000	(2,000)
Future income taxes	60,000	45,000	15,000
Common shares	944,000	844,000	100,000
Retained earnings	611,000	408,000	203,000
Total liabilities and shareholders' equity	$3,474,000	$2,638,000	$836,000

Additional Information:

- On January 2, 2004, Bergen sold all of its marketable investment securities for $95,000 cash.
- On March 10, 2004, Bergen paid a cash dividend of $30,000 on its common shares. No other dividends were paid or declared during 2004.

- On April 15, 2004, Bergen issued 2,000 common shares for land having a fair value of $100,000.
- On May 25, 2004, Bergen borrowed $450,000 from an insurance company. The underlying promissory note bears interest at 15% and is payable in three equal annual installments of $150,000. The first payment is due on May 25, 2005.
- On June 15, 2004, Bergen purchased equipment for $392,000 cash.
- On July 1, 2004, Bergen sold equipment costing $52,000, with a book value of $28,000, for $33,000 cash.
- On September 1, 2004, Bergen paid a $20,000 additional tax assessment for 2003 due to an error in tax calculation discovered by the Canada Customs and Revenue Agency. This payment was appropriately recorded by Bergen as a prior period adjustment.
- On December 31, 2004, Bergen leased equipment from Tilden Company, for a ten-year period. Equal payments under the lease are $25,000 and are due on December 31 each year. The first payment was made on December 31, 2004. The present value at December 31, 2004, of the ten lease payments is $158,000. Bergen appropriately recorded the lease as a capital lease. The $25,000 lease payment due on December 31, 2005, will consist of $9,000 principal and $16,000 interest.
- Bergen's net income for 2004 is $253,000.
- Bergen owns a 10% interest in the voting common shares of Mason Inc., which is appropriately accounted for by the cost method. Mason reported net income of $120,000 for the year ended December 31, 2004, and paid a common share dividend of $55,000 during 2004.

Required:

Prepare a cash flow statement for Bergen using the indirect method for 2004.

P17-5 Preparing and interpreting cash flow statements

Minto Boats Ltd. manufactures customized fibreglass boat shells. The company began operations early in January 2001. Presented next are the company's balance sheets and selected income statement information for the first three years of Minto's activities.

Balance Sheets

($000s)	December 31,		
	2003	2002	2001
Cash and cash equivalents	640	300	200
Accounts receivable	600	1,200	400
Inventories	1,350	600	600
Prepaid expenses	150	120	100
Capital assets—gross	2,400	2,000	2,000
Accumulated amortization	(1,200)	(800)	(400)
Intangible assets	220	40	60
Total Assets	4,160	3,460	2,960
Wages payable	200	200	0
Accounts payable	400	200	600
Taxes payable	100	0	0
Deferred revenue	100	200	200
Debt—current portion	200	200	200
Future income taxes	300	200	20
Debt	600	800	600
Common shares	1,260	960	940
Preferred shares	200	0	0
Retained earnings	800	700	400
Total Liabilities and Shareholders' Equity	4,160	3,460	2,960

Selected Income Statement Information:

- Depreciation each year was $400,000.
- Amortization of intangible assets each year was $20,000.

Required:

1. Prepare cash flow statements for Minto for 2001, 2002, and 2003. Since the company intends to attract new capital, the statements should be prepared in accordance with GAAP, because an audit might be necessary.
2. Comment critically on the company's cash flow experience and the operations generally.

P17-6 Analysis of cash flow statement

The financial statements of Cavalier Toy Stores (a merchandising company) are provided as follows:

Cavalier Toy Stores

Income Statement for the Year Ended December 31, 1998

Sales Revenue		$1,500,000
Cost of Goods Sold		(1,200,000)
Gross Margin		300,000
Other Expenses:		
Salaries Expense	$200,000	
Bad Debt Expense	100,000	
Insurance Expense	30,000	
Office Supplies Expense	55,000	
Amortization Expense—Office Building	30,000	
Amortization Expense—Office Equipment	45,000	
Interest Expense	90,000	550,000
Net Loss		$ (250,000)

Cavalier Toy Stores

Statement of Retained Earnings for the Year Ended December 31, 1998

Retained Earnings 1/1/98	$600,000
Net Loss for the Year	(250,000)
Dividends Paid	(300,000)
Retained Earnings 12/31/98	$ 50,000

Cavalier Toy Stores

Balance Sheets

	December 31,	
	1998	1997
Assets		
Current Assets:		
Cash	$ 30,000	$ 180,000
Accounts Receivable	100,000	525,000
Less: Allowance for Doubtful Accounts	(10,000)	(30,000)
Prepaid Insurance	5,000	35,000
Inventory	50,000	550,000
Noncurrent Assets:		
Office building	900,000	—
Less: Accumulated Amortization	(30,000)	—
Office Equipment	200,000	200,000
Less: Accumulated Amortization	(85,000)	(40,000)
Total Assets	$1,160,000	$1,420,000
Liabilities and Owners' Equity		
Current Liabilities:		
Salaries Payable	$ 100,000	$ 80,000
Interest Payable	8,000	16,000
Accounts Payable for inventory purchases	252,000	64,000
Dividends Payable	—	50,000
Noncurrent Liabilities:		
Loan from Thrifty Bank	700,000	560,000
Owners' Equity:		
Contributed Capital	50,000	50,000
Retained Earnings	50,000	600,000
Total of Liabilities and Owners' Equity	$1,160,000	$1,420,000

Required:

1. Prepare a cash flow statement using the indirect method.
2. Compute the following for the year ended December 31, 1998:
   (a) bad debts written off during the year
   (b) cash collected from the customers
   (c) purchases made during the year
   (d) cash paid to the suppliers for the purchase of inventory
   (e) cash paid for insurance
3. The following is an excerpt from the chief executive officer's (CEO's) letter to the shareholders that was included in the annual report of Cavalier Toy Stores:

> It feels real good to finish 1998 and be thankful that your company achieved its best year ever. I am sure that you are all puzzled by my statement given the net loss we have reported in the income statement. Let me explain. Although our gross margin has declined from last year's because of competitive pressures, we have set a company record in terms of sales revenue. You know quite well how accounting income can be manipulated. We don't play that game. We let cash flows tell our success story. Also,

we have very efficiently managed our receivables and inventory, and at the same time, taken advantage of all available credit from our suppliers. More importantly, I am sure all of you are very pleased with the dividends that you have received this year. Let me end this letter by proudly inviting you to visit our new executive office building. While touring the luxurious executive suites, please remember that your top management team did not burden you with one dollar of debt to buy this building.

Assume you are a commercial lending officer in Thrifty Bank. The working capital loan given to Cavalier Toy Stores (balance outstanding as of December 31, 1998, is $700,000) is repayable by April 1, 1999. The CEO has sent a loan proposal to Thrifty Bank requesting renewal of the loan for one more year and an increase in the credit limit to $1,000,000. Your job is to write a report to your boss with a specific recommendation on whether to accept or reject the proposal. Base your recommendation on the information available to you. In your report, please consider all the claims made by the CEO in the letter to the shareholders.

Cases

C17-1 Pan American Silver Corp: Cash flow information

PAN AMERICAN
SILVER CORP.
www.
panamericansilver.
com

SEDAR
www.sedar.com

Pan American Silver Corp (PASC) is a Vancouver-based silver mining company.

Required:

Part A
Access PASC's 2001 audited financial statements on the SEDAR website.

1. Does PASC use the direct or indirect method? Explain.
2. Prepare a brief memo (maximum 500 words) outlining the costs and benefits of using the direct and indirect methods in PASC's audited financial statements. The memo is to be presented at the next meeting of PASC's Audit Committee of the Board of Directors.
3. From an analyst's perspective, why is Note 12 of PASC's 2001 audited financials useful? Explain.
4. Analyze the pattern of cash flows that the company has reported over the three-year period up to 2001. Is the pattern of significance? Explain.

Part B
Access PASC's annual report on either the company's website or the SEDAR website.

1. Explain why PASC would hedge silver. Explain how this is done.
2. What impact, if any, does silver hedging have on PASC's cash flow?

C17-2 TrizecHahn Corporation: Measures of a real estate company's performance versus liquidity

TrizecHahn Corporation is (according to the inside cover of its 1998 annual report) "one of the largest real estate companies in North America and now expanding into Europe ... TrizecHahn's mandate is to become a leading real estate growth company with consistently superior financial performance." With total assets as at December 31, 1998, of US$7.6 billion, this Toronto-based company is a major integrated real estate developer and operator that owns, develops, and manages office buildings and mixed-use properties in the United States, Canada, and Europe. Properties include the World Apparel Center in New York City, the Watergate Office Building in Washington, D.C., Place Ville Marie in Montreal, Bankers Hall in Calgary, and the CN Tower in Toronto.

On pages 57 and 58 of TrizecHahn's 1998 annual report, the MD&A reads in part:

> The Corporation prepares its financial statements in accordance with Canadian generally accepted accounting principles ("GAAP"), with the major differences from U.S. GAAP described in Note 14 to the Consolidated financial statements. ...
>
> In the U.S., The National Association of Real Estate Investment Trusts ("NAREIT") has adopted a measurement called Funds from Operations ("FFO") to supplement net income as a measure of real operating performance. This measurement is considered to be a meaningful and useful measure of real estate operating performance. The Corporation's presentation of Cash Flow from Real Estate Operations is consistent with NAREIT's definition of FFO, except that FFO would include any increase or decrease in income due to straight-line revenue recognition. As described in Note 14 to the Consolidated Financial Statements, under U.S. GAAP, TrizecHahn's 1998 FFO would have been approximately $284 million (or $15 million higher) due to the impact of the straight-line rent method of revenue recognition. FFO does not represent cash flow from operations as defined by Canadian GAAP. This measure is not necessarily indicative of cash available to fund cash needs and should not be considered as an alternative to cash flow as a measure of liquidity.

Excerpts from TrizecHahn's 1998 consolidated financial statements, including the accounting policy note and note 6 ("Exchangeable Debentures"), are presented on the following pages.

Required:

1. Examine TrizecHahn's Consolidated Statements of Cash Flows. What does this examination reveal about the company?
2. What is the significance of the exchangeable debentures to measures of the company's financial performance?
3. The company presents Consolidated Statements of Cash Flow from Real Estate Operations.
   (a) Explain how Cash Flow from Real Estate Operations, as disclosed in the statement, differs from operating cash flow as disclosed in the company's Consolidated Statements of Cash Flows.
   (b) How are the measures in part (a) different from FFO, as FFO is described in the MD&A excerpt above? What is the purpose of each of these measures?
   (c) TrizecHahn's Cash Flow from Real Estate Operations (as defined by the company) increased by 53% from 1997 to 1998, but net income increased by a much more impressive 1,004%. Yet the company seems to insist that the former is a better, more reliable measure of its performance than the latter. Is this true, in your opinion?

   (d) Which of the two measures is more susceptible to manipulation, in your opinion? Is operating cash flow as defined in Section 1540 of the *CICA Handbook* better than both? Explain, with specific reference to TrizecHahn.

TrizecHahn Corporation

Consolidated Balance Sheets

(US$ millions)	Note	As at December 31, 1998	1997
Assets			
Properties	2	$6,310.8	$4,757.2
Cash and short-term investments		488.5	193.4
Other assets	3	556.3	372.4
Investment in Barrick	4	286.2	552.2
		$7,641.8	$5,875.2
Liabilities			
Long-term debt	5	$3,987.4	$3,029.4
Exchangeable debentures:			
Carrying amount	6	590.8	564.5
Deferred amount	6	284.2	310.5
Accounts payable and accrued liabilities		364.6	279.3
		5,227.0	4,183.7
Deferred Income Taxes		315.7	38.3
Shareholders' Equity	8	2,099.1	1,653.2
		$7,641.8	$5,875.2

See accompanying notes to consolidated financial statements.

TrizecHahn Corporation

Consolidated Statements of Income

For the Years Ended December 31 (US$ millions, except per share amounts)	Note	1998	1997	Pro Forma 1996	1996
Rental Operations				(Note 1)	
Rental revenue		$963.5	$713.7	$597.1	$112.1
Operating expenses		(313.6)	(243.3)	(202.3)	(35.8)
Property taxes		(107.5)	(74.3)	(56.2)	(13.5)
Rental Income		542.4	396.1	338.6	62.8
General and administrative expense		(35.4)	(29.4)	(28.6)	(12.0)
Interest expense, net	5	(230.8)	(186.1)	(180.5)	(12.5)
Real Estate Operating Income Before the Following Items		276.2	180.6	129.5	38.3
Depreciation expense		(73.8)	(50.1)	(39.9)	(8.0)
Exchangeable debentures interest expense, net		(23.8)	(19.9)	(28.4)	(28.4)
Gain on sale of properties, net		452.2	—	—	—
Gain on sale of Barrick shares		193.1	—	—	—
Income and other corporate taxes	7	(294.4)	(19.6)	44.5	67.5
Loss on early debt retirement and other, net	9	—	(25.1)	(69.8)	(69.8)
Share of net income of Barrick		—	—	31.4	31.4
Share of net income of Trizec		—	—	—	17.4
Exchangeable debentures revaluation	6	—	—	(35.0)	(35.0)
Income from Continuing Operations		529.5	65.9	32.3	13.4
Discontinued Operations of Clark	4				
Gain on sale/(operations)		—	5.0	(7.6)	(7.6)
Income taxes		—	(23.1)	—	—
		—	(18.1)	(7.6)	(7.6)
Net Income		$529.5	$ 47.8	$ 24.7	$ 5.8

See accompanying notes to consolidated financial statements.

TrizecHahn Corporation

Consolidated Statements of Cash Flow from Real Estate Operations

For the Years Ended December 31 (US$ millions, except per share amounts)	Note	1998	1997	Pro Forma 1996 (Note 1)	1996
Real Estate Operating Income		$276.2	$180.6	$129.5	$38.3
Current taxes	7	(6.9)	(4.4)	(3.7)	(0.7)
Cash Flow from Real Estate Operations		$269.3	$176.2	$125.8	$37.6
Cash Flow from Real Estate Operations per Share	1				
Basic		$1.76	$1.19	$0.92	
Fully diluted		$1.65	$1.16	$0.89	

See accompanying notes to consolidated financial statements.

TrizecHahn Corporation

Consolidated Statements of Cash Flows

For the Years Ended December 31 (US$ millions)	Note	1998	1997	Pro Forma 1996	1996
Cash flow from (applied to):				(Note 1)	
OPERATING ACTIVITIES					
Net income		$ 529.5	47.8	24.7	5.8
Non-cash items:					
Depreciation expense		73.8	50.1	39.9	8.0
Gain on sale of properties, net		(452.2)	—	—	—
Gain on sale of Barrick shares		(193.1)	—	—	—
Deferred income taxes	7	287.5	38.3	(48.2)	(68.2)
Discontinued operations of Clark		—	(5.0)	7.6	7.6
Share of affiliates' net income (net of dividends)		—	—	(23.2)	(40.6)
Dilution gains and other, net		—	—	69.8	69.8
Exchangeable debentures revaluation		—	—	35.0	35.0
Net change in operating working capital	3	9.3	(5.9)	(17.7)	10.2
Total operating cash flows		254.8	125.3	87.9	27.6
FINANCING ACTIVITIES					
Long-term debt:					
Acquisition financing		$1,467.6	$ 686.4	$205.0	$205.0
Development financing		87.5	24.2	99.7	5.6
Property financings		356.0	320.8	123.6	107.3
Unsecured debentures issued		188.5	395.7	—	—
Principal repayments		(324.5)	(757.5)	(339.7)	(263.4)
Financing of retail partnership interests		323.4	—	—	—
Repaid on dispositions		(1,142.1)	(36.0)	(206.9)	(147.8)
Exchangeable debentures issued	6	—	—	264.0	264.0
Issue of shares	8	8.1	293.8	12.9	12.9
Shares purchased and cancelled	8	(14.1)	—	—	—
Dividends paid		(46.0)	(36.4)	(7.3)	(7.3)
Total financing cash flows		904.4	891.0	151.3	176.3
Total Operating and Financing Activities		$1,159.2	$1,016.3	$239.2	$203.9

INVESTING ACTIVITIES

Properties:

Acquisitions		(2,896.2)	(1,188.2)	(333.2)	(333.2)
Development expenditures		(377.5)	(93.2)	(124.9)	(18.7)
Tenant installation costs		(100.9)	(45.6)	(41.7)	(10.0)
Capital expenditures		(26.8)	(16.2)	(15.6)	(6.2)
Acquisitions of retail partnership interests		(544.2)	—	—	—
Dispositions		2,772.9	86.1	330.0	221.7
Sale of Barrick shares	4	512.6	—	—	—
Barrick share sale installment receivable	4	(182.3)	—	—	—
Investment in Sears Tower	3	—	(70.0)	—	—
Proceeds from sale of investment in Clark		—	115.6	—	—
Funds invested in other assets and liabilities		(21.7)	(15.6)	29.8	9.3
Acquisition of Trizec	13	—	—	—	90.6
Total investing cash flows		(864.1)	(1,227.1)	(155.6)	(46.5)
Net Increase (Decrease) in Cash and Short-Term Investments		295.1	(210.8)	83.6	157.4
Cash and Short-Term Investments, Beginning of Year		193.4	404.2		246.8
Cash and Short-Term Investments, End of Year		$ 488.5	$ 193.4		$404.2

See accompanying notes to consolidated financial statements.

TrizecHahn Corporation

Excerpts from Notes to the Consolidated Financial Statements
For the Years Ended December 31, 1998, 1997 and 1996

(tabular amounts in US$ millions, except per share amounts)

---

1. Significant Accounting Policies

The consolidated financial statements of TrizecHahn Corporation ("TrizecHahn" or "the Corporation") are prepared in accordance with generally accepted accounting principles as recommended by the Canadian Institute of Chartered Accountants ("Canadian GAAP"). These principles differ in certain respects from those generally accepted in the United States ("U.S. GAAP") and to the extent that they affect the Corporation, these differences are described in Note 14 "Differences from United States Accounting Principles."

The Corporation's accounting policies and its standards of financial disclosure conform to the recommendations of the Canadian Institute of Public Real Estate Companies ("CIPREC"). In the United States, the National Association of Real Estate Investment Trusts ("NAREIT") has adopted a measurement called Funds From Operations ("FFO") to supplement net income as a measure of operating performance. This measurement is considered to be a meaningful and useful measure of real estate operating performance. TrizecHahn's and CIPREC's presentation of cash flow from real estate operations is consistent with NAREIT's definition of FFO. FFO does not represent cash flow from operations as defined by Canadian GAAP. This measure is not necessarily indicative of cash available to fund cash needs and should not be considered as an alternative to cash flow as a measure of liquidity.

The preparation of financial statements in accordance with generally accepted accounting principles requires management to make estimates and assumptions that affect the reported amounts of assets and liabilities and disclosure of contingent assets and liabilities at the date of the financial statements and the reported amounts of revenues and expenses during the reporting period. Actual results may differ from those estimates.

Certain comparatives have been reclassified to conform to the current year's presentation. ...

e. Income Recognition

i. Revenue from a rental property is recognized once the property is substantially completed and available for occupancy. Prior to this time, the property is categorized as a property under development. The Corporation has retained substantially all of the benefits and risks of ownership of its rental properties and therefore accounts for leases with its tenants as operating leases. Rental revenue includes minimum rents, participating percentage rents and recoveries of operating expenses and property, capital and large corporation taxes.

ii. Income from the sale of properties is recorded when the collection of the sale is reasonably assured and all other significant conditions and obligations are met. ...

h. Exchangeable Debentures

The carrying amount of the Corporation's exchangeable debentures is based on the market price, on the balance sheet date, of the underlying Barrick shares that would be exchanged to extinguish the debenture liability.

Where it is contemplated that delivery of the underlying Barrick shares will be made in satisfaction of the liability, hedge accounting is used whereby the difference between the carrying amount and the original issue amount of the debentures is recorded as a deferred charge until such time as there is a realization. Prior to December 31, 1996, where hedge accounting was not used, the difference between the carrying amount and the original issue amount was charged to net income in the period. ...

6. Exchangeable Debentures

	1998	1997
Carrying amount:		
$600 million, 3¼% Debentures, due 2018	$417.9	$399.2
$275 million, 3% Debentures, due 2021	172.9	165.3
	590.8	564.5
Deferred amount	284.2	310.5
	$875.0	$875.0

a. 3¼% Exchangeable Debentures

In December 1993, the Corporation issued $600 million of 3¼% Debentures due December 10, 2018. Interest is payable semi-annually. Each $1,000 principal amount of 3¼% Debentures is exchangeable at the option of the holder for 32.4675 common shares of Barrick, without payment of accrued interest. The 3¼% Debentures are redeemable at the option of the Corporation on or after December 10, 1998 at a price equal to the principal amount plus accrued interest. Upon notice of redemption by the Corporation or within 30 days prior to maturity, the holder has the option to exchange each $1,000 principal amount for between 32.4675 and 35.7143 Barrick common shares (depending upon the current market value of Barrick shares at such time), plus accrued interest payable in cash. The 3¼% Debentures are direct unsubordinated obligations of the Corporation. As of December 31, 1998 the Corporation has placed with a trustee 21,428,580 Barrick shares as collateral for its exchange obligation. This represents the maximum number of Barrick shares that are required to be pledged as collateral.

The Corporation's obligation related to any exchange or redemption can be satisfied through delivery of the cash equivalent of the current market value of Barrick shares at such time, the Barrick shares, or any combination thereof. Satisfaction of the liability with cash would retain the potential benefit of future equity appreciation related to the Barrick shares for the period subsequent to the retirement.

Prior to December 31, 1996, the Corporation carried the $600 million of 3¼% debentures at their face amount. To create consistency on a prospective basis with the accounting treatment mandated for the $275 million of 3% debentures issued in 1996, the $600 million 3¼% debentures were retroactively marked to market. This change in accounting policy resulted in the recording of a revaluation charge of $35 million for the year ended December 31, 1996. A deferred tax recovery of $15 million was recorded related to the revaluation charge resulting in a net charge to net income for the year ended December 31, 1996 of $20 million.

The carrying amount of the Corporation's 3¼% Debentures is based on the market price, on the balance sheet date, of the underlying Barrick shares that would be exchanged to extinguish the debenture liability, and approximates their fair market value.

Effective January 1, 1997, as it is contemplated that

delivery of the underlying Barrick shares will be made in satisfaction of the liability, hedge accounting has been applied, whereby the difference between the carrying amount and the original issue amount of the 3¼% Debentures is recorded as a deferred charge until such time as there is a realization.

b. 3% Exchangeable Debentures

In January 1996, the Corporation issued $275 million of 3% Debentures due January 29, 2021. The net proceeds from the issue amounted to $264.0 million. Interest is payable semi-annually. Each $1,000 principal amount of 3% Debentures is exchangeable at the option of the holder for 32.2581 common shares of Barrick, without payment of accrued interest. The 3% Debentures are redeemable at the option of the Corporation on or after January 29, 2006 at a price equal to the principal amount plus accrued interest. Upon notice of redemption by the Corporation or within 30 days prior to maturity, the holder has the option to exchange each $1,000 principal amount for 32.2581 Barrick common shares, plus accrued interest payable in cash. The 3% Debentures are direct unsubordinated obligations of the Corporation. As of December 31, 1998 the Corporation has placed with a

trustee a further 8,870,978 Barrick shares (see Note 6a above) as collateral for its exchange obligation. This represents the maximum number of Barrick shares that are required to be pledged as collateral under this issue.

The Corporation's obligation related to any exchange or redemption can be satisfied through delivery of the cash equivalent of the current market value of Barrick shares at such time, the Barrick shares, or any combination thereof. Satisfaction of the liability with cash would retain the potential benefit of future equity appreciation related to the Barrick shares for the period subsequent to the retirement.

The carrying amount of the Corporation's 3% Debentures is based on the market price, on the balance sheet date, of the underlying Barrick shares that would be exchanged to extinguish the debenture liability, and approximates their fair market value. As it is contemplated that delivery of the underlying Barrick shares will be made in satisfaction of the liability, hedge accounting has been applied, whereby the difference between the carrying amount and the original issue amount of the 3% Debentures is recorded as a deferred charge until such time as there is a realization.

7. Income and Other Corporate Taxes

a. The provision for income and other corporate taxes from continuing operations is as follows:

For the Years Ended December 31	1998	1997	1996	Pro Forma 1996
Income tax:			(Note 1)	
Current	$ (0.6)	$ (0.2)	$(0.4)	$ (0.4)
Deferred:				
Operations	(53.8)	(38.3)	(17.2)	2.8
Gain on sale of properties, net	(182.9)	—	—	—
Gain on sale of Barrick shares	(50.8)	—	—	—
Debenture revaluation (Note 6)	—	—	15.0	15.0
Valuation adjustment (Notes 9 and 13)	—	—	50.4	50.4
Other corporate tax—current	(6.3)	(4.2)	(3.3)	(0.3)
Utilization of tax-loss carry-forwards—Clark	—	23.1	—	—
Total tax (expense) recovery	$(294.4)	$(19.6)	$44.5	$67.5

Integrative Running Case Study
Bombardier on the Web

Examine Bombardier's consolidated statements of cash flows on page 72 of the company's annual report for the year ended January 31, 2002, located on the Companion Website for this text at **www.pearsoned.ca/revsine**.

1. Provide arguments in favour of Bombardier's disclosure of *both* consolidated cash flow statements and cash flow statements for its operating companies and BC separately.
2. Explain how each line item in note 22 to the company's financial statements affected the cash flows from operating activities.
3. Critically assess the company's cash flow information. What insight does it provide about the company, and its operating, investing, and financing decisions and policies?
4. Prepare, to the best of your ability, the cash flow statement for Bombardier Inc. consolidated (with BC), using the comparative balance sheets, income statements, and any other information (excluding, of course, the cash flow statements themselves). Compare the statement that you prepared with the company's published consolidated cash flow statement.

Collaborative Learning Cases
CL17-1 Best Buy Company, Inc. (KR): Analysis of financial performance from the cash flow statement and other information

The following are the consolidated cash flow statements of Best Buy Company Inc. The information provided in the annual report has been combined and abbreviated.

The following information is based on the information provided by the company in its SEC filings:

> Best Buy Co., Inc. is the nation's largest-volume specialty retailer of name brand consumer electronics, home office equipment, entertainment software, and appliances. Part of the company's strategy is to provide a large selection of brand name products comparable to retailers that specialize in the company's principal product categories, and it seeks to ensure a high level of product availability for customers. The company has experienced substantial growth over the last several years. The number of stores operated by the company increased from 151 at the end of 1994, to 204, 251, and 272 at the end of 1995, 1996, and 1997, respectively. When entering a major metropolitan market, the company establishes a district office, service centre, and major appliance warehouse. Each new store requires approximately [US]$3 million of working capital, depending on the size of the store, for merchandise inventory (net of vendor financing), leasehold improvements, fixtures, and equipment. Pre-opening costs of approximately [US]$300,000 per store are incurred in hiring and training new employees and in advertising and are expensed in the year the store is opened.

Required:

1. Using information provided in the cash flow statement, compare Best Buy's earnings and cash flows from operations for the last three years and provide an explanation for the dramatic differences between these two numbers within each year and from year to year. Which measure provides a better indication of Best

Buy's performance? Explain.

2. How have new store openings affected Best Buy's working capital needs over the last three years? Compare the company's actual changes in working capital to the working capital needed to support new store openings, and comment on any differences.

3. Comment on the rather dramatic year-to-year changes in inventories for the last three years and how these changes have been financed.

4. Comment on any insights gained from an analysis of the "Investing" and "Financing" sections of Best Buy's cash flow statement.

Best Buy Company Inc.

Consolidated Statements of Cash Flows

	For the Fiscal Years Ended:		
(US$ in thousands)	March 1, 1997	March 2, 1996	February 25, 1995
Operating Activities			
Net earnings	$ 1,748	$ 48,019	$ 57,651
Charges to earnings not affecting cash:			
Depreciation and amortization	66,844	54,862	38,570
Loss on disposal of property and equipment	468	1,267	760
Changes in operating assets and liabilities:			
Receivables	41,857	(36,998)	(31,496)
Merchandise inventories	69,083	(293,465)	(269,727)
Income taxes and prepaid expenses	8,174	(16,273)	(5,929)
Accounts payable	(186,050)	278,515	106,920
Other current liabilities	4,788	50,599	46,117
Deferred revenue and other liabilities	(27,262)	12,994	19,723
Total cash (used in) provided by operating activities	(20,350)	99,520	(37,411)
Investing Activities			
Additions to property and equipment	(87,593)	(126,201)	(118,118)
Other investment activities	72,752	(40,015)	(86,222)
(Increase) decrease in other assets	(5,593)	7,712	(11,676)
Proceeds from sale/leasebacks	—	—	24,060
Total cash used in investing activities	(20,434)	(158,504)	(191,956)
Financing Activities			
Increase in obligations under financing arrangements	33,559	12,196	70,599
Long-term debt borrowings	33,542	—	21,429
Long-term debt payments	(25,694)	(14,600)	(10,199)
Common stock issued	2,740	3,133	2,366
Proceeds from issuance of convertible preferred securities	—	—	230,000
Total cash provided by financing activities	44,147	729	314,195
Increase (Decrease) in Cash and Cash Equivalents	$ 3,363	$(58,255)	$ 84,828

Endnotes

1. H.S. Bailey, Jr., cited in R. Green, "Are More Chryslers in the Offing?" *Forbes*, February 2, 1981, p. 69.

2. The most recent Canadian pronouncement was issued in 1998. It modified Section 1540, "Statement of Changes in Financial Position," changing its title to "Cash Flow Statements," among other changes.

3. Section 1540, para. .32 requires that *"cash flows associated with extraordinary items … be classified as arising from operating, investing or financing activities. …"*

LEARNING OBJECTIVES

After studying this chapter, you should be able to:

1. Understand how financial reporting approaches worldwide fall into two categories—(1) those designed to reflect economic performance and (2) those that conform to tax or statutory law

2. Describe why financial reporting philosophies differ across countries

3. Briefly describe the various mechanisms that have evolved for coping with financial reporting diversity from country to country

4. Explain how compliance with GAAP is monitored in different countries

5. Understand that foreign countries with high inflation rates depart from the historical cost reporting model

6. Describe the two major approaches for adjusting financial reports for rapidly changing prices—current cost accounting and general price-level accounting

International investment in equity and debt securities has skyrocketed in recent years. For example, the Bank for International Settlements reported that back in 1975, total cross-border purchases and sales of bond and equity securities between residents and nonresidents of Canada were only 3% of that year's Canadian GDP, but by 1997 such transactions equalled 358% of 1997's Canadian GDP. For developed countries especially, there has been explosive growth in international bond and equity transactions from the mid-1970s to the present.

And indications of this high level of international investment are provided by other facts as well. For instance, stock exchanges across the world now have significant numbers of foreign companies listed:

BANK FOR
INTERNATIONAL
SETTLEMENTS
www.bis.org

Stock Exchange	Total Number of Companies Listed	Number of Domestic Companies Listed	Number of Foreign Companies Listed
Toronto Stock Exchange	1,456	1,410	46
New York Stock Exchange	2,592	2,187	405
NASDAQ	4,829	4,400	429
Germany	9,017	1,043	7,974
London	2,791	2,292	499
Paris	1,144	968	176

Source: International Accounting Standards Board's (IASB's) website data as of 1999.

Indeed, the Bank for International Settlements reported in its 72nd Annual Report (July 8, 2002) that the global financial system was very resilient in the aftermath of September 11, 2001, and other events (such as Enron).

Access to global capital as well as to global consumer markets allows companies from many countries to grow large. Table 18.1 shows the country of origin for the largest companies in eight selected industries for 2001. Investors who choose to concentrate on a specific industrial or commercial sector are compelled to think globally.

The growth of global investing has been fuelled by several factors. For example, many major industrial countries have relaxed their security market regulatory rules. Another example is improvements in telecommunications and computer technology. Finally, investors understand that portfolios based on a global investment strategy are less risky than portfolios comprising strictly domestic securities. That's because foreign issuers of securities are often subject to economic conditions that differ from those of domestic companies.

Global investment decisions are complicated by the diversity of financial reporting measurement and disclosure rules in different countries. Even the philosophy and objective of financial reporting differ considerably between countries. Investors reading foreign financial statements are frequently confronted with unfamiliar reporting rules, unique tax-driven financial statement items, and nuances specific to each country. An overview of some of these differences in financial reporting approaches is presented next.

An International Financial Reporting Map

There are numerous ways to classify international financial reporting approaches. In keeping with the philosophy of this book, our classification system stresses differences between countries in the nature of their financial reporting rules and how those differences are reflected in statement content and interpretation.

Two broad categories emerge from this perspective. First, there is a group of countries whose financial statements are intended (at least in principle) to capture and reflect the underlying economic performance of the reporting entity. Accounting principles in those countries are designed and selected to help achieve this objective and thereby aid external users' resource allocation decisions. Second, there is a large group of countries whose financial reporting rules do not try to capture (often elusive) "economic reality." Instead, the accounting reports simply conform to mandated laws or detailed tax rules designed to achieve purposes like raising tax revenues to fund government activities, or stimulating capital investment.

Disclosures Designed to Reflect Economic Performance

Canada is, of course, in this category. Brief comments on other prominent members of this category follow.

United Kingdom Financial reporting in the United Kingdom has influenced accounting in many other countries, such as Canada and other British Commonwealth members, as well as the United States.

Contemporary accounting principles in the United Kingdom are based on the *Companies Act 1985*—called "The Act"—as well as on a series of pronouncements—

TABLE 18.1 LARGEST GLOBAL COMPANIES IN EIGHT SELECTED INDUSTRIES (BY 2001 REVENUES)

Airlines
AMR (U.S.)

Banks: Commercial and Savings
Deutsche Bank (Germany)

Electronics, Electrical Equipment
Siemens (Germany)

Chemicals
BASF (Germany)

Food Consumer Products
Nestlé (Switzerland)

Forest and Paper Products
International Paper (U.S.)

Metals
Alcoa (U.S.)

Telecommunications
Nippon Telegraph and Telephone (Japan)

2001 FORTUNE GLOBAL 500
www.fortune.com/fortune/global500

Source: 2001 Fortune Global 500. Database and search engine on the Internet.

called Financial Reporting Standards—issued by the Accounting Standards Board, a private sector professional organization. The Act requires U.K. companies to distribute audited financial statements. While the Act does not contain detailed reporting rules, it does specify certain principles that companies must follow when preparing financial statements. For example, U.K. statements must be based on the accrual concept, the going concern perspective must be used, and the reporting rules must be consistently applied. Furthermore, the audit must ascertain whether the statements comply with the Act and whether they give a **true and fair view** of the company's state of affairs and profit or loss.[1]

The phrase "true and fair view" is central to financial reporting in the United Kingdom because it expresses the notion that financial statements must reflect the underlying economic conditions experienced by the reporting firm—that is, financial reporting rules in the United Kingdom are intended to do more than merely present an arbitrary, uniform set of numbers that may bear no correspondence to the existing market conditions under which the firm operates. The U.K. perspective that financial statements should capture a firm's underlying economic situation exerted great influence on the reporting philosophy that prevails in Canada, the United States, and other countries.

Exhibit 18.1 reproduces the directors' report and auditor's opinion from the 2001 annual report of BP Amoco. We have highlighted the phrases "the accounts give a true and fair view" and "prepared in accordance with the Companies Act 1985."

Before 1990, British GAAP were written by a predecessor group called the Accounting Standards Committee. Its pronouncements were known as "Statements of Standard Accounting Practice."

BP AMOCO
www.bp.com

United States

Following the Civil War, the United States experienced rapid industrialization and growth. This expansion was financed by a considerable amount of foreign capital—much of it from the United Kingdom. To review the accounts of their U.S. investments, U.K. investors frequently hired British auditors. These auditors came to the United States and exerted a strong influence on late 19th century U.S. accounting practices, which explains some of the parallels between modern financial reporting in the United States and in the United Kingdom.

The ultimate responsibility for formulating U.S. financial reporting rules resides in the governmental sector—with the Securities and Exchange Commission (SEC).[2] However, the SEC has delegated much of the detailed rule making to a private sector body—the Financial Accounting Standards Board (FASB).

Influenced by their British antecedents, U.S. financial reports are also intended to reflect the underlying economic events and activities of the reporting entity.

Exhibit 18.1 BP AMOCO

Statement of Directors' Responsibilities in Respect of the Accounts

Company law requires the directors to prepare accounts for each financial year which give a true and fair view of the state of affairs of the company and the group and of the profit or loss of the group for that period. In preparing those accounts, the directors are required:

- to select suitable accounting policies and then apply them consistently
- to make judgements and estimates that are reasonable and prudent
- to state whether applicable accounting standards have been followed, subject to any material departures disclosed and explained in the accounts
- to prepare the accounts on the going concern basis unless it is inappropriate to presume that the group will continue in business.

The directors are also responsible for keeping proper accounting records which disclose with reasonable accuracy at any time the financial position of the group and which enable them to ensure that the accounts comply with the Companies Act 1985. They are also responsible for taking reasonable steps to safeguard the assets of the group and to prevent and detect fraud and other irregularities.

The directors confirm that they have complied with these requirements, and, having a reasonable expectation that the company has adequate resources to continue in operational existence for the foreseeable future, continue to adopt the going concern basis in preparing the accounts.

Independent Auditors' Report

To the Members of BP p.l.c.

We have audited the group's accounts for the year ended 31 December 2001 which comprise the group income statement, balance sheets, group cash flow statement, statement of total recognized gains and losses and related notes 1 to 45. These accounts have been prepared on the basis of the accounting policies set out therein.

Respective responsibilities of directors and auditors

The directors' responsibilities for preparing the annual report and accounts in accordance with applicable United Kingdom law and accounting standards are set out in the statement of directors' responsibilities in respect of the accounts.

Our responsibility is to audit the accounts in accordance with relevant legal and regulatory requirements, United Kingdom Auditing Standards and the Listing Rules of the Financial Services Authority.

We report to you our opinion as to whether the accounts give a true and fair view and are properly prepared in accordance with the Companies Act 1985. We also report to you if, in our opinion, the Directors' Report, contained in *Annual Report 2001,* is not consistent with the accounts, if the company has not kept proper accounting records, if we have not received all the information and explanations we require for our audit, or if the information specified by law of the Listing Rules regarding directors' remuneration and transaction with the group is not disclosed.

We review whether the corporate governance statement contained in *Annual Report 2001* reflects the company's compliance with the seven provisions of the Combined Code specified for our review by the Listing Rules, and we report if it does not. We are not required to consider whether the board's statements on internal control cover all risks and controls, or form an opinion on the effectiveness of the group's corporate governance procedures or its risk and control procedures.

We read other information contained in *Annual Report 2001* and *Annual Accounts 2001* and consider whether it is consistent with the audited accounts. This other information comprises the supplementary information on oil and natural gas quantities and the Directors' Report, including the chairman's letter, group chief executive's review, financial and business performance review, corporate governance statement and executive directors' remuneration. We consider the implications for our report if we become aware of any misstatements or material inconsistencies with the accounts. Our responsibilities do not extend to any other information.

Basis of audit opinion

We conducted our audit in accordance with United Kingdom Auditing Standards issued by the Auditing Practices Board. An audit includes examination, on a test basis, of evidence relevant to the amounts and disclosures in the accounts. It also includes an assessment of the significant estimates and judgements made by the directors in the preparation of the accounts, and of whether the accounting policies are appropriate to the group's circumstances, consistently applied and adequately disclosed.

We planned and performed our audit so as to obtain all the information and explanations which we considered necessary in order to provide us with sufficient evidence to give reasonable assurance that the accounts are free from material misstatement, whether caused by fraud or other irregularity or error. In forming our opinion we also evaluated the overall adequacy of the presentation of information in the accounts.

Opinion

In our opinion the accounts give a true and fair view of the state of affairs of the company and of the group as at 31 December 2001 and of the profit of the group for the year then ended and have been properly prepared in accordance with the Companies Act 1985.

Ernst & Young LLP
Registered Auditor
London
12 February 2002

Statements that are prepared in accordance with this objective are said to "present fairly... in conformity with generally accepted accounting principles." Notice that the sidebar suggests that the auditor in the U.K. environment has more scope to focus on whether accounting standards seem appropriate. This greater onus on professional judgment has led to the suggestion that an Enron-like accounting failure might be more likely in the U.S. than in the U.K., since the former jurisdiction emphasizes compliance with specific accounting rules more than the latter does. This leads, it seems, to a mindset in which mere compliance with technical accounting rules could be an end in itself, rather than good reporting.

Other Countries

The United Kingdom also influenced the financial reporting philosophy and standards in Ireland, as well as in British Commonwealth countries (but see comment on Canada, below). Accounting statements in Australia, New Zealand, and India clearly display similarities to U.K. reporting. Although each of these countries' standards evolved independently after the initial British influence, their resemblance to U.K. accounting procedures is still recognizable today. For example, periodic writeups of fixed assets to reflect current appraised values—an accepted practice in the United Kingdom—is also permitted in Commonwealth Countries like Australia, New Zealand, India, and Zimbabwe. Furthermore, the notion that financial reporting is designed to capture underlying economic circumstances pervades these countries' procedures. Auditors' opinions in these countries also include the phrase "true and fair view."

By linking the U.K.'s "true and fair view" with the U.S.'s "present fairly," we only intend to show that each country's financial reporting is designed to capture underlying economic events. But there are *significant* differences between the two approaches. In the United States, "presents fairly" simply means that the statements conform to GAAP. Since U.S. GAAP are designed to reflect economic events, it is *presumed* that conformity to GAAP *automatically* means conformity to the economics of the events portrayed. This is not so in the U.K.'s application of the "true and fair view." There, if a firm's *unique* circumstances mean that U.K. GAAP will not reflect its economic position, departures from U.K. GAAP are permitted as long as the departure better reflects the "true and fair view" of the firm's operations. Despite this subtle difference, the two approaches share the characteristic that the reports are designed—in principle—to capture the underlying economic events the firm experienced. (See S.A. Zeff, "A Perspective on the U.S. Public/Private-Sector Approach to the Regulation of Financial Reporting," *Accounting Horizons*, March 1995, pp. 52–70.)

U.S. accounting principles have likewise had a wide impact on financial reporting in other countries. Examples include Mexico, Canada, and the Philippines. For example, Canadian auditors' reports include the phrase "these consolidated financial statements present fairly … in accordance with Canadian generally accepted accounting principles."

Netherlands[3] Dutch financial statements, like those in the United Kingdom and the United States, are also intended to reflect the underlying economic conditions experienced by the reporting entity. Interestingly, however, this "tell it like it is" goal for financial reporting in the Netherlands evolved independently of the Anglo-American tradition.

The evolution from reporting that was not designed to capture underlying economics to the modern Dutch approach proceeded slowly following the Second World War. Three factors appear to have shaped this transformation. First, the destruction caused by the Second World War as well as the prospect for postwar growth generated tremendous capital investment requirements and opportunities for Dutch companies. These enormous investment expenditures could only be undertaken with a large amount of foreign financing. As a result, improvements in financial reporting began to evolve as a way to attract foreign capital. Second, during the 1950s there was widespread debate in the Netherlands regarding whether or not shareholders had the right to receive expanded information about enterprise performance. Ultimately, these demands for improved disclosure emanating from employees, shareholders, and the general public prevailed; various quasi-public commissions over the next decade persistently recommended more realistic financial reporting. This emerging consensus caused leading companies to improve their financial reports voluntarily. The resulting reforms were ultimately made into law by the Dutch parliament in 1970. The third influence on Dutch reporting appears to have been driven by the activism of several leading influential Dutch companies, such as Unilever and Philips. Their financial reports became models that diffused throughout the business sector.

UNILEVER
www.unilever.com

PHILIPS
www.philips.com

While the philosophy of contemporary Dutch financial reporting is similar to the philosophy that underlies the Anglo-American-Canadian tradition, there are important differences. The main one is that Dutch GAAP permit more diversity in the financial reporting choices available to companies. Many companies in the Netherlands prepare financial reports that strive to capture the firm's underlying economics. However, due to the pervasive permissiveness of the Dutch environment, there are also some companies whose reports deviate from this philosophy. Accordingly, readers of Dutch financial statements must be prepared for greater diversity in financial reporting quality than is the norm in Canada.

Recap

As in Canada, GAAP in both the United Kingdom and the United States endeavour to capture underlying economic events. Because of the important historical influence of both of these countries, their reporting philosophies have been widely copied. Although numerous financial reporting differences exist among countries whose GAAP try to capture underlying economics, the similarities in reporting objectives and methods are numerous.

Disclosures That Do Not Necessarily Reflect Economic Performance

The British "true and fair view" and the Canadian and American "presents fairly" philosophy of financial reporting do not prevail everywhere. In many countries, public companies' financial statements are required to conform to tax law and/or to the existing commercial law governing accounting. Financial reports in these countries are not necessarily designed to reflect a firm's underlying economic performance. In France, Italy, and Belgium, financial reporting is heavily influenced by national tax laws; in Germany, Japan, and Switzerland, financial reporting is influenced by both commercial and tax laws.

Exhibit 18.2 shows the auditors' report from the 2001 Nestlé S.A. annual report. In this report, the auditors state that the figures "comply with Swiss law and the company's articles of incorporation." This level of assurance is very different from saying that the statements "present fairly." Readers accustomed to Canadian, U.S., or U.K. statements must be sensitive to a potentially wide range of divergence between reported amounts on such statements and underlying economics.

For example, balance sheet provisions for future losses are created in Germany in "good" earnings' years; the debit is charged to the income statement. This is a straightforward income smoothing device, since the balance sheet reserve is used to absorb losses in subsequent "bad" earnings years. An equally extreme opportunity for income smoothing exists in Finland, where companies in the past have been permitted to omit income statement amortization charges altogether in years of low earnings.

> Of course, financial reporting in Canada, the United States, and the United Kingdom is also influenced by law. However, there is a difference since each country also has standard-setting bodies whose role is to develop financial reporting procedures to capture underlying economic conditions, consistent with the philosophy of the law. In other countries, the law simply dictates report content without regard to whether the resulting numbers conform to economic circumstances.

Exhibit 18.2 NESTLÉ S.A.

Report of the Statutory Auditors

To the General Meeting of Nestlé S.A.

As statutory auditors, we have audited the accounting records and the financial statements (balance sheet, income statement and annex) of Nestlé S.A. for the year ended 31st December 2001.

These financial statements are the responsibility of the Board of Directors. Our responsibility is to express an opinion on these financial statements based on our audit. We confirm that we meet the legal requirements concerning professional qualification and independence.

Our audit was conducted in accordance with auditing standards promulgated by the Swiss profession, which require that an audit be planned and performed to obtain reasonable assurance about whether the financial statements are free from material misstatement. We have examined on a test basis evidence supporting the amounts and disclosures in the financial statements. We have also assessed the accounting principles used, significant estimates made and the overall financial statement presentation. We believe that our audit provides a reasonable basis for our opinion.

In our opinion, the accounting records, financial statements and the proposed appropriation of retained earnings comply with Swiss law and the company's articles of incorporation.

We recommend that the financial statements submitted to you be approved.

Klynveld Peat   Marwick Goerdeler SA

S.R. Cormack   B.A. Mathers
Chartered accountant   Chartered accountant

Auditors in charge
London and Zurich, 27th February 2002

NESTLÉ S.A.
www.nestle.com

These national accounting rules apply to financial statements prepared for distribution within the home country—in France, Germany, Italy, and numerous others. These statements are called **parent company** financial statements. However, the recent trend among European multinationals that have shares listed overseas is to use either standards of the International Accounting Standards Committee (IASC), now the International Accounting Standards Board (IASB), or U.S. GAAP in the consolidated statements that are prepared for foreign investors and others. (IASB standards are discussed later in the chapter.) This trend has begun to narrow the gap between these countries' consolidated reports and underlying economics.

To qualify for tax benefits in many countries, a company that claims deductions on the tax return must also include them in the published financial statements. ***This effectively requires conformity between tax and book amounts and greatly restricts the ability of financial statements to reflect economic performance.*** Regarding German accounting on this point, Frederick Choi and Gerhard Mueller state:

> *The second pervasive characteristic of accounting in Germany is its complete subordination to tax law. The so-called* **determination principle** *(Massgeblichkeitsprinzip) basically states that taxable income is determined by whatever is booked in a firm's financial records. Any available tax provisions can only be utilized if they are in fact fully booked. This means, among other things, that if any special or highly accelerated depreciation is to be used for tax purposes, it must be completely and fully booked for financial reporting purposes as well.*
>
> *The dominance of tax accounting rules means that there is literally no difference between financial statements prepared for tax purposes and financial statements published in financial reports. Since tax matters always dominate, there is literally no separate decision making concerning any accounting principles choice. Consequently, accounting standards or "generally accepted accounting principles" in the British-American sense do not exist in Germany. Financial reports reflect tax laws—not primarily the information needs of investors and other financial market participants.[4]*

Some elements of the Japanese income tax law are similar to those of Germany—that is, if a company wishes to gain certain tax deductions in Japan, its financial statements must reflect the same charges shown on the tax return. But the accounting used to make the financial reporting numbers conform to tax numbers in Japanese financial statements differs subtly from the procedures used in Germany. In Japan, the debit for the extra tax-driven deduction does not appear on the income statement. Instead, the debit is made to *retained earnings* and a credit is made to a special retained earnings reserve. (This credit can be thought of as a type of deferred income tax payable account, since the extra deductions in Japan reverse in future years.)

Recap

In countries like Germany and Japan, tax-driven amounts that may not bear any relation to underlying economic costs get reflected in reported financial results. Consequently, the underlying financial statements will not show—in many cases—the reporting firm's real performance during the period (i.e., to the extent that any GAAP-based accounting system is able to report a firm's "real" performance).

Why Do Reporting Philosophies Differ Across Countries?

What factors explain differences among countries' financial reporting concepts and rules? Why do certain countries' statements try to reflect underlying economics, while the statements in other countries merely conform to arbitrary legal formats?

A country's financial reporting rules represent one aspect of its legal, ethical, institutional, and financial customs, procedures, and social objectives. Differences in financial reporting philosophies reflect cross-country differences in underlying social mores and systems. When comparing countries, it is difficult to relate specific social differences to individual financial reporting differences, but certain basic links are apparent.

One link reflects the source of the financing used by companies. In countries where the bulk of the investment capital is attracted from a broad base of investors, these investors want comprehensive data to help them select appropriate securities. Here, there is a demand for a reporting system that captures underlying economics. The United States and Canada provide examples since an exceedingly large portion of firms' capital requirements are provided by individual debt and equity investors—either directly or indirectly through pension plans and mutual funds. The financial reporting environment in both countries has evolved to meet these information requirements.

By contrast, in countries like Japan and Germany, a small amount of firms' financing is provided by individual investors. The primary capital providers in Germany are several large banks—and the government itself. The German stock market is small. Similarly, six or eight large banks provide much of the financing in Japan; in addition, firms also raise capital from members of their associated corporate group.[5] As a consequence, external equity financing is also relatively unimportant in Japan. In countries like Japan and Germany, there are few important capital providers, and those that exist exert great power—such as the ability to acquire information directly from the firm seeking capital. Because of this power and because of the insignificance of the public market, the demand for economically realistic reporting standards has been low.

Sources of financing do shift over time. When this happens in a country, changes in the financial reporting environment will occur as well. This appears to be taking place in several European countries. As firms in these countries increasingly seek foreign capital, some feel the need to divorce their financial statements from tax rules and to conform more closely to an economic performance perspective. The hope is that by preparing their financial reports using procedures required by the countries in which potential investors reside, these statements will be more understandable to foreign investors. Consequently, a two-tiered financial reporting system is emerging in Europe. The rigid book/tax conformity rules are adhered to only at the parent company level. The parent is a financial (i.e., nonoperating) holding company that is an amalgamation of all the tax-paying entities the firm comprises. Legal rules are satisfied because the parent company statements conform to the tax law. But a second financial reporting tier evolved in the late 1990s. In this second tier, consolidated financial statements (described in Chapter 16) that encompass the legally separate operating subsidiaries are prepared. These statements—which are directed to potential investors—increasingly use either U.S. GAAP or IASB standards to report performance. This trend is especially evident in Germany, prompted by a 1998 law that allows German companies whose securities are publicly traded to use IAS or U.S. GAAP—rather than German GAAP—in their consolidated financial statements *for domestic reporting purposes*. So there is a clear international movement toward financial reports prepared in the Anglo-American tradition.

Coping with International Reporting Diversity

How should regulators respond to the diversity of financial reporting requirements for publicly traded securities across countries? What information requirements should be imposed by the securities regulatory commission in Country A if a firm from Country B wishes to sell securities in Country A?

There are at least four different approaches that regulatory commissions can use to deal with foreign issuers of securities. They can:

1. compel foreign issuers to use host country reporting regulations

"Traditionally, Japanese companies have been managed on behalf of their employees, not shareholders. The majority of a company's shares are likely to be held by banks and other companies for the purpose of maintaining a relationship, so there was little concern about shareholder returns and little fear of hostile takeovers. … [A]ccounting rules now under consideration would compel greater disclosure, making it harder for companies to sweep problems under the rug."
A. Pollack, "Japan Considers Opening the Veiled Corporate Ledger," *New York Times*, August 5, 1997.

2. create bilateral arrangements between a particular host country and a particular foreign country
3. allow every foreign issuer to use the foreign issuer's own financial reporting rules in a host country
4. require foreign issuers to use an internationally consistent set of reporting principles and procedures

We next briefly examine each of these alternatives.

Foreign Issuers Use Host Country Financial Reporting Rules

The United States requires foreign companies that wish to have securities traded on U.S. exchanges to reconcile their own reporting methods to U.S. GAAP. This reconciliation is mandated by the American SEC on Form 20-F. The disclosure is designed for the convenience of U.S. financial statement readers. This form provides U.S. investors with income and other statement numbers computed using familiar rules, allowing them to evaluate the performance of foreign issuers relative to U.S. companies using—on a common reporting basis—U.S. GAAP. However, this reconciliation is controversial from two perspectives.

One controversy relates to the competitive disadvantages that reconciliation may impose on U.S. markets; the other concerns whether the reconciliation accomplishes what it is supposed to—that is, whether it overcomes differences between U.S. and foreign GAAP.

U.S. stock exchanges contend that the Form 20-F reconciliation creates competitive disadvantages. The exchanges say that by imposing what they contend are burdensome disclosure requirements on foreign issuers, these issuers become reluctant to list their securities on U.S. exchanges. The U.S. exchanges believe it is costly for foreign firms to reconcile their statements to U.S. GAAP. To avoid this cost, the exchanges argue that some firms simply refuse to list and sell their securities in the United States. As a consequence, there's a dual loss—U.S. exchanges lose the business of listing foreign issues, and the cost of buying foreign securities is higher for U.S. investors since they must buy them abroad.

The other problem with the Form 20-F reconciliation is that even after a foreign company reconciles its numbers to U.S. GAAP, the information it provides may still not be truly comparable to the information provided by U.S. firms. The reason for this is that many U.S. GAAP procedures evolved from business and other institutional relationships that exist in the United States. These same relationships may not exist in the foreign issuer's country. Therefore, reconciliation to U.S. GAAP does not necessarily produce the desired comparability.

Consider the following example. The equity method of accounting for an investment in another company (Chapter 16) is required under U.S. GAAP when the percentage of share ownership is between 20% and 50%. This requirement is based on the fact that in the United States, this large proportionate ownership presumably gives the investor some degree of control over the investee's policies, *including its dividend policy*. Using the cost method in such circumstances would be inappropriate since control over dividend policy would allow the investor to manipulate income by altering dividend levels.

To see the flaw in the Form 20-F reconciliation approach, consider a Japanese company that reconciles its accounting to U.S. GAAP. Most larger Japanese companies are members of a **keiretsu**, a loosely interconnected corporate group. Members of the keiretsu typically own shares of other members of the keiretsu; this arrangement provides a source of financing and further aligns the group's incentives towards mutual benefits. Cross-ownerships in the 20% to 30% range are not unusual in these situations. But investment by one keiretsu member in another *conveys to the investor no control over the corporate affairs of the investee*. Yet Form 20-F would require the Japanese investor to account for the investee using the equity method. Once we understand the totally different institutional arrangements that govern intercorporate investments in Japan, it is evident that using the equity method to reflect such holdings above 20% will *not* capture underlying economics.

Interestingly, Form 20-F provides an important source of information for *Canadian* users of accounting information. For example, in his testimony before the Canadian Senate's Standing Committee on Banking, Trade and Commerce, on Wednesday, May 29, 2002, Brian Gibson of the Ontario Teachers' Pension Plan Board said:

> *When we look to invest in other countries around the world—Japan, or Germany, or Brazil, for example—we find that their standards are completely different from those to which we have become accustomed. We use a rather short-term solution to deal with that: We tend to focus on companies that are [SEC] registrants …. Therefore, we will get U.S. GAAP statements, which as Canadians we can understand."*

Source: Parliamentary Internet Parlementaire website of the Canadian Parliament at **www.parl.gc.ca**.

CANADIAN
PARLIAMENT
www.parl.gc.ca

Bilateral Multijurisdictional Agreements

Another method for dealing with international financial reporting diversity is "multijurisdictional disclosure," a procedure that is followed to an extent between Canada and the United States. Under this procedure, the Canadian securities commissions accept for registration purposes the American GAAP statements of an American firm seeking to issue debt or preferred stock, and in certain circumstances other equity issues like common shares (and vice versa).

The firm issuing financial statements benefits because it avoids the cost of reformulating its statements into another country's GAAP, but statement users must be knowledgeable about the financial reporting standards of *both* Canada and the United States. This cost is tempered by the fact that reporting methods in Canada and the United States are somewhat similar. Indeed, the multijurisdictional disclosure approach seems feasible only between countries with broadly similar accounting measurement and disclosure standards. However, "similar" is far from "identical," as the excerpt from BCE Inc.'s 2000 financials in Exhibit 18.3 shows.

BCE INC.
www.bce.ca

Issuer's Reporting Allowed

The third approach for coping with international reporting diversity is for a host country to allow foreign firms to use their own financial reporting rules. The host country could allow French firms to report their results using French accounting principles, Indian firms could report their results using Indian accounting principles, and so on. This approach imposes no costs on the reporting firm; however, it does place tremendous burdens on analysts in the host country, who need to be knowledgeable about a wide range of foreign financial reporting practices. Because of the high costs imposed on statement users, this approach for coping with financial reporting diversity is not widely advocated.

Foreign Issuers Use an International Standard

Progress is being made toward yet another approach, one in which the ultimate intent is that all firms use an internationally consistent set of reporting principles and procedures. The International Accounting Standards Board (IASB) is a privately funded accounting

INTERNATIONAL
ACCOUNTING
STANDARDS BOARD
www.iasc.org.uk

Exhibit 18.3 "SIMILAR" IS NOT "IDENTICAL": EXAMPLE FROM BCE'S 2000 AUDITED FINANCIAL STATEMENTS

21. RECONCILIATION OF EARNINGS REPORTED IN ACCORDANCE WITH CANADIAN GAAP WITH UNITED STATES GAAP

The significant differences between Canadian and United States GAAP affecting the consolidated financial statements of BCE are reconciled in the table below:

	2000		1999	
($ millions except per share amounts)	Net earnings applicable to common shares	Retained earnings	Net earnings applicable to common shares	Retained earnings
Canadian GAAP—				
Continuing operations	807	1,601	4,976	8,301
Adjustments				
Additional pick-up of non-controlling interest (a)	14	(66)	(80)	(80)
Pre-operating expenses and subscriber acquisition costs (b)	(100)	(221)	(17)	(121)
Foreign exchange (c)	(76)	(258)	(63)	(182)
Employee future benefits (d)	39	39	(69)	(477)
Income taxes (e)	45	45	252	(20)
Gain on exchange of investments (f)	—	99	99	99
Gain on disposal of investments and on reduction of ownership in subsidiary companies (g)	(31)	(276)	124	(245)
Other	(63)	(38)	(60)	25
U.S. GAAP—Continuing operations	635	925	5,162	7,300
Discontinued operations— U.S. GAAP (h)	(991)	(67)	231	(1,734)
U.S. GAAP	(356)	858	5,393	5,566
Other comprehensive earnings (loss) items:				
Change in currency translation adjustment	107		(467)	
Change in unrealized gain on investments, net (i)	2,788		8	
Comprehensive earnings—U.S. GAAP	2,539		4,934	

standard-setter based in the United Kingdom. It is the successor to the International Accounting Standards Committee (IASC), which began operation on July 1, 1973, following an agreement by professional accounting organizations in Australia, Canada, France, Germany, Japan, Mexico, the Netherlands, Ireland, the United Kingdom, and the United States. The objectives of the IASB were:

1. to formulate and publish in the public interest accounting standards to be observed in the presentation of financial statements and to promote their worldwide acceptance and observance

2. to work generally for the improvement and harmonization of regulations, accounting standards, and procedures relating to the presentation of financial statements[6] (Effective April 2001, the IASB took over the IASC's responsibilities, after restructuring.)

By 2002, the IASB had 34 accounting standards in effect. While these standards are not binding on participating countries, one of the objectives of the IASB is to "persuade governments and standard-setting bodies that published financial statements should comply with International Standards in all material respects."[7]

A heightened legitimacy for international standards seems to be emerging. However, at least one informed observer has misgivings about " 'political' pressures … [which] … could impede the effort to achieve convergence at a high level of quality."[8]

Recap

Several methods exist for coping with diverse international financial reporting standards. Many think that the best approach for overcoming reporting differences is a movement to an internationally consistent set of reporting principles developed by the IASB.

Monitoring Compliance

Financial reporting rules differ across countries, and so do the mechanisms for monitoring compliance with these rules. Different countries have different structures for determining whether the stated principles are actually being followed by firms. Of course, industrialized countries require firms to have audited financial statements. The independent auditor provides one mechanism for monitoring compliance with reporting rules. However, there have been instances in which auditors' independence and even adherence to professional standards were challenged. This is why a backup mechanism for monitoring financial reports is needed to provide additional safeguards for statement readers.

Across Canada, securities commissions have launched several initiatives intended to encourage compliance and to raise the level of financial reporting. For example, in its 1999 annual report, the British Columbia Securities Commission specifically mentioned the following, among others:

- harmonizing rules and policies for securities regulation across Canada
- improved mining company disclosures (a response to the Bre-X case)
- an increased emphasis on continuous disclosure

Also, the advent of securities sales and financial disclosure via the Internet has created new challenges.

In the United States, the SEC has the authority to challenge financial reports that it believes do not conform to GAAP. There have been many cases in which the SEC has objected to the accounting principles used in statements filed with the Commission. The reporting firms were compelled to alter their financial statements to bring them into compliance with the Commission's interpretation of GAAP. And recently—post-Enron, WorldCom, and others—the U.S. will require CEOs to certify that their companies' financial statements are "accurate and complete."

Currently, the SEC scrutinizes the financial statements for *all* new registrants—called initial public offerings (IPOs)—that are filed with the Commission. What

BRITISH COLUMBIA
SECURITIES
COMMISSION
www.bcsc.bc.ca

SEC
www.sec.gov

little remains of staff time is then used to review—on a sampling basis—the statements of longer-established registrants. The SEC compliance "safety net" is not exhaustive.

It can be worse in other countries.[9] For years in Australia, New Zealand, and the United Kingdom, the independent auditor represented the *only* monitoring and compliance force. This situation still persists in New Zealand. However, in Australia a new Australian Securities Commission has been established to expand monitoring. Similarly, in the United Kingdom a private sector agency called the Financial Reporting Review Panel has recently been formed. The U.K. parliament has delegated authority to this group to bring actions in civil court for perceived breaches of "true and fair view" reporting.

In the Netherlands, a type of "accounting court," which is called the Enterprise Chamber, was created by parliament in 1970. Interested parties can bring alleged violations of the financial reporting provisions of statute law to this group. However, the cost and inconvenience of this process has led to a decline in the number of actions initiated in recent years. The current effectiveness of the Dutch Enterprise Chamber as a compliance enforcement mechanism is unclear.

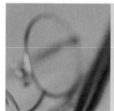

Recap

Users of foreign financial statements need to be aware of these monitoring mechanisms. Understanding that reporting rules differ across countries represents only one part of the story. It is also important to understand that there might be across-country differences in the adherence to the reporting rules that are supposed to be in effect.

Inflation Accounting

Inflation—a decline in the purchasing power of a country's currency—complicates analysis of international financial reports. Where inflation is high, historical-cost-based financial statements are misleading or totally irrelevant. Financial reporting standards in countries with high rates of inflation mandate some form of **inflation accounting** for both tax and financial statement reporting. Mexico is an example. Two forms of inflation accounting are required by Mexican GAAP: (1) specific price-change adjustments and (2) general price-level adjustments. Each of these inflation accounting approaches is explained and illustrated in this section.

Introduction: General Versus Specific Price Changes

All prices do not change at the same rate. Even during periods of severe inflation, it is not unusual for the prices of some goods and services to actually fall and move in the opposite direction to prices in general. Let us illustrate using Canadian data from Statistics Canada's website. Between 1992 and May 2002, the general level of consumer prices in Canada, as measured by the Consumer Price Index (CPI), increased by 18.6%. This includes all items in the CPI basket, for the country as a whole. However, over this same period, the average consumer price change for clothing and footwear increased by only 4.6%, and average consumer prices for transportation *increased* by 34.1%, considerably above the overall average of 18.6%.

These examples illustrate that significant differences are likely to arise between *average* rates of inflation for the economy as a whole and *specific* rates of price change for a given firm. Diversity in rates of price changes generates controversy regarding

STATISTICS CANADA
www.statcan.ca

the appropriate method for reflecting economic activity in these circumstances. Some believe that adjustments for changing prices should be based on the specific level of costs and prices experienced by each individual firm. This approach is called **current cost accounting.** The rationale for the current cost approach is that since each firm is unique, its own unique level of costs and prices should be reflected in its accounts.

Others believe that adjustments for changing prices should be based upon the general rate of inflation experienced in the economy as a whole. In this view, inflation adjustments would be derived from broad indices of overall price changes, such as the Consumer Price Index (CPI). This method of adjusting for inflation is called **general price-level accounting.**

First we'll explain and illustrate current cost accounting, and then we'll do the same for general price-level accounting.

Current Cost Accounting

Current cost refers to the market price that an individual firm would have to pay in order to replace the specific assets it owns. Current cost accounting (discussed briefly in Chapter 9 where LIFO and FIFO were contrasted) is designed to accomplish the following two objectives: (1) to reflect all nonmonetary assets like inventory, buildings, equipment, etc. at their current replacement cost as of the balance sheet date; and (2) to differentiate between (a) current cost income from continuing operations and (b) increases or decreases in current cost amounts (also called "holding gains" or "inventory profits").

These objectives are accomplished by first periodically increasing or decreasing the balance sheet asset carrying amount as current cost changes. Then, as the asset is sold or used up, this current cost carrying amount is written off the books and matched against the revenues from sales. These steps are illustrated in simplified form by the following example.

A firm purchases a unit of inventory for $100 at the beginning of 2001. The asset's current cost increases by $15 in 2001 and it is sold for $180 on January 1, 2002. Income statements and inventory carrying amounts for this example are shown in Exhibit 18.4.

There is controversy about how to treat increases in current cost. Are the increases to be included in net income? Alternatively, are they a direct (nonincome) equity increase?

If the firm wishes to maintain start-of-period equity capital expressed in nominal dollars, then the increase is included in net income. However, if the firm wants to maintain start-of-period equity expressed in dollars of physical productive capacity, then the $15 increase is not income—that is, it is a direct credit to owners' equity.[10]

Irrespective of which view is adopted, the cumulative change in owners' equity under the current cost approach for the two years combined ($80) is equal to the *total* equity change under the historical cost approach. However, although the total income is the same, the *timing* of income recognition and the *classification* of the income by causes differ.

Current cost income differentiates between operating profits and holding gains. In the example, $15 of the total $80 change in equity is attributable to increases in current cost amounts; these increases are recognized as they occur by increasing the inventory carrying amount. Assuming the increase is considered to be a direct credit to owners' equity, the accounting entry to recognize the inventory carrying amount change is:

Remember, current cost accounting for inventories is a departure from historical costing and is not allowed under GAAP in Canada.

In its 1999 annual report, Teléfonos de México SA describes its current cost adjustment process for nonmonetary assets as follows:

> *The appraised value of land, buildings and other fixed assets of domestic origin at December 31, 1996, and the cost of subsequent additions to such assets were restated based on the NCPI.*

Prior to 1997, Mexican accounting required appraisals of nonmonetary assets. But since January 1, 1997, the previous appraised values can be updated by applying the Mexican National Consumer Price Index (NCPI) to the December 31, 1996, appraisal amounts. *In accordance with Mexican GAAP, the restatement debit or credit offset is not included in income but is taken directly to owners' equity.* Inventory is also a nonmonetary asset. So Mexican GAAP illustrate the direct owners' equity (other comprehensive income) treatment of adjustments of all nonmonetary assets in a real-world setting.

Exhibit 18.4

Income Statements and Inventory Carrying Amounts—Current Cost Versus Historical Cost

	2001	2002	Total
Current Cost			
Sales revenues	–0–	$180	$180
Current cost of goods sold	–0–	$115[1]	115
Current cost income from continuing operations	–0–	65	65
Unrealized increase in current cost amount (or holding gain)	$ 15	–0–	15
Change in owners' equity	$ 15	$ 65	$ 80
Inventory carrying amount (end of year)	$115[1]	–0–	
[1]($100 + 15).			
Historical Cost			
Sales revenues	–0–	$180	$180
Historical cost of goods sold	–0–	100	100
Total historical cost income	–0–	$ 80	$ 80
Inventory carrying amount (end of year)	$100	–0–	

```
DR  Inventory                                        $15
    CR  Owners' equity—Unrealized increase in
        current cost amount                                    $15
```

When the sale is made in 2002, the new inventory carrying amount ($115) is matched against the selling price of $180 to yield the $65 current cost income from continuing operations. By contrast, historical cost procedures recognize no equity change as input costs increase. Instead, equity increases are deferred until the sale occurs in 2002. At that time, historical cost accounting reports the equity change as one lump-sum number ($80) and does not break this number into separate operating profit and holding gain components.

The failure of historical cost accounting to differentiate between operating profits and holding gains is a serious limitation of traditional accounting. Proponents of current cost accounting argue that the $80 profit number reported under historical cost accounting provides a misleading picture of current operating efficiency because it seems to imply that the spread between sales price and cost is $80. Statement readers might infer that each *future* sale would also generate a margin of $80. But this is incorrect. Because the current spread between selling price and replacement cost is only $65 ($180 – $115), current cost advocates contend that the $65 figure provides the better measure of existing *operating* efficiency and is also the proper starting point for analysts to use in developing estimates of future per-unit net operating cash inflows. Furthermore, the $15 difference between the current cost operating profit of $65 and total historical cost income of $80 is attributable to cost increases over the period that the inventory was held. These holding gains, it is argued, may or may not be sustainable, so they should be disclosed as a separate item to avoid unwarranted inferences. Since historical cost does not separately disclose operating profits and holding gains, critics claim that it obscures different elements of total profitability which may have different patterns of sustainability.

LIFO inventory accounting represents an attempt to separate operating profits from holding gains within the framework of the historical cost model. As discussed in Chapter 9, this separation is not achieved when LIFO dipping occurs because reported LIFO profit includes both current cost operating profits *and* realized holding gains. Furthermore, during periods of rising input costs, the LIFO inventory carrying amount can be far below the current economic cost of the assets that are tied up in inventory. Consequently, traditionally computed ratios (like return on assets [ROA]) will tend to be overstated because of the understatement of the denominator. A further distortion of return ratios exists when LIFO dipping occurs because the numerator—income—is inflated by the realized holding gains.

For several decades, accounting writers, accounting professional bodies, managers, financial analysts, governments, and other users of accounting information have wrestled with the problem of developing accounting that recognizes in some fashion the fact that prices are changing. This interest in accounting for changing prices becomes intense during times of significant inflation, and the 1970s was such a time. *Historical cost* accounting implicitly assumes that the monetary unit used to measure and report assets, liabilities, and all the other elements of financial statements has a constant value. During the 1970s and early 1980s, Australian, British, American, and Canadian authoritative bodies, among others, issued numerous exposure drafts and other documents approaching the "accounting for changing prices" issue from a variety of perspectives. For example, Section 4510 of the *CICA Handbook* ("Reporting the Effects of Changing Prices") was issued in late 1982 and urged (but did not require) larger Canadian companies to disclose supplementary current cost accounting information. Due to low inflation and lack of compliance, this Section was withdrawn from the *Handbook*. And between 1979 and 1985 in the United States, companies with inventories plus property, plant, and equipment exceeding $125 million were required by *SFAS No. 33* ("Financial Reporting and Changing Prices") to disclose certain supplementary information prepared on a current cost basis. But as of the late 1990s, all this activity has resulted in little change to the traditional historical cost financial accounting model that underlies much of the generally accepted accounting principles for these countries.

Exhibit 18.5 presents a representative current cost disclosure for Union Carbide which was taken from its 1985 annual report. For most companies, 1985 represents the latest disclosure, since these disclosures were made voluntary in 1986.[11]

Under the U.S. *Statement of Financial Accounting Standards (SFAS) No. 33* current cost rules, the only balance sheet accounts that were adjusted were the nonmonetary assets (such as inventory, buildings, and equipment). Actual market replacement costs were used wherever such data were available. When actual market replacement costs were not available, indices that reflected cost changes for the specific asset category being measured were employed. All monetary assets and liabilities were reported at their face value without adjustment. As shown in Exhibit 18.5, Union Carbide (UCC) displayed the current cost amounts for these balance sheet categories as well as their income statement effects on cost of sales and depreciation side-by-side with the historical cost amounts. UCC's historical cost income (US$75 million) became a current cost loss (US$71 million).

The UCC shareholders' equity number in Exhibit 18.5 was increased as a balancing item that resulted after the inventory and other assets were written up. Specifically:

DR	Inventories ($2,259 – $1,422)	$ 837	
DR	Property, etc. ($7,453 – $5,780)	1,673	
	CR Stockholders' equity ($6,529 – $4,019)		$2,510

Exhibit 18.5 UNION CARBIDE CORPORATION (UCC)

1985 Annual Report Supplemental Disclosure
Year Ended December 31, 1985

Data on Changing Prices
(US$ in millions)

Summary statement of income adjusted for changing prices	At Historical Cost— Nominal Dollars	Adjusted for Changes in Specific Prices Current Cost— Nominal Dollars
Net sales	$9,003	$9,003
Cost of sales	6,252	6,281
Depreciation	596	711
Other operating expense—net	1,708	1,708
Interest expense	292	292
Provision for income taxes	53	53
Minority share of income	27	29
Net income before unusual charges and extraordinary item	$ 75	$ (71)
Per share	$ 0.36	$ (0.34)
Summary balance sheet data adjusted for changing prices		
Inventories	$1,422	$2,259
Property, plant, and equipment, net of accumulated depreciation	5,780	7,453
UCC stockholders' equity	4,019	6,529

In countries like Mexico, where inflation is a continuing problem, current cost data for inventories can be determined from invoices received near the balance sheet date, from suppliers' end-of-period price lists, or from recently updated standard cost amounts. In all cases, the objective is to estimate the current cost that would be incurred to *replace* the actual asset in use. *Input costs that would be paid by the firm are used, not selling prices that would be charged to customers.*

Since inventories are purchased virtually continuously, actual market prices will usually be available at any date, making index adjustments rarely necessary for inventory. Land, buildings, and equipment are purchased sporadically, so actual current market costs will not always be available for these items. When fixed asset market costs *are* available—for example, from used equipment dealers' price lists—these market costs would be used to determine current cost balance sheet amounts. For custom-designed buildings and special purpose equipment, actual market replacement costs will seldom be determinable. In these cases, various market value **estimation techniques** must be utilized.

Market value estimation techniques may take several forms. For example, construction cost indices by geographical area are widely available. The construction cost index value would be applied to the historical book value of buildings to yield an estimated replacement cost. Special purpose price indices for equipment are also available. These price indices are reported both on an industry basis (e.g., an index specific to equipment used in the automotive industry) and by type of equipment (e.g., an index for general-purpose electronics equipment). Again, the index value would be multiplied by the historical book value of the equipment in order to obtain an estimated replacement cost. Market value estimation techniques can also be used to estimate land values. For example, real estate tax assessment data can form the basis for estimating the current cost of land.

Exhibit 18.5 indicates a US$146 million difference ($75 − [−$71]) between historical and current cost net income in 1985 for UCC. The exhibit shows that much more than 100% of UCC's 1985 historical cost income (US$75 million) comprised realized holding gains. We know that this is the case because in Exhibit 18.4 conventional historical cost income (US$80 million) comprised two components: (1) current cost income from continuing operations (US$65 million), and (2) realized holding gains (US$15 million). Examining the income statement disclosure in Exhibit 18.5 reveals that UCC's realized holding gains had three components: [US$ in millions]

To illustrate the procedure, let us assume that a building constructed in 1987 has the following book value at December 31, 1998:

Historical cost of building	$100,000,000
Accumulated amortization	30,000,000
Net book value	$ 70,000,000

Further assume that a construction cost index (base period 1977 = 100.0) for this type of building is available and has the following index values:

Average index value for 1987	246
Index value for December 31, 1998	396

The estimated replacement cost of the building at December 31, 1998, would be:

	Historical Cost Amounts	Index Adjustment	Estimated Current Cost Amounts
Cost of building	$100,000,000 ×	$\frac{396}{246}$	= $160,975,600
Accumulated amortization	$ 30,000,000 ×	$\frac{396}{246}$	= 48,292,680
Net book value	$ 70,000,000		$112,682,920

Cost-of-goods-sold difference	$ 29	($6,281 − $6,252)
Depreciation difference	115	($711 − $596)
Minority share difference[12]	2	($29 − $27)
Realized holding gains in 1985	$146	

This disclosure allows us to see the various components of UCC's historical cost income number: [US$ in millions]

Reported current cost loss from continuing operations	$ (71)	(Given)
Realized holding gains	146	*(Computed above)*
Historical cost income	$ 75	(Given)

General Price-Level Accounting

A currency unit such as the dollar possesses value because of the goods and services that it will buy. The real amount of goods and services that can be acquired at any moment is what determines the **purchasing power** of a currency.

Current costing, as we just discussed, is one way to measure purchasing power. It measures changes in the prices of the specific assets and liabilities of the firm. Current costing thus captures changes in *specific purchasing power*.

General price-level accounting, another way to measure purchasing power, makes no attempt to measure changes in specific prices. Instead, it focuses on changes in *general purchasing power*.

The general purchasing power approach uses an economy-wide price index. All indices are intended to price a market basket of goods and services at various points of time to determine how the price of the market basket has changed.

Overview of Adjustment Mechanics

Canadian GAAP financial statements record the dollar amount expended or incurred at the date of the original transaction. However, because the purchasing power of these dollars changes over time, the amounts stated in original (or "nominal") dollars are not comparable. In other words, historical cost statements ignore changes in the purchasing power of the currency. *The objective of general price-level accounting is to adjust all historical amounts into common purchasing power units using a broad purchasing power index.* Here's an example. Mitchel Corporation owns two assets. One was acquired on January 1, 1985, and the other on January 1, 1995:

Date	Original Transaction Amount	General Purchasing Power Index as of January 1
1985 (Asset 1)	$200,000	76
1995 (Asset 2)	200,000	193
2001	—	207
	$400,000	

The gross book value of $200,000 for each asset using historical cost does not reflect the difference in the purchasing power of the *nominal* dollars invested in each asset. That is, the $200,000 of 1985 dollars that were expended on asset 1 did not have the same purchasing power as the $200,000 of 1995 dollars that were expended on asset 2; nor does the sum of these amounts have the same purchasing power as $400,000 of January 1, 2001, dollars. *In order to reflect changes in the purchasing power of the measuring unit between 1985 and 2001, all amounts must be restated into dollars of uniform purchasing power.* If all amounts were restated in terms of the purchasing power of the January 1, 2001, dollar, the adjustment would be:

Asset Acquired In:	Restatement Amount		Restated into Factor		2001 Dollars
1985	$200,000	×	$\frac{207}{76}$	=	$544,737
1995	200,000	×	$\frac{207}{193}$	=	214,508
					$759,245

To understand these restated numbers, let's consider the $544,737 amount in 2001 dollars for the asset acquired in 1985. This number indicates that it would take $544,737 dollars on January 1, 2001, to have the same purchasing power that $200,000 had on January 1, 1985. Thus, the $200,000 invested in 1985 has a January 1, 2001, purchasing power equivalent of $544,737. The $200,000 invested on January 1, 1995, has a purchasing power equivalent in January 1, 2001, dollars of $214,508.

Generalizing from the example, to restate historical amounts into current purchasing power units, the nominal dollar amount is multiplied by a **restatement factor**, the ratio of price indices. The numerator of the ratio is the price index level of the current period, and the denominator of the ratio is the price index relating to the period of the original transaction amount. To restate 1985 dollars into what those dollars are equivalent to in 2001 purchasing power, we calculate:

$$\begin{array}{c}\text{1985 transaction} \\ \text{amount to be} \\ \text{restated}\end{array} \times \frac{\text{2001 General purchasing power index}}{\text{1985 General purchasing power index}} = \begin{array}{c}\text{2001 purchasing} \\ \text{power equivalent}\end{array}$$

In our example, the 1985 index value is 76 and the 2001 index value is 207, so the restatement factor is 207/76.

General price-level accounting is not intended to reflect current market values of assets and liabilities. This is not surprising, since the restatement factor relates to *overall* average purchasing power changes rather than to changes in the prices of the specific items being adjusted. The intent of general price-level accounting is simply to make historical currency amounts that are expended in different time periods comparable by adjusting all amounts to current purchasing power dollar equivalents. In this sense, general price-level accounting does not abandon the historical cost principle. Instead, nominal dollar historical costs are simply restated in dollars of constant purchasing power.

Overview of the Concepts General price-level accounting requires a clear distinction between monetary and nonmonetary items, because purchasing power changes affect each category differently. A **monetary item** is money, or a claim to receive or to pay a sum of money, which is fixed in amount. Examples include cash, accounts receivable, accounts payable, and bonds payable. What you should understand about these items is that they are stated in monetary units and that the claim or amount remains fixed even if the price level changes. By contrast, a **nonmonetary item** is not fixed in amount, and its price will likely change as the general level of prices changes. Examples of nonmonetary items include inventories, buildings, manufacturing equipment, and obligations under product warranties.

To illustrate the general concepts of constant dollar accounting, let's consider a firm that is financed entirely with equity. Suppose its only asset is land (a nonmonetary asset), which was purchased for $1,000 on January 1, 2001. By using the basic accounting equation, the firm would appear as follows on this date:

A	=	L	+	E
Land $1,000				Owners' equity $1,000

If we assume that the general level of prices rose by 4% during 2001 and that no transactions occurred during the year, the constant dollar basic accounting equation at the end of 2001 would reflect:

A	=	L	+	E
Land $1,040				Owners' equity $1,040

Notice that both amounts have been restated by the ratio 104/100 to reflect December 31, 2001, general purchasing power. In words, it takes $1,040 on December 31, 2001, to have the same general purchasing power that $1,000 had on January 1, 2001. All nonmonetary items would be adjusted in a similar manner in preparing general price-level financial statements.

Under such constant dollar accounting, the upward restatement of owners' equity is *not* considered to be income. An analogy makes it easy to understand why. Whether you express a temperature at 12° Celsius or at its equivalent of 54° Fahrenheit does not change the underlying real level of the temperature. So too with the adjustment from $1,000 January 1, 2001, dollars to $1,040 December 31, 2001, dollars. All that has happened is that the measurement unit has been changed. There is no income or loss.

By contrast, when the assets held are monetary, rather than nonmonetary, a gain or loss *does* occur. Let us illustrate this by assuming that the asset held on January 1, 2001, was cash rather than land. Cash, of course, is a monetary item. Since prices, on average, rose by 4% during 2001, to be in the same *real* position at the end of 2001 as it was at the beginning of 2001, the firm would have to possess a cash balance of $1,040. The reasoning is simple—it takes $1,040 end-of-year dollars to buy what $1,000 bought at the start of the year. If, however, there were no transactions during 2001 and if the ending cash balance is still $1,000, then the firm has suffered a real loss of $40 during 2001 because the purchasing power of its cash has declined. This would be reflected in the end-of-period general price-level accounting equation as follows:

A	=	L	+	E	
Cash $1,000				Owners' equity	$1,040
				Purchasing	
				power loss	(40)

When a firm holds *net* monetary assets during a period of inflation, a loss occurs since the purchasing power of the net monetary assets declines. Put somewhat differently, since monetary items are automatically expressed in end-of-period dollars, no adjustment of these items is necessary in constant dollar balance sheets; however, the implicit gain or loss that results from holding monetary items during a period of general inflation must be recognized. The purchasing power loss account would appear on the income statement and it would ultimately be closed to owners' equity.[13]

Summary

The objective of financial reporting rules differs across countries. In countries that follow a Canada/U.K./U.S. financial reporting tradition, financial reports are designed to reflect underlying economic performance. In countries such as Japan, Germany, and France, financial reporting rules either follow the tax law or are prescribed by statute. Reporting philosophies differ because of underlying differences in capital markets and other societal factors.

These differences in financial reporting rules complicate international investment analysis. Various mechanisms for coping with cross-country reporting diversity have evolved. In Canada, foreign companies must reconcile to Canadian GAAP. In the United States, foreign issuers are required to reconcile their home-country reporting rules to U.S. GAAP. Another approach that is gaining significant support is one in which companies are urged to use rules written by the IASB. These standards would then become a type of international accounting language. Mechanisms for monitoring compliance with GAAP also differ significantly from country to country—both in the form of the monitoring and its effectiveness.

Inflation is a serious problem in certain countries. Where this is the case, historical cost reporting becomes less meaningful and inflation accounting is often used. Two methods for reflecting changing prices are current cost accounting and general price-level accounting. Current cost accounting measures changes in the specific purchasing power of the company for which the financial statements are being prepared. By contrast, general price-level accounting strives to reflect overall, average changes in purchasing power.

For more Exercises, Problems/Discussion Questions, and Cases, visit the Companion Website for this textbook at **www.pearsoned.ca/revsine**.

Exercises

E18-1 Why do financial reporting rules differ?

Allocating resources in the most efficient manner maximizes the wealth of any country. It is generally acknowledged that financial information plays an important role in efficient resource allocation.

Required:

Given that both of the preceding statements are correct, why are the financial reporting rules in some countries designed to be helpful to external individual investors (e.g., in the United States and Canada) whereas in other countries (e.g., in Japan and Germany), they are less helpful?

E18-2 Overcoming reporting diversity

Some analysts contend that a single, standardized set of uniform financial reporting rules that would be required for all companies in all countries would improve interfirm comparisons and enhance financial analysis.

Required:

Do you agree that uniform reporting across many countries will always enhance the comparability of financial data and analyses? Why or why not?

E18-3 Alternative return measures

Telefonica de Espana, S.A. is a Spanish company that provides all types of public and private telecommunication services. Telefonica prepares its annual financial report in accordance with Spanish GAAP. In contrast to Canadian and U.S. GAAP, Spanish GAAP allow firms to revalue their assets. Since Telefonica's shares trade on the New York Stock Exchange (NYSE), Telefonica files Form 20-F with the SEC. Selected information from Telefonica's 1994 Form 20-F is as follows (in million pesetas):

Net income for the year reported in the Spanish Statutory Accounts	112,608
Approximate net income in accordance with U.S. GAAP	125,069
Reversal of net effect of revaluation of fixed assets and related accumulated amortization	(126,552)
Total net fixed assets (measured in accordance with Spanish GAAP)	3,109,222

Required:

Given that Telefonica's net increase in assets due to asset revaluations totalled 126,552 million pesetas, answer the following questions:

1. What is Telefonica's ROA when it reports in accordance with Spanish GAAP?
2. What is Telefonica's ROA under U.S. GAAP?
3. Which ROA measure is preferable? Explain.

E18-4 Current cost accounting

Highrate Company's 2001 historical cost income statement is as follows:

Sales	$20,000
Cost of sales	8,000
Gross margin	12,000
Amortization	2,000
Other operating expenses	8,000
Net income	$ 2,000

Highrate's management is concerned about the increase in inventory costs as well as the increasing costs of property, plant, and equipment. Management believes that the current cost of inventory sold is 25% higher than its historical cost at the time of sale. In addition, if property, plant, and equipment were valued at current costs, an additional $1,000 of amortization would be recorded.

Required:

1. Prepare a current cost income statement for Highrate Company.
2. Assume you are a shareholder of Highrate Company. Which net income figure do you think is more useful? Why?

E18-5 General price-level accounting

The following schedule shows the average general purchasing power index of the indicated years:

2000	100
2001	125
2002	150

Carl Corporation's plant and equipment consisted of the following totals at December 31, 2002:

Date Acquired	Percentage Amortized	Historical Cost
2000	30%	$30,000
2001	20	20,000
2002	10	10,000
		$60,000

Amortization is calculated at 10% per annum on a straight-line basis. A full year's amortization is charged in the year of acquisition. There were no disposals in 2002.

Required:

What amount of amortization expense should be included in a general price-level accounting income statement for the year 2002?

E18-6 Distinguishing between monetary and nonmonetary items

When computing purchasing power gain or loss on net monetary items, which of the following accounts would you classify as monetary? Why?

1. receivables under capitalized leases for a lessor
2. obligations under capitalized leases for a lessee

3. minority interest on a consolidated balance sheet
4. unamortized discount on bonds payable
5. long-term receivables
6. equity investment in unconsolidated subsidiaries
7. obligations under warranties
8. accumulated amortization of equipment
9. advances to unconsolidated subsidiaries
10. allowance for uncollectible accounts
11. unamortized premium on bonds payable

E18-7 General price-level accounting

Lewis Company was formed on January 1, 2000. Selected balances from the historical cost balance sheet at December 31, 2000, were as follows:

Land (purchased in 2000)	$120,000
Investment in nonconvertible bonds (purchased in 2000 and expected to be held to maturity)	60,000
Long-term debt	80,000

The general purchasing power index was 100 when the debt was issued and the land and bonds were purchased; it was 110 at December 31, 2001.

Required:

In a general price-level accounting balance sheet at December 31, 2001, at what amounts should the land, investment, and long-term debt be shown?

Problems/Discussion Questions

P18-1 Capital sources and disclosure differences

Accounting standards vary across national boundaries. As stated in the chapter, a specific country's financial reporting standards are a function of its legal environment, customs, and social objectives. In addition, the primary source of capital for companies within a country influences the country's financial reporting standards.

Required:

Assume there are two countries in the world. In the first country, Equityland, companies acquire capital through individual investors, who purchase equity shares on public stock exchanges. Companies in the second country, Debtland, acquire their capital from a few large banks. Answer the following questions on the basis of your understanding of the differences in the financial reporting incentives of firms domiciled in Equityland versus Debtland.

1. Who are the primary users of companies' financial reports?
2. What are the users concerned about when assessing companies' financial reports?
3. What financial ratios might financial statement users in the two countries employ when examining companies' economic performances?
4. What do you suppose are the disclosure demands of financial statement users in Equityland versus Debtland?

P18-2 Overcoming reporting diversity

EURO DISNEY S.C.A.
www.eurodisney.
com

Euro Disney S.C.A. began operations on April 12, 1992, by opening the Disneyland Paris Resort. Euro Disney operates the Disneyland Paris Theme Park, six hotels, and several other entertainment establishments. A partial income statement for Euro Disney that was prepared in accordance with French GAAP (measured in millions of French francs) follows:

	Year Ended September 30, 1994
Income (loss) before exceptional items	(1,282)
Exceptional income (loss)	(515)
Net income (loss)	(1,797)

In the footnotes to the financial statements, the "exceptional loss" of 515 million francs is detailed as follows:

Tax reimbursements	8
Provisions for risks and charges	(111)
Costs related to financial restructuring	(406)
Payable forgiveness	1,208
Reduction in carrying value of certain assets	(1,206)
Other	(8)
	(515)

Additional information provided in a footnote explains that the reduction in carrying value of certain assets represents the writedown of certain planning and development costs.

Required:

1. On the basis of your knowledge of Canadian GAAP, discuss how the "reduction in carrying value of certain assets" would be reported if Euro Disney followed Canadian GAAP.
2. Assume you subscribe to a global data service that provides only summary financial information limited to net income, total assets, and total shareholders' equity. How does this limit your analysis of international companies?
3. What adjustments would you make to approximate Euro Disney's income or loss from continuing operations on a Canadian GAAP basis?

P18-3 Overcoming reporting diversity

YIZHENG CHEMICAL
FIBRE COMPANY LTD.
www.english-
ycfc.com

Yizheng Chemical Fibre Company Ltd. is a company established in the People's Republic of China. In 1996, Yizheng Chemical prepared two financial reports, one in accordance with standards issued by the IASB and another in accordance with the accounting rules and regulations of the People's Republic of China (PRC). The operating sections of Yizheng's two income statements prepared under the alternative sets of accounting standards (reported in renminbi) follow:

Consolidated Profit and Loss Prepared Under IAS		Consolidated Profit and Loss Prepared Under PRC Accounting	
Turnover	6,999,118	Income from principal operations	6,999,118
Profit before tax	243,177	Less:	
Tax	(25,232)	Cost of sales	6,088,427
		Selling expenses	56,323
Profit after tax	217,945	Administrative expenses	386,622
		Financial expenses	233,574
		Business tax and surcharges	30,682
		Profit from principal operations	203,490

Required:

1. Identify various approaches that regulatory commissions can employ to bring uniformity to foreign issuers' financial reporting.
2. What approach to financial reporting uniformity has Yizheng Chemical taken?
3. After examining the partial income statements presented earlier, answer the following questions:
   (a) What is meant by "turnover"?
   (b) Which presentation form do you prefer? Why?
   (c) What might contribute to Yizheng Chemical's profit of 217,945 renminbi under IAS and 203,490 renminbi under PRC accounting standards?
   (d) As a user of Yizheng's financial reports, which profit figure will you use in your financial statement analysis? Why?

P18-4 Current cost ratio effects

TNT Ltd. is a multinational Australian company whose primary business activity is providing freight transportation services. TNT Ltd. prepares its annual financial report in accordance with Australian GAAP. Australian GAAP allow the revaluation of fixed assets. According to Australian GAAP, the revaluation of fixed assets is recorded by increasing the appropriate fixed asset accounts and by increasing shareholders' equity by means of a reserve account.

TNT LTD.
www.tnt.com.au

TNT states in its footnotes to the financial statements that "certain assets have been revalued at various times and are shown at their latest valuation. The basis for the revaluations is the recoverable value of the assets to the economic entity as a going concern." TNT also states, "Where assets have been revalued, depreciation is based on the revalued amount."

Required:

1. Assume you are a user of TNT's financial statements. Explain how the revaluation of fixed assets affects your time series analysis of TNT's economic performance.
2. How would the revaluation of fixed assets affect (i.e., improve or weaken) the following financial statement ratios?
   (a) total shareholders' equity to total assets
   (b) long-term debt to assets
   (c) current ratio
   (d) return on assets (ROA)

P18-5 Overcoming reporting diversity

SmithKline Beecham p.l.c. is a U.K. public limited company that conducts business worldwide by selling health-related consumer products. Selected data from its 1996 Form 20-F follows (in millions of pounds sterling):

Net income per U.K. GAAP	1,835
Net income per U.S. GAAP	800
Shareholders' equity per U.K. GAAP	1,369
Shareholders' equity per U.S. GAAP	4,735
Average number of ordinary shares outstanding (in millions)	3,252

Required:

1. What is SmithKline Beecham's return on equity (ROE) when it reports in accordance with U.K. GAAP? What is SmithKline Beecham's ROE under U.S. GAAP?
2. The difference between U.K. GAAP net income and U.S. GAAP net income is due in part to the accounting for goodwill. In accounting for business combinations, U.K. GAAP allow firms to write off the excess of the cost over the market value of assets acquired (i.e., goodwill) directly to shareholders' equity. According to U.S. GAAP, goodwill must be capitalized and amortized over a period not to exceed 40 years. SmithKline Beecham reported 97 million pounds sterling of goodwill amortization in its Form 20-F reconciliation. What impact does the amortization of goodwill have on earnings per share? How does the writeoff of goodwill at the time of purchase affect ROE in the current period and in future periods?
3. Assume the entire difference between U.K. GAAP net income and U.S. GAAP net income is due to the accounting for goodwill. Which ROE measure calculated in Question 1 better reflects the economic performance of SmithKline Beecham for the year ended 1996? Explain.

P18-6 Overcoming reporting diversity

Stork N.V., domiciled in Amsterdam, The Netherlands, is an industrial company with operations worldwide. In a footnote to its 1994 financial report, Stork disclosed the following current value information (in thousands of guilder):

	1994	1993
Fixed assets	858,000	825,000
Additional depreciation to be recorded under current value accounting	12,106	12,066

Information from Stork's profit and loss statement and balance sheet includes the following data:

Net income	81,257	55,906
Fixed assets	692,913	657,315
Shareholders' equity	778,364	749,093

Required:

1. Using the data reported on Stork's profit and loss statement and balance sheet, what is Stork's 1994 ROE?

2. If Stork N.V. were to book the revaluation of its fixed assets, what would be its 1994 ROE?
3. Which ROE is more relevant when comparing Stork's performance to the performance of an industrial firm domiciled in Canada? Explain.
4. Australian GAAP allow firms the option of revaluing their fixed assets. Which ROE measure is more relevant when comparing Stork's performance to the performance of an industrial firm domiciled in Australia? Explain.

P18-7 Overcoming reporting diversity

The 1993 income statement of Electrolux, a Swedish company that owns the U.S.-based appliance company Frigidaire, reports the following (in millions of Swedish kroner):

ELECTROLUX
www.electrolux.se

Sales	100,121
Operating expense	(92,594)
Share of income in associated companies	(10)
Operating income before depreciation	7,517

A footnote discloses that operating expense included the following items:

Capital gains on sales of real estate	114
Losses on sales of operations	(325)
Capital gains on sale of shares in Email Ltd.	204
Total included in operating expense	(7)

Required:

Describe how each of the items disclosed in the footnote would be reported if Electrolux prepared its financial statements in accordance with Canadian GAAP.

Cases

C18-1 Embratel: Brazilian GAAP—Reflecting the economic environment

Embratel Participações S.A., a Brazilian corporation organized as one of the 12 new telecommunications companies set up following the privatization of the huge Telebrás System in May 1998, has as its principal assets the shares of Embratel, its operating subsidiary. Embratel provides intraregional long-distance, interregional long-distance, and international long-distance services, as well as data communication, text, telex, sound and image transmission, Internet services, and mobile satellite and maritime communication. Following completion of the privatization of the Telebrás System, Embratel expects to face new competitors, but it will be able to offer certain services that it is currently prohibited from providing.

EMBRATEL
PARTICIPAÇÕES S.A.
www.embratel.net.
br

In the Form 20-F filed for the year ended December 31, 1998, with the American SEC, the company disclosed the following information:

Embratel Participações S.A.
Extract from Form 20-F Disclosures

Effects of Inflation, Devaluation and Interest Rates

In accordance with Brazilian GAAP, the Consolidated Financial Statements recognize certain effects of inflation and restate data from prior periods in constant *reais* of December 31, 1997 purchasing power. Such restatement has been effected in accordance with Brazilian GAAP using the integral restatement method (*correção integral*) through December 31, 1997. See "Selected Financial Data." In periods of inflation, monetary assets generate inflationary loss and monetary liabilities generate inflationary gain, due to the decline in purchasing power of the currency. In the Consolidated Financial Statements, inflationary gains or losses on monetary assets and liabilities have been allocated to their corresponding income or expense captions in the income statement. Inflationary gains or losses without a corresponding income or expense caption have been allocated to other net operating income (expense). See Note 2c to the Consolidated Financial Statements.

Until December 31, 1995, the relevant inflation index selected by the CVM and the one used for the constant currency method under Brazilian GAAP was the UFIR. Since January 1, 1996, the CVM has no longer required that the constant currency method of accounting be used in preparation of the financial statements of publicly traded Brazilian companies. Restatement in constant currency is now optional under CVM rules and any general price index may be used. The Brazilian Institute of Accountants has recommended that the IGP-M be used for this purpose. The Company's management believes that the IGP-M is the most appropriate measure of inflation in Brazil and has elected to use the IGP-M for purposes of preparing its Consolidated Financial Statements in accordance with the constant currency method effective January 1, 1996.

In July 1997, the three-year cumulative inflation rate for Brazil fell below 100% and, subsequently, totaled 1.7% for the year ended December 31, 1998. For these reasons, the Brazilian Institute of Accountants does not require inflation indexing of financial statements subsequent to December 31, 1997. Accordingly, the consolidated financial statements as of December 31, 1998 and for the year then ended have not been restated for inflation, and the restated balances of nonmonetary assets and related liabilities of the Company as of December 31, 1997 became the basis of accounting as from that date. Consequently, the amounts of the restatements of assets through that date are being depreciated over the useful lives of the assets, and the resulting depreciation expense, together with the related tax effect, is reflected in the consolidated statement of income for the year ended December 31, 1998.

Substantially all of the Company's revenues from international operations are denominated in U.S. dollars or other foreign currencies or equivalents, while the majority of its costs, other than payments to other international operators and interest paid on foreign denominated debt, are denominated in *reais.* The Company's results of operations are therefore affected by the relative movements of inflation and exchange rates.

The Company's financial condition and results of operations may be affected by changes in market rates of interest (primarily the London Interbank Offered Rate [LIBOR] and medium- and long-term U.S. interest rates). The Company is exposed to interest rate risk as a consequence of its floating rate debt and limited floating rate interest earning assets. At December 31, 1998, approximately 45.3% of the Company's interest bearing liabilities bore interest at floating rates. The Company has not entered into derivative contracts or made other arrangements to hedge against this risk. Accordingly, should market interest rates rise (principally LIBOR and U.S. medium- and long-term interest rates), the Company's financing expenses will increase. See "Quantitative and Qualitative Disclosures about Market Risk." . . .

Reconciliation to U.S. GAAP

The Company prepares its consolidated financial statements in accordance with Brazilian GAAP, which differs in significant respects from U.S. GAAP. The principal differences between Brazilian GAAP and U.S. GAAP as they affected the Company's results of operations during the reported periods are: (i) under Brazilian GAAP, loans and financing balances in default are not always classified as current liabilities while under U.S. GAAP, loans and financings in default or expected to be in default within a year of the balance sheet date are classified as current obligations unless creditors have provided the Company waivers for such defaults; a substantial portion of the Company's outstanding debt at December 31, 1998 is in default as a result of the Breakup of the Telebrás System and the Company's privatization (see "—Liquidity and Capital Resources"); (ii) under Brazilian GAAP, interest on loans to finance construction in progress is capitalized at the rate of 12% per annum of the total value of construction in progress, regardless of the amount of interest actually incurred on such loans while under U.S. GAAP, interest is capitalized at the interest rate of the debt incurred up to the lower of the amount of construction in progress and the total loans incurred; (iii) until December 31, 1993 capitalized interest under Brazilian GAAP was not added to individual assets but was capitalized separately and amortized over a time period different from the estimated useful lives of the related assets while under U.S. GAAP, capitalized interest is added to the cost of individual assets and is amortized over their estimated useful lives; (iv) the write-off of certain impaired, long-lived assets under U.S. GAAP; (v) adjustments to the Company's provision for pension and other post-retirement benefits resulting from the application of SFAS 87—"Employer's accounting for pensions" and SFAS 106—"Employer's accounting for post retirement benefits other than pensions" as required under U.S. GAAP; (vi) under Brazilian GAAP, the deferred tax liability arising from the indexation of assets and liabilities for financial reporting purposes was recorded against retained earnings while under U.S. GAAP such effects would be charged to income and social contribution taxes in the statement of income; (vii) under Brazilian GAAP, proposed dividends are accrued for in the consolidated financial statements in anticipation of their approval at the shareholders' meeting while under U.S. GAAP, dividends are not accrued until they are formally declared; (viii) under SEC rules, the differences between market price and grant price of Telebrás shares sold to employees must be recorded as compensation expense by each operating entity which was spun off from Telebrás; and (ix) under the SFAS No. 5, the Company is required to reverse the R$42.9 million COFINS-related tax credit taken in 1995 under Brazilian GAAP. The Company's income from continuing operations under U.S. GAAP would have been R$350.9 million, R$451.6 million and R$418.4 million for the years ended December 31, 1996, 1997 and 1998, respectively. In addition, under U.S. GAAP, Embratel is considered to be the continuing entity of the Telebrás System for financial reporting purposes through December 31, 1997. As a result, all operations of Telebrás and its subsidiaries, except for Embratel, are considered to be discontinued operations through December 31, 1997. Income from discontinued operations under U.S. GAAP amounted to R$1,976.4 million and R$3,127.9 million for the years ended December 31, 1996 and 1997, respectively. See Note 29 to the Consolidated Financial Statements, which also includes condensed financial statement schedules of the Company prepared in accordance with Brazilian GAAP, in a U.S. GAAP reporting format, reflecting discontinued operations.

Embratel provided a summary of differences between Brazilian GAAP (which it used) and U.S. GAAP in note 27 to the financial statements in Form 20-F (Note 27 is 13 pages long). A reconciliation included in the note was as follows:

Embratel Particip
Participaçôes S.A.
Extract from Reconciliation Included in Note to Form 20-F Financial Statements

Net Income Reconciliation of the Differences Between U.S. and Brazilian GAAP

	1998	1997	1996
Income as reported	11,735	376,497	414,927
Add (Deduct):			
Different criteria for:			
Capitalized interest	10,616	17,881	(18,378)
Amortization of capitalized interest	74,192	20,115	(20,969)
Impairment of long-lived assets:			
SFAS No. 121 impairment adjustment	—	119,447	(119,447)
Pension and other post-retirement benefits:			
SFAS No. 87 adjustment, including settlement and curtailment	366,474	(24,233)	(56,154)
SFAS No. 106 adjustment, including settlement and curtailment	105,687	(14,458)	(13,897)
Reversal of COFINS tax credit	—	42,900	—
Stock compensation	(52,000)	—	—
Items posted directly to shareholders' equity accounts:			
Deferred tax effect of the nondeductibility of the indexation increments to shareholders' equity	—	(138,120)	(163,203)
Effects of changes in income tax rates/tax effect on special reserve	1,614	2,917	83,081
Fiscal incentive investments/donations and grants	152	904	47
Interest on construction-in-progress	88,889	102,160	142,823
Deferred tax effect of the above adjustments	(183,800)	(53,346)	101,299
Effect of minority interest in the above adjustments	(5,147)	(1,114)	810
U.S. GAAP net income and income from continuing operations	418,412	451,550	350,939

An addition to the note, paragraph 27(n), was entitled "Price-Level Adjustments and the U.S. GAAP Presentation":

> The effects of price-level adjustments have not been eliminated in the reconciliation to U.S. GAAP nor has EMBRATEL reflected monetary gains or losses associated with the various U.S. GAAP adjustments separately identified, because the application of inflation restatement ... represents a comprehensive measure of the effect of price level changes in the Brazilian economy. As such, it is considered a more meaningful presentation than historic cost-based reporting for both Brazilian and U.S. accounting purposes.

Required:

1. Why do the Americans require companies like Embratel to reconcile their financial accounts to U.S. GAAP? What are the costs and benefits of such regulation?
2. How credible is note 27(n)?
3. Should there be one set of GAAP worldwide? If yes, should that set be U.S. GAAP? IASB GAAP?
4. On the basis of the Brazilian accounting disclosed in the case material, how appropriate is Brazilian GAAP for Brazilian companies?

5. Although the detailed support for the reconciling items has not been supplied in this case, suggest possible reasons why each reconciling item from Brazilian GAAP to U.S. GAAP causes the resulting income number to be of greater or lesser quality. (Alternatively, your instructor might suggest you visit the Embratel web site and examine note 27 in its entirety.)

C18-2 Pechiney: Choosing a new reporting currency for a multinational

Pechiney Group is a major aluminum production and packaging company headquartered in Paris, France.

Pechiney has decided to report its financial results in euros, as explained in the following excerpts from a recent financial report (Form 20-F, 1998, filed with the American SEC).

PECHINEY GROUP
www.pechiney.com

Pechiney Group
Excerpts from Financial Report

Presentation of Information

The Company publishes its Consolidated Financial Statements in euros ("euros" or "€"). The Company's financial statements for 1996, 1997 and 1998 were originally in French francs, and have been translated into euros for purposes of this document at the rate of FF6.55957 = €1.00, the applicable rate established on January 1, 1999. The euro did not exist during any of these periods, and the conversion rate used may not reflect the FF/euro exchange rate that would have applied if the euro had existed at such times. Solely for the convenience of the reader, this document contains translations of certain euro amounts into U.S. dollars at specified rates. These translations should not be construed as representations that the converted amounts actually represent such U.S. dollar amounts or could have been (at the relevant date) converted into U.S. dollars at the rates indicated or at any other rate. Unless otherwise stated, the translations of euros into dollars have been made at the rate published by the Banque de France (the "Banque de France Rate") of €1.00 = $1.17 (or $1.00 = €0.86) on December 31, 1998. See "—Exchange Rate Information" for information regarding the euro/dollar exchange rate from January 1, 1999 to the present. ...

Potential Impact for the Pechiney Group of the Conversion to the Euro and Measures Taken

Since the conversion to the euro affects the Group in a number of ways, Pechiney set up a euro pilot committee at the beginning of 1998. The Group studied its existing information systems and has installed euro-compatible equipment. Subsidiary accounting will be converted to euros at the beginning of the year 2000 on the basis of euro-compatible software to be installed during 1999. The Group has carried out training programs regarding the euro since 1998. During 1999, all employees within the euro zone will receive information on the introduction of the single currency.

The introduction of the euro will simplify the management of cash flows among Group entities located in the euro zone and will speed the reduction in the number of foreign currency bank accounts. The Group is currently studying the introduction of a Europe-wide cash management system. In May 1998, when fixed exchange rates for currencies of the future members of euro zone were introduced, the Group ended its hedging measures between these currencies. Since the euro will become the currency of intragroup billing, intragroup cash flows are expected to be progressively converted to euros during 1999 to enable the Group to adopt the euro as its internal currency of reference as of January 2000.

Pechiney estimates that it will incur costs of approximately €8 million in connection with the introduction of the euro. Of this amount, €2 million was incurred in 1998. These costs include principally information technology expenses, external assistance related to the establishment of a Group changeover plan, and the organization of training sessions.

The Group believes that the introduction of the euro will have no effect on profitability, since its principal markets and products are relatively insensitive to the increased price transparency between euro zone countries related to the introduction of the euro. ...

Use of the Euro by the Pechiney Group

Accounting and Financial Information

Pechiney has prepared its financial information in euros since January 1, 1999. On January 28, 1999, the board of directors decided that, subject to legal and regulatory restrictions (particularly tax matters), Pechiney's 1998 financial statements, and all future financial statements required by law, would be prepared and published in euros. Pursuant to the recommendations of the Commission des Opérations de Bourse, principal statement of income and balance sheet items will also be presented in French francs.

In addition, all of Pechiney's financial communications (including management reports, press releases and notices regarding financial operations) will be presented in euros.

As of January 1, 1999, all Pechiney Group companies are able to conduct commercial transactions in euros with customers and suppliers that so desire, without affecting billing systems.

The next two stages in the Group's changeover to the euro will be as follows:

→ on January 1, 2000, the euro will become the internal currency of reference for internal reporting and management control for all Group companies in the euro zone;

→ on or before January 1, 2002, the Group's human resources management and employee payroll within the euro zone will convert to euros. ...

Report of Independent Accountants

To the Board of Directors and the Shareholders of Pechiney

We have audited the consolidated balance sheet of Pechiney and its subsidiaries (together, the "Group") as of December 31, 1998, 1997 and 1996, and the related consolidated statements of income, of shareholders' equity and of cash flows for each of the three years in the period ended December 31, 1998, appearing on pages 119 through 161 of this document. These consolidated financial statements are the responsibility of the Group's management. Our responsibility is to express an opinion on these financial statements based on our audits.

We conducted our audits in accordance with United States generally accepted auditing standards. Those standards require that we plan and perform the audit to obtain reasonable assurance about whether the consolidated financial statements are free of material misstatement. An audit includes examining, on a test basis, evidence supporting the amounts and disclosures in the financial statements. An audit includes assessing the accounting principles used and significant estimates made by management, as well as evaluating the overall financial statement presentation. We believe that our audits provide a reasonable basis for our opinion.

In our opinion, the consolidated financial statements, audited by us, present fairly in all material respects, the financial position of Pechiney and its subsidiaries at December 31, 1998, 1997 and 1996, and the results of their operations and cash flows for each of the three years in the period ended December 31, 1998, in conformity with United States generally accepted accounting principles.

Paris, March 9, 1999

PricewaterhouseCoopers

Consolidated Statement of Income

Years Ended December 31, 1998, 1997 and 1996

(in millions of euros except per share amounts)	Notes	1998	1997	1996
Net sales		9,836	10,633	9,813
Other operating revenues		176	163	125
Cost of goods sold (excluding depreciation)		(8,442)	(9,328)	(8,692)
Selling, general and administrative expense		(529)	(527)	(534)
Research and development expense		(92)	(95)	(101)
Depreciation and amortization		(370)	(347)	(326)
Long-lived assets writedown	4-5	(8)	(36)	(79)
Restructuring expense	14	(7)	(18)	(264)
Other (expense) income	17	(3)	60	(250)
Income (loss) from operations		**561**	**505**	**(308)**
Financial expense, net	16	(142)	(176)	(151)
Income (loss) before income taxes		**419**	**329**	**(459)**
Income tax expense	18	(98)	(62)	(14)
Income (loss) from consolidated companies		**321**	**267**	**(473)**
Equity in net earnings of affiliates	7	10	20	18
Minority interests	13	(20)	(10)	1
Net income (loss)		**311**	**277**	**(454)**
Net income (loss) per common share "A" (in euros):	12			
Basic earnings (loss)		3.80	3.49	(5.90)
Diluted earnings (loss)		3.80	3.48	(5.90)

See Notes to the Consolidated Financial Statements.

All amounts in euros are translated using the official rate as of January 1, 1999 (see Note 1).

Consolidated Balance Sheet

December 31, 1998, 1997 and 1996

(in millions of euros)	Notes	1998	1997	1996
ASSETS				
Current assets				
Cash	15	971	431	534
Marketable securities	15	62	147	84
Accounts receivable—trade	11	1,087	1,155	1,023
Other receivables and prepaid expenses		202	157	134
Inventories, net	10	1,176	1,225	1,191
Deferred income taxes	18	103	121	115
Total current assets		**3,601**	**3,236**	**3,081**
Property, plant and equipment, net	4	2,770	2,787	2,719
Goodwill, net	5	1,485	1,662	1,469
Other intangible assets, net	6	191	212	198
Investments in equity affiliates	7	334	337	354
Long-term investments	8	63	93	125
Deferred income taxes	18	404	385	346
Other long-term assets	9	350	364	275
Total assets		**9,198**	**9,076**	**8,567**
LIABILITIES AND SHAREHOLDERS' EQUITY				
Current liabilities				
Accounts payable—trade		1,393	1,483	1,367
Other payables and accrued liabilities	20	517	611	550
Current portion of long-term debt	15	625	137	151
Short-term bank loans	15	1,188	1,030	1,458
Total current liabilities		**3,723**	**3,261**	**3,526**
Deferred income taxes	18	162	139	222
Other long-term liabilities	14	1,317	1,368	1,328
Long-term debt	15	1,307	1,695	1,261
Total liabilities		**6,509**	**6,463**	**6,337**
Minority interests	13	149	155	177
Contingencies	15-19-20	—	—	—

Consolidated Balance Sheet (cont.)

December 31, 1998, 1997 and 1996

(in millions of euros)	Notes	1998	1997	1996
Shareholders' equity				
Capital stock:				
Common shares "A"; par value € 15.24 per share, 163,364,343 shares authorized and 80,469,343 shares issued at December 31, 1998 and 1997; 77,278,258 shares issued at December 31, 1996		1,227	1,227	1,179
Preferred shares "B"; par value € 15.24 per share, 1,091,044 shares authorized and issued at December 31, 1998, 1997 and 1996		16	16	16
Share premium		833	833	741
Retained earnings		906	661	478
Accumulated other comprehensive income (loss)		(411)	(248)	(361)
Treasury shares (982,669 common shares "A" at December 31, 1998 and 982,320 at December 31, 1997)		(31)	(31)	—
Total shareholders' equity	12	**2,540**	**2,458**	**2,053**
TOTAL LIABILITIES AND SHAREHOLDERS' EQUITY		**9,198**	**9,076**	**8,567**

See Notes to the Consolidated Financial Statements.

All amounts in euros are translated using the official rate as of January 1, 1999 (see Note 1).

Consolidated Statement of Cash Flows

Years Ended December 1998, 1997, and 1996

(in millions of euros)	1998	1997	1996
CASH FLOWS FROM OPERATING ACTIVITIES			
Net income (loss)	311	277	(454)
Minority interests	20	10	(1)
Equity in net earnings of affiliates	(10)	(20)	(18)
Depreciation and amortization	370	347	326
Net gain on disposal of long-lived assets	(28)	(90)	(19)
Long-lived assets writedown	8	36	79
Restructuring provision	6	14	242
Other non-cash expense (income), net	67	(9)	224
Changes in assets and liabilities exclusive of effects of acquisitions, divestitures and translation adjustments:			
Decrease (increase) in inventories	19	(28)	183
Decrease (increase) in trade receivable	115	(208)	219
(Decrease) increase in trade payable	(60)	156	(191)
Restructuring expenditures	(66)	(74)	(37)
Other changes	(228)	(87)	(170)
Net cash provided by operating activities	**524**	**324**	**383**

Consolidated Statement of Cash Flows (cont.)

Years Ended December 1998, 1997, and 1996

(in millions of euros)	1998	1997	1996
CASH FLOWS FROM INVESTING ACTIVITIES			
Additions to property, plant and equipment	(389)	(300)	(306)
Increase in long-term investments	(21)	(57)	(112)
Increase in long-term receivables	(14)	(47)	(3)
Other (increase) decrease in long-lived assets	(15)	(7)	9
Proceeds from sales of other investments, net of cash of businesses sold	55	386	100
Other proceeds from sales of long-term assets	14	13	37
Receipts from other long-term receivables	16	6	34
Net cash used in investing activities	**(354)**	**(6)**	**(241)**
CASH FLOWS FROM FINANCING ACTIVITIES			
Addition to long-term debt	419	403	158
Decrease in other financial debt	(110)	(760)	(264)
Share capital increases:			
Pechiney	—	1	5
Subsidiaries (share of minority interests)	—	—	2
Dividends paid:			
By Pechiney	(66)	(18)	(33)
To minority interests in subsidiaries	(17)	(14)	(18)
Net cash provided by (used in) financing activities	**226**	**(388)**	**(150)**
Net effect of foreign currency translation on cash	59	28	(9)
Net increase (decrease) in cash and cash equivalents	455	(40)	(17)
Cash and cash equivalents at beginning of period	578	618	635
Cash and cash equivalents at end of period	**1,033**	**578**	**618**
Supplemental Disclosures			
Cash payments during the period for:			
Interest	(110)	(169)	(148)
Income taxes	(111)	(111)	(123)

See Notes to the Consolidated Financial Statements.

All amounts in euros are translated using the official rate as of January 1, 1999 (see Note 1).

Required:

1. Have Pechiney's results improved over the three-year period 1996 to 1998? Explain.
2. What are the costs and benefits of Pechiney's decision to adopt the euro?
3. Pechiney adopted the euro for purposes of preparing its financial statements as of January 1, 1999, and yet has presented euro-based statements for the two comparative years, 1996 and 1997. How meaningful is this, from a shareholder's perspective? From a Pechiney manager's perspective?

4. How should a company choose its reporting currency? Why do so many Canadian companies report in American dollars?

5. On August 11, 1999, Pechiney and two other major aluminum companies, Alcan (a Canadian company) and ALGROUP (a Swiss company), announced that they intended to merge. Suggest how a reporting currency for the merged entity should be chosen. Suggest how a set of GAAP for the merged entity should be chosen.

Integrative Running Case Study
Bombardier on the Web

Refer to the Bombardier Inc. annual report for the year ended January 31, 2002, available on the Companion Website for this text at **www.pearsoned.ca/revsine**.

Required:

1. Explain why the revenue numbers time series in the historical financial summary on pages 62–63 of the annual report would be misleading if used to assess the changes in Bombardier's scale of activities over time. How could this problem be partly corrected?

2. Examine the company's balance sheet information on page 69 (as well as the associated footnotes). Identify the monetary and nonmonetary items, and explain their significance to the company's income measurement when prices change.

3. Suppose general inflation for the year ended January 31, 2002 was 5%. On the basis of Bombardier's balance sheet, how would the company be affected? Would Bombardier (without the consolidation of BC) be affected differently from BC?

4. Examine Bombardier's income statement on page 71 (as well as the associated footnotes). Explain how each item might have to be adjusted if a current cost income statement were to be prepared. Which items might be expected to change the most?

5. Note 12 on pages 90–91 describes the company's long-term debt. As may be seen from the note, debt has been issued by the non-BC Bombardier entities as well as by the BC Bombardier entities. For each debt issue, estimate the carrying value of the debt if the company had accounted for its debt on the basis of the "market value" of the debt as of the year-end, assuming inflation for the year ended January 31, 2002 was 3%, and it has been 3% for several years and is expected to be 3% in the future. Should companies mark their debt to market (i.e., reset the carrying value of debt to its "current value") each year? Why or why not? If yes, how should the other side of the required journal entry be treated?

6. Examine note 23 on pages 98–100. Explain how the "fair value" information provided is related to information about current prices or market values. Also explain whether this information is useful; be specific.

7. Many people describe the existing GAAP-basis accounting model as "historical-cost." On the basis of your examination of the Bombardier financial statements, is this accurate?

Endnotes

1. See B.D.O. Binder, *The Accounting Profession in the United Kingdom*, 2nd ed., rev. (New York: American Institute of Certified Public Accountants, 1994).

2. These powers are given to the SEC in Section 19(a) of *The Securities Act of 1933 as Amended*: "... [T]he Commission shall have authority, for the purposes of this title, to prescribe the form or forms in which required information shall be set forth, the items or details to be shown in the balance sheet and earning statement, and the methods to be followed in the preparation of accounts, in the appraisal or valuation of assets and liabilities, in the determination of depreciation and depletion, in the differentiation of recurring and nonrecurring income, in the differentiation of investment and operating income, and in the preparation, where the Commission deems it necessary or desirable, of consolidated balance sheets or income accounts of any person directly or indirectly controlling or controlled by the issuer, or any person under direct or indirect common control with the issuer. The rules and regulations of the Commission shall be effective upon publication in the manner which the Commission shall prescribe" (U.S. Congress, "Securities Act of 1933 as Amended" [H.R. 5480], 73d Congress).

3. The material in this section relies heavily on S. A. Zeff, "The Regulation of Financial Reporting: Historical Development and Policy Recommendations," *De Accountant* [The Netherlands], November 1993, pp. 152–60.

4. F. D. S. Choi and G. G. Mueller, *International Accounting*, 2nd ed. (Englewood Cliffs, NJ: Prentice Hall, 1992), p. 96.

5. Large companies in Japan are often members of an associated corporate group, termed a *keiretsu*. The membership of the keiretsu typically comprises several different industry groups. Members of the group typically purchase inputs from one another and provide each other with equity financing. In addition, a keiretsu typically includes a large bank, which is another source of financing.

6. "Preface to Statements of International Accounting Standards," in *International Accounting Standards 1997* (London: IASC, 1997), pp. 29–30. Available on IASB website.

7. Ibid., p. 18.

8. S. A. Zeff, " 'Political' Lobbying on Proposed Standards: A Challenge to the IASB," *Accounting Horizons*, 16(1), March 2002, pp. 43–54; the quote is from page 44.

9. S. A. Zeff, "International Accounting Principles and Auditing Standards," *The European Accounting Review*, September 1993, pp. 403–10.

10. For a simple overview of different capital maintenance concepts, see L. Revsine, "A Capital Maintenance Approach to Income Measurement," *The Accounting Review*, April 1981, pp. 383–9.

11. See "Financial Reporting and Changing Prices," *SFAS No. 89* (Stamford, CT: FASB, 1986). The ostensible reason for altering the disclosure requirement was that, because inflation rates had abated, the disclosures were no longer essential. An unexpressed—but more plausible—explanation was that managers of capital-intensive firms opposed the disclosures, since they generated adverse reactions directed against managers by shareholders. For example, it is difficult to justify managerial bonuses tied to reported income when the supplemental disclosure indicated losses were being incurred on a current cost basis. The simplest financial reporting remedy for avoiding this conflict is to dispense with the disclosure altogether. Managers of firms aggressively lobbied the FASB to rescind *SFAS No. 33*. One explanation for why the FASB acquiesced to such efforts is developed in L. Revsine, "The Selective Financial Misrepresentation Hypothesis," *Accounting Horizons*, December 1991, pp. 16–27.

12. The minority share difference arises because the current cost income from those subsidiaries with minority shareholders was apparently *higher* than the historical cost income.

13. A loss on monetary items that is recognized while the asset carrying value is not changed might cause you to question how the balance sheet can still balance under such circumstances. The issue is best understood by considering the gain or loss on monetary items as a two-step computation. First, when 4% inflation occurs during 2001 for the all-cash firm in the example, the following entry might be made to put all amounts into end-of-period dollars:

DR Cash	$40	
CR Owners' equity		$40

After this entry is made, the end-of-period general price-level accounting equation is:

A	= L +	E
Cash $1,040		Owners' equity $1,040

Cash is now shown as $1,040 when, in reality, the December 31, 2001 balance is only $1,000. The difference, of course, is the purchasing power loss. To adjust cash to the proper year-end balance, the following entry must be made:

DR Owners' equity (purchasing power loss)	$40	
CR Cash		$40

After this entry is made, the basic accounting equation shows:

A	= L +	E	
Cash $1,000		Owners' equity	$1,040
		Purchasing power loss	(40)

Although formal journal entries are seldom employed when historical cost statements are adjusted to a general price-level basis, an understanding of the hypothetical journal entries described here makes it easier to grasp the mechanics of the purchasing power gain or loss on monetary items.

Appendix

Table 1 Present Value of $1

$$p = \frac{1}{(1+r)^n} = (1+r)^{-n}$$

(n) Periods	2%	3%	4%	5%	6%	7%	8%	9%	10%	11%	12%	15%	16%	17%
1	0.98039	0.97087	0.96154	0.95238	0.94340	0.93458	0.92593	0.91743	0.90909	0.90090	0.89286	0.86957	0.86207	0.85470
2	0.96117	0.94260	0.92456	0.90703	0.89000	0.87344	0.85734	0.84168	0.82645	0.81162	0.79719	0.75614	0.74316	0.73051
3	0.94232	0.91514	0.88900	0.86384	0.83962	0.81630	0.79383	0.77218	0.75132	0.73119	0.71178	0.65752	0.64066	0.62437
4	0.92385	0.88849	0.85480	0.82270	0.79209	0.76290	0.73503	0.70843	0.68301	0.65873	0.63552	0.57175	0.55229	0.53365
5	0.90573	0.86261	0.82193	0.78353	0.74726	0.71299	0.68058	0.64993	0.62092	0.59345	0.56743	0.49718	0.47611	0.45611
6	0.88797	0.83748	0.79031	0.74622	0.70496	0.66634	0.63017	0.59627	0.56447	0.53464	0.50663	0.43233	0.41044	0.38984
7	0.87056	0.81309	0.75992	0.71068	0.66506	0.62275	0.58349	0.54703	0.51316	0.48166	0.45235	0.37594	0.35383	0.33320
8	0.85349	0.78941	0.73069	0.67684	0.62741	0.58201	0.54027	0.50187	0.46651	0.43393	0.40388	0.32690	0.30503	0.28478
9	0.83676	0.76642	0.70259	0.64461	0.59190	0.54393	0.50025	0.46043	0.42410	0.39092	0.36061	0.28426	0.26295	0.24340
10	0.82035	0.74409	0.67556	0.61391	0.55839	0.50835	0.46319	0.42241	0.38554	0.35218	0.32197	0.24718	0.22668	0.20804
11	0.80426	0.72242	0.64958	0.58468	0.52679	0.47509	0.42888	0.38753	0.35049	0.31728	0.28748	0.21494	0.19542	0.17781
12	0.78849	0.70138	0.62460	0.55684	0.49697	0.44401	0.39711	0.35553	0.31863	0.28584	0.25668	0.18691	0.16846	0.15197
13	0.77303	0.68095	0.60057	0.53032	0.46884	0.41496	0.36770	0.32618	0.28966	0.25751	0.22917	0.16253	0.14523	0.12989
14	0.75788	0.66112	0.57748	0.50507	0.44230	0.38782	0.34046	0.29925	0.26333	0.23199	0.20462	0.14133	0.12520	0.11102
15	0.74301	0.64186	0.55526	0.48102	0.41727	0.36245	0.31524	0.27454	0.23939	0.20900	0.18270	0.12289	0.10793	0.09489
16	0.72845	0.62317	0.53391	0.45811	0.39365	0.33873	0.29189	0.25187	0.21763	0.18829	0.16312	0.10686	0.09304	0.08110
17	0.71416	0.60502	0.51337	0.43630	0.37136	0.31657	0.27027	0.23107	0.19784	0.16963	0.14564	0.09293	0.08021	0.06932
18	0.70016	0.58739	0.49363	0.41552	0.35034	0.29586	0.25025	0.21199	0.17986	0.15282	0.13004	0.08081	0.06914	0.05925
19	0.68643	0.57029	0.47464	0.39573	0.33051	0.27651	0.23171	0.19449	0.16351	0.13768	0.11611	0.07027	0.05961	0.05064
20	0.67297	0.55368	0.45639	0.37689	0.31180	0.25842	0.21455	0.17843	0.14864	0.12403	0.10367	0.06110	0.05139	0.04328
25	0.60953	0.47761	0.37512	0.29530	0.23300	0.18425	0.14602	0.11597	0.09230	0.07361	0.05882	0.03038	0.02447	0.01974
30	0.55207	0.41199	0.30832	0.23138	0.17411	0.13137	0.09938	0.07537	0.05731	0.04368	0.03338	0.01510	0.01165	0.00900
35	0.50003	0.35538	0.25342	0.18129	0.13011	0.09366	0.06763	0.04899	0.03558	0.02592	0.01894	0.00751	0.00555	0.00411
40	0.45289	0.30656	0.20829	0.14205	0.09722	0.06678	0.04603	0.03184	0.02209	0.01538	0.01075	0.00373	0.00264	0.00187

Table 2 Present Value of an Ordinary Annuity of $1

$$p_{OA} = \left(1 - \frac{1}{(1+r)^n}\right)/r$$

(n) Periods	2%	3%	4%	5%	6%	7%	8%	9%	10%	11%	12%	15%	16%	17%
1	0.98039	0.97087	0.96154	0.95238	0.94340	0.93458	0.92593	0.91743	0.90909	0.90090	0.89286	0.86957	0.86207	0.85470
2	1.94156	1.91347	1.88609	1.85941	1.83339	1.80802	1.78326	1.75911	1.73554	1.71252	1.69005	1.62571	1.60523	1.58521
3	2.88388	2.82861	2.77509	2.72325	2.67301	2.62432	2.57710	2.53129	2.48685	2.44371	2.40183	2.28323	2.24589	2.20958
4	3.80773	3.71710	3.62990	3.54595	3.46511	3.38721	3.31213	3.23972	3.16987	3.10245	3.03735	2.85498	2.79818	2.74324
5	4.71346	4.57971	4.45182	4.32948	4.21236	4.10020	3.99271	3.88965	3.79079	3.69590	3.60478	3.35216	3.27429	3.19935
6	5.60143	5.41719	5.24214	5.07569	4.91732	4.76654	4.62288	4.48592	4.35526	4.23054	4.11141	3.78448	3.68474	3.58918
7	6.47199	6.23028	6.00205	5.78637	5.58238	5.38929	5.20637	5.03295	4.86842	4.71220	4.56376	4.16042	4.03857	3.92238
8	7.32548	7.01969	6.73274	6.46321	6.20979	5.97130	5.74664	5.53482	5.33493	5.14612	4.96764	4.48732	4.34359	4.20716
9	8.16224	7.78611	7.43533	7.10782	6.80169	6.51523	6.24689	5.99525	5.75902	5.53705	5.32825	4.77158	4.60654	4.45057
10	8.98259	8.53020	8.11090	7.72173	7.36009	7.02358	6.71008	6.41766	6.14457	5.88923	5.65022	5.01877	4.83323	4.65860
11	9.78685	9.25262	8.76048	8.30641	7.88687	7.49867	7.13896	6.80519	6.49506	6.20652	5.93770	5.23371	5.02864	4.83641
12	10.57534	9.95400	9.38507	8.86325	8.38384	7.94269	7.53608	7.16073	6.81369	6.49236	6.19437	5.42062	5.19711	4.98839
13	11.34837	10.63496	9.98565	9.39357	8.85268	8.35765	7.90378	7.48690	7.10336	6.74987	6.42355	5.58315	5.34233	5.11828
14	12.10625	11.29607	10.56312	9.89864	9.29498	8.74547	8.24424	7.78615	7.36669	6.98187	6.62817	5.72448	5.46753	5.22930
15	12.84926	11.93794	11.11839	10.37966	9.71225	9.10791	8.55948	8.06069	7.60608	7.19087	6.81086	5.84737	5.57546	5.32419
16	13.57771	12.56110	11.65230	10.83777	10.10590	9.44665	8.85137	8.31256	7.82371	7.37916	6.97399	5.95423	5.66850	5.40529
17	14.29187	13.16612	12.16567	11.27407	10.47726	9.76322	9.12164	8.54363	8.02155	7.54879	7.11963	6.04716	5.74870	5.47461
18	14.99203	13.75351	12.65930	11.68959	10.82760	10.05909	9.37189	8.75563	8.20141	7.70162	7.24967	6.12797	5.81785	5.53385
19	15.67846	14.32380	13.13394	12.08532	11.15812	10.33560	9.60360	8.95011	8.36492	7.83929	7.36578	6.19823	5.87746	5.58449
20	16.35143	14.87747	13.59033	12.46221	11.46992	10.59401	9.81815	9.12855	8.51356	7.96333	7.46944	6.25933	5.92884	5.62777
25	19.52346	17.41315	15.62208	14.09394	12.78336	11.65358	10.67478	9.82258	9.07704	8.42174	7.84314	6.46415	6.09709	5.76623
30	22.39646	19.60044	17.29203	15.37245	13.76483	12.40904	11.25778	10.27365	9.42691	8.69379	8.05518	6.56598	6.17720	5.82939
35	24.99862	21.48722	18.66461	16.37419	14.49825	12.94767	11.65457	10.56682	9.64416	8.85524	8.17550	6.61661	6.21534	5.85820
40	27.35548	23.11477	19.79277	17.15909	15.04630	13.33171	11.92461	10.75736	9.77905	8.95105	8.24378	6.64178	6.23350	5.87133

Table 3 Present Value of an Annuity Due of $1

$$p_{AD} = 1 + \left(1 - \frac{1}{(1+r)^{n-1}}\right)/r$$

(n) Periods	2%	3%	4%	5%	6%	7%	8%	9%	10%	11%	12%	15%	16%	17%
1	1.00000	1.00000	1.00000	1.00000	1.00000	1.00000	1.00000	1.00000	1.00000	1.00000	1.00000	1.00000	1.00000	1.00000
2	1.98039	1.97087	1.96154	1.95238	1.94340	1.93458	1.92593	1.91743	1.90909	1.90090	1.89286	1.86957	1.86207	1.85470
3	2.94156	2.91347	2.88609	2.85941	2.83339	2.80802	2.78326	2.75911	2.73554	2.71252	2.69005	2.62571	2.60523	2.58521
4	3.88388	3.82861	3.77509	3.72325	3.67301	3.62432	3.57710	3.53129	3.48685	3.44371	3.40183	3.28323	3.24589	3.20958
5	4.80773	4.71710	4.62990	4.54595	4.46511	4.38721	4.31213	4.23972	4.16987	4.10245	4.03735	3.85498	3.79818	3.74324
6	5.71346	5.57971	5.45182	5.32948	5.21236	5.10020	4.99271	4.88965	4.79079	4.69590	4.60478	4.35216	4.27429	4.19935
7	6.60143	6.41719	6.24214	6.07569	5.91732	5.76654	5.62288	5.48592	5.35526	5.23054	5.11141	4.78448	4.68474	4.58918
8	7.47199	7.23028	7.00205	6.78637	6.58238	6.38929	6.20637	6.03295	5.86842	5.71220	5.56376	5.16042	5.03857	4.92238
9	8.32548	8.01969	7.73274	7.46321	7.20979	6.97130	6.74664	6.53482	6.33493	6.14612	5.96764	5.48732	5.34359	5.20716
10	9.16224	8.78611	8.43533	8.10782	7.80169	7.51523	7.24689	6.99525	6.75902	6.53705	6.32825	5.77158	5.60654	5.45057
11	9.98259	9.53020	9.11090	8.72173	8.36009	8.02358	7.71008	7.41766	7.14457	6.88923	6.65022	6.01877	5.83323	5.65860
12	10.78685	10.25262	9.76048	9.30641	8.88687	8.49867	8.13896	7.80519	7.49506	7.20652	6.93770	6.23371	6.02864	5.83641
13	11.57534	10.95400	10.38507	9.86325	9.38384	8.94269	8.53608	8.16073	7.81369	7.49236	7.19437	6.42062	6.19711	5.98839
14	12.34837	11.63496	10.98565	10.39357	9.85268	9.35765	8.90378	8.48690	8.10336	7.74987	7.42355	6.58315	6.34233	6.11828
15	13.10625	12.29607	11.56312	10.89864	10.29498	9.74547	9.24424	8.78615	8.36669	7.98187	7.62817	6.72448	6.46753	6.22930
16	13.84926	12.93794	12.11839	11.37966	10.71225	10.10791	9.55948	9.06069	8.60608	8.19087	7.81086	6.84737	6.57546	6.32419
17	14.57771	13.56110	12.65230	11.83777	11.10590	10.44665	9.85137	9.31256	8.82371	8.37916	7.97399	6.95423	6.66850	6.40529
18	15.29187	14.16612	13.16567	12.27407	11.47726	10.76322	10.12164	9.54363	9.02155	8.54879	8.11963	7.04716	6.74870	6.47461
19	15.99203	14.75351	13.65930	12.68959	11.82760	11.05909	10.37189	9.75563	9.20141	8.70162	8.24967	7.12797	6.81785	6.53385
20	16.67846	15.32380	14.13394	13.08532	12.15812	11.33560	10.60360	9.95011	9.36492	8.83929	8.36578	7.19823	6.87746	6.58449
25	19.91393	17.93554	16.24696	14.79864	13.55036	12.46933	11.52876	10.70661	9.98474	9.34814	8.78432	7.43377	7.07263	6.74649
30	22.84438	20.18845	17.98371	16.14107	14.59072	13.27767	12.15841	11.19828	10.36961	9.65011	9.02181	7.55088	7.16555	6.82039
35	25.49859	22.13184	19.41120	17.19290	15.36814	13.85401	12.58693	11.51784	10.60857	9.82932	9.15656	7.60910	7.20979	6.85409
40	27.90259	23.80822	20.58448	18.01704	15.94907	14.26493	12.87858	11.72552	10.75696	9.93567	9.23303	7.63805	7.23086	6.86946

Financial Reporting and Analysis

Common Financial Ratios

Profitability

$$\text{Return on Assets (ROA)} = \frac{\text{Net Income} + \text{Interest Expense (1 − Tax Rate)}}{\text{Average Total Assets}}$$

$$\text{Profit Margin for ROA} = \frac{\text{Net Income} + \text{Interest Expense (1 − Tax Rate)}}{\text{Sales}}$$

$$\text{Total Asset Turnover} = \frac{\text{Sales}}{\text{Average Total Assets}}$$

$$\text{Common Earnings Leverage} = \frac{\text{Net Income} − \text{Preferred Dividends}}{\text{Net Income} + \text{Interest Expense (1 − Tax Rate)}}$$

$$\text{Financial Structure Leverage} = \frac{\text{Average Total Assets}}{\text{Average Common Shareholders' Equity}}$$

$$\text{Return on Common Equity (ROCE)} = \frac{\text{Net Income} − \text{Preferred Dividends}}{\text{Average Common Shareholders' Equity}}$$

Asset Utilization

$$\text{Accounts Receivable Turnover} = \frac{\text{Net Credit Sales}}{\text{Average Accounts Receivable}}$$

$$\text{Inventory Turnover} = \frac{\text{Cost of Goods Sold}}{\text{Average Inventory}}$$

$$\text{Fixed Asset Turnover} = \frac{\text{Sales}}{\text{Average Fixed Assets}}$$